Morton Benson
Evelyn Benson
Robert Ilson

Student's Dictionary of Collocations

mit einem Vorwort von
F. J. Hausmann

Morton Benson, Evelyn Benson and Robert Ilson

Student's Dictionary of Collocations

mit einem Vorwort von Professor Dr. F. J. Hausmann, Universität Erlangen-Nürnberg

Das *Student's Dictionary of Collocations* basiert auf dem
BBI Combinatory Dictionary of English: A Guide to Word Combinations,
© Copyright 1986 – shared by Morton Benson, Evelyn Benson, Robert Ilson and John Benjamins B.V.

1. Auflage 1989

© 1989 Cornelsen Verlag, Berlin

ISBN 3-464-02324-9

Vertrieb: Cornelsen Verlagsgesellschaft, Bielefeld
Bestellnummer 23249

Inhaltsübersicht

Praktische Einführung in den Gebrauch des *Student's Dictionary of Collocations*

Vorbemerkung: Kollokationen und Konstruktionen

Das vorliegende Wörterbuch der lexikalischen und grammatikalischen Anschlüsse hat den englischen Titel *Dictionary of Collocations*. In der englischen Terminologie wird unterschieden zwischen *lexical collocations* und *grammatical collocations*. In einer verbreiteten deutschen Terminologie heißen die *lexical collocations* „Kollokationen" und die *grammatical collocations* „Konstruktionen". Das *Student's Dictionary of Collocations* ist also ein Wörterbuch der Kollokationen und Konstruktionen. Die folgende Einführung in Inhalt und Gebrauch des Wörterbuchs geht zuerst auf die Kollokationsangaben ein, sodann auf die Konstruktionsangaben. Danach schließen sich Hinweise an, die beide Angaben betreffen.

Das *Student's Dictionary of Collocations* als Kollokationswörterbuch

Was ist eine Kollokation?
Was heißt auf englisch „Hammer" und „Nagel"? Die Antwort ist einfach: *hammer* und *nail*. *Nail = Nagel*, das ist eine der Wortgleichungen, die man lernen muß, wenn man englischen Wortschatz lernt, und die man auch als Wortgleichung lernen d a r f, denn *nail* ist wirklich dasselbe wie *Nagel*.

Ganz andere Schwierigkeiten treten auf, wenn es darum geht, nicht den Gegenstand Nagel auf englisch zu benennen, sondern auch das Wort zu gebrauchen, z.B. weil man sagen will: „Er ist nicht fähig, einen Nagel einzuschlagen." Dann lautet die Frage nämlich nicht mehr: Was heißt auf englisch „einschlagen"? Denn diese Frage kann man nicht ohne weiteres beantworten. Damit auf die Frage eine Antwort gefunden werden kann, muß sie lauten: Was heißt „einen Nagel einschlagen"? Hier lautet die Antwort: *hammer a nail into (the wall)* oder *drive a nail into (the wall)*. Wer sich vom deutschen Wort *einschlagen* beeinflussen läßt und schreibt **beat a nail into the wall*, macht einen Fehler, genauso wie der Franzose, der, weil man in seiner Sprache sagt *planter un clou* (einen Nagel „einpflanzen"), meint, im Englischen heiße es **plant a nail*.

---

* Das Sternchen kennzeichnet fehlerhaftes Englisch.

Wie man sieht, gebrauchen die Sprachen ganz verschiedene Bilder und Ausdrucksweisen für die Beschreibung des gleichen Vorgangs. Im Deutschen „schlägt" man den Nagel in die Wand, im Französischen „pflanzt" man ihn hinein, im Englischen „hämmert" oder „treibt" man den Nagel in die Wand. Während man also beim Lernen von *nail* lediglich einen deutschen Wortkörper durch einen englischen ersetzt, muß man beim Lernen von *hammer a nail* oder *drive a nail* eine deutsche Vorstellung der Dinge, eine deutsche Analyse des Vorgangs, durch eine englische ersetzen. Genauso wie der Sprecher des Englischen, wenn er Deutsch lernt, lernen muß, daß man in dieser Sprache den Nagel „einschlägt".

Wir wollen nun solche der Sprache eigene und nicht automatisch in andere Sprachen übertragbare Wortkombinationen K o l l o k a t i o n e n nennen (von lateinisch *collocare* = con-locare „nebeneinandersetzen").

Kollokationen verstehen und Kollokationen bilden

Eine besondere und in gewissem Sinne trügerische Eigenschaft der Kollokationen besteht darin, daß man sie in der Regel versteht, wenn man sie antrifft, und daß sie einem nicht einmal besonders auffallen. Was gibt es schon Besonderes, möchte man meinen, an *hammer a nail into the wall*? Das Besondere daran ist versteckt, daß man nämlich nicht sagt: **beat a nail into the wall*. Wer sich das beim Lesen von *hammer a nail into the wall* nicht bewußtmacht, der wird später überrascht feststellen, daß er nicht weiß, wie er „einen Nagel einschlagen" auf englisch ausdrücken soll. Kurz, die Kollokationen werden vor allem dann zum Problem, wenn man sich mündlich oder schriftlich auf englisch ausdrücken will, nicht aber beim Verstehen.

Daraus ergibt sich nun wieder die Konsequenz, daß man die Kollokationen im Wörterbuch nicht unbedingt zu erklären braucht und auch nicht unbedingt zu übersetzen. Es reicht notfalls, sie zu nennen, zu verzeichnen, damit der Benutzer sie auffinden kann und so eine Antwort bekommt auf die Frage: Was sagt man in diesem Fall auf englisch? Oder auch: Sagt man das auf englisch? Der Beantwortung dieser Fragen widmet sich das Kollokationswörterbuch.

Wozu ein Kollokationswörterbuch?

Nun wird man fragen: Ist das nötig? Es gibt doch bereits die *learner's dictionaries*. Stehen die Kollokationen denn da nicht bereits hinreichend verzeichnet? Die Antwort muß in zwei Stufen gegeben werden, nämlich ja und nein.

Zuerst einmal müssen wir uns klarmachen, daß Kollokationen als Zweierkombinationen von Wörtern im Wörterbuch immer an zwei Stellen stehen können, in unserem Beispiel unter **nail** und unter **drive** (oder **hammer**). Der Nutzen – und das ist ein wichtiges Faktum – ist an beiden Stellen verschieden. Im Artikel **drive** (oder **hammer**) eines einsprachigen englischen Wörterbuchs nützt dem deutschen Benutzer die Kollokation nur dann, wenn er bereits daran gedacht hat, daß „Nagel einschlagen" möglicherweise *drive a nail* heißt, und nur noch überprüfen will, ob es auch stimmt (so wie er auch unter **beat** nachsehen kann und feststellen wird, daß sich diese Hypothese nicht bestätigt). Hat er hingegen noch nicht die richtige Vermutung – und das wird oft so sein –, dann nützt ihm das Wörterbuch nur, wenn es die Kollokation im Artikel **nail** verzeichnet. Es gibt also gute Gründe, die Kollokation im Artikel **hammer** oder **drive** einzusetzen, aber noch bessere, sie unter **nail** einzutragen.

Sehen wir uns nun an, wie sich die *learner's dictionaries* gegenüber den Kollokationen verhalten. Tragen sie die Kollokationen unter dem Substantiv (z.b. **nail**), unter den Verben (z.b. **drive**) oder unter beiden Wortarten ein? Und tragen sie überhaupt Kollokationen ein, und wenn ja, mit welchem Grad von Vollständigkeit?

Die Antwort lautet zuerst einmal: Diese Wörterbücher haben gar nicht den Platz, die Kollokationen mit einiger Vollständigkeit einzutragen. Wenn sie sie aber eintragen, dann überwiegend in den Verbartikeln, weil man diese Wörter (z.B. *drive*) ohne Kollokationen oft gar nicht erklären kann.

Hingegen finden sich die Kollokationen unter dem Substantiv nur sehr sporadisch. Wir haben aber gesehen, daß der deutsche Benutzer sie dort am dringendsten braucht. Es fehlt also neben dem allgemeinen einsprachigen *learner's dictionary* das Spezialwörterbuch der Kollokationen, das die Kollokationen in erster Linie unter den Substantiven verzeichnet (zusätzlich vielleicht auch unter dem Verb, obwohl das nicht in gleicher Weise dringlich ist). Diese Lücke füllt das vorliegende *Dictionary of Collocations*.

Welche Typen von Kollokationen gibt es?

Typ 1 Kennengelernt haben wir bereits die Kollokationen Verb + Substantiv (Objekt). Beispiel: *tackle a problem* (ein Problem angehen, anpacken).

Typ 2 Ebenso zahlreich sind die Verbindungen Adjektiv + Substantiv. Beispiel: *weak tea* (schwacher Tee, nicht **feeble tea*); *a knotty problem* (ein schwieriges, verwickeltes Problem).

Typ 3 Weniger zahlreich sind die Kollokationen Substantiv (Subjekt) + Verb. Beispiel: *the heart palpitates, throbs* (das Herz klopft heftig, pocht).

Typ 4 Zahlreicher sind wieder die Verbindungen zweier Substantive, oft mit der Präposition *of*: Substantiv + *of* + Substantiv. Beispiel: *a pack of dogs* (eine Hundemeute), *a pack of wolves* (ein Wolfsrudel), *a herd of buffalo* (eine Büffelherde), *a pride of lions* (ein Löwenrudel).

Typ 5 Adjektive verbinden sich mit passenden Adverbien: Adverb + Adjektiv. Beispiel: *keenly aware*.

Typ 6 Auch zu Verben gibt es passende Adverbien: Verb + Adverb. Beispiel: *hurt badly, seriously; deeply; slightly*.

Wo findet man die Kollokationen im Kollokationswörterbuch?

Wir haben schon erfahren, wie wichtig es ist, daß die Kollokationen Verb – Substantiv (Objekt) im Kollokationswörterbuch unter dem Substantiv aufzufinden sind, also *hammer a nail into* im Artikel **nail**. Warum? Weil man in der Regel das passende Verb zum bereits bekannten Substantiv sucht und nicht umgekehrt, z.B. zu dem Substantiv *Termin (deadline)* das passende Verb *einhalten (meet)* und nicht umgekehrt. Wir wollen das dadurch zum Ausdruck bringen, daß wir sagen: In der Verbindung Verb + Substantiv ist das Substantiv die *Basis* der Kollokation (und meinen damit das Wort von dem aus die Kollokation gebildet wird). Auch bei den anderen fünf Kollokationstypen läßt sich eine Basis erkennen. In der Kollokation Typ 2 Adjektiv + Substantiv ist die Basis wiederum das Substantiv, ebenso in Typ 3: Substantiv (Subjekt) + Verb. Man sucht zu dem Basiswort *Junggeselle (bachelor)* das passende Adjektiv *eingefleischt (confirmed)*. Oder man sucht zu dem Basiswort *Wind (wind)* das passende Verb *abflauen, nachlassen, sich legen (fall, subside)*. Auch in Typ 4 (Substantiv + Substantiv) läßt sich meist deutlich eine Basis erkennen. In *a pack of dogs* ist von Hunden die Rede (Basis: *dogs*), deren Gruppierung auszudrücken ist *(a pack)*, nicht etwa umgekehrt. In *a gust of wind* wird eine bestimmte Charakterisierung des Windes vorgenommen (Basis: *wind*), nicht umgekehrt. Was nun die Adverbien betrifft (Typen 5 und 6), so charakterisieren sie, wie hinreichend bekannt, Adjektive (z.B. *hopelessly addicted, thoroughly ashamed*) und Verben (z.B. *amuse thoroughly*). Adverbien sind also nie Basis, und Adjektive und Verben sind nur gegenüber den Adverbien Basis.

Nachdem wir nun in allen sechs Kollokationstypen die Basis ermittelt haben, können wir auf die Frage „Wo suche ich die Kollokation?" antworten: Unter dem Basiswort, d.h. im einzelnen:

Typ 1: Verb + Substantiv (Objekt) unter dem *Substantiv*
Typ 2: Adjektiv + Substantiv unter dem *Substantiv*

Typ 3: Substantiv (Subjekt) + Verb   unter dem *Substantiv*
Typ 4: Substantiv + Substantiv   unter dem *Basissubstantiv*
                                     (zumeist dem zweiten
                                     Substantiv)
Typ 5: Adverb + Adjektiv   unter dem *Adjektiv*
Typ 6: Verb + Adverb   unter dem *Verb*

Innerhalb eines Artikels sind die Kollokationen in der Reihenfolge der Typen von 1 – 6 aufgeführt. (Zum weiteren Aufbau der Artikel siehe unten, S. xvi).

Zusätzlich ist eine Auswahl von Kollokationen auch unter dem charakterisierenden Wort eingetragen, z.B. findet man *hammer a nail into a wall* sowohl unter **nail** als auch unter **hammer**.

Was findet man nicht im Kollokationswörterbuch?
Kehren wir noch einmal zum Ausgangspunkt unserer Überlegungen zurück. Nehmen wir an, der Nagel läßt sich nicht einschlagen. Ich sehe ihn mir genauer an *(I take a closer look at it)*. Er ist krumm *(bent)*. Warum finde ich im Artikel **nail** des Kollokationswörterbuchs nicht auch die Kombination *take a close look at a nail* und *bent nail*? Weil im Unterschied zum Einschlagen des Nagels das Betrachten des Nagels wie auch seine Verbogenheit nicht spezifisch zum Nagel dazugehören. Das Verbiegbare ist zahlreich und das Betrachtbare endlos. In solchen Fällen handelt es sich um freie Kombinationen von Wörtern, die man ohne Kontextbeschränkung lernt und dann richtig gebrauchen kann. Kein Wörterbuch der Welt kann alle möglichen freien Kombinationen zusammenstellen – und braucht es auch nicht, da sie ja frei bildbar sind. Das Kollokationswörterbuch beschreibt deshalb nur den gebundenen Wortgebrauch, die Kombinationen, die nicht frei bildbar sind, also die Kollokationen. In diesem Falle findet man unter dem Eintrag **look** z.B. *a close look* (und nicht *an *exact look*) oder *take/get/have a look at* und nicht **do/*make a look at* usw.

Freilich sind die Übergänge zwischen freiem und gebundenem Wortgebrauch fließend, und man kann dem Kollokationswörterbuch im Einzelfall vorwerfen, zu weit oder nicht weit genug gegangen zu sein. Dabei muß man bedenken, daß Vollständigkeit derzeit noch unmöglich ist. Man nehme nur den passenden Gebrauch von *broad* und *wide*, deren Anwendung sich in zahllosen Fällen überschneidet, in zahllosen anderen aber auch gegenseitig ausschließt. Diesem Problem ist derzeit kein Wörterbuch gewachsen.

Kollokationen und bildliche Redewendungen
Eigentlich sollte man meinen, daß bildliche Redewendungen *(idioms)* in einem Kollokationswörterbuch nichts zu suchen haben, weil ihnen die

Basis fehlt: *jemanden durch den Kakao ziehen* in einem deutschen Kollokationswörterbuch unter *Kakao* einzutragen, hilft nur dem, der die Wendung bereits kennt, aber nicht dem, der nachschlägt, wie man den Gedanken „sich über jemanden lustig machen" sonst noch ausdrücken kann. Wenn in dem vorliegenden Wörterbuch dennoch zahlreiche bildliche Wendungen eingetragen sind, z.B. *spill the beans* (ein Geheimnis ausplaudern) im Artikel **bean**, dann gibt es dafür zwei Gründe:
a) Zum einen gibt es zwischen den Sprachen viele bildliche Gemeinsamkeiten, aus denen sich doch so etwas wie eine – freilich künstliche – Basis herausschält. So bildet z.B. das Wort *foot* (Fuß) aus deutscher Sicht eine Basis in den beiden Redewendungen *get a foot in the door* (einen Fuß in/zwischen die Tür setzen) und *she always lands on her feet* (sie fällt immer wieder auf die Füße). Das Kollokationswörterbuch lehrt den deutschen Benutzer in diesen Fällen, die passenden Verben *get* und *land* einzusetzen. Ob es sich allerdings lohnt, im Falle von Redewendungen das Kollokationswörterbuch aufzuschlagen, hängt ganz vom Zufall der Einzelsprache ab. Bei *Kakao* lohnt es sich nicht, und unter *bean* wird spontan kein deutscher Benutzer nachschlagen, der über Geheimnisse schreiben will.
b) So wie die Kollokationen zum Teil auch im Artikel des zur Basis passenden Wortes eingetragen sind (z.B. *hammer a nail into* im Artikel **hammer**), weil manche Benutzer mit einer Kollokationshypothese an das Wörterbuch herantreten (Sagt man *hammer a nail into?*), so ist auch vorstellbar, daß Benutzer die Richtigkeit einer Redewendung überprüfen wollen (Wie heißt noch die Wendung mit *beans* im Sinne von „ausplaudern"?) und froh sind, sie unter dem Substantiv (*bean, foot* usw.) zu finden, denn in der Tat neigen auch hier die allgemeinen einsprachigen Wörterbücher dazu, die Wendung unter dem Verb einzutragen.

Das *Student's Dictionary of Collocations* als Konstruktionswörterbuch

Was sind Konstruktionen und wozu dienen sie?

Kommen wir noch einmal auf unser erstes Kollokationsbeispiel zurück. Wenn ich weiß, mit welchem Verb ich das Wort *nail* verbinden kann, z.B. mit dem Verb *drive*, muß ich darüber hinaus wissen, wie das Verb grammatisch an seine Umgebung anzuschließen ist, anders gesagt, wie es zu k o n s t r u i e r e n ist. Vor allem muß ich wissen, ob das Verb mit oder ohne Präposition benutzt wird und gegebenenfalls mit welcher. Das gilt nun für alle Verben, und vor allem gilt es auch außerhalb der Kollokationen, also im lexikalisch freien Wortgebrauch, z.B.:

I congratulated him on his promotion.
(Ich gratulierte ihm *zur* Beförderung.)
I agree with her about that.
(Ich stimme mit ihr *darin* überein.)
I agree on/to the compromise.
(Ich bin *mit* dem Kompromiß einverstanden.)

Auch bei den Konstruktionen ist es oft so, daß man sie zwar versteht, wenn man sie zum ersten Mal antrifft, sie aber dann bei der aktiven Sprachproduktion, beim Sprechen oder Schreiben, nicht zur Verfügung hat und Fehler macht.

Neben der Beherrschung der Kollokation ist deshalb die der Konstruktion für das Abfassen von Texten in der Fremdsprache unabdingbar. Das vorliegende Wörterbuch setzt sich deshalb zum Ziel, die wichtigen Konstruktionen des Englischen übersichtlich und leicht lesbar aufzuführen.

Die Konstruktionen des Verbs

Das *Student's Dictionary of Collocations* unterscheidet 19 verschiedene Verbkonstruktionen *(verb patterns)*, die in den Verbartikeln mit den Buchstaben A – S gekennzeichnet sind. Wer nun vor dieser Anzahl und der undurchsichtigen Kennzeichnung mit Buchstabenkodes erschrickt, dem sei gesagt, daß jedes Vorkommen eines *pattern* durch ein Beispiel in verständlichem Englisch erläutert wird, so daß der Artikel auch ohne Kenntnis des Patternkodes verständlich ist. Die Kodebuchstaben kennzeichnen vor allem die Reihenfolge der *patterns* im Artikel, denn die geht grundsätzlich von A bis S.

Wir wollen nun zuerst die *patterns* in einer Übersicht vorstellen und dann ihre Anwendung in einem Artikel überprüfen.

A subj + verb + obj¹ + *to* + obj²   o d e r   subj + verb + obj² + obj¹
He sent the book to his brother.   *He sent his brother the book.*
He sent the book to him.   *He sent him the book.*
He sent it to him.   *He sent him it.*
                               He sent it him. (British English)

B subj + verb + obj + *to* + obj
They mentioned the book to her. (Falsch ist: ~ **her the book*)
Weitere Verben: *return, describe*, Geräuschverben wie *scream*.

C subj + verb + obj¹ + *for* + obj²   o d e r   subj + verb + obj² + obj¹
She bought a shirt for her husband.   *She bought her husband a shirt.*
She bought a shirt for him.   *She bought him a shirt.*

D und d subj + verb + prep + obj o d e r subj + verb + obj + prep + obj
In den folgenden Beispielen kann das Präpositionalgefüge entfallen (D):
He forgot about the concert. (Auch: *He forgot.*)
She fortified herself with a shot of whisky. (Auch: *She fortified herself*)
In anderen Fällen wird das Verb normalerweise nur mit Präpositionalgefüge
konstruiert (d):
Our state consists of 30 counties. (Nicht: **Our state consists.*)
They based their conclusions on the available facts. (Nicht: **They based
their conclusions.*)
Die Patternbeispiele werden in der alphabetischen Reihenfolge der
Präpositionen vorgestellt, z.B. im Artikel **come** von *to come across* bis *to
come under.*

E subj + verb + *to* + inf
They began to speak.

F subj + verb + inf
We must work.

G subj + verb + verb-*ing*
They enjoy watching television.

H subj + verb + obj + *to* + inf
She asked me to come.
We advised them to be careful.
Passiv ist möglich: *I was asked to come*, außer bei folgenden Verben:
*beseech, bring, cable, cause, commit, get, have, intend, like, prefer,
telegraph, telephone, thank, trouble, want, wire, wish, write.*

I sub + verb + obj + inf
She heard them leave.

J subj + verb + obj + verb-*ing*
He kept me waiting for two hours.
Passiv ist möglich: *I was kept waiting for two hours.*

K subj + verb + possessive + verb-*ing*
This fact justifies Bob's coming late.

L subj + verb (+ obj) + *that*-clause
They admitted that they were wrong.
She assured me that she would arrive on time.

M subj + verb + obj + *to be* + complement (adjective or noun)
We consider her to be well-trained.
We consider her to be a competent engineer.

N subj + verb + obj + complement (adjective or noun)
He made his meaning clear.
She wants the brooch identified.
We appointed Bob secretary.

O subj + verb + obj + obj
The teacher asked the pupil a question.
Passiv ist möglich: *No questions were asked.*

P subj + verb (+ obj) + adverbial
The road runs South.
He carried himself well.
She put pressure on them.

Q subj + verb (+ obj) + *wh*-word (Fragewort)
She knew when to keep quiet.
She knew when it was best to keep quiet.
We told them what to do.
Fragewörter sind: *how, what, when, where, which, who, why.*

R *it* + verb + obj + *to* + inf   o d e r   *it* + verb + obj + *that*-clause
It surprised me to learn of   *It surprised me that our offer*
her decision.   *was rejected.*

S subj + verb + complement (adjective or noun)
She was enthusiastic.
She was a teacher.

s subj + verb + complement (adjective)
The food tastes good.

Der Artikel zum Verb *come* enthält zuerst zahlreiche Untereinträge des *pattern* D bzw. d mit Definition (in Anführungszeichen). Die *patterns* sind nach der alphabetischen Reihenfolge der Präpositionen geordnet und nach den definierten Untereinträgen durchgezählt von 1 – 15. So werden z.B. fünf Untereinträge *come to* unterschieden (10.–14.). Davon sind in Nr. 11 allein acht Beispielkontexte beigegeben. Die Untereinträge 16 und 17 folgen *pattern* D, 18 folgt *pattern* G, 19 *pattern* P, 20 *pattern* s. Unter Nr. 21 stehen idiomatische Sonderfälle.

Die *phrasal verbs*

Mit den Verbkonstruktionen nicht zu verwechseln sind die sogenannten *phrasal verbs* (auch *compound verbs* genannt). Man vergleiche die Sätze:
a) *I came across an old friend.*
(Ich traf zufällig einen alten Freund.)
b) *He comes across as being very intelligent.*
(Er wirkt sehr intelligent.)
In a) wird das Verb *come* mit der Präposition *across* konstruiert. In b) hingegen wird das (zusammengesetzte) Verb *come across* mit der Präposition *as* konstruiert.

Die *phrasal verbs* werden im vorliegenden Wörterbuch wie einfache Verben behandelt und an ihrer alphabetischen Stelle eingetragen (z.B. **come down** nach **comedian**).

Die Konstruktionen des Adjektivs

Beim Adjektiv unterscheidet das Wörterbuch drei Konstruktionstypen

adj + prep:	*They were angry at everyone.*
adj + *to* + inf:	*It was necessary (for him) to work.*
	She is ready to go.
adj + *that*-clause:	*She was afraid that she would fail the*
	examination.

Auf eine Kodierung der Konstruktionstypen wird verzichtet. Im Artikel **afraid** findet man deshalb nach den Kollokationen (1.) die Konstruktionen *afraid of* (2.), *afraid to* + inf (3.), *afraid that* + clause (4.) und einen idiomatischen Sonderfall (5.).

Die Konstruktionen des Substantivs

Beim Substantiv *(noun)* unterscheidet das Wörterbuch vier Konstruktionstypen:

noun + prep:	*He expressed his deep anger at being*
	mistreated.
noun + *to* + inf:	*They made an attempt to do it.*
noun + *that*-clause:	*He took an oath that he would do his duty.*
prep + noun:	*by accident*

Auf eine Kodierung der Typen wird auch hier verzichtet. Im Artikel **attempt** I *n.* findet man deshalb im Anschluß an die Kollokationen (1.–3.) die Konstruktionen *an attempt against, on* (4.), *an attempt at* (5.) und *an attempt to* + inf (6.).

Weitere Hinweise zur Benutzung des Wörterbuchs

Unterschiede zwischen amerikanischem und britischem Englisch

Das *Student's Dictionary of Collocations* legt besonderen Wert auf die Unterschiede zwischen amerikanischem Englisch (AE) und britischem Englisch (BE), sowohl bei den Kollokationen als auch bei den Konstruktionen. Wenn man unter **different** 2. findet: „~ from, than (AE), to (BE)", so bedeutet dies: die Konstruktion mit *from* ist im amerikanischen wie im britischen Englisch üblich (gelegentlich als CE = *Common English* markiert), *than* nur amerikanisch, *to* nur britisch.

Die *Usage Notes*

An vielen Stellen stehen unter dem Titel USAGE NOTE zusätzliche Erklärungen. Sie betreffen Zweifelsfälle der Kollokation, der Konstruktion, der Zugehörigkeit zum amerikanischen oder britischen Englisch und anderes mehr.

Der Gebrauch der Tilde

Die Tilde (~) vertritt im Artikel das Stichwort. Bei den *phrasal verbs* (z.B. *get away*) gilt das jedoch nur, wenn die beiden Elemente nebeneinander stehen *(~ from = get away from)*. Kommen die beiden Elemente des *phrasal verb* nicht nebeneinander zu stehen, so vertritt die Tilde nur den verbalen Teil und nicht die Partikel, z.B. für *take down: ~ testimony down in shorthand.*

Die Bedeutung von Komma und Strichpunkt (Semikolon)

Bei der Aneinanderreihung von Kollokationen und Konstruktionen trennt das Komma solche gleicher Bedeutung, der Strichpunkt solche verschiedener Bedeutung *(give, offer advice* bzw. *answerable for; to)*. Ferner steht der Strichpunkt, wenn Gebrauchsunterschiede verdeutlicht werden sollen.

Ist das *Student's Dictionary of Collocations* ein vollständiges Wörterbuch?

Das *Student's Dictionary of Collocations* ist kein allgemeines einsprachiges Wörterbuch, sondern ein Spezialwörterbuch, das denjenigen unterstützt, der englische Texte zu schreiben hat. Man kann es ein S c h r e i b wörterbuch nennen. Hingegen ist es nicht geeignet, wenn es darum geht, englische Texte zu verstehen. Wer es zu diesem Zweck gebrauchen wollte, müßte das Fehlen vieler Wörter, Bedeutungen und Wendungen bemängeln. Das *Student's Dictionary of Collocations* erhebt aber in keiner Weise den Anspruch, ein solches L e s e wörterbuch zu sein. Ebensowenig erhebt es den Anspruch, ein *learner's dictionary* nach Art des *Oxford Advanced Learner's Dictionary* zu sein. Allerdings kann es ein solches *learner's dictionary* sinnvoll ergänzen.

Kann man in dem *Dictionary of Collocations* englischen Wortschatz l e r n e n ? Ganz gewiß. Das Wörterbuch ist mehr als ein reines Nachschlagewerk. Weil der Wortschatz, durch Beispielsätze illustriert, in der lernpsychologisch wichtigen kontextuellen Verbindung dargeboten wird, lohnt es sich, einzelne Artikel durchzulesen und durchzuarbeiten. Man dringt dabei nicht nur auf sehr ökonomische Weise in den Geist der englischen Sprache ein, sondern man sammelt sich vor allem einen Schatz wiederverwendbarer Halbfertigprodukte der Sprache, durch deren Kenntnis ein differenzierter und korrekter Ausdruck im Englischen möglich wird.

Erlangen, im Juli 1988   *F. J. Hausmann*

Erklärung einzelner Wörterbuchartikel

appointment *n.* ['agreement to meet'] 1. to keep; make an ~ with 2. to break; cancel an ~ 3. by ~ (he will see you by ~) 4. an ~ to + inf. (she had an ~ to see the dean) ['selection'] 5. an ~ to (they announced her ~ to the commission) 6. an ~ as (an ~ as professor) ['position'] 7. to hold; receive an ~ 8. a permanent; temporary ~ ['designation'] 9. by ~ to Her Majesty

— Definition (in Anführungszeichen), bezieht sich auf 1. – 4.

— Definition, bezieht sich auf 5. – 6.
— Definition, bezieht sich auf 7. – 8.
— Definition, bezieht sich auf 9.

clock I *n.* 1. to regulate, set; wind a ~ 2. to advance a ~; or: to set, turn a ~ ahead (by one hour) 3. to set, turn a ~ back (by ten minutes) 4. an alarm; cuckoo; electric; grandfather; wall ~ 5. a biological ~ 6. a ~ is fast; right; slow 7. a ~ gains time; goes; keeps time; loses time; runs down; stops 8. a ~ strikes the hour 9. (misc.) to watch the ~ ('to wait impatiently for the end of the working day'); to work around the ~ ('to work without rest'); the ~ ran out ('the allotted time expired'); to stop the ~ ('to suspend play in a game so that the clock stops running')

— 1. – 8. = Kollokationen

9. = Idioms

concerned *adj.* 1. deeply, greatly ~ 2. ~ about, for, over; with (~ about safety) 3. (esp. BE) ~ to + inf. (~ to know your decision) 4. ~ that + clause (we are ~ that they might have missed the train) 5. (misc.) as far as I'm ~ USAGE NOTE: The phrases *concerned about, concerned over* and less frequently, *concerned for,* mean 'worried about' (concerned about your safety). The phrase *concerned with* means 'interested in' (concerned with establishing the truth).

— 2. – 4. = Konstruktionen

USAGE NOTE enthält eine zusätzliche Erklärung.

— Die Kollokation ist nur im amerikanischen Englisch üblich.

meat *n.* 1. to broil (AE), grill; cook; cure; fry; roast ~ 2. to carve, cut; slice ~ 3. dark; fatty; fresh; halal; kosher; lean; raw; tender; tough; white ~ 4. chopped (AE), ground (AE), minced (BE); soup ~ 5. ~ goes bad, spoils

— Die Kollokation ist nur im britischen Englisch üblich.

excited *adj.* 1. ~ about, at, over (to get ~ about smt.) 2. ~ to + inf. (she was ~ to learn the news) —— Beispielsatz

—————————————— *Phrasal Verb*-Artikel

come out *v.* 1. (d; intr.) to ~ against ('to oppose') (to ~ against a proposal) 2. (d; intr.) to ~ for ('to support') (to ~ for a bill) 3. (d; intr.) to ~ for ('to try out for') (are you ~ing out for the team?) 4. (d; intr.) to ~ with ('to publish') (to ~ with a new book) 5. (P; intr.) ('to end up'); ('to result') to ~ on top ('to be victorious') 6. (s) the pictures came out fine 7. (misc.) to ~ in spots ('to be covered with spots as a result of illness'); they came out from behind the bushes

Kodebuchstaben für die Konstruktion (vgl. S. x)

Vgl. auch das Verzeichnis der Abkürzungen.

Verzeichnis der Abkürzungen

adj.	adjective
adv.	adverb
AE	American English
Am.	American
anat.	anatomical
BE	British English
Br.	British
CE	Common English
cf.	compare („siehe")
colloq.	colloquial („umgangssprachlich")
comm.	commercial
derog.	derogatory („abschätzig")
esp.	especially
fig.	figurative („übertragen")
GB	Great Britain
imper.	imperative

inf.	infinitive
intr.	intransitive
ling.	linguistics
lit.	literary
math.	mathematics
med.	medicine, medical
mil.	military
misc.	miscellaneous („Verschiedenes")
mus.	music
n.	noun („Substantiv")
neg.	negative
obsol.	obsolete („veraltet")
occ.	occasionally („gelegentlich")
pol.	politics, political
pred.	predicative
prep.	preposition
refl.	reflexive
rel.	religion, religious
smb.	somebody
smt.	something
subj.	subjunctive („Konjunktiv")
(T)	Trademark („eingetragenes Warenzeichen")
tr.	transitive
usu.	usually
US	United States
v.	verb

* Das Sternchen kennzeichnet fehlerhaftes Englisch.

Die Buchstaben A, B, C, D, d, E, F, G, H, I, J, K, L, M, N, O, P, Q, R, S, s bezeichnen die verschiedenen Konstruktionstypen der Verben. Zur Erläuterung siehe S. x.

A

aback *adv.* taken ~ (I was taken ~) ('I was startled')

abacus *n.* to operate, use an ~

abandon I *n.* reckless, wild ~

abandon II *v.* (D; tr.) to ~ to (they ~ed us to our fate)

abbreviate *v.* (D; tr.) to ~ to (*Esquire* can be ~d to *Esq.*)

ABC *n.* as easy, simple as ~

abdicate *v.* (D; intr.) to ~ from (the king has ~d from the throne) USAGE NOTE: One can also say--the king has abdicated the throne; most frequently, one simply says--the king has abdicated.

abduct *v.* (D; tr.) to ~ from (to ~ a child from its home)

aberration *n.* a mental ~

abet *v.* (formal) (D; tr.) to ~ in (to ~ smb. in doing smt.; to aid and ~ smb. in doing smt.)

abeyance *n.* (formal) in, into ~ (to hold in ~; to fall into ~)

abhor *v.* 1. (G) he ~s being idle 2. (K) she ~s his smoking

abhorrent *adj.* (formal) ~ to (his behavior was ~ to everyone)

abide *v.* (d; intr.) 1. to ~ by ('to agree to, obey') (we must ~ by her decision) 2. (obsol. and formal) (d; intr.) ('to stay') to ~ with

ability *n.* 1. to demonstrate, display, exhibit, show ~ 2. to appreciate, recognize ~ 3. creative; exceptional, great, outstanding, remarkable; innate, natural; latent ~ 4. an ounce of ~ (he doesn't have an ounce of ~) 5. ~ at, in 6. the ~ to + inf. (the ~ to reason) 7. of ~ (a person of great ~; to the best of one's ~)

ablaze *adj.* 1. ~ with (the city was ~ with lights) 2. to set ~

able *adj.* ~ to + inf. (she was not ~ to reach him) USAGE NOTE: In passive constructions, *able* is replaced by the verb *can*-- he cannot be reached.

ablutions *n.* (formal) to perform one's ~

aboard *adv.* 1. to come; go ~ 2. all ~!

abode *n.* (formal) to take up one's ~

abortion *n.* 1. to do, perform an ~ on 2. to induce an ~ 3. to get, have an ~ 4. (a) criminal, illegal; induced; spontaneous; therapeutic ~; legalized ~

abound *v.* (formal) 1. (d; intr.) to ~ in (this country ~s in opportunities) 2. (d; intr.) to ~ with (the book ~s with misprints)

about I *adj.* (cannot stand alone) ['ready'] 1. ~ to + inf. (the performance is ~ to begin) ['willing'] (colloq.) (AE) 2. not ~ to + inf. (we are not ~ to stop now; we are not ~ to be taken in by their campaign promises) ['misc.'] 3. to set ~ doing smt.

about II *prep.* 1. be quick ~ it ('do it quickly') 2. how/what ~ us?

about-face *n.* (esp. AE) ['sudden change in attitude'] to do an ~

abreast *adj.* (usu. does not stand alone) ~ of (to be ~ of the news; to keep smb. ~ of the latest developments)

abroad *adv.* from ~ (he had to return from ~)

abscond *v.* (D; intr.) to ~ from; with (they ~ed from the country with the funds)

absence *n.* 1. an excused; unexcused ~ 2. ~ from (an unexcused ~ from school) 3. during, in smb.'s ~

absent I *adj.* ~ from (she was ~ from school)

absent II *v.* (D; refl.) to ~ from (to ~ oneself from a meeting)

absentia *n.* in ~ (to be tried in ~)

absolution *n.* (rel.) to grant, pronounce ~ from (to grant ~ from sin)

absolve *v.* (D; tr.) to ~ from (he was ~d from his promise)

absorb *v.* (D; tr.) to ~ into (the small firms were ~ed into large cartels)

absorbed *adj.* 1. deeply, completely, thoroughly, totally ~ 2. ~ by, with; in (she was ~ by/with the problem; the children were ~ in their homework; ~ in thought)

abstain *v.* (D; intr.) to ~ from (to ~ from alcohol)

abstinence *n.* 1. to practice ~ 2. complete, total ~ 3. ~ from (~ from alcohol)

abstract I *n.* in the ~

abstract II *v.* (technical) (D; tr.) to ~ from (to ~ iron from ore)

absurd *adj.* 1. patently; totally ~ 2. ~ to + inf. (it was ~ to leave such a large tip) 3. ~ that + clause (it's ~ that we have to get up so early)

absurdity *n.* it was the height of ~ (to insist on a refund)

abundance *n.* 1. an ~ of (there was an ~ of water power) 2. in ~ (we had food in ~) 3. of ~ (a life of ~)

abundant *adj.* (formal) ~ in (~ in natural resources)

abuse *n.* ['insulting language'] 1. to heap, shower ~ on, upon; to hurl ~ at 2. to take ~ (she took a lot of ~ from him) 3. verbal ~ 4. a shower, stream of ~ 5. a term of ~ ['rough use'] 6. to take ~ (this car has taken a lot of ~) ['mistreatment'] 7. child; personal; sexual ~ ['improper use'] 8. drug ~

abusive *adj.* ~ to (he became ~ to his guests)

abut *v.* (D; intr.) to ~ against, on, upon

abyss *n.* a gaping, yawning ~

academe *n.* (formal) the groves, halls of ~

academy *n.* 1. a military; naval; riding ~ 2. an ~ for (an ~ for boys) 3. at an ~

accede *v.* (D; intr.) to ~ to (they ~d to our demands)

accelerator *n.* 1. to depress, step on an ~ 2. to ease up, let up on an ~

accent *n.* ['pronunciation'] 1. to affect, assume, imitate, put on; cultivate an ~ 2. to speak with an ~ 3. to get rid of an ~ 4. a foreign; heavy, noticeable, pronounced, strong, thick; slight ~ ['stress'] 5. to place, put the ~ on (to place the ~ on a syllable) 6. (ling.) an acute; grave; pitch, tonic ~ (see also **stress)**

accept v. 1. to ~ blindly; fully; readily 2. (D; tr.) to ~ as (they ~ed us as their equals) 3. (formal) (BE) (L) I ~ that the proposal may be defeated

acceptable adj. 1. completely, fully; mutually ~ 2. ~ to (the conditions are ~ to all concerned)

acceptance n. 1. blind ~ (blind ~ of dogma) 2. universal ~ (to meet with universal ~)

access n. 1. to gain, get ~ 2. to deny ~ 3. direct; easy, free, unlimited; limited ~ 4. (computers) random ~ 5. ~ to (we gained/got ~ to the files; ~ to a building)

accessary (esp. BE) see **accessory 1, 2**

accessibility n. ~ to (the professor's ~ to all students)

accessible adj. 1. easily ~ 2. ~ to (the stacks are ~ to the public; the director is ~ to everyone)

accession n. 1. on one's ~ (on his ~ to the throne he inherited vast estates) 2. ~ to (her ~ to power)

accessory n. ['accomplice'] 1. an ~ to (an ~ to a crime) 2. (legal) an ~ before the fact; an ~ after the fact ['optional equipment'] 3. auto (AE); matching; skiing; smoking ~ries

accident n. ['unexpected, unpleasant event'] ['catastrophe'] 1. to have, meet with an ~ (they had an ~ during their trip) 2. to prevent ~s 3. an awful, bad, dreadful, frightful, horrible, nasty, serious, shocking; fatal; near; unavoidable; unfortunate ~ 4. an automobile (AE), motorcar (BE); hit-and-run; hunting; industrial; railroad (AE), railway (BE), train ~ 5. an ~ occurs, takes place (a bad ~ took place) 6. in an ~ (he was in a hunting ~) ['chance'] ['luck'] 7. pure, sheer ~ 8. an ~ that + clause (it was pure ~ that we met) 9. by ~ (we discovered it by ~; it was by pure ~ that we found the money)

acclaim v. (N; used with a noun) the mob ~ed him emperor

acclamation n. by ~ (to elect smb. by ~)

acclimate (AE) see **acclimatize**

acclimatize v. (D; intr., refl., tr.) to ~ to (we ~d quickly/~d ourselves quickly to the jungle; he became ~d to the new surroundings)

accolade n. 1. to bestow an ~ on 2. the ultimate ~

accommodate v. (D; intr., refl., tr.) to ~ to (they ~d easily to the new conditions)

accommodation I n. ['agreement'] ['adjustment'] 1. to come to, make; reach, work out an ~ 2. an ~ between; on; to; with (to make an ~ to wartime conditions; to reach an ~ with neighboring countries)

accommodation II (BE) see **accommodations**

accommodations n. (AE) ['place to live'] 1. to secure; seek ~ 2. deluxe; first-class; hotel; second-class; travel ~

accompaniment n. 1. an ~ to (a piano ~ to a song) 2. to the ~ of (to the ~ of soft music)

accompany v. (D; tr.) to ~ on (to ~ a singer on the piano)

accomplice n. 1. an unwitting ~ 2. an ~ in, to (an ~ in crime)

accomplished adj. ~ at

accomplishment n. 1. see **achievement 1** for adjective + noun collocations 2. no mean ~ 3. an

~ to + inf. (it was a real ~ to defeat them) 4. of ~ (a man, woman of many ~s)

accord I n. 1. to come to, reach an ~ 2. an ~ with smb. about smt. (we reached an ~ with the neighboring country about our common border) 3. an ~ that + clause (they came to an ~ that profits would be shared equally) 4. in ~ with 5. (formal) of one's own ~ (he participated of his own ~)

accord II v. (formal) 1. (A) we ~ed a hero's welcome to him; or: we ~ed him a hero's welcome 2. (rare) (d; intr.) to ~ with (our information does not ~ with his report)

accordance n. in ~ with (in ~ with your instructions)

account I n. ['description'] ['report'] 1. to give, render an ~ 2. an accurate, true; biased, one-sided; blow-by-blow, detailed, full; eyewitness; fictitious; first-hand; running; vivid ~ (she gave a detailed ~ of the incident) 3. newspaper, press ~s (according to press ~s) 4. by all ~s ['explanation'] 5. to call smb. to ~ ['consideration'] 6. to take ~ of smt; to take smt. into ~ ['business arrangement'] ['record of a business arrangement'] 7. to open an ~ 8. to keep an ~ (I keep an ~ in that bank) 9. to charge smb.'s ~ 10. to balance; close; settle an ~ 11. to overdraw an ~ 12. to pay smt. into an ~ 13. to charge smt. to an ~ 14. an active; blocked; charge (AE), credit (BE); checking (AE), current (BE); deposit (BE), savings; dollar; expense; inactive; individual retirement (AE); joint; money-market; outstanding ~ 15. in an ~ (the funds were in her ~) 16. on ~ (to put smt. on smb.'s ~) ['dispute'] 17. to settle an ~ (I have an ~ to settle with him) 18. an old ~ ['sake'] 19. on smb.'s ~ (do not refuse on my ~) 20. on ~ of (he did it on ~ of me) ['showing'] ['performance'] 21. to give a good ~ of oneself ['misc.'] 22. on no ~ ('under no circumstances')

account II v. 1. (d; intr.) to ~ for ('to explain') (he could not ~ for the missing funds; how do you ~ for the accident?) 2. (d; intr.) to ~ for ('to cause the destruction of') (our battery ~ed for three enemy planes)

accountable adj. 1. strictly ~ 2. ~ for; to (we are ~ to our parents for our actions) 3. to hold smb. ~ for smt.

accountant n. a certified public (AE), chartered (BE) ~

accounting n. 1. to give, render an ~ 2. a strict ~ 3. cost ~

accounts n. ['books'] 1. to keep ~ ['record of transactions'] 2. ~ payable; receivable ['differences'] 3. to settle, square ~

accredit v. (D; tr.) to ~ to (our envoy was ~ed to their new government)

accrue v. (D; intr.) to ~ to (the interest ~d to our account)

accuracy n. 1. historical; reasonable; scientific; strict, total ~ 2. ~ in

accurate adj. 1. fairly; strictly ~ 2. ~ to + inf. (it would be ~ to say that he is lazy)

accusation n. 1. to bring, make an ~ against (he brought an ~ of theft against Smith; more usu. is: he accused Smith of theft) 2. to deny; refute an ~

3. a damaging, grave; false, groundless, unfounded, unjust; sweeping ~ 4. an ~ against; of (an ~ of gross negligence) 5. an ~ that + clause (he denied the ~ that he had accepted bribes)

accuse v. (D; tr.) to ~ of (he was ~d of murder)

accused adj. to stand ~

accustom v. (d; refl., tr.) to ~ to (we had to ~ ourselves to the new working conditions; more usu. is: we had to get ~ed to the new working conditions)

accustomed adj. (cannot stand alone) ~ to (~ to hard work; ~ to walking long distances; he got ~ to the warm climate)

ace n. ['a serve that an opponent cannot touch'] (tennis) 1. to score an ~ ['expert combat pilot'] 2. a flying ~ ['misc.'] 3. within an ~ of ('very close to'); an ~ in the hole ('a concealed advantage')

ache I n. a dull; steady ~ (he felt a dull ~ in his shoulder) (see **backache, earache, headache, stomachache, toothache**)

ache II v. 1. (d; intr.) 1. to ~ for (to ~ for company) 2. (E) he is ~ing to get even

achievement n. 1. a brilliant, crowning, dazzling, epic, glorious, great, lasting, magnificent, major, memorable, monumental, notable, outstanding, phenomenal, remarkable, signal, superb, wonderful ~ 2. an ~ in (outstanding ~s in science)

acid n. 1. corrosive, strong ~ 2. boric; citric; hydrochloric; sulfuric ~ 3. ~ corrodes

acknowledge v. 1. to ~ gratefully 2. (B) the author ~d her debt to her research assistants 3. (D; tr.) to ~ as (she ~d him as her heir) 4. (G) he ~d being ignorant of the facts 5. (K) he ~d my being the first to think of it 6. (L; to) she ~d (to us) that she was to blame 7. (rare) (M) they ~d us to be the winners of the contest 8. (formal and rare) (N; used with a past participle) he ~d himself defeated

acknowledgment n. 1. to make an ~ of 2. a frank; grateful; public ~ 3. in ~ of

acme n. to attain, reach the ~ of

acquaint v. 1. to ~ thoroughly 2. (D; refl, tr.) to ~ with (the lawyer ~ed herself with the facts of the case)

acquaintance n. ['familiarity'] 1. to have an ~ with (he has some ~ with statistics) 2. a slight, superficial ~ 3. on ~ (on closer ~ he proved to be a nice person) 4. an ~ with ['casual friendship'] 5. to make smb.'s ~ 6. to keep up; renew; strike up an ~ with 7. a casual, nodding, passing, slight ~ (to have a nodding ~ with smb.) ['friend'] 8. a casual ~

acquaintanceship n. 1. to strike up an ~ with 2. a casual; close, intimate ~ 3. an ~ with

acquainted adj. 1. casually; closely, intimately, thoroughly ~ 2. ~ with (he got/became ~ with the situation; are you ~ with him?)

acquiesce v. (D; intr.) to ~ in, to (they ~d in the decision) USAGE NOTE: Some purists feel that the collocation *acquiesce to* is now old-fashioned.

acquiescence n. 1. complete, total ~ 2. ~ in, to (~ in a decision)

acquisition n. 1. to make an ~ 2. (BE) an ~ to (he is a valuable ~ to our firm)

acquit v. 1. (D; tr.) ('to exonerate') to ~ of (the jury ~ted her of all charges) 2. (P; refl.) ('to behave') she ~ted herself well; he ~ted himself like a veteran

acquittal n. (legal) to bring in an ~ (the jury brought in an ~)

acrimony n. bitter, sharp ~

acrobatics n. 1. to perform ~ 2. (fig.) mental ~

acronym n. to form an ~

act I n. ['action'] 1. to commit, perform an ~ 2. a barbaric, barbarous; courageous; criminal; foolish, rash; heroic, noble; humane; illegal; impulsive; justified; kind; overt; statesmanlike; thoughtful ~ (she performed an heroic ~) 3. an ~ of (an ~ of faith; he committed an ~ of folly) 4. in the ~ (caught in the ~) ['performance'] 5. a circus; nightclub; variety (BE), vaudeville (AE) ~ 6. (misc.) to put on an ~ ('to pretend') ['misc.'] 7. to get into the ~ ('to participate')

act II v. 1. to ~ impulsively; irresponsibly; responsibly 2. (d; intr.) ('to serve') to ~ as (she ~ed as our interpreter) 3. (d; intr.) to ~ for ('to replace') and esp. BE ('to represent as one's lawyer') 4. (d; intr.) ('to behave') to ~ like (the soldier ~ed like a real hero) 5. (D; intr.) ('to take action') to ~ on, upon (to ~ on smb.'s advice; to ~ on a request) 6. (d; intr.) ('to take action') to ~ out of (they ~ed out of fear) 7. (d; intr.) ('to behave') to ~ towards (how did they ~ towards you?) 8. (P; intr.) ('to behave') the soldier ~ed bravely

action n. ['activity'] ['act'] 1. to initiate; take ~; to go into ~ 2. to put smt. into ~ (we put our plan into ~) 3. to prod, spur smb. into ~ 4. concerted, united; decisive; direct; disciplinary; drastic; emergency; hasty, rash; immediate, prompt; remedial; vigorous ~ (we must take immediate ~) 5. (AE) affirmative ~ ('giving preference to members of minority groups') 6. industrial (BE), (E) job (AE) ~ ('a protest by workers') 7. congressional; political ~ 8. a reflex ~ ['combat; military or police activity'] 9. to go into ~ 10. to see ~ ('to participate in combat') 11. to break off ~ 12. to take evasive ~ ('to maneuver in order to escape enemy fire') 13. enemy ~; a delaying; holding; police; punitive; rearguard ~ 14. in ~ (killed in ~) 15. out of ~ (two tanks were put out of ~) ['lawsuit'] 16. to bring, institute, take ~ against smb. for smt. (he brought legal ~ against his neighbor) 17. to dismiss an ~ (the judge dismissed the ~) 18. a civil; class; legal ~ ['initiative'] ['enterprise'] 19. a man, woman of ~ ['plot of a play, novel'] 20. the ~ drags; picks up (the ~ picks up in the third act) ['misc.'] 21. (colloq.) a piece of the ~ ('participation in an activity') (he wants a piece of the ~)

activity n. 1. to engage in, participate in, take part in an ~ (all students take part in extracurricular ~ties) 2. to resume one's ~ties 3. to break off, terminate an ~ 4. to curb; paralyze ~ (business was paralyzed) 5. bustling, constant, feverish, furious, uninterrupted ~ 6. behind-the-scenes; business, economic; cultural; intellectual; physical; political; scientific; subversive; terrorist ~ 7. extracurricular; recreational; social; union ~ties

8. to buzz, hum with ~ 9. a burst of ~
actor, actress *n.* 1. to cast an ~ 2. a character ~
act up *v.* (D; intr.) ('to function badly') to ~ on (my leg has been ~ing up on me)
acuity *n.* mental; visual ~
acumen *n.* 1. to demonstrate, display ~ 2. business; legal ~ 3. the ~ to + inf. (she had enough ~ to see through the scheme)
acupuncture *n.* to do, perform ~
ad *n.* a classified, small (BE); help-wanted; want ~ (see also **advertisement)**
adage *n.* an old ~
adamant *adj.* 1. ~ about; in 2. ~ that + clause; subj. when the subjects of the clauses are different (he was ~ that he was fit to go; she was ~ that he not go)
adapt *v.* 1. (D; tr.) to ~ for; from (to ~ a novel for the stage; to ~ a film from a novel) 2. (D; intr., refl., tr.) to ~ to (we ~ed quickly to life in Paris; she had to ~ herself to local conditions)
adaptation *n.* 1. to make an ~ 2. an ~ for (an ~ of a novel for television)
add *v.* 1. (D; intr., tr.) to ~ to (we ~ed this amount to the bill; these changes ~ed to the confusion) 2. (L) she ~ed that she would not bring the children
addendum *n.* an ~ to
addict *n.* a confirmed; drug ~
addicted *adj.* 1. chronically, hopelessly ~ 2. ~ to (~ to drugs)
addiction *n.* 1. chronic, hopeless ~ 2. (an) ~ to (~ to drugs)
adding machine *n.* to operate, use an ~
addition *n.* ['adding of numbers'] 1. to do ~ ['part added'] 2. to make an ~ 3. an ~ to (an ~ to the family; an ~ to a report) 4. in ~ to (in ~ to his salary, he earns a lot from royalties)
add on *v.* (D; tr.) to ~ to (to ~ a garage to the house)
address I *n.* ['speech'] 1. to deliver, give an ~ 2. an eloquent, moving, stirring ~ 3. an inaugural; keynote ~ 4. an ~ about, concerning ['place of residence'] ['place for receiving mail'] 5. to change one's ~ 6. a business; forwarding; home; permanent; return; temporary ~ 7. at an ~ (at what ~ does she live?)
address II *v.* 1. (B) she ~ed her remarks to us; I ~ed the letter to him 2. (d; tr.) to ~ as (you should ~ him as 'sir') 3. (d; tr.) to ~ to (~ her mail to this post-office box) 4. (d; refl.) ('to refer') to ~ to (the candidates did not ~ themselves to the issues)
add up *v.* (d; intr.) to ~ to (it all ~s up to a hoax; the figures ~ to 50)
adept *adj.* ~ at, in (~ at solving crossword puzzles)
adequate *adj.* 1. ~ for (the food was ~ for all of us) 2. ~ to (she was ~ to the task) 3. ~ to + inf. (it would be ~ to list just the basic objections)
adhere *v.* 1. to ~ closely, doggedly, strictly, stubbornly, tenaciously 2. (d; intr.) to ~ to (to ~ strictly to a plan)
adherence *n.* 1. close, strict ~ 2. ~ to (strict ~ to a plan)
adieu *n.* to bid smb. ~

adjacent *adj.* ~ to (~ to our building)
adjective *n.* 1. to compare an ~ 2. an attributive; descriptive; possessive; predicate, predicative ~ 3. ~s modify nouns
adjourn *v.* 1. (D; intr.) ('to stop') to ~ for (to ~ for lunch) 2. (d; intr.) ('to move') (to ~ to the living room for brandy)
adjudge *v.* (formal) (M and N; used with an adjective) the court ~d him (to be) guilty
adjunct *n.* an ~ to (an adverb is usually an ~ to a verb)
adjure *v.* (formal) (H) to ~ smb. to tell the truth
adjust *v.* (D. intr., tr.) to ~ to (he had to ~ to the new climate; we ~ed our watches to local time)
adjuster *n.* an insurance ~
adjustment *n.* 1. to make an ~ 2. an ~ in, of (an ~ in/of his salary; an ~ of the brakes) 3. an ~ to (an ~ to a new environment)
adjutant *n.* an ~ general
administer *v.* 1. (B) ('to give') to ~ an oath to smb. 2. (d; intr.) to ~ to ('to help with') (to ~ to smb.'s needs)
administration *n.* ['management'] 1. business; public ~ ['government'] 2. a centralized; civil; colonial; decentralized; federal ~
administrator *n.* a civil; school ~
admiral *n.* a rear; vice ~; a fleet ~ (US); an ~ of the fleet (GB)
admiration *n.* 1. to arouse, win; command ~ 2. to express; feel ~ 3. blind; deep, great, sincere, strong, undying; grudging; mutual; ungrudging ~ 4. ~ for (he felt great ~ for them) 5. in, with ~ (to look at smb. with ~)
admire *v.* 1. to ~ greatly, very much 2. (D; tr.) to ~ for (we ~ her for her tact) 3. (K) they all ~d his behaving in that manner
admirer *n.* an ardent, devoted, enthusiastic, fervent, sincere; secret ~
admission *n.* ['access'] 1. to apply for; gain; seek ~ 2. to deny, refuse ~ 3. free, open; restricted, selective ~; rolling (esp. AE) ~s 4. ~ to (she applied for ~ to the university) ['confession'] 5. to make an ~ of (he made an ~ of guilt) 6. a damaging ~ 7. an ~ that + clause (his ~ that he had been at the scene of the crime led to his conviction) 8. by, on smb.'s own ~ ['entry fee'] 9. general ~
admit *v.* 1. to ~ readily 2. (B) ('to confess') the accused ~ted his guilt to the police 3. (D; tr.) ('to allow entry') to ~ into, to (the manager ~ted him to the theater; she was ~ted to the university) 4. (formal) (d; intr.) ('to tolerate') to ~ of (the situation ~s of no delay) 5. (formal) (d; intr.) ('to confess') to ~ to (he ~ted to his complicity in the crime; the boy ~ted to stealing the apples) 6. (G) ('to confess') the employee ~ted stealing the money 7. (L; to) ('to confess') the clerk ~ted (to the police) that he had taken the jewels
admittance *n.* 1. to gain ~ to 2. to deny ~ to (he was denied ~ to the concert)
admonish *v.* (formal) 1. (D; tr.) to ~ for (the teacher ~ed the child for coming late to school) 2. (H) to ~ smb. to do smt.
ado *n.* 1. to make (much) ~ about, over 2. without much ~

adopt *v.* (D; tr.) to ~ as (they ~ed the child as their heir)

adoption *n.* to put up for ~ (to put a child up for ~)

adore *v.* 1. (D; tr.) to ~ for (we ~ them for their generosity) 2. (G) she ~s visiting museums

adrift *adj., adv.* to cast, turn ~

adroit *adj.* ~ at, in (~ at staying out of trouble)

adroitness *n.* ~ at, in (~ at giving injections)

adultery *n.* to commit ~ with

adulthood *n.* to reach ~

adults *n.* consenting ~

advance I *n.* ['forward movement'] 1. (usu. mil.) to make; press an ~ 2. (usu. mil.) an ~ against, on, to, towards (our troops made an ~ against the enemy) 3. an ~ in (~ in science) 4. an ~ into (an ~ into new territory) ['early payment'] 5. to receive an ~ 6. to pay an ~ 7. an ~ on (to receive an ~ on royalties) ['misc.'] 8. she paid her rent in ~; in ~ of the main party

advance II *v.* 1. (A) we ~d a month's salary to him; or: we ~d him a month's salary 2. (D; intr.) to ~ against, on, to, towards (our troops ~d on the next town) 3. (D; tr.) to ~ to (he was ~d to the rank of corporal)

advanced *adj.* ~ in (~ in industrial development)

advancement *n.* 1. to further, speed smb.'s ~ 2. to block smb.'s ~ 3. professional ~ 4. rapid, slow ~

advances *n.* ['effort to become friendly or to enter into negotiations'] 1. to make ~ to (he made ~ to her; the Americans made ~ to the Russians) 2. to rebuff, reject smb.'s ~

advantage *n.* 1. to have an ~ of; over (our team had the ~ of experience; her connections gave her an ~ over the others) 2. to gain; press (home) an ~ 3. to take ~ of ('to exploit') 4. to outweigh an ~ 5. a clear, decided; mutual; unfair ~ 6. an ~ to (his wealth was an obvious ~ to us) 7. an ~ to + inf. (it was an ~ to have that team as our opponent in the first round = it was an ~ having that team as our opponent in the first round) 8. an ~ that + clause; subj. (it was to his ~ that she not participate) 9. to smb.'s ~; used to good ~ (see also 8) 10. at an ~ 11. (tennis) ~ in; ~ out 12. (misc.) (BE) you have the ~ of me ('you know more than I do')

advantageous *adj.* 1. clearly ~ 2. ~ to (his decision was ~ to us) 3. ~ to + inf. (it would be ~ to wait)

adventure *n.* 1. to have, meet with an ~ 2. a bold; breathtaking, exciting, real, thrilling ~; high ~ 3. an ~ to + inf. (it was an ~ to visit that place = it was an ~ visiting that place)

adventurer *n.* a bold, dauntless, intrepid ~

adverb *n.* an interrogative; negative ~

adversary *n.* a formidable, worthy ~

adverse *adj.* (formal) ~ to (~ to our interests)

adversity *n.* to face; overcome ~

advert I (BE) see **advertisement**

advert II *v.* (formal and rare) (d; intr.) ('to refer') to ~ to

advertise *v.* 1. (D; intr.) to ~ for (to ~ for a maid) 2. (L) they ~d that a position was open

advertisement *n.* 1. to place, publish, run an ~ for (to run an ~ for a used car) 2. a classified; full-

page ~

advertising *n.* classified; outdoor; word-of-mouth ~

advice *n.* 1. to give, offer ~ 2. to act on, follow, take ~ 3. to disregard, refuse, turn a deaf ear to ~ 4. friendly; good, sage, sensible, sound; misleading; parting; professional; unsolicited ~ 5. a bit, piece, word of ~ 6. ~ about, on 7. ~ to (my ~ to him was that...) 8. ~ to + inf. (we took his ~ to remain silent) 9. ~ that + clause; subj. (my ~ is that you see/should see a doctor) 10. against smb.'s ~ 11. on, upon smb.'s ~ (on ~ of counsel; I acted on her ~)

advisable *adj.* ~ to + inf. (it was ~ to leave immediately)

advise *v.* 1. to ~ strongly 2. (D; tr.) to ~ about, on 3. (d; intr., tr.) to ~ against (to ~ smb. against a course of action) 4. (formal) (d; tr.) to ~ of ('to ~ smb. of the facts) 5. (G) who ~d making that statement? 6. (H) she ~d us not to wait 7. (K) who ~d his making that statement? 8. (L; must have an object) she ~d us that we should leave 9. (Q; must have an object) he ~d us what to do

advisement *n.* (often legal) to take smt. under ~

adviser, advisor *n.* 1. an economic; financial; legal; political; senior; spiritual; technical ~ 2. an ~ on; to (an ~ on foreign affairs; an ~ to the president)

advisory *adj.* ~ to

advocate I *n.* 1. an aggressive, strong ~ 2. a client, patient; consumer ~ 3. the devil's ~

advocate II *v.* 1. (G) he ~d bringing legal action 2. (K) she ~d our withdrawing from the contest 3. (formal) (L; subj.) they ~d that one candidate withdraw

aegis *n.* under smb.'s ~

aerial *n.* (BE) a television, TV ~ (AE has **antenna**)

aeroplane (BE) see **airplane**

aether (BE) see **ether**

afar *adv.* from ~

affair *n.* ['romantic liaison'] 1. to carry on, have an ~ with 2. a casual; clandestine, secret; illicit; love; tempestuous ~ ['matter'] ['event'] 3. to investigate an ~ 4. to cover up, hush up an ~; to wash one's hands of an ~ 5. a delicate; private; sinister, sordid, ugly ~ 6. an ~ of honor ['social event'] 7. a dull; exciting; formal; gala; informal ~

affairs *n.* 1. to administer, conduct ~ (of state) 2. to arrange; manage; settle; straighten out one's ~ 3. civil; community; cultural; current; domestic, internal; external, foreign; international; legal; military; national; political; public; veterans ~

affect *v.* 1. to ~ smb. deeply, profoundly, strongly 2. (formal and rare) (BE) (E) he ~ed not to hear

affection *n.* 1. to demonstrate, display, show; return ~ 2. to feel ~ 3. to gain, win smb.'s ~ (she won the children's ~) 4. deep, strong, warm ~ 5. ~ for (to feel ~ for smb.)

affectionate *adj.* ~ to, towards, with (~ with children)

affections *n.* to alienate smb.'s ~

affidavit *n.* (legal) to file an ~ (the lawyer filed an ~ on behalf of her client)

affiliate v. (D; refl., tr.) to ~ to, with (to ~ oneself with a movement; they are ~d with the national committee; to become ~d with)

affiliation n. 1. to form an ~ with 2. business; labor; party, political ~s

affinity n. 1. to demonstrate, show (an) ~ 2. to feel; have (an) ~ 3. (a) close; elective; natural; strong ~ 4. ~ between; for; to; with (he always felt a close ~ with the underdog)

affirm v. 1. to ~ categorically 2. (L) the ministry ~ed that the visit had been postponed

affirmative n. to reply in the ~

affix v. (D; tr.) to ~ to (to ~ one's signature to a document)

afflicted adj. 1. grievously ~ 2. ~ with (~ with a disease)

affluence n. in ~ (to live in ~)

affluent adj. ~ in (~ in worldly goods)

afford v. 1. to well ~ 2. (formal) (A) it ~ed great pleasure to him; or: it ~ed him great pleasure 3.(E; preceded by the forms: can -- cannot -- can't -- could) we cannot ~ to buy a new house; we can ill ~ to lose this contract 4. (formal) (K; preceded by the forms: can -- cannot -- can't -- could) we could not ~ his signing up for another course

affront n. 1. (formal) to suffer an ~ 2. a shocking ~ 3. an ~ to (it was an ~ to common decency)

afloat adj. 1. to keep smt. ~ 2. to set (a ship) ~

aflutter adj. (colloq.) 1. all ~ 2. ~ with (~ with excitement)

afoul adv. to run ~ of (to run ~ of the law) (also **foul** II)

afraid adj. 1. deathly, terribly ~ 2. ~ of (the child was ~ of the dark) 3. ~ to + inf. (he was ~ to dive from the high board) 4. ~ that + clause (we were ~ that he would find out) 5. (misc.) is it true? I'm ~ so

after, afterwards adv. shortly ~

afterburners n. to activate, go to ~ (our interceptors had to go to ~)

aftermath n. 1. a grim ~ 2. an ~ of, to 3. in the ~ (in the ~ of/to that incident, he had to leave town)

afternoon n. in the ~; ~s (AE), on any ~; on Wednesday ~

aftershave n. to apply, put on; use ~

aftertaste n. 1. to leave an ~ 2. a nice, pleasant; unpleasant ~ (it left a pleasant ~)

agape adj. (formal) ['gaping'] ~ with (~ with excitement)

age n. ['stage of life'] 1. to live to, reach an ~ 2. an advanced, (ripe) old, venerable ~ (she lived to a ripe old ~) 3. an early, tender, young ~ (at an early ~; at a very young ~) 4. middle ~ 5. (a) college; high-school (AE); preschool; school ~ 6. (a) retirement, retiring (BE) ~ 7. a legal ~; the ~ of consent 8. at an ~ (at a tender ~; at the ~ of six) 9. of an ~ (people of all ~s) 10. (misc.) to come of ~ ('to reach one's majority'); to look one's ~ ('to not have a youthful appearance') ['era'] ['period'] 11. to usher in an ~ (to usher in the computer ~) 12. a golden; heroic ~ 13. the Dark; Middle ~s (during the Middle ~s) 14. the Bronze; Ice; Iron; nuclear; Stone ~ 15. in an ~ (in the nuclear ~) 16. for ~s 17. through the ~s

agency n. 1. an advertising; detective; employment; government; health-care; home-health; intelligence; law-enforcement; news; private; public; regulatory; ticket; travel; voluntary; watchdog; welfare ~ 2. at an ~ (she works at a travel ~)

agenda n. 1. to draw up, make up an ~ 2. to place, put smt. on the ~ (to put an item on the ~) 3. a hidden ~

agent n. ['representative'] 1. a double; enemy; estate (BE), land (BE), real-estate (AE); free; insurance; literary; press; purchasing; rental; secret, undercover; shipping; special; ticket (AE; BE has *booking clerk*) ~ 2. an ~ provocateur 3. an ~ for (an ~ for a large firm) ['substance'] 4. an asphyxiating; chemical ~

aggrandizement n. territorial ~

aggregate n. in the ~

aggression n. ['attack'] 1. to commit ~ against 2. to repel, repulse ~ 3. armed; brazen, naked, outright, stark, unprovoked ~ ['aggressiveness'] 4. to manifest ~ 5. to control, stifle ~ 6. deep-seated, hidden, deep-rooted ~ 7. an act of ~ (to commit an act of ~)

aghast adj. ~ at (~ at the very thought of going back to work)

agitate v. 1. to ~ strongly 2. (D; intr.) to ~ against; for (they were ~ing for reform)

agitation n. 1. political; student; subversive ~ 2. ~ against; for

agitator n. a political ~

aglow adj. ~ with (~ with happiness)

ago adv. ~ that + clause (it was five years ~ that we met)

agog adj. ~ over; with (she was all ~ over her new granddaughter)

agonize v. (D; intr.) to ~ over (to ~ over a decision)

agony n. 1. to experience, feel ~ 2. to prolong the ~ 3. acute, deep, great, indescribable, untold; mortal~ ~ 4. in ~ (in great ~)

agree v. 1. ('to concur') to ~ completely, entirely, fully, wholeheartedly; readily 2. (D; intr.) ('to concur') to ~ about; on, to; with (to ~ with smb. about smt.; to ~ on/to a compromise) 3. (d; intr.) (of food, climate) to ~ with ('to suit') (the food doesn't ~ with me) 4. (grammar) (D; intr.) ('to correspond') to ~ in; with (Latin adjectives ~ with nouns in gender) 5. (E) ('to consent') they ~d to help 6. (L) ('to concur') we ~d that everyone would receive an equal share

agreeable adj. 1. mutually ~ 2. ~ to (they were all ~ to our proposal; is this ~ to you?)

agreement n. ['contract, settlement, treaty'] 1. to come to, conclude, enter into, negotiate, reach, work out an ~ 2. to carry out an ~ 3. to break, violate; denounce an ~ 4. a binding; contractual; ironclad; legal; tacit; tentative ~ (we reached a tentative ~) 5. an armistice; ceasefire; sales; trade ~ 6. a bilateral; executive; gentleman's ~ 7. an ~ about, on; between; with (an ~ was worked out between them on all points) 8. an ~ to + inf. (we reached an ~ with them to cooperate fully at all times) 9. an ~ that + clause (the negotiatiors came to an ~ that all troops would be withdrawn) ['concord, harmony'] 10. to express; reach ~ 11. complete, full, solid; mutual; tacit ~ (they reached full ~ on all points) 12. ~ about, on 13. by ~ (by mutual ~) 14. in ~ (we were in full ~ with them on all points) ['grammatical concord'] 15. grammatical ~ 16. ~ in (~ in case, gender, and number)

aground *adj., adv.* to run ~ (the ship ran ~)

ahead *adj., adv.* 1. far ~ 2. ~ by (our team was ~ by three points) 3. ~ of (~ of one's competitors) 4. (misc.) straight ~; full speed ~

aid I *n.* 1. to extend, give, offer, provide, render ~ 2. to come to smb.'s ~ 3. to cut off, withdraw ~ 4. generous, unstinting ~ 5. audiovisual; teaching ~s 6. first ~ (first ~ to the injured) 7. a hearing ~ 8. economic; foreign; government ~ 9. legal ~ (for the poor) 10. (an) ~ for; in; to (an ~ to memorization; economic ~ to developing countries) 11. (misc.) to enlist smb.'s ~

aid II *v.* 1. (D; tr.) to ~ in (she ~ed him in his work) 2. (rare) (H) to ~ smb. to do smt. 3. (misc.) to ~ and abet

aide *n.* 1. a home (BE), home health (AE); presidential ~ 2. an ~ to

AIDS *n.* to contract, get ~

ailment *n.* a chronic; common; minor ~

aim I *n.* ['purpose'] ['goal'] 1. to achieve one's ~ 2. a chief; immediate; long-range ~ 3. idealistic, lofty ~s 4. an ~ to + inf. (it was our ~ to complete the work before the end of the month)['aiming of a weapon'] 5. to take ~ at 6. careful; steady ~ (she took careful ~ at the intruder)

aim II *v.* 1. (D; intr., tr.) to ~ at (he ~ed at me; I ~ed the revolver at the intruder) 2. (d; intr.) to ~ for (he ~ed for the heart; she was ~ing for a promotion) 3. (E) we ~ to please

air I *n.* ['atmosphere'] 1. to clear the ~ 2. to breathe, inhale ~ 3. to pollute the ~ 4. balmy, mild; bracing, brisk, crisp, refreshing; compressed; country; dry; foul; fresh; humid; polar; polluted; stale ~ 5. a breath of (fresh) ~; a blast of hot ~ 6. in the ~ (the decisive battles were fought in the ~) ['transportation by aircraft'] 7. by ~ (to travel by ~) ['medium through which radio signals are transmitted'] 8. on the ~ (to go on the ~; our station is on the ~) 9. off the ~ (that station never goes off the ~) ['appearance'] 10. to assume an ~ (to assume an ~ of innocence) 11. a detached; knowing; nonchalant; superior; triumphant ~ ['tune'] 12. a martial ~ (the band struck up a martial ~) ['misc.'] 13. in the ~ ('imminent'); to walk on ~ ('to be elated'); to give smb. the ~ ('to reject smb.'); up in the ~ ('unsettled'); to disappear into thin ~

air II *v.* (B) he is ready to ~ his views to anyone

air conditioner *n.* 1. to run; turn on an ~ 2. to turn off an ~ 3. a central; room ~ 4. the ~ was or, was running

air conditioning *n.* central ~

aircraft *n.* enemy; friendly; unidentified ~

airline *n.* a domestic; feeder; international; overseas; local ~

airmail *n.* by ~ (to send a letter by ~)

airplane, aeroplane *n.* 1. to board; take an ~ 2. to

bring down, land; ditch; fly, pilot; hijack; navigate an ~ (a pilot flies an ~) 3. to bring down, shoot down an ~ (our fire brought down an enemy ~) 4. a jet; propeller-driven ~ 5. an ~ crashes; cruises; flies; gains altitude; lands, touches down; levels off; loses altitude; reaches an altitude; taxes off; taxis along the runway

airport *n.* at an ~

air raid *n.* to carry out, conduct an ~ against

airs *n.* ['affected manners'] to give oneself, put on ~

air show *n.* to hold, put on, stage an ~

air superiority *n.* 1. to establish ~ 2. complete, overwhelming, total ~

aisle *n.* 1. to clear the ~s 2. in the ~ (don't stand in the ~) 3. on the ~ (to sit on the ~)

ajar *adj.* to leave ~ (she left the door ~)

akin *adj.* (formal) (usu. does not stand alone) ~ to (a feeling ~ to love)

alarm *n.* ['warning device'] ['warning'] 1. to activate; give, send in, set off, sound; set an ~ (she set the ~ to go off at five) 2. to deactivate, turn off an ~ 3. a burglar; fire; silent; smoke ~ 4. a false ~ 5. an ~ goes off, rings, sounds ['apprehension, fear'] 6. to express; feel ~ 7. to cause ~ (the incident caused great ~) 8. ~ at (to express ~ at the danger of war)

alarm clock *n.* 1. to set an ~ 2. an ~ goes off; rings, sounds

alarmed *adj.* ~ at, by (we were ~ at the news of the earthquake)

alarming *adj.* ~ to + inf. (it was ~ to think of the possible consequences)

album *n.* an autograph; photograph; stamp ~

alcohol *n.* 1. to distill, make ~ 2. to abstain from ~ 3. to reek of ~ 4. ethyl, grain; methyl, wood; pure, unadulterated; rubbing (AE; BE has *surgical spirit*) ~

alcoholic *n.* a chronic ~

alcoholism *n.* acute; chronic ~

alert I *adj.* ~ to (~ to danger)

alert II *n.* 1. to call an ~ 2. to place, put (troops) on ~ 3. to call off, cancel an ~ 4. (a) full; preliminary; red ~ (the troops were on full ~) 5. on (the) ~ (to be on the ~) 6. (misc.) in a state of ~

alert III *v.* (D; tr.) to ~ to (we must ~ the public to the danger)

A levels *n.* (BE) to sit one's ~

algebra *n.* to do ~

alias *n.* under an ~

alibi *n.* 1. to establish; provide an ~ for 2. to confirm smb.'s ~ 3. to break, disprove an ~ 4. an airtight, foolproof, unassailable ~ 5. his ~ held up

alien I *adj.* (formal) ~ to (such ideas are ~ to us)

alien II *n.* 1. to intern an ~ 2. an enemy; illegal ~

alienate *v.* (D; tr.) to ~ from (she was ~d from her family)

alienation *n.* ~ from (~ from one's old friends)

alight *v.* (formal) (D; intr.) to ~ from (to ~ from a vehicle)

align *v.* (D; refl., tr.) to ~ with (the wheels must be ~ed with the frame; he ~ed himself with the left wing of the party)

alignment *n.* in; out of ~ (the wheels are out of ~)

alimony *n.* to award ~ (the judge awarded the wife ~)

alive *adj.* 1. very much ~ 2. (cannot stand alone) ~ to (~ to the danger of becoming overconfident)

all *determiner, pronoun* ~ of (we saw ~ of them) USAGE NOTE: The use of the preposition *of* is necessary when a personal pronoun follows. When a noun follows, *of* is omitted--the dean saw all students ('the dean saw every student'). To express limited meaning, *of the* or *the* (very common in BE) can be inserted--the dean saw all students who had received poor grades = the dean saw all (of) the students who had received poor grades.

allegation *n.* ['assertion'] 1. to make an ~ 2. to drop, retract, withdraw an ~ 3. to deny; refute an ~ 4. a false; serious; unproved, unsubstantiated, unsupported; vague ~ 5. an ~ about; against (~s of fraud were made against him) 6. an ~ that + clause (their ~ that she had taken the money proved to be false)

allege *v.* (L) it has been ~d that you stole the money

allegiance *n.* 1. to give; pledge, swear ~ 2. to disavow, forsake one's ~ to 3. true, unfailing, unswerving ~ 4. ~ to (~ to a cause)

allergic *adj.* ~ to (~ to dust)

allergy *n.* to acquire, develop an ~ to

alliance *n.* 1. to enter into, form an ~ 2. to dissolve an ~ 3. a defense; military; political; unholy ~ 4. an ~ against; between; with (to form an ~ with one's neighbors against the common enemy) 5. an ~ to + inf. (an ~ to defend an area against any invader)

allied *adj.* ~ against; to, with (we were ~ with them against the aggressor)

allocate *v.* 1. (B; more rarely -- A) the dean ~d the funds to several students 2. (D; tr.) to ~ for (our committee ~d money for the memorial)

allocation *n.* 1. to make an ~ 2. a budget ~ 3. an ~ for; to

allot *v.* 1. (A) the city has ~ted space to us; or: the city has ~ted us space 2. (D; tr.) to ~ for

allow *v.* 1. (A; usu. without the preposition) ('to permit') he ~ed himself no meat 2. (d; intr.) ('to provide') to ~ for (we ~ed for the difference in age; you must ~ for shrinkage) 3. (D; tr.) ('to give') to ~ for (they ~ed an hour for lunch) 4. (formal) (d; intr.) to ~ of ('to permit') (our financial situation ~s of no unnecessary expenditures) 5. (H) ('to permit') we ~ed the children to go to the park 6. (formal) (L) ('to admit') I must ~ that he is capable

allowance *n.* ['taking into account'] 1. to make (an) ~ for (to make ~/an ~ for inexperience; to make ~s for wear and tear) ['sum granted'] 2. to grant an ~ 3. a cost-of-living; depletion; trade-in ~ 4. a daily; fixed; weekly ~

allude *v.* 1. to ~ vaguely 2. (d; intr.) to ~ to (the story ~d to a mystery in his past)

allusion *n.* 1. to make an ~ to (she made no ~ to the incident) 2. a vague ~

ally I *n.* a faithful, staunch ~

ally II *v.* (D; intr., refl.) to ~ against; to, with (we

~ied ourselves with our friends against the common enemy)

alms *n.* (formal) 1. to dispense, give ~ 2. ~ for (~ for the needy)

alone *adj.* to leave smb. ~

aloof *adj.* 1. to hold oneself, remain, stand ~ 2. ~ from (he remained ~ from the others)

alphabet *n.* 1. the Arabic; Cyrillic; Greek; Hebrew; Latin; Phoenician; Sanskrit ~ 2. a phonetic; runic ~

altar *n.* 1. at the ~ 2. to lead smb. to the ~

alteration *n.* 1. to make an ~ 2. a major; minor, slight ~

altercation *n.* 1. to have an ~ 2. an ~ about, over; between; with

alternate *v.* 1. (D; intr.) to ~ between (they ~ between supporting us and opposing us) 2. (D; intr.) to ~ in (we ~ in doing the household chores) 3. (d; intr., tr.) to ~ with (sunny weather ~d with rain; the coach ~d Jones with Wilson)

alternative *n.* 1. to propose an ~ 2. to fall back on an ~ 3. a viable ~ 4. an ~ to 5. no ~ but to + inf. (we have no ~ but to compromise)

altitude *n.* 1. to reach an ~ of 2. to lose ~ 3. a cruising ~ 4. at an ~ (at high ~s)

amalgamate *v.* (D; intr., tr.) to ~ with (our firm will be ~d with a Japanese company)

amateur *n.* a rank ~

amaze *v.* (R) it ~d me (to learn) that he had been promoted

amazed *adj.* 1. ~ at, by (he was ~ at what he saw) 2. ~ to + inf. (she was ~ to see the results of the research) 3. ~ that + clause (we were ~ that he agreed so quickly)

amazement *n.* 1. complete, total, utter 2. ~ at, with (they expressed their ~ at/with our performance) 3. in ~ (they stared in ~) 4. to one's ~ (to my utter ~, he arrived on time)

amazing *adj.* 1. ~ to + inf. (it was ~ to watch them perform) 2. ~ that + clause (it was ~ that she was able to solve the problem so quickly)

ambassador *n.* 1. to appoint an ~ 2. to recall an ~ 3. an ~ extraordinary; an ~ plenipotentiary; an ambassador-at-large 4. a goodwill; roving ~ 5. an ~ to (our ~ to Rome)

ambiguity *n.* 1. to clear up, remove an ~; to avoid ~ 2. an ~ about, concerning

ambition *n.* 1. to achieve, attain, fulfill, realize one's ~ 2. to spur, stir smb.'s ~ 3. to limit, restrain one's ~ 4. boundless, unbridled; overweening ~ 5. a burning, cherished; frustrated; unrealized ~ 6. territorial ~s (of an aggressor) 7. an ~ to + inf. (he achieved his ~ to become mayor)

ambitious *adj.* (formal) (esp. BE) ~ to + inf. (she is ~ to succeed)

ambivalent *adj.* ~ about

amble *v.* (P; intr.) to ~ along the road

ambush *n.* 1. to lay, set an ~ for 2. to draw smb. into an ~ 3. to lie in ~ (for) 4. to run into an ~ 5. from ~ (to attack from ~)

amen *n.* to say ~

amenable *adj.* ~ to (~ to compromise)

amendment *n.* 1. to adopt; propose; ratify an ~ 2. a constitutional ~ 3. an ~ to (an ~ to the constitution)

amends *n.* to make ~ for (he wanted to make ~ for the damage that he had caused)

amenities *n.* ['comforts'] 1. to provide the ~ for ['greetings'] 2. to exchange ~ ['proper manners'] 3. to observe the ~

American *n.* 1. a native ~ ('an American Indian') 2. General ~ ('the English spoken in most of the US')

amiss *adj., adv.* (formal) 1. to take smt. ~ 2. to go ~

ammunition *n.* 1. to provide ~ for (also fig.) 2. to issue ~ 3. blank; dummy; live; tracer ~

amnesty *n.* 1. to declare, grant, offer (an) ~ (he was granted ~) 2. a general; political ~ 3. an ~ for (the government declared a general ~ for political prisoners)

amok, amuck *adv.* to run ~

amorous *adj.* (rare) ~ of

amount I *n.* 1. an ample, considerable, enormous, huge, large, tremendous; moderate; negligible, paltry, small ~ 2. the full ~

amount II *v.* (d; intr.) to ~ to (it ~s to fraud; he'll never ~ to anything)

amuse *v.* 1. to ~ greatly, thoroughly, very much 2. (D; refl., tr.) to ~ by, with (she ~d the children with tricks; they ~d themselves by playing games) 3. (R) it ~d us to watch them play; it ~d me that they would never admit to being wrong

amused *adj.* 1. highly, thoroughly, vastly ~ 2. ~ at, by (she was ~ at/by that story) 3. ~ to + inf. (I was ~ to see him playing up to the boss) 4. to keep smb. ~ (he kept the children ~ by reading stories)

amusement *n.* 1. to provide ~ for 2. to find ~ in 3. to smb.'s ~ (much to my ~, everyone believed her story)

amusing *adj.* 1. highly ~ 2. ~ to (it was ~ to everyone) 3. ~ to + inf. (it was ~ to watch the trained elephants perform)

anaemia (BE) see **anemia**

anaesthesia (BE) see **anesthesia**

anaesthetic (BE) see **anesthetic**

analogous *adj.* ~ to, with

analogy *n.* 1. to draw, make an ~ 2. a close; superficial ~ (there is a close ~ between these two phenomena) 3. an ~ between; to, with 4. by ~ (to reason by ~) 5. on the ~ of (to say *thunk* on the analogy of *sunk)*

analysis *n.* ['examination of component parts'] 1. to make an ~ 2. a careful, painstaking, thorough; in-depth; penetrating ~ 3. (ling.) discourse ~ 4. (chemistry) qualitative; quantitative ~ 5. (math.) vector ~ 6. upon ~ (upon further ~, we concluded that...) 7. in the last, final, ultimate ~ ['psychoanalysis'] 8. to undergo ~

anarchy *n.* 1. complete, total, utter ~ 2. ~ reigns

anathema *n.* 1. to declare, pronounce an ~ on 2. to lift an ~ from 3. ~ to (his theories were ~ to his colleagues)

anatomy *n.* comparative; descriptive ~

ancestor *n.* a common; remote ~

ancestry *n.* 1. to trace one's ~ 2. of (a certain) ~ (to be of French ~)

anchor I *n.* 1. to cast, drop ~ 2. to raise, weigh ~

3. at ~ (to ride at ~)

anchor II *v.* to ~ firmly

anecdote *n.* 1. to relate, tell an ~ 2. a funny, witty; off-color ~

anemia, anaemia *n.* 1. to develop ~ 2. pernicious; sickle-cell ~

anesthesia, anaesthesia *n.* 1. to induce, produce ~ 2. to undergo ~ 3. general; local ~ 4. the ~ wears off

anesthetic, anaesthetic *n.* 1. to administer, give an ~ 2. to have, take an ~ 3. a general; local ~ 4. the ~ wears off 5. under (an) ~

angel *n.* (lit.) a guardian, ministering ~

anger I *n.* 1. to arouse, stir up ~ 2. to express; feel; show ~ 3. to allay, appease, calm smb.'s ~; to repress, swallow one's ~ 4. to vent one's ~ 5 blind, burning, deep, profound, seething; righteous; unbridled ~ 6. a blaze, fit, outburst of ~ 7. ~ at; towards, with (he finally expressed his deep ~ at being mistreated) 8. in; with ~ (she struck back in ~; burning with ~)

anger II *v.* (R) it ~ed me (to learn) that they had not kept their promise

angle I *n.* ['space between two straight lines that meet'] 1. an acute; alternate; complementary; exterior; interior; obtuse; right; solid ~ 2. a sharp ~ (at a sharp ~) 3. the side; vertex of an ~ ['deviation from a straight line'] 4. at an ~ (at an ~ of thirty degrees; at a rakish ~; at a right ~) ['viewpoint'] ['aspect'] 5. from an ~ (to examine a question from various ~s) ['motive; scheme'] (colloq.) (esp. AE) 6. to have an ~

angle II *v.* (d; intr.) to ~ for ('to try to obtain') (she was ~ing for an invitation)

angry *adj.* 1. to become, get ~ 2. ~ about; at, with; for (he was ~ at/with his neighbor about the noisy party; we were ~ at being disturbed; she was ~ at/with me for being late) 3. ~ to + inf. (I was ~ to learn of his refusal to help) 4. ~ that + clause (we were ~ that our request had been rejected)

anguish *n.* (formal) 1. to cause ~ 2. deep; mental ~ 3. ~ at, over 4. in ~ (in ~ over smb.'s death)

animadversion *n.* (formal) to make an ~ on, upon

animadvert *v.* (formal) (D; intr.) to ~ on, upon (to ~ on corruption)

animal *n.* 1. to domesticate an ~; to tame; train a wild ~ 2. to trap an ~ 3. to hunt wild ~s 4. to butcher, slaughter ~s (for food) 5. to skin an ~ 6. to stuff an ~ 7. to neuter an ~ 8. a carnivorous, flesh-eating; domestic; draft; herbivorous; pack; predatory; wild ~ 9. (misc.) like a caged ~; human beings are social ~s

animation *n.* suspended ~

animosity *n.* 1. to arouse, stir up ~ 2. to feel ~ 3. burning, deep, seething ~ 4. racial; religious ~ 5. ~ against, to, towards (she felt a burning ~ towards them)

ankle *n.* 1. to sprain, turn, twist one's ~ 2. a well-turned ('shapely') ~ 3. (misc.) ~ deep in mud

annex I **annexe** *n.* an ~ to (an ~ to the main building; an ~ to a treaty)

annex II *v.* (D; tr.) to ~ to (they ~ed the conquered territory to their country)

anniversary *n.* 1. to celebrate, commemorate,

mark, reach an ~ 2. a wedding ~ 3. a diamond; golden; silver ~ 4. on an ~ (on their tenth wedding ~)

annotation *n.* 1. to make an ~ (to make ~s on a text) 2. copious ~s

announce *v.* 1. (B) they ~d the news to the reporters 2. (L; to) the president of the firm ~d (to the employees) that there would be a bonus

announcement *n.* 1. to issue, make an ~ 2. a formal, official; public; spot ~ 3. an ~ about, of 4. an ~ that + clause (they made a public ~ that an amnesty would be declared)

announcer *n.* a radio; sports ~

annoy *v.* 1. to ~ greatly, very much 2. (R) it ~ed me to be kept waiting so long; it ~ed us that they took so long to answer

annoyance *n.* 1. to express; feel; show ~ 2. ~ at, over, with 3. ~ that + clause (his ~ that he had been awakened so early was evident) 4. to one's ~ (much to my ~, he was late)

annoyed *adj.* 1. ~ at, with (we were ~ at losing the order; he was ~ at/with the children) 2. ~ to + inf. (he was ~ to find his door unlocked) 3. ~ that + clause (she was ~ that the library was still closed)

annoying *adj.* 1. highly ~ 2. ~ to (it was ~ to everyone) 3. ~ to + inf. (it is ~ to read nothing but bad news) 4. ~ that + clause (it's ~ that there is no hot water)

annulment *n.* 1. to grant an ~ 2. to obtain an ~

anoint *v.* (N; used with a noun) they ~ed him king

answer I *n.* 1. to give, offer, provide an ~ 2. a blunt, curt; civil; diplomatic; direct; equivocal; evasive, vague; glib; ready; straight; wise; witty ~ 3. a negative; positive ~ 4. the right; wrong ~ 5. (BE) a dusty ('unsatisfactory') ~ 6. an ~ to 7. in ~ to (in ~ to your question)

answer II *v.* 1. ('to respond') to ~ glibly 2. (d; intr.) ('to be responsible') to ~ to smb. for smt. (the directors had to ~ to the stockholders for the loss) 3. (d; intr.) ('to respond') to ~ to (to ~ to a name; the child ~s only to its nickname) 4. (d; intr.) ('to correspond') to ~ to (she ~s to the description) 5. (L; may have an object) ('to respond') they ~ed (us) that they would come

answerable *adj.* ~ for; to (we are ~ to our superiors for our actions)

answer back *v.* (D; intr.) to ~ to (children should not ~ to their parents)

ant *n.* 1. army; carpenter; harvester; honey; leaf-cutter ~s 2. a colony of ~s

antagonism *n.* 1. to arouse, stir up ~ 2. to feel (an) ~ 3. deep, deep-rooted, profound, strong ~ 4. ~ between; to, towards (to feel a strong ~ towards smb.)

antagonist *n.* a formidable ~

antagonistic *adj.* ~ to, towards (he is very ~ to us)

antelope *n.* a herd of ~

antenna *n.* (AE) a loop; TV ~ (BE has *aerial*)

anterior *adj.* (formal) ~ to

anthem *n.* a national ~ (the band played/struck up the national ~)

anthropology *n.* cultural; physical; social ~

antibiotic *n.* 1. to prescribe an ~ 2. to take an ~ 3. a broad-spectrum ~

anticipate *v.* 1. (G) we ~ spending two weeks here 2. (K) we ~d his winning first prize 3. (L) I ~d that they would be late

anticipation *n.* 1. eager, keen ~ 2. in ~ of (an exhibit was scheduled in ~ of his visit) 3. with ~ (to look forward to smt. with eager ~)

anticlimax *n.* an ~ to (everything was an ~ to winning an Olympic gold medal)

antidote *n.* 1. to administer, give an ~ 2. to take an ~ 3. an ~ against, for, to (he took an ~ for the poison; an ~ to complacency)

antifreeze *n.* to add; drain ~

antipathy *n.* 1. to feel (an) ~ 2. (a) deep, strong; natural ~ 3. ~ to, towards (he felt strong/a strong ~ towards foreigners)

antique *n.* a genuine ~

antithesis *n.* 1. the direct, very ~ 2. an ~ between 3. an ~ of, to (the ~ to my theory)

antithetical *adj.* ~ to

antlers *n.* 1. to lock ~ 2. to shed ~ 3. a pair of ~

anxiety *n.* 1. to feel ~ 2. to relieve one's ~ 3. deep, grave, great, high ~ 4. ~ about; for (~ for smb.'s safety) 5. ~ to + inf. (in his ~ not to offend them, he agreed to concessions) 6. in ~ (see 5)

anxious *adj.* 1. ~ about (~ about the world situation) 2. ~ for (we were ~ for them to meet you) 3. ~ to + inf. (she is ~ to help) 4. ~ that + clause; subj. (he was very ~ that we meet/should meet)

any 1. *adv.* (used with the comparative form of adjectives and with *good*) ~ better (I wonder if they can work ~ better); ~ good (I don't think that this wine is ~ good); ~ easier (that doesn't make my job ~ easier); ~ more difficult (do not make my job ~ more difficult than it is now) 2. *determiner, pronoun* ~ to + inf. (we don't have ~ books to sell; we don't have ~ to sell) 3. *determiner, pronoun* ~ of (I did not see ~ of them) USAGE NOTE: The use of the preposition *of* is necessary when a pronoun follows. When a noun follows, the use of *of the* limits the meaning--did you see any students? did you see any of the students whom we had discussed earlier? (see the Usage Note for **something)**

anybody *pronoun* do you have ~ to talk to? (see the Usage Note for **something)**

anyone see **anybody**

anyplace (AE) see **anywhere**

anything *pronoun* 1. do you have ~ to say? 2. (misc.) ~ but ('not at all') (see the Usage Note for **something)**

anywhere *adv.* do you have ~ to go? (see the Usage Note for **something)**

apart *adj., adv.* 1. to fall ~ 2. to tell ~ 3. ~ from (~ from everything else) •

apartment *n.* (esp. AE) 1. to rent an ~ from 2. to rent (out) an ~ to 3. to furnish; redecorate; renovate an ~ 4. a duplex; efficiency; furnished; garden; high-rise; penthouse; studio; unfurnished ~

apathetic *adj.* ~ about; to, towards (he is ~ about everything)

apathy *n.* 1. to feel; show ~ towards 2. to cast off, shed, throw off one's ~ 3. ~ towards

apes *n.* the higher ~

aplomb *n.* 1. the ~ to + inf. (she had the necessary

~ to order the meal in French) 2. with great ~

apologetic *adj.* ~ about, for (she was ~ for her blunder)

apologist *n.* an ~ for

apologize *v.* 1. to ~ humbly 2. (D; intr.) to ~ for; to (he ~d to us for being late)

apology *n.* 1. to make, offer an ~ 2. to demand an ~ 3. an abject, humble; public; sincere ~ 4. an ~ for; to (Jim made an ~ to the teacher for his rude behavior)

apostasy *n.* (formal) (an) ~ from

apostate *n.* (formal) an ~ from (an ~ from the true faith)

appall, appal *v.* (R) it ~ed me to see such sloppy work; it ~ed them that no preparations had been made

appalled *adj.* 1. ~ at, by (we were ~ at/by the news) 2. ~ to + inf. (I was ~ to see the results of their work 3. ~ that + clause (everyone was ~ that the murderer had been released on parole)

appalling *adj.* 1. ~ to + inf. (it was ~ to see him in that condition) 2. ~ that + clause (it is ~ that so many people evade paying taxes)

apparel *n.* wearing ~

apparent *adj.* 1. clearly; increasingly ~ 2. ~ to 3. ~ that + clause (it was ~ to all that he was guilty)

apparition *n.* 1. a strange ~ 2. an ~ appears; disappears

appeal I *n.* ['request'] ['request for review'] 1. to make an ~ 2. (legal) to file, lodge, make; lose; win an ~ 3. (legal) to take an ~ to a higher court 4. (also legal) to deny, dismiss, reject, throw out an ~ 5. a desperate, urgent; eloquent, irresistible, ringing, stirring; emotional; final, last ~ 6. an ~ against, from; for; to (to file an ~ against a decision; to make an ~ to the public for donations; there is no ~ from a verdict of the higher court) ['attraction'] 7. box-office; sales; sex; snob ~

appeal II *v.* 1. (D; intr.) ('to request a review') to ~ against (to ~ against a decision) 2. (D; intr.) ('to request') to ~ for; to (they ~ed to us for help) 3. (d; intr.) ('to request') to ~ to smb. to + inf. (he ~ed to them to support his campaign) 4. (d; intr.) to ~ to ('to resort to') (to ~ to common sense) 5. (d; intr.) to ~ to ('to please') (he doesn't ~ to her)

appear *v.* 1. (D; intr.) to ~ against; for (she ~ed against him in court) 2. (D; intr.) to ~ to (she ~ed to him in a dream) 3. (E) she ~s to be well 4. (L; to) it ~s (to me) that they will not come 5. (esp. BE) (S) to ~ sad; to ~ a fool 6. (misc.) to ~ before a committee; to ~ in print; to ~ on the scene; to ~ on stage; to ~ in person; to ~ at the door; the story ~ed in the newspaper

appearance *n.* ['appearing'] 1. to make, put in an ~ (the policeman made a timely ~) 2. a guest; personal; public; TV ~ (the actor made a personal ~) 3. at one's ~ (the crowd went wild at their first ~ on stage) ['outward impression'] 4. a disheveled; immaculate, neat; shabby; unkempt, untidy ~ 5. in ~ (neat in ~) 6. at first ~

appearances *n.* ['outward looks'] 1. to keep up ~ 2. outward ~ 3. by ~ (to judge by ~) 4. for the sake of ~ 5. from, to all ~ (to all ~, the matter is closed)

append *v.* (D; tr.) to ~ to (to ~ a translation to a document)

appendage *n.* an ~ to

appendectomy *n.* 1. to do, perform an ~ on 2. to have an ~

appendix *n.* 1. (anatomical) an inflamed; ruptured ~ 2. (anatomical) an ~ bursts, ruptures 3. an ~ to (an ~ to a textbook)

appertain *v.* (formal) (d; intr.) to ~ to

appetite *n.* 1. to whet one's; to work up an ~ 2. to satisfy one's ~ 3. to curb, spoil, take away one's ~ 4. a good, healthy, hearty, ravenous, voracious, insatiable ~ 5. an ~ for

applaud *v.* to ~ heartily, loudly

applause *n.* 1. to draw, get, win ~ for 2. heavy, lengthy, prolonged; light, weak; loud, thunderous ~ 3. a burst; ripple; round of ~ 4. to (the) ~ (she appeared on stage to the thunderous ~ of her admirers)

apple *n.* 1. cooking; eating ~s 2. a baked; green; sour ~ 3. (misc.) a rotten ~ ('an undesirable person')

applicable *adj.* ~ to (~ to a case)

applicant *n.* an ~ for (an ~ for a position)

application *n.* ['request'] 1. to file, make, put in, send in, submit an ~ 2. to screen ~s 3. to reject, turn down; withdraw an ~ 4. a fellowship; membership ~ 5. a formal; written ~ 6. an ~ for an ~ for admission to a university) 7. an ~ to + inf. (he filed an ~ to be admitted to the intensive course) 8. by, on ~ ['putting to use'] 9. ~ to (the ~ of theory to practice) ['placing'] 10. ~ to (the ~ of ice to the forehead)

application form *n.* 1. to fill in (esp. BE), to fill out (AE), fill up (BE, rare) an ~ 2. to file, submit an ~

apply *v.* 1. (D; intr.) ('to request') to ~ for; to (we ~lied to the authorities for assistance; the captain ~lied to headquarters for a transfer; she ~lied for a fellowship) 2. (D; intr.) ('to seek admission to') to ~ to (she ~lied to three universities) 3. (D; intr.) ('to be relevant') to ~ to (the rule does not apply to this case) 4. (D; refl.) ('to concentrate one's efforts') to ~ to (she ~lied herself to her new duties with great energy) 5. (D; tr.) ('to put on') to ~ to (to ~ paint to a surface; to ~ ointment to a rash) 6. (D; tr.) ('to put to use') to ~ to (to ~ theory to practice) 7. (d; tr.) ('to channel') to ~ towards (to ~ money towards a purchase) 8. (E) ('to request') he ~lied to be transferred

appoint *v.* 1. (D; tr.) to ~ as (we ~ed him as treasurer) 2. (D; tr.) to ~ to (they ~ed her to the committee) 3. (H) they ~ed me to serve as secretary 4. (M and N; used with a noun) we ~ed her (to be) treasurer

appointment *n.* ['agreement to meet'] 1. to keep; make an ~ with 2. to break; cancel an ~ 3. by ~ (he will see you by ~) 4. an ~ to + inf. (she had an ~ to see the dean) ['selection'] 5. an ~ to (they announced her ~ to the commission) 6. an ~ as (an ~ as professor) ['position'] 7. to hold; receive an ~ 8. a permanent; temporary ~ ['designation'] 9. by ~ to Her Majesty

apportion v. (D; tr.) to ~ among, between (the funds were ~ed among the various departments)

apposition n. (grammar) in ~ to (the second noun is in ~ to the first)

appraisal n. 1. to give, make an ~ of 2. a down-to-earth; objective ~

appraise v. (D; tr.) to ~ at (the house was ~d at seventy thousand dollars)

appreciate v. 1. to ~ deeply, greatly, keenly, sincerely, very much 2. (K) we ~ your helping us 3. (misc.) we ~ the fact that you have helped us

appreciation n. 1. to demonstrate, display, show one's ~ for 2. to express; feel ~ 3. deep, keen, sincere ~ 4. in ~ of (he did this in ~ of the help that he had received)

appreciative adj. 1. deeply, keenly, sincerely ~ 2. ~ of (~ of help)

apprehension n. ['foreboding'] ['fear'] 1. to express; feel; show ~ 2. to allay one's ~(s) 3. grave ~ 4. ~ for (we felt ~ for their safety) ['conception'] 5. under an ~

apprehensive adj. 1. ~ about, for, of (~ about recent developments) 2. ~ that + clause (we were ~ that they might forget)

apprentice I n. an ~ to (he was an ~ to a master craftsman)

apprentice II v. (B) at an early age, I was ~d to a carpenter

apprenticeship n. to fill; serve an ~

apprise v. (formal) (d; tr.) to ~ of (he was ~d of the decision by his lawyer)

approach I n. 1. to make an ~ 2. to take an ~ (to take a judicious ~ to a problem) 3. a forthright; holistic; judicious; pragmatic; rational; scholarly; scientific ~ 4. with the ~ (with the ~ of spring, we began to feel better) 5. an ~ from; to (I like her ~ to the problem; the ~es to a stadium; the pilot began her ~ to the runway)

approach II v. 1. (D; tr.) to ~ about (I was afraid to ~ them about this matter) 2. (D; intr., tr.) to ~ from (to ~ from the other direction) 3. (d; tr.) to ~ with (to ~ smb. with a request)

appropriate I adj. 1. ~ for; to (~ for us; ~ to the occasion) 2. ~ to + inf. (it is not ~ to tip a bus driver) 3. ~ that + clause; subj. (it is ~ that he be/should be present)

appropriate II v. 1. (B) Congress ~d the funds to the states 2. (D; tr.) to ~ for (the committee ~d money for the memorial)

appropriation n. 1. to make an ~ for (our government made an ~ for the project) 2. defense; foreign-aid ~s

approval n. 1. to give one's ~ for 2. to nod; voice one's ~ 3. to meet with, win ~ 4. one's complete, unqualified; qualified; tacit ~ 5. final; public ~ 6. ~ to + inf. (we received their ~ to continue the research) 7. on ~ (we bought it on ~) 8. (misc.) to receive smb.'s stamp of ~

approve v. 1. to ~ of wholeheartedly 2. (D; intr.) to ~ of (we ~d of his decision)

approximate v. (BE) (D; intr.) ('to come near') to ~ to (to ~ to the truth)

apt adj. (cannot stand alone) ~ to + inf. (he is ~ to exaggerate)

aptitude n. 1. to demonstrate, display, show (an) ~ 2. (a) great, outstanding; natural; special ~ 3. mechanical; scholastic ~ 4. an ~ for, in (an ~ for painting)

arbitrate v. (D; intr.) to ~ between (to ~ between opposing parties)

arbitration n. 1. to conduct ~ 2. to go to; resort to ~ (the union and management went to ~; the dispute went to ~) 3. binding; voluntary ~ 4. ~ between; of

arcade n. an amusement (BE); penny; video-game ~

architecture n. Baroque; Byzantine; Colonial; Eastern; Gothic; Greek; Modern; Renaissance; Roman; Romanesque ~

ardor, ardour n. 1. to demonstrate, display ~ 2. to cool, dampen one's ~ 3. fervent, intense; patriotic ~ 4. ~ for

area n. 1. to close off, rope off an ~ 2. an assembly, staging; built-up; catchment; disaster; distressed; drainage; impacted ('crowded with federal employees'); metropolitan, urban; residential; rural; service ~ 3. (soccer) a penalty ~ 4. (meteorology) a high-pressure; low-pressure ~

arena n. a sports ~

arguable adj. ~ that + clause (it is ~ that some unemployment is necessary)

argue v. 1. to ~ calmly, logically, plausibly, sensibly; heatedly, passionately, strenuously, vehemently 2. (D; intr.) to ~ about, over; with (we ~d with them about the new law) 3. (d; intr.) to ~ against; for (to ~ against the amendment; to ~ for the new policy) 4. (d; tr.) to ~ out of (to ~ smb. out of doing smt.) 5. (L) she ~d logically that the new regulations would harm the poor

argument n. ['dispute'] 1. to get into, have an ~ 2. to break off, terminate; clinch, settle an ~ 3. an angry, bitter, heated, loud, violent ~ 4. an ~ breaks out 5. an ~ about, over; between; with (I had a bitter ~ with him about politics) ['statement'] 6. to drive home, press; offer, present, put forward an ~ 7. to confute, rebut, refute an ~ 8. an airtight, balanced, cogent, compelling, conclusive, convincing, irrefutable, logical, persuasive, rational, solid, sound, telling, trenchant, unassailable, valid ~ 9. a groundless; spurious; tenuous; weak ~ 10. an ~ about; against; for (she presented a convincing ~ against the proposal) 11. an ~ that + clause (I cannot accept his ~ that war is inevitable) 12. (misc.) (legal) to hear ~s against; for

aristocrat n. a born ~

arithmetic n. to do ~

arm I n. ['upper limb'] 1. to bend; cross; fold; lower; raise; stretch; swing; wave one's ~s 2. (misc.) to take smb. by the ~; to fling/put/throw one's ~s around smb.; to carry smt. under one's ~; to greet smb. with open/outstretched ~s; to walk ~ in ~ with; with ~s akimbo ['power'] 3. the long ~ of the law ['division'] 4. our naval air ~ ['attachment'] 5. a pickup, tone ~ ['misc.'] 6. to twist smb.'s ~ ('to exert pressure on smb.')

arm II v. (D; intr., refl., tr.) to ~ against (to ~ against a potential enemy)

armed *adj.* ~ to the teeth
armistice *n.* 1. to agree on, work out; declare; sign an ~ 2. to violate an ~ 3. to suspend an ~
armor, armour *n.* 1. heavy; light ~ 2. (misc.) to pierce ~
arms *n.* ['weapons'] 1. to bear; take up ~ 2. to call to ~ 3. (mil.) inspection; left shoulder; order; port; present; right shoulder; trail ~! 4. to lay down one's ~ 5. small ~ 6. under ~ ('armed') ['misc.'] 7. up in ~ ('stirred up')
arms race *n.* 1. to accelerate, step up the ~ 2. to curb the ~
army *n.* 1. to command, lead; drill, train; rally an ~ 2. to mobilize, raise an ~ 3. to equip, supply an ~ 4. to array, commit, deploy, field; concentrate, mass an ~ 5. to inspect, muster, review an ~ 6. to encircle, envelop, surround; outfight; outflank; outmaneuver; overrun; surprise an ~ 7. to crush, decimate, defeat, rout an ~; to put an ~ to flight 8. to demobilize, disband an ~ 9. a rebel; regular, standing; territorial; volunteer ~ 10. an advancing; conquering; defeated; occupation, occupying; retreating; victorious ~ 11. an ~ advances; attacks; conducts war, engages in combat, fights; pulls back, retreats, withdraws 12. (misc.) to join the ~
aroma *n.* 1. a delicate, delightful, fragrant, pleasant, pleasing; tantalizing ~ 2. an ~ emanates from
arouse *v.* (D; tr.) to ~ from (to ~ smb. from a deep sleep)
aroused *adj.* easily; sexually ~
arraignment *n.* 1. (legal) to hold an ~ for 2. a public ~
arrange *v.* 1. to ~ neatly; tastefully 2. (d; intr.) to ~ for (to ~ for a series of lectures; we ~d for him to give a concert) 3. (E) they ~d to leave early 4. (L) I ~d that they should be seated next to each other
arrangement *n.* 1. to make, work out an ~ 2. a floral; seating; working ~ 3. an ~ for; with 4. an ~ to + inf. (they made an ~/~s to meet secretly) 5. by ~ (by special ~) 6. under an ~ (under a special ~)
array I *n.* ['order'] 1. in battle ~; drawn up in full ~ ['display'] 2. an imposing, impressive ~
array II *v.* (D; tr.) to ~ against (~ed against the enemy)
arrears *n.* in ~ (he is in ~ with his rent)
arrest I *n.* ['detention'] 1. to make an ~ 2. to resist ~ 3. a citizen's; false ~; house ~ 4. an ~ for, on charges of (to make an ~ for murder) 5. under ~ (to be under ~; to place/put smb. under ~) ['stoppage'] 6. a cardiac ~
arrest II *v.* (D; tr.) to ~ for, on charges of (the police ~ed him for murder)
arrest warrant *n.* (AE) to issue an ~
arrival *n.* 1. an early; late ~ 2. an ~ at, in; from 3. on one's ~ (on our ~ in Chicago)
arrive *v.* 1. (D; intr.) to ~ at, in; from (they ~d from Paris) 2. (s) they ~d safe and sound 3. (misc.) to ~ early; late; on time
arrogance *n.* 1. to demonstrate, display, exhibit ~ 2. insufferable, overpowering, overwhelming ~ 3. the ~ to + inf. (he had the ~ to ask for more money)

arrogant *adj.* ~ towards
arrogate *v.* (formal) (B) to ~ a privilege to oneself
arrow *n.* 1. to shoot an ~ at 2. a poisoned; spent ~ 3. (misc.) as straight as an ~
arson *n.* to commit ~
art *n.* 1. to practice an ~ (to practice the occult ~ of the alchemist) 2. abstract; classical; folk; impressionist; modern; pop; primitive; verbal ~ 3. (the) applied; creative; fine; graphic; industrial; language; liberal; martial; performing; plastic ~s 4. an ~ to (there is an ~ to making a good omelet) 5. a work of ~
artefacts (BE) see **artifacts**
artery *n.* ['blood vessel'] 1. a blocked, occluded; coronary; pulmonary; ruptured ~ 2. (misc.) hardening of the ~ries ['channel'] 3. a major; traffic ~
arthritis *n.* to develop ~
article I *n.* ['essay'] 1. to write an ~ 2. (BE) a leading ~ 3. an ~ about (she wrote an ~ about her research) ['section'] 4. according to an ~ (according to ~ two of our constitution) ['object'] 5. secondhand; toilet ~s ['grammatical affix'] 6. to take an ~ (certain nouns always take the definite ~) 7. the definite; indefinite ~
article II *v.* (BE) (d; tr.) ('to apprentice') to ~ to, with (to ~ smb. to a firm of solicitors)
artifacts, artefacts *n.* ancient; cultural ~
artillery *n.* antiaircraft; coast; field; heavy light; long-range; medium; self-propelled ~
artist *n.* 1. a dramatic; gifted, talented; struggling ~ 2. a pavement (BE), sidewalk (AE) ~ 3. a con; escape; make-up; quick-change; trapeze ~
artistry *n.* brilliant ~
ascendancy *n.* 1. to attain, gain ~ over 2. (a) clear-cut; overwhelming ~
ascent *n.* 1. to make an ~ (to make the ~ of a mountain) 2. a gradual; steep ~
ascertain *v.* 1. (L) she ~ed that fraud had been committed 2. (Q) can you ~ who he is?
asceticism *n.* to practice ~
ascribe *v.* 1. (B) the painting was ~d to an unknown artist 2. (d; tr.) to ~ to (she ~d her success to hard work)
ash *n.* volcanic ~
ashamed *adj.* 1. thoroughly ~ 2. ~ of (he was ~ of himself) 3. ~ to + inf. (she was ~ to admit her mistake) 4. ~ that + clause (he was ~ that his family was poor)
ashes *n.* 1. to rake; spread ~ 2. to reduce to ~ 3. (misc.) to rise from the ~
ashore *adv.* 1. to put, set ~ 2. to come; go ~
aside *adv.* 1. to move; stand ~ 2. to push, shove; put; take ~
asinine *adj.* ~ to + inf. (it was ~ to behave like that)
ask *v.* 1. (D; intr., tr.) ('to inquire') to ~ about, after (BE) (they ~ed me about my work; he ~ed about/after her mother) 2. (d; intr., tr.) ('to request') to ~ for (she ~ed me politely for the book; the guest ~ed for the manager) 3. (D; tr.) ('to invite') to ~ to (we ~ed them to the party) 4. (D; tr.) ('to request') to ~ smt. of (I have a favor to ~ of you; he is ~ing a great deal of us) 5. (E)

('to request') she ~ed to be excused; we ~ed to see him 6. (H) ('to request') she ~ed us to come to the concert 7. (L; subj.) ('to request') the family ~ed that the story not be/should not be printed 8. (O; can be used with one object) ('to pose') he ~ed (her) a question (also possible is: he ~ed a question of her) 9. (Q; may have an object) ('to inquire of') he ~ed (his son) point-blank where he was going; she ~ed wistfully how she might help

askance *adv.* to look ~ at

asking *n.* (colloq.) for the ~ (it's yours for the ~)

asleep *adj.* 1. to be fast, sound ~ 2. to fall ~

aspect *n.* ['view'] ['side'] 1. a frightening; grim; humorous; serious ~ (the humorous ~ of the situation) 2. from an ~ (from this ~) 3. in an ~ (in all ~s)

aspersion *n.* to cast ~s on

aspirant *n.* an ~ for; to (an ~ to the throne)

aspiration *n.* (formal) 1. lofty, noble ~s 2. an ~ to (~s to independence)

aspire *v.* (formal) 1. (d; intr.) to ~ to (to ~ to success) 2. (E) she ~d to become a lawyer

aspirin *n.* 1. to take (an) ~ 2. an ~ tablet (he took two ~ tablets; or: he took two ~s)

ass *n.* ['fool'] 1. a pompous ~ ['donkey'] 2. ~es bray

assail *v.* (formal) to ~ bitterly

assassination *n.* 1. to carry out an ~ 2. a character; political ~

assault *n.* 1. (often mil.) to carry out, make; lead an ~ on (the troops carried out an ~ on the enemy position) 2. (legal) to commit ~ 3. (usu. legal) aggravated; bodily; criminal; indecent ~ 4. an all-out; armed; military ~ 5. (usu. mil.) by ~ (to take by ~)

assault and battery *n.* (legal) to commit ~

assembly *n.* 1. to convene an ~ 2. a constitutional; deliberative; general; legislative; national; public ~ 3. (misc.) the right of ~

assent I *n.* 1. to give; nod one's ~ (she gave her ~ to our plan) 2. by common ~

assent II *v.* (formal) (D; intr.) to ~ to (we ~ed to his proposal)

assert *v.* 1. to ~ boldly 2. (L) she ~ed that she was innocent

assertion *n.* 1. to make an ~ 2. to deny; refute an ~ 3. a bold; sweeping; unfounded ~ 4. an ~ that + clause (we do not believe his ~ that he is innocent)

assess *v.* (D; tr.) to ~ at (the value of this property was ~ed at one million dollars)

assessment *n.* to make an ~ (she made a careful ~ of the situation)

asset *n.* 1. an invaluable, valuable ~ 2. an ~ to (she was an invaluable ~ to our firm)

assets *n.* 1. to realize; unfreeze ~ 2. current; financial; frozen; hidden; intangible; liquid; tangible ~

asseverate *v.* (formal and rare) (L) they ~ed that they would never surrender

assign *v.* 1. (A) they ~ed a very difficult mission to us; or: they ~ed us a very difficult mission 2. (D; tr.) to ~ to (headquarters ~ed the soldiers to a different unit; an experienced detective was ~ed to the case; to ~ a painting to a certain century) 3.

(esp. BE) (H) we were ~ed to prepare a meal

assignation *n.* (formal) to make an ~

assignment *n.* ['task'] ['mission'] 1. to give smb. an ~ 2. to carry out an ~ (the ambassador carried out her ~ brilliantly) 3. a dangerous; difficult, rough, tough; easy ~ 4. an overseas; rush; special ~ 5. an ~ to + inf. (an ~ to guard the president) 6. on ~ ('on a mission') (the correspondent was on ~ in the Far East) ['homework'] (esp. AE) 7. to give, hand out an ~ 8. to do; hand in an ~ (the pupils did their ~) 9. a difficult; easy ~ ['appointment'] (esp. AE) 10. an ~ to (an ~ to a new job)

assimilate *v.* 1. (D; intr., tr.) to ~ into, to (the newcomers tried to ~ into the community; America has ~d millions of immigrants into its way of life) 2. (D; intr.) to ~ with (they did not ~ with the local population)

assimilation *n.* ~ into, to (their ~ into society was swift)

assist I *n.* (colloq.) with an ~ from

assist II *v.* 1. (D; intr., tr.) to ~ at, in, with (the young nurse was ~ing at her first operation; to ~ in the preparation of a report; to ~ with the editing of a manuscript) 2. (formal, rare) (H) to ~ smb. to do smt.

assistance *n.* 1. to give, offer, provide, render ~ 2. considerable, great ~ 3. clerical; directory (AE); economic, financial; legal; material; public; technical ~ 4. ~ to (economic ~ to underdeveloped countries) 5. of ~ (he was of considerable ~ to us)

assistant *n.* 1. a personal (BE; AE has *personal secretary);* research; shop (BE; AE has *sales-clerk);* teaching ~ 2. an ~ to (an ~ to the president)

associate *v.* (d; intr., tr.) to ~ with (we ~ with all sorts of people; one usually ~s poverty with misery)

association *n.* ['organization'] 1. to form an ~ 2. a bar ~ (AE; BE has *law society)* 3. a building and loan ~ (AE; BE has *building society)* ['connection'] 4. a close ~ 5. an ~ with 6. in ~ with ['connection in the mind'] 7. to bring up, call up an ~ 8. free ~

assortment *n.* a wide ~

assume *v.* 1. (L) we ~d that he was dead 2. (M) everyone ~d him to be dead

assumed *adj.* (cannot stand alone) ~ to + inf. (she was ~ to be out of the country)

assumption *n.* 1. to make an ~ 2. an erroneous, false; implicit; reasonable; safe; valid ~ 3. an ~ about; of (to make an ~ of guilt) 4. an ~ that + clause (we all made the ~ that the new company would fail) 5. on an ~ (we proceeded on the ~ that he would help)

assurance *n.* 1. to give an ~ that + clause (he gave every ~ that he would attend) 2. (BE) life ~ (see the Usage Note for **insurance)**

assurances *n.* 1. to give, provide ~ of 2. ~ that + clause (the contractor gave ~ that the work would be completed on time)

assure *v.* 1. (d; tr.) to ~ of (we ~ed her of our support) 2. (L; must have an object) they ~d us that they would not be late

astonish *v.* 1. to ~ greatly, very much 2. (R) it ~ed

me to learn that he was here; it ~ed us that they were able to survive

astonished adj. 1. greatly, very much ~ 2. ~ at, by (they were ~ at/by the news of his escape) 3. ~ + inf. (I was ~ to learn of his divorce) 4. ~ that + clause (she was ~ that he had survived)

astonishing adj. 1. ~ to 2. ~ to + inf (it was ~ to watch them perform) 3. ~ that + clause (it was ~ to everyone that the court had made such a decision)

astonishment n. 1. to express ~ 2. ~ at (he could not conceal his ~ at seeing them together) 3. ~ that + clause (they expressed ~ that I won the election) 4. in ~ (they gaped in ~) 5. to smb.'s ~ (to our ~, they arrived on time)

astound v. (R) it ~ed me to find the country so backward; it ~ed us that they came

astounded adj. 1. ~ at, by (~ at the news) 2. ~ to + inf. (everyone was ~ to learn of her exploits) 3. ~ that + clause (I was ~ that the mayor had taken bribes)

astounding adj. 1. ~ to + inf. (it was ~ to watch) 2. ~ that + clause (it was ~ that an experienced engineer had made such a miscalculation)

astray adv. 1. to lead smb. ~ 2. to go ~

astride adv. (formal) to sit ~ (to sit ~ smb.'s knee)

astute adj. (formal) ~ at (~ at conducting negotiations)

asunder adv. (formal) to rend, tear ~

asylum n. 1. to grant ~ to 2. to receive; seek ~ 3. to deny smb. ~ 4. political ~ (they were granted political ~)

athlete n. an all-around (AE), all-round; amateur; professional; weekend; world-class ~

athletics n. 1. (esp. BE) to go in for ~ 2. intercollegiate ~

atlas n. a dialect, linguistic; geographical ~

atmosphere n. 1. a formal; friendly; informal, relaxed; stifling, stultifying; tense ~ 2. a polluted; rarified ~ 3. the upper ~

atom n. to split the ~

atone v. (D; intr.) to ~ for (to ~ for one's sins)

atonement n. to make ~ for

atrocity n. 1. to commit an ~ 2. a dreadful, grisly, gruesome, horrible, horrid, monstrous, revolting, vile ~; death-camp ~ties

attach v. 1. (d; refl.) ('to join') to ~ to (she ~ed herself to our group) 2. (D; tr.) ('to fasten') to ~ to (she ~ed an aerial/antenna to the radio; a tag was ~ed to each article) 3. (d; tr.) ('to assign temporarily') to ~ to (the officer was ~ed to headquarters) 4. (d; tr.) ('to ascribe') to ~ to (we ~ed no significance to her statement)

attaché n. an air-force; commercial; cultural; military; naval; press ~

attached adj. 1. deeply, strongly ~ 2. ~ to

attachment n. 1. to feel; form an ~ 2. a close; lasting; sentimental; strong ~ 3. an ~ to (to form a lasting ~ to smb.)

attack I n. ['assault'] (also fig.) 1. to carry out, make; launch, mount; lead, spearhead; press an ~ 2. to provoke an ~ 3. to blunt; break up, repel, repulse an ~ 4. (often mil.) an all-out, concerted, full-scale; coordinated; mock; pre-emptive;

sneak, surprise ~ 5. (usu. mil.) an air; enemy; flank; frontal; torpedo ~ 6. a bitter, blistering, savage, scathing, sharp, violent; scurrilous, vicious; unprovoked; wanton ~ 7. an ~ fails, fizzles out; succeeds 8. an ~ against, on (our forces launched an all-out ~ against the enemy; he made a blistering ~ on his opponent) 9. under ~ ['onset of an ailment'] 10. to have an ~ (she had an ~ of hiccups) 11. an acute; light, slight; recurrent; sudden ~ 12. a fatal; heart ~

attack II v. to ~ viciously

attempt I n. 1. to make an ~ 2. to foil, thwart an ~ 3. an abortive, fruitless, futile, vain; all-out, concerted, last-ditch; bold, brazen, daring; crude; deliberate; feeble, halfhearted, weak; first; premature; successful ~; repeated ~s 4. an ~ against, on (an ~ on smb.'s life) 5. an ~ at (an ~ at being funny) 6. an ~ to + inf. (we made an ~ to get in touch with them)

attempt II v. 1. (E) she ~ed to find a job 2. (rare) (G) he ~ed walking 3. (misc.) to ~ smt. in vain

attend v. (d; intr.) to ~ to (to ~ to one's duties; to ~ to a customer)

attendance n. ['persons present'] ['number of persons present'] 1. to check ~; to take ~ (in school) 2. average; daily; low, poor; perfect ~ 3. ~ has gone up; ~ has fallen, gone down ['presence'] 4. ~ at (~ at a ceremony) 5. in ~ (a nurse was in ~) ['misc.'] 6. to dance ~ on smb. ('to fawn over smb.')

attendant n. 1. a flight; wedding ~ 2. an ~ to

attention n. ['concentration'] ['notice'] 1. to attract, capture, catch, command, draw get; hold, retain, rivet smb.'s ~ 2. to devote one's ~ to; to focus one's ~ on; to pay ~ to 3. to bring smt. to smb.'s ~ 4. to distract, divert smb.'s ~ 5. to escape one's ~ 6. close; meticulous; rapt; undivided ~ (this matter will require your undivided ~) 7. ~ to (meticulous ~ to detail) ['position of attention'] (usu. mil.) 8. to call smb. to ~ (the sergeant called his platoon to ~); to come to snap to ~; to stand at ~; or: to stand at the position of ~; or: (BE) to stand to ~ ['care'] 9. to give ~ to; to lavish ~ on 10. medical ~ (to receive medical ~) 11. individual; personal ~ (the manager gave me her personal ~; I lavished my individual ~ on him)

attentive adj. ~ to (~ to our needs)

attest v. (formal) (d; intr.) to ~ to (several witnesses can ~ to her good character)

attire n. 1. casual; civilian; formal ~ 2. in ~ (in formal ~)

attitude n. 1. to assume, strike, take an ~ 2. a belligerent, defiant, surly; casual; cavalier; condescending, patronizing; hands-off; holier-thanthou; irreverent; liberal; negative; positive; reverent; scornful ~ 3. an ~ about; of; to, towards (to assume an ~ of defiance towards all authority) 4. an ~ that + clause (I didn't like his ~ that he deserves special treatment)

attorney n. (esp. AE) 1. to hire, retain an ~ 2. a defense; district (AE; BE has *public prosecutor*); prosecuting ~ 3. an attorney-at-law 4. (CE) an ~ general 5. (CE) a power of ~

attract *v.* (D; tr.) to ~ to (a crowd was ~ed to the scene of the accident)

attracted *adj.* ~ to (he was ~ to her)

attraction *n.* ['charm'] 1. to feel an ~ to 2. an irresistible, strong; sexual ~ (she felt a strong ~ to him) ['something that attracts'] 3. a box-office; public; scenic; tourist ~

attractive *adj.* 1. physically; sexually ~ 2. ~ to (the offer is very ~ to us)

attributable *adj.* ~ to (the fire was ~ to carelessness)

attribute *v.* (d; tr.) to ~ to (we ~ this saying to Shakespeare; they ~d their success to hard work)

attrition *n.* 1. a rate of ~ 2. by ~ (the staff will be reduced by ~)

attune *v.* (D; refl., tr.) to ~ to (you will have to ~ your ears to this type of music)

atypical *adj.* ~ of (such behavior was ~ of him)

auction *n.* 1. to hold an ~ 2. an ~ takes place 3. to put smt. up for ~ 4. a public ~ 5. at (an) ~; by ~ (we bought these items at an ~; they sold their house by ~)

audacious *adj.* ~ to + inf. (it was ~ of her to try that)

audacity *n.* 1. to demonstrate, show ~ 2. sheer ~ 3. the ~ to + inf. (he had the ~ to ask for an increase in salary)

audience *n.* ['interview'] 1. to give, grant an ~ 2. to receive; seek an ~ with 3. at an ~ ['group of spectators'] 4. to attract, draw an ~ 5. to electrify, grip, move, stir, sway an ~ 6. an appreciative, enthusiastic, responsive; cold, passive, unresponsive; sympathetic; unsympathetic ~ 7. a capacity; captive; live; mass; select, standing-room-only; studio ~

audit *n.* 1. to carry out, conduct an ~ 2. a tax ~

audition I *n.* 1. to give smb. an ~ 2. to hold ~s

audition II *v.* 1. (D; intr., tr.) to ~ for (he ~ed for the role of the butler; they ~ed her for a part in the school play) 2. (E) she ~ed to play Juliet

auditorium *n.* 1. a main ~ 2. in an ~

augur *v.* (D; intr.; P) to ~ for (this ~s well for the future)

aura *n.* a glittering ~

auspices *n.* under the ~ of smt. (under the ~ of the mayor's office)

austerity *n.* 1. to practice ~ 2. strict; wartime ~

authenticate *v.* (D; tr.) to ~ as (the painting was ~ed as genuine)

authenticity *n.* 1. to establish, prove; vouch for the ~ of smt. 2. to doubt, question the ~ of smt.

author *n.* an anonymous; beginning; classic; contemporary; established, famous, noted, recognized, well-known; prolific; rising; talented; young ~

authorities *n.* ['governmental officials'] civil, civilian; government; local; military; occupation ~

authority *n.* ['control'] ['power'] 1. to assume; delegate; demonstrate, show; establish; exercise, wield; invoke ~ 2. to defy; deny, reject; undermine ~ 3. absolute, complete, full, supreme, unquestioned; parental ~ 4. ~ for; over (he assumed ~ for overseas operations; a commanding officer has complete ~ over her personnel) 5.

in ~ (who was in ~?) 6. of ~ (a man, woman of ~) 7. under smb.'s ~ (these employees are under my ~) ['legal power'] ['authorization'] 8. to abuse, overstep one's ~ 9. legal; ministerial; presidential; reviewing (mil.); royal ~ 10. by, on smb.'s ~ (by whose ~ were these funds spent? she did it on her own ~) 11. the ~ to + inf. (the police had the ~ to conduct a search) ['expert'] ['source'] 12. to cite, invoke an ~ 13. a competent, reliable; indisputable, irrefutable, unimpeachable, unquestioned; leading, respected ~; the greatest living ~ 14. an ~ on (an outstanding ~ on shipbuilding) 15. on ~ (on good ~; on the highest ~)

authorization *n.* 1. to give, grant ~ 2. to receive ~ 3. to revoke smb.'s ~ 4. official ~ 5. ~ for 6. (the) ~ to + inf. (we received ~ to begin demolition)

authorize *v.* 1. (H) the director ~d us to work in the laboratory 2. (K) she ~d his entering the vault

authorized *adj.* 1. (usu. does not stand alone) ~ to + inf. (we are not ~ to enter the restricted area)

authorship *n.* to establish ~ (to establish the ~ of an ancient mansucript)

automatic *adj.* fully ~

automatic pilot *n.* to engage; disengage the ~

automobile *n.* (AE) to drive, operate; park an ~ (see **car 1-9**)

autonomy *n.* 1. to grant ~ 2. to seek ~

autopsy *n.* to do, perform an ~ on

autumn *n.* (esp. BE) in (the) ~

auxiliary *n.* 1. (grammar) a modal ~ 2. (BE) a nursing ~

avail I *n.* (formal) ['aid'] 1. of little ~ 2. to no ~

avail II *v.* (formal) 1. intr. ('to help') to ~ against (nothing could ~ against the enemy attack) 2. (d; refl.) ('to make use') to ~ of (she ~ed herself of the offer)

available *adj.* 1. easily, readily ~ 2. to make oneself ~; to make smt. ~ 3. ~ to (the information is ~ to anyone) 4. ~ for (are you ~ for a meeting tomorrow?) 5. ~ to + inf. (is there anyone ~ to replace her?)

avenge *v.* (D; refl.) to ~ on, upon (to ~ oneself on an enemy)

avenue *n.* ['opportunity'] 1. to explore every ~ 2. an ~ to (an ~ to success) ['street'] 3. in (BE), on (AE) an ~

aver *v.* (formal) (L) he ~red that he was innocent

average *n.* 1. to calculate, work out an ~ 2. (misc.) above ~; below ~; on the ~ she works seven hours a day; (AE) he finished school with a B ~

average out *v.* (d; intr.) to ~ at, to (snowfall ~s out in this part of the country at/to twenty inches a year)

averse *adj.* (formal) ~ to (I would not be ~ to taking a drink)

aversion *n.* (formal) 1. to have; take an ~ to 2. a deep, deep-rooted, distinct, marked; pet ~ 3. an ~ to (an ~ to animals)

avert *v.* (formal) (D; tr.) to ~ from (he ~ed his eyes from the scene of the accident)

aviation *n.* civil; military ~

avid *adj.* (formal) (usu. does not stand alone) ~ for (~ for fame)

avoid *v.* 1. to ~ studiously 2. (G) she managed to

~ being punished

avow *v.* (formal) (M or N; used with a noun) he ~ed himself (to be) a socialist

avowal *n.* 1. to make an ~ 2. an ~ that − clause (she made a solemn ~ that she would never reveal the secret)

awake I *adj.* 1. wide ~ 2. ~ to (~ to the danger of inflation)

awake II *v.* 1. (D; intr.) to ~ from (she awoke from a deep sleep) 2. (d; intr.) to ~ to (I awoke to bright sunlight) 3. (E) they awoke to find the house in flames

awaken *v.* 1. see **awake** II 2. (formal and rare) (d; tr.) to ~ to (to ~ smb. to a sense of duty)

awakening *n.* a rude, sudden ~

award I *n.* 1. to grant, make, present an ~ 2. to receive an ~ 3. an ~ for

award II *v.* 1. (A) the judges ~ed the prize to her; or: the judges ~ed her the prize 2. (D; tr.) to ~ for (to ~ a prize for research)

aware *adj.* 1. keenly, painfully, very much ~ 2. (cannot stand alone) ~ of (they were ~ of the difficulties) 3. ~ that + clause (he was ~ that the deadline had passed)

awareness *n.* ~ that + clause (there is a general ~

that smoking is harmful)

away *adv.* ~ from (he is ~ from home)

awe I *n.* 1. to inspire ~ in (he inspired ~ in everyone) 2. to hold smb. in ~ 3. in ~ of (to stand in ~ of smb.)

awe II *v.* (D; tr.) to ~ into (to ~ smb. into silence)

awful *adj.* (colloq.) 1. ~ about (I feel ~ about it) 2. ~ for (the situation is ~ for all of us) 3. ~ to + inf. (it was ~ to work there = it was ~ working there) 4. ~ that + clause (it's ~ that they were reprimanded because of my mistake)

awkward *adj.* 1. ~ with (he is ~ with children) 2. (BE) ~ for (Monday is ~ for me) 3. ~ to + inf. (it is ~ to discuss such matters in public = it is ~ discussing such matters in public)

AWOL *adj.* to go ~

awry *adj., adv.* to go ~ (our plans have gone ~)

ax, axe *n.* 1. to swing, wield an ~ 2. (misc.) to have an ~ to grind ('to seek personal advantage')

axiom *n.* 1. to lay down an ~ 2. an ~ that + clause (we accept the ~ that a straight line is the shortest distance between two points)

axis *n.* on an ~ (to rotate on an ~)

B

babble I *n.* childish; confused; incessant ~
babble II *v.* 1. to ~ ceaselessly, incessantly 2. (B) he ~d a few words to her 3. (D; intr.) to ~ about
babe *n.* a ~ in the woods ('a naive person')
babel *n.* 1. above the ~ (his voice was heard above the ~) 2. a ~ of tongues
baboon *n.* a troop of ~s
baby *n.* 1. (of a woman) to have a ~ 2. (of a woman) to carry a ~ (a pregnant woman carries a ~ for nine months; to carry a ~ to term) 3. (of a mother) to nurse a ~ 4. (of a midwife, nurse, doctor) to deliver a ~ 5. (of a clergyman) to baptize a ~ 6. to change a ~ ('to change the baby's diaper/nappy') 7. to calm, comfort, hush a ~ 8. to lull; put; rock a ~ to sleep 9. to diaper (AE); swaddle a ~ 10. to wean a ~ 11. to bubble (AE), burp a ~ 12. a blue; full-term; newborn; premature; stillborn; test-tube; thalidomide ~ 13. a ~ babbles, coos; bawls; burps; crawls, creeps; cries; drools; teethes; throws up; toddles; whimpers
baby carriage *n.* (AE) to push, wheel a ~ (BE has *pram*)
baby-sit *v.* (D; intr.) to ~ for (who ~s for you?)
bachelor *n.* a confirmed; eligible ~
back I *adj., adv.* 1. ~ (things are ~ to normal) 2. way ~ (~ back in the eighteenth century) 3. (misc.) to go ~ on one's promise/word ('to fail to keep one's promise')
back II *n.* ['part of the body opposite to the front'] 1. to turn one's ~ to smb.; (usu. fig.) to turn one's ~ on smb. 2. to arch one's ~ (the cat arched its ~) 3. a broad ~ 4. on one's, smb.'s ~ (to lie on one's ~; a heavy bag was on his ~) 5. to stand ~ to ~; they stood with their ~s to the door ['rear part'] 6. at, in the ~ (of) (a room at the ~ of the house; we sat in the back of the car) 7. from the ~ ['area behind smt.'] 8. at the, in (AE) ~ of (BE: a garden at the ~ of the house = AE: a yard in ~ of the house) ['misc.'] 9. he did it behind my ~ ('he did it without my knowledge'); in the ~ of one's mind ('subconsciously'); to break one's ~ ('to work very hard'); to get one's ~ up ('to balk at smt.'); get off my ~ (colloq.) ('leave me alone'); if you scratch my ~, I'll scratch yours (colloq.) ('if you help me, I'll help you'); in ~ of (AE) ('behind'); to have one's ~ to the wall ('to be in a desperate position'); to break the ~ of a job ('to do most of a job'); to put some ~ into one's work ('to make a maximum physical effort'); who will sit in ~?
back III *v.* 1. (D; tr.) ('to support') to ~ against (the independents will ~ us against the majority party) 2. (D; tr.) to ~ for (we will ~ her for public office) 3. (d; intr., tr.) ('to move') to ~ into (to ~ into a garage; she ~ed the car into the driveway) 4. (d; intr., tr.) to ~ out of (he ~ed out of the driveway; to ~ a car out of a garage) 5. (D; intr.) ('to withdraw') to ~ out of (they ~ed out of the deal)
backache *n.* 1. to have ~ (BE)/ a ~ (AE) 2. (a)

chronic, nagging, persistent ~
back away *v.* (D; intr.) to ~ from
backbone *n.* ['courage'] the ~ to + inf. (will he have the ~ to tell the truth?)
backdate *v.* (D; tr.) to ~ to (to ~ an agreement to the beginning of the year)
back down *v.* (D; intr.) to ~ from (they had to ~ from their demands)
backdrop *n.* 1. to provide a ~ for 2. against a ~ of
backer *n.* a financial ~
back formation *n.* (ling.) a ~ from *(to burgle is a ~ from burglar)*
background *n.* ['one's experience, past'] 1. to check smb.'s ~ 2. a broad; narrow; rich; specialized ~ 3. one's academic, educational; cultural; religious ~ 4. a ~ for (to have the right ~ for a job) ['rear part of a picture, scene'] 5. against, on a ~ (against a dark ~) ['surroundings'] 6. an appropriate, fitting ~ 7. a ~ to (the music served as a ~ to the recitation of poetry) ['a less important position'] 8. to relegate smb. to the ~ 9. in the ~ (to remain in the ~) ['history, past'] 10. an historical ~ 11. a ~ to (do you know the ~ to this case?)
backing *n.* 1. financial ~ 2. ~ for (financial ~ for a project)
backlog *n.* 1. to accumulate, build up a ~ 2. to reduce a ~
back off *v.* (D; intr.) to ~ from (to ~ from one's demands)
backseat *n.* to take a ~ to smb. (she will not take a ~ to anyone)
backstroke *n.* to do, swim the ~
backup *n.* ['substitute'] a ~ for, to
back up *v.* (D; intr.) to ~ to (he ~ed up to the loading platform)
backwater *n.* a cultural ~
bacon *n.* 1. crisp; lean; smoked; streaky (BE) ~ 2. a rasher of ~ 3. (misc.) to bring home the ~ ('to succeed')
bacteria *n.* non-pathogenic; pathogenic; virulent ~
bad I *adj.* 1. ~ for (smoking is ~ for your health) 2. ~ to + inf. (it's ~ to lie) 3. ~ that + clause (it's too ~ that he was not able to attend the meeting) 4. (misc.) not ~ ('quite good'); not half ~ ('fairly good'); that's (just) too ~ ('nothing can be done about that')
bad II *n.* 1. (colloq.) to be in ~ with smb. ('to be on bad terms with smb.') 2. to go from ~ to worse
bad form *n.* (esp. BE) ~ to + inf. (it's ~ to be late)
badger *v.* 1. (D; tr.) to ~ into (they ~ed me into buying a new car) 2. (D; tr.) to ~ with (to ~ smb. with questions)
baffle *v.* 1. to ~ completely 2. (R) it ~d me that they rejected our offer
bag *n.* ['suitcase'] 1. to pack, unpack one's ~s 2. to check one's ~s ['container'] ['pouch'] 3. an air ~ (that inflates within a car on impact) 4. a barracks;

carrier (BE), shopping; duffel, kit (BE); flight; garment; ice; jiffy ('padded bag used for mailing'); musette (AE); overnight; paper; plastic; sleeping ~ 5. (BE) a sponge ~ ('bag for toilet articles') 6. (AE) a doggy ~ ('bag for leftover food given to a diner in a restaurant') 7. (AE) a grab ~ (BE has *lucky dip*) 8. a tea ~ ['leather ball'] 9. (AE) a punching ~ (BE has *punching ball*) ['misc.'] 10. in the ~ ('assured of success')

baggage *n.* 1. (esp. AE) to check; claim one's ~ 2. excess ~

bagpipes *n.* 1. to play the ~ 2. ~ wail

bail I *n.* 1. to grant, set ~ 2. to post, put up, stand ~ for; (colloq.) to go ~ for 3. to make, raise ~ 4. to deny smb. ~ 5. to forfeit, jump, skip ~ 6. on ~ (to release smb. on ~; to be set free on a thousand dollars ~)

bail II *v.* 1. (AE) (d; intr.) ('to parachute') to ~ out of (to ~ out of an airplane) 2. (d; tr.) ('to remove') to ~ out of (~ water out of a boat) 3. (d; tr.) ('to help') to ~ out of (to ~ smb. out of trouble)

bailiwick *n.* in one's own ~

bait *n.* 1. to hold out, offer; put out, set out ~ 2. to nibble at; swallow, take the ~ 3. to rise to the ~ 4. tempting ~

bake *v.* (C) he ~d a cake for us; or: he ~d us a cake

bakery *n.* at, in a ~ (she works at/in a ~)

balance I *n.* 1. to strike a ~ between 2. to keep; recover one's ~ 3. to lose one's ~ 4. to disturb, upset the ~; to throw smt. off ~ 5. a delicate ~ 6. (bookkeeping) a trial ~ 7. a bank; credit; debit; foreign-trade, trade ~ 8. a favorable; unfavorable ~ (a favorable trade ~) 9. the strategic ~ 10. (misc.) to hang in the ~ ('to be uncertain'); on ~ ('all in all')

balance II *v.* (d; tr.) to ~ against (to ~ one argument against the other)

balance of power *n.* to hold the ~

bale (BE) see **bail II 1**

balk *v.* (D; intr.) to ~ at (he ~ed at the price)

Balkans *n.* in the ~

ball I *n.* ['game'] 1. to play ~ ['round object used in a sport'] 2. to bat; bounce; catch; drop; fumble; hit; kick; throw a ~ 3. a ~ bounces 4. the ~ is dead ('the ball does not bounce') 5. a cue; medicine ~ 6. (BE) a punching ~ (AE has *punching bag*) 7. a baseball; basketball; football; golf; tennis ~; volleyball ['round mass'] 8. a cotton ~ 9. in a ~ to curl up in a ~) ['glass object used in fortune telling'] 10. a crystal ~ ['misc.'] 11. to start the ~ rolling ('to begin an activity'); (colloq.) on the ~ ('efficient'); (AE) to play ~ with ('to cooperate with')

ball II *n.* ['formal dance'] 1. to have, organize a ~ 2. a costume; fancy-dress; inaugural; masked ~ 3. at a ~ (to dance at a ~) 4. (misc.) (esp. AE; colloq.) to have a ~ ('to enjoy oneself')

ballad *n.* a folk; lewd, ribald ~

ballast *n.* 1. to take on ~ 2. to drop ~

ballet *n.* 1. to dance, perform; stage a ~ 2. classical; folk ~; (a) water ~

balloon *n.* 1. to fly; launch a ~ 2. to blow up, inflate; deflate a ~ 3. a ~ bursts 4. a barrage;

observation ~ 5. (fig.) a trial ~ (to send up a trial~)

ballot *n.* 1. to cast a ~ 2. to invalidate a ~ 3. an absentee; open; secret; straw; void ~ 4. a ~ against; for 5. by ~ (to vote by secret ~)

ballot box *n.* to stuff the ~es

balm *n.* 1. to apply a ~ 2. a healing, soothing ~

bamboozle *v.* (colloq.) ('to trick') 1. (D; tr.) to ~ into 2. to ~ out of

ban I *n.* 1. to impose, place put a ~ on 2. to lift a ~ from 3. a test ~ 4. a wartime ~ 5. a ~ on

ban II *v.* 1. (D; tr.) to ~ from (they were ~ned from attending) 2. (K) the police ~ned their demonstrating in the park

banana *n.* 1. to peel a ~ 2. a green; ripe; rotten ~

band I *n.* ['orchestra'] 1. to form a ~ 2. a brass; concert; dance; jazz; marching; military; regimental; school; string ~ 3. a big ~ 4. a ~ marches; performs, plays 5. (misc.) to strike up the ~ ['group'] 6. a predatory; roving ~ 7. a ~ of marauders

band II *n.* ['ring'] 1. a wedding ~ ['range of wavelengths'] 2. a wave ~ 3. a citizens ~ (cr: CB) ['circular strip'] 4. a brake; rubber ~

bandage *n.* 1. to apply, put on a ~ 2. to roll a ~ 3. to remove a ~ 4. to loosen; tighten a ~

Band-Aid (T) *n.* (esp. AE) to apply, put on a ~

bandit *n.* a masked ~

band together *v.* (D; intr., refl.) to ~ against (the liberals ~ed together against the new legislation)

bandwagon *n.* ['attractive cause'] to climb on, jump on the ~

bandy *v.* (D; tr.) to ~ with (to ~ words with smb.)

bang I *n.* with a ~ (the door slammed with a ~)

bang II *v.* 1. (d; intr.) to ~ against; into; on (she ~ed on the door; I ~ed into the wall) 2. (D; tr.) to ~ against, on (he ~ed his head on the low ceiling)

bang away *v.* (colloq.) (D; intr.) ('to shoot') to ~ at (we ~ed away at the enemy plane)

banish *v.* (D; tr.) to ~ from; to (she was ~ed from the country)

banjo *n.* to play; strum a ~

bank I *n.* ['financial establishment'] 1. to charter; establish a ~ 2. a central; commercial; credit; drive-in; land; national; people's, state; merchant (BE); reserve; savings ~ 3. a ~ closes, collapses, fails 4. at, in a ~ (she works at/in a ~) ['fund held in a gambling game'] 5. to break the ~ ['place of storage'] 6. a blood; corneal, eye; data; organ; soil; sperm ~ 7. a citation ~ (for dictionaries)

bank II *v.* (d; intr.) to ~ on ('to rely on') (we were ~ing on your support)

bank III *n.* ['shore'] 1. a rugged; sloping; steep ~ 2. a river ~ 3. on a ~

bank IV *n.* ['row'] ['tier'] an elevator (AE) ~

banker *n.* an international; investment; merchant (BE) ~

banking *n.* electronic; international ~

bankrupt *adj.* to go ~

bankruptcy *n.* to declare, go into, file for, petition for ~

banner *n.* 1. to plant; unfurl a ~ 2. a ~ flutters; waves 3. a regimental ~ 4. (fig.) under a ~

banns *n.* ['declaration of an impending marriage'] to publish the ~

banquet *n*. 1. to arrange, give, hold a ~ 2. to cater a ~ 3. an elaborate, lavish, sumptuous ~ 4. a farewell; formal; state ~ 5. a ~ for 6. at a ~

banter *n*. 1. to exchange ~ with 2. good-natured, light; witty ~

baptism *n*. 1. to administer ~ 2. to accept, receive, undergo ~ 3. (misc.) the ~ of fire

baptize *v*. (N; used with a noun) they ~d him Joseph

bar I *n*. ['counter or place where drinks are sold'] 1. to manage, operate, run a ~ 2. to stop at a ~ (on the way home); to drink at the ~; to drop into a ~ 3. a cash (AE); cocktail; coffee (BE); gay; open ('free'); public (BE); salad; saloon (BE); singles ~ ['barrier'] 4. the color ~ 5. a ~ to (a ~ to success) ['barrier in a law court'] 6. at the ~ (the prisoner at the ~; to be tried at the ~) 7. before the ~ (of justice) ['the profession of barrister, trial lawyer'] (esp. BE) 8. to be admitted, called to the ~ 9. to read for the ~ ['metal strip used as a barrier'] 10. behind ~s ['in prison'] (he was put behind ~s) ['strip used in gymnastics'] 11. a horizontal ~ 12. parallel ~s 13. on the ~ (to work out on the ~) ['handrail used by ballet dancers'] 14. at the ~ (to warm up at the ~) ['metal strip used in a suspension system'] 15. a torsion ~ ['lever on a typewriter'] 16. a space ~ ['oblong piece'] 17. a candy; chocolate ~ ['musical measure'] 18. to hum; play; sing a few ~s

bar II *v*. 1. (D; tr.) ('to exclude') to ~ from (he was ~red from the competition) 2. (K) ('to forbid') they ~red his participating

barb *n*. ['critical remark'] to sling ~s at

barbarism, barbarity *n*. 1. to demonstrate, display ~ 2. outright, unmitigated, utter ~

barbarous *adj*. ~ to + inf. (it was ~ to treat prisoners in that manner)

barbecue I *n*. ['party at which barbecued meat is served'] 1. to have a ~ 2. at a ~

barbecue II *v*. (C) she ~d a steak for me; or: she ~d me a steak

barbed wire, barbwire *n*. to string ~

barbell *n*. 1. to clean; lift; press a ~ 2. an adjustable ~

barber *n*. at the ~'s

barbershop *n*. (esp. AE) at, in a ~ (he is at/in the ~)

bare *adj*. 1. ~ of (the hills were ~ of vegetation) 2. (misc.) to lay smt. ~

bargain I *n*. ['agreement'] 1. to drive; make, strike; seal a ~ 2. to meet one's end of a ~ 3. a hard ~ (she drives a hard ~) 4. a ~ with (we struck a ~ with them) 5. a ~ to + inf. (they made a ~ not to cut prices) ['advantageous purchase'] 6. to find, get a ~ 7. to shop for ~s 8. a good, real ~ ['misc.'] 9. to make the best of a bad ~ ('to do one's best in a difficult situation')

bargain II *v*. 1. ('to negotiate') to ~ shrewdly 2. (D; intr.) ('to negotiate') to ~ for; over; with (we ~ed with them for the property) 3. (d; intr.) to ~ for (BE), on (AE) ('to count on') (I wasn't ~ing on any trouble)

bargaining *n*. collective; plea ~

barge I *n*. 1. to drive; float; tow a ~ 2. to load;

unload a ~

barge II *v*. (d; intr.) to ~ into (she ~d into the room)

barge in *v*. (D; intr.) to ~ on (to ~ on a conversation)

baritone *n*. to sing ~

bark I *n*. ['covering of a tree'] ~ peels

bark II *n*. ['the sound made by a dog'] a furious; loud, noisy ~

bark III *v*. 1. to ~ furiously 2. (B) the sergeant ~ed an order to his squad 3. (D; intr.) to ~ at (the dog ~ed at the jogger)

barn *n*. a car ~ (AE; BE has *waggon shed*)

barnacles *n*. ~ cling (to the bottom of a ship)

barometer *n*. 1. an aneroid; mercurial ~ 2. a ~ is steady; falls; rises

baron *n*. ['magnate'] a cattle; coal; oil; robber; steel ~

barracks *n*. 1. (AE) to GI the ~ 2. (AE) to police (up) the ~ 3. disciplinary ~ 4. restricted to ~

barrage *n*. 1. to lay down a ~ 2. to lift a ~ 3. a rolling ~ 4. an advertising; propaganda ~

barrel *n*. 1. to tap a ~ 2. (misc.) (colloq.) to have smb. over a ~ ('to have placed smb. in a difficult position')

barricade *n*. 1. to place, set up a ~ 2. to man the ~s 3. to remove, take down a ~ 4. a barbed-wire ~ 5. a ~ against

barrier *n*. 1. to erect, place, set up a ~ 2. to overcome, take a ~ (the horse took the ~ easily) 3. to break down; remove a ~ 4. the sonic, sound ~ (to break the sound ~) 5. a crush (BE), police ~ 6. a cultural; language; racial ~ (to break a racial ~) 7. a ~ between 8. a ~ to (a ~ to progress)

barrow *n*. to push a ~

barter I *n*. 1. to engage in ~ 2. ~ between; for; with

barter II *v*. 1. (D; intr., tr.) to ~ for (to ~ furs for tobacco) 2. (D; intr.) to ~ with

base I *n*. ['center of operations'] 1. to establish, set up a ~ 2. an advanced, forward; main ~ 3. an air, air-force; army; military; missile; naval ~ 4. (misc.) a power ~; a ~ of operations ['goal'] (AE) (baseball) 5. to reach; touch a ~ 6. to steal a ~ 7. (misc.) (slang) she couldn't get to first ~ with them ('she couldn't even begin to achieve any success with them') ['collection'] 8. a data ~ ['basic ingredient'] 9. an oil ~

base II *v*. (d; tr.) to ~ on, upon (we ~d our conclusions on facts)

baseball *n*. ['game'] 1. to play ~ 2. night ~ ['ball'] 3. to pitch a ~

basement *n*. 1. (AE) a finished; full ~ 2. (esp. AE) a bargain ~ (in a department store)

bash I *n*. (slang) (BE) ['attempt'] to have a ~ at smt.

bash II *v*. (D; tr.) to ~ against (he ~ed his head against the door)

bashful *adj*. ~ with

basic *adj*. ~ to

basic training *n*. (mil.) to go through, take ~

basin *n*. 1. a river; tidal ~ 2. a handbasin (BE), washbasin, wash-hand (BE) ~

basis *n*. 1. to form, provide a ~ for 2. a firm, solid,

sound; first-name; scientific; shaky ~ 3. on a ~
(on a solid ~; she was promoted on the ~ of her
accomplishments; to be paid on an hourly ~; to be
on a first-name ~)
bask *v.* to ~ in (to ~ in the sunshine; to ~ in the
adulation of one's followers)
basket *n.* ['receptacle'] 1. to make, weave a ~ 2. a
laundry, linen (BE); picnic; wastepaper; wicker ~
['goal in basketball'] 3. to make, score, sink a ~ 4.
to shoot at the ~ 5. to miss the ~
basketball *n.* ['game'] 1. to play ~ ['ball used in
the game of basketball'] 2. to dribble; pass a ~
bass *n.* 1. to sing ~ 2. a deep ~
bat I *n.* ['club'] 1. to swing a ~ 2. a baseball; cricket ~ ['one's turn batting'] 3. (AE) at ~ (who's at
~?) ['misc.'] 4. (colloq.) (BE) at full ~ ('very
fast')
bat II *n.* ['flying mammal'] 1. ~s fly at night 2.
(misc.) as blind as a ~
batch *n.* a fresh ~ (of dough)
bath *n.* 1. to have (BE), take a ~ 2. to draw, run
a ~ 3. (BE) a swimming ~ 4. a sitz; steam, Turkish; whirlpool ~ 5. (misc.) a blood ~ ('slaughter')
USAGE NOTE: In BE, one meaning of *bath* is
'bathtub'.
bathed *adj.* ~ in (~ in sunshine)
bather *n.* a sun ~
bathing *n.* sun ~
bathing suit *n.* (esp. AE) a one-piece; two-piece ~
bathroom see the Usage Note for **room**
baton *n.* 1. (in a relay race) to pass the ~ 2. (of a
drum major) to twirl a ~ 3. (of an orchestra
leader) to raise a ~
battalion *n.* to command a ~ (a major commands
a ~)
batter I *n.* ['mixture for baking'] to mix up; pour;
stir (a) ~
batter II *v.* (D; tr.) to ~ to (to ~ smt. to pieces)
batter III *n.* ['one whose turn it is to bat']
(baseball) a leadoff ~
battery *n.* ['a group of cells that store and furnish
current'] 1. to charge; recharge a ~ 2. to discharge, run down a ~ 3. a flashlight (AE), torch
(BE); storage ~ 4. a ~ charges (itself) 5. a ~ dis-
charges, runs (itself) down 6. a ~ is dead, flat (BE)
['artillery unit'] 7. to command a ~ (a captain
commands a ~) 8. a missile ~
battle I *n.* 1. to do, give, join ~ 2. to fight, wage;
lose; win a ~ 3. to break off, terminate a ~ 4. a
bloody; decisive; fierce, pitched; raging; losing;
running ~ 5. a naval ~ 6. a ~ royal 7. a ~ rages 8.
a ~ against; among, between; for, over; with (they
fought a ~ among themselves for domination of
the market; the ~ against inflation; to join ~ with
smb.; a ~ between two strong adversaries) 9. a ~
to + inf. (it was a real ~ to win the election) 10. at
a ~ (at the ~ of Gettysburg) 11. in ~ (to be killed
in ~)
battle II *v.* (D; intr.) to ~ against, with; for, over
battlefield *n.* on the ~ (to die on the ~)
battleship *n.* a pocket ~
battle station *n.* to take up one's ~
batty *adj.* (slang) ['mad'] to go ~ over
baulk (esp. BE) see **balk**

bay I *n.* 1. to hold, keep at ~ 2. to bring to ~
bay II *v.* (D; intr.) to ~ at (the hounds were ~ing
at the fox)
bayonet *n.* 1. to thrust a ~ into (smb.'s body) 2. to
fix; unfix ~s
bazaar *n.* 1. a charity ~ 2. at a ~
bazooka *n.* to fire; operate a ~
be *v.* 1. (E; usu. in the past) he was never to see his
family again; she was to become famous 2. (S) to
~ a teacher; to ~ happy
beach *n.* 1. an isolated; private; public; sandy ~ 2.
at, on the ~
beachhead *n.* to establish; hold; secure a ~
beacon *n.* 1. a homing; landing; radar; radio;
rotating ~ 2. (BE) a Belisha ~ ('a light marking a
pedestrian crossing') 3. a ~ to (to serve as a ~ to
others)
bead *n.* ['front sight'] to draw a ~ on
beads *n.* 1. (rel.) to say, count one's ~ 2. to string
~ 3. (rel.) prayer ~ 4. a string of ~
beam I *n.* ['shaft of light'] 1. to direct, shine a ~
at 2. a high; low ~ (on a car) 3. a ~ from; to ['signal'] 4. a radar; radio ~ 5. (also fig.) off the ~; on
the ~ ['piece of wood'] 6. a balance ~
beam II *v.* 1. (B) they ~ed the program to the
countries of Central America 2. (AE) (d; tr.) to ~
at (the sales campaign was ~ed at young profes-
sionals) 3. (D; intr.) to ~ with (to ~ with joy)
bean *n.* 1. broad; French (BE), haricot (BE), kidney; lima; navy; pinto; runner (BE), string wax
~s 2. baked ~s 3. (misc.) to spill the ~s (slang)
('to reveal a secret'); to use the old ~ (slang) ('to
use one's head'); full of ~s (slang) ('mistaken')
(AE); ('full of energy') (BE)
bear I *n.* 1. the black; brown; grizzly; Kodiak;
polar ~ 2. a teddy ~ 3. ~s hibernate
bear II *v.* 1. (formal) (A; the omission of *to* is
rare) ('to carry') the servants were ~ing food to
the guests 2. (A; used without *to*) ('to give birth
to') she bore him two children 3. (d; intr.) ('to pertain') to ~ on (these facts ~ on the case) 4. (d;
intr.) ('to move') to ~ to (we had to ~ to the right)
5. (d; intr.) ('to have patience') to ~ with (please
~ with me for a few minutes) 6. (E; preceded by:
can -- cannot -- can't) ('to stand, tolerate') she
can't ~ to watch them suffer 7. (G; often used
with: can -- cannot -- can't) ('to stand, tolerate') he
can't ~ being alone; her words ~ repeating 8. (K)
('to stand, tolerate') I cannot ~ his behaving in
that manner 9. (O; can be used with own inanimate
object) ('to feel') she ~s them a grudge; he ~s us)
no ill will 10. (P; refl.) ('to behave') she bore herself with dignity 11. (misc.) to bring to ~ on (she
brought her influence to ~ on the legislators)
beard *n.* 1. to grow a ~ 2. to shave off; trim one's
~ 3. to stroke one's ~ 4. a bushy, heavy, rough,
thick; light, sparse; neat, trim ~
bear down *v.* (d; intr.) to ~ on (our destroyers
bore down on the enemy carrier)
bearing *n.* ['relation'] 1. to have a ~ on (that fact
has no ~ on the case) 2. a direct ~ ['position'] 3. to
take a ~ on (we took a ~ on the hill) ['carriage']
['manner'] 4. a dignified; military; regal, royal ~
['machine part that supports'] 5. to burn out a ~ 6.

a ball; roller ~ ['charge on a coat of arms'] 7. a heraldic ~

bearings *n.* ['orientation'] 1. to get one's ~ 2. to lose one's ~

bear up *v.* (D; intr.) to ~ against, under (to ~ under pressure)

beast *n.* ['qualities of an animal'] 1. to bring out the ~ in smb. ['animal'] 2. a wild ~

beat I *n.* ['a regularly traversed round'] 1. to patrol, walk one's ~ 2. to cover one's ~ 3. a policeman's ~ ['rhythm'] 4. an irregular; regular, steady ~ 5. to a ~ (to dance to the ~ of jungle music) ['unit of rhythm'] 6. a ~ to (four ~s to a measure)

beat II *v.* 1. to ~ brutally, mercilessly, severely, viciously 2. (d; intr., tr.) ('to strike') to ~ against (the bird beat its wings against the bars of its cage; the waves ~ against the rocks) 3. (d; tr.) ('to hammer') to ~ into (to ~ facts into smb.'s head; to ~ swords into plowshares) 4. (d; tr.) ('to strike') to ~ into, to (to ~ smb. into submission; to ~ smb. to death) 5. (d; intr.) ('to strike') to ~ on (smb. was ~ing on the door) 6. (colloq.) (D; tr.) ('to arrive ahead of') to ~ to (I'll ~ you to the car!) 7. (N; used with an adjective) ('to strike') they beat him unconscious 8. (slang) (R) ('to astound') it ~s me that they turned down the invitation

beat down *v.* 1. (D; intr.) to ~ on (the sun beat down on us mercilessly) 2. (BE) (D; tr.) ('to persuade to reduce a price') to ~ to (I beat them down to ten pounds)

beating *n.* 1. to give smb. a ~ 2. to get, take a ~ 3. a brutal, good, merciless, severe, vicious ~ (he got a good ~)

beat out *v.* (D; tr.) to ~ for (we beat them out for the title by ten points)

beat up *v.* (slang) (AE) (d; intr.) to ~ on ('to beat') (to ~ on smb.)

beau *n.* (colloq.) a steady ~

beautiful *adj.* ~ to + inf. (it was ~ to watch)

beauty *n.* ['a beautiful person or thing'] 1. a dazzling, raving, striking ~ 2. a bathing ~ ['good looks'] 3. to enhance ~ 4. dazzling, striking, wholesome ~

beauty contest *n.* 1. to hold, stage a ~ 2. to enter a ~

beaver *n.* 1. a colony of ~s 2. (misc.) an eager ~ ('an overzealous person')

beaver away *v.* (slang) (BE) (D; intr.) ('to work hard') to ~ at

beck *n.* to be at smb.'s ~ and call

beckon *v.* 1. (D; intr.) to ~ to (he ~ed to her) 2. (H) she ~ed me to follow

become *v.* 1. (d; intr.) to ~ of (what became of her?) 2. (formal) (R) it doesn't ~ you to speak like that 3. (S) she became a teacher; to ~ depressed

becoming *adj.* (rare) ~ to (that is not ~ to you)

bed *n.* ['article of furniture for sleeping'] 1. to make, make up a ~ 2. to undo a ~ 3. to lie, stay in ~; to lie, sit on a ~ 4. to get out of ~ 5. to take to one's ~ ('to remain in bed because of illness') 6. a double; king-size; queen-size; single; twin ~ 7. a bunk; camp (BE); folding; hospital; rollaway; sofa; truckle (BE), trundle (AE); water ~ 8. an unmade ~ 9. a feather ~ ('a feather mattress')

['ground at the bottom of a body of water'] 10. a river ~ ['plot of ground'] 11. a flower ~

bedfellow *n.* strange ~s (politics make strange ~s)

bedroom *n.* a master; spare ~

bedside *n.* at smb.'s ~

bedsore *n.* 1. to develop, get a ~ 2. to prevent a ~

bee I *n.* ['insect'] 1. to keep ~s 2. a killer; queen; worker ~ 3. ~s buzz, hum; sting; swarm 4. a cluster; colony; swarm of ~s 5. (misc.) as busy as a ~

bee II *n.* (esp. AE) ['meeting to work or compete'] a quilting; sewing; spelling; spinning ~

beef I *n.* 1. to boil; braise; broil; cook; roast; stew ~ 2. chipped; corned; salt (BE) ~ 3. (AE) ~ Wellington 4. baby; prime ~ USAGE NOTE: Corned beef in the US is not the same as corned beef in GB.

beef II *v.* (D; intr.) ('to complain') to ~ about

beeline *n.* ['shortest route'] to make a ~ for ('to go directly toward')

beer *n.* 1. to brew ~ 2. cold; strong; weak ~ 3. ginger; light; near ~ 4. (AE) root ~ 5. a bottle; can; glass; mug, stein of ~

beet *n.* 1. a sugar ~ 2. (misc.) as red as a ~ (AE; BE has: as red as a beetroot)

beg *v.* 1. to ~ humbly 2. (D; intr.) to ~ for (to ~ for mercy) 3. (formal) (d; tr.) to ~ of (I must ~ a favor of you) 4. (E) they ~ged to be allowed to go; I ~ to differ 5. (H) they ~ged her to help 6. (L; subj.) he ~ged that his family be/should be spared 7. (misc.) to go ~ging ('to be unwanted') (those jobs went ~ging)

begging *n.* to live by ~

begin *v.* 1. (D; intr.) to ~ by, with (they began by saying a prayer; or: they began with a prayer) 2. (E) she began to work 3. (G) she began working

beginner *n.* a rank ~

beginning *n.* 1. to make a ~ 2. to mark a ~ 3. an auspicious, promising ~ 4. at, in the ~ 5. from (the) ~ (from ~ to end; from the very ~)

begrudge *v.* (O; can be used with one inanimate object) he ~s us our success

beguile *v.* (formal) 1. (D; tr.) to ~ into (he ~d me into lending him money) 2. (D; tr.) to ~ out of 3. (D; tr.) to ~ with (to ~ children with stories)

behalf *n.* in (AE), on smb.'s ~ USAGE NOTE: Some purists maintain that in AE *in smb.'s behalf* means 'for smb.'s benefit', whereas *on smb.'s behalf* means 'as smb.'s representative'.

behave *v.* 1. (d; intr.) to ~ like (he ~d like a gentleman) 2. (D; intr.) to ~ towards (how did they ~ towards you?)

behavior, behaviour *n.* 1. to exhibit ~ (to exhibit strange ~) 2. abnormal; asocial; criminal; diplomatic; disciplined; disruptive; inconsiderate; inexcusable; infantile; irrational; model; modest; neurotic; normal; obsequious; promiscuous; provocative; ruthless; scandalous; scurrilous; strange; sullen; undiplomatic; undisciplined; unorthodox; unruly; unsportsmanlike ~ 3. good ~ (in prison) 4. ~ towards, with 5. on one's ~ (to be on one's best ~)

behest *n.* at smb.'s ~

behind *adv., prep.* 1. to fall, lag ~ 2. to remain,

stay ~ 3. ~ by (our team is ~ by two points) 4. ~ in, with (he's ~ with his payments) 5. (misc.) to be solidly ~ smb. ('to support smb. wholeheartedly')

beholden adj. (cannot stand alone) ~ for; to (we are ~ to nobody for anything)

behoove, behove v. (R) (formal) it ~s them to help the needy

being n. 1. to come into ~ 2. an extraterrestrial; human; mortal; rational; supernatural ~

belch n. to emit, let out a ~

belief n. 1. to express; hold a ~ 2. to shake one's ~ 3. to give up, relinquish one's ~ 4. a basic; doctrinaire; erroneous, false, mistaken; firm, strong, unshakable; popular; prevalent; unpopular ~ 5. a ~ in (nothing will shake his ~ in ghosts) 6. a ~ that + clause (it is their firm ~ that the earth is flat) 7. beyond ~ 8. in the ~ that...

believe v. 1. to ~ firmly, sincerely, strongly; mistakenly 2. (D;intr.) to ~ in (to ~ in ghosts) 3. (D; tr.) to ~ of (I can't ~ it of him) 4. (L) we ~ that she will come 5. (M) they all ~ the story to be true 6. (misc.) I ~ so; I ~ not

believer n. 1. a firm, sincere, strong; true ~ 2. a ~ in (he's no ~ in miracles)

bell n. 1. to cast a ~ 2. to ring, sound a ~ 3. a church; door ~ 4. a diving ~ 5. wedding ~s 6. a ~ chimes, clangs, peals, rings, sounds, tolls 7. (misc.) (boxing) to come out for the ~

belligerency n. 1. to demonstrate, display, exhibit ~ 2. a state of ~ 3. ~ towards

belligerent adj. ~ towards

bellow v. 1. (B) he ~ed a command to his men 2. (L) he ~ed that he would fight any man at the bar

bellows n. to operate, use ~

bellyache v. (slang) (D; intr.) ('to complain') to ~ about

belong v. 1. (d; intr.) ('to deserve to be') to ~ in (he ~s in jail) 2. (d; intr.) to ~ to ('to be owned by') (the book ~s to her) 3. (d; intr.) to ~ to ('to be a member of') (to ~ to an organization) 4. (d; intr.) ('to be appropriate') to ~ under (this item ~s under a different heading)

belongings n. one's earthly; personal ~

below prep. ~ in (to be ~ smb. in rank)

belt I n. ['band'] 1. to buckle, fasten one's ~ 2. (also fig.) to tighten one's ~ 3. to loosen; undo one's ~ 4. a life; money; safety, seat, shoulder ~ 5. a cartridge; Sam Browne ~ 6. a garter (AE), suspender (BE) ~ 7. a chastity ~ 8. a conveyor ~ 9. (usu. fig.) below the ~ ('unfairly') ['zone'] (AE) 10. the Bible; corn; cotton ~ ['symbol of expertise in judo or karate'] 11. a black; brown; white ~ ['misc.'] 12. under one's ~ ('experienced, lived through')

belt II v. (colioq.) (O) I ~ed him one

bench n. ['judge's seat'] 1. to reprimand from the ~) 2. on the ~ (who will be on the ~ during her trial?) ['places in Parliament'] (BE) 3. the back; cross; front ~ ['place where reserve players sit'] 4. on the ~ (he spent ten minutes on the ~) ['table'] 5. a work ~

bench warrant n. to issue a ~

bend I n. 1. to make a ~ (the river makes a ~) 2. a horseshoe; sharp; slight ~ 3. a knee ~ 4. (misc.)

(colloq.) (BE) round the ~ ('mentally unsound')

bend II v. 1. (D; intr., tr.) to ~ to (the road ~s to the right; she cannot ~ them to her will) 2. (D; tr.) to ~ into (she bent the bar into the right shape)

bender n. (colloq.) ['drunken spree'] to go on a ~

benediction n. 1. to give, offer, pronounce the ~ 2. to pronounce a ~ over

beneficial adj. 1. ~ for, to (~ to health) 2. ~ to + inf. (it would be ~ to keep abreast of developments in Asia)

beneficiary n. to name a ~; to name smb. (as) (a) ~

benefit I n. 1. to derive, get, reap (a) ~ from 2. a death; fringe; sickness (BE); tax ~ 3. to be of ~ to 4. for smb.'s ~ 5. (misc.) to give smb. the ~ of the doubt; without ~ of clergy

benefit II v. (D; intr.) to ~ from (we all ~ed from her success)

benefits n. 1. to provide ~ 2. to collect; reap ~ 3. to withhold ~ 4. disability; fringe; health-care; old-age; retirement; strike; survivors' (AE); unemployment; veterans'; workers' ~

benevolent adj. ~ towards

bent I adj. (cannot stand alone) ['determined'] ~ on (he was ~ on getting himself hurt; ~ on mischief)

bent II n. ['propensity'] 1. to have; show a ~ for 2. to follow one's (own) ~ 3. an artistic; decided; natural ~

bequeath v. (formal) (A) she ~ed her fortune to him; or: she ~ed him her fortune

bequest n. 1. to make a ~ 2. a ~ to

berate v. (D; tr.) to ~ for

bereft adj. (cannot stand alone) ['stripped'] ~ of (~ of all hope; ~ of one's senses) USAGE NOTE: In the meaning 'having recently lost a dear one', the form bereaved is used--the bereaved parents.

berry n. to pick ~ies

berserk adj. to go ~

berth n. 1. to make up a ~ 2. a lower; sleeping; upper ~ 3. (misc.) to give smb. a wide ~ ('to avoid smb.')

beseech v. (formal) (H; no passive) to ~ smb. to show mercy

beset adj. (cannot stand alone) ~ by, with (~ by doubts)

beside prep. to be ~ oneself with (he was ~ himself with grief)

best I adj. 1. ~ to + inf. (it is ~ not to speak of it in public) 2. ~ that + clause; subj. (it is ~ that she say/should say nothing to the press)

best II n. 1. to do, give; try one's (level) ~ 2. to make the ~ (of smt.) 3. to get the ~ (of smb.) 4. to look one's ~ 5. one's level ~ 6. next, second ~ 7. one's ~ to + inf. (she tried her ~ to finish the job on time) 8. at one's ~ (she is not at her ~ in the morning) 9. for the ~ (it turned out for the ~) 10. in the ~ of (he's not in the ~ of health) 11. in one's Sunday ~ 12. to the ~ of (to the ~ of my ability) 13. (misc.) (colloq.) give my ~ to your family

bestir v. (formal and rare) (H; refl.) we must ~ ourselves to get there on time

bestow v. (formal) (d; tr.) to ~ on, upon (to ~ an honor on smb.)

bet I *n.* 1. to make a ~ 2. to place a ~ on 3. to accept, take a ~ 4. a side ~ 5. a ~ that + clause (she made a ~ that her team would win) 6. on a ~ (he did it on a ~) 7. (misc.) to hedge one's ~s ('to protect oneself by placing several bets')

bet II *v.* 1. (D; intr., tr.) to ~ on (he bet on that horse; he bet a month's salary on that horse) 2. (L; may have an object) I bet (her) that it would snow 3. (O; can be used with one, two, or three objects) we bet him; we bet ten pounds; we bet him ten pounds; we bet him ten pounds that it would rain

betake *v.* (formal and obsol.) (P; refl.) he betook himself to the fair

betray *v.* (B) the informer ~ed them to the police

betroth *v.* (rare) (B) they were ~ed to each other at an early age

betrothal *n.* 1. to announce a ~ 2. a ~ to

better I *adj.* 1. any ~ (is she any ~ today?) 2. ~ at (he is ~ at tennis than at squash) 3. ~ to + inf. (it is ~ to give than to receive) 4. ~ that + clause; subj. (it's ~ that she go/should go alone)

better II *n.* 1. to get the ~ of smb. 2. to think ~ of smt. 3. for the ~ (a change for the ~; to take a turn for the ~)

betting *n.* off-track; parimutuel ~

beverage *n.* an alcoholic; carbonated; intoxicating; non-alcoholic ~

beware *v.* (D; intr.; only in the imper.) ~ of (~ of the dog!)

bewildered *adj.* ~ to + inf. (she was ~ to find them gone)

bewildering *adj.* ~ to + inf. (it was ~ to contemplate all the possibilities)

bias *n.* ['prejudice'] 1. to demonstrate, display, exhibit, show ~ 2. to root out ~ 3. deep-rooted, strong ~ 4. a ~ against; for; towards ['diagonal line'] 5. on the ~ (to cut on the ~)

biased *adj.* 1. strongly ~ 2. ~ against; towards

Bible *n.* the Holy ~

bibliography *n.* 1. to compile, make up a ~ 2. an annotated; comprehensive; selective ~

bicentenary *n.* to celebrate, mark, observe a ~

bicentennial (esp. AE) see **bicentenary**

bicker *v.* (D; intr.) 1. to ~ constantly, incessantly 2. to ~ about, over; with

bickering *n.* constant, incessant ~

bicycle *n.* 1. to pedal, ride a ~ 2. to get on, mount a ~ 3. an exercise, stationary; racing ~ 4. by ~ (to go somewhere by ~)

bid I *n.* ['bidding of an amount'] 1. to enter, file, make, put in, submit a ~ 2. to call for, invite ~s 3. to raise one's ~ 4. to consider, entertain ~s 5. to recall a ~ 6. an opening; sealed ~ 7. the highest ~ 8. a ~ for, on (she made a ~ on the painting) ['attempt'] 9. to make a ~ 10. a desperate ~ 11. a ~ for (she made a ~ for the nomination) 12. a ~ to + inf. (he made a ~ to regain his former influence)

bid II *v.* 1. (D; tr.) to ~ for (she bid twenty pounds for the vase) 2. (esp. AE) (D; intr.) to ~ on (to ~ on a contract)

bid III *v.* 1. (formal) (A) she bade farewell to them; or: she bade them farewell 2. (obsol.) (H) to ~ smb. to do smt. 3. (obsol.) (I) to ~ smb. do smt.

bidder *n.* the highest; lowest ~

bidding *n.* ['offering of bids'] 1. to open the ~ 2. competitive; spirited ~ ['request'] 3. to do smb.'s ~ 4. at smb.'s ~

big *adj.* ['kind'] ['good'] (colloq., ironical) 1. ~ of (that's ~ of you) 2. ~ to + inf. (it was ~ of you to do that) ['older'] 3. a ~ boy; brother; girl; sister ['very powerful'] 4. ~ business; government; labor

bigamy *n.* to commit; practice ~

bigot *n.* a fanatical, ingrained, narrow-minded, vicious; religious ~

bigoted *adj.* 1. strongly ~ 2. ~ against 3. ~ to + inf. (it was ~ to say that)

bigotry *n.* 1. to arouse, stir up ~ 2. to demonstrate, display ~ 3. fanatical, ingrained, narrow-minded, vicious; religious ~ 4. ~ against

bike *n.* to ride a ~ (see **bicycle**)

bilk *v.* (D; tr.) to ~ out of (they ~ed us out of the money)

bill I *n.* ['proposed law'] 1. to draft; introduce, propose; oppose; pass; support a ~ 2. to move; railroad a ~ through a legislature 3. to quash, reject, vote down; veto a ~ 4. to shelve a ~ ['banknote'] (AE) 5. to break, change; pass a ~ 6. marked ~s ['statement of money owed'] ['debt'] 7. to run up a ~ 8. to foot (colloq.), pay; settle a ~ 9. a hospital, medical; hotel; telephone; utility (gas and electric; water) ~ 10. a ~ falls due, matures ['poster'] 11. to post, stick (BE) a ~ (post no ~s!) ['misc.'] 12. to fill, fit the ~ ('to meet all requirements')

bill II *v.* 1. (D; tr.) ('to charge') to ~ for (the doctor did not ~ them for the visit) 2. (H) ('to cast'); ('to announce') he was ~ed to appear as Hamlet

billet *n.* an officers' ~

billiards *n.* to play ~

billing *n.* ['prominence in advertising, promotion'] top ~ (to get top ~)

bill of health *n.* ['approval'] 1. to give smb. a clean ~ 2. to get, receive a clean ~

bill of sale *n.* to make up, prepare a ~

bin *n.* a storage ~

bind I *n.* ['trouble'] ['dilemma'] 1. a double ~ 2. in a ~

bind II *v.* 1. (D; tr.) ('to put together') to ~ in (to ~ a book in leather) 2. (D; tr.) ('to tie') to ~ to (they bound him to a post) 3. (D; tr.) ('to require') to ~ to (to ~ smb. to secrecy) 4. (H) ('to require') the contract ~s you to pay interest

binder *n.* ['deposit of money'] (esp. AE) 1. to place, put down a ~ on ['holder for sheets of paper'] 2. a loose-leaf; ring ~ ['broad bandage'] (AE) 3. to apply a ~ 4. an abdominal; breast; straight ~

binding I *adj.* ~ on, upon (the agreement is ~ on you)

binding II *n.* ['fastening of the sections of a book'] 1. a handsome; leather ~ 2. in a ~ (the book is in a leather ~) ['narrow strip of fabric'] 3. to sew on, tack on a ~

bind over *v.* (D; tr.) to ~ to (she was bound over to the grand jury)

binge *n.* (colloq.) 1. ['a drunken spree'] to go on a ~ ['unrestrained activity'] 2. a shopping ~

binoculars n. 1. to adjust, focus; train~ on 2. high-powered, powerful ~ 3. a pair of ~
biography n. an authorized; critical; unauthorized ~
biology n. molecular ~
bird n. 1. game; land; migratory; tropical; wading; water ~s 2. ~s of passage; ~s of prey 3. (usu. fig.) a rare ~ 4. ~s build nests; chirp, twitter, warble; flock together; fly; migrate; molt; sing; soar 5. a covey, flock of ~s 6. (misc.) to ring ~s (for scientific purposes); a ~ in the hand ('smt. already possessed'); ~s of a feather ('people with similar characteristics, tastes, and standards'); as free as a ~ ('absolutely free')
bird call n. to do, imitate a ~
birdwatching n. to go in for, take up ~ (as a hobby)
birth n. 1. to give ~ (she gave ~ to twins) 2. a breech; multiple; normal; premature ~ 3. at ~ (she weighed seven pounds at ~) 4. by ~ (he's Spanish by ~) 5. of ~ (of noble ~)
birth control n. to practice ~
birthday n. 1. to attain (formal), reach a ~ 2. to celebrate, mark a ~ 3. at, on a ~ (on her tenth ~) 4. happy ~!
birth pangs n. to endure, suffer ~
birthrate n. 1. a falling; high; low; rising; stable ~ 2. the crude ~
biscuit n. 1. to bake ~s 2. a sweet ~ (BE; AE has cookie) 3. a cream ~ (BE; AE has sandwich cookie) 4. baking-powder; soda; tea ~s 5. (misc.) to take the ~ ('to be the best or worst') (BE; CE has to take the cake)
bishop n. an Anglican, Episcopal; Catholic; Orthodox ~
bison n. a herd of ~
bit I n. ['share'] 1. to do one's ~ ['small piece'] 2. a tiny ~ ['misc.'] 3. every ~ ('completely'); ~ by ~ ('little by little'); he's a ~ of a snob ('he is something of a snob'); she's not the least ~ upset ('she's not at all upset'); wait a ~ ('wait a little')
bit II n. ['mouthpiece on a horse's bridle'] to take the ~ (between one's teeth) (also fig.)
bitch v. (slang; vulgar) (D; intr.) to ~ about (they're always ~ing about the food)
bitchy adj. (colloq.) ['nasty'] ~ about
bite I n. ['act of biting'] ['result of biting'] 1. to take a ~ (she took a ~ out of the apple) 2. an insect; mosquito; snake ~ ['ability to bite'] 3. a powerful ~ (the large dog has a powerful ~) ['snack'] 4. to grab, have a ~ 5. a quick ~ ['request for a loan'] (colloq.) 6. to put the ~ on smb. ['amount of money deducted'] (colloq.) 7. to take a ~ from, out of (the wage tax takes quite a ~ from his paycheck)
bite II v. 1. (D; intr.) to ~ at (also fig.) (to ~ at the bait) 2. (D; intr.) to ~ into, on (she bit into the apple)
bitter I adj. ~ about (he was ~ about his lot)
bitter II n. to take the ~ (with the sweet)
bitterness n. 1. to feel ~ 2. a touch of ~ 3. ~ about, over; towards
bivouac n. 1. to go on; set up a ~ 2. to be on ~
bizarre adj. ~ that + clause (it was ~ that we ran

into each other in such a remote corner of the world)
blabber v. (B) he ~ed everything to the press
black n. ['profit'] 1. in the ~ (to operate in the ~) ['sign of mourning'] 2. to wear ~ 3. jet ~
blackboard n. 1. to clean, wash; erase (esp. AE) a ~ 2. to write on the ~ 3. at the ~ (two pupils were at the ~) 4. (misc.) to send a pupil to the ~
blacklist n. on a ~
black magic n. to practice ~
blackmail I n. to commit; practice ~
blackmail II v. (D; tr.) to ~ into (to ~ smo. into doing smt.)
black market n. on the ~ (to buy smt. on the ~)
black-marketing, black-marketeering n. to engage in, to go in for ~
blackout n. ['extinguishing or concealment of all lights during wartime'] 1. to impose, order a ~ 2. to observe a ~ ['suppression of news'] 3. to impose, order a ~ 4. to lift a ~ 5. to violate a ~ 6. a news ~
bladder n. 1. to empty one's ~ 2. a full ~
blade n. 1. a blunt, dull; sharp ~ 2. a rotary ~ 3. a razor ~
blame I n. 1. to ascribe, assign, attribute (the) ~ to smb. 2. to lay, place, put the ~ on smb.; to lay the ~ at smb.'s door 3. to assess; fix the ~ 4. to shift the ~ to smb. (else) 5. to assume, bear, take the ~ for (she took the ~ for my mistake) 6. the ~ falls on smb.
blame II v. 1. to ~ unfairly, unjustly 2. (D; tr.) to ~ for (they ~d her for the accident) 3. (d; tr.) to ~ on (they ~d the accident on her) 4. to be to ~ for (I am not to ~ for the mistake)
blanch v. 1. (D; intr.) to ~ at (he ~ed at the sight of the mutilated corpse) 2. (D; intr.) to ~ with (to ~ with fear)
blank I adj. to go ~ (my mind went ~)
blank II n. 1. to draw a ~ ('to achieve no result') 2. a complete ~
blanket n. 1. a bath; receiving; saddle; sheet ~ 2. a security ~
blasé adj. ~ about (they were very ~ about winning first prize)
blaspheme v. (D; intr.) to ~ against (to ~ against God)
blasphemous adj. ~ to + inf. (it was ~ to speak in that manner)
blasphemy n. to commit; utter ~ against
blast n. ['explosion'] 1. to set off a ~ ['gust of wind'] 2. an icy ~ ['verbal attack'] 3. to issue a ~ against 4. a vicious, withering ~ ['misc.'] 5. at full ~ (the work was proceeding at full ~)
blather n. ['nonsense'] 1. sheer, utter ~ 2. ~ about
blaze n. to extinguish, put out a ~
blaze away v. (D; intr.) to ~ at (to ~ at the enemy)
blazes n. go to ~! ('damn you!')
bleach n. liquid ~
bleed v. 1. to ~ profusely, uncontrollably 2. (fig.) (D; intr.) to ~ for (my heart ~s for him) 3. (D; intr.) to ~ from (to ~ from the nose) 4. (N; used with an adjective) to ~ smb. white 5. (misc.) to ~ to death
bleeding n. 1. to staunch, stop (the) ~ 2. heavy,

profuse, uncontrollable ~ 3. internal; menopausal ~ 4. ~ from (~ from the rectum)

blemish *n.* a minor; ugly ~

blench *v.* (D; intr.) ('to flinch') to ~ at (he ~ed at the sight)

blend *v.* 1. to ~ together (their voices ~ together well) 2. (d; intr.) to ~ into (to ~ into the crowd) 3. (D; intr.) to ~ with (water does not ~ with oil)

blend in *v.* (D; intr.) to ~ with (she ~ed in with the crowd)

bless *v.* (D; tr.) to ~ with (we are ~ed with good health)

blessing *n.* 1. to give, make, pronounce, say a ~ over 2. to chant a ~ 3. to give one's ~ to; to bestow one's ~ on 4. a divine; priestly ~; God's ~ 5. a ~ for (it was a ~ for us) 6. a ~ that + clause (it was a ~ that we didn't have to make the trip) 7. (misc.) a mixed ~; a ~ in disguise; to count one's ~s

blight *n.* 1. to cast, put a ~ on, upon 2. a potato ~ 3. urban ~ 4. a ~ on (a ~ on one's honor)

blind I *adj.* ['sightless'] 1. legally ~ 2. (misc.) as ~ as a bat ['blinded'] (cannot stand alone) 3. ~ to (~ to danger) 4. ~ with (~ with rage)

blind II *v.* (D; tr.) to ~ to (his infatuation ~ed him to her faults)

blind III (BE) see **window shade**

blindness *n.* color; congenital; night; snow ~

blinds *n.* 1. to adjust; draw; lower; raise the ~ 2. venetian ~

blink *v.* (D; intr.) to ~ at ('to show surprise') (she didn't even ~ at his outrageous proposal)

bliss *n.* 1. to enjoy ~ 2. complete, pure, sheer, total, utter ~ 3. domestic, marital, nuptial, wedded ~ 4. ~ to + inf. (it was ~ to be without a telephone = it was ~ being without a telephone)

blister *n.* 1. to open a ~ 2. a fever ~ (AE; CE has *cold sore)* 3. a ~ bursts; forms

blizzard *n.* 1. a raging; winter ~ 2. a ~ rages; strikes 3. a ~ blows itself out

bloc *n.* 1. the Communist; eastern; NATO; Soviet ~ 2. a voting ~

block *n.* ['interruption'] ['obstacle'] 1. (Am. football) to throw a ~ at smb. 2. a mental ~ (when it comes to word games, I have a mental ~) 3. (med.) a heart; nerve; saddle ~ 4. a stumbling ~ ['street'] ['city square'] (AE) 5. a city ~ (the building occupies an entire city ~) 6. around the ~; in, on a ~ (they went around the ~; they live in this ~) ['apartment house'] (BE) 7. a council ~ 8. a tower ~ ('a high-rise apartment') 9. (misc.) a ~ of flats ['platform'] 10. a butcher's; chopping; headsman's ~ ['auctioneer's platform'] 11. the auction ~ 12. on the ~ ('being auctioned') ['group'] ['bloc'] 13. a trade ~ ['rectangular unit used in construction'] 14. a building; cinder; concrete ~ ['support'] ['brace'] 15. a starting ~ (for a runner) ['section of text'] (computers) 16. to copy; delete; end; move a ~

blockade *n.* 1. to impose; maintain a ~ 2. to break (through); lift; run a ~ 3. a ~ against; on

blocks *n.* to play with ~

blonde *n.* a natural; platinum ~

blood *n.* 1. to draw, let ~ 2. to lose; shed, spill ~ 3. to staunch the flow of ~ 4. to donate; type ~ 5.

blue; pure; royal ~ 6. whole ~ 7. hot ('fiery') ~ 8. ~ cakes; circulates, flows, runs; clots, coagulates, congeals, curdles; spurts (~ spurted from the wound) 9. (fig.) ~ boils; freezes; runs cold 10. (fig.) ~ tells 11. by ~ (related by ~) 12. of ~ (of royal ~) 13. (misc.) to run in the ~ ('to be hereditary '); in cold ~ ('without feeling'); to draw first ~ ('to score the first success'); fresh/ new ~ ('new personnel'); old ~ ('old personnel'); (colloq.) tired ~ ('rundown condition of the body')

blood cell *n.* a red; white ~

blood count *n.* 1. to do a ~ on 2. to have a ~ (done)

blood pressure *n.* 1. to take smb.'s ~ 2. elevated, high; labile; low; normal ~

blood test *n.* 1. to do a ~ 2. to have a ~ (done)

blood transfusion *n.* 1. to administer, (colloq.) do, give a ~ 2. to get, have a ~

blood vessel *n.* 1. an occluded ~ 2. a ~ bursts

bloom *n.* 1. to come into ~ 2. full ~ 3. in ~ (the tulips are in full ~)

bloomer (BE) see **blooper**

blooper *n.* (colloq.) (AE) ['blunder'] 1. to commit, make a ~ 2. a prize ~

blossom I *n.* in ~ (the trees are in ~)

blossom II *v.* (D; intr.) to ~ into (their friendship ~ed into true love)

blot *n.* 1. leave a ~ 2. a ~ on (his actions left a ~ on our name)

blotter *n.* ['blotting paper'] 1. a ~ absorbs (ink, water) ['record'] 2. a police ~

blouse *n.* a full; peasant; see-through ~

blow I *n.* 1. to deal, deliver, strike a ~ (he dealt us a severe ~) 2. to heap, rain ~s on smb. 3. to come to ~s; to exchange ~s 4. to take a ~ (the boxer took several ~s to the head) 5. to cushion; deflect, parry, ward off; dodge a ~ 6. a body; crushing, hard, heavy, powerful, resounding, severe, staggering, telling; decisive; fatal, mortal; glancing, light ~ 7. indiscriminate ~s (to rain indiscriminate ~s on one's victims) 8. a low ('illegal') ~ (also fig.) 9. an exchange of ~s 10. a ~ against, at (to strike a ~ against poverty) 11. a ~ for (to strike a ~ for freedom) 12. a ~ on, to (a ~ on the head; he took a ~ to the chin; a ~ to one's hopes) 13. under ~s (to reel under crushing ~s)

blow II *v.* 1. to ~ hard (the wind was ~ing hard) 2. (A; usu. without *to)* she blew him a kiss 3. (D; intr.) to ~ on (~ on the soup; it's too hot) 4. (misc.) (slang) he blew ('came') into town

blowout *n.* ['flat tire'] 1. to have a ~ 2. to fix a ~

bludgeon *v.* 1. (d; tr.) ('to force by beating') to ~ into (to ~ smb. into doing smt.) (also fig.) 2. (misc.) to ~ smb. to death

blue *n.* ['color'] 1. dark; light ~ ['something colored blue'] 2. a patch of ~ ['symbol of belonging to a team at Oxford or Cambridge'] (BE) 3. to get, win one's ~ ['misc.'] 4. out of the ~ ('unexpectedly')

blueprint *n.* 1. to draw up, make a ~ 2. a ~ for (fig.: a ~ for peace)

blues *n.* (colloq.) to sing the ~ ('to complain')

bluff I *n.* ['false threat'] 1. to call smb.'s ~ ('to challenge smb. to carry out a false threat') 2. to fall for smb.'s ~ ('to be deceived by a false threat')

bluff II v. 1. (D; tr.) to ~ into; out of (they ~ed him into making concessions) 2. to be caught ~ing

blunder I n. 1. to commit, make a ~ 2. a costly, egregious, fatal, glaring, grave, serious, stupid, terrible ~ 3. a ~ to + inf. (it was a ~ to invite them)

blunder II v. (d; intr.) to ~ on, upon ('to happen on')

blush I n. 1. a deep ~ 2. (misc.) at first ~ ('at first sight'); in the first ~ of youth ('as a youth') -

blush II v. 1. to ~ deeply; readily 2. (D; intr.) to ~ at (to ~ at the very suggestion) 3. (D; intr.) to ~ for, with (he ~ed with shame)

boar n. a wild ~

board n. ['ship's deck'] 1. to go on ~ ['commission'] 2. an advisory; draft (AE); editorial; liquor-control (AE); parole; school; zoning ~ 3. on a ~ (to serve on a ~) ['footboard'] 4. a running ~ (on a car) ['flat piece of wood or other material'] 5. a baseboard (AE), skirting (BE); bulletin (AE), notice (BE) ~; checkerboard; chessboard; cutting; dart; diving; drawing; emery; ironing ~ ['misc.'] 6. a sounding ~; across the ~ ('for everyone')

boarder n. to keep, take in ~s

boards n. (esp. AE) ['qualifying examination'] 1. to pass; take one's ~ 2. college; state ~

boast I n. 1. to make a ~ 2. an empty, idle, vain; proud ~

boast II v. 1. to ~ idly; proudly 2. (D; intr.) to ~ about, of (to ~ of one's success) 3. (L; to) she ~ed (to the reporters) that she would win the race

boastful adj. ~ about, of

boat n. 1. to row; sail; steer a ~ 2. to launch, lower a ~ 3. to overturn, swamp, upset a ~ 4. an assault; fishing; flying ~; gunboat; lifeboat; mosquito. PT (AE; BE has *MTB*); patrol ~; rowboat (AE), rowing (BE) ~; sailboat (AE), sailing (BE) ~; torpedo ~ 5. a ~ goes, sails; heaves; pitches; rolls 6. by ~ (to cross a river by ~) 7. (misc.) to be in the same ~ ('to be in the same circumstances'); to miss the ~ ('to let an opportunity slip by'); to push the ~ out (BE; colloq.) ('to make a special effort')

bobsled, bobsleigh n. to ride a ~; to race on ~s

bode v. 1. (D; intr.; P) to ~ for (these events ~ well for us) 2. (formal) (O) this ~s us no good

body n. ['substance'] ['firmness'] 1. to give ~ to ['group'] ['unit'] 2. an advisory; deliberative; elected; governing; student ~; the ~ politic 3. in a ~ (they presented their petition in a ~) ['physical object'] 4. a foreign ~ (to remove a foreign ~ from one's eye) 5. a gaseous; liquid; solid ~ 6. a celestial, heavenly ~ ['corpse'] 7. to cremate; embalm; exhume a ~ 8. a bloated; decomposing ~ ['physical structure of a person'] 9. to build up, condition, strengthen one's ~ 10. to sell one's ~ 11. a healthy ~ 12. (colloq.) the ~ beautiful

bog n. a peat ~

boggle v. (d; intr.) to ~ at (the mind ~s at the idea)

boil I n. ['state of boiling'] 1. to bring to a ~ (bring the milk to a ~) 2. to come to a ~ (the water must first come to a ~)

boil II v. 1. to ~ gently; hard 2. (C) he ~ed an egg for her; or: he ~ed her an egg 3. (D; intr.) to ~ with (to ~ with rage) ,

boil III n. ['furuncle'] 1. to lance a ~ 2. a ~ comes to a head 3. to apply hot compresses to a ~

boil down v. 1. (d; intr.) to ~ to (it all ~s down to one simple fact) 2. (D; tr.) to ~ to (she ~ed the whole story down to one paragraph)

boiler n. a ~ cracks, ruptures

boiling point n. to reach the ~

bold adj. (often used humorously) to be so ~ as to + inf. (may I be so ~ as to ask how old you are?)

boldface n. to print in ~

bolshy adj. (colloq.) (BE) ['rebellious'] ~ about

bolt I n. 1. a lightning ~ 2. (misc.) like a ~ out of the blue ('unexpectedly')

bolt II v. to ~ upright

bomb n. 1. to detonate, explode, set off; drop; fuse a ~ 2. to plant a ~ 3. to deactivate, defuse a ~ 4. to dispose of an unexploded ~ 5. an atom, atomic, fission, nuclear; fusion, hydrogen neutron ~ 6. a clean; dirty ~ 7. a buzz; car; fragmentation; high-explosive; incendiary; letter; napalm; petrol (esp. BE); pipe; plastic; smoke; stink; time ~ 8. a smart ('guided') ~ 9. (AE) a cherry ~ ('a type of firecracker') 10. a ~ explodes, goes off 11. (misc.) (colloq.) (BE) to go like a ~ ('to be very successful')

bombardment n. 1. to conduct a ~ 2. air; intensive ~

bomber n. 1. a dive-bomber; fighter; heavy; light; long-range; medium ~ 2. an enemy ~

bombing n. area; around-the-clock; carpet; dive; indiscriminate, random; pin-point, precision; saturation; shuttle; strategic; tactical ~

bombshell n. ['sensation'] to drop a ~

bond n. ['certificate'] 1. to issue a ~ 2. to cash (n), redeem a ~ 3. a debenture; development; government; long-term; municipal; negotiable; savings; serial; treasury; war ~ ['tie'] ['link'] 4. to ~ strengthen a ~ (of friendship) with 5. a close, firm, strong; spiritual ~ 6. a ~ between ['fetters'] 7. to break, cast off one's ~s ['guarantee'] ['obligation'] 8. to set ~ (the judge set ~ for him at two thousand dollars) 9. to furnish, post a ~ 10. to forfeit a ~ ['storage under supervision'] 11. in ~; out of ~ (bottled in ~; to take wine out of ~)

bondage n. 1. to sell into ~ 2. to deliver from ~ 3. in ~ to

bone n. ['part of a skeleton'] 1. to set a (broken) ~ 2. to break, fracture a ~ 3. a (broken) ~ knits 4. to the ~ (chilled/frozen to the ~) ['complaint'] (colloq.) 5. to pick a ~ with smb.

boner n. (slang) (AE) ['blunder'] to pull a ~

bone up v. (colloq.) (AE) (D; intr.) to ~ on (she had to ~ on her French)

bonfire n. 1. to build, light, make a ~ 2. to sit around/round a ~ 3. a blazing, roaring ~

bonnet (BE) see **hood**

bonus n. 1. to give, pay a ~ 2. to get, receive a ~ 3. an annual; Christmas; cost-of-living ~

booby trap n. 1. to set a ~ 2. to set off, trigger a ~ 3. to deactivate a ~ 4. a ~ explodes, goes off

book I n. 1. to bring out, publish, put out; write a

~ 2. to ban; censor; copyright; dedicate, inscribe; edit; expurgate; pirate; proofread; review; revise; translate a ~ 3. to bind a ~ 4. to set a ~ in type 5. to charge, check a ~ (out of a library) 6. to renew a ~ (borrowed from a library) 7. a children's; comic; complaint ~; cookbook (AE), cookery (BE) ~; handbook; illustrated; library; phrase; picture; prayer; rare; ration; reference; ring (BE) ~; schoolbook; telephone ~; textbook 8. (colloq.) the Good Book ('the Bible') 9. a ~ appears, comes out, is published 10. a ~ goes out of print; is sold out 11. a ~ about, on (a ~ about computers) 12. (misc.) to make ~ ('to make or accept bets'); a closed ~ ('an obscure matter, person'); ('a completed event, condition'); an open ~ ('an accessible subject, person'); (slang) to throw the ~ at smb. ('to punish an accused person severely'); to go by the ~ ('to adhere strictly to regulations')

book II v. (esp. BE) 1. (C) she ~ed a seat for me; or: she ~ed me a seat 2. (D; intr. tr.) to ~ through to (can we ~ a ticket through to Berlin?)

bookcase n. built-in ~s

bookends n. a pair of ~

booking n. (esp. BE) 1. to make a ~ 2. to cancel a ~

bookkeeping n. 1. to do the ~ 2. double-entry; single-entry ~

books n. ['financial records'] 1. to keep (the) ~ 2. to audit, go over, inspect the ~

book up v. to ~ fully, solid (the hotel is ~ed up solid = the hotel is fully ~ed up)

boom n. 1. a sonic ~ 2. a baby; business, economic; postwar; wartime ~

boomerang n. 1. to throw a ~ 2. a ~ always returns

boon n. a ~ to (a ~ to science)

boor n. an insufferable ~

boost n. 1. to give (smb.) a ~ 2. a big ~ 3. a ~ to (a ~ to their morale)

boot see the Usage Note for **trunk**

booth n. an information; phone, telephone; polling, voting; projection ~

boots n. 1. to put on; take off (one's) ~ 2. bovver (BE; slang; worn by young rowdies); hip; leather; riding ~ 3. a pair of ~ 4. (misc.) to lick smb.'s ~ ('to be overly subservient to smb.')

bootstraps n. to pull oneself up by one's own ~ ('to emerge from poverty through one's own efforts')

booty n. 1. to capture, seize, take ~ 2. war ~

border I n. 1. to draw, establish, fix a ~ 2. to cross, slip across a ~ 3. to patrol a ~ 4. a closed; common; disputed; fixed; open; recognized; unguarded ~ 5. a ~ between 6. across, over a ~ (to smuggle goods across a ~) 7. at, on the ~ 8. as far as, up to the ~ (she drove me as far as the ~) 9. (misc.) north of the ~; south of the ~

border II v. (d; intr.) to ~ on, upon (to ~ on the absurd)

borderline n. 1. a ~ between 2. on the ~

bore I n. a crashing, frightful, insufferable, utter ~

bore II v. 1. (D; intr., tr.) ('to dig') to ~ through (to ~ a hole through a board) 2. (D; tr.) ('to weary') to ~ to (he ~d us to death/to tears)

bored adj. 1. ~ to (~ to death/to tears) 2. ~ with; BE also has, esp. in children's language: ~ of (~ with life) 3. (misc.) he was ~ doing nothing

boredom n. 1. complete, sheer, utter ~ 2. out of ~ (he started drinking again out of ~)

boring adj. ~ to + inf. (it was ~ to sit there without anything to do)

born adj. 1. ~ of (~ of poor parents) 2. ~ to (~ to wealth; ~ to illiterate parents) 3. ~ to + inf. (he was ~ to rule) 4. (misc.) ~ free

borrow v. 1. (D; intr., tr.) to ~ from (she ~ed a book from me; they are always ~ing from us) 2. (D; tr.) to ~ from; into (the word was ~ed from English into German)

borrowing n. a ~ from (a ~ from French)

bosom n. 1. an ample ~ 2. (formal) in the ~ (in the ~ of one's family)

boss n. 1. an absolute, undisputed ~ 2. a straw ~ ('one who has little authority') 3. a party, political ~

both determiner, pronoun ~ of (we saw ~ of them) USAGE NOTE: The use of the preposition of is necessary when a pronoun follows. When a noun follows, two constructions are possible--we saw both of the students; we saw both students.

bother I n. 1. a ~ to (he was a ~ to everyone) 2. a ~ to + inf. (it was no ~ to take care of them) 3. (BE) a spot of ~ 4. (esp. BE) he had a lot of ~ finding our house

bother II v. 1. (D; intr., tr.) to ~ about, with (she didn't ~ me about/with the details) 2. (E; usu. in neg. sentences) he didn't ~ to shave; don't ~ to get up 3. (G; usu. in neg. sentences) he didn't ~ getting up 4. (R) it ~ed me (to learn) that she had not been promoted

bottle n. ['container for liquids'] 1. to break; empty; fill; rinse; uncork a ~ 2. a baby (AE), feeding (BE), nursing (AE); hot-water ~ 3. a Thermos ~ (AE; BE has Thermos flask) 4. a disposable, no-deposit, no-return; plastic; returnable, reusable ~ ['alcohol'] 5. to take to the ~ ('to begin to drink to excess') 6. to hit the ~ ('to drink to excess') 7. over a ~ ('while drinking') ['courage'] (slang) (BE) 8. to have a lot of ~ 9. the ~ to + inf. (she hasn't got the ~ to do it)

bottleneck n. 1. to form, produce a ~ 2. to be caught, trapped in a ~ 3. to eliminate a ~ 4. a ~ in

bottom n. 1. (usu. fig.) to scrape the ~ of the barrel ('to use one's last resources') 2. (fig.) to hit ('reach') ~ 3. to sink to the ~ 4. a double, false ~ 5. a ~ to (there's a false ~ to the suitcase) 6. at, on the ~ (at the ~ of the well; we never could find out what was at the ~ of the affair) 7. (misc.) to get to the ~ of an affair ('to clear up a matter)

bough n. 1. a slender ~ 2. ~s sway in the breeze

bounce I n. 1. a ~ to (there's a ~ to his walk) 2. on the ~ (to catch a ball on the ~; to hit on the first ~)

bounce II v. 1. (d; intr.) to ~ out of (she ~d out of the chair) 2. (d; intr.) to ~ to (he ~d to his feet) 3. (misc.) to ~ up and down (she ~d the ball up and down)

bounce back v. (D; intr.) to ~ from (our team ~d back from its defeat)

bound I adj. (cannot stand alone) ['headed'] 1. ~ for (~ for London) 2. homeward ~

bound II adj. ['covered'] ~ in (the book was ~ in leather)

bound III adj. ['sure'] (cannot stand alone) ~ to + inf. (she is ~ to find out)

bound IV v. (formal) (D; tr.) to ~ on, to (Germany ~s France on the east)

bound V n. see **bounds**

boundary n. 1. to draw, fix, set; redraw a ~ 2. to form a ~ 3. a common ~ 4. a ~ between

bounds n. 1. to set the ~ 2. out of ~ to 3. within ~ 4. (misc.) to know no ~ (her generosity knew no ~)

bound up adj. (cannot stand alone) ['connected'] ~ in; with (~ in one's work; her future is ~ with this firm)

bounty n. 1. to offer; pay a ~ 2. a cash ~ 3. a ~ for

bow I /bau/ n. ['bending of the head or body'] 1. to make; take a ~ (the actor took his ~) 2. a low ~ 3. a ~ to ['debut'] 4. to make one's ~

bow II v. 1. ('to bend the head or body') to ~ politely 2. (D; intr.) ('to bend the head or body') to ~ before; to (to ~ politely to one's host; to ~ before an emperor) 3. (d; intr.) ('to ~ out of ('to abandon') (to ~ out of politics)

bow III /bou/ n. ['device for shooting arrows'] 1. to draw a ~ (in order to shoot an arrow) ['decorative ribbon'] 2. to wear a ~ (in one's hair) ['knot'] 3. to tie a ~

bow down /bau/ v. (D; intr.) to ~ to

bowels n. 1. to move one's ~ 2. loose ~

bowl n. ['dish, vessel'] 1. a punch; salad; soup; sugar (AE); washing-up (BE) ~ ['championship football game'] (AE) 2. the Cotton; Rose; Sugar ~ ['region'] (esp. AE) 3. a dust; rice ~

bowling n. 1. to go in for ~ 2. to go ~

bowling alley n. at a ~ (she works at a ~)

bow out v. (D; intr.) ('to give up') to ~ as (he had to ~ as a contender)

bow tie /bou/ n. 1. to tie a ~ 2. to undo, untie a ~

box n. 1. a call (BE), telephone (BE) ~ 2. a letter (BE) ~, mailbox (AE), pillar (BE) ~ 3. a signal ~ (BE; AE has signal tower) 4. (ice hockey) a penalty ~ 5. a witness ~ (BE; AE has witness stand) 6. a music (AE), musical (BE) ~ 7. a prompt (BE), prompter's (AE) ~ 8. a shooting ~ (BE; CE has hunting lodge) 9. a black ~ ('electronic recording device') 10. a jewelry; lunch; spice ~ 11. a poor ~ (in a church) 12. a press ~ (for journalists) 13. a safe-deposit ~ 14. (BE) a Christmas ~ ('a Christmas gift') 15. a suggestion ~ 16. a fire-alarm ~ 17. (slang) (BE) on the ~ ('on television')

boxer n. 1. a clean; dirty ~ 2. ~s box; break; clinch 3. (misc.) to knock out a ~

boxing n. to go in for ~

boy n. 1. an altar; barrow (BE; CE has street vendor); bugle; cabin; chorus; college (esp. AE); delivery; messenger; newspaper; office; shoeshine; stock; water ~ 2. a best ~ ('assistant gaffer on a TV or film set') 3. a ball ~ (who retrieves tennis balls) 4. (AE; southern) a good old (ole) ~ ('a good fellow') 5. a mere ~ 6. a whipping ~ ('a scapegoat') 7. a blue-eyed (BE), fair-haired (AE) ~ ('a favorite') 8. (BE) a back-room ~ ('a scientist') USAGE NOTE: The meaning of 'non-white' servant', now obsolete, is considered offensive. The AE use of boy in the meaning of 'black male', now obsolete, is also considered offensive

boycott n. 1. to impose a ~ 2. to lift a ~ 3. an economic, trade; secondary ~ 4. a ~ of, or (they imposed a ~ on all imports; they lifted their ~ of imports

boyfriend n. a steady ~

brace I n. a back; leg; shoulder ~

brace II v. 1. (D; intr., refl.) to ~ for (to ~ for an attack) 2. (E; refl.) she ~d herself to hear what the doctor would say

braces (BE) see **suspenders**

bracket n. ['support'] 1. to put up ~s (on a wall) ['mark used to enclose'] 2. to enclose (a word) in ~s; to put (a word) into ~s 3. angle, broken; round; square ~s ['group with similar characteristics'] 4. an age; income; tax ~

brag v. (D; intr.) to ~ about

braid I n. gold; silver ~

braid II v. (D; tr.) to ~ into (to ~ one's hair into pigtails)

brain n. 1. to use one's ~ 2. to beat, rack one's ~ over (she racked her ~ over the problem) 3. to pick smb.'s ~ 4. (colloq.) on the ~ (he has nothing but rock music on the ~)

brains n. 1. to blow one's ~ out ('to shoot oneself through the head') 2. the ~ to + inf. (does he have enough ~ to figure it out?)

brainstorm n. (AE) ['sudden bright idea'] to have a ~ (see the Usage Note for **wave**)

brake n. 1. to apply, step on a ~; to pump the ~s; to put on the ~s; to jam on/slam on the ~s 2. to ride the ~s ('to use the brakes excessively') 3. (fig.) to put a ~ on (the government put a ~ on plans for expansion) 4. to release a ~ 5. an air; coaster; disk; electric; emergency; foot; hand; hydraulic; mechanical; power ~ 6. the ~s jammed, locked; faded; failed; held, worked; screeched

branch n. ['division'] 1. the executive; judicial; legislative ~ (of the government) ['limb of a tree'] 2. to trim ~es

branch off v. (D; intr.) to ~ from (the spur ~es off here from the main line)

branch out v. (D; intr.) to ~ from; into (our firm has ~ed out into various industries)

brand I n. 1. to put a ~ on (an animal) 2. a name, popular ~

brand II v. 1. (d; tr.) to ~ as (he was ~ed as a traitor) 2. (N; used with a noun) to be ~ed a traitor

brash, brassy adj. ~ to + inf. (it was ~ of him to demand more)

brass n. (colloq.) ['officers'] 1. air-force; army; navy; Pentagon ~ 2. the top ~ ['daring'] 3. the ~ to + inf. (she had the ~ to ask for a raise)

brat n. (colloq.) 1. a spoiled ~ 2. an Army ~ ('child in an Army family')

brave adj. ~ to + inf. (it was ~ of you to do that)

bravery *n.* to demonstrate, display, exhibit, show; inspire ~

brawl *n.* a barroom, drunken ~

breach *n.* ['violation'] 1. to commit a ~ (of etiquette, of the peace) 2. an egregious, flagrant ~ ['gap'] 3. to effect, make a ~ (in enemy lines) 4. to close, seal off a ~ 5. to fling oneself, throw oneself into the ~ ['break in friendly relations'] 6. to cause a ~ 7. to heal a ~

bread *n.* ['baked food'] 1. to bake ~ 2. to toast ~ 3. to break ~ with ('to eat with') 4. fresh; moldy; stale ~ 5. black; brown; corn; dark; leavened; rye; sliced; unleavened; wheat; white; whole meal (BE), whole wheat (AE) ~ 6. a crust; loaf; piece, slice of ~ ['living'] 7. to earn one's daily ~ 8. (misc.) to take the ~ out of smb.'s mouth

breadth *n.* (formal) in ~ (it is ten feet in ~)

break I *n.* ['dash'] 1. to make a ~ (for safety) ['escape'] 2. a mass; prison ~ ['interruption'] 3. to make a ~ 4. a ~ in, with (a ~ in the conversation; to make a ~ with tradition) ['rest'] 5. to have (esp. BE), take a ~ 6. a coffee; news; station (AE); tea (esp. BE) ~ 7. during, on a ~ ['opportunity'] (colloq.) 8. to give smb. a ~ ['good fortune'] 9. to get a ~ 10. a lucky; unexpected ~ 11. a tax ~

break II *v.* 1. (B) ('to communicate') I had to ~ the news to them 2. (D; intr.) ('to curl and fall') to ~ against, on (the waves were ~ing against the rocks) 3. (d; intr.) ('to dash') to ~ for (to ~ for cover) 4. (d; intr.) ('to take time') to ~ for (they broke for lunch) 5. (d; intr.) ('to enter forcibly') to ~ into (burglars broke into the house) 6. (d; intr.) ('to begin') to ~ into (to ~ into song) 7. (d; tr.) ('to cure') to ~ of (in time he was broken of his drug habit) 8. (D; tr.) ('to crack') to ~ on (she broke a tooth on a bone) 9. (d; intr.) ('to escape') to ~ out of (two prisoners broke out of jail; our troops broke out of the encirclement) 10. (d; intr.) ('to penetrate') to ~ through (to ~ through enemy lines) 11. (d; intr.) ('to end relations') to ~ with (I broke with them) 12. (D; tr.) ('to cut off') to ~ with (she broke all ties with her friends) 13. (misc.) to ~ loose; to ~ smb. on the wheel

break away *v.* (D; intr.) to ~ from (he broke away from his captors)

breakdown *n.* 1. to have, suffer a ~ (he had a nervous ~) 2. a complete; mental; nervous ~ 3. a ~ in communications

break down *v.* 1. (D; intr., tr.) to ~ into (to ~ a substance into its components) 2. (misc.) to ~ in tears

breaker *n.* a circuit ~

breakfast *n.* 1. to eat, have ~ 2. to make, prepare ~ 3. a continental; full; hurried; nutritious, wholesome; substantial ~ 4. at ~ (what did you discuss at ~?) 5. for ~ (to eat eggs for ~) 6. (misc.) to have ~ in bed; bed and ~ (as in a tourist home)

break free *v.* (D; intr.) to ~ from

break-in *n.* to commit a ~

break in *v.* (D; intr.) to ~ on (he broke in on their conversation)

breaking *n.* (the crime of) ~ and entering

break loose *v.* (D; intr.) to ~ from

break off *v.* (D; intr.) to ~ from (they broke off

from the main wing of the party)

breakout *n.* 1. to organize a ~ (from prison) 2. to achieve, effect a ~ (from an enemy encirclement)

break out *v.* 1. (D; intr.) to ~ in (he broke out in a rash) 2. (misc.) (Am. football) the back broke out in/into the open

breakthrough *n.* 1. to achieve, effect, make a ~ 2. a scientific ~

break through *v.* (D; intr.) to ~ to (they broke through to the encircled unit)

break up *v.* 1. (D; intr., tr.) to ~ into (they broke up the estate into small lots; our party broke up into several splinter groups) 2. (colloq.) (D; intr.) to ~ with (he broke up with his girlfriend) 3. (misc.) ~ it up! (esp. AE; slang) ('stop fighting/congregating and separate!')

breast *n.* 1. to beat one's ~ 2. to put a (newborn) infant to ~ 3. (of an infant) to take the ~ 4. a pigeon ~ ('a deformity of the chest') 5. (cul.) chicken ~s 6. (misc.) to make a clean ~ of smt. ('to confess smt.')

breaststroke *n.* to do, swim the ~

breath *n.* 1. to draw, take a ~ 2. to catch; hold one's ~ 3. to get one's ~ back 4. to lose one's ~ 5. a deep; long ~ (she took a deep ~) 6. out of ~ ('breathless') 7. (misc.) to spare, save one's ~ ('to avoid a futile conversation'); to waste one's ~ ('to speak in vain'); to take smb.'s ~ away ('to stun smb.'); in the same ~ ('at the same time'); to one's last ~ ('to the end of one's life'); under one's ~ ('in a whisper'); with bated ~ ('with the breath held, in suspense')

breathe *v.* 1. to ~ deeply 2. (B) he didn't ~ a word to anyone 3. (d; tr.) to ~ into (she ~d new life into the project)

breather *n.* ['rest'] to have (BE), take a ~

breathing *n.* 1. deep; heavy, labored, noisy; irregular; regular, steady ~ 2. (ling.) rough; smooth ~

breathtaking *adj.* ~ to + inf. (it was ~ to watch the acrobats perform)

breeches *n.* riding ~

breed *n.* 1. a ~ apart 2. a hardy; rare ~

breeder *n.* a cattle, livestock; horse; poultry ~

breeding *n.* 1. cattle, livestock; horse; poultry ~ 2. selective ~ 3. of ~ (a person of good ~)

breeze *n.* ['light wind'] 1. a ~ blows, comes up 2. a gentle, light, soft ~ ['easy task'] (slang) (AE) 3. a ~ to + inf. (it was a ~ to get him to agree = it was a ~ getting him to agree) ['misc.'] 4. (colloq.) (AE) to bat, shoot the ~ ('to chat')

brew I *n.* (a) home ~

brew II *v.* (C) she ~ed some tea for us; or: she ~ed us some tea

brew-up *n.* (BE) ['making tea'] to have a ~

bribe I *n.* 1. to give, offer a ~ 2. to accept, take a ~

bribe II *v.* 1. (D; tr.) to ~ into (to ~ smb. into collusion) 2. (H) they ~d him to overlook the violation

brick *n.* (colloq.) (BE) ['blunder'] to drop a ~

brickbats *n.* ['insults'] to hurl ~ at

bricks *n.* 1. to lay ~ (a bricklayer lays ~) 2. to point ~

bride *n.* 1. to take a ~ 2. a ~ takes a husband 3. a beautiful, lovely ~ 4. a child; war ~ 5. a bride-to-be; a future ~; one's intended ~

bridge I *n.* ['structure carrying a roadway'] 1. to build, construct, erect a ~ 2. to throw a ~ across a river 3. an arch; Bailey; bascule; cantilever; covered ~; drawbridge; footbridge; pontoon; railroad (AE), railway (BE); suspension; toll; truss ~ (to raise a drawbridge) 4. a jet ~ (at an airport) 5. a ~ collapses 6. a ~ across, over (a ~ across a river) 7. (misc.) our planes knocked out the enemy ~ ['partial denture'] 8. to make; put in a ~

bridge II *n.* ['card game'] auction; contract; duplicate ~

bridgehead *n.* 1. to establish a ~ 2. to develop, enlarge a ~

bridle I *n.* to put on a ~

bridle II *v.* (D; intr.) to ~ at (she ~d at her friend's nasty remark)

brief I *n.* ['summary of a legal case'] 1. to draw up; file a ~ ['brevity'] 2. in ~ ['misc.'] 3. to hold no ~ for ('not to argue for')

brief II *v.* (D; tr.) to ~ smb. about, on (he had to ~ his lawyer on the case)

briefing *n.* 1. to give smb. a ~ 2. to get, receive a ~ 3. a ~ about, on

brigade *n.* 1. a bucket; fire ~ (BE; AE has *fire department*) 2. (misc.) a brigadier (BE)/brigadier general (AE) commands a ~

brilliant *adj.* ~ + inf. (it was ~ of him to find a solution so quickly)

brim I *n.* to the ~ (to fill smt. to the ~)

brim II *v.* (D; intr.) to ~ with (she was ~ming with enthusiasm)

brim over *v.* (D; intr.) to ~ with (to ~ with enthusiasm)

bring *v.* 1. (A) ('to carry') she brought word to them; or: she brought them word 2. (C) ('to carry') he brought a book for me; or: he brought me a book 3. (d; tr.) ('to present') to ~ before (to ~ a proposal before a committee) 4. (d; tr.) ('to summon') to ~ before (he was brought before the court) 5. (d; tr.) ('to carry') to ~ into (she brought the chairs into the house) 6. (d; tr.) to ~ on ('to cause') (he brought trouble on himself) 7. (d; tr.) to ~ to ('to cause to reach') (to ~ water to a boil; her speech brought the crowd to its feet; we must ~ him to his senses; to ~ smb. to life) 8. (d; tr.) to ~ within ('to cause to reach') (another few feet will ~ them within range) 9. (H; no passive) ('to induce') we could not ~ him to share our views; she could not ~ herself to read the letter 10. (J) ('to cause to come') his last-minute appeal brought them rushing to his aid 11. (misc.) to ~ a child into the world

bring around *v.* (AE) (D; tr.) ('to convince') to ~ to (she brought them around to our point of view)

bring back *v.* 1. (C) bring back some coffee for me; or: bring me back some coffee 2. (D; tr.) ('to return') to ~ to (to ~ smb. back to life)

bring down *v.* 1. (mil.) (D; tr.) ('to call for') to ~ on (the artillery spotter brought down fire on the enemy tanks) 2. (D; tr.) ('to reduce') to ~ to (they finally brought the price down to a reasonable fig-

ure)

bring home *v.* (D; tr.) ('to make known') to ~ to (the bombing brought the war home to the civilian population)

bring in *v.* (D; tr.) ('to include') to ~ on (we must ~ them in on our plans)

bring out *v.* (D; intr.) ('to evoke') to ~ n (the crisis brought out the best in her)

bring over *v.* (D; tr.) ('to move') to ~ to (the incident brought them over to our side)

bring round (CE) see **bring around**

bring together *v.* (D; tr.) ('to unite') to ~ for (we brought them together for negotiations)

bring up *v.* 1. (B) I didn't want to ~ the subject to her at that time 2. (d; tr.) to ~ against ('to confront with') (the drought brought us up against serious difficulties) 3. (D; tr.) ('to raise') to ~ for (to ~ up a question for discussion) 4. (D; tr.) to ~ on ('to inculcate with') (they brought the children up on stories about the Old West) 5. (D; tr.) ('to lift') to ~ to (we brought their proficiency up to the required level) 6. (H) ('to educate, raise') our parents brought us up to respect others 7. (misc.) her scream brought us up short ('her scream startled us')

brink *n.* at, on the ~ (he teetered on the very ~ of disaster; at the ~ of war)

brinkmanship, brinksmanship *n.* to practice ~

bristle *v.* 1. (D; intr.) to ~ at (he ~d at the remark) 2. (D; intr.) to ~ with (she ~d with anger)

broach *v.* 1. (B) I would like to ~ the subject to him 2. (D; tr.) to ~ with (I didn't want to ~ the matter with her)

broadcast I *n.* 1. to carry a ~ 2. to beam a ~ to 3. to jam a ~ 4. a live ~

broadcast II *v.* 1. to ~ live 2. (B) they ~ the news to the local population every day 3. (N; used with an adjective) they broadcast the interview live

broadside *n.* to fire a ~ at

brogue *n.* 1. to speak (in, with) a ~ 2. a heavy, incomprehensible, thick ~

broil *v.* (C) he broiled a few steaks for us; or: he broiled us a few steaks

broiled *adj.* (AE) charcoal ~

broke *adj.* (colloq.) ['having no money'] 1. to go ~ 2. flat ~

broker *n.* 1. to act as a ~ for 2. an insurance; marriage; real-estate (AE; BE has *estate agent*) ~ 3. (AE) a power ~ 4. an honest ~

bromide *n.* (colloq.) ['platitude'] a (tired, old) ~ about

bronco *n.* 1. to ride a ~ 2. to break a ~

Bronx cheer *n.* (AE) to give, let out a ~

brood *v.* (D; intr.) to ~ about, over

brook *n.* a babbling ~

broth *n.* beef; chicken; clear ~

brother *n.* 1. a big, older; kid (colloq.), little, younger; twin ~ 2. a foster; half ~; stepbrother 3. a blood; lay; soul ~ 4. a ~ to (he was like a ~ to us) 5. (misc.) Big Brother ('government that exercises complete control')

brouhaha *n.* ['fuss'] a ~ over

brow *n.* to knit, wrinkle one's ~

browbeat v. (D; tr.) to ~ into (they could not ~ him into confessing)

browse v. (D; intr.) to ~ through (to ~ through books)

brunt n. to bear, take the ~ (our battalion bore the ~ of the attack)

brush I n. 1. to apply a ~ to 2. a bottle; clothes ~; hairbrush; nailbrush; paintbrush; scrub (AE); scrubbing (BE); shaving ~; toothbrush; upholstery ~

brush II v. 1. (d; intr.) to ~ against (she ~ed against the table) 2. (d; intr.) to ~ by, past (she ~ed by me) 3. (d; tr.) to ~ off (he ~ed the crumbs off the table) 4. (N; used with an adjective) she ~ed her coat clean

brush III n. ['brief encounter'] 1. to have a ~ with (to have a ~ with the authorities) 2. a close ~ (a close ~ with the law)

brush-off n. ['snub'] to give smb. the ~

brush up v. 1. (d; intr.) to ~ against (to ~ against a wall) 2. (D; intr.) to ~ on (to ~ on one's Latin)

brutal adj. ~ to + inf. (it was ~ of him to do that)

brutality n. 1. to demonstrate, display, exhibit ~ 2. extreme ~ 3. police ~ 4. an act of ~ 5. ~ to, towards, with

bubble n. 1. to blow ~s 2. to prick a ~ 3. to burst a ~ 4. a ~ bursts 5. soap ~s

bubble over v. (D; intr.) to ~ with (the children were ~ling over with excitement)

bubbling adj. ~ with (~ with enthusiasm)

buck I n. (colloq.) (AE) ['responsibility'] to pass the ~

buck II v. (colloq.) (AE) 1. (d; intr.) to ~ against ('to oppose') 2. (D; intr.) to ~ for (to ~ for a promotion)

bucket n. 1. a coal; fire; ice; water ~ 2. a metal; wooden ~ 3. an empty; full ~ 4. (misc.) (colloq.) to kick the ~ ('to die')

buckle I n. 1. to fasten a ~ 2. to undo, unfasten a ~ 3. a brass ~

buckle II v. (D; intr.) ('to collapse') to ~ under (to ~ under severe pressure)

buckle down v. (colloq.) (D; intr.) to ~ to (to ~ to work)

bud n. ['cell embedded in the tongue'] 1. a taste ~ ['early stage'] 2. to nip in the ~

buddy n. a bosom; old ~

budget I n. 1. to draw up a ~ 2. to submit a ~ 3. to balance a ~ 4. to adhere to; keep, remain within a ~ 5. to exceed ; stretch a ~ 6. to cut, reduce a ~ 7. an annual; federal; household; itemized; municipal; national; state ~ 8. an item in, on a ~

budget II v. 1. (d; intr.) to ~ for (they ~ed for a new copying machine) 2. (D; tr.) to ~ for (we ~ed a thousand dollars for new books)

buff n. ['the bare skin'] 1. in the ~ 2. (BE) to strip to the ~ ['devotee'] 3. a history; jazz; opera, theater ~

buffalo n. a herd of ~

buffer n. 1. to act as a ~ between 2. (misc.) a ~ state

buffet v. to be ~ed from pillar to post ('to be forced to go to many places')

buffoon n. to play the ~

bug n. ['listening device'] 1. to install a ~ 2. to remove, tear out a ~

bugle n. 1. to blow, play a ~ 2. a ~ sounds

build I n. ['figure'] a heavy; slight; slim; stocky; sturdy ~

build II v. 1. (C) they built a new library for us; or: they built us a new library 2. (D; tr.) to ~ into (he built cupboards into the walls) 3. (D; tr.) to ~ on (to ~ a relationship on trust) 4. (D; tr.) to ~ out of (they built a boat out of wood)

building n. 1. to build, erect, put up; renovate a ~ 2. to demolish, raze, tear down a ~ 3. to gut a ~ (fire gutted the ~) 4. a dilapidated, gutted, ramshackle, tumbledown; low; tall ~ 5. an apartment (AE); public ~

buildup n. a military ~

build up v. 1. (D; tr.) to ~ into (they built him up into a huge success) 2. (D; intr.) to ~ to (the tension built up to a climax)

built adj. (cannot stand alone) 1. ~ around (the whole story was ~ around one character) 2. ~ into (quality was ~ into their products) 3. (misc.) jerry ('cheaply') ~; purpose ~ (BE)

bulb n. ['light bulb'] 1. to change, put in, screw in (AE) a ~ 2. a ~ blows out; burns out 3. an electric; frosted; light; three-way ~ 4. the glare of a ~ ['tuber'] 5. a crocus; tulip ~

bulge v. (D; intr.) to ~ with (her suitcase was ~ing with presents)

bulk I n. 1. a lumbering ~ 2. in ~ (to sell smt. in ~)

bulk II v. (rare) to ~ large (the case ~ed large in his thoughts)

bull I n. n. ['adult male of a bovine animal'] 1. a ~ bellows; gores ['nonsense'] (colloq.) 2. to shoot the ~ ['misc.'] 3. to take the ~ by the horns ('to confront a problem boldly'); like a ~ in a china shop ('in a rough, crude, or clumsy manner')

bull II n. ['letter'] a papal ~

bulldoze v. to ~ through (they ~d their way through all obstacles)

bulldozer n. to operate a ~

bullet n. 1. to shoot a ~ 2. a stray; tracer ~ 3. a ~ ricochets 4. a ~ lodges somewhere (the ~ lodged in her shoulder) 5. a hail, volley of ~s 6. (misc.) to bite the ~ ('to perform a very unpleasant task')

bulletin n. 1. to issue a ~ about 2. an all-points ~ 3. a daily; news ~ 4. the ~ that + clause (we heard the ~ that the dam had burst)

bullfight n. to hold, stage a ~

bull's eye n. to hit, score a ~

bully I n. (colloq.) a big ~

bully II v. (D; tr.) to ~ into (they ~ied him into doing it)

bulwark n. a ~ against

bump v. 1. (d; intr.) to ~ against, into (she ~ed into me) 2. (D; tr.) to ~ against, on (she ~ed her arm against the table) 3. (colloq.) (AE) (D; tr.) ('to remove without warning') to ~ from (he was ~ed from the flight)

bumpkin n. a country ~

bump up v. (esp. AE) (d; intr.) to ~ against (he ~ed up against me)

bum's rush n. (colloq.) to give smb. the ~ ('to

eject smb.')

bun *n.* ['knot of hair that resembles a bun'] 1. in a ~ (she wore her hair in a ~) ['type of pastry'] 2. a cinnamon, sticky ~

bundle *n.* (slang) ['a large amount of money'] to make a ~

bundle off *v.* (D; tr.) to ~ to (we ~d the children off to school)

bundle up *v.* (D; intr., refl., tr.) to ~ against (they ~d up against the cold)

bungle *v.* to ~ completely (they completely ~d the job)

bunk *n.* (slang) (BE) to do a ~ ('to disappear')

buoy *n.* 1. to anchor a ~ 2. a bell; breeches, life ~

burden I *n.* 1. to bear, carry, shoulder a ~ 2. to impose, place a ~ on smb. 3. to alleviate, lighten, relieve a ~ 4. to share a ~ 5. to distribute a ~ equitably 6. a crushing, heavy, onerous ~ 7. a financial; tax ~ 8. a ~ on, to (he became a ~ to his family) 9. (misc.) it was a heavy ~ to bear

burden II *v.* (D; tr.) to ~ with (she didn't want to ~ us with her problems)

bureau *n.* a better-business (AE); credit; farm; missing-persons; news; service; speakers'; travel; weather (AE; BE has *meteorological office*) ~

bureaucracy *n.* a government; overgrown, swollen ~

burglar *n.* a cat ~

burglar alarm *n.* see **alarm**

burglary *n.* to commit (a) ~

burial *n.* a ~ takes place (the ~ took place at sea)

burn I *n.* 1. to receive a ~ 2. a brush, friction; first-degree; minor, superficial; second-degree, moderate; third-degree, severe ~ 3. (misc.) (esp. AE) a slow ~ ('increasing fury')

burn II *v.* (d; refl.) to ~ into (the incident ~ed itself into my memory) 2. (D; intr., tr.) to ~ to (he ~ed the meat to a crisp; the wood ~ed to ashes; she was ~ed to death) 3. (D; intr.) to ~ with (his cheeks ~ed with shame) 4. (N; used with a noun) to ~ smb. alive 5. (misc.) to ~ smb. at the stake; she ~ed her hand on the stove

burner *n.* 1. to light, turn on; turn off a ~ 2. a Bunsen; charcoal; gas; oil ~ 3. (misc.) (esp. AE) to put smt. on the back ~ ('to postpone action on smt.')

burnout *n.* (colloq.) (AE) ['exhaustion'] to experience, suffer ~

burn up *v.* (slang) (AE) (R) it ~ed me up that she was not promoted

burp *n.* 1. to let out, make a ~ 2. a loud, noisy ~

burrow *v.* (D; intr.) to ~ into (the moles ~ed into our lawn)

bursary *n.* (BE) 1. to award a ~ 2. to receive a ~

burst I *n.* ['series of shots'] 1. to fire a ~ at ['outbreak'] 2. a sudden ~ 3. in ~s ['misc.'] 4. she finally finished the job in/with a sudden ~ of energy

burst II *v.* 1. (d; intr.) to ~ into (the mob burst into the room; to ~ into flames; to ~ into tears) 2. (d; intr.) to ~ out of (to ~ out of a room) 3. (D; intr.) to ~ with (to ~ with pride; the granaries are ~ing with grain) 4. (E) she was ~ing to tell everyone the news

burst in *v.* (D; intr.) to ~ on, upon (we burst in on them without warning)

burst out *v.* (G) they burst out laughing

burton *n.* (slang) (BE) to go for a ~ ('to be lost; to be broken; to be killed, to fail')

bury *v.* 1. (d; refl., tr.) to ~ in (he ~ied himself in his work) 2. (N; used with an adjective) they ~ied him alive

bus *n.* 1. to drive a ~ 2. (as a passenger) to board, get on; catch a ~; get off a ~; to go by ~ to ride a ~; to ride in a ~; to take a ~ 3. a city; doubledecker; local; long-distance (AE; BE has *coach*); school; sightseeing ~ 4. by ~ (they came by ~)

bush *n.* 1. to prune, trim a ~ 2. (misc.) to beat about/around the ~ ('to speak indirectly')

bushel *n.* by the ~ ('to sell by the ~)

business *n.* ['commerce'] ['trade'] 1. to conduct, do, transact; drum up ~ (to do ~ with smb.) 2. to go into ~ 3. to go out of ~ 4. big; small ~ 5. a mailorder ~; show ~; the travel ~ 6. retail; wholesale ~ 7. (AE) a land-office ('brisk') ~ (to do a landoffice ~ in real estate) 8. ~ drops off; picks up 9. ~ is brisk, booming, flourishing, thriving; slack; ~ is at a standstill 10. in ~ (to be in ~ for oneself) 11. on ~ (to travel on ~) ['firm'] 12. to build up; establish; launch a ~ 13. to manage, operate, run a ~ 14. to buy into; buy out; take over a ~ ['work'] 15. to get down to ~ 16. to go about one's ~ 17. to talk ~ ['affairs'] 18. to mind one's (own) ~ 19. bad; dirty; funny; (colloq.) monkey ~ 20. company; personal; unfinished ~ ['misc.'] 21. he has no ~ leaving so early (he should not leave so early'); to know one's ~ ('to be competent in one's field'); to state one's ~ ('to explain what one is doing'); to mix ~ with pleasure ('to combine work and recreation'); to mean ~ ('to be serious about achieving one's ends'); to give smb. the ~ ('to deceive smb.'); it's none of your ~ ('the matter doesn't concern you')

busing *n.* (US) forced; school; voluntary ~

bust *n.* (colloq.) ['arrest'] 1. to make a ~ 2. a drug ~

bustle off *v.* (D; tr.) to ~ to (she ~ed the children off to school)

busy I *adj.* 1. ~ at, with (the children were ~ with their homework) 2. to be ~ doing smt. (she was getting dinner ready) 3. to keep smb. ~

busy II *v.* (d; refl.) to ~ by, with (he ~ied himself with various jobs)

butcher *n.* a family ~ (BE) ('a butcher's business run by a single family'); ('a butcher's business that sells retail rather than wholesale')

butt I *n.* a cigarette; rifle ~

butt II *v.* 1. (d; intr.) to ~ against 2. (colloq.) (d; intr.) to ~ into (to ~ into smb.'s business)

butter *n.* 1. to churn; cream; make ~ 2. ~ed ~ (on bread) 3. apple (AE); cocoa; peanut; prune; salted; sweet; whipped ~ 4. fresh; rancid ~ 5. a pat; stick of ~ 6. in ~ (to fry in ~)

butterfly *n.* 1. to collect ~flies 2. a ~ flits from flower to flower 3. (misc.) a social ~ ('one who leads an active social life')

butter up *v.* (colloq.) (d; intr.) to ~ to (he keeps ~ing up to the boss)

butt in *v.* (D; intr.) to ~ on (to ~ on a conversation)

button *n.* ['fastener'] 1. to sew on a ~ 2. to lose; rip off, tear off a ~ 3. a ~ comes off (my ~ came off) ['push button'] 4. to press, push a ~ 5. a panic (colloq.); push ~ ['badge'] 6. a campaign ~

buy I *n.* (colloq.) ['purchase'] a good ~

buy II *v.* 1. (C) we bought a book for her; or: we bought her a book 2. (D; tr.) to ~ from (she bought her car from a local dealer) 3. (d; intr.) to ~ into (to ~ into a business) 4. (misc.) to ~ as is ('to purchase with no guarantee of quality'); to ~ retail; to ~ wholesale; to ~ at a reasonable price

buy back *v.* (D; tr.) to ~ from

buyer *n.* a prospective ~

buying *n.* impulse; panic ~

buzz I *n.* (colloq.) ('telephone call') to give smb. a ~

buzz II *v.* 1. (D; intr.) to ~ for (to ~ for one's secretary) 2. (D; intr.) to ~ with (to ~ with activity)

buzzer *n.* 1. to press, sound a ~ 2. at the ~ (at the ~, stop work immediately!)

bye *n.* (sports) to draw a ~

by-election see **election**

bypass *n.* a coronary ~

byplay *n.* ~ between

bystander *n.* an innocent ~

C

cab *n*. 1. to call for; get; hail; hire; take a ~ 2. to drive a ~ (for a living) 3. a radio ~ 4. by ~; in a ~ (to go somewhere by ~)

cabbage *n*. 1. red; savoy; white ~ 2. boiled ~ 3. a head of ~ 4. (AE) corned beef and ~

cabin *n*. ['compartment'] 1. a first-class; second-class ~ ['small house'] 2. a log ~ 3. a tourist ~

cabinet *n*. ['case'] ['cupboard'] 1. a built-in; china; file, filing; kitchen ~ ['body of advisors'] 2. the president's ~ 3. a coalition; kitchen ('informal') ~ 4. a shadow ~ ('members of the opposition party who will form the next cabinet') 5. (misc.) a ~ minister (not US); a ~ reshuffle ['cabinet meeting'] (BE) 6. to hold a ~ 7. in ~ (to take a decision in ~)

cable I *n*. ['wire'] 1. to lay, string ~ 2. a submarine ~; the transatlantic ~ 3. an electric, power; telegraph; telephone ~ ['cablegram'] 4. to send a ~ 5. a ~ from; to

cable II *v*. 1. (A) we ~d the message to them; or: we ~d them the message 2. (d; intr., tr.) to ~ for (they ~d for immediate delivery) 3. (H) we ~d them to return home immediately 4. (L; may have an object) she ~d (us) that the manuscript had arrived 5. (Q; may have an object) they ~d (us) where to meet

cablegram *n*. 1. to send a ~ 2. to get, receive a ~ 3. a ~ from; to

cadence *n*. (usu. mil.) 1. to count ~ 2. in ~

cadet *n*. 1. an air-force; military; naval ~ 2. (slang) (AE) a space ~ ('an absent-minded person')

caesarean, caesarean section *n*. 1. to do, perform a ~ on 2. (misc.) to be delivered by ~

cafe *n*. a transport ~ (BE; AE has *truck stop*)

cafeteria *n*. a school ~

cage *n*. a bank teller's (AE) ~

cagey *adj*. (colloq.) ['sly'] ~ about

cahoots *n*. (esp. AE) in ~ with ('in partnership with')

cajole *v*. 1. (d; tr.) (with an inanimate object) to ~ from, out of (she ~d some money from him) 2. (d; tr.) to ~ into (he ~d me into signing over the property) 3. (d; tr.) (with an animate object) to ~ out of (they ~d him out of changing his will)

cake *n*. 1. to bake; frost (esp. AE), ice a ~ 2. a birthday; chocolate; coffee; honey; layer; Madeira (BE), pound (AE); marble; sponge; wedding; white ~ 3. a piece, slice of ~ 4. (misc.) a piece of ~ ('smt. very easy to do'); to take the ~ ('to be the best or worst')

calamity *n*. 1. to avert; ward off a ~ 2. to survive a ~ 3. a ~ befalls smb. 4. a crushing, dire, great; national ~

calculate *v*. (L) we ~d that the trip would take two days

calculated *adj*. 1. ill; well ~ 2. (usu. does not stand alone) ~ to + inf. (his actions were ~ to provoke his opponents)

calculations *n*. 1. to do ~ 2. mathematical ~

calculator *n*. 1. to use, operate a ~ 2. a pocket ~

calculus *n*. ['mathematical method'] 1. differential; integral; vector ~ ['deposit formed in an organ of the body'] 2. a renal; urinary ~

calendar *n*. ['chart that shows the days and months'] 1. the Chinese; Gregorian; Hindu; Islamic, Muslim; Jewish; Julian; Roman ~ 2. a perpetual ~ ['schedule'] 3. to clear one's ~ 4. a court; full; school; social ~ 5. on a ~ (what's on your ~ this week?)

calf *n*. 1. a ~ bleats 2. in ~ (the cow was in ~) 3. (misc.) the meat of the ~ is veal

caliber, calibre *n*. ['diameter of the barrel of a weapon'] 1. heavy; light ~ ['quality'] 2. high; low ~ 3. of a certain ~ (there are few workers eft of her ~)

calisthenics, callisthenics *n*. 1. to do ~ 2. daily; group, mass ~

call I *n*. ['appeal'] ['summons'] 1. to issue a ~ for (the government issued a ~ to the populace for voluntary contributions) 2. to answer, heed, respond to a ~ (to answer the ~ of duty) 3. a clarion ~ 4. a curtain ~ (the actor had five curtain ~s) 5. at smb.'s beck and ~ ['visit'] 6. to make, pay a ~ on smb. 7. to make a ~ at a place (the ships made ~s at several ports) 8. a business; courtesy; port; professional ~ 9. a house ~ (my doctor makes house ~s) 10. a ~ to (a ~ to arms) ['invitation'] 11. to accept a ~ ['telephone call'] 12. to give smb. a ~ 13. to make, place a ~ to smb. 14. to answer; return; take a ~ (who will take her ~?) 15. to put a ~ through (the operator put my ~ right through) 16. a business; collect (AE), transferred-charge (BE); conference; dial-direct (AE), direct-dialled (BE); emergency; local; long-distance, toll (AE), trunk (BE); operator-assisted; ordinary (BE), station-to-station (AE); personal (BE), person-to-person (AE); telephone; wake-up ~ 17. a ~ from; to ['signal'] 18. a bugle ~ ['reading aloud'] 19. a roll ~ ['duty'] 20. on ~ (which nurse is on ~?) ['need'] 21. a ~ for (there is no ~ for such behavior) 22. a ~ to + inf. (there was no ~ to complain) ['formation'] (AE) (usu. mil.) 23. sick ~ (to go on sick ~) ['misc.'] 24. a close ~ ('a narrow escape')

call II *v*. 1. (C) ('to summon') she ~ed a taxi for me; or: she ~ed me a taxi 2. (d; intr.) ('to visit') o ~ at (the ship will ~ at several ports) 3. (d; intr.) to ~ for ('to fetch') (I'll ~ for you at two o'clock) 4. (d; intr.) to ~ for ('to require') (the position ~s for an experienced engineer) 5. (d; intr.) to ~ for ('to seek') (to ~ for help) 6. (d; tr.) ('to summon') to ~ into (she was ~ed into the room) 7. (D; intr.) to ~ on ('to visit') (several friends ~ed on us) 8. (colloq.) (d; tr.) to ~ on ('to reprimand') (the boss ~ed me on my sloppy writing) 9. (d; tr.) ('to summon') to ~ out of (she was ~ed out of town or business) 10. (D; intr.) ('to shout') to ~ to (she

~ed to me in a loud voice) 11. (d; tr.) ('to summon') to ~ to (to ~ smb. to account; to ~ smt. to mind; the chair ~ed the delegates to order; to be ~ed to the bar) 12. (N; used with a noun or adjective) ('to describe as') she ~ed him a stuffed shirt; I ~ that mean 13. (O) ('to describe as ') to ~ smb. a bad name 14. (misc.) (esp. AE) ('to telephone') to ~ long-distance

call down v. 1. (D; tr.) ('to summon') to ~ on, upon (to ~ the wrath of God on smb.'s head) 2. (D; intr.) ('to shout') to ~ to (he ~ed down to us from the roof)

call on v. 1. (D; tr.) to ~ for (to ~ a pupil for an answer) 2. (H) the mayor ~ed on the people to remain calm

callous adj. 1. ~ to (~ to suffering) 2. ~ to + inf. (it was ~ of him to say that)

call out v. (D; intr., tr.) ('to shout') to ~ to (he ~ed smt. out to me)

call over v. (D; tr.) to ~ to (I ~ed him over to our table)

call up v. (D; intr.) ('to shout') to ~ from; to (she ~ed up to us from the basement)

call upon v. see **call on**

calm n. 1. to shatter the ~ 2. a dead, perfect ~ 3. (misc.) the ~ before the storm

calories n. 1. to count ~ 2. to burn ~ 3. empty ~ (in junk food)

calumny n. to heap ~ on

camel n. an Arabian, one-humped; Bactrian, two-humped ~

camera n. 1. to load a ~ 2. an automatic; box; cine (BE), motion-picture (AE), movie (AE); miniature; television, TV ~ 3. candid ~ ('taking pictures of people without their knowledge') 4. off ~ ('not being filmed') 5. on ~ ('being filmed') 6.(misc.) to face the ~ (in order to be photographed)

cameraman n. a motion-picture (AE); television ~

camouflage n. 1. to utilize ~ 2. natural ~ 3. by ~ (to conceal by ~)

camp n. 1. to make, pitch, set up a ~ 2. to break, strike ~ 3. an army; concentration; detention; displaced-persons, DP; internment; labor; prisoner-of-war, POW, PW (AE); refugee; repatriation; summer; training; work ~ 4. a trailer ~ (AE; BE has *caravan park*) 5. the enemy; rival ~ 6. an armed ~

campaign I n. 1. to carry on, conduct, wage; launch, mount, organize a ~ 2. an active, vigorous; feeble, weak; whirlwind ~ 3. an advertising; anti-smoking; educational; election, political; membership; military; national, nationwide; public-relations; smear; whispering; whistle-stop; write-in ~ 4. the ~ got off to a good start; the ~ fizzled (out) 5. a ~ against; for (the ~ against smoking; a ~ for equal rights) 6. a ~ to + inf. (a ~ to curb alcoholism)

campaign II v. 1. to ~ vigorously 2. (D; intr.) to ~ against; for

camp bed (BE) see **cot 1, 2**

camper n. a summer ~ (person)

campus n. (esp. AE) 1. a college, university ~ 2.

off; on ~ (to live on ~)

can I n. 1. (AE) an ash, garbage, trash ~ (BE has *dustbin*) 2. a milk; watering ~ 3. a tin ~

can II v. (F) she ~ work (see the Usage Note for **able**)

Canadian n. a French ~

canal n. 1. to build, construct, dig a ~ 2. an irrigation ~

canard n. 1. to circulate, spread a ~ 2. an absurd, preposterous ~

canary n. a ~ sings

cancer n. 1. to develop ~ 2. breast; colon, colorectal; lung; metastatic; rectal; skin; stomach ~ 3. inoperable; terminal ~ 4. ~ metastasizes; spreads

candid adj. 1. ~ about 2. ~ with

candidacy, candidature n. 1. to announce, file one's ~ 2. to withdraw one's ~

candidate n. 1. to put up a ~ (for office) 2. to adopt (BE); endorse a ~ 3. (BE) to de-select a ~ ('to refuse at the local level to support a party candidate adopted at the national level') 4. a party; write-in ~ 5. a defeated; handpicked; leading; successful; unsuccessful; victorious (a successful ~ for admission to the university; a victorious ~ for the party's nomination) 6. a ~ for (a ~ for the presidency)

candle n. 1. to dip ~s 2. to light a ~ 3. to blow out, extinguish, snuff out a ~ 4. the ~ was burning; was flickering; was going out; was sputtering 5. a wax ~ 6. the flame of a ~ 7. (misc.) to burn the ~ at both ends ('to dissipate one's energy by doing too much'); not to hold a ~ to smb. ('to be far inferior to smb.')

candlelight n. by ~ (to read by ~)

candlestick n. 1. brass; silver ~s 2. a pair of ~s

candor n. 1. complete; disarming ~ 2. the ~ to + inf. (she had enough ~ to tell them the truth)

candy n. (AE) 1. chocolate; cotton; hard ~ 2. a box; piece of ~ (BE has *sweets*)

cane n. ['walking stick'] 1. to carry; twirl a ~ ['plant'] 2. sugar ~

cannibalism n. to engage in, practice ~

cannon n. 1. to fire a ~ 2. to aim a ~ at; to train a ~ on 3. to load a ~ 4. a ~ booms, roars; fires 5. a water ~ (the police trained a ~ on the mob)

canoe n. to paddle a ~

canon n. ['dogma'] 1. to establish, lay down a ~ ['round'] (mus.) 2. to sing a ~

cap n. ['container holding an explosive charge'] 1. a percussion ~ ['head covering'] 2. to place, put a ~ on one's head 3. a baseball; bathing; dunce; forage (BE), garrison; overseas; service; skull ~ 4. (BE) a cricket; rugby ~ (showing that the wearer is a member of a certain team) 5. (fig.) a thinking ~ ['ceiling'] 6. to place a ~ on (to place a ~ on expenditures)

capability n. 1. to demonstrate one's ~ties 2. a defense; nuclear ~ 3. the ~ to + inf. (the ~ to win) 4. beyond; within one's ~ties

capable adj. ~ of (he is ~ of anything)

capacity n. ['ability to hold'] 1. to ~ (filled to ~) 2. lung; seating; storage ~ 3. a ~ of (a ~ of twenty gallons) ['ability'] 4. intellectual, mental ~ 5. one's earning ~ 6. a ~ for (a ~ for making friends)

7. the ~ to + inf. (she has the ~ to go all the way to the top) ['ability to produce'] 8. plant; productive ~ (our country's productive ~) 9. full, peak ~ 10. at ~ (to operate at peak ~) ['function'] 11. an administrative; advisory; official; professional; unofficial ~ 12. in a ~ (she acted in an advisory ~; in his ~ as legal advisor, he helped us a great deal)

caper n. 1. to cut a ~ 2. a childish ~

capital n. ['wealth'] 1. to borrow; raise ~ 2. to invest, put up; tie up ~ 3. to withdraw ~ 4. borrowed; circulating; working; fixed, permanent; foreign; idle ~ ['gain'] 5. to make ~ out of smt. 6. political ~ (they made political ~ out of the incident) ['official seat of government'] 7. to establish a ~ 8. a national; provincial; state ~ 9. foreign; world ~s ['main center'] 10. a diamond; fashion; film ~ (Hollywood is the film ~ of the world)

capitalize v. (d; intr.) to ~ on (to ~ on smb.'s mistakes)

capital punishment n. 1. to impose; re-introduce ~ 2. to abolish ~

capitulate v. (D; intr.) to ~ to (to ~ to the enemy)

capricious adj. ~ to + inf. (it was ~ to act in that manner)

capsule n. a space; time ~

captain n. 1. (AE) a bell ~ 2. a ship's; team ~ 3. (AE) a precinct ~ (in the police) 4. (mil.) a ~ commands a company or battery 5. (misc.) ~s of industry ['leading industrialists']

captive adj. to hold smb. ~

car n. ['automobile, motorcar'] 1. to drive, operate a ~ 2. to bring a ~ to a stop; to stop a ~ 3. to back a ~ (she backed the ~ into the garage) 4. to ride in a ~ 5. to go, travel by ~ 6. to hire (BE), rent a ~ 7. to break in (AE), run in (BE) a (new) ~ 8. to jack up; park; register; repair; road-test; service; tune up; winterize a ~ 9. to smash up, total, wreck a ~ 10. an armored; command; getaway; Panda (BE), patrol, police, prowl (AE), squad (AE); passenger; racing; scout; sports; stock ~ 11. an estate ~ (BE; AE has *station wagon*) 12. a new; secondhand, used ~ ['vehicle that moves on rails'] 13. (on a train) (AE; BE has carriage, wagon, van) a baggage; box; cattle; club, lounge, parlor; dining, restaurant (BE); flat; freight; mail; railroad; sleeping; tank ~ 14. a trolley ~ (AE; BE has *tram)* 15. a cable ~ 16. (misc.) to uncouple railroad/railway ~s

carbon n. radioactive ~

card n. 1. a boxing; calling, visiting; credit; filing; identity; index (AE), record (BE); library (AE); membership; playing; postal; race (BE), racing (AE); ration; time ~ 2. a boarding ~ (for boarding a plane) 3. a report ~ (AE; BE has *school report)* 4. a trump ~ (also fig.) ['advantage'] 5. a flash ~ (used as a teaching aid) 6. an anniversary; birthday; Christmas; confirmation; Easter; get-well; graduation; greeting; Hanukkah; New Year's; sympathy ~ 7. (misc.) a drawing ~ ('one who attracts large audiences')

cards n. 1. to play ~ 2. to cut; deal; shuffle the ~ 3. playing ~ 4. (misc.) to stack the ~ ('to prearrange conditions to one's own advantage') to hold all the ~ ('to be in a strong negotiating position');

to be in (AE), on (BE) the ~ ('to be destined by fate')

care I n. ['caution'] 1. to exercise, take ~ 2. great, meticulous, painstaking, scrupulous, utmost ~ 3. ~ to + inf. (she took ~ to avoid catching cold) 4. ~ that + clause (take ~ that you don't get involved) ['solicitude'] ['maintenance'] ['keep'] 5. to provide ~ for 6. to take ~ of 7. to entrust smb. to smb.'s ~; to put smb. in smb.'s ~ 8. (tender) loving; parental ~ 9. antenatal (BE), antepartal prenatal (AE); child; coronary; custodial; day; dental; domiciliary; emergency; extended; foster; health; hospice; in-patient; intensive; long-term; medical; nursing; out-patient; postnatal, postpartum; respite; special ~ (this patient requires intensive ~; day ~ for children) 10. primary (health) ~ 11. in smb.'s ~ (the children were left in my ~) 12. under smb.'s ~ (under a doctor's ~) 13. (misc.) a coronary-care unit; an intensive-care unit ['misc.'] 14. in ~ of ('at smb.'s address')

care II v. 1. (D; intr.) ('to be interested') to ~ about (she doesn't ~ about our opinions) 2. (D; intr.) ('to like') to ~ about, for (he ~s about us; she ~s a lot for you; would you ~ for some more coffee?) 3. (d; intr.) ('to take care of') to ~ for (she ~s for her elderly mother) 4. (E) ('to want') I don't ~ to attend

career n. 1. to carve out, make a ~ (for oneself) 2. to enter on; launch a ~ 3. to abandon, give up one's ~ 4. to cut short smb.'s ~ (the accident cut short her ~) 5. a brilliant, distinguished; checkered; promising; successful; turbulent ~ 6. an academic; amateur; diplomatic; literary; military; political; professional; public; stage ~ 7. a ~ as (to carve out a ~ as a diplomat) 8. a ~ in (she made a ~ for herself in politics)

careful adj. 1. ~ about, of (a good writer is ~ about details) 2. ~ in (to be ~ in negotiating a new trade agreement) 3. ~ with (we must be ~ with dynamite) 4. ~ to + inf. (she was ~ to avoid controversy)

careless adj. 1. ~ about, in, or, with (~ about one's appearance) 2. ~ to + inf. (it was ~ of you to leave the door unlocked)

carelessness n. ~ about, in, with

caress I n. a gentle ~

caress II v. to ~ gently

cargo n. 1. to carry, haul ~ 2. to load, take on; stow; transfer ~ 3. to unload ~ 4. contraband; general ~ 5. (misc.) a ~ plane; ship

caricature n. 1. to draw a ~ of 2. a bold, striking ~

carol I n. a Christmas ~

carol II v. to go ~ing

carp v. (D; intr.) to ~ at

carpet n. 1. to beat a ~ 2. to lay a ~ 3. to take up a ~ (the ~ must be taken up and cleaned) 4. (misc.) to roll out the red ~ for smb. ('to give smb. a warm reception'); a flying, magic ~; to call smb. on the ~ ('to call smb. to account for her/his actions')

carpeting n. ['floor covering'] 1. fitted (BE), wall-to-wall ~ ['severe reprimand'] (BE) 2. to give smb. a ~

carriage n. ['vehicle'] 1. see **baby carriage** 2. a

railway ~ (BE; AE has *railroad car)* 3. a horse-drawn ~ ['support'] 4. a gun; typewriter ~ ['bearing.'] 5. an erect; proud ~

carriageway *n.* a dual ~ (BE; AE has *divided highway)*

carrier *n.* 1. an aircraft; escort; personnel; troop ~ 2. a letter, mail ~ (AE; CE has *postman)* 3. a common, public ~ ('a transport service used by the public') 4. a chronic ~ (of a disease)

carrot *n.* 1. diced ~s 2. a bunch of ~s

carry *v.* 1. (B) she ~ied the books to me 2. (d; tr.) to ~ from; to (we ~ied the table from the door to the center of the room) 3. (d; tr.) to ~ into (~ the chairs into the house) 4. (d; tr.) to ~ out of (we ~ied the books out of the room) 5. (P; refl.) she ~ies herself well 6. (misc.) to ~ to excess, to an extreme ('to go too far')

carry back *v.* (B) he ~ied the books back to her

carry forward *v.* (D; tr.) to ~ to (the figures must be ~ied forward to the next page)

carry on *v.* 1. (D; intr.) ('to continue') to ~ with (~ with your work) 2. (D; intr.) ('to have an affair') to ~ with (he was ~ying on with a married woman) 3. (BE) (G) to ~ talking

carry-over *n.* a ~ from; to (a ~ from the past)

carry over *v.* (D; tr.) to ~ from; to (~ these figures over to the next page; to ~ a tradition from one generation to another)

cart *n.* 1. to draw, pull; push a ~ 2. a ~ creaks; lumbers 3. a shopping ~ (AE; BE has *trolley)* 4. (misc.) to put the ~ before the horse ('to do in the wrong order'); to upset the apple ~ ('to ruin smb.'s plans')

cartel *n.* 1. to form a ~ 2. to break up a ~ 3. an international, multinational ~

cartilage *n.* (a) torn ~

cart off *v.* (D; tr.) to ~ to (they ~ed him off to jail)

cartoon *n.* 1. to draw a ~ 2. an animated; political ~ 3. a strip ~ (BE; CE has *comic strip)*

cartridge *n.* a blank; practice; ruptured; spent ~

cartwheel *n.* to do, turn a ~

carve *v.* 1. (C) he ~d an ornament for me; or: he ~d me an ornament 2. (D; tr.) to ~ from, out of (to ~ a figure from ivory) 3. (d; intr.) to ~ in (to ~ in wood)

carving *n.* an ivory; wood ~

case I *n.* ['legal action'] ['argument'] 1. to hear, try a ~ (the court will not hear this ~) 2. to argue, plead a ~ (the lawyer argued the ~ skillfully) 3. to make (out), present, state; take a ~ (she made out a good ~ for her client; the president took his ~ to the people) 4. to lose; win a ~ 5. to decide; settle a ~ (they settled the ~ out of court) 6. to rest one's ~ ('to cease introducing evidence') (the defense lawyer rested her ~) 7. to dismiss, throw out a ~ (the judge dismissed the ~) 8. an airtight, ironclad, open-and-shut, watertight; clear; strong; weak ~ 9. a civil; criminal; pending; test ~ 10. a ~ goes to trial 11. a ~ against (we had an airtight ~ against him) 12. (misc.) to have a good ~ ('to have a convincing argument') (often ironic) ['crime, felony'] 13. to break, crack, solve a ~ (the detective broke the ~) 14. to investigate, work on a ~ (the police worked on the ~ for a year) ['in-

stance, occurrence, example'] 15. to cite a ~ 16. an attested; authenticated; borderline; celebrated; clear; flagrant; hypothetical; isolated, rare; open-and-shut ('easily settled'); similar; special ~ 17. (med.) an acute; advanced; chronic; hopeless; lingering; mild; terminal ~ 18. to be the ~ ('to be so') 19. in a certain ~ (in this ~; in any ~; in ~ of emergency) 20. a ~ in point ('a pertinent case') ['inflectional form'] 21. to govern, take a ~ (certain Russian verbs take the dative ~) 22. the ablative; accusative; dative; genitive; instrumental; locative; oblique; prepositional; vocative ~ ['misc.'] 23. a basket ~ ('smb. without arms or legs or who is in a completely hopeless situation'); as the ~ may be

case II *n.* ['container'] ['cover'] an attaché; display; jewelry; packing; pillow; watch ~

caseload *n.* 1. to carry a ~ 2. to increase; reduce smb.'s ~ 3. a heavy; light ~ (the social worker carries a heavy ~)

cash I *n.* 1. to pay (in) ~ 2. to run out of ~ 3. out of, short of ~ 4. cold, hard; loose; ready; spare ~ 5. petty ~ 6. (misc.) ~ on the barrel (esp. AE)/nail (BE) ('pay now in cash'); ~ on delivery ('pay when the order is delivered')

cash II *v.* (D; tr.) to ~ for (she ~ed the money order for me)

cash in *v.* (colloq.) (d; intr.) to ~ on (to ~ on one's sudden popularity)

casino *n.* a gambling ~

casserole *n.* 1. to bake a ~ 2. a meat; vegetable ~

cast I *n.* ['set of performers'] 1. to head a ~ 2. to select a ~ 3. an all-star; supporting ~ ['rigid dressing of gauze'] (med.) 4. to apply a ~ to; to put a ~ on (to put a ~ on a leg) 5. a plaster ~

cast II *v.* 1. (D; tr.) ('to assign to a role') to ~ as (he was cast as Hamlet) 2. (d; tr.) ('to throw') to ~ on (his actions have cast doubts on our entire campaign)

cast about *v.* (d; intr.) to ~ for ('to seek') (to ~ for a solution)

caste *n.* 1. a warrior ~ 2. a ~ system

cast in *v.* to ~ one's lot with smb. ('to join forces with smb.')

casual *adj.* ~ about (she was very ~ about winning the prize)

casualties *n.* 1. to inflict ~ on 2. to incur, suffer, take ~ 3. to report ~ 4. heavy, serious; light ~ (to inflict heavy ~ on the enemy) 5. civilian; military; traffic ~

cat *n.* 1. to neuter a ~; to spay a (female) ~ 2. an alley; stray ~ 3. an Angora; Burmese; Persian; Siamese ~ 4. ~s meow (AE), miaow (BE); purr; scratch 5. a young ~ is a kitten 6. a male ~ is a tomcat 7. (misc.) to let the ~ out of the bag ('to reveal a secret')

catalog, catalogue *n.* 1. to compile, make up a ~ 2. an author; card; subject; union ~ 3. a college, school, university; mail-order; museum ~

catapult *v.* (D; intr., tr.) to ~ to (he was ~ed to fame)

cataract *n.* (med.) 1. to develop a ~ 2. to remove a ~

catastrophe *n.* 1. to suffer a ~ 2. a financial;

major, overwhelming ~ 3. a ~ for, to (the fire was a ~ to everyone)

catch I *n.* ['hook'] 1. to fasten a ~ 2. a safety ~ ['smt. caught'] 3. a good ~ (the fishermen brought in a good ~) 4. the ~ of the day; the day's ~ ['act of catching'] 5. a running ~ (as in baseball)

catch II *v.* 1. to ~ red-handed, in the act 2. (C) she caught a small fish for me; or: she caught me a small fish 3. (D; tr.) to ~ from (she caught a cold from her brother) 4. (D; intr., tr.) to ~ in (the kite caught in a tree) 5. (D; intr., tr.) to ~ on (his shirt caught on a nail; he caught his shirt on a nail) 6. (J) we caught him stealing 7. (colloq.) (esp. BE) (O) she caught him one in the eye 8. (misc.) we caught him at his old tricks

catch on *v.* 1. (D; intr.) to ~ to ('to comprehend') (he caught on to what I said immediately) 2. (D; intr.) ('to become popular') to ~ with (to ~ with the public)

catch up *v.* 1. (D; intr.) to ~ on (to ~ on one's correspondence) 2. (D; intr.) to ~ to (AE), with (I'll ~ with you later; BE also has: I'll ~ you up later)

catechism *n.* (rel.) to recite the ~

category *n.* 1. to establish, set up a ~ 2. to assign to, put into a ~ 3. to fit into a ~

cater *v.* (d; intr.) to ~ for (BE), to (to ~ to all tastes) USAGE NOTE: In BE *cater to* is typically pejorative, meaning 'to pander to'.

cater-cornered, catty-cornered *adj., adv.* (AE) ~ to

catheter *n.* (med.) to change; insert; irrigate; remove a ~

Catholicism *n.* Roman ~

cattle *n.* 1. to breed; raise (esp. AE), rear (BE) ~ 2. to drive; graze; round up ~ 3. to brand ~ 4. dairy; prize ~ 5. ~ graze 6. a head of ~; a herd of ~ 7. young ~ are calves 8. female ~ are cows 9. male ~ are bulls

catty *adj.* (colloq.) ['malicious'] ~ about

catty-cornered see **cater-cornered**

caucus *n.* 1. to hold a ~ 2. a party ~

caught up *adj.* ['involved'] ~ in (~ in radical movements)

cause I *n.* ['movement'] ['objective'] 1. to advance, champion, fight for, promote; serve a ~ 2. to espouse, plead a ~ 3. to take up a ~ 4. a common; good, just, worthwhile, worthy ~ (to make common ~ with smb.) 5. a lost ~ ['reason'] 6. to give; show ~ for 7. (legal) probable ~ 8. a deep-rooted, root, underlying; immediate; leading, major; primary; secondary; ultimate ~ 9. natural ~s (to die of natural ~s) 10. (a) ~ for (there is no ~ for alarm) 11. ~ to + inf. (to find ~ to rejoice; there is no ~ to complain; she had good ~ to be disappointed)

cause II *v.* 1. (A; usu. without *to*) we ~d them a lot of trouble 2. (rare) (H; no passive) the incident ~d me to reflect

caution I *n.* 1. to exercise, use ~ 2. due; extreme, great ~ 3. with ~ (to view with ~) 4. (misc.) to fling/hurl/throw ~ to the winds

caution II *v.* 1. (D; tr.) to ~ about, against (they ~ed us against drinking the water) 2. (H) she ~ed us not to go

cautious *adj.* 1. ~ about, of (he was ~ about committing himself; she was ~ of strangers) 2. ~ in (~ in using firearms) 3. ~ with (be ~ with them)

cavalry *n.* 1. to commit ~ 2. heavy; light ~

cave *n.* 1. to explore a ~ 2. a deep ~

cavil *v.* (formal) (D; intr.) to ~ at

cavity *n.* 1. to fill a ~ (in a tooth) 2. the abdominal; chest; oral ~

cease *v.* 1. (E) the old empire has ~d to exist 2. (rare) (G) we ~d pretending

cease-fire *n.* 1. to declare; sign; work out a ~ 2. to honor, observe a ~ 3. to break, violate a ~ 4. a temporary ~ 5. the ~ has gone into effect

cede *v.* (A) France ~d the territory to them; or: France ceded them the territory

ceiling *n.* ['upper limit'] 1. to place, set a ~ (on prices) 2. to lower; raise a ~ 3. to abolish, lift a ~ (on prices) 4. a high; low ~ 5. a price; rent ~ ['top of a room'] 6. a high; low ~ ['misc.'] 7. (slang) to hit the ~ (AE; CE has *roof*) ('to lose one's temper')

celebrate *v.* to ~ formally; joyously; noisily, officially; privately; publicly; quietly; solemnly

celebrated *adj.* 1. ~ as (~ as a painter) 2. ~ for (~ for scientific research)

celebration *n.* 1. to hold a ~ 2. a formal; joyous; noisy; quiet; solemn ~ 3. a centenary; official; public; religious ~

celebrity *n.* ['famous person'] a film, Hollywood; international; literary; local; national; visiting ~

celery *n.* 1. crisp ~ 2. a bunch of ~

celibacy *n.* to practice ~

cell *n.* ['cubicle, small room'] 1. a jail, prison; monk's; padded ~ ['small mass of protoplasm'] 2. to form a ~ 3. a blood; cancer; egg; germ; nerve; sperm ~ ['receptacle containing electrodes and an electrocyte'] 4. a dry; photoelectric; primary; voltaic ~ ['smallest unit of an organization'] 5. to form a ~ 6. a local; party ~

cellar *n.* a cyclone, storm; wine ~

cellophane *n.* to wrap smt. in ~

cement I *n.* 1. to mix; pour ~ 2. Portland ~ 3. ~ sets

cement II *v.* to ~ smt. together

cemetery *n.* at, in a ~ (she works at/in the ~; to be buried in a ~)

censor *n.* a government; military ~

censorship *n.* 1. to impose, introduce ~ 2. to exercise, practice ~ 3. to abolish, lift ~ 4. rigid, strict ~ 5. film; government(al); military; press ~ 6. ~ of, over

censure I *n.* bitter, strong; public ~

censure II *v.* 1. to ~ bitterly, strongly 2. (D; tr.) to ~ as (they were ~d as traitors) 3. (D; tr.) to ~ for (the senator was ~d for income tax evasion)

census *n.* 1. to conduct, take a ~ 2. a national ~ 3. at, in a ~ (at the last ~)

cent *n.* (colloq.) not to have a red ~ ('to have no money at all')

center I **centre** *n.* ['point equally distant from all points on a circumference'] 1. dead ~ 2. at, in the ~ (at the ~ of a circle) ['central point'] 3. a storm ~ (also fig.) 4. at, in a ~ (at the ~ of operations; right in the ~ of activity) ['location where an activity takes place; focus of activity'] 5. an amusement; birthing (AE), childbearing (AE); business, commercial; civic; communications; community; convention; crisis; cultural; day-care; fashion; financial; health; industrial; job (BE); literary; manufacturing; medical; research; science; senior-citizen; separation (mil.); service; shopping; social; trade; wine-producing ~ 6. (fig.) a nerve; storm ~ 7. a national; world ~ ['group of nerve cells'] 8. a nerve ~

center II **centre** v. (d; intr., tr.) to ~ on, upon (attention ~ed on their opening statements)

central adj. (formal) (cannot stand alone) ~ to (such values are ~ to our way of life)

century n. 1. from; to a ~ (from the fifth to the tenth ~) 2. in a ~ (in the ninth ~) 3. over, through the ~ries

ceremony n. ['formal act'] 1. to conduct, hold, perform a ~ 2. a flag-raising; formal; funeral; marriage, wedding; opening; religious; solemn; wreath-laying ~ (to perform a religious ~) ['formality'] 3. to stand on ~ 4. appropriate ~ 5. with ~ (with appropriate ~) 6. without ~ (they all pitched in without ~)

certain adj. 1. absolutely, completely, totally; almost, nearly; quite; very ~ 2. far from ~ 3. for ~ 4. ~ about, of (we were ~ of his support) 5. ~ to + inf. (she is ~ to agree) 6. ~ that + clause (it is ~ that they will sign the contract; make ~ that all doors are locked; are you ~ that you turned the gas off?)

certainty n. 1. absolute, dead; mathematical; moral ~ 2. ~ of (there is no ~ of success) 3. ~ that + clause (there is no ~ that an agreement will be reached) 4. with ~ (to state with ~)

certificate n. 1. to issue a ~ 2. to cash (in) a ~ 3. a baptismal; birth; death; marriage; medical ~ 4. a money-market; savings; stock; tax-free; treasury ~ 5. a gift ~ 6. a teaching ~ (you cannot teach in this state without a teaching ~) 7. (BE) a school ~

certification n. 1. to grant ~ 2. to receive ~

certify v. 1. (esp. BE) (D; tr.) to ~ as (the psychiatrist ~fied him as insane) 2. (L) she ~fied that it was a true copy 3. (M) can you ~ this to be a true copy? 4. (esp. BE) (N; used with an adjective) he was ~fied insane

certitude n. 1. absolute, complete, utter ~ 2. ~ that + clause (it is with ~ that I can attest to her good character)

chafe v. (d; intr.) to ~ at, under (to ~ at the delay; to ~ under restrictions)

chaff n. to separate the (wheat from the) ~ (by threshing or winnowing)

chagrin n. 1. to express; feel ~ 2. deep, profound ~ 3. (formal) ~ at (to chafe ~ at being rejected) 4. ~ that + clause (she expressed her ~ that the bill had been voted down) 5. to smb.'s ~ (to my great ~, the trick did not work)

chagrined adj. 1. ~ at (~ at being rejected) 2. ~ to + inf. (she was ~ to learn of the outcome) 3. ~ that + clause (we are ~ that the meeting cannot take place)

chain I n. ['series of metal links'] 1. to keep (a dog) on a ~ 2. to put ~s on (the tires of a car) 3. a

bicycle; tire ~ 4. a link in a ~ ['measuring instrument'] 5. an engineer's; surveyor's ~ ['shackles'] 6. in ~s (the prisoners were in ~s) ['group of associated enterprises'] 7. a department-store; hotel; restaurant ~ ['misc.'] 8. a human ~; to pull the ~ (BE) ('to flush the toilet')

chain II v. (D; tr.) to ~ to (to ~ a dog to a fence)

chair n. ['piece of furniture for sitting'] 1. a camp (BE); folding; deck; easy; rocking; swivel ~ ['professorship'] 2. to endow; establish a ~ 3. to be appointed to, receive a ~ 4. to hold, occupy a ~ 5. to give up, relinquish a ~ 6. a university ~ ['position of chairperson'] 7. (esp. BE) to occupy; take the ~ 8. a rotating ~ ['chairperson'] 9. to address one's questions to the ~ ['misc.'] 10. an electric ~ ('a device for executing criminals')

chairman n. 1. a department(al) ~ 2. ~ of the board USAGE NOTE: BE usu. has *department head, head of (the) department*.

chairmanship n. a rotating ~

chairperson see **chairman 1**

chairwoman see **chairman 1**

chalet n. a Swiss ~

chalk n. 1. to write with ~ (on a blackboard) 2. a piece of ~

chalk up v. 1. (d; tr.) to ~ against (to ~ ten victories against two defeats) 2. (D; tr.) to ~ for (to ~ another victory for our team) 3. (d; tr.) to ~ to (to ~ smt. up to lack of experience)

challenge I n. ['dare'] 1. to issue, send a ~ 2. to accept, respond to, take up a ~ 3. to meet a ~ 4. a formidable, real ~ 5. a ~ to (it was a ~ to our very existence) 6. a ~ to + inf. (it was a ~ just to survive) ['demand for identification'] (usu. mil.) 7. to give the ~ (the sentry gave the ~) ['objection to a prospective juror'] (legal) 8. a peremptory ~ (to use one's peremptory ~)

challenge II v. 1. (D; tr.) to ~ to (to ~ smb. to a duel) 2. (H) he ~d me to fight

challenger n. to take on a ~

chamber n. 1. the lower; upper ~ 2. an assembly; council; parliamentary; senate ~ ['room'] ['compartment'] 3. a gas; torture ~ 4. a combustion; decompression ~

chameleon n. ~s change their color

champ v. 1. (d; intr.) to ~ at (to ~ at the bit) 2. (E) they were ~ing to get home

champagne n. to drink; quaff; sip ~

champion n. a defending; national; world ~

championship n. ['position of a champion'] 1. to hold; win a ~ 2. to regain; retain a ~ 3. to give up, lose, relinquish a ~ 4. an individual; national; team; world ~

championships n. ['contest'] 1. to hold ~ 2. (the) national; world ~

chance I n. ['opportunity'] ['possibility'] 1. to have, stand a ~ of (she has a good ~ of success; he doesn't have a ghost of a ~) 2. to let a ~ slip by; to miss one's ~ 3. an earthly, poor, slight, slim; even; fair; fighting; good; last; only; outside; sporting ~ (he doesn't have an earthly ~ of being elected) 4. little, small ~ (there is little ~ of that happening) 5. a ~ against (she doesn't stand a ~ against such strong competitors) 6. a ~ for (a ~ for success) 7.

a ~ to + inf. (she had a ~ to visit her family) 8. a ~ that + clause (there is no ~ that she will win) ['luck'] 9. to take a ~ on ('to try one's luck at'] 10. to leave smt. to ~ 11. pure, sheer ~ 12. a lucky ~ 13. by ~ (it was by pure ~ that we met)

chance II *v.* 1. (d; intr.) to ~ upon ('to find by chance') (to ~ upon a rare item) 2. (formal) (E) ('to happen') I ~d to be there when they arrived

chandelier *n.* a crystal ~

change I *n.* ['alteration'] ['transition'] 1. to bring about, effect, make a ~ 2. to undergo ~ 3. a drastic, great, marked, momentous, radical, striking, sweeping; long overdue, needed, welcome; quick; sudden ~; little ~ (there was little ~ in his condition) 4. a ~ occurs, takes place 5. a ~ for (a ~ for the better) 6. a ~ from; into, to (the ~ from spring to summer) 7. a ~ in, of (a ~ in the weather; ~s in personnel; a ~ of diet; the ~ of seasons) 8. for a ~ (let's eat out for a ~) ['money returned'] ['metal coins'] 9. to give; make; return ~ for (can you give me ~ for a pound?) 10. to count; get, take one's ~ 11. to keep the ~ 12. loose; small ~ ['change of clothing'] 13. to make a ~ 14. a quick ~ (to make a quick ~)

change II *v.* 1. to ~ drastically, radically 2. (D; intr.) ('to transfer') to ~ for (we must ~ at the next station for Chicago) 3. (D; tr.) ('to exchange') to ~ for (to ~ dollars for pounds) 4. (D; intr.) ('to put on different clothes') to ~ for (to ~ for dinner) 5. (D; intr., tr.) ('to be transformed; to transform') to ~ from; into (the disease ~d him from an athlete into an invalid; to ~ dollars into pounds) 6. (D; intr.) ('to put on different clothes') to ~ into (to ~ into smt. less formal) 7. (D; intr., tr.) ('to transfer') to ~ to (we must ~ to an express; she ~d the appointment to Monday) 8. (D; tr.) ('to exchange') to ~ with (I would not want to ~ places with her)

change back *v.* 1. (d; intr.) to ~ from; to (they ~d back to peacetime production) 2. (d; intr.) to ~ into (we ~d back into casual wear)

changeover *n.* 1. a complete, radical, thorough, total ~ 2. a ~ from; to (a ~ from a peacetime to a war economy)

change over *v.* (d; intr.) to ~ from; to (the country ~d over to a war economy; to ~ to the decimal system)

changer *n.* a coin; record ~

channel I *n.* 1. to change ~s 2. a television, TV ~

channel II *v.* (D; tr.) to ~ into (we had to ~ their energy into useful activities)

channels *n.* 1. diplomatic; military; regular ~ 2. through ~ (he sent his request for transfer through regular ~; to go through ~)

chaos *n.* 1. to cause, create ~ 2. complete, total, utter ~ 3. economic; political ~ 4. ~ ensues, results 5. a state of ~

chap *n.* (colloq.) a decent, fine, good, nice ~

chapel *n.* ['place of worship'] 1. (a) hospital; military; prison; ship's ~ ['Nonconformist place of worship'] (BE) (used as an adjective) 2. are you church or ~?

chaperon, chaperone *n.* to serve as a ~ (to serve as a ~ at a dance)

chaplain *n.* a hospital; military; prison; ship's ~

chapter *n.* 1. a closing; introductory, opening ~ 2. a ~ about, on 3. (misc.) a closed ~ in one's life ('smt. that belongs to the past'); to quote ~ and verse ('to cite an exact source')

character *n.* ['personality'] ['behavior'] 1. to form, mold one's ~ 2. to epitomize; reflect smb. ~ ~ 3. one's moral; true ~ 4. a bad, disreputable firm, strong; excellent, fine, good; impeccable, stainless; lovable; national; upright; weak ~ 5. of ~ (a person of good ~) ['role'] ['person playing a role'] 6. to assume; play, portray a ~ 7. to delineate, depict, draw; develop; kill off a ~ 8. a fictitious; leading, main, major, principal; minor, supporting ~ 9. in ~; out of ~ (his behavior was in ~ with his upbringing; her actions were out of ~) ['person, esp. dubious or eccentric'] 10. a dangerous; disreputable; historical; seedy, shady; strange, weird; suspicious; tough; underworld; unforgettable ~ ['letter, figure'] 11. to form, trace; write ~s 12. Arabic; Chinese; cuneiform; Cyrillic; Greek; Hebrew; Hindi; Latin; mathematical; special ~s ['nature'] 13. to have a ~ of one's own 14. an official; political; subversive; unofficial ~ (the statements were of a political ~)

characteristic I *adj.* ~ of

characteristic II *n.* 1. a distinctive, marked; distinguishing, identifying; dominant, outstanding; unique ~ 2. facial; individual; national; physical ~s

characterize *v.* (d; tr.) ('to describe') to ~ as (he can be ~d as a fanatic)

charades *n.* to play ~

charcoal *n.* to burn ~

charge I *n.* ['accusation'] 1. to bring, level, make a ~; to prefer, press ~s 2. to concoct, cook up, fabricate, trump up a ~ (they trumped up various ~s against her) 3. to prove, substantiate a ~ 4. to face a ~ 5. to dismiss, throw out a ~ (the judge dismissed all ~s) 6. to drop, retract, withdraw a ~ 7. to deny; refute; repudiate a ~ 8. a baseless, fabricated, false, trumped-up; frivolous ~ 9. a ~ against smb. (to bring ~s of forgery against smb.) 10. a ~ that (he denied the ~ that he had taken bribes) 11. on a ~ of (he was arraigned on a ~ of embezzlement; to be arrested on various ~s) 12. ['attack'] to lead; make a ~ against 13. to sound the ~ 14. to fight off, repel, repulse a ~ 15. a bayonet; cavalry; infantry ~ ['explosive'] 16. to set off a ~ 17. a depth ~ ['responsibility'] 18. to place, put smb. in ~ of smt. 19. to take ~ of smt. 20. to be in ~ of smt. ['custody'] 21. in smb.'s ~ (the child was in my ~) ['cost'] ['price'] 22. to make a ~ 23. to reverse, transfer (BE) (the) ~s (when telephoning) 24. an exorbitant; reasonable ~ 25. an admission; carrying; cover; minimum; service ~ 26. a ~ against, to (a ~ to smb.'s account) 27. a ~ for (there will be no ~ for installation) ['infusion of stored energy'] 28. to give (a battery) a ~ 29. an electric; quick; slow ~ ['thrill'] (slang) 30. to give smb. a big ~ 31. to get a ~ out of smt. 32. an emotional ~ ['instructions'] 33. to give one's ~ (the judge gave her ~ to the jury) 34. a ~ to (the judge's ~ to the jury)

charge II *v*. 1. ('to ask in payment') to ~ double 2. (D; intr.) ('to rush') to ~ at (the bull ~d at us) 3. (d; intr.) ('to ask payment') to ~ for (they didn't ~ for it) 4. (D; intr., tr.) to ~ for ('to ask in payment') (they ~d ten dollars for shipping our books; he ~s by the hour for laying a carpet) 5. (d; intr.) ('to rush') to ~ into; out of (to ~ into a room) 6. (D; tr.) to ~ out of ('to borrow from') (to ~ a book out of a library) 7. (D; tr.) ('to impose as an obligation') to ~ to (~ it to my account) 8. (D; tr.) ('to accuse') to ~ with (he was ~d with murder) 9. (D; tr.) ('to saturate') to ~ with (the air was ~d with tension) 10. (D; tr.) ('to assign') to ~ with (our agency has been ~d with the responsibility of gathering all pertinent information) 11. (L) ('to accuse') they ~d that he had cheated them 12. (O; may be used with one object) ('to ask payment') she ~d (me) fifty dollars for her services; how much did he ~? did they ~ you?

chargeable *adj*. ~ to

charitable *adj*. 1. ~ towards 2. ~ to + inf. (it was ~ of her to say that)

charity *n*. 1. to dispense, distribute, give ~ to; to bestow ~ on, upon 2. to accept ~ 3. to ask for, beg for, plead for ~ 4. an act of ~ 5. ~ for (~ for the needy) 6. (misc.) (proverb) ~ begins at home

charm *n*. ['amulet'] 1. to wear a ~ ['attractive quality'] 2. to turn on, use one's ~ 3. to exude; have, possess ~ 4. to lend ~ to 5. great, irresistible; natural; particular, special; unfailing ~ 6. the ~ to + inf. (she has enough ~ to win anyone over) ['misc.'] 7. it works like a ~ ('it works perfectly')

charmed *adj*. ~ to + inf. (I would be ~ to accept your invitation)

charmer *n*. 1. (to be) a real ~ 2. a snake ~

charming *adj*. 1. ~ to (she is ~ to everyone) 2. ~ to + inf. (it was ~ to watch them)

chart I *n*. 1. to compile a ~ 2. an aeronautical; clinical; eye; flow; genealogical; statistical; wall ~

chart II *v*. (D; tr.) to ~ for (he has ~ed a difficult course for us)

charter *n*. 1. to apply for; take out a ~ 2. to grant a ~ 3. to revoke a ~ 4. a ~ to + inf. (the company was granted a ~ to trade in the occupied territory)

charter flight *n*. to organize a ~

chary *adj*. 1. ~ about (~ about doing smt.) 2. ~ of (~ of strangers)

chase I *n*. 1. to give ~ to 2. to abandon, give up the ~ 3. a wild-goose ~ 4. in ~ of (in full ~) 5. (misc.) (AE) to lead smb. a merry ~ (BE has *to lead smb. a merry dance*)

chase II *v*. 1. (d; intr.) to ~ after (to ~ after fame) 2. (D; tr.) to ~ from, out of (~ the dog out of our yard!)

chaser *n*. 1. a submarine ~ 2. (misc.) (colloq.) an ambulance ~ (esp. AE) ('a lawyer who seeks clients among accident victims'); whiskey with a beer ~ ('whiskey served with a glass of beer')

chasm *n*. 1. to bridge a ~ 2. a gaping, yawning ~

chat I *n*. 1. to have a ~ 2. a friendly, nice, pleasant ~ 3. a ~ about; with (I had a pleasant ~ with them about our new grandchildren) 4. a ~ between

chat II *v*. 1. (D; intr.) to ~ about; to (BE), with

chatter I *n*. constant, endless, idle, incessant ~

chatter II *v*. 1. ('to talk fast') to ~ incessantly 2. (D; intr.) ('to talk fast') to ~ about 3. (D; intr.) ('to click') to ~ from, with (his teeth were ~ing with the cold)

cheap *adj*. 1. (colloq.) dirt ~ 2. ~ to + inf. (it's not ~ to live in the city; it is ~er to live in the south than in the north) 3. (misc.) to hold life ~

cheat I *n*. 1. a downright; notorious ~ 2. a tax ~

cheat II *v*. 1. (D; intr., tr.) to ~ at (to ~ at cards) 2. (D; intr.) to ~ on ('to deceive') (to ~ on one's wife) 3. (D; tr.) to ~ out of (he ~ed us out of our money) 4. (misc.) to ~ on an examination

check I *n*. ['order to a bank'] (BE has **cheque**) 1. to issue, make out, write out a ~ to 2. to draw a ~ against one's account; to draw a ~ on a bank 3. to cash; clear; deposit; present a ~ 4. to cover a ~ (by making a deposit) 5. to endorse; negotiate a ~ 6. to pass a (bad) ~; to kite a ~ (AE) ('to write a bad ~'); to raise ('increase fraudulently') a ~ 7. to stop payment of, on a ~ 8. a bad ('not covered'); blank; cashier's; certified; crossed (BE); negotiable; traveler's ~ 9. a ~ bounces; clears 10. by ~ (to pay by ~) ['verification'] ['control'] 11. to conduct, make, run a ~ of, on 12. a background; bed; loyalty; spot ~ (to run a background ~ on all new employees) ['endangered position of the king'] (chess) 13. to produce a ~ 14. to discover ~ 15. discovered; perpetual ~ 16. in ~ (your king is in ~) ['bill in a restaurant'] (AE) 17. to pay the ~ ['token of ownership, of a right'] 18. a baggage (AE); claim; hat; rain (AE) ~ ['blocking of an opponent'] (ice hockey) 19. a board; body; hook ~ ['device for braking'] 20. a door ~ ['restraint'] 21. to hold, keep in ~

check II *v*. 1. (D; intr.) to ~ into ('to verify') (to ~ into smb.'s story) 2. (d; intr.) to ~ into ('to register at') (to ~ into a hotel) 3. (d; intr.) to ~ on ('to verify') (to ~ on smb.'s story) 4. (d; intr.) to ~ out of ('to announce one's departure from') (to ~ out of a hotel) 5. (d; tr.) to ~ out of ('to borrow from') (she ~ed the book out of the library) 6. (D; intr.) to ~ through ('to look through') (to ~ through the files) 7. (AE) (d; tr.) to ~ through to ('to register as far as') (she ~ed her suitcase through to Chicago)

checkbook *n*. to reconcile a ~ with (a bank statement)

checkers *n*. 1. to play ~ 2. Chinese ~

check in *v*. (D; intr.) to ~ at (to ~ at a hotel)

checking account *n*. (AE) to balance a ~ (every month)

checklist *n*. 1. to compile, make up a ~ 2. to go down, go through a ~

check out *v*. (D; tr.) ('to borrow') to ~ from (she ~ed out a book from the library)

checkrein *n*. (rare) a ~ on, upon

checkup *n*. 1. to do, give a ~ (the doctor gave me a thorough ~) 2. to have a ~ (I had a ~ at the hospital yesterday) 3. an annual; careful; regular; thorough ~

check up *v*. (D; intr.) to ~ on (to ~ on smb.'s story)

cheek *n*. ['side of the face'] 1. to puff (out) one's ~s 2. burning, flushed; dimpled; full, rounded;

hollow, sunken; pale; rosy, ruddy ~s ['impudence'] (colloq.) 3. the ~ to + inf. (she had the ~ to phone me at home)
cheekbones *n.* high, prominent ~
cheeky *adj.* (colloq.) ['impudent'] ~ to + inf. (it was ~ of her to phone you at home)
cheer I *n.* ['rallying cry'] ['cry of approval'] 1. to give, shout a ~ (let's give him three ~s) 2. to draw a ~ (her performance drew ~s) 3. to acknowledge the ~s (of the crowd) 4. a loud, ringing, rousing ~ 5. a school ~ (let's give the school ~!) ['good mood'] 6. Christmas; good ~ 7. of ~ (to be of good ~)
cheer II *v.* 1. to ~ enthusiastically, loudly 2. (D; intr.) to ~ for (they ~ed loudly for their team) 3. (N; refl.; used with an adjective) they ~ed themselves hoarse
cheese *n.* 1. grated; grilled (AE), toasted (BE); hard; mild; semi-soft; sharp; smoked; soft ~ 2. (misc.) (colloq.) say ~! ('smile'!)
chemistry *n.* ['science that deals with substances'] 1. analytical; inorganic; organic; physical ~ ['personal feelings'] (colloq.) 2. personal ~; the right; wrong ~ 3. the ~ between
cheque (BE) see **check** I, 1-10
chequebook (BE) see **checkbook**
chess *n.* 1. to play ~ 2. (misc.) a ~ game; master; match
chest *n.* ['thorax'] 1. to beat; throw out one's ~ (with pride) 2. a barrel ~ ['box'] 3. a hope (AE; BE has *bottom drawer);* ice; medicine; silver; tool ~
chestnuts *n.* 1. to roast ~ 2. (misc.) to pull smb.'s ~ out of the fire ('to extricate smb. from an unpleasant situation')
chewing gum *n.* a piece; stick of ~
chic I *adj.* ['fashionable'] ~ to + inf. (it's very ~ to give up smoking)
chic II *n.* 1. an indefinable ~ 2. radical ~
chick *n.* 1. to hatch ~s 2. ~s cheep 3. a brood of ~s
chicken I *n.* 1. ~s cluck 2. a brood of ~s 3. a young ~ is a chick, cockerel (BE) 4. a female ~ is a hen 5. a male ~ is a cock (esp. BE)/rooster (esp. AE) 6. (misc.) to count one's ~s before they are hatched ('to rejoice prematurely')
chicken II *v.* (colloq.) (d; intr.) to ~ out of ('to abandon') (to ~ out of an agreement)
chickenpox *n.* to catch, come down with (the) ~
chide *v.* (D; tr.) to ~ for
chief *n.* 1. an Indian ~ 2. a fire; police (AE) ~
chieftain *n.* a tribal ~
child *n.* 1. to adopt; bear, give birth to, have a ~ (she had four children) 2. to carry a ~ (a mother carries a ~ for nine months) 3. to beget; conceive a ~ 4. to bring up, raise, rear a ~ 5. to feed; nurse; wean a ~ 6. to indulge, pamper, spoil a ~ 7. to toilet-train, train a ~ 8. to acknowledge a ~ (as one's own) 9. to marry off one's ~ 10. an adopted; foster; illegitimate; love, natural; legitimate; only; unwanted ~ 11. a delinquent; disobedient; incorrigible; mischievous; problem; recalcitrant; stubborn; unruly; self-willed, wilful; wayward ~ 12. an indulged, pampered, spoiled ~ 13. a disciplined, obedient, well-behaved ~ 14. a bright, gifted,

intelligent; sensitive ~ 15. a precocious; young ~ 16. a dull, slow; handicapped; retarded; underprivileged ~ 17. a flower (of the l960s); latchkey (who comes home to an empty house) ~ 18. a happy; loving; well-cared for ~ 19. an abused mistreated; neglected ~ 20. a ~ develops grows (into adulthood) 21. (misc.) to be with ~ (old-fashioned) ('to be pregnant')
childbirth *n.* 1. natural; prepared ~ 2. in ~ (she died in ~)
childhood *n.* 1. to spend one's ~ (somewhere) 2. one's second ~ 3. in one's ~ 4. since ~
childish *adj.* ~ to + inf. (it was ~ of him to do that)
child's play *n.* (colloq.) ['easy task'] 1. ~ to (that's ~ to him) 2. ~ to + inf. (it was ~ to solve that riddle)
chill I *n.* 1. (fig.) to cast a ~ on, over 2. to catch a ~ 3. to take the ~ off (take the ~ off the milk)
chill II *v.* 1. (C) ~ a glass for me; or (rare): ~ me a glass 2. (misc.) ~ed to the bone
chills *n.* to send ~ up one's spine ('to frighten smb.')
chime *v.* (d; intr.) to ~ into ('to join in') (she always ~s into a conversation)
chime in *v.* (D; intr.) to ~ with (to ~ with one's opinion)
chimes *n.* 1. to sound ~ 2. organ ~ 3. ~ sound
chimney *n.* 1. smoke goes up a ~ 2. smoke comes out of a ~
chin *n.* 1. a double; smooth ~ 2. a glass ('weak' ~ (of a boxer) 3. (misc.) to keep one's ~ up ('not to become discouraged'); to take it on the ~ ('to suffer a misfortune courageously')
china *n.* ['porcelain'] 1. fine ~ 2. a set of ~
chink *n.* a ~ in one's armor ('a weak point')
chip *n.* ['thin slice'] (AE) 1. a potato ~ (BE has *crisp)* ['semiconductor body'] 2. an integrated-circuit; silicon ~ ['misc.'] 3. a bargaining ~ ('smt. that can be used to win concessions'); a ~ off the old block ('a child who resembles its parent'); to have a ~ on one's shoulder ('to harbor resentment')
chip away *v.* (d; intr.) to ~ at (to ~ at a rock; the police kept ~ping away at their alibi)
chip in *v.* 1. (D; intr.) to ~ for (they all ~ped in for a present) 2. (D; intr.) to ~ with (we all ~ped in with our suggestions)
chips *n.* ['gambling tokens'] to cash in one's ~ (also fig.) ('to die')
chisel *v.* 1. (D; tr.) ('to shape with a chisel') to ~ from, out of (to ~ smt. from wood) 2. (colloq.) (D; tr.) to ~ out of ('to cheat out of') (he ~ed me out of my money)
chiseled *adj.* ['shaped'] finely ~
chloroform *n.* to administer, give ~ to
chock-full *adj.* (colloq.) ~ of
chocolate *n.* ['candy, sweet'] 1. dark; milk ~ 2. a bar of ~ ['beverage'] 3. hot ~ 4. a cup of ~
choice *n.* 1. to exercise, make a ~ 2. a bad, sorry, wrong; careful; difficult; first; good, happy, intelligent, judicious, wise; random; second; wide (she made the wrong ~) 3. (a) free; individual; limited ~ (to exercise individual ~) 4. a ~ among, between; of (a ~ between two jobs; a ~ of colors)

5. (misc.) we have a difficult ~ to make; take your ~; freedom of ~; Hobson's ('no') ~

choir n. 1. to form; lead a ~ 2. to sing in a ~

choke I n. (on a car) 1. to pull out; push in the ~ 2. an automatic; manual ~

choke II v. 1. (D; intr.) to ~ on (to ~ on a bone) 2. (d; intr.) to ~ with (to ~ with emotion) 3. (misc.) to ~ to death

choked adj. ['blocked'] ~ with (~ with weeds)

choked up adj. (all) ~ with (~ with emotion)

cholera n. 1. to come down with, contract ~ 2. (misc.) a ~ epidemic

cholesterol n. 1. to cut down on ~ 2. high; low in ~

choose v. 1. to ~ carefully, judiciously; to ~ at random 2. (D; intr.) to ~ among, between, from (to ~ between two offers) 3. (D; tr.) to ~ as (they chose her as their spokesperson) 4. (D; intr., tr.) to ~ by (to ~ by lot; to ~ by tossing a coin) 5. (D; tr.) to ~ for (~ a book for me) 6. (D; tr.) to ~ from (they chose us from a large number of candidates) 7. (E) she chose to remain at home 8. (H) they chose me to serve as their representative

choosey adj. (colloq.; esp. AE) ~ about

choosing n. of one's own ~

chop I n. ['cut of meat'] 1. a chump (BE); lamb; mutton; pork; veal ~ ['blow'] 2. a karate ~

chop II v. (C) ~ some wood for me; or: ~ me some wood

chopper n. a food; meat ~

chopsticks n. to use ~

chop up v. 1. (C) ~ some wood for me; or (colloq.): ~ me up some wood 2. (D; tr.) to ~ into (he ~ped the log up into firewood)

chord I n. ['combination of three or more musical notes'] 1. to play ~s 2. a dominant; major; minor ~

chord II n. ['feeling, emotion'] 1. to strike, touch a ~ 2. a popular; responsive, sensitive, sympathetic ~ (to strike a responsive ~)

chores n. 1. to do one's ~ 2. daily; routine ~

chortle v. 1. (D; intr.) to ~ about, over 2. (D; intr.) to ~ with (to ~ with glee)

chorus n. ['group of singers'] 1. a female; male; mixed ~ ['simultaneous utterance'] 2. to join in, swell the ~

chowder n. (AE) clam; corn; fish ~

christen v. (N; used with a noun) they ~ed the child Joseph

christening n. to perform a ~

Christian n. a believing (esp. BE); born-again; evangelical; fundamentalist; good; practicing ~

Christmas n. 1. to celebrate ~ 2. a white ~ 3. on ~ 4. on ~ day; on ~ eve; Merry ~

Christmas tree n. to decorate, trim a ~

chronicle n. 1. to keep a ~ 2. a daily; monthly; weekly ~ 3. (misc.) a ~ of events

chuck v. (colloq.) (usu. B) ~ the ball to me

chuckle I n. 1. to have; let out a ~ (we had a good ~); a hearty ~ 3. a ~ about, over

chuckle II v. 1. (D; intr.) to ~ about, over 2. (D; intr.) to ~ to (to ~ to oneself) 3. (D; intr.) to ~ with (to ~ with glee)

chum n. (colloq.) a childhood; old; school ~

chummy adj. (colloq.) ['friendly'] ~ with

chum up v. (D; intr.) to ~ with

church n. 1. to consecrate, dedicate a ~ 2. to attend, go to ~ 3. the Catholic; Christian; (Eastern) Orthodox; Protestant; Uniate ~ 4. the Anglican; Baptist; Christian Science; Congregational; Episcopal; Lutheran; Mennonite; Methodist; Mormon; Presbyterian; Seventh Day Adventist; Unitarian ~ 5. an evangelical; fundamentalist ~ 6. (esp. GB) an established ('official'); free ('Nonconformist') ~ 7. (esp. GB) The Church of England; Ireland; Scotland 8. at, in ~

churlish adj. ~ to + inf. (it would be ~ to offer such petty criticism)

cider n. hard (AE); sweet ~

cigar n. 1. to light (up); puff on; smoke a ~ 2. a Havana ~

cigarette n. 1. to light (up); puff on, smoke a ~ 2. to roll a ~ (he used to roll his own ~s) 3. to extinguish, put out, stub out a ~ 4. a live ~ 5. a filtertip; king-size; low-tar; mentholated ~ 6. a carton; pack (AE), packet (BE) of ~s

cinch n. (colloq.) ['certainty'] 1. ~ to + inf. (he's a ~ to be elected) 2. ~ that + clause (it's a ~ that he'll win)

cinders n. to spread ~ (on a snow-covered road)

cinema n. (BE) at, in the ~

cipher n. ['code'] 1. to break, solve a ~ 2. in ~

circle n. ['circular geometric figure'] 1. to describe, draw a ~ 2. to square a ~ (to square a ~ is impossible) 3. the Antarctic; Arctic; polar ~ (at the Arctic ~) 4. the great ~ (on the earth's surface) 5. a traffic ~ (AE; BE has *roundabout*) 6. (sports) the center ~; the winner's ~ (at a racecourse/racetrack) 7. the area; circumference; diameter; radius of a ~ ['group resembling the figure of a circle'] 8. to form a ~ 9. to join a ~ (she joined the ~ of dancers) ['group'] 10. academic; artistic; business, financial; court; diplomatic; exclusive, select; high; informed, well-informed; literary; official; political; professional; ruling ~s (to move in the highest ~s) 11. a charmed ('exclusive'); close, closed, inner, intimate, narrow; wide ~ (a close ~ of friends) 12. a linguistic; quilting; sewing ~ 13. a family ~ 14. in a ~ (in our ~ of friends; in informed ~s) ['cycle'] 15. to come full ~ ['misc.'] 16. a vicious ~ ('an insoluble, never-ending problem'); to go around in ~s ('to behave in a confused manner')

circuit n. ['path of an electric current'] 1. to break; close a ~ 2. a closed; integrated; printed; short ~ ['route traveled by a judge on tour'] 3. to make a ~ (the judge makes a ~ every year) 4. on ~ (the judge was on ~) ['series of similar events'] 5. the lecture; rodeo; talk-show ~

circuit breaker n. to trip a ~

circular n. 1. to send out a ~ 2. to distribute ~s

circulate v. 1. (D; intr.) to ~ among (the host ~d among the guests) 2. (D; intr.) to ~ through (blood ~s through the body)

circulation n. ['distribution'] 1. to put into ~ (to put more money into ~) 2. to withdraw from ~ (to withdraw old banknotes from ~) 3. enormous, large, wide; general; limited, small; national, nationwide ~ (this magazine has attained a wide

~) 4. in ~ (this money is no longer in ~) ['move-'ment'] 5. blood ~; or: ~ of the blood 6. good, healthy; poor ~

circumcision *n.* to do, perform a ~ (on)

circumference *n.* in ~ (ten feet in ~)

circumstances *n.* 1. adverse, difficult, trying ~ 2. reduced, straitened ~ 3. aggravating; extenuating, mitigating ~ 4. attendant; compelling; exceptional, special; favorable; suspicious; tragic; unavoidable; unforeseen ~ 5. a combination of ~ 6. due to ~ (our absence was due to ~ beyond our control) 7. in, under ~ (in certain ~, I would agree; she will not go under any ~; they lived in difficult ~)

circus *n.* 1. to present, put on a ~ 2. to go to the ~ 3. a three-ring; traveling ~ 4. at a ~ 5. (misc.) a three-ring ~ ('hectic activity')

citation *n.* ['reference'] 1. the earliest ~ (of the use of a word) 2. a ~ from ['summons'] 3. to issue a ~ for 4. a ~ to + inf. (she received a ~ to appear in court) ['mention of meritorious performance'] (AE) (mil.) 5. to write smb. up for a ~ 6. to receive a ~ (for bravery) 7. a unit ~

cite *v.* 1. (B) she ~d an interesting passage to us 2. (D; tr.) to ~ as (to ~ smt. as an example) 3. (AE) (mil.) (D; tr.) to ~ for (to ~ smb. for bravery)

citizen *n.* 1. a law-abiding; eminent, leading, prominent; respectable, solid ~ 2. a senior ~ 3. a private; second-class ~ 4. a native-born (esp. AE); naturalized, new ~

citizenry *n.* an informed ~

citizenship *n.* 1. to grant ~ 2. to acquire, receive ~ 3. to revoke smb.'s ~ 4. to give up, renounce one's ~ 5. dual ~

city *n.* 1. to govern, manage (AE), run a ~ 2. a capital; cosmopolitan; densely populated; free; garden (BE), planned; port; provincial; satellite ~; twin ~ties 3. (the) central; inner ~ 4. a beleaguered; open ~ (during wartime) 5. in a ~ (to live in the ~) (see the Usage Note for **town**)

civil *adj.* 1. ~ to (he wasn't even ~ to his guests) 2. (formal) ~ to + inf. (it was ~ of them to offer their help)

civil action *n.* (legal) to bring a ~

civilization *n.* 1. to introduce; spread ~ 2. to create a ~ 3. to destroy, stamp out ~ 4. an ancient; modern ~

clad *adj.* 1. fully; lightly, scantily; partially ~ 2. smartly ~

claim I *n.* 1. to enter, file, lodge, make, put forward, put in, submit; establish; press; substantiate a ~ (she filed a ~ for compensation) 2. to lay ~ to; to stake, stake out a ~ to 3. (esp. AE) to jump ('steal') smb.'s ~ 4. to contest; disallow, dismiss, reject; dispute a ~ 5. to forfeit; give up, renounce, waive, withdraw a ~ 6. to settle a ~ (they settled their ~ out of court) 7. an excessive, extravagant, unreasonable; fraudulent; legal; moral; outstanding; prior; specious; undisputed; unsubstantiated, unsupported ~; competing, conflicting, rival ~s 8. a disability; insurance ~ 9. a ~ against; for; on; to (she submitted a ~ for damages against the other driver; there are many ~s on my time; he has no ~ to the estate; a ~ to fame) 10. a ~ that +

clause (the ~ that he could reduce taxes proved to be false)

claim II *v.* 1. (E) she ~s to own this property 2. (L) he ~s that he was cheated

claimant *n.* a ~ to (a ~ to the estate)

clam *n.* baked ~s

clamber *v.* (P; intr.) to ~ into/onto a bus

clamor, clamour I *n.* 1. an insistent; loud; public ~ 2. a ~ against; for (a ~ against new taxes)

clamor, clamour II *v.* 1. (d; intr.) to ~ for (to ~ for justice) 2. (E) they were ~ing to see the senator

clamp *v.* (d; tr.) to ~ on, upon (to ~ controls on interest rates)

clampdown *n.* a ~ on

clamp down *v.* (D; intr.) to ~ on (to ~ on pickpockets)

clan *n.* a ~ gathers

clang *n.* a metallic ~

clanger *n.* (colloq.) (BE) ('blunder') to drop a ~

clank *v.* to ~ shut

clap *v.* ('to put') 1. (d; tr.) to ~ into (to ~ smb. into jail) 2. (d; tr.) to ~ on (to ~ a muzzle on a dog) 3. (d; tr.) to ~ to (he ~ped his hand to his mouth)

clarification *n.* to provide; seek ~

clash I *n.* 1. a bitter; bloody; violent ~ 2. a ~ between (there was a violent ~ between the two rivals) 3. a ~ with (a ~ with the police)

clash II *v.* 1. (D; intr.) ('to argue') to ~ over 2. (D; intr.) ('to struggle') to ~ with (the demonstrators ~ed with the police) 3. (D; intr.) ('not to match') to ~ with (red ~es with green)

clasp I *n.* a tie ~

clasp II *v.* (d; tr.) to ~ to (she ~ed the baby to her bosom)

class I *n.* ['lesson'] 1. to conduct, hold (a) ~; to give, meet one's ~; to schedule; reschedule a ~ 2. to attend, go to ~; to sit in on a ~ (esp. AE) 3. to cut (esp. AE); miss a ~ 4. to call off, cancel; dismiss a ~ 5. an advanced; beginners'; intermediate ~ (to sit in on an advanced English ~) ['group'] 6. to form a ~ 7. the educated; leisure; lower; middle; privileged; ruling; social; underprivileged; upper; working ~ 8. (misc.) out of one's ~ ('outclassed'); in a ~ of one's own ('unsurpassed'); ~ conflict/struggle ['division of travelers'] 9. cabin; economy; first; second; third; tourist ~ (to travel first-class) ['group of pupils, students graduating together'] (AE) 10. the freshman; junior; senior; sophomore ~

class II see **classify 1-4**

classification *n.* to make a ~

classify *v.* 1. (D; tr.) to ~ according to (the children were ~fied according to age) 2. (D; tr.) to ~ among, with 3. (D; tr.) to ~ as (she was ~fied as fit for service) 4. (D; tr.) to ~ by (to ~ books by subject) 5. (N; used with an adjective) to ~ information confidential

clatter *v.* (P; intr.) the cart ~ed over the cobblestones

clause *n.* ['group of words with a subject and predicate'] 1. a conditional; dependent, subordinate ~ independent, main; nonrestrictive; relative restrictive; verbless ~ ['provision'] ['article'] 2. (esp. AE) a grandfather ~ ('a clause that exempts those already engaged in an activity prohibited by new legislation') 3. an escalator; penalty ~ 4. a most-favored-nation ~

claw I *n.* 1. to retract one's ~s (cats retract their ~s) 2. sharp ~s 3. nonretractile; retractile ~s

claw II *v.* (d; tr.) to ~ to (to ~ one's way to the top)

clay *n.* 1. to model, shape, work ~ 2. to bake; temper ~ 3. modeling; potter's ~

clean I *adj., adv.* 1. immaculately, spotlessly ~ 2. (misc.) to come ~ ('to confess'); we're ~ out of food ('we're completely out of food')

clean II *v.* (D; tr.) to ~ out of (the store was ~ed out of cigarettes)

cleaner *n.* ['device'] 1. a pipe; vacuum ~ ['person'] 2. a street ~

cleaning *n.* 1. dry ~ 2. a spring; thorough ~

cleanliness *n.* personal ~

cleanse *v.* (formal) (D; tr.) to ~ of (to ~ one's thoughts of sin)

clean up *v.* (colloq.) (AE) (D; intr.) ('to make a profit') to ~ on (to ~ on a deal)

clear I *adj.* 1. crystal, perfectly; painfully ~ 2. (cannot stand alone) ~ about (are you ~ about the situation?) 3. ~ from (the answer is ~ from these facts) 4. ~ of (the roads were ~ of snow; to keep ~ of trouble) 5. ~ to (the situation is ~ to everyone) 6. ~ that + clause (it was ~ that they would not come; the teacher made it ~ that discipline would be maintained)

clear II *n.* ['uncoded language'] in the ~ (to send a message in the ~)

clear III *v.* 1. (D; tr.) ('to authorize'); ('to prepare') to ~ for (to ~ an article for export; our plane was ~ed for takeoff; to ~ a deck for action) 2. (D; tr.) ('to remove') to ~ from (to ~ the snow from the driveway) 3. (D; tr.) ('to free') to ~ of (to ~ a harbor of mines; to ~ smb. of guilt; to ~ land of trees) 4. (colloq.) (d; intr.) to ~ out of (to ~ leave') (to ~ out of town) 5. (d; tr.) ('to remove') to ~ out of (to ~ things out of a cupboard) 6. (D; tr.) ('to complete formalities for') to ~ with (to ~ a shipment with the authorities) 7. (H) ('to authorize') we were ~ed to land

clearance *n.* ['act of clearing away'] 1. slum ~ ['authorization'] 2. to give; receive ~ for 3. customs ~ 4. ~ to + inf. (the control tower gave the pilot ~ to land) ['space between parts'] 5. valve ~ ['certification of eligibility for access to classified material'] 6. to give; receive ~ 7. a security ~

clearinghouse *n.* a ~ for (a ~ for information)

clear off *v.* (D; intr.) ('to leave') to ~ of (~ of my property!)

cleavage *n.* ['division'] a sharp ~ between (a sharp ~ developed between the two factions)

cleave *v.* (formal) (d; intr.) ('to cling') to ~ to (to ~ to old customs)

cleaver *n.* a butcher's; meat ~

clemency *n.* 1. to show ~ 2. to beg for, seek ~ 3. to deny ~

clerk I *n.* 1. a booking ~ (BE; AE has *ticket agent*) 2. a desk (AE), reception (BE), room

(AE) ~ (in a hotel) 3. a bank (BE); city (AE), town; cipher, code; court; filing; mail, postal ~; salesclerk (AE; BE has *shop assistant)*; shipping; stockroom ~

clerk II *v.* (D; intr.) (legal) to ~ for (the budding lawyer was ~ing for a prominent judge)

clever *adj.* 1. ~ at, in (she is ~ at arranging furniture) 2. ~ with (he is ~ with his hands) 3. ~ to + inf. (it was ~ of her to think of that)

clew see **clue**

click *v.* (colloq.) (D; intr.) ('to be successful') to ~ with (the new show ~ed with the public)

client *n.* to serve a ~

clientele *n.* an exclusive ~

cliff *n.* 1. to climb, scale a ~ 2. a rugged; sheer, steep ~

climate *n.* 1. a friendly; hospitable; inhospitable; invigorating ~ 2. an arctic, frigid; continental; damp; dry; hot; humid; maritime; Mediterranean; mild, moderate, temperate; severe; subtropical; tropical; warm; wet ~

climax *n.* 1. to come to, reach a ~ 2. to bring smt. to a ~; to work up to a ~ 3. to mark a ~ 4. a dramatic, thrilling ~ 5. a sexual ~ 6. a ~ to (the ~ to our efforts)

climb I *n.* a difficult, hard; easy; gradual; rough, rugged; steep; tortuous ~

climb II *v.* 1. (d; intr.) to ~ aboard (to ~ aboard a raft) 2. (d; intr.) to ~ down (to ~ down a hill) 3. (d; intr.) to ~ onto, upon (the child ~ed onto her mother's lap) 4. (d; intr.) to ~ out of (to ~ out of a pit) 5. (D; intr.) to ~ to (to ~ to the top) 6. (D; intr.) to ~ up (to ~ up a hill)

climb-down *n.* (BE) ['retreat'] a ~ from (a ~ from an untenable position)

climb down *v.* 1. (D; intr.) to ~ from (to ~ from a tree) 2. (BE) (D; intr.) ('to retreat') to ~ from (to ~ from an untenable position)

climber *n.* 1. a mountain ~ 2. a social ~

clinch *n.* in a ~

cling *v.* 1. (d; intr.) to ~ to (to ~ to one's possessions; to ~ to old customs; they clung to the floating wreckage; he clung to my arm) 2. (misc.) to ~ together

clinic *n.* 1. to hold a ~ 2. an abortion; animal; dental; diagnostic; family-planning; mental health; outpatient; special; speech; well-child (AE) ~ 3. at, in a ~ (she works at the ~)

clip I *n.* ['device to hold cartridges'] 1. to insert a ~ 2. a cartridge ~ ['device that fastens'] 3. a paper; tie ~

clip II *n.* (colloq.) (esp. AE) ['speed'] at a ~ (to move at a fast ~)

clip III *v.* 1. (esp. AE) (D; tr.) to ~ from (to ~ articles from a newspaper) 2. (d; tr.) to ~ to (to ~ one page to another) 3. (N; used with an adjective) she ~ped his hair short

clipper *n.* 1. a nail ~ 2. a barber's ~s 3. a coupon ~ ('one whose income is derived from stocks and bonds')

clipping *n.* 1. a newspaper, press ~ (AE; BE has *press cutting)* 2. fingernail; toenail ~s

clique *n.* a court; military ~

cloak I *n.* ['shield'] under a ~ (under the ~ of

anonymity)

cloak II *v.* (d; tr.) to ~ in (~ed in secrecy)

cloakroom see the Usage Note for **room**

clock I *n.* 1. to regulate, set; wind a ~ 2. to advance a ~; or: to set, turn a ~ ahead (by one hour) 3. to set, turn a ~ back (by ten minutes) 4. an alarm; cuckoo; electric; grandfather; wall ~ 5. a biological ~ 6. a ~ is fast; right; slow 7. a ~ gains time; goes; keeps time; loses time; runs down; stops 8. a ~ strikes the hour 9. (misc.) to watch the ~ ('to wait impatiently for the end of the working day'); to work around the ~ ('to work without rest'); the ~ ran out ('the allotted time expired'); to stop the ~ ('to suspend play in a game so that the clock stops running')

clock II *v.* (D; tr.) ('to time') to ~ at (he was ~ed at a record speed)

clockwork *n.* (misc.) to work like ~ ('to work perfectly'); as regular as ~ ('completely regular')

close I *adj., adv.* /klous/ ['near'] 1. ~ to (~ to tears; we live ~ to town; ~ to the truth) ['stingy'] (colloq.) 2. ~ with (~ with one's money) ['secretive'] 3. ~ about (~ about one's past) ['on intimate terms'] 4. ~ to, with (~ with one's parents) ['misc.'] 5. to see smt. ~ to (BE), up

close II *n.* /klouz/ ['finish'] 1. to bring to a ~ 2. to come to, draw to a ~ ['end of a letter'] 3. the complimentary ~ (to a letter)

close III *v.* /klouz/ 1. (d; intr.) to ~ about, around, round ('to encircle') (night ~d around us) 2. (D; tr.) to ~ for (to ~ a store for renovations) 3. (d; intr.) to ~ on ('to get near to') (the police were ~ing on the fugitive) 4.(D; tr.) ('to shut') to ~ on (she ~d the door on him) 5. (D; tr.) ('to shut') to ~ to (they ~d their eyes to the truth) 6. (d; intr.) to ~ with ('to engage') (to ~ with the enemy) 7. (d; intr., tr.) ('to finish') to ~ with (they ~d the concert with a march) 8. (N; used with an adjective) ('to shut') she ~d the door tight 9. (s) stocks ~d strong; weak

closed *adj.* 1. ~ for (~ for repairs) 2. ~ to (the road was ~ to traffic; ~ to the public)

close in *v.* /klouz/ 1. (D; intr.) to ~ for ('to approach and prepare for') (to ~ for the kill) 2. (D; intr.) to ~ on ('to bring to bay') (the police ~d in on the fugitives)

closemouthed *adj.* ~ about

closeness *n.* ~ to

closet *n.* ['cupboard'] 1. a china; clothes; linen; walk in ~ ['toilet'] (esp. BE) 2. a water ~ ['misc.'] 3. to come out of the ~ ('to come out into the open about smt.')

closeted *adj.* ~ with (he was ~ with the mayor for an hour)

clot *n.* 1. to form a ~ 2. to dissolve a ~ 3. a blood ~ 4. a ~ forms

cloth *n.* 1. to weave ~ 2. homespun ~ 3. a drop ~ 4. a loin ~ 5. a bolt; strip of ~

clothe *v.* 1. (D; tr.) to ~ in (~d in wool) 2. (misc.) fully; partially ~d

clothes *n.* 1. to change; put on; take off; wear ~ 2. to launder, wash ~ 3. night; summer; swaddling; winter ~ 4. new; old ~.5. civilian ~ 6. in ~ (the soldier was in civilian ~)

clothesline *n.* to put up, string; take down a ~

clothing *n.* 1. to put on; wear ~ 2. to take off one's ~ 3. heavy; light; outer; protective; warm ~ 4. summer; winter ~ 5. custom-made, tailor-made; ready-to-wear; secondhand, used; shabby; trendy ~ 6. an article of ~ 7. (misc.) to model ~

cloture *n.* to apply, impose, invoke ~

cloud *n.* 1. to disperse ~s (the strong wind dispersed the ~s) 2. dark; heavy; thick; high; scattered; threatening ~s 3. rain, storm ~s; thunderclouds 4. a mushroom; radioactive ~ 5. ~s form; gather 6. ~s scud across the sky 7. (misc.) under a ~ (of suspicion); the gathering ~s of war in the ~s ('absorbed in one's fantasies'); to seed ~s (to produce rain)

cloudburst *n.* a sudden ~

cloudy *adj.* partly ~ (in weather forecasts)

clout *n.* (colloq.) (AE) ['influence'] ['power'] 1. to have, wield ~ 2. political ~ (he has a great deal of political ~)

clover *n.* ['plant'] 1. a four-leaf ~ ['prosperity'] 2. to roll in ~ ('to live in luxury')

clown I *n.* 1. to act, play the ~ 2. a circus ~

clown II *v.* (D; intr.) to ~ with

club *n.* ['association'] 1. to form, organize a ~ 2. to join a ~ 3. to break up, disband a ~ 4. an exclusive; private ~ 5. an athletic; book; country; fan; glee; jockey; tennis; yachting ~ 6. a ~ breaks up, disbands 7. a Christmas ~ (esp. AE) ('type of savings account to provide money for the purchase of Christmas presents'); a savings ~ ['piece of wood'] 8. a golf; Indian ~ ['misc.'] 9. (colloq.) join the ~! ('we are in the same situation!') (see the Usage Note for **team**)

clue *n.* 1. to discover, find, uncover a ~ 2. to furnish, provide, supply a ~ 3. an important, key, vital ~ 4. a ~ to (the police had no ~ to her identity)

clue in *v.* (colloq.) (D; tr.) to ~ on ('to inform about')

clumsy *adj.* 1. ~ at (he's ~ at sports) 2. ~ of (that was ~ of her) 3. ~ with (to be ~ with one's hands) 4. ~ to + inf. (it was ~ of you to make a mistake like that)

cluster I *n.* a consonant ~

cluster II *v.* 1. (d; intr.) to ~ around (the crowd ~ed around the entrance) 2. (P; intr.) they ~ed in small groups

clutch I *n.* ['device for engaging and disengaging a transmission'] 1. to engage, throw in the ~ ('to release the clutch pedal') 2. to work the ~ 3. to disengage the ~ ('to depress the clutch pedal') 4. to ride the ~ ('to keep the clutch pedal partially depressed') ['crisis'] 5. in a ~ (to count on smb. in a ~) ['misc.'] 6. a ~ hitter ('smb. who is called on to help in a crisis')

clutch II *v.* 1. (d; intr.) to ~ at (to ~ at a branch) 2. (d; tr.) to ~ to (she ~ed her children to her breast) 3. (misc.) to ~ at a straw ('to consider any possibility')

clutches *n.* ['power'] in smb.'s ~ (in the ~ of the enemy)

coach I *n.* ['trainer of an athlete or team'] 1. a basketball; crew; fencing; football; soccer; swimming; tennis; track-and-field; volleyball ~ ['trainer of a performer or troupe'] 2. a drama; voice ~ ['long-distance bus'] (esp. BE) 3. to go, travel by ~ ['airplane'] 4. an air ~

coach II *v.* 1. (D; tr.) to ~ for (to ~ a team for a championship match) 2. (D; tr.) to ~ in

coal *n.* 1. to mine, produce ~ 2. to burn, use ~ 3. to shovel ~ (into a furnace) 4. anthracite, hard; bituminous, soft; brown ~ 5. hot, live ~s (to cook meat over hot ~s) 6. a bed of ~s

coalesce *v.* (D; intr.) to ~ into

coalition *n.* (pol.) 1. to form a ~ 2. to break up, dissolve a ~ 3. a ~ breaks up, falls apart 4. a political ~ 5. (AE) a rainbow ~ ('a political coalition consisting of representatives of various ethnic groups') 6. a broadly based, umbrella ~ ('a group consisting of many diverse elements') 7. a ~ among, between, of

coast *n.* 1. a forbidding, inhospitable; rugged ~ 2. off a ~ (a ship sank right off the ~) 3. along, on the ~ (there are many fishing towns on the ~) 4. (AE) on the Coast ('on the Pacific Coast of the US')) (he's out on the Coast) 5. (misc.) the ~ is clear ('there is no danger in sight')

coastline *n.* a broken, jagged ~

coat *n.* ['sleeved outer garment'] 1. to have a ~ on, wear a ~ 2. to take off one's ~ 3. an all-weather; fur; fur-lined; mink ~; overcoat; raincoat; sheepskin; spring; trench; winter; zip-lined ~ ['layer of paint'] 4. to apply, put on a ~ (we had to put on a second ~)

coating *n.* an outer; protective ~

coat of arms *n.* a family ~

coax *v.* 1. (D; tr.) to ~ into; out of (she ~ed me into going) 2. (H) he ~ed me to do it

cobweb *n.* ['spider's network'] to spin a ~ (spiders spin ~s)

cobwebs *n.* (colloq.) ['confusion'] to clear, sweep the ~ from one's brain

cocaine *n.* to freebase; snort; shoot ~

cock *n.* ['rooster'] (esp. BE) 1. ~s cock-a-doodle-doo, crow ['water tap'] 2. a ball ~ ['opening of a water tap'] 3. full ~ (a water tap turned on full ~)

cocktail *n.* 1. to make, mix, prepare a ~ 2. fruit ~; a prawn (BE), shrimp (AE) ~ 3. a champagne ~

cocoon *n.* to spin a ~

code *n.* ['cryptographic system'] 1. to design, make up a ~ 2. to break, crack, decipher a ~ 3. a binary ~ 4. the Morse ~ 5. in ~ (to send a message in ~) ['body of laws, principles'] 6. to establish, formulate, lay down a ~ 7. a building; civil; criminal, penal; ethical, moral; sanitary; uniform; unwritten ~; a ~ of ethics ['system of symbols'] 8. an area (AE), dialling (BE) ~ 9. the genetic ~ 10. a postal (BE), zip (AE) ~

codicil *n.* (legal) 1. to draw up a ~ 2. a ~ to (a will)

coerce *v.* 1. (D; tr.) to ~ into (to ~ smb. into doing smt.) 2. (H) (rare) he was ~d to sign

coercion *n.* under ~ (to do smt. under ~)

coeval *adj.* (formal) ['contemporary'] ~ with

coexist *v.* 1. to ~ peacefully 2. (D; intr.) to ~ with

coexistence *n.* 1. peaceful ~ 2. ~ with

coffee *n.* 1. to brew; grind; make; percolate; strain ~ 2. to stir ~ (with a spoon) 3. to grow ~ 4. strong;

weak ~ 5. black; white (BE) ~, ~ with cream 6. decaffeinated; ersatz; fresh; instant; Irish; Turkish ~ 7. a cup of ~; one ~; or: one cup of ~; two ~s; or: two cups of ~ (bring us two cups of ~)

coffin *n.* to lower a ~ into a grave

cogitate *v.* (formal) (D; intr.) to ~ on

cognate *adj.* ~ to, with (Dutch is ~ to English and German)

cognizance *n.* (formal) ['notice'] to take ~ of

cognizant *adj.* (formal) (cannot stand alone) ~ of (~ of the danger)

cohabit *v.* (D; intr.) to ~ with

coherence *n.* to lack ~

cohesion *n.* ~ among, between

coil I *n.* an induction; primary ~

coil II *v.* 1. (d; intr., refl.) to ~ around/round (the snake ~ed around its victim) 2. (d; intr., refl.) to ~ into (to ~ into a ball)

coin *n.* 1. to mint, strike ~s 2. to drop a ~ (into a slot) 3. to spin a ~; or: to flip, throw, toss a ~ (in order to decide an issue) (they tossed a ~ to decide who would go first) 4. to collect ~s 5. antique; counterfeit; gold; metal; rare; silver; valuable ~s 6. (misc.) common ~ ('smt. that is widely known'); to pay back in the same ~ ('to treat smb. as he or she has treated others')

coincide *v.* (D; intr.) to ~ with

coincidence *n.* 1. mere, pure, sheer ~ 2. a happy; interesting; odd, strange; remarkable ~ 3. a ~ that + clause (it was pure ~ that we were seated together) 4. by ~ (we ended up in the same town by sheer ~)

coincidental *adj.* ~ with

cold I *adj.* ['of a low temperature'] 1. biting, bitter, bitterly ~ (it was bitter ~) 2. ~ to (~ to the touch) ['unfriendly'] 3. ~ towards

cold II *n.* ['low temperature'] 1. biting, bitter, extreme, intense, severe ~ 2. the ~ has let up ['illness'] 3. to catch, come down with, contract a ~ 4. to have; nurse a ~; to suffer from a ~ 5. to fight off, shake off, throw off a ~ 6. a bad, severe; lingering; slight ~ 7. the common ~; a chest; head ~

cold cream *n.* to apply ~

cold feet *n.* (colloq.) ['reluctance'] at the last minute he got ~ and withdrew from the deal

cold light *n.* ['clear view'] in the ~ of reality

cold shoulder *n.* (colloq.) ['snub'] to give smb. the ~

cold turkey *n.* (colloq.) ['abrupt cessation of the use of drugs and other harmful substances'] to go ~

collaborate *v.* (D; intr.) to ~ in, on; with (to ~ on a project with smb.)

collaboration *n.* 1. international ~ 2. in ~ with

collaborator *n.* (historical and pejorative) a wartime ~

collapse I *n.* 1. (an) economic ~ 2. an emotional, mental ~ 3. a total ~ (he was in a state of total ~)

collapse II *v.* 1. (d; intr.) to ~ from, with (to ~ from exhaustion) 2. (d; intr.) to ~ under (the weight of smt.)

collar *n.* 1. a button-down; stand-up; starched; stiff; turndown ~ 2. (misc.) hot under the ~ ('very angry')

collate v. (D; tr.) to ~ with (to ~ one edition with another edition)

collateral n. to put up ~ for

collect v. 1. (D; intr.) to ~ around (a crowd ~ed around them) 2. (D; tr.) to ~ from (to ~ money from one's colleagues) 3.(D; intr.) to ~ on (to ~ on one's insurance)

collection n. 1. to take up a ~ (of money) 2. to break up a ~ 3. an art; coin; private; stamp ~

collective n. a workers' ~

collector n. 1. an art; coin; rare-book; stamp ~ 2. a tax; ticket; toll ~ 3. (AE) a garbage, trash ~ (BE has *dustman*) 4. an ardent, avid, serious ~

college n. 1. to go to ~ 2. to apply for admission to (a) ~; to enroll, matriculate at (a) ~; to enter (a) ~ 3. to finish, graduate from ~ 4. to put smb. through ~ ('to pay for smb.'s college education') 5. to drop out of; fail out of (AE), flunk out of (AE; slang) ~ 6. a business (AE); community (AE); junior (AE); technical (BE); village (BE); war ~; a College of Further Education (BE) 7. (US) the Electoral College 8. at, in ~ (she's away at ~; he made many friends when he was in ~) USAGE NOTE: One says *to go to college*, but *to go to a good college*. (see the Usage Note for **university**)

collide v. 1. to ~ head-on 2. (D; intr.) to ~ with (they ~d with another ship)

collision n. 1. to cause a ~ 2. a head-on; midair ~ 3. a near ~ 4. a ~ between; with (the ~ between the ships was caused by fog)

collocate v. (D; intr.) to ~ with (some verbs ~ with certain nouns)

collocation n. a grammatical; lexical ~

colloquy n. (formal) a ~ between

collude v. 1. (D; intr.) to ~ with 2. (E) to ~ with smb. to do smt.

collusion n. 1. ~ between 2. in ~ with

colon n. (med.) the ascending; descending; transverse ~

colonel n. 1. a chicken (AE; slang), full; lieutenant ~ 2. a ~ commands a regiment

colony n. 1. to establish a ~ 2. to disband a ~ 3. a crown ~ 4. an artists'; leper; nudist; penal ~ 5. an ant ~

color, colour I n. ['hue'] 1. bright, brilliant; dark; dull; garish, gaudy, loud; harsh; natural; rich; soft; subdued; vivid; warm ~s 2. (usu. fig.) glowing ~s (to picture smt. in glowing ~s) 3. complementary; primary; secondary ~s 4. ~s clash; fade; match 5. in ~ (in natural ~) 6. a combination of ~s; a riot of ~ ['features'] 7. local ~ ['paint'] 8. oil; water ~s (to paint with oil ~s) ['vividness'] 9. to add, lend ~ (to a story) ['complexion'] 10. to change ~ ('to become pale; to blush') 11. (misc.) the fresh air brought the ~ back to his cheeks

color, colour II v. (N; used with an adjective) she ~ed her hair red

coloring, colouring n. artificial; natural; protective ~

color line, colour line n. ['social boundary between races of different color'] to cross the ~

colors, colours n. ['banner, flag'] 1. to display, show the ~ 2. to salute; troop the ~ 3. to dip; haul down, strike the ~ 4. college; regimental; school ~ ['armed forces'] 5. to be called to the ~ ['character'] 6. to show one's ~ 7. one's true ~ ['misc.'] 8. to come through with flying ~ ('to score an impressive success'); under false ~ ('passing oneself off as another'); to ride under the ~ of a certain stable

column n. ['series of articles'] 1. a syndicated ~ (in a newspaper) ['vertical division of a page'] 2. advertising (esp. BE) ~s; correspondence (esp. BE) ~s; a personal; society; sports ~ ['list of numbers'] 3. to add up a ~ ['shaft'] 4. a steering ~ (on a car) 5. (med.) the spinal, vertebral ~ ['row'] 6. a tank ~ ['misc.'] 7. a fifth ~ ('enemy supporters behind one's own lines')

columnist n. 1. a syndicated ~ 2. a fifth ~ ('an enemy agent operating behind one's own lines')

coma n. 1. to fall, lapse, slip into a ~ 2. to come out of a ~ 3. a deep; irreversible ~

comb n. a fine-tooth ~ (usu. fig.) (we went through the documents with a fine-tooth ~

combat n. 1. to engage in, go into ~ 2. to break off ~ 3. close, hand-to-hand; deadly, fierce, mortal ~ 4. ~ between

combination n. 1. a rare; strange ~ 2. (ling.) a fixed, recurrent; free ~

combine v. 1. (D; intr., tr.) to ~ against (to ~ forces against a common enemy) 2. (D; intr., tr.) to ~ with (hydrogen ~s with oxygen; to ~ initiative with caution; to ~ business with pleasure)

combo n. (colloq.) a jazz ~

combustion n. 1. to produce ~ 2. internal; spontaneous ~

come v. 1. (d; intr.) to ~ across ('to meet by chance') (to ~ across an old friend) 2. (d; intr.) to ~ at ('to attack') (he came at me with a knife) 3. (d; intr.) to ~ between ('to alienate'); ('to separate') (to ~ between two friends) 4. (d; intr.) ('to originate') to ~ from (she ~s from a different country); milk ~s from cows) 5. (d; intr.) ('to enter') to ~ into (to ~ into being; to ~ into use; to ~ into focus; to ~ into the open; to ~ into view) 6. (d; intr.) to ~ on, upon ('to meet') (to ~ upon a stranger; to ~ upon a shocking scene) 7. (d; intr.) to ~ on ('to begin'); ('to enter') (to ~ on duty; to ~ on the scene) 8. (d; intr.) to ~ out of ('to leave') (he came out of the room) 9. (d; intr.) to ~ over ('to affect') (what has come over you?) 10. (d; intr.) ('to amount') to ~ to (the bill came to twenty dollars) 11. (d; intr.) to ~ to ('to arrive at'); ('to reach') (the incident came to their attention; to ~ to grief; success came to her early; he came to his senses; it came to our knowledge that...; to ~ to terms; when it ~s to politics; to ~ to the point) 12. (D; intr.) ('to fall') to ~ under (to ~ under he jurisdiction of a court; to ~ under suspicion; to ~ under smb.'s influence; to ~ under fire) 16. (E) ('to occur') if it came to be known that...; to ~ to pass ('to happen') 17. (E) ('to begin') they finally came to consider me a friend 18. (G) to

(d; intr.) ('to begin') (to ~ into being; to ~ into use; to ~ into focus; to ~ into the open; to ~ into view) 13. (d; intr.) ('to happen') to ~ no harm came to them) 14. (d; intr.) to ~ to ('to be remembered by') (her name finally came to me) 15. (d; intr.) ('to fall') to ~ under ('to get what was ~ing to him)

approach') the children came running 19. (P; intr.) ('to occur in a certain order') Tuesday ~s after Monday 20. (s) to ~ true; the dressing came undone 21. (misc.) what will ~ ('become') of him? the years to ~; to ~ on strong ('to try to make a very strong impression'); to ~ into a fortune ('to inherit or acquire a fortune'); the case never did ~ before the court; he had it ~ing ('he deserved his punishment')

come across v. (d; intr.) to ~ as ('to appear') (he ~s across as being very intelligent)

come around v. (D; intr.) ('to change') to ~ to (she finally came around to our viewpoint)

come away v. (d; intr.) ('to leave') to ~ with (he came away with a favorable impression)

comeback n. ['recovery'] 1. to attempt, try; make a ~ 2. a successful; unsuccessful ~ ['retort'] 3. a snappy ~

come back v. (D; intr.) to ~ to ('to return') (they came back to their hometown; the details are ~ing back to me)

comedian n. an alternative (BE) ('anti-establishment'); nightclub; radio; stand-up; TV ~

come down v. 1. (BE) (D; intr.) to ~ from ('to leave') (to ~ from Oxford) 2. (d; intr.) to ~ from ('to originate from') (this statue has come down to us from the fifteenth century) 3. (d; intr.) to ~ on ('to treat') (the teacher came down hard on him for missing class) 4. (d; intr.) to ~ to ('to amount to') (it ~s down to the same old thing) 5. (d; intr.) to ~ with ('to catch, develop') (to ~ with a cold)

comedy n. black; light; musical; situation; slapstick ~

come forward v. (D; intr.) to ~ with ('to present') (to ~ with new evidence)

come in v. 1. (d; intr.) to ~ for ('to be subjected to') (to ~ for criticism) 2. (D; intr.) to ~ on ('to join') (to ~ on a project)

come out v. 1. (d; intr.) to ~ against ('to oppose') (to ~ against a proposal) 2. (d; intr.) to ~ for ('to support') (to ~ for a bill) 3. (d; intr.) to ~ for ('to try out for') (are you ~ing out for the team?) 4. (d; intr.) to ~ with ('to publish') (to ~ with a new book) 5. (P; intr.) ('to end up'); ('to result') to ~ on top ('to be victorious') 6. (s) the pictures came out fine 7. (misc.) to ~ in spots ('to be covered with spots as a result of illness'); they came out from behind the bushes

come over v. 1. (D; intr.) to ~ to ('to approach') (she came over to our table) 2. (D; intr.) ('to come') to ~ with (their ancestors came over with the Pilgrims) 3. (BE) (s) ('to begin to feel') to ~ faint; nervous

come round see **come around**

come through v. (D; intr.) to ~ with ('to provide') (he finally came through with the money)

come up v. 1. (d; intr.) to ~ against ('to meet') (to ~ against opposition) 2. (D; intr.) to ~ for ('to be brought up for') (the question finally came up for discussion) 3. (d; intr.) to ~ to ('to reach') (the water came up to our knees) 4. (d; intr.) to ~ to ('to approach') ('he came up to me and introduced himself') 5. (d; intr.) to ~ with ('to produce') (she came up with a good idea) 6. (misc.) to ~ to expec-

tations

comeuppance n. (colloq.) ['well-deserved misfortune'] to get one's ~

comfort n. 1. to bring, give, provide ~ 2. to derive ~ from; to find, take; seek ~ in (she finds ~ in helping others) 3. to enjoy the ~s (of life) 4. cold, little ~ 5. creature ~s; spiritual ~ 6. a ~ to (he was a great ~ to his parents) 7. a ~ to + inf. (it was a ~ to know that they were safe) 8. in ~ (to live in ~)

comfortable adj. (colloq.) ~ with (are you ~ with this decision?)

comforter n. (AE) a down ~

comforting adj. ~ to + inf. (it was ~ to be sure of their support)

coming n. the Second Coming

comma n. 1. to place, put in a ~ 2. inverted ~s (BE; CE has *quotation marks*)

command I n. ['authority'] ['control'] 1. to assume, take (over) ~ 2. to exercise ~ 3. to give up, relinquish; lose one's ~ 4. firm ~ 5. ~ of, over (he assumed ~ of the regiment) 6. in ~ of (he was put in ~ of the task force; who will be placed in ~ of the division?) 7. under smb.'s ~ (we were under her ~) 8. the chain of ~ ['headquarters'] 9. the high, supreme ~ 10. a unified ~ ['order'] 11. to carry out, execute; give, issue a ~ 12. a ~ that + clause; subj. (we obeyed their ~ that prisoners be/ should be treated properly) 13. at smb.'s ~ (at his ~ we opened fire) ['military unit'] 14. a combat; military ~ ['mastery'] 15. fluent, perfect ~ (fluent ~ of a language)

command II v. 1. (H) he ~ed his men to fire 2. (L; subj.) the captain ~ed that the company fall in/ should fall in

commandant n. (AE) (mil.) the ~ of the Marine Corps; the ~ of a service school

commander n. 1. a lieutenant; naval ~ 2. a battalion; camp; company; division; regimental; supreme ~ 3. a ~ commands a unit

commandment n. (rel.) 1. to keep the ~s 2. to violate a ~ 3. the Ten Commandments

commence v. (formal) 1. (D; intr.) to ~ with (we'll ~ with a reading of the minutes of the last meeting) 2. (rare) (G) (mil.) ~ firing!

commencement exercises n. (AE) to attend; hold ~

commend v. 1. to ~ highly 2. (formal) (B) I can ~ him to you 3. (D; tr.) to ~ for (she was ~ed for bravery)

commendable adj. ~ to + inf. (it is ~ to help others)

commendation n. a ~ for (a ~ for bravery)

commensurable adj. ~ to, with

commensurate adj. ~ to, with (a reward ~ with the results achieved)

comment I n. ['observation'] ['remark'] 1. to make a ~ 2. (an) appropriate, fitting; caustic, critical, scathing, unfavorable; cryptic; favorable; inappropriate; ironic, wry; nasty, vicious; off-the-record; passing; perceptive, shrewd; sarcastic ~ 3. (a) ~ about, on (there was no ~ about the incident in the press) 4. (a) ~ from (there was no ~ from the other party) 5. a ~ that + clause (her ~ that she would retire soon was greeted with dismay) 6. without further ~ ['gossip'] ['talk'] 7. to arouse, cause, evoke ~ 8. considerable; critical, scathing; favorable; unfavorable ~ (the incident evoked considerable ~ in the capitals of western Europe)

comment II *v.* 1. (D; intr.) to ~ about, on 2. (L) she ~ed that she was very happy to be a guest in their country

commentary *n.* 1. to give a ~ 2. a play-by-play, running ~ 3. (misc.) a sad ~ (on the world situation)

commentator *n.* a news; radio; TV ~

commerce *n.* 1. to carry on, engage in ~ 2. to develop, expand ~ 3. interstate; overseas ~ 4. ~ between; with (to carry on ~ with the countries of Central America)

commercial *n.* ['paid spoken advertisement'] 1. to sponsor a ~ 2. a radio; TV ~

commiserate *v.* (d; intr.) to ~ on; with (I ~ with you on your misfortune)

commissar *n.* a political ~

commission I *n.* ['committee'] ['council'] 1. to appoint, establish a ~ 2. to disband a ~ 3. a fact-finding; investigating; joint; planning; roving ~ 4. a ~ on (a ~ on the problems of alcoholism) ['certificate conferring rank'] (usu. mil.) 5. to award, confer a ~ 6. to earn, win a (battlefield) ~ 7. to resign one's ~ 8. a battlefield ~ ['fee'] 9. to charge; pay a ~ 10. to deduct; divide a ~ 11. a ~ for, on 12. on ~ (to work on ~) ['operating condition'] 13. to put out of ~ (the storm put all power lines out of ~) ['task'] (formal) 14. to execute a ~ 15. a ~ to (~ to serve)

commission II *v.* 1. (H) she ~ed an artist to paint her portrait 2. (N; used with a noun) she was ~ed a second lieutenant

commissioner *n.* 1. a high ~ for (the high ~ for occupied territories) 2. a fire; health; police; water ~ 3. (GB) the Canadian High Commissioner in London

commit *v.* 1. (d; refl.) ('to devote') to ~ to (to ~ oneself to a cause) 2. (D; tr.) ('to assign') to ~ to (to ~ funds to a project) 3. (D; tr.) ('to confine') to ~ to (to ~ smb. to a mental hospital; ~ted to prison) 4. (d; tr.) ('to place') (to ~ a child to a relative's care; to ~ a poem to memory; to ~ one's thoughts to paper) 5. (H; usu. refl.; no passive) ('to promise') he ~ted himself to support her parents

commitment *n.* ['promise'] 1. to make a ~ 2. to meet a ~ 3. a firm ~ 4. a ~ to + inf. (he made a ~ to pay off his debts) 5. a ~ that + clause (they reaffirmed their ~ that they would help) ['devotion'] 6. to demonstrate, display, show ~ 7. an all-out, total ~ 8. (a) ~ (to a cause)

committed *adj.* 1. ~ to (~ to his principles) 2. ~ + inf. (they are ~ to help us; or, more usu.: they are ~ to helping us)

committee *n.* 1. to appoint, establish, form, organize, set up a ~ 2. to disband a ~ 3. an ad-hoc; advisory; budget; credentials; executive; grievance; nominating; planning; program; select; special; standing; steering; strike; watchdog; ways-and-means ~; a ~ of the whole 4. a ~ on (a ~ on

problems of the elderly) 5. on a ~ (who is serving on the ~?) 6. (misc.) to report a bill out of ~

commodity *n.* 1. to trade in ~ties 2. a farm; marketable; staple ~

common I *adj.* 1. quite ~ 2. (cannot stand alone after a noun) ~ to (a heritage ~ to both our peoples)

common II *n.* in ~ with

commonplace I *adj.* ~ to + inf. (it was ~ for them to travel abroad)

commonplace II *n.* 1. to state a ~ 2. a ~ to + inf. (it's a ~ to say that people should work hard)

common sense *n.* 1. to apply, exercise, show, use ~ 2. the ~ to + inf. (he had the ~ to remain silent) 3. (misc.) good; plain ~ (just plain, good, old ~)

common touch *n.* to have; lose the ~

commotion *n.* 1. cause, create, raise a ~ 2. a ~ subsides 3. in a state of ~

commune *v.* (d; intr.) to ~ with (to ~ with nature)

communicate *v.* 1. to ~ officially; unofficially 2. (B) she tried to ~ her thoughts to her children 3. (D; intr.) to ~ with (to ~ with one's parents)

communication *n.* ['message'] 1. to address, direct, send (all) ~s (to a certain place) 2. a direct, official; personal; privileged ('confidential') ~ 3. a ~ from; to ['act, means of communicating'] 4. to establish ~ 5. to cut off ~s 6. mass ~s 7. radio; two-way ~ 8. ~ with (to establish ~ with the rescue team; to cut off all ~s with the mainland) 9. in ~ with (she has been in ~ with her family)

communication cord *n.* (BE) to pull a ~ (AE has *emergency cord)*

communion *n.* ['sharing'] 1. ~ with ['a Christian sacrament, the Eucharist'] 2. to administer, give ~ 3. to take ~ 4. Holy Communion

communiqué *n.* 1. to issue a ~ 2. a joint ~ 3. an official ~ 4. a ~ about, on (they issued a ~ on the results of the conference)

community *n.* ['group of persons with common interests'] 1. an (the) academic, college, university; business; gay; intelligence; religious; scientific; speech ~ ['group of persons who live together'] 2. a close-knit ~ 3. a life-care (AE); retirement ~

commute *v.* 1. (D; intr.) ('to travel regularly') to ~ between; from; to (to ~ between two cities; to ~ from the suburbs to the city) 2. (D; tr.) ('to change') to ~ to (to (the Governer ~d his death sentence to life imprisonment)

commuter *n.* 1. a suburban ~ 2. a ~ between; from; to

compact *n.* (formal) ['agreement'] 1. to make a ~ with 2. a ~ between; with

companion *n.* 1. a boon, close, inseparable ~ 2. a life; traveling ~ 3. a ~ for, to (she worked as a ~ to an elderly woman)

company *n.* ['military unit consisting of several platoons'] 1. to command a ~ (a captain commands a ~) 2. to deploy; form a ~ 3. a cannon; headquarters; infantry ~ ['companionship'] 4. to keep (smb.) ~; to seek smb.'s ~ 5. to part ~ with 6. (good) ~ for (the children were good ~ for us) ['guests'] 7. to have; invite ~ (we enjoy having ~) ['associates'] ['association'] ['gathering of per-

sons'] 8. to keep ~ with 9. mixed ~ (don't use that word in mixed ~) 10. (colloq.) bad, fast ~ ('reckless, wild associates') (he runs around in/with fast ~) 11. present ~ ('those present') (present ~ excepted) 12. in ~ (to behave appropriately in ~; in ~ with smb.) ['firm'] 13. to manage, operate, run a ~ 14. to establish, form a ~ 15. a finance; holding; insurance; investment; joint-stock; shipping; transport (esp. BE), transportation ~ 16. an opera; repertory (esp. BE), stock (AE); theatrical ~ 17. (BE) a (public) limited ~ (AE prefers *corporation*) 18. a ~ fails, goes bankrupt ['fire-fighting unit'] 19. an engine, hose; ladder ~
comparable *adj.* ~ to, with
compare I *n.* beyond ~
compare II *v.* 1. to ~ advantageously, favorably; unfavorably 2. (d; intr.) to ~ to, with (these roads cannot ~ with ours) 3. (d; tr.) to ~ to, with (how would you ~ this wine with a good French wine?) USAGE NOTE: The construction *to compare x to y* usually means 'to claim a similarity between x and y' (to compare New York to a beehive). The construction *to compare x with/and y* usually means 'to discuss similarities and differences between x and y' (to compare New York with/and London).
comparison *n.* 1. to draw, make a ~ 2. to hold up under ~ 3. to defy ~ 4. a favorable; unfavorable ~ 5. a ~ between; to, with (there is no ~ between them; she made a ~ of our literature to theirs; I would like to draw a ~ of recent events with those of the 1930s) 6. beyond ~ 7. by ~ (her works suffer by ~) 8. in ~ with USAGE NOTE: Note that there can be a difference in meaning between *a comparison of New York to a beehive* and *a comparison of New York with/and London.* See the Usage Note for **compare II.** The preposition *between* can be used in both meanings -- *a comparison between New York and a beehive* and *a comparison between New York and London.*
compartment *n.* 1. a glove ~ 2. a first-class; second-class ~ 3. a watertight ~
compartmentalize *v.* (D; tr.) to ~ into
compass *n.* 1. to box the ~ 2. to read a ~ 3. a magnetic; mariner's ~
compassion *n.* 1. to arouse ~ 2. to demonstrate, display, show; feel, have ~ 3. deep, profound, strong ~ 4. ~ for 5. out of ~ (to act out of ~)
compatibility *n.* ~ between, with
compatible *adj.* ~ with
compel *v.* (H) to ~ smb. to do smt.
compensate *v.* 1. (d; intr.) ('to make up for') to ~ for (I cannot ~ for my inferiority complex) 2. (D; tr.) ('to reimburse') to ~ for (to ~ smb. for damages)
compensation *n.* 1. to make, pay; offer ~ 2. to deny, refuse ~ 3. adequate, appropriate ~ 4. unemployment; workmen's (AE) ~ 5. ~ for (~ for the damage suffered)
compete *v.* 1. (d; intr.) to ~ against, with (that store ~s with us) 2. (D; intr.) to ~ for (to ~ for first prize) 3. (D; intr.) to ~ in (to ~ in a contest)
competence *n.* ['ability'] 1. to acquire, gain ~ 2. ~ for (does she have the necessary ~ for the posi-

tion?) 3. ~ in (~ in English) 4. the ~ to + inf. (do they have the ~ to cope with the job?) ['jurisdiction'] (legal) 5. beyond; within the ~ (the matter lay within the ~ of the court)
competent *adj.* 1. highly ~ 2. ~ as (he is ~ as a teacher) 3. ~ at, in (she is ~ in her field) 4. ~ to + inf. (she is ~ to teach history; ~ to stand trial)
competition *n.* ['rivalry'] ['opposition'] 1. to offer, provide ~ 2. to undercut, undersell the ~ 3. bitter, fierce, formidable, keen, stiff, strong; cutthroat, unfair, unscrupulous; fair; free, unfettered; healthy ~ 4. ~ among, between; with (stiff ~ among several firms) 5. ~ for (~ for control of the market) 6. in ~ with ['contest'] ['match'] 7. to hold, stage a ~ 8. a gymnastics; high-diving; speed-skating ~ 9. (an) open ~ 10. a ~ for (a ~ for the championship)
competitive *adj.* 1. fiercely, keenly ~ 2. ~ with (to be ~ with the best)
competitor *n.* a formidable, keen, strong; unscrupulous ~
compilation *n.* 1. to do, make a ~ 2. a ~ from (various sources)
compile *v.* (D; tr.) to ~ from (to ~ a dictionary from various sources)
complacency *n.* ~ about; towards
complacent *adj.* ~ about
complain *v.* 1. to ~ bitterly, loudly, vociferously; constantly 2. (D; intr.) to ~ about, of; to (I ~ed to the manager about the service; she ~ed of indigestion) 3. (L; to) she ~ed (to the manager) that there was no hot water
complainer *n.* a chronic ~
complaint *n.* 1. to bring, file, lodge, make, register a ~ 2. to express, voice a ~ 3. to act on, respond to a ~ 4. to disregard, ignore; reject a ~ 5. a bitter, loud, vociferous; justified; legitimate; unjustified ~ 6. a ~ about; with (she filed a ~ about the service with the manager) 7. a ~ against (they lodged a ~ against me) 8. a ~ to (our ~ to the dean was ignored) 9. a ~ that + clause (they rejected his ~ that proper procedures had not been followed) 10. (misc.) grounds for/a cause for ~
complement *n.* 1. a full ~ 2. (naval) a ship's ~ ('crew') 3. (grammar) a predicate ~ 4. a ~ to
complementary *adj.* ~ to
complete *adj.* ~ with (a turkey dinner ~ with all the trimmings)
completion *n.* 1. to near ~ 2. on ~ of (on ~ of this dictionary we will need a rest)
complex *n.* 1. an Electra; inferiority; Oedipus; persecution; superiority ~ 2. the military-industrial ~
complexion *n.* a clear; dark; fair; florid, ruddy; pasty; sallow ~
compliance *n.* 1. ~ with (~ with the law) 2. in ~ with (in ~ with regulations)
complication *n.* 1. to cause ~s 2. to avoid ~s 3. ~s arise, set in
complicity *n.* 1. ~ between 2. ~ in (a crime)
compliment I *n.* ['praise'] 1. to pay smb. a ~ 2. to lavish, shower ~s on 3. to return a ~ 4. to angle for, fish for ~s 5. to bandy ~s 6. a backhanded, dubious, left-handed; nice, pretty; sincere ~ 7. a

~ on (she paid him a nice ~ on his success)
compliment II *v.* (D; tr.) to ~ on (I ~ed him on his performance)
compliments *n.* ['greetings'] 1. to convey, present, send one's ~ 2. (misc.) with the author's ~; with the ~ of the management
comply *v.* (D; intr.) to ~ with (to ~ with the law; to ~ with smb.'s request)
component *n.* an essential ~
comport *v.* (formal) (P; refl.) to ~ oneself with dignity; to ~ oneself well
compose *v.* (B) to ~ an ode to an emperor
composed *adj.* (cannot stand alone'] ['consisting'] ~ of (the team was ~ of seasoned players) (see the Usage Note for **comprised)**
composer *n.* a major; minor; popular ~
composition *n.* ['essay'] 1. to do, write a ~ ['typesetting'] 2. to do ~ ['piece of music'] 3. to perform, play a ~
composure *n.* 1. to keep, retain; regain one's ~ 2. to lose one's ~
compound I *n.* ['result of mixing'] a chemical; organic ~
compound II *n.* ['enclosure'] a prison ~
comprehensible *adj.* ~ to
comprehension *n.* 1. to defy, elude ~ 2. beyond ~
comprehensives *n.* (AE) ['comprehensive examination'] to take one's ~
compress I *n.* 1. to apply a ~ to 2. a cold; dry; hot; wet ~
compress II *v.* (D; tr.) to ~ into (to ~ a whole paragraph into two sentences)
comprised *adj.* (cannot stand alone) ['consisting'] ~ of USAGE NOTE: Some purists prefer *composed of* to *comprised of.*
compromise I *n.* 1. to agree on, come to, reach, work out a ~ 2. to reject a ~ 3. an acceptable, reasonable ~ 4. a ~ between; with
compromise II *v.* (D; intr.) to ~ on, over; with (they ~d on certain items with us)
comptroller *n.* (AE) the Comptroller General
compulsion *n.* 1. to feel a ~ 2. (a) moral ~ 3. a ~ to + inf. (he felt no ~ to do it) 4. under ~ (to give in under ~)
compulsory *n.* ~ for
compunction *n.* 1. to feel, have; show ~ 2. ~ about (she felt no ~ about making us wait) 3. without ~ (he violated the law without the slightest ~)
computer *n.* 1. to operate, use a ~; to turn on; turn off a ~ 2. to program a ~ 3. an analog; digital; electronic; general-purpose; home; mainframe ~; microcomputer; minicomputer; parallel; personal; serial ~ 4. the ~ is down ('the computer is not functioning') 5. the ~ is up ('the computer is functioning') 6. a ~ bombs (AE), crashes 7. on a ~ (to run a program on a ~)
comrade *n.* 1. one's fallen ~s 2. a ~ in arms 3. an old ~
con *v.* (colloq.) ('to trick') 1. (D; tr.) to ~ into (to trick smb. into doing smt.) 2. (D; tr.) to ~ out of (he ~ned me out of my money)
conceal *v.* (D; tr.) to ~ from
concede *v.* 1. (B) he finally ~d the election to his opponent 2. (L; to) she ~d (to us) that she had

been mistaken
conceded *adj.* (cannot stand alone) ~ to + inf. (this painting is ~ to be her best work)
conceit *n.* insufferable, overwhelming ~
conceivable *adj.* ~ that + clause (it is ~ that they knew about it beforehand)
conceive *v.* 1. (d; intr.) to ~ of (can you ~ of such cruelty?) 2. (L) I could not ~ that he would do such a thing
concentrate *v.* (D; intr., tr.) to ~ on (to ~ all our efforts on solving the problem)
concentration *n.* 1. to disrupt, disturb one's ~ 2. deep ~ 3. ~ on 4. in ~ (in deep ~)
concept *n.* 1. to formulate, frame a ~ 2. to grasp a ~ 3. the ~ that + clause (the ~ that trade lessens international tensions is valid)
conception *n.* ['concept'] 1. a clear; vague ~ 2. the ~ that + clause (the ~ that the superpowers must fight is dangerous) ['becoming pregnant or being conceived'] 3. at ~
concern I *n.* ['interest'] ['apprehension'] 1. to arouse, cause, give ~ 2. to express, voice; feel; show ~ 3. considerable, deep, grave, serious; growing; national; overriding; particular; primary; public ~ 4. an object of ~ 5. ~ about, for, over, with (~ about debts; ~ for the children; ~ over the future) 6. (esp. BE) ~ to + inf. (~ to know the truth) 7. ~ that + clause (to express ~ that they might fail) 8. of ~ (to the matter was of deep ~ to us) 9. out of ~ (she did it out of ~ for her family) ['firm'] 10. to manage a ~ 11. (misc.) a going ('successful') ~
concern II *v.* 1. (d; refl.) to ~ oneself about, over with (she ~ed herself with the problem of illiteracy) 2. (misc.) to whom it may ~
concerned *adj.* 1. deeply, greatly ~ 2. ~ about, for, over; with (~ about safety) 3. (esp. BE) ~ to + inf. (~ to know your decision) 4. ~ that + clause (we are ~ that they might have missed the train) 5. (misc.) as far as I'm ~ USAGE NOTE: The phrases *concerned about, concerned over* and less frequently, *concerned, for,* mean 'worried about' (concerned about your safety). The phrase *concerned with* means 'interested in' (concerned with establishing the truth).
concert *n.* ['musical program'] 1. to give hold, stage a ~ 2. to cancel a ~ 3. a band; orchestral; pop, promenade (BE); rock; subscription ~ 4. at a ~ (we met at the ~) ['harmony, agreement~'] 5. in ~ ('together') (to work in ~; voices raised in ~)
concerto *n.* 1. to compose a ~ 2. to perform, play a ~ 3. a piano; violin ~
concession *n.* ['yielding'] 1. to grant, make a ~ 2. a ~ to ['right to conduct business'] 3. to grant; receive a ~ 4. a parking; refreshment ~ 5. a ~ to + inf. (their firm received a ~ to prospect for oil)
conclave *n.* ['meeting'] a party ~
conclude *v.* (L) we ~d that he would not come
conclusion *n.* 1. to arrive at, come to, draw, reach a ~; to jump to a ~ 2. to bring to a ~ 3. a correct; erroneous, invalid, wrong; foregone; hasty; inescapable, inevitable; reasonable, tenable, valid ~ 4. a ~ that + clause (their ~ that war is inevitable is disturbing) 5. at the ~ (at the ~ of the concert)

concoction *n.* (colloq.) to whip up a ~
concomitant *adj.* (formal) ~ with
concord *n.* (formal) in ~ with
concordance *n.* ['list of words'] 1. to compile a ~ ['harmony'] 2. in ~ with
concordat *n.* (rel.) 1. to conclude, draw up a ~ 2. a ~ between; with
concrete *n.* 1. to pour ~ 2. prestressed; ready-mix; reinforced ~ 3. a slab of ~
concubine *n.* 1. to have, keep a ~ 2. by one's ~ (he had many children by his ~s)
concur *v.* (formal) ('to agree') 1. to ~ completely, fully 2. (D; intr.) to ~ in (to ~ in supporting a cause) 3. (D; intr.) to ~ with (to ~ with an opinion; to ~ with smb.) 4. (L) we ~ that the practice should be halted
concurrence *n.* 1. complete, full ~ 2. ~ in 3. in ~ with 4. with the ~ of
concussion *n.* 1. to receive a ~ 2. a severe; slight ~ 3. a brain ~
condemn *v.* 1. to ~ bitterly, harshly, strongly; unfairly, unjustly 2. (D; tr.) to ~ as (they were ~ed as traitors) 3. (D; tr.) to ~ for (he was ~ed for stealing a horse) 4. (D; tr.) to ~ to (to ~ smb. to death; ~ed to hard labor) 5. (H) he was ~ed to spend the rest of his life in prison
condemnation *n.* 1. to issue a ~ 2. a bitter, harsh, scathing, strong; sweeping ~
condense *v.* (D; tr.) to ~ into (you must ~ your paper into a few paragraphs)
condescend *v.* (formal) 1. (d; intr.) to ~ to (to ~ to cheating) 2. (E) to ~ to mingle with the workers
condition I *n.* ['requirement'] 1. to impose, set; state, stipulate a ~ 2. to accept a ~ 3. to fulfill, meet, satisfy a ~ 4. an essential ~ 5. on ~ that + clause; subj. (she will join us on ~ that you also be there) ['state of repair'] 6. bad, poor, terrible; excellent, good ~ 7. operating, running ~ 8. in ~ (our house is in good ~; his car is in running ~; the roads are in terrible ~) ['good health'] ['fitness'] 9. to get into ~ 10. in ~; out of ~ (he never exercises and is out of ~) ['state of health'] 11. critical, poor; fair, satisfactory; good; serious; stable; weakened ~ 12. in ~ (the patient was in critical ~) ['ailment'] 13. a heart; lung ~ 14. an untreatable ~
condition II *v.* 1. (D; refl.) to ~ for 2. (formal) (D; tr.) to ~ on 3. (D; tr.) to ~ to (~ed to life in the jungle) 4. (H) to ~ smb. to do smt.
conditional *adj.* ~ on
conditioned *adj.* ~ to + inf. (the dog was ~ to attack at a certain signal)
conditioner *n.* a hair; skin ~
conditions *n.* ['circumstances'] 1. favorable; unfavorable ~ 2. difficult; normal; pitiful, squalid; repressive ~ 3. living; weather; working ~ (if weather ~ permit) 4. in ~ (they live in squalid ~) 5. under ~ (to work under difficult ~)
condolences *n.* 1. to convey, express, offer ~ 2. heartfelt, sincere ~ 3. ~ on (I conveyed our sincere ~ to them on the death of their mother)
condole with *v.* (esp. BE) (D; tr.) to ~ on (to ~ smb. on the death of a parent)
condone *v.* (K) I don't ~ his coming late to work
conducive *adj.* (cannot stand alone) ~ to (exercise is ~ to good health)

conduct I *n.* 1. appropriate; chivalrous; ethical; irreproachable; proper ~ 2. disorderly; improper; inappropriate, unbecoming; unethical ~ 3. (mil.) dishonorable (AE); good ~; ~ unbecoming an officer
conduct II *v.* 1. (d; refl.) to ~ like (he ~ed himself like a good soldier) 2. (P; refl.) to ~ oneself with dignity 3. (formal) (P; tr.) she was ~ed into the conference room; they ~ed us through the museum
conductor *n.* ['substance that conducts'] 1. a lightning ~ ['person who collects fares'] (BE) 2. a bus ~ ['director'] 3. a guest; orchestra ~
cone *n.* 1. an ice-cream ~ 2. a pine ~
confederacy *n.* 1. to form a ~ 2. a ~ among, between; with
confederate *v.* (D; intr.) to ~ with
confederation *n.* 1. to form a ~ 2. a ~ among, between; with 3. a loose, weak ~
confer *v.* 1. (D; intr.) ('to converse') to ~ about; with (we will ~ with them about this matter) 2. (D; tr.) ('to award') to ~ on (to ~ an award on smb.)
conference *n.* 1. to convene; hold a ~ 2. a news, press; peace; staff; summit ~ 3. a ~ between 4. a ~ on (to hold a ~ on disarmament) 5. at a ~ (you'll see her at the press ~) 6. in ~ (he is in ~ and cannot come to the telephone)
confess *v.* 1. to ~ frankly, honestly; willingly 2. (B) he confessed his crime to the police 3. (D; intr.) to ~ to (to ~ to a crime; to ~ to the police; he ~ed to cheating on the exam) 4. (L; to) he ~ed (to us) that he had lied
confession *n.* 1. to make a ~ 2. to extort, force a ~ from; to beat a ~ out of (the police beat a ~ out of him) 3. to repudiate, retract, take back, withdraw a ~ 4. a deathbed; forced; full; public; voluntary ~ 5. (rel.) to hear smb.'s ~ 6. (rel.) to go to ~ 7. a ~ that + clause (he made a public ~ that he had accepted bribes)
confetti *n.* to sprinkle, throw ~
confide *v.* 1. (B) he ~d his secret to us 2. (d; intr.) to ~ in (she ~s in her sister)
confidence *n.* ['trust'] ['reliance'] 1. to enjoy, have; gain, win smb.'s ~ 2. to inspire, instill ~ in smb. 3. to have; place one's ~ in smb. 4. to misplace one's ~ 5. to take smb. into one's ~ 6. to shake smb.'s ~ 7. to betray smb.'s ~ 8. absolute, every, perfect ~ (I have absolute ~ in her ability) 9. ~ in (my ~ in him was shaken) ['secrecy'] ['secret'] 10. to exchange ~s 11. to violate a ~ 12. strict ~ 13. in ~ (she told it to me in strictest ~) ['belief in one's own ability'] ['firm belief'] 14. to express; gain ~ 15. to exude, ooze ~ (he just oozes ~) 16. to shake smb.'s ~ 17. buoyant, unbounded ~ 18. the ~ to + inf. (he doesn't have enough ~ to proceed on his own) 19. ~ that + clause (nothing could shake her ~ that she would succeed)
confident *adj.* 1. ~ of (~ of success) 2. ~ that + clause (she was ~ that she would succeed)
confidential *adj.* strictly ~
confidentiality *n.* 1. to maintain ~ 2. to violate ~ 3. strict ~

confine *v.* (D; refl., tr.) to ~ to (~d to bed; ~d to quarters; the lecturer ~d herself to one topic; ~ yourself to the facts)
confinement *n.* ['imprisonment'] ['being confined'] 1. solitary ~ (they put him into solitary ~) 2. ~ to (~ to quarters) 3. in ~ (in solitary ~) ['lying-in'] (obsol.) 4. in ~ (before the birth of a child)
confirm *v.* (L) the president ~ed that a summit conference would take place
confirmation *n.* 1. official; unofficial ~ 2. ~ that + clause (we have received ~ that she will attend)
confiscate *v.* (D; tr.) to ~ from
conflagration *n.* a major ~
conflict I *n.* 1. to provoke a ~ 2. to come into ~ with 3. to resolve a ~ 4. armed; direct ~ 5. (a) ~ about, over; among, between; with (a ~ between neighboring countries over their common border; a ~ with one's relatives about the terms of a will) 6. in (a) ~ with (their stories are in ~ with each other)
conflict II *v.* (D; intr.) to ~ with (your version ~s with mine)
confluence *n.* at a ~ (the city lies at the ~ of three rivers)
conform *v.* (D; intr.) to ~ to, with (to ~ to specifications)
conformance *n.* in ~ with
conformity *n.* 1. strict ~ 2. ~ to 3. in ~ with
confront *v.* (D; tr.) to ~ with (to ~ a prisoner with a witness)
confrontation *n.* 1. to provoke a ~ 2. a direct ~ 3. a ~ with
confuse *v.* (d; tr.) to ~ with (I always ~ him with his brother)
confused *adj.* ~ to + inf. (I was ~ to learn of his latest decision)
confusing *adj.* ~ to + inf. (it was ~ to listen to the testimony)
confusion *n.* 1. to cause, create ~ 2. to clear up ~ 3. ~ arises; reigns 4. to throw into ~ (their unexpected arrival threw our plans into ~) 5. complete, general, utter ~ 6. a scene; state of ~ (it was a scene of utter ~) 7. ~ between
congestion *n.* 1. traffic ~ 2. nasal; lung, pulmonary ~
congratulate *v.* 1. to ~ heartily, sincerely, warmly 2. (D; refl. tr.) to ~ on, upon (to ~ smb. on her/his promotion)
congratulations *n.* 1. to extend, offer ~ on 2. deepest, heartiest, hearty, sincere, warm, warmest ~ 3. ~ on, upon (my warmest ~ on your promotion!)
congress *n.* 1. to convene, hold a ~ 2. an annual; biennial; party ~
congruence *n.* (formal or technical) ~ with
congruent *adj.* (formal or technical) ~ to, with
congruity *n.* (formal) ~ with
congruous *adj.* (formal) ~ to, with
conjecture I *n.* (formal) ['guess'] 1. to make a ~ 2. a ~ that + clause (her ~ that the election would be a landslide proved to be true)
conjecture II *v.* (formal) (L) ('to guess') the press ~d that a summit conference would take place

conjugation *n.* ['verb forms'] an irregular; regular ~
conjunction *n.* ['connecting word'] 1. a coordinating; subordinating ~ ['cooperation'] ['coincidence'] 2. in ~ with
connect *v.* 1. to ~ closely, intimately; loosely 2. (d; intr.) to ~ to, with (this bus is supposed to ~ with a train) 3. (D; tr.) to ~ to, with (are you ~ed with this firm? to ~ a TV set to an antenna)
connection, connexion *n.* ['association'] 1. to establish, make a ~ 2. to break, sever a ~ 3. a close, intimate; foreign; international; loose, tenuous ~ 4. a ~ between; to; with (there was no ~ between the two phenomena; to have a ~ with smb.) 5. in a certain ~ (in this ~; in ~ with the other matter) ['acquaintance'] ['tie'] 6. business; professional; social ~s ['transfer during a trip'] 7. to make; miss a ~ ['linking of two telephones'] 8. to get a ~ ['misc.'] 9. to have ~s ('to have influential supporters')
connect up *v.* (D; tr.) to ~ to, with (to ~ a telephone up to the exchange)
connexion (BE) see **connection**
connive *v.* 1. (D; intr.) to ~ at; with 2. (E) they ~d (with each other) to cheat her
conquest *n.* 1. to make a ~ 2. to consolidate extend one's ~s 3. world ~
conscience *n.* 1. to appeal to; arouse smb.'s ~ 2. to have smt. on one's ~ 3. to ease one's ~ 4. a clear; guilty ~ (to have a guilty ~) 5. a matter of ~ 6. in ~ (in all good ~)
conscientious *adj.* ~ about (she is ~ about her work)
conscious *adj.* 1. fully ~ 2. (cannot stand alone) ~ of (~ of danger) 3. ~ that + clause (she became ~ that everyone was staring at her)
consciousness *n.* ['conscious state'] 1. to lose; recover, regain ~ ['awareness'] 2. to raise smb.'s ~ 3. class; political; social ~ ['misc.'] 4. stream of ~
conscript *v.* (D; tr.) to ~ into (to ~ youths into the armed forces)
conscription *n.* 1. to introduce ~ 2. military; universal ~
consecrate *v.* 1. (d; tr.) to ~ to (she ~d her life to helping the poor) 2. (N; used with a noun) he was ~d archbishop
consecration *n.* ~ to
consensus *n.* 1. to reach a ~ 2. a ~ that + clause (there is a ~ that we should abstain)
consent I *n.* 1. to give one's ~ to 2. to refuse, withhold one's ~ 3. common; general; informed; mutual; parental; tacit; unanimous ~ 4. by ~ (by mutual ~) 5. (misc.) the age of ~
consent II *v.* 1. (D; intr.) to ~ to (to ~ to a proposal) 2. (E) she ~ed to help
consequence *n.* ['importance'] 1. of ~ (a matter of some ~) ['result'] 2. in ~ of
consequences *n.* ['results'] 1. to have ~ for 2. to accept, bear, face, suffer, take the ~ 3. far-reaching, fateful; grave, serious; inevitable; unforeseeable; unforeseen ~
conservation *n.* 1. forest; soil; water; wild-life ~ 2. (the) ~ of natural resources

conservative I *n.* a dyed-in-the-wool; political ~
conservative II *adj.* ~ in (~ in one's views)
conservatory *n.* a music ~
consider *v.* 1. ('to regard') to ~ favorably 2. (D; tr.) ('to regard'); ('to examine') to ~ as (we ~ed him as a possible candidate) 3. (D; tr.) ('to regard as a candidate') to ~ for (he cannot be ~ed for the job) 4. (G) ('to contemplate') she ~ed resigning 5. (M) ('to believe') we ~ her to be our friend 6. (N; used with an adjective, noun, past participle) ('to believe') we ~ her qualified; we ~ her a genius 7. (Q) ('to contemplate') they ~ed where to hide the money USAGE NOTE: Note the contrasts between *consider as* and *consider* in the following text -- In her book she considers ('examines') Shakespeare as a playwright and as a poet. She considers ('believes') Shakespeare (to be) both a great playwright and a great poet. However, she considers ('believes') Shakespeare (to be) even greater as a playwright than as a poet.
considerate *adj.* 1. ~ of (he was ~ of everyone) 2. ~ towards 3. ~ to + inf. (it was ~ of her to do that)
consideration *n.* ['thought'] ['concern'] 1. to give ~ to (to give some ~ to a matter) 2. to show ~ for 3. to take smt. into ~ 4. to deserve; require ~ (the matter requires careful ~) 5. careful; due; serious ~ 6. an overriding ~ 7. financial; humanitarian; personal ~s 8. for smb.'s ~ (I submit the enclosed proposal for your ~) 9. in ~ of (in ~ of past services) 10. on careful ~ of 11. out of ~ for smb. 12. under ~ (the matter is under ~) 13. with ~ for (with due ~ for your feelings, we must reject your request) ['fee'] 14. for a ~ (for a modest ~, he'll do anything)
consign *v.* 1. (B) they ~ed the shipment to us 2. (d; tr.) to ~ to (the paintings were ~ed to our care)
consignment *n.* ['a sale allowing the dealer to return unsold merchandise'] to sell; ship on ~
consist *v.* 1. (d; intr.) to ~ of ('to be composed of') (our state ~s of thirty counties) 2. (formal) (d; intr.) to ~ in ('to be equivalent to') (freedom ~s in the absence of oppressive laws)
consistent *adj.* ~ with (~ with our principles)
consistory *n.* (usu. rel.) to convoke, hold a ~
consolation *n.* 1. to afford, offer ~ 2. ~ to 3. a ~ to + inf. (it's a ~ to know that they are safe = it's a ~ knowing that they are safe) 4. a ~ that + clause (our only ~ was that no one was hurt seriously)
console *v.* 1. (D; tr.) to ~ on (to ~ smb. on the loss of a loved one) 2. (d; refl.) to ~ with (I ~d myself with the thought that the situation could be worse)
consommé *n.* 1. clear ~ 2. a bowl; cup of ~
consonance *n.* in ~ with
consonant I *adj.* (formal) ~ to, with
consonant II *n.* 1. to articulate, pronounce a ~ 2. a dental; double, geminate; final; guttural; hard; labial; liquid; soft; unvoiced; velar; voiced ~ 3. (misc.) a ~ cluster
consort *v.* (formal) (d; intr.) to ~ with
consortium *n.* to form, organize a ~
conspicuous *adj.* ~ for, in
conspiracy *n.* 1. to hatch, organize a ~ 2. to crush;

foil a ~ 3. (a) criminal ~ 4. a ~ against; with 5. a ~ to + inf. (a ~ to overthrow the government)
conspire *v.* 1. (D; intr.) to ~ against; with 2. (E) they ~d to overthrow the government
constable *n.* (BE) ['police officer'] a chief ~
consternation *n.* 1. to cause ~ 2. to express; feel ~ 3. in ~ 4. to smb.'s ~ (to our ~, the current was turned off)
constituent *n.* (ling.) an immediate; ultimate ~
constitute *v.* (formal and rare) (N; used with a noun) they ~d her chief justice
constitution *n.* ['basic law'] 1. to adopt, establish; ratify a ~ 2. to draw up, frame, write a ~ 3. to preserve, safeguard a ~ 4. to abrogate; amend a ~ 5. to violate a ~ 6. a written; unwritten ~ ['physical makeup'] 7. a feeble, frail; iron, rugged, strong ~
constitutional *adj.* ~ to + inf. (it is not ~ to censor the press)
constitutionality *n.* to challenge, question; establish the ~ (of a law)
constrain *v.* (formal) 1. (D; tr.) to ~ from 2. (H) to ~ smb. to do smt.
constrained *adj.* (formal) (cannot stand alone) ~ to + inf. (we were ~ to act)
constraint *n.* ['restriction'] 1. to impose, place, put a ~ on, upon 2. legal ~s ['control'] 3. to show ~ ['compulsion'] 4. under ~ (to act under ~)
construction *n.* ['building industry'] 1. in ~ (he is in ~) ['act of building'] 2. shoddy ~ 3. commercial; modular; residential ~ 4. under ~ (the new skyscraper is under ~) ['interpretation'] 5. to put a ~ on (he put the wrong ~ on my statement) ['syntactic phrase'] 6. an absolute; idiomatic ~
construe *v.* 1. (d; tr.) to ~ as (he ~d the statement as a threat) 2. (M) I ~d his speech to be a warning
consul *n.* a ~ general
consulate *n.* a ~ general
consult *v.* 1. (D; intr.) to ~ about; with (to ~ with smb. about a problem) 2. (D; tr.) to ~ about (to ~ smb. about smt.)
consultant *n.* 1. a business; legal; medical; nursing; political ~ 2. a ~ for, on; to (a ~ to the president on foreign policy) 3. (med.) a ~ in
consultation *n.* 1. to hold ~s 2. ~s about, on; with 3. in ~ (she is in ~ and cannot come to the phone)
consumption *n.* conspicuous; mass ~
contact *n.* ['being together'] ['connection'] 1. to come in, into ~; to establish, make ~ 2. to maintain, stay in ~ 3. to bring into ~ 4. to break off; lose ~ 5. (electrical) to break ~ 6. close, intimate; direct; eye; face-to-face; indirect ~ 7. cultural; personal; radar; radio ~ (the control tower was in radar ~ with the plane) 8. ~ with (to establish ~ with one's relatives; to stay in ~ with friends) 9. in ~ (have they been in ~?) 10. on ~ (the bomb exploded on ~ with the ground) 11. a point of ~ ['acquaintance'] ['tie'] 12. business; professional; international; social ~s
contagious *adj.* extremely, highly ~
contaminate *v.* (D; tr.) to ~ by, with (to ~ smb. with smt; a wound ~d by bacteria)
contemplate *v.* (G) he ~d resigning
contemplation *n.* 1. quiet ~ 2. lost in ~
contemporaneous *adj.* (formal) ~ with

contemporary adj. ~ with

contempt n. ['scorn'] 1. to demonstrate, display, show ~ for 2. bitter, deep, profound, total, unmitigated, utter ~ 3. ~ for 4. beneath ~ ['disrespect'] (legal) 5. to hold in ~ (to hold smb. in ~ of court) ('to accuse smb. of disrespect for a court') 6. civil; criminal ~

contemptible adj. ~ to + inf. (it was ~ of him to behave like that)

contemptuous adj. ~ of (he was ~ of all authority)

contend v. (formal) 1. (D; intr.) ('to compete') to ~ for; with (to ~ for a position) 2. (L) ('to claim') he ~ed that he had been cheated

contender n. 1. a leading; likely; presidential ~ 2. a ~ for (the leading ~ for the heavyweight crown)

content I adj. 1. ~ with (they were ~ with their lot) 2. ~ to + inf. (she was not ~ to remain at home)

content II n. to smb.'s heart's ~ ('to one's complete satisfaction')

content III v. (formal) (d; refl.) to ~ with (to ~ oneself with a simple life)

contention n. ['argument'] 1. to rebut, refute a ~ 2. a bone of ~ ('something contentious') 3. a ~ that + inf. (it is his ~ that taxes are too low) ['competition'] 4. in ~ with

contents n. 1. to divulge the ~ (of a letter) 2. a table of ~

contest n. 1. to hold, stage a ~ 2. to judge a ~ 3. to enter a ~ 4. a bitter, hard-fought; close; one-sided ~ 5. a baby; beauty; oratorical ~ 6. a ~ among, between; for

contestant n. a ~ for

contested adj. bitterly, hotly, vigorously ~

context n. 1. an historical ~ 2. in; out of ~; within a ~ (to cite a passage out of ~)

contiguous adj. ~ to, with

continent n. on a ~

contingency n. 1. to provide for every ~ 2. a ~ arises 3. an unforeseen ~

contingent adj. (pompous) (cannot stand alone) ~ on, upon (the time of his arrival is ~ on the weather)

continuance n. ['adjournment'] (legal) (AE) to grant a ~

continue v. 1. to ~ unabated 2. (D; intr.) to ~ by (she ~d by citing more facts) 3. (D; intr.) to ~ with (she ~d with her work) 4. (E) they ~d to write 5. (G) they ~d writing

continuity n. to break the ~

continuum n. 1. the health-illness ~ 2. along a ~

contraband n. 1. to smuggle ~ 2. to seize ~ 3. ~ of war

contraception n. to practice, use ~

contraceptive n. a chemical; oral; vaginal ~

contract I n. 1. to conclude, sign; negotiate; ratify a ~ 2. to carry out, execute a ~ 3. to draw up, write a ~ 4. to assign (after bidding), let; award a ~ 5. to abrogate, cancel, repudiate a ~ 6. to breach, break, violate a ~ 7. a legal, valid; void ~ 8. (colloq.) (AE) a sweetheart ~ ('an agreement favorable to the employer that was reached without the participation of the union members') 8. (AE) a yellow-dog ~ ('a contract that obligates

the workers not to join a union') 9. a marriage ~ 10. a ~ for; with 11. under ~ with (that player is under ~ with our team)

contract II v. 1. (d; intr.) to ~ for; with (the city ~ed for a new library with their firm) 2. (E) the firm ~ed to construct the bridge

contractions n. to time (labor) ~

contractor n. a building; defense; electrical; general; plumbing ~; a sub-contractor

contradiction n. 1. an apparent; basic; glaring; inherent ~ 2. a ~ between; to 3. in ~ with 4. (misc.) a ~ in terms

contradictory adj. ~ to

contradistinction n. (formal) in ~ to

contraption n. (colloq.) to build, put together; slap together a ~

contrary I adj. (cannot stand alone) ~ to (his actions are ~ to the rules)

contrary II n. 1. on, to the ~ (does your back feel any better? on the ~, it feels much worse) 2. to the ~ (I will come next month unless you write to the ~)

contrast I n. 1. to present a ~ 2. a harsh, sharp, startling, striking ~ 3. a ~ between, to, with 4. by ~ with 5. in ~ to (in ~ to their neighbors, they live modestly)

contrast II v. 1. to ~ sharply 2. (D; intr., tr.) to ~ with (their deeds ~ with their promises)

contravention n. (formal) in ~ of (to act in ~ of international law)

contribute v. 1. (D; tr.) to ~ for (we ~d clothing for the flood victims) 2. (D; intr., tr.) to ~ to, towards (to ~ to charity; she ~d a week's salary to the relief fund)

contribution n. 1. to make a ~ 2. to send in a ~ 3. a charitable; generous; monetary; token; voluntary ~ (to make a generous ~ to charity) 4. a brilliant, notable, outstanding, remarkable; key; major; valuable ~ (she made an outstanding ~ to science) 5. a ~ to, towards

contributor n. ['one who gives money'] 1. a generous; regular ~ 2. a ~ to (a generous ~ to charity) ['one who contributes scholarly works'] 3. a prolific; regular ~ 4. a ~ to (a regular ~ to a journal)

contrition n. 1. to show ~ 2. to express; feel ~ 3. an act of ~ 4. ~ for

contrive v. (E) she somehow ~d to arrange a meeting

control n. 1. to establish; exercise, exert ~ over 2. to assume, take ~ of 3. to bring smt. under ~ (the fire was finally brought under ~) 4. to wrest ~ from 5. to lose ~ of (she lost ~ of the car) 6. absolute; close, strict; full; government; lax, loose; parental; remote ~ (to exert strict ~ over smt.) 7. birth; communicable-disease; cost; damage; emissions; fire; flight; flood; gun; mission; pest; quality; stress; thought ~ 8. price; rent; wage ~(s) 9. ~ of, over (to establish ~ over prices) 10. in ~ of (she was in full ~ of the situation) 11. beyond, out of ~ (the car went out of ~; the fire got out of ~) 12. under ~ (the fire was finally brought under ~; the area was placed under the ~ of the military)

controller n. an air-traffic, flight ~

controls n. ['restrictions'] 1. to impose, introduce;

tighten ~ on 2. to lift, remove ~ from 3. price; rent; wage ~ ['regulating instruments'] 4. to take over the ~ (the copilot took over the ~)

controversial *adj.* bitterly, highly ~

controversy *n.* 1. to arouse, cause, fuel, stir up (a) ~ 2. to settle a ~ 3. a bitter, furious, heated, lively ~ 4. a ~ about, over 5. a ~ between, with

convalesce *v.* (D; intr.) to ~ from

convenience *n.* ['comfort'] 1. a ~ to + inf. (it's a great ~ to live in town = it's a great ~ living in town) 2. at one's ~ (answer at your ~) ['device that adds to comfort'] 3. modern ~s 4. (BE) a public ~ ('a public toilet')

convenient *adj.* 1. ~ for (will Tuesday be ~ for you?) 2. ~ to + inf. (it is very ~ to have the bus stop so close = it is very ~ having the bus stop so close) 3. ~ that + clause (it's very ~ that he can drive you to work)

convention *n.* ['assembly'] ['conference'] 1. to hold a ~ 2. an annual; national; party; political ~ ['agreement'] 3. a copyright ~

converge *v.* (d; intr.) to ~ on, upon; towards (to ~ on the speaker's platform)

conversant *adj.* (cannot stand alone) ['familiar'] 1. thoroughly ~ 2. ~ in 3. ~ with (~ with procedures)

conversation *n.* ['talk'] 1. to begin, strike up; carry on, have a ~ 2. to make ~ (we had little in common, and it was difficult to make ~) 3. to bug, monitor, tap a ~ 4. to monopolize; stimulate a ~ 5. to break off, terminate; interrupt a ~ 6. (an) animated, lively; intimate; light; serious ~ 7. (a) private; telephone ~ 8. fragments, scraps of a ~ (we overheard scraps of their ~) 9. (a) ~ about; with 10. in ~ (she was in ~ with a friend) ['sexual intercourse'] (legal) 11. criminal ~ ('adultery')

conversations *n.* ['negotiations'] 1. to hold ~ 2. to bug, monitor ~ 3. to break off ~ 4. ~ about; with

converse *v.* 1. to ~ fluently (to ~ fluently in a foreign language) 2. (D; intr.) to ~ about; with

conversion *n.* ['change'] 1. condo ~ 2. a ~ from; to ['a score made by a kick or pass after a goal has been scored'] (Am. football, rugby) 3. to make a ~ ['adoption of a religion'] 4. to undergo ~

convert I *n.* 1. to gain a ~ 2. a ~ to (a ~ to Buddhism)

convert II *v.* 1. (AE) (D; intr.) ('to change one's religion') to ~ from; to (they ~ed from Buddhism to Hinduism) 2. (D; intr., tr.) ('to change'); ('to change smb.'s religion') to ~ from; into, to (to ~ smb. to Islam; the plant ~ed to microchip production; they ~ed their money from marks into pounds; to ~ a barn into a garage)

converter *n.* a catalytic ~

convertible *adj.* 1. freely ~ 2. ~ into, to (~ into hard currency)

convey *v.* 1. (B) ('to give') ~ my best wishes to them 2. (D; tr.) ('to transfer') to ~ from; to (the title to the property was ~ed from them to you)

conveyance *n.* ['vehicle'] a public ~

convict *v.* (D; tr.) to ~ of (he was ~ed of murder)

conviction *n.* ['strong belief'] 1. to carry ~ (his story carries ~) 2. a burning, deep, firm, strong; lifelong ~ 3. a ~ that + clause (she expressed her

firm ~ that television was harmful to children) 4. by ~ (a pacifist by ~) ['guilty verdict'] 5. to get a ~ (the prosecutor got ten ~s last year) 6. to overturn a ~ (the appeals court overturned the ~) 7. a ~ for (a ~ for embezzlement)

convince *v.* 1. (D; tr.) to ~ of (he ~d me of his sincerity) 2. (slightly colloq.) (AE) (H) we ~ed ('persuaded') her to stay home 3. (L; must have an object) he ~d everyone that he was honest

convinced *adj.* 1. absolutely, completely, firmly, thoroughly ~ 2. ~ that + clause (we are ~ that our project will succeed)

convocation *n.* ['assembly'] 1. to hold a ~ ['assembly of graduates of a university'] (GB) 2. a member of ~

convoy *n.* 1. to form a ~ 2. in, under ~ (to travel in ~)

convulsions *n.* to go into ~

cook I *n.* 1. the chief, head ~ 2. (AE) a short-order ~

cook II *v.* (C) ~ some vegetables for us; or ~ us some vegetables

cooker *n.* a pressure ~

cookie *n.* 1. (AE) a homemade; sandwich ~ 2. a fortune ~

cooking *n.* 1. to do the ~ 2. home; home-style ~

cookout *n.* to have a ~

cool I *adj.* ['calm'] 1. to keep, remain, stay ~ ['indifferent'] ['unfriendly'] 2. ~ to, towards (she was ~ to the idea)

cool II *n.* (slang) ['composure'] to keep; lose one's ~

cool III *v.* (D; tr.) to ~ to (boil the mixture and then ~ it to room temperature)

coolant *n.* to add ~

coolness *n.* ['indifference'] ~ to, towards

coop *n.* 1. a chicken ~ 2. (misc.) (colloq.) to fly the ~ ('to escape')

cooperate *v.* (D; intr.) to ~ in, on; with (to ~ on a project with smb.)

cooperation *n.* 1. close; wholehearted ~ 2. ~ in; with (~ in a project with another university) 3. in ~ with (their dictionary was published in ~ with the Ministry of Education) 4. (misc.) to enlist smb.'s ~

cooperative, co-op, coop *n.* a consumers'; farmers'; producers'; workers' ~

coop up *v.* (D; tr.) to ~ in; with (we were ~ed up in a small room)

coordinate *v.* 1. to ~ closely 2. (D; tr.) to ~ with (we must ~ our operations with theirs)

coordination *n.* 1. close ~ 2. ~ among, between; with

cop *v.* (colloq.) (esp. AE) (D; intr.) to ~ out of ('to renege on') (to ~ out of a responsibility)

cope *v.* (D; intr.) to ~ with (to ~ with difficulties)

cop out *v.* (colloq.) (esp. AE) ('to renege') to ~ on (to ~ on a responsibility)

copulate *v.* (D; intr.) to ~ with

copy *n.* ['reproduction'] 1. to make, run off a ~ 2. to Xerox (T) a ~ 3. to print ~pies (the publisher decided to print ten thousand ~pies of the book) 4. to inscribe a ~ (the author inscribed a ~ of her book for him) 5. (a) clean, fair ~; hard ('readable') ~ (from a computer); a rough. true ~ 6. a backup; carbon; extra; master ~; photocopy; presentation; top (BE) ('original'); Xerox (T) ~ ['manuscript'] ['draft of material to be printed'] 7. to edit ~ ['issue'] 8. an advance; back ~ ['news'] 9. to make good ~ ('to be newsworthy')

copybook *n.* (BE) to blot one's ~ ('to ruin one's reputation')

copyright *n.* 1. (of a copyright office) to grant, register a ~ 2. (of an author, publisher) to apply for; claim; hold; secure a ~ 3. to infringe a ~ 4. an ad-interim; full-term; statutory ~ 5. a ~ on (a book) 6. under ~

cord *n.* a communication (BE), emergency (AE); electric (AE; BE has *flex);* extension; spinal; umbilical ~

cordial *adj.* ~ to, towards

cordon *n.* ['protective ring of police, soldiers'] 1. to form a ~ 2. to throw a ~ around (an area)

cords *n.* the vocal ~

core *n.* 1. the hard ~ 2. at the ~ (at the ~ of the problem) 3. to the ~ (rotten to the ~)

cork *n.* to pop, remove a ~

corn *n.* ['maize'] 1. to grow, raise; husk ~ 2. hybrid; Indian; sweet; young ~ 3. an ear of ~ 4. (misc.) ~ on the cob

corner *n.* 1. to round, turn a ~ 2. a blind ~ 3. (also fig.) around the ~ (they live around the ~; to go around the ~; prosperity is just around the ~) 4. at, on a ~ (of a street) 5. in the ~ (of a room) 6. (misc.) the four ~s of the globe; I could see her out of the ~ of my eye; (boxing) a neutral ~

cornerstone *n.* to lay a ~

corollary *n.* a ~ to

coronation *n.* to hold a ~

corporal *n.* a lance ~

corporation *n.* 1. to establish, form, set up a ~ 2. to manage, run a ~ 3. to dissolve a ~ 4. (BE) a public ~ 5. a multinational ~

corps *n.* 1. the diplomatic; press ~ 2. an air; army; marine ~

corpse *n.* 1. to bury; lay out a ~ 2. to dig up, exhume a ~ 3. a ~ decays, decomposes, rots

corpus *n.* (ling.) to collect, gather a ~

corpuscle *n.* a red; white ~

correct *adj.* ['true'] 1. ~ in (you are ~ in thinking that he is foolish) 2. ~ to + inf. (it would be ~ to say that we have committed a blunder) 3 ~ that + clause (is it ~ that he has resigned?)

correction *n.* 1. to make a ~ 2. to mark ~s (in a text)

correlate *v.* (d; intr., tr.) to ~ with (to ~ one set of data with another set)

correlation *n.* a ~ between

correspond *v.* 1. (D; intr.) ('to be equal) to ~ to (what German word ~s to *hound?)* 2. (BE) (D; intr.) ('to be in harmony') to ~ with (his actions do not ~ with his words; to ~ with one's needs) 3. (D; intr.) ('to write') to ~ about; with (they have been ~ing with each other about this matter for years)

correspondence *n.* ['exchange of letters'] 1. to carry on, conduct (a) ~ 2. to break off ~ 3. business, commercial; personal ~ 4. ~ about; between; with 5. in ~ with (to be in ~ with smb.)

about smt.) ['conformity'] 6. close ~ 7. ~ between (~ between theory and practice)

correspondent *n.* a foreign; special; war ~

corresponding *adj.* ~ to

corridor *n.* 1. an air; long; narrow; winding ~ 2. a ~ across; between; through

corruption *n.* political ~

cortex *n.* the cerebral ~

cosigner *n.* a ~ for (a ~ for a promissory note)

cosmetics *n.* to apply, put on; use ~

cost I *n.* 1. to bear a ~; to pay ~s; to spare no ~ 2. to cut, reduce ~s 3. to estimate; put, set a ~ at (he put the ~ at one hundred dollars) 4 court; direct; fixed; indirect; overhead ~s (who will pay the court ~s?) 5. a high ~ (the high ~ of energy) 6. a unit ~ 7. at a certain ~ (at any ~; at all ~s; at the ~ of his health; at a terrible ~; at no ~ to the taxpayer)

cost II *v.* 1. (O; may be used with one inanimate object) it cost us ten dollars; it cost ten dollars 2. (P; with an animate object) his blunder cost us dearly 3. (misc.) it ~s (us) five thousand dollars a year to maintain this house

co-star *v.* (D; intr.) to ~ with

costly *adj.* ~ to + inf. (it is ~ to run an air-conditioner all day)

costume *n.* 1. an academic; bathing (BE), swimming (BE) ~ 2. (a) folk, national, native ~ (they were all in native ~)

cot *n.* ['folding bed'] (AE; BE has *camp bed,* 1. to open up, unfold a ~ 2. a folding ~ ['child's bed'] (BE) 3. see **crib**

cottage *n.* a summer; weekend ~

cotton I *n.* 1. to gin; grow; pick; plant ~ 2. (AE) absorbent ~ 3. a bale of ~

cotton II *v.* (colloq.) (AE) (d; intr.) ('to take a liking') to ~ to

cotton on *v.* (colloq.) (BE) (D; intr.) ('to understand') to ~ to

cotton up *v.* (colloq.) (esp. AE) (d; intr.) ('to try to ingratiate oneself') to ~ to

couch I *n.* a studio ~

couch II *v.* (formal) (D; tr.) to ~ in (to ~ a request in tactful language)

cough I *n.* 1. to develop a ~ 2. to suppress a ~ 3. a bad, heavy; croupy; dry; hacking, persistent; smoker's ~

cough II *v.* to ~ loudly

coughing *n.* a fit of ~

could *v.* (F) he ~ not attend the meeting

council *n.* 1. to convene a ~ 2. a city (AE), local (BE); executive; student; township (AE) ~ 3. The Privy Council

counsel I *n.* ['advice'] 1. to give, offer, provide ~ 2. sage, wise ~ 3. ~ about, concerning ['lawyer'] 4. a legal ~ 5. ~ for (~ for the defense; ~ for the prosecution)

counsel II *v.* 1. (D; tr.) to ~ about, in 2. (D; tr.) to ~ against (I ~ed him against going) 3. (H; he ~ed us to wait

counseling *n.* family; guidance; marriage; pastoral; vocational ~

counselor, counsellor *n.* ['adviser'] 1. a guidance ~ 2. a ~ to (a ~ to the ambassador)

count I *n.* ['act of counting'] ['total, tally'] 1. to make, take a ~ 2. to keep ~ of 3. to lose ~ of 4. (boxing) to go down for the ~ ('to be counted out'); to take a ~ of ten 5. an accurate, correct ~ 6. a blood; body; cell; pollen ~ 7. the ~ stands at... 8. by smb.'s ~ (by my ~) ['issue'] 9. on a certain ~ (on all ~s) ['charge, accusation'] 10. on a certain ~ (he was guilty on all ~s)
count II *v.* 1. (d; intr.) ('to be taken into account') to ~ against (your previous convictions will ~ against you) 2. (d; intr., tr.) ('to be considered; to consider') to ~ as (the draw ~s as a victory; we ~ed the draw as a victory) 3. (d; intr.) ('to be valued') (his opinion ~s for very little) 4. (d; intr.) ('to rely') to ~ for; on, upon (she ~ed on us for help; she ~ed on us to help her) 5. (D; intr.) ('to name numbers') to ~ from; to (to ~ from one to ten) 6. (D; intr.) ('to be taken into account') to ~ towards (do associate members ~ towards a quorum?) 7. (N; refl.; used with an adjective) ('to consider') we must ~ ourselves lucky (to have escaped)
countdown *n.* 1. a final ~ 2. a ~ from; to (the ~ to zero has begun)
countenance *n.* (biblical) a shining ~
counter I *adj., adv.* to go ~ to
counter II *n.* ['surface, table over which business is conducted'] 1. a bargain; lunch; notions (AE) ~ 2. at a ~ ['misc.'] 3. over the ~ ('through a broker's office'); ('without a prescription'); under the ~ ('illicitly')
counter III *v.* 1. (D; intr., tr.) to ~ with (she ~ed with an even stronger argument; they ~ed our proposal with one of their own) 2. (L) she ~ed that her advice had not been heeded
counterattack *n.* 1. to launch, make a ~ 2. a ~ against
counterbalance *n.* a ~ to
counterblow *n.* 1. to deal, deliver a ~ 2. a ~ against, to
countercharge *n.* 1. to bring, file, make a ~ 2. a ~ against
counterclaim *n.* 1. to bring, enter, make a ~ 2. a ~ against
counterespionage *n.* 1. to conduct ~ 2. ~ against
counterfeit *n.* a crude; skillful ~
counterintelligence *n.* to conduct ~
countermeasures *n.* 1. to take ~ 2. ~ against
counteroffensive *n.* 1. to launch, undertake a ~ 2. to go over to the ~ 3. a ~ against
counteroffer *n.* to make a ~
counterpart *n.* 1. to have a ~ in 2. a ~ of, to
counterplot *n.* 1. to hatch a ~ 2. a ~ against
counterpoint *n.* ['accompanying melody'] 1. double; single; triple ~ 2. in ~ to ['contrasting element'] 3. to serve as a ~ to
counterproductive *adj.* ~ to
counterproposal *n.* to make, offer a ~ to
counterpunch *n.* to deliver, throw a ~
counterrevolution *n.* 1. to foment, stir up a ~ 2. to carry out; organize a ~ 3. a ~ against
countersign *n.* to give the ~
countersuit *n.* (legal) 1. to bring a ~ 2. a ~ against
counterweight *n.* a ~ to

country *n.* ['nation'] 1. to govern, rule, run a ~ 2. a civilized ~ 3. one's mother, native ~ 4. a host; neighboring ~ 5. developing; third-world; underdeveloped ~ies ['rural area'] 6. the back ~ 7. open; rough, rugged ~ (in open ~) 8. in the ~ (to live in the country) ['misc.'] 9. (BE) to go to the ~ ('to hold a general election')
count up *v.* (d; intr.) to ~ to (the child could ~ to twenty)
coup *n.* ['successful action'] to score a ~ (see also **coup d'état**)
coup de grâce *n.* ['finishing shot'] to deliver the ~
coup d'état *n.* ['sudden overthrow of a government'] 1. to carry out, stage a ~ 2. a bloodless; bloody ~
couple I *n.* a married; unmarried ~
couple II *v.* (D; tr.) to ~ to; with (to ~ a dining car to a train)
couplet *n.* a rhyming ~
coupon *n.* 1. to detach; redeem a ~ 2. to clip ~s ('to profit from stocks and bonds')
courage *n.* 1. to demonstrate, display, show ~ 2. to get up, muster, screw up, summon up ~ 3. to take ~ to + inf. (it takes ~ to tell the truth) 4. dauntless, indomitable; grim; moral; physical ~ 5. the ~ to + inf. (he lacked the ~ to do it) 6. of ~ (a person of great ~)
courageous *adj.* ~ to + inf. (it was ~ of her to volunteer)
courier *n.* 1. to dispatch a ~ 2. a diplomatic ~ 3. a ~ to
course I *n.* ['organized program of study'] 1. to conduct, give, offer, teach a ~ 2. to take a ~ 3. to audit, sit in on a ~ 4. to enroll for, register for, sign up for a ~ 5. to fail; pass a ~; to take a ~ pass-fail (AE) 6. to complete; drop; drop out of; withdraw from a ~ 7. to introduce; organize, plan a ~ 8. to cancel a ~ 9. a demanding, difficult, rigorous; easy, gut (colloq.) ~ 10. an advanced; beginning, elementary, introductory; intermediate ~ 11. (at a university) an elective; graduate, postgraduate (esp. BE); intensive; laboratory; lecture; non-credit; required; survey; undergraduate ~ 12. a correspondence; day-release (BE); extension (AE); makeup; refresher ~ 13. a ~ covers, deals with, treats a subject (our history ~ covered the nineteenth century) 14. a ~ in, on (she took a ~ in mathematics; I offered a ~ on lexicography) ['itinerary'] ['path'] 15. to chart, map out, mark out a ~ 16. to follow, pursue, take a ~ (the law must take its ~) 17. to set ~ for (we set ~ for the nearest port) 18. to change ~ (it's not good to change ~ in midstream) 19. to stay the ~ ('to persist until the end') 20. to run its ~ (the disease ran its expected ~) 21. a collision; middle; natural; zigzag ~ (events took their natural ~) 22. a ~ of action (to pursue a ~ of action) 23. off ~; on ~ (our ship was right on ~; to be on a collision ~; the plane was off ~) ['playing area'] 24. a golf ~; racecourse (esp. BE) ['training area'] 25. an obstacle ~ ['period'] 26. in the ~ of (in the ~ of an investigation; in the ~ of time; in due ~) ['misc.'] 27. of ~ ('naturally') (see the Usage Note for **track**)

course II *v.* (d; intr.) to ~ through (the blood ~d through her veins)

court *n.* ['place where justice is administered'] 1. to hold ~ 2. to adjourn; dismiss (a) ~ 3. to take smb. to ~ 4. to clog the ~s (with frivolous litigation) 5. an appeals (esp. BE), appellate; circuit; city, municipal; county; criminal; crown (BE); district (AE); domestic relations, family; federal (US); high; juvenile; kangaroo ('irregular'); magistrate's; moot; night; orphans'; police; probate; small-claims; superior; supreme; traffic; trial ~ 6. a ~ of appeals; a ~ of common pleas; a ~ of domestic relations; a ~ of law; a ~ of original jurisdiction 7. in ~ (to testify in ~; in open ~) 8. out of ~ (to settle a case out of ~) ['sovereign's residence'] 9. to hold ~ 10. at ~ (at the ~ cf Louis XIV) ['homage'] 11. to pay ~ to smb. ['sports arena'] 12. a basketball; clay (for tennis); grass (for tennis); squash; tennis; volleyball ~ ['motel'] (obsol.) (AE) 13. a motor, tourist ~

courteous *adj.* 1. ~ to, towards (she is ~ to everyone) 2. ~ to + inf. (it was ~ of him to do that)

courtesy *n.* 1. to demonstrate, extend, show ~ (they showed us every ~) 2. common; unfailing ~ 3. professional; senatorial (US) ~ 4. ~ to, towards (it was done as a ~ to you) 5. the ~ to + inf. (he didn't have the ~ to answer my letter) 6. (misc.) she did me the ~ of remaining silent; a basket of fruit was delivered to our door: ~ of the management

courthouse *n.* (esp. AE) a county; federal; state ~

court martial *n.* 1. to hold a ~ 2. a drumhead; general; special; summary ~

cousin *n.* 1. a first; second ~; a first ~ once removed 2. a ~ to (she is a first ~ to the count) 3. (colloq.) kissing ('friendly') ~s

covenant *n.* a ~ between

Coventry *n.* (esp. BE) to send to ~ ('to ostracize')

cover I *n.* ['shelter'] ['concealment'] 1. to seek; take ~ 2. to break ~ 3. (colloq.) to blow one's ~ ('to give oneself away') 4. under ~ (under ~ of darkness) ['covering'] 5. cloud ~ 6. a dust; mattress; pillow ~ ['defense'] 7. air ~ ['front'] 8. a ~ for (the whole operation was a ~ for foreign agents) ['envelope'] 9. under separate ~ ['binding'] 10. from ~ to ~ (to read a book from ~ to ~)

cover II *v.* 1. ('to report on') to ~ live (the event will be ~ed live by TV) 2. (D; refl., tr.) ('to protect') to ~ against (this policy will ~ you against flood damage) 3. (d; intr.) to ~ for ('to substitute for') (to ~ for a friend)

coverage *n.* ['insurance'] 1. to provide ~ for 2. comprehensive, full ~ ['reporting'] 3. to receive ~ 4. complete, extensive, full, wide ~ (the story received wide ~) 5. live; television ~

cover up *v.* (D; intr.) to ~ for ('to protect') (she ~ed up for me when I made that blunder)

covetous *adj.* ~ of

cow I *n.* 1. to milk a ~ 2. a dairy, milch ~ 3. ~s calve; low, moo 4. the meat of the ~ is beef 5. a young ~ is a calf 6. (misc.) (colloq.) holy ~! (AE); silly ~! (BE)

cow II *v.* (D; tr.) to ~ into (to ~ smb. into making

concessions)

coward *n.* an abject, dastardly, dirty ~

cowardice *n.* 1. to demonstrate, show ~ 2. abject, rank; moral ~ 3. (misc.) a streak of ~

cowardly *adj.* ~ to + inf. (it was ~ of them to behave like that)

coy *adj.* ~ about; with (don't be ~ with me about your past record)

cozen *v.* (formal) 1. (d; tr.) to ~ into 2. (d; tr.) to ~ out of (to ~ smb. out of his money)

cozy up *v.* (colloq.) (AE) (D; intr.) to ~ to

crab *n.* ['rower's defective stroke'] to catch a ~

crack *n.* ['remark'] (colloq.) 1. to make a ~ 2. a dirty, nasty ~ 3. a ~ that (her ~ that you are always late was unjustified) ['moment'] 4. at the ~ of dawn ['attempt'] 5. to have a ~ at (let's have a ~ at it)

crackdown *n.* 1. to launch a ~ 2. a ~ on (a ~ on drunk drivers)

crack down *v.* (D; intr.) to ~ on (to ~ on drug dealers)

cracked up *adj.* (colloq.) (cannot stand alone) ['reputed'] ~ to be (this hotel is not what it's ~ to be)

cracker *n.* (esp. AE) a graham; soda; unsalted ~

crackpot *n.* (colloq.) a ~ to + inf. (he was a ~ to do it)

cradle *n.* 1. to rock a ~ 2. (misc.) from the ~ to the grave ('during one's whole life')

craft *n.* ['occupation'] 1. to ply, practice a ~ 2. to learn, master a ~ ['boat'] 3. a landing ~ 4. (in plural) small ~

craftsman *n.* a master ~

cram *v.* 1. (D; intr.) ('to study hastily') to ~ for (to ~ for an exam) 2. (d; tr.) ('to jam') to ~ into (to ~ one's things into a suitcase)

cramp *n.* 1. to get a ~ (esp. AE)/get ~ (BE) 2. writer's ~ 3. (BE) seized with ~

cranberry *n.* to pick ~ries

crane *n.* to operate a ~

crank *n.* ['handle'] to turn, use a ~

crap game *n.* a floating ~

craps *n.* to play, shoot ~

crash I *n.* 1. a loud, resounding ~ 2. a plane; stockmarket ~

crash II *v.* 1. (d; intr.) to ~ into (the car ~ed into a pole) 2. (d; intr.) to ~ through (the car ~ed through the barrier) 3. (d; intr.) to ~ to (to ~ to the floor) 4. (misc.) the plane ~ed in flames

crass *adj.* ~ to + inf. (it was ~ of him to ask how much you earn)

crave *v.* to ~ strongly 2. (d; intr.) to ~ for ('to ~ for peace and quiet) USAGE NOTE: The phrase *to crave for smt.* is less common than *to crave smt.*

craving *n.* 1. to feel, have a ~ 2. a powerful, strong ~ 3. a ~ for

craw *n.* ['crop of a bird or insect'] to stick in smb.'s ~ ('to be distasteful to smb.')

crawl I *n.* ['swimming stroke'] 1. to swim the ~ ['act of crawling'] (also fig.) 2. to a ~ (traffic slowed to a ~)

crawl II *v.* 1. (d; intr.) to ~ into (to ~ into a hole) 2. (d; intr.) to ~ out of (to ~ out of the ruins) 3. (d;

intr.) to ~ with (the city is ~ing with reporters)
crawl out *v.* (D; intr.) to ~ from under (to ~ from under the ruins)
crayon *n.* colored ~s
craze *n.* 1. the current, latest, newest ~ 2. the ~ swept the country 3. a ~ for
crazy *adj.* (colloq.) ['infatuated'] 1. (cannot stand alone) ~ about (he is ~ about her) ['foolish'] 2. ~ to + inf. (it was ~ of her to do that; she was ~ to drive without headlights) 3. to drive smb. ~
cream *n.* ['component of milk'] 1. to whip ~ 2. clotted (BE); double (BE), whipping; ice; single (BE); sour, soured (BE); whipped ~ ['cosmetic'] 3. to apply ~ 4. cold; face; hand; shaving; skin; vanishing ~
crease *n.* to iron out, remove the ~s
credence *n.* 1. to attach, give, lend ~ to 2. to find; gain ~
credentials *n.* 1. to present one's ~ 2. to evaluate; examine smb.'s ~
credibility *n.* 1. to establish ~ 2. to lose one's ~ 3. (misc.) a ~ gap
credit I *n.* ['time given for payment'] 1. to allow, give, extend, offer ~ (this store does not give ~) 2. to deny, refuse smb. ~ 3. consumer ~ 4. on ~ (to buy smt. on ~) ['recognition'] ['honor'] 5. to do ~ to; to reflect ~ on (her work does ~ to her teachers) 6. to get, take ~ for (he took ~ for my work) 7. to give smb. ~ for (I give her ~ for being so sensible) 8. a ~ to (she is a ~ to her parents) 9. ~ that + clause (it was to her ~ that she never gave up) 10. to smb.'s ~ (to her ~, she was never late to work; with all due ~ to you) ['sum allowed, deducted'] 11. an energy (AE); tax ~ ['recognition that a student has completed a course or unit of study'] 12. to get, receive ~ for a course 13. advanced ~
credit II *v.* 1. (D; tr.) to ~ to (to ~ an amount to smb.'s account) 2. (d; tr.) to ~ with (to ~ smb. with common sense; to ~ an account with fifty dollars)
credit card *n.* to issue a ~
creditor *n.* to pay off one's ~s
credo *n.* a ~ that + clause (it is our ~ that everyone is equal)
credulity *n.* to strain smb.'s ~
creed *n.* 1. to adhere to a ~ 2. a political; religious ~ 3. a ~ that + clause (it is our ~ that we must help the poor) 4. (misc.) all races and ~s
creep *v.* (d; intr.) to ~ into (to ~ into a hole) 2. (d; intr.) to ~ out of (an insect crept out of the pipe) 3. (misc.) to ~ on all fours; to ~ out from under a bush
creeps *n.* (colloq.) ['fear'] it gives me the ~
creep up *v.* (D; intr.) to ~ on (he crept up on me in the dark)
creepy *adj.* (colloq.) ['weird'] ~ about (there is smt. ~ about him)
crescendo *n.* 1. to reach a ~ 2. a deafening ~
crest *n.* ['top'] 1. to ride the ~ (to ride the ~ of popularity) 2. at the ~ ['heraldic device'] 3. a family ~
crew *n.* ['group working together'] 1. a ground; gun; road; skeleton; stage; tank; work; wrecking

~ ['ship's personnel'] 2. a ship's ~ 3. a ~ mutinies 4. in a ~ ['rowing team'] 5. a varsity ~ 6. to go out for ~ ['misc.'] 7. a motley ~ ('a disparate group')
crib I *n.* (AE) 1. to assemble, put up a ~ 2. to dismantle a ~ (BE has *cot)*
crib II *v.* (colloq.) (D; intr., tr.) ('to plagiarize') to ~ from
cricket I *n.* ['game'] 1. to play ~ ['fair play'] (colloq.) 2. ~ to + inf. (it's not ~ to cheat at cards)
cricket II *n.* ['insect'] ~s chirp
crier *n.* a town ~
crime *n.* 1. to commit, perpetrate a ~ 2. to deter; eradicate, stamp out, wipe out; prevent ~ 3. an atrocious, brutal, heinous, horrible, infamous, outrageous, vicious ~ 4. a daring; economic; major, serious; minor, petty; perfect; political; victimless; violent; war ~; (a) white collar ~; a ~ of passion 5. organized ~ 6. a ~ against (a ~ against humanity) 7. a ~ to + inf. (it was a ~ to butcher French like that) 8. a ~ that + clause (it is a ~ that so many people go to bed hungry) 9. (misc.) to investigate a ~; to report a ~ (to the police); it's a ~ the way he behaves
criminal I *adj.* ~ to + inf. (it was ~ of him to do that) 2. ~ that + clause (it is ~ that he is allowed to remain in this country)
criminal II *n.* 1. to apprehend, arrest a ~; to bring a ~ to justice 2. to pardon; parole; release a ~ 3. to rehabilitate a ~ 4. a born; common; desperate; habitual, hardened, inveterate; infamous, notorious; master; war ~ 5. a band, gang of ~s
crimp *n.* (colloq.) (AE) ['obstacle'] to put a ~ in
crisis *n.* 1. to cause, precipitate, provoke, stir up a ~ 2. to aggravate a ~ 3. to avert, forestall a ~ 4. to defuse, overcome, settle a ~; to ride out a ~ 5. an acute, grave, serious; impending; mounting ~ 6. a cabinet; economic, financial; energy; food; housing; identity; mid-life; political ~ 7. a ~ concerning, over (there was a ~ over the budget deficit) 8. a ~ in (the ~ in health care) 9. in a ~
crisp *n.* burned to a ~
criterion *n.* 1. to apply; establish a ~ 2. to meet, satisfy criteria 3. a reliable, valid ~
critic *n.* 1. a harsh, severe, unkind; impartial ~ 2. an art; drama; literary; music; social ~
critical *adj.* ['criticizing'] 1. ~ of (he was ~ of my work) ['crucial'] 2. ~ to (~ to our work) 3. ~ that + clause; subj. (it is ~ that the work be/should be completed on time)
criticism *n.* 1. to arouse, provoke, stir up ~ 2. to express, offer ~; to level ~ at 3. to take ~ 4. to temper one's ~ 5. to subject smb. to ~ 6. adverse, biting, damaging, devastating, harsh, hostile, scathing, severe, sharp, sweeping, unsparing, withering ~ 7. constructive; fair; mild; nitpicking, petty; sober; valid ~ 8. textual ~ 9. (the) higher; lower ~ (of the Bible) 10. the barbs of ~
criticize *v.* 1. to ~ fairly; harshly, severely, sharply 2. (D; tr.) to ~ for (to ~ smb. for sloppy work)
critique *n.* to give, present a ~
crop I *n.* 1. to grow; plant a ~ 2. to gather, harvest, reap a ~ 3. to bear; yield a ~ 4. to rotate ~s 5. to dust, spray ~s 6. a bountiful, bumper; record; poor ~ 7. a cash; staple ~

crop II *v.* (N; used with an adjective) they ~ped the grass short
cropper *n.* ['failure'] to come a ~ ('to fail')
croquet *n.* to play ~
croquettes *n.* chicken; salmon ~s
cross I *adj.* ['irritable'] ~ at, with (~ at smt.; ~ with smb.)
cross II *n.* ['symbol of the Christian religion'] 1. to die on the ~ (said of Jesus Christ) 2. to bear one's ~ ('to bear a heavy burden') 3. to make the sign of the ~['figure of a cross'] 4. to make one's ~ (in place of a signature) 5. a Greek; Latin; Maltese ~ ['mixture'] 6. a ~ between (a ~ between two breeds)
cross III *v.* 1. (D; intr., tr.) ('to go') to ~ from; to (they ~ed from one bank of the river to the other; we ~ed the valley from one ridge to the other) 2. (D; tr.) ('to breed') to ~ with (to ~ one breed with another)
cross-examination *n.* 1. to conduct a ~ 2. to subject smb. to ~ 3. a rapid-fire ~ 4. under ~
cross-examine *v.* to ~ sharply
cross fire *n.* to be caught in a ~
crossing *n.* 1. to make a ~ 2. a rough; smooth ~ 3. a border ~ 4. a grade (AE), level (BE); Panda (BE), pedestrian, pelican (BE), zebra (BE); railroad (AE), railway (esp. BE) ~ 5. a transoceanic ~ 6. at a ~ (at the border ~)
cross over *v.* (D; intr.) to ~ into, to (she ~ed over to the other lane)
cross-purposes *n.* at ~ (to work at ~)
cross-refer *v.* (D; intr., tr.) to ~ to
cross-reference *n.* 1. to make a ~ 2. a ~ to
crossroads *n.* at a ~ (also fig.)
crossword (BE) see **crossword puzzle**
crossword puzzle *n.* (esp. AE) to do, work (out) a ~
crow I *n.* 1. ~s caw 2. (misc.) as the ~ flies ('in a straight line'); to eat ~ ('to be placed in a humiliating position')
crow II *v.* (colloq.) ('to exult') (d; intr.) to ~ about, over (to ~ about one's success; to ~ over an enemy's misfortune)
crowd I *n.* ['throng'] 1. to attract, draw a ~ 2. to disperse a ~ 3. an enormous, huge, tremendous; overflow ~ 4. a ~ collects, gathers; disperses; thins out 5. a ~ mills, swarms (around the entrance) ['audience'] 6. a capacity ~ ['group'] 7. a bad; fast, wild ~; the wrong ~ (to run around with a fast ~; she got in with the wrong ~)
crowd II *v.* 1. (d; intr.) to ~ around (to ~ around the entrance) 2. (d; intr.) to ~ into (to ~ into a small room) 3. (d; tr.) to ~ off, out of (they ~ed me off the road) 4. (d; intr.) to ~ through (they ~ed through the turnstiles) 5. (misc.) to ~ together
crown I *n.* ['part of a tooth'] 1. to put a ~ on (a tooth) ['monarch's headdress'] 2. to wear a ~ ['boxing title'] 3. to win the (heavyweight) ~
crown II *v.* 1. (d; tr.) to ~ with (their efforts were ~ed with success) 2. (N; used with a noun) they ~ed him emperor
crucial *adj.* 1. ~ for, to (these negotiations are ~ for/to the future of our firm) 2. ~ that + clause;

subj. (it is ~ that this matter remain/should remain secret)
crude *adj.* ~ to + inf. (it was ~ of him to say that)
cruel *adj.* 1. ~ to, towards (~ to animals) 2. ~ to + inf. (it was ~ of him to say that)
cruelty *n.* 1. to demonstrate, display ~ 2. consummate, deliberate, wanton ~ 3. mental ~ ~. ~ to, towards (~ to animals)
cruise I *n.* 1. to go on, take a ~ 2. a shakedown; world ~ 3. a ~ around (to take a ~ around the world)
cruise II *v.* (D; intr.) to ~ around (to ~ around the world)
cruiser *n.* a battle; heavy; light; medium ~
crumble *v.* (D; intr.) to ~ into
crunch *n.* (colloq.) (esp. AE) ['shortage'] 1. an energy ~ ['showdown'] 2. if it comes to a ~
crusade I *n.* 1. to conduct; launch a ~ 2. to embark on; engage in; go on; join a ~ 3. a one-man, one-woman ~ 4. a holy ~ 5. a ~ against; for (a ~ against smoking)
crusade II *v.* (D; intr.) to ~ against; for (to ~ against smoking)
crush I *n.* (colloq.) ['infatuation'] 1. a schoolboy; schoolgirl; youthful ~ 2. a ~ on (to have a ~ on smb.)
crush II *v.* 1. (d; intr.) to ~ against (the mob ~ed against the barriers) 2. (misc.) to ~ smb. to death
crust *n.* (colloq.) ['impudence'] the ~ to ~ inf. (she had the ~ to ask for a raise)
crutch *n.* 1. to walk on, with ~es 2. a pair of ~es
cry I *n.* 1. to give, raise (formal), utter a ~ 2. an anguished, plaintive; heart-rending; loud, lusty; piercing; rallying ~ 3. a battle, war ~ 4. a ~ for (a ~ for help) 5. (misc.) a far ~ from ('very far from')
cry II *v.* 1. to ~ loudly 2. (d; intr.) ('to appeal') to ~ for (to ~ for justice) 3. (d; intr.) ('to weep') to ~ for, with (to ~ for joy; to ~ with grief) 4. (d; intr.) ('to weep') to ~ over (to ~ over one's bad luck) 5. (d; intr.) to ~ to ('to complain to') (don't come ~ing to me) 6. (misc.) to ~ wolf ('to give a false alarm'); to ~ havoc ('to warn of disaster'); to ~ one's eyes out; to ~ over spilled/spilt milk ('to complain in vain'); she cried herself to sleep
cry out *v.* 1. (d; intr.) ('to appeal') to ~ against for (to ~ against injustice; to ~ for equal rights) 2. (d; intr., tr.) ('to shout') to ~ to (he cried out to us to stop)
crystal *n.* fine ~
cube *n.* an ice ~
cube root *n.* to find, extract the ~
cucumber *n.* 1. to peel; slice a ~ 2. (misc.) as cool as a ~
cuddle up *v.* (D; intr.) to ~ to (the twins ~d up to each other)
cudgels *n.* ['defense'] to take up the ~ for
cue *n.* ['signal'] 1. to give the ~ 2. to take one's ~ from smb. 3. to miss the ~ 4. on ~
cuff *n.* 1. a French ~ 2. (misc.) (esp. AE) on the ~ ('on credit')
cull *v.* (D; tr.) to ~ from
culminate *v.* (d; intr.) to ~ in (to ~ in victory)
cult *n.* 1. to join a ~ 2. a cargo; fertility; personality ~

cultivation *n.* under ~

culture *n.* ['enlightenment'] ['developed intellectual faculties'] 1. to develop a ~ 2. to bring ~ to 3. to disseminate, foster, spread ~ 4. ethnic; human; material ~ ['professional training'] 5. beauty ~ ['bacteria cultured for examination or vaccine production'] 6. to do, grow a ~

cunning I *adj.* ~ to + inf. (it was ~ of them to do that)

cunning II *n.* to show ~

cup *n.* ['prize'] 1. to lose; win a ~ 2. a challenge ~ ['small drinking vessel'] 3. to drain one's ~ 4. a coffee; drinking; paper; plastic ~; teacup 5. (misc.) to be in one's cups ('to be drunk')

cupboard *n.* 1. an airing (BE); built-in ~ 2. (usu. fig.) a bare ~

cupid *n.* to play ~

curb *n.* ['restraint'] a ~ on

curd *n.* soybean (AE), soya bean (BE) ~

cure I *n.* 1. to effect, provide, work a ~ 2. a certain, sure; complete; miraculous ~ 3. a rest; water ~ 4. a ~ for

cure II *v.* (D; tr.) to ~ of (to ~ smb. of a disease)

curfew *n.* 1. to impose a ~ 2. to lift a ~ 3. a midnight ~

curious *adj.* ['eager to know'] 1. ~ about (~ about smb.'s past) 2. ~ to + inf. (I would be ~ to know what really happened) ['odd'] 3. ~ that + clause (it is ~ that she didn't remember the incident)

curiosity *n.* 1. to arouse, excite, pique, whet (one's) ~ 2. to satisy one's ~ 3. healthy; idle; intellectual; natural; unquenchable ~ 4. ~ about 5. out of ~ (he did it out of ~)

curls *n.* natural ~

curl up *v.* (D; intr.) to ~ in, into (to ~ into a ball)

currency *n.* ['paper money'] 1. to issue; print ~ 2. to call in, withdraw ~ 3. convertible, hard; foreign; non-convertible, soft, weak; stable, strong ~ ['general use'] 4. to enjoy, have ~ (to enjoy wide ~)

current *n.* ['flow of electricity'] 1. alternating; direct; electric; high-tension; low-tension; oscillating ~ ['flow'] 2. an air ~ 3. an underwater ~ 4. against; with the ~

curriculum *n.* 1. to draw up, design a ~ 2. a college, university; school ~ 3. a basic, core ~ 4. a ~ in (the ~ in engineering)

curry *n.* 1. hot, mild ~ 2. fish; meat; vegetable ~

curse I *n.* 1. to pronounce, put a ~ on, upon smb. 2. to utter a ~ 3. to lift a ~ 4. under a ~

curse II *v.* (D; tr.) to ~ for (she ~d him for his clumsiness)

curtain *n.* 1. to draw; lower; raise a ~ 2. (in the theater) to ring down; ring up the ~ 3. to hang, put up ~s 4. a drop; shower; stage, theater ~ 5. (fig.) a bamboo; iron ~ 6. (in the theater) the ~ goes up, rises; comes down, drops, falls

curtain call *n.* to take a ~

curtains *n.* (colloq.) ['ruin'] ~ for (it will be ~ for him if he loses his job)

curtsy I *n.* to make a ~

curtsy II *v.* (D; intr.) to ~ to (to ~ to the Queen)

curve I *n.* 1. to describe, make a ~ (the road makes a ~ to the right) 2. to plot a ~ ('to locate a

curve by plotted points') 3. (teaching) to grade (AE), mark on a ~ 4. a hairpin, horseshoe; sharp ~

curve II *v.* 1. to ~ sharply 2. (D; intr.) to ~ to (to ~ to the right)

custody *n.* ['guardianship'] 1. to award, grant ~ 2. to receive, take ~ 3. joint ~ ['arrest'] 4. to take smb. into ~ 5. police; protective ~ 6. in ~ ('under arrest') (held in ~)

custom *n.* 1. to establish a ~ 2. to cherish, observe, practice a ~ 3. (a) local ~ 4. an ancient, old; pagan; quaint; tribal ~ 5. a ~ to + inf. (it is not our ~ to break the law) 6. a ~ that + clause (it is an old ~ that men tip their hats when greeting smb.)

customary *adj.* ~ to + inf. (it is ~ to tip the waiter)

customer *n.* 1. to attract ~s 2. an irate; prospective; satisfied; steady ~ 3. a cash ~ 4. (misc.) an ugly ~ ('a violent person')

customs *n.* 1. to clear, get through, go through, pass through ~ (we got through ~ very quickly) 2. to clear, get smt. through ~ (we got the toys through ~ without difficulty) 3. to declare smt. at ~

cut I *n.* ['wound made by smt. sharp'] 1. a clean; deep; superficial ~ ['reduction'] 2. to take a ~ 3. a budget; pay; personnel; tax ~ 4. a ~ in (we had to take a ~ in pay) ['haircut'] 5. a crew ~

cut II *v.* 1. ('to gash') to ~ deeply 2. (C) ('to sever') ~ a slice of cake for me; or: ~ me a slice of cake 3. (d; intr.) ('to go') to ~ across (to ~ across a field) 4. (D; tr.) ('to sever') to ~ from (to ~ a branch from a tree; he was cut from the team; she cut a thin slice from the loaf) 5. (d; intr.) ('to slice') to ~ into (she cut into the cake) 6. (D; tr.) ('to slice') to ~ into (he cut the meat into small pieces) 7. (D; refl.) ('to gash') to ~ on (she cut herself on a knife) 8. (D; tr.) ('to remove') to ~ out of (she was cut out of the will) 9. (d; intr.) ('to go') to ~ through (they cut through the woods; let's ~ through this building) 10. (D; tr.) ('to reduce') to ~ to (they cut the budget to the minimum) 11. (N; used with an adjective) ('to trim') she cut her hair short 12. (misc.) to ~ smb. short ('to interrupt smb.'); to ~ smb. to the quick ('to insult smb. deeply')

cut ahead *v.* (d; intr.) to ~ of ('to cut off') (the other runner cut ahead of her)

cut away *v.* (D; tr.) to ~ from

cutback *n.* a ~ in (a ~ in production)

cut back *v.* (D; intr.) to ~ on (to ~ on smoking)

cut down *v.* 1. (D; intr.) to ~ on (to ~ on smoking) 2. (misc.) to ~ smb. down to size ('to deflate smb.'s ego')

cut in *v.* 1. (D; intr.) to ~ on (he cut in on me when I was dancing) 2. (slang) (D; tr.) to ~ on (he cut me in on the deal)

cutlet *n.* a veal ~

cut off *v.* 1. (C) ('to slice') he cut off a slice for me; or: he cut me off a slice 2. (D; tr.) ('to separate') to ~ from (we were cut off from civilization)

cut out *adj.* ['suited'] 1. ~ for (she wasn't ~ for this job 2. ~ to + inf. (I wasn't ~ to be an administrator)

cut out *v.* (D; tr.) to ~ from (to ~ an article out from the newspaper)

cutter *n.* a cookie (AE); paper ~

cutting *n.* a press ~ (BE; AE has *press clipping)*

cut up *v.* (D; tr.) to ~ into (to ~ smt. up into pieces)

cycle *n.* 1. to complete a ~; to come full ~ 2. to go through, pass through a ~ 3. a business; economic; estrous (AE), oestrous (BE); life; menstrual ~ 4. (as on a washing machine) a delicate; normal; permanent-press ~ 5. in ~s (some epidemics occur in ~s)

cynical *adj.* ~ about (~ about smb.'s motives)

cypher (esp. BE) see **cipher**

czar *n.* a financial; gambling; shipbuilding ~ (BE spelling is *tsar)*

D

dab *v.* (d; intr.) to ~ at (to ~ at one's eyes with a handkerchief)

dabble *v.* (d; intr.) to ~ at, in (to ~ in politics; to ~ at painting)

dagger *n.* 1. to draw a ~ 2. to plunge a ~ into (smb.) 3. (misc.) to look ~s at ('to look angrily at')

daisy *n.* (misc.) as fresh as a ~

dally *v.* 1. (D; intr.) ('to be slow') to ~ over (to ~ over one's work) 2. (d; intr.) ('to play') to ~ with (to ~ with smb.'s affections)

dam *n.* 1. to build, construct, erect a ~ 2. a hydroelectric; storage ~ 3. a ~ bursts

damage I *n.* ['harm'] 1. to cause, do ~ to; to inflict ~ on 2. to suffer, sustain ~ 3. to repair, undo ~ 4. grave, great, extensive, irreparable, serious, severe; lasting, permanent; light, slight; widespread ~ 5. fire; flood; material; property; structural ~ 6. brain ~ (irreversible brain ~) 7. ~ from (~ from the fire) 8. ~ to (was there much ~ to the car? the ~ done to the house was extensive; grave ~ to one's reputation)

damage II *v.* 1. to ~ badly 2. easily ~d

damages *n.* ['compensation'] 1. to award ~ (the court awarded ~) 2. to claim; sue for ~ 3. to pay; receive, recover ~ 4. compensatory; exemplary, punitive; nominal ~ 5. ~ for

damn *n.* (colloq.) ['small amount'] not to give a (tinker's) ~ (I don't give a ~ for their opinions!)

damnedest, damndest *n.* (colloq.) ['utmost'] to do, try one's ~

damper *n.* ['deadening influence'] to put a ~ on

dance I *n.* 1. to do, perform a ~ 2. to have a ~ with 3. to sit out a ~ 4. (the) classical ~; modern ~ 5. a barn; belly; circle, round; folk; formal; square; sword; tap; war ~ 6. to go to a ~ 7. at a ~ (they met at a ~) 8. (misc.) (BE) to lead smb. a merry ~ (AE has *to lead smb. a merry chase*)

dance II *v.* 1. (D; intr.) to ~ to (to ~ to the music of a rock group) 2. (D; intr.) to ~ with 3. (misc.) to ~ for, with joy

dancer *n.* a ballet; ballroom; belly; folk; tap; taxi ~

dancing *n.* aerobic; ballroom, social; belly; break; folk; tap ~

dander *n.* ['temper'] to get one's ~ up

danger *n.* 1. to constitute, represent; create (a) ~ 2. to run a ~ 3. to expose to ~ 4. to face; sense (a) ~ 5. to avert (a) ~ 6. (a) deadly, grave, mortal; imminent, impending ~ 7. (legal) a clear and present ~ 8. a ~ to (a ~ to national security) 9. a ~ that + clause (there was a ~ that fire would break out) 10. in ~ (our lives were in ~; the building is in imminent ~ of collapsing) 11. out of ~

dangerous *adj.* 1. ~ to + inf. (it's ~ to play in the street) 2. ~ that + clause (it's ~ that so many people have guns)

dangle *v.* 1. (d; intr.) to ~ from (his keys ~d from a chain) 2. (d; tr.) to ~ before, in front of (to ~ bait in front of smb.)

dare *n.* to take a ~

dare II *v.* 1. (E) I don't ~ to protest 2. (F) I ~ not protest (formal); I don't ~ protest; she didn't ~ open her mouth; how ~ you speak to me like that? 3. (H) he ~d me to sue him USAGE NOTE: Some purists believe that *I don't dare protest* is an incorrect blend of *I don't dare to protest* and *I dare not protest*.

daring *adj.* ~ to + inf. (it was ~ to attempt the climb at night)

dark I *adj.* 1. pitch ('completely') ~ 2. (misc.) as ~ as night ('very dark'); to grow ~

dark II *n.* ['darkness'] 1. after ~ 2. in the ~ (to grope for the door in the ~) ['ignorance'] 3. to keep smb. in the ~

darkness *n.* 1. complete, pitch, total ~ 2. ~ falls

darn *n.* (colloq.) ['small amount'] not to give a ~ (I don't give a ~!)

dart *v.* 1. (D; tr.) to ~ at (to ~ a glance at smb.) 2. (P; intr.) the children ~ed into the room; the hare ~ed along the edge of the clearing

darts *n.* to play ~ USAGE NOTE: A singular verb is used with this noun--*darts is a popular game*.

dash I *n.* ['rush'] 1. to make a ~ for (to make a ~ for safety) 2. a frantic, mad ~

dash II *v.* (P; intr.) when the rain started, we ~ed for cover

data *n.* 1. to feed in; process; retrieve; store ~ 2. to cite; evaluate; gather ~ 3. biographical; raw; scientific; statistical ~ USAGE NOTE: Purists insist on *the data are available* and consider *the data is available* to be incorrect.

date I *n.* ['time'] 1. to fix, set a ~ 2. to bring (smb.) up to ~ 3. to bear a ~ (the letter bears no ~) 4. a significant ~ (in history) 5. a cut-off; due; target ~ 6. at a certain ~ (the meeting will be held at a later ~; at a future ~) 7. on a certain ~ (on this ~ in history) 8. to ~ (how many have returned their invitations to ~?) ['rendezvous'] 9. to have; make a ~ 10. to go out on a ~ 11. to break a ~ 12. a blind; double ~ 13. a ~ with ['misc.'] 14. out of ~; to go out of ~; up to ~; to bring a dictionary up to ~

date II *v.* (d; intr.) to ~ from (this custom ~s from the seventeenth century)

date back *v.* (d; intr.) to ~ to (the temple ~s back to the tenth century)

dating *n.* carbon ~

daughter *n.* 1. to adopt a ~ 2. to marry off a ~ 3. an only ~ 4. an adopted; foster ~; stepdaughter 5. a ~ to (she was like a ~ to me)

dawdle *v.* (D; intr.) ('to waste time') to ~ over

dawn *n.* 1. (formal) ~ breaks 2. at (the crack of) ~

dawn on *v.* 1. (L) it ~ed on me that the following day would be her birthday 2. (Q) it finally ~ed on us what must be done

day *n.* 1. a chilly, cool; clear, nice; cloudy; cold; foggy; gloomy; hot, stifling; rainy; sunny; warm ~

2. an eventful, field, memorable, red-letter ~ (we had a field ~ criticizing their report) 3 a holy; opening; visiting; wedding; working ~ (opening ~ of the baseball season) 4. ~ breaks, dawns (poetic) 5. by ~ (London by ~) 6. by the ~ (to be paid by the ~) 7. for a ~ (we are going to town for the ~) 8. in a ~ (we cannot do the whole job in a ~; back in the old ~s) 9. on a certain ~ (on the following ~; on New Year's Day) 10. within several ~s (within ten ~s) 11. (misc.) ~ after ~; ~ and night ('all the time'); D-day ('a day on which a significant event is scheduled to begin'); to take a ~ off; I rue the ~ ('I wish that that day had never been'); from ~ to ~; ~ in, ~ out; to carry the ~ ('to be victorious'); the other ~ ('recently'); his ~s are numbered ('he will die soon'); the dog ~s ('the hot days of July and August'); halcyon ~s; the good old ~s; it was a big ('successful') ~ for our team; to take one ~ at a time; judgment ~: on the ~ (BE; colloq.) ('when the time comes') USAGE NOTE: The collocation *by day* contrasts with *by night* (London by day is very different from London by night). (see the Usage Note for **night**)

daybreak *n.* at ~

daydream *v.* (D; intr.) to ~ about

daylight *n.* in broad ~

daylights *n.* (colloq.) ['insides'] 1. to beat, wallop the ~ out of smb. ['wits'] 2. to scare the (living) ~ out of smb.

daze *n.* in a ~ (he's always in a ~)

dazed *adj.* ~ at (~ at the sight of the carnage)

dead I *adj.* ['having died'] 1. to drop ~ (of a heart attack) 2. (misc.) to be left for ~; to rise from the ~; the quick and the ~; to play ~ ['unresponsive'] 3. (cannot stand alone) ~ to (he was ~ to the world)

dead II *n.* ['period of greatest quiet'] in the ~ of the night

dead horse *n.* (colloq.) ['a topic that has been exhausted'] to beat a ~

deadline *n.* 1. to establish, set a ~ 2. to meet a ~ 3. to extend a ~ 4. to miss a ~ 5. to work against a ~

deadlock *n.* 1. to reach a ~ 2. to break a ~

dead set I *adj.* ['resolutely'] ~ against

dead set II *n.* ['attack'] to make a ~ at

deaf *adj.* 1. stone ~ 2. (cannot stand alone) ~ to (they were ~ to all our pleas)

deafness *n.* acquired; congenital ~

deal I *n.* ['transaction'] 1. to close, wrap up (colloq.); do (BE), make (AE), strike a ~ with (we closed the ~ with them yesterday) ['treatment'] 2. a fair, square; raw (colloq.), rotten (colloq.), rough (colloq.) ~ (she got a raw ~ from her boss) ['arrangement'] 3. a package ~ ['amount'] 4. a good, great ~ ['misc.'] 5. (colloq.) a big ~ ('an impressive matter'); it means a great ~ to her ('it is very important to her')

deal II *v.* 1. (formal) (A) he dealt a deathblow to the enemy; or: he dealt the enemy a deathblow 2. (d; intr.) to ~ in (they ~ in furs) 3. (d; intr.) to ~ with (we ~ with many customers; to ~ with complaints; I'll ~ with the children later; this chapter ~s with the problem of inflation)

dealer *n.* 1. an art; book; car; junk ~ 2. ε ~ in (a ~ in rare books)

dealership *n.* an automobile (AE) ~

dealings *n.* ['business'] 1. straight; underhanded ~ 2. ~ with (I have had ~ with them)

dear *adj.* 1. (cannot stand alone) ~ to (this project is ~ to my heart) 2. (misc.) to hold smb. ~

death *n.* 1. to cause ~ 2. to face ~; to meet one's ~ 3. to feign ~ 4. to mourn smb.'s ~ 5. a certain, sure; heroine's, hero's; lingering; living; natural; painful; sudden, unexpected; untimely; violent ~ (to die a natural ~; to meet a violent ~) 6. brain ~ 7. cot (BE), crib (AE) ~ 8. ~ by (~ by drowning; fire; firing squad; hanging; lethal injection) 9. at one's ~ (at her ~ the estate was broken up) 10. to ~ (beaten; bored; burnt; frozen; put; shot; starved to ~) 11. (misc.) a fight to the ~; a ~ in the family; (sports) sudden ~ ('an overtime period ending when the first point or goal is scored'); ~ to tyrants!; in ~ as in life; till ~ do us part

deathblow *n.* to deal a ~ (they dealt the enemy a ~)

death knell *n.* to sound the ~

deathwatch *n.* to maintain a ~

debar *v.* (formal) (d; tr.) to ~ from

debate I *n.* 1. to conduct, hold; moderate a ~ 2. an acrimonious, bitter; heated, lively, sharp spirited ~ 3. a campaign; parliamentary ~ 4 a ~ about; with

debate II *v.* 1. to ~ heatedly, hotly 2. (D; intr.) to ~ about (to ~ about disarmament) 3. (D; intr.) to ~ with 4. (Q) we ~d what to do

debit *v.* ('to charge') 1. (D; tr.) to ~ against, to (to ~ a purchase against smb.'s account; to ~ an amount to smb.'s account) 2. (D; tr.) to ~ with (~ her account with the entire amount)

debris *n.* to clear ~

debt *n.* 1. to contract, incur, run up a ~; to get into, go into ~ 2. to collect, recover a ~ 3. to discharge, pay (off), settle; wipe out; write off a ~ 4. to cancel; repudiate a ~ 5. a bad; outstanding, unsettled ~ 6. a business; gambling; personal, private ~; the national ~ 7. in ~ for; to (he is in ~ to me for a large sum; deeply in ~) 8. out of ~ (to stay out of ~) 9. (misc.) a ~ of honor

debut *n.* 1. to make one's ~ 2. a ~ as (to make one's ~ as an actor)

decay *n.* 1. to fall into ~ 2. tooth ~ 3. radioactive ~ 4. moral ~

deceit *n.* 1. to practice ~ 2. to expose ~

deceitful *adj.* ~ to + inf. (it was ~ to say such things behind her back)

deceive *v.* (D; refl., tr.) to ~ into (to ~ smb. into doing smt.)

decency *n.* 1. common ~ 2. the ~ to + inf. (he didn't even have the ~ to call) 3. (misc.) to observe the ~cies; a spark of ~

decent *adj.* ~ to + inf. (it was ~ of her to help us)

deception *n.* 1. to practice ~ 2. (a) deliberate ~

decide *v.* 1. to ~ unanimously 2. (d; intr.) (to make a decision') to ~ against (to ~ against buying a car) 3. (d; intr.) ('to choose') to ~ between (it was difficult to ~ between the two) 4. (d; intr.) to ~ for ('to find for') (the jury ~d for the plaintiff)

5. (d; intr.) to ~ on ('to choose in favor of') (we have ~d on a new computer) 6. (E) ('to choose') we ~d to stay home 7. (L) ('to make a decision') she ~d that the children would stay home 8. (Q) ('to make a decision') we could not ~ what to do

decision n. ['act of deciding'] 1. to arrive at, make, reach, take (BE) a ~ 2. (esp. legal) to affirm; appeal; hand down (AE), render a ~ 3. (esp. legal) to overrule, reverse a ~ 4. to reconsider a ~ 5. an arbitrary; clear-cut; crucial; ethical; fair, just; favorable; final; firm; hasty, rash, snap; irreversible, irrevocable; landmark; momentous; unfair; unfavorable ~ 6. a court; split ('divided') ~ 7. a ~ about, on 8. a ~ to + inf. (we made the ~ to accept their offer) 9. the ~ that + clause (we applauded the ~ that taxes would be cut) ['decisiveness'] ['firmness'] 10. to lack ~ 11. of ~ (a man, woman of ~)

deck n. ['pack of playing cards'] (AE) 1. to cut; shuffle a ~ 2. to stack a ~ ('to arrange cards dishonestly') (also fig.) ['floor on a ship'] 3. to swab a ~ 4. a flight; main; poop; promenade; upper ~

deck out v. (D; refl., tr.) to ~ in (~ed out in their Sunday best)

declaration n. 1. to issue, make a ~ 2. a solemn ~ 3. a currency; customs ~

declare v. 1. (B) he ~d his love to her 2. (D; tr.) to ~ against, on (to ~ war on another country) 3. (L) the president ~d that the situation would improve 4. (M) the court ~d the law to be unconstitutional 5. (N; used with a noun, adjective, past participle) the court ~d the law unconstitutional; the government ~d him persona non grata

declension n. an adjective; noun; strong; weak ~

decline I n. 1. to go into, suffer a ~ 2. a gradual; sharp; steady; steep ~ 3. a ~ in (a ~ in trade) 4. on the ~

decline II v. (E) she ~d to address the delegates

decorate v. (D; tr.) ('to give a medal to') to ~ for (to ~ a soldier for valor)

decoration n. ['medal'] 1. to award a ~ 2. (AE) to write smb. up for a ~

decorations n. ['ornaments'] 1. to put up ~ 2. Christmas ~

decorator n. an interior ~

decorum n. 1. to display ~ 2. strict ~

decouple v. (D; tr.) ('to separate') to ~ from

decrease n. 1. a gradual; sharp; steady ~ 2. a ~ in 3. on the ~ (crime is on the ~)

decree I n. 1. to enact; issue a ~ 2. to rescind, revoke a ~ 3. a consent (legal); divorce; executive; government; royal ~ 4. a ~ that + clause; subj. (we had to obey the ~ that beards be/should be shaved off)

decree II v. (formal) (L; may be subj.) the government ~d that a new tax be/should be imposed; the government ~d that it was illegal to traffic in furs

decry v. (formal) (K) she decried their gambling and drinking

dedicate v. (d; refl., tr.) to ~ to (she ~d her life to science; the book was ~d to her husband; they ~d themselves to helping the poor)

dedication n. 1. to demonstrate, display, show ~

2. total ~ 3. ~ to (~ to the cause of freedom) 4. ~ to + inf. (they had the ~ to continue their research in spite of the obstacles)

deduce v. 1. (D; tr.) to ~ from (what can we ~ from these figures?) 2. (L) on the basis of the evidence we ~d that he was guilty 3. (Q) the police were able to ~ where the fugitive was hiding

deduct v. (D; tr.) to ~ from (to ~ a tax from one's wages)

deduction n. ['subtracting'] ['deducting'] 1. to make a ~ 2. a ~ for; from (our employer makes a deduction from our salary for the income tax) ['conclusion'] 3. to make a ~ 4. an illogical; logical ~ 5. a ~ about 6. the ~ that + clause (these events confirm my ~ that he was to blame)

deed I n. ['something done'] 1. to do, perform a ~ 2. a brave, daring, heroic; chivalrous; dirty (colloq.); great; illustrious; kind; noble; wicked ~ 3. in word and ~ ['legal instrument of transfer'] 4. to transfer a ~ 5. a title ~ 6. a ~ to (to hold a ~ to property) 7. by ~ (to transfer property by ~)

deed II v. (AE) (B) ('to transfer') he ~ed the property to his daughter

deem v. (formal) (N; used with an adjective, noun) we ~ her worthy of support

deep adj. 1. ~ in (~ in thought; ~ in the forest) 2. (misc.) the well was forty feet ~

deep water n. ['trouble'] in ~

deer n. 1. a herd of ~ 2. a young ~ is a fawn 3. a female ~ is a doe 4. a male ~ is a buck, stag 5. the meat of a ~ is venison

default I n. by ~ (to lose by ~)

default II v. (D; intr.) to ~ on (to ~ on a debt)

defeat I n. 1. to inflict (formal) a ~ on 2. to meet, suffer (a) ~ (at smb.'s hands) 3. to invite ~ 4. to admit ~ 5. a crushing, decisive, resounding, total, utter; ignominious, shameful ~

defeat II v. to ~ decisively

defect I n. 1. to correct a ~ 2. a glaring ~ 3. a birth, congenital; hearing; mechanical; mental; physical; speech; structural ~ 4. a ~ in (there was a ~ in the transmission)

defect II v. ('to desert') 1. (D; intr.) to ~ from (to ~ from the army) 2. (D; intr.) to ~ to (to ~ to the enemy)

defective adj. ~ in

defence (BE) see **defense**

defenceless (BE) see **defenseless**

defend v. 1. (D; refl., tr.) to ~ against, from (she ~ed herself against the attack) 2. (K) I cannot ~ his drinking on the job

defendant n. to arraign a ~

defender n. 1. a public ~ ('a lawyer who represents poor people at public expense') 2. a staunch ~ (of the faith)

defense, defence n. 1. to conduct, organize, put up a ~ 2. to overwhelm smb.'s ~s 3. an adequate; airtight, impenetrable; heroic; inadequate, weak; strong; stubborn ~ 4. civil; national ~; military ~s 5. (sports) a man-to-man; zone ~ 6. a legal ~ 7. a ~ against, for 8. in ~ of

defenseless, defenceless adj. ~ against (~ against any attack)

defense pact, defence pact n. a mutual ~

defensive I *adj.* ~ about (they were very ~ about their party's record on tax reform)
defensive II *n.* on the ~ (to put smb on the ~)
defer *v.* 1. (D; intr.) to ~ in; to (he ~red to his partner in everything) 2. (formal) (G) we ~red going
deference *n.* 1. to show ~ to 2. in ~ to 3. with all ~ to
deferential *adj.* ['respectful'] ~ to
defiance *n.* ['resistance'] 1. to glare in ~ 2. ~ towards (~ towards all authority) 3. in ~ of (to act in ~ of one's parents)
defiant *adj.* ~ towards
deficiency *n.* ['defect'] ['inadequacy'] 1. a hearing; iron; mental; mineral; vitamin ~ 2. (a) ~ in ['incompleted work'] (as in school) (AE) 3. to make up a ~
deficient *adj.* ~ in
deficit *n.* 1. to make up a ~ 2. an operating; trade ~ 3. a ~ in
define *v.* (D; tr.) to ~ as (we can ~ *burn-out* as *exhaustion*)
defined *adj.* ['outlined, delineated'] 1. sharply ~ 2. ~ against (sharply ~ against a light background)
definite *adj.* 1. ~ about (she was ~ about it) 2. ~ that + clause (is it ~ that they will sign the contract?)
definition *n.* 1. to formulate, give, provide, write a ~ 2. a dictionary; formulaic; referential; synonym ~
deflect *v.* (D; tr.) to ~ from
defraud *v.* (D; tr.) to ~ of (he ~ed them of their money)
defy *v.* (H; passive is rare) she ~fied them to prove her guilty
degenerate *v.* (D; intr.) to ~ from; into
degradation *n.* moral; public ~
degrading *adj.* ~ to + inf. (it was ~ to work in such conditions)
degree *n.* ['academic title'] 1. to award a ~ to; to confer a ~ on 2. to do (BE), earn, receive, take a ~ 3. an academic; advanced, graduate, postgraduate (esp. BE); college ~ 4. an earned; honorary ~ 5. a bachelor's; doctoral, doctor's; master's ~ 6. (BE) a good ~ ('a first or upper second at a British university') 7. a ~ in (to take a ~ in history) ['extent'] ['level'] 8. to achieve a ~ (to achieve a high ~ of proficiency) 9. a great, high, large; slight ~ 10. to a ~ (to a high ~) ['form of an adjective or adverb'] 11. the comparative; positive; superlative ~ ['misc.'] 12. by ~s ('gradually'); (BE; colloq.) to a ~ ('to a very high degree')
deicide *n.* (formal) to commit ~
deign *v.* (formal or humorous) (E) she ~ed to be interviewed
dejected *adj.* ~ to + inf. (he was ~ to learn that he had failed the examination)
dekko *n.* (slang) (BE) ['look'] to have a ~ at
delay I *n.* 1. to brook no ~ 2. a ~ in (she apologized for the ~ in answering)
delay II *v.* 1. (G) we ~ed sending the telegram 2. (K) he ~ed my calling the police

delaying action *n.* to fight a ~
delegate I *n.* 1. a party ~ 2. a ~ at large 3. a ~ to (a ~ to a convention)
delegate II *v.* 1. (B) he ~d his responsibilities to a deputy 2. (H) she was ~d to represent us
delegation *n.* 1. to head a ~ 2. an official, unofficial ~ 3. a ~ from; to
delete *v.* (D; tr.) to ~ from (to ~ smt. from a dossier)
deleterious *adj.* ~ to
deliberate I *adj.* ~ in (~ in one's speech)
deliberate II *v.* 1. (D; intr.) to ~ about, on, over 2. (rare) (Q) we ~d where to meet
deliberations *n.* ~ about
delicacy *n.* 1. extreme, great ~ 2. a matter of extreme ~
delicatessen *n.* kosher ~
delight I *n.* 1. to feel ~; to take ~ in (they took ~ in watching the children play) 2. great, intense, sheer; sardonic ~ 3. ~ at 4. a ~ to + inf. (it was a ~ to watch such fine acting) 5. to smb.'s ~ (to my great ~, our guests arrived on time)
delight II *v.* 1. (d; intr.) to ~ in (to ~ in the beauties of nature) 2. (R) it ~ed me (to learn) that you can attend
delighted *adj.* 1. ~ at, by, with 2. ~ to + inf. (we'll be ~ to come) 3. ~ that + clause (I'm ~ that you were able to visit us)
delightful *adj.* ~ to + inf (it was ~ to swim in the heated pool)
delinquency *n.* 1. juvenile ~ 2. ~ in
delinquent I *adj.* ~ in (~ in paying one's rent)
delinquent II *n.* a juvenile; tax ~
delirium *n.* in a ~
deliver *v.* 1. (B) they ~ed the merchandise to us 2. (formal) (D; tr.) to ~ from (~ us from evil) 3. (pompous) (D; refl.) to ~ of (to ~ oneself of an opinion)
deliverance *n.* (formal) ~ from (~ from captivity)
delivery *n.* ['act of delivering'] ['bringing'] 1. to make a ~ 2. to accept, take ~ 3. an emergency ~; (an) overnight; prompt ~ (we guarantee prompt ~) 4. general (AE); recorded (BE); rural-free (AE); special ~ 5. a ~ to 6. on ~ (payment on ~) ['childbirth'] 7. a breech; normal ~ ['manner of speaking or throwing'] 8. an effective ~
delude *v.* (D; refl., tr.) to ~ into
deluge *v.* (d; tr.) to ~ with (we were ~d with offers)
delusion *n.* 1. to cherish, cling to a ~ 2. a ~ that + clause (he was under a ~ that he would inherit money) 3. under a ~ (to labor under a ~) 4. (misc.) ~s of grandeur
delve *v.* (d; intr.) to ~ into (to ~ into the background of a case)
demand I *n.* ['urgent request'] 1. to make a ~ 2. to meet, satisfy a ~; to give in to, yield to a ~ 3. to reject a ~ 4. to drop a ~ 5. an excessive, exorbitant; inexorable; moderate, modest, reasonable; terroristic ~ 6. union; wage ~s 7. a ~ for; (a ~ for compensation; to make ~s on smb.'s time) 8. a ~ that + clause; subj. (they rejected our demand that no one be/should be punished) 9. at, on ~ (payment on ~) ['desire for a commodity'] 10. to

create a ~ 11. to meet, satisfy a ~ 12. (a) brisk, enormous, great, strong; limited ~ 13. a ~ for (there is a brisk ~ for home computers) 14. in ~ (small cars are in great ~) 15. consumer ~ ['misc.'] 16. the law of supply and ~

demand II v. 1. (D; tr.) to ~ from, of (to ~ an apology from smb.) 2. (E) she ~s to be informed of everything 3. (L; subj.) we ~ed that he help us

demanding adj. ~ of (she is very ~ of her employees)

demarcation n. a ~ between (lines of ~ between the two zones)

demarche n. 1. to make, present a ~ to 2. a diplomatic ~

demean I v. (formal) (D; refl.) ('to degrade') to ~ by (I will not ~ myself by cheating on the examination)

demean II v. (formal) (d; refl.) ('to behave') (he ~ed himself like a gentleman)

demerit n. a ~ for (a ~ for being late)

demobilization n. on, upon ~

democracy n. a constitutional; parliamentary; representative ~

Democrat n. (US) a registered ~

demonstrate v. 1. to ~ convincingly 2. (B) ('to explain by showing') they ~d the new invention to us 3. (D; intr.) ('to protest by marching') to ~ against (the students ~d against the government) 4. (D; intr.) ('to display support by marching') to ~ for (to ~ for lower taxes) 5. (L; to) ('to prove by showing') we ~d (to them) that a new computer would save considerable time 6. (Q) ('to explain by showing') she ~d how the computer works

demonstration n. ['explanation'] 1. to give, put on a ~ ['protest'] 2. to organize, stage a ~ 3. a mass; organized; public; spontaneous; staged; student ~ 4. a ~ against

demote v. (D; tr.) to ~ from; to (he was ~d to the rank of corporal)

demur v. (formal) (D; intr.) ('to object') to ~ at, to (to ~ at a proposal)

den n. a gambling; opium ~; a ~ of iniquity

denial n. 1. to issue a ~ 2. a flat; outright; strong; unqualified ~ 3. a ~ that + clause (they issued a ~ that their firm had been involved)

denomination n. ['group'] a religious ~ (to belong to a religious ~)

denominator n. 1. to find the lowest common ~ 2. a common ~

denounce v. 1. to ~ roundly 2. (B) to ~ smb. to the police 3. (D; tr.) to ~ as (to ~ smb. as an illegal alien) 4. (K) she ~d his drinking

density n. population; traffic ~

dent n. 1. to make a ~ in (he made a ~ in the door; to make a ~ in the backlog of work) 2. to hammer out, remove, straighten out a ~

denture n. a partial ~

denude v. (D; tr.) to ~ of (the hillside was ~d of trees)

denunciation n. 1. to issue, make a ~ 2. a bitter, scathing, strong, vehement; sweeping ~

deny v. 1. to ~ categorically, emphatically, fervently, flatly, strongly, vehemently 2. (A; usu. used without to) he ~ies himself nothing; they

were ~ied admittance; to ~ smb. bail; Everton's defence ~ied Liverpool the winning goal; he ~ies nothing to his family; or: he ~ies his family nothing 3. (G) she ~ied knowing anything 4. (L) she ~ied that she had been there 5. (rare) (M) he ~ied it to be the case

deodorant n. 1. to apply, put on a ~ 2. a cream; roll-on; spray; stick; underarm ~

depart v. 1. (D; intr.) to ~ for (to ~ for London) 2. (D; intr.) to ~ from (our train ~s from platform G)

department n. ['division of a school, of a university'] 1. a strong; weak ~ 2. an accounting; anthropology; astronomy; biology; chemistry; classics; economics; English; French; geology; German; history; Italian; linguistics; mathematics; music; nursing; philosophy; physics; political science; psychology; Slavic, Slavonic; sociology; Spanish ~ ['division of a company or government'] 3. an accounting; finance; fire (AE); health; personnel; police; recreation; sanitation; service ~ ['division of a hospital'] 4. a casualty (BE), emergency (AE) ~

departure n. 1. to mark a ~ from (this marks a ~ from established procedures) 2. a sudden ~ 3. a ~ for 4. a ~ from

depend see **depend on**

dependence n. 1. drug ~ 2. ~ on, upon

dependency n. 1. a colonial ~ 2. drug ~

dependent adj. ~ for; on, upon (he is ~ on his parents for support)

depend on, **depend upon** v. 1. (D; intr.) to ~ for (to ~ smb. for advice) 2. (H) you can ~ her to be there

depict v. 1. (B) they ~ed the situation to us in great detail 2. (d; tr.) to ~ as (he was ~ed as a traitor) 3. (J) the artist ~ed him strolling through a garden

deplete v. (D; tr.) to ~ of

deplorable adj. ~ that + clause (it is ~ that such corruption exists)

deplore v. 1. to ~ deeply, thoroughly 2. (K) we ~ their taking drugs

deport I v. (formal) ('to behave') 1. (d; refl.) to ~ like (he ~ed himself like a gentleman) 2. (P; refl.) to ~ oneself well

deport II v. (D; tr.) ('to send out of the country') to ~ from; to

depose v. (D; tr.) to ~ from

deposit I n. ['money put into a bank account'] 1. to make a ~ 2. a demand; time ~ 3. on ~ (the money was on ~ in a bank) ['down payment'] 4. to give, leave a ~ on 5. to forfeit one's ~

deposit II v. (D; tr.) to ~ in (to ~ money in a bank)

deposition n. (legal) 1. (of a witness) to make a ~ 2. (of a lawyer) to defend; notice; take a ~ 3. a sworn ~ 4. a ~ that (he made a ~ that he had witnessed the accident)

deposits n. coal; mineral; oil ~

depot n. an ammunition; freight (AE) ~

depreciate v. (D; intr.) to ~ in (to ~ in value)

depress v. (formal) (R) it ~ed everyone that no progress was made during the negotiations

depressed *adj.* 1. ~ at (~ at the bad news) 2. ~ to + inf. (she was ~ to learn of her illness)

depressing *adj.* 1. ~ to + inf. (it is ~ to read the headlines) 2. ~ that + clause (it's ~ that so many young people use drugs)

depression *n.* ['low economic activity'] 1. to cause a ~ 2. a major, severe; minor ~ 3. an economic ~ ['dejection'] 4. to cause ~ 5. chronic; deep, severe, total ~ (he was in a state of total ~)

depressor *n.* a tongue ~

deprivation *n.* to suffer ~

deprive *v.* (d; tr.) to ~ of (to ~ smb. of everything)

depth *n.* ['distance from the top to bottom'] ['distance from front to back'] 1. in ~ (the river is thirty feet in ~) ['place at the bottom of a body of water'] 2. to reach a ~ (the divers reached great ~s) ['capability'] 3. beyond, out of one's ~ ['worst part'] 4. in the ~s (in the ~s of the depression) ['misc.'] 5. in ~ ('thoroughly'); to plumb the ~s of smt. ('to get to the root of smt.'); in the ~s of despair; to lack ~ ('to be superficial')

depth charge *n.* to drop a ~

depute *v.* (formal) (BE) 1. (B) ('to assign') (he ~d the bookkeeping to me while he was away) 2. (H) ('to appoint as deputy') to ~ smb. to do smt.

deputize *v.* 1. (esp. AE) (D; tr.) ('to appoint') to ~ as (he ~d me as his assistant) 2. (BE) (D; intr.) to ~ for ('to replace') (to ~ for smb. as secretary) 3. (AE) (H) ('to appoint as deputy') to ~ smb. to do smt.

deputy *n.* a special ~

deranged *adj.* mentally ~

derelict I *adj.* ~ in (~ in one's duty)

derelict II *n.* a human ~

derision *n.* 1. to arouse, provoke ~ 2. an object of ~

derive *v.* 1. (d; intr.) ('to come') to ~ from (many words ~ from Latin) 2. (D; tr.) ('to trace') to ~ from (to ~ a word from a Latin root) 3. (D; tr.) ('to receive') to ~ from (to ~ pleasure from music)

derogatory *adj.* ~ of, to, towards

descend *v.* 1. (d; intr.) to ~ from ('to come down from') (do you know from whom you are ~ed?) 2. (d; intr.) ('to swoop down') to ~ on, upon (the guerrillas ~ed on the village) 3. (d; intr.) ('to stoop') to ~ to (to ~ to a life of petty crime)

descendant *n.* a direct ~

descended *adj.* (cannot stand alone) 1. directly ~ 2. ~ from (~ from a royal family)

descent *n.* ['origin'] 1. to trace one's ~ 2. direct ~ 3. ~ from 4. of a certain ~ ['decline'] 5. a gradual, steep ~

describe *v.* 1. to ~ minutely; vividly 2. (B) she ~d the scene to us 3. (D; refl., tr.) to ~ as (he was ~d as being very cruel) 4. (K) she ~d in detail their resisting the invaders 5. (Q) he ~d how we should proceed

description *n.* 1. to give, provide a ~ 2. to answer to a ~ (he answers to the ~ of the escaped convict) 3. to beggar, defy ~ 4. an accurate, correct, exact; blow-by-blow; clear; detailed; thorough; firsthand; glowing; lively, picturesque, vivid; mat-

ter-of-fact, objective; superficial ~ 5. a job ~

desensitize *v.* (D; tr.) to ~ to (to ~ smb. to suffering)

desert I *n.* 1. to reclaim a ~ 2. an arid; trackless ~ 3. a cultural ~

desert II *v.* 1. (D; tr.) to ~ for (to ~ the stage for Hollywood) 2. (D; intr.) to ~ from (he ~ed from his regiment) 3. (D; intr.) to ~ to (to ~ to the enemy)

deserts *n.* ['reward'] ['punishment'] to get one's just ~

deserve *v.* 1. to ~ richly 2. (E) she ~d to win 3. (G) he ~d being recommended for a decoration 4. (misc.) to ~ ill of; to ~ well of

deserving *adj.* 1. richly ~ 2. ~ of (~ of help)

design I *n.* ['plan'] 1. a ~ for (a ~ for a new library) ['intention'] 2. by ~ (was it by accident or by ~?)

design II *v.* 1. (C) he ~ed a beautiful house for us; or: he ~ed us a beautiful house 2. (d; tr.) to ~ as 3. (d; tr.) to ~ for (~ed for recreational purposes)

designate I *adj.* (placed after a noun) a minister ~

designate II *v.* 1. (D; tr.) to ~ as (the state was ~d as a disaster area) 2. (H) we ~d him to serve as our delegate 3. (N; used with a noun) the state was ~d a disaster area

designation *n.* a ~ as

designed *adj.* (cannot stand alone) 1. ~ for ~ for use in cold climates) 2. ~ to + inf. (the equipment is ~ to operate at any altitude)

designer *n.* an aircraft; fashion; interior ~

designs *n.* ['evil intentions'] 1. to have ~ against, on, upon (to have ~ on smb.'s money) 2. sinister ~

desirable *adj.* 1. ~ to + inf. (it is ~ to wait) 2. ~ that + clause; subj. (it is ~ that you be/should be there by two o'clock)

desire I *n.* 1. to arouse, create, whet (a) ~ 2. to express, voice a ~ 3. to feel a ~ 4. to satisfy a ~ 5. to stifle, suppress a ~ 6. (an) ardent, blind, burning, earnest, fervent, intense, keen, overwhelming, passionate, strong; sincere; unfulfilled ~ 7. animal; sexual ~s 8. a ~ for 9. a ~ to + inf. (a ~ to excel) 10. a ~ that + clause; subj. (it was her ~ that the estate be/should be divided evenly)

desire II *v.* 1. to deeply, fervently, strongly ~ 2. (E) she ~s to remain neutral in the dispute 3. (formal) (H) to ~ smb. to do smt. 4. (formal) (L; subj.) I ~ that he be present

desirous *adj.* (formal) 1. (cannot stand alone) ~ of (~ of fame) 2. ~ that; subj. (he is ~ that you be/ should be there)

desist *v.* (formal) (D; intr.) to ~ from (to ~ from further litigation)

desk *n.* ['counter'] 1. (in a hotel) a front (AE), reception (BE) ~ ['department'] 2. (at a newspaper) a city; copy ~ ['table for writing'] 3. to clear one's ~ 4. a cluttered ~ 5. a rolltop; writing ~ USAGE NOTE: In AE *copy desk* means 'local news desk'; in BE it means 'financial news desk'.

desolation *n.* complete, utter ~

despair I *n.* 1. to overcome ~ 2. deep, sheer, total, utter ~ 3. the depths of ~ 4. in ~ (in utter ~) 5. out of ~ (to do smt. out of ~)

despair II v. 1. to ~ deeply 2. (D; intr.) to ~ of (to ~ of success)

despatch (rare) (BE) see **dispatch**

desperate adj. ~ for (~ for help)

desperation n. in ~

despicable adj. ~ to + inf. (it was ~ of him to desert his family)

despise v. 1. to ~ utterly 2. (D; tr.) to ~ for (I ~d him for his cowardice) 3. (K) I ~ his refusing to accept responsibility

despoil v. (formal) (D; tr.) to ~ of

despondent adj. ~ about, over

despot n. an absolute; benevolent; enlightened ~

destination n. 1. to reach one's ~; to arrive at one's ~ 2. one's final, ultimate ~

destine v. 1. (d; tr.) to ~ for 2. (H) fate ~d her to go far in life

destined adj. (cannot stand alone) 1. ~ for (the shipment is ~ for New York) 2. ~ to + inf. (she was ~ from birth to become president)

destiny n. 1. to achieve, fulfill one's ~ 2. to decide, shape smb.'s ~ 3. Manifest Destiny 4. ~ to + inf. (it was her ~ to make an important medical discovery)

destitute adj. ~ of (~ of feeling)

destitution n. in ~ (to die in ~)

destroyer n. a tank ~

destruction n. 1. to carry out ~ (with a human subject: the soldiers carried out the total ~ of the village) 2. to cause ~ (with any subject: the flood caused great ~) 3. complete, total, utter; wanton ~

destructive adj. ~ of

detach v. (D; tr.) to ~ from (the officer was ~ed temporarily from his unit)

detail I n. ['small part'] ['minute treatment'] 1. to bring up, cite ~s 2. to go into ~; to fill in, furnish (the) ~s 3. essential, important; (a) graphic, gruesome, harrowing, lurid, revolting, sordid, unsavory; meticulous, microscopic, minute; petty ~; a mere, minor; technical ~ (they went into lurid ~; they brought up petty ~s; the newspapers wrote of the gruesome ~s; he described the event in graphic ~; only the police knew the sordid ~s of the crime; can you fill in the technical ~s?) 4. in ~ (to treat a topic in minute ~) ['detachment'] (usu. mil.) 5. to form a ~ 6. a fatigue, work ~

detail II v. (usu. mil.) (D; tr.) ('to assign') to ~ for (to ~ a unit for fatigue duty)

detained adj. unavoidably ~

detective n. an amateur; house (obsol.); private ~

detector n. a lie; mine; smoke ~

detention n. in ~ (he was kept in ~ for two hours)

deter v. (D; tr.) to ~ from

detergent n. (a) laundry; liquid ~

determination n. ['decisiveness'] 1. to show ~ 2. dogged, firm, great, iron, sheer, unflinching, unyielding ~ ['firm intention'] 3. ~ to + inf. (I admire her ~ to succeed) ['judicial decision'] 4. to come to a ~ (of a case) 5. the final ~ (of a case)

determine v. 1. (rare) (E) he ~d to learn English (more usu. is: he is ~d to learn English) 2. (L) the police ~d that no crime had been committed 3. (Q) we must ~ where the conference will take place

determined adj. ~ to + inf. (she is ~ to finish law school)

deterrent n. 1. a nuclear ~; the ultimate ~ 2. a ~ to

detest v. 1. (G) he ~s working 2. (K) we ~ his constantly lying

detestable adj. ~ to + inf. (it is ~ to speak like that; it was ~ of them to do that)

detour n. 1. to set up a ~ 2. to follow, make, take a ~ 3. a ~ around

detract v. (d; intr., tr.) to ~ from (the scandal will not ~ from his fame)

detriment n. 1. a ~ to 2. to the ~ of

detrimental adj. ~ to (smoking is ~ to health)

devastation n. 1. to cause ~ 2. complete, total, utter ~

develop v. (D; intr.) to ~ from; into (to ~ from a child into an adult)

developer n. a property (BE); real-estate (AE) ~

development n. 1. arrested; economic; historical; intellectual; physical ~ 2. a housing ~ 3. (BE) a ribbon ~ ('line of similar buildings constructed along roads leading out of a town')

deviate v. 1. to ~ sharply 2. (D; intr.) to ~ from

deviation n. 1. a sharp ~ 2. a ~ from

device n. 1. a detonating; intrauterine; flotation; labor-saving; listening; mnemonic ~ 2. a ~ for 3. (misc.) left to one's own ~s ('on one's own')

devil n. ['spirit of evil'] 1. go to the ~! ('damn you!') ['severe reprimand'] (esp. AE) 2. to catch the ~ ['fellow'] (colloq.) 3. a lucky; poor ~ ['disturbed state'] 4. in a ~ of a mess ['misc.'] 5. where in the ~ did she go?

devoid adj. (cannot stand alone) ~ of (~ of any redeeming features)

devolve v. (formal) (d; intr.) ('to be transferred') to ~ on, upon (his duties ~d on his deputy)

devote v. 1. to ~ oneself completely, entirely 2. (D; refl., tr.) to ~ to (he ~d himself to his work; we must ~ a lot of time to this project)

devoted adj. 1. blindly, completely, entirely ~ 2. ~ to (~ to one's family)

devotee n. a ~ of (a ~ of the theater)

devotion n. 1. to demonstrate, display, show ~ 2. absolute, blind, complete, deep, great, slavish, thorough, undying, unswerving, utter ~ 3. ~ to (blind ~ to the cause) 4. the ~ to + inf. (does she have enough ~ to serve without pay?)

devour v. to ~ eagerly, ravenously

dexterity n. 1. to demonstrate, display, show ~ 2. great; manual ~ 3. the ~ to + inf. (does he have enough ~ to cope with a job like that?)

diabetes n. to develop ~

diagnosis n. 1. to make a ~ 2. to confirm a ~ 3. (med.) differential ~ 4. a ~ that + clause (further studies confirmed the ~ that the tumor was benign)

diagonal I adj. ~ to

diagonal II n. on the ~ (to cut on the ~)

diagram n. to draw a ~

dial I n. to turn a ~

dial II v. to ~ direct, directly (she ~led London direct)

dialect *n.* 1. to speak (in) a ~ 2. a local, regional; social; standard ~

dialing, dialling *n.* direct ~

dialogue *n.* 1. to have a ~ with 2. a meaningful ~ 3. a ~ between; with

diamond *n.* 1. to cut; grind; polish; set a ~ 2. a cut; flawless, perfect; industrial; rough, uncut ~ 3. a ~ sparkles

diaper *n.* (AE) 1. to change, put on a ~ 2. disposable ~s (BE has *nappy*)

diaphragm *n.* ['contraceptive device'] to insert a ~

diarrhea, diarrhoea *n.* 1. to come down with; have ~ 2. severe ~ 3. an attack of ~

diary *n.* 1. to keep a ~ 2. a personal ~

diatribe *n.* 1. to utter a ~ 2. a bitter ~ 3. a ~ against

dice *n.* 1. to roll, throw (the) ~ 2. crooked, loaded ~ 3. a roll of the ~

dicker *v.* to ~ for; with

dictate *v.* 1. (D; intr., tr.) to ~ to (she was ~ing to her secretary; the conqueror ~s terms to the conquered) 2. (Q) they ~d how everything would be done

dictation *n.* 1. to give ~ 2. to take, take down ~

dictator *n.* an absolute; benevolent; brutal; military; ruthless ~

dictatorship *n.* 1. to establish, set up a ~ 2. an absolute; benevolent; brutal; military; ruthless ~

diction *n.* clear ~

dictionary *n.* 1. to compile a ~ 2. to expand; revise; update a ~ 3. to consult a ~ 4. an abridged, desk; bilingual; biographical; college, collegiate (AE); combinatorial, combinatory; dialect; etymological; general-use, general-purpose; historical; learner's; medical; monolingual; multivolume; names; orthographic, spelling; phonetic, pronouncing; pocket; reverse; technical; unabridged ~ 5. a ~ of abbreviations; collocations; foreign words; synonyms

die I *n.* the ~ is cast (fig.)

die II *v.* 1. to ~ hard; heroically (rumors ~ hard; he died heroically at the front) 2. (d; intr.) to ~ by (to ~ by the sword; to ~ by one's own hand) 3. (d; intr.) to ~ for (to ~ for one's beliefs) 4. (colloq.) (d; intr.) (only in the progressive) to ~ for ('to want') (she's dying for a cup of coffee) 5. to ~ from, of (he died of tuberculosis; to ~ of natural causes) 6. (colloq.) (E) (only in the progressive) ('to want') she's dying to find out 7. (misc.) to ~ in action; to ~ in battle; (fig.) to ~ laughing; (legal) to ~ intestate

diet *n.* 1. to be on, follow, stick to a ~; to go on a ~ 2. to prescribe a ~ 3. a balanced, well-balanced; bland; crash; reducing; special; starvation; steady; therapeutic ~ 4. a high-calorie; high-carbohydrate; high-fiber, high-fibre; high-protein; low-calorie; low-carbohydrate; low-cholesterol; low-residue; low-salt, low-sodium; salt-free ~

differ *v.* 1. (D; intr.) to ~ about, on 2. (D; intr.) to ~ from (this arrangement ~s from the one I had in mind) 3. (D; intr.) to ~ on; with (I ~ with you on that point)

difference *n.* 1. to make a ~ 2. to tell the ~ 3. to compose, reconcile, resolve, settle, thrash out ~s

4. to set aside ~s 5. to split the ~ ('to take an average') 6. a considerable, great, marked, noticeable, striking; essential; irreconcilable; minor, slight; radical; subtle; superficial ~ 7. a ~ among, between; from 8. a ~ in (a ~ in age) 9. a ~ to (that makes no ~ to me) 10. (misc.) a world of ~ ('a considerable difference')

different *adj.* 1. basically, entirely, radically ~ 2. ~ from, than (AE), to (BE) USAGE NOTE: Some purists consider only *different from* to be correct. Note that when a clause follows, *than* becomes a conjunction, but *from* and *to* remain prepositions--different than we thought; different from/to what we thought

differentiate *v.* 1. (d; intr.) to ~ between 2. (d; tr.) to ~ from

differentiation *n.* to make a ~ between

difficult *adj.* 1. ~ for (typing is ~ for me) 2. ~ to + inf. (it is ~ to please him = he is ~ to please = he is a ~ person to please; it is ~ to translate this book = this book is ~ to translate = this is a ~ book to translate; it is ~ for me to translate such material = such material is ~ for me to translate)

difficulty *n.* 1. to cause, create, make, present ~ties for 2. to come across, encounter, experience, face, meet, run into ~ties 3. to clear up, overcome, resolve, surmount a ~ 4. (a) grave, great, insurmountable, serious, severe ~ 5. economic, financial ~ties 6. a ~ arises 7. ~ in (she has ~ in breathing = she has ~ breathing) 8. in ~ (he is in serious ~)

diffuse *v.* (formal) (D; tr.) to ~ through (~d through the air)

dig I *n.* (colloq.) ['excavation'] 1. to go on a ~ 2. an archeological ~ ['poke'] 3. to give smb. a ~ (in the ribs)

dig II *v.* 1. (D; intr.) to ~ for ('to search for') (to ~ for gold) 2. (d; intr.) ('to delve') to ~ into (□ ~ into a report) 3. (d; intr., tr.) ('to jab') to ~ into (his elbow was ~ging into my ribs; he dug his spurs into the sides of the horse)

dignitary *n.* visiting ~ries

dignity *n.* 1. to possess ~ 2. to maintain one's ~ 3. the ~ to + inf. (does he have enough ~ to cope with a hostile press?) 4. (misc.) to live in ~; to die in/with ~

digress *v.* (D; intr.) to ~ from

digression *n.* ['act of digressing'] 1. a ~ from ['digressive remarks'] 2. a ~ on (he launched into a ~ on the need for more power plants)

dilate *v.* (formal) (d; intr.) ('to speak or write in detail') to ~ on, upon (to ~ upon a subject)

dilemma *n.* 1. to resolve a ~ 2. in a ~ 3. (misc.) on the horns of a ~

diligence *n.* 1. (legal) due ~ 2. the ~ to + inf. (does she have enough ~ to finish the job on time?)

diligent *adj.* ~ in (~ in one's work)

dillydally *v.* (D; intr.) to ~ with

dimension *n.* ['importance'] 1. to assume, take on a ~ (the issue assumed serious ~s) 2. (misc.) a problem of international ~s ['measurement'] (can be fig.) 3. a third ~ 4. in a ~ (in two ~s)

din *n.* ['noise'] 1. to make a ~ 2. above the ~

dine v. 1. (D; intr.) to ~ on ('to eat') (to ~ on steak) 2. (misc.) to ~ at home; to ~ out
dining n. congregate ~
dinner n. 1. to eat, have ~ 2. to make, prepare ~ 3. a TV ~ 4. at, during ~ 5. for ~ (what will we have for ~?)
dint n. by ~ of (by ~ of hard work)
dip I n. ['short swim'] 1. to have (BE), take a ~ ['semiliquid food'] 2. a cheese ~
dip II v. (d; intr.) to ~ into ('to withdraw from') (to ~ into one's savings)
diphtheria n. to come down with, contract; prevent ~
diploma n. 1. to award, confer, present a ~ 2. a college; high-school (AE) ~ 3. a ~ in (a ~ in Applied Linguistics)
diplomacy n. 1. to rely on, resort to ~ 2. dollar; gunboat; media; public; quiet; shuttle ~ 3. megaphone ~ (using public propaganda rather than negotiations)
diplomat n. a career, professional ~
diplomatic immunity n. 1. to grant ~ 2. to have ~ 3. to withdraw ~
direct v. 1. (d; tr.) ('to point') to ~ against, at (they ~ed the attacks against the enemy's seaports) 2. (d; tr.) ('to address') to ~ at, to (the remark was ~ed at you) 3. (D; tr.) ('to guide') to ~ to (can you ~ me to the post office?) 4. (d; tr.) ('to aim') to ~ to, towards (our efforts were ~ed towards the elimination of poverty) 5. (H) ('to order') he ~ed us to remain silent 6. (L; subj.) ('to order') the government ~ed that supplies be sent to the flooded areas
direction n. ['course'] 1. the opposite; right; wrong ~ ['supervision'] 2. under smb.'s ~ ['guidance'] 3. to give ~ to
directions n. ['instructions'] 1. to give, issue ~ 2. to follow ~ 3. ~ for 4. ~ that + clause; subj. (she gave ~ that her estate be given/should be given to charity)
directive n. 1. to issue a ~ 2. a ~ that + clause; may be used with the subj. (the government issued a ~ that all firearms be/must be handed in)
director n. an acting; athletic; casting; funeral; managing; music; program ~
directorate n. interlocking ~s
directory n. a city; telephone ~
dirge n. a funeral ~
dirt n. 1. in the ~ (to play in the ~) 2. (misc.) to hit the ~ ('to fall to the ground')
disability n. a learning; physical ~ (children with learning ~ties)
disabled adj., n. learning; physically ~ (learning ~ children; help for the learning ~)
disabuse v. (D; tr.) to ~ of
disadvantage n. 1. to offset, outweigh a ~ 2. a decided ~ 3. a ~ for, to 4. a ~ to + inf. (it was a ~ not to have a car available = it was a ~ not having a car available) 5. at a ~ (that places me at a decided ~)
disadvantageous adj. ~ to
disagree v. 1. to ~ completely; sharply 2. (D; intr.) to ~ about, on; with
disagreeable adj. ~ to

disagreement n. 1. to express a ~ 2. to resolve a ~ 3. a bitter, marked, serious, sharp; slight ~ 4. a ~ among, between, with 5. a ~ about, over
disappear v. 1. to ~ completely 2. (D; intr.) to ~ from (to ~ from view)
disappearance n. a mysterious; sudden ~
disappoint v. (formal) (R) it ~ed everyone that she did not win the prize
disappointed adj. 1. deeply ~ 2. ~ about, at, in, with (~ at/with the results; I was ~ in/with him) 3. ~ to + inf. (she was ~ to learn that she had failed the course) 4. ~ that + clause (we are ~ that you will not be able to attend)
disappointing adj. 1. ~ to + inf. (it is ~ to analyze the results) 2. ~ that + inf. (it's ~ that so few showed up)
disappointment n. 1. to express; feel ~ 2. (a) bitter, deep, great, keen, profound ~ 3. ~ about, at, over (she felt deep ~ at not getting the job) 4. ~ that + clause (he expressed keen ~ that the hearing had been postponed) 5. to smb.'s ~ (to our great ~, it started to rain)
disapproval n. 1. to express (one's) ~ 2. strong ~
disapprove v. 1. to ~ completely, strongly, thoroughly, utterly 2. (D; intr.) to ~ of (they ~d strongly of my proposal)
disarmament n. general, universal; multilateral; nuclear; phased; unilateral ~
disarray n. 1. total ~ 2. in ~ (to break up in total ~)
disassociate, dissociate v. (D; refl.) to ~ from USAGE NOTE: Some purists prefer dissociate.
disaster n. 1. to cause a ~ 2. to experience, meet, suffer (a) ~ 3. to court ~ 4. to cope with; recover from (a) ~ 5. to avert (a) ~ 6. a catastrophic, devastating, major, tragic, unqualified ~ 7. an impending; national; natural; near ~
disastrous adj. 1. ~ to 2. ~ to + inf. (it would be ~ to wait)
disbar v. (D; tr.) to ~ from (to ~ from practice)
disbelief n. 1. complete, total, utter ~ 2. ~ in
disburse v. (B) to ~ funds to the states
disc n. ['tag'] (BE) (mil.) 1. an identification ~ ['recording'] 2. to cut a ~ (see **disk**)
discharge I n. 1. a dishonorable; general; honorable; medical ~ (from the armed forces) 2. a ~ from (a ~ from the hospital)
discharge II v. 1. (D; tr.) to ~ from (to ~ smb. from hospital/from the hospital) 2. (D; tr.) to ~ into (to ~ waste into a river)
disciple n. an ardent, devoted; fanatical ~
discipline I n. 1. to establish; maintain ~ 2. to crack down on violations of ~ 3. to undermine ~ 4. to violate ~ 5. firm, harsh, iron, severe, stern, strict; lax, loose, slack; military; party ~ 6. the ~ to + inf. (they didn't have enough ~ to cope with the job)
discipline II v. 1. (D; tr.) to ~ for 2. (H; usu. refl.) (she ~d herself to exercise every day)
disciplined adj. highly ~
disclose v. 1. (B) the authorities finally ~d the facts to the press 2. (L) the report ~d that he had served time in prison
disclosure n. 1. to make a ~ 2. a financial; public;

sensational, startling ~ 3. a ~ that + clause (the ~ that he had been in prison ruined his chances for public office)

discomfort *n.* 1. to cause ~ 2. to bear ~ 3. to alleviate ~ 4. physical ~

disconcert *v.* (formal) (R) it ~ed us (to learn) that they had refused our offer

disconcerting *adj.* 1. ~ to + inf. (it is ~ to watch them make one mistake after the other) 2. ~ that + clause (it is ~ that so many pupils have dropped out of school)

disconnect *v.* (D; tr.) to ~ from

disconsolate *adj.* ~ about, at, over

discontent *n.* 1. to cause, stir up ~ 2. outspoken; widespread ~ 3. ~ about, at, with

discontinue *v.* (G) she ~d paying rent

discord *n.* 1. to arouse, generate, stir up; spread ~ 2. domestic, family ~ 3. ~ among, between 4. ~ in (~ in one's family relationships)

discount *n.* 1. to give a ~ 2. a cash ~ 3. a ~ on (to give a ~ on all purchases) 4. at a ~ (she sold it at a ~)

discourage *v.* (D; tr.) to ~ from

discouraged *adj.* 1. deeply ~ 2. ~ at, about, over 3. ~ to + inf. (we were ~ to see that many students had failed)

discouragement *n.* deep ~

discouraging *adj.* 1. deeply ~ 2. ~ to + inf. (it is ~ to read the newspapers) 3. ~ that + clause (it's ~ that so little progress has been made in banning nuclear weapons)

discourse I *n.* (grammar) direct; indirect ~

discourse II *v.* (formal) (D; intr.) to ~ upon

discourteous *adj.* 1. ~ to 2. ~ to + inf. (it was ~ of him to say that)

discourtesy *n.* 1. to show ~ 2. (a) grave ~

discover *v.* 1. (J) I ~ed them swimming in our pool 2. (L) we ~ed that he can cook 3. (rare) (M) we ~ed him to be a good cook 4. (Q) I never have ~ed how it works

discovery *n.* ['finding'] 1. to make a ~ 2. a dramatic; exciting, startling, world-shaking; scientific ~ 3. a ~ that + clause (we made the exciting ~ that exercise can be fun) ['pretrial disclosure of facts'] (legal) 4. to conduct ~

discredit *n.* 1. to bring ~ on, to 2. a ~ to (a ~ to one's family)

discreet *adj.* (it was not ~ of you to say that)

discrepancy *n.* 1. a glaring, striking, wide ~ 2. a ~ between; in

discretion *n.* 1. to exercise, show, use ~ in 2. complete, full, wide ~ 3. ~ to + inf. (she has full ~ to make decisions) 4. at one's ~ (to act at one's own ~) 5. with ~ (to proceed with ~)

discriminate *v.* 1. (D; intr.) to ~ against (to ~ against minorities) 2. (d; intr.) to ~ among, between 3. (d; tr.) to ~ from (to ~ right from wrong)

discrimination *n.* 1. to practice ~ 2. to subject smb. to ~ 3. age; racial; religious; reverse; sex ~ 4. ~ against

discus *n.* to throw the ~

discuss *v.* 1. (D; tr.) to ~ with (to ~ smt. with smb.) 2. (Q) we ~ed how we would do it

discussion *n.* 1. to arouse, provoke, stir up (a) ~ 2. to have; lead a ~ 3. to bring smt. up for ~; to come up for ~ 4. an animated, brisk, heated, lively, spirited; brief; candid, frank, open; lengthy; peaceful, quiet; serious ~ 5. a group; panel; round-table ~ (to lead a panel ~) 6. a ~ about, of 7. under ~ (their case is now under ~)

disdain *n.* ~ for (to have the greatest ~ for smt.)

disdainful *adj.* ~ of; towards

disease *n.* 1. to come down with, contract a ~ 2. to carry; spread (a) ~ 3. to cure; prevent (a) ~ 4. to eradicate, stamp out, wipe out (a) ~; to bring a ~ under control 5. an acute; common; deadly degenerative; fatal, terminal; incurable, untreatable; lingering; mild; protracted; rare; serious ~ 6. an acquired; chronic; communicable, contagious, infectious; congenital; mental; occupational; sexually transmitted, social, venereal; skin; tropical ~ 7. Addison's; Alzheimer's; caisson; foot-and-mouth; heart; Hodgkin's; Legionnaire's ~ 8. a ~ spreads 9. the outbreak of a ~

disembark *v.* (D; intr.) to ~ from

disengage *v.* (formal) (D; refl., tr.) to ~ from

disentangle *v.* (D; refl., tr.) to ~ from

disfavor, disfavour *n.* 1. to fall into ~ with 2. in ~

disfigured *adj.* badly ~

disgrace I *n.* 1. to bring; suffer ~ 2. deep; public ~ 3. a ~ to (he is a ~ to his family) 4. a ~ to ~ inf. (it was a ~ to behave like that = it was a ~ behaving like that) 5. a ~ that (it's a ~ that these roads are so poorly marked) 6. in ~ (he quit in ~ over the bribe)

disgrace II *v.* (D; refl., tr.) to ~ by (he ~d himself by getting drunk)

disgraceful *adj.* ~ to + inf. (it was ~ to behave like that = it was ~ behaving like that)

disgruntled *adj.* ~ at, over, with

disguise I *n.* 1. to assume a ~ 2. to shed, throw off a ~ 3. a clever ~ 4. in ~

disguise II *v.* 1. thinly ~d 2. (D; tr.) to ~ as (he was ~d as a waiter)

disgust I *n.* 1. to express; feel ~ 2. ~ at, with 3. in ~ (he left in great ~) 4. to one's ~ (to my ~ I discovered that...)

disgust II *v.* 1. to ~ thoroughly 2. (R) it ~ed everyone that he had taken bribes

disgusted *adj.* 1. ~ at, with 2. ~ to + inf. (she was ~ to see him drunk) 3. ~ that + clause (I am ~ that he is absent again)

disgusting *adj.* 1. ~ to + inf. (it was ~ to watch) 2. ~ that + clause (it's ~ that the crime rate is so high)

dish *n.* ['food served in a dish'] 1. a favorite; main; side ~ ['container for food'] 2. a chafing ~

disharmony *n.* to stir up ~

dishearten *v.* (formal) (R) it ~ed all of us (to learn) that she had been dismissed

disheartened *adj.* 1. ~ at 2. ~ to + inf. (he was ~ to learn of the bad news)

disheartening *adj.* 1. ~ to + inf. (it is ~ to read the daily press) 2. ~ that + clause (it was ~ that so few passed the test)

dishes *n.* ['dirty utensils left after a meal'] 1. to do, wash; rinse; stack the ~ 2. dirty ~ 3. plastic ~

['containers for holding food'] 4. a set of ~
USAGE NOTE: BE usu. uses *to wash up* rather
than *to do, wash the dishes.*
dishonest *adj.* ~ to + inf. (it is ~ to lie about one's
age)
dishonor, dishonour *n.* 1. to bring ~ on, to 2. a ~
to
dish out *v.* (B) he was ~ing out food to the women
dishwasher *n.* 1. to load, stack a ~ 2. an automatic
~
disinclined *adj.* (cannot stand alone) ~ to + inf.
(he seems ~ to put up resistance)
disk *n.* ['structure in a spinal column'] 1. to slip
('dislocate') a ~ 2. a slipped ~ ['flat plate for computer storage'] 3. to format; make a ~; to copy
onto a ~ 4. a back-up; fixed, hard; floppy ~
USAGE NOTE: BE prefers the spelling *disc* for
1 and 2.
diskette *n.* see **disk 3**
dislike I *n.* 1. to take a ~ to 2. to show a ~ for, of
3. an active, cordial, hearty, strong, violent ~
dislike II *v.* 1. to ~ deeply, very much 2. (G) he
~s going to the opera 3. (K) we ~ his hanging
around with that crowd
dislodge *v.* (D; tr.) to ~ from (the doctor ~d the
bone from her throat)
disloyal *adj.* ~ to
disloyalty *n.* to demonstrate ~ to
dismay I *n.* 1. to express; feel ~ 2. ~ at, with 3. to
smb.'s ~ (to my ~, he was absent again)
dismay II *v.* (formal) (R) it ~ed me to learn of her
actions; it ~ed us that the project had been canceled
dismayed *adj.* 1. ~ at, with 2. ~ to + inf. (he was
~ to see that he had a flat tire)
dismaying *adj.* ~ to + inf. (it is ~ to contemplate
the results of their incompetence)
dismiss *v.* 1. to ~ curtly, summarily; lightly 2. (D;
tr.) to ~ as (he was ~ed as incompetent) 3. (D; tr.)
to ~ for (I was ~ed for being late) 4. (D; tr.) to ~
from (he was ~ed from his job) 5. (misc.) (BE;
cricket) the bowler ~ed the next batsman for six
runs
dismissal *n.* 1. a curt; summary ~ 2. a ~ from
dismount *v.* (D; intr.) to ~ from
disobedience *n.* 1. willful ~ 2. civil ~ 3. ~ to (~ to
orders)
disobedient *adj.* ~ to
disorder *n.* ['lack of order'] 1. to throw into ~ 2. in
~ (to retreat in ~) ['riot'] 3. violent ~s 4. ~s broke
out ['ailment'] 5. a brain; circulatory; digestive,
intestinal; mental; minor; neurotic; personality;
respiratory ~
disoriented *adj.* ~ as to (~ as to time and place)
disparity *n.* 1. a great, wide ~ 2. a ~ between, in
dispatch I *n.* ['news item'] ['message'] 1. to file;
send a ~ 2. to dateline a ~ 3. a ~ from; to 4. a ~
that + clause (we read her ~ that war had been
declared) 5. (misc.) (BE; mil.) mentioned in ~es
(for bravery in combat) ['promptness'] 6. with
great ~
dispatch II *v.* (D; tr.) to ~ from; to (the message
was ~ed from battalion headquarters to each
company)

dispensation *n.* papal; special ~
dispense *v.* 1. (B) to ~ charity to the needy; to ~
equal justice to all 2. (d; intr.) to ~ with (to ~ with
the formalities)
dispenser *n.* a soap ~
dispersed *adj.* widely ~
display I *n.* 1. to make, put on a ~ (to make a vulgar ~ of one's wealth) 2. a dazzling, imposing,
impressive; lavish, ostentatious; modest; public;
spectacular ~ (to make a public ~ of grief; to put
on a dazzling ~ of one's skill) 3. a graphic ~ (of a
computer)
display II *v.* (B) he ~ed his ignorance to everyone
displeased *adj.* ~ at, with
displeasure *n.* 1. to incur smb.'s ~ 2. to show one's
~ with 3. to smb.'s ~
disposal *n.* ['availability'] 1. to have at one's ~ (I
had a huge car at my ~) 2. to place smt. at smb.'s
~ 3. at smb.'s ~ ['device used to grind up garbage'] 4. a garbage ~; or: a garbage-disposal unit
['elimination of refuse'] 5. waste ~
dispose *v.* 1. (d; intr.) to ~ of ('to deal with') (to ~
of the opposition) 2. (d; intr.) to ~ of ('to get rid
of') (to ~ of the rubbish) 3. (formal) (H) ('to
incline') what ~d him to do it?
disposed *adj.* (formal) ['inclined'] (cannot stand
alone) 1. ~ to, towards (he seems well ~ towards
us) 2. ~ to + inf. (she is ~ to accept our offer)
disposition *n.* ['inclination'] 1. a ~ to + inf. (a ~
to argue) ['personality'] 2. a bland; buoyant,
cheerful, genial, pleasant, sunny; mild; unpleasant ~
dispossess *v.* (D; tr.) to ~ of (they were ~ed of
their wealth)
disproportionate *adj.* ~ to
dispute I *n.* 1. to stir up a ~ about 2. to arbitrate;
resolve, settle a ~ (to settle a ~ out of court) 3. an
acrimonious, bitter, heated, sharp; public ~ 4. a
border; labor ~ 5. a ~ about, over; with 6. in ~
(this point is in ~)
dispute II *v.* (L) I do not ~ that he was there
disqualify *v.* (D; tr.) to ~ from
disregard I *n.* 1. to show ~ 2. willful ~ 3. ~ for
disregard II *v.* (K) we cannot ~ his coming late to
work so often
disrepair *n.* 1. a state of ~ 2. in ~ (the building is
in ~)
disrepute *n.* 1. to fall into ~ 2. to hold smb. in ~
disrespect *n.* 1. to show ~ 2. to intend, mean no ~
3. deep, profound ~ 4. ~ for (I meant no ~ for
your traditions)
disrespectful *adj.* 1. ~ to 2. ~ to + inf. (it was ~
of them to say that)
disruption *n.* 1. complete, total ~ 2. ~ in
dissatisfaction *n.* 1. to express, voice; feel ~ 2.
deep, keen, profound; growing; widespread ~ 3.
~ about, with (they expressed deep ~ with working conditions)
dissatisfactory *adj.* ~ to
dissatisfied *adj.* ~ with
dissension *n.* 1. to introduce; sow, stir up ~ 2.
deep ~ 3. ~ among, between
dissent I *n.* 1. to express ~ 2. to brook (formal),
tolerate no ~ 3. ~ from

dissent II v. (D; intr.) to ~ from
dissertation n. 1. to defend; write a ~ (to write a ~ under smb.'s supervision) 2. to supervise a ~ 3. a doctoral ~ 4. a ~ about, on USAGE NOTE: AE prefers a *doctoral dissertation, master's thesis;* BE prefers a *doctoral thesis, master's dissertation/ master's essay.*
disservice n. 1. to do smb. a ~ 2. a ~ to
dissident n. a political ~
dissimilarity n. a ~ between
dissociate v. (D; refl., tr.) to ~ from (we ~d ourselves from his views) (see the Usage Note for **disassociate)**
dissolve v. (D; intr., tr.) to ~ into
dissonance n. cognitive ~ ('the holding of beliefs that contradict accepted facts')
dissuade v. (D; tr.) to ~ from
distance I n. 1. to cover; run; travel; walk a ~ 2. to keep a ~ (to keep a safe ~ between cars) 3. to close the ~ between 4. a discreet; good, great, long; safe; short ~ (we traveled a short ~) 5. (a) shouting; striking; walking ~ (it's within easy walking ~) 6. (a) braking, stopping ~ 7. a ~ between; from; to (the ~ between New York and London is three thousand miles; the ~ from Philadelphia to Chicago is less than eight hundred miles) 8. at a ~ (at a discreet ~; we spotted them at a ~ of two hundred yards) 9. from a ~ (I spotted her from a ~) 10. in the ~ (the city was visible in the ~) (misc.) 11. to keep one's ~ ('to not allow familiarity'); a short ~ away; quite a ~
distance II v. (D; refl.) to ~ from
distant adj. ~ from
distaste n. 1. to develop; express; feel; show a ~ 2. a strong ~ 3. a ~ for
distasteful adj. 1. ~ to (his behavior was ~ to everyone) 2. ~ to + inf. (it was ~ for me to have to enforce discipline)
distil, distill v. (D; tr.) to ~ from (to ~ whiskey from grain)
distinct adj. ~ from
distinction n. ['differentiation'] 1. to draw, make a ~ 2. to blur a ~ 3. a clear-cut; dubious; fine; subtle ~ 4. a ~ between ['eminence'] ['superiority'] 5 to enjoy, have, hold a ~ (he holds the dubious ~ of being the first person to break the new speed limit) 6. a doubtful, dubious ~ 7. of ~ (an artist of ~) 8. with ~ (to serve with ~)
distinctive adj. ~ of
distinguish v. 1. (d; intr.) to ~ among, between 2. (D; tr.) to ~ from (to ~ good from evil)
distinguishable adj. 1. clearly, plainly ~ 2. ~ from
distinguished adj. ~ for
distortion n. a crude, gross; deliberate ~
distract v. (D; tr.) to ~ from (the music ~ed them from their studies)
distraught adj. ~ at, over, with
distress I n. 1. to feel; suffer ~ 2. to alleviate, ease ~ 3. deep, great, profound ~ 4. economic, financial ~ 5. ~ at, over, with 6. to smb.'s ~ (to our ~, her condition did not improve)
distress II v. (R) it ~ed me (to read) that a new epidemic had broken out
distressed adj. 1. deeply ~ 2. ~ at, by, with (~ at

the news) 3. ~ to + inf. (I was deeply ~ to learn of your loss)
distressing adj. 1. deeply ~ 2. ~ to + inf. (it is ~ to listen to the news) 3. ~ that + clause (it is ~ that nations constantly quarrel)
distribute v. 1. to ~ fairly; unfairly; widely 2. (B) the instructor ~d the test papers to the students 3. (D; tr.) to ~ among (to ~ food among the poor)
distribution n. 1. fair; unfair; wide ~ 2. (math.) normal ~ 3. (ling.) complementary ~ 4. ~ among (the ~ of surplus food among the needy)
district n. 1. the business (AE); financial, red-light; theater ~ 2. a health; school ~
distrustful adj. ~ of
disturb v. (R) it ~ed me (to read) that a new epidemic had broken out
disturbance n. 1. to cause, create, make a ~ 2. to quell, put down a ~
disturbed adj. 1. emotionally ~ 2. ~ about, at, by, over 3. ~ to + inf. (I am ~ to learn of this latest incident)
disturbing adj. 1. ~ to + inf. (it is ~ to find evidence of widespread corruption) 2. ~ that + clause (it's ~ that so few people vote)
disuse n. to fall into ~
ditch n. 1. to dig a ~ 2. a deep; shallow ~
ditty n. 1. to sing a ~ 2. a popular ~
dive I n. 1. to make a ~ 2. a swallow (BE), swan (AE) ~ 3. a back; headfirst; high ~ 4. a crash ~ (of a submarine) 5. a power ~ (of a plane) 6. a ~ for (they made a ~ for the ditch) 7. a ~ from; into 8. (misc.) (colloq.) to take a ~ ('to lose a contest deliberately')
dive II v. 1. to ~ headfirst 2. (D; intr.) to ~ from; into (she ~d into the pool from the high diving board)
diverge v. (D; intr.) to ~ from
diversion n. ['amusement'] a favorite; popular ~
divert v. (D; tr.) to ~ from; to
divest v. (formal) (d; refl., tr.) to ~ of (they ~ed themselves of all stocks and bonds)
divide I n. 1. a continental ~; (in North America) the Great Divide 2. (fig.) the great ~ ('death') to cross the great ~)
divide II v. 1. to ~ equally, evenly 2. (D; tr.) to ~ among, between; with (to ~ profits among the partners) 3. (D; tr.) to ~ by (to ~ six by three) 4. (D; refl., tr.) to ~ into (they ~d the loot into equal shares; to ~ three into six)
divided adj. 1. sharply ~ 2. ~ on, over (they are sharply ~ over the choice of a new chairperson)
dividend n. ['sum divided among stockholders'] 1. to declare a ~ 2. (also fig.) to pay a ~ 3. a stock ~
divide up v. (D; tr.) to ~ among, between; into (they ~d up the profits into equal shares)
dividing line n. 1. to draw a ~ between 2. to cross the ~
divisible adj. ~ by; into
division n. ['mathematical operation of dividing'] 1. to do ~ 2. long; short ~ ['major military unit'] 3. an airborne; armored; infantry; motorized ~ ['classification'] 4. to make a ~ 5. an arbitrary ~ ['dividing'] 6. an equal; sharp; unequal ~ 7. cell ~
divisor n. a common ~

divorce *n.* 1. to file for, sue for ~ 2. to get, receive a ~ 3. to grant a ~ 4. (a) no-fault ~; an uncontested ~; (a) ~ by mutual consent 5. (misc.) a ~ settlement

divorced *adj.* ~ from (he was ~d from his wife)

divulge *v.* (B) to ~ information to the press

dizzy *adj.* 1. ~ from (~ from the rays of the sun) 2. ~ with (~ with success)

do *v.* 1. (C) ('to perform') she did a favor for me; or: she did me a favor 2. (d; tr.) to ~ about ('to help improve') (what can we ~ about his schoolwork?) 3. (d; intr.) to ~ by ('to treat') (the firm did very well by her when she retired) 4. (BE) (d; intr.) to ~ for ('to act as housekeeper for') (she does for me twice a week) 5. (colloq.) (BE) (d; intr.) to ~ for ('to ruin') (that long hike nearly did for me) 6. (d; tr.) to ~ for ('to make arrangements for') (what did you ~ for light when the electricity was turned off?) 7. (D; tr.) to ~ for ('to help') (what can I ~ for you?) 8. (d; tr.) to ~ out of ('to cheat out of') (they did him out of his inheritance) 9. (d; tr.) to ~ to ('to inflict on') (what did they do to him?) 10. (d; tr.) to ~ with ('to use for') (what should we ~ with this old typewriter?) 11. (d; intr.) to ~ without ('to manage without') (we had to ~ without fresh fruit) 12. (AE) (G; only in the construction: he is done...) he is done talking 13. (P; intr.) ('to fare') she is ~ing very well

do away *v.* (d; intr.) to ~ with ('to eliminate') (they did away with that department several years ago)

dock I *n.* ['basin for ships'] 1. to go into ~ 2. a dry, floating ~ 3. at, in, on a ~ (there was labor trouble down on the ~s)

dock II *v.* 1. (D; intr.) to ~ at (the ship ~ed at Portsmouth) 2. (D; intr.) to ~ with (the spaceship ~ed with the satellite)

dock III *v.* (D; tr.) ('to deduct, take') to ~ from (they ~ed ten dollars from her wages)

docket *n.* ['agenda'] on the ~

doctor *n.* 1. a family ~ 2. a witch ~ 3. a barefoot ~ ('an auxiliary medical worker in a rural area, esp. in China') 4. ~s see; treat (their) patients 5. (misc.) to see ('consult') a ~

doctorate *n.* 1. to award, grant a ~ 2. to earn a ~ 3. an earned (AE); honorary ~ 4. a ~ in (a ~ in physics)

doctrine *n.* 1. to apply; preach a ~ 2. to establish a ~ 3. to disprove a ~ 4. a sound ~ 5. a basic; defense ~ 6. a ~ that + clause; subj. (it was their basic ~ that nothing interfere/should interfere with free trade)

document *n.* 1. to draw up a ~ 2. to file; store ~s 3. to classify; declassify a ~ 4. a classified; confidential; restricted; secret; top-secret ~ 5. an authentic ~ 6. a ~ about, concerning

documentation *n.* 1. to provide ~ for 2. strong; weak ~

dodge *v.* (D; intr.) to ~ behind (to ~ behind a door)

dodger *n.* ['evader'] a draft; tax ~

dog *n.* 1. to breed; keep ~s 2. to walk a ~ (on a leash) 3. to muzzle a ~ 4. to curb one's ~ 5. a mad, rabid; stray; vicious; wild ~ 6. a bird (AE), gun (BE); Eskimo; guard (BE); guide, seeing-eye; hunting; pet; police; sheep; toy ~; watchdog; working ~ 7. ~s bark; bite; growl; salivate; snap; snarl; whine; yelp 8. a pack of (wild) ~s 9. a young ~ is a puppy 10. a female ~ is a bitch 11. (misc.) a lucky ~ ('a lucky person'); a running ~ ('a lackey'); a ~'s life ('a wretched existence'); to work like a ~ ('to work very hard') USAGE NOTE: In CE a *police dog* is one used by the police; in AE it can also mean a breed of dog called a *German shepherd* in AE and an *Alsatian* in BE.

dogfight *n.* ['aerial combat'] to engage in a ~

doghouse *n.* (colloq.) ['disfavor'] in the ~

dogma *n.* 1. political; religious ~ 2. the ~ that + clause (they rejected the ~ that the earth is the center of the universe)

doily *n.* a lace; linen; paper ~

doldrums *n.* (colloq.) ['stagnation'] in the ~

dole *n.* (colloq.) (BE) ['unemployment insurance'] on the ~ (to be on the ~; to go on/sign on the ~)

dole out *v.* (B) to ~ food to the needy

doll *n.* a paper; rag ~

dollar *n.* a half; silver ~

doll up *v.* (colloq.) (D; refl., tr.) to ~ for (she ~ed herself up for the party)

dolphin *n.* 1. a school of ~s 2. a young ~ is a calf 3. a female ~ is a cow 4. a male ~ is a bull

domain *n.* ['sector'] the public ~ (in the public ~)

dominance *n.* 1. ~ in 2. ~ over

domination *n.* 1. world ~ 2. ~ over 3. under smb.'s ~

dominion *n.* ~ over

donate *v.* (B) she ~d her books to the library

donation *n.* 1. to make a ~ 2. a voluntary ~ 3. a ~ to

done *adj.* 1. (AE) ~ with (we're ~ with the chores) 2. (BE) to have ~ with (we've ~ with the plates) 3. (misc.) after that hike, I'm ~ for ('I'm completely exhausted')

donkey *n.* ~s bray, go heehaw, heehaw

donor *n.* 1. an anonymous ~ 2. a blood; organ ~

doom I *n.* 1. to seal smb.'s ~ 2. (misc.) the crack of ~

doom II *v.* (D; tr.) to ~ to (he was ~ed to oblivion)

doomed *adj.* 1. ~ to (~ to failure) 2. ~ to + inf. (he is ~ to eke out a miserable existence)

door *n.* 1. to hang a ~ 2. to close, shut; lock; open; slam; unlock a ~ 3. to break down, force a ~ 4. to knock on a ~ 5. the ~ is ajar; closed; locked; open; unlocked 6. a back; double; French (AE; BE has *French window*); front, main; revolving; screen; side; sliding; stage; storm (esp. AE) ~ 7. a ~ to (the ~ to this room is never locked) 8. at the ~ (who is at the ~?) 9. (misc.) behind closed ~s ('in secret'); they live next ~ to us; to sell from ~ to ~; to close the ~ on any compromise ('to rule out the possibility of any compromise'); at death's ~ ('almost dead'); to show smb. the ~ ('to ask smb. to leave')

doorbell *n.* to ring a ~

doornail *n.* (misc.) as dead as a ~

doorway *n.* 1. (fig.) the ~ to (the ~ to freedom) 2.

in the ~ (she stood in the ~)
dope *n.* (colloq.) ['drugs'] to take ~
dormancy *n.* a state of ~
dormant *adj.* to lie ~
dose *n.* 1. to administer, give; measure out a ~ 2. to take a ~ 3. a fatal, lethal ~
dotage *n.* to be in one's ~
dote *v.* (d; intr.) to ~ on, upon (she ~s on her grandchildren)
double I *n.* ['double time, accelerated marching cadence'] (usu. mil.) 1. at, on the ~ ['misc.'] 2. (colloq.) on the ~ ('very quickly')
double II *v.* (D; intr.) ('to do smt. additional') to ~ as (the gardener ~d as the chauffeur)
doubles *n.* (tennis) men's; mixed; women's ~
double take *n.* (colloq.) ['delayed reaction'] to do a ~
double up *v.* 1. (D; intr.) ('to share living accommodations') to ~ with 2. (misc.) to ~ in pain
doubt I *n.* 1. to raise (a) ~ (her proposal raised serious ~s in my mind) 2. to cast ~ on 3. to feel ~; to entertain, harbor ~s about 4. to express, voice (a) ~ 5. to dispel, resolve a ~ 6. a deep, serious, strong; gnawing; lingering; reasonable; slight ~ 7. ~s appear, arise 8. a ~ about, of 9. a ~ that + clause (he expressed serious ~ that he could finish the job on time) 10. beyond (a shadow of) a ~; without a ~ 11. in ~ (the result was never in serious ~) 12. (misc.) to give smb. the benefit of the ~; (colloq.) there is no ~ about it: she's the best USAGE NOTE: Some purists recommend that *whether* or the more informal *if* be used with the noun *doubt*, especially in the meaning 'uncertainty'--she expressed doubt (about/as to) whether they would finish on time ('she was not certain whether they would finish on time'). In the meaning of 'disbelief', the conjunction *that* is common--she expressed doubt that they would finish on time ('she did not believe that they would finish on time'). Note that in interrogative sentences the use of *that* prevails--is there any doubt that they will finish on time? In negative sentences the conjunction *that* must be used--there is no doubt that they will finish on time.
doubt II *v.* 1. to ~ strongly, very much 2. (L) I ~ that (if, whether) she will want to participate USAGE NOTE: See the Usage Note for **doubt I**. Thus, to express 'uncertainty', one can say--she doubted whether they would finish on time. To express 'disbelief', one can say--she doubted that they would finish on time. In negative sentences, only *that* is used--she doesn't doubt that they will finish on time.
doubtful *adj.* 1. ~ of 2. ~ that + inf. (it's ~ that she will be present) USAGE NOTE: See the Usage Note for **doubt I**. Thus, to express 'uncertainty', one can say--it is doubtful whether they will finish on time. To express 'disbelief', one can say--it is doubtful that they will finish on time.
dough *n.* 1. to knead, mix, roll, work ~ 2. flaky; firm; stiff ~ 3. ~ rises
doughnuts *n.* 1. to make ~ 2. glazed; jelly ~
dove *n.* 1. a gentle ~ 2. ~s coo
dovetail *v.* (D; tr., intr.) ('to fit') to ~ into

down *adj.* (colloq.) ['angry'] ~ on (he's ~ on us)
downfall *n.* 1. to bring about smb.'s ~ 2. to head for a ~
downgrade *v.* (D; tr.) to ~ to (the embassy was ~d to a legation)
down payment *n.* 1. to make a ~ 2. a ~ on
downpour *n.* a brief; steady; sudden; torrential ~
dowry *n.* to provide a ~ for
dozen *n.* a baker's; round ~
draft I *n.* ['rough copy'] 1. to make, prepare a ~ 2. a final, polished; preliminary, rough; working ~ ['conscription'] (AE) 3. to introduce the ~ 4. to dodge, evade the ~ ['current of air'] 5. to sit in a ~ ['order for payment'] 6. to honor a ~ 7. a bank ~ 8. a ~ for; on (a ~ on the Paris branch of our bank for one thousand pounds) ['drawing of liquid'] 9. on ~ (beer on ~) USAGE NOTE: BE prefers the spelling *draught* in senses 5 and 9.
draft II *v.* (AE) (D; tr.) ('to conscript') to ~ into (to ~ young people into the army) 2. (H) the ~ ~ed her to serve as their delegate
drag I *n.* ['puff'] 1. to take a ~ (on a cigarette) ['obstacle'] (colloq.) 2. a ~ on (a ~ on the economy) ['street'] (colloq.) 3. the main ~ ['women's clothing worn by a male transvestite'] (slang) 4. in ~ 5. (misc.) a ~ queen
drag II *v.* 1. (d; intr.) ('to search at the bottom of a lake, river, sea') to ~ for (to ~ for a body) 2. (D; tr.) ('to search') to ~ for (they ~ged the lake for the body) 3. (d; tr.) ('to pull') to ~ into (they ~ged the tables into the garden; to be ~ged into a war) 4. (d; intr.) ('to draw deeply') to ~ on (to ~ on a pipe) 5. (d; tr.) ('to pull') to ~ out of (we ~ged the old sofa out of the house) 6. (D; tr.) ('to pull') to ~ through (they ~ged the logs through the forest) 7. (D; tr.) ('to pull') to ~ (over) to (they ~ged him to the door)
drag down *v.* (usu. fig.) (D; tr.) to ~ into (to ~ smb. down into the gutter)
dragnet *n.* ['network'] a police ~
dragoon *v.* (rare) (d; intr.) ('to coerce') to ~ into
drag over *v.* (D; tr.) ('to pull') to ~ to (they ~ged her over to the car)
drain I *n.* 1. to clean out, clear, unblock, unclog a ~ 2. to block, clog a ~ 3. (misc.) a brain ~
drain II *v.* 1. (d; intr.) to ~ from (the blood ~ed from his face when he heard the news) 2. (D; tr.) to ~ of (~ the tank of all water) 3. (N; used with an adjective) they ~ed the swamps dry
drama *n.* 1. a courtroom; epic ~ 2. high ~ 3. a ~ unfolds
dramatics *n.* to study ~
drapes *n.* (AE; BE has *curtains*) 1. to hang ~ 2. to draw; open the ~ 3. window ~
draught (BE) see **draft 5, 9**
draw I *n.* ['act of drawing a weapon'] 1. on the ~ (quick on the ~) 2. (misc.) to beat smb. to the ~ ['lottery'] (esp. BE) 3. to hold a ~ (AE has *drawing*)
draw II *v.* 1. (C) ('to sketch') ~ a picture for me; or: ~ me a picture 2. (D; tr.) to ~ against, on ('to take from') (to ~ a check/cheque against an account) 3. (D; intr.) ('to pick a number at random') to ~ for (to ~ for a prize) 4. (D; tr.) to

remove') to ~ from (to ~ money from an account; to ~ water from a well) 5. (D; tr.) ('to elicit') to ~ from (to ~ applause from an audience) 6. (d; tr.) ('to bring') to ~ into (to ~ smb. into a quarrel) 7. (d; intr.) ('to puff') to ~ on (to ~ on a pipe) 8. (d; intr.) to ~ on, upon ('to take from') (to ~ on one's reserves; to ~ on an account) 9. (D; tr.) ('to attract') to ~ to (to ~ smb.'s attention to smt.) 10. (J) ('to sketch') the artist drew her looking out at the sea 11. (N; used with an adjective) ('to pull') ~ the rope tight 12. (misc.) he drew a gun on his opponent; to ~ to a close; sharply drawn

draw away v. (D; intr.) to ~ from ('to increase the distance from') (the leader drew away from the pack)

drawbridge n. to lower; raise a ~

drawer n. 1. to close, push in a ~ 2. to open, pull out a ~

drawing n. ['picture'] 1. to do, make a ~ 2. a composite ~ ['representation by lines'] 3. mechanical ~ 4. (a) freehand; line ~ ['lottery'] (esp. AE) 5. to hold a ~ (BE has *draw*)

drawing board n. ['planning stage'] 1. on the ~ 2. (misc.) back to the ~

dread v. 1. (rare) (E) I ~ to see him again 2. (G) she ~s going to the dentist

dreadful adj. ~ to + inf. (it is ~ to contemplate the possibility of another war)

dream I n. ['image seen while sleeping'] 1. to have a ~ 2. to interpret ~s 3. a bad; recurring; wet; wild ~ 4. a ~ about, of ['hope'] ['goal'] 5. to achieve one's ~s 6. a childhood; visionary; wild ~ 7. a ~ comes true 8. a ~ of 9. a ~ to + inf. (it was his ~ to become a teacher) 10. a ~ that + clause (it was only a ~ that he might be elected) 11. beyond one's wildest ~s

dream II v. 1. (D; intr.) to ~ about, of 2. (L) she never ~ed that she would someday write dictionaries

dreary adj. it was very ~ to do the same job every day = it was very ~ doing the same job every day

dregs n. the ~ of society

drench v. 1. to ~ thoroughly 2. (D; tr.) to ~ to (we were ~ed to the skin)

dress I n. ['clothing'] 1. casual, informal; evening, formal; native ~ 2. improper; proper ~ 3. in ~ (in informal ~) ['woman's frock'] 4. a casual; cocktail; evening (esp. BE); low-cut; maternity; summer ~ 5. a ~ is long; short; tight 6. a ~ fits (well) 7. in a ~ (she was in a summer ~) ['garment for sleeping'] (BE) 8. a nightdress

dress II v. 1. to ~ elegantly, smartly; lightly; warmly 2. (d; intr., tr.) to ~ as (he was ~ed as a sailor) 3. (d; intr.) to ~ for (to ~ for dinner) 4. (d; intr., tr.) to ~ in (to ~ in black)

dressing n. ['bandage'] 1. to apply, put on a ~ (to apply a ~ to a wound) 2. to remove; replace a ~ 3. a sterile ~ ['sauce'] 4. a salad ~ (blue cheese; creamy Italian; French; Italian; Roquefort; Russian; Thousand Island; vinegar-and-oil ~)

dress up v. (D; intr., tr.) to ~ as (he ~ed up as a cowboy; they ~ed her up as a ballerina)

dribble n. (basketball) a double ~

drift I n. (colloq.) ['meaning'] to get the ~

drift II v. 1. (d; intr.) to ~ into (to ~ into a life of crime) 2. (D; intr.) to ~ with (to ~ with the current)

drift away v. (D; intr.) to ~ from

drift back v. (D; intr.) to ~ to (the strikers ~ed back to work)

drill I n. ['boring tool'] 1. to operate, use a ~ 2. an electric, power; hand; rotary ~ ['exercise'] 3. to conduct a ~ 4. (mil.) close-order ~ 5. an air-raid; evacuation; fire ~

drill II v. 1. (D; intr.) ('to prospect') to ~ for (to ~ for oil) 2. (D; tr.) ('to train') to ~ in (to ~ students in pronunciation) 3. (d; tr.) ('to instill') to ~ into (to ~ discipline into cadets)

drink I n. 1. to fix, make, mix a ~ 2. to pour a ~ 3. to have, take; nurse; toss off a ~ 4. a fizzy (BE); potent, stiff, strong; still (BE) ('not sparkling'); weak ~ 5. a mixed; soft ~ 6. (misc.) to drown one's sorrows in ~

drink II v. 1. (d; intr.) to ~ from (I always ~ tea from a glass) 2. (d; intr.) to ~ to (let's ~ to good health) 3. (D; tr.) to ~ to (to ~ a toast to smb.) 4. (misc.) to ~ oneself to death; to ~ smb. under the table

drinker n. a hard, heavy ~

drinking n. 1. excessive; hard, heavy ~ 2. a bout of ~

drip I n. a steady ~

drip II v. 1. (D; intr.) to ~ from (the water was ~ping from the tap) 2. (D; intr.) to ~ with

drive I n. ['trip in a vehicle'] 1. to go for, go on, have (BE), take a ~ 2. an easy ~ (it's an easy half hour ~ to their place) 3. a test ~ ['campaign'] 4. to initiate, launch a ~ for (to launch a ~ for flood relief) 5. a charity; fund-raising ~ ['energy'] 6. the ~ to + inf. (does she have enough ~ to finish the job?) ['impulse'] 7. an elemental ~ ['type of propulsion'] 8. a chain; disc (BE); disk (AE); fluid; four-wheel; front-wheel; rear-wheel ~ (see also **driveway**)

drive II v. 1. (d; intr.) to ~ at ('to suggest') (what is she ~ing at?) 2. (d; tr.) ('to direct') to ~ through (to ~ a nail through a wall) 3. (D; tr.) ('to transport') to ~ to (she drove me to the station; who ~s the children to school?) 4. (d; tr.) to ~ to ('to bring to') (to ~ smb. to despair) 5. (H) ('to force') he was driven by necessity to steal 6. (N; used with an adjective) ('to make') he drove me crazy

drive down v. (D; intr.) to ~ to (let's ~ to the beach)

drive home v. 1. (B) to ~ a point home to smb. 2. (L) he could not ~ to her that we cannot afford a new car 3. (Q) we must ~ to him where the difficulties lie

driver n. 1. a lorry (BE), truck; mule; tractor ~ 2. (BE) an engine ~ (AE has *engineer*) 3. a learner (BE), student (AE) ~ 4. a hit-and-run ~

driver's license n. (AE) 1. to issue a ~ 2. to revoke; suspend a ~

driveway n. (esp. AE; BE prefers *drive*) 1. to pave, surface a ~ 2. a ~ between (a ~ between two houses)

driving n. city; defensive; drunken; highway (AE), motorway (BE); reckless; rush-hour; safe;

stop-and-go; turnpike ~

driving licence n. (BE) 1. to issue a ~ 2. to revoke; suspend a ~

drool v. (colloq.) (D; intr.) ('to show pleasure') to ~ over (they were ~ing over their new grandchild)

drop I n. ['fall'] 1. a sharp; sheer; sudden ~ 2. a ~ in (a sharp ~ in the interest rate) ['depository'] 3. a mail ~

drop II v. 1. (A; used without to) ('to write') ~ me a line when you get there 2. (d; intr.) ('to lag') to ~ behind (he ~ped behind the other runners) 3. (D; intr., tr.) ('to fall; to let fall') to ~ from (the book ~ped from her hand; his name was ~ped from the list) 4. (d; intr., tr.) ('to fall; to let fall') to ~ into (the stone ~ped into the water; I ~ped a coin into the slot) 5. (D; tr.) ('to let fall') to ~ on, to (she ~ped a book on the floor) 6. (d; intr.) to ~ out of ('to abandon') (to ~ of school) 7. (c; intr.) to ~ out of ('to disappear') (to ~ out of sight) 8. (D; intr.) ('to fall') to ~ to (prices ~ped to the lowest point in a year; everyone ~ped to the ground) 9. (misc.) to ~ dead

drop behind v. (D; intr.) to ~ in (to ~ in one's work)

drop in v. (D; intr.) to ~ on (~ on me at any time)

drop off v. 1. (D; tr.) ('to leave') to ~ at (could you ~ the books at the library?) 2. (misc.) to ~ to sleep

droppings n. animal ~

drops n. (med.) 1. to put in ~ 2. cough; eye; knockout; nose ~

drudgery n. sheer ~

drug n. 1. to administer; prescribe a ~ 2. to take a ~ 3. a mild; powerful, strong; weak ~ 4. a generic; habit-forming; miracle, wonder; non-addictive; nonprescription, over-the-counter; prescription; proprietary; sulfa (AE), sulpha (BE); toxic ~ 5. (misc.) a ~ on the market ('smt. for which there is little demand'); a ~ addict; a ~ dealer/pusher

drugs n. 1. to take ~ 2. to peddle, push, sell, traffic in (illicit) ~ 3. hard; soft ~ 4. illegal, illicit ~

drugstore n. (esp. AE; BE has chemist's) at, in a ~ (he works at/in a ~)

drum I n. ['percussion instrument'] 1. to beat, play; roll a ~ 2. a bass ~; kettledrum; snare ~ 3. muffled ~s 4. the ~s roll ['cylinder'] 5. a brake ~

drum II v. (d; tr.) to ~ into (to ~ smt. into smb.'s head)

drumfire n. ['barrage'] to keep up an incessant ~

drum up v. (D; tr.) to ~ for (he ~med up some business for us)

drunk I adj. 1. dead, roaring, stinking ~ 2. to get ~ on (he got ~ on cheap wine) 3. ~ with (~ with power)

drunk II n. to roll ('rob') a ~

drunkard n. an habitual ~

dry adj. to go, run ~ (the well ran ~)

dry run n. (esp. AE) to do, make a ~

dub I v. (N; used with a noun) ('to name') they ~bed him Bud

dub II v. (d; tr.) ('to provide with a new sound track') to ~ into (to ~ a film into English)

dubious adj. 1. ~ about, of 2. ~ if, that, whether

+ clause (it's ~ if they'll come)

duck I n. 1. ~s quack; waddle 2. a young ~ is a duckling 3. a male ~ is a drake 4. (misc.) to take to like a ~ takes to water ('to adapt to smt. quickly and easily')

duck II v. 1. (d; intr.) ('to move quickly') to ~ into (we ~ed into the nearest building) 2. (d; intr.) to ~ out of ('to evade') (to ~ out of an obligation)

ducking n. to give smb. a ~

dudgeon n. ['indignation'] in high ~

due I adj. 1. (cannot stand alone) ~ for (~ for a promotion) 2. (cannot stand alone) ~ to (her absence was ~ to illness) 3. to come, fall ~ (the note has fallen ~) 4. ~ to + inf. (the train is ~ to arrive at ten o'clock) USAGE NOTE: Purists prefer to use due to as an adjectival predicate phrase modifying the subject--her absence was due to illness. Otherwise, because of or owing to is preferred--she was absent because of illness; owing to illness she was absent.

due II n. ['recognition'] to give smb. her/his ~

duel n. 1. to fight a ~ 2. to challenge smb. to a ~ 3. a ~ to the death

due process n. (legal) to observe ~

dues n. 1. to pay ~ 2. annual; membership ~

duet n. to play; sing a ~

dukes n. (colloq.) ['fists'] to put up one's ~

dumb adj. (colloq.) (esp. AE) ['stupid'] 1. to play ~ 2. ~ to + inf. (it was ~ of you to say that)

dumbfounded adj. 1. completely ~ 2. ~ at (~ at the news) 3. ~ to + inf. (he was ~ to learn that his wife had left him)

dummy n. (slang) ['stupid person'] a ~ to + inf. (he was a ~ to agree) (see also **pacifier**)

dummy run (BE) see **dry run**

dump I n. ['place for dumping'] (esp. AE) 1. a garbage, trash ~; the town ~ (BE prefers refuse tip) ['dilapidated place'] (colloq.) 2. a real ~ (this town is a real ~)

dump II v. (slang) (AE) to ~ on ('to project bad experiences or feelings on') (I have enough troubles of my own--don't ~ on me)

dun v. (D; tr.) to ~ for (to ~ smb. for payment)

dupe v. (D; tr.) to ~ into (he was ~d into signing)

duplicate n. 1. to make a ~ 2. in ~

duplicity n. ~ in

duration n. 1. long; moderate; short ~ 2. of a certain ~ (of short ~) 3. for the ~ (of the war)

duress n. under ~ (to sign a confession under ~)

dusk n. at ~

dust n. 1. to gather; raise ~ 2. fine, powdery ~ 3. cosmic; gold; radioactive; volcanic ~ 4. a cloud; layer; particle of ~ 5. ~ collects; settles 6. (misc.) from ~ to ~

duster see the Usage Note for **eraser**

dusting n. a light ~ (of snow)

Dutch n. (colloq.) (may be derog.) 1. in ~ ('in trouble') 2. to go ~ ('to eat or drink with everyone paying her/his own way')

duty n. ['obligation'] ['service'] 1. to assume, take on a ~ 2. to carry out, discharge, do, perform one's ~ 3. to shirk one's ~ 4. an ethical, moral; legal; painful, unpleasant; pleasant ~ 5. a civic; official; patriotic; professional ~; supervisory

~ties 6. (esp. mil.) active; detached; fatigue; guard; light; overseas; sea; special; temporary ~ (to see active ~) 7. a ~ to (a ~ to one's country) 8. a ~ to + inf. (physicians have a ~ to report such cases) 9. on ~; off ~ (who was on ~ yesterday? when do you get off ~?) 10. (misc.) a sense of ~; in line of ~; ~ calls ['tariff'] ['tax'] 11. to impose a ~ on 12. to pay ~ on 13. to lift a ~ from 14. to exempt smt. from ~ 15. (BE) a death ~ (AE has *inheritance tax*)

dwell *v.* (d; intr.) to ~ on (to ~ on a question; to ~ on one's personal problems)

dweller *n.* a cave; cliff; lake ~

dwindle *v.* (D; intr.) to ~ (away) to (to ~ to nothing)

dye I *n.* 1. to apply ~ to 2. natural; synthetic ~s

dye II *v.* (N; used with an adjective) she ~d the dress blue

dynamite *n.* 1. ~ explodes 2. a stick of ~

dynasty *n.* 1. to establish, found a ~ 2. to overthrow a ~

dysentery *n.* 1. to come down with ~ 2. an attack of ~ 3. amebic ~

E

each *determiner, pronoun* ~ of (~ of them)
USAGE NOTE: The use of the preposition *of* is
necessary when a pronoun follows. When a noun
follows, two constructions are possible—we saw
each student; we saw each of the students.
eager *adj.* 1. ~ for (~ for success) 2. ~ to + inf.
(she's ~ to help)
eagerness *n.* ~ to + inf. (we appreciate his ~ to
help)
eagle *n.* 1. a bald; golden ~ 2. ~s scream, soar 3.
a young ~ is an eaglet
ear *n.* 1. to perk up, prick up; wiggle one's ~s 2. to
pierce smb.'s ~ 3. a musical ~ 4. the inner; middle; outer ~ 5. one's ~s perk up, prick up; ring 6.
an ~ for (to have an ~ for music) 7. by ~ (to play
music by ~) 8. (misc.) to lend an ~ to ('to pay
attention to'); to turn a deaf ~ to ('to pay no attention to'); to fall on deaf ~s ('to be disregarded'); a
cauliflower ~ ('an ear deformed by repeated
blows'); to have smb.'s ~ ('to have access to smb.
who is superior in rank'); to box smb.'s ~s ('to
strike smb. on the head'); the loud music grated on
our ~s; up to one's ~s in debt ('heavily in debt');
to play it by ~ ('to improvise')
earache *n.* to have an ~ (AE), to have ~ (BE)
eardrum *n.* a perforated ~
earmark *v.* (d; tr.) to ~ for (money has been ~ed
for the new library)
earmarks *n.* ['characteristics'] to have all the ~ of
earn *v.* (C) his accomplishments ~ed respect for
him; or: his accomplishments ~ed him respect
earnest I *adj.* ~ about
earnest II *n.* in ~ about
earnings *n.* annual; average; gross; net ~
earplug *n.* to insert an ~
earshot *n.* out of ~; within ~
earth *n.* 1. to circle; orbit the ~ 2. the ~ revolves
around the sun; rotates on its axis 3. on (the) ~ (is
there more land or water on ~?) 4. (misc.) down
to ~ ('practical'); who on ~ would ever do that?
what on ~ is that?
earthquake *n.* 1. to record an ~ 2. a devastating;
light; severe ~ 3. an ~ strikes (a severe ~ struck
the area) 4. the magnitude of an ~
earwax *n.* to remove ~
ease I *n.* 1. at ~ (to put smb. at ~; ill at ~) 2. at
~ with (she feels at ~ with us) 3. (formal) for ~ in
(for ~ in sleeping) 4. with ~ (he can lift a hundred
pounds with great ~)
ease II *v.* (P; refl., tr.) they ~d the piano through
the window
easement *n.* ['right of way'] (legal) to grant an ~
ease up *v.* (D; intr.) to ~ on (you should ~ on your
workers: you've been pushing them too hard)
east I *adj., adv.* ~ of
east II *n.* 1. in, to the ~ 2. (AE) back ~ ('in the
eastern part of the US') 3. (BE) out ~ ('in, to
Asia') 4. the Far; Middle; Near ~ USAGE
NOTE: The *Far East* refers to the countries of

eastern Asia. The *Middle East* refers to the countries of the eastern Mediterranean. The *Near East*
is now generally a synonym of the preceding term;
formerly it referred to the Balkans and the Otto-
man Empire.
easy *adj.* ['not difficult'] 1. ~ for (that job was ~
for her) ['lenient'] 2. (cannot stand alone) ~ on
(you are too ~ on the children; go ~ on him: he's
been sick) ['showing moderation'] 3. (cannot
stand alone) ~ on (go ~ on the hot peppers) ['not
difficult'] 4. (cannot stand alone) ~ to + inf. (this
book is ~ to translate = it is ~ to translate this
book = this is an ~ book to translate; Bob is ~ to
please = it is ~ to please Bob; it is not ~ to be a
parent = it is not ~ being a parent; it is ~ for you
to say that)
eat *v.* 1. to ~ heartily, voraciously 2. (d; intr.) to
~ into (acid ~s into metal) 3. (d; intr., tr.) to ~
out of (our cat ~s out of her own dish)
eat away *v.* (d; intr.) to ~ at (the waves ~ at the
shore)
eater *n.* a heavy; light ~
eavesdrop *v.* (D; intr.) to ~ on (to ~ on a conversation)
ebb *n.* 1. at a low ~ 2. on the ~ (the tide is on the
~)
eccentric *adj.* ~ in (~ in one's habits)
echelon *n.* 1. (mil.) the forward; rear ~ 2. the
higher, top, upper ~s of society
echo *n.* to produce an ~
eclipse *n.* ['obscuring of the moon or sun'] 1. a full,
total; lunar; partial; solar ~ ['dimming of one's
influence'] 2. in ~
ecology *n.* deep; human ~
economical *adj.* ['inexpensive'] ~ to + inf. (it's
more ~ to go by bus = it's more ~ going by bus)
economics *n.* supply-side; trickle-down ~
economize *v.* (D; intr.) to ~ on (to ~ on fuel)
economy *n.* ['frugality'] 1. to practice ~ 2. strict ~
['economic structure'] 3. a free-market; national;
peacetime; planned; shaky; sound; wartime ~
['the science of economics'] 4. political ~
ecstasy *n.* 1. pure, sheer ~ 2. in ~ over
ecstatic *adj.* ~ about, at, over (~ at being
selected)
edge I *n.* ['margin, border'] (also fig.) 1. a cutting;
jagged, ragged ~ 2. at, on an ~ (she stood at the
~ of the crater) ['advantage'] (colloq.) (esp. AE)
3. an ~ on (to gain a competitive ~ on smb.)
['misc.'] 4. to take the ~ off one's appetite ('to
satisfy one's appetite partially'); to be on ~ ('to be
tense')
edge II *v.* (P; intr., tr.) to ~ one's way through a
crowd
edgy *adj.* (colloq.) ['nervous'] ~ about
edict *n.* 1. to issue an ~ 2. to recall, rescind an ~
3. a royal; solemn ~ 4. an ~ that + clause (the
government issued an ~ that all prisoners would
be released)

edition *n.* 1. to bring out, publish an ~ (to bring out a new ~) 2. (of a book, dictionary) an abridged; annotated; corrected; critical; deluxe; expanded; first; hardback; limited; paperback; revised; thumb-indexed; unabridged; unexpurgated; variorum ~ 3. (of a newspaper) a city, home; evening; final; morning; special ~ 4. (misc.) (BE) an omnibus ~ ('the rebroadcast of the week's episodes of a soap opera or of a series')

editor *n.* 1. a city ~ 2. a copy; managing; news; technical ~ USAGE NOTE: In AE, *city editor* means 'local news editor'; in BE it means 'London financial editor'.

editorial *n.* 1. to write an ~ 2. an ~ about

editorship *n.* under the ~ of

educate *v.* 1. (D; tr.) to ~ for, to (~d to one's responsibilities) 2. (H) to ~ smb. to do smt.

educated *adj.* highly, well; poorly ~

education *n.* 1. to provide an ~ 2. compulsory; free ~ 3. elementary (esp. AE), primary; higher; secondary ~; a college, university ~ 4. adult (AE), continuing, further (BE); health; in-service; physical; pre-professional; professional; remedial; sex; special; vocational ~ 5. a broad, general; liberal ~; (a) progressive ~ 6. the ~ to + inf. (does she have enough ~ to cope with the job?)

eel *n.* 1. a conger; electric ~ 2. (misc.) as slippery as an ~

effect *n.* ['efficacy'] ['influence'] 1. to have, produce an ~ on 2. to heighten an ~ 3. to take ~ (the drug took ~) 4. to feel an ~ (I feel the ~ of the narcotic) 5. to mar; negate, nullify; sleep off the ~ (of smt.) 6. an adverse; beneficial, salutary; calculated; cumulative; deleterious, harmful; desired; dramatic; exhilarating; far-reaching; hypnotic; limited, marginal; minimal; net; practical; profound ~ 7. a domino; greenhouse ('warming of the earth's surface'); halo ('overly favorable judgment based on irrelevant factors'); knock-on (BE) ('additional'); placebo; retroactive; ripple ('gradually spreading influence'); side ~ 8. an ~ wears off 9. to little ~ ['operation'] 10. to put into ~ (to put new regulations into ~) 11. to go into, take ~ (when does the new law take ~?) 12. in ~ (the ordinance is still in ~) ['desired impression'] 13. for ~ (she said that purely for ~) ['meaning'] 14. to the ~ (he said smt. to the ~ that he might be late; words to that ~) ['reality'] ['practice'] 15. in ~

effective *adj.* 1. ~ against (~ against the common cold) 2. ~ in (~ in fighting forest fires) 3. ~ to + inf. (it would be more ~ not to respond to the charges)

effects *n.* ['belongings'] 1. household; personal ~ ['impressions'] 2. sound; special ~ ['results'] 3. ill ~

efficiency *n.* 1. to impair ~ 2. fighting; maximum, peak ~ 3. ~ in (~ in combating absenteeism) 4. at a certain ~ (at peak ~)

efficient *adj.* 1. ~ in (she was very ~ in reducing waste) 2. ~ to + inf. (it is not ~ to hire poorly trained workers)

effigy *n.* to burn; hang smb. in ~

effort *n.* 1. to make, put forth an ~ ~ 2. to redouble one's ~s 3. to spare no ~ 4. to foil, stymie, thwart smb.'s ~s 5. an abortive; all-out, furious, gallant, great, Herculean, heroic, massive, maximum, painstaking, strenuous, valiant; collaborative, joint; concerted; conscious; desperate, frantic; minimal; sincere; studious; superhuman; useless, vain ~; ceaseless, unceasing; unsparing, untiring; wasted ~s 6. a team ~; the war ~ 7. an ~ to + inf. (they made an all-out ~ to finish the work on time)

effrontery *n.* the ~ to + inf. (he had the ~ to demand more money)

egg I *n.* 1. to hatch; incubate; lay ~s 2. to beat (AE), whisk (BE); boil; fry; poach an ~ 3. to candle ~s 4. an addled, bad, rotten ~; boiled; devilled; fried; hard-boiled; poached; raw; Scotch (BE); scrambled; soft-boiled ~s 5. (misc.) a bad/rotten ~ ('a bad person'); a good ~ ('a good person'); to have ~ on one's face ('to be in an embarrassing position'); (BE) to teach one's grandmother to suck ~s ('to try to tell smb. smt. that they already know')

egg II *v.* (d; tr.) to ~ into (to ~ smb. into doing smt.)

egg on *v.* (H) to ~ smb. on to do smt.

ego *n.* 1. to feed, flatter smb.'s ~ 2. an inflated, overbearing, overwhelming ~ 3. an alter ~

either *determiner, pronoun* ~ of (~ of the two; ~ of them) USAGE NOTE: The use of the preposition *of* is necessary when *two* or a pronoun follows. When a noun follows, the following constructions are used--either student will know the answer; either of the students will know the answer.

eject *v.* (D; intr., tr.) to ~ from (to ~ from a disabled plane; they were ~ed from the room for disorderly conduct)

elaborate *v.* (D; intr.) to ~ on

elated *adj.* ~ about, at, over (~ at the good news)

elbow I *n.* 1. a tennis ~ ('an elbow that hurts because of excessive exercise') 2. at smb.'s ~ ('close to smb.')

elbow II *v.* (d; intr., tr.) to ~ through (to ~ one's way through a crowd)

elbowroom *n.* 1. to give smb. ~ 2. ~ for

elect *v.* 1. to ~ unanimously 2. (D; tr.) to ~ as 3. (D; tr.) to ~ to (he was ~ed to the state legislature) 4. (formal) (E) he ~ed to become a physician 5. (H) she was ~ed to represent us 6. (N; used with a noun) the nation ~ed her vice-president

election *n.* 1. to hold, schedule an ~ 2. to carry, win an ~ 3. to decide, swing an ~ (her last speech swung the ~ in her favor) 4. to concede; lose an ~ 5. to fix, rig an ~ 6. a close, hotly contested; rigged ~ 7. a free; general; local; national; primary; runoff ~ 8. smb.'s ~ to (her ~ to the senate was welcome news) 9. (misc.) ~ fever ('excitement before an election'); (BE) the runup to an ~ ('an election campaign')

electrician *n.* to call (in) an ~

electricity *n.* 1. to generate; induce ~ 2. to conduct ~ 3. static ~ 4. ~ flows

electrocardiogram *n.* to do; have an ~

elegance *n.* 1. faded; sheer ~ 2. sartorial ~

element *n.* ['component'] 1. a basic, essential, vital ~ ['group'] 2. a foreign ~ 3. criminal; extremist; subversive; undesirable ~s ['substance'] 4. chemical ~s ['natural environment'] 5. in one's ~; out of one's ~ ['factor'] 6. the human ~

elephant *n.* 1. a rogue ('wild') ~ 2. ~s trumpet 3. a herd of ~s 4. a young ~ is a calf 5. a female ~ is a cow 6. a male ~ is a bull

elevate *v.* (formal) (D; tr.) to ~ to (to ~ smb. to the peerage)

elevator *n.* (AE for 1-6; BE has *lift*) ['device for raising and lowering people and freight'] 1. to operate an ~ (an ~ operator operates an ~) 2. to take an ~ (we took the ~ to the tenth floor) 3. a down; express; self-service; up ~ 4. a freight ~ 5. a service ~ 6. a bank of ~s ['storage building'] 7. a grain ~

elicit *v.* (D; tr.) to ~ from

eligibility *n.* ~ for

eligible *adj.* 1. ~ for (~ for promotion) 2. ~ to + inf. (she is ~ to vote)

eliminate *v.* (D; tr.) to ~ from

elimination *n.* ~ from

elite *n.* a party; power; social ~

elixir *n.* the ~ of life

elk *n.* 1. a herd of ~ 2. a female ~ is a cow 3. a male ~ is a bull USAGE NOTE: The European *elk* is the North American *moose*. The North American *elk* resembles the European *red deer*, but is larger.

elope *v.* (D; intr.) to ~ with (she ~d with her childhood sweetheart)

eloquence *n.* flowery ~

eloquent *adj.* to wax ~

emanate *v.* (d; intr.) to ~ from

emancipate *v.* (D; tr.) to ~ from (to ~ serfs from bondage)

emancipation *n.* ~ from

embankment *n.* a railroad, railway ~

embargo *n.* 1. to impose an ~ 2. to place, put an ~ on 3. to lift, remove an ~ from 4. a trade ~ 5. an ~ against, on 6. under ~

embark *v.* 1. (D; intr.) to ~ for (to ~ for France) 2. (d; intr.) to ~ on (to ~ on a new career)

embarrass *v.* (R) it ~ed him to be caught cheating

embarrassed *adj.* 1. ~ about, at, over 2. ~ to + inf. (he was ~ to see his name in print)

embarrassing *adj.* 1. ~ to + inf. (it was ~ to fail the exam) 2. ~ that + clause (it's ~ that our streets are so dirty)

embarrassment *n.* 1. to cause ~ 2. to feel ~ 3. ~ about, at, over (we felt ~ about the disclosure) 4. an ~ to (his outburst was an ~ to his family) 5. to smb.'s ~ (to my ~, she accepted the invitation)

embassy *n.* 1. a foreign ~ 2. at, in an ~ (she works at/in the ~)

embed *v.* (D; refl., tr.) to ~ in

embers *n.* 1. burning; live ~ 2. the glow of (burning) ~

embezzle *v.* (D; intr., tr.) to ~ from

embezzlement *n.* 1. to commit ~ 2. ~ from

emblazoned *adj.* ~ with

emblem *n.* a national ~

embodiment *n.* a living ~ (of an ideal)

embody *v.* (D; tr.) to ~ in

embolden *v.* (formal) (H) what ~ed him to make the attempt?

embolism *n.* a coronary ~

embrace *n.* a loving, tender, warm; passionate; tight ~

embroider *v.* (D; tr.) to ~ for (she ~ed a towel for me)

embroil *v.* (D; tr.) to ~ in

embryo *n.* an ~ develops

emerge *v.* 1. (d; intr.) to ~ as (he ~d as the leading contender) 2. (D; intr.) to ~ from (the sun ~d from behind the clouds; to ~ from the shadows)

emergency *n.* 1. to cause, create; declare an ~ 2. a grave, serious; life-and-death; life-threatening; national ~ 3. a state of ~ 4. in case of an ~ (esp AE); in (the event of) an ~

emergency cord *n.* (AE) to pull an ~ (BE has *communication cord*)

emigrate *v.* (D; intr.) to ~ from; to

eminence *n.* of ~ (a person of great ~)

eminent *adj.* ~ in

emissary *n.* an ~ to

emission *n.* 1. to control ~s 2. sulfur (AE), sulphur ~s 3. a nocturnal ~

emit *v.* (D; tr.) to ~ into (to ~ smoke into the air)

emotion *n.* 1. to stir up, whip up ~(s) 2. to express; show ~ 3. deep, sincere; pent-up; strong ~(s) 4. conflicting, mixed ~s 5. with ~ (to speak with deep ~)

empathize *v.* (D; intr.) to ~ with

empathy *n.* 1. to feel; show ~ 2. ~ with

emphasis *n.* 1. to lay, place, put ~ on 2. particular, special ~

emphasize *v.* 1. (B) she ~d its importance to me 2. (L) I ~d that everyone should come on time

emphatic *adj.* ~ about, in

empire *n.* 1. to govern, rule an ~ 2. to build up; consolidate an ~ 3. to break up an ~ 4. a colonial; commercial; publishing ~

emplacement *n.* an antiaircraft; concealed; gun ~

employ *v.* 1. to ~ gainfully 2. (D; tr.) to ~ as (she was ~ed as a programmer)

employee *n.* 1. to engage (esp. BE), hire (esp. AE), take on an ~ 2. to dismiss, fire, sack (colloq.) an ~; (BE) to make an ~ redundant 3. a government; white-collar ~ 4. a full-time; part-time ~ 5. a fellow ~

employer *n.* an equal-opportunities (BE), equal-opportunity ~

employment *n.* 1. to give, provide ~ 2. to find; seek ~ 3. casual (BE); full-time; part-time; seasonal; steady ~ 4. ~ peaks; rises 5. ~ is down; up 6. ~ as (to find ~ as a mechanic)

empower *v.* (H) to ~ smb. to do smt.

empty I *adj.* ~ of (~ of meaning)

empty II *v.* 1. (d; intr.) ('to flow') to ~ into (the Danube ~ties into the Black Sea) 2. (D; tr.) to ~ of

enable *v.* (H) to ~ smb. to do smt.

enamored *adj.* 1. deeply ~ 2. ~ of

encase *v.* (D; tr.) to ~ in

enclose *v.* (D; tr.) to ~ in

encore *n.* to do; play; sing an ~
encounter *n.* a brief, fleeting; casual; chance; close ~
encourage *v.* 1. (H) she ~d me to leave 2. (K) who ~d his taking drugs? 3. (R) it ~d me (to learn) that they had promised to help
encouraged *adj.* 1. ~ at, by (~ at the news) 2. ~ to + inf. (I was ~ to see such excellent results)
encouragement *n.* 1. to give, offer, provide ~ 2. to find ~ in 3. warm ~
encouraging *adj.* 1. ~ to + inf. (it is ~ to read that illiteracy is declining) 2. ~ that + clause (it's ~ that the inflation rate has dropped)
encroach *v.* (d; intr.) to ~ on, upon (to ~ on smb.'s territory)
encrusted *adj.* ~ with
encumber *v.* (D; tr.) to ~ with
encyclopedia, encyclopaedia *n.* 1. to compile an ~ 2. (humorous) a walking ~
end I *n.* ['finish'] 1. to put an ~ to smt. 2. at the ~ (at the ~ of the word) 3. by the ~ (by the ~ of the year) 4. to the ~ (to the bitter ~) ['outer part'] 5. the opposite ~ 6. from ~ to ~; from the beginning to the ~ ['purpose'] 7. to accomplish, achieve one's ~s ['misc.'] 8. to be on the receiving ~ ('to be a recipient'); to make both ~s meet ('to manage to get along on one's income'); to the ~s of the earth ('to the most remote parts of the earth'); in the ~ ('finally')
end II *v.* 1. (d; intr., tr.) to ~ by (he ~ed his remarks by quoting Lincoln) 2. (d; intr.) to ~ in (the word ~s in a consonant; to ~ in a draw; to ~ in disaster) 3. (D; intr., tr.) to ~ with (we ~ed our meal with a nice dessert)
endear *v.* (D; refl., tr.) to ~ to (she ~ed herself to everyone)
endeavor, endeavour *v.* (formal) (E) he ~ed to remain calm
endemic *adj.* ~ in, to
ending *n.* 1. a happy; sad; surprise ~ (to have a happy ~) 2. (grammar) a feminine; grammatical; inflectional; masculine; neuter ~
endorsement *n.* ['approval'] 1. to give one's ~ 2. to receive smb.'s ~ 3. to withdraw one's ~ 4. a qualified; unqualified ~
endow *v.* 1. to ~ richly 2. (d; tr.) to ~ with
endowment *n.* to provide an ~ for
end up *v.* 1. (d; intr.) to ~ as (she ~ed up as governor of the state) 2. (d; intr.) to ~ by (she ~ed up by going to law school) 3. (d; intr.) to ~ with (I ~ed up with the estate) 4. (J) he ~ed up robbing banks 5. (S) she ~ed up governor of the state; to ~ rich
endurance *n.* 1. to test smb.'s ~ 2. physical ~ 3. the ~ to + inf. (does she have enough ~ to run the entire distance?) 4. beyond ~ 5. (misc.) smb.'s powers of ~
endure *v.* 1. (G) she cannot ~ seeing hungry children 2. (K) I cannot ~ his suffering 3. (misc.) to ~ to the bitter end
enema *n.* 1. to administer, give an ~ 2. to get, have an ~
enemy *n.* 1. to conquer, overcome, rout an ~ 2. to confront, face an ~ 3. an arch, avowed, bitter,

implacable, mortal, sworn; common; formidable, powerful; insidious; mutual; natural; political; secret ~ 4. a public ~ 5. (misc.) to be one's own worst ~
energy *n.* ['capacity'] 1. to apply, expend one's ~; to redirect one's ~gies 2. to dissipate; sap smb.'s ~ 3. boundless, limitless, unflagging; latent; misguided; unharnessed ~ 4. a burst of ~ 5. the ~ to + inf. (does she have enough ~ to get all of these jobs done?) ['usable power'] 6. to provide ~ for 7. to harness ~ (to harness solar ~) 8. atomic, nuclear; kinetic; solar ~ 9. sources of ~ 10. (misc.) an ~ crisis
enforce *v.* to ~ rigidly, strictly, stringently
enforcement *n.* 1. rigid, strict, stringent ~ 2. law ~
engage *v.* 1. (D; tr.) to ~ as (to ~ smb. as a guide) 2. (d; intr., tr.) to ~ in (to ~ in sports; to ~ smb. in conversation) 3. (d; intr.) to ~ with (the first gear ~s with the second) 4. (H) we ~d him to drive us around the city
engaged *adj.* ['busy'] 1. actively; directly ~ 2. ~ in, on (esp. BE) (we are ~ in compiling a dictionary) ['betrothed'] 3. ~ to (Bill is ~ to Betty) ['hired'] 4. ~ to + inf. (she was ~ to work in public relations)
engagement *n.* ['betrothal'] 1. to announce an ~ 2. to break (off) an ~ 3. an ~ to (her ~ to him was announced in the local paper) ['appointment'] ['obligation'] 4. to cancel an ~ 5. a luncheon; previous, prior; social; speaking ~ ['battle'] 6. to break off an ~ 7. a naval ~
engine *n.* ['motor'] 1. to crank, start; operate, run; rev up an ~ 2. to lubricate; repair; service; tune up an ~ 3. to cut, kill, turn off; warm up an ~ 4. an air-cooled; aircraft; diesel; donkey; electric; internal-combustion; jet; radial; reciprocating; rotary; steam; turbojet; V-8; valve-in-head ~ 5. an ~ breaks down; floods; functions, runs, works; gets overheated; idles; knocks, sputters; stalls 6. an ~ burns gasoline (AE), petrol (BE) 7. an ~ runs on electric power; solar energy ['vehicle'] 8. a fire ~
engineer *n.* ['skilled specialist in a branch of engineering'] 1. a chemical; civil; electrical; flight; graduate; highway; marine; mechanical; metallurgical; mining; operating; sanitary; systems; transportation ~ ['driver'] 2. a locomotive ~ (AE; BE has *engine driver*) ['technician'] 3. an operating; radio; sound ~
engineering *n.* chemical; civil; electrical; genetic; highway; hydraulic; marine; mechanical; metallurgical; sanitary; systems; traffic; transportation ~
English *n.* 1. American; Australian; Basic; Black; British; Canadian; Common, World; Indian; Middle; Modern; Old ~ 2. BBC; broken, fractured; colloquial; idiomatic; the King's, the Queen's; nonstandard; pidgin; Shakespearean; spoken; standard; substandard; written ~ 3. in fluent; good; plain ~
engrave *v.* 1. (d; refl., tr.) to ~ on (the events ~d themselves on my memory) 2. (D; tr.) to ~ with
engrossed *adj.* 1. deeply ~ 2. ~ in (~ in one's work)

engulf *v.* (D; tr.) to ~ in

enigma *n.* an ~ to

enjoin *v.* (formal) 1. (esp. AE) (d; tr.) ('to forbid') to ~ from 2. (d; tr.) ('to order') to ~ on (to ~ a duty on smb.) 3. (H) ('to order') to ~ smb. to obey the law

enjoy *v.* 1. to ~ enormously, greatly, immensely, very much 2. (G) she ~s swimming 3. (K) they ~ his singing

enjoyable *adj.* 1. highly ~ 2. ~ to + inf. (it is ~ to swim in the ocean)

enjoyment *n.* 1. to give, provide ~ 2 to derive ~ from 3. full, great ~

enlarge *v.* (d; intr.) to ~ on, upon ('to discuss in detail')

enlargement *n.* to make an ~ (of a photograph)

enlighten *v.* (D; tr.) to ~ about, on (can you ~ me on this subject?)

enlightening *adj.* 1. thoroughly ~ 2. ~ to + inf. (it was ~ to read the old newspaper accounts of the incident)

enlist *v.* 1. (D; intr.) to ~ for (to ~ for three years) 2. (D; intr.) to ~ in (to ~ in the army) 3. (H) we ~ed them to help

enlistment *n.* to extend one's ~

enmeshed *adj.* (cannot stand alone) ~ in (~ in legal details)

enmity *n.* 1. to stir up ~ 2. to incur smb.'s ~ 3. bitter ~ 4. ~ against, towards; among, between

enough *adj., determiner, pronoun* 1. ~ for ('that's ~ for me) 2. ~ to + inf. (it's ~ to know that they are safe; we've had ~ excitement to last a lifetime) 3. ~ of (~ of them) USAGE NOTE: The use of the preposition *of* is necessary when a pronoun follows. When a noun follows, the use of *of the* limits the meaning--we have seen enough documentaries; we have seen enough of the documentaries that we had discussed earlier.

enquire (BE) see **inquire**

enquiries *n.* (BE) 1. directory ~ (AE has *directory assistance* or *information*) 2. long-distance, trunk ~ (AE has *long-distance information)*

enrage *v.* (R) (rare) it ~d me (to learn) that he had embezzled company funds

enraged *adj.* 1. ~ at, by, over 2. ~ to + inf. (she was ~ to learn that her friends had left without her)

enroll, enrol *v.* (D; intr., refl., tr.) to ~ for, in (to ~ for a course; to ~ students in a course)

enrollment, enrolment *n.* 1. heavy; light ~ 2. open ('unrestricted') ~ 3. ~ in (the ~ in several courses went up)

en route *adv.* ~ from; to (they are ~ to London)

ensconced *adj.* ~ in (~ in an easy chair)

ensue *v.* (D; intr.) to ~ from

ensure *v.* (formal) 1. (A; usu. used without *to)* the present contract cannot ~ you a job 2. (d; tr.) to ~ against (to ~ workers against accidents) 3. (K) I cannot ~ his being on time 4. (L) no one can ~ that he'll come

entail *v.* 1. (G) it ~s moving to another city 2. (K) this job would ~ your learning how to use a computer

entangle *v.* (D; tr.) to ~ in, with

entanglement *n.* ~ in, with

enter *v.* 1. (D; intr.) ('to come in') to ~ by (to ~ by the rear door) 2. (D; tr.) ('to enroll') to ~ in (to ~ smb. in a contest) 3. (d; intr.) to ~ into ('to participate in') (to ~ into negotiations) 4. (D; intr.) to ~ on, upon ('to begin') to ~ upon a new career

enterprise *n.* ['initiative'] 1. free; private ~ 2. a joint ~ 3. of ~ (a person of great ~) ['firm'] 4. a commercial ~

entertain *v.* (D; tr.) to ~ with (to ~ children with funny stories)

entertaining *adj.* ~ to + inf. (it's ~ to watch people in a restaurant)

entertainment *n.* 1. to provide ~ 2. live ~ 3. ~ to + inf. (it was pure ~ to watch them dance) 4. to smb.'s ~ (to everyone's ~, he showed up in a clown's costume) 5. ~ for

enthralling *adj.* ~ to + inf. (it was ~ to watch the ballet)

enthuse *v.* (colloq.) (D; intr.) to ~ about, over

enthusiasm *n.* 1. to arouse, kindle, stir up ~ 2. to demonstrate, display, show; radiate ~ 3. to dampen smb.'s ~ 4. boundless, great, unbounded unbridled, wild ~ 5. ~ for 6. the ~ to + inf. (they had enough ~ to continue the campaign in spite of the difficulties)

enthusiastic *adj.* ~ about, at, over

entice *v.* 1. (D; tr.) to ~ into (to ~ smb. into a life of crime) 2. (D; tr.) to ~ with (they ~d the children with candy)

entirety *n.* in its ~

entitle *v.* 1. (d; tr.) to ~ to (your years of service ~ you to a pension) 2. (H) to ~ smb. to do smt.

entitled *adj.* (cannot stand alone) 1. ~ to (she is fully ~ to benefits) 2. ~ to + inf. (we are ~ to attend all concerts free)

entrance *n.* 1. to make one's ~ 2. a back rear; front, main; service; side ~ 3. a grand, triumphal ~ (to make a grand ~) 4. an ~ from; into, to (the ~ to this building) 5. at an ~ (wait for me at the ~)

entranced *adj.* ~ at, over, with

entrap *v.* (D; tr.) to ~ in, into

entreat *v.* (formal) (H) to ~ smb. to do smt.

entree *n.* ['access'] to gain ~ into, to

entrepreneur *n.* an independent; private ~

entrust *v.* 1. (B) he ~ed his money to me 2. (d; tr.) to ~ with (she ~ed me with her watch)

entrusted *adj.* (cannot stand alone) ~ with

entry *n.* ['headword and definition'] (in a dictionary) 1. to give, include an ~ 2. a run-on ~ 3. at, in, under an ~ ['act of entering'] 4. to make an ~ (to make a triumphal ~; to make an ~ in a diary) 5. to gain ~ to (they gained ~ to his apartment) 6. forced ~ (of a burglar) 7. an ~ into (she announced her ~ into the presidential race; our ~ into the war) ['bookkeeping procedure'] 8. to make an ~ for 9. double; single ~

entry blank, entry form *n.* to send in, submit an ~ for

enumerate *v.* (B) to ~ the facts to smb.

enunciate *v.* 1. to ~ clearly 2. (B) he ~d his theory to his colleagues

envelop *v.* (D; intr.) to ~ in

envelope *n.* 1. to address; seal an ~ 2. a pay ~

(AE; BE has *pay packet*) 3. a self-addressed; stamped; window ~ USAGE NOTE: AE has *stamped self-addressed envelope;* BE has *stamped addressed envelope.*
envious *adj.* ~ of
environment *n.* 1. to clean up; preserve, protect the ~ 2. to pollute the ~ 3. a healthy ~
envisage *v.* 1. (d; tr.) to ~ as (we ~ this dictionary as a handboook for serious students) 2. (L) we had not ~d that the situation would get so bad
envision (AE) see **envisage**
envoy *n.* 1. to dispatch an ~ 2. a personal ~ 3. an ~ extraordinary 4. an ~ to (our ~ to Paris)
envy I *n.* 1. to arouse, stir up ~ of 2. to feel ~ 3. to show ~ 4. out of ~ (he did it out of ~) 5. ~ at 6. (misc.) an object of ~; consumed/green with ~
envy II *v.* (O) they ~ us our new house
epic *n.* a folk ~
epicenter, epicentre *n.* at the ~
epidemic *n.* 1. to touch off, trigger an ~ 2. to contain, control an ~ 3. an ~ breaks out; spreads 4. a cholera; flu; measles; typhoid; typhus ~
epigram *n.* to compose; deliver an ~
epilepsy *n.* to have ~
epilogue *n.* an ~ to
episode *n.* a dramatic; humorous; thrilling; touching; tragic ~
epithet *n.* a harsh, offensive, vile ~
epoch *n.* 1. to mark; usher in an ~ 2. a glacial; revolutionary ~
equal I *adj.* 1. ~ in (~ in price) 2. ~ to (one kilometer is ~ to five eighths of a mile; ~ to the occasion)
equal II *n.* an ~ in (to have no ~ in political cunning)
equal III *v.* (D; tr.) to ~ in
equality *n.* 1. to achieve, attain ~ 2. racial; religious; total ~ 3. ~ among, between (~ between the sexes) 4. ~ in (~ in pay) 5. ~ of (~ of opportunity)
equanimity *n.* to upset smb.'s ~
equate *v.* (D; tr.) to ~ with (one should not ~ wealth with happiness)
equation *n.* 1. to formulate, state an ~ 2. to solve, work (esp. AE) an ~ 3. a differential; first-degree; identical; integral; linear; quadratic; simple ~; an ~ in one unknown; an ~ in two unknowns 4. (misc.) the human ~
equator *n.* above; at, on; below the ~
equidistant *adj.* ~ from
equilibrium *n.* 1. to maintain one's ~ 2. to lose one's ~ 3. to upset the ~
equinox *n.* the autumnal; vernal ~
equip *v.* 1. (d; tr.) to ~ for; with 2. (H) her training ~ped her to cope with the new job
equipment *n.* 1. hunting; military; office; sports ~ 2. (the) ~ for (~ for road construction) 3. the ~ to + inf. (do you have enough ~ to do the job?)
equipped *adj.* 1. ~ for; with 2. ~ to + inf. (our hospital is ~ to handle emergency cases)
equity *n.* ['supplementary system of justice'] in ~ (a suit in ~)
equivalent I *adj.* ~ in; to
equivalent II *n.* an approximate; exact ~
equivocal *adj.* ~ about

era *n.* 1. to introduce, usher in an ~ 2. the Christian, Common; Roman Era 3. the horse-and-buggy ~ 4. in an ~ (in the Roman Era) USAGE NOTE: The *Common Era* is abbreviated as C.E.; thus, *1920 C.E.* equals *1920 A.D.*
erase *v.* (D; tr.) to ~ from
eraser *n.* a blackboard; ink ~ USAGE NOTE: In BE an *eraser* is usu. called a *rubber;* a *blackboard eraser* may be called a *duster.*
erect *adj.* to stand ~
erosion *n.* glacial; soil ~
errand *n.* 1. to do, run an ~; to go on an ~ 2. personal ~s 3. a fool's ('useless') ~ 4. an ~ for (could you run an ~ for me?) 5. (misc.) an ~ of mercy
erroneous *adj.* ~ to + inf. (it's ~ to assume that the press always prints the truth)
error *n.* 1. to commit, make an ~ 2. to compound an ~ 3. to correct, rectify an ~ 4. to admit to (making) an ~ 5. a cardinal, costly, egregious, flagrant, glaring, grievous, serious ~ 6. a clerical; grammatical; printer's, typographical; tactical; typing ~ 7. (statistics) (a) random ~ 8. an ~ in (an ~ in judgment) 9. an ~ to + inf. (it was an ~ to invite them) 10. by, through ~ (her name was omitted by ~)
erudition *n.* 1. to display; flaunt one's ~ 2. great ~
erupt *v.* (D; intr.) to ~ into (the demonstrations ~ed into violence)
eruption *n.* 1. a volcanic ~ 2. a skin ~
escalate *v.* (D; intr.) to ~ into (the local war ~d into a major conflict)
escalator *n.* a down; up ~
escapade *n.* a childish, schoolboy; wild ~
escape I *n.* ['act of escaping'] 1. to make, organize an ~; to make good one's ~ 2. to foil, thwart an ~ 3. a clean; hairbreadth, narrow ~ 4. an ~ from (an ~ from prison) ['misc.'] 5. a fire ~ ('an emergency staircase')
escape II *v.* 1. (D; intr.) to ~ from; to (to ~ from prison) 2. (G) a famous actor cannot ~ being recognized
escort I *n.* 1. to provide an ~ for 2. an armed; motorcycle; police ~ 3. an ~ for 4. under ~
escort II *v.* (D; tr.) to ~ from; to
escrow *n.* to hold in ~
escutcheon *n.* 1. an armorial ~ 2. (misc.) (humorous) a blot on one's ~
espionage *n.* 1. to conduct, engage in ~ 2. industrial; military ~
esprit de corps *n.* 1. to develop (an) ~ 2. (a) strong ~
essay *n.* 1. to write an ~ about, on 2. a critical ~ (see the Usage Note for **dissertation**)
essence *n.* 1. the very ~ of smt. 2. in ~
essential *adj.* 1. ~ for; to 2. ~ to + inf. (it is ~ to work hard) 3. ~ that + clause; subj. (it is ~ that all be present)
essentials *n.* the bare, basic ~
establish *v.* 1. (d; refl., tr.) to ~ as (the press ~ed him as the leading contender) 2. (L) the police ~ed that she was innocent
estate *n.* 1. to administer, manage an ~ 2. (BE) a housing ~ 3. (BE) an industrial ~ 4. (misc.) to come into an ~ ('to inherit smt.')
esteem I *n.* 1. to hold smb. in high ~ 2. to fall; rise

in smb.'s ~ 3. high ~

esteem II *v.* to ~ highly

estimate I *n.* 1. to give, make; submit an ~ (the contractors had to submit ~s) 2. (colloq.) (AE) a ballpark ('approximate') ~ 3. an approximate, rough; conservative; long-range; preliminary; short-range; written ~ 4. an ~ that + clause (it's my ~ that the interest rate will drop by two percent) 5. by smb.'s ~ (by my ~)

estimate II *v.* 1. (L) I ~ that we'll arrive at about two o'clock 2. (M) we ~ the cost to be five thousand dollars

estimation *n.* in smb.'s ~ (in my ~ the situation is not critical)

estrange *v.* (D; tr.) to ~ from (~d from his wife)

estrangement *n.* (an) ~ between; from

etch *v.* 1. to ~ sharply 2. (D; tr.) to ~ into (sharply ~ed into my memory)

ether *n.* under ~

ethic *n.* the work ~

ethical *adj.* ~ to + inf. (it is not ~ to plagiarize)

ethics *n.* professional ~

etiquette *n.* 1. to prescribe ~ 2. courtroom; military; social ~

etymology *n.* 1. to ascertain, determine, trace an ~ 2. folk ~ (the professor explained the origin of a word by folk ~)

Eucharist *n.* to celebrate; give; receive the ~

eulogy *n.* 1. to deliver a ~ for 2. a touching ~

euphoria *n.* a feeling; state of ~

evacuate *v.* (D; tr.) to ~ from; to (the civilians were ~d from the city to farms)

evacuation *n.* 1. to carry out an ~ 2. a mass ~ 3. an ~ from; to

evade *v.* (G) they ~ paying taxes by living abroad

evaluate *v.* (D; tr.) to ~ as (he was ~d as unfit for military service)

evaluation *n.* 1. to make an ~ 2. a critical; fair, objective ~

evasion *n.* tax ~

eve *n.* 1. Christmas; New Year's Eve (on New Year's Eve) 2. on the ~ (on the ~ of the wedding) USAGE NOTE: In AE *Christmas Eve* means the 'night before Christmas'; in BE it can also mean 'the entire day before Christmas'.

even *adj.* 1. ~ with (the water was ~ with the roof) 2. to get ~ with smb. ('to avenge oneself on smb.'); to break ~ (when betting)

evening *n.* 1. in the ~; (AE) ~s (he works in the ~; or AE: he works ~s) 2. on a certain ~ (on that evening)

event *n.* 1. a disastrous; dramatic; historical; literary; major; outstanding; sensational; significant; social; spectacular; sporting; tragic ~ 2. a media ~ (to stage a media ~) 3. a blessed ~ ('a birth') 4. current ~s 5. (sports) field ~s 6. an ~ occurs, takes place 7. in the ~ that + clause (in the ~ that they come) 8. in an ~ (in the ~ of fire; in any ~) 9. (misc.) the media sometimes manipulate ~s

ever *adv.* ~ so much

evict *v.* (D; tr.) to ~ from

eviction *n.* an ~ from

evidence *n.* 1. to furnish, give, introduce, produce, provide ~ 2. to dig up, find, turn up,

unearth; gather ~; to piece together ~ 3. to plant ~ (on smb.) 4. to suppress; withhold ~ 5. to turn King's (BE), Queen's (BE), state's (AE) ~ 6. admissible; ample; circumstantial; cogent, compelling, convincing; conclusive; concrete, hard; damaging; direct; documentary; hearsay; inadmissible; incontestable, indisputable, irrefutable, undeniable, unquestionable; material; prima facie; reliable, trustworthy; satisfactory; strong; substantial; telltale ~ 7. a body of ~; a piece; scrap, shred of ~ 9. ~ against 10. ~ that + clause (the lawyer produced conclusive ~ that the accused could not have been at the scene of the crime) 11. in ~ (they were very much in ~) 12. (misc.) the bulk of the ~

evident *adj.* 1. ~ to 2. ~ that + clause (it is ~ that she will be elected)

evil I *adj.* ~ to + inf. (it is ~ to kill)

evil II *n.* 1. to do ~ 2. to root out ~ 3. an unmitigated; necessary ~ 4. (misc.) the lesser of two ~s

evocative *adj.* (formal) (cannot stand alone) ~ of

evolution *n.* 1. a gradual; historical ~ 2. an ~ from; into, to

evolve *v.* (d; intr.) to ~ from, out of; into

exact I *adj.* ~ in

exact II *v.* (formal) (D; tr.) to ~ from (to ~ tribute from the population)

exaggerate *v.* to ~ greatly, grossly

exaggerated *adj.* greatly, grossly ~

exaggeration *n.* 1. a gross ~ 2. ~ to + inf. (it's an ~ to claim that inflation has been controlled)

exam *n.* ['test'] 1. see **examination** 2. (colloq.) (AE) to ace an ~

examination *n.* ['test'] ['set of questions'] 1. to administer, conduct, give an ~ 2. to draw up, make up an ~ 3. to monitor, proctor, supervise an ~ 4. to sit (BE), take an ~ 5. to fail; pass an ~ 6. a difficult, stiff; easy ~ 7. a bar; civil-service; competitive; comprehensive; doctoral; entrance; external; final; makeup; master's; multiple-choice; open-book; oral; placement; qualifying; state-board (AE); true-false; written ~ 8. an ~ in, on (an ~ in physics; an ~ on irregular verbs) ['inspection'] ['scrutiny'] 9. to do, make an ~ 10. a careful, close, complete, in-depth, thorough; cursory, perfunctory, superficial ~ 11. a physical ~ (the doctor did a thorough physical ~ of/on the patient) 12. on ~ (on close ~ of the facts, she discovered that...)

examine *v.* 1. to ~ carefully, closely, thoroughly 2. (D; tr.) to ~ for (to ~ a car for defects) 3. (D; tr.) to ~ in (to ~ students in physics)

examiner *n.* a bank; medical ~

example *n.* 1. to cite, give, provide an ~ 2. to set an ~ for 3. to make an ~ of 4. to follow smb.'s ~ 5. a classic; concrete; extreme; glaring, striking; illustrative; impressive; prime, shining; typical ~ 6. (misc.) to lead by personal ~

exasperate *v.* (R) it ~s me that they never keep their promises

exasperated *adj.* 1. ~ at, by 2. ~ to + inf. (she was ~ to find nobody at home)

exasperating *adj.* 1. ~ to 2. ~ to + inf. (it is ~ to teach in a school like that one) 3. ~ that + clause

(it's ~ that we cannot find any spare parts)

excavations *n.* to carry out archeological ~

exceed *v.* (D; tr.) to ~ in (to ~ smb. in productivity)

excel *v.* (D; intr.) to ~ at, in (to ~ at sports)

excellence *n.* ~ at, in

exception *n.* ['exclusion'] 1. to make an ~ for 2. an ~ to (an ~ to the rule) ['objection'] 3. to take ~ to (she took strong ~ to what he said)

excerpt I *n.* 1. to quote an ~ 2. an ~ from

excerpt II *v.* (D; tr.) to ~ from (to ~ a passage from a work)

excess *n.* 1. in ~ of 2. to ~ (to drink to ~)

exchange I *n.* ['act of exchanging'] 1. to agree to; make an ~ 2. a cultural ~ 3. in ~ for 4. an ~ between ['place where items are bought or sold'] 5. a commodity; corn (BE), grain (AE); farmers'; post (AE); stock ~ ['central office'] 6. an employment (BE), labour (BE); telephone ~ ['currency'] 7. foreign ~ USAGE NOTE: The BE terms *employment exchange* and *labour exchange* have been largely superseded by *Job Centre*.

exchange II *v.* 1. (D; tr.) to ~ for (I ~d the defective tire for a good one) 2. (D; tr.) to ~ with (to ~ places with smb.)

exchange rate *n.* 1. to set an ~ 2. to apply an ~

excited *adj.* 1. ~ about, at, over (to get ~ about smt.) 2. ~ to + inf. (she was ~ to learn the news)

excitement *n.* 1. to arouse, create, stir up ~ 2. to feel ~ 3. considerable, great, intense; mounting ~ 4. ~ builds (to a climax); mounts 5. ~ about, at, over

exciting *adj.* ~ to + inf. (it's ~ to read adventure stories)

exclaim *v.* (formal) (L) he ~ed that he was innocent

exclude *v.* (D; tr.) to ~ from

exclusion *n.* ~ from

exclusive *adj.* mutually ~

excommunication *n.* to decree, order, pronounce (an) ~

exculpate *v.* (formal) (D; tr.) to ~ from

excursion *n.* 1. to go on an ~ 2. an ~ to

excursus *n.* an ~ into

excuse I *n.* 1. to find; make; make up an ~ for 2. to accept an ~ 3. to reject an ~ 4. an acceptable, good; convincing; feeble, flimsy, lame, poor, weak; glib; plausible; ready-made; unacceptable; valid ~ 5. an ~ for (an ~ for being late) 6. an ~ to + inf. (it was just an ~ to leave early) 7. an ~ that + clause (they accepted the ~ that I had been ill) 8. (misc.) a poor ~ for something

excuse II *v.* 1. (D; tr.) to ~ as (he was ~d as physically unfit for duty) 2. (D; tr.) to ~ for (to ~ smb. for coming late) 3. (D; tr.) to ~ from (he was ~d from drill; BE also has: he was ~d drill) 4. (G) we will never ~ taking innocent hostages 5. (K) please ~ my arriving late

execute *v.* (D; tr.) to ~ as (he was ~d as a deserter)

execution *n.* 1. to carry out an ~ 2. a mass; public ~ 3. ~ by (~ by firing squad)

executive *n.* a chief ~

exempt I *adj.* ~ from

exempt II *v.* (D; tr.) to ~ from

exemption *n.* 1. to claim an ~ 2. to grant an ~ 3. a draft (AE); tax ~ 4. an ~ for (he received an ~ for his elderly parents) 5. an ~ from (an ~ from the draft)

exercise I *n.* 1. to engage in, go in for ~ 2. to do ~s 3. hard, strenuous, vigorous; regular ~ 4. (an) aerobic; flexibility; isometric; relaxation; setting-up; warming-up ~ 5. physical ~ 6. a form of ~ (brisk walking is an excellent form of aerobic ~) 7. (fig.) an ~ in (an ~ in futility)

exercise II *v.* to ~ hard, strenuously, vigorously

exercised *adj.* ['upset'] ~ about, over

exercises *n.* ['ceremony'] to hold ~

exertion *n.* physical; strenuous ~

exhaustion *n.* 1. heat; nervous; total ~ 2. a state of ~

exhibit I *n.* ['exhibition'] 1. to mount, organize an ~ 2. an art; photo; traveling ~ 3. on ~ ['piece of evidence shown in court'] (legal) 4. ~ A

exhibit II *v.* (B) she ~ed her paintings to the public

exhibition *n.* 1. to put on, stage an ~ 2. to close; open an ~ 3. an art; international; photo; trade ~ 4. (misc.) to make an ~ of oneself (by behaving badly)

exhilarating *adj.* ~ to + inf. (it's ~ to climb mountains)

exhort *v.* 1. (D; tr.) to ~ to (to ~ smb. to action) 2. (H) to ~ students to work harder

exile I *n.* 1. to send smb. into ~ 2. in ~ (to live in ~)

exile II *v.* (D; tr.) to ~ from; to

exist *v.* (D; intr.) to ~ on (to ~ on bread and water)

existence *n.* 1. to lead a certain ~ (to lead a drab ~) 2. to eke out a (miserable) ~ 3. a drab, miserable; precarious ~

exit I *n.* 1. to make one's (she made a hasty ~) 2. (in a plane) an emergency; tail; window; wing ~ 3. an ~ from; to 4. (misc.) no ~!

exit II *v.* (D; intr.) to ~ from; to (to ~ to the system on a computer)

exodus *n.* 1. a mass ~ (there is a mass ~ from Paris every August) 2. an ~ from

exonerate *v.* (D; tr.) to ~ from

exorcise *v.* (D; tr.) to ~ from

expand *v.* 1. (D; intr., tr.) ('to become larger') ('to make larger') to ~ into (to ~ an article into a book) 2. (d; intr.) to ~ on ('to explain in detail') (to ~ on a topic)

expanse *n.* a broad, wide ~

expatiate *v.* (formal) (d; intr.) to ~ on, upon ('to discuss in detail')

expatriate *v.* (D; tr.) to ~ from; to

expect *v.* 1. (D; tr.) to ~ from, of (we ~ed more from him) 2. (E) she ~s to leave tomorrow 3. (H) we ~ed them to wait 4. (L) I ~ that the weather will be nice

expectancy *n.* life ~

expectation *n.* in ~ of

expectations *n.* 1. to come up to, meet ~ 2. to exceed, surpass ~ 3. to fall short of ~ 4. great, high ~ 5. ~ for (they had great ~ for their daughter) 6. beyond ~ (to succeed beyond all ~)

expedient *adj.* ~ to + inf. (sometimes it is ~ to make concessions)

expedition *n.* 1. to launch, mount, organize; lead an ~ 2. to go on an ~ 3. an archeological; hunting; military; mountain-climbing; punitive; scientific ~ 4. an ~ into, to (to lead an ~ to the Amazon) 5. (misc.) a fishing ~ ('an attempt to obtain information')

expel *v.* (D; tr.) to ~ from (to ~ a child from school)

expend *v.* (D; tr.) to ~ for, on (to ~ considerable funds on a new skating rink)

expenditure *n.* 1. to curb, curtail, cut down (on), reduce ~s 2. a capital ~ 3. an ~ for

expense *n.* 1. to incur, run up an ~ 2. to go to great ~; to spare no ~; to put smb. to great ~ 3. to curb, curtail, cut down (on), reduce ~s 4. to spare no ~ 5. to defray ~s 6. to reimburse ~s 7. to share ~s 8. business; entertainment; incidental; legal; operating; overhead; personal; traveling ~ 9. at smb.'s ~ (at my ~; at government ~)

expense account *n.* to pad an ~

expensive *adj.* ~ to + inf. (it's more ~ to live in the city than in the country)

experience *n.* ['practice'] ['participation'] 1. to acquire, gain, gather, get ~ from 2. broad, wide; direct, firsthand; hands-on; practical; previous ~ 3. a learning ~ 4. ~ to + inf. (they don't have enough ~ to do the job) 5. by, from ~ (to know from previous ~) ['adventure'] ['event'] 6. to have; share an ~ (I had quite an ~) 7. an enlightening; ennobling; harrowing, painful, unnerving, unpleasant; interesting; memorable; pleasant; rewarding; unforgettable ~

experienced *adj.* ~ at, in

experiment I *n.* 1. to carry out, conduct, perform, run an ~ on 2. a control; controlled ~ 3. a chemistry; physics ~

experiment II *v.* (D; intr.) to ~ on, upon, with

expert I *adj.* ~ at, in

expert II *n.* 1. a demolition; efficiency; self-styled; technical ~ 2. an ~ at, in, on (an ~ at troubleshooting; an ~ in computer science)

expertise *n.* 1. technical ~ 2. ~ in 3. the ~ to + inf. (does she have the ~ to do the job?)

expiration *n.* at, on the ~ (what will he do at the ~ of his term in office?)

explain *v.* 1. to ~ satisfactorily 2. (B) she ~ed the problem to me 3. (L; to) he ~ed (to us) that the examination would take place later 4. (Q) he ~ed why he was late

explanation *n.* 1. to give, offer, provide an ~ 2. to accept an ~ 3. a lucid; rational; satisfactory; simple; unsatisfactory ~ 4. an ~ for 5. an ~ that + clause (they accepted her ~ that she had been unavoidably detained)

expletive *n.* ~ deleted

explicit *adj.* 1. sexually ~ 2. ~ about

explode *v.* (D; intr.) to ~ with (to ~ with rage)

exploit *n.* 1. to perform an ~ 2. a fantastic; heroic ~

exploitation *n.* commercial ~

exploration *n.* space ~

explore *v.* to ~ carefully, gingerly (they had to ~ this possibility very gingerly)

explorer *n.* a brave; intrepid ~

explosion *n.* 1. to set off, touch off an ~ 2. a deafening, loud ~ 3. a population ~

explosive *n.* 1. to set off an ~ 2. to plant an ~ 3. (a) high; plastic ~

exponent *n.* ['champion'] a leading ~ (a leading ~ of reform)

export *v.* (D; intr., tr.) to ~ from; to (we ~ to many countries; they ~ tractors from the West Coast to several Asian countries)

expose *v.* (D; refl., tr.) to ~ to (to ~ smb. to danger; on; with ~d to the elements)

exposé *n.* to publish an ~

exposition *n.* 1. to hold an ~ 2. an international ~

expostulate *v.* (formal) (D; intr.) ('to argue') to ~ about, on; with

exposure *n.* ['being exposed'] 1. ~ to (~ to the elements) 2. of ~ (to die of ~) ['time during which film is exposed'] 3. a double; time ~ ['baring one's private parts'] 4. indecent ~ ['location in relation to the sun'] 5. a southern ~ (a house with a southern ~) ['publicity'] 6. wide ~

expound *v.* (formal) 1. (B) she ~ed her theory to her colleagues 2. (d; intr.) to ~ on (to ~ on one's favorite subject)

express *v.* 1. to ~ clearly; forcefully 2. (B) he ~ed his sympathy to the bereaved family 3. (D; refl., tr.) to ~ in (to ~ oneself in good English)

expression *n.* ['phrase'] 1. a colloquial; common; elliptical; figurative; fixed; hackneyed, trite; idiomatic; technical ~ ['look'] 2. an angry; deadpan; grave, serious; happy; intense; pained; pleasant; puzzled, quizzical; vacuous ~ (she had a pained ~ on her face)

expressive *adj.* ~ of

expropriate *v.* (D; tr.) to ~ from (to ~ land from the absentee owners)

expulsion *n.* ~ from

expunge *v.* (D; tr.) to ~ from

expurgate *v.* (D; tr.) to ~ from

extend *v.* 1. (A) ('to convey') they ~ed a warm welcome to us; or: they ~ed us a warm welcome 2. (d; intr.) ('to reach') to ~ beyond (the forest ~s beyond the border) 3. (d; intr.) ('to reach') to ~ from; to (the border ~s to the river) 4. (D; tr.) ('to prolong') to ~ from; to (we ~ed the fence to the edge of our property) 5. (d; intr.) ('to continue') to ~ into (the cold wave ~ed into March) 6. (d; intr., tr.) ('to spread') to ~ over (his power ~s over the whole country) 7. (P; intr.) ('to stretch') the plateau ~s for many miles

extension *n.* ['increase in time allowed'] 1. to grant an ~ 2. to ask for, request; get, receive an ~ ['branch'] (AE) 3. a university ~

extent *n.* to a certain ~ (to a great ~; they were emaciated to such an ~ that they required special treatment)

exterior *n.* a stern ~ (a soft heart under a stern ~)

extermination *n.* complete, total ~

external *adj.* ~ to (formal)

extinguisher *n.* a fire ~

extoll *v.* (D; tr.) to ~ as (they were ~ed as heroes)

extort *v.* (D; tr.) to ~ from (to ~ money from merchants)

extortion *n.* to commit; practice ~

extra *n.* ['special edition of a newspaper'] to issue, publish, put out an ~

extract I *n.* lemon; vanilla ~

extract II *v.* (D; tr.) to ~ from (to ~ information from smb.)

extraction *n.* ['origin'] of a certain ~ (a family of Irish ~)

extradite *v.* (D; tr.) to ~ from; to

extradition *n.* 1. to ask for ~ 2. to grant smb.'s ~ 3. to fight, oppose ~ 4. to waive ~ ('to agree to be extradited')

extraneous *adj.* ~ to

extraordinary *adj.* ~ that (it was ~ that no one reported the incident to the police)

extrapolate *v.* (D; intr., tr.) to ~ from, on the basis of

extravagance *n.* ~ in

extravagant *adj.* ~ in (~ in spending their father's money)

extreme *n.* 1. to go to an ~ (to go from one ~ to the other) 2. at an ~ (at the other ~) 3. in the ~ ('extremely')

extreme unction *n.* to administer, give ~ (see the Usage Note for **unction**)

extremist *n.* a political; religious ~

extremities *n.* ['limbs'] the lower; upper ~

extricate *v.* (D; refl., tr.) to ~ from (she ~d herself from a difficult situation)

extrinsic *adj.* (formal) ~ to

exult *v.* (D; intr.) to ~ at, in, over

exultation *n.* ~ at, in, over

eye *n.* ['organ of sight'] 1. to blink; close, shut; open; roll; squint one's ~s 2. to drop, lower; lift, raise one's ~s 3. to rest; strain one's ~s 4. to lay, set one's ~s on smt. ('to see smt.') 5. to keep one's ~s open, peeled (esp. AE), skinned (BE) ('to be watchful') 6. the naked ~ (the meteor could be seen with the naked ~) 7. bulging; glassy ~s 8. ~s twinkle; twitch 9. a pair of ~s 10. in one's ~s (tears were in his ~s; fear could be seen in their ~s) ['vision, sight'] 11. good, strong; weak ~s 12. an eagle ~ ('keen sight') ['area around the eyes'] 13. (also fig.) a black ~ (to give smb. a black ~) ['look, glance'] 14. to cast an ~ on smt.; to run one's ~ over smt.; to fix one's ~ on smt. 15. to take one's ~s off (they could not take their ~s off Hannah) 16. an anxious; critical; sharp, watchful; weather; suspicious ~ 17. a jaundiced ~ ('an envious, hostile look') 18. (of one who flirts) bedroom ('seductive') ~s; a roving, wandering ~ (he has a roving ~) 19. curious, prying; piercing ~s ['attention'] ['interest'] ['observation'] 20. to catch smb.'s ~ 21. to open smb.'s ~s (to the truth) 22. to close, shut one's ~s (to the truth); to turn a blind ~ to smt. ('to let smt. pass as if unnoticed') 23. to keep an ~ on smt. ('to keep smt. under observation') 24. to keep an ~ out for smt. ('to watch for smt. attentively') 25. the public ~ (to be constantly in the public ~) 26. with an ~ to (with an ~ to public opinion) ['judgment'] ['viewpoint'] 27. a good, keen ~ 28. an ~ for (she has a good ~ for distances) 29. to the trained ~ 30. in smb.'s ~s (in the ~s of the law, he is innocent until proved guilty) ['perception'] ['appreciation'] 31. to open smb.'s ~s to smt. 32. an ~ for (an ~ for beauty; to have an ~ for a good bargain) ['device that detects'] 33. an electric ~ ['detective'] (colloq.) 34. a private ~ ['prosthesis for an eye'] 35. an artificial, glass ~ ['misc.'] 36. an ~ for an ~ ('an equivalent retaliation'); to feast one's ~s on smt. ('to look at smt. with great pleasure'); to give smb. the ~ ('to flirt with smb.') or ('to give smb. a visual signal'); to make ~s at smb. ('to look lovingly at smb.'); to see ~ to ~ with ('to agree with'); the mind's ~ ('the visual recollection of past events'); the evil ~ ('a look intended to inflict harm'); his ~ fell on a bargain ('he discovered a bargain'); under the teacher's watchful ~; without batting an ~ (esp. AE) ('while remaining calm'); easy on the ~s ('pretty'); more than meets the ~ ('more than is seen'); to look someone in the ~ ('to look at someone directly'); before one's ~s

eyebrow *n.* 1. to pluck, tweeze one's ~s 2. bushy ~s 3. (misc.) to lift, raise an ~ ('to express one's surprise')

eyeglasses *n.* (AE: CE has *glasses*) a pair of ~

eyelash see **eyelid 2**

eyelid *n.* 1. drooping ~s 2. (misc.) without batting an ~ (esp. BE) ('while remaining calm') (AE has *without batting an eyelash*)

eye shadow *n.* to apply, put on ~

eyesight *n.* keen; poor, weak ~

eyeteeth *n.* to cut one's ~ on smt. ('to become knowledgeable while doing smt.')

eye witness *n.* an ~ to (there was an ~ to the crime)

F

fable *n.* a ~ about
fabric *n.* ['material'] 1. to weave a ~ 2. a cotton; rayon; silk; synthetic; woolen; wrinkle-free ~ ['structure'] 3. a basic; social ~ (the basic ~ of the country)
fabrication *n.* an outright, total ~
face I *n.* ['grimace'] 1. to make, pull (BE) a ~ (at) ['prestige'] 2. to save ~ 3. to lose ~ ['front part of the head'] 4. to press one's ~ (against a window) 5. (fig.) to show one's ~ (he didn't dare show his ~) 6. to powder one's ~ 7. a beautiful, handsome, pretty; familiar; oval; round; ruddy; strange; ugly ~ 8. (misc.) to come/meet ~ to ~; to bring ~ to ~; to look smb. in the ~; I would never say that to her ~; to laugh in smb.'s ~; ~ down ['expression'] 9. an angry; funny; happy; poker, straight; sad; serious ~ (to keep a straight ~) ['makeup'] (colloq.) 10. to put one's ~ on ['misc.'] 11. in the ~ of serious difficulties ('facing serious difficulties'); on the ~ of it ('judging by appearances'); to disappear from the ~ of the earth; to fly in the ~ of smt. ('to defy smt. energetically')
face II *v.* 1. to ~ squarely 2. (d; tr.) to ~ with (to ~ smb. with irrefutable evidence) 3. (G) I could not ~ going there alone 4. (P; intr.) to ~ east
face up *v.* (d; intr.) to ~ to (to ~ to reality)
facial *n.* 1. to do a ~ 2. to get a ~
facilities *n.* ['installations'] 1. to provide ~ for 2. ample; excellent; modern; outmoded; poor; rundown ~ 3. dining, eating; educational; hotel; medical; port; public; public health; recreational; research; storage; transportation ~ (our city has excellent port ~) 4. ~ for
facility *n.* ['skill'] 1. a ~ for, in, with (to have a ~ for languages) ['installation'] 2. to operate a ~
fact *n.* ['something that is true'] 1. to ascertain, establish a ~ 2. to check, confirm, verify a ~ 3. to cite; collect, gather, marshal; present (the) ~s 4. to classify; evaluate, interpret (the) ~s 5. to face (the) ~s 6. to distort, twist; embellish, embroider (the) ~s 7. to ignore a ~ 8. an accepted, established; cold, dry, hard, incontestable, incontrovertible, indisputable, irrefutable, unquestionable; firsthand ~ 9. a basic, essential; historic; proven; statistical; well-known ~; the bare ~s 10. a ~ that + clause (it's a ~ that some officials are corrupt) ['reality'] 11. to distinguish ~ from fiction 12. in ~ ['misc.'] 13. a question of ~; the ~s of life
faction *n.* a contending; extremist; opposing; rebel ~
factor *n.* 1. a contributing; critical, deciding, determining, essential, major ~ 2. (math. and fig.) a common ~ 3. (meteorology) a wind-chill ~ 4. a safety ~ 5. a ~ in
factory *n.* 1. to manage, operate a ~ 2. to open a ~ 3. to close, shut down a ~ 4. an automobile (AE), motorcar (BE); clothing; munitions; shoe; textile ~ 5. at, in a ~ (she works at/in a ~)
faculty *n.* ['division of a university'] (esp. BE; CE has *school*) 1. a ~ of education; law; medicine; science ['teaching staff'] (esp. AE) 2. on the ~ (she is on the ~) 3. a college, university; school ~ 4. the standing ('permanent') ~ ['ability'] 5. a ~ for (a ~ for learning languages)
fad *n.* 1. the latest, newest ~ 2. a passing ~
faddism *n.* food ~
fade *v.* 1. (d; intr.) (usu. fig.) to ~ from, out of (to ~ from the picture) 2. (d; intr.) to ~ into (to ~ into obscurity) 3. (misc.) (AE) to ~ in the stretch ('to drop out of contention near the end of a contest')
fail I *n.* without ~
fail II *v.* 1. to ~ dismally, miserably 2. (D; intr.) to ~ in (to ~ in business) 3. (D; tr.) to ~ on (to ~ a student on an examination) 4. (E) he ~ed to comprehend the seriousness of the problem
failure *n.* 1. to experience ~ 2. an abject complete, dismal, hopeless, miserable, outright ~ 3. a box-office; crop ~ 4. heart ~ 5. a power ~ 6. a ~ to + inf. (the patient's ~ to respond to treatment was discouraging)
faint I *adj.* to feel ~ from (she felt ~ from lack of air)
faint II *n.* 1. to fall into a ~ 2. a dead ~ (to fall into a dead ~)
faint III *v.* (D; intr.) to ~ from (to ~ from loss of blood)
fair I *adj.* 1. scrupulously ~ 2. ~ to (he's ~ to his employees) 3. ~ to + inf. (it's ~ to say that she deserved the promotion) 4. ~ that + clause (it's not ~ that our application was rejected)
fair II *n.* an annual; book; county; health; livestock; state (US); trade; world's ~
faith *n.* ['firm belief, trust'] 1. to have ~ in; to place one's ~ in 2. to lose ~ in 3. to shake smb.'s ~ in 4. an abiding, enduring, steadfast; deep, strong, unshakable ~ 5. on ~ (to accept on ~) ['fidelity to one's promises'] 6. to keep ~ with 7. to demonstrate, show good ~ 8. in good ~; in bad ~ (she acted in good ~) ['religion'] 9. to adhere to, practice a ~ 10. to abjure, recant, renounce one's ~ 11. the true ~ (brought up in the true ~) 12. by ~ (she is a Buddhist by ~)
faithful I *adj.* ~ in; to
faithful II *n.* (plural) the party ~
faithfulness *n.* ~ to
faithless *adj.* (formal) ~ to
fake *v.* (esp. AE) (usu. sports) (d; tr.) to ~ out of (to ~ an opposing player out of position)
fall I *n.* ['dropping, coming down'] 1. to have, take a ~ 2. to break a ~ 3. a bad, nasty ~ (she had a bad ~ and broke her ankle) 4. a free ~ (of a parachutist); crop ~ 5. a ~ from (a ~ from a horse) ['autumn'] (AE) 6. an early; late ~ 7. in (the) ~ (we have a lot of rain in the ~)
fall II *v.* 1. ('to drop') to ~ flat, headlong; short 2. (colloq.) (d; intr.) to ~ for ('to become infatuated with') (he fell for her) 3. (D; intr.) ('to drop') to ~

from (to ~ from a tree; to ~ from grace) 4. (d; intr.) ('to come'); ('to drop') to ~ into (to ~ into disfavor; to ~ into disrepute; to ~ into place; to ~ into a trap) 5. (d; intr.) ('to be divided') to ~ into (to ~ into three categories) 6. (D; intr.) ('to drop') to ~ off (to ~ off a table) 7. (D; intr.) ('to drop') to ~ on (to ~ on one's back; the stress ~s on the last syllable) 8. (d; intr.) ('to come') to ~ on (the holiday fell on a Monday) 9. (d; intr.) ('to drop') to ~ out of (to ~ out of bed; to ~ out of favor) 10. (d; intr.) to ~ over (she fell over the side of the ship) 11. (formal) (d; intr.) ('to devolve') to ~ to (it fell to me to break the news) 12. (D; intr.) ('to drop') to ~ to (he fell to his knees; the book fell to the floor) 13. (d; intr.) ('to drop') ('to come') to ~ under (to ~ under a train; to ~ under smb.'s influence) 14. (misc.) to ~ asleep; to ~ due; to ~ foul of the law; to ~ ill; to ~ in love with smb.; to ~ in battle; to ~ silent; to ~ on hard times; to ~ to pieces; to ~ into step

fallacy n. 1. a ~ to + inf. (it's a ~ to assume that he will help) 2. a ~ that (it's a ~ that all politicians are corrupt

fall back v. 1. (D; intr.) to ~ into (to ~ into an easy chair) 2. (D; intr.) to ~ on, to (the troops fell back to their defensive positions)

fall behind v. (D; intr.) to ~ in, with (to ~ with the rent)

fall in v. (d; intr.) to ~ with (to ~ with the wrong crowd)

falling out n. (colloq.) ['quarrel'] to have a ~ with

fallout n. 1. radioactive ~ 2. ~ from (also fig.)

fall out v. 1. (D; intr.) ('to quarrel') to ~ with (to ~ with smb.) 2. (misc.) the platoon fell out on the company street

fallow adj. ['uncultivated'] to lie ~ (the field lay ~)

fall short v. (D; intr.) to ~ of (they fell short of their goal)

fall to v. (G) he fell to brooding

false front n. ['deceptive manner'] to put up a ~

falsehood n. 1. to tell, utter a ~ 2. an absolute, downright, utter ~

falsetto n. to sing ~

falter v. (D; intr.) to ~ in (to ~ in one's determination)

fame n. 1. to achieve, attain, win; seek ~ 2. international; undying ~ 3. at the height of one's ~

familiar adj. ['known'] 1. ~ to (is this area ~ to you?) 2. (misc.) all too ~ ['acquainted'] 3. thoroughly ~ 4. ~ with (are you ~ with the details?)

familiarity n. 1. thorough ~ 2. ~ with

familiarize v. (d; refl., tr.) to ~ with (she had to ~ herself with the facts of the case)

family n. ['social unit traditionally consisting of parents and children'] 1. to start a ~ 2. to clothe; feed; raise; support a ~ 3. the close, immediate; extended; nuclear ~ 4. a good ('respected') ~ (he comes from a good ~) 5. a blended; broken ~ 6. the head of a ~; a member of a ~ 7. in the ~ (poor vision runs in the ~) 8. (misc.) ~ planning ('birth control'); (old-fashioned) in the ~ way ('pregnant') ['group of related languages'] 9. a language

~ (in the same language ~)

family style adv. (esp. AE) to serve (a meal) ~

famine n. 1. ~ strikes (~ struck several provinces) 2. widespread ~

famous adj. 1. ~ as (he is ~ as an actor) 2. ~ for (the city is ~ for its museums)

fan I n. ['electrical device for cooling'] 1. to turn on; turn off a ~ 2. a ceiling; exhaust (AE), extractor (BE) ~ ['paper or cloth fan'] 3. to wave a ~

fan II n. ['admirer'] ['supporter'] 1. an ardent ~ 2. (AE) a ~ roots (for a team) USAGE NOTE: In CE one can be a *fan* of a certain sport--a football fan. In AE one can also be a fan of a certain team-- a Dodger fan. In BE, however, one would usu. be called a *supporter* of a team.

fanatic n. 1. a religious ~ 2. a ~ to + inf. (he had to be a ~ to do that)

fancy I n. 1. to take a ~ to 2. to catch, strike, take (BE), tickle smb.'s ~ 3. a passing ~ 4. a flight of ~

fancy II v. 1. (d; tr.) ('to like') to ~ as (I don't ~ him as an actor) 2. (G) ('to like') I don't ~ going there 3. (G) ('to imagine') just ~ winning first prize 4. (L) ('to imagine') she ~cied that she heard footsteps

fanfare n. with great ~

fangs n. an animal bares its ~

fan out v. to ~ in all directions

fantasize v. (D; intr.) to ~ about

fantastic adj. (colloq.) ['very good'] ~ to + inf. (it's ~ to work with them = it's ~ working with them)

fantasy n. 1. to act out a ~ 2. to indulge in ~ 3. a childhood; sexual ~ 4. (misc.) (to live in) a world of ~/~ world

far adj., adv. 1. ~ from (~ from the city; the problem is ~ from being solved) 2. by ~ (she is by ~ the better player) 3. (misc.) to go ~ on one's connections; ~ be it from me to criticize, but... USAGE NOTE: The phrases *by far* and *far and away* mean 'very much'--she is by far/far and away the better player. In nonstandard BE the two phrases are blended to produce *by far and away*.

farce n. a ~ to + inf. (it was a ~ to conduct a trial under such conditions)

fare I n. ['payment for transportation'] 1. to charge; pay a ~ 2. a full; half; reduced ~ 3. at a ~ (at a reduced ~) ['food'] 4. simple ~

fare II v. (formal) (P; intr.) she ~d well in the big city

farewell n. 1. to make one's ~s 2. to bid smb. ~ 3. a fond; sad ~ 4. a ~ to

farm n. 1. to manage, operate, run, work a ~ 2. a chicken; collective; dairy; poultry; private; sheep; stock; truck (AE) ~ 3. on a ~ (to work on a ~)

farmer n. a dirt (AE); tenant ~

farming n. 1. to be engaged in ~ 2. chicken; collective; cooperative; dairy; pig; poultry; sheep; state; stock; subsistence; truck ~

farmland n. to cultivate, work ~

farm out v. (B) the work was ~ed out to several associates

farsighted adj. ~ to + inf. (it was ~ of her to buy up this property)

farsightedness *n.* the ~ to + inf. (they had enough ~ to provide for their old age)

fascinated *adj.* 1. ~ at, with (~ at the spectacle of a rocket launching) 2. ~ to + inf. (I was ~ to learn of their work

fascinating *adj.* 1. ~ to + inf. (it's ~ to listen to her) 2. ~ that + clause (it's ~ that migratory birds never get lost)

fascination *n.* 1. to have, hold a ~ for (the Himalayas have/hold a special ~ for climbers) 2. a morbid; special ~ 3. ~ with

fashion I *n.* ['vogue'] 1. to set a ~ 2. to come into ~; to go out of ~ 3. current ~(s); the latest ~(s) 4. high ~ 5. in ~ (big hats are no longer in ~) ['manner'] 6. in a ~ (she behaved in a strange ~)

fashion II *v.* 1. (D; tr.) to ~ from, out of (to ~ a pipe out of clay) 2. (d; tr.) to ~ into (to ~ clay into a pipe)

fashion show *n.* to hold, organize a ~

fast I *adv.* to hold ~ to (they held ~ to their beliefs)

fast II *n.* 1. to observe a ~ 2. to break a ~

fasten *v.* (D; tr.) to ~ onto, to

fastidious *adj.* ~ about (~ about one's appearance)

fast-talk *v.* (colloq.) (D; tr.) to ~ into; out of (to ~ smb. into doing smt.)

fat *n.* 1. to trim (away) the ~ 2. animal; deep; excess; polyunsaturated; vegetable ~ (to fry in deep ~) 3. subcutaneous ~ 4. (misc.) (colloq.) to live off the ~ of the land ('to live very well'); to chew the ~ ('to chat')

fatal *adj.* (formal) 1. ~ to + inf. (it would be ~ to hesitate)

fatalities *n.* 1. to cause ~ 2. highway (AE), motorway (BE), traffic ~

fate *n.* 1. to decide, seal smb.'s ~ 2. to tempt ~ 3. to meet one's ~ 4. blind; cruel; inexorable ~ 5. ~ decreed (that we would win the lottery) 6. a stroke of ~

fated *adj.* (formal) 1. ~ to + inf. (they were ~ never to meet) 2. ~ that + clause (it was ~ that they should never meet again)

father *n.* 1. an expectant; proud ~ 2. a foster ~; stepfather 3. a ~ to (he was like a ~ to them) 4. (misc.) the city ~s; a founding ~

fatigue *n.* 1. to feel ~ 2. battle, combat; mental ~ 3. metal ~ 4. a state of ~ (she was in a state of complete ~)

faucet *n.* (AE) 1. to turn on a ~ 2. a ~ leaks 3. a leaky ~ (CE has *tap*)

fault I *n.* 1. to find ~ with 2. to correct a ~ 3. to overlook smb.'s ~s 4. a grievous; human ~ 5. a ~ that + clause (it was not my ~ that he was late) 6. at ~ (we were all at ~) 7. through smb.'s ~ 8. to a ~ (she is fastidious to a ~)

fault II *v.* (D; tr.) ('to blame') to ~ for

faux pas *n.* 1. to commit, make a ~ 2. a grave ~

favor I **favour** *n.* ['friendly act, service'] 1. to do, grant (smb.) a ~ 2. to perform a ~ (for smb.) ['approval'] ['liking'] 3. to curry ~ with; to vie for smb.'s ~ 4. to find, gain ~ with; to find ~ in smb.'s eyes 5. to lose ~ 6. universal ~ 7. in ~ with 8. out of ~ (to fall out of ~) 9. to look with ~ on smt. ['support'] 10. in ~ of (these facts speak in ~ of his

acquittal; we are in ~ of reform) 11. in smb.'s ~ (the odds are in her ~)

favor II **favour** *v.* 1. (formal) (D; tr.) to ~ with (she will now ~ us with a song) 2. (G) he ~s raising taxes

favorable, favourable *adj.* ~ for, to

favored, favoured *adj.* 1. heavily ~ 2. ~ to + inf. (our team is heavily ~ to win)

favorite, favourite *n.* a heavy, strong ~

favoritism, favouritism *n.* 1. to show ~ 2. strong ~

favors, favours *n.* ['sexual privileges'] to grant one's ~ to smb.; to bestow one's ~s on

fawn *v.* (d; intr.) to ~ on, over

fear I *n.* 1. to arouse, inspire, instill, kindle ~ 2. to express; feel; show ~ (she felt ~ for their safety) 3. to confirm one's ~s 4. to allay, dispel, overcome ~ 5. grave, mortal, strong; groundless idle; inarticulate; lingering; sudden ~ 6. ~ that + clause (there are ~s that no compromise can be worked out) 7. for ~ of (he lied for ~ of being punished) 8. in ~ of (he is in ~ of his life) 9. out of ~ (he did it out of ~) 10. (misc.) to strike ~ into smb.'s heart

fear II *v.* 1. to ~ greatly, very much 2. (d; intr.) to ~ for (I ~ for his safety) 3. (E) I ~ to think what may happen 4. (K) he ~s my getting involved 5. (L) we ~ that we will not be able to attend

fearful *adj.* 1. ~ of 2. ~ that + clause (they were ~ that the river would flood)

feasible *adj.* ~ to + inf. (it was not ~ to build a bridge at that point)

feast I *n.* a royal, sumptuous ~

feast II *v.* (formal) (D; intr., tr.) to ~ on, upon (to ~ on Chateaubriand; to ~ one's eyes on beautiful scenery)

feat *n.* 1. to accomplish, perform a ~ 2. a brave, heroic; brilliant, notable, noteworthy, outstanding, remarkable ~ (to perform a remarkable ~) 3. no mean, small ~ (it was no mean ~ to get him to agree)

feather *n.* 1. to pluck ~s (from a chicken) 2. (misc.) as light as a ~ ('very light'); a ~ in one's cap ('a symbol of accomplishment'); to smooth smb.'s ruffled ~s ('to calm smb.')

feature I *n.* ['quality'] 1. a characteristic, distinctive, distinguishing; notable; noteworthy; special ~ 2. a redeeming ~ ['contour'] ['line'] 3. coarse; delicate, fine; prominent; regular; sharp; soft; striking ~s ['main film'] 4. a double ~ ('a program consisting of two films in a movie theater') ['special item'] 5. an optional ~ (we chose several optional ~s for our new car)

feature II *v.* (D; tr.) to ~ as (she was ~d as a dancer)

federate *v.* (D; tr.) to ~ into

federation *n.* 1. to form a ~ 2. a ~ among, between

fed up *adj.* ~ of (BE), with

fee *n.* 1. to charge a ~ 2. to split ~s (as of lawyers, doctors) 3. to waive one's ~ 4. a fat, large; nominal ~ 5. an admission, entrance; contingency; laboratory; membership; registration ~ 6. a ~ for (a ~ for service) 7. for a ~ (for a nominal ~)

feed *v.* 1. (A) they fed erroneous information to

us; or: they fed us erroneous information 2. (d; tr.) to ~ into, to (to ~ data into a computer) 3. (D; intr.) to ~ on (certain animals ~ on insects)
feedback n. negative; positive ~
feeding n. breast; communal; forced; intravenous ~
feel I n. (colloq.) to have a (good) ~ for
feel II v. 1. ('to believe') to ~ keenly, strongly 2. (D; intr.) ('to have an opinion') to ~ about (how do you ~ about this problem?) 3. (d; intr.) ('to grope') to ~ (around) for (he felt in his pockets for his keys) 4. (colloq.) (d; intr.) to ~ for ('to sympathize with') (I ~ for them) 5. (D; tr.) ('to experience') to ~ for (to ~ pity for smb.) 6. (I) ('to sense') he could ~ his heart beat 7. (J) ('to sense') he could ~ his heart beating 8. (L) ('to believe') we ~ that you should return home 9. (s) to ~ comfortable; I ~ cheated; to ~ sorry about smt.; to ~ good ('happy'); to ~ fine/well ('healthy'); to ~ bad ('unwell') or ('sad') 10. (BE) (S) I ~ such a fool 11. (misc.) it ~s good to be on vacation; it felt nice to swim in the heated pool; she felt proud of her children; to ~ bad/badly ('sad') about smt.
feeler n. ['probe'] to put out, throw out a ~
feeling n. ['emotional reaction'] 1. to arouse, stir up ~ ['appreciation'] 2. to develop a ~ for (to develop a ~ for classical music) ['sentiment'] ['sensation'] 3. to express; show one's ~s 4. to experience, have a ~ 5. to harbor ~s (to harbor warm ~s of friendship towards smb.) 6. to hide, mask; repress one's ~s 7. to lose ~ (he lost all ~ in his foot) 8. a deep, strong; eery, strange; friendly, tender, warm; gloomy, sad; hostile; intangible; intense; queasy; satisfied; sick; sinking; sneaking; uneasy ~ 9. (colloq.) a gut ('instinctive') ~ 10. one's innermost, intimate; pent-up ~s 11. hard ~s (we have no hard ~s ('we are not angry') 12. a ~ that + clause (I had an eery ~ that I had been there before) ['attitude'] ['opinion'] 13. definite; strong ~s (we have strong ~s about this matter) 14. popular ~ (popular ~ was running against the president) 15. ~s about, on (to have definite ~s on a subject) ['sensitivity'] 16. to hurt smb.'s ~s 17. delicate, sensitive ~s ['premonition'] 18. a ~ that + clause (I had a ~ that she would show up)
feel like v. 1. (G) she ~s like resting 2. (S; used only with nouns) to ~ a fool; it ~s like satin
feel up v. (d; intr.) to ~ to ('to feel capable of') (do you ~ to a drive to town?)
feign v. (formal) (L) he ~ed that he was sick
feint n. to make a ~
fellow n. ['scholar'] ['fellowship holder'] 1. a research; senior; teaching ~ ['man'] 2. a good; honest; nice, regular; young ~
fellowship n. ['stipend; support for studies'] 1. to award, grant; establish a ~ 2. to receive, win a ~ 3. a graduate, postgraduate (esp. BE); postdoctoral ~ ['community of interest'] 4. to foster, promote (good) ~ 5. ~ with
felony n. 1. to commit, perpetrate a ~ 2. to compound a ~ ('to waive prosecution in return for compensation')
feminist n. an ardent, dedicated, devoted; moderate; radical ~

fence n. 1. to build, erect, put up a ~ 2. a high; low ~ 3. a barbed-wire; chain-link; picket; rail; snow; wrought-iron ~ 4. a ~ around 5. (misc.) to mend ~s ('to set things right'); on the ~ ('uncommitted')
fend v. (d; intr.) to ~ for (to ~ for oneself)
fender n. (AE) a dented ~ (BE has wing)
ferment n. 1. intellectual; social ~ 2. in ~ (the country was in ~)
ferry I n. 1. to board; take a ~ 2. by ~ (to cross a river by ~)
ferry II v. (d; tr.) to ~ across (to ~ troops across a river)
fertilizer n. 1. to spread ~ 2. artificial; chemical; natural ~
fervor, fervour n. (a) messianic; religious ~
festival n. 1. to hold a ~ 2. a dance; drama; folk; music ~
fetch v. (C) please ~ my pipe for me; or: please ~ me my pipe
fête n. (esp. BE) 1. to hold a ~ 2. a church; village ~
fetish n. to make a ~ of smt. (they made a ~ of good grooming)
fetus, foetus n. 1. to abort a ~ 2. a viable ~ 3. an unborn ~
feud I n. 1. to stir up a ~ 2. a blood; family, internecine; personal ~ 3. a ~ between, with
feud II v. (D; intr.) to ~ over; with
fever n. ['elevated temperature of the body'] 1. to come down with, develop a ~ 2. a constant; high; intermittent; mild, slight; recurrent; remittent ~ 3. a ~ breaks, subsides ['disease or condition'] 4. glandular; hay; relapsing; rheumatic; Rocky Mountain spotted; scarlet; trench; typhoid; undulant; yellow ~
fever pitch n. 1. to reach (a) ~ 2. at (a) ~
few I determiner, n., pronoun 1. relatively ~ 2. a ~ of (we saw a ~ of them) USAGE NOTE: The use of the preposition of is necessary when a pronoun follows. Compare the following constructions with nouns--we saw very few students; we saw a few ('several') students.
few II n. 1. (a) precious, very ~ 2. (misc.) to have a ~ too many ('to drink too much'); ~ and far between ('rare'); just a ~, only a ~
fiasco n. 1. to end in a ~ 2. a complete, total, utter ~
fib n. to tell a ~
fiber, fibre n. 1. coarse; synthetic; wool ~ 2. moral ~ 3. nerve ~
fiction n. 1. pure ~ (her story was pure ~) 2. science ~
fiddle n. 1. to play the ~ 2. (colloq.; AE) a bass ~ (CE has double bass) 3. (misc.) as fit as a ~ ('very healthy')
fidelity n. ['loyalty'] 1. to swear ~ 2. ~ to ['quality of electronic reproduction'] 3. high ~
fidget v. (D; intr.) to ~ with
field n. ['cultivated area'] 1. to plow; till, work a ~ 2. a corn; wheat ~ 3. in a ~ (farmers were working in the ~s) ['area used for athletic events'] 4. to take the ~ 5. a baseball; football, soccer (BE often

has *pitch*); playing ~ 6. on the ~ (how many players were on the football ~?) ['area used as a landing strip'] 7. a flying, landing ~ 8. on the ~ ['area used for practical work'] 9. to work (out) in the ~ ['unbroken expanse'] ['space'] 10. an open ~ 11. a visual ~ ['area producing a natural resource'] 12. a coal; gold; oil ~ ['space in which electric lines of force are present'] (physics) 13. an electromagnetic, magnetic ~ ['area of activity'] 14. in a ~ (in the ~ of science) ['misc.'] 15. on the ~ of honor

field day *n.* ['a great success'] to have a ~ (they had a ~ with the reporters)

field glasses *n.* to focus, train ~ on

fieldwork *n.* to do ~

fiend *n.* a sex ~

Fifth *n.* (colloq.) (AE) ['the Fifth Amendment protecting witnesses against self-incrimination'] to invoke, take the ~

fight I *n.* ['struggle'] 1. to pick, provoke, start a ~ (he picked a ~ with me) 2. to put up, wage a ~ (to wage a ~ against corruption) 3. to get into a ~ (to get into a ~ with a neighbor about the property line) 4. a bitter, desperate, fierce, hard, stubborn; clean, fair; dirty, unfair; last-ditch ~; a ~ to the death (to put up a last-ditch ~) 5. a fist ~ 6. a ~ breaks out, starts 7. a ~ about, over; against; among, between; for; with (a ~ for justice; a ~ between local politicians) 8. a ~ to + inf. (we joined the ~ to reduce waste) ['boxing match'] 9. to hold, stage a ~ 10. to fix a ~ ('to influence the results of a ~ illegally') 11. a clean; dirty ~ 12. (misc.) the big ~ (everyone was talking about the big ~)

fight II *v.* 1. to ~ bravely, heroically; clean; desperately, hard, stubbornly; dirty, unfairly; fair, fairly 2. (D; intr., tr.) to ~ about, over; against; among; for; with (he was always ~ing with his neighbors about the noise; Great Britain fought with Turkey against Russia; they are always ~ing among themselves; the United States fought a war with Mexico over their common border; the war was fought for a just cause; the dogs were ~ing over a bone) 3. (D; intr.) to ~ like (they fought like heroes) 4. (misc.) to ~ to the finish; to ~ with one's fists

fighter *n.* ['pugilist'] 1. a clean; dirty ~ ['fighting aircraft'] 2. a long-range; medium-range ~ ['misc.'] 3. a firefighter

fighting *n.* 1. to step up the ~ 2. bitter, fierce, hard, heavy; hand-to-hand ~ 3. clean; dirty ~ 4. street ~ 5. breaks out; rages

figure I *n.* ['impression'] ['appearance'] 1. to cut a (fine) ~ ('to make a strong impression') 2. a conspicuous, dashing, fine, handsome, imposing, striking, trim ~ (to cut a dashing ~) 3. a ridiculous, sorry ~ ['person'] ['personage'] 4. a familiar; national; political; prominent, well-known; public; religious; underworld ~ 5. a father; mother; parental ~ ['number'] 6. to bandy ~s 7. approximate, ball-park (AE; colloq.), round; available; exact; official; reliable ~s 8. in ~s (in round ~s)

figure II *v.* 1. (d; intr.) ('to play a role') to ~ in (she ~d prominently in history) 2. (colloq.) (esp.

AE) ('to estimate') (L) we ~d that he would arrive at around two o'clock 3. (colloq.) (esp. AE) (M) ('to estimate') I ~d him to be worth a few hundred thousand

figure on *v.* (colloq.) (esp. AE) (G) ('to intend') I ~d on staying a few days

figure out *v.* (colloq.) (AE) 1. (L) he ~d out that we could not possibly get there on time 2. (Q) she could not ~ how to do it

filch *v.* (d; tr.) ('to steal') to ~ from

file I *n.* ['dossier'] ['folder'] 1. to make up, open a ~ 2. to keep a ~ 3. to close a ~ 4. official ~s 5. a vertical ~ 6. a ~ on (to keep a ~ on smb.) 7. on ~ (these documents are kept on ~) ['collection of data in a computer'] 8. to copy; create; delete, erase; edit; print a ~

file II *v.* 1. (D; tr.) ('to apply') to ~ for (to ~ for divorce) 2. (D; tr.) ('to submit') to ~ with (she ~d an application with several employment agencies)

file III *n.* ['row'] 1. Indian, single ~ 2. in single ~

file IV *v.* ('to move in a line') 1. (d; intr.) to ~ by past (to ~ past a coffin) 2. (d; intr.) to ~ into; out of (to ~ into an auditorium; the jury ~d out of the courtroom)

file V *n.* ['tool for smoothing surfaces'] a rail ~

filibuster *n.* to carry on, conduct, engage in, wage a ~

filing *n.* ['storage of data'] to do ~

fill I *n.* ['what is necessary to satisfy'] to drink; eat; have one's ~

fill II *v.* 1. (D; tr.) to ~ to (the auditorium was ~ed to capacity; to ~ to overflowing) 2. (D intr., tr.) to ~ with (the lecture hall ~ed with people; to ~ a hole with sand)

fill in *v.* (D; intr.) to ~ for ('to replace') (to ~ for a friend)

filling *n.* (dental) 1. to put in a ~ 2. to cement a ~ 3. a broken, cracked ~ 4. a permanent; temporary ~ 5. a ~ breaks, cracks; chips; falls out

film *n.* ['cinema picture, motion picture'] 1. to edit; make, produce, shoot a ~ (the ~ was shot on location) 2. to release; show a ~ 3. to ban; censor a ~ 4. to rate; review a ~ 5. an action; adult, blue (BE), X-rated; adventure; children's; color; documentary; educational; feature; gangster; instructional; propaganda; silent; sound; television, TV; training; travel ~ 6. (misc.) (BE) to work in ~s ('to work in the film industry') ['roll of material used to take photographs'] 7. to insert, load; remove; rewind; wind ~ 8. to develop ~ 9. to splice ~ 10. black-and-white; color; fast; 16-millimeter; 35-millimeter ~

filter I *n.* 1. to pass smt. through a ~ 2. a cloth; sand ~

filter II *v.* 1. (d; intr.) to ~ into (foreign influence began to ~ into the country) 2. (d; tr.) to ~ through

filth *n.* in ~ (to live in ~)

fin *n.* a caudal; dorsal; pectoral; pelvic ~

finale *n.* the grand ~

finals *n.* (AE) ['final examinations'] to take one's ~

finance *n.* high; public ~

financing *n.* deficit; private; public ~

find I *n.* 1. an archeological ~ 2. a lucky; rare ~

find II *v.* 1. (C) ~ an interesting book for me; or: ~ me an interesting book 2. (legal) (d; intr.) ('to decide') to ~ against; for (to ~ for the plaintiff) 3. (D; tr.) ('to discover') to ~ for (have you found a suitable candidate for the job?) 4. (J) ('to discover') we found her working on her book 5. (L) ('to discover') we found that she was always ready to help 6. (M) ('to discover') we found London to be a fascinating city 7. (N; used with an adjective, past participle) we found Alaska interesting; to ~ smb. wanting; the soldiers found the village destroyed; she was found guilty by the jury

finding *n.* 1. ~ that + clause (it was the court's ~ that no crime had been committed) 2. (misc.) to rubber-stamp a committee's ~s

find out *v.* 1. (D; intr.) to ~ about (we found out about the accident yesterday) 2. (D; intr.) to ~ for (she found out about the concert for me) 3. (D; intr.) to ~ from (we found out from the reporter that the fire had been started by an arsonist) 4. (L) we found out that the train would be late 5. (Q) I finally found out how to operate the new computer

fine I *adj.* ~ to + inf. (it's ~ to reduce taxes, but the deficit will be increased)

fine II *n.* 1. to impose, levy a ~ on smb. 2. (colloq.) to slap a ~ on smb. 3. to pay a ~ 4. a heavy, stiff ~ 5. a mandatory ~ 6. a ~ for (a ~ for illegal parking)

fine III *v.* 1. (D; tr.) to ~ for (to ~ smb. for illegal parking) 2. (O; can be used with one animate object) the police ~d him twenty dollars; the police ~d him

finery *n.* ['showy clothing'] in all one's ~ (dressed up in all their ~)

finger I *n.* 1. to point a ~ at 2. (usu. fig.) to snap one's ~s (I jump when she snaps her ~s)('I obey her commands without question') 3. an accusing; warning ~ (to point an accusing ~ at smb.) 4. an index; little; middle; ring; trigger ~ 5. (misc.) to prick a ~; she jammed her ~ in the door; to lay a ~ on smb. ('to harm smb.'); I can't lay/put my ~ on what is wrong ('I cannot discover what is wrong'); to count on one's ~s; to keep one's ~s crossed ('to hope for smt.'); to lift a ~ ('to make an effort'); to have one's ~ in smt. ('to be involved in smt.'); the ~ of suspicion points at/to you ('you are under suspicion') to have smb. wrapped around one's little ~ ('to have smb.'s complete devotion')

finger II *v.* (colloq.) (D; tr.) ('to identify') to ~ as (he was ~ed as one of the escaped convicts)

fingerprints *n.* 1. to take smb.'s ~ 2. telltale ~ 3. a set of ~ (the police got a clean set of ~)

fingertips *n.* at one's ~ (to have information at one's ~)

finicky *adj.* ~ about

finish I *n.* ['end'] 1. a hairbreadth, photo ~ 2. at the ~ 3. to the ~ (to fight to the ~) ['polish'] 4. a dull; glazed; glossy ~

finish II *v.* 1. (D; intr., tr.) to ~ by, with (they ~ed their performance by singing a song/with a song; are you ~ed with your work?) 2. (G) they ~ed working at four o'clock

finish line *n.* to cross; reach the ~

finish up *v.* (D; intr., tr.) to ~ by, with (we ~ed up the year with no profit; they ~ed up by scrubbing the floor)

fire I *n.* ['destructive burning'] 1. to set, start a ~; to set ~ to (they set ~ to the barn) 2. to catch ~ (the house caught ~) 3. to contain; extinguish, put out; stamp out a ~; to bring a ~ under control 4. a raging, roaring ~ 5. a brush; electrical; forest ~ 6. a ~ breaks out; burns; goes out; smoulders; spreads (the ~ burned out of control for two hours) 7. on ~ (the house was on ~) ['burning, combustion'] 8. to build, kindle, light, make a ~; to strike ~ 9. to fuel; poke, stir; stoke a ~ 10. to bank; douse, extinguish, put out a ~ 11. a ~ burns 12. (misc.) the ~ is out; the glow of a ~ ['shooting'] 13. to commence, open ~ (to open ~ on the enemy) 14. to exchange ~ (with the enemy) 15. to call down ~ on 16. to attract, draw ~ 17. to cease ~ (cease ~!); to hold one's ~ 18. concentrated, fierce, heavy, murderous; cross; harassing; hostile; incoming; interdictory; rapid ~ 19. artillery; automatic; machine-gun; rifle; semiautomatic; small-arms ~ 20. under ~ (also fig.) 21. (misc.) the baptism of ~ ['misc.'] 22. to play with ~ ('to take a risk'); to fight ~ with ~ ('to use extreme measures as a counterattack'); to set the Thames (BE)/the world on ~ ('to be very successful')

fire II *v.* 1. to ~ point-blank 2. (B) the quarterback ~d a pass to an end 3. (D; intr., tr.) to ~ at (he ~d at me; he ~d his pistol at me) 4. (D; intr., tr.) to ~ into (to ~ into the air; to ~ into a crowd)

fire alarm *n.* 1. to set a ~ 2. to activate, set off, trigger a ~ 3. a ~ goes off, rings

fire away *v.* (D; intr.) to ~ at (to ~ at the enemy)

fire back *v.* (D; intr.) to ~ at

firecracker *n.* 1. to light, set off a ~ 2. a ~ goes off

fire drill *n.* to conduct, hold a ~

fired up *adj.* ['excited'] ~ with

fire extinguisher *n.* 1. to train a ~ (on a fire) 2. to operate a ~ 3. to recharge a ~

fire sale *n.* to hold a ~

fireworks *n.* a spectacular display of ~

firing line *n.* ['line from which soldiers fire their weapons'] in (BE), on (AE) the ~ (also fig.)

firm I *adj.* ['competitive, strong'] 1. ~ against (the pound was ~ against the dollar) ['strict'] 2. ~ with (~ with the children)

firm II *n.* ['company'] 1. to establish; manage, operate, run a ~ 2. an advertising; business; manufacturing; shipping ~

first *adj., n.* 1. to come in ~ (in a race) 2. the ~ to + inf. (she was the ~ to arrive) 3. among the ~ 4. at ~

first aid *n.* 1. to administer, give ~ 2. to get ~

first-class *adv.* to travel ~

first strike *n.* 1. to carry out, make a ~ 2. (misc.) a first-strike capability

fish I *n.* 1. to catch (a) ~ 2. baked; broiled; dried; filleted; fresh; freshwater; fried; frozen; saltwater; smoked ~ 3. tropical ~ 4. ~ bite at bait; swim 5. a school, shoal of ~ 6. (misc.) to drink like a ~ ('to drink excessive amounts of alcohol'); a queer

~ ('a strange person')

fish II v. 1. (d; intr.) to ~ for (to ~ for compliments) 2. to go ~ing

fish fry n. to have a ~

fishing n. 1. to go in for ~ 2. deep-sea ~ USAGE NOTE: Compare to go in for fishing with to go fishing.

fishy adj. (colloq.) ~ about (there is smt. ~ about them)

fission n. binary; nuclear ~

fist n. 1. to make a ~ 2. to clench; raise; shake one's ~ 3. a tight ~ 4. (misc.) an iron ~ ('a harsh policy'); a mailed ~ ('a threat of armed force')

fisticuffs n. to engage in ~

fit I n. ['emotional reaction'] 1. to have, throw a ~ ['misc.'] 2. by ~s and starts ('in irregular bursts of activity')

fit II adj. ['qualified'] ['physically capable'] 1. physically ~ 2. ~ for (~ for duty) 3. ~ to + inf. (he is not ~ to work) 4. to keep ~ ['suitable'] 5. to see, think ~ to + inf. (they saw ~ to employ smb. else)

fit III n. ['manner of fitting'] a good; loose; snug, tight ~

fit IV v. 1. to ~ together 2. (D; tr.) to ~ for (to ~ a customer for a new suit) 3. (D; intr.) to ~ into (everything fit into the suitcase) 4. (d; tr.) to ~ into (she was able to ~ all the books into one carton) USAGE NOTE: In BE the past and past participle of fit are usu. fitted. AE usu. has fit when the verb cannot be used in the passive form-- the tailor fitted the customer carefully (CE); the suit was fitted carefully by the tailor (CE); the suit fit me a year ago (AE).

fit in v. (D; intr.) to ~ with ('to blend in') (she fit right in with our crowd)

fitness n. 1. physical ~ 2. ~ for

fit out v. (d; tr.) to ~ as (the ship was ~ted out as a tender)

fitting I adj. 1. ~ to + inf. (it is ~ to pay tribute to the early pioneers) 2. ~ that + clause; subj. (it is ~ that she be/should be honored)

fitting II n. ['small part'] 1. an electrical; female; gas; male ~ ['trying on of a garment'] 2. to go for a ~ 3. (misc.) a ~ room

fix I n. (colloq.) ['difficult situation'] 1. to be in a ~ 2. a fine, nice, pretty ~ ['injection of a narcotic'] (slang) 3. to get; need a ~

fix II v. 1. (esp. AE) (C) ('to prepare') ~ a drink for me; or: ~ me a drink 2. (d; tr.) to ~ on (she ~ed her gaze on him) 3. (colloq.) (esp. AE) (E) ('to get ready') they're ~ing to eat

fixation n. ['obsession'] a ~ on (to have a ~ on smt.)

fixing n. 1. price ~ 2. (misc.) (colloq.) a turkey with all the ~s

fixture n. a lighting; plumbing; shop (esp. BE), store (esp. AE) ~

fix up v. (D; tr.) (colloq.) to ~ with ('to match with') (to ~ smb. up with a good job; my friends ~ed me up with her)

flag n. 1. to display, fly; hang out; hoist, raise, run up, unfurl; wave a ~ 2. to dip, lower a ~; to strike the ~ 3. a garrison; holiday; national ~ 4. the white ~ ('symbol of surrender') 5. a ~ flies, flut-

ters (the ~ was flying at half-mast) 6. under a ~ (the ship sailed under the Panamanian ~) 7. (misc.) to show/wave the ~ ('to demonstrate one's patriotism'); (under) a ~ of truce

flair n. 1. to develop; show a ~ for 2. a distinctive ~

flame n. 1. (also fig.) to kindle a ~ 2. (fig.) to stir the ~s (of racism) 3. to burst into ~ 4. a clear; open ~ 5. a ~ burns 6. in ~s (the house was in ~s) 7. (misc.) an (the) eternal ~; the Olympic ~; my old ~ ('my old love')

flank n. 1. to turn ('go around') a ~ (to turn the enemy's ~) 2. on a ~ (on the left ~) 3. (misc.) a ~ attack

flap n. (slang) ['commotion'] 1. a political ~ 2. in a ~ about, over

flare n. 1. to light; shoot up a ~ 2. to set out; set up a ~ (they set up ~s along the runway) 3. a parachute ~

flare up v. (D; intr.) to ~ at (to ~ at the slightest provocation)

flash I n. 1. an electronic ~ (for a camera) 2. a hot ~ (AE; BE has hot flush) 3. a news ~ 4. in a ~ ('quickly')

flash II v. 1. (usu. B; rarely A) ('to convey by light') they ~ed a signal to the crew 2. (D; tr.) ('to shine') to ~ at (the driver ~ed his lights at us) 3. (d; intr.) ('to come suddenly') to ~ into (a brilliant idea ~ed into her mind) 4. (d; intr.) ('to pass') to ~ through (a thought ~ed through my mind) 5. (D; intr.) ('to glow') to ~ with (her eyes ~ed with anger)

flashback n. 1. to insert, interject, put in a ~ (as part of a film) 2. a ~ to (a ~ to smb.'s childhood)

flashlight n. (AE; BE has torch) 1. to turn on a ~ 2. to shine a ~ on

flask n. a Thermos (BE), vacuum (BE) ~ (AE has Thermos bottle)

flat adj. ['flavorless, stale'] 1. to go ~ (the beer has gone ~) ['extended at full length'] 2. (also fig.) to fall ~ (as an actor he fell ~) ['exact'] 3. she ran a mile in seven minutes ~

flat II n. ['deflated tire'] (esp. AE; BE prefers flat tyre or puncture) 1. to have a ~ 2. to change; fix a ~ ['apartment'] (esp. BE) 3. to rent a ~ from 4. to let a ~ to 5. to furnish; redecorate; renovate a ~ 6. a cold-water (esp. AE; obsol.); council; service; studio ~ 7. converted; purpose-built ~s 8. a block of ~s (AE has apartment house)

flatter v. 1. (D; refl.) to ~ on (to ~ oneself on one's knowledge of history) 2. (D; tr.) to ~ smb. about, on

flattered adj. 1. ~ at, by (~ at the invitation) 2. ~ to + inf. (she was ~ to be invited) 3. ~ that + clause (we were ~ that she came to visit us)

flattering adj. 1. ~ to + inf. (it is ~ to be interviewed on TV) 2. ~ that + clause (it's ~ that we've been chosen)

flattery n. to resort to, use ~

flavor, flavour n. ['characteristic quality'] 1. to impart a ~ to 2. a colloquial; foreign; old-world ~ ['taste'] 3. a bitter; delicate; pleasant; strong; art ~ 4. an artificial; natural ~

flaw *n.* 1. a fatal ~ 2. a ~ in (there's a ~ in your reasoning)

flea *n.* ~s bite

flee *v.* (D; intr.) to ~ from; to

fleece *v.* (D; tr.) to ~ of

fleet *adj.* ~ of foot

flesh *n.* 1. to mortify the ~ 2. proud ~

flesh out *v.* (D; tr.) to ~ with (to ~ a report with greater detail)

flexibility *n.* 1. to demonstrate, show ~ 2. ~ in; towards 3. the ~ to + inf. (he has enough ~ to cope with the job)

flexible *adj.* ~ in; towards

flick *v.* (D; intr.) to ~ through ('to go through quickly') (to ~ through a report)

flies (BE) see **fly III**

flight I *n.* ['flying'] 1. to take a ~ 2. to overbook a ~ 3. a chartered; coast-to-coast; connecting; cross-country; direct; domestic; international; maiden; manned; nonstop; reconnaissance; round-the-world; scheduled; shakedown; solo; space; suborbital; test; unmanned ~ 4. a bumpy, rough; smooth ~ 5. a ~ from; to (a ~ from Philadelphia to Frankfurt) 6. a ~ over (a ~ over the South Pole) 7. in ~ (at that moment the plane was in ~ over the Mediterranean) 8. on a ~ (on the ~ to Chicago)

flight II *n.* ['fleeing'] 1. to take ~ 2. to put to ~ (their army was put to ~) 3. full, headlong ~ (the enemy was in full ~) 4. in ~

flinch *v.* (D; intr.) to ~ from

fling I *n.* (colloq.) ['attempt'] 1. to have, take (esp. BE) a ~ at smt. ['period of self-indulgence'] 2. to have a last ~

fling II *v.* 1. (D; tr.) to ~ at (to ~ a stone at smb.) 2. (d; tr.) to ~ to (they flung their rifles to the ground) 3. (N; used with an adjective) we flung the doors open 4. (P; tr.) they flung their hats into the air; to ~ caution to the winds

flip *v.* 1. (slang) (D; intr.) ('to lose one's mind') to ~ over (he ~ped over her) 2. (d; intr.) to ~ through ('to go through quickly') (to ~ through an article)

flirt I *n.* an incorrigible; terrible ~

flirt II *v.* (D; intr.) to ~ with

flirtation *n.* to carry on, engage in a ~ with

flit *v.* (P; intr.) bees ~ from flower to flower; the idea ~ted into his brain

flock I *n.* to tend a ~ (of sheep)

flock II *v.* (P; intr.) the crowd ~ed around the speaker; customers ~ed into the store; to ~ together

floe *n.* an ice ~

flood I *n.* 1. a flash; raging ~ 2. the ~ inundated; struck (several cities) 3. a ~ subsides

flood II *v.* (D; tr.) to ~ with (to ~ the market with cheap goods)

floodlight *n.* to focus; shine a ~ on

floodwaters *n.* 1. raging; rising ~ 2. ~ subside

floor *n.* ['story'] 1. the first; ground; lower; main; second; top; upper ~ 2. on a ~ (on the second ~) ['lower surface of a room'] 3. a dirt (AE), earth (BE); inlaid; parquet; tile; wooden ~ 4. on a ~ (he was sleeping on the ~) 5. (misc.) to buff; mop;

scrub; sweep; wax a ~ ['right to speak'] 6. to ask for; get, take the ~ 7. to give smb. the ~ 8. to yield the ~ ['place where members sit'] 9. from the ~ (a motion was made from the ~) ['misc.'] 10. the ocean ~

flop I *n.* a ~ as

flop II *v.* (D; intr.) to ~ as (she ~ped as a stage actress)

flora *n.* 1. intestinal ~ 2. (misc.) ~ and fauna ('plants and animals')

floss *n.* 1. dental ~ 2. candy ~ (BE; AE has *cotton candy*)

flour *n.* 1. to mix ~ with; to sift ~ 2. bleached; cake; enriched; self-rising (AE), self-raising (BE); unbleached; white ~ 3. (BE) corn ~ (AE has *cornstarch*)

flow I *n.* 1. to regulate a ~ 2. to staunch the ~ (of blood) 3. a smooth; steady ~ 4. a cash ~ 5. a lava ~ 6. a ~ from; to (the ~ of traffic to the city)

flow II *v.* 1. (D; intr.) to ~ from, out of (water ~ed from the pipe) 2. (D; intr.) to ~ from; to (the river ~s from east to west) 3. (D; intr.) to ~ into, to (rivers ~ into the sea)

flower *n.* ['plant'] 1. to grow; plant ~s 2. to pick, pluck ~s 3. a fragrant ~ 4. artificial; cut ~s 5. ~s bloom; fade, wither, wilt 6. (misc.) a bouquet, spray of ~s

flu *n.* 1. to come down with (the) ~ 2. intestinal ~ 3. a strain of ~ (virus) 4. an attack, bout; outbreak; touch of (the) ~

fluctuate *v.* 1. (D; intr.) to ~ between 2. (D; intr.) to ~ with (his mood ~s with the weather)

fluency *n.* 1. to acquire ~ 2. to demonstrate, display ~ 3. ~ in (~ in a foreign language) 4. ~ to + inf. (she has enough ~ to order a meal in English)

fluent *adj.* ~ in (~ in English)

fluids *n.* 1. (med.) to force; measure; restrict; withhold ~ 2. to drink, take ~ 3. body; clear; cold; hot ~

fluke *n.* (colloq.) ['stroke of luck'] 1. a pure ~ 2. by a ~ (he won by a ~)

flunk *v.* (colloq.) (esp. AE) (D; intr.) to ~ out of (he ~d out of school)

flush I *adj.* ~ with (~ with the ground)

flush II *n.* 1. a hot ~ (BE; AE has *hot flash*) 2. the first ~ (of success)

flush III *v.* (D; intr.) to ~ with (to ~ with pride)

flush IV *v.* (d; tr.) ('to chase') to ~ from, out of (they were ~ed from their hiding place)

flute *n.* to play the ~

flux *n.* in ~

fly I *n.* 1. to swat a ~ 2. a fruit; tsetse ~

fly II *v.* 1. (D; intr.) to ~ across, over (to ~ across the ocean) 2. (d; intr.) to ~ at ('to attack') 3. (D; intr., tr.) ('to travel by plane') ('to pilot') to ~ from; to (she flew from New York to London; he flew his private plane to Florida) 4. (d; intr.) to ~ into ('to arrive by plane') (to ~ into Chicago) 5. (d; intr.) to ~ into ('to go into') (to ~ into a rage) 6. (d; intr.) to ~ out of ('to depart by plane') (to ~ out of Chicago) 7. (misc.) to ~ blind ('to ~ a plane solely with the help of instruments'); to ~ high ('to be elated'); to ~ nonstop; to ~ in the face of tradition ('to defy tradition'); to ~ off the handle ('to become angry')

fly III *n.* ['opening on trousers'] 1. to close, do up (BE), zip up one's ~ 2. to open, unzip one's ~

flying *n.* blind; formation; instrument; stunt ~

flying colors, flying colours *n.* ['success'] to come through with ~

flyover (BE) see **overpass**

fob off *v.* (colloq.) 1. (D; tr.) ('to get rid of by deceit') to ~ on (to ~ cheap merchandise on customers) 2. (BE) (D; tr.) ('to deceive') to ~ with (to ~ customers with cheap merchandise)

focus I *n.* 1. to bring smt. into ~ 2. in ~; out of ~

focus II *v.* (D; intr., tr.) to ~ on (we must ~ our attention on two major problems)

fodder *n.* 1. cannon ~ 2. ~ for

foe *n.* 1. a bitter, implacable; formidable; sworn ~ 2. a political ~ 3. (misc.) to vanquish a ~

foetus (BE) see **fetus**

fog *n.* 1. (a) dense, heavy, thick; light ~ 2. a ground ~ 3. a ~ clears, lets up, lifts 4. a patch of ~ 5. (misc.) in a ~ ('bewildered')

foible *n.* a human ~

foil *n.* aluminium (BE), aluminum (AE); gold; silver ~; tinfoil

foist off *v.* (D; tr.) to ~ on (to ~ inferior merchandise on a customer)

fold *v.* (D; tr.) to ~ into (she ~ed the newspaper into a hat)

folder *n.* a manila ~

fold up *v.* (D; intr., tr.) to ~ into (the bed ~s up into the wall)

follow *v.* 1. to ~ blindly; closely; faithfully 2. (d; intr.) to ~ in (to ~ in smb.'s footsteps) 3. (L) it ~s from what has been said that he cannot be considered for the job

follower *n.* a faithful ~

following *n.* ['followers'] a large ~

follow through *v.* (D; intr.) ('to continue') to ~ with

follow-up *n.* 1. to do a ~ on (the reporter did a ~ on her first story) 2. a ~ to (this letter is the ~ to our telephone conversation)

follow up *v.* 1. (D; intr.) to ~ on (to ~ on a story) 2. (D; intr., tr.) to ~ with (we should ~ with a letter)

folly *n.* ~ to + inf. (it was ~ to persist)

fond *adj.* (cannot stand alone) ~ of (she is ~ of him)

fondness *n.* ~ for

font *n.* ['bowl'] a baptismal ~

food *n.* 1. to cook, prepare; heat; reheat ~ 2. to bolt, gulp (down); eat; swallow ~ 3. appetizing, delicious, tasty; coarse; exotic; fine; heavy; light; nourishing, wholesome; plain; rich; simple; spicy ~ 4. frozen; gourmet; health; junk; kosher; soul (AE) ~ 5. scraps of ~ 6. (misc.) ~ for thought

fool I *n.* 1. to play the ~ 2. to make a ~ of smb. 3. a big; doddering (old); poor; silly; stupid; utter; young ~ 4. a ~ to + inf. (I was a ~ to trust him)

fool II *v.* (D; intr.) to ~ with

fool about (BE) see **fool around**

fool around *v.* (D; intr.) to ~ with (don't ~ with fire)

foolhardy *adj.* ~ to + inf. (it was ~ of him to even try)

foolish *adj.* ~ to + inf. (it was ~ to take the test without preparation; he was ~ to try)

foolishness *n.* ~ to + inf. (it was ~ to do it)

foot *n.* ['lower extremity of a leg'] 1. to stamp; tap one's ~; to shuffle one's feet 2. to gain, get to one's feet 3. to set ~ on (she has never set ~ on foreign soil) 4. flat feet 5. in one's stocking feet 6. at one's feet (the dog lay at his feet) 7. on ~ (they came on ~) 8. (misc.) to drag one's feet ('to move very slowly') or ('to refuse to act'); fast/quick on one's feet; to put one's best ~ forward ('to attempt to make a good impression'); to put one's ~ down ('to act firmly'); to get a ~ in the door ('to make an initial step'); underfoot ('beneath one's feet'); to put one's ~ in one's mouth ('to make an inappropriate statement'); she always lands on her feet ('she always manages to get out of difficulty') ['bottom, end'] 9. at the ~ of (at the ~ of the bed) ['unit of measurement equalling twelve inches'] 10. a cubic; square ~

football *n.* 1. to play ~ 2. a ~ game (AE), match (BE) 3. association ~ ('soccer')

foot fault *n.* (tennis) to commit a ~

foothold *n.* 1. to establish, gain, secure, win a ~ 2. a firm ~

footing *n.* 1. to keep one's ~ 2. to lose one's ~ 3. an equal; solid, sure; unequal ~ 4. on a certain ~ (to be on a friendly ~ with smb.; to place a country on a war ~)

footnote *n.* a ~ to (the ~s to a chapter)

footprint *n.* to leave a ~ (in the snow)

footrace *n.* to run a ~

footsie *n.* (slang) ['collusion'] ['flirting'] to play ~ with

footstep *n.* 1. to dog smb.'s ~s 2. to follow in smb.'s ~s

footwork *n.* fancy ~ (as of a boxer)

forage *v.* (D; intr.) to ~ for (to ~ for food)

foray *n.* 1. to make a ~ 2. a bold ~ 3. a ~ into

forbid *v.* (formal) 1. to ~ categorically, expressly, outright 2. (H) she has forbidden him to smoke in her presence; I ~ you to take the car

force I *n.* ['compulsion'] ['violence'] 1. to apply, resort to, use ~ 2. to renounce (the use of) ~ 3. armed; brute; deadly; moral; physical; spiritual ~ ['military power'] 4. to marshal, muster, rally one's ~s; to join ~s with 5. armed, military; ground; naval ~s (strong naval ~s began to shell the enemy positions) 6. an air ~ 7. an expeditionary; guerrilla; occupation; peacekeeping; task ~ (a naval task ~) 8. a show of ~ ['organized body, group'] 9. a labor, work; police; sales ~ 10. in full ~ (the police were out in full ~) ['energy'] ['power'] 11. to spend one's ~ (the storm has spent its ~) 12. centrifugal; centripetal ~ 13. an explosive; irresistible; magnetic; motivating ~ 14. the vital ~ ('basic force') ['effect'] 15. in ~ (the regulation is still in ~)

force II *v.* 1. (d; tr.) to ~ into (they ~d their way into the building) 2. (d; tr.) to ~ off (we were ~d off the road) 3. (d; refl., tr.) to ~ on (she tried to ~ her views on us) 4. (d; tr.) to ~ through (to ~ one's way through a crowd) 5. (H) they ~d her to sign 6. (N; used with an adjective) he ~d the door open

foreboding *n*. 1. a gloomy ~ 2. a ~ that + clause (I have a ~ that there will be a bad storm)

forecast I *n*. 1. to make a ~ 2. a long-range; short-range; weather ~ (to give the weather ~)

forecast II *v*. (L) she forecast that an earthquake would occur

foreclose *v*. (D; intr.) to ~ on (they will ~ on us) ('they will foreclose our mortgage')

foredoomed *adj*. ~ to (~ to failure)

forefront *n*. in the ~

foreground *n*. in the ~

forehead *n*. a high ~

foreign *adj*. ~ to

forerunner *n*. ['precursor'] a ~ of, to

foresee *v*. 1. (K) nobody could ~ his running away 2. (L) he foresaw that prices would drop 3. (Q) who can ~ what should be done?

foresight *n*. the ~ to + inf. (he had the ~ to provide for the education of his children)

forest *n*. 1. to clear a ~ 2. a dense, thick; impenetrable; luxuriant; primeval; virgin ~ 3. a broad-leaf; coniferous; deciduous; evergreen; (tropical) rain ~ 4. a national; state (US) ~ 5. the ~ stretches for miles

forethought *n*. the ~ to + inf. (she had the ~ to save money)

forewarn *v*. (D; tr.) to ~ of

foreword *n*. a ~ to

forfeit *v*. (B) he ~ed the game to his opponent

forge *v*. (d; intr.) ('to move ahead') to ~ into the lead

forgery *n*. 1. to commit ~ 2. a clever; crude; skillful ~

forget *v*. 1. to ~ completely, utterly 2. (D; intr.) to ~ about (she forgot about the concert) 3. (E) I forgot to call 4. (G; usu. in neg. and interrogative constructions) the children will never ~ visiting this park 5. (K) the audience will not ~ his singing this role 6. (L) don't ~ that we are going out this evening 7. (Q) a person never ~s how to swim USAGE NOTE: The sentence *she forgot to buy a newspaper* means that she did not buy a newspaper. The sentence *she forgot about buying a newspaper* may mean either that she did not buy a newspaper or that she bought a newspaper but does not remember buying it.

forgetful *adj*. ~ of (he has become ~ of things)

forgive *v*. 1. (D; tr.) to ~ for (to ~ smb. for a mistake) 2. (biblical) (O; may be used with one object) ~ us our sins

fork *n*. ['pronged device'] 1. a tuning ~ ['division into branches'] 2. at a ~ in the road ['implememt for eating'] 3. a dinner; salad ~

fork over *v*. (colloq.) (B) we had to ~ our savings to our creditors

form I *n*. ['printed document'] 1. to fill in (BE), fill out (esp. AE), fill up (obsol. BE) a ~ 2. an application; tax ~ ['shape'] ['manner'] 3. to assume, take (on) a ~ (to assume human ~) 4. an abridged, condensed; comprehensive; concise; convenient, handy; revised ~ 5. in a ~ (the book came out in abridged ~; we reject fraud in any ~;

a fiend in human ~) ['grammatical element'] 6. a bound; colloquial; combining; diminutive; free; inflectional; obsolete; plural; singular; surface; underlying; verbal ~ ['behavior'] 7. bad; good, proper ~ (it's bad ~ to come late to a formal reception) ['condition'] 8. bad; excellent, good, superb ~ 9. in (certain) ~ (she was in superb ~ today -- she didn't lose a single match) ['good condition'] 10. in ~ (I'm not in ~ today) 11. off ~ ['table giving information'] 12. a racing ~ ['school class'] (BE) 13. in a ~ (in the fourth ~)

form II *v*. 1. (D; tr.) to ~ from, out of (they ~ed an army out of rabble) 2. (d; tr.) to ~ into (to ~ chopped beef into patties)

formal *adj*. ~ with (he is always ~ with his colleagues)

formalities *n*. 1. to complete, go through the ~ 2. bureaucratic; legal ~; (the) usual ~

format *n*. a suitable ~

formation *n*. ['arrangement of troops, ships, aircraft'] 1. to break ~ 2. close; tight ~ 3. battle ~ (drawn up in battle ~) 4. in ~ (to fly in close ~) ['structure'] ['grouping'] 5. a cloud; rock ~ 6. (ling.) a back ~

formula *n*. ['milk mixture for infant feeding'] 1. to make up, prepare ~ ['symbolic representation'] ['method'] 2. to devise a ~ 3. a scientific ~ 4. a ~ for 5. a ~ to + inf. (a ~ to change lead into gold)

form up *v*. (D; intr.) to ~ in (to ~ in three ranks)

fort *n*. 1. a strong ~ 2. a ~ falls; holds out 3. (misc.) to hold the ~ ('to bear responsibility in the absence of others')

fortify *v*. 1. (D; tr.) to ~ against 2. (D; refl., tr.) to ~ with (he ~ied himself with a shot of whiskey)

fortitude *n*. 1. to demonstrate, display, show ~ 2. (humorous) intestinal ~ ('great courage') 3. moral ~ 4. the ~ to + inf. (they had enough ~ to finish the job)

fortress *n*. 1. to besiege; storm, take a ~ 2. an impregnable; strong ~ 3. a ~ falls, surrenders; holds out

fortunate *adj*. 1. ~ in (we are ~ in having such a nice house) 2. ~ to + inf. (she is ~ to have influential friends) 3. ~ that + clause (it is ~ that we can all meet tomorrow)

fortune *n*. ['wealth'] 1. to accumulate, amass, make a ~ 2. to come into, inherit a ~ 3. to dissipate, run through, squander a ~ 4. an enormous, large, vast ~ 5. a family ~ ['luck'] 6. to try one's ~ 7. the (bad; good) ~ to + inf. (they had the good ~ to find a suitable house quickly; we had the bad fortune to get caught in a storm) 8. (bad; good) ~ that + clause (it was our good ~ that it did not rain) 9. ~ smiled on us 10. a stroke of good ~ ['fate'] 11. to tell smb.'s ~

forum *n*. 1. to conduct, hold a ~ 2. an open, public ~ 3. a ~ about, on

forward *v*. 1. (usu. B; occasionally A) they always ~ my mail to me 2. (D; tr.) to ~ from; to (to ~ letters to a new address; the books were ~ed from Amsterdam to Tokyo)

foul I *adv*. 1. see **afoul** 2. to fall ~ of (to fall ~ of the law)

foul II *n*. 1. to commit a ~ 2. a personal; team;

technical ~
foul III *v.* (esp. basketball) (D; intr.) to ~ out of
(to ~ out of a game)
foul out *v.* (esp. basketball) (D; intr.) to ~ on (he
~ed out on five personals)
foul play *n.* ['violence'] to meet with ~
found *v.* (D; tr.) to ~ on (our country was ~ed on
certain principles)
foundation *n.* ['underlying base'] 1. to lay a ~ 2.
to undermine a ~ 3. a firm, solid, sound, strong ~
4. the ~ (of a building) settles ['an endowed
institution'] 5. a charitable, philanthropic; educational ~
fountain *n.* 1. a drinking, water ~ 2. (esp. AE) a
soda ~
fours *n.* ['two hands and two feet'] on all ~
fox *n.* 1. an arctic, white; desert; red; silver ~ 2. a
~ yelps 3. a young ~ is a cub, pup 4. a female ~ is
a vixen 5. (misc.) as sly as a ~
fraction *n.* 1. to reduce a ~ 2. a common; complex, compound; decimal; improper; irreducible;
partial; proper; simple, vulgar ~
fracture *n.* 1. to reduce, set a ~ 2. a compound;
compression; greenstick; hairline; simple; stress
~
frailty *n.* human ~
frame *n.* a mirror; picture ~
framework *n.* 1. a conceptual ~ 2. within a ~
franchise *n.* ['the right to vote'] 1. to exercise one's
~ ['the license to sell a product or services in a certain area'] 2. to grant a ~ 3. to have, hold a ~ 4. to
withdraw a ~
frank *adj.* 1. brutally, perfectly ~ 2. ~ about; with
(she was ~ with us about everything)
frankness *n.* 1. disarming ~ 2. ~ about
fraternity *n.* (US) 1. to pledge a ~ ('to agree to
join a fraternity') 2. a college ~ (see also **sorority**)
fraternize *v.* (D; intr.) to ~ with
fratricide *n.* to commit ~
fraud *n.* 1. to commit ~; to perpetrate (a) ~ 2. to
expose (a) ~ 3. mail; vote ~
fraudulent *adj.* ~ to + inf. (it was ~ to claim an
exemption of that type)
fraught *adj.* (cannot stand alone) ~ with (the situation was ~ with danger)
fray *n.* to enter, join the ~
frazzle *n.* burnt to a ~ ('completely burnt')
freak out *v.* (slang) (D; intr., tr.) to ~ on (to ~ on
drugs)
free I *adj.* 1. ~ from, of (~ from pain; ~ of debt)
2. ~ with (~ with advice) 3. ~ to + inf. (I am ~ to
accept your invitation) 4. (misc.) to set, turn smb.
~
free II *v.* (D; tr.) to ~ from
freedom *n.* 1. to gain, secure, win ~ 2. to abridge,
curtail (a) ~ 3. academic; political; religious ~ 4.
~ of assembly; of the press; of religion, worship;
of speech 5. ~ from (~ from want) 6. the ~ to +
inf. (we have the ~ to do what we want)
free hand *n.* ['freedom of action'] 1. to give smb. a
~ 2. to get; have a ~
free throw *n.* (basketball) to make a ~
freeze I *n.* ['frost'] ['freezing'] 1. a deep, hard ~
['freezer'] (BE) 2. a deep ~ ['fixing at a certain

level'] 3. to impose a ~ 4. a nuclear; wage, wages
(BE) ~ 5. a ~ on
freeze II *v.* 1. to ~ hard, solid (it froze hard last
night) 2. (D; intr.) to ~ to (his exposed skin froze
to the metal; to ~ to death)
freezer *n.* 1. a home ~ 2. (misc.) a ~ compartment
(in a refrigerator)
freight *n.* ['goods, cargo'] 1. to carry; handle; ship
~ ['freight train'] (colloq.) 2. to hop jump
('board') a ~
French *n.* Canadian ~ (natives of Quebec speak
Canadian ~)
French leave *n.* (obsol.) ['leaving without saying
goodbye'] to take ~
French toast *n.* to make ~
frenzy *n.* 1. a wild ~ 2. in a ~ (in a ~ of despair)
frequency *n.* ['number of repetitions'] 1. alarming; great, high; low ~ 2. with ~ (with alarming ~)
['number of periodic waves per unit of time']
(physics) 3. high; low; medium ~ 4. a radio ~ 5.
on a ~
fresco *n.* to paint a ~
fresh I *adj.* ['recent'] ['new'] ~ from, out of (~
out of school)
fresh II *adj.* (colloq.) (AE) ['bold'] ['impudent']
~ with (don't get ~ with me)
freshener *n.* an air, room ~
fret *v.* 1. (D; intr.) to ~ about, over 2. (misc.) to
~ and fume
friction *n.* 1. to create, generate, produce ~ 2. ~
among, between; with (there has been some ~
between the union and management)
friend *n.* 1. to make a ~; to make ~s with smb. 2.
a bosom, close, good, intimate; fair-weather;
faithful, fast, loyal, staunch, strong, true; false;
lifelong; mutual; personal; special ~ 3. inseparable ~s 4. a pen ~ (BE; CE has *pen pal*) 5. a ~ to
(she was a good ~ to us) 5. (misc.) my good ~
friendliness *n.* ~ to, towards
friendly *adj.* 1. ~ of (that was ~ of you) 2. ~ to,
towards, with 3. ~ to + inf. (it was ~ of him to
offer his help)
friendship *n.* 1. to cement, develop, make, strike
up a ~ 2. to cherish, cultivate a ~ 3. to promote
(international) ~ 4. to break up, destroy a ~ 5. a
close, firm, intimate, strong, warm; lifelong; long
~ 6. the bonds of ~ 7. (a) ~ among, between; with
fright *n.* 1. to give smb. a ~ 2. a nasty; sudden ~
3. stage ~ 4. in, with ~ (to scream with ~)
frighten *v.* 1. (d; tr.) to ~ into (to ~ smb. into submission) 2. (d; tr.) to ~ out of (to ~ smb. out of
doing smt.) 3. (misc.) to ~ smb. to death
frightened *adj.* ~ about, at, of (~ at the very
thought)
frightening *adj.* 1. ~ to + inf. (it's ~ to even contemplate such a possibility) 2. ~ that + clause (it's
~ that a war could break out at any time)
frightful *adj.* see **frightening**
fringe *n.* 1. the lunatic ~ 2. on the ~s (of society)
fringe benefits *n.* to get; provide ~
fritter away *v.* (D; tr.) to ~ on (to ~ one's time
away on trifles)
frivolous *adj.* ~ to + inf. (it was ~ of him to make
such an accusation)

frog *n.* 1. a grass; green; wood ~ 2. ~s croak; jump 3. (misc.) to have a ~ in one's throat ('to be hoarse')

front I *adv.* to face ~

front II *n.* ['front line'] (mil.) 1. at, on the ~ (the war correspondents spent two days at the ~; there has been no activity on this ~) ['area of activity'] 2. the home; political ~ 3. on a ~ (on the home ~) ['advanced part'] 4. at the ~ of; in ~ of ['movement'] ['campaign'] 5. a popular; united ~ (to present a united ~) ['boundary'] (meteorology) 6. a cold; occluded; stationary; warm ~ ['walk, road along a body of water'] (BE) 7. a river; sea ~ 8. along a ~ (to walk along the sea ~) 9. on a ~ (is there a hotel on the sea ~?) ['behavior'] 10. to put on, put up a ~ 11. a bold, brazen ~ (to put on a bold ~) ['facade'] 12. a ~ for (the store was a ~ for illegal drug sales)

front III *v.* 1. (d; intr.) to ~ for (to ~ for the mob) 2. (d; intr.) to ~ on (our building ~s on the main road)

frontage *n.* ocean; river ~

frontier *n.* 1. to advance, extend a ~ (to extend the ~s of science) 2. to cross a ~ 3. on a ~

front line *n.* at, in, on the ~

frost *n.* 1. a hard, heavy, severe; light, slight ~ 2. eternal ~, permafrost 3. a touch of ~

frown *v.* 1. (D; intr.) to ~ at ('to look with displeasure at') (the teacher ~ed at the noisy children) 2. (d; intr.) to ~ on, upon ('to disapprove of') (they ~ on all forms of affection in public)

frozen *adj.* ~ hard, solid

frugal *adj.* (formal) ~ of (esp. BE), with (~ of one's money)

frugality *n.* to practice ~

fruit *n.* 1. to grow ~ 2. (also fig.) to bear ~ (not all trees bear ~) 3. ripe; unripe ~ 4. fresh; luscious; young ~ 5. citrus; tropical ~ (our country exports citrus ~) 6. (fig.) forbidden ~ 7. canned (AE), tinned (BE); dried; fresh; frozen ~ 8. (misc.) (fig.) the ~s of one's labor

fruitcake *n.* (misc.) (colloq.) as nutty as a ~ ('completely insane')

fruition *n.* 1. to bring smt. to ~ 2. to come to ~

frustrated *adj.* ~ to + inf. (he was ~ to find no support among his friends)

frustrating *adj.* 1. ~ to + inf. (it's ~ for me to work in a place like that) 2. ~ that + clause (it is ~ that so few people support this worthy cause)

frustration *n.* to vent one's ~ on

fry *v.* (C) ~ an egg for me; or: ~ me an egg

fry-up *n.* (colloq.) (BE) ['frying of foods'] to do, have a ~

fudge *v.* (D; intr.) ('to hedge') to ~ on (to ~ on an issue)

fuel *n.* 1. to take on ~ 2. to run out of ~ 3. jet; liquid; nuclear; solid ~ 4. fossil; synthetic ~s 5. (misc.) (usu. fig.) to add ~ to the fire

fugitive *n.* 1. to track down a ~ 2. a ~ from (a ~ from justice)

fulfillment, fulfilment *n.* 1. personal ~ (a sense of personal ~) 2. partial ~ (of the requirements for a doctoral degree)

full *adj.* ~ of (~ of wine)

fulminate *v.* (D; intr.) to ~ against

fumble I *n.* to make a ~

fumble II *v.* 1. (d; intr.) ('to grope') to ~ for (he was ~ling in his pocket for the key) 2. (d; intr.) to ~ with ('to handle clumsily') (she was ~ling with the lock)

fume *v.* (D; intr.) to ~ about; at, over (to ~ at the delay) (see also **fret**)

fumes *n.* 1. to inhale ~ 2. cigar; cigarette; gas ~

fun *n.* 1. to have ~ (we had a lot of ~) 2. to make ~ of smb.; to poke ~ at smb. 3. to spoil the ~ 4. ~ to + inf. (it was ~ to go on the roller coaster = it was ~ going on the roller coaster) 5. for, in ~ (to play for ~)

function *n.* ['characteristic action'] 1. to fulfill, perform a ~ 2. a grammatical ~ 3. the bodily ~s ['mathematical correspondence'] 4. an exponential; inverse; linear; trigonometric ~ ['social event'] 5. to attend a ~ 6. an annual; social ~

fund *n.* 1. to establish, set up a ~ 2. to administer, manage a ~ 3. an inexhaustible ~ 4. a contingency, emergency; pension; secret; sinking; slush; strike; trust ~ 5. a mutual ~ (AE; BE has *unit trust*)

fundamental *adj.* ~ to

funds *n.* 1. to raise ~ 2. to disburse, pay out ~ 3. matching; private; public ~ 4. (stamped on a check) insufficient ~ (AE; BE has *refer to drawer*) 5. ~ dry up, run out 6. the ~ to + inf. (we have enough ~ to complete the work)

funeral *n.* 1. to conduct; hold a ~ 2. a military; state ~

funk *n.* ['depressed state'] (colloq.) a blue ~ (in a blue ~)

funny *adj.* (colloq.) ['strange'] ['interesting'] 1. ~ about (there's smt. ~ about that affair) 2. ~ to + inf. (it's ~ to watch how people order in a restaurant = it's ~ watching how people order in a restaurant) 3. ~ that + clause (it's ~ that they didn't call)

funny bone *n.* to tickle smb.'s ~

furious *adj.* 1. ~ about, at, over smt. 2. ~ at (esp. AE), with smb. 3. ~ to + inf. (he was ~ to learn that his pay check had been lost) 4. ~ that + clause (she was ~ that the information had been leaked)

furlough *n.* (esp. AE) on ~

furnace *n.* 1. to stoke a ~ 2. a blast; coal; coke; gas; hot-air; oil; open-hearth ~

furnish *v.* 1. to ~ elegantly; luxuriously; plainly; tastefully 2. (D; tr.) ('to provide') to ~ for (to ~ blankets for the refugees) 3. (D; tr.) ('to provide') to ~ with (can you ~ us with the necessary information?) 4. (D; tr.) ('to supply with furniture') to ~ with (they ~ed the room with very expensive tables, chairs, and drapes)

furniture *n.* 1. to upholster ~ 2. antique; garden, lawn, outdoor, patio; modern; office; period; secondhand, used; unfinished (esp. AE) ~ 3. an article, piece, stick of ~

furor, furore *n.* to create a ~

furrow *n.* 1. to make, turn a ~ 2. an even, straight ~

furtherance *n.* in ~ of

fury *n.* 1. to vent one's ~ on, upon 2. pent-up; savage, unbridled ~

fuse I *n.* ['tube, wick used to set off an explosive charge'] 1. to light a ~ 2. a slow ~ (also fig.)

fuse II *n.* ['safety device'] 1. to blow, blow out (esp. AE) a ~ 2. to change a ~ 3. a safety ~ 4. a ~ blows, blows out (esp. AE) 5. (misc.) to blow a ~ ('to get very angry')

fuse III *n.* (CE) ['detonating device'] 1. to arm, set a ~ 2. a contact; delayed; percussion; proximity; time ~ (AE also has **fuze**)

fuse IV *v.* (D; intr.) to ~ with

fusion *n.* nuclear ~

fuss I *n.* 1. to kick up, make a ~ 2. a ~ about, over

fuss II *v.* 1. (D; intr.) to ~ about, over 2. (D; intr.) to ~ with

fussy *adj.* ~ about

futile *adj.* ~ to + inf. (it's ~ to speculate about what might have been = it's ~ speculating about what might have been)

futility *n.* an exercise in ~

future *n.* 1. to predict the ~ 2. to plan (out) the ~ 3. to face the ~; to look into the ~ 4. a bleak; bright, promising, rosy; unforeseeable ~ 5. the distant; foreseeable; immediate, near ~ 6. a ~ for (there is no ~ for them here) 7. in the ~ (in the near ~) 8. (BE) in ~ ('from now on') (be more careful in ~) 9. (misc.) what will the ~ bring?

fuze (AE) see **fuse III**

G

gadfly *n.* ['annoying person'] a ~ to (the reporter was a constant ~ to the government)

gadget *n.* 1. a ~ for (they have a ~ for everything) 2. a ~ to + inf. (a ~ to clean windows)

gaff *n.* (slang) (BE) to blow the ~ ('to reveal a secret')

gaffe *n.* ['blunder'] to make a ~

gag I *n.* (colloq.) ['joke'] as, for a ~ (she did it as/for a ~)

gag II *v.* (D; intr.) to ~ on (to ~ on food)

gaga *adv.* (colloq.) ['enthusiastic'] to go ~ over smt.

gage see **gauge**

gain I *n.* 1. to make ~s (in recent years minority groups have made considerable political ~s) 2. to consolidate one's ~s 3. to nullify a ~ 4. a considerable, enormous, notable, substantial, tremendous; tangible ~ 5. ill-gotten ~s 6. (economics) capital ~s 7. a ~ to (a ~ to our profession)

gain II *v.* 1. to ~ in ('to acquire') (to ~ in experience) 2. (D; intr.) to ~ on ('to move faster than') (the police were ~ing on the fugitive; to ~ on one's pursuers)

gait *n.* 1. a steady; unsteady ~ 2. at a certain ~ (at a steady ~)

gale *n.* 1. a heavy, raging, severe, strong; sudden ~ 2. a ~ blows itself out; rages

gall *n.* (colloq.) ['impudence'] 1. unmitigated ~ 2. the ~ to + inf. (he had the ~ to sue for damages)

gallant *adj.* ~ to + inf. (it was ~ of him to say that)

gallantry *n.* to display ~

gallery *n.* an art; fresco; press; shooting ~

galling *adj.* 1. ~ to 2. ~ to + inf. (it's ~ to watch him deceive everyone)

gallon *n.* an imperial ~

gallop *n.* at a ~

gallows *n.* to be sent to the ~

galvanize *v.* (d; tr.) to ~ into (to ~ smb. into action)

gambit *n.* (chess) 1. to play a ~ 2. to accept; decline a ~ 3. an opening ~

gamble *v.* (D; intr.) ('to risk') to ~ on (to ~ on smb.'s cooperation)

gambler *n.* a compulsive, inveterate; professional ~

gambling *n.* compulsive; illegal; legal ~

game *n.* ['contest, match'] 1. to play; win a ~ 2. to lose a ~ 3. (AE) to call ('cancel') a (baseball) ~ 4. to throw ('purposely lose') a ~ 5. a close; crucial; fair ~ 6. a bowl (Am. football); championship; home; match (tennis); practice; wild-card (Am. professional football) ~ ['form of recreation'] 7. to play a ~ 8. a ball; board; children's; numbers; parlor; video; word ~ 9. a ~ of chance; a ~ of skill ['deception'] 10. to see through smb.'s ~ 11. (AE) a con, confidence ~ ['tactic, strategy'] 12. a waiting ~ 13. a cat-and-mouse ~ ['hunted animals'] 14. to hunt; stalk ~ 15. big; small ~ 16. (fig.) fair ~ ('a legitimate object of attack') (to be fair ~ for

smb.) 17. (misc.) a ~ preserve, refuge ['prostitution'] (colloq.) (BE) 18. on the ~ ['misc.'] 19. the mating ~ (see the Usage Note for **match)**

games *n.* ['competition'] ['maneuvers'] 1. to hold ~ 2. war ~ 3. the Commonwealth; Olympic; summer; winter ~

gamut *n.* 1. to run the ~ from; to 2. the whole ~ (her performance ran the whole ~ from outstanding to terrible)

gander *n.* (colloq.) ['look'] to take a ~ at

gang *n.* 1. to form a ~ 2. to join a ~ 3. to break up, bust (up) a ~ 4. a chain; section; street; work ~ 5. an inner-city; juvenile ~

gangrene *n.* ~ sets in

gang up *v.* (d; intr.) to ~ against, on

gaol (BE) see **jail**

gap *n.* 1. to leave a ~ 2. to bridge, close, fill a ~ 3. a sorely felt, unbridgeable, wide ~ 4. a communications; credibility; generation; trade ~ 5. the gender ~ 6. a ~ between 7. a ~ in

gape *v.* (D; intr.) to ~ at

garage *n.* 1. a parking ~ 2. (misc.) to park a car in a ~

garage sale *n.* (AE) to have, hold a ~

garb I *n.* 1. formal ~ 2. in (formal) ~

garb II *v.* (d; refl.) to ~ in (they ~ed themselves in colorful costumes)

garbage *n.* (esp. AE) 1. to collect, pick up the ~ 2. to dispose of; dump ~

garden *n.* 1. to lay out; plant a ~ 2. to maintain a ~ 3. to water; weed a ~ 4. a botanical; formal; market (BE); rock; sunken; terraced; vegetable; zoological ~ (see the Usage Note for **yard)**

gardening *n.* 1. to do, go in for ~ 2. landscape; market (BE) ~

garlic *n.* 1. a clove of ~ 2. a whiff of ~

garment *n.* a foundation ~

gas *n.* ['accelerator'] 1. to step on the ~ ['combustible gaseous mixture'] 2. to light, turn on the ~ 3. to turn off the ~ 4. coal; natural ~ ['substance dispersed through the air to disable the enemy'] 5. mustard; nerve; poison, toxic; tear ~ ['misc.'] 6. laughing ~ ('nitrous oxide') (see also **gasoline)**

gash *n.* 1. to make a ~ 2. a deep ~

gasoline *n.* (AE) high-octane; leaded; lead-free, unleaded; premium; regular ~ (BE has *petrol)*

gasp I *n.* 1. to emit, give, let out a ~ 2. an audible ~ 3. a ~ for (a ~ for breath) 4. (misc.) the last ~ ('the last effort')

gasp II *v.* 1. (d; intr.) to ~ at ('to express surprise at') (they ~ed at our offer) 2. (D; intr.) ('to breathe with difficulty') to ~ for (to ~ for breath)

gas range *n.* to light, turn on a ~

gate *n.* 1. a starting ~ (at a racetrack) 2. at a ~ 3. (misc.) (colloq.) to give smb. the ~ ('to reject smb.')

gateway *n.* a ~ to (the ~ to the west)

gather *v.* 1. (d; intr.) ('to assemble') to ~ around (they ~ed around the speaker) 2. (d; tr.) ('to conclude') to ~ from (I ~ from the expression on your face that you don't like the proposal) 3. (L) ('to conclude') I ~ that you don't like him

gathering *n.* a public; social ~

gauge *n.* ['measuring device'] 1. a fuel; oil; pressure; rain; tire-pressure; water; wind ~ ['distance between rails'] 2. broad, wide; narrow; standard ~

gauntlet I *n.* ['challenge'] 1. to throw down the ~ 2. to pick up, take up the ~

gauntlet II *n.* ['ordeal'] to run a ~ (to run the ~ of reporters)

gavel I *n.* 1. to rap a ~ 2. a rap of the ~

gavel II *v.* (d; tr.) to ~ into (he ~led the protesters into silence)

gawk *v.* (colloq.) (D; intr.) to ~ at

gaze I *n.* an admiring; intense, rapt, steady, unblinking; wistful ~

gaze II *v.* 1. to ~ intently 2. (d; intr.) to ~ at

gear I *n.* ['toothed wheel as part of a transmission'] 1. to change (BE), shift ~s 2. to reverse ~s 3. to strip ~s 4. bottom (BE), low; high (AE), top (BE); reverse ~ 5. a worm ~ 6. ~s clash, grind; jam, lock, stick; mesh 7. in ~; out of ~ ['equipment'] 8. fishing; hunting; skiing ~ ['clothing'] (colloq.) (BE) 9. trendy ~

gear II *v.* (d; tr.) to ~ to (the whole economy is ~ed to the tourist trade)

gear up *v.* (d; intr., tr.) to ~ for (we are ~ing up for increased production)

gender *n.* 1. grammatical ~ 2. (the) feminine; masculine; neuter ~ (many languages have no neuter ~)

gene *n.* 1. to transfer, transplant ~s 2. to cut; splice ~s 3. a dominant; recessive ~

general *n.* 1. a brigadier (US); commanding; four-star; lieutenant; major ~ 2. (US) a ~ of the Army

generality *n.* 1. a broad, sweeping ~ 2. (to speak) in ~ties

generalization *n.* 1. to make a ~ 2. a broad, sweeping; valid ~ 3. a ~ about 4. a ~ that + clause (it is a valid ~ that exercise promotes good health)

generalize *v.* (D; intr.) to ~ about

general quarters *n.* to sound ~

generation *n.* 1. the coming, next; new; older; present; younger ~ 2. future; past ~s 3. a lost ~ 4. (misc.) a ~ gap

generosity *n.* 1. to demonstrate, display, show ~ 2. great, lavish, magnanimous, unstinting ~ 3. (misc.) to abuse smb.'s ~

generous *adj.* 1. ~ in; with (~ with money) 2. ~ to + inf. (it was ~ of her to contribute such a large sum)

genial *adj.* ~ towards

genitalia *n.* (plural) female; male ~

genius *n.* ['great mental capacity, ability'] 1. to demonstrate, show ~'2. an inventive; rare ~ 3. a spark of ~ ['ability'] 4. a ~ for (he has a ~ for getting into trouble) ['person of great mental capacity, ability'] 5. an artistic; budding; inventive; mathematical; mechanical; military; musical; rare; real ~ 6. a ~ to + inf. (she was a ~ to think of that)

genocide *n.* to commit, perpetrate ~

gentle *adj.* ~ with

gentleman *n.* 1. the complete, perfect, real, true ~ 2. a country ~ 3. (misc.) every inch a ~; a ~ of the old school

gentry *n.* the landed; local ~

gen up *v.* (slang) (BE) (D; tr.) ('to inform') to ~ about, on (they ~ned me up on the situation)

geography *n.* dialect, linguistic; economic; physical; political ~

geometry *n.* descriptive; Euclidean; plane; projective; solid ~

germ *n.* ['microorganism'] 1. ~s multiply 2. (some) ~s cause disease

germane *adj.* ~ to (~ to the discussion)

German measles *n.* ['rubella'] to catch, come down with ~

gestation *n.* period of ~

gesticulate *v.* to ~ frantically, wildly

gesture *n.* 1. to make a ~ 2. a bold; conciliatory; frantic; friendly; glorious, grand, grandiose, magnificent; habitual; humane, kind; imperious ~

get *v.* 1. (B) ('to deliver') I have to ~ a message to her 2. (C) ('to obtain') she got a newspaper for me; or: she got me a newspaper 3. (d; intr., tr.) to ~ across ('to cross'); ('to cause to cross') (to ~ across a bridge; the general finally got his troops across the river) 4. (d; intr.) to ~ after ('to exert pressure on') (you'll have to ~ after them: they are coming to work late every day) 5. (d; intr.) to ~ around ('to evade') (we cannot ~ around the regulations) 6. (d; intr.) to ~ at ('to suggest') (what are you ~ting at?) 7. (d; intr.) to ~ at ('to reach') (I hope that the children cannot ~ at the medicine; you're safe here: your enemies cannot ~ at you; to ~ at the truth) 8. (esp. AE) (d; intr.) to ~ behind ('to support') (we must ~ behind her campaign) 9. (d; intr.) to ~ between ('to try to separate') (never ~ between fighting dogs) 10. (d; intr., refl., tr.) to ~ into ('to enter'); ('to cause to enter') (to ~ into trouble; to ~ oneself into debt; to ~ smb. into trouble; to ~ into a fight) 11. (d; intr.) to ~ into ('to affect') (what got into him?) 12. (d; intr.) to ~ off ('to leave') (to ~ off a train) 13. (d; intr.) to ~ on ('to climb onto') (to ~ on a train) 14. (d; intr.) to ~ on ('to affect') (to ~ on smb.'s nerves) 15. (d; tr.) to ~ on ('to cause to enter') (he finally got the whole group on the train) 16. (d; intr.) to ~ onto ('to enter') (she could not ~ onto the train) 17. (d; intr.) to ~ onto ('to take up for discussion') (we got onto a very interesting topic) 18. (colloq.) (esp. AE) (d; intr.) to ~ onto ('to become aware of') (we finally got onto her schemes) 19. (d; intr., tr.) to ~ out of ('to leave'); ('to extricate'); ('to extricate oneself from') (to ~ out of a car; I got him out of trouble; to ~ out of trouble; when did he ~ out of prison?) 20. (d; intr.) to ~ over ('to overcome') (you'll have to ~ over your fear of speaking in public) 21. (d; intr.) to ~ over ('to recover from') (has she got/gotten over the shock?) 22. (d; intr.) to ~ past ('to slip by') (we got past the guard) 23. (d; intr.) ('to be unnoticed') to ~ past (the error got past him) 24. (d; intr., tr.) ('to pass'); ('to cause to pass') to ~ through (to ~ through a door; we could not ~ the piano through the window) 25. (d; intr.) to ~ to ('to reach') (to ~ to a telephone; to ~ to the point; we got to the theater late) 26. (colloq.) (d; intr.) to ~ to ('to affect') (her pleas got to me) 27. (colloq.) (d; intr.) to ~ to ('to bribe') (they got to the mayor himself) 28. (d; tr.) ('to deliver') to ~ to (to ~ smb. to a hospital) 29. (d; intr.) to ~ within ('to come') (don't ~ within range of the enemy artillery) 30. (E) ('to succeed in') if you can ~ to see her, you may receive some help; if you ~ to know her, you'll like her 31. (colloq.) (E; used in the perfect tense) ('to be obliged to') she's got to finish the work by tomorrow 32. (G) ('to begin') he finally got going 33. (H; no passive) ('to bring about') she finally got the television to work; I got a gardener to cut the grass 34. (J; more usu. is H) ('to bring about') she finally got the television working 35. (N; used with an adjective, past participle) ('to make') we got our tools ready; he got us involved; try to ~ them interested 36. (P; intr.) ('to arrive') he finally got home 37. (s) ('to become') to ~ angry; to ~ drunk; to ~ loose; to ~ rid of; to ~ even with smb. 38. (misc.) to ~ cracking ('to start moving'); to ~ in touch with smb.; to ~ nowhere ('to be unsuccessful'); to ~ somewhere ('to score a success') USAGE NOTE: In AE, the past participle of *to get* is usu. *gotten*--they'd gotten everything ready. In BE, it is *got*--they'd got everything ready. (Note that *ill-gotten gains* is CE.) However, AE does use *have got* especially in the meaning 'must'. Thus, the sentence *I've got to go* is CE. Only BE uses *had got* to form the past tense of this construction--*I'd got to do it yesterday* 'I had to do it yesterday'. BE also has *he'd got work* 'he had work'.

get across *v.* (B) ('to make clear') she tried to ~ her ideas across to us

get after *v.* (H) ('to induce') you'll have to ~ him to trim the bushes

get ahead *v.* (d; intr.) to ~ of ('to occupy a position in front of') (try to ~ of him)

get along *v.* 1. (D; intr.) ('to manage') to ~ on (we cannot ~ on his salary) 2. (D; intr.) ('to relate') to ~ with (how does she ~ with her brother?)

get around *v.* (d; intr.) ('to find time') to ~ to (we finally got around to answering our correspondence)

getaway *n.* 1. to make (good) one's ~ 2. a quick ~

get away *v.* 1. (D; intr.) ('to escape') to ~ from (to ~ from one's pursuers) 2. (D; intr.) ('to escape') to ~ with (the thieves got away with the loot) 3. (d; intr.) to ~ with ('to succeed in') (they didn't ~ with their scheme)

get back *v.* 1. (d; intr.) ('to get revenge') to ~ at; for (we got back at him for his insult) 2. (d; intr.) to ~ to ('to resume') (to ~ to work)

get behind *v.* (D; intr.) ('to be late') to ~ in, with (to ~ with one's payments)

get by *v.* 1. (D; intr.) ('to manage') to ~ on (to ~ on very little) 2. (D; intr.) ('to manage') to ~ with (we'll have to ~ with one car)

get down *v.* 1. (D; intr.) ('to dismount') to ~ from (to ~ from a horse) 2. (D; tr.) ('to bring down') to ~ from (she got the book down from the shelf) 3.

(d; intr.) to ~ to ('to begin'); ('to take up') (to ~ to work; to ~ to details)

get in *v.* ('to join') 1. (d; intr.) to ~ on (to ~ on the act) ('to participate in'); (to ~ on the ground floor) ('to join at the very beginning') 2. (d; intr.) to ~ with (to ~ with the wrong crowd)

get off *v.* 1. (d; intr.) to ~ to ('to begin with') (to ~ to a good start) 2. (D; intr.) ('to escape') to ~ with (he got off with a light sentence; to ~ with a few scratches)

get on *v.* 1. (d; intr.) ('to advance') to ~ in (to ~ in years) 2. (d; intr.) ('to continue') to ~ with (to ~ with one's work) 3. (esp. BE) (d; intr.) ('to get along') to ~ with (how does she ~ with her brother?)

get out of *v.* (E) I couldn't ~ doing it

get over *v.* (D; intr.) ('to pass') to ~ to (to ~ to the other side)

get round (BE) see **get around**

get through *v.* 1. (B) ('to deliver') (she finally got the message through to them) 2. (D; intr.) ('to reach') to ~ to (we could not ~ to her)

get-together *n.* to have a ~

get together *v.* 1. (d; intr.) to ~ on ('to agree on') (we finally got together on a compromise) 2. (D; intr.) ('to meet') to ~ with (we got together with some friends last night)

get-up *n.* ['outfit'] an elaborate ~

get up *v.* (D; intr.) ('to rise') to ~ from (to ~ from the table)

ghastly *adj.* ~ to + inf. (it was ~ of him to say that)

ghetto *n.* an inner-city, urban ~

ghost *n.* ['apparition'] 1. to see a ~ 2. a ~ appears 3. to believe in ~s

gibe I *n.* a ~ about, at

gibe II *v.* (D; intr.) to ~ at

gift *n.* ['present'] 1. to give, present a ~ to 2. to heap, lavish ~s on 3. an extravagant, lavish; generous; outright ~ 4. a farewell; graduation; shower; wedding ~ ['talent'] 5. a ~ for (a ~ for languages)

gifted *adj.* intellectually; physically ~

giggle I *n.* a nervous; silly ~

giggle II *v.* (D; intr.) to ~ at

gimmick *n.* an advertising, promotional ~

girder *n.* a steel ~

girdle *n.* 1. a tight, trim ~ 2. a panty ~

girl *n.* 1. a career; chorus; college (esp. AE); dancing; flower; office; pinup; working ~ 2. a ball ~ (who retrieves tennis balls) 3. (old-fashioned) a good ('virtuous') ~ 4. a call ~ ('prostitute who can be summoned by telephone') USAGE NOTE: It can be offensive to call a woman a *girl*. Thus, *career woman* and *working woman* are considered by many to be more acceptable than *career girl* and *working girl*. (See the Usage Note for **woman.**) In some circles, *working girl* can be a euphemism for *prostitute*. In addition, the former use of *girl* in the meaning of 'black female' is considered offensive. (See also the Usage Note for **boy.**)

girlfriend *n.* a steady ~

girth *n.* to measure the ~ of

gist *n.* (colloq.) ['main meaning'] to get the ~ of

give v. 1. (A) she gave the book to me; or: she gave me the book 2. (D; tr.) to ~ for (she gave the money for a new health center) 3. (H) she gave us to understand that she would attend

giveaway n. (colloq.) ['unintentional revelation'] a dead ~

give back v. (usu. B; sometimes A) she gave the money back to us

give in v. (D; intr.) ('to yield') to ~ to (we had to ~ to their demands)

given adj. (cannot stand alone) ~ to (~ to exaggeration)

give out v. (B) we gave the food out to those who needed it

give over v. (colloq.) (BE) (used in the imper.) (G) ('to stop') ~ hitting the child

give up v. 1. (B) ('to yield') he gave up his seat to a man on crutches 2. (D; intr.) ('to lose hope') to ~ on (we have given up on him) 3. (G) ('to stop') she gave up attempting to influence them

give way v. (d; intr.) ('to yield') to ~ to (reason gave way to hysteria)

glad adj. 1. ~ about, of 2. ~ to + inf. (I will be ~ to help) 3. ~ that + clause (we are ~ that they are coming)

gladiator n. a Roman ~

glance I n. 1. to cast, dart, shoot; steal a ~ at 2. to exchange ~s 3. an admiring; amused; casual, cursory, fleeting, passing; conspiratorial; disapproving, indignant; furtive, stolen, surreptitious; imploring; knowing; meaningful, significant; penetrating, probing, searching; quizzical; shy; sidelong; suspicious; wistful; withering ~ 4. at a ~ (I recognized her at a ~)

glance II v. 1. ('to look') to ~ admiringly; casually; furtively, surreptitiously; imploringly; indignantly; knowingly; meaningfully; quizzically; shyly; suspiciously 2. (d; intr.) ('to look') to ~ at 3. (d; intr.) ('to ricochet') to ~ off (the rock ~d off the window)

gland n. 1. the pituitary; prostate; thyroid ~ 2. the adrenal; eccrine, sweat; endocrine; lachrymal; lymph; mammary; salivary ~s 3. swollen ~s

glare I n. in the ~ (in the ~ of publicity)

glare II v. (D; intr.) to ~ at

glass n. ['transparent substance'] 1. to blow, make ~ 2. cut; ground; plate; safety; sheet; stained ~ 3. a pane of ~ ['tumbler'] ['container'] 4. to drink a ~ (of water) 5. to drain; fill a ~ 6. to raise one's ~ (to give a toast) 7. to clink, touch ~es (when giving a toast) 8. a champagne; cocktail; drinking; shot; water; wine ~ 9. a measuring ~ ['optical instrument'] 10. a magnifying ~

glasses n. ['spectacles'] 1. dark, sun; reading ~ ['binoculars'] 2. field; opera ~ ['misc.'] 3. to see life through rose-colored ~ ('to see only the good in life')

gleam I n. 1. a faint ~ 2. a wild ~ (there was a wild ~ in his eyes)

gleam II v. (D; intr.) to ~ with

glean v. (D; tr.) to ~ from

glee n. 1. to express ~ 2. with ~ (to dance with ~)

glider n. 1. to fly a ~ 2. to launch; tow a ~ 3. a ~ flies; glides; soars

glimmer n. a faint, pale, slight, weak ~

glimpse n. 1. to catch a ~ of 2. a brief, fleeting ~ 3. a ~ into (a ~ into the life of a coal miner)

glint v. (D; intr.) to ~ with

glisten v. (D; intr.) to ~ with

glitch n. (slang) ['mishap'] an unexpected ~

glitter v. 1. (D; intr.) to ~ in (to ~ in the sunlight) 2. (D; intr.) to ~ with

gloat v. (D; intr.) to ~ over

globe n. to circle, girdle the ~

gloom n. 1. to express ~ 2. (an) all-pervading, deep ~ 3. ~ about, over (to express ~ over the situation)

gloomy adj. ~ about, over

glorious adj. ~ to + inf. (it would be ~ to live in a peaceful world)

glory I n. 1. to achieve, win ~ 2. to bring ~ to 3. to reflect ~ on 4. eternal, everlasting ~ 5. military ~ 6. a blaze of ~ 7. ~ to (eternal ~ to our heroes!) 8. in (one's) ~ (to bask in smb.'s ~; to be in one's ~)

glory II v. (d; intr.) to ~ in (to ~ in one's triumph)

gloss I n. ['luster'] a high ~

gloss II v. (d; intr.) to ~ over ('to cover up') (to ~ over one's mistakes)

glove n. 1. boxing; kid; lace; leather; rubber; suede; work ~s 2. an oven ~ (esp. BE; AE has pot holder) 3. a pair of ~s 4. (misc.) to fit like a ~ ('to fit perfectly')

glow I n. 1. to cast, emit a ~ 2. an eerie ~ 3. a soft; warm ~

glow II v. (D; intr.) to ~ with (to ~ with pride)

glower v. (D; intr.) to ~ at

glued adj. (cannot stand alone) ~ to (he was ~ to his TV set; her eyes were ~ to the door)

glum adj. ~ about

glut I n. a ~ on the market

glut II v. (D; refl., tr.) to ~ with (to ~ the market with cheap goods)

glutton n. a ~ for punishment

gnaw v. (d; intr.) to ~ (away) at

go I n. (colloq.) ['attempt'] 1. a ~ at (let's have a ~ at it) ['misc.'] 2. to make a ~ of it ('to get along'); always on the ~

go II v. 1. (d; intr.) ('to proceed') to ~ about (to ~ about one's business) 2. (d; intr.) to ~ across ('to cross') (to ~ across a river) 3. (d; intr.) to ~ against ('to be opposed to'); ('to be unfavorable to') (this ~es against my principles; to ~ against the grain; the war began to ~ against them) 4. (d; intr.) to ~ beyond ('to exceed') (to ~ beyond the call of duty) 5. (d; intr.) ('to pass') to ~ by (to ~ by smb.'s house) 6. (d; intr.) to ~ by ('to follow') (to ~ by the rules) 7. (d; intr.) ('to be known') to ~ by (he used to ~ by another name) 8. (d; intr.) to ~ down ('to descend') (to ~ down a hill) 9. (d; intr.) ('to leave') to ~ for (to ~ for a drive; to ~ for a walk; to ~ for the doctor) 10. (d; intr.) ('to be spent') to ~ for (half our money ~es for food) (see also 21) 11. (d; intr.) ('to be sold') to ~ for (the painting went for a hundred dollars) 12. (d; intr.) to ~ for ('to attack') (he went straight for me; to ~ for the jugular) 13. (d; intr.) ('to try') to ~ for (she went for the first prize) 14. (d; intr.) to ~ for ('to concern') (what he said ~es for you too) 15. (colloq.) (d; intr.) to ~ for ('to like') (I could ~ for her; we could ~ for a drink) 16. (d; intr. ('to move') to ~ from; to (to ~ from the ridiculous to the sublime) 17. (d; intr.) to ~ into ('to enter') (to ~ into town; to ~ into the army; to ~ into detail) 18. (d; intr.) to ~ off ('to leave') (to ~ off duty; the train went off the tracks; to ~ off the air) 19. (d; intr.) to ~ on ('to leave') (to ~ on a trip) 20. (colloq.) (d; intr.) to ~ on ('to judge by'); ('to rely on') (we must ~ on the assumption that he'll agree; we don't have much to ~ on) 21. (esp. BE) (d; intr.) to ~ on ('to be spent for') (half our money ~es on food) (see also 10) 22. (d; intr.) to ~ out of ('to leave') (to ~ out of the house) 23. (d; intr.) to ~ over ('to examine') (to ~ over the books) 24. (d; intr.) to ~ through ('to be sold out in') (the dictionary went through three printings) 25. (d; intr.) ('to pass') to ~ through (to ~ through a red light; to ~ through a door) 26. (d; intr.) to ~ through ('to endure') (she went through a lot) 27. (d; intr.) to ~ through ('to spend, squander') (he went through his inheritance in six months) 28. (d; intr.) to ~ through ('to repeat') (to ~ through the main points again) 29. (d; intr.) to ~ through ('to conduct') (to ~ through a ceremony) 30. (d; intr.) to ~ through ('to examine') (to ~ through the books) 31. (d; intr.) ('to travel') to ~ to (we went to Alaska) 32. (d; intr.) ('to move') to ~ to (she went to the door) 33. (d; intr.) to ~ to ('to attend') (to ~ to school; to ~ to college) 34. (d; intr.) to ~ to ('to be received by') (the estate went to her; first prize went to my cousin) 35. (d; intr.) to ~ to ('to reach') (this road ~es to town; the railway ~es to the border) 36. (d; intr.) ('to move') to ~ towards (she went towards the exit) 37. (d; intr.) to ~ towards ('to be devoted to') (our contributions went towards setting up a shelter for the homeless) 38. (d; intr.) to ~ up ('to ascend') (to ~ up a hill) 39. (d; intr.) to ~ with ('to date'); ('to be a companion to') (Jim ~es with Nancy) 40. (d; intr.) ('to combine') to ~ with (what verb ~es with that noun?) 41. (E; usu. in progressive tenses) ('to intend, plan') we are ~ing to see them; that just ~es to show you that I'm right 42. (G) to ~ shopping 43. (s) to ~ unnoticed; everything went wrong 44. (misc.) to ~ abroad; to ~ bad ('to be corrupted'); ('to turn sour'); to ~ bankrupt; to ~ to bed; to ~ begging ('to be in little demand'); to ~ broke ('to run out of money'); (BE) to ~ to the country ('to hold a general election'); to ~ easy on smb. ('to treat smb. leniently'); to ~ to great expense ('to spend a great deal'); to ~ to extremes; to ~ native ('to behave like the natives'); to ~ overboard ('to exaggerate'); to ~ to pieces ('to disintegrate'); to ~ to press ('to be printed'); to ~ to sea ('to become a sailor'); to ~ steady (esp. AE) ('to be a boyfriend or girlfriend'); to ~ to trial (the case went to trial); to ~ to waste ('to be wasted'); to ~ wrong ('to be corrupted'); she has a lot ~ing for her ('she has many advantages')

goad v. 1. (D; tr.) to ~ into (to ~ smb. into doing smt.) 2. (H) he kept ~ing me to fight

go-ahead n. 1. to give smb. the ~ 2. to get the ~ 3. the ~ to + inf. (we got the ~ to proceed with the investigation)

go ahead v. (D; intr.) ('to proceed') to ~ with (to ~ with one's plans)

goal n. 1. to set a ~ 2. to achieve, attain, reach, realize a ~ 3. (sports) to kick, make, score a ~ 4. (sports) to nullify a ~ 5. an immediate; long-range, long-term; ultimate ~ 6. (sports) a field ~ 7. (BE) (soccer) an own ~ ('a goal scored by a player against his own team')

go along v. (D; intr.) to ~ with ('to agree to') (to ~ with a compromise)

goat n. 1. to keep (BE), raise (esp. AE) ~s 2. a mountain ~ 3. ~s baa, bleat 4. a herd of ~s 5. a young ~ is a kid 6. a female ~ is a doe or nanny goat 7. a male ~ is a buck or billy goat 8. (misc.) to get smb.'s ~ ('to irritate smb.')

go away v. (D; intr.) to ~ for (to ~ for a rest)

go back v. 1. (d; intr.) ('to renege') to ~ on (to ~ on one's promise) 2. (D; intr.) ('to return') to ~ to (he went back to his home)

God n. 1. to bless; praise; worship ~ 2. to believe in ~ 3. (misc.) in praise of ~

go down v. 1. (d; intr.) ('to become known') to ~ in as (to ~ in history as a great ruler) 2. (D; intr.) ('to descend') to ~ into (to ~ into a mine) 3. (d; intr.) ('to descend') to ~ to (to ~ to the river) 4. (misc.) to ~ to defeat

godsend n. 1. a real ~ 2. a ~ to

godspeed n. (old-fashioned) to bid, wish smb. ~

go forward v. (d; intr.) ('to proceed') to ~ with (to ~ with one's plans)

goggle n. (D; intr.) to ~ at

go in v. 1. (d; intr.) ('to occupy oneself') to ~ for (to ~ for gardening) 2. (d; intr.) to ~ with ('to join') (he agreed to ~ with them)

going n. ['progress'] rough, slow ~

gold n. 1. to mine; prospect for ~ 2. to strike ~ (also fig.) ('to discover smt. valuable') 3. pure, solid ~ 4. a bar of ~ 5. (misc.) as good as ~ ('very good')

gold standard n. 1. to adopt the ~ 2. to go off the ~

golf n. 1. to play ~ 2. clock (BE); miniature ~ 3. a round of ~ (to play a round of ~)

golf ball n. to drive; putt a ~

gong n. to sound a ~

gonorrhea n. to catch, contract ~

good I adj. 1. any ~ (is he any ~ at chess?) 2. ~ at, in (she is ~ at/in mathematics) 3. ~ for (exercise is ~ for you) 4. ~ to (he is ~ to his parents) 5. ~ with (he is ~ with his hands) 6. ~ to + inf. (it's ~ to be home again; it was ~ of you to come) 7. ~ that + clause (it's ~ that we don't have to work tomorrow)

good II n. ['something useful'] 1. to do ~ 2. the common; highest ~ ['positive qualities'] 3. to bring out the ~ in smb. ['favor'] 4. in ~ with smb. ['favorable result'] 5. to come to no ~ ['restitution'] 6. to make ~

goods n. 1. capital; consumer; dry (esp. AE), soft

(esp. BE); durable; manufactured; yard ~ 2. (misc.) to have the ~ on (colloq.) ('to have evidence against'); one's worldly ~

goodwill *n.* to show ~

go on *v.* 1. (d; intr.) ('to advance') to ~ to (to ~ to greater accomplishments) 2. (D; intr.) ('to continue') to ~ with (they went on with their work) 3. (E) ('to advance') she went on to become dean 4. (G) ('to continue') he went right on typing

goose *n.* 1. geese cackle, honk 2. a flock, gaggle of geese 3. a young ~ is a gosling 4. a male ~ is a gander

go out *v.* 1. (D; intr.) ('to leave') to ~ for (to ~ for a walk) 2. (D; intr.) ('to try out') to ~ for (to ~ for a team) 3. (D; intr.) ('to go steady') to ~ with (Olga has been ~ing out with Joe) 4. (misc.) our hearts ~ to the bereaved ('we have deep sympathy for the bereaved'); to ~ into the world ('to become independent')

go over *v.* 1. (d; intr.) ('to pass') to ~ to (to ~ to the attack) 2. (d; intr.) to ~ to ('to desert to') (to ~ to the enemy)

Gordian knot *n.* to cut the ~

gorge *v.* (D; refl.) to ~ on, with (to ~ oneself on sweets)

gospel, Gospel *n.* 1. to preach; spread the ~ 2. to believe in the ~ 3. the ~ truth

gossip I *n.* 1. to spread ~ 2. common; idle; malicious, vicious; silly ~ 3. a piece, tidbit (AE), titbit (BE) of ~ 4. ~ about 5. ~ that + clause (have you heard the ~ that he intends to resign?)

gossip II *v.* (D; intr.) to ~ about

go through *v.* (d; intr.) ('to proceed') to ~ with (to ~ with one's plans)

goulash *n.* Hungarian ~

go up *v.* 1. (d; intr.) to ~ to ('to approach') (she went up to him and said something) 2. (D; intr.) ('to ascend') (to ~ to the top)

governess *n.* a ~ for, to (she served as a ~ to three small children)

government *n.* 1. to form a ~ 2. to head; operate, run a ~ 3. to destabilize, subvert; dissolve; overthrow; seize a ~ 4. (a) clean; corrupt; strong; weak ~ 5. a caretaker; civil; coalition; military; provisional ~ 6. an authoritarian; communist; conservative; democratic; dictatorial; liberal; minority; parliamentary; reactionary; shadow; socialist; totalitarian ~ 7. (a) central; federal; local; municipal; national; provincial ~ 8. a student ~ 9. a ~ falls 10. under a ~ (to live under a democratic ~) 11. (misc.) (BE) ~ and opposition; the ~ benches

governor *n.* 1. to appoint; elect smb. ~ 2. a deputy, lieutenant; military ~ 3. a ~ general

gown *n.* a dressing; evening (AE); formal; hospital ~; nightgown (esp. AE); wedding ~

grab *v.* 1. (C) ~ a few for me; or: ~ me a few 2. (d; intr.) to ~ for (she ~bed for his pistol)

grace *n.* ['short prayer'] 1. to say ~ ['sense'] ['decency'] 2. the ~ to + inf. (she had the good ~ to concede defeat) ['favor'] 3. divine ~ 4. to fall from ~ 5. by the ~ of God 6. in smb.'s good ~s 7. (rel.) a state of ~ ['willingness'] 8. with bad; good ~ ['attractiveness'] 9. effortless ~ ['feature'] 10. a saving ~

gracious *adj.* 1. ~ to, towards (she is ~ to all) 2. ~ to + inf. (it was ~ of him to make the offer; she was ~ enough to introduce me to them)

gradation *n.* 1. (ling.) vowel ~ 2. a ~ in

grade *n.* ['mark, rating'] (esp. AE) 1. to make out ~s; to give a ~ 2. to get, receive a ~ 3. an excellent, high; failing; fair, mediocre; low; passing ~ 4. (a student's) average ~s ['standard'] 5. to make the ~ 6. a high; low; medium; prime ~ ['degree of descent, rise'] 7. a slight; steep ~

graduate I *n.* a college (AE); university; high-school (AE) ~

graduate II *v.* 1. (D; intr.) to ~ from (to ~ from college) 2. (misc.) to ~ with honors, cum laude

graduate studies *n.* to pursue ~

graduate work *n.* to do ~

graduation *n.* 1. a college; high-school (AE) ~ 2. ~ from (~ from college) 3. on ~ (on ~ from college, she got a good job)

graduation exercises *n.* to hold ~

graft I *n.* ['act of grafting, inserting'] 1. to do a ~ 2. a bone; skin ~ 3. a (skin) ~ takes ['bribes'] 4. ~ and corruption ['work'] (colloq.) (BE) 5. hard ~

graft II *v.* (D; tr.) to ~ on to, onto

grain *n.* ['food plants'] 1. to grow ~ 2. to store ~ ['texture'] 3. a fine; rough; smooth ~ 4. against the ~; with the ~ ['misc.'] 5. to take smt. with a ~ of salt ('to be skeptical about smt.')

grammar *n.* comparative; descriptive; functional; generative; historical; prescriptive; structuralist; systemic; transformational ~

grand *adj.* see **great**

grandeur *n.* delusions of ~

grant I *n.* 1. to award, give a ~ 2. a block; cash; categorical (AE); federal (AE); government; matching; research ~ 3. a ~ for (a ~ for research on folklore) 4. a ~ to + inf. (we received a ~ to attend the conference)

grant II *v.* 1. (A) the government ~ed a pension to her; or: the government ~ed her a pension 2. (L; may have an object) I ~ (you) that this is true 3. (formal) (M) I ~ this to be true

granted *adj.* 1. to take smb. for ~ ('to assume that smb. will agree, cooperate') 2. to take smt. for ~ ('to assume that smt. is certain to happen')

grapefruit *n.* 1. pink; seedless; white ~ 2. (misc.) half a ~; a ~ section

grapes *n.* 1. to pick ~ 2. to press ~ 3. seedless; sweet ~ 4. a bunch of ~ 5. (usu. fig.) sour ~

grapevine *n.* ['circulation of rumors, gossip'] by, through the ~ (to hear news through the ~)

graphics *n.* computer ~

grapple *v.* 1. (d; intr.) to ~ for (they ~d for the key) 2. (d; intr.) to ~ with (to ~ with a problem)

grasp I *n.* ['comprehension'] 1. a firm; thorough ~ 2. an intuitive ~ ['reach'] 3. beyond one's ~; within one's ~

grasp II *v.* 1. (d; intr.) to ~ at, for 2. (D; tr.) to ~ by (to ~ smb. by the arm)

grass *n.* 1. to cut, mow (the) ~ 2. high, tall ~ 3. a blade; tuft of

grasshopper *n.* 1. ~s jump, leap 2. ~s chirp

grass on *v.* (slang) (BE) (D; intr.) ('to inform on')

to ~ to (he ~ed on them to the police)

grate v. (D; intr.) to ~ on (the noise ~s on my ears)

grateful adj. 1. ~ for; to (I am ~ to you for your help) 2. ~ that + clause (I'm ~ that you can help)

gratification n. 1. to express ~ 2. deep, profound; instant ~ 3. smb.'s ~ at

gratified adj. 1. ~ at, by, over, with (~ at the outcome) 2. ~ to + inf. (we were ~ to learn that our proposal has been accepted) 3. ~ that + clause (I am ~ that you can come)

gratifying adj. 1. ~ to + inf. (it was ~ to see the results of the exam) 2. ~ that + clause (it was ~ that she lived to see the fruits of her labor)

gratitude n. 1. to express; feel; show ~ 2. deep, profound, sincere, undying; everlasting ~ 3. ~ for (she expressed her ~ for our help)

grave n. 1. to dig a ~ 2. to desecrate a ~ 3. a mass; pauper's; unmarked; watery ~ 4. at a ~ (to pray at a ~) 5. (misc.) a gravedigger

gravitate v. (d; intr.) to ~ to, towards

gravity n. ['seriousness'] 1. to grasp the ~ (of a situation) ['weight'] 2. specific; zero ~ 3. the center; force of ~

gravy n. thick; watery ~

gray (AE) see **grey**

graze v. (d; intr.) to ~ against (he ~d against the table)

grease n. 1. to cut, dissolve ~ 2. axle ~ 3. a spot of ~ 4. (misc.) (colloq.) elbow ~ ('hard work')

great adj. (colloq.) 1. ~ to + inf. (it was ~ of you to help; it was ~ to see everyone again = it was ~ seeing everyone again) 2. ~ that + clause (it was ~ that we could finally meet)

great divide n. to cross the ~ ('to die')

great guns n. (colloq.) to go ~ ('to have great energy')

greatness n. to achieve ~

great one n. (colloq.) ['enthusiast'] a ~ for (he's a ~ for telling fibs)

greed n. 1. to demonstrate, display ~ 2. insatiable ~ 3. ~ for 4. consumed with ~

greedy adj. 1. ~ for 2. ~ to + inf. (it was ~ of them to eat up all the candy)

Greek n. (colloq.) it was (all) ~ to me ('it was incomprehensible to me')

green I adj. (cannot stand alone) ~ with (envy)

green II n. ['color'] 1. bright; dark; light ~ ['green light'] 2. on ~ (turn on ~ only)

green light n. ['permission to continue'] 1. to give smb. the ~ 2. to get the ~

greeting n. 1. to exchange; extend, send ~s 2. to extend a ~ 3. a cordial, friendly, sincere, warm ~ 4. cordial, friendly, sincere, warm, warmest ~s 5. an official ~; official ~s 6. holiday, season's ~s (see also **regards**)

grenade n. 1. to launch; lob, throw a ~ 2. a hand; percussion; rifle ~ 3. (misc.) to pull the pin on a ~

grey n. dark; light ~

grief n. 1. to express; feel, suffer ~ 2. to come to ~ 3. bitter, deep, inconsolable, overwhelming, profound ~ 4. ~ at, over 5. of ~ (to die of ~) 6. (misc.) good ~! (exclamation expressing mild dismay)

grievance n. 1. to air, vent a ~ 2. to file, submit a (formal) ~ 3. to hear a ~ (the committee heard the ~) 4. to nurse a ~ 5. to redress; settle a ~ 6. a justified, legitimate, valid; unjustified ~ 7. a ~ against

grieve v. 1. to ~ deeply 2. (D; intr.) to ~ for, over 3. (R) it ~d me (to learn) that she had been severely injured

grill I n. 1. a charcoal ~ 2. mixed ~

grill II v. (C) ~ a hamburger for me; or: ~ me a hamburger

grimace n. to give, make a ~

grin I n. a broad; contagious, infectious; foolish, silly; sardonic ~

grin II v. (D; intr.) to ~ at

grind v. 1. (C) ~ a pound of coffee for me; or: ~ me a pound of coffee 2. (D; tr.) to ~ into (to ~ wheat into flour) 3. (N; used with an adjective) I ground the coffee very fine

grinder n. (AE) a meat ~ (BE has *mincing machine, mincer*)

grip n. ['grasp'] ['hold'] 1. to get a ~ on 2. to lose one's ~ 3. to relax, release; tighten one's ~ 4. a firm, iron, strong, tight, vise-like; loose, weak ~ ['control'] 5. to get a ~ on oneself 6. to lose one's ~ 7. in the ~ of (in the ~ of a general strike) ['device that grips'] 8. a hair ~ (BE; AE has *bobby pin*) ['stagehand'] 9. a first, key ~

gripe I n. (colloq.) ['complaint'] 1. a legitimate ~ (he has a legitimate ~) 2. a ~ about

gripe II v. (colloq.) (D; intr.) ('to complain') to ~ about, at

grips n. (colloq.) to come to ~ with smt. (esp. AE) ('to confront')

grist n. ~ for smb.'s mill ('smt. used to good advantage')

grit n. ['courage, perseverance'] (colloq.) 1. to display, show ~ 2. true ~ 3. the ~ to + inf. (they had enough ~ to hold out in the face of real hardship)

groan I n. 1. to emit, heave, utter a ~ 2. a loud ~

groan II v. 1. (D; intr.) to ~ about, over (to ~ over new taxes) 2. (D; intr.) to ~ with (to ~ with frustration) 3. (L) he ~ed that he had been shot 4. (misc.) to ~ under the weight of oppression

groom v. 1. (d; tr.) to ~ as (she was ~ed as our next candidate) 2. (d; tr.) to ~ for (to ~ smb. for the presidency)

grooming n. good ~

grope v. 1. (D; intr.) to ~ for (to ~ for one's keys) 2. (P; intr.) to ~ around (in the dark)

grotesque adj. ~ to + inf. (it was ~ of him to come dressed like that)

ground n. ['contested area'] 1. to gain ~ on 2. to hold, stand one's ~ 3. to give ~ 4. to lose, yield ~ ['soil'] ['terrain'] 5. to cover ~ 6. firm, hard, solid; frozen; high; soft ~ 7. hallowed, holy ~ 8. on the ~ ['interest'] 9. common ~ ['area used for a specific purpose'] 10. a breeding; burial; dumping; hunting; parade; picnic; proving; recreation (BE) ~ ['area of knowledge'] 11. to cover ~ ['misc.'] 12. to break ~ ('to begin building'); to get off the ~ ('to get started'); from the ~ up ('from the very beginning'); on delicate ~ ('in a situation that demands great tact'); to get off the ~ ('to get

started'); on shaky ~ ('without a firm basis'); one's favorite stamping ~ ('one's favorite spot')
grounded *adj.* (usu. does not stand alone) ~ in (she is well ~ in grammar)
grounding *n.* a ~ in (a good ~ in physics)
grounds *n.* ['basis, foundation'] 1. to give smb. ~ 2. ample; solid ~ 3. ~ for (~ for divorce) 4. ~ to + inf. (we had sufficient ~ to sue; there were no ~ to deny bail) 5. on ~ (on what ~?) ['sediment'] 6. coffee ~ ['area used for a specific purpose'] 7. hospital ~ 8. on the (hospital) ~
groundwork *n.* to do, lay the ~ for
group I *n.* 1. an affinity; age; control; discussion; encounter; ethnic, minority; peer; pressure; social; special-interest; splinter ~ 2. (BE) a ginger ~ ('a group of activists') 3. a blood ~
group II *v.* 1. (d; intr.) to ~ around (the scouts ~ed around their leader) 2. (d; tr.) to ~ under (to ~ several types under one heading)
grouse *v.* (D; intr.) to ~ about
grove *n.* an olive; orange ~
grovel *v.* 1. (D; intr.) to ~ to (she will not ~ to anyone) 2. (misc.) to ~ in the dirt
grow *v.* 1. (d; intr.) ('to develop') to ~ from (oaks ~ from acorns) 2. (d; intr.) ('to develop') to ~ into (the small shop grew into a large firm) 3. (colloq.) (d; intr.) to ~ on ('to become likable') (the strange new sculpture just ~s on you) 4. (d; intr) to ~ out of ('to become too large for') (the children grew out of their clothes) 5. (d; intr.) ('to develop') to ~ out of (the city grew out of a small village) 6. (d; intr.) ('to develop') to ~ to (to ~ to adulthood; to ~ to one's full height) 7. (E) ('to begin') we grew to love them 8. (s) ('to become') to ~ longer; old; older; taller (in the autumn/fall the days ~ longer) USAGE NOTE: The verb *grow* 'to become' often suggests a gradual process rather than a sudden change. Compare *to grow cold* (gradually) and *to turn cold* (suddenly).
growl *v.* 1. (B) he ~ed a few words to us 2. (D; intr.) to ~ at (the dog ~ed at the jogger) 3. (L; to) he ~ed (to us) that he would be late
growth *n.* 1. to foster, promote ~ 2. to retard, stunt ~ 3. rapid; untrammeled; zero ~ 4. economic; population ~ (zero population ~) 5. (med.) a cancerous, malignant; inoperable; non-cancerous, non-malignant ~ 6. (biology) cell ~ 7. ~ in 8. (misc.) a scraggly ~ (of beard)
grow up *v.* (E) she grew up to be an able politician
grub *v.* (d; intr.) ('to rummage') to ~ for (to ~ for food)
grudge *n.* 1. to bear, harbor, hold, nurse a ~ 2. a bitter; deep-seated ~ 3. a ~ against
grumble *v.* 1. to ~ constantly 2. (D; intr.) to ~ about, at, over; to (to ~ at new taxes) 3 (L; to) they ~d (to us) that the decision was not fair
grumbler *n.* a chronic, constant ~
grumbling *n.* chronic, constant ~
grumpy *adj.* (colloq.) ~ about
grunt I *n.* to utter a ~
grunt II *v.* 1. (B) she ~ed a few words to them 2. (L; to) he ~ed (to her) that he would get up later 3. (misc.) to ~ and groan
guarantee I *n.* ['assurance of quality'] 1. to give,

offer, provide a ~ 2. a written ~ 3. a ~ against (a ~ against mechanical defects) ['assurance, pledge'] 4. to give a ~ 5. a firm ~ 6. a ~ that — clause (we have a firm ~ that the work will be finished on time)
guarantee II *v.* 1. to ~ fully 2. (A; usu. without *to*) we cannot ~ you regular hours 3. (D; intr.) to ~ against (to ~ a new car against rust) 4. (H) it's ~d to last five years 5. (L) she can ~ that you will be satisfied 6. (formal) (M) the owner ~d the coins to be genuine
guard I *n.* ['group of sentries'] ['sentry'] 1. to call out the ~ 2. to mount, post the ~ 3. to change, relieve the ~ 4. an advance; armed; color; honor; palace; police; rear; security ~ (they slipped past the palace ~) 5. under ~ ['guard duty'] 6. to stand ~ over 7. on ~ (to go on ~) ['militia'] 8. a home ~ ['police officer'] ['auxiliary police officer'] 9. (AE) a crossing ~ 10. a prison ~ (AE; BE has *warder, wardress*) ['alertness'] ['readiness to fight'] 11. off ~; on ~ (to be caught off ~) 12. to put smb. on one's ~ 13. to keep one's ~ up ['protective article of clothing'] 14. a knee; nose; shin ~ (see the Usage Note for **warden**)
guard II *v.* 1. to ~ closely (the player was ~ed closely by her opponent) 2. (d; intr.) to ~ against (to ~ against catching cold) 3. (D; tr.) to ~ against (to ~ an embassy against intruders) 4. (D; ~.) to ~ from (to ~ smb. from harm)
guardian *n.* 1. to appoint smb. ~ 2. (often fig.) a self-appointed ~
guerrilla *n.* 1. an armed ~ 2. (misc.) a ~ band
guess I *n.* 1. to hazard, make a ~ 2. a lucky; random, wild; rough; shrewd ~ 3. a ~ that + clause (it is only a ~ that she will be appointed)
guess II *v.* 1. to ~ shrewdly; wildly 2. (D; intr.) to ~ at (to ~ at smb.'s age) 3. (colloq.) (AE) (L; I ~ that he'll be late 4. (Q) ~ where the money is
guest *n.* 1. to have ~s (for dinner) 2. an invited; unexpected; unwelcome; wedding; weekend; welcome ~ 3. a regular ~ (at a hotel)
guff *n.* (colloq.) ['back talk'] to take ~ (I will not take any of your ~)
guffaw *n.* 1. to emit, give, let out a ~ 2. a loud ~
guidance *n.* 1. to provide ~ for 2. friendly; parental; vocational ~ 3. under smb.'s ~
guide I *n.* ['guidebook'] 1. a handy ~ 2. a ~ to (this handbook is a good ~ to London) ['person who guides'] 3. a tour ~
guide II *v.* (D; tr.) to ~ around, through (to ~ smb. around a city)
guidelines *n.* 1. to draw up ~ for 2. to adhere to, follow ~ 3. to violate ~
guilt *n.* 1. to establish smb.'s ~ 2. to bear ~ for 3. to admit; expiate one's ~ 4. (misc.) ~ by association
guiltless *adj.* ~ of
guilty *adj.* 1. to find; pronounce ~ of (the jury found him ~ of murder) 2. (misc.) to plead ~; to plead not ~; ~ as charged
guise *n.* in, under the ~ of (under the ~ of friendship)
guitar *n.* 1. to play the (a) ~ 2. to strum a ~ 3. an acoustic; electric, steel; Hawaiian ~

gulf *n.* 1. a wide, yawning ~ 2. a ~ between (a wide ~ between generations)

gull *v.* (D; tr.) ('to trick') to ~ into

gulp *n.* at, in a ~ (she swallowed the whole spoonful at one ~)

gum *n.* 1. to chew ~ 2. bubble; chewing ~ 3. a stick of ~

gumption *n.* (colloq.) ['courage'] the ~ to + inf. (will she have enough ~ to refuse?)

gun I *n.* 1. to aim; fire; point a ~ at smb. 2. to turn a ~ on smb. 3. to draw a ~ 4. to hold a ~ on smb.; to hold a ~ to smb.'s head 5. to load; unload a ~ 6. to man a ~ 7. (artillery) to lay ('adjust') a ~ 8. to carry, pack (AE, colloq.) a ~ 9. to silence an enemy ~ 10. to spike ('make unusable') a ~ 11. an antiaircraft; antitank; BB; burp (colloq.), submachine, Tommy (colloq.); field; heavy; machine; ray; riot ~; shotgun; starter's; stun; zip (AE) ~ 12. a grease; spray ~ 13. a ~ fires, goes off; jams; misfires 14. (misc.) to jump the ~ ('to start too early')

gun II *v.* (d; intr.) to ~ for ('to search for with a gun') (also fig.)

gunfire *n.* 1. heavy, murderous ~ 2. under ~

gung ho *adj.* (slang) (AE) ['enthusiastic'] ~ about

gunpoint *n.* to hold smb. at ~

gunpowder *n.* 1. smokeless ~ 2. a grain of ~

gurgle *v.* (D; tr.) to ~ to (the baby ~d a few sounds to us)

gush *v.* (d; intr.) to ~ from (a column of oil ~ed from the ground)

gusher *n.* ['oil well from which oil gushes'] to hit a ~

gush forth *v.* (D; intr.) to ~ from

gust *n.* fitful; strong ~s (the wind was blowing in fitful ~s)

gusto *n.* with ~ (with great ~)

gutless *adj.* (colloq.) ~ to + inf. (it was ~ of him to lie)

guts *n.* (colloq.) 1. the ~ to + inf. (he doesn't have the ~ to do it) 2. (misc.) to hate smb.'s ~ ('to hate smb. very much')

gutter *n.* (fig.) 1. to get down into the ~ 2. to drag smb. down into the ~

guy *n.* (colloq.) 1. a great, nice, regular ~ 2. a bad; good ~ USAGE NOTE: In AE *you guys* (colloq.) can now be used in speaking not only to a group of men, but also to a group of men and women, and even to a group of women only.

gymnastics *n.* to do ~

gyp *v.* (slang) (D; tr.) to ~ out of (he ~ped me out of my share)

gyrate *v.* to ~ wildly

H

habit *n.* ['custom'] ['usual manner'] 1. to acquire, develop, form a ~ 2. to make a ~ of smt. 3. to get into a ~ 4. to break a ~; to get out of a ~; (slang) to kick the ~ 5. to break smb. of a ~ 6. an annoying; bad; entrenched, ingrained; filthy; good; incurable; nasty; repulsive ~ 7. irregular; regular ~s 8. a ~ of (he has a bad ~ of interrupting people) 9. by force of ~ 10. out of ~ (I did it out of ~) ['costume'] 11. a monk's; nun's; riding ~

habitat *n.* a natural ~

hack I *n.* ['hireling'] a party ~

hack II *v.* ('to chop') 1. (d; intr.) to ~ at (to ~ at a tree) 2. (misc.) they ~ed their way through the forest; to ~ (a body) to pieces

hackles *n.* ['anger'] to raise smb.'s ~

haggle *v.* (D; intr.) to ~ about, over; with

hail *v.* 1. (C) ('to summon') ~ a taxi for me; or: ~ me a taxi 2. (esp. AE) (d; intr.) to ~ from ('to be from') (where do you ~ from?) 3. (D; tr.) ('to proclaim') to ~ as (she was ~ed as a heroine) 4. (rare) (N; used with a noun) ('to name') to ~ smb. emperor

hailstones *n.* ~ fall

hair *n.* 1. to brush; comb ~ 2. to backcomb (BE), tease (AE); braid; do; set; style ~ 3. to cut; trim ~ 4. to shampoo, wash ~ 5. to color; dye; tint ~ 6. to part one's ~ (he parts his ~ in the middle, and I part mine on the side) 7. to stroke smb.'s ~ 8. to lose, shed one's ~ (people lose their ~; animals shed their ~) 9. curly; kinky; straight; wavy ~ 10. long; short; thick; thinning ~ 11. unmanageable, unruly ~ 12. dark; light ~ 13. black; blond; brown; grey; red; white ~ 14. pubic ~ 15. ~ falls out; grows 16. a single ~ 17. a curl, lock; strand of ~ 18. a head; shock of ~ (he has a thick head of ~) 19. (misc.) to split ~s ('to nitpick'); to get in smb.'s ~ ('to annoy smb.'); to let one's ~ down ('to lose one's inhibitions'); by a ~ ('by a small margin')

haircut *n.* 1. to get a ~ 2. to give smb. a ~ 3. a short ~

hairline *n.* a receding ~

half *determiner, pronoun* 1. (in telling time) ~ past the hour (it's ~ past four) 2. ~ of (~ of them) 3. (misc.) it's not ~ bad ('it's fairly good') USAGE NOTE: The use of the preposition *of* is necessary when a pronoun follows. When a noun follows, the *of* may be omitted--half (of) the students; half (of) the audience. However, compare-- she spent half (of) the money; she spent her half of the money. Note the constructions--a half hour, half an hour.

half-mast *n.* at ~ (the flags were flying at ~)

half price *n.* at ~ (to admit children at ~)

halfway *adj., adv.* 1. ~ between 2. (misc.) to meet smb. ~ ('to compromise with smb.')

hall *n.* a concert; dance; entrance; lecture; music; pool; study; town ~

halo *n.* a ~ around (the sun, moon)

halt *n.* 1. to call a ~ 2. to bring smt. to a ~ 3. to

come to a ~ 4. a complete; grinding, screeching ~

halter *n.* to put a ~ on an animal

ham *n.* baked; cured; honey-roast (BE), sugar-cured (AE) ~

hamburger *n.* to grill a ~

hammer I *n.* 1. to swing a ~ 2. (sports) to throw the ~ 3. a drop ~ 4. to come under the (auctioneer's) ~ ('to be sold at auction')

hammer II *v.* 1. (d; intr.) to ~ at (to ~ at enemy positions) 2. (D; tr.) to ~ into (to ~ a nail into a wall; to ~ an idea into smb.'s head)

hammer and tongs *adv.* to go at smb. ~ ('to attack smb. with great energy')

hammer away *v.* (d; intr.) to ~ at (to ~ at a compromise; to ~ at the enemy)

hamper *v.* (D; tr.) to ~ in

hand I *n.* ['part of the arm below the wrist'] 1. to shake smb.'s ~; to shake ~s with smb. 2. to clasp, grab, grasp; take smb.'s ~ 3. to hold; join ~s 4. to lay one's ~s on 5. to cup one's ~s 6. to clap one's ~s 7. to wring one's ~s 8. to lower; raise one's ~ 9. bare; delicate; dishpan (esp. AE); gentle ~s (he grasped the hot metal with his bare ~s) 10. a pair of ~s 11. by ~ (to do smt. by ~) 12. by the ~ (to lead smb. by the ~; to take smb. by the ~) 13. ~s off; ~s up ['help'] ['active participation'] 14. to give, lend smb. a ~ 15. to lift a ~ (he would not lift a ~ to help) 16. to have a ~ in 17. a guiding; helping ~ (to lend a helping ~) 18. a ~ at, in with (give me a ~ with the dishes) ['worker'] (esp. AE) 19. a hired; ranch ~ ['specialist'] 20. an old ~ (at smt.) ['pointer on a clock'] 21. an hour; minute; second, sweep-second ~ ['ability'] 22. to try one's ~ at smt. ['control'] 23. to get out of ~ 24. to take smb. in ~ 25. a firm; iron ~ ['pledge of betrothal'] (formal) 26. to ask for smb.'s ~ ['cards held by a player'] (also fig.) 27. to show, tip one's ~ 28. to have, hold a ~ 29. a good, strong; weak ~ (she held a strong ~) ['possession'] ['ownership'] 30. to fall into smb.'s ~s 31. to change ~s 32. enemy; private ~s (the documents fell into enemy ~s) ['source'] 33. at first ~ ('directly') 34. at second ~ ('indirectly') ['viewpoint'] 35. on one ~ ('from one viewpoint'); on the other ~ ('from the other viewpoint') ['closeness'] 36. at, on ~ (near at ~) ['misc.'] 37. to lay a ~ on smb. ('to harm smb.'); from ~ to mouth ('barely existing'); to have one's ~s full ('to be very busy'); to get out of smb.'s ~ ('to be subservient to smb.'); to force smb.'s ~ ('to compel smb. to act'); to throw up one's ~s ('to give up'); to wash one's ~s of smt. ('to shed all responsibility for smt.'); with a heavy ~ ('crudely'); to suffer at smb.'s ~s; with clean ~s ('innocent'); to go ~ in ~ ('to go together'); to win ~s down ('to win easily'); all ~s on deck! ('all sailors on deck'); to have time on one's ~s ('to have free time'); to have worthless property on one's ~s ('to be burdened by worthless property')

hand II *v.* (A) ~ the salt to me; or: ~ me the salt

hand back v. (usu. B; occ. A) she ~ed the documents back to me

handball n. team ~

handbook n. a ~ for (a ~ for beginners)

handcuffs n. 1. to put (the) ~ on smb. 2. to remove ~

hand down v. (D; tr.) to ~ from; to (to ~ a tradition to the next generation; to ~ old clothes from one child to the next)

handicap n. ['assigned advantage or disadvantage'] 1. to assign, give a ~ ['hindrance'] 2. to overcome a ~ 3. a ~ to 4. under a ~

hand in v. (B) to ~ homework in to the teacher

handle n. ['part grasped by the hand'] 1. (BE) a starting ~ ['misc.'] (colloq.) 2. to fly off the ~ ('to lose one's temper'); to get a ~ on smt. ('to comprehend smt.')

handler n. a baggage; food ~

handling n. 1. delicate; gentle; rough; tactful ~ (the matter requires delicate ~) 2. special ~ (by the post office)

hand on v. (D; tr.) to ~ to (to ~ traditions to the next generation)

hand organ n. to grind, play a ~

handout n. (colloq.) ['alms'] 1. to give smb. a ~ 2. to ask for a ~

hand out v. (B) to ~ food to the needy

hand over v. (B) to ~ a criminal to the police

handpicked adj. 1. ~ for 2. ~ to + inf. (she was ~ to do the job)

handrail n. 1. to grasp a ~ 2. to hold on to a ~

handshake n. 1. a firm; warm ~ 2. (misc.) a golden ~ ('a gift presented to smb. who is retiring')

handspring n. to do, turn a ~

handwriting n. 1. illegible; legible ~ 2. (misc.) to see the ~ on the wall ('to foresee an impending disaster')

handy adj. 1. ~ at; with (she's ~ with tools) 2. ~ for (this tool is ~ for various jobs) 3. ~ to + inf. (it's ~ to have a pharmacy so close = it's ~ having a pharmacy so close)

hang I n. (colloq.) ['knack'] to get the ~ of smt.

hang II v. 1. ('to be suspended'); ('to fall') to ~ limp; loose, loosely 2. (colloq.) (d; intr.) to ~ around ('to frequent') (to ~ around a bar) 3. (D; intr.) ('to be suspended') to ~ by (to ~ by a thread) (see also 16) 4. (D; tr.) ('to execute by hanging') to ~ for (he was ~ed for murder ~) 5. (d; intr.) ('to be suspended') to ~ from (flags hung from the windows) 6. (d; intr.) ('to cling') to ~ on (to ~ on smb.'s arm) 7. (d; intr.) to ~ on, upon ('to listen closely to') (they hung on every word) 8. (d; intr.) to ~ on ('to depend on') (the outcome ~s on the results of the election) 9. (d; intr.) to ~ on ('to be oppressive') time ~s on their hands) 10. (d; intr., tr.) ('to be suspended'); ('to suspend') to ~ on (she hung the picture on the wall) 11. (d; intr.) ('to cling') to ~ onto (he hung onto my arm) 12. (colloq.) (d; intr.) to ~ onto ('to keep, retain') (we intend to ~ onto this property; they hung onto their customs) 13. (d; intr.) ('to lean') to ~ out of (to ~ out of a window) 14. (d; intr.) ('to be suspended') to ~ over (the coat was ~ing over the chair; the threat of war hung over the country) 15.

(d; tr.) ('to drape, suspend') to ~ over (she hung the wet towel over the tub) 16. (misc.) to ~ by a thread ('to be in a critical situation') USAGE NOTE: The past and past participle of *hang* are *hung* or *hanged*. The form *hanged* is more usual in the sense 'killed by hanging'. In other senses the form *hung* is usual.

hang around v. (colloq.) (d; intr.) ('to spend time') to ~ with (he likes to ~ with the boys down at the bar)

hang back v. (D; intr.) to ~ from (to ~ from giving information)

hang down v. (D; intr.) to ~ from; to (to ~ from a branch)

hanger n. a coat ~

hang on v. 1. (D; intr.) to ~ to ('to grasp') (to ~ to the rail) 2. (D; intr.) to ~ to ('to keep') (to ~ to one's privileges)

hangout n. (colloq.) ['gathering place'] a ~ for

hang out v. (slang) (D; intr.) ('to spend time') to ~ with (to ~ with one's friends)

hang up v. (D; intr.) to ~ on (she hung up on me) ('she broke off her telephone conversation with me')

hanker v. (colloq.) (esp. AE) 1. (d; intr.) to ~ after, for ('to want') (to ~ for a good steak) 2. (E) ('to want') she ~ed to go south

hankering n. (colloq.) 1. a ~ for 2. a ~ to + inf. (a ~ to travel)

happen v. 1. (D; intr.) to ~ to (what ~ed to you?) 2. (E) she ~ed to be there when we arrived

happiness n. 1. personal ~ 2. a feeling, glow of ~

happy adj. 1. ~ about; with 2. (colloq.) ~ for (we are ~ for them) 3. ~ to + inf. (I'll be ~ to attend the meeting; she'll be ~ to work here = she'll be ~ working here) 4. ~ that + clause (they are very ~ that the proposal was accepted)

harakiri n. to commit ~

harangue n. to deliver, launch into a ~

harassment n. 1. to engage in ~ 2. police; sexual ~

harbor, harbour n. 1. to clear a ~ 2. to blockade; mine a ~ 3. a natural ~ 4. a safe ~ (also fig.)

hard adj. ['demanding'] 1. (cannot stand alone) ~ on (she's very ~ on herself) ['difficult'] 2. ~ to + inf. (this book is ~ to translate = it is ~ to translate this book = it is a ~ book to translate; she is ~ to understand = it is ~ to understand her; it is ~ to get them to participate = it is ~ getting them to participate) 3. ~ for (this job will be ~ for me; it is ~ for us to concentrate) ['misc.'] 4. to play ~ to get ('to pretend to be uninterested in an invitation or proposal')

hardened adj. (cannot stand alone) ~ to (~ to suffering)

hard line n. (pol.) to adopt, take; follow a ~

hard put adj. ['facing difficulties'] ~ to + inf. (she was ~ to pay her rent)

hardship n. 1. to bear, suffer, undergo ~ 2. to overcome a ~ 3. a ~ to + inf. (it was a real ~ for her to get to work on time)

hard time n. (colloq.) 1. to give smb. a ~ ('to make things difficult for smb.') 2. (misc.) we had a ~ finding her

hard up adj. (colloq.) ('in need of') ~ for (they are

~ for new ideas)
hark back *v.* (d; intr.) ('to revert') to ~ to (to ~ to the old days)
harm *n.* 1. to cause, do ~ 2. to undo ~ 3. considerable, grave, great, immeasurable, irreparable, severe ~ 4. (grievous) bodily ~ 5. ~ in; to (there is no ~ in doing that; was any ~ done to the children?)
harmful *adj.* 1. ~ to (~ to one's health) 2. ~ to + inf. (it's ~ to smoke)
harmless *adj.* 1. ~ to 2. ~ to + inf. (it's ~ to daydream)
harmonica *n.* (esp. AE) to play a ~
harmonize *v.* (D; intr.) to ~ with
harmony *n.* ['concord, agreement'] 1. to achieve ~ 2. in ~ with ['congruity'] (ling.) 3. vowel ~
harness *v.* (D; tr.) to ~ to (to ~ horses to a coach)
harp I *n.* to play the ~
harp II *v.* (d; intr.) to ~ on (to keep ~ing on the same old theme)
harpoon *n.* to hurl, throw; shoot a ~
harsh *adj.* ~ to, with (he's too ~ with the children)
harvest *n.* 1. to bring in, reap a ~ 2. an abundant, bountiful, rich; poor ~
hash *v.* (colloq.) (AE) (d; intr.) to ~ over ('to discuss') (to ~ over a question)
hassle I *n.* ['struggle'] a ~ to + inf. (it was a ~ to get a visa = it was a ~ getting a visa)
hassle II *v.* (D; tr.) to ~ about, over
haste *n.* 1. to make ~ ('to hurry') 2. in ~ (they acted in great ~)
hasten *v.* (E) he ~ed to apologize
hat *n.* 1. to doff; don; tip a ~ 2. a cardinal's; fur; straw; ten-gallon; top ~ 3. (misc.) to pass the ~ ('to collect money'); to take one's ~ off to ('to congratulate smb.'); to talk through one's ~ ('to say foolish things'); to throw one's ~ into the ring ('to enter a political campaign'); to take one's ~ off to smb. ('to feel respect for smb.')
hatch *n.* 1. to batten down the ~es 2. an escape ~
hate I see **hatred**
hate II *v.* 1. to ~ deeply, intensely, utterly 2. (E) he ~s to work 3. (G) she ~s going to school 4. (rare) (J) he ~s people watching when he practices 5. (K) she ~s his staying out late
hateful *adj.* 1. ~ to 2. ~ to + inf. (it was ~ of him to say that)
hatred *n.* 1. to arouse, stir up ~ 2. to instill ~ 3. to incur ~ 4. to develop; express; feel; show ~ 5. blind, deep-rooted, implacable, intense, profound, violent, virulent ~ 6. ~ for, towards 7. consumed with, filled with ~
hat trick *n.* to do a ~
haul I *n.* ['distance'] a long; short ~ (also fig.)
haul II *v.* (D; tr.) to ~ from; to (to ~ coal from the mines to the city)
haul up *v.* (D; tr.) to ~ before (to ~ smb. up before a magistrate)
haunt *n.* a favorite; quiet ~
have *v.* 1. (d; tr.) ('to keep') ~ about (BE), around (it's dangerous to ~ a gun around the house) 2. (d; tr.) to ~ against ('to consider as grounds for rejection, dislike') (I ~ nothing against him) 3. (d; tr.) to ~ for ('to consume')

(what are we ~ing for dinner?) 4. (colloq.) (d; tr.) to ~ on ('to possess evidence against') (you ~ nothing on me) 5. (E) ('to be obligated') we ~ to leave 6. (H; usu. with words such as *nothing, something*) I ~ nothing to say to her; I ~ nothing to wear; we ~ smt. to tell you 7. (esp. AE) (I) ('to cause') he had a gardener cut the grass (CE also has: he got a gardener to cut the grass); she had her research assistant look up the information; what would you have me do? 8. (J) we soon had them all laughing 9. (N; used with an adjective; past participle) ('to consume'); ('to cause') I'll have my martini dry; we had a meal sent up to our room; they had the building torn down; he had his hair cut; she had her tonsils removed 10. (misc.) he had two children by his first wife; to ~ it in for smb. ('to have a grudge against smb.'); she had a strange thing happen to her ('a strange thing happened to her')
haven *n.* a tax ~
havoc *n.* to play, raise, wreak ~ with
hay *n.* 1. to make ~ 2. to bundle, gather, stack ~ 3. a haystack 4. (misc.) (AE; colloq.) to hit the ~ ('to go to sleep')
haymaker *n.* (colloq.) ['punch'] to throw a ~
hayride *n.* to go on a ~
haywire *adj.* (colloq.) to go ~ ('to be ruined')
hazard *n.* 1. a fire; occupational ~ 2. a ~ to (a ~ to health)
hazardous *adj.* 1. ~ to (~ to one's health) 2. ~ to + inf. (it is ~ to work at that height = it is ~ working at that height)
hazy *adj.* ~ about (she's ~ about the details)
head I *n.* ['upper part of the body'] 1. to nod; shake one's ~ 2. to bare; bow; drop, hang, lower; lift, raise; move, poke, stick; scratch; toss turn one's ~ (to scratch one's ~ in amazement; to poke one's ~ around the corner) 3. to hold one's ~ high ('to be proud') 4. from ~ to foot ['length of a horse's head'] 5. by a ~ (our horse won by a ~) ['poise'] 6. to lose one's ~ 7. a cool, level ~ (to keep a level ~) ['person'] 8. to count ~s ['brain'] 9. to use one's ~ 10. to cram, fill, stuff smb.'s ~ (with nonsense) 11. a clear ~ 12. to have a ~ for (figures) ['climax'] 13. to bring to a ~ ['boil'] 14. to come to a ~ (the boil came to a ~; when will the crisis come to a ~?) ['front part'] 15. at the ~ (of a column) ['leader'] 16. a titular ~ ['chairperson'] (esp. BE) 17. a department ~, a ~ of (the) department (AE usu. has *chairman, chairperson*) ['misc.'] 18. a thick ~ of hair; success went to his ~ ('his success made him conceited'); over heels ('completely'); ~s up ('watch out'); to get smt. through one's ~ ('to finally comprehend smt.'); to hang one's ~ in shame ('to be greatly embarrassed'); to be ~ and shoulders above smb. ('to be greatly superior to smb.'); to keep one's ~ above water ('to survive barely'); over one's ~ ('incomprehensible'); out of one's ~ ('delirious'); to make ~ or tail of ('to comprehend'); he took it into his ~ to leave ('he decided suddenly to leave')
head II *v.* 1. (d; intr.) ('to go') to ~ for (to ~ for

the city; to ~ for a downfall) 2. (P; intr., tr.) they ~ed (their boat) east

headache *n.* 1. to have a ~ 2. a bad, racking, severe, splitting; migraine; sick (esp. AE); slight ~

heading *n.* 1. a chapter ~ 2. under a ~

headlights *n.* to dim (one's) ~

headline *n.* 1. to carry a ~ 2. banner; front-page; screaming ~s 3. in (banner) ~s

headlock *n.* ['wrestling hold'] to put a ~ on smb.

headquarters *n.* 1. to set up ~ 2. supreme ~ 3. at ~

headstart *n.* to have a ~ on, over

headway *n.* to gain, make ~ against

healer *n.* a faith ~

healing *n.* faith ~

health *n.* ['condition of the body and mind'] 1. to enjoy good ~ 2. to promote (good) ~ 3. to recover, regain one's ~ 4. to ruin, undermine smb.'s ~ 5. bad, broken, failing, feeble, fragile, frail, ill, poor; delicate; good, robust ~ 6. holistic; mental; physical ~ 7. for one's ~ (she swims for her ~) 8. (misc.) the state of one's ~ ['science of protecting the health of the community'] 9. community, public; occupational ~ ['misc.'] 10. here's to your (good) ~!

healthy *adj.* ['promoting health'] 1. ~ for (smoking is not ~ for you) ['safe'] (colloq.) 2. ~ to + inf. (it's not ~ to walk there at night = it's not ~ walking there at night)

heap I *n.* a compost; dump; scrap ~

heap II *v.* (d; tr.) to ~ on, upon (to ~ gifts on smb.)

hear *v.* 1. (d; intr.) ('to learn') to ~ about, of (we have heard of her; have you heard about the earthquake?) 2. (d; intr.) ('to receive word') to ~ from (I have not heard from him about this matter) 3. (I) ('to perceive by ear') I heard them go out 4. (J) ('to perceive by ear') we heard him coming up the stairs 5. (L) ('to learn') we have heard that he is in town 6. (N; used with a past participle) ('to listen to') we heard the aria sung in Italian 7. (Q) ('to learn') we heard why she left

hearing *n.* ['perception of sounds'] 1. acute, keen ~ 2. defective, impaired ~ 3. hard of ~; ~ impaired ['session of a committee, court'] 4. to conduct, hold a ~ 5. a fair, impartial; open ~ (he got a fair ~) 6. Congressional ~s 7. an administrative; judicial; pre-trial; public ~ 8. at a ~ (to testify at a ~)

heart *n.* ['organ that circulates the blood'] 1. to transplant a ~ 2. a healthy, strong; weak ~ 3. an artificial ~ 4. a ~ beats; fails, stops; palpitates, throbs; pumps blood ['the heart as the center of emotions'] 5. to gladden; harden smb.'s ~ 6. to break; steal, win smb.'s ~ 7. my ~ aches, bleeds (for her) 8. from the ~ (to speak from the ~) 9. in one's ~ (in my ~ I know that she is right) ['disposition'] 10. a cold, cruel, hard; good, kind, soft, tender, warm; stout ~ (she has a kind ~); a ~ of gold ['liking'] 11. to have a ~ for (she has no ~ for this type of work) 12. after one's own ~ (he's a man after my own ~) ['sympathy'] 13. to have a ~ (have a ~ and lend me some money) ['essence']

14. to get to the ~ of smt. 15. at ~ (he's not bad at ~) ['feeling'] 16. a heavy; light ~ 17. with a (heavy) ~ ['courage'] 18. to take ~ from (he took ~ from her example) 19. to lose ~ 20. a brave; faint ~ 21. the ~ to + inf. (I didn't have the ~ to tell her) ['memory'] 22. by ~ (to know a poem by ~) ['resolve'] 23. to set one's ~ (on doing smt.) 24. a change of ~ ['misc.'] 25. a bleeding ~ ('one who always supports the underdog'); to eat one's ~ out ('to brood'); to lose one's ~ to ('to fall in love with'); from the bottom of one's ~ ('sincerely'); to have one's ~ in the right place ('to have good intentions'); to do smb.'s ~ good ('to make one happy'); with all one's ~ ('wholeheartedly'); to take smt. to ~ ('to take smt. seriously'); the way to smb.'s ~

heart attack *n.* 1. to have a ~ 2. a fatal; massive; mild; severe; sudden ~

heartbroken *adj.* 1. ~ about, at, over (~ over a friend's death) 2. ~ to + inf. (she was ~ to learn of the verdict) 3. ~ that + clause (I'm ~ that he cannot come)

heart failure *n.* congestive; massive ~

heartless *adj.* ~ to + inf. (it was ~ of him to say that)

heartstrings *n.* ['deep feelings'] to tug at smb.'s ~

heat I *n.* ['warmth'] 1. to generate, produce; radiate ~ 2. to alleviate the ~ 3. blistering, extreme, great, intense, oppressive, scorching, stifling, sweltering, unbearable ~ 4. dry; penetrating; radiant; red; white ~ 5. animal; body ~ 6. ~ emanates from (an oven) ['excitement'] 7. in the ~ (of battle) ['estrus, sexual excitement'] 8. in (AE), on (BE) ~ (the bitch was in ~) ['heating system'] 9. to turn on the ~ 10. to turn off the ~ 11. electric; gas; steam ~ ['preliminary race, race'] 12. to run a dead ~ 13. a qualifying ~ ['pressure'] (colloq.) 14. to put the ~ on (the police were putting the ~ on him)

heat II *v.* 1. (C) ~ some water for me; or: ~ me some water 2. (D; tr.) to ~ to (she ~ed the oven to two hundred degrees)

heater *n.* an electric; hot-water, immersion (BE); kerosene (AE), paraffin (BE); oil; space ~

heating *n.* central; forced-air; space ~

heave *v.* (P; tr.) ('to throw') they ~d the trash into the pit

heave-ho *n.* (colloq.) ['ejection'] to give smb. the (old) ~

heaven *n.* 1. in ~ 2. (misc.) in seventh ~ ('in a state of bliss'); to move ~ and earth ('to make a maximum effort')

hedge *n.* ['row of shrubs'] 1. to crop, trim a ~ ['protection against loss'] 2. a ~ against (a ~ against inflation)

heed *n.* to pay ~ to; to take ~ of

heedful *adj.* (cannot stand alone) ~ of (~ of advice)

heedless *adj.* (cannot stand alone) ~ of (~ of danger)

heel *n.* ['tyrannical oppression'] 1. under the ~ (under the ~ of the occupier) ['misc.'] 2. smb.'s Achilles' ~ ('smb.'s vulnerable point')

heels *n.* 1. to click one's ~ 2. built-up; high; low ~

3. to be at, on smb.'s ~ ('to follow smb. closely')
4. (misc.) to cool one's ~ ('to be kept waiting'); down at the ~ ('shabby'); to kick up one's ~ ('to be very lively'); to show one's ~ ('to flee'); to take to one's ~ ('to flee'); hard on smb.'s ~ ('close to smb.')

hegemony *n.* ~ over

height *n.* 1. to attain, reach a ~ 2. to clear; scale a ~ 3. a dizzy, precipitous, vertiginous ~; dizzying ~s 4. a ~ above; below (at a ~ of two hundred feet above sea level) 5. at a ~ (at the ~ of one's success; to fly at a ~ of ten thousand feet) 6. in ~ (ten feet in ~)

heir *n.* 1. to fall ~ (to fall ~ to a large estate) 2. an ~ apparent; an ~ presumptive 3. an immediate; rightful ~ 4. ~ to

heirloom *n.* a family; priceless ~

helicopter *n.* to fly, pilot a ~ (see also **airplane**)

hell *n.* (colloq.) ['the netherworld'] 1. go to ~! ['scolding'] 2. to catch, get ~ 3. to give smb. ~ ['misc.'] 4. a ~ of a team ('an excellent team'); for the ~ of it ('for no real reason'); to be ~ on ('to be harmful to'); (BE; slang) bloody ~

hell-bent *adj.* (cannot stand alone) ['determined'] 1. ~ for, on (~ on balancing the budget) 2. ~ to + inf. (~ to balance the budget)

helm *n.* 1. to take (over) the ~ 2. at the ~

helmet *n.* 1. a crash, safety; sun (AE) ~ 2. a steel ~

help I *n.* 1. to give, offer, provide ~ 2. to call for, seek ~ 3. a big, great ~ (she was a big ~ to us) 4. domestic ~ 5. (BE) a home ~ 6. of ~ to (she was of great ~ to us) 7. (misc.) ~ wanted (as in a newspaper advertisement)

help II *v.* 1. (D; tr.) ('to assist') to ~ in (we ~ed them in their work; she ~ed me with the translation) 2. (D; tr.) ('to assist in moving') to ~ into; off; out of (~ them into the house; ~ her off the train; ~ him out of the car) 3. (D; refl.) ('to serve oneself') to ~ to (she ~ed herself to the dessert) 4. (D; tr.) ('to serve') to ~ to (can I ~ you to some food?) 5. (E) they ~ed to cook the meal 6. (esp. AE) (F) ('to assist') she ~ed move the furniture 7. (G; often used with: cannot -- can't -- couldn't) ('to keep from') we couldn't ~ laughing 8. (H) she ~ed us to move the furniture 9. (esp. AE) (I) she ~ed us move the furniture 10. (misc.) I couldn't ~ but laugh

helpful *adj.* 1. ~ in; (she's been very ~ to us) 2. ~ to + inf. (it's always ~ to be well-informed)

helping *n.* a generous; second ~

hem *n.* 1. to let out; lower; raise a ~ 2. to pin up; shorten, take up; straighten a ~

hemisphere *n.* the eastern; northern; southern; western ~

hemmed in *adj.* ~ on all sides

hemorrhage *n.* a cerebral; internal ~

hen *n.* 1. ~s cackle, cluck 2. ~s lay eggs

hepatitis *n.* infectious; serum ~

herbs *n.* medicinal ~

herd *n.* 1. to drive; round up a ~ 2. to tend a ~ 3. (misc.) to ride ~ on ('to control')

here *adv.* from ~

heresy *n.* 1. to be be guilty of ~ 2. to preach ~ 3.

~ to + inf. (it was ~ to talk like that)

heritage *n.* 1. to cherish one's ~ 2. to repudiate one's ~ 3. a priceless, proud, rich ~ 4. a cultural; family; religious ~

hernia *n.* a hiatal; inguinal ~

hero *n.* a conquering; folk; local; military, war; national; popular; unsung ~

heroic *adj.* ~ to + inf. (it was ~ of them to oppose the invader)

heroin *n.* to do (colloq.), inject, shoot (colloq.) ~

heroine see **hero**

heroism *n.* to demonstrate, display ~

herpes *n.* 1. to come down with, contract, get ~ 2. genital ~

hesitancy *n.* 1. to show ~ 2. ~ about, in

hesitant *adj.* ~ about (they are ~ about signing a contract)

hesitate *v.* 1. (D; intr.) to ~ over (to ~ over a choice) 2. (E) she ~d to act; do not ~ to call me

hesitation *n.* 1. to show ~ 2. momentary ~ 3. ~ about, in (I have no ~ about throwing him out)

hew *v.* (d; intr.) ('to adhere') (AE) to ~ to (to ~ to the party line)

hex *n.* (AE) to put a ~ on smb.

hide I *n.* 1. to tan a ~ 2. (misc.) to save smb.'s ~ ('to save smb.'s life'); to tan smb.'s ~ ('to spank smb.')

hide II *v.* 1. (D; intr.) to ~ behind (to ~ behind a legal technicality) 2. (D; intr., tr.) to ~ from

hide-and-seek *n.* to play ~

hideaway *n.* a secret ~

hideous *adj.* ~ to + inf. (it was ~ to watch)

hideout *n.* a secret ~

hide out *v.* to ~ from (to ~ from the police)

hiding *n.* 1. to go into ~ 2. to come out of ~ 3. in ~

hierarchy *n.* 1. to rise in the ~ 2. an academic; church; corporate; military; ruling ~

high I *adj.* 1. ~ in (~ in iron) 2. (misc.) (colloq.) to get ~ on (a drug)

high II *n.* ['acme'] 1. an all-time ~ ['state of euphoria'] (slang) 2. to reach a ~

highball *n.* ['type of drink'] to make, mix a ~

highhanded *adj.* ~ to + inf. (it was ~ of him to remove the equipment without permission)

high horse *n.* (colloq.) ['arrogance'] to get on one's ~

highness *n.* (her, his, your) royal ~

high-pressure *v.* (D; tr.) to ~ into (she was ~d into signing)

high sign *n.* (esp. AE) ['signal'] 1. to give smb the ~ 2. to get the ~

high time *n.* ~ to + inf. (it's ~ to leave)

high treason *n.* to commit ~

highway *n.* (AE) 1. a divided ~ 2. a belt; limited-access ~

hijacking *n.* 1. to carry out, commit a ~ 2. to foil, thwart a ~

hike *n.* 1. to go on; organize a ~ 2. a long; short ~ (they went on a long ~) 3. an overnight ~ (as of Boy Scouts)

hill *n.* 1. to come down; go up a ~ 2. rolling ~s a steep ~ 3. in the ~s (to live in the ~s) 4. on a ~ (the house stood on a ~) 5. (misc.) (colloq.) to take to the ~s ('to take refuge in the hills')

hilt *n.* ['limit'] to the ~

hinder *v.* 1. (D; tr.) to ~ from 2. (D; tr.) to ~ in

hindrance *n.* a ~ to

hinge *v.* (d; intr.) ('to depend') to ~ on, upon

hint I *n.* 1. to drop, give a ~ 2. to take a ~ 3. a broad, obvious; delicate, gentle, subtle ~ 4. the merest ~ 5. a ~ about, of (a ~ about the answer; a ~ of suspicion) 6. a ~ that + clause (she dropped a ~ that she would retire soon) 7. at a ~ (they fled at the first ~ of trouble)

hint II *v.* 1. (d; intr.) to ~ at 2. (L; to) he ~ed (to us) that an agreement had been reached

hip I *adj.* (slang) ['aware'] ~ to

hip II *n.* to shake, sway, wiggle one's ~s

hire I *n.* for ~

hire II *v.* (H) we ~d her to mow our lawn

hired *adj.* ~ to + inf. (he was ~ to work as a gardener)

hire out *v.* (D; refl., tr.) to ~ as; to (he ~d himself out as a mercenary to the highest bidder)

hire purchase *n.* (BE) on ~ (to buy smt. on ~)

hiss *v.* (D; intr.) to ~ at (the crowd ~ed at the delay)

history *n.* 1. to make ~ 2. to trace the ~ of smt. 3. to distort; revise, rewrite ~ 4. to go down in ~ as (he went down in ~ as a tyrant) 5. ancient; cultural; medieval; military; modern; natural ~ 6. a case; personal ~ 7. oral ~ 8. (misc.) ~ repeats itself; a page in ~

hit I *n.* ['blow that strikes the target'] 1. to score a ~ 2. to take a ~ (our ship took several direct ~s) 3. a direct ~ ['success'] (colloq.) 4. to make a ~ with (she made quite a ~ with the audience) 5. a smash ~

hit II *v.* 1. ('to strike') to ~ hard 2. (d; intr.) ('to strike') to ~ against, on (he hit his head on the ceiling) 3. (d; intr.) to ~ at ('to attack') (the press hit hard at governmental corruption) 4. (slang) (AE) (d; tr.) to ~ for ('to make a request of') (he hit me for twenty dollars) 5. (D; tr.) ('to strike') to ~ in (to ~ smb. in the face) 6. (d; intr.) to ~ on, upon ('to discover') (they finally hit on an acceptable compromise) 7. (BE) (O; can be used with one animate object) ('to strike') he hit me a hard blow

hit back *v.* (D; intr.) to ~ at

hitch I *n.* (colloq.) ['obstacle'] ['stoppage'] 1. a slight ~ 2. a ~ in (there's been a slight ~ in our plans) 3. without a ~ (it went off without a ~) ['period of military service'] (esp. AE) 4. to do a ~ 5. to sign up for another ~

hitch II *v.* 1. (D; tr.) to ~ to (to ~ horses to a cart)

hitch up *v.* (D; tr.) to ~ to (to ~ horses to a cart)

hit off *v.* to hit it off with smb. ('to get along well with smb.')

hit up *v.* (slang) (d; tr.) ('to request') to ~ for (he hit me up for a loan)

hoax *n.* 1. to perpetrate a ~ 2. to play a ~ on smb. 3. a literary ~

hobby *n.* to have, go in for, pursue a ~

hobnob *v.* (d; intr.) to ~ with

hock *n.* (colloq.) in ~ ('pawned')

hockey *n.* 1. to play ~ 2. field; ice ~

hold I *n.* ['grip'] 1. to catch, get, grab, lay, seize,

take ~ of 2. to keep ~ of 3. to relax one's ~ 4. a firm, strong ~ ['type of wrestling grip'] 5. to break a ~ ['control, domination'] 6. to relinquish one's ~ 7. a ~ over (they refused to relinquish their ~ over this area) ['waiting, esp. on the telephone'] 8. to put smb. on ~

hold II *v.* 1. ('to keep') to ~ high (to ~ one's head high; also fig.) 2. (d; tr.) to ~ against ('to take into account') (we will not ~ your past blunders against you; they held his criminal record against him) 3. (d; intr.) to ~ onto ('to seize and cling to') (~ onto my arm) 4. (d; intr.) to ~ to (to ~ to the terms of a contract) 5. (d; tr.) ('to make smb. adhere') to ~ to (they held us to the terms of the contract) 6. (d; tr.) ('to restrict') to ~ to (we held the visiting team to a tie) 7. (d; intr.) ('to agree') to ~ with (I don't ~ with his ideas) 8. (L) ('to assert') we ~ that these truths are self-evident 9. (M) ('to consider') we ~ him to be responsible 10. (N; used with an adjective) ('to consider'); ('to keep') to ~ smb. responsible; she held the ladder steady; they ~ life cheap

hold III *n.* ['interior of a ship below decks'] in the ~

hold back *v.* 1. (D; tr.) ('to keep') to ~ from (lack of education held him back from promotion) 2. (d; intr.) to ~ with (to ~ with one's reserves)

holder *n.* 1. a cigarette; napkin ~ 2. (AE) a pot ~

holdings *n.* ['investments'] 1. to diversify one's ~ 2. far-flung ~

hold out *v.* 1. (B) ('to offer') they didn't ~ much hope to us 2. (D; intr.) to ~ against ('to resist') (they held out against the enemy for a month) 3. (D; intr.) to ~ for ('to demand') (they held out for better terms) 4. (d; intr.) to ~ on ('to keep information from') (don't ~ on me)

holdover *n.* a ~ from (a ~ from the old days)

hold up *v.* 1. (d; tr.) to ~ as (to ~ as an example 2. (esp. AE) (D; intr.) to ~ on (they had to ~ on their travel plans) 3. (d; tr.) to ~ to (to ~ smt. up to ridicule)

hole *n.* 1. to bore; dig a ~ 2. to fill in a ~ 3. a deep; gaping, yawning ~ 4. a rabbit; watering ~ 5. (misc.) to pick ~s in smt. ('to find flaws in smt.'); to poke a ~ in smb.'s argument; (golf) to shoot a ~ in one

hole up *v.* (colloq.) (D; intr., tr.) to ~ in (they were ~d up in an old farmhouse)

holiday *n.* ['day set aside for the suspension of business, labor'] 1. to celebrate, observe a ~ 2. a bank (BE), legal (AE), public; national; religious ~ ['period of rest'] (esp. BE; AE prefers *vacation*) 3. to take a ~ 4. to go on ~ 5. a summer ~ 6. a ~ from 7. on ~ (she was away on ~) ['misc.'] 8. a busman's ~ ('a holiday spent in doing one's usual work') (see the Usage Note for **vacation**)

hollow *v.* (d; tr.) to ~ out of (to ~ a canoe out of a log)

holster *n.* a shoulder ~

holy water *n.* to sprinkle ~

homage *n.* 1. to pay ~ to 2. in ~ to

home *n.* ['establishment providing care or service'] 1. to manage, operate, run a ~ 2. a convalescent; detention; funeral (AE); nursing; remand

(BE); rest; retirement ~ ['residence'] 3. to build; establish a ~ 4. to provide a ~ for 5. to make one's ~ at, in 6. an ancestral; country; mobile; summer; winter ~ 7. a ~ for, to (San Francisco was ~ to them for years) 8. at ~ (she is never at ~; AE also has: she is never ~) ['family'] 9. a broken; foster; good ~ ['misc.'] 10. to romp ~ ('to score an easy victory'); she is at ~ in Greek literature; to go ~ USAGE NOTE: In many instances *home* is used as an adverb--to go home; to romp home, etc.

home in v. (D; intr.) to ~ on (to ~ on a target)

home run n. (AE; baseball and fig.) ['hit that allows the batter to score a run'] to hit a ~

homesick adj. ~ for

home visit n. to go on, make a ~

homework n. 1. to do ~ 2. to hand in ~ 3. to correct; grade ~

homicide n. 1. to commit ~ 2. excusable; felonious; justifiable ~

homily n. to deliver a ~

honest adj. 1. ~ about; with (be ~ about this matter with us) 2. ~ to + inf. (it's not ~ to discuss company affairs with outsiders)

honesty n. 1. to impugn smb.'s ~ 2. ~ in 3. the ~ to + inf. (she had the ~ to report the bribe)

honey n. 1. to gather ~ 2. (misc.) as sweet as ~

honeycombed adj. (cannot stand alone) ~ with

honeymoon n. 1. to go on a ~ 2. to spend a ~ (they spent their ~ in Hawaii)

honk v. (D; intr.) to ~ at

honor I **honour** n. ['respect'] ['credit'] 1. to bring, do ~ to (she brought ~ to her family) 2. an ~ to (he is an ~ to his school) 3. in smb.'s ~; in ~ of (to give a reception in smb.'s ~) ['distinction'] ['recognition'] 4. to win (an) ~ 5. to confer an ~ on 6. a dubious; great, high ~ 7. an ~ that + clause (it was a great ~ that we were chosen) 8. (to graduate) with ~s ['privilege'] 9. to have the ~ (may I have the ~ of your company?) 10. an ~ to + inf. (it was an ~ to serve with you) ['integrity'] ['reputation'] 11. to stake one's ~ on smt. 12. one's word of ~; an affair of ~ 13. on one's (word of) ~ ['rite'] 14. to do the ~s ('to serve as host') 15. military ~s (to be buried with full military ~s) ['misc.'] 16. a (military) guard of ~

honor II **honour** v. 1. (D; tr.) to ~ as (she was ~ed as a community leader) 2. (D; tr.) to ~ with

honorable, honourable adj. ~ to + inf. (it is not ~ to deceive them with false promises)

honorarium n. to pay; receive an ~

honored, honoured adj. 1. ~ to + inf. (he was ~ to be invited) 2. ~ that + clause (I am ~ that you have decided to offer me the position)

hood n. (AE) ['cover over an engine'] to check under the ~ (of a car) (BE has *bonnet*)

hoodwink v. 1. (D; tr.) to ~ into 2. (D; tr.) to ~ out of

hoof n. 1. a cloven ~ 2. on the ~ (to buy cattle on the ~)

hook n. ['curved piece of metal, wood'] 1. a crochet; meat; pruning ~ ['blow delivered with bent arm'] 2. to deliver a ~ (he delivered a right ~ to his opponent's jaw) ['misc.'] (slang) 3. off the ~ ('relieved of responsibility')

hooked adj. (slang) ['addicted'] ~ on (~ on drugs)

hookey, hooky n. (colloq.) (AE) ['unexcused absence from school'] to play ~

hooks and eyes n. ['type of fastening'] to sew on ~

hook up v. 1. (D; tr.) to ~ to (to ~ a telephone up to the cable) 2. (D; intr.) to ~ with ('to join')

hoop n. to roll a ~

hoopla n. (slang) (AE) ['bustle, noise, fuss'] the ~ subsides

hoot I n. (colloq.) ['slightest care'] not to give a ~

hoot II v. (D; intr.) ('to shout') to ~ at

hop I n. ['short flight'] 1. a short ~ 2. a ~ from; to (it's a short ~ from Detroit to Cleveland)

hop II v. 1. (d; intr.) to ~ into (the children ~ped into their nice warm beds) 2. (d; intr.) to ~ out of (to ~ out of a chair)

hope I n. 1. to arouse, inspire, stir up ~ 2. to raise smb.'s ~s 3. to express, voice a ~ 4. to cherish, entertain, nurse a ~ 5. to pin, place, put one's ~s on 6. to dash, deflate, dispel; thwart smb.'s ~s 7 to abandon, give up ~ 8. an ardent, fervent fond; faint, slender, slight; false; high; idle, illusory, vain; real; realistic, reasonable; unrealistic, unreasonable ~ 9. ~s come true; fade 10. a flicker, glimmer, ray, spark of ~ 11. ~ for, in, of (~ of recovery; we had high ~s for their) 12. a ~ that + clause (it was our ~ that they would settle near us; there was little ~ that she would be elected) 13. in, with the ~ (we returned to the park in the ~ of finding her wallet) 14. beyond, past ~

hope II v. 1. to ~ fervently, sincerely, very much 2. (D; intr.) to ~ for (to ~ for an improvement) 3. (E) she ~s to see them soon 4. (L) we ~ that you are comfortable 5. (misc.) I ~ so; I ~ not

hopeful I adj. 1. ~ of 2. ~ that + clause (we are ~ that they will agree)

hopeful II n. a presidential ~

hopeless adj. 1. ~ at (he's ~ at balancing the checkbook) 2. ~ to + inf. (it's ~ to expect him to help)

hopper n. ['container for bills that are being considered'] a legislative ~

hopscotch n. to play ~

horizon n. 1. (fig.) to broaden one's ~s 2. on the ~ (to appear on the ~)

hormone n. a growth; sex ~

horn n. 1. to blow, sound a ~ 2. (misc.) on the ~s of a dilemma ('in a dilemma'); to lock ~s with ('to come into conflict with'); to take the bull by the ~s ('to confront a problem boldly'); (AE) to blow/toot one's own ~ ('to boast')

hornet n. ~s sting

hornet's nest n. ['angry reaction'] to stir up a ~

horn in v. (D; intr.) to ~ on ('to interrupt')

Horn of Africa n. in, on the ~

horoscope n. to read smb.'s ~

horrible adj. 1. ~ to + inf. (it is ~ to work there = it is ~ working there) 2. ~ that + clause (it's ~ that he was fired)

horrid adj. 1. ~ to 2. ~ to + inf. (it's ~ of you to tease them like that)

horrified adj. 1. ~ at (~ at the prospect of losing one's job) 2. ~ to + inf. (she was ~ to learn the news) 3. ~ that + clause (we were ~ u..t he had been chosen)

horrify v. (R) it ~fied us (to learn) that their house had burned down

horrifying adj. ~ to + inf. (it is ~ to contemplate that possibility)

horror n. 1. to express; feel ~ 2. to have a ~ of 3. indescribable, unspeakable ~ 4. ~ at (she expressed her ~ at the crime) 5. in ~ (to scream in ~) 6. to one's ~ (to his ~, the bus caught fire)

horror-stricken adj. ~ at

horse n. ['animal'] 1. to mount; ride; walk a ~; to lead a ~ by the bridle 2. to curry; harness; hobble; saddle; shoe a ~ 3. to break (in) a ~ 4. to breed, raise ~s 5. a cart (BE), draft (AE), dray; race; saddle; thoroughbred; wild ~; a workhorse (usu. fig.) 6. ~s canter; gallop; neigh; snicker; trot; whinny 7. an unbroken ~ bucks 8. a herd of (wild) ~s; a pair; team of ~s 9. a young ~ is a foal 10. a female ~ is a mare 11. a male ~ is a stallion; a castrated male ~ is a gelding 12. a young female ~ is a filly 13. a young male ~ is a colt ['padded block'] (gymnastics) 14. a pommel, side (AE); vaulting ~ ['misc.'] 15. to back the wrong ~ ('to support the losing side'); to beat/flog a dead ~ ('to discuss an issue that has already been settled'); from the ~'s mouth ('from an original source'); to hold one's ~s ('to behave more carefully'); a ~ of a diferent color ('an entirely different matter'); on one's high ~ ('behaving arrogantly'); to eat like a ~ ('to eat a great deal'); to work like a ~ ('to work very hard'); to play the ~s ('to bet on horse races')

horse around v. (slang) (AE) (D; intr.) to ~ with

horseback n. on ~

hose n. ['flexible tube'] 1. to play, train a ~ on 2. a fire; garden; rubber; water ~ ['stockings'] 3. mesh ~; pantyhose (AE); stretch; support ~

hosiery n. support ~

hospitable adj. ~ to

hospital n. 1. to establish, found a ~ 2. to go to ~ (BE)/to go to the ~ (AE) 3. a base; children's; city, municipal; community, non-profit; cottage (BE); evacuation; field; general; mental; military; private, proprietary (AE); state; station; teaching; veterans ~ 4. at, in a ~ (she works at/in the ~) 5. in ~ (BE)/in the ~ (AE) (she's ill and has been in/in the ~ for a week) USAGE NOTE: In BE, the phrases *to go to hospital, to be in hospital* mean 'to be hospitalized'; in AE one says *to go to the hospital, to be in the hospital.*

hospitality n. 1. to extend, offer, show ~ 2. to abuse smb.'s ~ 3. warm ~

host n. 1. to play ~ to (who will play ~ to the next Olympic Games?) 2. a congenial ~ 3. ~ to (which city will be ~ to the next World's Fair?)

hostage n. 1. to take smb. ~ 2. to seize, take ~s 3. to hold smb. (as a) ~

hostel n. a youth ~

hostess n. 1. an air (BE), airline (AE) ~ 2. a dance-hall; nightclub ~ USAGE NOTE: The term *flight attendant* has almost completely replaced *air hostess* and *airline hostess.*

hostile adj. 1. openly ~ 2. ~ to, towards

hostilities n. ['war'] 1. to open ~ 2. to suspend ~

3. ~ break out 4. an outbreak of ~ 5. ~ between

hostility n. 1. to arouse, stir up ~ 2. to display, show ~ 3. to express; feel ~ 4. bitter, deep, profound; open ~ 5. ~ against, to, towards 6. ~ between

hot adj. piping, scalding; unbearably ~

hotel n. 1. to manage, operate, run a ~ 2. a deluxe, five-star, luxury; first-class; four-star; rundown, seedy; swanky (colloq.); three-star ~ 3. at, in a ~ (she works at/in a ~) 4. (misc.) to check in, register at a ~; to check out of a ~

hot line n. 1. to establish, set up a ~ 2. a ~ between

hot pursuit n. in ~ (they crossed the border in ~ of the terrorists)

hound I n. ['hunting dog'] 1. a pack of ~s 2. (esp. BE) to ride to ~s, to follow the ~s ('to hunt on horseback with dogs') ['enthusiast'] 3. autograph ~s

hound II v. 1. (d; tr.) to ~ from, out of (they ~ed her out of office) 2. (d; tr.) to ~ into (to ~ smb. into doing smt.) 3. (H) they kept ~ing me to get a haircut

hour n. 1. to show, tell the ~ (my watch shows the minute and ~) 2. a solid ('full') ~ (the police grilled him for three solid ~s) 3. an ungodly ('very early'); ('very late') ~ (she called at an ungodly ~) 4. the decisive ~; or: the ~ of decision 5. the cocktail ~ 6. office; peak; visiting ~s (during peak ~s more trains run) 7. the rush ~ (traffic is very heavy during the rush ~) 8. at a certain ~ (at the appointed ~) 9. by the ~ (to pay workers by the ~) 10. in a certain ~ (in one's ~ of need) 11. in, inside, within an ~ (she'll be here in an ~) 12. on the ~ ('every hour') 13. (misc.) to keep late ~s ('to go to bed late'); one's finest ~ ('the noblest period in one's life'); in the wee ~s of the morning ('late at night'); after ~s ('after work'); (a) happy ~ ('period in which a bar sells alcoholic drinks at a reduced price'); H-hour/zero ~ ('time at which a significant event is scheduled to begin')

house n. ['building'] ['home'] 1. to build, put up a ~ 2. to redecorate, refurbish, remodel, renovate a ~ 3. to demolish, raze, tear down a ~ 4. to rent a ~ from smb. 5. to let (BE), rent out (AE) a ~ to smb. 6. a dilapidated, ramshackle ~ 7. an apartment (AE); brick; clapboard; country; detached; frame; manor (esp. BE); one-family, single; prefabricated; ranch (AE); rooming; row (AE); terraced (BE); semidetached; summer; town ~ 8. a haunted ~ 9. (AE) a fraternity; sorority ~ ['housekeeping'] 10. to keep ~ for smb. ['theater'] 11. to bring the ~ down ('to win thunderous approval') 12. an empty; full, packed ~ (to play to a packed ~) 13. an opera ~ ['chamber of a parliament'] 14. a lower; upper ~ ['firm'] 15. a banking; discount; gambling; mail-order; pharmaceutical; publishing ~; slaughterhouse ['place providing a public service'] 16. a boarding; halfway; safe; settlement ~ ['bar'] (BE) 17. a free; public; tied ~ ['shelter'] 18. a reptile ~ (at a zoo) ['misc.'] 19. a ~ of correction/detention ('a prison'); a disorderly ~ ('a brothel'); (AE) a station ~ ('a police station'); drinks are on the ~ ('drinks are served

free'); an open ~ ('informal hospitality'); ('a residence being sold or rented out that is open for
inspection')
house arrest *n.* to place, put smb. under ~
household *n.* 1. to establish, set up a ~ 2. to run a
~
housekeeping *n.* 1. to do ~ 2. light ~
housework *n.* to do ~
housing *n.* council (BE), public (AE); fair (AE),
open (AE); low-cost, low-income; off-campus;
student; subsidized; substandard ~
hovel *n.* a miserable, wretched ~
hover *v.* 1. (d; intr.) to ~ around (we ~ed around
our guide) 2. (d; intr.) to ~ between (to ~
between life and death) 3. (d; intr.) to ~ over (the
fear of a new war ~ed over us)
howl I *n.* to let out a ~
howl II *v.* 1. (D; intr.) to ~ at 2. (D; intr.) to ~ in,
with (to ~ with pain)
Hoyle *n.* according to ~ ('according to the rules')
hub *n.* ['focal point'] at the ~ (at the ~ of activity)
huddle I *n.* 1. to go into a ~ 2. in a ~
huddle II *v.* (usu. P; intr.) to ~ around a fire; to
~ together
hue *n.* to raise a ~ and cry
huff *n.* (to leave) in a ~
hug *n.* to give smb. a ~
hum *v.* 1. (usu. B; occ. A) ~ the tune to me 2. (D;
tr.) to ~ for (to ~ a song for smb.)
human *adj.* ~ to + inf. (it's only ~ to seek a better
life)
humanism *n.* secular ~
humanity *n.* ['quality of being humane'] 1. to display ~ 2. common ~ ['the human race'] 3. a crime
against ~
humble pie *n.* (forced) to eat ~
humiliating *adj.* 1. ~ to + inf. (it is ~ to take
orders from him) 2. ~ that + clause (it's ~ that we
may not make our own decisions)
humiliation *n.* 1. to suffer ~ 2. abject ~
humility *n.* to demonstrate, display ~
humor, humour *n.* ['something funny'] 1. bitter,
caustic; black; deadpan, dry, straight; earthy; gallows; infectious; irrepressible; slapstick; sly, wry;
subtle ~ 2. a sense of ~ 3. a dash, trace, vein of ~
['mood'] 4. (a) bad; good ~ (she's in good ~
today) 5. a ~ to + inf. (he's in no ~ to be fooled
with) 6. in a certain ~ (in bad ~)
hump *n.* ['fit of depression'] (colloq.) (BE) 1. it
gives me the ~ ('it depresses me') ['worst part']
(colloq.) 2. over the ~
hunch *n.* (colloq.) ['feeling'] ['suspicion'] 1. to
play a ~ ('to act on the basis of a hunch') 2. a ~
that (I have a ~ that she will not come) 3. on a ~
(she did it on a ~)
hunger I *n.* 1. (formal) to allay, alleviate, appease
one's ~ 2. to satisfy one's ~; to gratify one's ~
(fig.) 3. ravenous ~ 4. ~ for (~ for knowledge) 5.
of ~ (to die of ~)
hunger II *v.* (D; intr.) to ~ after, for
hungry *adj.* 1. (cannot stand alone) ~ for (~ for
news) 2. to go ~
hunt I *n.* 1. to organize, stage a ~ 2. a ~ for (a ~
for big game)

hunt II *v.* (D; intr.) to ~ for (to ~ for big game)
hunter *n.* a bargain; big-game; bounty; fortune;
head; souvenir ~
hurdle *n.* 1. to clear, take a ~ 2. to hit, knock
down a ~ 3. high; low ~s
hurl *v.* (d; refl., tr.) to ~ at (to ~ oneself at the
enemy; to ~ insults at smb.)
hurrah *n.* the last ~ ('a last attempt')
hurricane *n.* 1. a severe, violent ~ 2. a ~ hits,
strikes (the ~ struck several cities) 3. a ~ blows
itself out 4. the eye of a ~
hurry I *n.* 1. in a ~ 2. a ~ to + inf. (we were in a
~ to finish)
hurry II *v.* (E) he ~ied to respond to her letter
hurry back *v.* (D; intr.) to ~ to (she ~ried back to
her desk)
hurt I *adj.* ['insulted'] 1. deeply ~ ['injured'] 2.
badly ~
hurt II *v.* 1. to ~ badly, seriously; deeply; slightly
2. (R) it ~s me to cough; it ~s me to see her ruin
her life
hurtle *v.* (P; intr.) to ~ through the air (a large
rock came ~ling through the air)
husband *n.* 1. to leave one's ~ 2. a common-law;
cuckolded; estranged ~; ex-husband, former;
faithful; henpecked; jealous; philandering,
unfaithful ~ 3. (misc.) she had two children by her
first ~
husbandry *n.* animal ~
hush *n.* a ~ fell (over the crowd)
hustings *n.* ['route of an election campaign'] to go
out on the ~
hustle I *n.* (slang) ['quick movement'] to get a ~
on (AE)
hustle II *v.* (P; tr.) the police ~d the prisoner in to
a cell
hut *n.* 1. a bamboo; thatched ~ 2. a Nissen (BE),
Quonset (AE) ~
hutch *n.* a rabbit ~
hydrant *n.* 1. to open, turn on a ~ 2. a fire ~
hyena *n.* 1. a brown; laughing; spotted; striped ~
2. a clan, pack of ~s
hygiene *n.* 1. to practice (good) ~ 2. dental;
feminine; field; industrial; mental; personal; sexual; social ~
hygienist *n.* a dental (AE), oral (BE) ~
hymen *n.* to rupture a ~
hymn *n.* 1. to chant, sing a ~ 2. a rousing; solemn
~ 3. a ~ to (a ~ to freedom)
hypersensitive *adj.* ~ about, to
hypertension *n.* essential; malignant; mild; severe
~
hypnosis *n.* 1. to induce, produce ~ 2. to put smb.
under ~ 3. under ~
hypnotism *n.* to practice ~
hypocrisy *n.* to display ~
hypocritical *adj.* 1. ~ about 2. ~ to + inf. (it was
~ of her to make the offer)
hypothesis *n.* 1. to advance, formulate, propose a
~ 2. to confirm a ~ 3. a null; working ~ 4. the ~
that + clause (she advanced the ~ that the disease
was spread by rodents)
hypothesize *v.* 1. (D; intr.) to ~ about 2. (L) they
~d that the disease was spread by rodents

hysterectomy *n.* 1. to do, perform a ~ on 2. to have a ~

hysteria *n.* 1. to produce ~ 2. mass ~ 3. an attack, fit of ~

hysterical *adj.* ~ about

hysterics *n.* a fit of ~ (to have a fit of ~)

I

ice *n.* 1. to form, make, produce ~ 2. to melt ~ 3. hard; soft ~ 4. cracked; crushed; dry; water ~ 5. pack ~ 6. ~ forms; melts 7. on the ~ (to slip on the ~) 8. (misc.) to break the ~ ('to create a more relaxed atmosphere'); to cut no ~ ('to have no effect'); on thin ~ ('in a dangerous situation'); on ~ ('in reserve')
iceberg *n.* 1. to hit, strike an ~ (the ship struck an ~) 2. (misc.) (fig.) the tip of the ~
icebox *n.* (colloq.) to raid the ~ ('to eat heartily esp. during the night')
ice cream *n.* 1. to make ~ 2. hand-dipped ~ 3. chocolate; strawberry; vanilla ~
icicle *n.* an ~ forms; hangs down
icon *n.* to paint an ~
idea *n.* 1. to get, hit upon an ~ 2. to develop; entertain, toy with an ~ 3. to communicate, disseminate ~s; to market, package an ~ 4. to implement an ~ 5. to endorse, favor an ~ 6. to dismiss, reject an ~ 7. a bright, brilliant, clever, ingenious; logical ~ 8. an absurd, crazy, fantastic, far-fetched; desperate; silly, stupid; strange ~ 9. a fresh, new, novel ~ 10. a daring; grandiose ~ 11. an old, outmoded, stale, warmed-over ~ 12. an approximate, rough; clear; fixed; general; main; vague ~ 13. the faintest, slightest ~ (she didn't have the faintest ~ of what I meant) 14. the ~ that + clause (I had no ~ that she would attend the meeting) 15. (misc.) he didn't get the ~ ('he did not understand')
ideal I *adj.* ~ for
ideal II *n.* 1. to attain; realize an ~ 2 a lofty, noble ~; high ~s
idealistic *adj.* ~ about
identical *adj.* ~ to, with (his hat is ~ to mine)
identification *n.* 1. to make an ~ 2. positive ~
identify *v.* 1. (B) she ~fied the intruder to the police 2. (D; refl., tr.) to ~ as; to (he ~fied himself as an old friend of the family; she ~fied him to the police as the intruder) 3. (d.; intr., refl., tr.) to ~ with (she always ~fies with the underdog; he didn't want to be ~fied with the liberals)
identity *n.* 1. to establish smb.'s ~ 2. mistaken ~ (it was a case of mistaken ~)
ideology *n.* to embrace; espouse an ~
idiocy *n.* 1. congenital ~ 2. ~ to + inf. (it was sheer ~ for him to arrive late)
idiot *n.* 1. a blithering, blooming, driveling ~ 2. the local, village ~ 3. an ~ to + inf. (he was an ~ to agree)
idiotic *adj.* ~ to + inf. (they were ~ to do that)
idle *adj.* to stand ~ (the machinery stood ~ for a month)
idol *n.* 1. to worship an ~ 2. (fig.) a fallen; matinee; national; popular ~
idolize *v.* (D; tr.) to ~ as (she was ~d as a movie star)
ignition *n.* (in a car) 1. to turn on the ~ 2. to turn off the ~

ignorance *n.* 1. to betray, demonstrate, display, show ~ 2. abysmal, blatant, crass, profound, total; blissful ~ 3. ~ about; of 4. in ~ of
ignorant *adj.* 1. blissfully ~ 2. ~ in; of (~ of the facts)
ignore *v.* 1. to ~ completely, totally 2. (K) you'll have to ~ their talking so loud
ilk *n.* ['kind'] of a certain ~
ill *adj.* 1. to be taken ~ 2 to fall ~ 3. desperately, gravely, seriously; incurably, terminally ~ 4. emotionally; mentally; physically ~ 5. ~ with (she is ~ with a tropical disease) 6. (misc.) ~ at ease ('uncomfortable')
ill-advised *adj.* ~ to + inf. (you would be ~ not to invite both of them)
ill-disposed *adj.* (formal) (cannot stand alone) ~ to, towards (they are ~ towards me)
illegal *adj.* ~ to + inf. (it is ~ to drive while intoxicated)
ill feeling *n.* 1. to stir up ~ 2. ~ over (there was a great deal of ~ stirred up over the appointment)
illiteracy *n.* 1. to eliminate, stamp out ~ 2. functional; widespread ~
illiterate *n.* a functional ~
illness *n.* 1. to get over an ~ 2. a fatal; grave, major, serious; incurable; lingering; slight; sudden; terminal; untreatable ~ 3. mental ~
illogical *adj.* ~ to + inf. (it's ~ to assume that)
illuminating *adj.* ~ to + inf. (it was ~ to read the candidate's earlier speeches)
illusion *n.* 1. to create, produce an ~ 2. to cherish, harbor an ~ 3. to dispel an ~ 4. an optical ~ 5 an ~ about 6. an ~ to + inf. (it's an ~ to think that...) 7. an ~ that + clause (it is an ~ that appeasement will deter an aggressor) 8. under an ~
illustration *n.* ['example'] 1. to give, offer, provide an ~ ['picture'] 2. to draw an ~
illustrative *adj.* ~ of (~ of one's views)
ill will *n.* 1. to stir up ~ 2. to bear, harbor ~ towards smb. 3. ~ about, over; between
image *n.* 1. to project an ~ 2. a public; tarnished ~ 3. a spitting ~, spit and ~ (a spitting ~ of George Washington) 4. (misc.) to be created in the ~ of God
imagery *n.* vivid ~
imagination *n.* 1. to excite, fire smb.'s ~ 2. to use one's ~ 3. to defy, stagger, stir smb.'s ~ 4. an active, lively, vivid; creative; feeble; wild ~ 5. a figment of smb.'s ~ 6. the ~ to + inf. (does she have the ~ to figure out what happened?) 7. in one's ~ 8. (misc.) by no stretch of the ~
imagine *v.* 1. (d; tr.) to ~ as (can you ~ her as an actress?) 2. (G) I can't ~ going to the party without an invitation 3. (J) can you ~ me becoming a teacher? 4. (K) it is difficult to ~ his marrying anyone 5. (L) I ~ that they will be delighted to hear from you 6. (N; used with an adjective, noun, past participle) can you ~ him president?
imbalance *n.* 1. to correct, redress an ~ 2. an ~

between

imbecile *n.* an ~ to + inf. (he was an ~ to sign a contract with them)

imbecilic *adj.* ~ to + inf. (it was ~ to do that)

imbued *adj.* (cannot stand alone) 1. deeply, profoundly, thoroughly ~ 2. ~ with (~ with a fighting spirit)

imitation *n.* 1. to do an ~ of smb. 2. a pale ~ 3. in ~ of

imitative *adj.* (formal) ~ of

immaterial *adj.* 1. wholly ~ 2. ~ to

immature *adj.* ~ to + inf. (it was ~ of her to do that)

immaturity *n.* to display ~

immerse *v.* 1. to ~ deeply 2. (D; refl., tr.) to ~ in (she ~d herself in the water; ~d in one's work)

immersion *n.* 1. total ~ 2. ~ in (total ~ in one's work)

immigrant *n.* 1. an illegal ~ 2. an ~ from; to (~s to Canada)

immigrate *v.* (D; intr.) to ~ from; into, to (to ~ into a country)

immigration *n.* ~ from; into, to

immodest *adj.* ~ to + inf. (it was ~ of me to say that)

immoral *adj.* ~ to + inf. (it's ~ to steal)

immune *adj.* ['exempt'] 1. ~ from (~ from prosecution; her prestige made her ~ from criticism) ['unaffected'] 2. ~ to (~ to a disease; his self-confidence made him ~ to criticism)

immunity *n.* 1. to acquire, develop ~ 2. acquired; natural ~ 3. active; passive ~ 4. diplomatic ~ 5. ~ from, to (~ from prosecution; ~ to a disease)

immunization *n.* 1. to carry out a (mass) ~ against 2. active; passive ~

immunize *v.* (D; tr.) to ~ against (the children have been ~d against poliomyelitis)

impact I *n.* 1. to have an ~ on, upon 2. a considerable, strong; dramatic; emotional ~ 3. on ~ (the pole collapses on ~)

impact II *v.* (esp. AE) (d; intr.) to ~ on

impaired *adj.* hearing; visually ~

impairment *n.* (a) hearing; memory; mental; physical; speech; visual ~

impale *v.* (D; tr.) to ~ on, upon (the driver was thrown from the car and ~d on a fence)

impart *v.* (B) to ~ knowledge to students

impartiality *n.* 1. to demonstrate, display, show ~ 2. ~ in

impasse *n.* 1. to reach an ~ 2. to break an ~ 3. at an ~ (negotiations were at an ~)

impatience *n.* 1. to display, show ~ 2. ~ with 3. ~ to + inf. (we noted her ~ to begin)

impatient *adj.* 1. ~ at, with (~ at the delay; ~ with children) 2. ~ for (I was ~ for the trip to start) 3. ~ to + inf. (we were ~ to leave)

impeach *v.* (D; tr.) to ~ for (to ~ smb. for taking bribes)

impediment *n.* 1. a speech ~ 2. an ~ to (an ~ to progress)

impel *v.* (formal) 1. (d; tr.) to ~ into, to 2. (H) to ~ smb. to do smt.

impelled *adj.* (cannot stand alone) ~ to + inf. (she felt ~ to intercede)

imperative I *adj.* 1. ~ to + inf. (it is ~ to act now) 2. ~ that + clause; subj. (it is ~ that you be/should be present)

imperative II *n.* 1. a moral ~ 2. an ~ that + clause; subj. (it is a moral ~ that no concessions be/should be made)

imperceptible *adj.* ~ to (~ to the touch)

imperfection *n.* a slight ~

impersonation *n.* to do an ~

impertinence *n.* the ~ to + inf. (he had the ~ to demand a raise)

impertinent *adj.* 1. ~ to 2. ~ to + inf. (it was ~ of him to behave like that)

impervious *adj.* ~ to (~ to criticism)

impetuous *adj.* ~ to + inf. (it was ~ of her to do that)

impetus *n.* 1. to give, provide an ~ 2. to gain ~ 3. an ~ to 4. an ~ to + inf. (there was no ~ to work harder)

impinge *v.* (formal) (d; intr.) to ~ on, upon (to ~ on smb.'s rights)

impingement *n.* an ~ on, upon

implant I *n.* a breast; heart; kidney ~

implant II *v.* (d; tr.) to ~ in (to ~ respect for democracy in the younger generation)

implicate *v.* (D; tr.) to ~ in (to ~ smb. in a scandal)

implication *n.* 1. a derogatory, negative; subtle ~ 2. an ~ for 3. an ~ that + clause (I resent your ~ that my work is unsatisfactory) 4. by ~

implicit *adj.* 1. ~ in (~ in the contract) 2. ~ that + clause (it is ~ in our agreement that she will be a partner)

implore *v.* (formal) (H) they ~d her to help

imply *v.* (L; to) she ~lied (to us) that she knew more than she had told the reporters

impolite *adj.* ~ to + inf. (it is ~ to interrupt someone who is speaking)

import *v.* (D; tr.) to ~ from; into (to ~ goods from abroad)

importance *n.* 1. to acquire, assume ~ 2. to attach, attribute ~ to 3. great, paramount, utmost, vital ~ (the matter assumed paramount ~) 4. ~ for, to 5. of ~ (it was a question of great ~ to us)

important *adj.* 1. ~ for (irrigation is ~ for farming) 2. ~ to (winning the contest was very ~ to her) 3. ~ to + inf. (it is ~ to study hard) 4. ~ that + clause; subj. (it is ~ that everyone attend/should attend)

importune *v.* (formal) 1. (D; tr.) to ~ for 2. (H) to ~ smb. to do smt.

impose *v.* 1. (D; intr., refl.) to ~ on, upon ('to take advantage of') (to ~ on smb.'s good nature; don't ~ yourself on them) 2. (D; tr.) ('to levy') to ~ on (to ~ a new tax on cigarettes)

impossible *adj.* 1. almost, practically, virtually, well-nigh ~ 2. ~ for (it's ~ for me to help) 3. ~ to + inf. (it is ~ to predict the future; that child is ~ to control = it is ~ to control that child) 4. (misc.) to attempt; do the ~

impractical *adj.* ~ to + inf. (it's ~ to live in one city and work in another)

impregnate *v.* (d; tr.) to ~ with

impress *v.* 1. to ~ deeply; favorably 2. (D; tr.) to

~ as (she ~ed me as a scholar) 3. (d; tr.) to ~ on, upon (he tried to ~ on them the importance of being punctual) 4. (D; tr.) to ~ with (she ~ed me with her grasp of the subject) 5. (R) it ~ed me that they cooperated so willingly

impressed *adj.* 1. easily ~ 2. deeply, greatly, highly, strongly ~

impression *n.* 1. to create an ~ 2. to make an ~ on, upon 3. to gain an ~ 4. an accurate; deep, indelible, lasting, profound, strong; erroneous, false, inaccurate, wrong; excellent; favorable; first; fleeting; general; good; painful; personal; pleasant; unfavorable, unpleasant; vivid ~ 5. an ~ that + clause (she created the erroneous ~ that her family is wealthy) 6. under an ~ (I was under the ~ that you would come)

imprimatur *n.* the royal ~

imprint *n.* 1. to bear an ~ (to bear the ~ of genius) 2. to leave one's ~ on

imprisonment *n.* life ~

improbable *adj.* 1. highly ~ 2. ~ that + clause (it's ~ that she'll accept the invitation)

improper *adj.* 1. ~ for 2. ~ to + inf. (it was ~ to do that)

impropriety *n.* crass ~

improve *v.* 1. (D; intr.) to ~ in (she has ~d in English) 2. (d; intr.) to ~ on, upon (I cannot ~ on her performance)

improvement *n.* 1. to bring about an ~ 2. to show (an) ~ 3. a decided, distinct, marked, substantial; minor ~ 4. an ~ in, of (an ~ in her work; an ~ of service) 5. an ~ on, over, upon (this edition is an ~ over the previous one)

improvisation *n.* to do an ~

imprudent *adj.* ~ to + inf. (it was ~ of them to speculate on the stock exchange)

impudence *n.* 1. brazen ~ 2. the ~ to + inf. (he had the ~ to breach the contract)

impudent *adj.* ~ to + inf. (it was ~ of her to answer like that; she was ~ to answer like that)

impulse *n.* ['driving force'] 1. to feel an ~ 2. to curb, resist an ~ 3. an irresistible ~ 4. an ~ to + inf. (he felt an irresistible ~ to buy a new TV set) 5. on, under (an) ~ (to act on ~) ['stimulus'] 6. to convey, transmit an ~ 7. a nerve ~

impute *v.* (formal) (d; tr.) to ~ to (to ~ base motives to smb.)

in I *adv.* (colloq.) 1. ~ for ('facing') (they are ~ for trouble) 2. ~ with ('on intimate terms with') (they are ~ with highly influential people)

in II *n.* (colloq.) ['influence'] to have an ~ with smb.

in III *prep.* ~ smb. to + inf. (it's not ~ me to lie; she doesn't have it ~ her to break her word)

inability *n.* ~ to + inf. (her ~ to pay caused trouble)

inaccessible *adj.* ~ to (~ to students)

inaccuracy *n.* a glaring ~

inaccurate *adj.* ~ to + inf. (it is ~ to say that she was dismissed)

inadequate *adj.* 1. ~ for; to (the supply of water is ~ for the trip; ~ to the occasion) 2. ~ to + inf. (the supply is ~ to meet the demand)

inapplicable *adj.* ~ to

inappropriate *adj.* 1. ~ for, to (~ to the occasion) 2. ~ to + inf. (it is ~ for you to wear shorts at a formal reception) 3. ~ that + clause; subj. (it is ~ that he be/should be present)

inattention *n.* ~ to (~ to detail)

inattentive *adj.* ~ to

inaudible *adj.* ~ to

inaugurate *v.* (D; tr.) to ~ as (to be ~d as president)

inauguration *n.* to hold an ~

incantation *n.* to chant, utter an ~

incapable *adj.* (cannot stand alone) ~ of (she is ~ of cheating)

incense *n.* to burn ~

incensed *adj.* 1. ~ about, at, over 2. ~ to + inf. (she was ~ to learn of the accusation)

incentive *n.* 1. to offer an ~ 2. a powerful, strong ~ 3. an ~ to (an ~ to investment) 4. an ~ to + inf. (they have no ~ to work harder)

inception *n.* from smt.'s ~

incest *n.* to commit ~ (with)

inch I *n.* 1. to contest, fight for every ~ of one's land 2. a cubic; square ~ 3. every ~ ('to the utmost degree') (she is every ~ a champion) 4. within an ~ ('almost') (he was beaten within an ~ of his life) 5. (misc.) ~ by ~

inch II *v.* (P; intr.) to ~ forward slowly

incidence *n.* a high; low ~ (a high ~ of crime)

incident I *adj.* (formal) (cannot stand alone) ~ to (the risks ~ to military service)

incident II *n.* 1. to provoke an ~ 2. to cover up, suppress an ~ 3. an amusing, funny, humorous; curious; painful, unpleasant; pleasant; strange; touching; ugly ~ 4. a border ~ 5. an ~ occurs, takes place

incidental *adj.* ~ to (problems ~ to growing up)

incision *n.* 1. to make an ~ 2. a deep ~

incisors *n.* central; lateral ~

incite *v.* 1. (D; tr.) to ~ to (to ~ workers to rebellion) 2. (H) to ~ the populace to riot

incitement *n.* ~ to (~ to riot)

inclination *n.* 1. to feel an ~ 2. a natural; strong ~ 3. an ~ for, to, towards 4. an ~ to + inf. (the carburetor has an ~ to flood)

incline *v.* (BE) 1. (d; intr.) to ~ to, towards (he ~s to laziness) 2. (d; tr.) to ~ to (it ~d me to anger) 3. (E) I ~ to believe that she is innocent 4. (E) the news ~d me to leave at once

inclined *adj.* (cannot stand alone) ~ to + inf. (I am ~ to agree)

include *v.* (D; tr.) to ~ among, in (to ~ smb in a list of candidates; who was ~d among the guests?)

inclusive *adj.* ~ of

incognito *adv.* to go, travel ~

incognizant *adj.* ~ of

income *n.* 1. to earn an ~ 2. an annual; earned; fixed; gross; independent; monthly; net; taxable; unearned; weekly ~ 3. per capita ~ 4. beyond one's ~ (they live beyond their ~) 5. within one's ~ (to live within one's ~)

incommensurable *adj.* ~ with

incommensurate *adj.* ~ to, with

incommunicado *adv.* to hold smb. ~

incompatibility *n.* ~ with

incompatible *adj.* ~ with
incompetence *n.* ~ at, in
incompetent *adj.* 1. ~ at, in 2. ~ to + inf. (he is ~ to judge)
incomplete *n.* ['academic deficiency'] to make up an ~ (the student had to make up three ~s)
incomprehensible *adj.* 1. ~ to 2. ~ that + clause (it is ~ that they were admitted to the program)
inconceivable *adj.* 1. ~ to 2. ~ that + clause (it is ~ that she could be considered for the job)
incongruous *adj.* ~ with
inconsiderate *adj.* 1. ~ of (he's ~ of her feelings) 2. ~ to + inf. (it was ~ of you to say that)
inconsistent *adj.* ~ with
inconvenience *n.* 1. to cause ~ 2. to put up with (an) ~ 3. (a) considerable, great; slight ~
inconvenient *adj.* 1. ~ for 2. ~ to + inf. (it is ~ to meet tomorrow)
incorporate *v.* (D; tr.) to ~ into
incorrect *adj.* 1. ~ in 2. ~ to + inf. (it's ~ to say that he is a good administrator)
increase I *n.* 1. a considerable, large, sharp, sizable, substantial; moderate; slight; steady ~ 2. a rate ~ 3. an ~ in (an ~ in coal consumption) 4. on the ~
increase II *v.* 1. (D; intr., tr.) to ~ by (production ~d by ten percent) 2. (D; intr., tr.) to ~ from; to (the physician ~d the dosage from one to four)
incredible *adj.* ~ that + clause (it was ~ that nobody paid attention to the new invention)
increment *n.* an ~ in (an ~ in salary)
incriminate *v.* (D; tr.) to ~ in
inculcate *v.* (D; tr.) to ~ in, into (to ~ ideas in the minds of young people)
incumbent *adj.* (cannot stand alone) ~ on, upon + to + inf. (it's ~ on you to warn them)
incursion *n.* 1. to make an ~ 2. an armed ~ 3. an ~ into (to make an ~ into enemy territory)
indebted *adj.* 1. deeply ~ 2. (cannot stand alone) ~ for; to (we are ~ to her for her help)
indecent *adj.* ~ to + inf. (it was ~ of him to do that)
indecisive *adj.* ~ about
indemnification *n.* to pay ~ for
indemnify *v.* (D; tr.) to ~ for
indemnity *n.* 1. to pay an ~ 2. double ~
indent *v.* (BE) (d; intr.) ('to request officially') to ~ for; on (we had to ~ on the company for new typewriters)
indentation *n.* to make an ~
independence *n.* 1. to achieve, gain, win ~ from 2. to declare one's ~ from 3. to lose one's ~ 4. political ~
independent *adj.* 1. fiercely ~ 2. ~ of
index *n.* ['alphabetical list'] 1. to compile, do, make an ~ 2. an author; cumulative; subject ~ 3. an ~ to (an ~ to a book) ['indicator'] 4. a consumer-price, cost-of-living; price ~ 5. an ~ to (an ~ to economic progress) ['ratio of one dimension to another'] 6. a cephalic; cranial; facial ~
Indian *n.* an American ~ USAGE NOTE: To somebody from Canada and the United States, the primary meaning of *Indian* is 'American Indian'. To somebody from other English-speaking countries, the primary meaning is 'native of India'. Note that a *West Indian* is always somebody from the West Indies.
indicate *v.* 1. (B) she ~d her reasons to us 2. (L; to) they ~d (to us) that they would sign the contract
indication *n.* 1. to give an ~ 2. an ~ that + clause (there is every ~ that she will recover)
indicative *adj.* ~ of
indict *v.* (D; tr.) to ~ for (to ~ smb. for murder)
indictment *n.* (usu. legal) 1. to hand up, issue, present, return an ~ 2. to waive (the) ~ 3. to quash an ~ 4. (fig.) a stinging; sweeping ~ 5. an ~ against 6. an ~ for 7. on ~ (to try a case on ~)
indifference *n.* 1. to affect, feign ~ 2. to display, show ~ 3. marked; studied ~ 4. ~ about, concerning 5. ~ to, towards
indifferent *adj.* 1. to remain ~ 2. ~ about, concerning 3. ~ to, towards
indigenous *adj.* ~ to
indigestion *n.* 1. to cause ~ 2. to give smb. ~ (pickles give me ~) 3. acute, severe; chronic ~ 4. an attack, touch of ~
indignant *adj.* 1. ~ about, at, over 2. (misc.) to wax ~ (over smt.)
indignation *n.* 1. to arouse ~ 2. to express; feel, show ~ 3. burning; helpless; public; righteous ~ 4. ~ about, at, over (to feel ~ at gross injustice) 5. to smb.'s ~
indignity *n.* 1. to inflict an ~ on 2. to suffer ~ties
indiscreet *adj.* ~ to + inf. (it was ~ of her to say that)
indiscretion *n.* 1. to commit an ~ 2. a youthful ~
indiscriminate *adj.* ~ in
indispensable *adj.* ~ for, to (~ to life)
indisposed *adj.* (formal) ~ to + inf. (she appears ~ to go)
indistinguishable *adj.* ~ from
individualism *n.* rugged ~
individuality *n.* to express one's ~
indoctrinate *v.* (D; tr.) to ~ against; in; with
indoctrination *n.* ~ against; in; with
induce *v.* (H) we could not ~ her to come
inducement *n.* 1. to offer, provide an ~ 2. a strong ~ 3. an ~ to 4. an ~ to + inf. (we had no ~ to work harder)
induct *v.* (D; tr.) to ~ into (to ~ smb. into the armed forces)
induction *n.* ~ into (~ into the armed forces)
indulge *v.* (d; intr., refl., tr.) to ~ in (to ~ in the luxury of a nice, warm bath; he ~s her in everything)
indulgence *n.* to ask for smb.'s ~
indulgent *adj.* ~ towards
industry *n.* 1. to build up, develop (an) ~ 2. (an) ~ springs up 3. a basic, key ~ 4. a cottage; defense; high-tech ~ 5. heavy; light ~ 6. the film; machine-tool; meat-packing; pharmaceutical; steel; textile; tourist, travel; trucking (esp. AE) ~ 7. a smokestack ('old, obsolete') ~ 8. (misc.) government often regulates ~; a branch of ~
inelegant *adj.* ~ to + inf. (it was ~ to phrase the request in that manner)
ineligibility *n.* ~ for

129 **inhere**

ineligible *adj.* 1. ~ for 2. ~ to + inf. (she is still ~ to vote)

inept *adj.* ~ at, in

ineptitude *n.* 1. to demonstrate, display ~ 2. ~ at, in

inequality *n.* ~ between

inertia *n.* 1. sheer ~ 2. through ~

inevitable *adj.* ~ that + clause (it was ~ that she would find out)

inexcusable *adj.* 1. ~ to + inf. (it was ~ of him to blurt that out) 2. ~ that + clause (it is ~ that she was left out)

inexperienced *adj.* ~ at, in

infallibility *n.* 1. papal ~ 2. ~ in

infallible *adj.* ~ in

infancy *n.* ['first stage'] in one's ~ (the industry was still in its ~)

infant *n.* 1. to nurse, suckle; wean an ~ 2. a newborn; premature ~ 3. (misc.) ~ mortality (see also **baby 7-11, 13**)

infanticide *n.* to commit ~

infantile *adj.* ~ to + inf. (it was ~ to behave like that)

infantry *n.* light; motorized; mountain ~

infatuated *adj.* ~ with

infatuation *n.* ~ with

infection *n.* 1. to pass on, spread, transmit (an) ~ 2. a latent; localized; primary; secondary; serious, severe; slight, superficial; systemic ~

infer *v.* 1. (D; tr.) to ~ from (to ~ a conclusion from the facts) 2. (L) I ~ that my proposal has been accepted 3. (Q) we had to ~ what she meant

inference *n.* 1. to draw, make an ~ from 2. an invalid; valid ~ 3. an ~ that + clause (we made the ~ that she had been wrongly accused)

inferior *adj.* 1. ~ in (~ in rank) 2. ~ to (he felt ~ to them)

inferiority *n.* 1. a feeling of ~ 2. ~ to

inferno *n.* a blazing, raging, roaring ~

infidelity *n.* 1. conjugal, marital ~ 2. ~ to (~ to one's ideals)

infighting *n.* ~ among, between

infiltrate *v.* (D; intr.) to ~ into

infiltration *n.* ~ into; through (enemy ~ into our lines)

infinitive *n.* 1. to split an ~ 2. a split ~

infinity *n.* to ~

inflammation *n.* 1. to cause (an) ~ 2. (an) ~ subsides

inflation *n.* 1. to cause ~ 2. to control, curb ~ 3. creeping; double-digit; galloping, rampant, runaway, uncontrolled ~

inflection, inflexion *n.* a falling; rising ~

inflexibility *n.* ~ in

inflexible *adj.* ~ in

inflict *v.* (D; tr.) to ~ on (to ~ heavy losses on the enemy)

influence I *n.* 1. to exert ~ on 2. to use one's ~ 3. to wield ~ 4. to bring ~ to bear 5. to flaunt one's ~ 6. (colloq.) to peddle ~ 7. to consolidate, strengthen one's ~ 8. to counteract, curb, neutralize smb.'s ~ 9. (a) bad, baleful, baneful, far-reaching; good; leavening, moderating; negative; pernicious; positive; powerful, profound, strong;

salutary; undue; unwholesome ~ 10. cultural; moral ~ 11. an ~ for (an ~ for good) 12. the ~ to + inf. (they have enough ~ to get the bill passed) 13. under smb.'s ~; under the ~ of (to come under smb.'s ~; to drive under the ~ of alcohol) 14. (misc.) outside ~s; a sphere of ~; an ~ peddler

influence II *v.* 1. to ~ deeply, profoundly, strongly 2. (D; tr.) to ~ in 3. (H) who ~d her to do that?

influential *adj.* ~ in

influx *n.* an ~ from; into

inform *v.* 1. (D; tr.) to ~ about, of (we ~ed them of the incident) 2. (d; intr.) to ~ against, on (he ~ed on his accomplices) 3. (L; must have an object) she ~ed them that she would come 4. (Q; must have an object) the thief ~ed the police where the money was hidden

informal *adj.* ~ with (she's ~ with everyone)

informant *n.* a native ~

information *n.* 1. to furnish, give, offer, provide ~ 2. to collect, dig up, find, gather; extract ~ 3. to classify ~ 4. to divulge, leak ~ 5. to declassify ~ 6. to feed ~ (into a computer) 7. to retrieve ~ (from a computer) 8. to cover up, suppress, withhold ~ 9. classified, confidential; detailed; firsthand; inside; misleading; reliable; secondhand; secret ~ 10. (AE) long-distance ~ (BE has *long-distance enquiries, trunk enquiries*) 11. ~ about, on 12. ~ that + clause (we have ~ that she has returned to this country) 13. for smb.'s ~ (for your ~)

informative *adj.* ~ to + inf. (it was ~ to read the latest statistics)

informed *adj.* 1. to keep smb. ~ 2. ~ about

informer *n.* 1. to turn ('become') ~ 2. a police ~

inform on *v.* (D; intr.) to ~ to (he ~ed on them to the police)

infraction *n.* 1. to commit an ~ 2. a minor ~

infringe *v.* (d; intr.) to ~ on, upon (to ~ on smb.'s rights)

infringement *n.* an ~ of, on (an ~ of smb.'s rights)

infuriate *v.* (R) it ~d me (to read) that he had been indicted

infuriated *adj.* 1. ~ about, at, over; with 2. ~ to + inf. (he was ~ to find his seat occupied)

infuriating *adj.* 1. ~ to + inf. (it's ~ to pay such prices for inferior merchandise) 2. ~ that + clause (it's ~ that these items are so expensive)

infuse *v.* (d; tr.) to ~ into (to ~ new life into the troops)

infusion *n.* 1. an intravenous ~ 2. an ~ into

ingenious *adj.* ~ to + inf. (it was ~ of her to solve the problem so quickly)

ingenuity *n.* 1. human ~ 2. the ~ to + inf. (she had the ~ to succeed where everyone else had failed)

ingrained *adj.* deeply ~

ingratiate *v.* (D; refl.) to ~ with (she ~d herself with the boss)

ingratitude *n.* 1. to demonstrate, display, show ~ 2. base, rank ~

ingredients *n.* 1. to combine ~ (in baking) 2. basic; principal ~ 3. (misc.) the book has all the ~ of a best-seller

inhale *v.* to ~ deeply

inhere *v.* (formal) to ~ in

inherent *adj.* ~ in, to
inherit *v.* (D; tr.) to ~ from (to ~ a fortune from an uncle)
inhibit *v.* (D; tr.) to ~ from
inhospitable *adj.* 1. ~ to 2. ~ to + inf. (it is ~ to turn a stranger away)
inhumanity *n.* man's ~ to man
inimical *adj.* (formal) ~ to (actions ~ to the maintenance of friendly relations between our countries)
initiate *v.* (d; tr.) to ~ into (to ~ students into the mysteries of linguistics)
initiation *n.* 1. to conduct an ~ 2. an ~ into (an ~ into a fraternity)
initiative *n.* 1. to demonstrate, display, exercise, show ~ 2. to take the ~ 3. to stifle ~ 4. private ~ 5. the ~ to + inf. (does she have enough ~ to get this job done?) 6. on one's (own) ~ (she made the decision on her own ~)
inject *v.* (D; tr.) to ~ into (to ~ a note of humor into the proceedings)
injection *n.* 1. to administer, give an ~ 2. to get an ~ 3. a lethal ~ 4. a hypodermic; intradermal; intramuscular; intravenous; subcutaneous ~
injudicious *adj.* (formal) ~ to + inf. (it was ~ of you to speak to the press)
injunction *n.* 1. to grant, hand down, issue an ~ 2. to deliver an ~ 3. an ~ against (an ~ against picketing) 4. a permanent; temporary ~ 5. an ~ to + inf. (an ~ to prevent picketing) 6. an ~ that + clause; subj. (the court issued an ~ that picketing not take/should not take place)
injure *v.* to ~ badly, seriously, severely; slightly
injurious *adj.* ~ to
injury *n.* 1. to inflict (an) ~ on 2. to receive, suffer, sustain an ~ 3. a fatal; minor, slight; serious, severe ~ 4. bodily ~; an internal ~ 5. an ~ to (an ~ to the head) 6. (misc.) to add insult to ~
injustice *n.* 1. to do an ~ to 2. to commit an ~ 3. to redress an ~ 4. (a) blatant, gross, rank ~ 5. an ~ to
ink *n.* 1. indelible; India (AE), Indian (BE); invisible; marking; permanent; printer's; secret; washable ~ 2. a blob, drop of ~
inkling *n.* 1. the faintest, slightest ~ 2. an ~ that + clause (I didn't have the slightest ~ that he was ill)
inland *adv.* to go, travel ~
inmate *n.* a prison ~
innate *adj.* ~ in
innocence *n.* 1. to maintain; prove, show one's ~ 2. (misc.) an air of injured ~
innocent *adj.* ~ of
innovation *n.* 1. a daring ~ 2. an ~ in
innuendo *n.* 1. to cast, make an ~ 2. an ~ about 3. an ~ that + clause (she made an ~ that he had a prison record)
inoculate *v.* (D; tr.) to ~ against (to ~ a dog against rabies)
inoculation *n.* 1. to give an ~ 2. an ~ against (an ~ against tetanus)
input *n.* ~ into
inquest *n.* 1. to conduct, hold an ~ 2. a coroner's; formal ~ 3. an ~ into
inquire *v.* 1. (D; intr.) to ~ about, after; into 2.

(Q) he ~d where we were to meet USAGE NOTE: In BE, the spelling *enquire* is also used-- we enquired about her health.
inquiry *n.* 1. to conduct, make; launch an ~ 2. a discreet; exhaustive, thorough; official ~ 3. an ~ about (to make ~ries about a matter) 4. an ~ into (an official ~ into the incident was launched) USAGE NOTE: The noun *inquiry* can mean 'question' or 'investigation'. In BE, the spelling *enquiry* is often recommended for the meaning 'question'--an enquiry about her health. Compare--an official inquiry into the incident.
inquisition *n.* 1. to carry out, conduct an ~ 2. a cruel, senseless ~
inquisitive *adj.* ~ about
inroads *n.* 1. to make ~ 2. deep ~ 3. ~ in, into, on, upon (to make ~ on the freedom of the press)
insane *adj.* ~ to + inf. (it was ~ of him to risk everything)
insanity *n.* 1. (legal) to plead ~ 2. outright, pure, sheer ~ 3. (legal) temporary ~ 4. ~ to + inf. (it was sheer ~ to steal the money)
inscribe *v.* (D; tr.) to ~ for (to ~ a book for smb.)
inscription *n.* 1. to bear an ~ 2. to decipher an ~
insecticide *n.* to spray, spread, use an ~
insects *n.* 1. ~ bite; crawl, creep; fly 2. a swarm of (flying) ~
insecure *adj.* ~ about; in
insecurity *n.* a feeling of ~
insemination *n.* artificial ~
insensibility *n.* 1. to display, show ~ 2. ~ to
insensible *adj.* ~ to
insensitive *adj.* 1. ~ to (~ to the feelings of others) 2. ~ to + inf. (it was ~ of her to bring that up)
insensitivity *n.* 1. to display, show ~ 2. ~ to
inseparable *adj.* ~ from
insert *v.* (D; tr.) to ~ into (to ~ a new sentence into a paragraph; to ~ a key into a lock)
inside I *adv.* ~ out ('with the inner surface facing out'); ('thoroughly') (to know a subject ~ out) USAGE NOTE: The compound preposition *inside of* can refer to time or space. Referring to time, it is colloq. CE--to finish a job inside of an hour; referring to space, it is colloq. AE--inside of a building.
inside II *n.* (colloq.) ['confidential information'] 1. to have the ~ on ['position of trust'] 2. to be on the ~
insight *n.* 1. to gain; have (an) ~ into 2. to provide (an) ~ 3. a deep ~ 4. the ~ to + inf. (she had the ~ to predict what would happen)
insignia *n.* military; royal ~
insinuate *v.* 1. (d; refl.) ('to ingratiate') to ~ into (to ~ oneself into smb.'s good graces) 2. (L; to) ('to suggest') she ~ (to us) that her partner had embezzled funds
insinuation *n.* 1. to make an ~ 2. an ~ that + clause (she didn't like his ~ that she had cheated)
insist *v.* 1. to ~ absolutely, definitely, positively; stubbornly 2. (D; intr.) to ~ on (they ~ on more money; she ~ed on coming with us) 3. (L; can be used with the subj.) she ~ed that everyone attend; he ~ed that the accused was innocent
insistence *n.* 1. dogged, firm, stubborn ~ 2. ~ on

(~ on an increase in salary) 3. ~ that + clause; subj. (we resent your ~ that the debt be/should be paid at once)

insistent *adj.* 1. ~ on, upon 2. ~ that + clause; subj. (~ that the debt be/should be paid)

insolence *n.* 1. to display ~ 2. the ~ to + inf. (they had the ~ to file a complaint)

insolent *adj.* 1. ~ in (~ in their manner) 2. ~ to, towards 3. ~ to + inf. (it was ~ of them to demand special treatment)

insolvency *n.* to force into ~

insomnia *n.* to suffer from ~

inspection *n.* 1. to carry out, conduct, make an ~ 2. a close, thorough; cursory, perfunctory; visual ~ 3. a technical ~ 4. on ~ (on closer ~ the money turned out to be counterfeit)

inspector *n.* 1. a customs; fire; health mine; police ~ 2. the ~ general

inspiration *n.* 1. to give, offer, provide ~ 2. to derive, draw ~ from 3. divine ~ 4. ~ comes (from many sources) 5. a flash, spark of ~ 6. an ~ for (what provided the ~ for the statue?) 7. an ~ to (her example was an ~ to young people) 8. the ~ to + inf. (what gave him the ~ to do it?)

inspire *v.* 1. (D; tr.) to ~ in, with (formal) (to ~ awe in smb.; to ~ smb. with awe) 2. (H) to ~ smb. to do smt.

inspiring *adj.* ~ to + inf. (it was ~ to watch)

install *v.* (d; tr.) to ~ as (to ~ smb. as president)

installations *n.* military; naval; port ~

installment, instalment *n.* 1. to pay an ~ 2. monthly; quarterly ~s 3. in ~s (the book came out in ~s; to pay in ~s)

installment plan *n.* on the ~ (to buy smt. on the ~)

instance *n.* ['example'] 1. to cite, give an ~ 2. an isolated, rare ~ 3. for ~ 4. in an ~ (in rare ~s; in a few isolated ~s)

instant *n.* at a certain ~ (at that ~ I realized who had planned the whole scheme)

instigate *v.* (esp. BE) (H) to ~ smb. to do smt.

instigation *n.* at smb.'s ~

instill, instil *v.* 1. to ~ deeply, firmly 2. (D; tr.) to ~ in, into (to ~ respect for the law in the younger generation)

instinct *n.* 1. to arouse an ~ 2. a basic; destructive; herd; human; killer; maternal; natural ~ 3 animal; predatory ~s 4. an unerring ~ 5. an ~ for 6. the ~ to + inf. (nothing can destroy the ~ to survive)

institute *n.* 1. a research ~ 2. an ~ for (an ~ for theoretical research) 3. at an ~ (to work at an ~)

institution *n.* 1. to endow; support an ~ 2. a charitable; educational; financial; penal; philanthropic; social; state-supported ~ 3. a heavily endowed ~ 4. (misc.) an ~ of higher learning; the ~ of marriage

instruct *v.* 1. (D; tr.) ('to teach') to ~ in (to ~ soldiers in field hygiene) 2. (H) ('to order') she ~ed us to begin work at once 3. (L; must have an object) ('to inform') we have been ~ed that the matter has been settled by our lawyers 4. (Q; must have an object) ('to order') we were ~ed where to meet

instruction *n.* 1. to conduct, give, provide ~ 2. to

take ~ (before converting to a religion) 3. advanced; beginning, elementary; bilingual; intermediate; remedial ~ 4. computer-assisted ~ 5. ~ in (to provide advanced ~ in mathematics)

instructions *n.* 1. to give, issue ~ 2. to leave ~ (for smb.) 3. to carry out, follow ~ 4. to await (further) ~ 5. verbal; written ~ 6. ~ for 7. ~ to + inf. (we had ~ to report to her) 8. ~ that + clause; subj. (she left ~ that her estate be/should be divided evenly) 9. on ~ (we acted on your ~)

instructive *adj.* ~ to + inf. (it will be ~ to analyze the results)

instructor *n.* an ~ in, of (an ~ in physics)

instrument *n.* ['implement'] 1. a blunt; delicate; sharp ~ 2. surgical ~s; ~s of torture 3. an ~ for (an ~ for good) ['device for producing a musical sound'] 4. to play an ~ 5. a brass; musical; percussion; stringed; wind; woodwind ~

instrumental *adj.* (cannot stand alone) ~ in (her help was ~ in tracking down the criminal)

insubordinate *adj.* ~ to

insubordination *n.* 1. rank ~ 2. ~ to (~ to authority)

insufficient *adj.* 1. ~ for; in 2. ~ to + inf. (it's ~ to cite only one example)

insulate *v.* (D; tr.) to ~ against, from

insulation *n.* ~ against, from

insult *n.* 1. to fling, hurl an ~ at 2. to swallow, take an ~ 3. to avenge an ~ 4. a gratuitous; imaginary; nasty, vicious ~ 5. an ~ to (an ~ to smb.'s intelligence) 6. (misc.) a stream of ~s; to add ~ to injury

insulted *adj.* deeply ~

insurance *n.* 1. to provide ~ for 2. to sell, write; underwrite ~ 3. to carry; take out ~ (our firm carries fire ~) 4. to cancel; renew ~ 5. accident; automobile (AE), motor (BE), motor-car (BE); collision; comprehensive; compulsory; disability; endowment; fire; flight; flood; group; health; homeowner's; hospitalization; hurricane; liability (AE), third party (BE); life; major-medical (AE); marine; no-fault; property; term (esp. AE); title; whole life ~ 6. (GB) National Insurance 7. social; unemployment ~ 8. ~ against; on (~ against loss from flood; ~ on one's personal effects) 9. (misc.) an ~ policy USAGE NOTE: BE has traditionally distinguished between *insurance* (to provide compensation for what may happen) and *assurance* (to provide compensation for what will happen); thus-- *fire insurance* and *life assurance*. However, nowadays, *life insurance* is also used in BE.

insure *v.* (D; refl., tr.) to ~ against; for (to ~ one's home against loss from fire; to ~ one's life for fifty thousand dollars)

insured *adj.* fully; heavily ~

insurrection *n.* 1. to foment, stir up an ~ 2. to crush, put down, quell, suppress an ~

insusceptible *adj.* ~ to

integrate *v.* (D; intr., tr.) to ~ into; with

integration *n.* 1. economic; racial; school; token ~ 2. ~ into

integrity *n.* 1. to display, show ~ 2. great ~ 3. the ~ to + inf. (he had the ~ not to accept bribes) 4. (misc.) a person of ~

intellect *n.* 1. (a) keen, sharp, superior ~ 2. of ~ (a person of keen ~)

intelligence *n.* ['ability to comprehend, learn'] 1. to demonstrate, show ~ 2. great, high, keen; limited; low; normal; outstanding, remarkable ~ 3. artificial; native ~ 4. the ~ to + inf. (she had the ~ to see through their scheme) 5. of a certain ~ (a person of considerable ~) ['information'] 6. to collect, gather ~ 7. classified; combat, military; industrial; secret ~

intelligent *adj.* ~ to + inf. (it would not be ~ to provoke her)

intelligible *adj.* ~ to

intend *v.* 1. (d; tr.) ('to design') to ~ as (it was ~ed as a joke) 2. (d; tr.) ('to design') to ~ for (the book is ~ed for children) 3. (E) ('to plan') she ~s to file suit 4. (G) ('to plan') what do you ~ doing? 5. (BE) (H) ('to want') we ~ them to do it 6. (L; subj.) ('to want') we never ~ed that she get/ should get involved

intended *adj.* (cannot stand alone) ~ for (this dictionary is ~ for serious students)

intent I *adj.* (cannot stand alone) ~ on, upon (she is ~ on getting the job done quickly)

intent II *n.* 1. criminal ~ 2. ~ to + inf. (with ~ to kill) 3. by ~ 4. (misc.) to all ~s and purposes ('practically'); (legal) loitering with ~ (to commit a crime)

intention *n.* 1. to announce, declare, state one's ~ 2. to make one's ~s clear 3. every; no ~ (she has every ~ of accepting the invitation) 4. honorable ~s 5. the ~ to + inf. (have you heard of her ~ to resign?)

interact *v.* (d; intr.) to ~ with

interaction *n.* ~ among, between; with

intercede *v.* (D; intr.) to ~ for; with (to ~ with the authorities for smb.)

interchangeable *adj.* ~ with

intercourse *n.* 1. to have ~ with 2. anal; heterosexual; oral; sexual ~ 3. social ~ 4. ~ among, between; with

interest I *n.* ['concern'] ['curiosity'] 1. to arouse, generate, pique, stir up; revive ~ (in) 2. to hold smb.'s ~ 3. to demonstrate, display, evince, manifest, show ~ 4. to express; take an ~ in (she took a keen ~ in the project) 5. to lose ~ (in) 6. an academic; active; deep, intense, keen, lively, profound, serious, strong; passing; vested ~ 7. broad; common, mutual; narrow ~s 8. human ~ (this story has a lot of human ~) 9. personal; popular ~ 10. the national; (the) public ~ 11. ~ flags; peaks; picks up; wanes 12. a conflict of ~(s) 13. ~ in (to show no ~ in financial matters) 14. ~ to + inf. (it's in/to our ~ to have stable prices) 15. in smb.'s ~ (to act in one's own ~) 16. in a certain ~ (in the national ~; in the public ~) 17. in the ~s of (in the ~s of safety; in the ~s of our organization) 18. of ~ to (this story will be of ~ to us) 19. to smb.'s ~ (see 14) ['money paid for the use of money'] 20. to bear, pay, yield ~ 21. to draw; receive ~ 22. to add; calculate; charge; compound ~ 23. compound; simple ~ 24. ~ accrues (to an account) 25. ~ on (~ on a loan; six percent ~ is paid on all accounts) 26. at a certain (rate of) ~ (at six percent ~) ['share'] 27. to own an ~ (in a business) 28. a half ~ (see also **interests**)

interest II *v.* 1. to ~ greatly, very much 2. (D; tr.) to ~ in (could I ~ you in this project?)

interested *adj.* 1. deeply, greatly, highly, keenly, very much ~ 2. ~ in (we are ~ in politics) 3. ~ to + inf. (you will be ~ to know that an agreement has been reached)

interesting *adj.* 1. highly ~ 2. ~ for; to 3. ~ to + inf. (he's ~ to watch = it's ~ to watch him) 4. ~ that + clause (it's ~ that the incident was not reported in the newspapers)

interests *n.* ['stakes, investments'] 1. to have ~ (to have ~ throughout the world) 2. to advance, further, promote one's ~ 3. to defend, guard, look after, protect one's ~ 4. to serve smb.'s ~ (it serves their ~ to have stability in the area) 5. far-flung; international; worldwide ~ 6. ~ clash; coincide ['groups having a common concern'] 7. banking; business, commercial; competing; controlling; shipping; special; steel; vested ~

interface I *n.* an ~ between; with

interface II *v.* (D; intr., tr.) to ~ with (to ~ a machine with a computer)

interfere *v.* (D; intr.) to ~ in; with USAGE NOTE: In BE, *to interfere with smb.* often means 'to molest smb. sexually'.

interference *n.* 1. to brook no ~ 2. unwarranted ~ 3. ~ in, with 4. (misc.) (esp. Am. football) to run ~ for

interim *n.* in the ~

interject *v.* (D; tr.) to ~ into

interjection *n.* an ~ into (the ~ of new issues into a campaign)

interlace *v.* (d; tr.) to ~ with

interlard *v.* (formal) (d; tr.) to ~ with (to ~ a speech with local expressions)

interlibrary loan *n.* to borrow, get a book on/ through ~

interlude *n.* 1. a romantic ~ 2. a musical ~

intermarriage *n.* ~ between, with

intermarry *v.* (D; intr.) to ~ with (to ~ with the local population)

intermediary *n.* an ~ between (an ~ between the warring groups)

intermingle *v.* (d; intr.) to ~ with (to ~ with the crowd)

intermission *n.* an ~ between USAGE NOTE: In AE, *intermission* has the meaning 'pause between parts of a theatrical performance'. In BE, *interval* is used in this meaning.

internship *n.* (AE) to serve one's ~

interplay *n.* ~ among, between

interpolate *v.* (D; tr.) to ~ into

interpose *v.* (D; refl., tr.) to ~ among, between

interpret *v.* 1. (B) I had to ~ the passage to them 2. (d; tr.) to ~ as (they ~ed his response as an admission of guilt) 3. (D; intr.) to ~ for (to ~ for foreign visitors)

interpretation *n.* 1. to make an ~ 2. a free, liberal, loose; strict ~ (of the law)

interpreter *n.* 1. to serve (smb.) as an ~ 2. a conference; court; simultaneous ~

interpreting *n.* conference; simultaneous ~

interrogation *n.* to conduct an ~

interrogator *n.* 1. to serve as an ~ 2. a prisoner-of-war ~

interrogatory *n.* (legal) to file; serve an ~

intersection *n.* 1. a busy; dangerous ~ 2. at an ~

intersperse *v.* (P; tr.) to ~ anecdotes throughout a speech

intertwine *v.* (D; intr.) to ~ with

interval *n.* ['space of time between events'] 1. a brief, short; irregular; regular ~ 2. a lucid ~ 3. at a certain ~ (at regular ~s) ['distance'] ['gap'] 4. to maintain an ~ (the proper ~ should be maintained between vehicles) 5. an ~ between (see the Usage Note for **intermission**)

intervene *v.* 1. (D; intr.) to ~ between 2. (D; intr.) to ~ in; with (to ~ in smb.'s affairs; to ~ with the authorities)

intervention *n.* 1. armed, military; government ~ 2. nursing; surgical ~ 3. divine ~

interview I *n.* 1. to conduct an ~ 2. to give, grant an ~ 3. an exclusive; job; personal; taped; telephone; television, TV ~ 4. an ~ for; with (an ~ with the personnel director for a job)

interview II *v.* (D; tr.) to ~ for (to ~ smb. for a job)

interwoven *adj.* ~ with

intestine *n.* the large; small ~

intimacy *n.* ~ between; with

intimate I *adj.* ~ with

intimate II *v.* 1. (B) she ~d her wishes to us 2. (L; to) they ~d (to us) that an agreement would be worked out soon 3. (Q) they would not ~ how the problem could be solved

intimation *n.* 1. to give an ~ 2. ~ that + clause (there was no ~ that she would retire)

intimidate *v.* (D; tr.) to ~ into (to ~ smb. into doing smt.)

intolerable *adj.* 1. ~ to 2. ~ to + inf. (it's ~ to allow hardened criminals to roam our streets) 3. ~ that + clause (it is ~ that such excesses are allowed)

intolerance *n.* ['lack of tolerance'] 1. to display, show ~ 2. to stir up ~ against 3. racial; religious ~ ['sensitivity'] 4. ~ to (drugs)

intolerant *adj.* ~ of

intonation *n.* a falling; rising ~

intoxication *n.* a state of ~

intransigence *n.* ~ about

intransigent *adj.* ~ about

intrigue I *n.* 1. to carry on, engage in (an) ~ 2. high; petty ~ 3. a hotbed; web of ~

intrigue II *v.* (d; intr.) to ~ against; with (to ~ against the government)

intrinsic *adj.* ~ in, to

introduce *v.* 1. (B) she ~d me to her friends 2. (D; tr.) to ~ into (to ~ new methods into an industry) 3. (d; tr.) to ~ to (to ~ students to the elements of computer science)

introduction *n.* 1. to make an ~ 2. to serve as an ~ 3. a formal ~ 4. an ~ into, to (an ~ to a book) 5. (misc.) a letter of ~

introductory *adj.* (formal) ~ to

intrude *v.* 1. (D; intr.) to ~ into 2. (D; intr.) to ~ on, upon (to ~ on smb.'s privacy)

intrusion *n.* 1. to make an ~ 2. an unwarranted; unwelcome ~ 3. an ~ into (to make an ~ into enemy territory) 4. an ~ on (an ~ on my time) 5. (misc.) pardon my ~

intuition *n.* by ~ (she sensed what was wrong by ~)

inure *v.* (formal) (d; tr.) to ~ to (to ~ smb. to hardship; ~d to danger)

invalid *v.* (BE) 1. (d; tr.) to ~ home 2. (c; tr.) to ~ out of (to be ~ed out of the army)

invaluable *adj.* ~ to

invasion *n.* 1. to carry out; launch an ~ 2. to repel, repulse an ~

invective *n.* 1. to hurl ~/~s at 2. bitter; coarse, vulgar ~ 3. a stream, torrent of ~/~s 4. ~ against

inveigh *v.* (formal) (d; intr.) to ~ against

inveigle *v.* (d; tr.) to ~ into; out of (to ~ smb. into doing smt.)

invention *n.* 1. to come up with an ~ 2. to patent, register an ~ 3. to market, promote an ~ 4. an ingenious ~

inventory *n.* 1. to make an ~ (of); to take (an) ~ (of) 2. to reduce (an) ~ (by having a sale) 3. an annual ~ 4. closed for ~

invest *v.* 1. ('to place money') to ~ heavily 2. (D; intr., tr.) ('to place money') to ~ in (to ~ heavily in municipal bonds; to ~ surplus funds in stocks) 3. (formal) (d; tr.) ('to entrust') to ~ with (to ~ smb. with authority)

invested *adj.* (formal) (cannot stand alone) ~ with (~ with broad powers)

investigation *n.* 1. to carry out, conduct, make; launch an ~ 2. a cursory, perfunctory; impartial; painstaking, thorough ~ 3. a criminal; police ~ 4. an ~ into, of (to launch an ~ into charges of corruption) 5. on, upon ~ (on closer ~ we discovered the cause of the fire) 6. under ~ (the incident is under ~)

investigator *n.* a government; private ~

investment *n.* 1. to make an ~ 2. a bad, poor; good, lucrative, profitable; solid, sound ~ 3. heavy; long-term; overseas ~s 4. an ~ in (~ in oil stocks)

investor *n.* a heavy; large; small; speculative ~

invigorating *adj.* ~ to + inf. (it's ~ to swim in the sea)

invisible *adj.* ~ to (~ to the naked eye)

invitation *n.* 1. to extend, issue, send an ~ 2. to send out ~s 3. to decline, spurn an ~ 4. a cordial; kind; formal; informal ~ 5. an ~ to a party) 6. an ~ to + inf. (she has received an ~ to attend the reception) 7. by ~ (participation is by ~ only)

invite *v.* 1. to ~ cordially (everyone is cordially ~d) 2. (D; tr.) to ~ to (we ~d them to our party) 3. (H) they ~d us to participate

invite over *v.* (D; tr.) to ~ for; to (we ~d them over to our place for a drink)

invocation *n.* to offer, pronounce the ~

invoice *n.* 1. to issue; send an ~ 2. a duplicate; original ~

involve *v.* 1. (D; tr.) to ~ in; with (to ~ smb. in a project; we were ~d with the technical details) 2. (K) that job would ~ my traveling a great deal

involved *adj.* 1. emotionally ~ with 2. ~ in; with (I got her ~ in the planning; to become ~ with smb.)
involvement *n.* 1. an emotional ~ 2. ~ in; with
invulnerable *adj.* ~ to
inward *adv.* ~ bound
IQ *n.* 1. to test smb.'s ~ 2. an average, normal; high; low ~ 3. an ~ of (an ~ of one hundred; the ~ of a genius) 4. (misc.) an ~ test
irate *adj.* ~ about
ire *n.* to arouse, rouse smb.'s ~
irk *v.* (R) it ~s her to have to get up so early; it ~s me that they get all the credit
irksome *adj.* (formal) ~ to + inf. (it is ~ to listen to his constant complaints)
iron *n.* ['type of metal'] 1. to mine; smelt ~ 2. cast; corrugated; crude; pig; scrap; wrought ~ ['device for pressing clothes'] 3. to plug in an ~ 4. to unplug an ~ 5. an electric; steam ~ ['rodlike device used for branding'] 6. a branding ~ ['tool used to apply solder'] 7. a soldering ~ ['instrument used to curl hair'] 8. a curling ~ ['hook'] 9. a climbing; grappling ~ ['utensil for making waffles'] 10. a waffle ~
ironic, ironical *adj.* ~ that + clause (it's ~ that the weakest student in mathematics was elected class treasurer)
ironing *n.* to do the ~
irons *n.* ['shackles'] 1. to put smb. into ~ 2. in ~
irony *n.* 1. bitter ~ 2. dramatic, tragic ~ 3. a touch of ~ 4. an ~ that + clause (it was a tragic ~ that he was killed in a traffic accident after the war)
irrational *adj.* ~ to + inf. (it was ~ to react in that manner)
irregular *adj.* grossly, highly ~
irregularity *n.* 1. a gross ~ 2. ~ in (an ~ in the accounts)
irrelevant *adj.* 1. ~ to 2. ~ to + inf. (it's ~ to cite such outdated evidence) 3. ~ that + clause (it's ~ that she was out of town)
irrespective *adj.* ~ of
irresponsible *adj.* ~ to + inf. (it was ~ of him to speak to reporters)
irritant *n.* an ~ to
irritate *v.* 1. to ~ greatly, very much 2. (R) it ~d me (to learn) that she had been promoted
irritated *adj.* 1. ~ at (~ at being awakened so early) 2. ~ to + inf. (he was ~ to see her dancing with someone else)

irritating *adj.* 1. ~ to + inf. (it's ~ to see them waste so much time) 2. ~ that + clause (it's ~ that he got off so easy)
irritation *n.* 1. to express; feel ~ 2. ~ at, with 3. ~ that + clause (he could not hide his ~ that he had not been invited)
irrupt *v.* (D; intr.) to ~ in; into (to ~ in a frenzied demonstration)
irruption *n.* an ~ into
island *n.* 1. a deserted, uninhabited; tropical ~ 2. a safety (AE), traffic ~ 3. on an ~
isolate *v.* (D; tr.) to ~ from
isolated *adj.* ~ from
isotope *n.* a radioactive ~
issue I *n.* ['number of a journal'] 1. to bring out, publish an ~ 2. a back; current ~ 3. an ~ comes out, is published ['question'] 4. to bring up, raise an ~ 5. to address; face; straddle an ~ 6. to settle an ~ 7. a burning; collateral, side; dead; divisive; moral; political; sensitive; substantive ~ 8. at ~ (the point at ~) 9. (misc.) to force the ~; to take ~ with smb. on smt. ('to disagree with smb. about smt.') ['progeny'] 10. without ~ (to die without ~)
issue II *v.* 1. (B) ('to distribute') the army ~d new rifles to the troops 2. (esp. BE) (d; intr.) ('to come') to ~ from (blood ~d from the wound; smoke ~d from the chimneys) 3. (rare) (BE) (d; tr.) to ~ with (the school ~d the pupils with new textbooks)
it *pronoun* of ~ (they made a mess of ~; to have had a hard time of ~)
itch I *n.* ['itchy feeling'] 1. to relieve an ~ 2. ['wish'] (colloq.) an ~ to + inf. (she has an ~ to go out west)
itch II *v.* (colloq.) (d; intr.) ('to yearn') to ~ for (to ~ for a fight)
itching I *adj.* (colloq.) (cannot stand alone) 1. ~ for (he's ~ for a fight) 2. ~ to + inf. (he's ~ to get into action)
itching II *n.* 1. to cause ~ 2. to alleviate, relieve (the) ~
item *n.* 1. a luxury ~ 2. a budget ~ 3. a collector's ~ (BE has *collector's piece*) 4. ~ by ~ (she answered all objections ~ by ~)
itinerary *n.* 1. to plan (out), prepare an ~ 2. a tentative ~ 3. according to an ~
ivy *n.* 1. ~ climbs 2. (misc.) (US) poison ~

J

jab I *n.* ['short punch'] 1. to throw a ~ 2. a left; right ~ 3. a ~ to (a left ~ to the head)

jab II *v.* 1. (D; intr.) to ~ at (he ~bed at the other boxer with his left) 2. (D; tr.) to ~ in (she ~bed me in the ribs)

jabber *v.* (D; intr.) to ~ about

jack *n.* (esp. BE) (colloq.) ['human being'] every man ~

jackal *n.* a pack of ~s

jackass *n.* a damned; stupid ~

jacket *n.* ['garment for the upper body'] 1. a dinner; field; flak; life; pea; smoking; sport (AE), sports ~ ['cover'] 2. (AE) a record ~ 3. a dust ~ ('cover for a book') ['potato skin'] 4. to cook potatoes in their ~s

jackpot *n.* to hit the ~ (also fig.)

jacks *n.* to play (a game of) ~

jag *n.* (colloq.) ['state of intoxication'] 1. to have a ~ on ['spell'] 2. a crying ~

jail *n.* 1. to go to ~ (he went to ~ for his crime) 2. to be sent to ~ (she was sent to ~ for shoplifting) 3. to serve time in ~ 4. to break ~; to break out of ~

jailbreak *n.* 1. to attempt; make a ~ 2. a daring; mass ~

jam I *n.* ['food made by boiling fruit with sugar'] 1. to spread ~ (on bread) 2. apricot; grape; peach; plum; red raspberry; strawberry ~

jam II *n.* ['blockage'] 1. a log; traffic ~ ['difficult situation'] 2. (to be) in a ~

jam III *v.* 1. to ~ full 2. (D; tr.) to ~ in (she ~med her fingers in the door; or: she got her fingers ~med in the door) 3. (d; intr., tr.) to ~ into (they all tried to ~ into the small room; he ~med everything into one suitcase) 4. (d; tr.) to ~ on (he ~med a hat on his head) 5. (D; tr.) to ~ with (the street was ~med with traffic) 6. (N; used with an adjective) to ~ smt. full

jamboree *n.* a boy scout; girl scout ~

jam-packed *adj.* ~ with

jangle *v.* (D; intr.) to ~ on ('to irritate') (to ~ on smb.'s nerves)

jar I *n.* ['jolt'] 1. to feel a ~ 2. a slight ~

jar II *v.* 1. (d; intr.) to ~ against ('to strike') (I ~red against the table) 2. (d; intr.) to ~ on ('to irritate') (the noise ~red on my nerves) 3. (esp. BE) (d; intr.) ('to clash') to ~ with 4. (N; used with an adjective) to ~ a tooth loose

jar III *n.* ['container'] 1. a biscuit (BE), cookie (AE) ~ 2. an earthenware; glass; Mason (esp. AE); plastic; stone ~

jargon *n.* 1. to speak in, use ~ 2. professional, technical, trade ~

jaunt *n.* ['pleasure trip'] 1. to go on a ~ 2. a ~ through; to

javelin *n.* to hurl, throw a ~

jaw I *n.* 1. to move one's ~ (his ~ was broken and he could not move it) 2. to set one's ~ (she set her ~ in determination) 3. to dislocate one's ~ 4. the lower; upper ~ 5. (misc.) snatched from the ~s of death

jaw II *v.* (colloq.) (D; intr.) ('to speak angrily') to ~ about; at

jealous *adj.* 1. bitterly, blindly, violently ~ 2. ~ of

jealousy *n.* 1. to arouse ~ 2. to feel ~ 3. bitter, blind; fierce; groundless, unfounded; petty ~ 4. interservice; professional ~ 5. a fit of ~ 6. ~ towards

jeans *n.* blue (AE); designer ~

jeer *v.* (D; intr.) to ~ at

jelly *n.* ['food made from boiled fruit juice'] apple; blackberry; cherry; currant; grape; mint; peach plum; quince; strawberry ~

jeopardy *n.* 1. to place, put (smb.) in ~ 2. ('legal') double ~ 3. in ~ (our lives were in ~)

jerk *n.* ['sudden movement'] with a ~ (the train started with a ~)

jest I *n.* (formal) 1. an idle ~ 2. in ~ (that was said in ~)

jest II *v.* (formal) (D; intr.) to ~ about; with

jester *n.* a court ~

jet I *n.* to fly, pilot a ~ (see **airplane 1, 2**)

jet II *v.* (d; intr.) ('to fly by jet') to ~ from; to (to ~ to London)

jewel *n.* 1. to mount a ~ 2. crown; precious; priceless ~s

jewelry, jewellery *n.* antique; costume; imitation; junk; precious ~

jibe *v.* (colloq.) (esp. AE) (D; intr.) to ~ with (his story doesn't ~ with yours)

jiffy *n.* (colloq.) ['short time'] in a ~

jig *n.* to dance, do a ~

jigsaw (BE) see **jigsaw puzzle**

jigsaw puzzle *n.* (AE) to do, put together a ~

jingle *n.* 1. to compose, make up a ~ 2. an advertising; rhyming ~

jinx *n.* to put a ~ on smb.

jitters *n.* (colloq.) ['panic'] 1. to have the ~ 2. to give smb. the ~ 3. a case of the ~ (she had a bad case of the ~)

job *n.* ['task'] 1. to do a ~ 2. to take on a ~ 3. a backbreaking; difficult, hard ~ 4. odd ~s (he does odd ~s) 5. a ~ to + inf. (it was quite a ~ to find him = it was quite a ~ finding him = we had quite a ~ finding him) ['employment'] 6. to get, land, take a ~ 7. to hunt for, look for a ~ 8. to hold, hold down a ~ 9. to give up, quit; lose a ~ 10. a cushy, easy, soft; demanding; menial; steady ~ 11. a desk; full-time; part-time; summer ~ 12. at a ~ (she was working at two ~s) 13. on the ~ (he is always on the ~) (also fig.) ['criminal act'] (colloq.) 14. to do, pull a ~ 15. an inside ~ ['misc.'] 16. a snow ~ (AE) ('deceit'); to do a hatchet ~ on smb. ('to criticize smb. harshly'); a put-up ~ ('a prearranged scheme'); he really did a ~ on his opponent ('he inflicted a crushing defeat on his opponent') USAGE NOTE: In colloq. BE, *on the job* can also mean 'having sex'.

jockey I *n.* a disc (BE), disk (AE) ~
jockey II *v.* 1. (D; intr.) to ~ for (to ~ for position) 2. (d; tr.) to ~ into (to ~ smb. into position)
jogging *n.* to go in for ~
join *v.* 1. (D; tr.) to ~ for (would you ~ us for a drink?) 2. (d; intr.) to ~ in (they all ~ed in singing the national anthem) 3. (D; tr.) to ~ in (to ~ smb. in a drink) 4. (D; tr.) to ~ to, with (to ~ one wire to another; they all ~ed hands with each other; to ~ forces with one's allies) 5. (D; intr.) to ~ with (we must ~ with them in fighting tyranny)
join in *v.* 1. (D; intr.) to ~ as (she ~ed in as a volunteer) 2. (D; intr.) to ~ with
joint *n.* 1. (med.) to dislocate a ~ 2. (anatomical) an elbow; hip; knee; shoulder ~ 3. (technical) a ball-and-socket; mortise; riveted; toggle; universal; welded ~ 4. (misc.) (slang) to case a ~ ('to inspect a place before robbing it') (also fig.)
join up *v.* (D; intr.) to ~ with (we'll ~ with you in the next town)
joke I *n.* 1. to crack, tell a ~ 2. to ad-lib a ~ 3. to play a ~ on 4. to carry a ~ too far 5. to take a ~ (he can't take a ~) 6. to make a ~ of smt. 7. a clean; coarse, crude; dirty, obscene, off-color, smutty; old, stale; practical; sick ~ 8. the butt, object of a ~ 9. a ~ about 10. (colloq.) no ~ to + inf. (it's no ~ to oppose smb. like her = it's no ~ opposing smb. like her) 11. (misc.) as a ~; to turn smt. into a ~; the ~ was on me
joke II *v.* (D; intr.) to ~ about; with (I was ~ing with her about her latest escapade)
joker *n.* 1. a practical ~ 2. (cards) ~s wild; a ~ in the pack (also fig.)
joking *n.* ~ aside
jolt I *n.* ['shock'] 1. a severe ~ 2. a ~ to (it was a ~ to her pride)
jolt II *v.* (D; tr.) to ~ out of (she was finally ~ed out of her depression)
jostle *v.* 1. (d; intr.) to ~ for (to ~ for position) 2. (d; intr.) to ~ with (the children were ~ling with each other)
journal *n.* ['diary'] 1. to keep a ~ ['magazine'] 2. to publish, put out a ~ 3. to edit a ~ 4. to subscribe to, take (esp. BE; old-fashioned) a ~ 5. a professional; scholarly ~
journalism *n.* advocacy; yellow ~
journey I *n.* 1. to go on, make, set out on, undertake a ~ 2. a long; pleasant; safe; sentimental; tiring ~ (we had a pleasant ~) 3. a round-the-world ~ 4. a ~ into; through; to
journey II *v.* (d; intr.) to ~ from; to
jowls *n.* heavy ~
joy *n.* 1. to express; feel ~ 2. to find, take ~ 3. to radiate ~ 4. boundless, great, indescribable, ineffable, overwhelming, sheer, unbounded, unbridled ~ 5. ~ in (they found ~ in helping others) 6. a ~ to + inf. (it was a ~ to behold) 7. ~ that + clause (she could not hide her ~ that everyone was safe) 8. for, with ~ (to dance with ~)
joyful *adj.* ~ about, over
joyride *n.* to go for, on a ~
jubilant *adj.* ~ about, at, over (they were ~ over their victory)
jubilation *n.* 1. to express; feel ~ 2. ~ about, at,
over (~ over a victory)
jubilee *n.* a diamond; golden; silver ~
Judaism *n.* Conservative; Liberal (BE), Progressive (BE); Orthodox; Reform ~ USAGE NOTE: *Liberal Judaism* and *Progressive Judaism* in Great Britain are approximately equivalent to *Reform Judaism* in North America. *Reform Judaism* in Great Britain is approximately equivalent to *Conservative Judaism* in North America.
judge I *n.* 1. a fair, impartial; harsh, severe; lenient ~ 2. a hanging ('severe') ~ 3. an administrative; circuit; district; itinerant; trial ~ 4. (sports) a field ~ 5. (mil.) a ~ advocate; a ~ advocate general
judge II *v.* 1. to ~ fairly, impartially; harshly, severely, sternly; leniently 2. (d; intr.) to ~ by, from (to ~ by appearances; to ~ from the facts) 3. (colloq.) (L) we ~ that she is the best candidate 4. (M) I ~ her to be about twenty years old 5. (Q) we cannot ~ whether she is guilty
judgment, judgement *n.* 1. to display, exercise, show ~ (she always exercises good ~) 2. to form, make a ~ 3. to hand down, pass, pronounce, render ~ on 4. to sit in ~ on 5. to reserve ~ 6. good; impaired; poor; sober; sound ~ (to display poor ~) 7. a value ~ 8. a ~ against; for 9. a ~ that + clause (I repeat my ~ that he was to blame) 10. in smb.'s ~ (in my ~, she is not guilty)
judiciary *n.* the federal (US) ~
judicious *adj.* (formal) ~ to + inf. (it would be ~ to remain silent)
jugular *n.* ['jugular vein'] to go for the ~ (colloq.) ('to attempt to finish off')
juice *n.* 1. digestive, gastric ~s 2. apple; fruit; grapefruit; lemon; orange; tomato; vegetable ~
jump I *n.* 1. to take a ~ (on horseback) 2. to make a ~ (with a parachute) 3. (sports) the broad (AE); long; high; ski; triple ~ 4. (sports) a water ~ 5. a delayed (parachute) ~ 6. (basketball) the center ~ 7. a quantum ~ 8. a ~ from; to 9. (misc.) to get the ~ on smb. ('to anticipate smb.')
jump II *v.* 1. (d; intr.) to ~ across (to ~ across a stream) 2. (d; intr.) to ~ at ('to be eager for') (she ~ed at the chance) 3. (d; intr.) to ~ for, with (to ~ for joy) 4. (d; intr.) to ~ from, off (he ~ed off the roof) 5. (d; intr.) to ~ from; to (to ~ from one topic to another) 6. (d; intr.) ('to leap') to ~ into; onto (the child ~ed into bed; the dog ~ed onto the sofa) 7. (d; intr.) to ~ on ('to attack') (he ~ed on his opponent) 8. (d; intr.) to ~ out of (to ~ out of a window) 9. (d; intr.) to ~ over (to ~ over a fence) 10. (d; intr.) to ~ to (to ~ to one's feet) 11. (d; intr.) ('to rush') to ~ to (to ~ to conclusions; to ~ to smb.'s defense) 12. (misc.) to ~ down smb.'s throat ('to berate smb.'); to ~ up and down (for joy)
jump clear *v.* (D; intr.) to ~ of (she ~ed clear of the wreckage)
jump down *v.* (D; intr.) to ~ from (he ~ed down from the roof)
jump off *v.* (d; intr.) to ~ to (she ~ed off to a good start)
jump up *v.* 1. (D; intr.) to ~ from (to ~ from one's seat) 2. (D; intr.) to ~ on, onto (to ~ onto the

table)
jumpy *adj.* (colloq.) ['nervous'] ~ about
juncture *n.* 1. (ling.) close; open; terminal ~ 2. (misc.) at this ~ ('in this situation')
jungle *n.* ['tropical forest'] 1. a dense; tropical ~ ['dangerous place'] 2. an asphalt, concrete; blackboard ~
junior I *adj.* 1. ~ in (~ in rank) 2. ~ to (he is ~ to me by three years)
junior II *n.* ~ by (he is my ~ by four years)
junket *n.* ['pleasure trip'] 1. to go on a ~ 2. a fact-finding ~ 3. a ~ to (the legislators went on a ~ to Hawaii)
junta *n.* 1. a military; revolutionary; ruling ~ 2. by ~ (government by ~)
jurisdiction *n.* 1. to have ~ 2. local ~ 3. original; primary ~ (a court of original ~) 4. ~ over (to have ~ over a case) 5. outside; under; within a ~ (that case is under the ~ of this court)
jurisprudence *n.* analytical; medical ~
juror *n.* 1. to challenge a (prospective) ~ 2. an alternate; prospective ~
jury *n.* 1. to empanel, swear in a ~ 2. to charge, instruct; sequester a ~ (the judge charged the ~) 3. to dismiss a ~ 4. to fix ('corrupt') a ~ 5. to serve on a ~ 6. a hung ('deadlocked') ~ 7. a grand; petit; trial ~ 8. a blue-ribbon ('special') ~ 9. a ~ comes to, reaches a verdict 10. (misc.) the ~ is still out ('the jury is still deliberating'); the ~ is still out

on him (AE) ('a final decision has still not been reached concerning him'); (a) trial by ~
jury trial *n.* to waive a ~
just *adj.* ~ to, towards
justice *n.* ['rules of law'] ['administration of law'] 1. to administer, dispense, mete out, render ~ 2. to obstruct ~ 3. to pervert ~ 4. divine; frontier (US); poetic; summary ~ 5. ~ prevails 6. a miscarriage; travesty of ~ 7. (misc.) to bring (a criminal) to ~; to temper ~ with mercy ['recognition appreciation'] 8. to do ~ to (her portrait does not do ~ to her) 9. in ~ to ['judge'] 10. an associate (esp. US); chief (esp. US) ~; Lord Chief Justice (GB); a supreme court ~ ['magistrate'] 11. a traffic court ~; a ~ of the peace USAGE NOTE: The plural of *Lord Chief Justice* is *Lords Chief Justice*.
justification *n.* to find ~ for
justified *adj.* ~ in (we are ~ in assuming that she will attend)
justify *v.* 1. (B) can you ~ your actions to me? 2. (G) nothing ~fies cheating on an exam 3. (K) what ~fied her being late?
jut out *v.* 1. (D; intr.) to ~ from; over (the balcony ~s out over the swimming pool) 2. (D; intr.) to ~ into (to ~ into the sea)
juxtapose *v.* (D; tr.) to ~ with
juxtaposed *adj.* ~ with
juxtaposition *n.* in ~ with

K

kangaroo *n.* 1. ~s hop, leap 2. (Australian) a mob of ~s

kayak *n.* to paddle a ~

keel *n.* on an even ~ ('well-balanced')

keel over *v.* (D; intr.) to ~ from (to ~ from the heat)

keen *adj.* ['very interested'] (esp. BE) 1. ~ on (she's ~ on music; he's ~ on her) ['eager'] (BE) 2. ~ to + inf. (she is ~ to pass the examination)

keep I *n.* ['maintenance'] to earn one's ~

keep II *v.* 1. (D; tr.) ('to have') to ~ about (esp. BE), around (do you ~ a screwdriver around the house?) 2. (d; intr.) to ~ after ('to keep persuading') (~ after the children: they are still too untidy) 3. (d; tr.) to ~ at ('to hold') (she kept them at their studies) 4. (d; tr.) ('to hold') to ~ for (the librarian will ~ the book for you) 5. (d; intr., refl.) to ~ from ('to refrain') (she could not ~ from talking) 6. (d; tr.) ('to conceal') to ~ from (to ~ a secret from smb.) 7. (d; tr.) ('to hold back'); ('to prevent') to ~ from (the rain kept us from going; don't ~ her from her work) 8. (d; intr.) to ~ off (~ off the grass) 9. (d; tr.) ('to hold') to ~ off (~ the children off the street) 10. (d; intr.) ('to remain') to ~ out of (~ out of my way; I kept out of their quarrel) 11. (d; tr.) ('to hold') to ~ out of (~ the guests out of the house) 12. (d; intr.) ('to be confined') to ~ to (she kept to her room) 13. (d; intr.) ('to continue') to ~ to (~ to the right) 14. (D; tr.) ('to reserve') to ~ to (to ~ a secret to oneself) 15. (G) ('to continue') she kept reading 16. (J) ('to cause') he kept us waiting 17. (N; used with an adjective, noun, past participle) ('to maintain'); ('to hold') she kept us busy; they kept him prisoner; the fire kept us warm; she kept the children amused with her stories 18. (P; intr., tr.) ('to continue'); ('to hold') to ~ right; to ~ a car in a garage 19. (s) ('to remain') to ~ quiet; to ~ warm

keep abreast *v.* 1. (d; intr.) ('to be informed') to ~ of (she kept abreast of the news) 2. (D; tr.) ('to inform') to ~ of (they kept me abreast of the latest developments)

keep after *v.* (H) ('to keep urging') they kept after me to buy a new car

keep ahead *v.* (D; intr.) ('to remain in front') to ~ of (he kept ahead of his rivals)

keep aloof *v.* (D; intr.) to ~ from ('to remain at a distance from') (she kept aloof from the others)

keep away *v.* (D; intr., tr.) to ~ from (he kept away from us; she kept the dogs away from the children)

keep back *v.* (D; tr.) to ~ from (they kept her back from the crowd)

keep clear *v.* (D; intr., tr.) to ~ of (~ of him; they kept the roads clear of snow)

keeping *n.* ['care'] 1. in ~ (in safe ~) ['conformity'] 2. in ~ with (in ~ with regulations) 3. out of ~ with

keep on *v.* (G) ('to continue') she kept on working

keep up *v.* (D; intr.) to ~ with ('to remain on the same level with') (I ran to ~ with the others; she worked hard to ~ with the other students)

keg *n.* a powder ~

kelter (BE) see **kilter**

ken *n.* ['understanding'] beyond; within one's ~

kettle *n.* 1. to put a ~ up to boil 2. a teakettle 3. a ~ boils; whistles 4. (misc.) (colloq.) a fine ~ of fish ('a mess')

kettledrum *n.* to play a ~

key I *n.* ['device for turning the bolt of a door'] 1. to duplicate; make a ~ 2. to insert; turn a ~ 3. to fit, match a ~ 4. a duplicate; master; skeleton ~ 5. ~s dangle (on a chain) 6. a bunch of ~s 7. a ~ to (a ~ to a door) ['solution'] 8. a ~ to (to hold the ~ to a mystery; a ~ to the exercises in a textbook) ['system of notes'] (mus.) 9. a high; low; major; minor ~ 10. in a (certain) ~ (played in the ~ of C) 11. off ~ ['button on a keyboard'] 12. to press, strike a ~ 13. to jam a ~ 14. to de-jam a ~ 15. (on a typewriter) a backspace; dead; de-jammer; shift ~ 16. (on a computer) a function, soft ~

key II *v.* see **keyed**

keyboard *n.* a standard ~

keyed *adj.* (esp. BE) (cannot stand alone) ~ to (~ to the needs of our armed forces; our plants are ~ to producing civilian aircraft)

keyed up *adj.* ['psychologically ready'] ~ for, over (~ for the big game)

keyhole *n.* to look through, peep through a ~

keypunch *n.* to operate a ~

keystone *n.* a ~ to (the ~ to success is hard work)

kibosh *n.* (colloq.) ['end'] to put the ~ on smt.

kick *n.* ['blow delivered with the foot'] 1. to give smb. a ~ 2. a nasty, vicious ~ 3. (soccer) a free; penalty ~ 4. a ~ in (a ~ in the groin) ['thrill'] (slang) 5. to get a ~ out of smt. ['strong effect'] (slang) 6. a ~ to (this vodka has a ~ to it)

kicks *n.* (colloq.) ['thrill'] for ~ (they did it for ~)

kid *v.* (colloq.) (D; tr.) ('to tease good-naturedly') to ~ about (they ~ded him about his paunch)

kid around *v.* (colloq.) (D; intr.) ('to fool') to ~ with

kid gloves *n.* to treat smb. with ~ ('to treat smb. with great deference or mildness')

kidney *n.* 1. to transplant a ~ 2. an artificial; floating ~

kill I *n.* 1. to make a ~ (the lion made the ~) 2. at the ~ (to be in at the ~) 3. (misc.) to go in for the ~

kill II *v.* 1. to ~ (smb.) outright 2. (usu. mil.) ~ed in action

killer *n.* ['murderer'] 1. a multiple, serial; psychopathic ~ 2. a ~ strikes

killing *n.* ['putting to death'] 1. (a) mercy ~ ['large profit'] (colloq.) 2. to make a ~

kilter *n.* ['order'] out of ~

kind I *adj.* 1. ~ of (that was very ~ of you) 2. ~

to (~ to animals) 3. ~ to + inf. (it was ~ of you to help us)

kind II *n.* ['sort'] 1. of a ~ (of all ~s; of several ~s; two of a ~) ['same manner'] 2. in ~ (to be paid back in ~; to respond in ~) ['goods'] 3. in ~ (to pay smb. back in ~) ['misc.'] (colloq.) 4. ~ of ('somewhat')

kindergarten *n.* to attend, go to ~

kindly *adv.* ['readily'] to take ~ to ('to accept readily')

kindness *n.* ['quality of being good, kind'] 1. to display, show ~ 2. human ~ 3. ~ to, towards 4. out of ~ (she did it out of ~) ['good, kind act'] 5. to do smb. a ~ 6. to repay, return a ~

king *n.* 1. to crown a ~ 2. to crown; proclaim smb. ~ 3. to depose, dethrone a ~ 4. (chess) to checkmate a ~ 5. a despotic; popular; strong; weak ~ 6. a ~ mounts a throne 7. a ~ abdicates (a throne) 8. (misc.) to toast the ~

kingdom *n.* the animal; mineral; plant, vegetable ~

king's evidence *n.* (BE) to turn ~ (see also **queen's evidence, state's evidence)**

kink *n.* ['imperfection'] to iron out the ~s

kinship *n.* to feel (a) ~ with smb.

kiosk *n.* a telephone ~ (BE; CE has *telephone booth)*

kiss I *n.* 1. to blow, throw; give (smb.) a ~ 2. to steal a ~ 3. a fervent, passionate; French; loving, tender ~ 4. a ~ on (a ~ on the cheek) 5. (misc.) the ~ of death

kiss II *v.* 1. to ~ passionately; tenderly 2. (D; tr.) to ~ on (she ~ed the baby on the cheek) 3. (O; can be used with one animate object) (she ~ed him goodnight)

kit *n.* ['equipment'] 1. a first-aid; instruction; mess; sewing; shaving; survival ~ ['clothing and equipment'] (BE) 2. camping; travelling ~ 3. (misc.) (mil.) a ~ bag

kitchen *n.* a field; soup ~

kite *n.* 1. to fly a ~ 2. (misc.) (AE; colloq.) go fly a ~! ('go away')

kith *n.* ['friends and relatives'] ~ and kin

kitty *n.* ['fund, pool'] in the ~ (how much is in the ~?)

knack *n.* ['skill'] 1. to get, have the ~ of smt. 2. an uncanny ~ 3. a ~ for (she has a ~ for getting into trouble) 4. a ~ to (there's a ~ to baking a good cake)

knee *n.* 1. to bend one's ~s 2. to dislocate; wrench one's ~ 3. a trick ('defective') ~ 4. (fig.) at smb.'s ~ (she learned the language at her mother's ~) 5. (usu. fig.) on bended ~ (s)

kneel *v.* (D; intr.) to ~ before

knell *n.* to sound, toll the ~

knife *n.* ['instrument for cutting'] 1. to plunge a ~ into smb. 2. to pull a ~ (on smb.) 3. to stab smb. with a ~ 4. to sharpen a ~ 5. a dull; sharp ~ 6. a bowie; boy-scout; bread; butcher (esp. AE), butcher's (esp. BE); clasp; electric; flic (BE; AE has *switchblade);* hunting; kitchen; paper (BE; AE has *letter opener);* paring; pocket; sheath; steak; trench ~ ['surgery'] 7. under the ~ (she was under the ~ for two hours)

knight *n.* to dub smb. ~

knighthood *n.* to bestow a ~ on, upon

knit *v.* (C) ~ a scarf for me; or: ~ me a scarf

knitting *n.* ['action of knitting'] 1. to do ~ ['one's own business'] (colloq.) (esp. AE) 2. to mind, stick to, tend to one's (own) ~

knob *n.* 1. to turn a ~ 2. a control ~

knock I *n.* ['thumping noise'] 1. engine ~ 2. a gentle; loud ~ 3. a ~ at, on (a ~ at/on the door) ['blow'] (colloq.) 4. hard ~s (she has taken some hard ~s in her life)

knock II *v.* 1. ('to rap') to ~ loudly 2. (colloq.) (d; intr.) ('to wander') to ~ about, around (he ~ed around the western part of the state for a few months) 3. (d; intr., tr.) ('to strike') to ~ against (she ~ed her head against the ceiling) 4. (D; intr.) ('to rap') to ~ at, on (to ~ at/on the door) 5. (d; tr.) ('to pound') to ~ into (to ~ some sense into smb.'s head) 6. (d; tr.) to ~ off ('to fell') (he ~ed me off my feet) 7. (d; tr.) ('to remove') to ~ out of (the impact ~ed two teeth out of his mouth) 8. (N; used with an adjective) ('to render by striking') to ~ smb. cold 9. (P; tr.) ('to render by striking') she ~ed me down 10. (misc.) ~ it off! (slang) ('stop!')

knock down *v.* (colloq.) (BE) (D; tr.) ('to persuade to reduce a price') to ~ to (I ~ed him down to ten pounds)

knockout *n.* 1. to score a ~ 2. a technical ~

knot *n.* 1. to tie; tighten a ~ 2. to loosen; undo, untie a ~ 3. the Gordian ~ (to cut the Gordian ~) 4. a loose; tight ~ 5. a bowline; granny; reef (esp. BE), square ~

know *v.* 1. (D; intr.) to ~ about, of (we knew about the incident) 2. (D; tr.) to ~ as (I knew her as a colleague) 3. (d; tr.) to ~ by (to ~ a poem by heart; to ~ smb. by name; I knew her by sight only) 4. (d; tr.) to ~ from ('to be able to differentiate') (the little child doesn't ~ a dog from a cat) 5. (H; only in the past and perfect) (I've known her to lose her temper) 6. (BE) (I; only in the past and perfect) I've known her lose her temper 7. (L) we ~ that they will come 8. (formal) (M) I ~ him to be a fool 9. (Q) she ~s how to drive 10. (misc.) to ~ smt. for a fact ('to know smt. to be true'); to ~ smt. by heart; to ~ smt. inside out = to ~ smt. backwards and forwards

know-how *n.* 1. the necessary ~ (he doesn't have the necessary ~ for the job) 2. the ~ to + inf. (she has the ~ to do the job)

knowing *n.* there is no ~ (what they will do)

knowledge *n.* 1. to acquire, accumulate, gain ~ 2. to demonstrate, display, show; flaunt, parade one's ~ (of a subject) 3. to communicate, disseminate; impart ~ 4. to absorb, assimilate, soak up ~ 5. (esp. BE) to bring smt. to smb.'s ~ 6. to brush up (on) one's ~ (of a subject) 7. to deny ~ (of smt.) 8. direct; extensive; inside, intimate; intuitive; profound, thorough; rudimentary, slight, superficial ~ 9. fluent; reading; speaking; working ~ (to have fluent ~ of English; to have reading/a reading ~ of several languages) 10. common ~ 11. carnal ~ (to have carnal ~ of) 12. ~ about, of 13. the ~ to + inf. (she has enough ~ about the subject to write a good book) 14. the ~ that + clause (it is common ~ that he has spent time in prison) 15. to smb.'s ~ (to my ~, she has never been here) 16. (esp. BE) to come to smb.'s ~ (it came to our ~ that she had left town) 17. (misc.) to the best of one's ~

knowledgeable *adj.* ~ about

known *adj.* 1. ~ as (~ as a patron of the arts) 2. ~ for (~ for being witty) 3. ~ to (~ to everyone) 4. (cannot stand alone) ~ to + inf. (he is ~ to frequent that bar; she is ~ to be a patron of the arts) 5. ~ that + clause (it is ~ that she has a criminal record)

knuckle *n.* 1. to rap smb. on, over the ~s 2. to crack one's ~s 3. brass ~s (AE; BE has *knuckle duster*)

knuckle down *v.* (D; intr.) to ~ to (to ~ to work)

knuckle under *v.* (D; intr.) ('to submit') to ~ to (to ~ to an aggressor)

kowtow *v.* (d; intr.) to ~ to ('to fawn over') (to ~ to the boss)

kudos *n.* (colloq.) ['praise'] 1. ~ to smb. for smt. (~ to our mayor for reducing taxes) 2. (BE) to get ~ for

L

label I *n*. ['sticker'] 1. to attach, put on, stick on; sew on a ~ 2. to bear, carry, have a ~ 3. to remove, take off a ~ 4. an adhesive, gummed ~ 5. a brand; designer; manufacturers'; union ~ (on a garment) ['descriptive phrase in a dictionary entry'] 6. to apply, use a ~ 7. a field; regional; stylistic; temporal; usage; warning ~ ['recording company'] 8. on, under a ~ (on what ~ was the song recorded?) ['misc.'] 9. to pin a ~ on smo. ('to assign smb. to a category')
label II *v*. 1. (d; tr.) to ~ as (he was ~ed as a delinquent) 2. (D; tr.) to ~ with (all items should be ~ed with a price) 3. (N; used with a noun) her story was ~ed a hoax
labor I **labour** *n*. ['work'] 1. to do, perform ~ 2. manual, physical; menial; painstaking; productive; sweated (BE), sweatshop; skilled; unskilled ~ 3. a division of ~ 4. (misc.) (a) division of ~; a ~ of love ['servitude'] 5. forced; hard; slave ~ (he got ten years at hard ~; democratic countries forbid forced ~; slave ~ has been outlawed) ['work force'] 6. child; migrant; organized; seasonal; skilled; unskilled ~ ['giving birth'] 7. to induce ~ 8. to go into ~ 9. difficult, prolonged, protracted; easy; false ~ 10. in ~ (she was in ~ for five hours)
labor II **labour** *v*. 1. (d; intr.) to ~ as (to ~ as a migrant worker) 2. (d; intr.) to ~ under (to ~ under a misconception)
laboratory *n*. a chemistry; crime; language; physics; research ~
laborer, labourer *n*. 1. a common; day; immigrant; itinerant; skilled; unskilled ~ 2. (BE) an agricultural labourer (CE has *farm worker*) 3. (BE) a casual labourer (AE has *transient worker*)
lace I *n*. delicate; exquisite; fine ~
lace II *v*. 1. (d; intr.) to ~ into ('to attack verbally') (they ~d into her for being late) 2. (D; tr.) to ~ with ('to add to') (they ~d the punch with rum)
laceration *n*. a deep; minor, superficial; severe ~
lack I *n*. for ~ of (for ~ of fuel, their planes were grounded)
lack II *v*. (D; intr.) to ~ for (formal) (we don't ~ for anything)
lacking *adj*. 1. badly, completely, sadly, totally, utterly ~ 2. ~ in (~ in common sense)
lacquer *n*. to apply ~
lad *n*. a young ~
ladder *n*. ['framework with rungs for climbing'] 1. to put up a ~ 2. to steady a ~ 3. to lean a ~ (against a wall) 4. to climb, go up, mount a ~ 5. to come down, descend a ~ 6. an aerial; extension; rope ~ 7. an accommodation ~ (over the side of a ship) ['unraveled stitches in a stocking'] (BE; AE has *runner*) 8. to get, have a ~ ['path'] 9. the ~ to success ['hierarchy'] 10. the social ~
laden *adj*. 1. fully ~ 2. ~ with
lady *n*. 1. a leading; young ~ 2. (esp. AE) the first ~ ('wife of the President or of a state governor') 3.

(esp. AE) a bag ~ ('a destitute woman living on the streets') 4. (misc.) the first ~ of the American theater
lag I *n*. 1. a cultural; time ~ 2. jet ~
lag II *v*. (D; intr.) to ~ behind; in (she ~ged behind the others)
lag behind *v*. (D; intr.) to ~ in (to ~ in one's work)
laid up *adj*. ~ with (~ with the flu)
lake *n*. 1. a deep; dry ~ 2. at, on a ~ (they have a summer bungalow at/on the ~)
lam I *n*. (slang) ['flight'] on the ~ (she took it on the ~) ('she fled')
lam II *v*. (slang) (d; intr.) to ~ into ('to attack')
lamb *n*. 1. a sacrificial ~ 2. ~s bleat 3. (misc.) as gentle as a ~; like a ~ to (the) slaughter
lambchops *n*. 1. to broil (AE), grill ~ 2. a rack of ~
lame *adj*. ~ in (~in one leg)
lament I *n*. 1. a bitter ~ 2. a ~ for
lament II *v*. 1. to ~ bitterly, deeply 2. (D; intr.) to ~ for, over
lamp *n*. 1. to plug in a ~ 2. to turn on a ~ 3. to light a ~ 4. to unplug a ~ 5. to turn off a ~ 6. an anglepoise (BE); electric; floor (AE), standard (BE); fluorescent; gooseneck; incandescent; neon; reading; safety ~; sunlamp; table; ultraviolet; wall ~ 7. a kerosene (AE), paraffin (BE); oil; spirit ~
lance *n*. to throw a ~
land I *n*. ['soil'] ['ground'] 1. to clear ~ (to clear ~ of trees and brush) 2. to cultivate; irrigate, redistribute ~ 3. arable; barren; fertile; grazing; marginal ~ 4. private; public ~ 5. a plot of ~ ['solid surface of the earth'] 6. to raise, sight ~ (from a ship) 7. to reach ~ 8. dry ~ 9. a body of ~ 10. by ~ (to travel by ~) 11. on (the) ~ ['rural area'] 12. to go back to the ~ ['country'] ['domain'] 13. one's native ~ 14. a promised ~ (we were in the promised ~) ['area'] 15. no man's ~ (in no man's ~) ['misc.'] 16. the Holy Land
land II *v*. (colloq.) (O) ('to punch') she ~ed him one in the eye
landfill *n*. a sanitary ~
landing *n*. ['coming down to earth'] 1. to make a ~ 2. a belly; bumpy; crash; emergency; forced; hard; instrument; pancake; safe; smooth; soft; three-point ~ 3. a parachute ~ ['level part of a staircase'] 4. on a ~
landing gear *n*. 1. to raise, retract a ~ 2. to let down, lower a ~ 3. a retractable ~
landlord *n*. an absentee; slum ~
landscape *n*. a beautiful; bleak, gloomy ~
lane *n*. 1. to shift ~s 2. to cross over into, get over into the other ~ 3. the fast (also fig.); inside; outside; passing; slow ~ 4. (BE) the nearside ('left'); offside ('right') ~ 5. an air; sea; shipping ~
language *n*. ['linguistic system of communication'] 1. to use a ~ 2. to plan; standardize a ~ 3. to learn, master a ~ 4. to speak (in) a ~ 5. to butcher, mu-

der; enrich; purify a ~ 6. (the) spoken; written ~ 7. one's native ~ 8. a foreign; international, world; national; official; second; universal ~ 9. colloquial, informal; formal; idiomatic; literary; standard; nontechnical; substandard; technical ~ 10. an ancient; artificial; classical; creolized; dead, extinct; living; modern; natural; sign; trade ~ 11. an agglutinative; inflecting; isolating; synthetic; tone ~ 12. an object, target; source ~ ['style of speaking or writing'] 13. abusive; bad, coarse, crude, dirty, foul, nasty, obscene, offensive, unprintable, vile, vulgar; rough, strong, vitupera- tive ~ 14. elegant; everyday, plain, simple; flow- ery; polite; rich ~ 15. children's; diplomatic ~ ['system of signs, symbols used by a computer'] 16. a computer, machine, programming ~ ['misc.'] 17. ~ acquisition; ~ maintenance

languish v. (D; intr.) (to ~ in prison)

lantern n. 1. to light a ~ 2. to shine a ~ on 3. a bat- tery-operated; kerosene (AE), paraffin (BE); propane ~ 4. a ~ flashes; gleams; shines

lap I n. ['complete circuit around a track'] 1. on a ~ (they are on the last ~) ['part of the body from the knees to waist of a sitting person'] 2. in, on smb.'s ~ (the little girl sat in her mother's ~) 3. (misc.) in the ~ of the gods ('with an uncertain future')

lap II v. (d; intr.) to ~ against (the waves ~ped against the sides of the boat)

lapse I n. 1. a momentary, temporary ~ (of mem- ory) 2. a linguistic ~ 3. a ~ in (a ~ in judgment)

lapse II v. (d; intr.) to ~ into (to ~ into a coma)

larceny n. 1. to commit ~ 2. aggravated; grand; petty; simple ~

lard n. to render ~

larder n. a full, well-stocked ~

large 1. at ~ ('uncaptured') (the prisoner was still at ~) 2. an assemblywoman at ~ ('an assemblywo- man who represents several or all districts') 3. by and ~ ('in general')

lark I n. ['prank'] for a ~ (he did it just for a ~)

lark II n. ['type of bird'] ~s sing, warble

lash v. 1. (d; intr.) to ~ against (the rain ~ed against the roof) 2. (d; intr.) to ~ at, into (the speakers ~ed into the government) 3. (d; tr.) to ~ into (to ~ a crowd into a fury)

lash back v. (D; intr.) to ~ at, against (to ~ at one's critics)

lash out v. (D; intr.) to ~ against, at

lasso n. 1. to throw a ~ 2. to catch with a ~

last I adj., adv. 1. to come in ~ (in a race) 2. the ~ to + inf. (she was the ~ to finish) 3. at ~; at long ~

last II n. to breathe one's ~

last III v. 1. (d; intr.) to ~ from; to, until (the meeting ~ed from one to three) 2. (P; intr.) the examination ~ed two hours; the food will ~ (us) (for) a week; the meeting ~ed (for) an hour

last rites n. to administer (the) ~

last word n. to get in, have the ~ (she had the ~ in the argument)

latch v. (colloq.) (d; intr.) to ~ onto (since he didn't know anyone else, he ~ed onto us)

late adj. 1. ~ for (she was ~ for class) 2. ~ in (we

were ~ in filing our tax return; I was ~ in getting up) 3. ~ with (they are ~ with the rent) 4. of ~ ('recently')

later adv. ~ on

lathe n. 1. to operate a ~ 2. a turret; vertical ~

lather n. ['sweating'] to work oneself into a ~

latitude n. ['freedom of action'] 1. to allow smb. ~ in (we are allowed quite a bit of ~ in selecting our subjects) ['distance measured in degrees north or south of the equator'] 2. high; low ~s 3. at a ~ (at a ~ of ten degrees north)

laudable adj. (formal) ~ to + inf. (it was ~ of you to help them)

laugh I n. 1. to get a ~ (the joke got a big ~) 2. to stifle, suppress a ~ 3. a belly; derisive; forced; hearty, loud; infectious; sardonic; subdued ~ 4. (misc.) to have the last ~ on smb.; to do smt. for a ~ (for ~s)

laugh II v. 1. (D; intr.) to ~ about ('to show one's amusement by laughing') (everyone ~ed about the incident) 2. (D; intr.) to ~ at ('to respond to smt. funny by laughter') (to ~ at a joke) 3. (D; intr.) to ~ at ('to show one's derision') (they ~ed at our efforts; she ~ed at our warnings) 4. (d; tr.) to ~ out of ('to drive out by laughter') (he was ~ed out of court) 5. (N; used with an adjective) he ~ed himself hoarse 6. (misc.) to ~ up one's sleeve ('to laugh secretly'); to burst out ~ing

laughingstock n. to make a ~ of smb.

laughter n. 1. to cause, provoke ~ 2. contagious, infectious; convulsive; derisive; hearty, loud, raucous, uproarious; sardonic; subdued ~ 3. a burst, fit, gale; ripple of ~ 4. (misc.) to double up with ~

launch v. 1. (D; tr.) ('to fire') to ~ against, at (the missiles were ~ed against enemy targets) 2. (d; intr.) to ~ into ('to begin') (to ~ into a tirade)

laundry n. ['clothes, linens that are to be washed or have been washed'] 1. to do the ~ 2. to dry; fold; iron the ~ 3. clean; dirty ~ ['establishment for washing clothes, linens'] 4. a self-service ~ 5. at, in a ~ (they work at a ~)

laurels n. to rest on one's ~

lava n. ~ flows

lavish I adj. ~ in, with (~ with praise; ~ in donat- ing money to charity)

lavish II v. (d; tr.) to ~ on (to ~ gifts on smb.)

law n. ['statute, regulation'] 1. to administer, apply, enforce a ~ 2. to adopt, enact, pass; draft; promulgate a ~ 3. to obey, observe a ~ 4. to inter- pret a ~ (courts interpret ~s) 5. to annul, repeal, revoke a ~; to declare a ~ unconstitutional (US) 6. to break, flout, violate a ~ 7. to challenge, test; cite; strike down a ~ (in the courts) 8. a fair, just; stringent; unfair ~ 9. a blue (US); dietary; ex post facto; lemon (US); shield (US); sunset (US); sun- shine (US); sus (GB); unwritten; zoning ~; the licensing ~s (GB) 10. a ~ against (there is no ~ against fishing) 11. a ~ that + clause (there is a ~ that all income must be reported) ['body of sta- tutes, regulations'] 12. to administer, apply, enforce the ~ 13. to obey the ~ 14. to interpret the ~ (courts interpret the ~) 15. to break; flout the ~ 16. administrative; antitrust; business, commercial; canon; case; civil; common; constitutional; copyright; corporate; criminal; environmental; family; marriage; feudal; immigration; international; Islamic; labor; lynch; maritime; military; Mosaic; natural; occupation; parliamentary; patent; private; public; Roman; statutory; substantive ~ 17. the supreme ~ (of the land) 18. according to the ~ 19. against the ~ (it is against the ~ to smoke in an elevator) ['jurisprudence'] ['lawyer's profession'] 20. to practice ~ 21. to study ~ ['principle'] 22. Mendel's; Newton's; periodic ~ 23. the ~ of diminishing returns; the ~ of gravity; the ~ of motion; the ~ of supply and demand; (also fig.) the ~ of the jungle ['misc.'] 24. to take the ~ into one's own hands; to lay down the ~; in the eyes of the ~; an attorney at ~ (AE); everyone is equal under the ~; the letter of the ~; the spirit of the ~; a higher ('divine') ~

law and order *n.* to maintain ~

lawful *adj.* ~ to + inf. (is it ~ to hunt deer in this state?)

lawn *n.* to mow, trim a ~

lawn mower *n.* to operate, work a ~

lawsuit *n.* 1. to bring, file, institute; lose; settle; win a ~ 2. a ~ against; over

lawyer *n.* 1. to hire, retain a ~ 2. a practicing ~ 3. a civil-rights; corporation; criminal; trial ~ 4. a Philadelphia ('shrewd') ~ 5. (humorous; usu. mil.) a barrack-room (esp. BE), guardhouse (esp. AE) ~ ('a soldier who claims to know all about military law')

lax *adj.* 1. ~ about (they are ~ about their appearance) 2. ~ in (the police were ~ in enforcing the law)

laxative *n.* 1. to take a ~ 2. to prescribe a ~ 3. an effective; mild; strong ~

lay *v.* 1. (N; used with an adjective) ('to render'); ('to place') she laid her soul bare; they laid the boards flat 2. (colloq.) (O; can be used with two or three objects) ('to bet') he laid me ten dollars (that it would not rain) 3. (P; tr.) ('to place') we laid the books on the table

layaway plan *n.* (esp. AE) (to buy smt.) on the ~

layer *n.* 1. the bottom; outer; top ~ 2. an even; uneven ~ 3. a protective ~ 4. in ~s (to dress in ~s)

lay off *v.* (D; tr.) to ~ from (she was laid off from her job at the factory)

layout *n.* ['design'] an artist's; typographer's ~

layover *n.* a ~ between (a ~ between planes)

leach out *v.* (D; tr.) ('to dissolve') to ~ from

lead I /liyd/ *n.* ['position in front'] ['leading position'] 1. to assume, take the ~ in 2. to build up, increase one's ~ 3. to hold, maintain the ~ 4. to follow smb.'s ~ 5. to give up, lose, relinquish the ~ 6. a commanding ~ 7. a ~ over (she built up a commanding ~ over her closest rivals) ['principal role'] 8. to play the ~ 9. the female; male ~ ['clue'] 10. to run down, track down a ~ ['leash'] (BE) 11. see **leash 1, 2**

lead II /liyd/ *v.* 1. (D; tr.) ('to guide') to ~ against (to ~ troops against the enemy) 2. (D; tr.) ('to guide') to ~ by (to ~ smb. by the hand; to ~ a horse by the bridle) 3. (d; intr.) ('to go') to ~ from; to (the path ~s from the house to the river;

all roads ~ to Rome) 4. (d; tr.) ('to guide') to ~ from; to (she led the group from the bus to the auditorium) 5. (D; tr.) to ~ in (to ~ the students in a cheer) 6. (d; intr.) ('to guide') to ~ into (the prisoners were led into the courtroom) 7. (d; tr.) ('to guide') to ~ off (he led the team off the field) 8. (d; tr.) ('to guide') to ~ out of (the fire fighters led them out of the burning building) 9. (d; tr.) ('to guide') to ~ through (to ~ smb. through the fog) 10. (d; intr.) to ~ to ('to result in') (the infection led to gangrene; these evening courses will ~ to an academic degree) 11. (d; intr.) ('to begin') to ~ with (the boxer led with a left jab) 12. (H) ('to induce') what led her to resign? I was led to believe that she would accept our offer 13. (P; intr.) ('to go') the road ~s nowhere 14. (misc.) to ~ smb. a merry chase (AE) = to ~ smb. a merry/pretty dance (BE)

lead back *v.* (D; intr., tr.) ('to return') to ~ to (the road ~s back to town; she led us back to the starting point)

lead down *v.* 1. (d; intr.) ('to go') to ~ to (the path ~s down to the main road) 2. (d; tr.) ('to guide') to ~ to (they led us down to the river)

leader *n.* 1. a born, natural; undisputed ~ 2. (in a legislature) a floor; majority; minority; opposition ~ 3. a labor; military; political; troop ~ 4. a squadron ~ 5. a ~ in

leadership *n.* 1. to assume, take on, take over the ~ 2. to exercise ~ 3. to relinquish, surrender ~ 4. collective; party ~ 5. ~ in

lead off *v.* (D; intr.) ('to begin') to ~ with (she led off with a lively song)

lead up *v.* 1. (d; intr.) ('to go up') to ~ to (the path ~s up to the top) 2. (d; intr.) to ~ to ('to precede and cause') (can you describe the events that led up to your decision?) 3. (D; tr.) ('to guide') to ~ to (he led us up to the top)

leaf I *n.* 1. a fig ~ (also fig.) 2. a bay; tea ~ 3. gold ~ 4. autumn; deciduous leaves 5. leaves fall; rustle; turn (the leaves were turning yellow) 6. (misc.) to turn over a new ~ ('to make a fresh start'); to take a ~ from smb.'s book ('to follow smb.'s example')

leaf II *v.* (d; intr.) to ~ through ('to look through superficially') (to ~ through a book)

leaflet *n.* propaganda ~s (to drop propaganda ~s over enemy lines)

league *n.* ['alliance'] 1. to form a ~ 2. in ~ with ['group of teams'] 3. to form a ~ 4. (esp. Am. baseball) a big, major; bush (colloq.), minor ~

leak I *n.* 1. to spring a ~ 2. to plug, stop a ~

leak II *v.* 1. (B) ('to divulge') they ~ed the news to the press 2. (d; intr.) ('to enter by flowing') to ~ into (water ~ed into the basement) 3. (D; intr.) ('to escape by flowing') to ~ out of (the oil ~ed out of the tank) 4. (D; intr.) ('to be divulged') to ~ to (the news ~ed to the press)

leak out *v.* (D; intr.) to ~ to (the news ~ed out to the press)

lean *v.* 1. (d; intr.) to ~ across, over (to ~ across a table) 2. (d; intr.) to ~ against, on (to ~ against a wall; to ~ on a desk) 3. (d; intr.) to ~ on ('to rely on') (they had to ~ on their friends for help) 4.

(colloq.) (d; intr.) to ~ on ('to exert pressure on') 5. (d; intr.) to ~ out of (to ~ out of a window) 6. (d; intr.) to ~ to (to ~ to one side) 7. (d; intr.) ('to tend') to ~ to, towards (they are now ~ing to our position) 8. (misc.) to ~ over backwards to help smb. ('to make a maximum effort to help smb.')

leaning *n.* 1. a strong ~ 2. a ~ towards (to have a strong ~ towards political conservatism)

leap I *n.* 1. a quantum ~ 2. a ~ forward

leap II *v.* 1. (d; intr.) to ~ at ('to be eager for') (to ~ at an opportunity) 2. (d; intr.) to ~ out of (the dolphin ~ed out of the water) 3. (d; intr.) to ~ over (to ~ over a fence) 4. (misc.) to ~ to smb.'s defense ('to defend smb. with enthusiasm')

leap down *v.* (D; intr.) to ~ from (to ~ from a tree)

leapfrog I *n.* to play ~

leapfrog II *v.* (d; intr.) to ~ from; to (American forces ~ged from one island to another)

learn *v.* 1. (d; intr.) to ~ about, of 2. (d; intr.) to ~ by (to ~ by experience) 3. (D; intr., tr.) to ~ from (to ~ from experience; she ~ed everything from me) 4. (E) she is ~ing to drive 5. (L) we have ~ed that he has found a job 6. (Q) they are ~ing how to dance

learning *n.* book (colloq.); higher; programmed ~

lease I *n.* 1. to take a ~ 2. to lose; renew a ~ 3. to cancel a ~ 4. mining; (off-shore) oil ~s 5. a ~ expires, runs out 6. under (a) ~ (to hold land under ~) 7. (misc.) a new ~ of (BE), on (AE) life ('a new chance to lead a happy life')

lease II *v.* 1. (usu. B; occ. A) to ~ property to smb. 2. (D; tr.) to ~ as (they ~d the building as a warehouse) 3. (D; tr.) to ~ from (to ~ property from smb.)

lease out *v.* (B) to ~ property to smb.

leash *n.* ['strap'] 1. to slip ('get free of') a ~ 2. on a ~ (to walk a dog on a ~) ['control'] ['restraint'] 3. to hold in ~ 4. to strain at the ~ ('to attempt to cast off controls')

least *n.* at the ~

leather *n.* composition; genuine; imitation; patent; saddle ~

leave I *n.* ['period of absence from duty, work'] 1. to give, grant a ~ 2. to extend smb.'s ~ 3. to go on ~; to take a ~ 4. to overstay one's ~ 5. to cancel smb.'s ~ 6. an annual; compassionate; maternity; research; sabbatical; shore; sick; terminal ~; a ~ of absence 7. on ~ (she was on maternity ~) ['permission'] (formal) 8. to ask ~ (to do smt.) 9. by smb.'s ~ ['departure'] (formal) 10. to take ~ of ['misc.'] 11. to take ~ of one's senses ('to act irrationally') (see the Usage Note for **vacation)**

leave II *v.* 1. (A) ('to bequeath') he left his estate to her; or: he left her his estate 2. (C) ('to entrust') she left the report for me; or: she left me the report 3. (D; intr.) ('to depart') to ~ for (they have left for London) 4. (D; tr.) ('to abandon') to ~ for (she left her comfortable home for a rugged life in the desert; he was left for dead on the battlefield; to ~ Paris for London) 5. (d; tr.) to ~ out of ('to omit') (we had to ~ this paragraph out of the text) 6. (d; tr.) ('to abandon') to ~ to (we left them to their own devices; I ~ the decision to your judg-

ment) 7. (d; tr.) ('to cause to remain') to ~ with (they left the children with her mother; she left her books with us) 8. (H) ('to take leave of') we left them to muddle through on their own 9. (J) ('to abandon') I left him working in the garden 10. (N; used with an adjective, past participle, noun) ('to cause to be in a certain state or condition') they left the fields fallow; the film left me cold; the flood left them homeless; ~ me alone; the enemy left the countryside devastated; the war left her an orphan 11. (P; tr.) ('to forget') I left my books at home

leave of absence *n.* see **leave I**

leave up *v.* (B) we left this decision up to her

lecture I *n.* ['formal talk'] 1. to deliver, give a ~ 2. to attend; follow ('understand') a ~ 3. a ~ about, on 4. at a ~ ['reprimand'] 5. to give smb. a ~ (about smt.)

lecture II *v.* 1. (D; intr.) ('to discuss formally') to ~ about, on 2. (D; tr.) ('to reprimand') to ~ for (she ~d the boys for being late) 3. (d; intr.) ('to discuss formally') to ~ to (to ~ to advanced students)

lecturer *n.* 1. a senior ~ (BE) 2. a ~ in, on (a ~ in English) (see the Usage Note for **professor)**

leech *n.* to apply ~es to

leer *v.* (D; intr.) to ~ at

leery *adj.* ~ of

leeway *n.* to give, provide ~

left *n.* ['left side'] 1. on the ~; to the ~ ['radical, leftist group'] 2. the extreme, far ~ ['punch delivered with the left hand'] 3. to deliver, throw a ~ 4. a hard, stiff ~ 5. a ~ to (a ~ to the head) ['turn to the left'] (colloq.) 6. to take a ~

leftovers *n.* to eat up; use up ~

leg *n.* 1. to bend; cross; kick; lift, raise; lower; spread; straighten; stretch one's ~s 2. a game, gammy (BE) ('lame') ~ 3. an artificial, wooden ~ 4. (an animal's) front; hind ~s 5. (misc.) he doesn't have a ~ to stand on ('he has no defense'); to pull smb.'s ~ ('to deceive smb.'); on one's last ~s ('near collapse'); to get a ~ up on smt. (AE) slang) ('to be in command of a situation')

legacy *n.* 1. to hand down a ~ 2. a lasting ~ 3. a ~ to

legal *adj.* ~ to + inf. (is it ~ to own a pistol in this state?)

legend *n.* ['inscription'] ['wording'] 1. to bear a ~ ['myth, story'] 2. a ~ arises 3. a living; local; popular ~ 4. a ~ to (her exploits were a ~ to millions) ['notable person'] 5. to become a ~ (in one's own time)

legislation *n.* ['statutes, laws'] 1. to adopt, enact, pass; draft ~ 2. to veto; vote down ~ 3. to abrogate, repeal ~ 4. emergency; progressive; remedial; social ~

legislature *n.* 1. to convene a ~ 2. to disband, dismiss, dissolve a ~ 3. a bicameral ~

legitimacy *n.* 1. to confirm; establish the ~ (of smt.) 2. to challenge, question the ~ (of smt.)

legitimate *adj.* ~ to + inf. (is it ~ to pose such questions?)

legwork *n.* (colloq.) to do the ~

leisure *n.* at one's ~

lend *v.* 1. (A) she lent the money to him: or: she lent him the money 2. (d; refl.) to ~ to ('to be suitable for') (it ~s itself to satire) (see the Usage Note for **loan II**)

length *n.* 1. at ~ (she described each event at great ~) 2. in ~ (ten feet in ~) 3. (misc.) to keep smb. at arm's ~ ('to keep smb. at a certain distance'); to go to great ~s to do smt. ('to make a great effort to do smt.')

leniency *n.* 1. to show ~ 2. ~ towards, with

lenient *adj.* ~ towards, with

lens *n.* 1. to grind a ~ 2. a concave; convex; crystalline; telephoto, telescopic ~ 3. contact; corrective ~es

leopard *n.* 1. a snow ~ 2. a young ~ is a cub 3. a female ~ is a leopardess

leprosy *n.* 1. to develop ~ 2. to have, suffer from ~

lese majesty *n.* ~ against

lesion *n.* an open ~

lesson *n.* ['instruction'] 1. to take ~s (to take ~s in English) 2. to study one's ~s 3. a ~ in ['something that should be known'] 4. to learn a ~ 5. to teach smb. a ~ 6. a moral; object ~ 7. a ~ to (let that be a ~ to you)

let *v.* 1. (esp. BE; AE has *to rent out*) (B) ('to give the use of in return for payment') they ~ rooms to students 2. (I) ('to allow') we cannot ~ them go 3. (esp. BE) (N; used with an adjective) ('to leave') ~ it alone

lethargy *n.* (in) a state of ~

let in *v.* 1. (D; refl.) to ~ for ('to cause') (you'll ~ yourself in for a lot of trouble if you take her in as a partner) 2. (d; tr.) to ~ on ('to share') (to ~ smb. in on a secret)

let off *v.* (D; tr.) ('to release') to ~ with (he was let off with a small fine)

let on *v.* 1. (D; intr.) to ~ about ('to reveal') (she did not ~ about her promotion) 2. (L; to) ('to indicate') he let on (to the accused) that he could be bribed

let out *v.* (esp. BE) (B) to ~ rooms to students (see also **rent out**)

let's (verbal form) (F) ~ continue; ~ go

letter *n.* ['written message'] 1. to type; write a ~ 2. to mail, post (BE), send a ~ 3. to drop a ~ into a mailbox (AE), letter box (BE) 4. to certify; register a ~ 5. to take (down), transcribe a ~ 6. to dictate a ~ 7. to deliver; forward a ~ 8. to get, receive a ~ 9. a brief; detailed; long; rambling ~ 10. an anonymous; business; chain; fan; follow-up; form; love; open; pastoral; personal; poison-pen ~ 11. an airmail; certified; dead; express; registered; special-delivery ~ 12. the ~s crossed in the mail (esp. AE), post (BE) 13. a ~ about 14. a ~ from; to (we received a ~ from her about the incident) 15. in a ~ ['unit of an alphabet'] 16. a block; capital, large, upper-case; lower-case, small ~ ['first letter of the name of a school, college denoting membership on a sports team'] (AE) 17. to earn, win one's ~ 18. a school ~

lettuce *n.* 1. crisp ~ 2. bib; iceberg; leaf ~ 3. a head of ~

letup *n.* a ~ in (there was no ~ in the bickering)

let up *v.* (D; intr.) ('to ease up') to ~ on (she should ~ on the children)

leukemia, leukaemia *n.* 1. to develop ~ 2. to have, suffer from ~ 3. acute ~

level I *adj.* ~ with (to draw ~ with; ~ with the street)

level II *n.* ['height'] ['plane'] 1. to reach a ~ 2. a high; low ~ 3. an energy; poverty ~ 4. eye; ground; sea; water ~ 5. the federal (US), national; international; local; state (US) ~ 6. at, on a ~ (at sea ~; at the highest ~s; on the international ~) ['instrument for determining a horizontal plane'] 7. a spirit ~

level III *v.* 1. (d; tr.) to ~ against (to ~ charges against smb.) 2. (D; tr.) to ~ to (the village was ~ed to the ground) 3. (colloq.) (d; intr.) to ~ with ('to tell the truth to') (she ~ed with me)

level best *n.* to do one's ~

lever *n.* 1. (in a polling booth) to pull a ~ 2. a gear ~ (BE; AE has *gearshift*)

levy I *n.* to impose a ~ (on)

levy II *v.* (D; tr.) to ~ on (to ~ a tax on rum)

lexicon *n.* to compile a ~

liability *n.* 1. to accept, acknowledge, assume incur, take on a ~ 2. full; limited ~ 3. a ~ for (we assumed full ~ for our children's debts)

liable *adj.* ['legally obligated'] 1. ~ for; to (she is ~ to them for her children's debts) ['likely'] 2. (cannot stand alone) ~ to + inf. (she is ~ to show up at any time)

liaise *v.* (BE) (D; intr.) ('to mediate') to ~ between; with

liaison *n.* ['communication'] 1. to establish; maintain ~ 2. a ~ between; with ['adulterous relationship'] 3. to have a ~ with

liar *n.* an abject, congenital, consummate, incorrigible, inveterate, outright, pathological ~

lib *n.* (colloq.) women's ~ (see **liberation 1**)

libel *n.* 1. to commit ~ 2. (a) ~ against

liberal I *adj.* ~ in; with

liberal II *n.* a bleeding-heart; knee-jerk; staunch ~

liberate *v.* (D; tr.) to ~ from

liberation *n.* 1. women's ~ 2. ~ from

liberties *n.* ['undue familiarity'] to take ~ with

liberty *n.* ['freedom'] 1. to gain ~ 2. individual, personal; political; religious ~ 3. civil ~ties ['permission'] 4. to take the ~ (of doing smt.) (may I take the ~ of reminding you of your promise?) ['authorized absence'] (AE) (naval) 5. on ~ ['misc.'] 6. are you at ~ to give us any information?

library *n.* 1. to accumulate, build up a ~ 2. to computerize a ~ 3. a children's; circulating; lending; law; mobile; municipal; music; public; reference; rental; research; school; university ~ 4. at, in (she works at/in the ~)

license I **licence** *n.* 1. to grant, issue a ~ 2. to apply for; receive; renew a ~ 3. to revoke; suspend a ~ 4. a driver's (AE), driving (BE); dog; hunting; liquor (esp. AE); marriage; state (esp. US) ~ 5. poetic ~ 6. a ~ to + inf. (we had a ~ to sell beer)

license II *v.* (H) she is ~d to practice nursing

lick v. 1. (d; intr.) to ~ at (the flames ~ed at the roof of the next house) 2. (N; used with an adjective) she ~ed the plate clean

lid n. ['cover'] 1. to cover smt. with a ~ 2. to put a ~ on smb. ['curb'] 3. to clamp, clap, put a ~ on smt.

lie I n. ['falsehood'] 1. to tell a ~ 2. to give the ~ to ('to prove to be false') 3. a bald-faced, barefaced, blatant, brazen, deliberate, downright, monstrous, outright, transparent, whopping; white ~ 4. a pack, tissue, web of ~s 5. (misc.) to live a ~ ('to continue to do something which is felt to be dishonest')

lie II v. 1. to ~ flatly, outright 2. (D; intr.) ('to tell a falsehood') to ~ to (he lied to the judge)

lie III v. 1. ('to be') to ~ ahead 2. ('to be in a reclining position') to ~ flat; still 3. (P; intr.) ('to be located') to ~ in bed; Mexico ~s to the south 4. (s) to ~ fallow (the field lay fallow) 5. (misc.) to ~ in wait for

lie-detector test n. 1. to administer, give a ~ 2. to subject smb. to a ~ 3. to take a ~ 4. to fail; pass a ~

lie down v. (misc.) to take smt. lying down ('to accept smt. without protest'); to ~ on the job ('to work very little')

lief adv. (obsol.) ['willingly'] ~ + inf. (I would as ~ remain at home)

lien n. ['legal claim'] 1. to put, slap (esp. AE; colloq.) a ~ on smt. 2. to have a ~ on smt.

lie to v. (D; intr.) to ~ about (she ~d to me about the incident)

lieutenant n. 1. a first; flight (GB); second ~ 2. a ~ junior grade (US)

life n. 1. to lead a ~ (to lead a busy ~) 2. to prolong; save a ~ 3. to devote one's ~ (to smt.) 4. to spend one's ~ (doing smt.) 5. to give, lay down, sacrifice; risk one's ~ 6. to claim, snuff out, take a ~ (she took her own ~; the accident claimed many lives) 7. to ruin smb.'s ~ 8. to bring; restore smb. to ~ 9. to come to ~; to take on ~ (the statue took on ~ in the sculptor's skilled hands) 10. an active; ascetic, austere; busy, hectic; charmed; cloistered; difficult, hard, miserable, tough; dissipated, dissolute, dull; easy, exciting; full; happy; idyllic; lonely, solitary; long; monastic; peaceful, quiet, serene; short; simple; stormy, turbulent ~ 11. campus (esp. AE); city; civilian; country, rural; married; modern; nomadic; political; public ~ (in civilian ~ the sergeant was a teacher; married ~ seems to agree with them; the hunters led a nomadic ~) 12. smb.'s family, home; love; personal; private; sex; social ~ (to lead a hectic social ~; in private ~ she was very easygoing) 13. animal; bird; human; marine; plant ~ 14. smb.'s adult ~ 15. the shelf ~ (of smt. being sold in a store) 16. in ~ (early in ~) 17. (misc.) in the prime of ~; the facts of ~; the accused got ~ ('the accused was sentenced to life imprisonment'); to show signs of ~; (to hang on) for dear ~ ('with all one's energy'); not on your ~ ('not for anything in the world'); to start a new ~; to make a new ~ for oneself; to breathe (new) ~ into smt.; to bring back to ~; to stake one's ~ on smt.; a way of ~

lifeboat n. 1. to launch, lower a ~ 2. to swamp a ~ (the ~ was swamped in the surf) 3. (misc.) to take to the ~s

life insurance n. to take out ~ on

lifeline n. ['rope used to save a life'] 1. to throw smb. a ~ ['vital route'] 2. to cut a ~ 3. a ~ to

lifestyle n. a sedentary ~

lifetime n. 1. to devote a ~ (to smt.) 2. in one's ~ 3. (misc.) to last a ~

lift I n. ['device for raising and lowering people and freight'] (BE; AE has *elevator*) 1. to operate a ~ (a liftboy or liftman operates a ~) 2. to take a ~ (we took the ~ to the tenth floor) 3. a service ~ (see also **elevator 1-6**) ['conveyor suspended from a cable'] 4. a chair, ski ~ ['ride'] (colloq.) 5. to bum; get a ~ (from smb.) 6. to give smb. a ~ ['boost, inspiration'] (colloq.) 7. to get a ~ (from smb. or smt.) 8. to give smb. a ~ (your words of encouragement gave us a real ~)

lift II v. 1. (D; tr.) ('to raise') to ~ from (she did not ~ her head from the TV set) 2. (d; tr.) ('to steal') to ~ from (the material was ~ed from smb.'s dissertation)

lift up v. (D; tr.) to ~ to (he ~ed the child up to the ceiling)

ligament n. to strain; tear a ~

light I adj. 1. to make ~ of ('to attach little importance to') 2. ~ of foot

light II n. ['illumination'] ['source of brightness'] 1. to put on, switch on, turn on a ~ 2. to shine a ~ on smt. 3. to cast, shed ~ on smt. 4. to extinguish, turn off, turn out a ~ 5. to dim the ~s, turn the ~s down; to turn the ~s up 6. a bright, strong; dull, faint; harsh; soft ~; moonlight; sunlight 7. an electric; klieg; landing; neon; overhead; pilot; strobe; traffic ~ 8. (on a car) a backup (AE), reversing (BE); dome; instrument; parking ~; taillight 9. a ~ flickers; goes on; goes out; the ~s are off, out; the ~s are on 10. ~ travels (very fast) 11. (BE) the ~s have fused ('a fuse has blown') 12. by the ~ of (to read by the ~ of a candle) ['traffic light'] 13. to go through a ~ 14. against a ~ (to cross against the ~) 15. at a ~ (to stop at a ~) ['flame used to light a cigarette'] 16. to give smb. a ~ ['misc.'] 17. in ~ of ('in view of'); in the harsh ~of reality; a guiding ~ ('one who sets an example'); to see the ~ ('to comprehend the truth'); to bring smt. to ~ ('to make smt. known'); to come to ~ ('to become known'); she wanted to see her name in ~s ('she wanted to succeed on the stage and become famous'); the northern ~s; the southern ~s

light III v. (D; intr.) (to ~ on, upon ('to come across') (to ~ on a rare dictionary)

light bulb n. see **bulb 1-4**

lighter n. a cigarette ~

lighting n. 1. direct; indirect; soft ~ 2. electric ~

lightning n. 1. ball; forked; heat, sheet ~ 2. ~ flashes; strikes 3. a bolt, flash, stroke of ~

light out v. (colloq.) (esp. AE) (D; intr.) to ~ for ('to leave for') USAGE NOTE: The past and past participle of this verb are usu. *lit out*--she lit out for home.

light up v. (D; intr.) to ~ with (her face lit up with pleasure)

like I *prep.* (colloq.) ~ to + inf. (it was ~ them to be late)

like II *v.* 1. to ~ a great deal, a lot, very much 2. (E) he ~s to read 3. (G) she ~s reading 4. (H; no passive) (often with the conditional) I'd ~ him to go; I ~ people to tell me the truth; I'd ~ you to go; AE also has, slightly colloq.: I'd ~ for you to go 5. (M) we ~ our friends to be honest 6. (N; used with an adjective) I ~ my steak rare USAGE NOTE: The verb *like* can be used with *it* + clause--I like it when you smile; I'd like it if you smiled.

likelihood *n.* 1. great; little ~ 2. ~ that + inf. (there is every ~ that she'll come) 3. in all ~

likely *adj.* 1. (cannot stand alone) ~ to + inf. (she is ~ to show up; it is not ~ to snow) 2. ~ that + clause (it is ~ that there will be more rain)

liken *v.* (d; tr.) ('to compare') to ~ to (her estate could be ~ed to a fortress)

likeness *n.* 1. to catch a ~ (the artist caught the ~) 2. to bear a ~ 3. a striking, uncanny ~ 4. a family ~ 5. a ~ between; to

likewise *adv.* to do ~

liking *n.* 1. to take a ~ to 2. to develop a ~ for 3. to one's ~ (that is not to my ~)

limb *n.* 1. an artificial ~ 2. the lower; upper ~s 3. (misc.) out on a ~ ('in a precarious position')

limbo *n.* in ~ (in political ~)

limelight *n.* 1. to hold the ~ 2. to hog the ~ 3. in the (public) ~

limit I *n.* 1. to place, put, set a ~ on 2. to disregard, exceed a ~ 3. an age; speed; time; weight ~ 4. a ~ on, to 5. within ~s 6. (misc.) to push smb. to the ~

limit II *v.* (D; refl., tr.) to ~ to (she had to ~ herself to twenty minutes)

limitations *n.* 1. to put ~ on 2. budgetary, financial ~ 3. within certain ~

limited *adj.* 1. ~ in (~ in resources) 2. ~ to

limits *n.* 1. city ~ 2. (AE) (esp. mil.) off ~ to; on ~ to (the bar was put off ~ to all military personnel) 3. within (reasonable) ~ ,

limousine *n.* 1. to hire; take a ~ 2. an airport; bulletproof ~

limp *n.* 1. to have a ~ 2. a decided, marked, pronounced; slight ~

line *n.* ['long, thin mark'] 1. to draw a ~ 2. a broken; contour; crooked; curved; dotted; fine, thin; heavy, thick; horizontal; parallel; perpendicular; solid, unbroken; straight; vertical; wavy ~ ['queue'] (AE) 3. to form a ~ 4. to buck ('push into') a ~ 5. to get into ~; to wait in ~ 6. a checkout; chow ~ ['row'] 7. to form a ~ 8. a picket; police; receiving ~ ['row of characters'] 9. to indent; insert a ~ 10. (fig.) to read between the ~s ['text'] ['unit of text'] 11. to deliver a ~ 12. to go over, rehearse one's ~s (the actors had to rehearse their ~s several times) 13. to fluff one's ~s 14. a dull; witty ~ (there isn't a dull ~ in the whole play) ['route'] 15. to introduce a (new) ~ 16. to discontinue a ~ 17. a feeder; main ~ 18. a bus; commuter; high-speed; steamship; streetcar (AE), tram (BE) ~ 19. supply ~s (to cut enemy supply ~s) ['path'] 20. to follow a ~ (to follow a ~ of reasoning; to follow the ~ of least resistance)

['telephone connection'] 21. to get a ~; to give smb. a ~ 22. the ~ is busy (AE), engaged (BE) 23. an outside; party ('shared') ~ 24. a hot ~ (the hot ~ between Washington and Moscow; a hot ~ for missing children) ['note'] 25. to drop smb. a ~ ['information'] 26. to get a ~ on smb. ['type of merchandise'] 27. to carry; handle; introduce a ~ 28. to discontinue, drop a ~ 29. a complete, full ~ ['policy'] 30. to adhere to, follow, hew to, pursue, take a ~ 31. a firm, hard; official; party ~ (to hew to the official ~) ['flattering talk'] (colloq.) 32. to give, hand smb. a ~ ['wire'] ['pipe'] ['conduit'] 33. a fuel; oil; sewage; steam; telegraph; telephone ~ 34. high-voltage; power ~s (the power ~s are down) ['boundary'] 35. a city; county; snow; squall; state; township; tree ~ 36. (sports) a base; end; foul; goal; service ~; sideline 37. at, on a ~ (at the goal ~; on the base ~; on the sidelines) ['established position along a front'] ['boundary '] (mil.) 38. to hold a ~ 39. a battle; cease-fire; firing; front ~ 40. (the) enemy ~s (behind enemy ~s) 41. at, on a ~ (on the cease-fire ~) ['conveyor belt'] 42. an assembly, production ~ (to work on an assembly ~) ['occupation'] ['field of interest'] 43. what ~ are you in? ['contour'] 44. the ~s of a ship ['limit'] 45. to hold the ~ (on prices) 46. to draw the ~ ('to set a limit') ['turn'] ['order'] 47. in ~ for (she is next in ~ for promotion) ['alignment'] 48. in ~; out of ~ (the wheels are out of ~) ['conformity'] 49. to toe the ~ 50. to bring smb. into ~; to keep smb. in ~ 51. to get into ~; to get out of ~ 52. in ~ with (in ~ with your stated policy) ['cord, device for catching fish'] 53. to cast a ~ 54. to reel in; reel out a ~ 55. a fishing ~ ['rope'] 56. to throw a ~ to smb. (who is in the water) 57. a plumb ~ ['division'] 58. to cross a ~ 59. a color ~ (to cross the color ~) ['tendency'] 60. along, on certain ~s (along modern ~s) ['dynasty'] 61. to establish, found a ~ 62. an unbroken ~ ['distinction'] 63. a fine, nebulous, thin ~ ['misc.'] 64. the bottom ~ ('the final result'); to be on the firing ~ ('to be at the center of activity'); to sign on the dotted ~ ('to sign an agreement'); credit ~ ('amount of credit allowed'); to walk a straight ~; to put smt. on the ~ ('to risk smt.'); to lay it on the ~ ('to speak candidly'); on ~ ('in operation'); in (the) ~ of duty

linen *n.* 1. to change the (bed) ~ 2. fresh ~ 3. bed; fine; table ~

liner I *n.* ['steamship'] a luxury; ocean; passenger; transatlantic ~

liner II *n.* ['lining'] a helmet ~

lineup *n.* 1. a police ~ (AE; BE has *identification parade*) 2. (AE) to be in a ~ (as a suspect)

line up *v.* (D; intr.) to ~ in (to ~ in three ranks)

linger *v.* (d; intr.) to ~ over ('to take one's time with') (don't ~ over your coffee)

lingo *n.* (colloq.) ['language, dialect'] to speak the ~

linguistics *n.* applied; comparative; contrastive; descriptive; general; generative; historical ~; psycholinguistics; sociolinguistics; structural; transformational ~

liniment *n.* to apply, rub in ~

lining *n.* 1. a brake; coat ~ 2. a zip-in ~ 3. (misc.) a silver ~ ('the bright side of a problem')

link I *n.* 1. to constitute a ~ 2. a close; strong; weak ~ 3. a connecting ~ 4. the missing ~ 5. a cuff ~ 6. a ~ between; to, with (he has ~s to the underworld) 7. (misc.) (GB) the fixed ~ (under the Channel)

link II *v.* (D; tr.) to ~ to, with (these events are ~ed to each other)

linkage *n.* ~ between, to, with

links *n.* ['golf course'] (out) on the ~

link up *v.* (D; intr.) to ~ with (we ~ed up with their forces on the Danube)

linoleum *n.* inlaid ~

lion *n.* 1. a mountain ~ 2. ~s roar 3. a pride of ~s 4. a young ~ is a cub 5. a female ~ is a lioness 6. (misc.) the ~ is the king of beasts

lip *n.* 1. to lick; move; part; pucker; purse one's ~s 2. to press one's ~s to (she pressed her ~s to the baby's forehead) 3. chapped; dry; moist; thick; thin ~s 4. the lower; upper ~ 5. from smb.'s ~s (I heard it from his ~s) 6. on one's ~s (she died with a prayer on her ~s) 7. on everyone's ~s (his name was on everyone's ~s) 8. (misc.) to bite one's ~ ('to restrain oneself'); to moisten one's ~s; to lick/smack one's ~s ('to anticipate or remember with pleasure'); to keep a stiff upper ~ ('to refuse to become discouraged'); don't give me any of your ~ ('don't be impudent with me'); to seal smb.'s ~s ('to induce smb. to remain silent'); to read ~s

lip service *n.* ['meaningless promise'] to pay ~ to

lipstick *n.* to apply, put on; remove, wipe off ~

liquid *n.* 1. (a) clear; cloudy ~ 2. (a) dishwashing ~

liquor *n.* ['alcoholic drinks'] (esp. AE) 1. to ply smb. with ~ 2. to hold one's ~ 3. hard, strong ~ 4. malt ~

list I *n.* ['catalog, roll'] 1. to compile, draw up, make (up) a ~ 2. to head a ~ 3. to go down, read down a ~ 4. an alphabetical ~; checklist; dean's (AE); guest; mailing; shopping; waiting ~ (to go down a checklist) 5. a short ~ (of candidates) 6. a casualty ~ 7. on a ~ (she was third on the ~; high on the ~ of priorities)

list II *v.* ('to include') 1. (d; intr.) to ~ among (to be ~ed among the casualties) 2. (d; refl., tr.) to ~ as (she ~ed herself as an independent voter; he was ~ed as missing)

list III *n.* ['tilt'] a ~ to (a ~ to starboard)

list IV *v.* (D; intr.) ('to tilt') to ~ to (to ~ to starboard)

listen *v.* 1. (d; intr.) to ~ for (to ~ for a signal) 2. (D; intr.) to ~ to (to ~ to advice)

listen in *v.* (D; intr.) to ~ on, to (to ~ on smb.'s conversation)

listen to *v.* 1. (esp. AE) (I) we ~ed to them sing 2. (J) we ~ed to them singing

listing *n.* an exclusive ~ (of a property being sold)

list price *n.* (to sell smt.) at a ~

lists *n.* ['combat arena'] to enter the ~

literate *adj.* ~ in

literature *n.* 1. to produce (a) ~ 2. (an) extensive, voluminous ~ 3. belletristic; classical; contemporary; modern; professional; pulp ~ 4. compara-

tive ~ 5. a body of ~ (a considerable body of ~) 6. ~ about, on (there was extensive ~ on the topic)

litigation *n.* 1. to initiate, start ~ 2. ~ over; with 3. in ~ (the case was in ~)

little *adv.* 1. precious ~ 2. ~ by ~ ('gradually')

liturgy *n.* to chant; offer; recite the ~

live I /layv/ *adv.* ['directly'] to come ~ (this telecast is coming to you ~ from Wimbledon)

live II /liv/ *v.* 1. to ~ dangerously; high 2. (d; intr.) to ~ by ('to adhere to') (to ~ by certain principles) 3. (d; intr.) ('to exist') to ~ for (they ~ only for their children) 4. (d; intr.) ('to subsist') to ~ off, on (they ~ on her salary; you cannot ~ on love alone; to ~ off one's parents) 5. (D; intr.) ('to survive') to ~ to (she ~d to ninety) 6. (d; intr.) ('to cohabit') to ~ with (they ~ with each other) 7. (colloq.) (d; intr.) to ~ with ('to tolerate') (can you ~ with this arrangement?) 8. (E) she ~d to regret her decision; he ~d to be ninety 9. (P; intr.) ('to reside') to ~ in the country 10. (misc.) they ~ beyond their means ('they spend more than they earn'); to ~ from hand to mouth ('to eke out a bare living'); to ~ from day to day ('to be concerned only with the present'); to ~ together ('to cohabit')

livelihood *n.* to earn one's ~

livestock *n.* to graze ~

live up *v.* 1. (d; intr.) to ~ to ('to satisfy') (to ~ to expectations) 2. (misc.) (colloq.) to ~ it up ('to enjoy oneself ostentatiously')

livid *adj.* ~ with (~ with rage)

living *n.* ['livelihood'] 1. to earn, get (BE), make a ~ 2. to eke out a ~ (to eke out a precarious ~) 3. a comfortable; honest ~ (to earn a comfortable ~) ['manner of existence'] 4. communal; high; suburban ~ 5. a standard of ~

living room *n.* a sunken ~

load I *n.* 1. to carry, transport a ~ 2. to lessen, lighten a load (also fig.) 3. a heavy; light ~ 4. a capacity, maximum, peak ~ 5. a case; work ~

load II *v.* 1. (D; tr.) to ~ into, onto (to ~ coal into a ship) 2. (d; tr.) to ~ (to ~ a ship to full capacity) 3. (D; tr.) to ~ with (to ~ a ship with coal)

load down *v.* (d; tr.) to ~ with

loaf *n.* 1. a fish; meat ~ 2. a ~ of bread

loan I *n.* 1. to float, negotiate, raise a ~ 2. to make a ~ 3. to get, receive a ~ 4. to secure; underwrite a ~ 5. to pay off, repay a ~ 6. an interest-free; long-term; low-interest; short-term ~ 7. interlibrary ~ (she got the book on/through interlibrary ~) 8. a ~ to 9. on ~ from; to (the painting was on ~ to the National Gallery from the Louvre)

loan II *v.* (A) she ~ed the money to me; or: she ~ed me the money USAGE NOTE: When *to loan* means 'to lend officially', it is CE--the Louvre has loaned a painting to the National Gallery. When it means 'to lend', it is esp. AE--she loaned me the money.

loanword *n.* 1. to adopt a ~ 2. a ~ from (a ~ from French)

loath *adj.* (pompous or lit.) (cannot stand alone) ~ to + inf. (we are ~ to summon the authorities)

loathe *v.* 1. to ~ deeply, intensely 2. (G) he ~s

working

loathing *n.* 1. deep, intense ~ 2. ~ for

lob *v.* (D; tr.) to ~ at (to ~ a ball at smt.)

lobby I *n.* ['pressure group'] 1. an education; farm; labor; oil ~ ['large hall'] 2. a hotel; theater ~ 3. in the ~ (let's meet in the ~)

lobby II *v.* 1. to ~ actively 2. (D; intr.) to ~ against; for (to ~ against higher taxes; to ~ for a bill)

locate *v.* (esp. AE) (P; tr.) ('to place') we ~d our firm in Florida

location *n.* 1. to pinpoint a ~ 2. at a ~ (at an undisclosed ~) 3. on ~ (to shoot a film on ~)

lock I *n.* 1. to pick a ~ 2. a combination; deadbolt; double; mortise; safety; time; Yale ~ 3. under ~ and key ('locked up securely')

lock II *v.* (d; intr.) to ~ on, onto ('to sight and track') (to ~ onto a target)

locked *adj.* ['bound'] (cannot stand alone) ~ in (~ in mortal combat)

locket *n.* a gold; silver ~

locomotive *n.* 1. to drive a ~ 2. a diesel; electric; steam ~

locusts *n.* 1. ~ swarm 2. a swarm of ~

lodge I *n.* ['house'] 1. a hunting; ski ~ ['organization, society'] 2. a fraternal; Masonic ~ ['motel'] (AE) 3. a motor ~

lodge II *v.* 1. (D; tr.) to ~ against; with (to ~ a complaint against a neighbor with the police) 2. (d; intr.) to ~ in (the bullet ~d in his shoulder)

lodger *n.* to take in ~s

lodgings *n.* to find; seek ~

log *n.* ['record'] ['diary'] 1. to keep a ~ 2. a ship's ~ ['piece of timber'] 3. to float ~s (down a river) 4. to split a ~; to saw a ~ in two ['misc.'] 5. to sleep like a ~ ('to sleep very soundly')

logarithm *n.* a common; natural ~

loggerheads *n.* at ~ with ('in disagreement with')

logic *n.* 1. to apply, use ~ 2. clear; cold; irrefutable; simple ~ 3. deductive; formal; inductive; symbolic ~ 4. ~ in (there is no ~ in their policy)

logical *adj.* ~ to + inf. (it is ~ to assume that they will attend)

logjam *n.* 1. to break (up), clear a ~ 2. (fig.) (esp. AE) a legislative ~

loins *n.* ['power'] to gird one's ~ ('to prepare oneself for a difficult task')

lollipop *n.* to lick, suck a ~

lonely *adj.* ~ for

lonesome *adj.* (AE) ~ for

long I *adj.* (colloq.) ['strong'] ~ on (~ on common sense)

long II *adv.* 1. ~ ago 2. ~ before

long III *v.* 1. (d; intr.) to ~ for (to ~ for peace) 2. (E) she ~ed to return home; (rare) I ~ed for them to return

long chalk (BE) see **long shot**

long-distance *adv.* to call, telephone ~

long division *n.* to do ~

long haul see **long run**

longing *n.* 1. to feel a ~ 2. a ~ for

longitude *n.* at a ~ (at a ~ of ten degrees west)

long run *n.* ['long-range outlook'] in, over the ~

long shot *n.* ['slight chance'] not by a ~ (AE) ('absolutely not')

look I *n.* ['glance'] ['expression'] 1. to get, have, take a ~ 2. to dart, shoot; steal a ~ 3. to give smb. a ~ 4. a blank, distant, faraway, vacant ~ (she had a faraway ~ in her eyes) 5. an anxious, worried; baleful; close, hard; come-hither, inviting; curious, strange; dirty, nasty, vicious; disapproving, stern; eloquent, meaningful; furtive; grim; haggard; hungry; inquiring, searching; knowing; penetrating; pensive, thoughtful; piercing; pleading; provocative; puzzled; rapt; scathing; sharp; sinister; skeptical; steady; sullen; suspicious; tender; troubled; withering ~ (she gave us a dirty ~) 6. a second ~ (to take a second ~ at smt.) ['appearance'] 7. a tailored ~ ['misc.'] 8. good ~s

look II *v.* 1. (d; intr.) to ~ after ('to watch') (to ~ after the children) 2. (D; intr.) to ~ at ('to examine') (to ~ at a painting) 3. (D; intr.) to ~ for ('to seek') (to ~ for a job) 4. (d; intr.) to ~ into ('to investigate') (to ~ into a complaint) 5. (d. intr.) to ~ like ('to resemble') (this horse ~s like a winner; BE also has: this horse ~s a winner) 6. (d; intr.) ('to appear') to ~ like (it ~s like rain = it ~s as if/as though it will rain) 7. (D; intr.) ('to watch') to ~ out (AE), out of (to ~ out of a window) 8. (d; intr.) to ~ through ('to direct one's gaze through') (to ~ through a telescope) 9. (d. intr.) to ~ through ('to examine') (to ~ through one's files) 10. (d; intr.) to ~ to ('to turn to') (to ~ to one's parents for help) 11. (s) she ~s terrible 12. (misc.) to ~ smb. squarely in the eye; to ~ from one to the other; to ~ one's age

look about (BE) see **look around**

look ahead *v.* (D; intr.) to ~ to (to ~ to a bright future)

look around *v.* (d; intr.) to ~ for ('to seek') (to ~ for a job)

look at *v.* 1. (AE) (I) ~ him jump 2. (J) ~ him jumping

look back *v.* (D; intr.) to ~ at, on (to ~ at the past year)

look down *v.* 1. (d; intr.) to ~ at; from ('to direct one's gaze down at') (to ~ at the beach from the balcony of the hotel) 2. (d; intr.) to ~ on ('to despise') (to ~ on all forms of corruption)

look forward *v.* (d; intr.) to ~ to (to ~ to spring; to ~ to a meeting with eager anticipation; I ~ to going)

look in *v.* (D; intr.) to ~ on (to ~ on the children)

look on *v.* (D; tr.) to ~ as (we ~ her as a friend)

lookout *n.* 1. to keep a (sharp) ~ for 2. on the ~

look out *v.* 1. (d; intr.) to ~ for ('to watch for') (the police were ~ing out for burglars) 2. (d; intr.) to ~ for ('to protect') (to ~ for one's own interests) 3. (d; intr.) to ~ on, onto ('to face') (our windows ~ onto the square)

look round (BE) see **look around**

looks *n.* ['appearance'] good ~

look up *v.* (d; intr.) to ~ to ('to respect') (children ~ to their parents)

look upon see **look on**

loom I *n.* a hand ~

loom II *v.* 1. (P; intr.) a ship ~ed out of the fog 2. (misc.) to ~ large (her possible candidacy ~ed large in the future plans of the party)

loop *n.* 1. to make a ~ 2. to loop the ~ (in an airplane) 3. (misc.) to throw smb. for a ~ ('to shock smb.')

loophole *n.* 1. to find a ~ 2. to close a ~ 3. a tax ~ 4. a ~ in

loose I *adj.* 1. to cut (smb.) ~ 2. to let, set, turn (smb.) ~

loose II *n.* on the ~

loose end (BE) at a ~ (see **loose ends**)

loose ends *n.* (AE) at ~ ('with no definite obligations')

looting *n.* to engage in ~

lope *v.* (P; intr.) she ~d through the park

lord I *n.* a feudal ~

lord II *v.* to ~ it over smb. ('to flaunt one's superiority over smb.')

lorry *n.* (BE) 1. to drive, operate a ~ (CE has *truck*) 2. an articulated ~ (AE has *trailer truck*) 3. a breakdown ~ (AE has *tow truck*) 4. a tipper ~ (AE has *dump truck*)

lose *v.* 1. (B) we lost the match to them 2. (D; intr.) to ~ to (our team lost to them by three points) 3. (O) his errors lost him the match

lose out *v.* 1. (D; intr.) to ~ on (to ~ on a deal) 2. (D; intr.) to ~ to (she lost out to her rival)

loser *n.* a bad, poor; born; good ~

loss *n.* 1. to inflict ~es on (our forces inflicted heavy ~es on the enemy) 2. (sports) to hand smb. a ~ (they handed our team its first ~ of the season) 3. to incur, suffer, sustain, take ~es (to take heavy ~es) 4. to make up, offset, recoup, replace a ~ (to recoup one's gambling ~es) 5. heavy; light ~es 6. an irreparable, irreplaceable, irretrievable ~ 7. a hearing; heat; memory ~ 8. ~es in (~es in dead and wounded) 9. a ~ to (an irreplaceable ~ to our nation) 10. at a ~ (to be at a ~ for words)

lost *adj.* 1. irretrievably; totally ~ 2. to get ~ (the small child got ~) 3. (misc.) (slang) get ~! ('go away!')

lot *n.* ['one's fortune'] 1. to cast, throw in one's ~ with 2. a happy; sorry, unhappy ~ 3. one's ~ to + inf. (it fell to her ~ to break the sad news) ['object used in deciding by chance'] 4. by ~ (to choose by ~) ['plot of ground'] (esp. AE) 5. an empty, vacant ~ 6. a parking ~ (AE; BE has *car park)* 7. a used-car ~

lotion *n.* 1. to apply, rub in (a) ~ 2. an after-shave; body; hand; skin; suntan ~

lots *n.* to cast, draw ~

lottery *n.* 1. to hold a ~ 2. a daily; weekly ~ 3. a state ~

loudspeaker *n.* (to speak) over a ~

lounge I *n.* 1. a cocktail ~ 2. a sun ~ (BE; AE has *sun porch)* 3. a transit ~ (at an airport) 4. a VIP ~ (at an airport)

lounge II *v.* (P; intr.) she enjoys ~ing around the pool

lour see **lower**

louse *n.* a plant; wood ~

lousy *adj.* (slang) ~ to + inf. (it's ~ to be without work = it's ~ being without work)

lout *n.* a stupid ~

love I *n.* ['deep affection'] 1. to inspire ~ for 2.

blind; deep, profound, sincere, true; platonic; undying; unrequited ~ 3. ~ for, of (~ for one's country; to have no ~ for smb.) 4. for, out of ~ (to do smt. for ~) 5. in ~ with (to fall in ~ with smb.; to be hopelessly in ~ with smb.; head over heels in ~ with smb.) ['expression of deep affection'] 6. to give; send one's ~ (give them our ~) ['sexual activity'] 7. to make ~ ('to pet'); ('to have intercourse') 8. free ~

love II *v.* 1. to ~ blindly; dearly; deeply; passionately; really, very much (I would dearly ~ to see them again) 2. (E) she ~s to swim 3. (G) she ~s swimming 4. (N; used with an adjective) she ~s her steak rare 5. (misc.) (colloq.) I ~ *jt* when you smile; I'd ~ you to come over and see our new hi-fi

lovely *adj.* (colloq.) ~ to + inf. (it was ~ of you to arrange this party)

lover *n.* 1. to take a ~ 2. to jilt a ~ 3. an impetuous; lousy (colloq.) ~

low *adj.* ['lacking'] (cannot stand alone) ~ in, on (she is ~ in funds; they were ~ on ammunition)

lower *v.* (D; intr.) ('to frown') to ~ at

low profile *n.* to keep, maintain a ~

loyal *adj.* ~ to

loyalty *n.* 1. to command ~ 2. to demonstrate, show ~ 3. to swear ~ 4. deep-rooted, deep-seated, strong, unquestioned, unshakable, undying ~ 5. party ~ 6. divided ~ties 7. ~ to (unswerving ~ to one's friends)

luck *n.* ['success'] ['good fortune'] 1. to bring ~ 2. to try one's ~ (at smt.) 3. to press, push one's ~ 4. pure, sheer ~ 5. beginner's ~ 6. one's ~ improves, turns; runs out 7. a bit, stroke of ~ 8. ~ at, in (~ at gambling) 9. the ~ to + inf. (she had the good ~ to hold the winning ticket; it was pure ~ to find him = it was pure ~ finding him) 10. ~ that + clause (it was sheer ~ that we met) 11. in ~ (you are in ~ to find them at home) 12. down on one's ~; out of ~ ['fate'] ['chance'] 13. to trust to ~ 14. to try one's ~ (at smt.) 15. bad, hard, tough; good; pure, sheer ~ (we had bad ~) 16. the ~ to + inf. (we had the bad ~ to get there at the wrong time) 17. ~ that + clause (it was bad ~ that he broke his leg)

lucky *adj.* 1. ~ in (~ in love) 2. ~ to + inf. (you are ~ to be alive) 3. ~ that + clause (it's ~ that we got here early)

ludicrous *adj.* 1. ~ to + inf. (it's ~ to dress like that) 2. ~ that + clause (it's ~ that we have to show our pass each time)

luggage *n.* 1. to check, register (esp. BE) one's ~ 2. to check one's ~ through (to the final destination) 3. to claim one's ~ 4. carry-on, hand ~ 5. personalized ~ 6. unclaimed ~ 7. a piece of ~

lukewarm *adj.* ['halfhearted'] ~ about, to (~ about a proposal; ~ to an idea) ['tepid'] 2. ~ to (~ to the touch)

lull I *n.* 1. a momentary, temporary ~ 2. a ~ in (a momentary ~ in the fighting)

lull II *v.* 1. (d; tr.) to ~ into (to ~ smb. into a false sense of security) 2. (d; tr.) to ~ to (to ~ a child to sleep)

lullaby *n.* to hum; sing a ~ to

lumbar puncture *n.* to do, perform a ~

lumber I *n.* (esp. AE) green; seasoned ~ (CE has *timber*)

lumber II *v.* (P; intr.) the bear ~ed through the forest

lumber III *v.* (colloq.) (BE) (D; tr.) ('to burden') to ~ with (I've been ~ed with all their problems)

lumps *n.* (colloq.) ['punishment'] to take one's ~

lunacy *n.* 1. sheer ~ 2. ~ to + inf. (it was ~ to climb that mountain)

lunatic *n.* a ~ to + inf. (he was a ~ to try that)

lunch *n.* 1. to eat, have ~ 2. a business, working; three-martini (AE; colloq.) ~ 3. a box; picnic ~ 4. at ~ (they were all at ~)

lung *n.* 1. an iron ~ 2. congested ~s

lunge I *n.* 1. to make a ~ 2. a ~ at, towards

lunge II *v.* (D; intr.) to ~ at, for

lurch I *n.* ['sudden movement'] to give a ~ (the stricken ship gave a ~)

lurch II *v.* (P; intr.) he ~ed towards me

lurch III *n.* ['vulnerable position'] in the ~ (to leave smb. in the ~)

lure *v.* (d; tr.) to ~ into (to ~ smb. into a trap)

lurk *v.* (P; intr.) to ~ in the shadows

lust I *n.* 1. to arouse ~ 2. to feel ~ 3. to gratify, satisfy one's ~ 4. insatiable, unquenchable ~ 5. ~ for (~ for power)

lust II *v.* (d; intr.) to ~ after, for

luster, lustre *n.* ['glory'] 1. to add ~ to 2. to take on a new ~

luxuriate *v.* (D; intr.) to ~ in (to ~ a newly acquired wealth)

luxury *n.* 1. to enjoy (a) ~ (to enjoy the ~ of a hot bath) 2. to afford a ~ (can we afford the ~ of a second car?) 3. pure, sheer; unaccustomed ~ 4. ~ to + inf. (it was sheer ~ to relax on the beach = it was sheer ~ relaxing on the beach) 5. in ~ (they lived in ~; to wallow in ~) 6. (misc.) in the lap of ~

lyre *n.* to play the ~

M

mace *n.* ['staff used as a symbol of authority'] a ceremonial ~

machete *n.* to brandish, wield a ~

machine *n.* 1. to operate, run, work a ~ 2. to shut down a ~ 3. an adding; answering; calculating; composing, linotype, typesetting; copy, copying, duplicating; earth-moving; heart-lung; milking; milling; money access (AE); sanding; sewing; threshing; video-game; voting; washing; x-ray ~ 4. a mincing ~ (BE; AE has *meat grinder)* 5. a fruit (BE), pinball, slot (AE) ~ (to play a pinball ~) (BE also has *pintable)* 6. a slot (BE), vending ~ 7. a party; political ~ 8. a ~ functions, runs; breaks down

machine gun *n.* 1. to fire, operate a ~ 2. a heavy; light; medium ~ 3. an air-cooled; water-cooled ~ 4. a ~ jams

machine-gun nest *n.* to clean out, wipe out a ~

machinery *n.* ['machines'] 1. to operate, run ~ 2. to maintain ~ ['apparatus'] 3. administrative; law-enforcement; propaganda ~ 4. ~ for (~ for negotiations)

mad *adj.* ['infatuated'] (colloq.) 1. (cannot stand alone) ~ about (they are ~ about each other) ['angry'] (colloq.) (esp. AE) 2. happing ~ 3. to get ~ 4. ~ at (she's ~ at him; to get ~ at smb.) ['insane'] 5. stark raving ~ 6. to go ~ 7. to drive smb. ~ 8. ~ with (~ with pain) 9. ~ to + inf. (he was ~ to try it)

maddening *adj.* 1. ~ to + inf. (it's ~ to have to wait here) 2. ~ that + clause (it's ~ that they never answer the telephone)

made *adj.* (cannot stand alone) ~ from, of, out of; with USAGE NOTE: Compare these examples, which illustrate general tendencies--1. *a stew can be made with vegetables* (vegetables are not the only ingredient). 2. *a stew can be made of/out of vegetables; a chair can be made of/out of wood; shoes are usually made of/out of leather* (only one major substance or ingredient is used). 3. *synthetic rubber can be made from petroleum; paper can be made from wood* (the basic substance has been greatly changed). (see **make II)**

made-to-order *adj.* ~ for

madness *n.* 1. sheer, utter ~ 2. ~ to + inf. (it was sheer ~ to do it)

magazine *n.* ['supply depot'] 1. a powder ~ ['journal'] 2. an alumni (AE); fashion; glossy; illustrated; popular ~

maggots *n.* crawling with ~

magic *n.* 1. to perform ~ 2. black ~ 3. by ~ (the medicine worked as if by ~)

magistrate *n.* a police ~ (esp. AE)

magnanimity *n.* 1. to display, show ~ towards 2. great ~

magnanimous *adj.* 1. ~ towards 2. ~ to + inf. (it was ~ of you to make the offer)

magnate *n.* a coal; steel; tobacco ~

magnetism *n.* animal; personal; physical ~

magnitude *n.* 1. considerable, great ~ 2. of a certain ~ (of considerable ~)

magpie *n.* ~s chatter

maid *n.* ['female servant'] a chambermaid; kitchen; lady's ~; parlormaid

mail I *n.* (esp. AE; BE usu. has *post* for 1-5, 8) ['letters'] ['postal system'] 1. to address; send out (the) ~ 2. to deliver the ~ 3. to forward; sort (the) ~ 4. incoming; outgoing; return ~ 5. airmail; certified; domestic; electronic; express; first-class; foreign; franked; registered; second-class; special-delivery; surface; third-class ~ 6. fan; hate; junk ~ 7. (esp. AE) a piece of ~ 8. by return ~ (BE has *by return of post)*

mail II *v.* (esp. AE; BE has *post)* (A) she ~ed the package to me; or: she ~ed me the package 2. (D; tr.) to ~ from; to (the letter was ~ed from Oregon to Pennsylvania) (for BE see **post II)**

mail III *n.* ['armor'] chain ~

main *n.* ['main pipe, duct'] 1. an electric; gas; sewer; water ~ 2. the water ~ burst

mainland *n.* 1. from; to the ~ 2. on the ~

mainstream *n.* in the ~ of politics

maintain *v.* (L) she ~s that the accusation is groundless

maintenance *n.* 1. preventive; routine ~ 2. building; health ~

majesty *n.* ['sovereign'] 1. Her; His; Your ~ ['grandeur'] 2. in all its ~

major I *n.* ['academic specialization'] (AE) 1. to give, offer a ~ (our department gives a literature ~) 2. a ~ in (our department offers a ~ in literature) ['student who is specializing'] (AE) 3. a ~ in (she is a ~ in English; or: she is an English ~) ['officer'] 4. a ~ commands a battalion

major II *v.* (AE) (d; intr.) ('to specialize') to ~ in (to ~ in Russian)

majority *n.* ['number greater than half'] (AE); ['greater number'] (BE) 1. to get, receive a ~ 2. to have, hold a ~ (the Democrats have a slim ~ in the House) 3. a bare, narrow, slim, small; clear; large; overwhelming, vast ~ 4. an absolute ~ (BE; AE has *majority)* 5. a relative ~ (BE; AE has *plurality)* 6. a simple; two-thirds; working ~ 7. the silent ~ (i.e., those who have moderate or conservative views but do not voice them) 8. by a ~ (to win by an overwhelming ~) 9. in a ~ (in the ~ of cases) ['full legal age'] 10. to attain, reach one's ~ USAGE NOTE: Compare the verbs in the following constructions--the majority of the (two hundred) votes were for peace; a majority of two hundred votes was enough to win.

make I *n.* (colloq.) ['search for gain or sexual favors'] on the ~ (he's always on the ~)

make II *v.* 1. (A) ('to propose') she made an offer to us; or: she made us an offer 2. (C) ('to prepare') ~ an omelet for me; or: ~ me an omelet 3. (d; intr.) to ~ for ('to head for') (she made for the exit; the ship made for the open sea) 4. (d; intr.) to

~ for ('to lead to') (willingness to compromise ~s for success in negotiations) 5. (D; tr.) ('to provide') to ~ for (to ~ room for smb.) 6. (D; tr.) ('to create') to ~ from, of, out of (to ~ butter from cream; she made a table out of wood; tires can be made from/of/out of synthetic rubber) 7. (d; tr.) ('to transform') to ~ into (to ~ a novel into a film; the experience made her into a skeptic) 8. (slang) (AE) (d; intr.) to ~ like ('to imitate') (to ~ like a clown) 9. (d; tr.) to ~ of ('to interpret') (what do you ~ of their offer?) 10. (d; tr.) ('to create') to ~ of, out of (to ~ a fool of smb.; the army made a man out of him) 11. (D; tr.) ('to create') to ~ with (you ~ a stew with meat and vegetables) 12. (I) ('to cause'); ('to force') she made the children clean their room; we made them wait; the police could not ~ him talk 13. (N; used with an adjective, noun, past participle) ('to cause to become') the news made us happy; the rough sea made them seasick; we made our position clear; he made me his deputy; she could not ~ herself understood 14. (S; used with nouns) ('to prove to be') she made a good deputy 15. (misc.) (AE; colloq.) he finally made colonel ('he was finally promoted to the rank of colonel') USAGE NOTE: When pattern I is put into the passive, to is inserted--they were made to wait. (see the Usage Note for **made**)

make away see **make off**

make do v. (D; intr.) to ~ with ('to manage with') (we'll have to ~ with this stove)

make off v. (d; intr.) to ~ with ('to steal and take away') (the thieves made off with the silverware)

make out v. (colloq.) ('to have success') (D; intr.) to ~ with (how did you ~ with the new boss?)

make over v. (esp. BE) (B) ('to transfer legally') she made the bonds over to me

maker n. 1. an auto ~; policymaker 2. (misc.) to meet one's ~ ('to die and go to heaven')

makeup n. ['cosmetics'] 1. to apply, put on ~ 2. to remove ~

make up v. 1. (d; intr.) to ~ for ('to recoup') (to ~ for lost time) 2. (colloq.) (d; intr.) to ~ to ('to gain favor with') (you should try to ~ to your boss) 3. (D; intr.) ('to become reconciled') to ~ with (she made up with her sister)

making n. ['evolution'] 1. in the ~ (a revolution in the ~) ['creation'] 2. not of one's own ~

maladjustment n. an emotional ~

malady n. (lit.) a fatal; serious; strange ~

malaria n. 1. to come down with, develop ~ 2. to eradicate, stamp out ~

malarkey n. (slang) ['nonsense'] (just) plain; pure, sheer ~

malevolence n. pure ~

malformation n. a congenital ~

malice n. 1. to bear ~ towards 2. (legal) with ~ aforethought

malicious adj. ~ towards

mall n. 1. a pedestrian; shopping ~ 2. at a ~ (she works at a shopping ~)

malpractice n. legal; medical; professional ~

mammals n. the higher; lower ~

man n. 1. an average; fat; grown; handsome; middle-aged; old; short; tall; thin; ugly; wise; young ~

2. Cro-Magnon; Heidelberg; Java; Neanderthal; Paleolithic; Peking; Piltdown ~ 3. a divorced; family; married; single ~ 4. a con, confidence; fancy (esp. BE); hatchet; hit (esp. AE); idea; ladies'; marked; organization; party (pol.); professional; Renaissance; right-hand; self-made; straight; straw ~; yes-man 5. an anchorman; businessman; leading ~; liftman (BE); maintenance ~; newspaperman; rewrite; stunt ~; weatherman 6. a moving (AE), removal (BE) ~ 7. a second-story ~ (AE; CE has cat burglar) 8. (pol.) (AE) an advance ~ 9. enlisted men (AE; BE has other ranks) 10. a university ~ (BE; AE has college graduate) 11. a lollipop ~ (BE; AE has crossing guard) 12. a best ~ (at a wedding) 13. the common ~, the ~ in the street 14. a ~ on horseback ('a potential dictator') 15. to a ~ ('everyone') 16. (misc.) he's a ~ of his word; ~ is mortal (esp. BE) every ~ jack ('every man'); a dirty old ~ (pejor.) ('an immoral man'); a medicine ~; the ~ of the year; a ~ of letters; a ~ of action; a ~ of the world

manage v. 1. (colloq.) (D; intr.) ('to cope') to ~ with (we cannot ~ with the children) 2. (D; intr.) ('to cope') to ~ without (we cannot ~ without a car) 3. (E) ('to succeed') she somehow ~d to see him

management n. 1. efficient ~ 2. middle ~ 3. under ~ (under new ~)

manager n. 1. an assistant. branch; business; campaign; city; credit; general; hotel; office; sales; service; stage ~ 2. a baseball ~ USAGE NOTE: For other sports coach is used.

mandate I n. ['order'] 1. to carry out a ~ 2. a clear ~ 3. a ~ to + inf. (we had a ~ to eliminate illiteracy) 4. under a ~ (to do smt.) ['assignment to administer an area'] 5. a ~ over 6. under (a) ~

mandate II v. (formal) (L; subj.) the constitution ~s that the president carry out the laws

mane n. a horse's; lion's ~

maneuver I manoeuvre n. 1. to carry out, conduct, execute a ~ 2. (mil.) to conduct, hold ~s 3. a clever; military; political; tactical ~

maneuver II manoeuvre v. 1. (d; intr.) to ~ for (to ~ for position) 2. (d; tr.) to ~ into (we ~ed them into a compromise) 3. (d; tr.) to ~ out of (the player was ~ed out of position)

mangle v. to ~ beyond recognition

manhole n. an open ~

manhood n. to grow to, reach ~

manhunt n. 1. to carry out, conduct; launch, organize a ~ 2. a ~ for

mania n. a ~ for

maniac n. a homicidal; sex ~

manicure n. 1. to give smb. a ~ 2. to get a ~

manifest n. 1. a plane's; ship's ~ 2. on a ~

manifesto n. 1. to issue a ~ 2. a political ~

manner n. 1. an arrogant, cavalier, imperious, overbearing; awkward; boorish; businesslike; casual, hit-or-miss, offhand, relaxed; charming; cloying; coarse, crude, rude, uncouth; courteous, polite; cursory; debonair; flippant; forthcoming; friendly; gentle, mild; gracious; grand; ingratiating; intriguing; lively; matter-of-fact; obnoxious;

polished; pretentious; prim; professional; servile; sheepish; slipshod, sloppy; statesmanlike; stern; suave; sullen, surly; unctuous ~ 2. bad; good ~s 3. (a doctor's) bedside ~ 4. in a certain ~ (they behaved in a statesmanlike ~; she was businesslike in her ~; in the grand ~; in an awkward ~; everything was done in a well organized ~) 5. (misc.) to the ~ born ('born to an elevated social position'); in a ~ of speaking ('as it were'); to mind one's ~s ('to behave properly')

manoeuvre (BE) see **maneuver**

mansion *n.* (US) a governor's ~

manslaughter *n.* 1. to commit ~ 2. involuntary; voluntary ~

mantle *n.* ['symbol of authority'] to assume; inherit; wear the ~ (of power)

manual *n.* an instruction; laboratory; owner's; teacher's ~

manufacturer *n.* an aircraft; automobile (AE); motorcar (BE); clothing; computer; drug; furniture; radio; shoe; television ~

manure *n.* to spread ~

manuscript *n.* 1. to edit; proofread; revise a ~ 2. to submit a ~ (for publication) 3. to accept; reject a ~ 4. an authentic; unpublished ~

many *determiner, pronoun* ~ of (~ of them) USAGE NOTE: The use of the preposition *of* is necessary when a pronoun follows. When a noun follows, the use of *of the* limits the meaning--we saw many students; we saw many of the students whom we had met earlier.

map *n.* 1. to draw; trace a ~ 2. to consult; read a ~ 3. a large-scale; small-scale ~ 4. a contour; dialect; military; Ordnance-Survey (GB); relief; road; strip; weather ~ 5. on a ~ (to find a village on a ~) 6. (misc.) to put a place on the ~ ('to make a place well-known'); to wipe smt. off the ~ ('to destroy smt.')

marathon *n.* 1. to organize, stage a ~ 2. to run a ~ 3. a dance ~

marauder *n.* a band of ~s

marble *n.* a slab of ~

marbles *n.* 1. to play ~ 2. a game of ~ 3. (misc.) (colloq.) to lose one's ~ ('to lose one's mind')

march I *n.* ['procession'] 1. a death; forced; hunger; peace ~ 2. a ~ from; into, to 3. on the ~ (science is on the ~) ['music that accompanies marching'] 4. to compose; play; strike up a ~ 5. a funeral; military; wedding ~ ['misc.'] 6. to steal a ~ on smb. ('to outwit smb.')

march II *v.* 1. (d; intr.) to ~ against (to ~ against the enemy) 2. (D; intr., tr.) to ~ from; to (the battalion ~ed from the barracks to the parade ground) 3. (d; intr., tr.) to ~ into (the troops ~ed into town) 4. (d; intr.) to ~ on, to, towards (to ~ on the next town)

marching orders *n.* ['notice of dismissal'] (colloq.) (BE) to give smb. her/his ~ (AE has *walking papers*)

march off *v.* (D; intr., tr.) to ~ to (they were ~ed off to prison)

mare *n.* a brood, stock ~

margin *n.* 1. to adjust; set a ~ (when typing) 2. to justify a ~ (in setting type, in word processing) 3.

a comfortable, handsome, large, wide; narrow, slender, slim, small; safe ~ 4. by a ~ (they won by a slim ~) 5. in, on a ~ (to make notes in the ~s) 6. (misc.) a ~ of error; a ~ of safety

marina *n.* a municipal, public ~

marine *n.* a mercantile (BE), merchant (AE) ~

marionette *n.* to manipulate a ~

mark I *n.* ['sign, symbol'] 1. to make one's ~ ('to make a cross in place of a signature') 2. an accent, stress; diacritical; exclamation (BE; AE has *exclamation point);* punctuation; question; quotation ~ 3. (mil.) a hash ~ 4. a laundry ~ ['impression, imprint'] 5. to leave, make one's ~ (they will leave their ~ on history) 6. a distinguishing; indelible ~ ['target'] 7. to find, hit the ~ (the bullet found its ~) 8. to miss; overshoot the ~ 9. to fall short of the ~ 10. off the ~; wide of the ~ ['skin blemish'] 11. a strawberry ~ (esp. BE; CE has *birthmark)* ['victim'] 12. an easy ~ ['starting line of a race'] 13. on your ~s! ['misc.'] 14. to toe the ~ ('to adhere to the rules'); to bear the ~ of Cain (see also **grade 1-4**)

mark II *v.* 1. (D; tr.) to ~ as (these items were ~ed as acceptable) 2. (d; tr.) to ~ for (~ed for death) 3. (K) this birthday ~s his coming of age 4. (N; used with an adjective) she ~ed the documents secret

market *n.* ['store, shop'] 1. a fish; food ~; hypermarket (BE); meat; open-air ~; supermarket 2. at a ~ (to shop at the ~) ['place where trade is conducted'] 3. a stock ~ 4. a flea; open; overseas; spot ~ 5. on a ~ (to buy oil on the spot ~; to put a new product on the ~; a new computer has just come out on the ~) ['stock market'] 6. to play the ~ ('to speculate') 7. to depress the ~ 8. a bear ('falling'); bull ('rising') ~ 9. the ~ is active; depressed; falling; firm, steady; rising; sluggish 10. the ~ closes strong; weak 11. the ~ opens strong; weak ['supply of goods, services'] 12. to capture, corner, monopolize a ~ 13. to flood, glut a ~ 14. the housing; labor ~ 15. a buyer's; seller's ~ ['demand'] 16. to create a ~ 17. to study the ~ 18. to depress a ~ 19. a ~ for (there is no ~ for large cars) 20. in the ~ for (we're in the ~ for a new house) 21. a drug on the ~ ('smt. for which there is little demand') ['trade'] 22. the bond; commodities; securities; stock; used-car; wheat ~

marketplace *n.* in the ~

marksman, markswoman *n.* a crack, skilled ~

marmalade *n.* orange ~

marriage *n.* 1. to enter into a ~ 2. to announce a ~ 3. to consummate a ~ 4. to arrange a ~ 5. to propose ~ 6. to annul a ~ 7. to break up, dissolve a ~ 8. a bad, unhappy; broken; good; happy ~ 9. an arranged; civil; common-law; communal; group; morganatic; open; proxy; secret; trial ~ 10. an interfaith; interracial; mixed ~ 11. a ~ of convenience 12. a ~ into (a family) 13. a ~ to (smb.) 14. (misc.) to give (one's child) in ~

marriage ceremony *n.* to perform a ~

married *adj.* ~ to

marrow *n.* 1. bone ~ 2. vegetable ~ (BE; AE has *squash)*

marry *v.* 1. (d; intr.) to ~ into (to ~ into a good

family) 2. see **marry off**

marry off v. (D; tr.) to ~ to

marshal n. a field ~

marshmallow n. to roast, toast ~s

martial law n. 1. to impose, invoke ~ 2. to rescind; suspend ~

martini n. 1. to fix, make, mix a ~ 2. a dry ~

martyr n. 1. to make a ~ (of smb.) 2. a ~ to (a ~ to tyranny) 3. (misc.) to burn a ~ at the stake; to play the ~

martyrdom n. to suffer ~

marvel I n. 1. to do ~s 2. a ~ to 3. a ~ that + clause (it's a ~ to me that he received the award)

marvel II v. (d; intr.) to ~ at (to ~ at smb.'s skill)

marvelous, marvellous adj. 1. ~ to + inf. (it's ~ to have a day off = it's ~ having a day off) 2. ~ that + clause (it's ~ that we could see each other again)

mascara n. 1. to apply, put on ~ 2. to remove, wipe off ~

mask n. a death; gas; oxygen; ski; stocking surgical ~

masquerade v. (D; intr.) to ~ as (to ~ as a policeman)

mass I n. ['body of matter'] 1. a plastic; shapeless; sticky ~ 2. a land ~ 3. critical ~ 4. atomic ~ 5. a dense ~ (of smoke) 6. (med.) a fixed; hard; irregular; movable; nodular; palpable ~

mass II n. ['celebration of the Eucharist'] 1. to celebrate, offer, say (a, the) ~ 2. to attend, hear ~ 3. high; low; pontifical; requiem; solemn; votive ~ 4. a ~ for

massacre n. to carry out, perpetrate a ~

massage n. 1. to give (smb.) a ~ 2. to get a ~ 3. a back; body; facial; therapeutic ~

mast n. 1. at half ~ 2. (misc.) (lit.) before the ~ ('at sea as a sailor')

master I n. 1. to find one's ~ ('to find one who is superior') 2. a question ~ (BE; AE has *quizmaster*) 3. (chess) a grand ~ 4. a past ~ 5. a ~ at, of (a ~ of deceit)

master II v. to ~ completely, thoroughly

masterpiece n. 1. to create a ~ 2. an enduring ~

mastery n. 1. to demonstrate, display ~ 2. to acquire ~ 3. (a) complete; thorough ~ 4. ~ of; over (~ of one's subject; ~ over other people)

mat n. 1. to weave a ~ 2. an exercise; place; welcome ~

match I n. ['slender piece of wood that catches fire when struck'] 1. to light, strike a ~ 2. to light, put, set a ~ to 3. a safety ~ 4. a book; box of ~es

match II n. ['marriage'] ['marriage partner'] 1. to make a ~ 2. a good ~ 3. a ~ for ['contest'] 4. to promote, stage a ~ 5. a championship; crucial; play-off; return; test (BE) ('international') ~ 6. a football ~ (esp. BE; AE has *football game*) 7. a boxing; cricket; fencing; golf; hockey; polo; tennis; wrestling ~ 8. a ~ between; with (a wrestling ~ between two strong competitors) ['equal competitor'] 9. to meet one's ~ 10. no ~ for (she proved to be no ~ for me; I was no ~ for him) 11. a ~ in (she was more than my ~ in ability) ['pair'] 12. a good; perfect ~ 13. a ~ for USAGE NOTE: When two teams compete before spectators, BE usu. has *match* (a football match); AE usu. has *game* (a football game). However, when the team game is of American origin, BE often uses *game* too (a basketball game). A *chess match* is CE.

match III v. 1. (D; tr.) to ~ against, with ('to pit against') (he was ~ed against a formidable opponent) 2. (D; tr.) ('to equal') to ~ in (no one can ~ him in speed and agility) 3. (D; tr.) to ~ with ('to find the equivalent of') (she wants to ~ this candlestick with a similar one)

matchmaker n. a professional ~

match up v. (D; intr.) to ~ to, with (he doesn't ~ to his opponent)

mate I n. ['petty officer'] (naval) 1. a boatswain's; machinist's ~ ['junior partner'] 2. (BE) a plumber's ~ 3. (US; pol.) smb.'s running ~

mate II v. (D; intr., tr.) to ~ with (zebras don't ~ with donkeys; to ~ a donkey with a mare)

material I adj. ~ to (this evidence is ~ to our case)

material II n. ['data'] 1. to collect, gather ~ 2. source ~ 3. about, on (to gather ~ about the case) 4. ~ for (to gather ~ for a dictionary) ['matter'] 5. radioactive; raw ~ 6. promotional; reading ~; writing ~s 7. packing ~ ['cloth'] 8. a swatch of ~

materialism n. dialectal; historical ~

mathematics n. elementary; higher ~

matrimony n. the state of ~

matron n. 1. a dignified ~ 2. a ~ of honor (at a wedding)

matter I n. ['affair'] 1. to pursue, take up a ~ 2. to arrange; clear up, settle, straighten out; complicate; simplify ~s 3. to give a ~ (attention, thought) (we have given this ~ considerable thought) 4. to not mince ~s (she never minces ~s) ('she always speaks candidly') 5. an important, pressing, serious; petty, trifling ~ 6. no easy; laughing ~ (it's no easy ~ to find a house in this city = it's no easy ~ finding a house in this city; being accused of assault is no laughing ~) 7. ~s came to a head 8. a ~ of (a ~ of grave importance) 9. in ~s of (in ~s of finance) 10. (misc.) as a ~ of fact ('really'); to take ~s into one's own hands; the fact of the ~ is that...; no ~ ('it's not important'); a ~ of record (legal); for that ~ ('concerning that'); a ~ of a few minutes; a ~ of personal opinion; a ~ of some urgency; a ~ of life and death; the crux/heart of the ~ ['material'] ['substance'] 11. printed; reading; subject ~ 12. gaseous; liquid; organic; solid; vegetable ~ 13. gray ~ ('brains') 14. the front ~ (of a book) ['misc.'] 15. what's the ~ with you?

matter II v. 1. (D; intr.) to ~ to (her financial status doesn't ~ to us) 2. (L; to) it doesn't ~ (to us) that we are not rich

mattress n. 1. a firm; soft ~ 2. a double, full; king-size; queen-size; single, twin ~

maturity n. to reach ~

maxim n. a ~ that + clause (it is a valid ~ that competition increases productivity)

maximum n. 1. to set a ~ 2. at a ~ (excitement was at its ~)

may v. (F) she ~ still show up

mayhem n. to commit ~

meadow *n.* in a ~

meal I *n.* ['repast'] 1. to cook, fix (esp. AE; colloq.), prepare a ~ 2. to eat, have; enjoy a ~ 3. to make a ~ of (to make a ~ of soup) 4. to order; serve a ~ 5. a big, heavy; decent, hearty, solid, square; sumptuous ~ (to have a square ~) 6. a light, small; simple; skimpy ~ 7. a main ~ (the main ~ of the day) ['misc.'] 8. (BE; colloq.) to make a ~ of smt. ('to behave as if smt. easy were difficult')

meal II *n.* ['ground seeds'] Indian ~ (BE; AE has *cornmeal*)

mean I *adj.* 1. ~ about (he was very ~about the loan) 2. ~ to (he's ~ to everyone) 3. ~ to + inf. (it was ~ of her to say that)

mean II *n.* ['mathematical value'] 1. to find a ~ 2. an arithmetic; harmonic ~ ['middle point'] 3. a golden ~

mean III *v.* 1. (A; usu. used without *to)* she meant them no harm 2. (d; tr.) to ~ as (it was meant as a favor) 3. (d; tr.) to ~ for (his remark was meant for you) 4. (D; tr.) to ~ to (her words meant nothing to me) 5. (E) I meant to write 6. (L) she really meant that she wanted us to leave 7. (misc.) they never knew what it meant to be hungry

meander *v.* (P; intr.) the brook ~s through the valley

meaning *n.* 1. to misconstrue a ~ 2. an accepted; basic; clear; connotative; double, equivocal; figurative; literal; obscure ~ 3. grammatical; lexical; referential ~ 4. in a ~ (in the accepted ~ of the word)

meanness *n.* 1. ~ to 2. out of ~ (he did it out of ~)

means *n.* ['method'] 1. fair; foul ~ 2. an effective ~ 3. by any ~ 4. (misc.) the end does not justify the ~; a ~ to an end ['resources'] ['wealth'] 5. independent; moderate ~ 6. the ~ to + inf. (do they have the ~ to buy such a large house?) 7. according to, within one's ~ (to live within one's ~) 8. beyond one's ~ (to live beyond one's ~) 9. of ~ (a person of moderate ~) ['misc.'] 10. by all ~ ('without fail'); by no ~ ('in no way')

meant *adj.* (cannot stand alone) ['destined'] 1. ~ for (they were ~ for each other) ['intended'] 2. ~ to + inf. (her remark was ~ to be a compliment) ['supposed'] (colloq.) (BE) 3. ~ to + inf. (Brighton is ~ to be lovely in summer)

meantime, meanwhile *n.* in the ~

measles *n.* 1. to catch, come down with (the) ~ 2. an epidemic; outbreak of ~

measure I *n.* 1. a cubic; dry; liquid; metric ~ 2. a tape ~ 3. in a certain ~ (in large ~) 4. (misc.) for good ~ ('as smt. extra'); made to ~ ('custom-made'); to take smb.'s ~ ('to evaluate smb.') (see also **measures**)

measure II *v.* 1. (d; tr.) to ~ against (to ~ one's accomplishments against smb. else's) 2. (P; intr.) the room ~s twenty feet by ten

measurement *n.* 1. to take a ~; to take smb.'s ~s 2. exact ~s 3. a metric ~ 4. a scientific ~ 5. chest; waist ~s

measures *n.* 1. to carry out, take ~ 2. coercive; compulsory; draconian; drastic, harsh, stern,

stringent; emergency; extreme, radical; preventive, prophylactic; safety, security; stopgap, temporary ~ 3. ~ to + inf. (we took ~ to insure their safety) 4. ~ against (to take ~ against smuggling)

measure up *v.* (D; intr.) to ~ to (he didn't ~ to his opponent)

meat *n.* 1. to broil (AE), grill; cook; cure; fry; roast ~ 2. to carve, cut; slice ~ 3. dark; fatty; fresh; halal; kosher; lean; raw; tender; tough; white ~ 4. chopped (AE), ground (AE), minced (BE); soup ~ 5. ~ goes bad, spoils

mechanic *n.* an automobile (AE), motorcar (BE); master ~

mechanics *n.* celestial; fluid; quantum ~

mechanism *n.* 1. to trigger a ~ 2. a defense; escape ~

medal *n.* 1. to award, give a ~ 2. to earn a ~ 3. to strike ('make') a ~ 4. a bronze; gold; silver ~ (as a prize) 5. a ~ for (to earn a ~ for bravery)

meddle *v.* (D; intr.) to ~ in; with (don't ~ in their affairs)

media *n.* the mass; news ~

mediate *v.* (D; intr.) to ~ between (to ~ between the warring parties)

mediation *n.* 1. to offer ~ 2. to go to ~ 3. ~ between

mediator *n.* 1. to appoint a ~ 2. a government ~ 3. a ~ between

medication *n.* 1. to take (a) ~ 2. to administer, dispense, give (a) ~ 3. to order; prescribe (a) ~ 4. to put smb. on ~ 5. to discontinue (a) ~ 6. to take smb. off ~ 7. (an) effective; mild; potent, strong ~ 8. (an) intramuscular; intravenous; oral; parenteral; topical ~

medicine *n.* ['method, science of treating disease'] 1. to practice ~ 2. to study ~ 3. aerospace, space; allopathic; alternative (BE); complementary (BE); fringe (BE); aviation; ayurvedic; clinical; community, social; defensive; family; folk; forensic, legal; group; homeopathic; industrial, occupational; internal; military; molecular; nuclear; osteopathic; physical; preventive; socialized; sports; traditional; tropical; veterinary ~ ['remedy'] 4. to take (a) ~ (to take ~ for a cold) 5. to prescribe (a) ~ 6. a cough; nonprescription, over-the-counter; patent; proprietary ~ 7. strong ~ (also fig.) 8. ~ for ['punishment'] (colloq.) 9. to take one's ~ ('to accept one's punishment')

meditate *v.* 1. to ~ deeply 2. (D; intr.) to ~ on, upon

meditation *n.* 1. to go in for, practice ~ 2. transcendental ~ 3. deep, profound ~ 4. (deep) in ~

medium *n.* ['middle degree'] 1. a happy ~ ['system'] 2. a ~ of instruction

meet I *n.* (esp. AE) (sports) 1. to hold, organize a ~ 2. a dual; swim, swimming; track, track-and-field ~

meet II *v.* 1. (d; intr.) to ~ with ('to encounter') (to ~ with approval; they met with an accident) 2. (esp. AE) (d; intr.) to ~ with ('to have a meeting with') (our negotiators will ~ with them tomorrow) 3. (misc.) to ~ smb. halfway ('to compromise with smb.') to ~ face to face; to ~ head-on

meeting *n.* 1. to call, convene a ~ 2. to arrange,

hold, organize a ~ 3. to chair, conduct, preside over a ~ 4. to adjourn; break up a ~ 5. to call off, cancel a ~ 6. a chance; clandestine, secret; closed; mass; open; private; protest; public ~ 7. a board; business; cabinet; committee; departmental; faculty; prayer; staff; town ~ 8. an athletics ~ (BE; AE has *track meet*) 9. a race ~ (BE AE has *racing card*) 10. a ~ between, of 11. at a ~ (I saw her at the ~) 12. (misc.) to call a ~ to order

meet up *v.* (AE) (D; intr.) to ~ with

megaphone *n.* (to speak) through a ~

melody *n.* 1. to hum; play; sing a ~ 2. a haunting ~

melon *n.* a juicy; ripe; tasty ~

melt *v.* (d; intr.) to ~ into (to ~ into the crowd)

member *n.* 1. an active; associate; card-carrying; charter (AE), founder (BE); honorary; life; ranking; sustaining ~ 2. a corresponding ~ (of the Academy of Sciences) 3. (misc.) to admit new ~s into an organization

membership *n.* 1. to apply for ~ 2. to grant ~ 3. to drop, resign one's ~ 4. closed; open ~ 5. (an) agency, institutional; associate; full; honorary; individual; life ~ 6. ~ in (AE), of (BE) (~ in/of an organization)

membrane *n.* 1. mucous ~ 2. ~s rupture

memo *n.* 1. an interoffice; office ~ 2. a ~ from; to (see also **memorandum**)

memoirs *n.* to publish; write one's ~

memorandum *n.* 1. to draw up, prepare a ~ 2. to send around a ~ (in an office) 3. to initial a ~ 4. a confidential, secret; diplomatic; interoffice; official; private ~ 5. a ~ about, on 6. a ~ from; to

memorial *n.* 1. to build, erect, put up a ~ 2. to unveil a ~ 3. a war ~ 4. a ~ to

memory *n.* ['power of recalling'] 1. to jog smb.'s ~ 2. to commit smt. to ~ 3. to slip smb.'s ~ (the date has slipped my ~) 4. to lose one's ~ 5. an infallible; photographic; powerful; retentive; short ~ 6. (med.) long-term; short-term; visual ~ 7. a ~ for (a good ~ for names) 8. (to speak) from ~ 9. (misc.) a lapse of ~ ['something recalled, recollection'] 10. to evoke, stir up a ~ 11. to blot out a ~ 12. bitter; dim, vague; enduring; fond; haunting, poignant; pleasant; unpleasant ~ries ['collective remembrance'] 13. to honor, venerate smb.'s ~ 14. a blessed, sacred ~ 15. in ~ of (to erect a memorial in smb.'s ~) 16. in living ~ 17. of blessed, sacred ~ 18. (misc.) dedicated to smb.'s ~ ['capacity for storing information in a computer'] 19. (a) random-access; read-only ~

menace *n.* 1. to constitute a ~ 2. a ~ to

mend *n.* on the ~ ('improving')

mending *n.* invisible ~

menopause *n.* to go through ~

mention I *n.* 1. to make ~ of 2. to deserve ~ 3. honorable ~ (conferred in a contest for an accomplishment of merit that does not win a prize) 4. at the ~ (at the very ~ of his name I shuddered)

mention II *v.* 1. (B) she ~ed the book to me 2. (K) he failed to ~ my being late twice last week 3. (L; to) they ~ed (to her) that they would bring a guest 4. (Q) she forgot to ~ where we should meet 5. (misc.) to ~ smb. by name

menu *n.* ['bill of fare'] 1. to bring a ~ (the waiter

brought the ~) 2. on a ~ (what's on the ~?) ['list of commands for a computer program'] 3. an edit; main; print ~

mercenary *n.* a foreign ~

merchandise *n.* 1. to buy, purchase; order ~ 2. to hawk, sell ~ 3. to ship ~ 4. to carry (a line of) ~ 5. assorted; first-class, high-quality; general ~

merciful *adj.* 1. ~ to 2. ~ to + inf. (it was ~ of her to offer help)

merciless *adj.* ~ to; towards

mercy *n.* 1. to have ~ on 2. to show ~ to, towards 3. to beg for ~ 4. to throw oneself at smb.'s ~ 5. divine; infinite ~; smb.'s tender ~cies (ironic) 6. at smb.'s ~ 7. (misc.) we turned him over to the tender ~cies of the student court

merge *v.* 1. to ~ gradually; imperceptibly 2. (D; intr., tr.) to ~ into (to ~ several small companies into one large one) 3. (D; intr.) to ~ with (our bank ~d with theirs)

merger *n.* 1. to carry out, effect a ~ 2. a ~ between, of; with

merit *n.* 1. intrinsic ~ 2. relative ~s 3. according to, on (the basis of) ~ (to decide a case on its ~s)

merry-go-round *n.* to ride (on) a ~

mesh *v.* (D; intr.) to ~ with (the gears ~ with each other)

mess I *n.* ['untidy condition'] 1. to make a ~ 2. to leave a ~ 3. to clean away, clean up, clear up, sweep up a ~ 4. in a ~ (to leave things in a real ~) ['dining hall'] (mil.) 5. an enlisted (AE); officers' ~ 6. at, in a ~ (they ate at the company ~)

mess II *v.* (colloq.) to ~ with (don't ~ with him)

mess about (BE) see **mess around**

message *n.* 1. to convey; relay; send, transmit a ~ 2. to deliver a ~ 3. to get; receive a ~ 4. to garble; scramble; unscramble a ~ 5. a clear; coded; garbled ~ 6. a ~ from; to 7. a ~ that + clause (we received a ~ that we were to return at once) 8. in a ~ 9. (misc.) to get the ~ ('to grasp the situation'); a divine ~ (from God)

mess around *v.* (colloq.) (AE) (D; intr.) to ~ with

messenger *n.* to dispatch a ~

Messiah *n.* to await the ~

metabolism *n.* 1. to disturb, upset smb.'s ~ 2. basal ~

metal *n.* 1. scrap ~ (to recycle scrap ~) 2. a base; ferrous; nonferrous; precious ~; sheet ~ 3. ~ corrodes, rusts

metamorphose *v.* (D; tr.) to ~ into

metamorphosis *n.* 1. to undergo ~ 2. a ~ into

metaphor *n.* a mixed ~

mete out *v.* (B) to ~ justice to everyone

meter I metre *n.* ['verse rhythm'] ['arrangement of syllables'] 1. anapaestic, anapestic; dactylic; heroic; iambic; trochaic ~ ['unit of length'] 2. a cubic; square ~

meter II *n.* ['instrument for measuring'] 1. to read a ~ (she came to read the gas ~) 2. an electric; exposure; gas; parking; postage; water ~

method *n.* 1. to apply, employ, use a ~ 2. to adopt a ~ 3. to give up, scrap a ~ 4. an antiquated, obsolete; crude; infallible, sure; modern, up-to-date; refined, sophisticated; sound; unorthodox ~ 5. the case; deductive; inductive; scientific; Socratic

~ 6. Madison Avenue ('high-pressure') ~s 7. the audiovisual; direct, oral; grammar-translation ~ (of foreign language instruction); the tutorial ~ (of instruction) 8. teaching ~s 9. the rhythm ~ (of contraception) 10. a ~ for; in, to (a ~ for learning languages; there is a definite ~ in her manner of interrogation)

methodical adj. ~ in (~ in one's work)

meticulous adj. ~ about, in (she is ~ in her dress)

mettle n. 1. to prove, show one's ~ 2. to put smb. on one's ~

mezzanine n. (AE) ['first rows of a balcony in a theater'] in the ~

mickey, Mickey Finn n. (slang) ['a drink to which a strong drug or narcotic has been added'] to slip smb. a ~

microcosm n. in ~ (the whole nation in ~)

microphone n. 1. to hook up, set up a ~ 2. to speak into, through a ~ 3. a concealed; throat ~

microscope n. 1. a compound; electron; optical ~ 2. under a ~

middle n. at, in the ~ (at the ~ of the last century; in the ~ of the room)

middle ground n. the ~ between

midmorning n. at ~

midnight n. at ~

midnight oil n. (colloq.) to burn the ~ ('to work or study late at night')

midpoint n. 1. to reach a ~ 2. at (the) ~

midriff n. 1. to expose one's ~ 2. a bare ~

midsemester n. (AE) at ~

midst n. in the ~ of

midstream n. 1. to reach ~ 2. in ~ (also fig.)

midway adj., adv. ~ between

midyear n. at ~

mien n. (lit.) an impassive; proud ~

might I n. 1. armed ~ 2. with all one's ~

might II v. (F) I ~ do that

migraine n. 1. a severe ~ 2. an attack of ~

migrate v. 1. (d; intr.) to ~ between 2. (D; intr.) to ~ from; to

migration n. 1. internal; mass ~ 2. annual ~ (the annual ~ of birds) 3. ~ from; to

mildew n. ~ forms

mile n. 1. a land, statute; nautical, sea ~ 2. (misc.) to miss by a ~ ('to miss by a great deal')

mileage n. to get ~ (I get good ~ with this small car; to get good ~ out of tires)

milestone n. to reach a ~ (usu. fig.)

military n. to call in the ~

military service n. universal ~

militate v. (d; intr.) to ~ against (see the Usage Note for *mitigate*)

militia n. to call out, mobilize the ~

milk I n. 1. to boil; express ~ 2. curdled, sour; fresh ~ 3. attested (BE), certified; chocolate; condensed; evaporated; fermented; fortified; fresh; homogenized; long-life (BE); low-fat; non-fat; pasteurized; powdered; raw; reconstituted; skim (AE), skimmed; whole ~ 4. cow's; goat's ~

milk II v. (N; used with an adjective) to ~ smt. dry

mill I n. ['machine for grinding'] 1. a coffee; pepper ~ ['factory'] 2. a flour; lumber; paper; rolling;

steel; textile ~ ['place where results are achieved in a quick, routine way'] 3. a diploma; divorce; marriage; propaganda ~ ['misc.'] 4. to go through the ~ ('to acquire experience under difficult conditions')

mill II v. (d; intr.) to ~ about, around (to ~ around the entrance)

millstone n. ['heavy burden'] to have a ~ around one's neck

mincemeat n. to make ~ of ('to defeat decisively')

mind I n. 1. to make up one's ~ 2. to make up one's ~ to do smt. 3. to cultivate, develop one's ~ 4. to speak one's ~ 5. to change one's ~ 6. to bear, keep smt. in ~ 7. to bring, call smt. to ~ 8. to keep one's ~ on smt. 9. to put, set one's ~ to smt. 10. to set one's ~ at ease 11. to take one's ~ off smt. 12. to cross one's ~ (it crossed my ~ that the store would be closed at five o'clock) 13. to know one's own ~ 14. to lose one's ~ 15. a clear; closed; disciplined; inquiring, inquisitive; keen, sharp; narrow; nimble, quick; one-track; open; scientific; uncluttered ~ 16. a deranged, twisted, unbalanced, unsound; sound ~ 17. in one's ~ (in one's right ~; in one's subconscious ~) 18. on one's ~ (what's on your ~?) 19. out of one's ~ (to go out of one's ~) 20. (misc.) I have half a ~ to vote for smb. else ('I may well vote for smb. else'); to give smb. a piece of one's ~ ('to state one's views to smb. very bluntly'); a meeting of the ~s; we were all of the same ~ ('we all had the same opinion'); a state of ~

mind II v. 1. (G) I don't ~ waiting; would you ~ opening the window? 2. (K) he didn't ~ her smoking; would you ~ my opening the window? 3. (Q) (esp. BE) ~ how you go! 4. (misc.) never ~ about that

mindful adj. (cannot stand alone) ~ of (~ of one's responsibilities)

mind's eye n. in one's ~

mine n. ['excavation from which minerals are taken'] 1. to open (up); operate, run, work a ~ 2. to close down a ~ 3. a coal; copper; diamond; gold; iron; lead; salt; silver; tin; zinc ~ 4. an abandoned; strip ~ ['explosive charge'] 5. to arm; lay a ~ 6. to hit, strike a ~ 7. to detonate, set off a ~ 8. to clear, remove, sweep ~s 9. to detect; disarm a ~ 10. a ~ blows up, explodes 11. an antipersonnel; antitank; contact; drifting, floating; land; magnetic; pressure; submarine ~

minerals n. metallic; nonmetallic; rock ~

mingle v. (D; intr.) to ~ with

miniature n. in ~

minimal pair n. (ling.) to produce; represent a ~

mining n. open-cast (BE), open-pit (AE), strip (AE); shaft ~

minister I n. 1. to accredit a ~ 2. a ~ plenipotentiary; a ~ without portfolio 3. a cabinet; foreign; prime ~ 4. a ~ from; to

minister II v. (d; intr.) to ~ to (to ~ to smb.'s needs)

ministry n. (rel.) a lay ~

minor I n. to serve ~s (this bar does not serve ~s)

minor II v. (AE) (d; intr.) to ~ in (to ~ in French) ('to have French as a secondary subject')

minority *n.* in a ~ (we were in the ~; in a ~ of cases)

minstrel *n.* a wandering ~

minuet *n.* to dance; play a ~

minus see **plus**

minute *n.* ['sixtieth part of an hour'] 1. in a ~ (she'll be here in a ~) ['instant'] 2. the last ~ (at the last ~) ['present time'] 3. this ~ 4. up to the ~

minutes *n.* ['official record'] 1. to keep, take ~ 2. to accept; read the ~ 3. to reject the ~

miracle *n.* 1. to accomplish, perform, work a ~ 2. a ~ that + clause (it's a ~ that she was not killed) 3. by a ~ (we survived by a ~) 4. (misc.) a ~ worker

miraculous *adj.* ~ that + clause (it's ~ that they were rescued)

mirage *n.* 1. to see a ~ 2. a ~ disappears

mire *n.* (to be stuck) in the ~

mired *adj.* to get ~ (in the mud)

mired down (esp. AE) see **mired**

mirror *n.* 1. to hang a ~ 2. a full-length; hand; pocket; rear-view ~

mirth *n.* 1. to provoke ~ 2. general ~

misapprehension *n.* 1. (to labor) under a ~ 2. a ~ that + clause (we labored under the ~ that we would receive help)

miscalculate *v.* to ~ badly

miscalculation *n.* 1. to make a ~ 2. to correct a ~ 3. a bad, glaring, serious ~ 4. a ~ about

miscarriage *n.* ['abortion'] 1. to have a ~ ['failure'] 2. a gross ~ (of justice)

mischief *n.* 1. to cause, do, make ~ 2. to be up to, get into ~ 3. malicious ~ 4. out of ~ (to stay out of ~; to keep children out of ~) 5. full of ~ 6. up to ~

misconception *n.* a popular ~

misconduct *n.* gross; professional ~

miscount *n.* to make a ~

misdeed *n.* 1. to commit a ~ 2. to rectify a ~ 3. a glaring ~

misdemeanor, misdemeanour *n.* to commit a ~

miserable *adj.* ~ to + inf. (it is ~ to work there = it is ~ working there)

misery *n.* 1. to cause ~ 2. to alleviate, relieve ~ 3. abject, deep; sheer, untold ~ 4. ~ to + inf. (it was sheer ~ to live there = it was sheer ~ living there) 5. in ~ (to live in ~)

misfortune *n.* 1. to have, suffer (a) ~ 2. the ~ to + inf. (she had the ~ to get there at the wrong moment)

misgivings *n.* 1. to have ~ about 2. to express one's ~ 3. ~ that + clause (we had ~ that he would back out of the agreement)

mishap *n.* (formal) 1. to have a ~ 2. a ~ befell us

misinformation *n.* 1. to give, peddle, plant, spread ~ 2. to correct ~ 3. ~ about

misinformed *adj.* 1. grossly ~ 2. ~ about

misjudge *v.* to ~ badly, completely

mislead *v.* (D; tr.) to ~ about (we were misled about this matter)

misleading *adj.* 1. grossly ~ 2. ~ to + inf. (it is ~ to cite only certain sources)

mismanagement *n.* gross ~

misnomer *n.* a ~ to + inf. (it's a ~ to call this vil-

lage a city)

mispronounced *adj.* commonly, frequently ~

misrepresentation *n.* gross ~

miss I *n.* a clean; near ~

miss II *v.* 1. to ~ terribly, very much 2. (G) I ~ walking in the park

missed *adj.* sorely ~

missile *n.* 1. to fire, launch; guide a ~ 2. to intercept a ~ 3. an air-to-air; air-to-ground, air-to-surface; antiaircraft, ground-to-air, surface to-air; antimissile; ballistic; cruise; ground-to-ground, surface-to-surface; guided; intercontinental ballistic; intermediate-range, medium-range long-range, strategic; nuclear; short-range, tactical; submarine-launched ~

missing *adj.* 1. ~ from (~ from a group) 2. (misc.) ~ in action (mil.); to turn up ~

missing link *n.* a ~ between

mission *n.* ['task'] 1. to accomplish, carry out, perform; undertake a ~ 2. (mil.) to fly a ~ 3. (usu. mil.) to cancel, scratch, scrub a ~ 4. a dangerous; pioneering; suicide ~ 5. a combat; diplomatic; goodwill; rescue; search-and-destroy; training ~ 6. on a ~ (they went on a goodwill ~ to Asia) 7. a ~ to + inf. (our ~ was to work out a trade agreement) 8. (misc.) ~ impossible (often humorous) ['group sent to perform a task'] 9. a diplomatic; military; trade ~ 10. a ~ from; to (a trade ~ to Africa)

missionary *n.* 1. a foreign. medical ~ 2. a ~ from; to

miss out *v.* (D; intr.) to ~ on (to ~ on a profitable deal)

misstatement *n.* to make a ~

mistake I *n.* 1. to make a ~ 2. to correct, rectify a ~ 3. to excuse, forgive a ~ 4. a bad, costly, glaring, serious; fatal; foolish; minor, slight ~ 5. ~s abound (on every page) 6. a ~ about; in (we made a ~ about that; she made a ~ in counting on their help) 7. a ~ to + inf. (it was a ~ to appoint her = it was a ~ appointing her) 8. by ~ (to do smt. by ~)

mistake II *v.* (d; tr.) to ~ for (he mistook me for my brother)

mistaken *adj.* 1. ~ about; in 2. ~ for (she was ~ for her sister)

mistletoe *n.* ['Christmas decoration'] to stand under the ~ ('to indicate one's willingness to be kissed, during the Christmas season')

mistrial *n.* (legal) to declare a ~

mistrust *n.* 1. to arouse ~ 2. deep, profound ~ 3. ~ towards

mistrustful *adj.* ~ of

misunderstanding *n.* 1. to cause, lead to a ~ 2. to clear up a ~ 3. a ~ about, over; between

mitigate *v.* (pompous) (d; intr.) to ~ against ('to make difficult') USAGE NOTE: Many consider the use of *mitigate* in place of *militate* to be substandard.

mitt *n.* ['glove'] 1. an oven ~ 2. (baseball) a catcher's; first baseman's ~

mix I *n.* ['mixture'] a cake; cement; pancake; soup ~

mix II *v.* 1. (B) ~ a nice drink for me; or: ~ me a

nice drink 2. (D; intr., tr.) to ~ with (he doesn't ~ with people like that; she ~ed the brandy with wine)

mixed up *adj.* 1. ~ in (~ in a scandal) 2. ~ with (she got herself ~ with criminals)

mixer *n.* ['informal dance, party'] 1. to give, hold a ~ ['device for mixing'] 2. a cement, concrete; electric ~

mix-up *n.* 1. to cause a ~ 2. a ~ about, in, over

mix up *v.* (D; tr.) to ~ with (he always ~es me up with my brother)

moan I *n.* 1. to emit a ~ 2. a barely audible, feeble, weak; loud ~

moan II *v.* 1. to ~ feebly; loudly 2. (D: intr.) to ~ about, over (to ~ over new taxes) 3. (D; intr.) to ~ with (to moan ~ pain)

mob *n.* 1. to inflame, stir up a ~ 2. to control, subdue a ~ 3. to disperse a ~ 4. an angry; undisciplined, unruly, wild ~ 5. a ~ disperses; gathers; runs amok, runs wild

mobile *adj.* upwardly ~

mobility *n.* upward ~

mobilization *n.* 1. to order (a) ~ 2. to carry out ~ 3. full, general; partial ~

mockery *n.* 1. to make a ~ of 2. a mere ~

mock-up *n.* ['model'] to do, prepare a ~

mode *n.* an access; insert ~ (on a computer)

model I *n.* 1. to take as a ~ 2. to pose; serve as a ~ 3. a role ~ 4. an artist's; photographer's ~ 5. a ~ for

model II *v.* 1. (d; refl., tr.) to ~ after, on (the academy was ~ed after a British public school) 2. (d; intr., tr.) to ~ in (to ~ in clay)

moderate *adj.* ~ in (they were ~ in their demands)

moderation *n.* 1. to display, show ~ 2. ~ in (~ in the consumption of alcohol) 3. in ~ (to drink in ~)

modest *adj.* 1. ~ about (she was ~ about her achievements) 2. ~ in

modesty *n.* 1. to affect; display ~ 2. false ~ (without false ~) 3. ~ about

modification *n.* 1. to make a ~ in 2. behavior ~

modifier *n.* a dangling (esp. AE); noun ~

modulation *n.* frequency ~

module *n.* a command; lunar; service ~

modus operandi *n.* to establish, work out a ~

modus vivendi *n.* to establish, work out a ~

mogul *n.* a movie (AE) ~

molar *n.* 1. to cut a ~ 2. an impacted ~ 3. a first; second; third ~

mold I **mould** *n.* ['furry growth'] to gather ~

mold II **mould** *n.* 1. a jello (AE), jelly (BE); plaster ~ 2. in a ~ (to be cast in a ~)

mold III **mould** *v.* (D; tr.) to ~ from, in, out of (to ~ a figure in/out of clay)

mole *n.* ['burrowing insectivore'] 1. ~s burrow ['spy'] 2. to plant a ~

molestation *n.* child; sexual ~

moment *n.* 1. to savor the ~ 2. a crucial; opportune, propitious; unpropitious ~ 3. a rash ~ (in a rash ~) 4. the psychological ~ ('the most favorable time') 5. at a ~ (at that ~) ('then'); (at the/this ~) ('now') 6. for the ~ (for the ~ let us drop this subject) 7. in a ~ (she'll be here in a ~; in a crucial

~ of one's life)

momentum *n.* to gain, gather ~

monarch *n.* an absolute; constitutional ~

monarchy *n.* 1. to establish, set up a ~ 2. to overthrow a ~ 3. an absolute; constitutional; hereditary; limited ~

money *n.* 1. to coin, make, produce; counterfeit ~ 2. to circulate ~ 3. to earn, make ~ 4. to bank; change; deposit; put up; raise; refund, return; save; spend; squander, throw away; tie up; withdraw ~ 5. to borrow; lend ~ 6. to invest ~ in; to put ~ into (they invested their ~ in stocks and bonds; she put her ~ into municipal bonds) 7. (colloq.) to sink (a lot of) ~ into (a venture) 8. to launder (illegally acquired) ~ 9. counterfeit; earnest; easy; hush; marked; paper; pin, pocket, spending; prize; seed; tight; well-spent ~ 10. blood; conscience ~ 11. tax ~ (politicians should not waste tax ~) 12. mad ~ ('small amount of money carried for emergency use') 13. for ~ (to do smt. for ~) 14. out of ~ (we are out of ~) 15. (misc.) to have ~ to burn ('to have a great deal of money')

money order *n.* 1. to make out a ~ 2. to send a ~ 3. to cash a ~

monitor I *n.* 1. an electronic; heart ~ 2. a video ~ (for a computer)

monitor II *v.* to ~ closely

monkey *n.* 1. a howler; rhesus; ring-tailed; spider ~ 2. a horde, troop of ~s 3. (misc.) (colloq.) to make a ~ (out) of smb. ('to make a fool of smb.')

monkey around *v.* (colloq.) (AE) (D; intr.) to ~ with

monkey wrench *n.* (colloq.) (esp. AE) ['disruption'] to throw a ~ into smt. ('to disrupt smt.')

monogamy *n.* to practice ~

monologue, monolog *n.* to recite a ~

mononucleosis *n.* (AE) infectious ~ (CE has *glandular fever*)

monopoly *n.* 1. to establish, gain a ~ 2. to have, hold a ~ 3. to break (up) a ~ 4. a government, state ~ 5. a ~ of, on, over 6. (misc.) to play Monopoly (T)

monotone *n.* in a ~

monotonous *adj.* ~ to + inf. (it is ~ to watch television every day = it is ~ watching television every day)

monotony *n.* to break, relieve the ~

monoxide *n.* carbon ~

monstrous *adj.* 1. ~ to + inf. (it is ~ to preach hatred) 2. ~ that + clause (it's ~ that innocent children throughout the world go hungry)

month *n.* 1. last; next; this ~ 2. by the ~ (she is paid by the ~) 3. for a ~ (he'll be here for a ~) 4. in a ~ (they will arrive in a ~) 5. in, to (colloq.) a ~ (there are four weeks in a ~)

monument *n.* 1. to build, erect a ~ 2. an ancient; literary; national ~ 3. a ~ to

mooch *v.* (slang) (AE) 1. (D; tr.) ('to beg for') to ~ from (he ~ed a cigarette from me) 2. (d; intr.) ('to sponge') to ~ off of, on (to ~ on one's friends)

mood I *n.* ['state of mind'] 1. an angry; bad, foul; bellicose; bilious; festive, holiday; genial, good, happy, jovial, joyful; melancholy; mellow; mercurial; nostalgic; pensive; resentful; sullen; tranquil ~ 2. in a ~ (in a good ~)

mood II *n.* ['verb form'] the conditional; imperative; indicative; subjunctive ~

moon I *n.* 1. a full; half; harvest; new; quarter ~ 2. the ~ wanes; waxes 3. the ~ comes out 4. on the ~ (astronauts have walked on the ~)

moon II *v.* (D; intr.) to ~ over

moonlight *n.* 1. by ~ 2. in the ~

moonlight flit *n.* (colloq.) (BE) ['moving without paying one's rent, debts'] to do a ~

moor *v.* (D; tr.) to ~ to (to ~ a boat to a pier)

moose *n.* 1. a band, herd of ~ 2. a young ~ is a calf 3. a female ~ is a cow 4. a male ~ is a bull (see the Usage Note for **elk)**

mop I *n.* a dry, dust, wet ~

mop II *v.* (N; used with an adjective) we ~ped the floor clean

moped *n.* to ride a ~

moral *n.* a ~ to (there's a ~ to the story)

morale *n.* 1. to boost, lift, raise ~ 2. to destroy, undermine ~ 3. high; low ~

moral fiber, moral fibre *n.* the ~ to + inf. (does she have the ~ to adhere to principle?)

moralize *v.* (D; intr.) to ~ about, on, over, upon

morals *n.* 1. to protect, safeguard (public) ~ 2. to corrupt smb.'s ~ 3. lax, loose; strict ~ 4. public ~

morass *n.* to get bogged down in a ~

moratorium *n.* 1. to declare a ~ 2. to lift a ~ 3. a ~ on

morbid *adj.* ~ about (don't be ~ about the future)

more *determiner, pronoun* ~ of (~ of them) USAGE NOTE: The use of the preposition *of* is necessary when a pronoun follows. When a noun follows, the use of *of the* limits the meaning--we drank more wine; we drank more of the wine that you brought yesterday.

morgue *n.* 1. a city (esp. AE); newspaper ~ 2. in a ~ (to work in a ~)

morning *n.* 1. early; late ~ 2. in the ~; (AE) ~s (she works in the ~; or AE: she works ~s) 3. from ~ (from ~ to night) 4. on a ~ (on a cold ~ last month; on the ~ of July 20)

moron *n.* (colloq.) a ~ to + inf. (I was a ~ to accept his offer)

Morse code *n.* 1. to tap out, use the ~ 2. to send (a message) in ~

mortality *n.* infant; maternal ~

mortar *n.* ['type of cannon'] 1. a trench ~ ['bowl'] 2. a ~ and pestle

mortgage *n.* 1. to give a ~ 2. to hold; receive; take out a ~ on 3. to pay off a ~ 4. to finance; foreclose; refinance a ~ 5. a chattel; conventional; first; second ~

mortification *n.* 1. deep ~ 2. to one's ~ (to my everlasting ~)

mortified *adj.* ['embarrassed'] 1. deeply ~ 2. ~ to + inf. (I was ~ to learn that my account was overdrawn) 3. ~ that + clause (we were ~ that our manuscript was rejected)

mortuary *n.* at, in a ~

Moses *n.* holy ~! (esp. AE; colloq.; *interjection)*

Moslem see **Muslim**

mosquito *n.* 1. ~s bite; fly; hum 2. ~s carry,

spread disease

most *determiner, n., pronoun* 1. to get the ~ (out of life) 2. to make the ~ (of one's opportunities) 3. ~ of (~ of them) 4. at (the) ~ USAGE NOTE: The use of the preposition *of* is necessary when a pronoun follows. When a noun follows, the following constructions are used--most American wine comes from California; most of the wines that we import come from Europe; we like most students; we like most of the students who study in this department.

motel *n.* to check into; out of a ~

mothballs *n.* ['protective storage'] 1. to put into ~ (to put ships into ~) 2. to take out of ~

mother *n.* 1. an expectant; nursing; surrogate; unwed; welfare; working ~ 2. a foster ~; step-mother 3. a ~ to (she was like a ~ to them) 4. (misc.) a den ~; a ~ superior

motif *n.* a guiding, leading ~

motion I *n.* ['proposal'] 1. to make a ~ 2. to second a ~ 3. to accept; defeat, vote down a ~ 4. to vote on a ~ 5. (AE) to table a ~ ('to postpone voting on a proposal') 6. (BE) to table a ~ ('to call for a vote on a proposal') 7. to withdraw a ~ 8. the ~ carried, passed 9. a ~ to + inf. (she made a ~ to adjourn) 10. a ~ that + clause; subj. (she made a ~ that debate be/should be stopped) 11. on a ~ (on my ~ they brought up the question of admitting new members) ['movement'] 12. to set smt. in ~ 13. harmonic; perpetual ~

motion II *v.* 1. (D; intr.) to ~ to (she ~ed to us) 2. (H) he ~ed (to) us to come closer

motivate *v.* (H) what ~d her to leave home?

motivation *n.* the ~ to + inf. (she has the ~ to master English)

motive *n.* 1. to establish, find a ~ 2. to question smb.'s ~s 3. altruistic; base; honorable; humane; noble; selfish; ulterior ~s; the highest ~s (to have nothing but the highest ~s) 4. the profit ~ 5. an underlying ~ 6. a ~ behind, for (the police could not find a ~ for the murder) 7. a ~ to + inf. (she had no ~ to commit the crime)

motor I *n.* 1. to start a ~ 2. to turn off a ~ 3. an outboard ~ 4. a ~ runs, works; stalls (see also **engine 1-7)**

motor II *v.* (d; intr.) to ~ to (they ~ed to to ~n)

motorbike *n.* to drive, ride a ~

motorcar *n.* (BE) to drive; park a ~ (see **car 1-3)**

motorcycle *n.* 1. to drive, ride a ~ 2. to ride in a ~ (as a passenger)

motor scooter *n.* to drive, ride a ~

motorway (BE) see **highway**

motto *n.* to coin a ~

mound *n.* 1. a burial ~ 2. (baseball) (AE) to take the ~

mount *n.* an engine ~

mountain *n.* 1. to climb, scale a ~ 2. high; rugged; snow-covered ~s 3. block; folded; volcanic ~s 4. a chain, range of ~s 5. (misc.) the elevation, height of a ~; to make a ~ out of a molehill ('to exaggerate')

mourn *v.* (D; intr.) to ~ for, over

mourning *n.* 1. to declare, proclaim (a period of) ~ 2. to go into ~ 3. deep ~ 4. national ~ 5. in ~

for

mouse *n.* 1. to catch mice 2. a field; house; meadow; white ~ 3. mice gnaw 4. (misc.) as quiet as a ~

moustache *n.* 1. to grow a ~ 2. to trim a ~ 3. to finger, twist one's ~ 4. a handlebar ~

mouth *n.* 1. to close, shut; open one's ~ 2. to cram, stuff one's ~ (with food) 3. to rinse one's ~ 4. (misc.) (colloq.) a big ~ ('a gossip'); to shoot off one's ~ ('to talk too much'); to make smb.'s ~ water ('to tempt smb.')

mouthful *n.* (colloq.) ['something true'] to say a ~

mouthpiece *n.* ['spokesperson'] to act, serve as a ~ for

move I *n.* ['act'] 1. to make a ~ (who will make the first ~?) 2. a false ~ (one false ~ would be costly) 3. a brilliant; clever, smart; decisive ~ ['moving of a piece in chess, checkers'] 4. to make a ~ 5. a brilliant; stupid, wrong ~ 6. an opening ~ (also fig.) ['act of moving'] 7. a ~ to (our firm's ~ to the Coast) 8. (misc.) (colloq.) to get a ~ on ('to go faster'); on the ~

move II *v.* 1. ('to stir') to ~ deeply, profoundly 2. ('to change the position of') to ~ bodily 3. (d; intr.) ('to request') to ~ for (to ~ for a new trial) 4. (D; intr., tr.) ('to change or cause to change one's position, place of residence, place of work') to ~ from; into, to; out of (let's ~ from this table to that one; they ~d from the city to the suburbs; the firm is ~ing to California; let's ~ the chair from/out of this room to that one; he ~d his family from/out of an old house into a new apartment; we are ~ing our main office from/out of the city to a small town) 5. (D; tr.) ('to stir') to ~ to (she was ~d to tears) 6. (d; intr.) ('to change one's position') to ~ towards (to ~ towards the exit) 7. (H) ('to induce') what ~d her to make such a gesture? 8. (L; subj.) ('to propose') she ~d that the resolution be/should be approved

move in *v.* 1. (d; intr.) ('to close in') to ~ for (to ~ for the kill) 2. (D; intr.) to ~ on ('to close in on') (the police ~d in on the fugitives) 3. (D; intr.) to ~ on ('to establish control of') (organized crime was ~ing in on the industry) 4. (D; intr.) to ~ on, with ('to take up residence with') (her relatives wanted to ~ with her)

movement *n.* ['organized effort to attain a goal'] 1. to launch a ~ 2. to support a ~ 3. to oppose; suppress a ~ 4. a civil-rights; consumer; feminist, women's; labor; peace; political; radical; revolutionary; social ~ 5. a ~ against; for (the ~ for equal pay) ['division of a musical composition'] 6. to perform a ~ ['military maneuver'] 7. a pincers ~ ['move'] 8. a downward; upward ~ 9. jerky; rhythmic; uncoordinated ~s 10. a ~ towards ['evacuation'] 11. a bowel ~ (to have a bowel ~)

move up *v.* 1. (D; intr.) to ~ into, to (she has ~d up to the position of general manager) 2. (D; intr.) to ~ through (to ~ through the ranks)

movie *n.* (esp. AE) ['film'] 1. to make, produce a ~ 2. (CE) a home ~ ['cinema'] 3. a drive-in ~

movies *n.* (AE) ['cinema'] to go to the ~

mower *n.* 1. to operate, work a ~ 2. a hand; lawn;

power ~

much *determiner, n., pronoun* 1. to make ~ of smt. 2. ~ of (we did not believe ~ of what we heard; he isn't ~ of an artist) 3. ~ to + inf. (she has ~ to say; we have ~ to learn) 4. (misc.) ~ as we want to help USAGE NOTE: The use of the preposition *of* is necessary when a pronoun follows--we did not believe much of what we heard. When a noun follows, the use of *of the* limits the meaning--much sorrow is caused by drug abuse; much of the sorrow that is caused by drug abuse could be avoided.

muck about *v.* (colloq.) (BE) to ~ with ('to mess around with')

mucus *n.* 1. to secrete ~ 2. nasal ~

mud *n.* ['wet earth'] 1. to spatter ~ 2. ~ oozes, squishes 3. ~ cakes 4. a layer of ~ 5. (misc.) to spatter smb. with ~ ['malicious charges'] 6. to sling, throw ~ at smb.

muddle *n.* ['confusion'] in a ~

mufti *n.* ['civilian clothes'] in ~

mug *n.* a shaving ~

mulct *v.* (rare) (D; tr.) ('to defraud') to ~ of (to ~ smb. of her/his money)

mule *n.* 1. to drive; ride a ~ 2. ~s bray 3. a team of ~s 4. (misc.) as stubborn as a ~

mull *v.* (d; intr.) to ~ over (to ~ over a new proposal)

multiplication *n.* to do ~

mum *adj.* to remain ~

mumble *v.* (L; to) he ~d (to us) that he would get up later

mumps *n.* to catch, come down with the ~

murder *n.* ['homicide'] 1. to commit ~ 2. a brutal, cold-blooded, grisly, heinous, vicious, wanton; premeditated; ritual ~ 3. (AE) (a) first-degree; second-degree ~ 4. mass ~ 5. multiple, serial ~s ['ruinous influence'] (colloq.) 6. ~ on (the rainy weather has been ~ on business)

murderer *n.* a mass; serial ~

murmur *n.* ['complaint'] 1. to let out a ~ (she didn't let out a ~) ['abnormal sound'] (med.) 2. a heart ~

muscle *n.* 1. to contract; flex, tense; move; pull, strain; relax; wrench a ~ 2. to develop one's ~s 3. involuntary; smooth; striated; voluntary ~s 4. ~s ache

muscle in *v.* (colloq.) (D; intr.) to ~ on (to ~ on smb.'s territory)

muse *v.* (D; intr.) to ~ about, over, upon

museum *n.* 1. an art (esp. AE; BE prefers *art gallery*); ethnographic; public; science; wax ~ 2. at, in a ~ (to work at a ~)

mushroom I *n.* 1. to pick ~s 2. an edible ~

mushroom II *v.* (D; intr.) to ~ from; into, to

music *n.* 1. to compose, write ~ 2. to perform, play ~ 3. to set smt. to ~ 4. to read ~ 5. background; band; chamber; choral; classical; country, hillbilly; dance; folk; funky; incidental; instrumental; light; martial; modern; organ; popular; rock; sacred; serious; soul ~ 6. sheet ~ 7. a piece of ~ 8. (fig.) ~ to (what she said was ~ to my ears) 9. to ~ (to dance to the ~ of a big band) 10. (misc.) to face the ~ ('to accept one's punish-

ment')
musical *n.* to produce, stage a ~
musical chairs *n.* to play ~
musician *n.* an accomplished; natural; strolling ~
Muslim *n.* a Black; Shiite; Sunni ~
muslin *n.* bleached; unbleached ~
must *v.* 1. (F) we ~ go 2. (misc.) I really ~ go; you surely ~ know
mustache see **moustache**
muster I *n.* to pass ~
muster II *v.* 1. (d; tr.) to ~ into (to ~ smb. into the army) 2. (d; tr.) to ~ out of ('to discharge from') (to be ~ed out of the army)
mutation *n.* 1. to induce a ~ 2. a gene ~
mute *adj.* to stand ~ ('to remain silent during an arraignment')
mutiny I *n.* 1. to foment, incite, stir up; organize a ~ 2. to crush, put down, quell a ~ 3. a ~ breaks

out
mutiny II *v.* (D; intr.) to ~ against
mutter *v.* 1. (B) she ~ed a few words to us 2. (D; intr.) to ~ about 3. (L; to) she ~ed (to him) that she would catch up later
mysterious *adj.* ~ about (~ about one's past)
mystery *n.* 1. to pose a ~ (her disappearance poses a real ~) 2. to clear up; fathom, solve, unravel a ~ 3. an unsolved ~ 4. a murder ~ 5. a ~ deepens 6. a ~ to (it was a ~ to me) 7. (misc.) shrouded, wrapped in ~
mystified *adj.* ~ to + inf. (she was ~ to find her watch gone)
mystifying *adj.* ~ that + clause (it's ~ that the matter was never investigated)
myth *n.* 1. to create a ~ 2. to debunk. dispel; explode a ~ 3. a ~ that + clause (we dispelled the ~ that their army was invincible)

N

nadir *n*. 1. to reach a ~ 2. at a ~

nag *v*. 1. (D; intr.) to ~ at (he kept ~ging at her) 2. (H) he kept ~ging her to buy a new sofa

nail I *n*. ['tapered piece of metal'] 1. to drive, hammer a ~ (he drove a ~ into the board) 2. to remove a ~ 3. a loose ~ ['horny substance growing at the ends of fingers and toes'] 4. to cut, pare, trim; do; file; manicure; polish one's ~s 5. to break a ~ 6. to bite one's ~s 7. a fingernail; toenail ['misc.'] 8. as hard/tough as ~s

nail II *v*. (D; tr.) to ~ to (she ~ed the plaque to the wall)

naive *adj*. 1. ~ of (that was ~ of you) 2. ~ to + inf. (it's ~ to trust everyone; you are ~ to believe them)

naked *adj*. 1. stark ~ 2. (misc.) to walk around ~

naked eye *n*. to the ~ (visible to the ~)

name I *n*. ['appellation'] 1. to adopt, assume; bear; use a ~ 2. to give smb. a ~ 3. to call smb. a (bad) ~ 4. to immortalize smb.'s ~ 5. to invoke God's ~ 6. an assumed; Christian (esp. BE), first, given; code; dirty; family ~, surname; fancy; geographic; legal; maiden; married; middle; personal; pet; professional; proper; stage ~ (she uses her middle ~) 7. a brand, proprietary, trade ~ 8. a common, vernacular ('not technical') ~ 9. a ~ for (there is no ~ for such conduct) 10. by ~ (to know smb. by ~ only) 11. in ~ (she is the chairperson in ~ only) 12. in smb.'s ~ (the book was charged out in your ~) 13. under a ~ (under an assumed ~) ['reputation'] 14. to make a ~ (for oneself) 15. to clear one's ~ 16. to besmirch, smear smb.'s (good) ~ 17. to give smb. a bad ~ 18. a bad; good ~ ['misc.'] 19. to drop ~s ('to boast of one's connections'); in the ~ of the law

name II *v*. 1. (d; tr.) to ~ after, for (AE) (Hannah was ~d after her great-grandmother) 2. (d; tr.) to ~ as (she was ~d as the winner) 3. (H) they ~d me to head the commission 4. (N; used with a noun) she was ~d winner of the contest

name-calling *n*. to engage in, go in for, resort to ~

nameless *adj*. to remain ~

nap *n*. to have, take a ~

napkin *n*. 1. to fold a ~ 2. to tuck a ~ (under one's chin) 3. a cocktail; dinner; linen; paper ~

nappy (BE) see **diaper**

narcosis *n*. 1. to produce (a state of) ~ 2. (a) ~ wears off 3. under ~

narcotics *n*. to smuggle ~ (into a country)

narrate *v*. (B) she ~d her story to us

narration *n*. a graphic; gripping ~

narrow down *v*. (D; tr.) to ~ to (the choice was ~ed down to a few candidates)

narrow-minded *adj*. ~ + inf. (it was ~ of her to say that)

nasal passages *n*. blocked, congested ~

nasty *adj*. 1. ~ about (they were very ~ about the whole incident) 2. ~ to (he is ~ to everyone) 3. ~ to + inf. (it was ~ of them to do that)

nation *n*. 1. to build; establish a ~ 2. a civilized; friendly; independent; peace-loving; sovereign ~ 3. belligerent, warring ~s 4. across the ~ (there were strikes across the ~) 5. (misc.) a member ~ (of the UN)

national anthem *n*. to play; sing; strike up the ~

National Guard *n*. (US) to call out; federalize the ~

nationalism *n*. 1. to foster ~ 2. extreme; rampant ~

nationhood *n*. to achieve ~

native I *adj*. 1. ~ to (this flower is ~ to our state) 2. (misc.) to go ~ ('to behave like the local population when in a foreign country')

native II *n*. friendly; hostile ~s

natter *v*. (colloq.) (BE) (D; intr.) ('to chatter') to ~ about; to (to ~ on to smb. about smt.)

natural I *adj*. 1. (AE) ~ to (that comes ~ to me) 2. ~ to + inf. (it's ~ to want a nice car) 3. ~ that + clause (it's perfectly ~ that children love ice cream)

natural II *n*. (colloq.) ['person who seems to be destined for success'] a ~ to + inf. (she's a ~ to win the election)

nature *n*. ['character, quality'] 1. an impetuous; placid ~ 2. human ~ (it's only human ~ to want to live well) 3. second ~ 4. one's true ~ 5. by ~ (she is friendly by ~) 6. in one's ~ (it was not in his ~ to complain) 7. of a certain ~ (wounds of a serious ~) ['physical universe'] 8. to harness (the forces of) ~ 9. (misc.) mother ~; a freak of ~; back to ~

naught *n*. (lit.) 1. to come to ~ 2. all for ~

naughty *adj*. 1. ~ of 2. ~ to + inf. (it was ~ to do that)

nausea *n*. 1. to cause ~ 2. a wave of ~ (came over her)

nauseated *adj*. to feel ~

nauseating *adj*. 1. ~ to 2. ~ to + inf. (it was ~ to watch them)

nauseous *adj*. to feel ~ USAGE NOTE: Some purists still claim that *nauseous* means only 'nauseating'. In fact, most speakers now use it as a synonym of *nauseated*.

navigation *n*. celestial; electronic ~

navy *n*. 1. a merchant ~ (BE; AE has *merchant marine*) 2. the Royal Navy

near *adv*. (rare) ~ to (she came ~ to winning the title)

nearer, nearest *adj., adv*. ~ to (the park is nearer to our hotel than it is to yours; which stop is nearest to Albert Hall?) USAGE NOTE: When *near* is an adjective, it is not used in the collocation *near to*. (Compare *close to*.)

nearness *n*. ~ to

neat *adj*. ~ in (~ in one's habits)

necessary *adj*. 1. absolutely ~ 2. ~ for; to 3. ~ + inf. (it is ~ to sleep) 4. ~ that + clause; subj. (it is ~ that we all be/should be there)

necessitate *v*. 1. (G) working for that firm would

~ living abroad 2. (K) going to school would ~ his moving to the city

necessity *n.* 1. to obviate a ~ 2. an absolute, dire; military ~ 3. the bare; daily ~ties 4. a ~ for 5. of ~ (you will of ~ remain silent) 6. (misc.) the ~ties of life

neck I *n.* 1. to crane one's ~ 2. to twist, wring smb.'s ~ 3. (misc.) to risk one's ~ ('to risk one's life'); to break one's ~ trying to do smt. ('to make a maximum effort to get smt. done'); to stick one's ~ out ('to expose oneself to danger'); by a ~ ('by a close margin'); up to one's ~ in work ('swamped with work'); ~ and ~ ('even')

neck II *v.* (colloq.) (D; intr.) ('to hug and kiss') to ~ with

neckline *n.* a high; low, plunging; sweetheart ~

necktie *n.* (AE) 1. to tie a ~ 2. a loud ~ (CE has *tie)*

need I *n.* 1. to create a ~ 2. to feel a ~ 3. to fill, meet, obviate a ~ 4. to satisfy a ~ 5. to minister to smb.'s ~s 6. an acute, crying, desperate, dire, pressing, urgent ~ 7. a basic, fundamental; biological; emotional, psychological; personal; physical; physiological; spiritual; unfulfilled, unmet; universal ~ 8. bodily; emergency; material ~s 9. a ~ for (there is no ~ for violence) 10. a ~ to + inf. (there was a pressing ~ to act immediately; there was no ~ for you to go) 11. in ~ (to live in dire ~; badly in ~) 12. in ~ of (in crying ~ of food) USAGE NOTE: The sentence *she needn't have gone* implies that she did go (though there was no need for her to go). The sentence *she didn't need to go* does not indicate if she went or not.

need II *v.* 1. to ~ badly, desperately, sorely 2. (E) we all ~ to work 3. (F; in neg. and occ. in interrogative sentences) she ~ not work; or: she doesn't ~ to work; ~ she go? or: does she ~ to go? 4. (G) the house needs painting

needle *n.* 1. to thread a ~ 2. a crochet; darning; hypodermic; knitting; phonograph; sewing ~ 3. (misc.) a ~ in a haystack ('smt. that is impossible to find')

needlepoint *n.* to do ~

needlework *n.* to do ~

negative *n.* ['exposed film'] 1. to develop a ~ ['phrase that rejects'] 2. in the ~ (to reply in the ~) ['expression that contains negation'] 3. a double ~

neglect I *n.* 1. benign; complete; total; parental ~ 2. child ~ 3. a state of ~

neglect II *v.* 1. to ~ willfully 2. (E) she ~ed to pay the fine

neglectful *adj.* ~ of

negligence *n.* 1. contributory; criminal; rank; willful ~ 2. (legal) gross; ordinary; slight ~

negligent *adj.* 1. grossly ~ 2. ~ about; in

negotiate *v.* 1. (D; intr.) to ~ about, over 2. (D; intr.) to ~ for 3. (D; intr.) to ~ with (we ~d with them for release of the prisoners; to ~ with smb. about a common border)

negotiations *n.* 1. to conduct; enter into ~ 2. to break off ~ 3. delicate; direct; fruitless, unsuccessful; high-level; marathon; round-the-clock; successful; top-level ~ 4. diplomatic; peace ~ 5. ~

between 6. ~ for

negotiator *n.* a management; union ~

neighbor I **neighbour** *n.* 1. a next-door ~ 2. a ~ to (she was a good ~ to us)

neighbor II **neighbour** *v.* (esp. BE) (D; ntr.) to ~ on

neighborhood, neighbourhood *n.* 1. a bad ('unsafe'); changing; friendly; good, nice, pleasant ~ 2. an ethnic; residential ~ 3. in a ~ (we live in a nice ~)

neighborly, neighbourly *adj.* ~ to + inf. (it was ~ of you to do that)

neither *determiner, pronoun* ~ of (~ of the two; ~ of them) USAGE NOTE: The use of the preposition *of* is necessary when *two* or a pronoun follows. When a noun follows, two constructions are possible--neither student knew the answer; neither of the students knew the answer.

nelson *n.* ['type of wrestling hold'] a full; half ~

nemesis *n.* to meet one's ~

neologism *n.* to coin a ~

nerve *n.* ['assurance'] ['gall'] (colloq.) 1. to display, have ~ 2. the ~ to + inf. (she had the ~ to ask for another day off) ['self-confidence'] 3. to lose one's ~ ['sensitivity'] 4. a raw ~ (his remark hit a raw ~) ['band of nervous tissue'] 5. the cranial ~s

nerves *n.* ['nervousness'] 1. an attack; bundle of ~ ['mental state'] 2. to fray, frazzle smb.'s ~; to get on smb.'s ~ 3. to calm, settle one's ~ 4. frayed frazzled; steady; strong; taut; weak ~ ['misc.'] 5. to have ~ of steel ('to be very strong emotionally')

nervous *adj.* ~ about, of (BE) (we were ~ about the recent reports of local violence)

nest *n.* 1. to build, make a ~ 2. a machine-gun ~ 3. (misc.) a hornets' ~ ('an angry reaction')

nest egg *n.* ['money set aside as a reserve'] to accumulate; set aside a ~

nestle *v.* 1. (d; intr., tr.) to ~ against (the children ~d against their mother) 2. (P; intr.) the small village ~d in the green hills

nestle up *v.* (d; intr.) to ~ to (the children ~d up to their mother)

net *n.* 1. to weave a ~ 2. to cast, spread a ~ 3. a butterfly; fishing; mosquito ~ 4. a life (esp. AE), safety (also fig.) ~ 5. in a ~ (to catch fish in a ~)

netting *n.* mosquito ~

nettles *n.* ~ sting

network *n.* 1. an old-boy; old-girl ~ 2. a communications; road ~ 3. a national ~ (of radio, TV stations) 4. over a ~ (over a national ~)

neurosis *n.* mild; severe ~

neutral I *adj.* ~ in (~ in a dispute)

neutral II *n.* ['position of disengaged gears'] in ~ (to run an engine while in ~)

neutrality *n.* 1. to maintain, observe ~ 2. to declare one's ~ 3. armed; strict ~

new *adj.* 1. ~ at, in (I'm ~ at this) 2. ~ to (this procedure is ~ to us)

newcomer *n.* a ~ to

new leaf *n.* to turn over a ~ ('to begin a new way of life')

news *n.* ['new information'] 1. to announce, give; break, flash; cover the ~ 2. to spread (the) ~ 3. to censor; control; cover up, suppress (the) ~ 4. to color, distort, twist (the) ~ 5. bad; good; interesting; sensational; shocking; startling; unexpected; welcome ~ 6. local; international; national; political ~ 7. the latest ~ (have you heard the latest ~?) 8. ~ spreads, travels 9. a bit, item, piece of ~; a ~ item 10. ~ about, of (~ about the earthquake; is there any news of them?) 11. the ~ that + clause (have you heard the ~ that the border has been closed?) ['newscast'] 12. to listen to; turn on; watch the ~ 13. the late; morning; nightly ~ (on TV) 14. on the ~ (we heard that item on the late ~) 15. (misc.) to make (the) ~ ('to be newsworthy')

news conference *n.* to hold a ~

newspaper *n.* 1. to edit; print; publish a ~ 2. a daily; evening; morning; weekly ~ 3. a ~ comes out, is published 4. (misc.) to make the ~s ('to be printed in the newspapers')

New Year *n.* to greet, ring in the ~

next *adj., adv.* 1. (cannot stand alone) ~ to (there's a newsstand ~ to the hotel) 2. (misc.) ~ of kin; ~ in line

nibble *v.* (D; intr.) to ~ at

nibble away *v.* (D; intr.) to ~ at

nice *adj.* 1. ~ to, with (he's ~ to the children) 2. ~ to + inf. (it's ~ just to sit and relax = it's ~ just sitting and relaxing; she is ~ to work with = it is ~ to work with her = it is nice working with her) 3. ~ that + clause (it's ~ that we could all get together)

niche *n.* ['position'] 1. to carve out a ~ (she has carved out a ~ for herself in her field) 2. to occupy a ~ (she occupies a special ~ in her field)

nick *n.* (misc.) in the ~ of time ('precisely when needed')

nickname *v.* (N; used with a noun) he was ~d *Butch*

niggardly *adj.* (lit.) ~ in

niggle *v.* (D; intr.) to ~ about, over (to ~ over every sentence)

nigh *adv.* (old-fashioned) ['near'] ~ on, onto, unto (~ onto ten years)

night *n.* 1. to spend a ~ (we spent a restless ~ waiting for news) 2. a clear; dark, murky; overcast; starlit; stormy ~ 3. a restless, sleepless ~ 4. a first, opening ~ (of a play) 5. a wedding ~ 6. last; tomorrow ~; tonight 7. at ~ (to work at ~; late at ~) 8. by ~ (London by ~) 9. for a ~ (to put smb. up for the ~) 10. on a certain ~ (on the ~ of December first; on that ~) 11. throughout the ~ 12. (misc.) to bid, wish smb. good ~; (AE) to work ~s; in the dead of the ~ USAGE NOTE: The collocation *at night* is usu. used with verbs (she works at night) and contrasts with *during the day.* The collocation *by night* is usu. used with nouns (London by night) and contrasts with *by day.* (see the Usage Note for **day**)

nightcap *n.* ['last drink of the night'] 1. to have a ~ 2. (misc.) to invite smb. in for a ~; to join smb. in a ~

nightclub *n.* at, in a ~ (to work at/in a ~)

nightfall *n.* at ~

nightingale *n.* ~s sing, warble

nightmare *n.* 1. to have a ~ 2. a horrible, terrible

~ 3. a ~ about

nightshift *n.* 1. to work the ~ 2. (to work) on the ~

nip I *n.* ['stinging cold'] (there is) a ~ in the air

nip II *v.* (colloq.) (BE) (P; intr.) ('to move quickly') she ~ped out and bought some bread

nipples *n.* cracked; sore, tender~

nitpick *v.* (colloq.) (D; intr.) to ~ at

noble *adj.* ~ to + inf. (it was ~ of him to make the sacrifice)

nobody *pronoun* we had ~ to talk to = we had ~ that we could talk to

nod I *n.* ['movement of the head'] 1. an approving ~ 2. a ~ to 3. (misc.) (BE) the proposal was approved on the ~ (without the need for a vote) ['awarding of a decision'] (usu. sports) 4. to get the ~

nod II *v.* (D; intr., tr.) to ~ at, to (when she entered the room, she ~ded to us)

node *n.* a lymph ~

noise *n.* 1. to make, produce (a) ~ 2. to cut (AE; colloq.), cut down on, reduce the ~ 3. constant, persistent; deafening; loud; shrill ~ 4. a ~ abates, dies down

nominate *v.* 1. (D; tr.) to ~ as (she was ~d as our candidate) 2. (D; tr.) to ~ for (to ~ smb. for the presidency) 3. (H) they ~d her to serve as chairperson

nomination *n.* 1. to place, put smb. (smb.'s name) in ~ 2. to accept; reject a ~ 3. a ~ to (a ~ to a committee)

nominative *n.* (grammar) the ~ absolute

nonconformity *n.* ~ in, to

none *determiner, n., pronoun* ~ of (~ of them) USAGE NOTE: The use of the preposition *of* is necessary when a pronoun follows. When a noun follows, the use of *of the* limits the meaning; *no* replaces *none* when the meaning is not limited-- we saw none of the students whom we had discussed earlier; we drank none of the wine that you brought; we saw no students; we drank no wine.

nonsense *n.* 1. to speak, talk ~ 2. to put up with, tolerate ~ 3. (colloq.) (AE) to cut the ~ 4. arrant (lit.), complete, outright, perfect, pure, sheer, total, utter ~ 5. ~ to + inf. (it was sheer ~ to trust them) 6. (misc.) (BE) to make ~ of ('to spoil') (the recession made ~ of our plans for expansion)

nonsensical *adj.* ~ to + inf. (it's ~ to trust her)

nook *n.* 1. a cozy ~ 2. a breakfast ~ 3. (misc.) every ~ and cranny

noon *n.* 1. high ~ 2. at ~ 3. from ~ (to evening)

no one see **nobody**

noose *n.* 1. to tighten a ~ around (they tightened the ~ around his neck) 2. a hangman's ~

norm *n.* ['standard'] 1. to establish, set a ~ ['average'] 2. above; below the ~

normal *adj.* 1. ~ to + inf. (it's ~ to want a steady job) 2. ~ that + clause (it's only ~ that we should expect equal pay)

north I *adj., adv.* 1. ~ of 2. up ~

north II *n.* 1. magnetic; true ~ 2. in, to the ~

northeast *n.* in; to, towards the ~

North Pole *n.* at the ~

northwest *n.* in; to, towards the ~

nose I *n.* 1. to blow; wipe one's ~ 2. to pick one's

~ 3. an aquiline, Roman; bulbous; pug, snub, turned-up ~ 4. a bloody; running, runny ~ (the child has a runny ~) 5. through the ~ (to breathe through the ~) 6. a ~ bleeds; runs 7. (misc.) to bury one's ~ in a book ('to become absorbed in a book'); to count ~s ('to count those present'); to cut off one's ~ to spite one's face ('to harm one's own interests'); to lead smb. by the ~ ('to order smb. around'); to pay through the ~ ('to pay an exorbitant price'); to keep one's ~ out of smb. else's business; to poke, stick one's ~ into smb. else's business; to thumb one's ~ at smb. ('to defy smb.'); to keep one's ~ to the grindstone ('to work long and hard'); under smb.'s (very) ~ ('in smb.'s plain sight'); to turn up one's ~ at ('to sneer at'); on the ~ (AE; colloq.) ('exactly'); a ~ for scandal ('an ability to ferret out scandal'); by a ~ ('by a small margin'); to follow one's ~ ('to go straight forward'); to tweak ('pinch') smb.'s ~

nose II v. 1. (colloq.) (D: intr.) to ~ into (to ~ into smb.'s affairs) 2. (P; tr.) she ~d the car into the street

nosebleed n. 1. to have a ~ 2. to stop a ~ 3. a light; severe ~

nose dive n. 1. (also fig.) to go into, take a ~ (stocks took a ~) 2. to come out of a ~

nostalgia n. 1. to feel ~ 2. ~ for

nostrils n. flaring, wide ~

nosy adj. (colloq.) ~ about

notable adj. ~ for

notch n. ['cut'] 1. to make a ~ 2. a ~ in

notch up v. (esp. BE) (d; tr.) ('to score') to ~ against (our team has ~ed up seven victories against them)

note I n. ['memorandum'] ['record'] 1. to make a ~ of (she made a ~ of the exact time) 2. to take ~ of ['short letter'] ['official letter'] 3. to compose, write a ~ 4. to address; deliver a ~ 5. to drop, send smb. a ~ 6. a diplomatic; protest ~ 7. a ~ from; to ['musical tone'] 8. to hit, strike a ~ (she hit the high ~ beautifully) 9. a false ~ (also fig.) 10. a high; low ~ 11. (AE) an eighth; half; quarter; whole ~ ['characteristic feature'] 12. to strike a ~ (to strike a sour ~) 13. a discordant; false; festive; fresh; jarring; optimistic; personal; pessimistic; sour; triumphant ~ 14. on a ~ (the meeting ended on an optimistic ~) ['document relating to a debt'] 15. to discount a ~ 16. a demand; promissory; treasury ~ 17. a ~ matures ['paper money'] 18. a banknote; pound ~

note II v. 1. (L) we ~d that she was late again 2. (Q) ~ how it is done

notebook n. a loose-leaf ~ (AE)

noted adj. (cannot stand alone) ~ for (our city is ~ for its fine restaurants)

notes n. ['condensed record'] 1. to make, take ~ (our students always take copious ~) 2. (usu. fig.) to compare ~

nothing n. 1. to ask (for) ~ (to ask ~ in return) 2. to gain ~ by (we will gain ~ by ignoring the regulations) 3. ~ about (we know ~ about it) 4. ~ to (they are ~ to us) 5. ~ to + inf. (we have ~ to lose) 6. (misc.) to leave ~ to chance; to make ~ of being awarded an honor; we expect ~ of him; you

can expect nothing from them; good for ~; ~ doing ('definitely not'); we have ~ that we can discuss

notice I n. ['heed'] 1. to take ~ of 2. to attract ~ 3. to escape ~ 4. scant ~ (to attract scant ~) ['sign'] 5. to place, pose, put up a ~ ['announcement'] ['notification'] 6. to serve ~ on 7. advance ~ 8. a ~ that + clause (we read the ~ that the water would be turned off for two hours) 9. at, on short ~ 10. until further ~ ['warning of one's intention to end an agreement'] 11. to give ~ 12. to put smb. on ~ 13. a month's; week's ~ 14. (colloq.) ~ to + inf. (the landlady gave him ~ to move) 15. subject to ~ ['review''] 16. to get rave ~s (the play got rave ~s) ['mention'] 17. a brief ~ 18. a book ~

notice II v. 1. (I) we ~d him leave the house 2. (J) we ~d him leaving the house 3. (L) we ~d that she had left

notification n. 1. to send ~ 2. to get, receive ~ 3. ~ that + clause (we read the ~ that our building had been sold) 4. pending (further) ~

notify v. 1. (BE) (B) to ~ a crime to the police 2. (D; tr.) to ~ about, of (we ~fied the police of the incident) 3. (BE) (H) we'll ~ her to draw up a contract 4. (L; must have an object) she ~fied us that she would accept the position 5. (formal) (Q) he will ~ us where we are to meet

notion n. 1. to have a ~ 2. to dispel a ~ 3. a foggy, hazy, vague; ludicrous; odd, strange; precorceived; widespread ~ 4. a ~ about, of (he didn't have the slightest ~ of what I meant) 5. a ~ that ~ clause (we tried to dispel the ~ that benefits would be curtailed)

notoriety n. 1. to enjoy ~ 2. ~ for (~ for being corrupt) 3. ~ surrounding (the ~ surrounding the published accounts of bribery in high places)

notorious adj. 1. ~ as (he was ~ as an outlaw) 2. ~ for (our town is ~ for its gambling casinos)

noun n. 1. to decline, inflect a ~ 2. an abstract; attributive; collective; common; count; mass, uncountable; predicate; proper; verbal ~ 3. a feminine; masculine; neuter ~

nourishment n. 1. to take ~ 2. to give ~ 3. ~ for

novel n. 1. to publish; write a ~ 2. a detective, mystery; dime; historical ~ 3. (misc.) to make a ~ into a film

novelty n. 1. to outgrow smt.'s ~ (it outgrew its ~) 2. a ~ wears off 3. a ~ for, to

novice n. 1. a rank ~ 2. a ~ at, in

now adv. 1. just; right ~ 2. until, up to ~

nowhere adv. 1. to get, go ~ ('to fail to arrive at a result') 2. ~ to + inf. (we had ~ to go) 3. (misc.) from, out of ~

nuance n. a fine, subtle ~

nucleus n. ['core'] to form a ~

nude n. in the ~ (to pose in the ~)

nugget n. a gold ~

nuisance n. 1. to cause, create a ~ 2. to make a ~ of oneself 3. a confounded, damned, perpetual ~ 4. a public ~ 5. a ~ to 6. a ~ to + inf. (it was a ~ to move during the semester) 7. a ~ that (it's a ~ that there's no hot water)

nuisance value n. 1. to have a ~ 2. a high ~

null *adj.* (misc.) ~ and void
numb *adj.* ~ with (~ with cold)
number I *n.* ['symbol indicating quantity'] 1. an even; odd ~ 2. a high; low ~ 3. an algebraic; cardinal; complex; compound; decimal; imaginary; infinite; irrational; mass; mixed; natural; negative; ordinal; positive; prime; quantum; whole ~ 4. (misc.) the call ~ (of a book); the daily; lucky; winning ~ (of a lottery); a serial ~ (of a product, part); a serial ~ (of a soldier) ['quantity'] 5. to decrease, reduce; increase a ~ (to reduce the ~ of traffic accidents) 6. an approximate, round; certain; enormous, untold; growing; large; small ~ 7. (misc.) our school has doubled its ~s ['telephone number'] 8. to call; dial a ~ 9. a telephone ~; an unlisted ~ (AE; BE has *ex-directory listing/number*) ['issue'] 10. a back ~ ['single selection in a program of entertainment'] 11. to do a ~ ['misc.'] 12. to carry a ~ (when adding)
number II *v.* (d; intr.) to ~ in (our books ~ in the thousands)
numbers *n.* ['form of gambling'] 1. to play the ~ ['large group'] 2. in ~ (there is safety in ~) ['misc.'] 3. by the ~ ('done to a specific count')
numeral *n.* an Arabic; Roman ~
nuptials *n.* to officiate at, perform (the) ~
nurse I *n.* 1. a community-health (AE), public-health (AE) ~ (BE is approximately *health visitor*) 2. a community (BE), district (BE), visiting (AE) ~ 3. a general-duty; head; industrial, occupational-health; operating-room (AE); practical; school; supervising ~ 4. a graduate (AE); Licensed Practical (AE), State Enrolled (BE); professional; Registered (AE), State Registered (BE) ~ 5. (misc.) a ~ practitioner
nurse II *v.* (d; tr.) to ~ back to (to ~ smb. back to health)
nursery *n.* 1. a day ~ 2. at, in a ~
nursing *n.* 1. to study ~ 2. community-health, public-health ~ (AE; BE has *health-visitor service*) 3. geriatric, gerontological; maternal-child health; medical-surgical; obstetric; operating room; pediatric; practical; primary; professional; psychiatric ~
nut *n.* 1. to crack a ~ 2. to shell ~s 3. (misc.) a hard/tough ~ to crack ('a difficult problem to deal with')
nutrients *n.* basic, essential ~
nuts *adj.* (colloq.) ['infatuated'] 1. ~ about (he's ~ about her) ['crazy'] 2. to go ~
nutshell *n.* (colloq.) ['brief form'] in a ~ (to put smt. in a ~) ('to state smt. very succinctly')
nutty *adj.* (slang) 1. ~ to + inf. (it's ~ to behave like that) 2. (misc.) as ~ as a fruitcake
nuzzle up *v.* (D; intr.) to ~ against; to (the dog ~d up against her)
nylon *n.* 1. sheer ~ 2. a pair of ~s ('a pair of nylon stockings')

O

oaf *n.* a stupid ~ (you stupid ~!)
oar *n.* to feather; peak ~s
oath *n.* ['solemn promise; solemn promise to tell the truth'] 1. to administer an ~ to smb. 2. to put smb. under ~ 3. to swear, take an ~ 4. to violate an ~ 5. a solemn ~ 6. a loyalty ~ 7. an ~ to + inf. (she took an ~ to do her duty) 8. an ~ that + clause (I took an ~ that I would obey all regulations) 9. on (BE), under ~ (to testify under ~ to tell the truth) ['swearword'] 10. to mutter, utter an ~ 11. a mild; strong ~ 12. a string of ~s
oatmeal *n.* to cook ~
obedience *n.* 1. to demand, exact ~ from 2. to instill ~ in 3. to pledge, swear ~ to 4. blind, strict ~ 5. ~ to
obedient *adj.* ~ to
obeisance *n.* (formal) ['curtsy'] to make one's ~s
obituary *n.* 1. to send in; write an ~ 2. to print, publish an ~ 3. (misc.) to read the ~ries
object I *n.* 1. a material, physical ~ 2. a sex ~ 3. (grammar) a direct; indirect ~ 4. (misc.) an ~ of derision; an unidentified flying ~ (= UFO)
object II *v.* 1. to ~ strenuously, strongly, violently 2. (D; intr.) to ~ to (to ~ to new taxes) 3. (L) she ~ed that the accusation was based on hearsay
objection *n.* 1. to lodge, make, raise an ~ 2. to deal with, meet an ~ 3. to overrule; sustain an ~ 4. to withdraw an ~ 5. a serious, strenuous, strong, violent, vociferous; valid ~ 6. (legal) ~ overruled; ~ sustained 7. an ~ to (to raise an ~ to a proposal; we have no objections to your going) 8. an ~ that + clause (the judge overruled their ~ that illegal evidence had been introduced) 9. over smb.'s ~s (the resolution was adopted over the vociferous ~s of the opposition)
objectionable *adj.* ~ to
objective *n.* 1. to attain, gain, win an ~ 2. an economic; long-range; military ~
objectivity *n.* in all ~
objector *n.* a conscientious ~
obligate *v.* (H) what does the agreement ~ us to do?
obligated *adj.* 1. ~ to (I'm ~ to you) 2. ~ to + inf. (he is ~ to pay off all debts by the end of the year)
obligation *n.* 1. to assume, take on an ~ 2. to discharge, fulfill, meet an ~ 3. to discharge, fulfill, meet an ~ 4. a legal; moral; social ~; family ~s 5. a military ~ ('required military service') 6. an ~ to (an ~ to one's parents) 7. an ~ to + inf. (we have an ~ to help them) 8. under (an) ~
obligatory *adj.* 1. ~ for 2. (formal) ~ on, upon (doing one's duty is ~ on a soldier)
oblige *v.* 1. (d; tr.) to ~ by (you would ~ me by not smoking) 2. (H) the contract ~s us to pay a penalty if we finish late
obliged *adj.* 1. ~ to (I'm ~ to you) 2. ~ to + inf. (we are ~ to attend all classes)
obliterate *v.* 1. to ~ completely, entirely, totally,

utterly 2. (D; tr.) to ~ from
oblivion *n.* to sink into ~
oblivious *adj.* (cannot stand alone) ~ of, to (~ of one's surroundings; she was ~ to what was going on)
obnoxious *adj.* 1. ~ to 2. ~ to + inf. (it was ~ of them to do that)
oboe *n.* to play the ~
obscene *adj.* ~ to + inf. (it's ~ to make such a comparison)
obscure *adj.* ~ to (the meaning was ~ to me)
obscurity *n.* 1. to emerge from ~ 2. to sink into ~
observance *n.* a religious ~
observant *adj.* ~ of
observation *n.* ['comment'] 1. to make an ~ 2. an astute, keen, penetrating, shrewd ~ 3. a personal ~ 4. an ~ about 5. an ~ that + clause (she made the astute ~ that the whole matter had been exaggerated) ['condition of being observed' 6. to keep; place smb. under ~ 7. to be under ~ ['act of observing'] 8. (an) empirical; scientific ~
observe *v.* 1. to ~ attentively, carefully, closely 2. (I) we ~d them enter the building 3. (J) we ~d them entering the building 4. (L) ('to comment') several commentators have ~d that the rate of inflation has eased 5. (Q) I ~d how it was done
observer *n.* 1. a casual; impartial; keen, perceptive; outside; shrewd; skilled ~ 2. a military ~
obsessed *adj.* ~ by, with (~ by greed; ~ with fear)
obsession *n.* an ~ for; with
obsolescence *n.* built-in; planned ~
obstacle *n.* 1. to pose an ~ 2. to come across, encounter an ~ 3. to clear, overcome, surmount an ~ 4. (of a horse) to take an ~ 5. to remove an ~ 6. a formidable; insurmountable ~ 7. an artificial; natural ~ 8. an ~ to (an ~ to progress)
obstinate *adj.* ~ about; in
obstruction *n.* 1. to remove an ~ 2. an intestinal; respiratory ~ 3. an ~ to
obtrude *v.* (formal) (d; intr.) ('to intrude') to ~ on, upon
obvious I *adj.* 1. ~ to (her disappointment was ~ to everyone) 2. ~ that + clause (it's ~ that he is drunk)
obvious II *n.* to state the ~
occasion *n.* ['opportunity'] 1. to have; take an ~ (to do smt.) 2. a propitious ~ 3. an ~ for 4. an ~ to + inf. (I had no ~ to speak with them; there was no ~ for me to tell her) 5. an ~ arises ['happening'] ['event'] 6. to celebrate; mark, observe an ~ 7. a festive, gala; fitting, propitious; happy, joyful, joyous; memorable; official; special; unforgettable ~ 8. on an ~ (on this ~; on numerous ~s) ['challenge'] 9. to rise to the ~ ['reason'] 10. an ~ for (there is no ~ for alarm) ['misc.'] 11. on ~ ('sometimes')
Occident *n.* in the ~
occlusion *n.* a coronary ~
occupation *n.* ['profession'] 1. a profitable,

rewarding ~ 2. by ~ (she is a waitress by ~) ['act of occupying'] 3. a military ~ 4. under ~

occupied *adj.* 1. deeply; solely ~ 2. ~ in; with (they are ~ with their own concerns)

occupy *v.* (d; refl., tr.) to ~ with (she ~pied them with minor chores)

occur *v.* (d; intr.) ('to come to mind') to ~ to (an idea ~red to her)

occurrence *n.* a common, daily, regular; unusual ~

ocean *n.* 1. across the ~ (to fly across the ~) 2. in the ~

o'clock *adv.* at (ten) ~

odd *adj.* 1. ~ to + inf. (it was ~ of her to do that) 2. ~ that + clause (it's ~ that she is not at home)

odds *n.* ['allowance designed to equalize a bettor's chances'] 1. to give, lay ~ 2. to accept, take ~ 3. to buck ('oppose') the ~ ['disadvantages'] 4. to beat the ~ 5. considerable, formidable, great, heavy, hopeless, long, overwhelming ~ 6. ~ against (all the ~ were against us) 7. against ~ (to struggle against formidable ~) ['advantages'] 8. ~ in favor of ['disagreement'] 9. at ~ over; with ['possibility'] 10. the ~ that + clause (what are the ~ that they will show up?) ['misc.'] 11. by all ~ ('without question'); ~ and ends

ode *n.* 1. to compose an ~ 2. an ~ to (an ~ to joy)

odious *adj.* ~ to

odor, odour *n.* ['smell'] 1. to emit, exude, give off, produce an ~ 2. to perceive; recognize an ~ 3. a faint, slight; fetid, foul, rank, unpleasant; heavy; musty; pleasant; pungent, strong ~ 4. an ~ emanates from ['repute'] (BE) 5. in bad; good ~

off *adv.* ['situated'] 1. comfortably; well ~ ['not exact'] 2. far, way (esp. AE) ~ 3. ~ in (he's way ~ in his calculations)

off-balance *adj., adv.* caught ~

offend *v.* to ~ deeply, gravely

offender *n.* a chronic; first ~

offense, offence *n.* ['infraction'] 1. to commit an ~ 2. a minor, petty, trivial; serious ~ 3. a capital; impeachable; indictable ~ 4. an ~ against ['feeling of outrage'] 5. to take ~ at (she takes ~ at every remark) ['insult'] (formal) 6. to give ~

offensive I *adj.* 1. ~ to (his actions were ~ to everyone) 2. ~ to + inf. (it's ~ to read such things in the newspaper)

offensive II *n.* 1. to assume, go over to, take the ~ 2. to launch, mount an ~ 3. (usu. mil.) to carry out, undertake an ~ 4. to break off an ~ 5. an economic; military; peace ~ 6. on the ~

offer I *n.* 1. to make an ~ 2. to accept, agree to; consider an ~ 3. to decline, refuse, reject, spurn an ~ 4. to withdraw an ~ 5. a firm; reasonable; tempting; tentative ~ 6. an introductory; job; trial ~ 7. an ~ to + inf. (her ~ to help was accepted gratefully) 8. (BE) on ~ ('available')

offer II *v.* 1. (A) she ~ed the job to me; or: she ~ed me the job 2. (D; refl., tr.) to ~ as (the money was ~ed as an inducement) 3. (E) they ~ed to compromise

offering *n.* 1. to make an ~ 2. a burnt; peace; sacrificial ~ 3. an ~ to

offer up *v.* (d; tr.) to ~ as (to ~ as a sacrifice)

office *n.* ['function'] ['place where a function is performed'] 1. to assume (an) ~ 2. to hold; take ~ 3. to seek (public) ~ 4. (pol.) to run for (AE), stand for (BE) ~ 5. to resign from (an) ~ 6. (pol.) (an) appointive; elective; high; public ~ 7. a branch; head, home, main ~ 8. a booking; box, ticket; business; dead-letter; dentist's (AE); doctor's (AE); lawyer's; left-luggage (BE); lost-and-found (AE), lost property (BE); met (BE), meteorological (BE); patent; post; printing ~ 9. at, in an ~ (she works at our ~) 10. (pol.) in; out of ~ (our party is out of ~) ['ministry'] (BE) 11. the Foreign; Home ~ ['misc.'] 12. smb.'s good ~s ('smb.'s services as a mediator') USAGE NOTE: In North America, doctors and dentists have *offices;* in Great Britain, they have *surgeries.*

officer *n.* ['person holding a certain rank in the armed forces'] 1. to commission an ~ 2. to promote an ~ 3. to break, demote; dismiss an ~ 4. a commissioned; non-commissioned; petty; warrant ~ 5. a commanding; company-grade (AE); · field-grade (AE); flag; general; high-ranking; line; senior; staff; top-ranking ~ 6. an air-force; army; military; naval ~ 7. a duty; executive; intelligence; liaison; line; public-relations; staff ~; ~ of the day; ~ of the deck ['person holding a position of authority'] 8. a correctional (AE); executive; juvenile; medical; peace, police; personnel; probation; public-relations; revenue (BE); senior nursing (BE); truant (AE) ~

official *n.* 1. a high, high-ranking, top-ranking; responsible ~ 2. an appointed; elected ~ 3. a church; city; county; customs; federal (US); government; health; law-enforcement, police; local; postal; public; state ~

officiate *v.* (D; intr.) to ~ at (to ~ at a ceremony)

offing *n.* in the ~ ('forthcoming')

offspring *n.* to produce ~

ogle *v.* (d; intr.) to ~ at

oil *n.* 1. to drill for; hit, strike ~ 2. to pump ~ 3. to produce; refine ~ 4. crude; refined ~ 5. household; lubricating; machine; motor ~ 6. castor; coconut; cod-liver; cooking; corn; cottonseed; linseed; mineral; olive; palm; peanut; poppyseed; safflower; salad; sardine; sunflower; vegetable ~ 7. coal ~ ('kerosene-AE, paraffin-BE'); shale ~ 8. a film of ~ 9. (misc.) to burn the midnight ~ ('to work very late at night'); ~ and water do not mix

oils *n.* to paint in ~ ,

ointment *n.* 1. to apply, rub in, rub on an ~ 2. a skin ~

OK I *adj.* (colloq.) ~ to + inf. (it is ~ to bring your lunch with you)

OK II *n.* (colloq.) ['approval'] 1. to give one's ~ 2. to get the ~ 3. the ~ to + inf. (we got the ~ to continue)

old age *n.* to live to a ripe ~

olive branch *n.* ['symbol of peace'] to extend, hold out, offer the ~

Olympic Games *n.* to hold the ~

omelet *n.* 1. to make an ~ 2. a cheese; mushroom; plain; Spanish; Western ~

omen *n.* 1. a bad; good ~ 2. an ~ for

omission *n.* 1. to correct, rectify an ~ 2. a glaring

~ 3. (misc.) sins of ~

omit *v.* (E) (BE) he ~ted to explain why he had been late

on *prep.* 1. to have smt. ~ smb. ('to have evidence against smb.') 2. the fire went out ~ me ('the fire went out through no fault of mine') 3. we were ~ to what was happening ('we were aware of what was happening') 4. well ~ in years ('rather old')

once *adv.* at ~

one *determiner, pronoun* 1. ~ by ~ 2. ~ of (~ of them; ~ of the students)

ooze *v.* 1. (d; intr.) to ~ from, out of; into (blood was ~ing from the wound) 2. (d; intr.) to ~ with (to ~ with charm)

open I *adj.* 1. ~ for (~ for business) 2. (cannot stand alone) ~ to (~ to the public; I'm ~ to suggestions) 3. (misc.) to lay oneself ~ to criticism; to bring smt. out into the ~

open II *v.* 1. to ~ wide 2. (D; intr., tr.) to ~ by, with (we ~ed our meeting by singing a song; we ~ed our meeting with a song) 3. (D; tr.) to ~ for (to ~ new land for development) 4. (D; tr.) to ~ to (they ~ed their meetings to the public) 5. (N; used with an adjective) ~ your mouth wide

opener *n.* ['device that opens'] 1. a bottle; can (AE), tin (BE) ~ 2. a letter ~ (AE; BE has *paper knife*)

open house *n.* to have, hold an ~

opening *n.* ['vacancy'] 1. an ~ for (we have an ~ for an engineer) ['putting into operation'] 2. a grand ~ (the grand ~ of a new supermarket)

open season *n.* an ~ on (an ~ on deer)

open up *v.* (D; intr., tr.) to ~ to (the government has ~ed up the files to the public; he finally ~ed up to the press)

opera *n.* 1. to perform, stage an ~ 2. (a) comic; grand; light ~ 3. a soap ~ 4. a horse ~ ('western film') 5. at the ~

operate *v.* 1. (d; intr.) to ~ against (their troops were ~ing against the guerrillas) 2. (med.) (D; intr.) to ~ for; on (the surgeon ~d on her for appendicitis; she was ~d on for appendicitis)

operating system *n.* to boot up; reboot the ~ (of a computer)

operation *n.* ['surgical procedure'] 1. to perform an ~ 2. to have, undergo an ~ 3. an exploratory; major; minor ~ 4. an ~ for (an ~ for the removal of gallstones) ['military activity, movement'] 5. to conduct; launch an ~ 6. guerrilla; joint; large-scale; mine-sweeping; mopping-up ~s ['state of being functional'] 7. to put into ~ (the plant has been put into ~) 8. in ~ (the factory is in ~) ['project'] 9. a cloak-and-dagger, covert, secret; rescue; sting (AE) ~

operations *n.* 1. to conduct ~ 2. drilling, joint; military; mining; offensive; salvage ~ 3. (mil.) a theater of ~

operator *n.* 1. a computer; crane; elevator (AE); ham, radio; machine (AE); radar; switchboard (AE), telephone (AE); tour ~ 2. (colloq.) a slick, smooth ~

opinion *n.* 1. to air, express, give, offer, pass, state, venture, voice an ~ 2. to form an ~ about (I still have not formed an ~ about the candidates) 3.

to mold (public) ~ 4. to entertain, have, hold an ~ 5. (legal) (AE) to hand down an ~ (the court handed down an ~) 6. a conflicting; considered; dissenting; frank, honest; informed; negative; opposing; personal; positive; prevailing, prevalent; strong ~ (she has strong ~s about everything) 7. a high; low ~ of (he has a high ~ of himself) 8. (an) expert; lay ~ 9. public ~ 10. a second ~ (as given by a doctor) 11. shades of ~ 12. an ~ about, on 13. the ~ that + clause (she expressed her ~ that a compromise would be reached) 14. in smb.'s ~ (in my humble ~) 15. of an ~ (she is of the ~ that nothing will help)

opponent *n.* 1. a formidable, strong; weak ~ 2. (ironical) my worthy ~

opportunity *n.* 1. to grab, seize, take an ~ 2. to afford, give, offer an ~ 3. to find; have an ~ 4. to lose an ~ 5. a fleeting; lost, missed ~ ≤ (AE) equal ~ ('government policy of giving all citizens an equal chance') 7. an ~ for 8. an ~ to + inf. (we had an ~ to visit our parents) 9. (misc.) ~ knocks ('appears')

oppose *v.* 1. to ~ resolutely, strongly, vehemently 2. (K) I ~d his dropping out of college

opposed *adj.* 1. diametrically; strongly, vehemently ~ 2. ~ to

opposite I *adj.* (BE) ~ to USAGE NOTE. When *opposite* means 'facing', it can be an adjective in BE--her house is opposite to ours. More usu., *opposite* is used as a preposition in both BE and AE--her house is opposite ours. When *opposite* means 'diametrically opposed', it is used only in BE as an adjective--her opinions are opposite to ours.

opposite II *n.* 1. a direct ~ 2. an ~ of, to 3. (misc.) ~s attract

opposition *n.* 1. to arouse, stir up ~ 2. to offer, put up ~ 3. to crush, overcome ~ 4. to come across, meet, run up against ~ 5. (ling.) to neutralize an ~ 6. determined, fierce, stiff, strong, unbending, unyielding, vehement ~ 7. ~ to (~ to new taxes) 8. against, despite, in spite of, over (the) ~ (we adopted the resolution over the ~ of the other party) 9. in ~ to

oppression *n.* under ~ (to live under ~)

opt *v.* 1. (d; intr.) to ~ for 2. (rare) (E) they ~ed to decline the invitation

optimism *n.* 1. to display, show; express ~ 2. incurable, unflagging ~ 3. ~ about, over

optimist *n.* an incurable ~

optimistic *adj.* 1. cautiously; incurably ~ 2. ~ about, over 3. ~ that + clause (we are ~ that the results will be favorable)

option *n.* 1. to exercise an ~ 2. an exclusive; first ~ 3. a local ~ (of a political subdivision) 4. a stock ~ 5. an ~ on 6. an ~ to + inf. (they had an ~ to buy the team) 7. (misc.) to have no ~ but to...

oracle *n.* ['authority'] to consult an ~

orange *n.* 1. a mandarin; navel ~ 2. (misc.) to squeeze an ~

oration *n.* 1. to deliver an ~ 2. a funeral ~

oratory *n.* 1. eloquent; inflammatory, moving, rabble-rousing ~ 2. campaign ~

orbit *n.* 1. to make an ~ around, of, round (the

spaceship made five ~s of the moon) 2. in; into ~ (to put a satellite into ~)

orchard *n.* an apple; cherry; peach ~

orchestra *n.* 1. to conduct, direct, lead (esp. AE) an ~ 2. a chamber; dance; philharmonic, symphony; pops; string ~

ordain *v.* (formal) 1. (L; subj.) the emperor ~ed that all foreigners be expelled 2. (N; used with a noun) he was ~ed priest

ordeal *n.* 1. to undergo an ~ 2. a terrible, trying ~ 3. (an) ~ by fire; water

order I *n.* ['request for merchandise or services'] 1. to give, place, put in; make out, write out an ~ 2. to fill; take an ~ (has the waiter taken your ~?) 3. to cancel an ~ 4. a prepublication; rush; shipping; side (esp. AE); standing ~ 5. (new) ~s are falling off 6. on ~ (the merchandise is on ~) 7. to ~ (made to ~) 8. (misc.) a tall ~ to fill ('a difficult task to carry out') ['command'] 9. to give, hand down (AE), issue an ~ 10. to carry out, execute an ~; to obey, take ~s 11. to cancel, countermand, rescind, revoke; violate an ~ 12. a direct; executive ~ 13. doctor's; marching; sealed; verbal; written ~s 14. an ~ to + inf. (we received an ~ to attack) 15. an ~ that + clause; subj. (headquarters issued an ~ that the attack be/should be resumed) 16. by smb.'s ~ (by whose ~ was this done?) 17. under ~s (we were under ~s to remain indoors) ['court decree'] 18. to issue an ~ 19. an affiliation (BE); cease-and-desist; court; gag; maintenance (BE), support (AE); restraining ~ ['association, group'] 20. a cloistered; Masonic; mendicant; monastic; secret ~ ['system'] 21. an economic; pecking; social ~ (he's at the bottom of the pecking ~) ['proper procedure'] 22. a point of ~ 23. in ~; out of ~ (the senator was out of ~) 24. to call a meeting to ~ ['state of peace'] 25. to establish; maintain; restore ~ ['state in which everything is in its proper place or condition'] 26. good, shipshape ~ 27. in; out of ~ (everything is in good ~; this machine is out of ~ again) ['condition'] 28. working ~ (in working ~) ['sequence'] 29. alphabetical; chronological; numerical ~ 30. in; out of ~ (in ~ of importance; in alphabetical ~; these entries are out of ~) ['military formation'] 31. close; extended; open ~ ['instructions to pay'] 32. a money, postal (BE) ~ ['misc.'] 33. law and ~; a new ~; an old ~

order II *v.* 1. (C) ~ a copy for me; or: ~ me a copy 2. (D; tr.) to ~ from (to ~ merchandise from a mail-order house) 3. (d; tr.) to ~ from, out of (she ~ed him out of the house) 4. (d; tr.) to ~ off (the referee ~ed the player off the field) 5. (H) the sergeant ~ed his platoon to fall in 6. (L; subj.) the mayor ~ed that free food be/should be distributed 7. (esp. AE) (N; used with a past participle) the judge ~ed the prisoner transferred to the county jail 8. (misc.) the doctor ~ed her to bed

`orders *n.* ['ordination'] to receive (holy) ~

ordinance *n.* ['local law'] 1. to adopt, enact, pass; issue an ~ 2. to apply, enforce an ~ 3. to obey, observe an ~ 4. to repeal, rescind, revoke an ~ 5. a city, municipal; township ~ 6. an ~ that + clause; subj. (the town issued an ~ that all dogs

be/should be muzzled)

ordnance *n.* naval ~

ore *n.* copper; iron ~

organ *n.* ['part of the body'] 1. body; major; reproductive; sense, sensory; sexual; speech; vital ~s ['large wind instrument'] 2. to play the ~ 3. a barrel; electronic; hand; pipe; reed ~ ['periodical'] 4. a government; official; party ~

organism *n.* 1. a dead; healthy; living ~ 2. a deadly; harmful; infectious ~ 3. microorganisms; minute ~s

organization *n.* 1. to establish, form an ~ 2. to disband, dissolve an ~ 3. a charitable, philanthropic; civic; community; government; health-maintenance (AE); international; local; national; non-profit, not-for-profit (AE); official; professional; profit-making, proprietary; religious; state; student; UN; voluntary; women's; youth ~ 4. a front ~ for

orgasm *n.* to achieve ~; to have, reach an ~

orgy *n.* 1. to engage in, stage an ~ 2. a drunken ~

Orient *n.* in the ~

orient, orientate *v.* (D; refl., tr.) to ~ to (to ~ oneself to one's surroundings)

orientation *n.* ['introduction'] 1. to give, offer smb. (an) ~ to 2. to get, go through, receive (an) ~

origin *n.* 1. in ~ (the documents were Norse in ~) 2. of ~ (she is of humble ~; the fire was of undetermined ~)

original *n.* in the ~ (to read a text in the ~)

originality *n.* 1. to display, show ~ 2. ~ in

originate *v.* (d; intr.) to ~ from; in; with (the idea ~d with her)

orphan *n.* 1. to be left an ~ 2. a war ~

orthodoxy *n.* strict ~

oscillate *v.* (D; intr.) to ~ between

osmosis *n.* by ~ (to absorb by ~)

other *adj.* ['second'] every ~ (I jog every ~ day)

ought *v.* (E) you ~ to help

oust *v.* (D; tr.) to ~ from

out *adj., adv.* ['unconscious'] 1. ~ cold ('completely unconscious') ['intent on'] 2. ~ to + inf. (she is ~ to get revenge) ['gone'] 3. ~ to (~ to lunch) ['misc.'] 4. over and ~ (used at the end of a radio message); to turn smt. inside ~; down and ~ ('destitute')

outage *n.* (AE) ['failure'] a power ~

outburst *n.* an angry; furious; spontaneous; sudden; violent ~

outcome *n.* 1. to decide the (final) ~ of 2. (AE) to measure ~s ('to evaluate results')

outcry *n.* 1. to make, raise an ~ 2. a public ~ 3. an ~ against; for

outgrowth *n.* a direct ~

outing *n.* to go on an ~

outlay *n.* ['spending of money'] 1. to make ~s for 2. a capital; huge; large; modest; small ~

outlet *n.* ['passage'] 1. an ~ to (an ~ to the sea) ['means of expression'] 2. to find an ~ for (to find an ~ for one's emotions) 3. to provide an ~ for ['retail store'] 4. a factory ~

outline I *n.* 1. to draw up, make an ~ 2. a bare; broad, general; rough ~ 3. in ~ (to draw in ~; to

present a project in broad ~)
outline II *v.* 1. (B) they ~d the project to us 2. (d;
tr.) to ~ against (the ship was ~d against the horizon)
outlook *n.* ['viewpoint'] 1. to have an ~ on (she
has a healthy ~ on life) 2. a healthy; negative, pessimistic; optimistic, positive ~ ['prospects'] 3. a
bright; dismal, gloomy ~ 4. the long-range, long-
term; short-range, short-term ~ 5. an ~ for (the ~
for the future is bright)
outpost *n.* a military ~
output *n.* 1. to increase, step up ~ 2. to curtail, cut
back, reduce ~ 3. annual; daily; monthly ~
outrage *n.* 1. to express; feel ~ 2. to spark (AE),
spark off (BE), stir up ~ 3. an ~ against (an ~
against public morality) 4. an ~ to + inf. (it was an
~ to take innocent civilians hostage) 5. an ~ that
+ clause (it was an ~ that her name was omitted)
outrageous *adj.* 1. ~ to + inf. (it's ~ to permit
such behavior) 2. ~ that + clause (it's ~ that such
practices are allowed)
outs *n.* (colloq.) to be on the ~ with smb. ('to be
on bad terms with smb.')
outset *n.* at; from the ~
outsider *n.* a rank ~
outskirts *n.* on the ~ (of a city)
outspoken *adj.* ~ in (~ in their opposition to new
taxes)
outstanding *adj.* ~ in (~ in scientific achievement)
outward *adv.* ~ bound
ovation *n.* 1. to get, receive an ~ 2. a standing;
thunderous, tremendous ~ 3. to an ~ (they
walked out on the stage to a thunderous ~)
oven *n.* 1. to light, turn on an ~ 2. to turn off an ~
3. an electric; gas; microwave; self-cleaning ~
over *adj.* ['finished'] ~ between; with (it's all ~
between them)
overboard *adv.* 1. to fall ~ 2. (misc.) man ~! to go
~ over smt. ('to carry smt. to excess')
overdose I *n.* a fatal, lethal ~
overdose II *v.* (D; intr.) to ~ on (to ~ on a medication)
overflow *v.* (D; intr.) to ~ into (the mob ~ed into

the street)
overgrown *adj.* ~ with
overhaul I *n.* ['repairs'] a complete; major;
thorough ~ (our car needs a major ~)
overhaul II *v.* to ~ completely; thoroughly
overindulgence *n.* ~ in
overjoyed *adj.* ~ to + inf. (we were ~ to learn of
the good news)
overpass *n.* (esp. AE) an ~ over (an ~ over a
road) (BE has *flyover*)
overrated *adj.* vastly ~
overrun *adj.* ~ with (~ with weeds)
overseas *adv.* to go ~
oversight *n.* 1. an ~ that + clause (it was through
an ~ that you were not invited) 2. by, through an
~ (her name was omitted through an ~)
overtime *n.* 1. to earn; work ~ 2. (sports) a sud-
den-death ~
overtones *n.* political; racial ~
overture *n.* ['musical introduction'] 1. to compose; perform, play an ~ 2. an ~ to ['introductory
proposal'] 3. to make an ~; to make ~s to 4. to
spurn smb.'s ~s
owe *v.* 1. (A) she ~s ten dollars to her sister; or:
she ~s her sister ten dollars (the *to* is usu. not
used when the indirect object is a pronoun: she
owes her ten dollars) 2. (D; tr.) to ~ for (we still ~
one hundred dollars for the car)
owing *adj.* ~ to
owl *n.* ~s hoot
own *n.* and *pronoun* 1. to hold one's ~ ('to continue to survive') 2. to come into one's ~ ('to
receive recognition') 3. on one's ~ ('independently') 4. of one's ~ (for reasons of one's ~) ('for
one's own reasons')
owner *n.* 1. a part ~ 2. the lawful, rightful ~
ownership *n.* communal; joint; private; public;
state ~
own up *v.* (colloq.) (D; intr.) ('to confess') to ~ to
(he ~ed up to stealing the watch)
ox *n.* 1. oxen bellow 2. a pair; team; yoke of oxen
3. (misc.) as strong as an ~
oxygen *n.* 1. to administer ~; to give smb. ~ 2. to
get, receive ~ 3. liquid ~

P

pace I *n*. ['rate of movement'] 1. to set the ~ 2. to keep ~ with 3. to change ~; to slacken the ~ 4. a brisk, fast, rapid; even, steady; frantic, hectic; grueling, killing ~ 5. a slack, slow, sluggish; snail's ('extremely slow') ~ 6. at a certain ~ (at a fast ~) 7. off the ~ 8. (misc.) a change of ~ (also fig.) ['step'] (esp. mil.) 9. to take a ~ (to take three ~s forward) ['misc.'] 10. to put smb. through the ~s ('to subject smb. to a test of skill')

pace II *v*. (P; intr.) she was ~ing back and forth

pacemaker *n*. (med.) to insert a ~

pacifier *n*. (AE) to suck on a ~ (BE has *dummy*)

pack I *n*. ['deck of playing cards'] 1. to cut; shuffle a ~ ['load, bundle'] 2. a back; full field (mil.); parachute ~ ['mass'] 3. an ice ~

pack II *v*. 1. (C) ~ a sandwich for me; or: ~ me a sandwich 2. (d; intr.) to ~ into (they all ~ed into the auditorium) 3. (D; tr.) to ~ into (I ~ed everything into one suitcase) 4. (N; used with an adjective) ~ everything tight

package *n*. 1. to deliver a ~ 2. to mail (esp. AE), post (BE); send; unwrap; wrap a ~ 3. a bulky; neat ~ 4. (misc.) a ~ deal

packaging *n*. tamper-proof; tamper-resistant ~

packed *adj*. 1. loosely; tightly ~ 2. vacuum ~

packer *n*. a meat ~

packet *n*. a pay ~ (BE; AE has *pay envelope*)

packing *n*. ['act of packing'] to do the ~

pack off *v*. (D; tr.) to ~ to (to ~ the children off to camp)

pact *n*. 1. to agree to, make; sign a ~ 2. to denounce a ~ 3. a formal; informal ~ 4. a defense; mutual-assistance; nonaggression; trade ~ 5. a ~ to + inf. (we had a ~ not to reveal the facts of the case) 6. a ~ that + clause (the two governments signed a ~ that they would jointly defend their borders)

pad *n*. ['cushion'] 1. a heating; heel; knee; shoulder ~ ['piece of material'] 2. a gauze; quilted; scouring ~ ['connected sheets of paper'] 3. a scratch; writing ~ ['airstrip'] 4. a helicopter; launch, launching ~ ['one's residence'] (slang) 5. at one's ~

paean *n*. (lit.) ['hymn of praise'] 1. to sing a ~ 2. a ~ to (to sing a ~ to smb.'s glory)

page I *n*. ['leaf of a book, journal, newspaper'] 1. to turn a ~ 2. to turn down a ~ 3. to cite a (volume and) ~ 4. to set a ~ (in type) 5. a title ~ (in a book) 6. an amusement; editorial; society; sports ~ (in a newspaper) 7. (misc.) you will not find a dull ~ in the whole book; a glorious ~ in our history; it reads like a ~ from real life ['one side of a sheet of paper'] 8. a blank ~

page II *n*. ['youth who serves'] 1. (BE) a hotel ~ 2. (US) a congressional ~

page III *v*. to ~ smb. over a loudspeaker

pageant *n*. a beauty; colorful ~

paid *adj*. highly, well ~

pail *n*. a garbage (AE); ice; lunch; milk ~

pain I *n*. ['sensation of suffering'] 1. to cause ~ 2.

to inflict ~ on 3. to bear, endure, stand, take ~ (she cannot stand any ~) 4. to feel, experience, suffer ~ (she experienced constant ~) 5. to allay, alleviate, dull, ease, kill, relieve, soothe ~ 6. (an) acute, excruciating, great, intense, maddening, piercing, severe, sharp ~ 7. (a) chronic, constant, gnawing, persistent, steady; dull; intractable, stubborn; nagging; referred; shooting; slight; stabbing; sudden; throbbing ~ 8. (a) back; chest; physical (he felt sharp chest ~s and went to see the doctor) 9. ~ appears; disappears, wears off 10. a spasm; stab; twinge of ~ 11. in ~ (to be in chronic ~) ['penalty'] 12. on, under, upon ~ of (mass meetings were forbidden on ~ of death) ['bother'] 13. (colloq.) a ~ to + inf. (it's a ~ to get up so early in the morning = it's a ~ getting up so early in the morning)

pain II *v*. 1. to ~ badly, deeply 2. (R) it ~ed me to watch them quarrel; it ~ed me that he did not keep his promise

pained *adj*. (cannot stand alone) ~ to + inf. (I was ~ to learn of his refusal to help)

painful *adj*. 1. ~ to 2. ~ to + inf. (it's ~ to read of such things)

pains *n*. ['trouble'] 1. to go to, spare no, take ~ to + inf. (she took great ~ to get her message across) ['physical suffering'] 2. (med.) labor ~ 3. growing ~

paint I *n*. 1. to apply, spread ~ (to apply ~ to a surface; to spread ~ evenly) 2. to spray ~ (to spray ~ on a wall) 3. to daub ~ (to daub ~ on a wall) 4. to dilute ~ 5. to mix ~s 6. to scrape ~ 7. exterior; flat; floor; house; latex; lead-based; metallic; oil-based; wall ~ 8. grease; war ~ 9. wet ~! 10. ~ chips; peels 11. a blob, speck; splash of ~ 12. a coat of ~ (to apply a second coat of ~) 13. a set of (oil) ~s

paint II *v*. 1. (usu. D; C occurs occ.) to ~ for (she ~ed a beautiful portrait for us) 2. (d; intr.) to ~ in (to ~ in oils) 3. (J) the artist ~ed her strolling through her garden 4. (N: used with an adjective) to ~ a house white 5. (misc.) to ~ the town red ('to go on a binge')

painter *n*. 1. a house; sign ~ 2. a landscape; portrait ~

painting *n*. 1. to do; restore a ~ 2. to authenticate a ~ 3. a finger; oil; water-color ~ 4. a ~ depicts, portrays, shows (smt.)

pair *n*. (ling.) a minimal ~

pair off *v*. (D; intr., tr.) to ~ with

pair up *v*. (D; intr., tr.) to ~ with

pajamas, pyjamas *n*. a pair of ~

pal *n*. a pen ~ (BE also has *pen friend*)

palace *n*. an imperial; presidential (not US); royal ~

palatable *adj*. ~ to

palate *n*. 1. a cleft; perforated ~ 2. the hard; soft ~ 3. (misc.) to tickle the ~ ('to be very tasty')

pale I *adj*. ['devoid of color'] 1. deathly ~ 2. to go,

turn ~ 3. ~ with (rage)
pale II *v.* 1. (d; intr.) ('to become devoid of color') to ~ at ('to ~ at the sight of blood') 2. (d; intr.) ('to become less important') to ~ before, beside (everything ~d before the possibility of war) 3. (d; intr.) ('to fade') to ~ into (to ~ into insignificance)
pale III *n.* ['prescribed area'] beyond, outside the ~
pall I *n.* ['blanket of gloom'] to cast a ~ over
pall II *v.* (D; intr.) ('to become less attractive') to ~ on, upon (her constant preaching began to ~ on everyone)
palm I *n.* ['part of the hand'] 1. to read smb.'s ~ ('to tell smb.'s fortune') 2. (misc.) to have an itching ~ ('to have a great desire for money, bribes'); to grease smb.'s ~ ('to bribe smb.')
palm II *n.* a potted; royal ~
palm off *v.* 1. (D; tr.) to ~ as (he ~ed off the copy as an original) 2. (D; tr.) to ~ on (to ~ inferior merchandise on smb.)
palpable *adj.* ~ to
palsy *n.* cerebral ~
pan I *n.* 1. to grease a ~ a baking; cake; frying ~ 2. (misc.) to scour pots and ~s
pan II *v.* (d; intr.) to ~ for (to ~ for gold)
panacea *n.* 1. to find a ~ 2. a universal ~ 3. a ~ for
panache *n.* (with) great ~
pancake *n.* 1. to make a ~ 2. (misc.) as flat as a ~
pandemonium *n.* to cause, create, stir up ~
pander *v.* (d; intr.) to ~ to (to ~ to the worst elements in society)
panegyric *n.* to deliver a ~
panel *n.* ['board'] 1. a control, instrument ~ ['group that discusses or investigates a topic'] 2. to select a ~ 3. to serve on a ~ 4. an impartial ~ 5. an advisory; consumer; fact-finding; government ~ 6. a ~ on (a ~ on drug addiction)
panel discussion *n.* to hold; lead, moderate a ~
paneling, panelling *n.* wood ~
pangs *n.* 1. birth ~ 2. ~ of conscience; hunger (she felt ~ of conscience)
panic I *n.* 1. to cause, create; spread ~ 2. to feel ~ at (they felt ~ at the thought of leaving their family) 3. to avert, prevent ~ 4. ~ spreads; subsides 5. in a ~ over
panic II *v.* (D; intr.) to ~ at (to ~ at the outbreak of fire)
panic button *n.* to press, push the ~
panicky *adj.* to get ~ over
pant *v.* (D; intr.) to ~ for (to ~ for breath)
pants *n.* 1. (esp. AE) see **trousers** 2. ski; sweat ~
paper *n.* ['lecture, treatise'] ['essay'] 1. to deliver, give, offer, present, read a ~ 2. to publish; write a ~ 3. (in a school, at a university) to do, write; hand in a ~ (the pupils did a ~ on the problem of air pollution; the students were required to hand in their ~s by the end of the semester) 4. an invited; position; term; test ~ 5. a ~ about, on 6. a ~ for (I had to do a ~ for my history course) ['document'] 7. a green (BE); white ~ ['negotiable instruments'] 8. commercial; negotiable ~ ['material made from wood pulp'] 9. to recycle (scrap) ~ 10. blank; blotting; bond; carbon; cigarette; filter; glossy; graph;

lined; litmus; manila; scrap; scratch (esp. AE); tar; tissue; toilet; tracing; typing; wax, waxed; wrapping; writing ~ 11. (misc.) a ream of ~ ['sheet of writing material'] 12. to line ~ 13. a piece, sheet; scrap of ~ 14. on ~ ('in written form') ['newspaper'] 15 to get a ~ out, publish a ~ 16. a school; trade ~ (see also **newspaper**)
papers *n.* ['documents'] 1. to show one's ~ 2. (US) to take out first ~ ('to begin the process of becoming a naturalized citizen') 3. first (US); naturalization; second (US); ship's; working ~ ['school work'] 4. to correct, grade (esp. AE), mark ~ ['articles sent by mail'] 5. printed ~ (BE; CE has *printed matter)*
par *n.* ['nominal value'] 1. at ~ ['common level'] 2. on a ~ with ['average'] 3. above, over; below ~ 4 up to ~ (to feel up to ~)
parachute jump *n.* to make a ~
parade I *n.* 1. to have, hold, stage a ~ 2. a church (BE); identification (BE; AE has *police lineup),* inaugural; military; sick (BE; AE has *sick call);* ticker-tape ~
parade II *v.* (P; intr.) to ~ in front of an audience
parade rest *n.* at ~ (the platoon was at ~)
paradise *n.* an earthly ~
paradox *n.* a ~ that + clause (it's a ~ that such good friends cannot work together)
paradoxical *adj.* ~ that + clause (it's ~ that we feel cold in warm weather)
parallel I *adj.* ~ to, with
parallel II *n.* 1. to draw a ~ between; with 2. to find ~s among, between 3. a striking ~ 4. (misc.) without ~ (in history)
paralysis *n.* 1. complete; creeping; partial ~ 2. infantile ~
paramount *adj.* ~ over
paranoid *adj.* ~ about
paratroops *n.* to commit, deploy; drop ~
parcel *n.* 1. to deliver a ~ 2. to address; mail (esp. AE), post (BE); send a ~ 3. to get, receive a ~ 4. to open, unwrap; wrap a ~
parcel out *v.* (B) she ~ed out the work to us
pardon I *n.* 1. to grant a ~ 2. to beg smb.'s ~ 3. a full ~
pardon II *v.* (D; tr.) to ~ smb. for
pare down *v.* (D; tr.) to ~ to (to ~ expenses to the minimum)
parent *n.* 1. to obey one's ~s 2. a loving; permissive; unfit ~ 3. an adoptive; foster; natural; single ~; stepparent
parentheses *n.* (esp. AE; BE prefers *brackets)* 1. to put smt. in, into ~ 2. between, in ~
parenthood *n.* planned ~
parity *n.* ['equality'] 1. to achieve, attain, establish ~ 2. ~ among, between ['equivalence in value] 3. at ~
park *n.* 1. to lay out a ~ 2. an amusement; city; national; public; state ~ 3. a caravan (BE), trailer (AE); theme ~ 4. a car ~ (BE; AE has *parking lot)* 5. (BE) a coach ~ 6. an industrial ~ (AE; BE has *industrial estate)*
parlay *v.* (d; tr.) ('to convert') to ~ into (to ~ a small investment into a fortune)
parley I *n.* to hold a ~ with

parley II *v.* (D; intr.) to ~ with
parliament *n.* 1. to convene, convoke (a) ~ 2. to adjourn; disband, dissolve (a) ~ 3. a bicameral; national; provincial; unicameral ~ 4. a rump ~ 5. a ~ adjourns; convenes, meets; disbands 6. a house of ~ 7. in ~ (to sit in ~) 8. (misc.) to stand for (BE) ~; a member of ~ (in GB abbreviated as MP) USAGE NOTE: In Great Britain, the Queen or King *opens* (a *session* of) Parliament. After the *State Opening*, Parliament is *in session*. Parliament *sits* until the session is over and then it *rises*.
parlor, parlour *n.* 1. a beauty; funeral; massage ~ 2. a sun ~ (AE; BE has *sun lounge*) USAGE NOTE: The services offered by a *massage parlor* are often sexual rather than therapeutic.
parody *n.* 1. to compose a ~ 2. a ~ of, on
parole I *n.* ['conditional release from prison'] 1. to grant a ~ 2. to violate (one's) ~ 3. early ~ 4. on ~ (to release smb. on ~)
parole II *v.* (D; tr.) to ~ from (to ~ smb. from prison)
part I *n.* ['share'] 1. to do one's ~ ['viewpoint, position'] 2. for, on one's ~ (for my ~, I will say no more) ['participation'] 3. to take ~ in 4. an active ~ ['role'] 5. to play a ~ (to play the ~ of Hamlet) 6. to act; look the ~ 7. to learn, memorize, study one's ~; to understudy a ~ 8. a bit; leading, major; speaking; walk-on ~ (she had a bit ~ in the play) ['element, portion'] 9. to spend a ~ of (they spent the major ~ of their life in England) 10. an essential; important, significant; insignificant, minor, small; large, major ~ 11. the (a) better ('greater'); good ('large') ~ (the better ~ of an hour) 12. a component, constituent, integral ~ 13. for the most ~ ('mostly') 14. in ~ ('partly'); (in great ~) ['component of a machine'] 15. a defective ~ 16. automobile (AE), motorcar (BE); spare ~s ['division'] 17. in ~s (a story in five ~s) ['side'] 18. to take smb.'s ~ (in a dispute) 19. (legal) of a ~ (the party of the first ~) ['dividing line in hair'] (AE; BE has *parting*) 20. to make a ~ (in one's hair) ['physical organ'] 21. the private ~s ['area'] 22. a remote ~ (in a remote ~ of the country)
part II *v.* 1. (D; intr.) to ~ as (to ~ as friends) 2. (d; intr., tr.) to ~ from (the children were ~ed from their parents) 3. (d; intr.) to ~ with (she hates to ~ with her money)
partake *v.* (d; intr.) to ~ of (to ~ of food and drink)
partial *adj.* (colloq.) ['fond of'] (cannot stand alone) ~ to
participant *n.* 1. an active; reluctant; willing ~ 2. a ~ in
participate *v.* 1. to ~ actively 2. (D; intr.) to ~ in
participation *n.* 1. active ~ 2. ~ in
participle *n.* (grammar) an active; dangling (esp. AE); misrelated (BE); passive; past; perfect; present ~
particle *n.* 1. a dust; minute ~ 2. (physics) an alpha; elementary; subatomic ~
particular I *adj.* ~ about (~ about one's appearance)

particular II *n.* ['detail'] 1. in every ~; in all ~s ['misc.'] 2. in ~ ('especially')
partition *v.* (D; tr.) to ~ into (the area was ~ed into two countries)
partner *n.* 1. an active; full; junior; senior ~ 2. a silent (AE), sleeping (BE) ~ 3. (boxing) a sparring ~ 4. (misc.) a ~ in (~s in crime)
partnership *n.* 1. to form a ~ 2. to dissolve a ~ 3. a ~ between 4. a ~ in 5. in ~ with
partridge *n.* a covey of ~s
parts *n.* (grammar) the principal ~ (of a verb)
party I *adj.* ['participating'] ~ to (~ to an arrangement)
party II *n.* ['social gathering'] 1. to arrange, give, have, throw; host a ~ for 2. to attend; crash a ~ 3. a birthday; Christmas; cocktail; coming-out; dinner; farewell; garden; going-away; lavish; New Year's Eve; pajama, slumber; singles; stag; surprise; tea ~ 4. a ~ breaks up (the ~ broke up at midnight) 5. at a ~ (we had a good time at the ~) ['political organization'] 6. to establish, form a ~ 7. to break up, disband, dissolve a ~ 8. a centrist; communist; conservative; labor; left-wing; liberal; majority; minority; political; populist; progressive; radical; reactionary; right-wing; ruling; socialist; splinter ~; the ~ in power ['participant'] ['litigant'] (legal) 9. an aggrieved; disinterested; innocent; third ~ 10. the interested ~ties 11. a ~ to (a lawsuit) 12. (misc.) the ~ of the first, second part ['group sent on a mission'] 13. a boarding; landing; raiding; rescue; search; stretcher; surveying ~
party line *n.* 1. to follow, hew to the ~ 2. to deviate from, veer from the ~
pass I *n.* ['permission'] ['leave of absence'] 1. to issue a ~ 2. to cancel, revoke a ~ 3. a ~ to (we got a ~ to town) 4. on ~ (they are in the city on ~) ['flight'] 5. to make a ~ (over a target) ['aggressive attempt to become friendly'] 6. to make a ~ (at smb.) ['transfer of a ball, puck'] 7. to complete; throw a ~ 8. to block; intercept a ~ 9. (Am. football) a forward; incomplete; lateral; touchdown ~ ['ticket'] 10. a free ~ 11. a ~ to (we got free ~es to the concert) ['misc.'] 12. things came to a pretty ~ ('the situation became very complicated')
pass II *v.* 1. (A) ('to hand') ('to throw') ~ the sugar to me; or: ~ me the sugar; my teammate ~ed the ball to me; or my teammate ~ed me the ball 2. (D; intr.) to ~ as, for ('to be accepted as') (he can ~ as/for a Frenchman) 3. (d; intr.) to ~ between ('to be exchanged') (a significant look ~ed between them) 4. (d; intr.) ('to shift') to ~ from; to (to ~ from one subject to another) 5. (d; intr.) to ~ on, upon ('to judge') (to ~ on the merits of a case) 6. (D; tr.) ('to deliver') to ~ on, upon (the judge ~ed sentence on the accused; to ~ judgment on smb.) 7. (d; intr.) ('to go'); ('to fly') to ~ over (several planes ~ed over our house; to ~ over a bridge) 8. (d; intr.) to ~ over ('to disregard') (they ~ed over her when promotions were handed out) 9. (d; intr.) ('to go') to ~ through (she was just ~ing through town) 10. (d; tr.) ('to insert') to ~ through (he ~ed the cable through the loop) 11. (s) to ~ unnoticed 12. (misc.) (BE)

to be ~ed fit for service

pass III *n*. ['passage'] 1. to clear a ~ 2. to block a ~ 3. a mountain ~ 4. a ~ between; over; through (a ~ through the mountains)

passage *n*. ['accommodations'] 1. to book ~ (on a ship) ['section'] 2. an obscure ~ (in a text) ['way, channel'] 3. to clear; force a ~ 4. a secret ~ ['channel in the body'] 5. nasal ~s 6. (BE) the back ~ ('the rectum') ['transition'] 7. a ~ from; to 8. (misc.) a rite of ~ ['trip'] 9. an outward ~

passageway *n*. a ~ between

pass along *v*. (B) ~ the message along to the others

pass around *v*. (B) ~ the chocolate around to the children

pass down *v*. (B) to ~ a tradition down to the next generation

passenger *n*. 1. to carry ~s (trains carry many ~s every day) 2. to pick up, take on ~s 3. to drop (off), leave off ~s 4. a first-class; second-class; steerage; tourist-class; transit ~ 5. a ~ for (~s for the next flight should go to the last gate)

passing *n*. ['death'] 1. to mourn smb.'s ~ ['misc.'] 2. in ~ ('incidentally')

passion *n*. 1. to arouse, excite, inflame, stir up ~ 2. to gratify, satisfy one's ~ 3. to curb, restrain one's ~ 4. animal, deep, frenzied, wild ~ 5. ~s run high 6. a ~ for (a ~ for gambling) 7. (misc.) to fly into a ~; his eyes blazed with ~

pass off *v*. (d; refl., tr.) to ~ as (he ~ed himself off as a doctor)

pass on *v*. 1. (B) they ~ed the information on to us 2. (d; intr.) to ~ to (let's ~ to another topic)

pass out *v*. (AE) (B) they ~ed the food out to all who came

passport *n*. 1. to issue; renew a ~ 2. to apply for a ~ 3. to falsify, forge a ~ 4. to revoke a ~ 5. a diplomatic; Nansen ~ 6. a ~ expires 7. (fig.) a ~ to (a ~ to happiness)

pass round see **pass around**

password *n*. to give the ~

past *n*. ['time preceding the present'] 1. a checkered (AE), chequered (BE); dark, murky ~ 2. in the ~ 3. (misc.) to recapture the ~

paste *n*. to make, mix a ~

pastime *n*. the national ~ (in America the national ~ is baseball)

pastry *n*. 1. to bake, make ~ 2. light; puff (BE) ~ 3. (a) Danish ~

pat I *adj., adv.* (colloq.) to stand ~ ('to refuse to change')

pat II *n*. to give smb. a ~ (on the back)

patch *n*. ['piece of material used to cover a hole'] 1. to sew on a ~ ['insignia'] 2. a shoulder ~ ['plot of ground'] (esp. AE) 3. a cabbage; potato ~

patent *n*. 1. to grant, issue a ~ 2. to apply for; obtain, take out a ~ 3. to hold a ~ 4. to infringe a ~ 5. ~ pending ('a patent has been applied for') 6. a ~ on (she took out a ~ on her invention)

paternity *n*. to establish ~

path *n*. 1. to beat, blaze, clear, make a ~ (to clear a ~ through a jungle) 2. to cross smb.'s ~ 3. a beaten ~ 4. a bridle ~ 5. a ~ goes, leads somewhere 6. a ~ to (the ~ to success) 7. (misc.) to lead

smb. up the garden ~ ('to deceive smb.') to lead smb. down the primrose ~ ('to lead smb. in an ill-advised search for pleasure')

pathetic *adj.* 1. ~ to + inf. (it was ~ to watch her condition deteriorate day by day) 2. ~ that ~ clause (it's ~ that he has sunk so low)

pathway *n*. a ~ to

patience *n*. ['quality of being patient'] 1. to display, show ~ 2. to tax, try smb.'s ~ 3. to lose one's ~; to run out of ~ 4. endless, inexhaustible, infinite ~ 5. one's ~ wears thin 6. ~ for; with (she has endless ~ with the children) 7. the ~ to + inf. (do you have the ~ to do this job?) 8. out of ~ with ['card game'] (BE) 9. to play ~ (AE has *solitaire*)

patient I *adj.* ~ with

patient II *n*. 1. to cure; handle; treat a ~ 2. to discharge a ~ (from a hospital) 3. an ambulatory; cardiac; comatose; hospital; mental; private ~

patriot *n*. an ardent, fervent; sincere ~

patriotism *n*. 1. to display, show ~ 2. (an) ardent, fervent, strong; sincere ~

patrol *n*. 1. a highway (AE), motorway (BE); military; police; reconnaissance ~ 2. (naval) a shore ~ 3. on ~ (they are out on ~)

patron *n*. 1. a regular, steady ~ 2. (misc.) a ~ of the arts

patronage *n*. political ~

patter *v*. (d; intr.) to ~ against, on (the rain was ~ing on the windows)

pattern I *n*. 1. to establish, set a ~ 2. an intricate, overall; underlying ~ 3. a holding; traffic ~ (our plane was in a holding ~) 4. (ling.) an intonation speech ~ 5. a behavior; personality ~

pattern II *v*. (d; tr.) to ~ after, on, upon (we ~ed our road system on theirs)

pause *n*. ['temporary stop'] 1. an awkward; long prolonged; pregnant; short ~ 2. a ~ in ['reason or cause for hesitating'] 3. to give smb. ~

pavement *n*. ['paved surface'] 1. to tear up the ~ (in order to lay pipes) 2. the ~ buckles 3. (misc.) to pound the ~ ('to walk about aimlessly or with determination') USAGE NOTE: In BE, *pavement* also means 'sidewalk'.

pawn *n*. a helpless ~

pay I *n*. 1. to draw, receive ~ 2. back; equal; incentive; mustering-out (mil.); overtime; severance (AE; BE has *redundancy payment*); retroactive; sick; strike; take-home ~ 3. ~ for (equal ~ for equal work) 4. in smb.'s ~ (he was in the ~ of the enemy)

pay II *v*. 1. to ~ handsomely, highly, well 2. (A) she paid the money to me; or: she paid me the money 3. (D; intr.) to ~ by (to ~ by check) 4. (D; intr., tr.) to ~ for (have you paid for the book? I paid ten dollars for this record) 5. (D; intr., tr.) to ~ into (we have been ~ing into a pension fund; the money was paid into her account) 6. (d; intr., tr.) to ~ out of (she paid out of her own pocket) 7. (E) it doesn't ~ to economize on essentials 8. (H) he paid us to watch his house

payable *adj.* 1. ~ to 2. (misc.) ~ at sight ~ on demand

pay back *v*. 1. (B) we must pay the money back to her 2. (D; tr.) to ~ for (she paid me back for the

tickets)
paycheck *n.* a monthly; weekly ~
pay dirt *n.* (colloq.) (AE) ['success'] to hit, strike
~
payment *n.* 1. to make (a) ~ 2. to stop ~ (of, on a
check) 3. to suspend ~s 4. a cash; down ('initial');
redundancy (BE; AE has *severance pay); token
~ 5. (a) ~ for, on 6. in full ~ (of a bill)
payoff *n.* to make a ~
pay out *v.* (B) the benefits have been paid out to
the workers
payroll *n.* 1. to meet (esp. AE) a ~ 2. a monthly;
weekly ~
peace *n.* 1. to achieve, bring about ~ 2. to make ~
with 3. to negotiate (a) ~ with 4. to impose a ~ on
5. to keep the ~ 6. to break, disturb, shatter the ~
7. a durable, lasting, permanent; fragile ~ 8. ~
reigns 9. at ~ with (we were at ~ with our
neighbors) 10. in ~ (to live in ~) 11. (misc.) a
breach of the ~; ~ and quiet; a ~ march
peacetime *n.* in ~
peacock *n.* (misc.) as proud as a ~
peak *n.* 1. to reach a ~ 2. to scale the ~ (of a
mountain) 3. at the ~ (at the ~ of her success)
pearls *n.* 1. to string ~ 2. cultured; imitation; natural ~ 3. a string of ~
peas *n.* 1. split ~ 2. (misc.) as like as two ~ in a
pod
peck *v.* (d; intr.) to ~ at (to ~ at one's food)
pecker *n.* (colloq.) (BE) ['spirits'] ['courage'] to
keep one's ~ up
peculiar *adj.* 1. ~ to 2. ~ that + inf. (it's ~ that he
never answers his phone)
pedal *n.* 1. to depress, step on a ~ 2. a brake;
clutch; gas (AE) ~
peddler, pedlar *n.* an influence; itinerant; smut ~
pedestal *n.* on a ~ ('held in high esteem')
peek I *n.* to take a ~
peek II *v.* 1. (D; intr.) to ~ at; through (to ~ at
smt. through a window) 2. (d; intr.) to ~ into (to
~ into the files) 3. (d; intr.) to ~ under (to ~
under the bed)
peek in *v.* 1. (D; intr.) to ~ at 2. (misc.) she ~ed
in from behind the bushes
peek out *v.* 1. (D; intr.) to ~ at 2. (D; intr.) to ~
from behind (to ~ from behind the shades) 3. (D;
intr.) to ~ from under (to ~ from under the bed)
peel I *n.* a banana; lemon; potato ~ (see the
Usage Note for **rind**)
peel II *v.* (C) ~ a banana for me; or: ~ me a
banana
peep I *n.* ['sound'] 1. to let out a ~ 2. a ~ out of
(we didn't hear a ~ out of him)
peep II *v.* ('to look') 1. (D; intr.) to ~ at; through
(to ~ at smb. through a keyhole) 2. (d; intr.) to ~
into (to ~ into smb.'s dossier) 3. (d; intr.) to ~
under (to ~ under the bed)
peep out *v.* 1. (D; intr.) to ~ at 2. (D; intr.) to ~
from behind (to ~ from behind the blinds) 3. (D;
intr.) to ~ from under (to ~ from under the bed)
peer *v.* 1. (d; intr.) to ~ at; through (to ~ at smb.
through a window) 2. (d; intr.) to ~ into (to ~ into
smb.'s eyes)
peerage *n.* (GB) to raise smb. to the ~

peer out *v.* 1. (D; intr.) to ~ at 2. (D; intr.) to ~
from behind (to ~ from behind the curtains) 3.
(D; intr.) to ~ from under (to ~ from under a car)
peeve *n.* one's pet ~
peevish *adj.* ['irritable'] ~ about
peg *n.* ['degree, step'] (fig.) to come down a ~; to
bring smb. down a ~
pelt *v.* (d; tr.) to ~ with (to ~ smb. with rocks)
pelt down *v.* (D; intr.) to ~ on (the rain ~ed down
on the roof)
pen I *n.* ['enclosure'] 1. a pig ~ ['dock'] 2. a submarine ~
pen II *n.* ['device for writing'] 1. a ballpoint; felt-
tip (AE), fibre-tip (BE); flair; fountain ~ 2.
(misc.) with a stroke of the ~, the new law was
enacted
penalize *v.* (D; tr.) to ~ for
penalty *n.* 1. to impose, mete out a ~ 2. to pay a ~
(to pay the full ~ for one's mistakes) 3. to rescind
a ~ 4. a light, mild; maximum; minimum; severe,
stiff, strict ~ 5. the death ~ 6. a ~ for 7. on, under
~ (of death)
penance *n.* to do, perform ~ for
penchant *n.* a ~ for
pencil *n.* 1. an indelible; lead ~ 2. a cosmetic,
eyebrow ~ 3. a styptic ~
pendulum *n.* 1. to swing a ~ 2. a ~ swings
penetrate *v.* 1. to ~ deeply 2. (D; intr.) to ~ into
(our troops ~d deeply into enemy lines)
penetration *n.* 1. a deep ~ 2. (mil.) a ~ in depth
penicillin *n.* 1. oral ~ 2. an injection, jab (BE; colloq.), shot of ~
penitence *n.* true ~ for
penitent *adj.* ~ for
pen name *n.* under a ~ (to write under a ~)
pennant *n.* ['baseball championship'] (AE) to
lose; win the ~
penny *n.* 1. to pinch ~nies ('to be frugal') 2.
(misc.) a pretty ~ ('a large sum of money'); (BE;
colloq.) the ~ drops ('somebody finally under-
stands'); (BE; colloq.) to spend a ~ ('to use a
toilet')
pension *n.* 1. to award, grant a ~ 2. to draw,
receive a ~ 3. to revoke a ~ 4. a disability; old-
age; survivor's ~ 5. on a ~ (to live on a ~; to retire
on a ~) 6. (misc.) a ~ plan
people *n.* 1. average, common, plain; working ~
2. old; young ~ 3. the chosen ~ 4. boat ~ ('destitute refugees traveling in boats') 5. city; country;
little, ordinary; primitive ~
pepper I *n.* ['spice'] 1. black; hot; red; white ~ 2.
a dash of ~ ['vegetable'] 3. (a) green; red; sweet ~
4. stuffed ~s
pepper II *v.* (d; tr.) ('to shower') to ~ with (she
was ~ed with questions)
pepper away *v.* (D; intr.) to ~ at
pep talk *n.* to give a ~ (the coach gave the team a
~)
perceive *v.* (formal) 1. (d; tr.) to ~ as (I ~d her
statement as a threat) 2. (L) we ~d that the situation was critical
percentage *n.* ['profit'] (colloq.) ~ in (there is no
~ in investing more money)
perceptible *adj.* 1. barely ~ 2. ~ to

perception *n.* 1. to have a ~ 2. clear; keen ~ 3. color; depth; extrasensory ~ 4. the ~ that + clause (events confirmed our ~ that she had been treated unfairly)

perceptive *adj.* 1. ~ of (that observation was very ~ of her) 2. ~ to + inf. (it was ~ of them to grasp our meaning)

perceptiveness *n.* the ~ to + inf. (she had the ~ to know what would happen)

perch I *n.* a high ~

perch II *v.* (P; intr.) the birds ~ed on the wire

per diem *n.* ['daily allowance for expenses'] 1. to pay (a) ~ 2. to receive (a) ~

perfect I *adj.* ~ for (she would be ~ for the job)

perfect II *n.* (grammar) the future; past; present ~

perfection *n.* 1. to achieve, attain ~ 2. the acme of ~ 3. to ~ (cooked to ~)

perfidy *n.* (formal) an act of ~

perform *v.* to ~ live

performance *n.* ['act of performing'] 1. to deliver, give, put on a ~ 2. a breathtaking, inspired, superb; listless; uneven ~ 3. a benefit; command; gala; live; repeat; request ~ ['functioning of a machine'] 4. engine ~

performer *n.* a star ~

perfume *n.* 1. to dab on, put on, spray on; use ~ 2. to reek of (derog.); smell of ~ 3. (a) strong ~

peril *n.* 1. to face a ~ 2. to avert a ~ 3. at one's ~ 4. in ~ (our lives were in ~)

perimeter *n.* ['boundary'] 1. (mi..) to guard a ~ 2. on a ~

period *n.* ['portion of time'] 1. a cooling-off; incubation; prehistoric; question-and-answer; rest; transitional; trial; waiting ~ 2. (sports) an extra ~ 3. for a ~ 4. in a certain ~ (in that ~ of history) ['menstruation'] 5. to have a ~ 6. a monthly ~ ['punctuation mark'] (esp. AE; BE prefers *full stop)* 7. to place, put a ~ (at the end of a sentence)

periodical *n.* 1. a current ~ (where does the library keep current ~s?) 2. bound ~s

peripheral *adj.* ~ to

periphery *n.* on the ~

periscope *n.* 1. to lower; raise a ~ 2. (as commands) ~ down; ~ up

perish *v.* (formal) 1. (D; intr.) to ~ by (to ~ by the sword) 2. (D; intr.) to ~ from, of (to ~ from disease)

perjury *n.* to commit ~

perm *n.* ['permanent wave'] 1. to give smb. a ~ 2. to get a ~

permeated *adj.* (cannot stand alone) ~ with (~ with idealism)

permissible *adj.* ~ to + inf. (it is not ~ to smoke in the library)

permission *n.* 1. to give, grant ~ 2. planning ~ (BE; AE has *building permit)* 3. ~ to + inf. (we had ~ to leave early)

permit I *n.* 1. to grant, give a ~ 2. to cancel, rescind, revoke a ~ 3. a building (AE; BE has *planning permission);* work ~

permit II *v.* 1. (H) they ~ted her to leave 2. (K) who ~ted their leaving early?

pernickety (esp. BE) see **persnickety**

perpendicular *adj.* ~ to

perpetuity *n.* in ~ ('forever')

perplex *v.* (R) it ~ed me to learn of his decision; it ~ed me that they refused the offer

perplexed *adj.* 1. ~ about, at, by, over 2. ~ to + inf. (we were ~ to learn of your decision)

perplexing *adj.* ~ to + inf. (it was ~ to read so many contradictory accounts of the incident)

persecute *v.* (D; tr.) to ~ for (they were ~d for their religious beliefs)

persecution *n.* 1. to suffer ~ 2. bloody; relentless ~ 3. political; racial; religious ~

perseverance *n.* 1. to display ~ 2. ~ at, in 3. the ~ to + inf. (she had enough ~ to finish)

persevere *v.* (D; intr.) to ~ at, in

persist *v.* (D; intr.) to ~ in (to ~ in doing smt.)

persistence *n.* 1. to display, show ~ 2. dogged ~ 3. ~ in 4. the ~ to + inf. (will you have the ~ to stick it out?)

persistent *adj.* 1. doggedly ~ 2. ~ in

persnickety *adj.* (colloq.) (esp. AE) ['fussy'] ~ about

person *n.* 1. a juridical; real ~ 2. a displaced; missing ~ 3. (legal) a ~ aggrieved 4. (grammar) the first; second; third ~ 5. in ~ (to appear in ~)

personal history *n.* to record, take down smb.'s ~

personality *n.* ['noted person'] 1. a celebrated ~ ['behavioral characteristics'] 2. a charismatic, charming; dynamic, forceful, magnetic, striking, strong ~ 3. a dual, split; multiple ~ ['misc.'] 4. to indulge in ~ties ('to make impolite remarks about people')

personnel *n.* enlisted (AE; BE has *other ranks);* government; indigenous; military; qualified ~

perspective *n.* 1. to put smt. into ~ 2. the proper, right, true; wrong ~ 3. from a ~ (to view a situation from a new ~) 4. in ~ (to look at, see smt. in ~)

perspicacity *n.* the ~ to + inf. (she had enough ~ to see through their schemes)

perspiration *n.* 1. profuse ~ 2. beads of ~ (ran down my face)

perspire *v.* to ~ profusely

persuade *v.* 1. (D; tr.) to ~ of (we had to ~ them of the need to evacuate their house) 2. (H) we ~d them to leave 3. (L; must have an object) we ~d her that it would be best to wait

persuasion *n.* 1. friendly ~ 2. (humorous) religious ~ (what is their religious ~?)

persuasiveness *n.* the ~ to + inf. (she has enough ~ to convince anyone)

pertain *v.* (d; intr.) to ~ to (these facts ~ to the case)

pertaining *adj.* (cannot stand alone) ~ to

pertinent *adj.* 1. ~ to 2. ~ to + inf. (is it ~ to cite those facts?)

perturb *v.* (R) it ~ed me (to learn) that she was late again

perturbed *adj.* 1. ~ about, at, by, over 2. ~ to + inf. (we were ~ to learn of the bad news from the front)

perturbing *adj.* ~ to + inf. (it's ~ to read such distortions of fact in the press)

pervaded *adj.* (cannot stand alone) ~ with (~ with

cynicism)

perverse *adj.* ~ to + inf. (it was ~ to behave like that)

perversion *n.* sexual ~

pervert *n.* a sexual ~

pessimism *n.* 1. to display ~ 2. to overcome ~ 3. ~ about, at, over

pessimistic *adj.* ~ about, at, over

pester *v.* 1. (D; tr.) to ~ about, for (he kept ~ing me for his money) 2. (D; tr.) to ~ into (they ~ed me into going) 3. (H) they kept ~ing me to buy a new car

pet *n.* 1. a household ~ 2. a teacher's ~ 3. (misc.) a ~ animal

petition I *n.* 1. to circulate; file, present a ~ 2. to grant a ~ 3. to withdraw a ~ 4. to deny, reject a ~ 5. a ~ about; against; for

petition II *v.* 1. (D; intr., tr.) to ~ for (to ~ for a new trial; they ~ed the government for tax relief) 2. (H) we have ~ed city council to provide more teachers 3. (formal) (L; subj.) they ~ed that the case be/should be retried

petrol (BE) see **gasoline**

petting *n.* heavy ~ (old-fashioned)

petty *adj.* ~ to + inf. (it was ~ of him to do that)

phalanx *n.* ['formation'] to form a (solid) ~

pharmacy *n.* 1. a hospital ~ 2. at, in a ~ (she works down at the ~)

phase *n.* 1. to begin, enter a ~ 2. to go through a ~ 3. a closing, final; critical, crucial; initial, new, opening ~ (the war was entering its final ~)

phenomenon *n.* 1. an isolated ~ 2. a natural ~

philander *v.* (D; intr.) to ~ with

philosophy *n.* ['belief'] ~ that + clause (it was her ~ that people should help each other)

phone see **telephone**

phoneme *n.* (ling.) an independent, separate ~

phooey *interjection* (expresses disgust) ~ on!

photo see **photograph**

photocopy *n.* to make a ~

photofinish *n.* (to end) in a ~

photograph I *n.* 1. to take a ~ 2. to develop; touch up a ~ 3. to blow up, enlarge a ~ 4. to mount a ~ 5. an aerial; family; group; still ~ 6. (misc.) to pose for a ~

photograph II *v.* (P; intr.) she ~s well

photography *n.* color; still; trick ~

phrase *n.* 1. to coin; turn a ~ 2. a colloquial; empty; glib; hackneyed, trite; well-turned ~ 3. (grammar) a noun; participial; prepositional; verb ~

physical, physical examinaton *n.* 1. to do a ~ 2. to get, have a ~

physician *n.* 1. an attending; family; house; practicing ~ 2. an allopathic; homeopathic; osteopathic ~

physics *n.* classical, Newtonian; high-energy, particle; nuclear; solid-state; theoretical ~

physique *n.* a burly, muscular, powerful ~

pianist *n.* a concert ~

piano *n.* 1. to play the ~ 2. to tune a ~ 3. a baby grand; grand; upright ~ 4. (misc.) a ~ is in tune or out of tune

piazza *n.* ['open square'] on a ~

pick I *n.* ['tool for breaking'] an ice ~

pick II *n.* (colloq.) ['selection'] to take one's ~

pick III *v.* 1. (C) ('to select') ~ a nice melon for me; or: ~ me a nice melon 2. (d; intr.) to ~ at ('to eat sparingly') (to ~ at one's food) 3. (D; tr.) ('to select') to ~ from, out of (she ~ed this album from our record library) 4. (colloq.) (d; intr.) to ~ on ('to find fault with') (she's always ~ing on me) 5. (H) ('to select') they ~ed me to serve as secretary 6. (N; used with an adjective) the animals ~ed the carcass clean

picketing *n.* informational ~ (esp. AE); mass ~

pickings *n.* (colloq.) ['choice'] lean, slim ~

pickle *n.* 1. a dill; sour; sweet ~ 2. (BE) mustard ~; ~s and chutney 3. (misc.) in a ~ ('in trouble') USAGE NOTE: In the United States, a pickle is a pickled cucumber. In Great Britain, the typical pickle is a thick sauce of pickled vegetables.

pick out *v.* 1. (C) ~ a nice melon for me; or: ~ me out a nice melon 2. (D; tr.) ('to select') to ~ for (we must ~ the best candidate for the job) 3. (H) I ~ed out a nice tie to go with this shirt

pick up *v.* 1. (d; intr.) to ~ after ('to clean up for') (I was always ~ing up after them) 2. (slang) (d; intr.) to ~ on ('to continue'); ('to become aware of')

picnic *n.* ['outing with a meal'] 1. to go on, have a ~ ['picnic meal'] (BE) 2. to make; pack a ~ ['pleasure'] (colloq.) 3. a ~ to + inf. (it's no ~ to work there = it's no ~ working there)

picture I *n.* ['photograph'] 1. to snap, take a ~ ['drawing, image, painting'] 2. to draw; paint; retouch a ~ 3. to frame; hang a ~ 4. (BE) an Identikit (T) ~ 5. in a ~ (did you see the animals in the ~?) 6. (misc.) as pretty as a ~ ['film'] 7. a motion (AE), moving (esp. AE) ~ 8. in a ~ (who played in that ~?) 9. (esp. BE) to go to the ~s ['description'] 10. to draw, paint a ~ 11. a clear; detailed; gloomy; realistic ~ 12. (misc.) (colloq.) to get the ~ ('to comprehend the situation')

picture II *v.* 1. (d; tr.) to ~ as (I cannot ~ her as an actress) 2. (J) can you ~ them leading a demonstration?

pie *n.* 1. to bake a ~ 2. an apple; blueberry; cherry; lemon-meringue; meat; mince; pecan; pumpkin; shepherd's ~ 3. a piece, slice, wedge of ~ 4. (misc.) as easy as ~

piece *n.* ['figure used in a game'] 1. chess ~s ['coin'] 2. a fifty-cent; gold; ten-cent ~ ['an artistic work'] 3. a collector's ~ (BE; CE has *collector's item*) 4. a conversation ~ 5. a ~ of music ['unit'] 6. by the ~ ['fragment'] 7. to break into ~s (the vase fell and broke into small ~s; she broke the dish into ~s) ['misc.'] 8. to go to ~s ('to fall apart'); a solid ~ of work ('high-quality work'); to give smb. a ~ of one's mind ('to tell smb. brusquely what one thinks'); to speak one's ~ ('to state one's opinion frankly'); a ~ of news; (BE; colloq.) a nasty ~ of work ('a nasty person'); to pick a theory to ~s ('to disprove a theory')

piecemeal *adv.* to do smt. ~

piecework *n.* to do ~

pier *n.* at, on a ~ (to meet smb. at the ~)

pig *n.* ['swine'] 1. a sucking (BE), suckling (AE) ~

2. ~s grunt, oink, squeal 3. a young ~ is a piglet 4. a female ~ is a sow 5. a male ~ is a boar ['glutton'] (colloq.) 6. to make a ~ of oneself ['misc.'] 7. as fat as a ~; a male chauvinist ~; to buy a ~ in a poke ('to buy, accept smt. with no previous inspection')

pigeon *n.* 1. a carrier, homing ~ 2. a clay ~ 3. ~s coo

piggyback *adv.* to carry smb. ~ ('to carry smb. on one's shoulders')

pigheaded *adj.* ~ of (that was ~ of him)

pig out *v.* (slang) (AE) (D; intr.) to ~ on (to ~ on ice cream)

pigtails *n.* in ~ (little girls in ~)

pile I *n.* ['concrete post'] to sink a ~

pile II *n.* ['soft raised surface on a rug'] shaggy; smooth; soft; thick ~

pile III *n.* ['fortune'] 1. to make a ~ ['reactor'] 2. an atomic ~

pile IV *v.* (P; intr.) ('to crowd') the children ~d into the car

pilfer *v.* (D; tr.) to ~ from

pilgrimage *n.* 1. to go on, make a ~ 2. a ~ to (they went on a ~ to Jerusalem) 3. on a ~

pill *n.* ['tablet of medicine'] 1. to swallow, take a ~ 2. (colloq.) to pop ~s 3. a headache; sleeping ~ ['oral contraceptive'] 4. to take the ~ 5. to be on the ~ ['misc.'] 6. it was a bitter ~ to swallow ('it was very difficult to experience failure')

pillbox *n.* to storm; take a ~

pillow *n.* to fluff up a ~

pilot *n.* ['person who flies aircraft'] 1. an air-force; airline, commercial; fighter; glider; helicopter; kamikaze; licensed; test ~ ['person who guides ships into and out of a port'] 2. to drop; take on the ~ 3. a harbor ~ ['device for steering'] 4. an automatic ~

pin I *n.* ['metal fastener'] 1. a safety; straight ~ 2. a bobby ~ (AE; BE has *hair grip*) 3. a drawing ~ (BE; AE has *thumbtack*) 4. a ~ pricks 5. (misc.) the head of a ~ ['tube-shaped piece of wood'] 6. a rolling ~ ['target in bowling'] 7. to spot ('place') ~s

pin II *v.* 1. (D; tr.) ('to trap') to ~ against (~ned against the wall) 2. (D; tr.) ('to trap') to ~ beneath, underneath (he was ~ned beneath the car) 3. (d; tr.) ('to place') to ~ on (we ~ned our hopes on her) 4. (d; tr.) to ~ to (her arms were ~ned to her sides)

pinball machine *n.* (BE also has *pintable*) to play; tilt a ~

pincers *n.* a pair of ~

pinch I *n.* ['painful squeeze'] 1. to give smb. a ~ ['emergency'] (colloq.) 2. at (BE), in (esp. AE) a ~ ['arrest'] (colloq.) 3. to make a ~

pinch II *v.* (colloq.) (D; tr.) ('to arrest') to ~ for (~ed for speeding)

pinch-hit *v.* (AE) (from baseball) (D; intr.) to ~ for ('to replace')

pine *v.* 1. (d; intr.) to ~ after, for (to ~ for home) 2. (E) they were ~ing to return home

pink *n.* (colloq.) ['good health'] in the ~ (of condition)

pinnacle *n.* 1. to reach a ~ (to reach the ~ of one's

power) 2. at a ~ (at the ~ of one's success)

pintable (BE) see **machine 5**

pipe I *n.* ['device for smoking'] 1. to light a ~ 2. to puff on, smoke a ~ 3. to fill one's ~ 4. a peace ~ ['long tube'] 5. a drain; exhaust; overflow; water ~

pipe II *v.* (D; tr.) to ~ from; into, to (to ~ water from a stream to a house)

pipeline *n.* in a ~ (also fig.)

pique *n.* a fit of ~

piracy *n.* 1. to commit ~ 2. air; literary ~; ~ on the high seas 3. an act of ~

pistol *n.* 1. to cock; fire a ~ 2. to aim, point; level a ~ at 3. to load a ~ 4. to draw, whip out a ~ 5. an automatic; dueling; starting; toy; water ~ 6. the ~ fired, went off; jammed; misfired

pit I *n.* an orchestra ~

pit II *v.* (d; tr.) to ~ against (we were ~ted against a formidable opponent)

pitch I *n.* ['high-pressure sales talk'] (colloq.) 1. to deliver a ~ 2. a sales ~ ['blade angle'] 3. a propeller ~ 4. reverse ~ ['intensity'] 5. a fever; high; low ~ (to reach a fever ~) ['throw of a baseball'] (esp. AE) 6. to throw a ~ 7. an underhand; wild ~ (to uncork a wild ~)

pitch II *v.* 1. (A) ('to throw') ~ the ball to me; or: ~ me the ball 2. (d; intr.) to ~ into ('to begin to work together enthusiastically') (let's all ~ into this job)

pitfall *n.* 1. to avoid a ~ 2. a hidden ~

pitiful *adj.* ~ to + inf. (it's ~ to see such suffering)

pittance *n.* (formal) a mere, small ~

pity *n.* 1. to arouse ~ 2. to feel; show ~ 3. to have, take ~ on smb. 4. ~ for 5. a ~ + inf. (it's a ~ to see what has happened) 6. a ~ that + clause (it's a ~ that the meeting was canceled) 7. out of ~ (he agreed out of ~ for her children) 8. (misc.) for ~'s sake; a sense of ~

pivot *v.* (D; intr.) to ~ on (the dancer ~ed on the ball of her foot; the future ~s on what we decide now)

placard *n.* to carry a ~

place I *n.* ['space occupied at a table'] 1. to lay (BE), set (esp. AE) a ~ for smb. ['position'] 2. to take smb.'s ~ 3. to trade ~s 4. (misc.) to know one's ~ (in life); to give up one's ~ in line in a queue; to occupy a prominent ~ in world literature ['point in space'] 5. a meeting ~ 6. at, in a ~ (at the same old ~) ['dwelling'] 7. at smb.'s ~ (let's meet at your ~) ['appropriate position'] 8. in; out of ~ (everything was in ~) ['seat'] 9. to take one's ~ (they took their ~s) ['standing in a competition'] 10. to take a ~ (she took second ~ in the competition) 11. a ~ goes to (first ~ went to Smith) ['duty, function'] 12. one's ~ to + inf. (it's not my ~ to criticize them) ['stage'] ['step'] 13. in a ~ (in the first ~) ['misc.'] 14. to take ~ ('to happen'); to go ~s ('to be successful'); all over the ~ ('everywhere'); in ~ of ('instead of')

place II *v.* 1. (d; tr.) ('to put') to ~ above (to ~ one's family above all other concerns) 2. (d; tr.) ('to put') to ~ at (she ~d her car at our disposal) 3. (d; tr.) ('to present') to ~ before (to ~ evidence before a grand jury) 4. (d; tr.) ('to put') to ~ in (to

~ one's confidence in smb.) 5. (D; tr.) to ~ with ('to find a home for') (to ~ a child with a family) 6. (P; tr.) ('to put') to ~ books on a table)

placebo *n.* 1. to administer, give a ~ 2. (misc.) a ~ effect

plagiarism *n.* to be guilty of ~

plague *n.* 1. bubonic ~ 2. a ~ spreads 3. (misc.) to avoid smb. like the ~

plain I *adj.* 1. ~ to (the truth is ~ to everybody) 2. ~ to + inf. (the facts are ~ to see) 3. ~ that + clause (it's ~ to everyone that she will never return) 4. (misc.) as ~ as day; or: as ~ as the nose on your face

plain II *n.* 1. a broad; coastal ~ 2. on a ~

plain clothes *n.* in ~ (the police officer was in ~)

plan I *n.* 1. to concoct, devise a ~ 2. to draw up, formulate, map out a ~ 3. to make ~s 4. to outline; unveil a ~ 5. to accept; carry out, execute, implement a ~; to put a ~ into operation 6. to present, propose a ~ 7. to foil, frustrate, thwart; reject; shelve a ~ 8. a brilliant, ingenious; complicated, elaborate; feasible; grandiose, sweeping; impracticable; impractical; realistic; secret; well-laid, well-thought-out ~ 9. a contingency; five-year; long-term; master; security; short-term ~ 10. (on) the installment ~ (AE; BE has *hire-purchase*) 11. a flight; floor ~ 12. a health ~ ('health insurance'); a pension, retirement ~ 13. an easy-payment ~ 14. a ~ calls for (smt.) 15. ~s materialize 16. a ~ for 17. a ~ to + inf. (the mayor had a ~ to reduce traffic congestion)

plan II *v.* 1. (d; intr.) to ~ for (to ~ for one's old age) 2. (d; intr.) to ~ on (to ~ on early retirement) 3. (E) we ~ to visit them soon 4. (Q) they ~ned very carefully how they would accomplish their mission

plane I *n.* see **airplane**

plane II *n.* 1. an inclined ~ 2. on a lofty ~

plane III *v.* (N; used with an adjective) to ~ a board smooth

plank *n.* ['board extending from a ship'] to walk the ~ ('to go to one's death') (see the Usage Note for **platform**)

planning *n.* 1. grandiose; long-range, long-term; short-range, short-term ~ 2. city; discharge; family ~

plan on *v.* (G) we ~ned on spending a month in Europe

plant I *n.* ['shrub, bush'] 1. to grow ~s 2. to water a ~ 3. an annual; biennial; climbing; decorative; exotic; perennial; tropical ~ 4. a ~ grows ['factory'] ['utility'] 5. to manage, operate, run a ~ 6. a power ~ ['buildings'] ['equipment'] 7. (the) physical ~ (of an institution)

plant II *v.* 1. (D; tr.) to ~ with (to ~ a field with rye) 2. (misc.) to ~ an idea in smb.'s head

plantation *n.* a coffee; cotton; rubber; sugar; tea ~

plaque *n.* ['filmy deposit on teeth'] 1. to remove ~ (from teeth) 2. dental ~ 3. ~ accumulates, builds up ['tablet'] 4. to put up a ~ (in smb.'s honor) 5. a memorial ~

plaster *n.* ['pasty composition'] 1. to apply ~ (to apply ~ to a wall) 2. to daub ~ (to daub ~ on a

wall) 3. crumbling, falling ~ 4. ~ comes off, falls off (a wall) ['pastelike mixture used for healing purposes'] 5. a mustard ~ ['tape'] 6. (BE) (a) sticking ~

plastic *n.* laminated ~

plate *n.* ['dish'] 1. a cake; dinner; salad; soup ~ ['denture'] 2. a dental; lower; upper ~ ['tag'] 3. a license (AE), number (BE) ~ ['thin layer'] 4. armor; silver ~ ['container passed around for donations of money'] 5. to pass the ~ 6. a collection ~

plateau *n.* 1. a high ~ 2. (misc.) to reach a ~ ('to cease making progress')

platform *n.* ['raised stage'] 1. to mount ('ascend') a ~ 2. from a ~ (to speak from a ~) 3. a launching ~ ['statement of policies'] (esp. AE; BE prefers *manifesto*) 4. to draft, draw up a ~ 5. to adopt a ~ 6. a party; political ~ USAGE NOTE: A political platform consists of various statements that are called planks.

platitude *n.* 1. to mouth, utter a ~ (he's always mouthing ~s) 2. in ~s (to speak in ~s)

platoon *n.* 1. to form a ~ 2. to deploy a ~

plaudits *n.* to earn, receive, win ~

plausible *adj.* 1. ~ to + inf. (it is ~ to assume that they will not accept our invitation) 2. ~ that + clause (it's ~ that most of the voters will not support this referendum)

play I *n.* ['stage presentation'] 1. to present, produce, put on, stage; revive; write a ~ 2. to perform; rehearse a ~ 3. to review a ~ 4. to criticize, pan (colloq.) a ~ 5. a miracle; morality; mystery; nativity; one-act; passion ~ 6. a ~ closes; opens; runs (the ~ ran for two years on Broadway) 7. (misc.) the ~ got rave reviews ['action, activity'] 8. to bring into ~ (to bring various factors into ~) 9. to come into ~ ['competition, playing'] 10. fair; foul; rough; team ~ 11. in; into; out of ~ (to put the ball into ~) ['attempt to attract'] (colloq.) (esp. AE) 12. to make a ~ for (he made a ~ for her) ['misc.'] 13. a ~ on words ('a pun')

play II *v.* 1. ('to compete') to ~ fair; foul; rough 2. (C) ('to perform') ~ a nice song for me; or: ~ me a nice song 3. (d; intr.) ('to compete') to ~ against (to ~ against a strong opponent) 4. (d; intr.) ('to gamble') to ~ for (to ~ for money) 5. (d; intr.) ('to perform') to ~ for (she ~s for our team) 6. (d; intr.) to ~ for ('to attempt to obtain') (to ~ for time) 7. (d; intr.) to ~ on, upon ('to exploit') (to ~ on smb.'s fears) 8. (d; intr.) to ~ on ('to pun') (to ~ on words) 9. (D; tr.) ('to do, make') to ~ on (they ~ed a joke on us; she ~ed a trick on me) 10. (d; intr.) ('to perform') to ~ to (to ~ to a full house) 11. (esp. tennis) (d; intr.) ('to direct one's strokes') to ~ to (to ~ to an opponent's forehand) 12. (D; intr.) ('to amuse oneself') to ~ with (to ~ with matches) 13. (L) (esp. in children's language) ('to pretend') let's ~ that I'm the teacher and you're the pupil 14. (O; can be used with one object) ('to oppose in') I'll ~ you a game of cards 15. (s) ('to feign') they ~ed dead 16. (misc.) to ~ smb. for a fool ('to ridicule smb.')

play about (BE) see **play around**

play around *v.* (D; intr.) to ~ with

play back v. (B) she ~ed the tape back to us

player n. ['athlete'] 1. a clean; dirty ~ 2. a key ~ ['electronic instrument'] 3. a record ~

playgoer n. a habitual ~

playground n. 1. (BE) an adventure ~ ('children's playground designed for spontaneous play') 2. a city, public ~

playing n. clean; dirty ~

play off v. (d; tr.) to ~ against ('to set against') (to ~ one side off against the other)

play up v. (d; intr.) to ~ to ('to flatter') (to ~ to the boss)

plea n. 1. to enter, make, put forward a ~ 2. to answer, respond to a ~ 3. to deny, reject a ~ 4. (slang) to cop a ~ ('to plead guilty to a lesser charge') 5. an ardent, fervent, impassioned, moving, passionate; urgent ~ 6. (to enter) a guilty ~; (to enter) a ~ of not guilty; more usu. is: to plead guilty; to plead not guilty 7. a ~ for (a ~ for mercy) 8. (misc.) ~ bargaining

plead v. 1. to ~ fervently 2. (D; intr.) to ~ for; with (to ~ with the judge for mercy) 3. (legal) to ~ guilty (to a charge) 4. (legal) to ~ not guilty (to a charge)

pleasant adj. ~ to + inf. (it's ~ to lie in the sun = it's ~ lying in the sun; she is ~ to work with = it is ~ to work with her = it is ~ working with her = she is a ~ person to work with)

please v. 1. to ~ greatly, highly 2. (R) it ~d us to learn of your success; it ~d us greatly that you could accept our invitation

pleased adj. 1. greatly, highly ~ 2. ~ about, at, by, with 3. ~ to + inf. (we are ~ to be here; I am ~ to meet you) 4. ~ that + clause (she was ~ that the proposal had been accepted)

pleasure n. 1. to afford, give ~ (it gives me great ~ to present the next speaker) 2. to feel; find, take ~ in 3. to derive ~ from 4. to forgo a ~ 5. a genuine, real; rare ~ 6. a ~ to + inf. (it's a ~ to work with them = it's a ~ working with them = they are a ~ to work with; it is a ~ to teach these children = it is a ~ teaching these children = these children are a ~ to teach)

plebiscite n. 1. to conduct, hold a ~ 2. a ~ to + inf. (a ~ to determine the status of a territory)

pledge I n. 1. to make, take a ~ 2. to give smb. one's ~ 3. to honor, redeem one's ~ 4. a solemn ~ 5. a campaign ~ 6. a ~ to + inf. (she made a solemn ~ to contribute fifty pounds) 7. a ~ that + clause (he took a ~ that he would stop smoking) 8. (misc.) to take the ~ ('to vow to stop drinking')

pledge II v. 1. (A) she ~d her support to us; or: she ~d us her support 2. (D; tr.) to ~ to (she was ~d to secrecy) 3. (E) they ~d to return 4. (L) he ~d that he would repay the debt within a month

plenty determiner, n., pronoun 1. ~ of (~ of money) 2. ~ to + inf. (she gave us ~ to do) 3. (formal) in ~ (to live in ~) 4. (formal) of ~ (a time of ~)

pliers n. a pair of ~

plod v. 1. (d; intr.) to ~ through ('to go through laboriously') (to ~ through a long reading list) 2. (P; intr.) ('to move') they ~ded slowly along the road

plot I n. ['conspiracy'] 1. to devise, hatch; weave a ~ 2. to foil, thwart a ~ 3. to expose a ~ 4. a cunning, diabolic; sinister ~ 5. a ~ against 6. a ~ to + inf. (to expose a ~ to overthrow the government) ['story'] 7. to build, construct the ~ (of a novel) 8. a contrived; intricate; simple ~ 9. a ~ thickens ['piece of ground'] 10. a cemetery; garden ~; a ~ of land

plot II v. 1. (D; intr.) to ~ against (to ~ against the government) 2. (E) they ~ted to overthrow the government 3. (Q) they were ~ting how to obtain the necessary information

plow I **plough** n. to pull a ~

plow II **plough** v. 1. (d; intr.) to ~ into ('to strike') (the racing car skidded and ~ed into the crowd) 2. (d; intr.) to ~ through ('to go through laboriously') (to ~ through a long reading list; to ~ through a crowd) ('to ~ through deep snow')

ploy n. 1. to resort to, use a ~ 2. a clever, ingenious ~ 3. a ~ to + inf. (it was a ~ to get money)

pluck I n. ['courage'] the ~ to + inf. (he had enough ~ to stand up to the boss)

pluck II v. 1. (d; intr.) ('to tug') to ~ at 2. (D; tr.) ('to pull') to ~ from (to ~ feathers from a chicken)

plug I n. ['electrical fitting'] 1. to insert, put a ~ into a socket 2. a ~ fits into a socket ['device carrying an electric current'] 3. a spark (AE); sparking (BE) ~ ['word of praise'] (colloq.) 4. to put in a ~ for ['misc.'] (colloq.) (esp. AE) 5. to pull the ~ ('to cut off a life-support system'); to pull the ~ on smt. ('to put an end to smt.')

plug II v. (d; intr., tr.) to ~ into (the lamp ~s into this receptacle)

plug away v. (D; intr.) to ~ at ('to work at laboriously') (to ~ at a job)

plumber n. 1. to call (in) a ~ 2. a master ~

plummet v. (d; intr.) to ~ to (to ~ to earth)

plump I adj. pleasingly ~

plump II v. (colloq.) (D; intr.) to ~ for ('to support')

plunge I n. ['risk'] (colloq.) to take the ~

plunge II v. 1. (d; intr.) ('to throw oneself') to ~ from; to (to ~ to one's death from a cliff) 2. (d; intr.) ('to dive'); ('to rush') to ~ into (to ~ into the water; to ~ into war) 3. (d; tr.) ('to throw'); ('to thrust') to ~ into (the room was ~ed into darkness; to ~ a dagger into smb.'s heart)

plural n. in the ~

plus n. to weigh the ~es and the minuses

ply v. 1. (d; intr.) ('to travel') to ~ between (these ships ~ between the two cities) 2. (d; tr.) ('to provide') to ~ with (they plied him with liquor)

pneumonia n. 1. to come down with, contract, develop ~ 2. bronchial; viral ~

poach v. (D; intr.) ('to trespass') to ~ on, upon

pocket n. 1. to turn out one's ~s 2. to pick smb.'s ~ 3. a back; coat; hip; inside; shirt; side; watch ~ 4. an air ~

pocketbook n. (AE) ['handbag'] to carry a ~

podium n. from; on a ~

poem n. 1. to compose, write; memorize; recite a ~ 2. a dramatic; epic, heroic; lyric; narrative ~

poet n. ~ laureate

poetry n. 1. to compose, write ~ 2. to memorize;

read; recite; scan ~ 3. dramatic; epic, heroic; lyric; narrative ~

pogrom *n.* to carry out; instigate; organize a ~

point I *n.* ['location, position, place, spot'] 1. to arrive at, reach a ~ 2. an assembly; cutoff; focal; jumping-off; pressure; rallying; salient; starting; turning; vanishing; vantage ~ 3. the ~ of no return 4. at a ~ (at that ~ in history) 5. for a ~ (for all ~s east) 6. from; to a ~ (from this ~ to that ~) ['level'] ['degree'] 7. to arrive at, reach a ~ 8. a high; low ~ (she has reached the high ~ of her career) 9. the boiling; breaking; freezing; melting; saturation ~ 10. (up) to a ~ (to a certain ~ they are right) ['step, stage'] 11. at, on the ~ (they were on the ~ of leaving) ['argument'] ['topic'] 12. to bring up, make, raise a ~ 13. to argue; cover, discuss; emphasize, stress, underscore; explain; illustrate; review; win a ~ 14. to belabor, labor; strain, stretch a ~ 15. to drive, hammer, press a ~ home; to make one's ~ 16. to concede, yield a ~ 17. a controversial; crucial; fine; major; minor; moot; selling; sore; sticking; subtle; talking; telling ~ 18. the ~ that + clause (she made the ~ that further resistance was useless) 19. beside the ~ (her remarks were beside the ~) 20. on a ~ (on that ~ we disagree) 21. to the ~ (to speak to the ~) 22. (misc.) to come to the ~; ~ by ~; a good ('convincing') ~; to have a ~ ('to have a convincing argument') ['core, essence'] 23. to see the ~ (he never did see the ~ of the joke) 24. to get to the ~ ['emphasis'] 25. to make a ~ of (he made a ~ of repeating her name several times) ['distinguishing feature'] 26. smb.'s bad, weak; good, strong ~s ['punctuation mark'] 27. a decimal; exclamation (AE) ~ ['scoring unit'] 28. to score a ~ (also fig.) 29. to shave ~s ('to manipulate the results of a contest for illegal purposes') 30. (esp. tennis) a game; match; set ~ 31. by ~s (to lead by five ~s) 32. (boxing) on ~s (to win on ~s) ['regard'] 33. in ~ of (in ~ of law; in ~ of fact) ['aim, object, purpose, reason'] 34. to get, see the ~ 35. a ~ in (there is no ~ in complaining = there is no ~ complaining) 36. a ~ to (there is no ~ to your going) 37. (misc.) what's the ~? ['tapered end'] 38. a sharp ~ (this pencil has a sharp ~) ['misc.'] 39. a ~ of view; at the ~ of a gun; a Brownie ~ (colloq.) ('ingratiation in the eyes of a superior') (to make Brownie ~s); a case in ~ ('a pertinent case'); a ~ of order

point II *v.* 1. (D; intr.) to ~ at, to ('to draw attention to') (she ~ed at me) 2. (d; tr.) ('to aim') to ~ at (to ~ a gun at smb.) 3. (D; intr.) to ~ to ('to cite') (they ~ed to poverty as a major problem; the evidence ~s to him as the criminal)

pointers *n.* ['advice'] 1. to give smb. ~ on 2. to ask for; get ~ on

pointless *adj.* ~ to + inf. (it's ~ to continue the discussion)

point out *v.* 1. (B) she ~ed out the sights to us 2. (L; to) they ~ed out (to us) that such investments would be risky

poise I *n.* 1. to keep, maintain one's ~ 2. to lose one's ~ 3. the ~ to + inf. (do you have enough ~ to speak without notes?)

poise II *v.* (D; refl.) ('to brace oneself') to ~ for (she ~d herself for the ordeal)

poison *n.* 1. to administer, give (a) ~ 2. to swallow, take ~ 3. (a) lethal; slow; strong ~ 4. rat ~ (to spread rat ~)

poison gas *n.* to use ~ against

poisoning *n.* blood; food; lead; ptomaine ~

poke I *n.* ['punch'] (colloq.) to give smb. a ~ (in the eye)

poke II *v.* 1. (d; intr.) to ~ at ('to jab') (he kept ~ing at me) 2. (D; tr.) ('to jab') to ~ in (to ~ smb. in the ribs) 3. (d; tr.) ('to extend') to ~ out of (to ~ one's head out of the window) 4. (d; tr.) ('to produce by piercing') to ~ through (to ~ a hole through a wall) 5. (P; tr.) ('to thrust') to ~ one's head through a window 6. (misc.) to ~ fun at smb.

poke about see **poke around**

poke around *v.* (colloq.) (D; intr.) to ~ in ('to look through') (stop ~ing around in my desk)

poker *n.* to play ~

polarization *n.* ~ between

polarize *v.* (D; intr., tr.) to ~ into (~d into opposing camps)

pole I *n.* ['long, slender piece of wood, metal'] 1. to put up a ~ 2. a breakaway; fishing; ski; tent; totem; trolley ~ 3. a telegraph; telephone (AE); utility (AE) ~

pole II *n.* ['end of the earth's axis'] 1. the North; South Pole 2. a celestial; magnetic ~ ['terminal of a battery'] 3. a negative; positive ~ ['misc.'] 4. ~s apart; or: at opposite ~s ('diametrically opposed')

police *n.* border; campus (US); city, municipal; local; military; mounted; secret; security; state ~

police car *n.* an unmarked ~

policeman *n.* 1. a military ~ (abbreviated as *MP*) 2. see **police officer**

police officer *n.* an off-duty; plainclothes; uniformed ~

policewoman see **police officer**

policy I *n.* ['plan'] ['principle'] 1. to adopt, establish, formulate, set a ~ 2. to adhere to, follow, pursue; carry out, implement a ~ 3. to form, shape a ~ 4. a cautious; clear, clear-cut; conciliatory; deliberate; established, set; firm; flexible; foolish; friendly; prudent; rigid; sound, wise ~ 5. (a) company; economic; foreign; government; public; long-range, long-term; military; monetary; national; official; open-door; personnel; population; scorched-earth; service; short-range, short-term; standard; wait-and-see; written ~ 6. a ~ to + inf. (it is our established ~ to treat everyone fairly) 7. a ~ that + clause; subj. (it is company ~ that all workers be/should be paid according to the same criteria)

policy II *n.* ['contract for insurance'] 1. to take out a ~ 2. to issue, write up a ~ 3. to reinstate a ~ 4. to cancel a ~ 5. an endowment; homeowner's; insurance; lifetime; straight life; term ~

polio, poliomyelitis *n.* to contract, develop ~

polish *n.* ['gloss'] 1. to apply ~ 2. French (BE); furniture ~ 3. nail ~ (AE; BE has *nail varnish*)

polite *adj.* 1. ~ to 2. ~ to + inf. (it was not ~ to say that)

politeness *n.* 1. studied ~ 2. ~ to

politic *adj.* (formal) ['expedient'] ~ to + inf. (it would not be ~ to get involved in their affairs)

political fences *n.* ['political standing'] to mend one's ~

politician *n.* an astute, shrewd; crooked; glib; great; hack; honest ~

politics *n.* 1. to go in for ~ 2. to play ~ 3. to talk ~ 4. local, parish-pump (BE); national; partisan, party; power; practical ~

poll *n.* 1. to conduct, take a ~ 2. (AE) an exit ~ (taken of voters leaving the voting booths) 3. (esp. AE) a straw ('unofficial') ~ 4. a public-opinion ~ 5. a ~ among (to conduct a ~ among students)

pollination *n.* cross ~

pollution *n.* 1. to control ~ 2. air; environmental; noise, sound; water ~

polo *n.* to play ~

polyandry *n.* to practice ~

polygamy *n.* to practice ~

polyp *n.* 1. to remove a ~ 2. a benign; malignant ~

pomp *n.* ceremonial ~

pond *n.* to drain a ~

ponder *v.* (d; intr.) to ~ on, over, upon (to ~ over a problem)

pontificate *v.* (D; intr.) to ~ on

pony *n.* a polo ~

pool I *n.* ['joint enterprise'] 1. to form a ~ 2. a car; stenographic, typing ~ ['group of vehicles'] 3. a motor ~ ['total of money bet by gamblers'] 4. a football ~ (BE has *pools*) ['billiards'] 5. to shoot ~ ['stock, supply'] 6. a gene ~

pool II *n.* ['basin'] 1. an indoor; outdoor; paddling (BE), wading (AE); swimming ~ ['small body of water'] 2. deep; shallow; stagnant ~

pools see **pool I 4**

poor *adj.* ~ in (the country is ~ in natural resources)

pop I *adv.* (colloq.) to go ~ ('to make a short explosive sound')

pop II *v.* (P; intr., tr.) we have to ~ into the store for a minute; ~ your head out of the window and see if it's raining; to ~ round the corner

popular *adj.* 1. ~ as (she was ~ as a nightclub singer) 2. ~ with (~ with teenagers)

popularity *n.* 1. to acquire, gain, win ~ 2. to enjoy ~ 3. to lose ~ 4. ~ with

populated *adj.* densely, heavily; sparsely ~

population *n.* 1. a decreasing, shrinking; dense; excess, overflow; expanding, growing, increasing, rising; sparse; stable; transient ~ 2. an aging; civilian; foreign-born; indigenous; local; native-born; rural; urban ~ 3. (misc.) a ~ explosion

porch *n.* 1. (AE) a back; front ~ (BE uses *veranda*) 2. (AE) a sun ~ (BE has *sun lounge*) 3. (AE) a screened, screened-in ~ (BE uses *veranda*) 4. (BE) a church ~

pore *v.* (d; intr.) to ~ over ('to examine') (to ~ over a document)

pores *n.* blocked, clogged, closed; open ~

pornography *n.* explicit, hard-core; soft, soft-core ~

porpoise *n.* 1. a school of ~s 2. a young ~ is a calf 3. a female ~ is a cow 4. a male ~ is a bull

porridge *n.* (esp. BE) 1. to cook, make ~ 2.

(misc.) a bowl of ~; (BE; slang) to do ~ ('to spend time in prison')

port *n.* 1. to clear ('leave') a ~ 2. to make ~ ('to arrive at a port') 3. to call at a ~ 4. a free; home ~ 5. in; into ~ (to put into ~)

portion *n.* 1. an individual ~ 2. equal ~s

portion out *v.* (B) they ~ed the food out to the needy

portrait *n.* 1. to make, paint a ~ 2. to commission a ~ 3. a family; full-length; group ~ 4. (misc.) to pose for, sit for one's ~

portray *v.* (d; tr.) to ~ as (to ~ smb. as a hero)

pose I *n.* to assume, strike a ~

pose II *v.* 1. (B) ('to put') she ~d a question to the speaker 2. (d; intr.) to ~ as ('to pretend to be') (to ~ as an expert) 3. (D; intr.) to ~ for ('to serve as a model for') (to ~ for an artist)

position *n.* ['posture'] 1. to assume, take a ~ 2. an awkward, uncomfortable; comfortable ~ 3. a kneeling; lotus; lying; prone; sitting; squatting; straddle; supine ~ 4. the fetal, foetal ~ ['attitude'] 5. to assume, take a ~ 6. a firm; radical; strong; untenable; weak ~ 7. an official; unofficial ~ 8. a ~ on (to take a ~ on foreign aid) 9. a ~ that + clause (they took the ~ that further resistance would be useless) ['site'] ['military site'] 10. to attack, storm a ~ 11. to hold, maintain; occupy, take up; regain a ~ 12. to give up, lose, surrender a ~ 13. a defensive; dominant; enemy; fortified; impregnable; strong; unfortified; untenable, vulnerable, weak ~ 14. a ~ of strength 15. from a ~ (to negotiate from a ~ of strength) ['place'] ['situation'] 16. to occupy a ~ 17. an embarrassing; ludicrous ~ 18. a high, leading, prominent; unique ~ (to occupy a prominent ~) 19. in a ~ (she is in a ~ to know) ['proper place'] 20. in ~ (the players were in ~) 21. out of ~ ['job'] 22. to apply for, look for, seek; find a ~ 23. a permanent; temporary; tenured ~ 24. a government; managerial; official; teaching ~

positive *adj.* ~ about

possess *v.* what ~ed you to do it?

possession *n.* 1. to get, take ~ of 2. material ~s 3. in ~ of

possibility *n.* 1. to raise a ~ 2. to exclude, rule out a ~ 3. a good, strong; remote, slim ~ 4. a ~ of (there is a strong ~ of snow) 5. a ~ that + clause (there's a strong ~ that the concert will be canceled)

possible *adj.* 1. easily, perfectly; humanly ~ 2. ~ to + inf. (it is ~ to rent a boat) 3. ~ that + clause (it is ~ that we might be able to attend)

possum *n.* (colloq.) to play ~ ('to pretend to be asleep')

post I *n.* ['mail'] 1. (BE) see **mail I** 2. (BE) free ~ 3. (CE) parcel ~ 4. (BE) by return of ~ (AE has *by return mail*)

post II *v.* (BE) 1. (A) she ~ed the book to me or: she ~ed me the book 2. (D; tr.) to ~ from; to ~ the letter was ~ed from London to Edinburgh) (AE has **mail II**)

post III *n.* ['station'] 1. a command; listening; observation; trading ~ ['place of duty'] 2. to leave; quit one's ~ 3. at one's ~ (to be asleep at one's ~)

post IV *v.* (esp. BE) (d; tr.) ('to station') to ~ to (she was ~ed to Bonn)

post V *n.* ['pole'] 1. a starting ~ (at a horse race) 2. (colloq.) (BE) a telegraph ~ 3. (misc.) from pillar to ~ ('from one situation to another without letup'); (BE) to pip at the ~ ('to overtake and defeat at the very end')

postage *n.* 1. to pay the ~ 2. the return ~

postcard *n.* 1. to send a ~ 2. to drop smb. a ~ 3. a picture ~

poster *n.* 1. to put up a ~ 2. a campaign ~

postmaster *n.* the ~ general

postpone *v.* 1. (D; tr.) to ~ to, until (the concert has been ~d to Wednesday) 2. (G) they ~d leaving because of the weather

postscript *n.* 1. to add a ~ 2. a ~ to

postulate I *n.* (formal) a ~ that + clause (his ~ that the area was uninhabited proved to be true)

postulate II *v.* (formal) (L) they ~d that the collision had been caused by fog

posture I *n.* 1. to assume a ~ 2. an erect; good ~ 3. a defense; political ~

posture II *v.* (D; intr.) ('to pretend') to ~ as

pot *n.* 1. (fig.) a melting ~ 2. a pepper ~ (BE; AE has *pepper shaker*) 3. a chamber ~ 4. (misc.) to scour ~s and pans

potato *n.* 1. to bake; boil; fry; mash; peel ~es 2. a baked ~ 3. chipped (BE), French-fried (AE); mashed; scalloped ~es

potential *n.* 1. to develop; realize one's ~ 2. a ~ for

potion *n.* a love ~

potluck *n.* ['whatever is offered'] to take ~

potshot *n.* (colloq.) ['critical remark'] to take a ~ at

potter *v.* (BE) (d; intr.) to ~ about (to ~ about the house) (AE has *putter*)

pottery *n.* to glaze ~

potty *adj.* (colloq.) (esp. BE) ['infatuated'] ~ about

pouch *n.* diplomatic ~ (the letter was sent by diplomatic ~)

poultice *n.* to apply a ~

pounce *v.* (d; intr.) to ~ on, upon (the cat ~d on the mouse)

pound I *n.* ['enclosure'] a dog ~

pound II *v.* 1. (d; intr.) to ~ at (to ~ at the door; our artillery was ~ing at the enemy positions) 2. (d; tr.) to ~ into (I've been trying to ~ some facts into their heads) 3. (d; intr.) to ~ on (to ~ on a table)

pour *v.* 1. (C) ~ a cool drink for me; or: ~ me a cool drink 2. (d; intr.) to ~ down (tears ~ed down her cheeks) 3. (d; intr., tr.) to ~ from (blood ~ed from the gaping wound) 4. (d; intr., tr.) to ~ into (water ~ed into the pit) 5. (d; intr., tr.) to ~ out of (oil ~ed out of the tank) 6. (d; tr.) to ~ over (to ~ gravy over meat)

pout *v.* (D; intr.) to ~ about

poverty *n.* 1. to breed ~ (illiteracy breeds ~) 2. to eliminate, eradicate, wipe out ~ 3. abject, dire, extreme, grinding, severe ~ 4. in ~ (to live in grinding ~)

powder *n.* 1. to put on ~ 2. baby; baking; bleach-ing; curry; dusting; face; garlic; scouring; talcum; tooth ~ 3. gunpowder; smokeless ~ 4. (misc.) (slang) to take a ~ ('to run off unexpectedly'); (colloq.) to keep one's ~ dry ('to remain calm')

power *n.* ['authority'] 1. to assume, take; exercise, wield; seize; transfer ~ 2. emergency; executive; political ~ 3. discretionary ~s 4. ~ over (they seized ~ over several provinces) 5. the ~ to + inf. (the prime minister has the ~ to dissolve parliament) 6. in; into ~ (the government in ~; to come into ~) ['dominance'] 7. the balance of ~ ['nation'] 8. the great, world ~s; a superpower 9. (the) warring ~s 10. a foreign; occupying ~ ['capability'] 11. to develop one's ~s (of observation) 12. bargaining; earning; healing; purchasing ~; recuperative; staying; supernatural ~s ['military force, police force'] 13. air; military; naval, sea; police ~ 14. fire ~ ['source of energy'] 15. to turn on the ~ 16. to cut off, turn off the ~ 17. electric; hydroelectric; nuclear; water ~ ['motive force'] 18. under one's own ~ ['exponent'] (math.) 19. to raise to a ~ (to raise five to the third ~)

powerless *adj.* ~ to + inf. (she was ~ to help)

power line *n.* to down a ~ (several ~s were downed during the storm)

power mower *n.* to operate, work a ~

power of attorney *n.* a ~ to + inf. (we had a ~ to conduct her business)

powwow *n.* (colloq.) ['conference'] to hold a ~

pox *n.* ['plague'] a ~ on

practicable *adj.* ['feasible'] ~ to + inf. (it was not ~ to put up a new building there)

practical *adj.* ['sensible'] ~ to + inf. (it is not ~ to do that)

practice I **practise** *n.* ['habit'] 1. to make a ~ of smt. 2. a common, usual; local; universal ~ 3. a ~ to + inf. (it was her ~ to drink a glass of wine every evening) ['exercise'] 4. to have ~ (we have ~ today at four o'clock) 5. target ~ 6. ~ at, in (~ at tying knots) 7. the ~ to + inf. (I've had enough ~ to pass the test) ['professional activity'] 8. (a) legal; medical; nursing; professional ~ 9. (of doctors) a general; group; private ~ 10. a lucrative ~ ['application'] 11. in; into ~ (to put a theory into ~; in theory and in ~) ['method of conducting business'] 12. sharp, unethical, unfair, unscrupulous ~s 13. (esp. AE) fair-trade ~s USAGE NOTE: In Great Britain, *private practice* refers to a practice that is not under the National Health Service.

practice II **practise** *v.* 1. (D; intr.) to ~ on (you can ~ mouth-to-mouth resuscitation on me) 2. (G) the boy ~d throwing the lasso

practitioner *n.* a family, general; nurse (esp. US) ~

prairie *n.* 1. a rolling; windswept ~ 2. on the ~

praise I *n.* 1. to earn ~ 2. to bestow, heap, lavish ~ on smb. 3. to give ~ to smb. 4. to sing smb.'s ~s 5. faint; fulsome; glowing, high, strong, unrestrained, unstinting ~ 6. ~ for 7. in ~ of 8. (misc.) a chorus of ~

praise II *v.* 1. to ~ highly, strongly 2. (D; tr.) to ~ for

praiseworthy *adj.* (formal) ~ to + inf. (it is ~ to

do volunteer work)
pram *n.* (BE) to push, wheel a ~ (AE has *baby carriage, carriage*)
prance *v.* (P; intr.) to ~ around the room
prank *n.* 1. to play a ~ on smb. 2. a childish; foolish; innocent; mischievous; wanton ~
prate see **prattle**
prattle *v.* 1. to ~ endlessly 2. (D; intr.) to ~ (on) about (he ~d on endlessly about his operation)
pray *v.* 1. to ~ devoutly, fervently; silently 2. (D; intr.) to ~ for; to (to ~ to God for good health) 3. (L; to) we ~ed (to God) that they would be safe
prayer *n.* 1. to offer; say; utter a ~ 2. to answer a ~ 3. a fervent; silent ~ 4. (a) communal; daily; evening; morning ~ 5. a ~ for (to offer a ~ for peace) 6. a ~ that + clause; subj. (our ~ that peace be/should be restored was heard) 7. (misc.) the answer to all our ~s
preach *v.* 1. (D; intr.) to ~ against (to ~ against sin) 2. (colloq.) (D; intr.) to ~ at (stop ~ing at me) 3. (D; intr.) to ~ to (to ~ to one's congregation) 4. (L) to ~ that the end of the world is near
preacher *n.* an itinerant; lay ~
preamble *n.* a ~ to
precaution *n.* 1. to take ~s 2. elaborate ~s 3. a ~ against
precedence *n.* to have, take ~ over
precedent *n.* 1. to create, establish, set a ~ 2. to cite a ~ 3. to break (a) ~ 4. a ~ for
precept *n.* a ~ that + clause (we adhere to the ~ that all criminals can be rehabilitated)
preceptor *n.* a ~ to
precinct *n.* a pedestrian (BE); police; voting ~
precious *adj.* ~ to
precipitate *v.* to ~ into (to ~ a country into war)
precipitation *n.* heavy; light ~
precise *adj.* ~ about
precision *n.* great, utmost; military; surgical; unerring ~
preclude *v.* (formal) (d; tr.) to ~ from (to ~ smb. from doing smt.)
precondition *n.* to set ~s
precursor *n.* a ~ of, to
predecessor *n.* smb.'s immediate ~
predestined *adj.* (cannot stand alone) 1. ~ to (~ to glory) 2. ~ to + inf. (she was ~ to go far in life) 3. ~ that + clause (it was ~ that they would never meet again)
predicament *n.* 1. an awkward; dire ~ (to get into an awkward ~) 2. in a ~
predicate *v.* (d; tr.) ('to base') to ~ on, upon (to ~ a theory on certain facts)
predict *v.* 1. (K) I ~ed their getting into trouble 2. (L) she ~ed that it would rain 3. (Q) who can ~ how the elections will turn out?
prediction *n.* 1. to make a ~ 2. a ~ comes true
predilection *n.* a ~ for
predispose *v.* (formal) 1. (d; tr.) to ~ to 2. (H) what ~d you to go?
predisposed *adj.* (cannot stand alone) 1. ~ to (~ to violence) 2. ~ to + inf. (~ to act rashly)
predisposition *n.* 1. a ~ to 2. a ~ to + inf. (a ~ to act rashly)

predominance *n.* ~ over
predominate I *adj.* ~ over
predominate II *v.* (D; intr.) to ~ over
preeminence *n.* ~ in
preen *v.* (formal) (d; refl.) to ~ oneself on ('to pride oneself on')
preface *n.* a ~ to (a ~ to a book)
prefer *v.* 1. (D; tr.) ('to bring') to ~ against (to ~ charges against smb.) 2. (D; tr.) to ~ to (she ~s fish to meat) 3. (E) we ~ to remain at home 4. (G) I ~red going to a concert 5. (esp. BE) (H; no passive) I'd ~ you to stay out of the dispute 6. (K) I would ~ your staying out of the dispute 7. (L; subj.) she ~s that he not get/should not get involved 8. (misc.) I (very) much ~ living in the suburbs USAGE NOTE: This verb can be used in several ways to express preference--I prefer walking to riding; I prefer to walk rather than to ride; I prefer not to ride.
preferable *adj.* 1. ~ to 2. ~ to + inf. (it is ~ to remain silent) 3. ~ that + clause; subj. (it is ~ that she go alone) USAGE NOTE: This adjective can be used in several ways--walking is preferable to riding; it's preferable to walk rather than to ride.
preference *n.* 1. to give ~ to 2. to demonstrate, display, show; express a ~ 3. a decided individual; marked ~ 4. (US) (a) veterans' ~ 5. a ~ for (she showed a decided ~ for classical music) 6. in ~ to
prefix *v.* (d; tr.) to ~ to (to ~ a title to a name)
pregnancy *n.* 1. to terminate a ~ 2. an ectopic; false; full-term; normal ~
prejudice I *n.* ['bias'] 1. to arouse, stir up ~ 2. to have, hold (a) ~ 3. to break down, eliminate ~ 4. (a) deep, deep-rooted, deep-seated, ingrained, strong ~ 5. race, racial; religious ~ 6. ~ against ['harm'] 7. without ~ to (without ~ to our claims)
prejudice II *v.* (D; tr.) to ~ against
prejudicial *adj.* ~ to
preliminary I *adj.* ~ to
preliminary II *n.* ~ to
prelude *n.* a ~ to
premature *adj.* ~ to + inf. (it is ~ to celebrate)
premiere *n.* 1. to give, stage a ~ 2. to attend a ~ 3. a lavish; world ~
premise *n.* ['proposition'] (logic) 1. the major; minor ~ ['assumption'] 2. the ~ that + clause her ~ that the results of the election were already decided proved to be true)
premises *n.* ['property'] on the ~ (to be consumed on the ~)
premium *n.* ['high value'] 1. to put a ~ on ['additional sum'] 2. to pay a ~ 3. at a ~ (to sell at a ~) ['fee paid to an insurance company'] 4. an insurance ~
premonition *n.* 1. to have a ~ 2. a ~ that + clause (she had a ~ that an accident would happen)
preoccupation *n.* a ~ with
preoccupied *adj.* ~ with
preordained *adj.* ~ that + clause; subj. (it was ~ that they meet/should meet)
preparation *n.* in ~ for (we are resting in ~ for the strenuous journey)
preparations *n.* 1. to make ~ 2. ~ for

preparatory *adj.* ~ to

prepare *v.* 1. to ~ carefully, thoroughly 2. (D; intr., refl., tr.) to ~ for (she was ~ing for the examination; they ~d themselves for unpleasant news; she is ~ing a paper for presentation at the national meeting) 3. (E) they were ~ing to leave 4. (H) parents should ~ children to cope with life

prepared *adj.* ~ to + inf. (we are ~ to leave)

preposition *n.* a compound; simple ~

preposterous *adj.* ~ to + inf. (it's ~ to speak of such things)

prerequisite I *adj.* (usu. does not stand alone) ~ to

prerequisite II *n.* a ~ for, to

prerogative *n.* 1. to exercise one's ~ 2. the royal ~ 3. smb.'s ~ to + inf. (it's our ~ to order an investigation)

prescribe *v.* 1. (D; tr.) to ~ for (to ~ a remedy for the common cold) 2. (formal) (L; subj.) regulations ~ that a lawyer draw up/should draw up the papers

prescription *n.* 1. to fill (AE), make up a ~ 2. a ~ for 3. by ~; on a ~ (to obtain a drug on a doctor's ~; by ~ only)

presence *n.* 1. to make one's ~ felt, known ('to make others notice one's presence') 2. in smb.'s ~

presence of mind *n.* to display ~

present I *n.* ['present time'] 1. at ~ 2. for the ~ ['present tense of a verb'] 3. in the ~

present II *n.* ['gift'] 1. an anniversary; birthday; Christmas; graduation; wedding ~ 2. a ~ for

present III *v.* 1. (B) ('to give') they ~ed an award to her 2. (D; tr.) ('to introduce') to ~ to (the new employees were ~ed to the rest of the staff) 3. (d; tr.) to ~ with ('to give a gift to') (he ~ed her with a beautiful bouquet of roses) 4. (med.) the patient ~ed with ('complained of') severe pains

presentable *adj.* to make oneself ~

presentation *n.* ['position of a fetus'] (med.) 1. a breech; face ~ ['act of presenting'] 2. to make a ~ 3. an oral ~ (of a report)

presentiment *n.* (formal) ['foreboding'] a ~ that + clause (she had a ~ that an accident would take place)

preservative *n.* a food ~

preserve I *n.* 1. a forest; game, wild-life ~ 2. (BE) see **preserves**

preserve II *v.* 1. (D; tr.) to ~ against, from (to ~ the environment from the ravages of pollution) 2. (D; tr.) to ~ for (to ~ a tradition for coming generations)

preserver *n.* a life ~ USAGE NOTE: In AE, *life preserver* means 'life belt', 'life jacket'; in BE, it means 'club used for self-defence'.

preserves *n.* ['fruit preserved by cooking with sugar'] apricot; blueberry; cherry; grape; peach; raspberry; strawberry ~

preside *v.* (D; intr.) to ~ over

presidency *n.* 1. to gain the ~ 2. a rotating ~

president *n.* 1. a vice ~ 2. an incoming; outgoing ~ 3. a ~ elect

press I *n.* ['instrument for crushing, shaping, squeezing'] 1. a cider; cookie (AE); hydraulic; wine ~ ['publishing house'] 2. a university; vanity ~ ['device for printing'] 3. a printing ~ 4. the ~es roll 5. (misc.) to go to ~ 6. in ~ (our book is now in ~) ['newspapers, magazines'] ['reporters'] 7. to censor; control; muzzle the ~ 8. a free ~ 9. the foreign; gutter; yellow; local ~ ['publicity'] 10. a bad; good ~ (we got a bad ~) ['smoothness of a fabric'] 11. (a) permanent ~ ['aggressive defense used in basketball'] 12. a full-court ~ ['type of lift used by weight lifters'] 13. to do a ~ 14. a bench; military ~

press II *v.* 1. to ~ hard 2. (d; intr., tr.) ('to push') to ~ against (to ~ against a door) 3. (d; intr., tr.) to ~ for ('to urge') (to ~ for reform; to ~ the authorities for information) 4. (D; tr.) ('to shape') to ~ into (to ~ clay into various forms) 5. (d; tr.) ('to place') to ~ into (to ~ all equipment into service) 6. (D; intr.) ('to squeeze') to ~ on (to ~ on a button) 7. (H) ('to urge') they were ~ing me to agree to the compromise

press conference *n.* to hold a ~

pressed *adj.* ~ for time

press on *v.* (D; intr.) to ~ with (the police ~ed on with the investigation)

press-up *n.* (BE) to do a ~ (see also **push-up**)

pressure I *n.* 1. to exert, place, put ~ on smb. 2. to bring ~ to bear on smb. 3. to build up, increase (the) ~ 4. to feel ~ 5. to ease, relieve (the) ~ 6. to face; resist ~ (to resist ~ from extremist groups) 7. inexorable, intense, maximum, relentless, strong, unrelieved ~ 8. financial; outside; parental; peer; population; public ~ (to resist public ~) 9. air; blood; oil; water ~ 10. (esp. meteorology) atmospheric; barometric; high; low ~ 11. ~ builds up, increases, rises; eases, falls 12. ~ for (~ for tax reform) 13. ~ from (to face inexorable ~ from the media) 14. under ~ (under relentless ~)

pressure II *v.* (AE) 1. (D; tr.) to ~ into (to ~ smb. into doing smt.) 2. (H) to ~ smb. to do smt.

pressurize *v.* (BE) see **pressure II**

prestige *n.* 1. to enjoy, have; gain ~ 2. to damage smb.'s ~ 3. great, high; little, low ~ 4. the ~ to + inf. (does she have enough ~ to get the party nomination?) 5. of ~ (of little ~)

presume *v.* (formal) 1. (d; intr.) to ~ on, upon (to ~ upon smb.'s good nature) 2. (E) I will not ~ to give you advice 3. (L) we can ~ that she will return 4. (M) we must ~ her to be innocent 5. (N; used with an adjective) we must ~ her innocent; she must be ~d innocent until proven guilty

presumption *n.* a ~ that + clause (our decision was based on the ~ that they would agree)

presumptuous *adj.* ~ to + inf. (it's ~ of you to make such claims)

pretence see **pretense**

pretend *v.* 1. (E) ('to feign'); ('to make believe') she ~ed not to notice; I ~ed to be busy; the children ~ed to be cowboys 2. (L) ('to feign'); ('to make believe') she ~ed that she was asleep; they ~ed that they were tourists

pretender *n.* a ~ to (a ~ to a throne)

pretense, pretence *n.* ['simulation'] ['false show'] 1. to make a ~ (he made no ~ of being objective) 2. to see through smb.'s ~ 3. under a ~ (under the ~ of patriotism; under false ~s) 4. without ~ (a person without ~) ['unsupported claim'] 5. to see through smb.'s ~ 6. a ~ that + clause (he saw through the ~ that lower taxes would cause unemployment) ['appearance'] 7. to keep, maintain a ~ (to maintain some ~ of legality) ['attempt'] 8. a ~ at (without any ~ at objectivity)

pretext *n.* 1. to find a ~ for 2. a flimsy; mere ~ 3. a ~ to + inf. (it was a ~ to occupy more territory) 4. a ~ that + clause (she refused to attend on the ~ that she would be out of town) 5. at, on, under a ~ (he would call for help at/on the slightest ~; under what ~ did she approach them?)

pretty *adj.* to be sitting ~ ('to be well off')

prevail *v.* 1. (D; intr.) to ~ against, over (to ~ against overwhelming odds) 2. (d; intr.) to ~ on, upon smb. to do smt. (they ~ed on me to buy a new television set)

prevent *v.* 1. (D; tr.) to ~ from (nothing can ~ this disease from spreading) 2. (BE) (J) nothing can ~ this disease spreading 3. (K) you cannot ~ her getting married

prevention *n.* 1. (health care) primary; secondary ~ 2. accident; fire ~

preview *n.* 1. to give a ~ 2. a sneak ~ (of a film)

prey I *n.* 1. to fall ~ to 2. easy ~

prey II *v.* (d; intr.) to ~ on (to ~ on small game)

price I *n.* 1. to fix, set a ~ 2. to hike (AE; colloq.), increase, mark up, raise ~s 3. to freeze; hold down, keep down; maintain ~s 4. to pay a ~ 5. to place, put a ~ on smt.; to quote a ~ 6. bring, command, fetch, get a ~ (icons bring a high ~) 7. to bring down ~s; to undercut (smb.'s) ~s (the latest news brought down oil ~s) 8. to cut, lower, mark down, reduce, roll back, slash ~s 9. an exorbitant, high, inflated, outrageous, prohibitive, steep stiff ~ 10. an attractive, bargain, fair, low, moderate, popular, reasonable, reduced ~ 11. an asking; buying, purchase; discount; going; list market; reduced; regular; resale; retail; sale; selling; unit; wholesale ~ 12. (at an auction) a reserve (esp. BE), upset (esp. AE) ~ 13. ~s drop, fall, go down, slump 14. ~s go up, rise, shoot up, skyrocket 15. a ~ for (to pay an exorbitant ~ for smt.) 16. at a certain ~ (to sell merchandise at reduced ~s) 17. (misc.) what ~ an economic recovery now? (BE) ('what are the chances of an economic recovery now?'); what ~ glory if you die in the trenches? (BE) ('what is the good of glory if you die in the trenches?'); to place a ~ on smb.'s head ('to post a reward for apprehending or killing smb.')

price II *v.* (D; refl., tr.) to ~ out of (they ~d themselves out of the market)

price index *n.* a consumer; retail ~

prick *n.* a pin ~

pride I *n.* 1. to take ~ in 2. to hurt smb.'s ~ 3. civic; fierce, great, strong; injured, wounded ~ (to take great ~ in one's children) 4. the ~ to + inf. (do they have enough ~ to defend their principles?) 5. (misc.) to appeal to smb.'s ~; to burst with ~; to pocket, swallow one's ~

pride II *v.* (d; refl.) to ~ on (to ~ oneself on one's strength)

priest *n.* 1. to ordain a ~ 2. to defrock, unfrock a

~ 3. an Anglican; Catholic; Episcopalian; Mormon; Orthodox ~ 4. a high; parish ~

priesthood *n.* to enter the ~

primary *n.* ['party election'] (AE) 1. to hold a ~ 2. a closed; direct; open; preferential; presidentia ; runoff ~

prime *n.* 1. to reach one's ~ 2. to pass one's ~ 3. in one's ~

primed *adj.* 1. ~ for (~ for the big game) 2. ~ to + inf. (we are ~ to begin)

prince *n.* 1. a crown ~ 2. (misc.) a ~ consort

princess *n.* a crown ~

principal *n.* a school ~ (esp. AE)

principle *n.* 1. to establish, formulate, lay down a ~ 2. to adhere to, apply a ~ 3. to betray, compromise one's ~s 4. a basic; general; guiding; high; sound; strict ~ 5. the ~ that + clause (we adhere to the ~ that everyone should be treated fairly) 6. in ~ (to agree in ~) 7. (misc.) a matter, question; person of ~

print I *n.* ['photograph'] 1. to develop; make a ~ ['printed state'] 2. in ~; out of ~ (I have not seen the story in ~; the book is out of ~) ['text of a contract'] 3. the fine, small ~ (people should always read the fine ~) ['printed letters'] 4. clear; large; small ~ ['impression made by type'] 5. dark; light ~

print II *v.* to ~ smt. (in) boldface; in italics; in Roman

printer *n.* ['device for printing computer data'] a daisy wheel; dot-matrix; laser; letter-quality; serial; thermal ~

printing *n.* offset ~

prior *adj.* (cannot stand alone) ~ to

priority *n.* 1. to establish, set a ~ 2. to take ~ over 3. (misc.) to reexamine, rethink; reorder, sort out one's ~ties

prise (BE) see **pry 2, 3**

prison *n.* 1. to go, be sent, be sentenced to ~ 2. to spend time in ~ 3. to be released from ~ 4. to break out of, escape from ~ 5. a maximum-security, minimum-security ~

prisoner *n.* 1. to take smb. ~; to take a ~ (we took many ~s) 2. a political ~

prisoner of war *n.* to interrogate; repatriate prisoners of war

privacy *n.* 1. to violate smb.'s ~ 2. an invasion of one's ~

private *n.* ['common soldier'] 1. a buck ~ 2. (US) a ~ first-class (the British Army has *lance corporal*)

privilege *n.* 1. to award, give, grant a ~ 2. to enjoy, exercise; have a ~ (to enjoy guest ~s) 3. to abuse a ~ 4. to revoke; suspend a ~ 5. a class; exclusive; special ~ 6. franking; guest; kitchen ~s 7. executive ~ 8. a ~ to + inf. (it was a ~ to work with them = it was a ~ working with them)

privileged *adj.* (usu. does not stand alone) ~ to + inf. (we are ~ to live in a democracy)

prize I *n.* 1. to award, give a ~ 2. to distribute ~s 3. to receive, win a ~ 4. a booby; consolation; door ~

prize II (BE) see **pry 2, 3**

pro see **professional**

probability *n.* in all ~

probable *adj.* ~ that + clause (it's ~ that she will not arrive until tomorrow; more usu. is: she'll probably not arrive until tomorrow)

probate *n.* 1. to grant ~ 2. to prove a will at ~

probation *n.* 1. to release smb. on ~ 2. to violate (the terms of one's) ~ 3. on ~ (he's out on ~)

probe I *n.* 1. to conduct; launch a ~ 2. an exhaustive, thorough ~ 3. an interplanetary, space ~ 4. a police ~ 5. a ~ into, of (a police ~ into racketeering)

probe II *v.* 1. to ~ deeply, thoroughly 2. (d; tr.) to ~ about, on (to ~ smb. on a matter) 3. (D; intr.) to ~ for (to ~ for weak spots) 4. (D; intr.) to ~ into (to ~ into the facts)

problem *n.* ['unsettled question'] ['source of difficulty'] 1. to cause, create, pose, present a ~ 2. to address, tackle; bring up, raise; resolve, settle, solve a ~ 3. an acute, difficult, major, pressing, serious; insoluble, insurmountable ~ 4. a complicated, involved, knotty, thorny ~ 5. a delicate, ticklish ~ 6. a minor, petty ~ 7. an emotional; physical; psychological; social ~ 8. a perennial ~ 9. a ~ to + inf. (it's a ~ to make ends meet = it's a ~ making ends meet) 10. (misc.) the crux of a ~; to get to the heart of a ~ ['mathematical statement requiring a solution'] 11. to do, solve a ~ 12. a complicated; difficult; easy; simple ~

procedure *n.* 1. to establish a ~ 2. to follow a ~ 3. (a) normal, proper, regular, standard ~ (to follow regular ~s) 4. a scientific; surgical ~ 5. (surgery) a major; minor ~ 6. parliamentary ~s

proceed *v.* 1. (d; intr.) to ~ against (to ~ against smb. in court) 2. (d; intr.) to ~ from; to (to ~ from New York to Philadelphia) 3. (d; intr.) to ~ with (to ~ with one's research) 4. (E) she ~ed to tell us every detail

proceedings *n.* (often legal) 1. to conduct; initiate, institute ~ against (to initiate legal ~ against a competitor) 2. judicial, legal ~ 3. divorce ~ (to institute divorce ~)

proceeds *n.* ['profit'] 1. net ~ 2. ~ from (~ from the sale of surplus property)

process *n.* 1. the judicial ~ 2. mental ~es

processing *n.* data; food ~

procession *n.* 1. to lead a ~ 2. a ceremonial; funeral; torchlight ~ 3. in (a) ~ (to march in a ~)

processor *n.* a food; word ~

proclaim *v.* (formal) 1. (L; to) the president ~ed (to the nation) that new currency would be issued 2. (N; used with a noun) the entire state was ~ed a disaster area

proclamation *n.* 1. to issue, make a ~ 2. a ~ that + clause (the government issued a ~ that all prisoners would be pardoned)

proclivity *n.* (formal) a ~ for; to, towards

procure *v.* (D; tr.) to ~ for

prod *v.* 1. (D; tr.) to ~ into (to ~ smb. into doing smt.) 2. (H) they kept ~ding me to buy a new car

prodigy *n.* a child; infant ~

produce I *n.* ['fruits and vegetables'] farm ~

produce II *v.* 1. (d; tr.) to ~ as (she ~d several letters as evidence) 2. (D; tr.) to ~ for (to ~ food for export)

producer *n.* an executive; film, movie; steel; television, TV ~

product *n.* 1. to promote a (new) ~ 2. a by-product; an end, finished ~ 3. a waste ~ 4. the gross national ~ (= GNP)

production *n.* ['work presented on the stage, radio, TV, etc.'] 1. to put on a ~ 2. a Hollywood; stage, theatrical; TV ~ ['process of producing'] 3. to increase, speed up, step up ~ 4. to decrease, roll back ~ 5. mass ~ 6. coal; oil; steel ~ 7. (misc.) the means of ~ ['misc.'] 8. (slang) to make a big ~ out of smt. ('to make a big fuss over smt.')

productive *adj.* ~ of

products *n.* dairy ~

profess *v.* (formal) (E) he ~ed to know nothing about the matter

profession *n.* 1. to practice a ~ 2. the legal; medical; nursing; teaching ~ 3. by ~ (she's a lawyer by ~)

professional, pro *adj.* and *n.* 1. (usu. sports) to turn ~ (he turned ~ at the age of twenty) 2. a real, true ~ (she is a real ~) ('she does her work seriously and well') USAGE NOTE: A *professional tennis player* and a *professional golfer* compete for money. A *tennis professional* and a *golf pro* coach for money, usu. at clubs.

professor *n.* 1. (AE) an adjunct; assistant; associate; full ~ 2. (GB) a Regius ~ (appointed by the Crown) 3. a research; visiting ~ 4. a ~ emeritus, an emeritus ~ 5. a college (esp. US); university ~ 6. (misc.) an absent-minded ~ USAGE NOTE: We speak of a professor *of* Latin, but of a lecturer or reader *in* Latin.

professorship *n.* 1. to hold a ~ 2. an endowed ~

proficiency *n.* 1. to demonstrate, display ~ 2. language ~ 3. ~ at, in

proficient *adj.* ~ at, in

profile *n.* ['public exposure'] 1. to keep a high; low ~ ['side view'] 2. in ~

profit I *n.* 1. to clear, earn, make, realize, reap, turn a ~ 2. to bring (in), yield a ~ 3. a handsome, large; marginal, small; quick ~ 4. an excess, exorbitant ~ 5. a clear; net; gross ~ 6. a ~ on (to make a ~ on a deal) 7. at a ~ (to operate at a ~)

profit II *v.* (D; intr.) to ~ by, from

profitable *adj.* ~ to + inf. (is it ~ to work this mine?)

profiteer *n.* a war ~

profuse *adj.* (cannot stand alone) ~ in (~ in one's apologies)

profusion *n.* in ~

prognosis *n.* to make a ~

program I *n.* ['plan'] 1. to chart, draw up a ~ 2. to carry out, implement; evaluate; introduce; launch; phase out, terminate a ~ 3. a long-range; pilot; short-range ~ 4. a building; development; political ~ 5. a ~ to + inf. (to launch a ~ to reduce crime) ['schedule'] 6. on one's ~ (what's on your ~ today?) ['entertainment'] 7. to put on a ~ ['broadcast, telecast'] 8. a call-in (AE), phone-in (BE); radio; television ~ ['coded instructions for a computer'] 9. to boot up; debug; execute; load; reboot; run; write a ~ 10. a user-friendly ~ 11. a computer; software; word processing ~

['academic course of study'] 12. a graduate, post-graduate (esp. BE); honors; training; under-graduate ~ 13. a ~ in (a ~ in linguistics) ['organized activities'] 14. an orientation; outreach (esp. AE); recreation; work-study (AE) ~ ['misc.'] 15. a reading ~ (for a dictionary) USAGE NOTE: The BE spelling is *programme*, except for the computer uses, 9-11.

program II v. (H) to ~ a computer to store certain information USAGE NOTE: Except when referring to the computer, the BE spelling is *programme*-- to programme an alarm system.

programme see Usage Notes for **program I, II**

progress I n. 1. to make ~ 2. to facilitate ~ 3. to hinder, impede, obstruct ~ 4. considerable, good, great, material; rapid; slow; smooth; spotty; steady ~ 5. economic; scientific; significant; technological ~ 6. ~ in (to make ~ in solving the problems of air pollution) 7. ~ towards (~ towards peace) 8. in ~ (negotiations are in ~)

progress II v. (D; intr.) to ~ to

progression n. an arithmetic; geometric; harmonic ~

prohibit v. 1. (D; tr.) to ~ from 2. (rare) (K) you cannot ~ their going out

prohibition n. 1. to repeal (a) ~ 2. a ~ against

project n. ['organized undertaking'] 1. to conceive; draw up a ~ 2. to carry out a ~ 3. to shelve a ~ 4. an irrigation; land-reclamation; pilot ('experimental'); public-works; water-conservation ~ ['publicly financed housing'] (AE) 5. a housing ~ (BE has *council block, housing estate*)

projectile n. to fire; launch a ~

projection n. ['estimate'] 1. to make a ~ 2. a computer ~ ['system of presenting a map'] 3. a homolosine; isometric; Mercator; sinusoidal ~

projector n. 1. to operate, work a ~ 2. a cine-projector (BE); film, motion-picture (AE); opaque; overhead; slide ~

proliferation n. nuclear ~

prologue n. a ~ to

prom n. (AE) ['formal school dance'] 1. the junior; senior ~ 2. at the ~ 3. (misc.) to go to the ~; to take smb. to the ~ USAGE NOTE: In BE, *prom* means 'a promenade concert'.

prominence n. 1. to acquire, gain ~ 2. to give ~ to (to give ~ to a story)

promiscuity n. sexual ~

promise I n. ['vow'] 1. to give, make a ~ 2. to fulfill, keep a ~ 3. to break, renege on, repudiate a ~ 4. a broken; empty, hollow; rash; sacred, solemn ~ 5. a campaign ~ (politicians sometimes break campaign ~s) 6. a ~ to + inf. (she made a ~ to write every week) 7. a ~ that + clause (they kept their ~ that the debt would be repaid promptly) 8. (misc.) to hold smb. to a ~ ['basis for hope'] 9. to show ~ (the young boxer showed real ~) 10. of ~ (a young boxer of ~)

promise II v. 1. (A) he ~d the book to me; or: he ~d me the book 2.(E) she ~d to return early; it ~s to be an exciting year 3. (H; often used in neg. constructions) he ~d me never to show up late again 4. (L; may have an object) he ~d (me) that he would never show up late again 5. (misc.) (BE) I ~

you ('I assure you')

promote v. 1. (D; tr.) to ~ from; to (she was ~d from captain to major) 2. (old-fashioned) (BE) (N; used with a noun) she was ~d major

promotion n. ['advancement in rank'] 1. to put smb. in for ~; to recommend smb. for ~ 2. to make, win one's ~ (he made his ~ to major) ('he was promoted to major') 3. a ~ from; to (a ~ to captain; a ~ to the rank of professor) ['furtherance, fostering'] 4. health ~ ['advertising'] 5. prepublication ~ 6. in ~ (she is in ~)

prompt I adj. 1. ~ at, in (~ in fulfilling one's obligations) 2. ~ to + inf. (~ to respond)

prompt II v. (H) what ~ed you to say that?

promptness n. ~ at, in

prone adj. ['likely'] (cannot stand alone) 1. ~ to (~ to exaggeration) 2. ~ to + inf. (he is ~ to exaggerate)

pronoun n. a demonstrative; indefinite; interrogative; personal; possessive; reflexive; relative ~

pronounce v. 1. (D; intr., tr.) to ~ after (~ after me) 2. (formal) (M) the physician ~d him to be healthy 3. (N; used with an adjective, noun) she was officially ~d dead; they were ~d husband and wife

pronouncement n. 1. to issue, make a ~ 2. a ~ that + clause (the government issued a ~ that taxes would be lowered)

pronunciamento n. (derog.) 1. to issue, make a ~ 2. a ~ that + clause (they issued a ~ that only their theories would be acceptable)

pronunciation n. 1. to acquire a (good) ~ 2. a native ~ (of a language) 3. (a) spelling ~ 4. BBC, Received ~

proof n. ['conclusive evidence'] 1. to furnish, give, offer, present, produce, provide ~ 2. ample, clear, conclusive, convincing, definite, incontestable, indisputable, irrefutable, positive, undeniable, unquestionable ~ 3. documentary; mathematical ~ 4. ~ that + clause (the prosecutor furnished convincing ~ that the accused could have been at the scene of the crime) 5. (misc.) the burden of ~ ['composed type'] 6. to correct, read ~ 7. galley; page; reproduction ~s

prop v. 1. (d; tr.) to ~ against (~ a chair against the door) 2. (N; used with an adjective) ~ the window open

propaganda n. 1. to engage in, spread ~ 2. to counteract, neutralize ~ 3. enemy; ideological; vicious ~ 4. ~ against

propensity n. (formal) 1. a ~ for (a ~ for exaggerating) 2. a ~ to + inf. (he has a ~ to exaggerate)

proper adj. 1. ~ to + inf. (it is not ~ to enter that restaurant without a jacket) 2. ~ that + clause; subj. (it is ~ that she state/should state her own opinion)

property n. 1. to confiscate, seize ~ 2. to buy; inherit; lease; rent; sell; transfer ~ 3. to reclaim; recover (stolen) ~ 4. (an) abandoned; commercial ~ 5. common; communal; government; individual; joint; movable; personal; private; public; real ~ 6. community ~ ('property held jointly by two spouses') 7. a piece of ~

prophecy *n.* 1. to make a ~ 2. a gloomy; self-fulfilling ~ 3. a ~ comes true; turns out to be true 4. a ~ about

prophesy *v.* 1. (K) no one could ~ your becoming governor 2. (L) I ~sied that she would succeed

prophet *n.* 1. a false ~ 2. (rel.) a major; minor ~

propinquity *n.* (formal) ~ to

propitious *adj.* ~ for, to

proportion *n.* 1. (a) direct; inverse ~ 2. in ~ to 3. out of ~ to (the punishment was out of ~ to the crime)

proportional *adj.* ~ to

proportionate *adj.* ~ to

proportions *n.* ['extent'] 1. to assume, take on ~ 2. epic; epidemic; menacing ~ (the outbreak assumed epidemic ~)

proposal *n.* 1. to make, present, put forth, put forward a ~ 2. to accept, adopt a ~ 3. to consider, entertain; receive a ~ 4. to kill (colloq.), reject, turn down a ~ 5. a concrete ~ 6. a ~ falls through 7. a ~ for 8. a ~ to + inf. (the committee rejected the ~ to reduce taxes) 9. a ~ that + clause; subj. (they presented a ~ that all workers be/should be given free dental care)

propose *v.* 1. (B) she ~d a new plan to us 2. (D; intr.) to ~ to ('to offer marriage to') 3. (E) I ~ to leave very early 4. (G) she ~d leaving very early 5. (K) she ~d his going in my place 6. (L; subj.; to) we ~d (to them) that she be/should be appointed

proposition *n.* ['unethical, immoral proposal'] (colloq.) 1. to make (smb.) a ~ ['subject, question to be discussed'] 2. the ~ that + clause (we debated the ~ that war should be outlawed)

proprieties *n.* ['accepted behavior'] to observe the ~

propriety *n.* ['conformity with accepted standards of behavior'] to doubt the ~ of smt.

propulsion *n.* jet; nuclear; rocket ~

prop up *v.* (D; tr.) to ~ against (she ~ped up the chair against the door)

pros and cons *n.* to weigh the ~

prose *n.* to write (in) ~

prosecute *v.* 1. to ~ vigorously 2. (D; tr.) to ~ for (to ~ smb. for murder)

prosecution *n.* 1. to conduct a ~ 2. to face ~ 3. a vigorous ~ 4. criminal ~ 5. ~ for 6. (misc.) subject to (criminal) ~

prosecutor *n.* a public ~ (esp BE; AE has *district attorney*)

proseminar *n.* 1. to give, hold a ~ 2. a ~ on

prospect I *n.* ['anticipated outcome'] a bleak, grim; inviting; rosy ~

prospect II *v.* (D; intr.) to ~ for (to ~ for gold)

prospects *n.* ['chances'] 1. to have ~ for (to have ~ for the future?) 2. ~ that + clause (~ are that the situation will improve) ['financial expectations'] 3. with; without ~

prosperity *n.* 1. to create ~ 2. to enjoy ~

prostitution *n.* 1. to engage in ~ 2. to decriminalize, legalize ~ 3. to ban, outlaw ~

prostrate *v.* (D; refl.) to ~ oneself before

prostration *n.* heat; nervous ~

protect *v.* (D; tr.) to ~ against, from

protection *n.* 1. to afford, give, provide ~ 2. government; police ~ 3. ~ against, from 4. under smb.'s ~ (she was placed under our ~)

protective *adj.* ~ of, towards

protector *n.* a chest; surge ~

protein *n.* 1. to furnish, provide ~ (of food) 2. (a) complete; incomplete; simple; total ~

protest I *n.* ['complaint'] ['dissent'] 1. to enter, file, lodge, register a ~ 2. to express, voice a ~ 3. to cause, draw, spark (AE), spark off (BE), trigger a ~ 4. to dismiss, reject a ~ 5. a strong, vigorous; weak ~ (we lodged a strong ~ with their government) 6. a ~ against 7. a ~ that + clause (the court rejected their ~ that due process had not been observed) 8. in ~ (to resign in ~) 9. under ~ (they complied with the order under ~) ['public demonstration of disapproval'] 10. to organize, stage a ~ 11. to put down, quell a ~ 12. a noisy; public ~ 13. a ~ against

protest II *v.* 1. to ~ strongly, vigorously 2. (D; intr.) to ~ about, against (to ~ against a war; AE also has: to ~ a war) 3. (K) we ~ed his being released 4. (L; to) we ~ed (to the mayor) that taxes were too high

protocol *n.* ['minutes'] ['statement'] 1. to draw up a ~ ['official code of conduct'] 2. diplomatic; military ~

protrude *v.* (D; intr.) to ~ from

proud *adj.* 1. justly ~ 2. ~ of (~ of one's children) 3. ~ to + inf. (she will be ~ to serve) 4. ~ that + clause (he is ~ that he served in the army)

prove *v.* 1. to ~ conclusively 2. (B) she was able to ~ her innocence to us 3. (E) she ~d to be a good worker 4. (L; to) he ~d (to everyone) that he could cope with the job 5. (M) history ~d her to be right 6. (N; used with an adjective, past participle) the evidence ~d him guilty

proverb *n.* a ~ goes, runs

provide *v.* 1. (d; intr.) to ~ for (to ~ for one's family; to ~ for every contingency) 2. (D; tr.) to ~ for (to ~ blankets for the refugees) 3. (d; tr.) to ~ with (they were ~d with the proper equipment; we ~d the refugees with blankets) 4. (L; subj.) this bill ~s that money be/should be allocated for flood control

providence *n.* divine ~

province *n.* (esp. in Canada) 1. an inland; maritime ~ 2. the Province of Alberta, Quebec, etc.

provision *n.* ['preparations'] 1. to make ~ for ['clause in a legal document'] 2. to violate a ~ (of a contract)

proviso *n.* 1. to add a ~ 2. with a ~ that + clause; subj. (we will agree to the proposal with the ~ that overtime be/should be paid)

provocation *n.* 1. extreme, gross ~ 2. ~ for (there was no ~ for such behavior) 3. at a ~ (he loses his temper at the slightest ~) 4. under ~ (he did use strong language, but only under extreme ~)

provocative *adj.* highly ~

provoke *v.* 1. (D; tr.) to ~ into (to ~ smb. into doing smt.) 2. (rare) (H) to ~ smb. to do smt.

prowess *n.* 1. to demonstrate, display ~ 2. athletic; military ~ 3. ~ in

prowl *n.* on the ~

proximate *adj.* (cannot stand alone) ~ to
proximity *n.* 1. close ~ 2. ~ to 3. in ~ to (in close ~ to the scene of the crime)
proxy *n.* 1. to hold smb.'s ~ 2. a ~ to + inf. (he had a ~ to vote for me) 3. by ~ (to vote by ~)
prudent *adj.* ~ to + inf. (it was ~ of you to sell that property)
prudish *adj.* ~ about
pry *v.* 1. (D; intr.) to ~ into (to ~ into smb.'s affairs) 2. (D; tr.) to ~ out of (to ~ information out of smb.) 3. (N; used with an adjective) they pried the door open USAGE NOTE: For senses two and three, BE uses *prise* or *prize*.
p's and q's *n.* ['manners'] to mind one's ~
pseudonym *n.* 1. to adopt; use a ~ 2. under a ~ (to write under a ~)
psychology *n.* ['science of the mind'] 1. abnormal; applied; behavioral; child; clinical; developmental; educational; experimental; general; Gestalt; social ~ ['attitudes'] 2. group; mob ~ ['knowledge of a person's habits, reactions'] (colloq.) 3. to use ~
psychosis *n.* a manic-depressive ~
puberty *n.* 1. to reach (the state of) ~ 2. at ~
public *n.* 1. to educate, enlighten the ~ 2. to fool, mislead the ~ 3. the general; great British (BE; humorous); reading; theatergoing; traveling ~ 4. in ~
publication *n.* ['act of publishing'] 1. to begin, start ~ 2. to suspend ~ ['printed work'] 3. a government; official ~
publicity *n.* 1. to give, provide ~ 2. to gain, receive; seek ~ 3. to avoid, shun ~ 4. extensive, wide ~ 5. ~ for 6. (misc.) a blaze of ~ (they left for Europe in a blaze of ~)
public opinion *n.* 1. to arouse, stir up ~ 2. to form, mold ~ 3. to affect, influence; manipulate ~ 4. to express ~ 5. to canvass, poll, probe, sound out ~
public welfare see **welfare**
puff I *n.* a powder ~
puff II *v.* (d; intr.) to ~ on (to ~ on a pipe)
pull I *n.* ['force'] 1. gravitational ~ ['influence'] (colloq.) 2. to use one's ~ 3. the ~ to + inf. (she had enough ~ to avoid paying the fine)
pull II *v.* 1. to ~ hard 2. (AE; colloq.) (d; intr.) to ~ for ('to support') (we were ~ing for the home team; they were ~ing for our team to win) 3. (d; intr.) ('to move') to ~ into (the train ~ed into the station) 4. (d; intr.) to ~ off ('to turn off') (to ~ off the road) 5. (D; intr.) ('to tug') to ~ on (to ~ on a rope) 6. (d; intr.) ('to move') to ~ out of (the train ~ed out of the station; to ~ out of a dive) 7. (d; tr.) ('to lift') to ~ out of (they ~ed her out of the water) 8. (misc.) to ~ a gun on smb.
pull ahead *v.* (D; intr.) to ~ of (to ~ of the other runners)
pull alongside *v.* (AE) (D; intr.) to ~ of (to ~ of the other car)
pull away *v.* (D; intr., tr.) to ~ from (to ~ from the curb; she ~ed the child away from the fire)
pull back *v.* (D; intr.) to ~ from (to ~ from the others)
pull down *v.* (D; tr.) to ~ over (she ~ed her hat down over her eyes)

pulley *n.* a fixed; movable ~
pull over *v.* (D; intr.) to ~ to (to ~ to the curb)
pull up *v.* (D; intr.) to ~ to (to ~ to the curb)
pulp *n.* to beat smb. to a ~
pulpit *n.* 1. to ascend, mount the ~ 2. from. on the ~ (to denounce wrongdoing from the ~)
pulse *n.* 1. to take ('measure') smb.'s ~ 2. to quicken smb.'s ~ (the excitement quickened his ~) 3. an erratic, irregular, unsteady; normal; rapid; regular, steady; strong; weak ~
pump I *n.* 1. to prime; work a ~ 2. a gasoline (AE), petrol (BE) ~ 3. a centrifugal; heat; stomach; suction; sump ~
pump II *v.* 1. (d; tr.) to ~ into (to ~ investments into a company; to ~ water into a tank) 2. (D; tr.) to ~ out of (to ~ water out of a flooded basement) 3. (N; used with an adjective) we ~ed the basement dry
punch I *n.* ['blow'] 1. to deliver, give, land, throw a ~ 2. to pull ('soften') one's ~es (also fig.) 3. to roll with a ~ 4. a one-two; rabbit; solid; Sunday ~ 5. a ~ in, on, to (a ~ in the face; a ~ on the nose) ['misc.'] 6. to pack a ~ ('to be powerful'); to beat smb. to the ~
punch II *v.* (D; tr.) to ~ in, on (I ~ed him in/on the jaw)
punch III *n.* ['mixed drink usu. consisting of fruit juice, liquor, etc.'] 1. to make ~ 2. to spike ('add alcohol to') the ~ 3. to water down the ~
Punch *n.* as pleased as ~ ('very pleased')
punctilious *adj.* ~ about
punctual *adj.* ~ in (~ in paying one's rent)
punctuality *n.* ~ in
punctuation mark *n.* to place, put a ~ somewhere
puncture *n.* to patch, repair a ~
pundit *n.* a political ~
punish *v.* 1. to ~ cruelly; harshly, severely; lightly, mildly; summarily 2. (D; tr.) to ~ for (they were ~ed harshly for their crime)
punishable *adj.* ~ by (~ by death)
punishment *n.* 1. to administer, mete out ~ to 2. to impose, inflict ~ on 3. to escape; suffer, take ~ 4. cruel, cruel and unusual; harsh, severe; just; light, mild ~ 5. capital; corporal; summary ~ 6. (mil.) company ~ 7. ~ for 8. as, in ~ for
pupil I *n.* ['opening in the iris of the eye'] constricted; dilated ~s
pupil II see the Usage Note for **student**
puppet *n.* 1. to manipulate, move a ~ 2. a hand ~
purchase I *n.* ['act of buying'] to make a ~
purchase II *v.* 1. (D; tr.) to ~ for 2. (D; tr.) to ~ from
purge I *n.* 1. to carry out, conduct a ~ 2. a radical, sweeping ~
purge II *v.* 1. (D; tr.) ('to remove') to ~ from (all dissidents were ~d from the party) 2. (D; tr.) ('to cleanse') to ~ of (the party was ~d of all disloyal elements)
purify *v.* (D; tr.) to ~ of
purity *n.* moral ~
purple I *adj.* ['livid'] ~ with (~ with rage)
purple II *n.* dark; light ~
purport *v.* (formal) (E) ('to claim') they ~ to be our friends

purported *adj.* (cannot stand alone) ~ to + inf. (they are ~ to be wealthy)

purpose *n.* 1. to accomplish, achieve, fulfill a ~ 2. to serve a ~ 3. to put smt. to a good ~ 4. for a ~ (it was done for a good ~; we arranged the meeting for the ~ of preventing a strike) 5. (misc.) for all practical ~s ('in reality'); on ~ ('purposely')

purse strings *n.* ['finances'] to control, hold the ~

pursuance *n.* (formal) in ~ of (in ~ of one's duties)

pursuant *adj.* (formal) (cannot stand alone) ~ to

pursuit *n.* ['chase'] 1. dogged, relentless; hot ~ 2. in ~ of (in hot ~ of the terrorists) ['hobby'] 3. one's favorite ~

pus *n.* 1. to discharge ~ 2. ~ forms

push I *n.* ['act of pushing'] 1. to give smb. a ~ (our car was stuck and they gave us a ~) ['attack'] 2. a big ~ 3. a ~ to (a ~ to the sea)

push II *v.* 1. (d; intr.) ('to shove') to ~ against (to ~ against the door) 2. (d; intr.) to ~ for ('to urge') (to ~ for reform) 3. (d; intr.) to ~ into ('to force one's way') (to ~ into a crowded bus) 4. (D; tr.) ('to force to move') to ~ into (we ~ed the stalled car into the garage) 5. (d; intr.) ('to press') to ~ on (to ~ on a handle) 6. (d; intr., tr.) to ~ through ('to force one's way through') (to ~ through a crowd; to ~ one's way through a crowd) 7. (d; intr.) ('to move') to ~ to, towards (our troops ~ed towards the next village) 8. (H) ('to urge') to ~ smb. to do smt. 9. (N; used with an adjective) ~ the chair closer 10. (misc.) the army was ~ed to the breaking point

push down *v.* (D; intr.) to ~ on (to ~ on a lid)

push on *v.* (D; intr.) ('to continue') to ~ to (we ~ed on to the next town)

pushover *n.* ['easy target'] a ~ for

push-up *n.* (esp. AE) to do a ~ (see also **press-up**)

push up *v.* (D; intr.) to ~ on (to ~ on a handle)

put I *adv.* (colloq.) ['remaining in one place'] to stay ~

put II *v.* 1. (B) ('to pose') to ~ a question to smb. 2. (d; tr.) ('to place') to ~ before (to ~ a proposal before a committee) 3. (d; tr.) ('to place') to ~ in; into (to ~ milk in/into the refrigerator; to ~ new equipment into service; to ~ a criminal in prison; to ~ money in/into circulation; to ~ a plan into operation; to ~ one's affairs in order; to ~ a theory into practice; to ~ wood into a stove; to ~ sugar in/into tea; to ~ a car into a garage; to ~ words into smb.'s mouth; to ~ one's faith in smb.; ~ yourself in my place) 4. (d; intr.) ('to move') to ~ into (the ship put into port) 5. (d; tr.) ('to express') to ~ into (to ~ one's feelings into words) 6. (d; tr.) ('to place') to ~ on (to ~ books on a table; to ~ a stamp on a letter; to ~ smb.'s name on a list; the doctor put the patient on a diet) 7. (d; tr.) ('to bet') to ~ on (to ~ money on a horse) 8. (d; tr.) ('to place') to ~ out of (to ~ an enemy tank

out of action) 9. (d; tr.) ('to assign') to ~ to (we put them all to work) 10. (d; tr.) ('to place') to ~ to (she put her fingers to her lips) 11. (d; tr.) ('to set') to ~ to (to ~ words to music) 12. (L; to) ('to suggest') I put it to them that the plan should be revised 13. (P; tr.) ('to place') ~ your shoes near the door; ~ the skis next to the fire; ~ the children to bed; ~ your things under the bed 14. (misc.) to ~ a question to a vote; to ~ smb. to shame; to ~ smb. under arrest; to ~ smb. to great expense; to ~ smb. through one's paces ('to subject smb. to a test of skill'); to ~ oneself in smb.'s place; the ship put out to sea

put down *v.* 1. (d; tr.) ('to consider') to ~ as (we can ~ this trip down as a business expense) 2. (d; tr.) to ~ for ('to enter a pledge for') (I'll ~ you down for five tickets) 3. (BE) (d; tr.) ('to enter') to ~ for (to ~ one's son for Eton) 4. (d; tr.) ('to attribute') to ~ to (to ~ a blunder down to inexperience)

put in *v.* (D; tr.) to ~ for ('to submit') (to ~ a claim for damages)

put off *v.* ('to postpone') 1. (D; tr.) to ~ until (she put the trip off until next week) 2. (G) we put off leaving because of the snow

put out *v.* 1. (D; refl.) ('to disturb') to ~ oneself out for (don't ~ yourself out for us) 2. (misc.) to ~ to sea

put over *v.* (D; tr.) ('to fob off') to put smt. over on (he put his scheme over on the unsuspecting investors)

putter *v.* (AE) (d; intr.) to ~ around (to ~ around the house) (BE has *potter*)

put through *v.* (D; tr.) ('to connect') to ~ to (she was finally put through to her number)

put up *v.* 1. (B) ('to propose') I'll put the idea up to the whole committee 2. (old-fashioned) (BE) (d; intr.) ('to stay') to ~ at; with (to ~ at a hotel; to ~ with friends in Exeter) 3. (d; tr.) ('to offer') to ~ for (to ~ smt. up for sale) 4. (d; tr.) ('to provide') to ~ for (she put up the money for the flowers) 5. (D; tr.) ('to give shelter to') to ~ for (to ~ smb. up for a night) 6. (d; intr.) to ~ with ('to tolerate') (we will not ~ with such behavior) 7. (H) ('to place') to ~ water up to boil; he put the meal up to cook

puzzle I *n.* 1. to solve a ~ 2. a crossword ~; jigsaw ~ (AE; BE has *jigsaw*) 3. a ~ to (the whole matter was a ~ to the police)

puzzle II *v.* 1. (d; intr.) to ~ over (to ~ over a problem) 2. (R) it ~d me that they never answered the telephone

puzzled *adj.* ~ to + inf. (we were ~ to learn of her decision)

puzzling *adj.* 1. ~ to (her behavior was ~ to everybody) 2. ~ that + inf. (it was ~ that he went straight home)

pyjamas (BE) see **pajamas**

pyre *n.* a funeral ~

Q

quagmire *n.* in a ~ of
quail I *n.* a bevy, covey of ~
quail II *v.* (d; intr.) ('to lose courage') to ~ at, before (we ~ed at the thought of getting lost in the forest)
quake *v.* (D; intr.) to ~ with (to ~ with fear)
qualifications *n.* ['qualities, attributes'] 1. excellent, fine, outstanding, strong ~ 2. the necessary ~ 3. educational; physical; professional ~ 4. the ~ for (she has the ~ for the job) 5. the ~ to + inf. (this engineer has outstanding ~ to build the bridge)
qualified *adj.* 1. eminently, fully, highly ~; well-qualified 2. ~ as (~ as an engineer) 3. ~ by (~ by education and experience for the position) 4. ~ for (she is highly ~ for the job) 5. ~ to + inf. (he is ~ to pass judgment on this matter)
qualify *v.* 1. (D; intr.) to ~ as (she ~fied as a teacher of the handicapped) 2. (D; intr.) to ~ for (she ~fied for the position) 3. (E) he ~fied to teach mathematics 4. (H) what ~fies her to represent us?
quality *n.* ['feature'] 1. admirable; endearing; moral; personal; redeeming ~ties (he has no redeeming ~ties) 2. (misc.) there was a rhapsodic ~ about her playing ['degree of excellence'] 3. excellent, superior; fine, good, high; low, poor ~ 4. of a certain ~ (of good ~)
qualms *n.* 1. to feel, have ~ 2. ~ about (I have no ~ about borrowing money) 3. without (any) ~
quandary *n.* 1. a hopeless ~ 2. in a ~ (we were in a hopeless ~)
quantity *n.* ['amount'] 1. a considerable, large; negligible, small; sufficient ~ 2. in (large) ~ties ['factor'] 3. an unknown ~
quarantine *n.* 1. to impose, institute a ~ 2. to lift a ~ 3. strict ~ 4. in, under ~ (to place under ~)
quarrel I *n.* 1. to cause, lead to a ~ (their political differences led to a bitter ~) 2. to have, pick, provoke, start a ~ (he picked a ~ with his neighbor) 3. to patch up, settle a ~ 4. a bitter, furious, violent; long-standing; never-ending ~ 5. a domestic, family ~ 6. a ~ breaks out, ensues 7. a ~ about, over; between; with (a bitter ~ broke out between them over the use of the telephone; he had a violent ~ with me about the money that he had borrowed)
quarrel II *v.* 1. to ~ bitterly, furiously, violently 2. (D; intr.) to ~ about, over; with (she ~ed with her neighbor about the noise)
quarry I *n.* ['prey'] 1. to stalk one's ~ 2. to bring one's ~ to bay 3. hunted ~
quarry II *n.* ['open excavation'] 1. to work a ~ 2. an abandoned ~ 3. a marble; stone ~
quarter I *n.* ['mercy'] 1. to give, show ~ (the mercenaries gave no ~) 2. to ask for; receive ~ ['one fourth'] 3. (in telling time) (a) ~ of (AE), to (the hour) (it was a ~ to five) 4. (a) ~ after (AE), past (the hour) (it is a ~ past five)

quarter II *v.* (esp. mil.) (D; tr.) ('to assign to a lodging place') to ~ on, upon (to ~ troops on the local population)
quarters *n.* ['housing'] 1. to find ~ 2. bachelor; officers' ~ 3. ('misc.') confined to ~ ['assigned stations on a ship'] 4. battle, general ~ ['sources'] 5. from certain ~ (from the highest ~) ['misc.'] 6. at close ~ ('close together')
quartet *n.* 1. to play a ~ 2. a piano; string, wood-wind ~
quay *n.* at, on a ~
queasy *adj.* ['uneasy'] ~ about (to feel ~ about smt.)
queen *n.* 1. to crown a ~ 2. to crown; proclaim smb. ~ 3. to depose, dethrone a ~ 4. a despotic; popular; strong; weak ~ 5. a ~ mounts the throne 6. a ~ abdicates (a throne) 7. a ~ consort; mother 8. (misc.) to toast the ~; a beauty ~; a drag ~ (colloq. and derog.) ('a male transvestite')
queen's evidence *n.* (BE) to turn ~ (see also **king's evidence, state's evidence**)
queer I *adj.* 1. ~ about (there is smt. ~ about them) 2. ~ to + inf. (it's ~ to be speaking of the heat in January) 3. ~ that + clause (it's ~ that he hasn't arrived yet)
queer II *v.* (colloq.) (d; refl.) ('to put oneself in a bad light') to ~ with (he ~ed himself with all his professors)
query *n.* 1. to put a ~ to 2. to respond to a ~ 3. a ~ about
quest *n.* 1. a ~ for 2. in ~ of
question I *n.* ['query'] 1. to ask (smb.) a ~ to ask a ~ of smb. 2. to address, pose, put a ~ to smb. 3. to bring up, raise a ~ 4. to answer, field, reply to, respond to a ~ (the senator fielded all ~s expertly) 5. to beg ('evade') the ~ 6. to parry smb.'s ~s 7. an academic, hypothetical, rhetorical; awkward, embarrassing, sticky, ticklish; blunt, direct; civil ('polite'); debatable, moot; irrelevant; leading; loaded, tricky; pointed, probing; relevant; thorny ~ 8. an essay ~ (on an examination) 9. an examination, test ~ 10. a ~ about, as to, concerning ['matter being discussed'] 11. to put the ~ ('to vote on the matter being discussed') 12. a burning; controversial; crucial; explosive; open; vexed (esp. BE) ~ 13. (misc.) (colloq.) to pop the ~ ('to propose marriage') ['vote'] (parliamentary procedure) 14. to put a matter to the ~ ['doubt'] ['dispute'] 15. to clear up, resolve a ~ 16. beyond all ~ 17. in, into ~ (to come into ~; to call smt. into ~) ['misc.'] 18. out of the ~ ('impossible')
question II *v.* (D; tr.) to ~ about (the police ~ed her about her activities)
questionable *adj.* highly ~
questioning *n.* 1. close ('intensive') ~ 2. under ~ (under close ~ by the district attorney)
questionnaire *n.* 1. to draw up, formulate a ~ 2. to circulate, distribute, send out a ~ 3. to answer, fill

in, fill out (esp. AE), fill up (BE; old-fashioned) a
~

queue I *n.* (esp. BE) 1. to form a ~ 2. to join; jump the ~ 3. in a ~ (to stand in a ~)

queue II *v.* see **queue up**

queue up *v.* (esp. BE) (D; intr.) to ~ for (they had to ~ for fresh fruit)

quibble I *n.* a minor ~

quibble II *v.* (D; intr.) to ~ about, over; with (to ~ about trifles)

quick I *adj.* 1. ~ about (be ~ about it) 2. ~ at (~ at picking up a new language) 3. ~ with (~ with one's hands) 4. (cannot stand alone) ~ to + inf. (she is ~ to learn; he is ~ to take offense) 5. (misc.) ~ on (~ on one's feet)

quick II *n.* 1. to cut smb. to the ~ ('to offend smb. gravely') 2. (misc.) the ~ and the dead

quicksand *n.* a bed of ~

quiet *n.* to shatter the ~

quilt *n.* a crazy; down; patchwork ~

quip I *n.* to make a ~ about

quip II *v.* 1. (D; intr.) to ~ about; at 2. (L) she ~ped that being without a telephone for a few days would be nice

quirk *n.* a strange ~

quit *v.* 1. (D; intr., tr.) to ~ because of, over (he quit his job in disgrace over the bribe) 2. (colloq.) (D; intr.) ('to stop') to ~ on (the engine quit on us) 3. (G) she quit smoking

quits *n.* (colloq.) to call it ~ ('to cease doing smt.')

quiver *v.* (D; intr.) to ~ with (to ~ with fear)

quiz I *n.* ['short test'] 1. to give; make up a ~ 2. to take a ~ 3. an oral; unannounced; written ~

quiz II *v.* (D; tr.) to ~ about (the police ~zed the neighbors about the incident)

quoits *n.* to pitch, play ~

quorum *n.* 1. to constitute, make (up) a ~ 2. to have; lack a ~

quota *n.* 1. to assign, establish, fix, set a ~ 2. to fill, fulfill, meet a ~ 3. to exceed one's ~ 4. an import; production; racial ~

quotation *n.* 1. to give a ~ from 2. a direct ~

quote I see **quotation**

quote II *v.* 1. to ~ directly 2. (A) she ~d several verses to us; or: she ~d us several verses 3. (d; intr.) to ~ from (she loves to ~ from Shakespeare) 4. (D; tr.) to ~ from (to ~ a passage from the Bible)

quotient *n.* an intelligence ~ (= IQ)

R

r *n.* 1. to roll, trill an ~ 2. a retroflex; rolled, trilled; uvular ~
rabbi *n.* a chief; Conservative; Orthodox; Reform ~.
rabbit *n.* ~s breed quickly; burrow
rabid *adj.* ['fanatical'] ~ about, on (~ on a certain subject)
rabies *n.* to come down with, get ~
race I *n.* ['group distinguished by certain physical traits'] 1. the Caucasoid; Mongoloid; Negroid ~ 2. the human ~ 3. the (so-called) master ~
race II *n.* ['contest of speed'] ['competition'] 1. to organize, stage a ~ 2. to drive; row; run a ~ 3. to lose; win a ~ 4. to fix (the results of) a ~ 5. to scratch ('cancel') a ~ (at a racetrack) 5. a close, even, hotly contested, tight; grueling; uneven ~ 7. an automobile (AE), motor (esp. BE); boat; cross-country; dog; drag ('acceleration') ~; foot-race; horse; relay ~ 8. (pol.) a congressional; governor's, gubernatorial; political; presidential ~ 9. the arms ~ 10. a ~ against, with; between; pfor the ~ for the presidency was run between well qualified candidates; a ~ against time) 11. a ~ to + inf. (the ~ to conquer space) ['misc.'] 12. a rat ~ ('very hectic activity')
race III *v.* 1. (D; intr.) to ~ against, with (to ~ against time) 2. (D; intr.) to ~ for (to ~ for a prize) 3. (D; intr., tr.) to ~ to (let's ~ to school; I'll ~ you to the car)
racialism (BE) see **racism**
racing *n.* auto (AE), motor (esp. BE); harness; horse ~
racism *n.* 1. to stamp out ~ 2. blatant, rampant, vicious, virulent ~
rack I *n.* ['framework, stand'] 1. a bomb; clothes; hat; luggage (AE), roof (BE); rifle; towel ~ ['instrument of torture'] 2. on the ~
rack II *n.* (obsol.) ['destruction'] to go to ~ and ruin
racket I *n.* ['noise'] 1. to make a ~ 2. a terrible ~ ['dishonest practice'] 3. to operate, run a ~ 4. a numbers; protection ~
racket II **racquet** *n.* ['bat used to play tennis'] 1. to swing a ~ 2. to string a ~ 3. a badminton; tennis ~
racketeer *n.* a big-time; petty ~
radar *n.* early-warning ~
radiant *adj.* ~ with (~ with joy)
radiate *v.* (D; intr.) to ~ from
radiation *n.* 1. to emit ~ 2. nuclear ~
radio *n.* ['radio receiving set'] 1. to put on, switch on, turn on a ~ 2. to switch off, turn off a ~ 3. to turn down; turn up a ~ 4. to listen to the ~ 5. an AM; clock; FM; shortwave; transistor ~ 6. on, over the ~ (I heard the bad news over the ~) ['radio broadcasting industry'] 7. (to be) in ~
radioactivity *n.* 1. to emit, generate, produce ~ 2. (a) dangerous (level of) ~
radishes *n.* a bunch of ~

radius *n.* 1. a cruising ~ 2. in, within a ~ of (within a ~ of fifty miles)
raffle *n.* 1. to hold a ~ 2. a ~ for
raft *n.* 1. to launch a ~ 2. a life ~
rafting *n.* white-water ~
rag I *n.* to chew the ~ (slang) ('to chat')
rag II *v.* (slang) (D; tr.) to ~ about (they ~ged him about his beard)
rage I *n.* ['anger'] 1. to provoke, stir up smb.'s ~ 2. to express; feel ~ 3. to fly into a ~ 4. (a) blind, towering, ungovernable, violent; jealous; sudden ~ 5. a fit, outburst of ~ 6. a ~ against 7. in a ~ 8. (misc.) to quiver with ~ ['fashion'] (colloq.) 9. the latest ~ 10. a ~ for 11. (misc.) it's all the ~
rage II *v.* 1. (D; intr.) to ~ against, at 2. (misc.) to ~ out of control (the fire ~d out of control)
ragged *adj.* to run smb. ~
rags *n.* 1. a bundle of ~ 2. (dressed) in ~ 3. (misc.) from ~ to riches ('from poverty to prosperity')
raid *n.* 1. to carry out, conduct a ~ 2. an air; border; guerrilla; police; retaliatory; suicide ~ 3. a ~ into (a ~ into enemy territory) 4. a ~ on, upon (a ~ on an illegal gambling casino)
rail I *n.* ['barrier, handrail'] 1. at the ~ (to stand at the ~) 2. (to jump) over the ~ 3. (misc.) to hold on to a ~
rail II *v.* (d; intr.) ('to complain') to ~ against at
railroad I *n.* (esp. AE) 1. to manage, run, operate a ~ 2. a double-track; elevated; single-track ~ 3. a ~ from; to
railroad II *v.* (colloq.) (d; tr.) ('to force') to ~ through (to ~ a bill through a legislature)
rails *n.* 1. to go off, jump the ~ 2. to ride the ~ (see **rod 5**)
railway *n.* 1. (esp. BE) see **railroad I** 2. a scenic ~ (BE) 3. a cog; rack ~ 4. a narrow-gauge; normal-gauge ~
rain I *n.* 1. to make, produce ~ 2. (a) driving, heavy, pouring, soaking, torrential; freezing; intermittent; light; steady ~ 3. acid ~ 4. ~ falls; freezes; lets up; pours; starts; stops 5. ~ beats, patters (against the windows) 6. (misc.) the ~ came down in buckets; to get caught in the ~
rain II *v.* to ~ hard
rainbow *n.* a ~ appears, comes out
rain check *n.* (AE) ['offer to accept an invitation at a later date'] to take a ~ on
raindrops *n.* ~ fall
rainfall *n.* 1. to measure ~ 2. annual, yearly; average; heavy; light; measurable; normal ~
rain in *v.* (D; intr.) to ~ on (it was ~ing in on us)
rainwater *n.* to catch ~ (in a barrel)
raise I *n.* (AE) 1. to give smb. a ~ (in salary) 2. to deserve; get a ~ 3. an across-the-board; annual ~ (BE has *rise*)
raise II *v.* 1. (D; tr.) ('to lift') to ~ from; to (to ~ a sunken ship from the bottom of the sea to the surface) 2. (d; tr.) ('to elevate') to ~ to (to ~ smb. to the peerage) 3. (esp. AE) (H) ('to bring up')

they ~d their children to respect the rights of other people

raising *n.* consciousness ~

raisins *n.* seeded; seedless ~

rake *v.* (D; tr.) to ~ into (to ~ hay into piles)

rally I *n.* ['mass meeting'] 1. to hold, organize a ~ 2. a peace; pep; political ~ ['competition, race between cars'] (also spelled **rallye)** 3. to hold, organize a ~

rally II *v.* 1. (d; intr., tr.) to ~ around, round (to ~ around a leader) 2. (d; intr., tr.) to ~ for (the commander ~ied his troops for a counterattack) 3. (d; intr., tr.) to ~ to (they ~ied to the support of their country)

ram I *n.* a battering ~

ram II *v.* 1. (d; tr.) to ~ into (to ~ piles into a river bed) 2. (misc.) to ~ smt. down smb.'s throat ('to force smb. to accept smt.')

ramble on *v.* (D; intr.) ('to talk in a disorganized manner') to ~ about (she ~d on about her childhood)

ramp *n.* 1. a steep ~ 2. (misc.) to go down a ~; to go up a ~

rampage *n.* to go on a ~

ramparts *n.* to storm the ~

ranch *n.* 1. a cattle; dude ~ 2. at, on a ~ (he works at the ~; to live on a ~)

rancher *n.* a cattle ~

rancor, rancour *n.* 1. to stir up ~ 2. to express; feel; show ~ 3. deep-seated ~ 4. ~ against, towards (to feel ~ towards smb.)

random *n.* at ~ (to choose at ~)

random sample *n.* to select, take a ~

range I *n.* ['series of connecting mountains'] 1. a mountain ~ ['distance that a gun fires, can fire'] 2. close; long; point-blank ~ 3. artillery; rifle ~ 4. at a certain ~ (at close ~) 5. in, within ~ 6. out of ~ ['place where shooting is practiced'] 7. an artillery; firing; rifle; rocket ~ 8. at, on a ~ ['extent, scope'] 9. a narrow; wide ~ 10. within a ~ (within a narrow ~) ['cooking stove'] 11. an electric; gas ~ ['open region on which livestock graze'] 12. to ride the ~ 13. on the ~ ['misc.'] 14. a driving ~ (where one practices driving golf balls)

range II *v.* 1. (d; tr.) ('to align') to ~ against (they were all ~d against us) 2. (d; intr.) ('to extend') to ~ from; to (prices ~ from ten dollars to thirty dollars)

ranger *n.* a forest ~

rank I *n.* ['row'] (esp. mil.) 1. to form a ~ 2. to break ~s (also fig.) 3. (misc.) to come up, rise from the ~s ['position, grade'] 4. to hold a ~ (to hold the ~ of captain) 5. to pull (colloq.), use one's ~ 6. high; junior; low; senior ~ 7. (mil.) permanent (AE), substantive (BE) ~ 8. (mil.) other ~s (BE; AE has *enlisted personnel)* 9. cabinet ~ 10. by, in ~ (to be seated by ~) 11. of ~ (of cabinet ~; of high ~) ['misc.'] 12. to close ~s ('to unite'); a taxi ~ (BE; AE has *taxi stand);* to come up from the ~s ('to work one's way up to a high position'); the ~ and file ('everyone')

rank II *v.* 1. (d; intr., tr.) ('to be rated; to rate') to ~ above (nobody ~s above Shakespeare; we do not ~ anyone above him) 2. (d; intr.) to ~ among

(she ~s among our best instructors) 3. (d; intr., tr.) to ~ as (to ~ as an outstanding chess player; we ~ you as our best candidate) 4. (d; intr., tr.) to ~ with (Pushkin ~s with Tolstoy)

rankle *v.* (R) it ~d me that they got all the credit

ransom *n.* 1. to pay (a) ~ for 2. to demand; exact a ~ from 3. to hold smb. for ~

rant *v.* 1. (D; intr.) to ~ at 2. (misc.) to ~ and rave (at smb.)

rap I *n.* (colloq.) (AE) ['blame'] 1. to take the ~ for 2. a bad, bum ~ (she got a bum ~) ('she was punished for smb. else's misdeeds') ['charge'] 3. to beat the ~ 4. on a ~ (he was sent to prison on a murder ~)

rap II *v.* 1. (d; intr.) ('to strike') to ~ at, on (to ~ on the window) 2. (d; tr.) ('to strike') to ~ over (she ~ped him over the knuckles)

rap III *v.* (colloq.) (AE) (D; intr.) ('to converse') to ~ about; with

rape *n.* 1. to commit ~ 2. attempted ~ 3. acquaintance, date; gang; marital; statutory ~

rapidity *n.* (with) lightning ~

rapids *n.* to ride, shoot ('pass by') (the) ~

rapport *n.* 1. to establish ~ 2. close ~ 3. in ~ with (they worked in close ~ with us)

rapprochement *n.* to bring about a ~ between

rapture *n.* 1. complete, total, utter ~ 2. in ~ over

rare *adj.* 1. ~ to + inf. (it's ~ to see snow in September) 2. ~ that + clause (it is ~ that he gets home before dark)

raring *adj.* (colloq.) ['eager'] (cannot stand alone) ~ to + inf. (we are ~ to go)

rash I *adj.* ~ to + inf. (it was ~ of her to try that)

rash II *n.* 1. a diaper (AE), nappy (BE); heat (the baby has heat ~) 2. nettle ~ 3. a ~ breaks out 4. (misc.) to break out in a ~

raspberry *n.* (slang) ['contemptuous noise'] to give smb. the ~

rat I *n.* 1. the black; brown; water ~ 2. (misc.) to smell a ~ ('to suspect that the truth is not being told'); a dirty ~ ('a contemptible person')

rat II *v.* (colloq.) (D; intr.) ('to inform') to ~ on

rate I *n.* ['amount in relation to something else'] 1. to fix, set a ~ 2. a fast; flat; high; low; moderate; slow; steady ~ 3. bargain; reasonable; reduced; regular ~s 4. an accident; birth; crime; death; divorce; fertility; growth; marriage; morbidity; mortality ~ 5. a discount; exchange; group; inflation; interest; primary; tax ~ 6. a metabolic; pulse; respiration ~ 7. an annual; hourly; monthly; seasonal; weekly ~ 8. at a certain ~ (at a steady ~; she borrowed money at a high interest ~) ['misc.'] 9. at any ~ ('in any case'); first ~ ('top quality')

rate II *v.* 1. to ~ high; low 2. (d; intr., tr.) ('to be ranked; to rank') to ~ among (that player is ~d among the very best) 3. (d; intr., tr.) ('to be ranked; to rank') to ~ as (this wine ~s as excellent; she is ~d as one of the best tennis players in the country) 4. (d; intr.) ('to compare') to ~ with (this wine ~s with the very best) 5. (colloq.) (AE) (D; intr.) ('to enjoy a favored status') to ~ with (she really ~s with them) 6. (P; tr.) ('to rank') this restaurant is ~d very highly 7. (GB) (P; tr.) ('to assess for tax purposes') their flat is ~d at eight hundred pounds this year 8. (misc.) on a scale of one to ten, we would ~ this restaurant eight

rather *adv.* 1. ~ + inf. + than (she would ~ play tennis than watch TV) 2. (colloq.) ~ + clause + than (I would ~ you stayed home than go out in this blizzard; she would ~ you did your homework than watched TV) 3. ~ + inf. (she would ~ not watch TV) 4.(colloq.) ~ + clause (she would ~ you didn't watch TV) 5. (misc.) I prefer to walk ~ than to ride; I prefer walking ~ than riding

rating *n.* ['classification'] ['limit'] 1. a high; low ~ 2. a credit; efficiency; octane; power ~ ['ordinary seaman'] (BE) 3. a naval ~

ratio *n.* 1. a compression ~ 2. an inverse ~ 3. a ~ between 4. at a ~ of; to (at a ~ of three to one)

ration I *n.* ['fixed allowance'] 1. a daily; monthly; weekly ~ 2. a food; gasoline (AE), petrol (BE) ~

ration II *v.* 1. to ~ strictly 2. (D; tr.) to ~ to (we were ~ed to ten gallons of gasoline/petrol a month)

rational *adj.* ~ to + inf. (it is not ~ to expect miracles)

rationalization *n.* ['excuse'] 1. a mere ~ 2. a ~ for (a ~ for refusing to contribute) 3. a ~ to + inf. (it was a ~ to argue that increased spending would spur the economy) 4. a ~ that + clause (their ~ that increased spending is bad has been disproved)

rationing *n.* 1. to introduce ~ 2. to end, terminate ~ 3. food; gasoline (AE), petrol (BE) ~ 4. emergency; wartime ~

ration out *v.* (D; tr.) to ~ among, to

rations *n.* 1. to issue ~ 2. army; emergency; short ~ 3. on ~ (we were on short ~)

rattle I *n.* ['noise in the throat caused by air passing through mucus'] 1. the death ~ ['device producing a rattling sound'] 2. a baby's ~

rattle II *v.* (colloq.) (R) it ~d me to realize how close we had been to a real catastrophe

rattlesnake *n.* a ~ bites, strikes

ravages *n.* ['destruction'] to repair the ~ (wrought by war)

rave *v.* (D; intr.) to ~ about, over; to (she was ~ing to us about her grandchild)

ravine *n.* a deep ~

raw *n.* ['natural state'] in the ~

ray *n.* 1. to emit, send forth, send out ~s 2. a cathode; cosmic; death; gamma; infrared; ultraviolet; X ~ 3. heat; light ~s

raze *v.* (D; tr.) to ~ to (to ~ a building to the ground)

razor *n.* 1. to hone, set, sharpen a ~ 2. a dull; keen, sharp ~ 3. a double-edged; electric; safety; single-edged; straight ~

reach I *n.* 1. beyond, out of ~ 2. in, within ~ (to bring smt. within ~) 3. (misc.) a boardinghouse ('very long') ~; the vast ~es (of the western plains)

reach II *v.* 1. (A; used without *to*) ('to pass') ~ me the salt 2. (d; intr.) ('to extend one's hand') to ~ for (she ~ed for a cigarette) 3. (d; intr.) ('to extend one's hand') to ~ into (she ~ed into her pocket for her keys) 4. (D; intr.) ('to extend') to ~ to (the rope doesn't ~ to the ground)

reach out *v.* 1. (d; intr.) to ~ for ('to attempt to

obtain') (to ~ for mutual understanding) 2. (D; tr.) ('to extend') to ~ for (she ~ed out her hand for the change) 3. (d; intr.) to ~ into, to ('to attempt to help') (to ~ to the local community) 4. (D; tr.) ('to extend') to ~ to (~ your hand to me)

react *v.* 1. to ~ strongly 2. (D; intr.) to ~ against (to ~ against unfair treatment) 3. (D; intr.) to ~ to (to ~ to a stimulus; to ~ to a provocation)

reaction *n.* 1. to cause, trigger a ~ 2. to encounter, meet with a ~ 3. an adverse, negative; favorable, positive; strong; weak ~ 4. an allergic chain; chemical; delayed; knee-jerk (usu. fig.); natural, normal; nuclear; physiological ~ 5. a ~ against, to (a natural ~ to provocation) 6. in ~ to

reactionary *n.* a dyed-in-the-wool ~

reactor *n.* an atomic, nuclear; breeder; fission ~

read *v.* 1. (A) she read a nice story to the children; or: she read the children a nice story 2. (D; intr.) to ~ about 3. (d; intr., tr.) to ~ for (she used to ~ for the patients in the nursing home; could you ~ that material for me?) 4. (esp. BE) (d; intr.) ('to study') to ~ for (to ~ for a degree; to ~ for the bar) 5. (d; tr.) to ~ into ('to attribute') (don't try to ~ anything else into her letter) 6. (AE) (d; tr) to ~ out of ('to exclude') (he was read out of the party) 7. (d; intr.) to ~ to (she loves to ~ to the children) 8. (misc.) to ~ by candlelight; to ~ a language fluently; to ~ between the lines; to ~ aloud; the letter ~s like an accusation; the cablegram ~s as follows...; to ~ a child to sleep; to ~ smb. like a book ('to comprehend smb.'s motives very clearly')

reader *n.* ['one who reads'] 1. an avid, voracious ~ 2. a regular ~ (of a newspaper) 3. a copy ~ (AE; BE has *subeditor*) 4. (rel.) a lay ~ ['university teacher below the rank of professor'] (BE) 5. a ~ in (a ~ in physics) ['practice book for reading'] 6. a basic ~ ['supervisor of a dissertation, thesis'] 7. a first; second ~ ['misc.'] 8. a mind ~ (see the Usage Note for **professor**)

readiness *n.* 1. ~ to + inf. (her ~ to help was appreciated) 2. (to hold oneself) in ~

reading *n.* ['act of reading'] 1. light; remedial; responsive; serious; solid ~ 2. a dramatic; poetry ~ 3. assigned; suggested ~(s) (have you done the assigned ~ for the course?) 4. at a ~ (at the first ~) 5. in a ~ (you will not be able to absorb the material in one ~) ['interpretation'] 6. a new ~ of (Shakespeare)

readjust *v.* (D; intr., refl., tr.) to ~ to

read up *v.* (d; intr.) to ~ on (to ~ on a subject)

ready *adj.* 1. ~ for (~ for any emergency) 2. ~ with (she is always ~ with an answer) 3. ~ to + inf (we are ~ to begin) 4. (misc.) to get (smb.) ~ for at the ~

reaffirm *v.* (L) she ~ed that she would serve as treasurer

realism *n.* to lend ~ (the sound effects lend ~ to the scene)

realist *n.* a down-to-earth, hardheaded ~

realistic *adj.* ~ to + inf (is it ~ to expect such results?)

reality *n.* 1. (the) grim, harsh, sober ~ (the harsh ~ of life) 2. in ~ 3. (misc.) to accept ~; to deny ~

realization *n.* 1. to come to the ~ 2. the ~ that + clause (the ~ that a catastrophe could occur at any time sobered them up)
realize *v.* 1. to ~ fully 2. (L) she ~d that she had been cheated 3. (Q) I ~d how my words had been distorted
reaper *n.* the grim ~ ('death')
reapply *v.* (D; intr.) to ~ for; to (to ~ for admission to a university)
reappoint *v.* 1. (D; tr.) to ~ as (to ~ smb. as chairperson) 2. (D; tr.) to ~ to (to ~ smb. to a committee) 3. (H) to ~ smb. to serve as secretary 4. (N; used with a noun) we ~ed her treasurer
reappraisal *n.* to do, make a ~
rear I *n.* 1. to bring up the ~ 2. at, from, in the ~ (the column was attacked from the ~)
rear II *v.* (H) we ~ed our chldren to help others
reason I *n.* ['cause, justification'] 1. to cite, give a ~ 2. a cogent, compelling, convincing, plausible, sound, strong, urgent ~ 3. a logical; personal; underlying; valid ~ 4. every ~; (a) sufficient ~ 5. a ~ against; behind; for (the real ~ behind their decision was never made public; to have a ~ for not going) 6. a ~ to + inf. (we had every ~ to complain; there is sufficient ~ to be concerned) 7. a ~ that + clause (the ~ that/why she did it is a mystery) 8. for a ~ (he quit for personal ~s) ['logic'] 9. to listen to; see ~ 10. to stand to ~ ('to be logical') (it stands to ~ that the majority party will be reelected) ['reasonable limits'] 11. within ~ (I'll do anything for you within ~) ['sanity'] 12. to lose one's ~
reason II *v.* 1. (D; intr.) to ~ with ('to attempt to persuade') (you can't ~ with him) 2. (L) ('to argue') they ~ed that any new proposal would fail
reasonable *adj.* 1. ~ about (let's be ~ about this) 2. ~ to + inf. (it is not ~ to demand so much from them)
reasoning *n.* 1. cogent, logical, plausible, solid, sound ~ 2. faulty; shrewd; specious ~ 3. deductive; inductive ~ 4. ~ that + clause (her ~ that the crime had been committed elsewhere proved to be true)
reassign *v.* (D; tr.) to ~ to (to ~ smb. to headquarters)
reassure *v.* 1. (D; tr.) to ~ about, of (they ~d us of their support) 2. (L; must have an object) we ~d them that we would not be late
reassuring *adj.* 1. ~ to + inf. (it is ~ to note that airport security has been improved) 2. ~ that + clause (it is ~ that airport security has been improved)
rebate *n.* 1. to give a ~ 2. to get, receive a ~
rebel I *n.* a ~ against
rebel II *v.* (D; intr.) to ~ against, at (to ~ against tyranny; they ~led at the thought of getting up before dawn)
rebellion *n.* 1. to foment, stir up a ~ 2. to crush, put down, quash, quell a ~ 3. open ~ 4. a ~ breaks out 5. a ~ against 6. in ~ (in open ~)
rebound I *n.* 1. (basketball) to grab a ~ 2. (misc.) on the ~ (right after her divorce she married smb. on the~)
rebound II *v.* (D; intr.) to ~ from (to ~ from a

setback)
rebuff *n.* 1. to meet with a ~ 2. a polite; sharp ~
rebuke I *n.* 1. to administer, deliver, give a ~ 2. to draw, receive a ~ 3. a mild; scathing, sharp, stern, stinging ~ 4. a ~ to
rebuke II *v.* 1. to ~ mildly; sharply, sternly 2. (D; tr.) to ~ for (to ~ smb. for sloppy work)
rebuttal *n.* to make a ~
recall I *n.* ['remembrance'] 1. beyond ~ ['memory'] 2. complete, total ~ ['signal recalling troops'] 3. to sound the ~
recall II *v.* 1. ('to remember') to ~ distinctly, vividly 2. (d; tr.) ('to remember') to ~ as (I ~ him as a very bashful child) 3. (D; tr.) ('to call back') to ~ from; to (to ~ smb. from retirement to active duty) 4. (G) ('to remember') she ~ed seeing him 5. (K) ('to remember') I ~ed their visiting us 6. (L) ('to remember') she ~ed that she had an appointment 7. (Q) ('to remember') I could not ~ where we had agreed to meet
recede *v.* (D; intr.) to ~ from
receipt *n.* ['receiving'] 1. to acknowledge ~ of 2. on ~ of ['written acknowledgment of something received'] 3. to give, make out, write out a ~ 4. to get a ~ 5. (esp. AE) a return ~ (for registered mail) 6. a ~ for
receive *v.* 1. to ~ smb. coldly, coolly; favorably; warmly 2. (d; tr.) to ~ as (the astronauts were ~d as conquering heroes) 3. (D; tr.) to ~ from (he ~d a letter from her) 4. (d; tr.) to ~ into (to ~ smb. into a church)
receiver *n.* ['part of a telephone'] 1. to pick up the ~ 2. to hang up, put down, replace a ~ 3. a telephone ~ ['radio'] 4. a shortwave ~ ['one who catches a forward pass'] (Am. football) 5. to hit; spot a ~ (to spot a ~ down the field)
receivership *n.* 1. to put a firm into ~ 2. in ~
reception *n.* ['social gathering'] 1. to give, hold; host a ~ 2. a diplomatic; formal; informal; official; wedding ~ 3. a ~ for (a ~ for graduating students) 4. at a ~ (we met at the ~) ['reaction, response'] ['greeting'] 5. to get, meet with a ~ 6. to accord, give (smb.) a ~ 7. a chilly, cold, cool; cordial, friendly, warm; emotional; enthusiastic; favorable; lavish; mixed; rousing; unfriendly ~ (their proposal got a mixed ~; they gave us a warm ~; the book received a favorable ~) ['registration desk in a hotel'] (BE) 8. at ~ (leave your key at ~) ['receiving of broadcasts'] 9. good, strong; poor, weak ~
receptive *adj.* ~ to (~ to any reasonable offer)
recess *n.* 1. to take a ~ 2. a spring; summer; winter ~ 3. in ~ (parliament was in ~)
recession *n.* 1. a business, economic ~ 2. (misc.) to come out of a ~; to go into a ~
recipe *n.* a ~ for
recipient *n.* a worthy ~
reciprocate *v.* (D; intr.) to ~ by; for; with
reciprocity *n.* 1. ~ between 2. (misc.) on a basis of ~
recital *n.* 1. to give a ~ 2. an organ; piano; violin ~
recite *v.* (B) she ~d her poetry to the audience
reckless *adj.* ~ to + inf. (it was ~ of them to go out alone at night)

reckon v. 1. (colloq. in AE) (d; intr.) ('to depend') to ~ on (you can always ~ on my support) 2. (colloq. in AE) (d; intr.) ('to deal') to ~ with (we'll have to ~ with him later) 3. (colloq.) (L) I ~ we'll have to see them eventually
reckoning n. ['navigation'] 1. dead ~ ['calculations'] 2. by smb.'s ~ (by my ~)
reclaim v. (D; tr.) to ~ from
reclamation n. land; water ~
recluse n. an aging; virtual ~
recognition n. 1. to give, grant ~ 2. to gain, receive, win ~ 3. general, universal; growing; official; public; tacit; wide ~ (to receive universal ~) 4. (diplomatic) de facto; de jure ~ 5. ~ for; from (to receive ~ for one's accomplishments from one's colleagues) 6. beyond ~ (burned beyond ~) 7. in ~ of 8. (misc.) to give/show no signs of ~
recognizance n. (legal) on one's own ~ (she was released on her own ~)
recognize v. 1. to ~ generally, universally; officially; widely 2. (D; tr.) to ~ as (she is universally ~d as an authority on the subject) 3. (L) we ~d that the situation was hopeless
recoil v. 1. (D; intr.) to ~ at, from 2. (misc.) to ~ in horror
recollect v. 1. (G) she could not ~ being there 2. (K) can you ~ my calling you? 3. (L) I ~ that the weather was cold 4. (Q) can anyone ~ how the alarm is deactivated?
recollection n. 1. to have a ~ of 2. a hazy, vague; painful; vivid ~
recommend v. 1. to ~ enthusiastically, highly, strongly 2. (BE) (A) she ~ed a good dictionary to me; or: she ~ed me a good dictionary 3. (B) she ~ed a good dictionary to me 4. (D; tr.) to ~ as (she was ~ed as a suitable candidate for the job) 5. (D; tr.) to ~ for (to ~ smb. for a job) 6. (G) he ~ed waiting 7. (BE) (H; no passive) I ~ you to buy this book 8. (K) he ~ed their investing in railroad stocks 9. (L; subj.; to) she ~ed (to us) that our trip be/should be postponed
recommendation n. 1. to give smb. a ~ 2. to provide, write a ~ for smb. 3. to make a ~ 4. to act on, carry out, implement a ~ 5. a lukewarm; negative; positive; strong; weak ~ for 6. a ~ for 7. a ~ to (her ~ to us was to postpone the trip) 8. a ~ to + inf. (we ignored her ~ to postpone the trip) 9. a ~ that + clause; subj. (we ignored her ~ that our trip be/ should be postponed) 10. at, on smb.'s ~ (we hired him on her ~)
recommit v. (D; tr.) ('to confine again') to ~ to (he was ~ted to the mental hospital)
recompense I n. (formal) ~ for
recompense II v. (formal) (D; tr.) to ~ for
reconcile v. 1. (D; refl., tr.) to ~ to (he had to ~ himself to his fate) 2. (d; tr.) to ~ with (we tried to ~ her with her family; to ~ a checkbook with a bank statement)
reconciliation n. 1. to bring about, effect a ~ 2. a ~ with
reconnaissance n. 1. to carry out, conduct ~ 2. aerial ~ 3. (a) ~ in force
record I n. ['best performance'] 1. to establish, set a (new) ~ 2. to equal, tie a ~ 3. to beat, better,

break, surpass a ~ 4. to hold a ~ 5. an unbroken ~ 6. an attendance; speed ~ 7. a national Olympic; world ~ 8. ~s fall ['account of events'] ['file'] 9. to keep; make a ~ (to keep a ~ of events) 10. to close; open up a ~ 11. to destroy ~s 12. an accurate; detailed; official; sketchy; verbatim ~ 13. public ~ (a matter of public ~) 14. medical ~s 15. of; on ~ (the coldest day on ~) 16. (misc.) to set the ~ straight ('to correct a misunderstanding') ['past performance'] 17. (to have) a clean; good ~ 18. an academic; distinguished; excellent; mediocre, spotty; safety; service ~ (her academic ~ is excellent; he's been in jail and has a police ~; this airline's safety ~ is impeccable; she has a distinguished ~ as a public official) ['recorded crimes'] 19. to have a ~ (he's been in jail and has a ~) 20. a criminal, police ~ ['publication'] ['public disclosure'] 21. to go on ~ 22. for the ~ (was his statement for the ~?) 23. off the ~ (what she told the reporters was off the ~) ['grooved disc'] 24. to cut (AE), make a ~ 25. to play a ~ 26. a gramophone (BE), phonograph (AE); long-playing ~
record II v. 1. to ~ live 2. (L) ('to report') the newspapers ~ed that a new era in international cooperation had begun
recorder n. a tape; voice ~
recording n. 1. to make a ~ 2. to play a ~ 3. a tape ~
records n. ['recorded information'] 1. to file; keep ~ 2. accurate ~
recount I n. to do, make a ~ (of votes)
recount II v. (B) to ~ a story to smb.
recourse n. to have ~ to
recover v. (D; intr., tr.) to ~ from (to ~ from an illness; the police ~ed the missing items from the bottom of the river)
recovery n. 1. to make a ~ 2. a quick, rapid, speedy; remarkable; slow ~ (the patient made a quick ~) 3. an economic ~ 4. a ~ from 5. (misc.) to wish smb. a speedy ~
recreation n. for ~ (what do you do for ~?)
recruit I n. a fresh, green, raw ~
recruit II v. 1. (D; tr.) to ~ for (to ~ volunteers for charitable work) 2. (D; tr.) to ~ from (to ~ volunteers from friendly countries) 3. (H) to ~ mercenaries to serve in the army
recruiter n. an air force; army; marine; navy ~
recuperate v. (D; intr.) to ~ from (to ~ from the flu)
recuperation n. ~ from
recur v. (D; intr.) ('to come again to mind') to ~ to (that thought keeps ~ring to me)
red n. ['color'] 1. bright; dark; light ~ 2. (misc. as ~ as a beet (AE), beetroot (BE) ['red light'] 3. on ~ (no turn on ~) ['debt'] 4. in the ~ (to operate in the ~)
red carpet n. ['warm reception'] to put out, roll out the ~ for smb.
rededicate v. (d; refl., tr.) to ~ to (we must ~ ourselves to our cause)
rededication n. ~ to
redeem v. (D; tr.) to ~ from
redemption n. 1. ~ from 2. beyond, past ~

redeploy *v.* (D; tr.) to ~ from; to (troops were being ~ed from Europe to Asia)

redeployment *n.* 1. large-scale ~ (the large-scale ~ of troops) 2. ~ from; to

redevelopment *n.* urban ~

red-faced *adj.* ~ with (~ with shame)

red light *n.* 1. to go through, run (AE) a ~ (she ran a ~ and was fined) 2. at a ~ (to stop at a ~)

redolent *adj.* (formal) ~ of, with (~ of honeysuckle)

redound *v.* (formal) (d; intr.) to ~ to ('to affect') (her success ~s to the credit of her teachers)

redress *n.* legal ~

red tape *n.* 1. to get caught up in, get involved in ~ 2. to cut, eliminate (the) ~

reduce *v.* 1. (d; tr.) to ~ in (he was ~d in rank) 2. (d; tr.) to ~ to (she was ~d to poverty; the corporal was ~d to the rank of private)

reduction *n.* 1. to take a ~ (in salary) 2. to make a (price) ~ 3. a ~ in (a ~ in salary) 4. a ~ to 5. at a ~ (to sell merchandise at a substantial ~)

reef *n.* 1. to strike a ~ (the ship struck a ~) 2. a barrier; coral ~

reek *v.* 1. (d; intr.) to ~ of (to ~ of alcohol) 2. (d; intr.) to ~ with (to ~ with sweat)

reel *v.* (D; intr.) ('to stagger') to ~ under (to ~ under blows)

reeling *adj.* to send smb. ~

reentry *n.* a ~ into (a spaceship's ~ into the atmosphere)

refer *v.* (d; intr., tr.) to ~ to (in her autobiography she never ~red to her parents; the problem was ~red to a committee; they ~red me to the manager)

referable *adj.* ~ to

refer back *v.* (d; tr.) to ~ to (the report was ~red back to the committee)

reference *n.* ['mention, allusion'] 1. to make (a) ~ (she made no ~s to her opponents) 2. to contain a ~ (the statement contains several ~s to me) 3. a direct; indirect, oblique ~ 4. a ~ to (without ~ to age) ['regard, relation'] 5. in, with ~ to 6. a frame of ~ ['recommendation'] ['statement'] 7. to give, provide a ~ 8. a good, positive, satisfactory; negative ~ ['consultation'] ['source of information'] 9. further; quick ~ 10. for ~ (to file for future ~)

referendum *n.* to conduct, hold a ~ on

referral *n.* 1. to make a ~ 2. a ~ from; to

refill *n.* 1. to give smb. a ~ 2. a ~ for (a ~ for a ballpoint pen)

refine *v.* (d; intr.) to ~ on, upon ('to improve') (to ~ on a method)

refinery *n.* an oil; sugar ~

reflect *v.* 1. ('to think about') to ~ closely; seriously 2. (D; intr.) to ~ on, upon ('to think about') (to ~ on one's past mistakes) 3. (d; intr.) to ~ on ('to discredit') (her unfounded accusations ~ed on her credibility) 4. (d; intr.) to ~ on ('to show') (her unselfish act ~s well on her upbringing) 5. (d; tr.) to ~ on ('to bring to') (the team's victory ~ed credit on the coach)

reflection *n.* ['criticism'] 1. a ~ on (this is no ~ on your qualifications) ['meditation, thought'] 2. quiet; serious; sober ~ 3. ~ on (~s on the war) 4.

after, on ~ (on further ~ she saw her mistake)

reflex *n.* 1. to test one's ~es 2. a conditioned ~ 3. abnormal; diminished; hyperactive; normal ~es

reform *n.* 1. carry out, effect a ~ 2. a far-reaching; radical, sweeping ~ 3. (an) agrarian, land; economic; labor; orthographic, spelling; penal; social ~

reformatory *n.* (now AE; obsol.) at, in a ~ (he spent time at/in a ~)

reformer *n.* an economic; social ~

refraction *n.* ['eye examination'] to do a ~ (the oculist did a ~)

refrain I *n.* to sing a ~

refrain II *v.* (D; intr.) to ~ from (to ~ from smoking)

refreshments *n.* 1. to offer ~ 2. light; liquid ~

refrigeration *n.* under ~ (to keep food under ~)

refrigerator *n.* 1. to defrost a ~ 2. a frostfree ~ 3. an electric; gas ~ 4. (misc.) to raid the ~ ('to consume large quantities of food from the refrigerator, esp. at night')

refueling, refuelling *n.* inflight, midair ~

refuge *n.* 1. to give, provide ~ 2. to find, take; seek ~ 3. a wildlife ~ 4. a place of ~ 5. ~ from (to take ~ from the storm)

refugee *n.* 1. a political ~ 2. a ~ from

refund I *n.* 1. to give, pay a ~ 2. to get, receive a ~ 3. a tax ~

refund II *v.* (B) the manager ~ed the purchase price to the customer

refusal *n.* 1. an adamant, curt, flat, outright, point-blank, unyielding ~ 2. a first ~ (BE; CE has *first option*) 3. a ~ to + inf. (I could not comprehend her ~ to help) 4. (misc.) to meet with a ~

refuse I *n.* (BE) to collect the ~ (see also **garbage, trash**)

refuse II *v.* 1. to ~ categorically, completely, outright, point-blank 2. (E) she ~d to see him 3. (O; can be used with one object) he ~d them nothing

refute *v.* to ~ completely

regain *v.* (D; tr.) to ~ from

regale *v.* (d; tr.) to ~ with (to ~ one's guests with funny stories)

regard I *n.* ['consideration'] 1. to show ~ 2. ~ for (he shows no ~ for the feelings of others; you must have ~ for our safety) ['esteem'] 3. high; low ~ (to hold smb. in high ~) ['aspect, relation'] 4. in a ~ (in this ~) 5. in, with ~ to (in ~ to your request, no decision has been made)

regard II *v.* 1. to ~ highly (highly ~ed in the scientific community) 2. (d; tr.) to ~ as (to ~ smb. as a friend) 3. (d; tr.) to ~ with (to ~ smb. with contempt)

regardless *adj.* ~ of

regards *n.* ['greetings'] 1. to convey smb.'s ~; to send one's ~ 2. to give smb. one's ~ 3. best, cordial, friendly, kind, kindest, sincere, warm, warmest; personal ~ (with best personal ~)

regatta *n.* an annual ~

regime *n.* 1. to establish a ~ 2. to overthrow a ~ 3. a puppet; totalitarian ~

regiment *n.* 1. a Guards (GB); infantry ~ 2. a colonel commands a ~

region *n.* a border; mountainous; outlying,

remote; polar; unpopulated ~
register I *n*. ['record, record book'] 1. to keep a ~ 2. a case; hotel ~ ['roster'] 3. the Social Register ['machine that registers the amount of each sale'] 4. a cash ~
register II *v*. 1. (D; intr., tr.) to ~ as (she ~ed as a Republican; he was not ~ed as a voter) 2. (D; intr., tr.) to ~ for (she ~ed for two courses; our departmental secretary has ~ed ten students for the seminar) 3. (D; tr.) to ~ in (how many ~ed in the course?) 4. (D; intr., tr.) to ~ with (he had to ~ with the authorities; to ~ a pistol with the police)
registration *n*. 1. to conduct ~ 2. gun; voter ~
regress *v*. (D; intr.) to ~ to (to ~ to one's childhood)
regret I *n*. 1. to express ~(s) 2. to fee ; show ~ 3. deep, keen ~ 4. a token of (one's) ~ 5. ~ at, over; for (to express ~ at not being able to accept an invitation; ~ for one's mistake)
regret II *v*. 1. to ~ deeply, very much 2. (formal) (E) we ~ to inform you that your position has been eliminated 3. (G) I ~ having to leave so early 4. (K) everyone ~ted his being dismissed 5. (L) we ~ that we cannot accept your invitation
regrets *n*. ['expression of regret at declining an invitation'] 1. to send ~ 2. ~ only (appears on invitations instructing recipients to respond only if they are unable to accept)
regulation *n*. 1. to adopt, enact a ~ 2. to apply, enforce a ~ 3. to obey, observe a ~ 4. to ignore; violate a ~ 5. rigid, strict ~s 6. army; government; health; police; security; traffic ~s 7. a ~ that + clause; subj. (we obeyed the ~ that no cars be/ should be parked there)
rehabilitation *n*. physical ~
rehearsal *n*. 1. to conduct, hold; schedule a ~ 2. a dress, final ~ 3. a ~ for 4. at a ~ (I'll see you at the dress ~)
rehearse *v*. (D; intr., tr.) to ~ for (to ~ for a concert)
reign I *n*. during smb.'s ~
reign II *v*. 1. (D; intr.) to ~ over 2. (s) to ~ supreme
reimburse *v*. 1. to ~ amply, fully, generously 2. (rare) (B) all expenses will be ~d to you 3. (D; tr.) to ~ for (you will be ~d for all expenses)
reimbursement *n*. ~ for
rein I *n*. ['control'] 1. to keep a ~ on 2. to give free, full ~ to ('to remove restraints on') 3. a tight ~ (to keep a tight ~ on smb.) 4. (misc.) to seize the ~s of government
rein II *v*. (D; tr.) to ~ to (to ~ a horse to the left)
reinforcements *n*. to bring up; commit; send ~
reins *n*. ['straps used to control an animal'] to draw in, tighten the ~
reinstate *v*. 1. (D; tr.) to ~ as (she was ~d as treasurer) 2. (D; tr.) to ~ in (to ~ smb. in her/his former position)
reissue *v*. (B) the supply sergeant ~d ammunition to the platoon
reiterate *v*. 1. (B) she ~d her story to the police 2. (L) he ~d that he would resign
reject *v*. to ~ completely, flatly, outright, totally

rejection *n*. complete, flat, outright, total ~
rejoice *v*. (D; intr.) to ~ at, in, over (they ~d at the good news)
rejoinder *n*. 1. a sharp; telling ~ 2. a ~ to
relapse *n*. 1. to have, suffer a ~ 2. a complete, total ~
relate *v*. 1. (B) she ~d her version of the incident to the police 2. (d; intr.) to ~ to (this law does not ~ to your case; how do they ~ to each other?)
related *adj*. ~ by; to (I am ~ to him by marriage)
relation *n*. 1. a ~ between 2. in ~ to
relations *n*. 1. to establish; have, maintain; normalize; renew ~ 2. to cement, improve, promote, strengthen ~ 3. to break off, sever; strain ~ (to break off diplomatic ~ with a country) 4. close intimate; friendly; strained, troubled ~ 5. business, commercial, economic, trade; diplomatic; extramarital; foreign; international; labor; marital; premarital; public; race; sexual ~ (to have sexual ~ with smb.) 6. ~ among, between; with 7. (misc.) friends and ~ ('friends and relatives')
relationship *n*. 1. to cement; establish a ~ (to establish a ~ with smb.) 2. to bear, have a ~ (to bear a ~ to smt.) 3. to break off a ~ (to break off a ~ with smb.) 4. a casual; close, intimate; direct; indirect; meaningful; solid; tenuous; warm ~ 5. a doctor-patient ~ 6. an extramarital; incestuous ~; interpersonal; spatial ~s 7. an inverse ~ & a ~ between; to, towards; with
relative I *adj*. ~ to
relative II *n*. a blood; close; distant ~; one's nearest ~s
relaxant *n*. a muscle ~
relaxation *n*. for ~ (what do you do for ~?)
relaxing *adj*. ~ to + inf. (it is ~ to spend a few days camping out)
relay I *n*. to run a ~
relay II *v*. (B) she ~ed the information to us
release I *n*. ['liberation'] 1. to bring about, effect smb.'s ~ 2. a ~ from (a ~ from prison) ['surrender of a claim or right'] (legal) 3. to agree to; sign a ~ ['handing over'] 4. ~ to (the ~ of information to the press) 5. a news ~
release II *v*. 1. (D; tr.) to ~ from (he has been ~d from prison) 2. (D; tr.) to ~ to (the judge ~ the youthful culprit to his parents; the film has been ~d to various movie theaters; the information was ~d to the press)
relegate *v*. 1. (d; tr.) to ~ to (to ~ smb. to second-class status) 2. (misc.) (GB) to ~ a team to the second division
relevance *n*. 1. to have ~ to 2. of ~ to (his testimony is of no ~ to the case)
relevant *adj*. ~ to (the evidence is ~ to the case)
reliance *n*. ~ on
reliant *adj*. ~ on
relics *n*. ancient; holy ~; ~ of the past
relief *n*. ['easing of pain, of a burden'] 1. to bring; give ~ 2. to express; feel ~ 3. to find; receive; seek ~ (they found ~ in looking at their son's photographs) 4. great, immense; instant; permanent; temporary ~ 5. (esp. BE) tax ~ 6. ~ from (the rain brought instant ~ from the heat) 7. ~ to (the news was a great ~ to us) 8. a ~ to + inf. (it was a

~ to get home) 9. ~ that + clause (they expressed ~ that the crisis was over) 10. to smb.'s ~ (to my ~ they got there safely) ['welfare, government aid'] (esp. AE; obsol.) 11. on ~ (in the l930s they were on ~) ['comic scenes'] 12. comic; mock ~ ['differences in height'] 13. in ~ (to show terrain in ~) ['sharpness of outline'] 14. in bold ~ against (a light background)

relieve *v.* 1. (D; tr.) to ~ of (the general was ~d of his command) 2. (R) it ~d me to learn that they were safe

relieved *adj.* 1. ~ at (we were ~ at the news) 2. ~ to + inf. (we were ~ to learn that they had arrived safely) 3. ~ that + clause (we were ~ that they had arrived safely)

religion *n.* ['formal belief in a divine power'] 1. to practice a ~ 2. to abjure a ~ 3. a fundamentalist; monotheistic; polytheistic ~ 4. (an) established, organized ~ 5. a personal; state ~ ['study of systems of worship'] 6. comparative ~(s)

religious *adj.* deeply, profoundly ~

relinquish *v.* (B) ('to yield') he ~ed his business interests to his children

relish I *n.* ['enjoyment'] to show ~ for

relish II *v.* 1. (G) I don't ~ confronting him 2. (K) no one ~es his coming here

reluctance *n.* 1. to display, show ~ 2. extreme, great ~ 3. ~ to + inf. (her ~ to get involved was understandable)

reluctant *adj.* (usu. does not stand alone) ~ to + inf. (we were ~ to act)

rely *v.* (d; intr.) to ~ on, upon (to ~ on smb. for advice)

remain *v.* 1. (D; intr.) to ~ of (did anything ~ of the wreckage?) 2. (E) that ~s to be seen 3. (S) she ~ed a widow for the rest of her life; to ~ silent

remains *n.* human, mortal ~

remand *v.* (d; tr.) ('to send') to ~ to (the judge ~ed the accused to the county jail)

remark I *n.* 1. to drop, make a ~ 2. a biting, catty, caustic, cutting, nasty, scathing ~ 3. a casual; complimentary; cryptic; derogatory; facetious; flattering; impertinent; inane; indiscreet; off-the-cuff; passing; pithy; pointed; reassuring; sarcastic; slanderous; snide; suggestive; sullen; timely; trite; trivial; witty ~ 4. one's closing, concluding, opening ~s 5. a ~ that + clause (she made the ~ that being interviewed was boring)

remark II *v.* 1. (d; intr.) to ~ on, upon (the visitors ~ed on the excellent condition of the streets) 2. (L; to) she ~ed (to us) that she found our story very strange

remarkable *adj.* 1. ~ for 2. ~ to + inf. (it's ~ to see such clean streets) 3. ~ that + clause (it's ~ that the streets are so clean after the parade)

remedy *n.* 1. to resort to a ~ 2. to prescribe a ~ 3. (legal) to pursue a (legal) ~ 4. (legal) to exhaust all (legal) ~ies 5. a certain, reliable, sure; effective, efficacious ~ 6. a cold; cough ~ 7. a folk; homeopathic ~ 8. a ~ for

remember *v.* 1. (B; colloq. the direct object is always a personal pronoun) please ~ me to your family ('please give my regards to your family') 2. (D; tr.) to ~ as (I ~ him as a young man) 3. (D; tr.)

to ~ of (what do you ~ of them?) 4. (E) she ~ed to buy a newspaper 5. (G) she ~ed buying the newspaper 6. (J) I ~ him being very generous 7. (K) I ~ his being very generous 8. (L) she ~ed that she had an appointment 9. (Q) I could not ~ how to open the safe USAGE NOTE: The sentence *she didn't remember to buy a newspaper* means 'she forgot to buy a newspaper'. The sentence *she didn't remember buying a newspaper* means 'she had no memory of buying a newspaper', whether she bought one or not.

remembrance *n.* in ~ of

remind *v.* 1. (d; tr.) ('to cause to remember') to ~ about, of (he ~ed me of my promise) 2. (d; tr.) ('to call to mind') to ~ of (he ~s me of my cousin) 3. (H) she ~ed me to buy a newspaper 4. (L; must have an object) we ~ed them that the meeting had been postponed

reminder *n.* 1. a bitter; final; gentle; grim ~ 2. a ~ that + clause (we received a ~ that the rent was due)

reminisce *v.* (D; intr.) to ~ about

reminiscences *n.* 1. personal ~ 2. ~ about

reminiscent *adj.* (cannot stand alone) ~ of (that melody is ~ of the old days)

remiss *adj.* (formal) ~ about, in (~ in performing one's duties)

remission *n.* ['lessening of the effects of a disease'] (med.) in ~

remit I *n.* (BE) ['assignment, area of responsibility'] 1. a limited; wide ~ 2. a ~ to + inf. (they have a ~ to investigate the company's affairs)

remit II *v.* 1. (BE) (A) they ~ted the money to us; or: they ~ted us the money 2. (AE) (B) they ~ted the money to us

remittance *n.* 1. to enclose; send a ~ 2. (obsol.) (BE) a ~ man ('one living abroad on money sent from home')

remonstrate *v.* (formal) (D; intr.) to ~ about; with (they ~d with the neighbors about the noise)

remorse *n.* 1. to display, show ~ 2. to express; feel ~ 3. bitter, deep, profound ~ 4. a feeling; twinge of ~ 5. ~ for, over (he displayed no ~ for his crimes)

remote *adj.* ~ from

removal *n.* 1. snow ~ 2. (BE) furniture ~ 3. ~ from

remove *v.* (D; tr.) to ~ from; to (to ~ a patient from a respirator)

removed *adj.* 1. easily ~ 2. once; twice ~ (a first cousin once ~)

remover *n.* (a) nail-polish (AE), nail-varnish (BE); paint; spot ~

remunerate *v.* (formal) (D; tr.) to ~ for

remuneration *n.* 1. to offer ~ 2. to accept ~ 3. ~ for

rend *v.* (D; tr.) ('to tear') to ~ into (to ~ one's clothes into shreds)

render *v.* 1. (A) she ~ed a valuable service to me; or; she ~ed me a valuable service 2. (formal) (D; tr.) to ~ into (to ~ a text into English) 3. (N; used with an adjective) her remark ~ed me speechless

rendezvous *n.* 1. to have; make a ~ with 2. a secret ~

rendition *n.* 1. to give a ~ 2. a letter-perfect (AE), word-perfect (BE) ~

renege *v.* (D; intr.) to ~ on (to ~ on a commitment)

renewal *n.* urban ~

renounce *v.* (D; tr.) to ~ for (to ~ wealth for happiness)

renovations *n.* to make ~

renown *n.* (formal) 1. to achieve, attain ~ 2. great, wide ~ 3. of ~ (an artist of great ~)

renowned *adj.* ~ as; for (~ as a pianist; ~ for one's inventions)

rent I *n.* 1. to pay ~ for 2. to raise the ~ 3. (AE) for ~ (the house is for ~) (BE has *the house is to let*) 4. (misc.) ~ control

rent II *v.* 1. (esp. AE) (A) she ~ed a room to me; or: she ~ed me a room 2. (D; tr.) to ~ from (to ~ a house from smb.) 3. (esp. AE) (d; intr.) to ~ to (she ~s to students)

rental *n.* 1. car; film; office ~ 2. ~ to

rent out *v.* (esp. AE) (B) to ~ rooms to students (see also **let out**)

reorganization *n.* to undergo ~

repair I *n.* ['process of restoring to working order'] 1. to do, make a ~ (we have done the necessary ~s) 2. extensive, major; minor; necessary ~s 3. ~s to (the ~s to our roof cost one hundred dollars) 4. under ~ (the road is under ~) ['condition'] 5. in ~ (to keep a car in good ~; in poor ~)

repair II *v.* (formal or humorous) (d; intr.) ('to go') to ~ to (to ~ to the drawing room)

reparations *n.* 1. to pay ~ 2. war ~ 3. ~ for

repartee *n.* witty ~

repast *n.* a light, meager ~

repatriate *v.* (D; tr.) to ~ from; to

repatriation *n.* 1. forced ~ 2. ~ from; to

repay *v.* 1. (A) she repaid the money to me; or: she repaid me the money 2. (D; tr.) to ~ for (I repaid him for his expenses) 3. (D; tr.) to ~ to (to ~ one's debt to society)

repeat *v.* 1. (B) she ~ed her story to us 2. (D; intr.) ('to cause an unpleasant aftertaste') to ~ on (this type of food ~s on me) 3. (L; to) he ~ed (to me) that he would buy some stamps 4. (misc.) ~ after me

repellent I *adj.* ~ to

repellent II *n.* an insect, mosquito ~

repent *v.* 1. to ~ sincerely 2. (D; intr.) to ~ of (to ~ of one's sins) 3. (rare) (G) he ~ed having stolen the car

repentance *n.* 1. to show ~ for 2. genuine, sincere ~

repercussions *n.* 1. to have ~ on 2. far-reaching ~

repertory *n.* in ~ (to play in ~)

replace *v.* (D; tr.) to ~ by, with

replacement *n.* 1. to make a ~ 2. to get, receive a ~ for 3. (misc.) the ~ of smt. by smt. else

replay *n.* action (BE), instant (AE) ~

replenish *v.* (D; tr.) to ~ with

replete *adj.* (cannot stand alone) ~ with

reply I *n.* 1. to give, make; send a ~ 2. to draw; elicit a ~ 3. a curt, gruff; immediate, prompt; stinging; succinct; sullen; terse; witty ~ 4. in ~ (to

nod in ~) 5. in ~ to (in ~ to your letter)

reply II *v.* 1. to ~ immediately, promptly 2. (D; intr.) to ~ to (she did not ~ to my letter) 3. (L) she replied that she would be happy to accept our invitation

report I *n.* 1. to file, give, make, present, submit a ~ 2. to draw up, make out, write, write out, write up a ~ 3. to confirm a ~ 4. an accurate; biased, slanted; confirmed; detailed, exhaustive; favorable, positive; firsthand; negative, unfavorable; objective; unconfirmed ~ 5. an annual; daily; incident; interim; majority; minority; monthly; morning; newspaper; oral; status; traffic; weather; weekly; written ~ 6. a classified; confidential; restricted; secret; top secret ~ 7. a school ~ (BE; AE has *report card*) 8. a ~ about, on; to (she filed a ~ about the incident; the annual ~ to stockholders) 9. a ~ that + clause (we have heard ~s that the road is closed)

report II *v.* 1. (B) ('to relate') we ~ed the information to the authorities 2. (D; intr.) to ~ about, on ('to describe') (the correspondent ~ed on the situation at the front) 3. (D; intr.) ('to present oneself') to ~ for; to (to ~ to headquarters for duty) 4. (D; tr.) ('to inform on') to ~ for; to ('to ~ smb. to the police for violating an ordinance) 5. (pol.) (AE) (d; tr.) to ~ out of ('to return smt. for further action') (to ~ a bill out of committee) 6. (D; intr.) to ~ to ('to answer to') (she ~s directly to the dean) 7. (G) ('to make known') several people ~ed having seen the stolen car 8. (K) ('to make known') smb. ~ed their leaving early 9. (L; to) ('to relate') she ~ed (to us) that she had accomplished her mission 10. (M) ('to describe') the fire was ~ed to be burning out of control 11. (N; used with an adjective, past participle) ('to describe') the patrol ~ed the entire area clear/cleared; he was ~ed missing in action 12. (Q) ('to describe') they ~ed how the incident took place 13. (esp. BE) (s) to ~ sick

report back *v.* (D; intr.) to ~ to (you will ~ to the chairperson of the committee)

reported *adj.* (cannot stand alone) 1. ~ to + inf. (they were ~ to be safe) 2. ~ that + clause (it was ~ed that they were safe)

reporter *n.* a court; cub; financial; investigative; news; police; roving; science; society; sports; TV ~

report in *v.* (AE) (s) to ~ sick

repose *n.* in (a state of) ~

represent *v.* 1. ('to depict') to ~ graphically 2. (B) ('to be the equivalent of') this room ~ed home to them 3. (esp. BE) (B) ('to convey') to ~ one's grievances to the authorities 4. (d; tr.) ('to depict') to ~ as (she was ~ed as a hero)

representation *n.* ['statement'] ['protest'] 1. to make ~s to (our ambassador made ~s to their government) ['act of representing'] 2. proportional ~

representative I *adj.* ~ of

representative II *n.* 1. a sales ~ (BE also has *commercial traveller*) 2. an elected ~

repression *n.* (to live) under ~

repressive *adj.* ~ of

reprieve *n.* 1. to give, grant a ~ 2. to get, receive a ~ 3. a ~ from

reprimand I *n.* 1. to administer, issue a ~ (the judge issued a ~ from the bench) 2. to receive a ~ 3. a mild; severe, sharp, stern ~ 4. an oral; written ~

reprimand II *v.* (D; tr.) to ~ for (to ~ an employee for being late)

reprint *n.* to issue a ~ (of a book)

reprisal *n.* 1. to carry out ~s 2. a harsh ~ 3. a ~ against, on 4. in ~ for 5. (misc.) by way of ~

reproach I *n.* 1. a term of ~ 2. above, beyond ~

reproach II *v.* (D; refl., tr.) to ~ for

reproduce *v.* (D; tr.) to ~ from (to ~ a photograph from an old negative)

reproduction *n.* ['copy'] 1. (a) high-fidelity; stereophonic ~ ['biological process of reproducing'] 2. animal; human; plant ~

reprove *v.* (formal) (D; tr.) to ~ for

reptile *n.* ~s crawl, creep, slither

republic *n.* 1. to establish a ~ 2. an autonomous; banana (obsol.); democratic; people's ~

Republican *n.* (US) a registered ~

repugnance *n.* 1. to feel ~ 2. (a) deep, profound ~

repugnant *adj.* ~ to

repulsive *adj.* ~ to

reputation *n.* 1. to acquire, establish a ~ 2. to have, hold a ~ (he had the ~ of being a heavy drinker) 3. to guard, protect one's ~ 4. to compromise, destroy, ruin, tarnish smb.'s ~ 5. an enviable, excellent, fine, good, impeccable, spotless, unblemished, unsullied, untarnished ~ 6. a tainted, tarnished, unenviable ~ 7. an international, worldwide; local; national ~ 8. a ~ as, for (that judge has a ~ for being fair) 9. by ~ (to know smb. by ~) 10. (misc.) to live up to one's ~; to stake one's ~ on smt.

repute *n.* ill, low ~ (a place of ill ~; to be held in low ~)

reputed *adj.* (cannot stand alone) 1. generally, widely ~ 2. ~ to + inf. (she is ~ to be very generous)

request I *n.* 1. to file, make, submit a ~ (to file a ~ with the appropriate authorities; she has a ~ to make of us; to submit a ~ to the mayor's office) 2. to act on; honor a ~ 3. to deny, reject a ~ 4. a desperate, urgent; moderate, modest; reasonable; unreasonable ~ 5. a formal; informal; oral; unofficial; written ~ 6. a ~ for (to make a ~ for more money) 7. a ~ to + inf. (a ~ to be allowed to leave) 8. a ~ that + clause; subj. (we submitted a ~ that lights be/should be installed on our street) 9. at smb.'s ~ (she did it at my ~) 10. by, on, upon ~ (brochures are mailed out on ~)

request II *v.* 1. (D; tr.) to ~ from; of (to ~ a favor of smb.) 2. (rare) (H) to ~ smb. to do smt. 3. (L; subj.) she ~ed that I be/should be there

require *v.* 1. (D; tr.) to ~ from, of (she ~s a term paper of each student) 2. (esp. BE) (G) the house ~s painting 3. (H) we ~ all incoming students to take placement examinations 4. (K) this position ~s your getting here on time every day 5. (L; subj.) she ~d that everyone attend/should attend the meeting

requirement *n.* 1. to establish, set ~s 2. to fill, fulfill, meet, satisfy a ~ 3. to waive a ~ 4. admission, entrance; distributional (AE); legal; minimum; physical ~s 5. a ~ that + clause; subj. (this candidate does not meet the ~ that secondary school be/should be completed)

requisite *n.* a ~ for

requisition I *n.* 1. to make out, send in, submit a ~ 2. to fill a ~ 3. a ~ for 4. on ~ (that item is on ~)

requisition II *v.* (D; tr.) to ~ for

rerun *n.* to show a ~ (that channel keeps showing ~s of old TV programs)

rescue I *n.* 1. to attempt; effect, make, mount a ~ 2. a daring, heroic ~ 3. a ~ from

rescue II *v.* (D; tr.) to ~ from

research *n.* 1. to conduct, do, pursue ~ 2. detailed, laborious, painstaking, solid, thorough; independent; original ~ 3. animal; market; medical; operations; scientific; space ~ 4. ~ in, into, on (~ on the development of an electric engine)

researcher *n.* an independent ~

resemblance *n.* 1. to bear a ~ to 2. a close, strong; remote; striking ~ 3. a family ~ 4. a ~ between; to

resemble *v.* to ~ closely

resent *v.* 1. to ~ bitterly, strongly 2. (G) she ~s having to wait 3. (J) we ~ him being the center of attraction 4. (K) we ~ed his being the center of attraction

resentful *adj.* 1. bitterly ~ 2. ~ about, at, of

resentment *n.* 1. to arouse, stir up ~ 2. to bear, feel, harbor ~ 3. to express, voice ~ 4. bitter, deep, profound, sullen ~ 5. ~ about; against; at, towards 6. ~ that + clause (they felt ~ that nobody paid attention to their request)

reservation *n.* ['booking'] 1. to make a ~ (we made a ~ at a very good hotel) 2. to confirm a ~ 3. to cancel a ~ 4. an advance; hotel, motel ~ ['qualification'] 5. a mental ~ 6. without ~ ['tract of land'] 7. an Indian; military ~

reservations *n.* ['doubts'] 1. to have ~ 2. deep, strong ~ 3. ~ about (do you have any ~ about the agreement?)

reserve I *n.* ['restraint, coolness'] 1. to display, show ~ 2. to break down smb.'s ~ ['limitation, restriction'] 3. without ~ (to accept a proposal without ~) ['availability'] 4. in ~ (to hold/keep smt. in ~) ['tract of land'] 5. a nature ~ ['military force kept available for future use'] 6. the active; inactive ~

reserve II *v.* 1. (D; tr.) ('to set aside') to ~ for (these seats are ~d for the handicapped) 2. (esp. AE) (D; tr.) ('to order in advance') to ~ for (we have ~d a room for you) (BE usu. has *to book*)

reserved *adj.* ['restrained, reticent'] 1. ~ about 2. ~ towards, with

reserves *n.* ['forces kept available for future use'] (usu. mil. and sports) 1. to call out, call up the ~ 2. to commit one's ~ 3. limited; limitless ~

reservoir *n.* an artificial; natural ~

reside *v.* (P; intr.) they ~ in London

residence *n.* ['home, abode'] 1. to establish, take up ~ 2. to change one's (place of) ~ 3. one's legal; permanent ~ ['state of being officially present'] 4. in ~ (a poet in ~)

resign v. 1. (D; intr.) to ~ from (she ~ed from her job) 2. (d; refl.) to ~ to (he ~ed himself to his fate)

resignation n. ['act of resigning'] 1. to hand in, offer, submit, tender; withdraw one's ~ 2. to accept; reject smb.'s ~ 3. a ~ from ['acceptance, submission'] 4. ~ to (one's fate)

resigned adj. ['submissive'] ~ to (~ to one's fate)

resist v. (G) they couldn't ~ making fun of him

resistance n. 1. to offer, put up ~ 2. to break down, crush, overcome, overpower, put down, smash, wear down ~ 3. determined, fierce, stiff, strong, stubborn, valiant ~ 4. armed; non-violent, passive; spotty; weak ~ 5. ~ to (~ to a disease)

resistant adj. ~ to (~ to change)

resolute adj. ~ in (~ in one's decision to do smt.)

resolution n. ['decision'] 1. to propose a ~ 2. to adopt, pass a ~ 3. a joint ~ (of Congress) 4. a ~ to + inf. (they adopted a ~ to increase membership dues) 5. a ~ that + clause; subj. (a ~ was passed that aid to farmers be/should be increased) ['vow'] 6. to make a (New Year's) ~ ['resolve'] 7. firm ~ ['fine detail'] (optics) 8. sharp ~

resolve I n. 1. to display, show ~ 2. to strengthen one's ~ 3. (a) firm ~

resolve II v. 1. (D; tr.) to ~ into (to ~ an issue into several component parts) 2. (E) she ~d to work harder 3. (L) we ~d that we would resist to the end

resolved adj. (usu. does not stand alone) 1. firmly ~ 2. ~ to + inf. (we are ~ to finish the work on time) 3. (formal) ~ that + clause; subj. (be it ~ that an official delegation be/should be sent)

resort I n. ['recourse'] 1. (formal) to have ~ to 2. a last ~ (as a last ~) ['recreational center'] 3. a health; holiday, vacation (esp. AE); summer; winter ~

resort II v. (d; intr.) to ~ to (to ~ to trickery)

resources n. 1. to develop; exploit, tap ~ 2. to husband; marshall; pool, share one's ~ 3. economic; natural; untapped ~ (to exploit natural ~) 4. the ~ to + inf. (we have the ~ to do the job)

respect I n. ['esteem'] 1. to pay, show ~ to 2. to command, inspire ~ (she commands ~ from everyone = she commands everyone's ~) 3. to earn, win; lose smb.'s ~ 4. deep, profound, sincere; due; grudging; mutual ~ 5. ~ for (~ for the law) 6. out of ~ (she did it out of ~ for her parents) 7. in ~ (to hold smb. in ~) 8. with ~ (with all due ~, I disagree) ['regard'] 9. in a ~ (in this ~; in all ~s) 10. in, with ~ to

respect II v. (D; tr.) to ~ as (to ~ smb. as a scholar)

respectful adj. ~ of, to (~ of one's elders)

respects n. to pay; send one's ~

respiration n. artificial; labored; normal ~ (to give smb. artificial ~)

respite n. 1. to allow, give ~ (we allowed them no ~) 2. a brief, temporary ~ 3. a ~ from (there was no ~ from the cold) 4. without ~

respond v. 1. (D; intr.) ('to react') to ~ by (they ~ed by walking out) 2. (D; intr.) to ~ to ('to answer') to ~ to a letter 3. (D; intr.) ('to react') to ~ to (to ~ to treatment)

response n. 1. to elicit, evoke a ~ 2. to give a ~ 3. a glib; sullen; witty ~ 4. a lukewarm ~ 5. a ~ to 6. in ~ to

responsibility n. ['accountability'] ['obligation'] 1. to accept, assume, shoulder, take, take on (a) ~ 2. to bear, exercise; share (the) ~ 3. to dodge, evade, shirk ~ 4. an awesome; clear; grave, great, heavy, terrible (colloq.) ~ 5. collective; personal ~ 6. the ultimate ~ 7. ~ lies with smb. 8. ~ for (to bear the ~ for the smooth operation of the assembly line) 9. the ~ to + inf. (everyone has the ~ to pay taxes) 10. ~ that + clause; subj. (it was her ~ that all members be/should be notified) 11. on one's ~ (she did it on her own ~) ['blame'] 12. to lay the ~ at smb.'s door 13. to admit, claim ~ (a shadowy group claimed ~ for the hijacking) 14. to disclaim ~ 15. ~ for

responsible adj. ~ for; to (politicians are ~ to the voters; people are ~ for their actions)

responsive adj. ~ to (~ to flattery)

responsiveness n. ~ to

rest I n. ['repose'] 1. to have, take a ~ 2. a well-earned ~ 3. bed; complete ~ 4. ~ from 5. at ~ 6. (misc.) to go to one's eternal ~ ('to die'); laid to ~ ('buried'); at parade ~ (mil.); to set one's mind at ~ ['support'] 7. an armrest; chin ~

rest II v. 1. (d; intr.) ('to stand') to ~ on (the statue ~s on a pedestal) 2. (d; intr.) ('to depend') to ~ with (the decision ~s with the court)

restaurant n. 1. to manage, operate, run a ~ 2. an elegant, first-class ~ 3. a dairy; fast-food ~ 4. (BE) a licensed ~ (that may sell alcoholic drinks)

restful adj. ~ to + inf. (it's ~ just to sit and read = it's ~ just sitting and reading)

restitution n. 1. to make; offer ~ 2. ~ for 3. ~ to

restore v. (d; tr.) to ~ to (to ~ smb. to her/his former position)

restrain v. (D; refl., tr.) to ~ from (to ~ smb. from committing violence)

restraint n. ['control'] ['act of restraining'] 1. to display, exercise, show ~ 2. to cast off, fling off, shake off (all) ~ 3. (legal) prior ~ 4. ~ in (they showed ~ in responding to the provocation) 5. in ~ of (in ~ of trade) ['device for restraining'] 6. to apply, put on ~s

restrict v. (D; refl., tr.) to ~ to (the chair ~ed discussion to items on the official agenda; she ~ed herself to two meals a day)

restriction n. 1. to impose, place, put ~s or 2. to lift a ~ 3. ~s on

result I n. 1. to achieve, produce ~s 2. to evaluate, measure; tabulate ~s 3. to negate, nullify, undo a ~ 4. a direct; final; lasting; logical; negative; net; positive; striking; surprising ~ 5. overall; surefire ~s

result II v. 1. (d; intr.) to ~ from (her death ~ed from an overdose of pills) 2. (d; intr.) to ~ in (the argument ~ed in a fight)

resume v. (G) she ~d working

resurrect v. (D; tr.) to ~ from (to ~ smb. from the dead)

resuscitation n. 1. to give ~ (the victim was given mouth-to-mouth ~) 2. cardiopulmonary (= CPR); mouth-to-mouth ~

retail I *adv.* to buy; sell ~

retail II *v.* to ~ for (it ~s for fifty dollars)

retainer *n.* ['advance fee'] to put down a ~

retaliate *v.* (D; intr.) to ~ against; for (to ~ against the enemy for shelling civilian targets)

retaliation *n.* 1. massive ~ 2. an act of ~ 3. in ~ for

retardant *n.* a fire; rust ~

retardation *n.* mental ~

retarded *adj.* mentally ~

retell *v.* (usu. B; occ. A) she has retold the story to us many times

reticence *n.* 1. to display ~ 2. ~ about

reticent *adj.* ~ about

retina *n.* a detached ~

retire *v.* 1. (D; intr.) ('to end one's working career') to ~ from (to ~ from one's job) 2. (D; intr.) ('to withdraw') to ~ to (the troops ~d to safer positions; let's ~ to the drawing room)

retirement *n.* 1. to go into ~ 2. to come out of ~ 3. compulsory, forced; early ~; semi-retirement; voluntary ~ 4. in ~ (to live in~)

retool *v.* 1. (D; intr., tr.) to ~ for (to ~ for wartime production) 2. (H) to ~ a plant to build prefabricated houses

retort I *n.* 1. to make a ~ 2. a ~ to

retort II *v.* (L) he ~ed heatedly that he needed no favors

retraction *n.* to issue a ~

retreat I *n.* ['withdrawal'] 1. to beat, carry out, make a ~ (they made good their ~; the regiment carried out its ~ in good order) 2. a hasty, precipitate ~ 3. full ~ (in full ~) 4. a strategic; tactical ~ ['signal for withdrawal'] 5. to sound ~ ['music for a flag-lowering ceremony'] (mil.) 6. to play, sound ~ ['secluded gathering'] 7. to go on (a) ~ 8. a religious; weekend ~ ['secluded spot'] 9. a country ~

retreat II *v.* (D; intr.) to ~ from; to (our troops ~ed from the border to safer positions; our government has ~ed from its hard-line position)

retribution *n.* 1. to exact ~ from; to visit ~ on 2. divine ~

retrieval *n.* data, information ~

retrieve *v.* (D; tr.) to ~ from (to ~ data from a computer)

retroactive *adj.* ~ to

retrorocket *n.* to activate, fire a ~

retrospect *n.* in ~

retrospection *n.* in ~

return I *n.* ['statement about income'] 1. to file a (tax) ~ 2. a joint; tax ~ ['going back, coming back'] 3. a ~ from; to (his ~ to civilian life) 4. on smb.'s ~ (on their ~ from a trip abroad) 5. the point of no ~ ['profit'] 6. to yield a ~ (this investment will yield a ~ of ten percent) ['compensation'] 7. in ~ (to give smt. in ~) 8. in ~ for

return II *v.* 1. (B) she ~ed the money to me 2. (D; intr., tr.) to ~ from; to (to ~ from a holiday/vacation; she ~ed to her home; to ~ books to the library)

returns *n.* ['election results'] 1. early; election; final; late ~ ['misc.'] 2. many happy ~ of the day ('happy birthday')

reunion *n.* 1. to hold a ~ 2. a touching ~ 3. an annual; class; family ~

reunite *v.* (D; tr.) to ~ with (to ~ smb. with her/his family)

reveal *v.* 1. (B) she ~ed the secret to us 2. (L; to) he ~ed (to us) that he had been ill for years 3. (M) the document ~ed her to be a conscientious employee

reveille *n.* (mil.) 1. to play, sound ~ 2. to fall out for ~

revel *v.* (D; intr.) to ~ in

revelation *n.* 1. to make a ~ 2. an amazing, astonishing, astounding, startling, stunning, surprising ~ 3. (a) divine ~ 4. a ~ to (the story was a ~ to us) 5. a ~ that + clause (the ~ that she had been in prison surprised everybody)

revenge I *n.* 1. to exact, get, have, take ~ on 2. sweet ~ 3. ~ for; on (to take ~ on smb. for smt.) 4. in ~ for

revenge II (BE) see **avenge**

revenue *n.* ['income'] 1. to generate, produce, yield ~ 2. to collect ~ 3. government ~ 4. Inland (BE), Internal (AE) Revenue 5. one's annual, yearly; monthly; weekly ~

reverberate *v.* (D; intr.) to ~ through (the cheers ~d through the arena)

revere *v.* (D; tr.) to ~ for

reverence *n.* 1. to feel ~ 2. to show ~ 3. deep, profound ~ 4. ~ for 5. in ~ (to hold smb. in ~)

reverie *n.* 1. to indulge in ~s 2. to be lost in ~

reverse *n.* ['setback'] 1. to suffer, sustain a ~ 2. a serious; slight; tactical ~ 3. financial ~s ['reverse gear'] 4. to put a transmission into ~ 5. to go into, shift into ~ 6. in ~ ['reversing mechanism'] 7. an (automatic) ribbon ~ (on a typewriter)

reversion *n.* ~ to

revert *v.* (d; intr.) to ~ to (her property ~ed to the state; to ~ to enlisted status)

review I *n.* ['renewed study'] (AE) 1. to do a ~ 2. a comprehensive ~ ['military ceremony'] 3. to hold a ~ (of troops) 4. to pass in ~ ['critical evaluation'] 5. to do, write a ~ (of a book) 6. to get, receive a ~ 7. a favorable, positive, rave; negative, unfavorable ~ (the play got rave ~s) 8. a book ~ 9. (legal) judicial ~ 10. under ~ (the entire matter is under ~)

review II *v.* (AE) (D; intr., tr.) ('to study again') to ~ for (to ~ for an exam)

revise (BE) see **review II**

revision *n.* ['renewed study'] (BE) 1. to do ~ (he had to do some ~ for the examination) ['revised version'] 2. to make a ~

revolt I *n.* 1. to incite, stir up a ~ 2. to crush, put down, quash, quell a ~ 3. a peasant ~ 4. a ~ breaks out, erupts 5. a ~ against

revolt II *v.* (D; intr.) to ~ against, at

revolting *adj.* 1. ~ to 2. ~ to + inf. (it's ~ to contemplate such a possibility) 3. ~ that + clause (it's ~ that they use such obscene language)

revolution *n.* ['overthrow of a regime'] 1. to foment, stir up a ~ 2. to carry out, conduct, fight; organize a ~ 3. to crush, defeat, put down a ~ 4. a cultural; industrial; palace; political; sexual; social ~ ['complete orbital turn'] 5. to make a ~ 6. a ~ about, around, round

revolve v. (D; intr.) to ~ about, around, round (the earth ~s around the sun)

revolver see **pistol 1-4, 6**

revue n. to produce, put on, stage a ~

revulsion n. 1. to express; feel ~ 2. deep, utmost ~ 3. a feeling of ~ 4. ~ against, at, towards

reward I n. 1. to offer, post; pay a ~ 2. to claim; reap; receive a ~ 3. a just; tangible; well-deserved ~ 4. a ~ for

reward II v. (D; tr.) to ~ for; with (she was ~ed with a bonus for her outstanding work)

rhapsody n. to compose; play a ~

rhetoric n. 1. to resort to, spout ~ 2. eloquent; impassioned, passionate; soothing ~

rheumatism n. 1. to develop ~ 2. to suffer from ~ 3. chronic ~

rhubarb n. (slang) ['argument'] 1. to get into a ~ 2. a ~ about

rhyme I n. 1. a nursery ~ 2. (poetry) a feminine; masculine ~ 3. (misc.) without ~ or reason ('with no apparent reason')

rhyme II v. (D; intr., tr.) to ~ with (this word ~s with that word; to ~ one word with another)

rhythm n. 1. (a) frenzied; pulsating; steady; undulating ~ 2. to a ~ (to dance to the ~ of drums)

rib n. 1. to poke smb. in the ~s 2. a false; floating ~ 3. (misc.) to break, fracture a ~

ribbing n. ['teasing'] to take a ~

ribbon n. ['strip of ink-impregnated cloth on a typewriter'] 1. to change a ~ 2. a typewriter ~ 3. the ~ reverses (automatically) ['misc.'] 4. a blue ~ ('a first prize'); to cut to ~s ('to destroy completely')

rice n. 1. to mill, winnow ~ 2. brown; enriched; polished; quick-cooking; wild ~

rich I adj. ~ in (~ in coal deposits)

rich II n. the idle ~

riches n. to amass ~

ricksha, rickshaw n. 1. to pedal; pull a ~ 2. to ride in a ~

ricochet v. (D; intr.) to ~ off

rid II v. 1. (d; refl., tr.) to ~ of (to ~ the town of rats) 2. to get ~ of

riddance n. (colloq.) ['act of getting rid of smt.'] good ~! (good ~ to bad rubbish!)

riddle n. 1. to solve a ~ 2. (misc.) to speak in ~s

ride I n. ['short trip by vehicle, on horseback'] 1. to catch, get; go for, go on, have (BE), take a ~ 2. (colloq.) to bum, hitch, thumb a ~ (as a hitchhiker) 3. to give (smb.) a ~; to take (smb) for a ~ 4. a joy; train ~ (to go on a joy ~ in a stolen car) ['attraction'] (in an amusement park) 5. to go on the ~s ['misc.'] 6. to take smb. for a ~ ('to victimize smb.')

ride II v. 1. (d; intr.) to ~ at (the ship was ~ing at anchor) 2. (d; intr.) to ~ by, in, on (to ~ in/on a bus) 3. (d; intr.) to ~ from; to (we ~ to work by bus) 4. (d; intr.) to ~ on ('to be wagered on') (a lot of money was ~ing on one horse) 5. (misc.) to ~ sidesaddle; to ~ roughshod over smb. ('to treat smb. in an abusive manner')

ride out v. (d; intr.) to ~ to (he rode out to the procession)

rider n. ['amendment, addition'] to attach a ~ to (a bill)

ridicule n. 1. draw, incur ~ 2. to heap, pour ~ on smb. 3. (misc.) to hold smb. up to ~

ridiculous adj. 1. ~ to + inf. (it's ~ to apply for that position) 2. ~ that + clause (it's ~ that they could not receive visas)

rife adj. ['abounding in'] 1. (cannot stand alone) ~ with (the city was ~ with rumors) ['misc.'] 2. to run ~ ('to be out of control') (rumors about them are running ~)

rifle I n. 1. to fire a ~ 2. to aim, point; level a ~ 3. to load a ~ 4. to handle, operate a ~ 5. to assemble; disassemble a ~ 6. an air; automatic; high-powered; hunting; recoilless; semiautomatic ~ 7. a ~ fires, goes off; jams; misfires

rifle II v. (d; intr.) to ~ through ('to search') to ~ through the drawers)

rift n. 1. to cause a ~ 2. to heal a ~ 3. an ideological ~ 4. a ~ among, between

rig n. ['large vehicle'] 1. to drive a ~ ['equipment'] 2. an oil-drilling ~

right I adj. 1. ~ about (to be ~ about smt.) 2. ~ in (you were ~ in assuming that) 3. ~ to + inf. (it was ~ of her to refuse = she was ~ to refuse) 4. ~ that + clause (it's not ~ that they should be treated in that manner) 5. (misc.) all ~; just ~; she is the ~ person for the job = she is ~ for the job (colloq.); to be in one's ~ mind ('to be sane'); to put things ~ ('to straighten things out')

right II n. ['that which is due'] 1. to achieve; gain a ~ (to achieve full civil ~s) 2. to enjoy, exercise, have a ~ 3. to assert, claim a ~ 4. to protect, safeguard smb.'s ~s 5. to abdicate, relinquish, renounce, sign away, waive a ~ 6. to deny (smb.) a ~ 7. a divine; exclusive, sole; inalienable; inherent; legal; natural; vested ~ 8. civil; conjugal; consumers'; film; grazing; human; individual; mineral; patients'; political; property; squatters'; states'; veterans'; voting; women's ~s 9. the ~ of assembly; asylum; a free press; free speech 10. a ~ to (the ~ to privacy) 11. the ~ to + inf. (the ~ to exist; you have the ~ to remain silent) 12. within one's ~s 13. (misc.) a bill of ~s ['right side'] 14. on, to the ~ ['conservative group'] 15. the extreme, far ~ ['punch delivered with the right hand'] 16. to deliver, throw a ~ 17. a hard, stiff ~ 18. a ~ to (a ~ to the jaw) ['turn to the right'] 19. to take a ~ ['misc.'] 20. in the ~ ('in accordance with the truth, accepted standards'); she has a promising career in her own ~; as of (BE), by ~ ('properly'); by ~ of (by ~ of conquest); ~ and wrong; within one's ~s (you are within your ~s not to answer); by ~s ('ideally')

right-of-way n. 1. to have the ~ 2. to give, yield the ~ 3. the ~ over (ambulances have the ~ over other vehicles)

rigid adj. ~ about, on (~ on points of procedure)

rigor mortis n. ~ sets in

rile v. (R) it ~d me that they were paying no taxes

riled adj. (colloq.) ['annoyed'] 1. ~ at 2. ~ that + clause (she was ~ that nobody believed her story)

rim n. along; on; up to a ~ (on the ~ of a crater)

rind n. lemon; melon ~ USAGE NOTE: One

usu. speaks of the *rind* of a melon, the *peel* or
the *rind* of a lemon, and the *peel* of an orange.
ring I *n*. ['circular band'] 1. a diamond; gold; sap-
phire ~ 2. an earring; engagement; signet; wedding ~ 3. a key; napkin; teething ~ 4. a piston ~
5. smoke ~s (to blow smoke ~s) 6. (misc.) to wear
a ~ on one's finger ['group'] 7. a smuggling; spy ~
['enclosed square area'] 8. the prize ~ ['misc.'] 9.
to run ~s around smb. ('to far outperform smb.')
ring II *n*. ['sound'] a false, hollow ~ (there was a
false ~ to his words)
ring III *v*. 1. (D; tr.) to ~ for ('to call by ringing')
(to ~ for the maid) 2. (s) to ~ false; hollow (her
words ~ false)
ringside *n*. at ~
ring up *v*. (D; tr.) ('to record') to ~ on (to ~ a bill
on a cash register)
rink *n*. 1. an ice-hockey; ice-skating; roller-skat-
ing ~ 2. at a ~
riot *n*. 1. to cause, foment, incite, instigate, spark
(AE), spark off (BE), stir up, touch off a ~ 2. to
crush, put down, quell a ~ 3. a communal; food;
race ~ 4. a ~ breaks out, erupts 5. (misc.) to run
~ ('to act wildly')
riot act *n*. ['stern warning'] to read the ~ to
rioting *n*. communal ~
rip *v*. (colloq.) (d; intr.) to ~ into ('to attack') (the
politician ~ped into her opponent)
ripe *adj*. ~ for (~ for the picking; the time is ~ for
action)
ripen *v*. (d; intr.) to ~ into (their friendship ~ed
into love)
ripple *v*. (P; intr.) applause ~d through the
auditorium
rise I *n*. ['origin'] 1. to give ~ to ['angry reaction']
2. to get a ~ out of smb. ['pay increase'] (BE) 3. an
across-the-board ~ 4. a ~ in (wages) (AE has
raise) ['increase'] 5. a sharp ~ 6. a ~ in (a ~ in
prices) 7. on the ~ (prices are on the ~) ['success']
8. a meteoric ~
rise II *v*. 1. (D; intr.) ('to revolt') to ~ against (to
~ against tyranny) 2. (D; intr.) ('to ascend') to ~
from (smoke rose from the chimney) 3. (d; intr.)
('to be resurrected') to ~ from (to ~ from the
dead; to ~ from the ashes) 4. (d; intr.) ('to
ascend') to ~ to (to ~ to the surface; to ~ to one's
feet) 5. (d; intr.) ('to be equal') to ~ to (to ~ to the
challenge; can you ~ to the occasion?)
risk I *n*. 1. to assume, incur, run, take; face;
spread a ~ (to run the ~ of being outvoted) 2. to
outweigh a ~ (the advantages outweigh the ~s) 3.
a calculated; grave, great, high; low; security ~
(to take a calculated ~; he is a security ~) 4. a ~
to (a ~ to safety) 5. a ~ to + inf. (it was a ~ to
enter that area) 6. at (a) ~ (at one's own ~; at the
~ of being ridiculed)
risk II *v*. 1. (G) she ~ed losing everything 2. (K)
he ~ed their turning against him
risky *adj*. ~ to + inf. (it's ~ to play with fire)
rite *n*. 1. to perform a ~ 2. a pagan; religious; solemn ~ 3. last ~s (to administer last ~s) 4. fertility
~s
ritual *n*. 1. to go through; perform a ~ 2. to make
a ~ of smt. 3. a pagan; religious; solemn ~

rival I *n*. a ~ for; in
rival II *v*. (D; tr.) to ~ in (to ~ smb. in skill)
rivalry *n*. 1. to stir up ~ 2. intense, keen, strong ~
3. sibling ~ 4. ~ among, between; for; in; with
(keen ~ between them for the award)
river *n*. 1. to cross; ford a ~ 2. to dredge a ~ 3. a
~ floods; flows (into the sea); overflows (its
banks); recedes; rises 4. down ~; up ~ 5. (misc.)
to sell down the ~ ('to betray')
rivet *n*. to drive a ~ (into metal)
riveted *adj*. (cannot stand alone) ~ on, to (all eyes
were ~ on the door; she stood ~ to the spot)
road *n*. 1. to resurface; surface a ~ 2. an impassa-
ble; rocky (also fig.); rough (also fig.); smooth
(also fig.); straight; winding ~ 3. a back, country;
dirt (AE), unpaved; macadam; main, trunk (BE);
mountain; paved, surfaced; ring (BE); secondary;
service; slip (BE); toll ~ 4. intersecting; merging
~s 5. a ~ goes, leads, runs somewhere 6. a ~
curves, winds 7. a ~ from; to (the ~ to town) 8. in,
on a ~ 9. (also fig.) on the ~ (on the ~ to recovery) 10. (misc.) to take a ~ (they took the wrong
~); one for the ~ ('a final drink')
road block *n*. 1. to establish, set up a ~ 2. to
remove a ~ 3. to break through, crash through,
run a ~
roadhouse *n*. (AE) at a ~ (to stop at a ~ for a
drink)
roadside *n*. on the ~
road sign *n*. to put up a ~
roadster *n*. (obsol.) to drive a ~
roadwork *n*. ['running'] to do ~ (the boxer did ~
every day)
roam *v*. (P; intr.) to ~ around town
roar I *n*. a deep ~
roar II *v*. 1. (D; intr.) to ~ at 2. (D; intr.) to ~
with (to ~ with laughter)
roast *n*. 1. to make a ~ 2. a chuck; eye; lamb;
pork; pot; rib; veal ~
rob *v*. (D; tr.) to ~ of (the bandits ~bed the pas-
sengers of their money)
robbery *n*. 1. to commit (a) ~ 2. armed; bank;
daylight (BE) ('overcharging'); highway (fig.) ~
rock I *n*. ['stone'] 1. to throw a ~ at (see Usage
Note) 2. jagged; rugged ~s 3. (misc.) solid as a ~
USAGE NOTE: In BE, a *rock* is usu. too big to
be thrown. Thus, *to throw a rock at smb.* is esp.
AE.
rock II *n*. ['type of music'] punk ~; rock-and-roll
rock III *v*. (D; tr.) ('to lull') to ~ to (to ~ a baby
to sleep)
rocket *n*. ['device propelled by a rocket engine or
explosives'] 1. to fire; launch a ~ 2. a booster;
liquid-fuel; long-range; multistage; solid-fuel ~
['reprimand'] (colloq.) (BE) 3. to give smb. a ~ 4.
to get a ~
rocket ship see the Usage Note for **ship**
rocks *n*. 1. on the ~ ('with ice') (scotch on the ~)
2. on the ~ ('ruined')
rod *n*. ['bar, shaft'] 1. a connecting; divining; lightning; piston ~; ramrod ['pistol'] (slang) (AE) 2. to
pack ('carry') a ~ ['metal track'] 3. a curtain;
traverse ~ ['pole'] 4. a fishing ~ ['misc.'] 5. to ride
the ~s (AE) ('to ride illegally in the framework

below a railroad car')
rodent *n.* ~s gnaw
rodeo *n.* to hold, stage a ~
roe *n.* 1. to spawn ~ 2. hard; soft ~
role *n.* 1. to assume, take (on) a ~ 2. to assign, hand out ~s 3. to interpret; perform, play; understudy a ~ 4. an active; key; leading; passive; secondary; starring; supporting; title ~ 5. (misc.) cast in the ~ of
roll I *n.* ['list of names'] 1. to call, take the ~ 2. an honor ~ (AE; BE has *roll of honour*) ['small cake or bread'] 3. to bake ~s 4. a hamburger; jelly (AE), swiss (BE); kaiser (esp. AE); poppyseed; sweet ~
roll II *v.* 1. (A) ~ the ball to me; or: ~ me the ball 2. (C) ~ a cigarette for me; or: ~ me a cigarette 3. (d; intr., tr.) to ~ down (the children ~ed down the hill; we ~ed the barrels down the incline) 4. (d; intr.) to ~ in (to ~ in the mud) 5. (d; intr.) to ~ off (the football ~ed off the field; new cars ~ed off the assembly line) 6. (d; intr.) to ~ with ('to lessen the impact by moving in the same direction') (he ~ed with the punch)
rollaway, rollaway bed *n.* to fold up; open up a ~
roll up *v.* 1. (d; tr.) to ~ in (to ~ smt. up in a blanket) 2. (D; intr., tr.) to ~ into (to ~ smt. into a ball) 3. (D; intr., tr.) to ~ to (the ball ~ed up to me)
romance *n.* 1. to find ~ 2. a whirlwind ~
romanticize *v.* (D; intr.) to ~ about
romp *v.* (D; intr.) to ~ with
roof *n.* 1. to install a ~ 2. a gabled; shingle; slate ~ 3. a ~ leaks 4. (misc.) to raise the ~ ('to complain vociferously'); to hit the ~ (AE) ('to lose one's temper')
room *n.* ['partitioned part of a building'] 1. to rent a ~ from 2. to let (BE), let out (BE), rent, rent out (AE) a ~ to 3. to book (BE), reserve a ~ 4. an adjoining; back; baggage (AE); banquet ~; bathroom; bedroom; board; changing (BE), dressing; common (BE); dining; double; drawing, front (BE), living, sitting; family; game, recreation, rumpus (AE); guest; locker; lumber (BE), storage; reading ~; showroom; single; spare; utility; waiting ~ 5. (in a hospital) a delivery; emergency (AE); hospital; operating (esp. AE; BE prefers *operating theatre*); private; recovery; semiprivate ~ 6. a ladies', powder; men's (AE); rest (AE) ~; (BE; euphemism) the smallest ~ ('the room with the toilet') 7. a furnished; rented ~; (a) ~ to let (now BE) ['space'] 8. to make ~ for 9 to occupy, take up ~ 10. headroom; legroom 11. (in a theater) standing ~ only 12. ~ for (there is ~ for another bed) 13. ~ to + inf. (the children have ~ to play) ['possibility'] 14. ~ for (there is no ~ for doubt) USAGE NOTE: In the US, a *bathroom* usu. contains a toilet, sink, and bathtub or shower. In GB, it must contain a bath or shower and may have a toilet and washbasin. In CE, a *cloakroom* is a place in a public building where coats, umbrellas, etc. may be left temporarily. In GB, it can also denote a small room on the ground floor of a house near the front door: this room often contains a toilet and a place for hanging coats.

rooster *n.* (esp. AE) a ~ cock-a-doodle-does, crows, goes cock-a-doodle-doo (BE has *cock*)
root I *n.* 1. to take ~ 2. to put down ~s; to strike ~(s) 3. deep ~s 4. (mathematics) a cube; square ~ 5. by the ~s (to pull smt. up by the ~s) 6. (misc.) at the ~ of the matter; to go back to, search for one's ~s; to get at the ~ of smt. ('to tackle smt. at the source'); (BE) ~ and branch ('wholly' ; the ~ of all evil; her ~s are in Canada; a ~ cause
root II *v.* (AE) (D; intr.) to ~ for ('to support') (to ~ for a team)
root about, root around *v.* (D; intr.) to ~ for ('to search for') (to ~ in a stack of papers for a specific document)
rooted *adj.* 1. deeply ~ 2. ~ in (~ in poverty) 3. ~ to (~ to the spot)
rooter *n.* (AE) an ardent ~
rope I *n.* 1. to jump, skip ~ 2. to ease up on; tighten a ~ 3. a loose, slack; tight ~ 4. a length; piece of ~ 5. by a ~ (to lower smt. by a ~) 6. (misc.) (boxing and fig.) on the ~s ('in a weak, vulnerable position')
rope II *v.* (colloq.) (d; tr.) to ~ into ('to induce') (to ~ smb. into doing smt.)
rosary *n.* to pray, recite, say the ~
rose *n.* 1. a long-stemmed; rambling; wild ~ 2. a bouquet of ~s
roster *n.* 1. to make up a ~ 2. a duty; personnel ~
rostrum *n.* 1. to get up on, mount the ~ 2. from; on a ~
rot *n.* 1. black; creeping; dry ~ 2. (misc.) to talk ~ ('to talk nonsense')
rotate *v.* (D; intr.) to ~ on (the earth ~s on its axis)
rotation *n.* 1. to make a ~ 2. crop ~
rote *n.* ['repetition'] by ~ (to learn by ~)
rotten *adj.* (colloq.) ~ to + inf. (it was ~ of him to do that)
rouge *n.* to apply, put on ~
rough I *adj.* (colloq.) ['not gentle'] 1. ~ on (you've been pretty ~ on the children) ['difficult'] 2. ~ to + inf. (it's ~ to work at night = it's ~ working at night) 3. (misc.) it was ~ on him, losing his job like that
rough II *n.* ['unpolished condition'] in the ~ (a diamond in the ~)
roughshod *adv.* to ride ~ over smb. ('to treat smb. in an inconsiderate manner')
roulette *n.* 1. to play ~ 2. Russian ~
round *n.* ['unit of ammunition'] 1. to fire a ~; to get a ~ off 2. an incoming ~ (of artillery fire) 3. the ~ jammed ['drinks served to everyone in a group'] 4. to buy; order a ~ (of drinks) ['complete game'] 5. to play, shoot a ~ (of golf) ['song sung in unison in which each part is repeated'] 6. to sing a ~
roundabout *n.* to ride a ~ (BE; CE has *merry-go-round*)
roundhouse *n.* ['type of blow'] to throw a ~
rounds *n.* to make one's ~ (the doctor was making her ~)
rouse *v.* (D; tr.) to ~ from, out of (to ~ smb. out of bed)

rouser *n.* a rabble ~

rout I *n.* a complete, utter ~

rout II *v.* to ~ completely, utterly

route I *n.* 1. to map out, plan a ~ 2. to follow, take a ~ 3. a circuitous; devious; direct; indirect; scenic ~ (to take the scenic ~) 4. a bus; newspaper; streetcar (AE), tram (BE); truck (AE) ~ 5. an overland; sea; trade ~

route II *v.* (d; tr.) to ~ to (to ~ a memorandum to the appropriate persons)

routine *n.* (a) daily, ordinary; dull ~

row I /rou/ *n.* ['arrangement in a straight line'] 1. an even, straight ~ 2. in a ['misc.'] 3. death ~ ('cell block where prisoners await execution') (on death ~); skid ~ (AE) ('area in a city where destitute persons congregate') (on skid ~)

row II /rau/ *n.* 1. to kick up, make, raise a ~ 2. to have a ~ 3. a ~ about, over; with (to have a ~ with smb. about a trifle)

row III /rau/ *v.* (D; intr.) to ~ about, over; with

rowboat *n.* (AE) to row a ~

rowing *n.* 1. to go ~ 2. to go in for ~

rowing-boat (BE) see **rowboat**

row out *v.* (d; intr.) to ~ to (to ~ to an island)

royalty *n.* ['percentage of revenue'] 1. to pay a ~/ ~ties on (the publisher paid them ~ties on their dictionaries) 2. to bring in, earn ~ties (the book brings in handsome ~ties) 3. author's ~ties

rub *v.* 1. (D; intr., tr.) to ~ against (one part was ~bing against the other; ~ your hand against this surface) 2. (d; tr.) to ~ into (to ~ lotion into one's skin) 3. (N; used with an adjective) ~ it dry

rubber *n.* 1. crude; foam; sponge; synthetic ~ 2. ~ stretches (see the Usage Note for **eraser)**

rubbers *n.* (AE) ['rubber overshoes'] 1. to put on; wear ~ 2. a pair of ~

rubbish *n.* an accumulation, heap, pile of ~

rubble *n.* 1. a heap, pile of ~ 2. (misc.) to reduce smt. to ~

rubdown *n.* to give smb. a ~

Rubicon *n.* to cross the ~ ('to commit oneself irrevocably')

rub off *v.* 1. (D; intr.) to ~ on, onto (the paint ~bed off on my shirt) 2. (colloq.) (D; intr.) to ~ on, onto ('to affect') (we hoped that some of these cultural activities would ~ on our children)

rub up *v.* 1. (d; intr.) to ~ against ('to touch') (don't let the wire ~ against the pipe) 2. (colloq.) (d; intr.) to ~ against ('to have contact with') (he used to ~ against many famous movie stars)

ruck *n.* (esp. BE) ['mass of undistinguished people'] 1. the common ~ 2. above; out of the ~

ruckus *n.* to raise a ~

rude *adj.* 1. ~ of (that was ~ of him) 2. ~ to 3. ~ to + inf. (it's ~ to talk during a concert)

rudeness *n.* 1. to display, show ~ 2. ~ to

rug *n.* 1. to weave a ~ 2. to clean; shampoo; vacuum a ~ 3. a scatter, throw; shag ~

ruin I *n.* 1. complete, utter ~ 2. financial ~ (to face financial ~)

ruin II *v.* to ~ completely, utterly

ruins *n.* 1. ancient; charred, smoking ~ 2. a heap, pile of ~ 3. (misc.) to sift through the ~; to lie in ~

rule I *n.* ['regulation'] ['principle'] 1. to establish,

lay down, make (the) ~s 2. to formulate a ~ 3. to adopt a ~ 4. to apply, enforce a ~ 5. to obey, observe a ~ 6. to break, violate a ~ 7. to bend, stretch a ~ 8. to rescind, revoke a ~ 9. a firm, hard-and-fast, inflexible, strict ~ 10. a general; ground ~; the Golden Rule 11. an exclusionary (AE); gag; parliamentary ~ 12. (ling.) a deletion; rewrite; substitution ~ 13. a ~ against 14. a ~ for 15. a ~ to + inf. (it's our ~ not to smoke at staff conferences) 16. a ~ that + clause (they established a ~ that everyone must share the expenses) 17. (to be) against, in violation of the ~s 18. (misc.) the golden ~; a ~ of thumb; as a ~ ('generally'); the ~ of law ['government, reign'] 19. to establish; extend one's ~ 20. to overthrow smb.'s ~ 21. benevolent; despotic; foreign; home; majority; minority; mob; popular ~ 22. ~ over 23. under smb.'s ~ (under foreign ~) ['straightedge, ruler'] 24. a slide ~

rule II *v.* 1. (d; intr.) to ~ against (the judge ~d against the plaintiff) 2. (D; intr.) to ~ on (to ~ on a question) 3. (D; intr.) to ~ over (to ~ over a country) 4. (L; subj.) the court ~d that the witness be/should be disqualified 5. (M) the judge ~d her to be out of order 6. (N; used with an adjective) the judge ~d him incompetent to stand trial

ruler *n.* ['person who rules'] 1. to put a ~ into power 2. to overthrow, unseat a ~ 3. an absolute, despotic, dictatorial; strong; weak ~

ruling *n.* 1. to hand down (AE), make a ~ (the court handed down a ~) 2. a fair, just; unfair, unjust ~ 3. a court ~ 4. a ~ about, on 5. a ~ that + clause (the court's ~ that the company had violated the law was appealed)

rumblings *n.* ['rumors'] ~ about; of (~ of discontent were heard)

ruminate *v.* (D; intr.) ('to reflect') to ~ about, on

rummage *v.* (D; intr.) to ~ through (to ~ through old clothes)

rumor, rumour *n.* 1. to circulate, spread a ~ 2. to confirm a ~ 3. to deny; dispel, spike a ~ 4. an idle, unfounded, wild ~ 5. an unconfirmed; vague ~ 6. ~s circulate, fly, spread 7. a ~ that + clause (we heard a ~ that she was back in town) 8. a ~ about 9. (misc.) ~ has it that she will be getting married soon

rumored *adj.* (cannot stand alone) 1. ~ to + inf. (he is ~ to have escaped to Canada) 2. ~ that + clause (it is ~ that she has returned home)

rumpus *n.* (colloq.) to raise a ~

run I *n.* ['course'] 1. a ski ~ ['freedom of movement'] 2. to have free ~ of the house ['race'] 3. a cross-country ~; the mile ~ ['series of demands'] 4. a ~ on a bank ['running away'] 5. on the ~ ['trial'] 6. a dry, dummy (BE) ~ ['flight'] 7. to make a ~ (over a target) 8. a bombing ~ ['point scored'] (baseball, cricket) 9. to score a ~ 10. (baseball) a home ~ ['unraveled stitches in a stocking'] (BE often has *ladder*) 11. to get, have a ~ (in a stocking) ['duration'] 12. in the long; short ~

run II *v.* 1. (C) ('to fill') ~ a bath for me; or ~ me a bath 2. (d; intr.) to ~ across ('to meet by chance') (to ~ across an old friend) 3. (d; intr.) to

~ after ('to chase') (to ~ after a bus) 4. (esp. AE) (d; intr.) to ~ against ('to oppose') (I would not like to ~ against her in the senatorial race; popular feeling was ~ning against the president) 5. (d; intr.) ('to ply') to ~ between (this train ~s between New York and Philadelphia) 6. (d; intr.) to ~ down ('to descend quickly'); ('to pour') (to ~ down the stairs; tears ran down her face) 7. (esp. AE; BE has *stand*) (D; intr.) ('to be a candidate') to ~ for (to ~ for office; to ~ for Congress) 8. (d; intr.) ('to extend') to ~ from; to (the sale will ~ from the first of the month to the tenth; the fence ~s from the house to the road) 9. (d; intr.) to ~ in ('to be present') (ability for languages ~s in their blood; talent ~s in the family) 10. (d; intr.) to ~ into ('to meet') (to ~ into an old friend; to ~ into trouble) 11. (d; intr.) to ~ into ('to hit') (he ran into a pole) 12. (d; intr.) to ~ into ('to enter quickly') (to ~ into the house) 13. (d; intr.) to ~ into ('to amount to') (the expenses will ~ into thousands of dollars) 14. (d; intr.) ('to move quickly') to ~ off (the car ran off the road) 15. (d; tr.) ('to force') to ~ off (she ran the other car off the road) 16. (d; intr., tr.) to ~ on ('to operate') (the engine ~s on diesel oil; they ran the business on borrowed money) 17. (d; intr.) to ~ out of ('to use up') (she ran out of money) 18. (d; intr.) to ~ out of ('to leave quickly') (to ~ out of the room) 19. (d; intr.) ('to pass') to ~ through (a blue thread ~s through the cloth; a strange thought ran through her mind) 20. (d; intr.) to ~ through ('to examine') (let's ~ through the material again) 21. (d; tr.) to ~ through ('to process') (~ the data through the computer again) 22. (d; intr.) ('to go quickly') to ~ to (she ran to the doctor) 23. (d; intr.) to ~ to ('to seek help from') (he keeps ~ning to his mother; don't ~ to the police) 24. (d; intr.) to ~ to ('to amount') (the dictionary ~s to a thousand pages) 25. (d; tr.) ('to drive') to ~ to (I'll ~ you to the station) 26. (d; intr.) to ~ up ('to ascend quickly') (to ~ up the stairs) 27. (P; intr.) ('to go') the road ~s south 28. (s) supplies are ~ning low; the differences ~ deep 29. (misc.) to ~ rampant ('to run wild'); (colloq.) ~ that by me again ('repeat that for me')

run afoul *v.* (d; intr.) to ~ of (to ~ of the law)

run aground *v.* (D; intr.) to ~ on (the boat ran aground on a sandbank)

runaround *n.* (colloq.) ['delaying action'] to give smb. the ~

run around *v.* (D; intr.) to ~ with (he ~s around with a fast crowd)

run away *v.* 1. (D; intr.) to ~ from (to ~ from home) 2. (D; intr.) to ~ with

run back *v.* (D; intr.) to ~ to (he ran back to his room)

run counter *v.* (d; intr.) to ~ to (their actions ~ to their promises)

rundown *n.* ['summary'] to give smb. a ~

run down *v.* 1. (d; intr.) ('to go') to ~ to (to ~ to the grocery store) 2. (D; intr.) ('to descend quickly') to ~ to (to ~ to the bottom of the hill)

run foul *v.* see **run afoul**

rung *n.* the bottom, lowest; highest, top ~ (of a ladder)

run low *v.* (D; intr.) to ~ on (to ~ on fuel)

runner *n.* ['one who runs'] 1. a distance, long-distance ~ ['unraveled stitches in a stocking'] 2. see **run I 11**

runner-up *n.* a ~ to

running *n.* ['competition'] 1. in the ~ 2. out of the ~

run off *v.* (D; intr.) to ~ with (he ran off with his company's funds)

run out *v.* 1. (D; intr.) to ~ into (to ~ into the street) 2. (D; intr.) to ~ on ('to abandon') (he ran out on his family)

run over *v.* (d; intr.) to ~ to (she ran over to her friend's place)

run short *v.* (d; intr.) to ~ of (they never ~ of money)

run-up *n.* (BE) ['preparatory period'] a ~ to (the ~ to the election)

run up *v.* 1. (d; intr.) to ~ against ('to encounter') (to ~ against strong competition; to ~ against difficulties) 2. (D; intr.) to ~ to ('to approach quickly') (she ran up to me)

ruse *n.* a clever ~

rush I *n.* 1. a gold ~ 2. a ~ to + inf. (there was a ~ to buy tickets for the concert) 3. in a ~

rush II *v.* 1. to ~ headlong, pell-mell 2. (d; intr.) to ~ at ('to attack') 3. (D; intr.) to ~ into (to ~ headlong into a business deal) 4. (d; intr., tr.) to ~ to (to ~ to the office; to ~ to smb.'s assistance; to ~ smb. to the hospital)

rut *n.* ['groove, furrow'] 1. a deep ~ (in a road) ['dreary routine'] 2. in a ~

ruthless *adj.* ~ in (he is ~ in his methods)

rye *n.* 1. winter ~ 2. a sheaf of ~

S

sabbath *n.* 1. to keep, observe the ~ 2. to desecrate, violate the ~

sabbatical *n.* 1. to give, grant a ~ 2. to get; have; take a ~ 3. (to be, go) on a ~ (she was on a ~)

saber, sabre *n.* 1. to draw one's ~ 2. to brandish a ~ 3. (misc.) to rattle one's ~ ('to threaten to wage war')

sabotage *n.* 1. to commit ~ 2. an act of ~

sack *n.* ['bag'] 1. a mail ~ ['bed'] (colloq.) 2. to hit the ~ ('to go to bed') ['dismissal'] (colloq.) 3. to get the ~ 4. to give smb. the ~

sackcloth *n.* ['mourning'] in ~ and ashes

sacrament *n.* 1. to administer a ~ 2. to receive a ~

sacred *adj.* ~ to (the shrines were ~ to them

sacrifice I *n.* 1. to make; offer a ~ 2. a great; heroic; personal ~ 3. a human ~ 4. the supreme, ultimate ~ 5. a ~ to 6. at (a) ~ (we achieved our success at great personal ~)

sacrifice II *v.* 1. (D; refl., tr.) to ~ for (to ~ oneself for a just cause) 2. (D; refl., tr.) to ~ to (to ~ an animal to the gods)

sacrilege *n.* 1. to commit (a) ~ 2. (a) ~ to + inf. (it was ~ to speak like that)

sacrilegious *adj.* ~ to + inf. (it's ~ to speak like that)

sad *adj.* 1. ~ about (we felt ~ about the accident) 2. ~ to + inf. (it is ~ to be alone) 3. ~ that + clause (it's ~ that we could not see each other)

sadden *v.* (R) it ~ed me to watch him turn into an alcoholic; it ~ed her that she would never see them again

saddened *adj.* ~ to + inf. (we were ~ to learn of her death)

saddle I *n.* 1. to put a ~ on (a horse) 2. an English; stock, western ~ 3. in the ~

saddle II *v.* 1. (D; tr.) to ~ for (they ~d a gentle pony for the child) 2. (d; tr.) to ~ with (to ~ smb. with an unpleasant task

saddle sore *n.* to develop ~s

sadism *n.* to display ~

sadness *n.* 1. to express; feel ~ 2. deep, profound ~ 3. ~ over

sad sack *n.* (slang) (AE) ['inept person'] a hopeless ~

safari *n.* 1. to organize a ~ 2. to go on a ~ 3. a ~ to

safe I *adj.* 1. absolutely ~ 2. ~ for (~ for children) 3. ~ from (~ safe from attack) 4. ~ to + inf. (it is not ~ to lean out of the window)

safe II *n.* 1. to open; unlock a ~ 2. to close; lock a ~ 3. to break open, crack a ~ 4. a wall ~

safe-conduct *n.* to issue a ~

safeguard *n.* 1. built-in ~s 2. a ~ against

safekeeping *n.* in ~

safety *n.* ['security'] 1. to assure smb.'s ~ 2. to jeopardize smb.'s ~ 3. industrial; public ~ 4. in ~ (to live in ~) 5. (misc.) a margin of ~; ~ first! ['device that prevents accidental discharge of a firearm'] 6. to set the ~ 7. to release the ~

safety factor *n.* a built-in ~

sag *v.* 1. (D; intr.) to ~ to (to ~ to one side) 2. (D; intr.) to ~ under (the floor ~ged under the weight)

saga *n.* a ~ about, of

sagacity *n.* the ~ to + inf. (she had the ~ to diversify her investments)

said *adj.* 1. ~ to + inf. (she is ~ to be very wise) 2. ~ that + clause (it is ~ that they own five cars)

sail I *n.* 1. to hoist, raise the ~s; to make ~ 2. to let out the ~s 3. to furl, take in a ~; to reduce; slacken ~ 4. to trim ('adjust') the ~s 5. to lower, strike the ~s 6. (misc.) to set ~ for ('to leave for by ship, boat'); to make ~ ('to set out on a voyage')

sail II *v.* 1. (d; intr.) to ~ along (to ~ along the coast) 2. (d; intr.) to ~ around, round (to ~ around the world) 3. (d; intr.) to ~ down (to ~ down a river) 4. (d; intr.) to ~ for (to ~ for Europe) 5. (d; intr.) to ~ from; to (~ from New York to Liverpool) 6. (d; intr.) to ~ into (the ship ~ed into port) 7. (colloq.) (d; intr.) to ~ into ('to attack') (the opposing candidates ~ed into each other) 8. (d; intr.) to ~ through (to ~ through the straits) 9. (colloq.) (d; intr.) to ~ through ('to cope with easily') (she just ~ed through her finals) 10. (d; intr.) to ~ up (to ~ up the river)

sailing *n.* smooth ~ ('unimpeded progress')

saint *n.* a patron ~

sake *n.* 1. for smb.'s ~ (do it for my ~) 2. for old times' ~ 3. for pity's ~

salad *n.* 1. to make a ~ 2. to garnish; season a ~ 3. a fruit; green; mixed; potato; tossed ~

salad dressing *n.* to make a ~

salary *n.* 1. to pay a ~ 2. to command, draw, get, receive; earn a ~ 3. (colloq.) to pull down (AE), pull in (BE) a ~ 4. to boost, raise ~ries 5. to cut, reduce, slash ~ries 6. to attach smb.'s ~ 7. an annual; fixed; handsome; meager; modest ~ 8. (misc.) to negotiate a ~

sale *n.* ['selling'] 1. to make a ~ 2. a cash ~ 3. for, on ~ ('being sold') (house for ~; the book will be on ~ next month) ['selling at reduced prices'] 4. to conduct, have, hold, run (colloq.) a ~ 5. an annual; clearance; closeout; fire; garage (AE), yard (AE); going-out-of-business; jumble (BE), rummage (AE); storewide; warehouse ~ 6. on ~ (AE) = at, in a ~ (BE) ('being sold at a reduced price')

sales *n.* 1. brisk ~ 2. gross; net ~ 3. (misc.) all ~ are final

salesman *n.* 1. a door-to-door ~ 2. a traveling ~ (BE also has *commercial traveller*)

salesmanship *n.* high-pressure ~

salient *n.* (mil.) 1. to form a ~ 2. a ~ juts out (into enemy lines)

saliva *n.* ~ dribbles

sally *n.* ['sortie'] 1. to make a ~ against ['trip'] 2. a ~ into (a ~ into strange territory)

salmon *n.* pink; red ~

salon *n.* a beauty; literary ~

salt *n.* 1. to pour ~ 2. common, table; fine; garlic; mineral; onion ~ 3. a dash, pinch; grain of ~ 4. a spoonful of ~ 5. (misc.) to take smt. with a grain of ~ ('to regard smt. with skepticism'); the ~ of the earth ('the very best')

salts *n.* bath; smelling ~

salute I *n.* 1. to fire; give a ~ (the president was given a 21-gun ~) 2. to return; take a ~ 3. a smart, snappy ~ 4. a military; naval; 19-gun; rifle; royal; 21-gun ~ 5. a ~ to

salute II *v.* to ~ smartly (the soldier ~d smartly)

salvage *v.* (D; tr.) to ~ from (to ~ records from a fire)

salvation *n.* 1. to bring; preach ~ 2. to seek ~ 3. ~ from

salve *n.* 1. to apply a ~ 2. a ~ for; to

salvo *n.* to fire a ~

Samaritan *n.* a good ~ ('a person who helps those in need')

same *n.* it's all the ~ to me ('it makes no difference to me')

sample *n.* ['representative item'] 1. to distribute, hand out (free) ~s 2. a floor; free ~ ['selected segment'] (statistics) 3. a random ~

sampler *n.* ['needlework'] to work a ~

sampling *n.* (a) random ~

sanction I *n.* ['approval'] 1. to give ~ to 2. to receive ~ 3. legal ~

sanction II *v.* (K) no one ~ed his smoking marijuana

sanctions *n.* ['coercive measures'] 1. to apply, impose ~ 2. to lift ~ 3. economic, trade ~ 4. ~ against

sanctuary *n.* 1. to give, offer, provide (a) ~ 2. to find; seek ~ 3. a bird; wildlife ~ 4. a ~ for 5. a ~ from

sanctum *n.* an inner ~

sand *n.* 1. to scatter, spread, sprinkle, strew ~ 2. coarse; fine ~ 3. a grain of ~

sandals *n.* 1. beach ~ 2. a pair of ~

sandwich I *n.* 1. to make a ~ out of 2. a cheese; club (AE); corned-beef; double-decker; grilled-cheese (AE), toasted-cheese (BE); ham; open-face; tomato-and-lettuce; tuna ~

sandwich II *v.* (d; tr.) to ~ between (to ~ a meeting between a staff conference and lunch)

sanitation *n.* environmental ~

sanity *n.* 1. to keep, maintain, preserve, retain one's ~ 2. to lose one's ~

sarcasm *n.* 1. biting, devastating, keen, piercing, scathing, withering; mild ~ 2. ~ about 3. (misc.) dripping with ~ (her remarks were dripping with ~)

sardines *n.* 1. a can (AE), tin (BE) of ~ 2. (misc.) to pack in like ~

sashay *v.* (colloq.) (AE) (P; intr.) ('to stroll') they ~ed down to the beach

satellite *n.* 1. to launch; orbit a ~ 2. an artificial (earth); communications; spy; weather ~

satire *n.* 1. (a) biting, scathing ~ 2. a ~ on

satisfaction *n.* ['act of satisfying'] ['state of being satisfied'] 1. to afford, give ~ to 2. to express; feel ~ 3. to find, take ~ in 4. deep, profound; quiet ~ 5. ~ that + clause (they felt ~ that a fair com-promise had been reached) 6. ~ about, with 7. to smb.'s ~ (the work was done to my ~) ['compensation for a wrong or injury'] 8. to demand; seek ~ 9. to get, receive; have ~ 10. ~ for (to receive ~ for an insult)

satisfactory *adj.* 1. highly ~ 2. ~ to

satisfied *adj.* 1. completely, greatly, perfectly, thoroughly ~ 2. ~ with (we are ~ with the results) 3. ~ to + inf. (she is not ~ to spend her days doing nothing) 4. ~ that + clause (we are ~ that all requirements have been met)

satisfy *v.* 1. to ~ completely, thoroughly 2. (L; refl.) she ~fied herself that all doors were locked

SATS *n.* (US) ['Standard Achievement Tests] (for admission to US universities) to take the ~

saturate *v.* (D; tr.) to ~ with

sauce *n.* apple; barbecue; cranberry; soy; steak; tomato ~

saunter *v.* (P; intr.) to ~ along the street

sausage *n.* liver ~ (BE; AE has *liverwurst*)

savage *n.* the noble ~

savagery *n.* 1. to display, show ~ 2. an outburst of ~

save I *n.* ['action that prevents an opponent from scoring'] 1. to make a ~ 2. a brilliant, spectacular ~

save II *v.* 1. (C) ~ a place for me; or: ~ me a place 2. (D; intr., tr.) to ~ for (they are ~ing for a new car; to ~ money for a new TV) 3. (D; tr.) to ~ from (to ~ valuable records from destruct on) 4. (D; intr.) to ~ on (during the mild winter we ~d on fuel) 5. (O) it will ~ you the trouble of making a second trip; the computer will ~ us a lot of time

save up *v.* (D; intr.) to ~ for (to ~ for a new tape recorder)

savings *n.* 1. to set aside ~ 2. to deposit; invest one's ~ 3. to withdraw one's ~ (from a bank) 4. to dip into; squander one's ~

savings bond *n.* (AE) 1. to issue a ~ 2. to cash (in) redeem a ~ 3. to roll over a ~

savings certificate *n.* 1. to issue a ~ 2. to cash (in) redeem a ~ 3. (AE) to roll over a ~

savour *v.* (BE) (d; intr.) to ~ of ('to suggest') (to ~ of treason)

savvy *n.* ['knowledge'] (colloq.) 1. to demonstrate ~ 2. political ~ (to demonstrate considerable political ~)

saw *n.* 1. to set ('put an edge on') a ~ 2. a band; buzz (AE), circular (BE), carpenter's; chair; coping; hand; power ~

say I *n.* ['decision'] 1. to have the final ~ ['opportunity to speak'] 2. to have one's ~

say II *v.* 1. (B) ('to utter') she said a few words to us 2. (d; tr.) ('to state') to ~ about, of (what did they ~ about our offer?) 3. (d; tr.) to ~ for ('to say in justification of') (what can you ~ for yourself?) 4. (d; tr.) to ~ to ('to respond to') (what do you ~ to the charges?) 5. (colloq.) (E) ('to state') the instructions ~ to take one tablet every morning 6. (L; to) ('to state') they said (to us) that they would be late 7. (Q) ('to state') she did not ~ when our next meeting would be 8. (misc.) to ~ smt. in jest; to ~ smt. under one's breath

saying *n.* 1. a common, old, popular, wise ~ 2.

(misc.) it goes without ~ that we will help
scab *n.* a ~ falls off; forms
scabies *n.* to catch, get ~
scaffolding *n.* 1. to erect, put up ~ 2. to take down ~
scale I *n.* ['series of notes arranged in a certain sequence'] (mus.) 1. to play; sing a ~ 2. a chromatic; diatonic; major; minor; natural ~ ['system of classifying in a series of steps'] 3. a sliding; social ~ 4. a pay, salary, wage; union ~ ['relative size'] 5. an enormous, grand, large; moderate; monumental; small ~ 6. on a certain ~ (everything was planned on a monumental ~; on a ~ of one to ten) 7. (misc.) drawn to ~
scale II *n.* ['weighing machine'] 1. a bathroom; beam; kitchen; spring; table ~ 2. on a ~ (to weigh smt. on a ~)
scale down *v.* (D; tr.) to ~ to (to ~ production to decreased demand)
scales *n.* ['weighing machine'] 1. see **scale II** 2. a pair of ~ 3. (misc.) to tip the ~ at one hundred fifty pounds ['decisive influence'] 4. to tip, turn the ~ ('to have a decisive influence')
scallions *n.* (esp. AE; BE prefers *spring onions*) a bunch of ~
scalp *n.* a dry; itchy; oily ~
scamper *v.* (P; intr.) to ~ across the field
scan *n.* ['radiographic image'] 1. to do, perform; interpret a ~ 2. to have, undergo a ~ 3. a bone; CAT; heart; liver; lung ~
scandal *n.* 1. to cause, create a ~ 2. to cover up, hush up; uncover a ~ 3. a juicy, sensational ~ 4. an open; political; public ~ 5. a ~ bursts, erupts 6. a breath, hint, suggestion of ~ 7. a ~ that + clause (it's a ~ that the buses are always so late)
scandalize *v.* (R) it ~d public opinion that the mayor had taken bribes
scandalous *adj.* 1. ~ to + inf. (it is ~ to behave like that) 2. ~ that + clause (it is ~ that this road has so many potholes)
scapegoat *n.* to make a ~ of smb.
scar *n.* 1. to leave a ~ 2. to bear, carry a ~ 3. a hideous, ugly; identifying; noticeable, prominent; permanent; psychological ~
scarcity *n.* 1. to cause a ~ 2. a severe ~
scare I *n.* (colloq.) 1. to give smb. a ~; to put, throw a ~ into smb. 2. to get a ~
scare II *v.* (colloq.) 1. (D; tr.) to ~ into (to ~ smb. into doing smt.) 2. (D; tr.) to ~ out of (she ~d me out of my wits) 3. (N; used with an adjective) to ~ smb. stiff 4. (R) it ~d us that no one answered the doorbell 5. (misc.) to ~ smb. to death
scared *adj.* (colloq.) 1. ~ at (~ at the sound of the air raid siren) 2. ~ to + inf. (they are ~ to say anything)
scarf *n.* 1. to knit a ~ 2. to wear a ~ (around the neck) 3. a knitted; silk; woolen ~
scarlet fever *n.* to develop; have ~
scar tissue *n.* ~ forms
scavenge *v.* (D; intr.) to ~ for
scenario *n.* ['film script'] 1. to write a ~ 2. a film ~ ['potential situation'] 3. a worst-case ~ (in the worst-case ~)

scene *n.* ['division of a play'] 1. to play; rehearse a ~ 2. to steal ('dominate') a ~ ['display of anger, feelings'] 3. to make a ~ 4. an awkward, painful ~ ['location'] 5. at, on a ~ (she was at the ~ of the crime) 6. on the national ~ ['spectacle, picture'] 7. to depict a ~ 8. a beautiful; disgraceful, shameful; distressing; familiar; funny; gruesome; revolting; ridiculous; tragic ~ ['misc.'] 9. behind the ~s ('in secret')
scenery *n.* ['stage props'] 1. to set up ~ 2. to move, shift ~ 3. to dismantle ~ 4. stage ~ ['landscape'] 5. beautiful, majestic, picturesque; wild ~ 6. (misc.) (usu. fig.) a change of ~
scent *n.* ['track, trail'] 1. to have; follow; pick up a (the) ~ (the dogs picked up the ~) 2. to leave a ~ 3. a cold; false; hot ~ 4. (misc.) to throw smb. off the ~ ['intuition'] 5. a ~ for (a ~ for news) ['odor'] 6. a faint; pungent ~ ['sense of smell'] 7. a keen ~
sceptical see **skeptical**
scepticism see **skepticism**
schedule *n.* 1. to draw up, make out, make up, plan a ~ 2. a fixed; flexible; full; heavy; rigid; rotating ~ 3. (esp. AE) an airline; bus; train ~ (BE prefers *timetable*) 4. a production ~ 5. a ~ for 6. according to, on; ahead of; behind ~ (our work is coming along according to/on ~)
scheduled *adj.* (cannot stand alone) ~ to + inf. (we're ~ to arrive at one o'clock)
scheme I *n.* 1. to concoct, cook up, devise, think up a ~ 2. to foil, thwart a ~ 3. a diabolical; fantastic; get-rich-quick; grandiose; nefarious; preposterous, wild-eyed ~ 4. a ~ to + inf. (she concocted a ~ to get publicity) 5. (misc.) in the overall ~ of things USAGE NOTE: In CE, a *scheme* can be dishonest or crafty; this connotation is probably encountered more frequently in AE than in BE.
scheme II *v.* (derog.) (E) they are ~ing to take over the government
schism *n.* 1. to cause, create a ~ 2. a ~ between
scholar *n.* an eminent; productive ~
scholarship *n.* ['systematized knowledge, research'] 1. to foster, promote ~ 2. productive; scientific; solid, sound, thorough ~ ['aid to a student, researcher, writer'] 3. to establish, found a ~ 4. to award, grant a ~ 5. to apply for; get, receive, win; hold a ~ 6. a ~ for (to receive a ~ for language study) 7. a ~ to + inf. (she won a ~ to study abroad)
school I *n.* ['educational institution'] 1. to direct; operate a ~ 2. to attend, go to ~; to enter (a) ~ (they go to a good ~) 3. to accredit a ~ 4. to finish, graduate from (AE), leave (BE) ~ (she left ~ and went to university) 5. to drop out of, leave, quit ~ 6. (by level) an elementary, grade (AE), grammar (AE), primary; first (BE); infant (BE); junior (BE); nursery ~ 7. (by level) a junior high (AE); middle ~ 8. (by level) a comprehensive (BE), high (esp. AE), secondary; grammar (BE); public (BE) ('private secondary'); secondary modern (BE; now rare) ~ 9. (by level) a graduate, postgraduate (esp. BE); undergraduate ~ 10. (by subject) an art; ballet; beauty; business; dancing; divinity; driving; fencing; military; naval; riding; secretarial; technical; trade, vocational ~ 11. (by

type) a boarding; church; consolidated; correspondence; council (BE; now rare); public (AE), state (BE); day; evening; finishing; magnet (AE); night; parochial; preparatory; private; reform (AE; now rare); religious; segregated; summer; Sunday ~ 12. (at a university; see also **faculty 1)** a dental; engineering; law; medical; nursing (AE; CE has *school of nursing);* professional ~ 13. at, in (a) ~ (she works at/in a ~; their son is still at ~; AE also has: their son is still in ~) 14. a ~ for (a ~ for gifted children) 15. (misc.) to be kept after ~; late for ~ ['group of persons holding similar views'] 16. an avant-garde ~ of artists; a radical ~ of economists 17. a ~ of opinion, thought 18. (misc.) of the old ~ ('adhering to established traditions') ['misc.'] 19. the ~ of hard knocks ('life with all its difficulties') USAGE NOTE: One says *to attend school* and *to go to school,* but with a modifier an article must be included-- *to attend a good school, to go to a good school, they go to the school of their choice.* Note that one can say either *they go to a school in California* or *they go to school in California.* (see the Usage Note for **university)**
school II *v.* 1. to ~ thoroughly 2. (D; tr.) to ~ in (to ~ smb. in the martial arts) 3. (H) they were ~ed to obey instantaneously
schooled *adj.* ~ in (well ~ in military tactics)
schooling *n.* 1. to receive one's ~ 2. formal ~ 3. ~ in
schoolwork *n.* to do one's ~
science *n.* 1. to advance, foster, promote ~ 2. an exact ~ 3. applied; basic; behavioral; domestic; information; library; linguistic; military; natural; naval; physical; political; popular; social; space ~
scientist *n.* a nuclear; political; social ~
scissors *n.* 1. to use ~ 2. to sharpen ~ 3. bandage (AE); manicure; nail ~ 4. a pair of ~
sclerosis *n.* multiple ~
scoff *v.* (D; intr.) to ~ at
scold I *n.* ['person who constantly complains'] a common ~
scold II *v.* (D; intr.) to ~ about, for (they ~ed me for being late)
scolding *n.* 1. to give smb. a ~ 2. to get, receive a ~
scoop I *n.* ['utensil for scooping'] 1. a coal; flour; grain; ice-cream ~ ['hot news item'] (colloq.) 2. to get the latest ~
scoop II *v.* (d; tr.) to ~ out of
scoot *v.* (P; intr.) the boys ~ed out of the room
scooter *n.* 1. to ride a ~ 2. a motor ~
score I *n.* ['tally'] (usu. sports) 1. to keep ~ 2. a close; even; lopsided ~ 3. (AE) (usu. baseball) a box ~ 4. a ~ stands (the ~ stood five to three = the ~ stood five--three = the ~ stood at five to three; how does the ~ stand?) 5. by a ~ (we won by a lopsided ~) ['points'] (sports) 6. (esp. AE) to run up a ~ 7. a lopsided ~ (our team ran up a lopsided ~) ['grievance'] ['matter'] 8. to pay off, settle a ~ 9. an old ~ (they had some old ~s to settle) 10. a ~ between (there are some old ~s between them) ['musical composition'] 11. to play; write a ~ ['copy of a musical composition'] 12. a full;

orchestra; piano; vocal ~ ['matter'] 13. or a certain ~ (we are even on that ~) ['facts of a situation'] (colloq.) 14. to know the ~
score II *v.* 1. (D; intr., tr.) ('to make a score') to ~ against (to ~ against a team; they ~d five points against the visiting team) 2. (D; intr., tr.) ('to make a score') to ~ for (she ~d ten points for her team; who ~d for their team?) 3. (d; intr.) ('to write music') to ~ for (to ~ for full orchestra) 4. (colloq.) (BE) (d; intr.) to ~ off ('to beat in an argument') (it's difficult to ~ off him in an argument) 5. (colloq.) (D; intr.) ('to achieve success') to ~ with (I really ~d with the boss) 6. (s) to ~ high; low (they ~d high in/on the proficiency tests)
scoreboard *n.* an electronic ~
scorecard *n.* to keep a ~
scorer *n.* (sports) a high; low ~ (who was the game's high ~?)
scorn I *n.* 1. to express; feel ~ 2. to heap ~ on 3. ~ for (to feel ~ for smb.)
scorn II *v.* (formal) 1. (BE) (E) she ~s to compromise 2. (G) she ~s compromising
scornful *adj.* ~ of
scorpion *n.* ~s sting
scot-free *adj.* to get off, go ~
scourge *n.* a ~ to (a ~ to the human race)
scout *n.* 1. a boy ~ (esp. AE; BE usu. has *scout)* 2. a girl ~ (AE; BE has *girl guide)* 3. a talent ~
scout about, scout around *v.* (D; intr.) to ~ for (to ~ for new talent)
scowl *v.* (D; intr.) to ~ at
Scrabble *n.* (T) ['game'] to play ~
scramble I *n.* 1. a mad, wild ~ 2. a ~ for (a wild ~ for tickets) 3. a ~ to + inf. (there was a ~ to buy tickets)
scramble II *v.* 1. (C) ~ a couple of eggs for me; or: ~ me a couple of eggs 2. (d; intr.) to ~ for, over (to ~ for government subsidies)
scrap I *n.* ['waste metal'] to sell (smt.) for ~
scrap II *n.* (colloq.) ['fight'] to put up a (good) ~
scrap III *v.* (colloq.) (D; intr.) ('to fight') to ~ over
scrapbook *n.* to keep a ~
scrape I *n.* ['awkward predicament'] ['fight'] to get into a ~
scrape II *v.* 1. (D; tr.) to ~ off (to ~ paint off furniture) 2. (D; intr.) to ~ through ('to manage to get through') (to ~ through a crisis) 3. (N; used with an adjective) (she ~d the dishes clean) 4. (misc.) to bow and ~ ('to be obsequious')
scrape along *v.* (D; intr.) to ~ on, with (to ~ on a small salary)
scratch I *n.* ['injury produced by scratching'] 1. (to come through a battle) without a ~ ['beginning'] 2. from ~ ['prescribed level'] 3. up to ~
scratch II *v.* 1. (d; intr.) to ~ at (the cat was ~ing at the door) 2. (misc.) (AE; colloq.) to ~ for oneself ('to eke out one's living independently')
scrawl *n.* ['bad handwriting'] 1. to decipher a ~ 2. an illegible ~ (to write in an illegible ~)
scream I *n.* a bloodcurdling, shrill ~
scream II *v.* 1. (B) she ~ed a few words to me 2. (D; intr.) to ~ at; for (he ~ed at the children for

making noise) 3. (d; intr.) to ~ for (to ~ for help) 4. (D; intr.) to ~ with (to ~ with pain) 5. (L) she ~ed that the house was on fire 6. (N; used with a reflexive pronoun and an adjective) (she ~ed herself hoarse)

screen I *n.* 1. to put up a ~ 2. a radar; smoke; television, TV ~ 3. a ~ between 4. on a ~ (there was no picture on the TV ~)

screen II *v.* (d; tr.) to ~ from

screening *n.* 1. to do a ~ 2. (a) mass ~

screen test *n.* 1. to get, have a ~ 2. to give smb. a ~

screw I *v.* 1. to tighten; turn a ~ 2. a loose ~

screw II *v.* 1. (d; tr.) to ~ into (to ~ a bracket into a wall) 2. (slang) (D; tr.) to ~ out of ('to cheat out of') (they ~ed him out of his bonus)

screw around *v.* (colloq.) (D; intr.) ('to fool around') to ~ with USAGE NOTE: This verb also has an obscene meaning.

screw on *v.* (N; used with an adjective) ~ the cap on tight

scrimp *v.* 1. (D; intr.) ('to be frugal') to ~ on (to ~ on food) 2. (misc.) to ~ and save

script *n.* ['alphabet'] phonetic ~ (transcribed in phonetic ~)

Scriptures *n.* Holy ~ (to be found in the Holy ~)

scrounge *v.* (colloq.) 1. (D; intr.) ('to scavenge') to ~ for 2. (D; tr.) ('to wheedle') to ~ from (he ~d a cigarette from me)

scrounge around *v.* (colloq.) (D; intr.) ('to scavenge') to ~ for

scrub *v.* (N; used with an adjective) we ~bed the tables clean

scruff *n.* (to take smb.) by the ~ of the neck

scruples *n.* 1. to have ~ 2. moral ~ 3. ~ about

scrupulous *adj.* ~ in (she was ~ in avoiding references to her opponent)

scrutinize *v.* to ~ closely, thoroughly

scrutiny *n.* 1. to bear ~ (his record will not bear close ~) 2. close, strict; constant ~ 3. open to ~ 4. under ~ (under constant ~)

scud *v.* (P; intr.) the clouds ~ded across the sky

scuffle *v.* (D; intr.) to ~ with

sculpture *n.* 1. to create, produce a ~ 2. to cast a ~

scurry *v.* 1. (d; intr.) to ~ for (to ~ for cover) 2. (P; intr.) to ~ along the street

sea *n.* 1. to sail the ~s 2. a calm, smooth; choppy, heavy, high, raging, rough, stormy, turbulent; open ~ 3. at ~ (buried at ~) 4. (misc.) to drift out to ~; to go to ~ ('to become a sailor'); to put out to ~; at ~ ('bewildered'); to sail the seven ~s ('to travel the world as a sailor')

seaboard *n.* (esp. AE) 1. the eastern ~ 2. on the (eastern) ~

seal I *n.* ['sea mammal'] 1. ~s bark 2. a colony of ~s 3. a young ~ is a pup 4. a female ~ is a cow 5. a male ~ is a bull

seal II *n.* ['piece of molten wax'] 1. a privy; wax ~ ['closure'] 2. to break a ~ ['stamp, symbol'] 3. to affix a ~ 4. a ~ of approval

seal *v.* 1. to ~ hermetically 2. (N; used with an adjective) they ~ed the area shut

sea level *n.* above; at; below ~

sea lion *n.* a colony of ~s

seam *n.* 1. to let out; rip open, tear open a ~ 2.

(misc.) (to come apart) at the ~s (also fig.)

seaman *n.* an able, able-bodied; junior (BE), ordinary; merchant ~

seance *n.* 1. to conduct, hold a ~ 2. at a ~

seaport *n.* a bustling, busy ~

search I *n.* 1. to conduct, make a ~ 2. a careful, exhaustive, painstaking, thorough ~ 3. a fruitless ~ 4. a body; literature ~ 5. a ~ for (the ~ for truth) 6. in ~ of 7. (misc.) (legal) unwarranted ~ and seizure

search II *v.* 1. to ~ carefully, thoroughly 2. (D; intr.) to ~ for (to ~ for a lost child) 3. (d; intr.) to ~ through (she ~ed through her purse for the keys)

searchlight *n.* 1. to direct, focus, shine a ~ 2. ~s play on (a wall)

search party *n.* to organize; send out a ~

search warrant *n.* to issue a ~

seas *n.* 1. the high ~ (on the high ~) 2. see **sea 2;** calm, smooth; choppy, etc. ~

seashore *n.* at the ~

seasick *adj.* to get; feel ~

seaside *n.* (BE) at, by the ~ (a holiday at the ~) (AE has **shore)**

season *n.* 1. to open, usher in the (a) ~ 2. to close, usher out the (a) ~ 3. the dead, low, off, slack; high ~ 4. (sports) the baseball; basketball; fishing; football; hunting; open ~ 5. the dry; harvest; holiday; hurricane; mating, rutting; monsoon; planting; rainy; tourist ~ 6. at a ~ (at that ~ of the year) 7. in ~; out of ~ 8. (misc.) it's open ~ on members of the opposition ('members of the opposition are being subjected to attack')

seasoned *adj.* highly; lightly ~

seat *n.* ['place to sit'] 1. to take one's ~ 2. to assign ~s 3. to book (esp. BE), reserve a ~ 4. to give up, relinquish; keep one's ~ 5. a box; bucket; car; front-row; jump; ringside ~ 6. a rumble ~ (AE; BE has *dicky)* 7. the driver's (AE), driving (BE) ~ 8. (misc.) please have a ~ ('please sit down') ['right to sit'] ['public office'] 9. to hold; win a ~ 10. to lose one's ~ ['administrative center'] 11. a county ~ (AE; BE has *county town)* ['dominant position'] 12. the catbird (AE), driver's (AE), driving (BE) ~

seated *adj.* 1. be ~ 2. to remain ~

secateurs *n.* a pair of ~

secede *v.* (D; intr.) to ~ from (a township cannot ~ from a county)

secession *n.* ~ from

seclude *v.* (D; refl., tr.) to ~ from

seclusion *n.* in ~

second I *adj.* ['inferior'] 1. ~ to (~ to none) ['placing after the first'] 2. to come in ~ (in a race)

second II *n.* ['one who ranks after the first'] 1. a close ~ ['assistant'] 2. a ~ to smb. 3. (misc.) ~s away! (in wrestling); ~s out! (in boxing) ['second gear'] 4. in ~ (don't start in ~) ['vote of endorsement'] 5. (do I hear) a ~ to (the motion?)

second III *n.* ['sixtieth part of a minute'] 1. a split ~ 2. for a ~ (I'm stepping out into the corridor for a ~) 3. in a ~ (she'll be here in a ~) 4. (misc.) wait a ~; it will take a ~

second IV /si'kond/ *v.* (BE) (D; tr.) ('to assign

temporarily') to ~ from; to (she was ~ed from the British Council to a university)

secondary adj. ~ to

second best adj. to come off ~

second-class adv. to travel ~

second fiddle n. ['subordinate role'] to play ~ to

second hand n. at ~ ('indirectly')

secondment n. (BE) on ~ from; to

second opinion n. to get a ~

seconds n. ['second portion of food'] to ask for ~

second thought n. 1. to have ~s about smt. 2. on ~ (AE)/on ~s (BE) ('after reconsideration') 3. (misc.) without giving the matter a ~

second wind n. to get one's ~

secrecy n. 1. to ensure ~ 2. strict ~ 3. ~ in (~ in conducting negotiations) 4. in ~ (to meet in ~) (the meetings were held in the strictest ~) 5. (misc.) to swear smb. to ~

secret I adj. 1. strictly ~ 2. most; top ~ 3. to keep smt. ~ (from smb.)

secret II n. 1. to make a ~ of smt. 2. to guard, keep a ~ 3. to betray, blurt out, divulge, reveal a ~ 4. to ferret out, uncover a ~ 5. a closely guarded; military; open; state; trade ~ 6. in ~ (to meet in ~)

secretary n. ['administrative assistant'] 1. a corresponding; executive; personal; press; recording; social ~ 2. a private ~ (AE; BE has *personal assistant*) 3. a ~ of, to ['company official'] (BE) 4. a company ~ ['officer supervising a government department'] 5. a defense; foreign; Home (GB); labor ~; the Secretary of State (US)

secretion n. 1. an internal ~ 2. a ~ from

secretive adj. ~ about (~ about one's plans)

sect n. a religious ~

section n. ['division of a newspaper'] 1. the business; classified; news; sports; travel ~ ['plane figure'] (geometry) 2. a conical; cross; vertical ~ ['group of instruments'] 3. a brass; percussion; string; woodwind ~ 4. in a ~ (to play in the woodwind ~) ['group'] 5. a cheering ~ (in a grandstand) ['surgical cutting'] 6. an abdominal; cesarean ~ ['area'] 7. a business; residential ~ ['department'] 8. the political ~ (of an embassy) ['part'] 9. in ~s (the bookcases come in ~s)

sector n. 1. the private; public ~ 2. in a ~ (in the private ~)

secure I adj. 1. ~ against, from (~ against attack) 2. ~ in (~ in one's beliefs)

secure II v. (D; refl., tr.) to ~ against (to ~ borders against attack)

securities n. 1. to issue; register ~ 2. corporate; gilt-edged; government; negotiable ~

security n. ['safety'] 1. to ensure, provide ~ 2. to strengthen, tighten ~ 3. to compromise; undermine ~ 4. collective; internal; maximum; national; personal ~ (to compromise national ~) 5. ~ against (~ against attack) 6. (misc.) a feeling, sense of ~ ['system of insurance'] 7. social ~ USAGE NOTE: The social security systems are quite different in the United States and Britain.

sedative n. 1. to administer, give a ~ 2. to take a ~ 3. a mild; strong ~

sediment n. to deposit ~

sedition n. 1. to foment, incite, stir up ~ 2. an act of ~

see v. 1. (d; intr.) to ~ about, after ('to take care of') (to ~ about an important matter) 2. (c; tr.) to ~ as ('to visualize'); ('to consider acceptable') (I can't ~ them as members of our organization; can you ~ him as Hamlet?) 3. (d; tr.) ('to find attractive') to ~ in (what does she ~ in him?) 4. (d; tr.) to ~ of ('to encounter') (we haven't seen much of you recently; you haven't seen the last of them) 5. (d; intr.) to ~ through ('to comprehend') (she saw through the scheme immediately) 6. (d; tr.) to ~ through ('to assist, guide') (to ~ a book through the press; they saw me through my period of grief) 7. (d; tr.) ('to accompany') to ~ to (she saw him to the door) 8. (d; intr.) to ~ to ('to attend to') (I had to ~ to the arrangements) 9. (d; tr.) to ~ (through) ('to be sufficient for') (this money will have to ~ us through to the end of the month) 10. (I) we saw him enter the building 11. (J) we saw him entering the building 12. (L) ('to perceive') they saw that further resistance was hopeless 13. (L) ('to make certain') ~ that you get there on time 14. (N; used with a past participle) ('to watch') we saw the play performed in New York 15. (Q) ('to perceive') I could not ~ how the trick is done 16. (P; tr.) ('to accompany') I'll ~ you home 17. (misc.) they are ~ing each other regularly ('they are dating each other'); I ~ by the newspapers that...

seed n. 1. to plant, sow, spread ~s 2. ~s germinate, sprout; grow 3. (misc.) to go to ~ ('to be neglected and become useless')

seeding n. cloud ~

seek v. (E) she sought to help

seeker n. a status ~

seem v. 1. (d; intr.) to ~ like (she ~s like a reasonable person) 2. (E) they ~ to be pleasant; they ~ to like me 3. (L; to) it ~s (to me) that there will be more rain 4. (S) they ~ pleasant; it ~ed a waste of time

seep v. (P; intr.) the water ~ed into the basement

seesaw v. (d; intr.) ('to alternate') to ~ between (the lead ~ed between the two teams)

seethe v. (D; intr.) to ~ with (to ~ with rage)

see to v. (L) he saw to it that the same mistake didn't happen again

segregate v. 1. (D; tr.) to ~ from (to ~ one group from another) 2. (D; tr.) to ~ into (to ~ people into different groups)

segregation n. 1. to maintain, practice ~ 2. racial; religious ~

seize v. (d; intr.) to ~ on, upon (to ~ upon a chance remark)

seized adj. ~ with (an acute illness)

seizure n. ['convulsion, paroxysm'] 1. to have a ~ 2. a cardiac, heart; epileptic; uncontrollable ~ ['act of seizing'] 3. search and ~

select v. 1. (D; tr.) to ~ from among (we ~ed her from among many candidates) 2. (H) we ~ed her to represent us

selection n. ['choice'] 1. to make a ~ 2. natural ~ ['selected piece of music'] 3. to play a ~ 4. a musical ~

self *n.* 1. one's real, true ~ 2. one's old ~ (she performed like her old ~)

self-assurance see **self-confidence**

self-confidence *n.* 1. to acquire, gain; display, show; have ~ 2. to instill ~ 3. to restore smb.'s ~ 4. to undermine smb.'s ~ 5. the ~ to + inf. (she doesn't have the ~ to run for public office)

self-conscious *adj.* ~ about

self-consciousness *n.* 1. to display ~ in 2. ~ about

self-control *n.* 1. to display; exercise ~ 2. to lose ~ 3. admirable, complete, total ~

self-defense, self-defence *n.* 1. in ~ (to kill smb. in ~) 2. the art of ~

self-denial *n.* to exercise, practice ~

self-determination *n.* 1. to give, grant ~ 2. to achieve, realize ~

self-discipline *n.* 1. to display, exhibit; exercise; have ~ 2. the ~ to + inf. (who has the ~ to write a dictionary?)

self-examination *n.* 1. to do, make a ~ 2. a frank, honest ~

self-flattery *n.* to indulge in ~

self-fulfillment, self-fulfilment *n.* to achieve; seek ~

self-government *n.* 1. to grant ~ 2. to enjoy ~

self-interest *n.* 1. enlightened ~ 2. in one's own ~

selfish *adj.* ~ to + inf. (it was ~ of them to do that)

self-management *n.* workers' ~

self-pity *n.* to indulge in ~

self-portrait *n.* to do, paint a ~

self-respect *n.* to keep one's ~

self-restraint *n.* to display, exercise, practice, show ~

self-rule *n.* 1. to grant ~ 2. to enjoy ~

self-sufficiency *n.* 1. to achieve, attain ~ 2. economic ~

self-treatment *n.* to resort to ~

sell I *n.* (colloq.) ['method of selling'] a hard; soft ~

sell II *v.* 1. to ~ retail; wholesale 2. (A) we sold our old car to him; or: we sold him our old car 3. (d; intr., tr.) to ~ for (it sold for ten pounds; we sold the car to them for three thousand dollars) 4. (colloq.) (d; tr.) to ~ on ('to convince of') (to ~ smb. on an idea) 5. (misc.) to ~ as is ('to sell with no guarantee as to quality'); to ~ smt. at a loss; to ~ by the dozen; to ~ in bulk; to sell like hot cakes ('to be sold very quickly in large quantities'); to ~ smb. down the river ('to betray and ruin smb.')

selling *n.* panic ~

sell out *v.* (D; intr., tr.) to ~ to (she sold out to her partner)

semantics *n.* general; generative ~

semester *n.* (esp. US) the fall; spring; summer ~

semicircle *n.* 1. to form a ~ 2. in a ~

semicolon *n.* to place, put in a ~

seminar *n.* 1. to conduct, hold a ~ 2. a ~ on

seminary *n.* a theological ~

senate *n.* 1. to convene, convoke a ~ 2. to disband, dissolve a ~ 3. a ~ meets, is in session 4. a ~ adjourns

senator *n.* a junior; senior ~

send *v.* 1. (A) we sent the manuscript to her; or: we sent her the manuscript 2. (D; tr.) to ~ as (he was sent as our representative) 3. (D; tr.) to ~ by (to ~ a letter by airmail) 4. (d; intr.) to ~ for ('to ask to come') (to ~ for the doctor) 5. (d; tr.) to ~ for ('to send smt.') (she sent me for some beer) 6. (d; tr.) ('to insert') to ~ into (the coach sent some new players into the game) 7. (d; tr.) to ~ on (to ~ students on a field trip) 8. (d; tr.) to ~ out of (the teacher sent the unruly pupils out of the room) 9. (d; tr.) to ~ to (her parents sent her to camp) 10. (H) we sent him to buy beer 11. (J) the explosion sent things flying; we sent him packing ('we dismissed him summarily')

send away *v.* (d; intr.) to ~ for; to (we had to ~ to the factory for spare parts)

send down *v.* (BE) (D; tr.) ('to expel') to ~ from (he was sent down from Oxford)

send in *v.* (D; intr., tr.) to ~ for (the children sent in box tops for prizes)

send-off *n.* to give smb. a (big) ~ (they gave her quite a ~)

send out *v.* 1. (B) they sent out invitations to many people 2. (d; tr.) to ~ as (they were sent out as our representatives) 3. (d; intr., tr.) to ~ for (to ~ for pizza; they sent him out for beer) 4. (d; tr.) to ~ on (the young reporter was sent out on her first assignment)

senior I *adj.* ~ to (she is ~ to me by one year)

senior II *n.* (AE) a college; graduating; high-school (AE) ~

seniority *n.* according to, by ~ (to promote according to ~)

sensation *n.* ['excitement'] 1. to cause, create a ~ ['feeling'] 2. a burning; choking; numbing; pleasant; unpleasant ~

sense I *n.* ['judgment'] 1. to display, show ~ 2. common, good, horse (colloq.) ~ 3. a grain of ~ 4. the ~ to + inf. (they don't have the ~ to admit defeat) 5. (misc.) to bring smb. to her/his ~s; to come to one's ~s; to take leave of one's ~s ['logic'] 6. to make ~ (her choice makes ~; it makes ~ to file an application; can you make any ~ out of this?) ['reaction to stimuli'] 7. to sharpen the ~s 8. to dull the ~s 9. an intuitive; keen ~ 10. the five ~s 11. the sixth ~ ('intuition') ['feeling'] 12. (to have) a false ~ (of security) 13. (misc.) a ~ of humor ['meaning'] 14. a figurative; literal, narrow, strict ~ 15. in a ~ (in the literal ~ of the word; in every ~ of the word) ['appreciation'] 16. a ~ of beauty

sense II *v.* (L) she ~d immediately that smt. was wrong

senseless *adj.* ~ to + inf. (it was ~ to lie)

sense of humor *n.* 1. to demonstrate, display a ~ 2. a wry ~

sensible *adj.* ['reasonable'] 1. ~ to + inf. (it was ~ of her to postpone the trip) ['aware'] (formal) (BE) 2. ~ of (they were ~ of the danger that they faced)

sensitive *adj.* ~ to (~ to charges of corruption; ~ to criticism)

sensitivity *n.* ~ to (~ to criticism)

sensitize *v.* (D; tr.) to ~ to

sensor *n.* to trip a ~

sentence I *n.* ['judgment of a court'] 1. to impose,

pass, pronounce (a) ~ 2. to carry out, execute a ~ 3. to serve (out) a ~ 4. to commute; reduce; suspend; vacate a ~ 5. a harsh, severe, stiff; light ~ 6. a death; indefinite, indeterminate; life; prison; suspended ~ 7. under ~ 8. (misc.) to get off with a light ~ ['independent group of words'] 9. to form, formulate, make up; generate a ~ 10. an affirmative; complex; compound; declarative; elliptical; embedded; exclamatory; impersonal; interrogative; negative; simple ~

sentence II *v.* (D; tr.) to ~ for; to (the judge ~d him to five years for theft; the convicted murderer was ~d to death)

sentiment *n.* ['feeling'] 1. to express a ~ 2. to display, show ~ 3. a growing; lofty; patriotic; shocking; strong ~ 4. ~ against; for, in favor of (there is growing ~ in favor of a tax reduction) 5. ~ that + clause (there was strong ~ that the government should step down)

sentimental *adj.* ~ about, over

sentimentality *n.* 1. maudlin, mawkish ~ 2. ~ about

sentimentalize *v.* (D; intr.) to ~ about, over

sentry *n.* 1. to post a ~ 2. to relieve a ~

separate I *adj.* ~ from (to keep ~ from)

separate II *v.* (D; intr., tr.) to ~ from (she was ~d from her family; to be ~d from the service)

separation *n.* ~ from

separatism *n.* political; racial; religious ~

sequel *n.* a ~ to

sequence *n.* 1. a chronological; natural ~ 2. in ~

serenade *n.* 1. to play, sing a ~ 2. a ~ to

sergeant *n.* 1. a buck; color; drill; first, top; flight (BE); gunnery; master; platoon; recruiting; staff; technical ~ 2. a ~ major

series *n.* ['sequence'] (math.) 1. an alternating; convergent; divergent; geometric; harmonic; infinite ~ ['succession'] 2. an unbroken ~ ['cycle of programs, publications'] 3. a miniseries; TV ~

serious *adj.* 1. deadly ~ 2. ~ about (she is ~ about her work)

sermon *n.* 1. to deliver, give, preach a ~ 2. a lay ~

servant *n.* 1. a domestic; personal; public ~ 2. a faithful, loyal, trusted ~ 3. a ~ to

serve I *n.* (tennis) 1. the ~ was good; long; out 2. a ~ to (a ~ to the backhand)

serve II *v.* 1. (A) ('to bring') she ~d dinner to us; or: she ~d us dinner 2. (d; intr.) to ~ as ('to fulfill the functions of') (his illness ~d as an excuse; to ~ as mayor) 3. (D; intr.) to ~ on ('to be a member of') (to ~ on a jury) 4. (D; tr.) to ~ on ('to deliver to') (to ~ a summons on smb.) 5. (tennis) (D; intr.) ('to put the ball in play') to ~ to (I hate to ~ to her -- she always returns the ball to my backhand) 6. (D; intr.) ('to be in service') to ~ under (he ~d directly under a general) 7. (d; tr.) to ~ with ('to deliver to') (to ~ smb. with a summons) 8. (E) ('to have an effect') it ~d to calm everyone's nerves 9. (misc.) it ~s him right ('he got what he deserved')

service *n.* ['work done for others'] 1. to do, offer, perform, provide, render a ~ 2. custom; meritorious; public; yeoman ('loyal') ~ 3. professional; social (BE) ~s (a fee for professional ~s) 4. ~ to

(she received an award for meritorious ~ to the community) 5. (misc.) to press smb. into ~ ['facility that satisfies a need'] 6. to introduce; offer, provide; restore ~ 7. to suspend a ~ 8. an ambulance; answering; bus; clipping (AE); press-cutting (BE); customer; dating; delivery; diaper (AE); door-to-door; employment (esp. AE); express; ferry; health-visitor (BE), visiting-nurse (AE); janitorial (AE); laundry; limousine (esp. AE); news, wire; placement; postal; repair room; telephone; towing ~ ['operation, use'] 9. to see ~ (this equipment has seen plenty of ~) 10. in; out of ~ (the bus was not in ~) 11. (misc.) to put smt. into ~ ['disposal'] 12. to be at smb.'s ~ ['help, benefit'] 13. to be of ~ to ['religious ceremony'] 14. to hold a ~; to hold ~s 15. a burial; marriage; memorial; prayer, religious ~ 16. an evening; morning; noontime; sunrise ~ (they hold sunrise ~s once a week) ['set of utensils'] 17. a coffee; dinner; tea ~ 18. a ~ for ['administrative division of government'] 19. the civil; consular; diplomatic foreign; intelligence, secret ~ 20. human ~s ('social services') ['game during which one serves'] (tennis) 21. to hold ('win'); lose one's ~ 22. to break smb.'s ~ ['duty in the armed forces'] 23. to see ~ (she saw ~ during the Second World War) 24. military; national (BE), selective (AE) ~ 25. active; inactive ~ 26. in the ~ ['position as a servant'] (esp. BE) 27. domestic ~ 28. to be in ~ to go into ~ ['scheduled routes, flights'] 29. to introduce; offer, provide ~ 30. to suspend ~ 31. daily; regular ~ 32. ~ between; from; to (regular ~ between two cities; that airline provides daily ~ from New York to London) ['manner of dealing with customers'] 33. fast; fine; slow ~ ['misc.'] 34. lip ~ ('meaningless promises')

serving *n.* ['portion'] a generous, liberal; second; small ~

servitude *n.* involuntary; penal ~

session *n.* 1. to hold a ~ 2. a briefing; bull (AE; colloq.), rap (AE; colloq.); jam; joint; legislative; plenary; practice; rap; special; summer; winter; working ~ 3. (colloq.) (AE) a stroking ~ ('an attempt at conciliation') 4. a ~ on (to hold a special ~ on problems of air pollution) 5. in ~ (in secret ~; the court was in ~)

set I *adj.* ['opposed'] 1. (cannot stand alone) ~ against (her parents were dead ~ against the marriage) ['ready'] 2. ~ for (we are ~ for the big celebration) 3. ~ to + inf. (we are ~ to begin) 4. (misc.) to get ~ for; (before a race) get ready, get ~, go! (AE; BE has *ready, steady, go!*)

set II *n.* ['collection of things used together'] 1. to make up a ~ 2. to break, break up a ~ 3. a carving; chemistry; chess; tea ~ ['group of six or more games'] (tennis) 4. to play a ~ 5. to lose; win a ~ ['apparatus'] 6. a radio; television, TV ~ ['clique'] 7. the fast (old-fashioned); international; jet; smart (old-fashioned) ~ (to belong to the jet ~) ['stage, film scenery'] 8. to dismantle, strike a ~ ['misc.'] 9. to make a dead ~ at smb. ('to attack smb.'); ('to attempt to win smb.'s favor')

set III *v.* 1. (BE) (C) ('to assign') the teacher set several problems for the pupils; or: the teacher set

the pupils several problems 2. (d; tr.) ('to place') to ~ against (to ~ a ladder against a wall) 3. (d; tr.) ('to pit') to ~ against (to ~ brother against brother) 4. (D; tr.) ('to arrange') to ~ for (to ~ the stage for smt.; to ~ a trap for smb.; to ~ a date for a wedding) 5. (d; tr.) ('to incite') to ~ on (to ~ dogs on a trespasser) 6. (D; tr.) ('to put') to ~ on (to ~ a price on an article) 7. (d; tr.) ('to attach') to ~ on (to ~ one's eyes on smt.) 8. (d; tr.) ('to adapt') to ~ to (to ~ a poem to music) 9. (d; intr.) to ~ upon ('to attack') (the wolves set upon the sheep) 10. (BE) (H) ('to assign as a task') she set them to write reports; I set myself to study these problems 11. (J) ('to compel') that set me thinking 12. (N; used with an adjective) to ~ smb. free 13. (P; tr.) ('to place') she set the lamp on the table 14. (misc.) to ~ an example for smb.; to ~ smt. apart; to ~ a price on smb. ('to rely on smb.'); to ~ fire to ('to ignite'); to ~ a match to ('to ignite'); to ~ one's mind to do smt. ('to resolve to do smt.'); to ~ smt. in motion; to ~ one's sights on ('to aspire to') to ~ sail for ('to leave by ship for')
set about v. 1. (E) ('to begin') he set about to undo the damage that he had caused 2. (G) ('to begin') we set about working on the project
set apart v. (D; tr.) to ~ from (certain traits ~ them apart from the others)
set aside v. (D; tr.) to ~ for (to ~ money for one's old age)
setback n. 1. to have, receive, suffer a ~ 2. a serious; unexpected ~ 3. a business; diplomatic; financial; military; personal; political; professional ~
set off v. (D; intr.) ('to start') to ~ for, on (to ~ for home; to ~ on a trip)
set out v. 1. (D; intr.) ('to leave') to ~ for; from (to ~ for town) 2. (d; intr.) to ~ on ('to begin') (to ~ on a new career) 3. (E) ('to resolve') he has set out to get revenge 4. (misc.) to ~ in search of smt.
setting n. ['set of tableware'] 1. a place ~ for ['frame in which a gem is set'] 2. a fashion a ~ for ['surroundings'] 3. a natural ~ ['arrangement of stage props'] 4. a stage ~ ['point at which a measuring device is set'] 5. to adjust, change the ~ (of a thermostat)
settle v. 1. to ~ peacefully (to ~ a dispute peacefully) 2. (d; intr.) to ~ for ('to be content with') (they had to ~ for a very modest house with no garage) 3. (d; intr.) ('to decide') to ~ on (have you ~d on a place for your vacation?) 4. (D; intr., tr.) ('to adjust accounts; to adjust') to ~ with (to ~ with one's creditors; we have ~d our accounts with our creditors) 5. (misc.) to ~ (a case) out of court; to ~ oneself in an armchair; to ~ on the land; to ~ into a routine
settled adj. to get ~
settle down v. 1. (D; intr.) to ~ into, to (to ~ into a routine; to ~ to family life) 2. (E) to ~ to study 3. (misc.) to ~ for the night
settlement n. 1. to come to, make, negotiate, reach a ~ on 2. a fair, reasonable; tentative ~ 3. a lump-sum; marriage; out-of-court ~
set up v. 1. (d; refl., tr.) ('to establish') to ~ as (she set herself up as a real estate agent) 2. (D; tr.) ('to

establish') to ~ in (to set smb. up in business)
several determiner, pronoun ~ of (~ of them) USAGE NOTE: The use of the preposition of is necessary when a pronoun follows. When a noun follows, the use of of the limits the meaning--we saw several students; we saw several of the students whom we had discussed earlier.
sew v. (C) she ~ed a dress for me; or: she ~ed me a dress
sewage n. 1. to treat ~ 2. raw, untreated ~
sewer n. a sanitary; storm ~
sex n. ['sexual relations'] 1. to have ~ with smb. 2. explicit; illicit; kinky (slang), perverse; premarital ~ ['division of organisms into male and female'] 3. the fair; female; male ~ 4. a member of the opposite ~
sex organs n. female; male ~
sexual intercourse n. to have ~ with
sexuality n. human ~
shack n. a dilapidated, run-down; jerry-built ~
shackle v. (d; tr.) to ~ to (the prisoner was ~d to the bars)
shackles n. to cast off, throw off one's ~
shack up v. (slang.) (D; intr.) to ~ with (he ~ed up with his girlfriend)
shade I n. ['gradation of color'] 1. a delicate, pale, pastel, soft ~ 2. a dark; light ~ ['window cover'] (AE; BE has blinds) 3. to draw, pull down; raise the ~s 4. a window ~ ['shaded place'] 5. in the ~ ['misc.'] 6. a lampshade
shade II v. (d; intr.) to ~ into (the colors ~ into each other)
shadow n. 1. to cast, produce, throw a ~ (the setting sun cast long ~s) 2. ~s fall 3. (misc.) a mere ~ of one's former self; beyond a ~ of a doubt; to walk in smb.'s ~ ('to be subservient to smb.)
shaft n. 1. to bore, sink a ~ 2. a cardan (BE), drive (AE) ~ 3. an air; elevator (AE), lift (BE) ~
shake I n. ['act of shaking'] 1. to give smb. or smt. a ~ (she gave the rug a good ~) ['opportunity'] (colloq.) (AE) 2. a fair ~ (she got a fair ~)
shake II v. 1. to ~ vigorously; violently 2. (d; tr.) to ~ from, out of (to ~ apples from a tree) 3. (D; intr.) to ~ with (to ~ with fear) 4. (misc.) ~ well before using
shake down v. (D; tr.) to ~ from (to ~ fruit down from a tree)
shaken adj. easily; visibly ~
shaker n. 1. a cocktail ~ 2. a pepper ~ (AE; BE has pepper pot)
shake-up n. a personnel ~
shall v. (F) we ~ see
shambles n. 1. to make a ~ of; to turn smt. into a ~ 2. in (a) ~ (their economy is in ~)
shame I n. 1. to bring ~ on, to, upon 2. to feel ~ at (they felt ~ at accepting bribes) 3. (colloq.) an awful, crying, dirty ~ 4. a ~ to + inf. (it's a ~ to waste so much time = it's a ~ wasting so much time) 5. a ~ that + clause (it was a ~ that they could not come) 6. for, in ~ ('to hang one's head in ~') 7. to smb.'s ~ (to my ~, I never did help them) 8. with ~ (his cheeks burned with ~) 9. (misc.) to put smb. to ~; a damned ~; ~ on you!
shame II v. 1. (d; tr.) to ~ into (to ~ smb. into

doing smt.) 2. (d; tr.) to ~ out of

shameful *adj.* 1. ~ to + inf. (it was ~ of them to surrender 2. ~ that + clause (it was ~ that they surrendered)

shameless *adj.* ~ to + inf. (it was ~ of them to do that)

shampoo *n.* ['washing of the hair'] 1. to give smb. a ~ 2. to get a ~

shape I *n.* ['form'] 1. to give ~ to 2. to assume a ~; to take ~; to take the ~ of (our plans are beginning to take ~; to take the ~ of a human being) ['good physical condition'] 3. to get (oneself) into ~ 4. to keep (oneself) in ~ ['physical condition'] 5. bad; good ~ 6. in ~ (to be in bad ~) 7. (misc.) she is in no ~ to give a speech

shape II *v.* (d; tr.) to ~ into (to ~ clay into a jug)

share I *n.* 1. to do one's ~ 2. an equal; fair; full; large, lion's, major ~ 3. ordinary ~s (BE; AE has *common stock*) 4. preference ~s (BE; AE has *preferred stock*) 5. a ~ in (to have a ~ in the profits)

share II *v.* 1. (D; tr.) to ~ among (the thieves ~d the loot among themselves) 2. (D; intr.) to ~ in (to ~ in the profits; to ~ in using the computer) 3. (D; tr.) to ~ with (we ~d our food with them)

sharing *n.* 1. profit ~ 2. revenue ~ (by the states)

shark *n.* 1. a man-eating ~ 2. (fig.) a loan ~

sharp *adj.* razor ~

sharpener *n.* a pencil ~

shave I *n.* 1. to give smb. a ~ 2. a close ~ 3. (misc.) a close ~ ('a narrow escape')

shave II *v.* (N; used with an adjective) she ~d me close; he ~d his head bald

shavings *n.* wood ~

shears *n.* 1. pinking; pruning ~ 2. a pair of ~

shed *v.* (D; tr.) to ~ on (to ~ light on a mystery) ('to clear up a mystery')

sheen *n.* ['brightness'] a high ~

sheep *n.* 1. to raise, rear (BE) ~ 2. to shear ~ 3. ~ baa, bleat, go baa 4. a flock, herd of ~ 5. the meat of the ~ is mutton 6. a young ~ is a lamb; its meat is lamb 7. a female ~ is a ewe 8. a male ~ is a ram 9. (misc.) ~ are tended by a shepherd

sheet *n.* ['piece of bed linen'] 1. a bed; cotton; percale ~ 2. a double; fitted; flat; king-sized; queen-sized; single; twin ~ 3. (misc.) to change the ~s = to put on clean ~s ['financial statement'] ['record'] 4. a balance ~ 5. (BE) a wages ~ ['diagram'] 6. a flow ~ ['piece of paper'] 7. a blank ~ ['news-paper'] (colloq.) 8. a scandal ~ ['statement'] 9. a charge ~ ('a statement of charges brought against an accused person') ['pan'] 10. a cookie ~

shelf *n.* 1. to build, put up a ~ 2. adjustable; built-in shelves 3. a continental ~ 4. (misc.) on the ~ ('no longer in demand'); to stock shelves with supplies

shell *n.* 1. to fire a ~ at 2. to fuse a ~ 3. to lob a ~ (our artillery was lobbing ~s into enemy positions) 4. an armor-piercing; high-explosive; hollow-charge; incendiary; mortar; smoke ~ 5. ~s burst

shellacking *n.* ['beating'] (colloq.) (AE) 1. to give smb. a ~ 2. to get, take a ~

shelling *n.* constant, round-the-clock; heavy, in-

tensive ; light ~

shell out *v.* (colloq.) (B) ('to pay') they have to ~ money to their creditors

shelter I *n.* 1. to afford, give, offer, provide ~ 2. to seek; take ~ from 3. an air-raid, bomb; fallout; tax ~

shelter II *v.* (D; tr.) to ~ from

shelving *n.* to put up ~

sheriff *n.* a deputy ~

sherry *n.* dry; sweet ~

shield *v.* (D; tr.) to ~ against, from

shift I *n.* ['change'] 1. to bring about, produce a ~ in 2. (ling.) a consonant; functional; vowel ~ ['work period'] 3. a day; eight-hour; night; split; swing ~ (she works the night ~; to make an eight-hour ~) ['transmission'] 4. an automatic; standard, stick ~

shift II *v.* 1. (D; intr., tr.) to ~ from; to (to ~ from first to second gear; to ~ responsibility to smb. else) 2. (D; intr.) to ~ into (to ~ into neutral) 3. (misc.) to ~ for oneself ('to live independently')

shift key *n.* (on a typewriter) to press a ~

shin *n.* to bark ('scrape') one's ~s

shine I *n.* ['liking'] (colloq.) (esp. AE) 1. to take a ~ to ['shining of shoes'] 2. to give smb. a ~ ('to shine smb.'s shoes')

shine II *v.* 1. (D; intr.) ('to give light') to ~ on (the hot sun was ~ing directly on our heads) 2. (d; tr.) ('to direct') to ~ on (~ the floodlights on this part of the field)

shiner *n.* ['black eye'] (colloq.) (old-fashioned) 1. to give smb. a ~ 2. to sport a ~

shingle *n.* ['small sign designating a professional office'] (colloq.) (AE) to hang out one's ~

shingles I *n.* ['building material on a roof'] to lay ~

shingles II *n.* ['herpes zoster'] to develop ~

ship I *n.* 1. to build; refit a ~ 2. to christen; launch a ~ 3. to navigate; sail a ~ 4. to scuttle; sink; torpedo a ~ 5. to abandon ~ (when it is sinking) 6. to jump ~ ('to desert from a ship's crew') 7. to raise a sunken ~ 8. to load; unload a ~ 9. a battleship; capital; hospital; merchant; oceangoing; passenger; rocket; sailing ~; spaceship; steamship; supply ~; warship; weather ~ 10. a ~ heaves; pitches; rolls 11. (misc.) to board a ~; to disembark from a ~; to run a tight ~ ('to operate efficiently') USAGE NOTE: The term *rocket ship* is now used chiefly in science fiction. The terms *spacecraft* and *space vehicle* are now used for the real thing. The term *spaceship* is sometimes used for 'manned spacecraft'.

ship II *v.* (A) they have ~ped the merchandise to us; or: they have ~ped us the merchandise

ship off *v.* (D; tr.) to ~ to (they ~ped their children off to camp)

shipping *n.* merchant ~

shipwreck *n.* to experience, suffer (a) ~

shipyard *n.* a naval ~

shirk *v.* (G) no one should ~ doing her/his duty

shirt *n.* 1. to put on; take off a ~ 2. a body; dress; hair; polo; sport; wash-and-wear ~ 3. (misc.) to lose one's ~ ('to lose everything')

shiver I *n.* a ~ went up and down my spine

shiver II *v*. 1. (D; intr.) to ~ at (she ~ed at the thought of getting up) 2. (D; intr.) to ~ from, with (to ~ from the cold)

shock I *n*. 1. to give smb. a ~ 2. to express; feel; get, have a ~ 3. to absorb a ~ 4. an emotional; mild, slight; profound, rude, severe, terrible ~ 5. (a) culture; electric; future; insulin; shell (old-fashioned) ~ 6. a ~ to (his arrest was a ~ to everybody) 7. a ~ to + inf. (it was a ~ to learn of his death = it was a ~ learning of his death) 8. a ~ that + clause (it came as a ~ that he had been released from prison) 9. ~ at (everyone expressed ~ at the hijacking)

shock II *v*. 1. (D; tr.) to ~ into (to ~ smb. into doing smt.) 2. (R) it ~ed me (to learn) that he had been in prison

shocked *adj*. 1. ~ at (~ at the results) 2. ~ to + inf. (we were ~ to learn that he had been fired) 3. ~ that + clause (everyone was ~ that he had been arrested)

shocking *adj*. 1. ~ to + inf. (it is ~ to read of such crimes) 2. ~ that + clause (it's ~ that the article was censored)

shock therapy *n*. 1. to administer ~ 2. to get, receive ~

shock wave *n*. to send a ~ (the uprising sent ~s through the country)

shoelace *n*. 1. to tie; untie a ~ 2. to knot a ~

shoes *n*. 1. to put on; wear ~ 2. to slip off, take off ~ 3. to break in (new) ~ 4. to lace (one's) ~ 5. to polish, shine ~ 6. to fix, mend (esp. BE), repair ~ 7. tight; well-fitting ~ 8. basketball; earth; gym ~; overshoes; running; saddle ~; snowshoes; sports; tennis; track ~ 9. ~ fit; pinch 10. (misc.) to fill smb.'s ~ ('to replace smb.')

shoestring *n*. (colloq.) ['limited funds'] on a ~ (to operate a business on a ~)

shoot I *n*. ['young plant'] 1. a bamboo ~ ['hunting trip'] (esp. BE) 2. (to go on) a tiger ~

shoot II *v*. 1. (D; tr.) ('to execute by shooting') to ~ as (he was shot as a deserter) 2. (D; intr.) ('to fire') to ~ at (to ~ at smb.) 3. (colloq.) (esp. AE) (d; intr.) ('to aim') to ~ for (to ~ for the top) 4. (D; intr., tr.) ('to fire') to ~ into (to ~ into the air) 5. (N; used with an adjective) ('to hit with gunfire') to ~ smb. dead 6. (P; intr.) ('to move quickly') they shot past us in a sports car

shop I *n*. ['store'] 1. to manage, operate a ~ 2. an antique ~; barbershop (esp. AE), barber's ~ (BE); bookshop; butcher (AE), butcher's (BE); chemist's (BE); duty-free; gift; novelty; pastry ~; sweetshop (BE); thrift; toy ~ 3. a draper's ~ (BE; AE has *dry-goods store*) 4. at, in (she works in a ~) ['workshop'] 5. a beauty (esp. AE); body; machine; paint; printing ~ ['place of work'] 6. a closed ~ ('firm that hires only union members') 7. an open ~ ('firm that hires union members and non-union members') 8. a union ~ ('firm that hires only workers who will join the union if they are not already members') ['misc.'] 9. to close down (a) ~ ('to stop operations'); to set up ~ ('to begin operations'); to talk ~ ('to discuss one's work while not at work'); a coffee ~ (AE; BE has *coffee bar)*; a betting ~ (BE; CE has *book-*

maker's) USAGE NOTE: *Shop* and *store* are CE. In BE, *store* tends to be used for a very large retail establishment *(department store)* and *shop* for the others *(bookshop, sweetshop)*. In AE, *store* is used for all, regardless of size *(department store, book store, candy store)*. However, AE can also use *shop* for a small specialized store *(bookshop, millinery shop)*.

shop II *v*. 1. (D: intr.) to ~ for (to ~ for food) 2. (misc.) to go ~ping; let's go window ~ping; to ~ smb. to the police (BE; slang) ('to inform on smb. to the police')

shop around *v*. (D; intr.) to ~ for (to ~ for bargains)

shopper *n*. a Christmas; comparison; window ~

shopping *n*. 1. to do the ~ 2. Christmas; comparison; window ~ (to do the Christmas ~; to do comparison ~)

shore *n*. 1. (AE; BE has *seaside)* at the ~ (a vacation at the ~) 2. off ~ (two miles off ~) 3. on a ~ (smb. was standing on the ~)

short *adj*. 1. ~ in (~ in stature) 2. ~ of (~ of funds; to run ~ of food; to fall ~ of one's goal) 3. (misc.) to be caught ~ ('to find oneself in acute need'); and: (BE; colloq.) ('to feel the need to go to the toilet')

shortage *n*. 1. an acute ~ 2. a food; housing; labor; teacher ~; wartime ~s

shortcut *n*. 1. to take a ~ 2. a ~ to (a ~ to success)

shorten *v*. 1. (D; tr.) to ~ by (to ~ trousers by two inches) 2. (D; tr.) to ~ to (to ~ a manuscript to acceptable length)

shortening *n*. (esp. AE) vegetable ~

shorthand *n*. (to take smt. down) in ~

short haul (esp. AE) see **short run**

short run *n*. ['brief period'] in the ~

shorts *n*. 1. Bermuda; boxer ~ 2. a pair of ~

short shrift *n*. ['quick work'] 1. to make ~ of ('to finish with quickly') 2. to give smb. ~ ('to deal with smb. summarily') 3. to get ~ from smb. ('to be treated summarily by smb.')

shortsighted *adj*. ~ to + inf. (it was ~ of her not to make a reservation)

short term see **short run**

shot *n*. ['act of shooting'] 1. to fire, take a ~ at (she took a ~ at him) 2. a random; warning ~ 3. a pistol; rifle ~ ['marksman'] 4. a bad; crack, good ~ ['throw, kick of the ball to score points'] 5. (esp. basketball) to make, sink; miss; take a ~ (to take a ~ at the basket) 6. (basketball) a dunk, stuff; foul; jump; lay-up ~ 7. (tennis) a drop; passing ~ 8. (ice hockey) a penalty ~ ['metal ball used in the shot put'] 9. to put the ~ ['injection'] 10. to give smb. a ~ 11. to get a ~ 12. a booster ~ ['critical remark'] 13. a cheap; parting ~ ['attempt'] (colloq.) 14. to get; have a ~ at (the boxer never got a ~ at the title) ['chance'] (colloq.) (AE) 15. a ~ that + clause (it's a five to one ~ that she'll find out) ['misc.'] 16. to call the ~s ('to direct matters'); a ~ in the arm ('a stimulus'); a ~ in the dark ('a wild guess')

shotgun *n*. a sawed-off (AE), sawn-off (BE) ~ (see also **gun 1, 2, 4, 5**)

should *v*. (F) she ~ help

shoulder I *n.* 1. to shrug one's ~s 2. to square one's ~s 3. broad, square ~s 4. (misc.) ~ to ~ (to work ~ to ~) ('to work closely together'); to give smb. a cold ~ ('to be unfriendly to smb.'); to put one's ~ to the wheel ('to work very hard'); to rub ~s with ('to associate with'); straight from the ~ ('in a direct manner')

shoulder II *v.* (d; tr.) to ~ through (he ~ed his way through the crowd)

shout I *n.* 1. to give a ~ 2. a loud; piercing; triumphant ~

shout II *v.* 1. (B) she ~ed a few words to me 2. (D; intr.) to ~ at (don't ~ at me) 3. (L; to) he ~ed (to us) that we should call the police 4. (N; refl.; used with an adjective) he ~ed himself hoarse

shove *n.* to give smb. a ~

shovel *n.* a steam ~

show I *n.* ['theatrical presentation'] ['performance'] ['program'] 1. to direct; do, produce, put on, stage; promote; sponsor a ~ 2. to catch (colloq.), see, take in a ~ 3. a chat (BE), talk; floor; ice; peep; Punch-and-Judy; sound-and-light; talent; TV; variety ~ (to sponsor a TV ~) ['display, exhibition'] 4. an air; auto (AE), motor (BE); flower; horse; ice ~ ['misc.'] 5. for ~ ('designed to make an impression'); head ~ ('very bad'); good ~ ('very good'); to put on a ~ ('to pretend'); to steal the ~ ('to draw the most attention'); to stop the ~ ('to receive a great deal of applause, attention'); a ~ of strength; who is running this ~? ('who is in charge here?'); to get the ~ on the road (slang) ('to get things going')

show II *v.* 1. (A) ('to display') ~ the book to me; or: show me the book 2. (d; tr.) ('to guide') to ~ around, over, round (esp. BE), through (she ~ed me through the museum) 3. (d; tr.) to ~ for ('to have as a result of') (what can we ~ for our efforts?) 4. (d; tr.) ('to guide') to ~ to (I ~ed her to her seat) 5. (J) ('to display') the photograph ~ed them conversing 6. (L; may have an object) ('to demonstrate') the research ~ed (us) that our theory was correct 7. (M) ('to demonstrate') she ~ed herself to be an excellent worker; history ~ed her to be a prophet 8. (Q; usu. has an object) ('to demonstrate') can you ~ me how to operate the copying machine? 9. (misc.) to ~ to advantage ('to show in the best light'); to ~ oneself in public

showdown *n.* to come to, have; force a ~ with

shower I *n.* ['bath using an overhead spray'] 1. to have (BE), take a ~ ['short period of rain'] ['brief downpour'] 2. a heavy; light ~ 3. April; passing; scattered ~s 4. a meteor; rain; thunder ~ 5. a sun ~ (esp. AE) ('rain that falls while the sun is shining') ['party to which the guests are expected to bring gifts'] (AE) 6. to make a ~ for smb. 7. a baby; bridal ~

shower II *v.* 1. (d; tr.) to ~ on, upon (to ~ gifts on smb.) 2. (d; tr.) to ~ with (to ~ smb. with gifts)

showing *n.* ['performance'] 1. to make a ~ 2. a good; poor ~ (he made a poor ~)

show up *v.* 1. (D; tr.) to ~ as (the incident ~ed him up as a charlatan) 2. (s) he ~ed up drunk

shrapnel *n.* to catch a piece of ~ (in the leg)

shreds *n.* to rip, tear smt. to ~

shrewd *adj.* 1. ~ at 2. ~ to + inf. (it was ~ of her to do that)

shrewdness *n.* 1. to display ~ 2. ~ at 3. the ~ to + inf. (she had the ~ to buy real estate when the market was depressed)

shriek I *n.* 1. to let out a ~ 2. a loud ~

shriek II *v.* 1. (D; intr.) to ~ at 2. (D; intr.) to ~ with (to ~ with laughter)

shrine *n.* 1. to consecrate; create, establish a ~ 2. to desecrate a ~ 3. a sacred ~ 4. a ~ to 5. at a ~ (to pray at a ~)

shrink *v.* (d; intr.) to ~ from (to ~ from responsibility)

shrouded *adj.* ~ in (~ in mystery)

shrubbery, shrubs *n.* to prune; trim ~

shrug I *n.* with a ~ (of the shoulders)

shrug II *v.* (D; intr.) to ~ at ('to express indifference to') (she ~ged at the suggestion)

shudder I *n.* a ~ ran (through the audience)

shudder II *v.* 1. (D; intr.) to ~ at (to ~ at the thought of going back to work) 2. (E) I ~ed to contemplate what lay ahead

shufty *n.* (slang) (BE) ['quick look'] to have, take a ~ at

shunt *v.* (d; tr.) to ~ onto, to (to ~ a train onto a siding)

shut *v.* 1. (D; tr.) to ~ on (to ~ the door on smb.) 2. (D; tr.) to ~ to (they shut their eyes to poverty)

shut off *v.* (D; tr.) to ~ from

shutter *n.* ['shield in a camera'] 1. to release the ~ ['window cover'] 2. to close; open the ~s

shuttle I *n.* ['vehicle used on an established route'] 1. to take a ~ 2. a space ~ 3. a ~ between

shuttle II *v.* (d; intr.) to ~ between (these ships ~ between the two ports)

shy I *adj.* ['wary'] 1. ~ about, of (BE) ['lacking'] (esp. AE) 2. ~ of (we are still a little ~ of our quota)

shy II *v.* (D; intr.) to ~ at (the horse shied at the noise)

shy away *v.* (d; intr.) to ~ from (they shied away from going through with the deal)

sic *v.* (D; tr.) ('to urge to attack') to ~ on (to ~ a dog on smb.)

sick *adj.* 1. ~ at (~ at heart; ~ at the prospect of leaving home) 2. ~ of (we are ~ of the red tape) 3. (misc.) ~ to one's stomach; worried ~; to be ~ and tired of smt.

sick call *n.* (mil.) to go on ~

sicken *v.* (R) it ~ed me to watch him drink himself to death

sickening *adj.* ~ to + inf. (it was ~ to watch them bicker constantly)

sickness *n.* 1. altitude, mountain; car; decompression; morning; motion, travel; radiation; sea; sleeping ~ 2. in ~ (and in health)

side I *n.* ['right or left part'] 1. the left; right ~ 2. the credit; debit ~ (of a ledger) 3. on a ~ (on the sunny ~ of the street) ['faction, party'] 4. to take smb.'s ~; to take ~s ('to support a faction') 5. the losing; right; winning; wrong ~ 6. on smb.'s ~ (of a dispute) ['direction'] 7. from a ~ (from the other ~; from all ~s) 8. (to turn) to one ~ ['surface'] ['part'] 9. a far; near; reverse ~ 10. the east; north;

south; west ~ 11. on a ~ (on the other ~; on the north ~ of the town square) ['aspect'] 12. the bright; dark, gloomy; humorous; practical ~ (of things); the seamy ~ of life 13. a ~ to (there are two ~s to every question) 14. (misc.) to study all ~s of a problem ['area near a person'] 15. at, by smb.'s ~ (she sat at my ~) ['shore, bank'] 16. on a ~ (on the other ~ of the river) ['arrogance'] (slang) (BE) 17. to put on ~ ['misc.'] 18. to tutor smb. on the ~ ('to tutor smb. part-time'); we split our ~s laughing ('we laughed long and hard'); time is on our ~ ('time is working for us'); on smb.'s ~ (of the family); he's a bit on the short ~ (see the Usage Note for **team)**

side II *v.* (d; intr.) to ~ against; with

sidelines *n.* on the ~ ('out of action')

sidestroke *n.* to do, swim the ~

siding *n.* ['material attached to the outside of a building'] (AE) 1. to install ~ 2. aluminum ~ ['short stretch of railway track'] 3. a railway ~ 4. on a ~

sidle up *v.* (d; intr.) to ~ to (she ~d up to me)

siege *n.* 1. to conduct a ~ of; to lay ~ to 2. to lift, raise a ~ 3. a state of ~ (in a state of ~) 4. at, during a ~ (he was killed at the ~ of Leningrad) 5. under ~ (a city under ~)

siesta *n.* to have a ~

sieve *n.* to pass smt. through a ~

sift *v.* 1. to ~ carefully 2. (d; tr.) to ~ from (to ~ fact from fiction) 3. (d; intr.) to ~ through (to ~ through the debris)

sigh *n.* 1. to breathe, heave a ~ (of relief) 2. a deep, profound ~

sight *n.* ['view'] 1. to catch; keep ~ of 2. to lose ~ of 3. at (the) ~ (to faint at the ~ of blood; to fall in love at first ~) 4. by ~ (to know smb. by ~) 5. in, within ~ (the ship was no longer in ~) 6. on ~ (to shoot looters on ~) 7. out of ~ 8. (misc.) to come into ~ ['something seen'] 9. a beautiful; comical, funny; disturbing; familiar; horrendous, horrible; memorable; pitiful; pleasant; sorry; thrilling; ugly; unpleasant ~ ['device used to aim a gun'] 10. to adjust one's ~s 11. to line up one's ~s 12. a front; panoramic; peep; rear; telescopic ~ 13. (misc.) to have smb. in one's ~s ['ability to see'] 14. keen ~

sighting *n.* a confirmed; radar; visual ~

sights *n.* ['aspirations'] 1. to set one's ~ on (she set her ~ on a career in politics) 2. to lower; raise one's ~ 3. (misc.) to set one's ~ high ['something worth seeing'] 4. to see, take in the ~ (the tourists took in the ~)

sign *n.* ['indication'] 1. to give, show a ~ (he showed ~s of advanced emphysema; they showed no ~s of life) 2. an encouraging; sure, telltale, unmistakable ~ 3. vital ~s ['basic indications of life'] 4. a ~ that + clause (there had been no ~ that the volcano would erupt) ['mark, symbol'] 5. a minus; plus ~ 6. a dollar ~ 7. a call ~ ('identifying letters of a radio station') ['marker'] ['placard'] 8. to post, put up; set up a ~ 9. a for sale; no trespassing; road, traffic ~ 10. (esp. AE) a ~ that + clause (the police put up a ~ that the road was closed) ['misc.'] 11. to make the ~ of the cross

signal I *n.* ['sign'] ['message'] 1. to flash, give, send a ~ 2. a clear, unmistakable ~ 3. a smoke ~ (Indians used to send up smoke ~s) 4. a turn ~ (AE; BE has *traffic indicator)* 5. (AE) a traffic ~ 6. a storm ~ 7. a ~ from; to 8. a ~ to + inf. (the ~ to attack) 9. a ~ that + clause (the troops received the ~ that the attack was to begin) 10. at, on a ~ (the raid began at a given ~) 11. (misc.) (Am. football) to call the ~s (also fig.) ['electrical impulses'] 12. a radar; shortwave ~

signal II *v.* 1. to ~ wildly 2. (B) they ~ed their position to us 3. (d; intr.) to ~ for (to ~ for help) 4. (H) he ~ed us to come closer 5. (L; to; may have an object) the radio operator ~ed (to us)/ ~ed (us) that the ship was in distress 6. (misc.) she ~ed for us to come closer

signature *n.* 1. to affix; scrawl one's ~ 2. to forge smb.'s ~

significance *n.* 1. to acquire; have ~ for 2. to be of ~ to

significant *adj.* 1. ~ for, to 2. ~ to + inf. (it was ~ to note that the story did not appear in the newspapers) 3. ~ that + clause (it is ~ that our ambassador was not invited)

signify *v.* (L) their statements ~ that no action will be taken

sign on *v.* 1. (D; intr.) to ~ as (to ~ as a seaman) 2. (misc.) (BE) to ~ for the dole

sign over *v.* (B) she ~ed over the property to her children

sign up *v.* 1. (D; intr.) to ~ as (to ~ as a volunteer) 2. (D; intr., tr.) to ~ for (she ~ed up for an evening course; to ~ smb. up for a course) 3. (D; intr., tr.) to ~ with (they ~ed up with the volunteers) 4. (E) they ~ed up to serve as volunteers 5. (H) they ~ed us up to serve as volunteers

silence *n.* 1. to impose ~ 2. to keep, maintain, observe ~ 3. to break (the) ~ 4. (an) awkward; dead; eerie; hushed; ominous; prolonged; stony ~ 5. (a) complete, perfect, total, utter; stony; stunned ~ 6. ~ reigns 7. in ~ (we were received in ~) 8. (misc.) radio ~

silent *adj.* to keep, remain ~

silhouetted *adj.* ~ against, on (~ against a light background)

silk *n.* ['fine fabric'] 1. to spin ~ 2. fine ~ 3. natural; synthetic ~ ['misc.'] (BE) to take ~ ('to become a King's Counsel or Queen's Counsel)

silkworm *n.* 1. to keep (BE), raise (esp. AE), rear (BE) ~s 2. ~s spin cocoons

silly *adj.* 1. ~ about 2. ~ to + inf. (it was ~ of her to say that) 3. (misc.) to make smb. look ~

silver *n.* sterling ~

similar *adj.* 1. strikingly ~ 2. ~ in (~ in outlook) 3. ~ to (this specimen is ~ to that one)

similarity *n.* 1. to bear (a) ~ 2. a striking ~ 3. a ~ among, between; to

simple *adj.* ~ to + inf. (it was ~ to do the job = it was a ~ job to do)

simultaneous *adj.* ~ with

sin I *n.* 1. to commit a ~ 2. to expiate; recant a ~ 3. to forgive smb.'s ~ 4. a deadly; inexpiable; mortal; unforgivable, unpardonable; venial ~ 5. original ~ 6. a ~ against 7. a ~ to + inf. (it's a ~ to tell a lie) 8. a ~ that + clause (it's a ~ that her talents are being wasted) 9. (misc.) (obsol.) to live in ~ ('to live together without being married')

sin II *v.* (D; intr.) to ~ against

sincerity *n.* 1. to demonstrate, show ~ 2. (misc.) to doubt smb.'s ~; in all ~

sinful *adj.* ~ to + inf. (it is ~ to waste so much food)

sing *v.* 1. (C; more rarely A) ~ a song for/to us; or: ~ us a song 2. (D; intr.) to ~ about, of 3. (D; intr.) to ~ to (to ~ to a piano accompan ment) 4. (D; intr.) to ~ with 5. (misc.) to ~ in tune; to ~ out of tune; to ~ a baby to sleep

singer *n.* a folk ~

single file *n.* (to walk) in ~

single out *v.* (D; tr.) to ~ for (to ~ smb. out for special treatment)

singular *n.* in the ~

sink I *n.* the bathroom (AE; BE has *handbasin, wash-hand basin);* kitchen ~

sink II *v.* 1. (d; intr.) to ~ below (to ~ below the surface) 2. (d; intr., tr.) to ~ into (to ~ into oblivion; to ~ one's teeth into a good steak) 3. (D; intr.) to ~ to (to ~ to the bottom)

sip *n.* to take a ~

siren *n.* 1. to sound, turn on a ~ 2. an air-raid; ambulance ~ 3. a ~ goes off, rings, sounds, wails

sister *n.* 1. a big, older; kid (colloq), little, younger; twin ~ 2. a foster; half ~; stepsister 3. a lay; soul ~ 4. a ~ to (she was like a ~ to us)

sit *v.* 1. to ~ quietly, still 2. (d; intr.) ('to pose') to ~ for (to ~ for a portrait) 3. (d; intr.) to ~ on ('to be a member of') (to ~ on a committee) 4. (d; intr.) to ~ through (we had to ~ through the whole boring speech) 5. (misc.) to ~ tight ('to refrain from taking action'); to ~ for an examination/to ~ an examination (BE) ('to take an examination'); to ~ on the bench ('to be a judge'); to be ~ting pretty ('to be well off')

sit down *v.* 1. to ~ hard 2. (d; intr.) to ~ to (to ~ to a meal)

site *n.* a battlefield; camping; construction ~

sit-in *n.* to conduct, hold; organize, stage a ~

sit in *v.* 1. (D; intr.) ('to attend') to ~ as (she sat in as our representative) 2. (D; intr.) to ~ for ('to replace') (she sat in for me while I was out of town) 3. (D; intr.) to ~ on ('to attend') (we sat in on a few meetings)

sitter *n.* a baby; house ~

sitting duck *n.* ['easy target'] a ~ for

situation *n.* 1. to comprehend, grasp, take in a ~ 2. to accept a ~ 3. an awkward; crisis, emergency; critical; delicate; desperate; embarrassing; explosive; fluid; hopeless, no-win (colloq); intolerable; life-and-death; stable; tricky; unpleasant ~ 4. the housing; international, world; political ~ 5. (misc.) to take stock of the ~ USAGE NOTE: Some purists prefer the simple words *crisis* and *emergency* to phrases such as *crisis situation* and *emergency situation.*

sit-up *n.* ['exercise'] to do ~s

sit up *v.* (D; intr.) to ~ with (to ~ with a sick child)

sit well *v.* (D; intr.) to ~ with ('to be accepted by') (such behavior doesn't ~ with them)

six-shooter *n.* see **pistol 1-4, 6**

size *n.* 1. to take (colloq.), wear (a) certain ~ (what ~ do you wear?) 2. an enormous, tremendous; large; moderate; small ~ 3. the right; wrong ~ (they gave me the wrong ~) 4. boys'; children's; girls'; junior; men's; misses'; women's ~s 5. life ~ 6. of a certain ~ (of tremendous ~) 7. (misc.) what ~ shirt do you wear?

skate *n.* 1. an ice; roller ~ 2. a pair of ~s

skate over *n.* (D; intr.) to ~ to (she ~d over to us)

skater *n.* a figure; speed ~

skating *n.* figure; ice; roller; speed ~

skeleton *n.* a human ~

skeptical, sceptical *adj.* ~ about, of

skepticism, scepticism *n.* 1. to demonstrate, display ~ 2. to maintain (a) ~ 3. ~ about (to maintain a healthy ~ about smt.) 4. (misc.) an air of ~

sketch *n.* ['drawing'] 1. to draw, make a ~ 2. a composite ~ 3. a rough ~ ['short essay'] 4. a brief, thumbnail ~ 5. a biographical ~

skid *v.* (D; intr.) to ~ on (cars often ~ on ice)

skid row see **row I 3**

skill *n.* 1. to acquire; master; hone a ~ 2. to demonstrate, display, show ~ 3. consummate, great ~ 4. diplomatic; professional; technical ~ 5. marketable ~s 6. ~ at; in; with (~ at/in using a computer; ~ with one's hands) 7. the ~ to + inf. (she had the ~ to cope with a difficult job) 8. (misc.) to market one's ~s

skilled *adj.* 1. highly ~ 2. ~ at, in; with

skillful, skilful, *adj.* ~ at, in; with (~ at tying knots; ~ with one's hands)

skim *v.* 1. (d; intr.) to ~ through ('to read quickly') (to ~ through an article) 2. (P; intr., tr.) ('to bounce') the boy ~med stones along the surface of the water

skimp *v.* (D; intr.) to ~ on (to ~ on food)

skin I *n.* 1. to tan a ~ 2. to cast, shed, slip one's ~ (the snake shed its ~) 3. chapped; coarse, rough; dark; delicate; dry; fair; fine; irritated; light; oily; sensitive; smooth; soft ~ 4. human ~ 5. (after sunburn) ~ blisters; peels 6. (misc.) to save one's ~ ('to save one's life'); a thick ~ ('insensitivity'); a thin ~ ('excessive sensitivity'); to get under smb.'s ~ ('to irritate smb.')

skin II *v.* (N; used with an adjective) to ~ smb. alive ('to punish smb. severely')

skirmish I *n.* 1. a border; minor ~ 2. a ~ between; with

skirmish II *v.* (D; intr.) to ~ with

skirt *n.* 1. to hem; lengthen; shorten a ~ 2. a divided; full; gored ~; miniskirt; pleated; slit; wraparound ~

skis *n.* water ~

skit *n.* to do a ~ on

skunk *n.* (misc.) to smell a ~ (esp. AE; colloq.) ('to sense trouble')

sky *n.* 1. a blue, clear, cloudless; cloudy; dull, gray, overcast, sullen; starry ~ 2. a ~ clears up; clouds up, clouds over 3. a patch of (blue) ~ 4. in the ~

skyline *n.* an imposing; jagged ~

slab *n.* a concrete; marble; mortuary; stone ~

slack *n.* ['part that hangs loose'] to take up the ~

(of a rope)

slacks *n.* a pair of ~

slander *n.* to spread ~

slang *n.* student; underworld ~

slanted *adj.* ['biased'] ~ against; towards (the article was ~ against our viewpoint)

slap I *n.* 1. to give smb. a ~ (in the face) 2. (misc.) a ~ in the face ('a direct insult'); a ~ on the wrist ('a gentle reprimand')

slap II *v.* 1. (d; intr.) ('to strike') to ~ against (the waves were ~ping against the sides of the boat) 2. (D; tr.) ('to strike') to ~ in (to ~ smb. in the face) 3. (d; tr.) ('to impose') to ~ on (to ~ new restrictions on exporters) 4. (misc.) to ~ smb. on the wrist ('to reprimand smb. gently')

slash *v.* (D; intr.) to ~ at (to ~ at smb. with a knife)

slate I *n.* ['record of past performance'] a clean ~ (to start off with a clean ~)

slate II *v.* (colloq.) (BE) (D; tr.) ('to criticize severely') to ~ for (the play was ~d for its dialogue)

slated *adj.* (AE) ['scheduled'] (cannot stand alone) 1. ~ for (~ for promotion) 2. ~ to + inf. (she is ~ to be promoted soon)

slaughter *n.* indiscriminate, mass, wanton, wholesale ~

slave I *n.* 1. to free, liberate a ~ 2. a fugitive, runaway ~ 3. (fig.) a ~ to (a ~ to a habit) 4. (misc.) to buy; sell ~s

slave II *v.* (d; intr.) to ~ over (to ~ over a hot stove)

slave away *v.* (D; intr.) to ~ at; over (to ~ over a hot stove)

slavery *n.* 1. to establish, introduce ~ 2. to abolish ~ 3. white ~

sledding *n.* (colloq.) (AE) ['progress'] rough, tough ~

sleep I *n.* 1. to induce ~ 2. to get (enough) ~ 3. deep, heavy, profound, sound; fitful; light; restful ~ 4. (misc.) to go to ~; to walk in one's ~; to put to ~ ('to kill'); ('to make unconscious'); to lose ~ over ('to worry a great deal about'); one's beauty ~; to get/have a good night's ~

sleep II *v.* 1. to ~ fitfully; lightly; soundly 2. (D; intr.) to ~ on ('to postpone for a day') (to ~ on a decision) 3. (d; intr.) to ~ with ('to have sexual relations with') 4. (misc.) my foot went to ~

sleeper *n.* a heavy, sound; light ~

sleeve *n.* 1. to roll up one's ~s 2. (misc.) to have smt. up one's ~ ('to have a secret'); to roll up one's ~s and get down to work ('to get down to serious work')

slice I *n.* 1. to cut off a ~ of 2. a thick; thin ~

slice II *v.* 1. (C) ~ a piece of meat for me; or: ~ me a piece of meat 2. (d; intr.) to ~ into (to ~ into the bread) 3. (d; intr.) to ~ through (the icebreaker ~d through the ice) 4. (N; used with an adjective) she ~d the bread thin

slick *n.* an oil ~

slide I *n.* a hair ~ (BE; AE has *barrette*)

slide II *v.* 1. (d; intr.) to ~ down (to ~ down a hill) 2. (d; intr.) to ~ from, out of (the glass slid from her hand) 3. (d; intr.) to ~ into (the car skid-

ded and slid into a ditch) 4. (AE) (baseball) (D; intr.) to ~ into ('to occupy by sliding') (he slid into second base)

slide rule *n.* to operate, use a ~

slides *n.* 1. to project, show ~ 2. to mount ~

slight *n.* (lit.) ['slur'] a ~ on, to (a ~ on smb.'s honor)

slime *n.* ~ oozes

sling I *n.* in a ~ (her arm was in a ~)

sling II *v.* 1. (D; tr.) to ~ at (to ~ stones at smb. 2. (misc.) to ~ mud at smb.) ('to slander smb.')

slink *v.* (P; intr.) to ~ through the bushes

slip I *n.* ['error'] 1. to make a ~ (of the tongue) 2. a Freudian ~ ['escape'] (colloq.) 3. to give smb. the ~ ['piece of paper'] 4. a credit (BE), deposit ~ (in a bank); a sales ~ (AE) 5. a call ~ ('request for a library book') 6. a pink ~ ('notice of termination of employment') 7. a rejection ~ ('notification that a manuscript has been rejected by a publisher')

slip II *v.* 1. (A) ('to hand') she ~ped a note to me; or: she ~ped me a note 2. (d; intr.) to ~ by, past ('to get by unnoticed') (they easily ~ped by the roadblock) 3. (D; intr.) to ~ from, out of ('to fall from') (the glass ~ped out of her hand) 4. (d; intr.) ('to move quickly') to ~ into (to ~ into a room) 5. (d; intr.) to ~ into ('to change into') (to ~ into smt. more comfortable; to ~ into a dressing gown) 6. (d; tr.) to ~ into ('to insert surreptitiously') (to ~ a clause into a contract; she ~ped a note into his hand) 7. (D; intr.) ('to slide and fall') to ~ on (he ~ped on a banana peel) 8. (d; intr.) ('to move quickly') to ~ out of (to ~ out of a house) 9. (d; intr.) to ~ out of ('to take off') (he ~ped out of his sweat suit) 10. (d; intr., tr.) to ~ through ('to pass through; to cause to pass through') (several scouts ~ped through their lines; we were able to ~ an agent through their security net; the opportunity ~ped through his fingers)

slipcovers *n.* (AE) 1. to make ~ 2. to put on ~ 3. custom-made ~

slippers *n.* 1. house ~ 2. a pair of ~

slip up *v.* (D; intr.) ('to blunder') to ~ on (she ~ped up on the last question)

slit I *n.* a narrow ~

slit II *v.* (N; used with an adjective) she slit the envelope open

slither *v.* (P; intr.) to ~ along the ground

slobber *v.* (colloq.) to ~ all over smb.

slog *v.* (P; intr.) to ~ through the mud

slogan *n.* 1. to coin a ~ 2. a catchy ~

slog away *v.* (D; intr.) to ~ at (to keep ~ging away at one's homework)

slope I *n.* a gentle, gradual ~

slope II *v.* 1. to ~ gently, gradually 2. (P; intr.) the river bank ~s to the east

slosh *v.* (P; intr.) to ~ through the snow

slot *n.* (colloq.) ['position'] to fill; fit into a ~

slot machine *n.* (AE) ['gambling device'] to play a ~ (BE has *fruit machine*)

slouch *n.* (colloq.) ['incompetent person'] no ~ at (she is no ~ at getting things done)

slouch down *v.* (D; intr.) to ~ behind (she ~ed

down behind the steering wheel)

slow *adj.* 1. ~ at, in (she was ~ in reacting) 2. ~ to + inf. (she was ~ to react)

slow burn *n.* (slang) (AE) to do a ~ ('to become angry gradually')

slowdown *n.* an economic ~

slow motion *n.* ['slow-motion photography'] in ~ (they showed the finish in ~)

sludge *n.* activated ~

slug *v.* (colloq.) (O) (can be used with one animate object) ('to punch') I'll ~ you one

slum *v.* to go ~ming

slumber *n.* deep ~

slump I *n.* a business, economic ~

slump II *v.* (D; intr.) to ~ to (the ground)

slums *n.* 1. to clean up, clear away, tear down ~ 2. festering; inner-city, urban ~

slur I *n.* ['insult'] 1. to cast a ~ 2. an ethnic, racial ~ 3. a ~ on (his remark was a ~ on my character)

slur II *v.* (d; intr.) to ~ over ('to minimize') (to ~ over a blunder)

slut *n.* a common ~

smack I *v.* (colloq.) (O) (can be used with one animate object) I'll ~ you one

smack II *v.* (d; intr.) to ~ of ('to suggest') (to ~ of treason)

smallpox *n.* 1. to contract, develop ~ 2. a ~ epidemic (there have been no ~ epidemics for many years)

small talk *n.* to make ~

smart I *adj.* ['impudent'] (colloq.) 1. to get ~ with (don't get ~ with me) ['shrewd'] 2. ~ to + inf. (she was ~ to refuse; it was ~ of him to reinvest his money)

smart II *v.* 1. (D; intr.) to ~ at, over (to ~ at an insult) 2. (D; intr.) to ~ under (to ~ under injustice)

smash *v.* 1. (d; intr.) to ~ into (to ~ into another car) 2. (d; intr.) to ~ through (to ~ through a fence)

smattering *n.* to acquire, pick up a ~ of (they have picked up a ~ of the language)

smear *n.* (med.) 1. to do, take a ~ 2. a Pap ~ (they did a Pap ~ on each patient)

smell I *n.* 1. to give off a ~ 2. an acrid; bad, disagreeable, foul; faint, slight; persistent; rank; strong; sweet ~ 3. a ~ of (the ~ of paint)

smell II *v.* 1. (D; intr.) to ~ like, of (to ~ of fish) 2. (J) we ~ed smt. burning 3. (s) the food ~s good

smile I *n.* 1. to crack, flash a ~ at 2. to give smb. a ~ 3. to evoke a ~ 4. to hide, repress a ~ 5. a beguiling, intriguing; cheerful, happy; disarming; fixed; forced; infectious; radiant; ready; sardonic; sunny; supercilious ~ 6. (misc.) they are all ~s at the good news

smile II *v.* 1. (D; intr.) to ~ at (she ~d at me) 2. (D; intr.) to ~ on ('to favor') (fortune ~d on us) 3. (misc.) to ~ from ear to ear

smirk *v.* (D; intr.) to ~ at

smite *v.* (rare; formal) (N; used with an adjective) to ~ smb. dead

smithereens *n.* to break, smash smt. into, to ~

smitten *adj.* ['affected'] (formal) 1. ~ by, with (~ by disease) ['infatuated'] (colloq.) 2. ~ by, with

(he was totally ~ with her)

smoke *n.* ['gaseous products of burning'] 1. to belch, emit, give off ~ (chimneys belch ~) 2. to inhale ~ 3. heavy, thick, light ~ 4. ~ pours from (a chimney) 5. ~ eddies, spirals (upward) in a column; pall; puff; wisp of ~ ['act of smoking'] 7. to have a ~ 8. (to go out) for a ~

smoker *n.* a chain; habitual, heavy, inveterate ~

smoke screen *n.* to lay (down) a ~

smooth *adj.* 1. ~ to (~ to the touch) 2. (misc.) as ~ as silk

smuggle *v.* 1. (D; tr.) to ~ across (to ~ goods across a border) 2. (D; tr.) to ~ by, past, through (to ~ a diamond past customs) 3. (D; tr.) to ~ into (to ~ currency into a country) 4. (D; tr.) to ~ out of (to ~ stolen goods out of a country)

smuggling *n.* to engage in ~

smut *n.* (esp. AE) a ~ peddler

snack *n.* 1. to have a ~ 2. to fix ('prepare') a ~ 3. a between-meal; midnight ~; party ~s

snag *n.* ['obstacle'] (colloq.) 1. to hit a ~ ['jagged tear'] 2. to get a ~ (in one's stocking)

snake I *n.* 1. a poisonous, venomous ~ 2. ~s bite; strike; coil; crawl; hibernate; hiss; molt; shed skin 3. (misc.) a ~ in the grass ('a treacherous person')

snake II *v.* (colloq.) he ~d his way through the crowd

snap I *n.* ['spell of weather'] 1. a cold ~ ['something easy'] (colloq.) 2. a ~ to + inf. (it was a ~ to find information about that author = it was a ~ finding information about that author)

snap II *v.* 1. (D; intr.) to ~ at (the dog ~ped at him; to ~ at the bait) 2. (misc.) to ~ to attention; to ~ out of a bad mood

snapshot *n.* to take a ~

snarl *v.* 1. (B) he ~ed a few words to me 2. (D; intr.) to ~ at

snatch I *n.* ['fragment'] to catch ~es (of conversation)

snatch II *v.* 1. (d; intr.) to ~ at (she ~ed at the line that the sailors threw to her) 2. (D; tr.) to ~ from, out of (he ~ed the purse from her hand)

sneak *v.* (P; intr.) the boy ~ed into the theater; to ~ around in the bushes

sneak up *v.* (D; intr.) to ~ on, to (he ~ed up to them)

sneaky *adj.* (colloq.) ~ of (that was ~ of him)

sneer *v.* (D; intr.) to ~ at

sneeze *v.* (colloq.) (d; intr.) to ~ at ('to consider lightly') (don't ~ at their offer)

sniff *v.* (D; intr.) to ~ at (the dog ~ed at her)

snipe *v.* (D; intr.) to ~ at (the press keeps ~ing at her)

snit *n.* (colloq.) (AE) ['state of agitation'] in a ~

snook *n.* (colloq.) (BE) to cock a ~ at ('to thumb one's nose at')

snore I *n.* a loud ~

snore II *v.* to ~ loudly

snow I *n.* 1. drifting; driving, heavy; light ~ 2. crisp; new-fallen ~ 3. ~ falls; melts; sticks 4. a blanket of ~ 5. in the ~ (to play in the ~) 6. (misc.) to shovel ~; as white as ~

snow II *v.* to ~ hard, heavily; lightly

snowball I *n.* to throw a ~ at

snowball II *v.* (D; intr.) ('to expand') to ~ into
snowball fight *n.* to have a ~
snowfall *n.* a heavy; light ~
snow job *n.* (colloq.) ['deception, flattery'] to give smb. a ~
snowman *n.* to build, make a ~
snowshoes *n.* 1. a pair of ~ 2. (to walk) on ~
snowstorm *n.* see **storm** I 2
snub *n.* a deliberate; obvious ~
snuff *n.* 1. to take ~ 2. a pinch of ~ 3. (misc.) not up to ~ ('not up to an acceptable standard')
snuggle *v.* (d; intr.) to ~ against (the children ~d against each other)
snuggle up *v.* (d; intr.) to ~ to (the little girl ~d up to her doll)
soak *v.* (d; intr.) to ~ into (the water ~ed into the soil)
soap *n.* 1. face; laundry; liquid; powdered; saddle; scented; toilet ~ 2. a bar, cake of ~
sob I *n.* a bitter ~
sob II *v.* 1. to ~ bitterly 2. (B) the child ~bed a few words to us 3. (misc.) to ~ oneself to sleep
sober *adj.* cold, stone ~
socialism *n.* 1. Fabian; utopian 2. under ~ (to live under ~)
social work *n.* to do ~
society *n.* ['group, association'] 1. to establish, found, set up a ~ 2. to disband, dissolve a ~ 3. a burial; historical; honor; humane; learned; literary; medical; musical; secret ~ 4. a friendly (BE), mutual-aid (AE) ~ 5. a building ~ (BE; AE has *building and loan association*) ['community'] 6. to polarize; unite a ~ 7. an advanced; affluent; civilized; closed; open; pluralistic; primitive ~ ['class'] 8. high; polite ~ 9. in ~ (such words are not used in polite ~)
sock I *n.* 1. to knit ~s 2. to darn, mend a ~ 3. athletic; knee; stretch; tube ~s 4. a pair of ~s
sock II *v.* (colloq.) to ~ it to smb. ('to speak to smb., act towards smb. in a very forceful manner')
socket *n.* a wall ~
soda *n.* ['form of sodium'] 1. baking; caustic; washing ~ ['beverage'] 2. (a) club; cream; ice-cream ~ ['soda water'] 3. a dash of ~ 4. (misc.) (a) whiskey and ~
sodomy *n.* to commit, practice ~
soft *adj.* (colloq.) ['attracted'] 1. ~ on (he is ~ on her) ['lenient'] 2. ~ on (this judge is not ~ on drunk drivers)
soft spot *n.* ['weakness'] to have a ~ for
software *n.* computer; proprietary; public-domain ~
soil *n.* 1. to cultivate, till, work the ~ 2. to fertilize; irrigate the ~ 3. barren; poor; fertile; firm; packed; sandy; soggy; swampy ~
solace *n.* 1. to find ~ in 2. a ~ to (she was a ~ to her parents)
solder *n.* to apply; melt ~
soldier *n.* 1. an armed; common; foot; professional; seasoned ~ 2. a ~ defects, deserts; enlists; fights; goes AWOL; reenlists; serves; trains 3. (misc.) the Unknown Soldier
sole I *n.* ['bottom part of a shoe'] 1. to put (new) ~s on shoes 2. a half ~

sole II *n.* ['type of fish'] fillet of ~
solicitor *n.* 1. The Solicitor General ('the assistant attorney general') 2. (GB) barristers and ~s
solicitous *adj.* ~ about, of
solicitude *n.* to show ~ for
solid *adj.* to be in ~ with smb.
solidarity *n.* 1. to express; feel; show ~ 2. ~ with (to express one's ~ with the protestors)
solitaire *n.* (AE) ['card game'] to play ~ (BE has *patience*)
solitary confinement *n.* 1. to put smb. into ~ 2. in ~
solitude *n.* 1. complete, utter ~ 2. in ~ (to live in complete ~)
solo I *adj.* to dance; fly; perform; play; sing ~
solo II *n.* to perform a ~
solstice *n.* the summer; winter ~
solution *n.* ['answer'] ['explanation'] 1. to find a ~ 2. to apply a ~ 3. an easy; glib; ideal; ingenious; neat; satisfactory ~ 4. a ~ for, to (a ~ to a problem) ['mixture'] 5. a strong; weak ~ 6. a saline ~
some *pronoun, determiner* 1. ~ to + inf. (we have ~ to sell; we have ~ books to sell) 2. ~ of (~ of them) USAGE NOTE: The use of the preposition *of* is necessary when a pronoun follows. When a noun follows, the use of *of the* limits the meaning--we saw some people; we saw some of the people whom we had discussed earlier. (see also the Usage Note for **something)**
somebody *pronoun* ~ to + inf. (we have ~ to talk to) (see also the Usage Note for **something)**
someone see **somebody**
someplace (AE) see **somewhere**
somersault *n.* to do, execute, turn a ~
something *n., pronoun* 1. an indefinable, inde-scribable, intangible ~ 2. ~ for (she has ~ for you) 3. ~ to + inf. (we have ~ to say) 4. (misc.) to make ~ of oneself ('to have success in life'); ('slang') I don't know if he wants to make ~ of it ('I don't know if he wants to make an issue of it'); there is ~ unusual about them; she is ~ of a celebrity USAGE NOTE: The form *some* and its com-pounds are often used in affirmative statements, whereas *any* and its compounds are often used in neg. and interrogative statements. Compare *we have some books to sell--we don't have any books to sell; we have something to say--do you have any-thing to say?* We have somebody to talk to--we don't have anybody to talk to; we have somewhere to go--do you have anywhere to go? However, in the meaning 'no matter', *any* and its compounds occur in affirmative statements--we will take any of these; they can say anything they want; we will talk to anyone; we will go anywhere. *Some* and its compounds can occur in questions, especially when an affirmative answer is expected--don't you have something to say to me? would you like some brandy?
somewhere *adv.* ~ to + inf. (we have ~ to go) (see also the Usage Note for **something)**
son *n.* 1. to adopt a ~ 2. to marry off a ~ 3. an only ~ 4. an adopted; foster ~; stepson 5. a ~ to (he was like a ~ to them) 6. (misc.) a favorite ~ (AE; pol.); a prodigal ~ (fig.)

song *n.* 1. to compose, write a ~ 2. to belt out (colloq.), sing; hum; play; whistle a ~ (the orchestra was playing our ~) 3. a drinking; folk; love; marching; theme ~ 4. a swan ('farewell') ~ 5. (misc.) the same old ~ ('the same story, complaint')

sonic barrier *n.* to break the ~

sonic boom *n.* to cause, generate, produce a ~

sonnet *n.* 1. to compose, write a ~ 2. an Italian, Petrarchan; Shakespearean; Spenserian ~

sop *n.* ['concession'] to throw a ~ to

sophistication *n.* the ~ to + inf. (will she have enough ~ to deal with their questions?)

sophistry *n.* 1. pure ~ 2. ~ to + inf. (it's pure ~ to rationalize such behavior)

soprano *n.* to sing ~

sorcery *n.* to practice ~

sore I *adj.* ['angry'] (colloq.) (esp. AE) 1. ~ at (why is she ~ at me?) 2. ~ over (~ over smb.'s remark) ['hurt'] 3. ~ from (~ from riding horseback)

sore II *n.* a bedsore; canker; cold; open, running; saddle ~

sore throat *n.* to come down with; have a ~

sorority *n.* (US) 1. to pledge a ~ ('to agree to join a sorority') 2. a college ~ (see also **fraternity**)

sorrow *n.* 1. to cause ~ 2. to express; feel; show ~ 3. to alleviate smb.'s ~ 4. deep, great, inexpressible, keen, profound ~ 5. personal ~ 6. ~ at (to feel deep ~ at the death of a friend) 7. to smb.'s ~ (to my great ~ I never saw them again)

sorry *adj.* 1. dreadfully, terribly ~ 2. ~ about 3. ~ for (she is ~ for him; we are ~ for being late) 4. ~ to + inf. (I am ~ to inform you that your application has been rejected) 5. ~ that + clause (we are ~ that you weren't able to come)

sort *n.* a bad; curious; good ~ (a curious ~ of a life)

sortie *n.* 1. to carry out, make a ~ 2. to fly a ~

sort of *adv.* (colloq.) ['more or less'] I ~ expected it (to happen)

SOS *n.* to broadcast, send an ~

soul *n.* 1. to save smb.'s ~ 2. an artistic; immortal; kindly; kindred; lost; poor; timid ~

sound I *adj.* ['healthy'] ~ in, of (~ in mind and body)

sound II *n.* 1. to emit, make, produce, utter; transmit a ~ 2. to articulate. enunciate, pronounce a ~ 3. to turn down; turn up the ~ (on a radio, TV set) 4. to carry ~ (air carries ~s) 5. a faint; hollow; loud; rasping; soft ~ 6. ~ travels (much slower than light) 7. a ~ rings out 8. to a ~ (to the ~ of music)

sound III *v.* 1. (d; intr.) to ~ like (that ~s like a great idea) 2. (BE) (S) that ~s a great idea 3. (s) their excuse ~ed reasonable

sound barrier *n.* to break the ~

sound off *v.* (colloq.) (D; intr.) to ~ against ('to criticize') (to ~ against an idea)

soup *n.* 1. to eat; make ~ 2. clear; cold; hot; thick; warm ~ 3. cabbage; celery; chicken; onion; pea; tomato; vegetable ~ 4. a bowl; cup of ~

sour *adj.* to go, turn ~ (things went ~; the whole affair turned ~)

source *n.* 1. to tap a ~ 2. to cite; disclose, indicate, reveal one's ~s 3. an impeccable, unimpeachable; reliable, reputable, trustworthy; unreliable ~ 4. an undisclosed, unnamed ~ 5. an original ~ 6. an energy ~ 7. ~s dry up 8. at a ~ (it is best to make inquiries at the original ~s) 9. (misc.) ~s close to the government revealed that...

south I *adj., adv.* 1. directly, straight ~ 2. ~ of (~ of the city) 3. (misc.) to go/head ~

south II *n.* 1. in, to the ~ 2. (misc.) down ~

South Pole *n.* at the ~

sovereignty *n.* 1. to grant ~ 2. to establish ~ 3. to violate a country's ~ 4. ~ over

space *n.* 1. to save ~ 2. breathing ~; (an) empty ~ 3. a crawl; parking ~ 4. office; storage ~ 5. airspace; interplanetary, interstellar, outer ~ 6. (a) ~ between 7. ~ for 8. (misc.) the (wide) open ~s; to indent several ~s; to violate a country's airspace

space bar *n.* (on a typewriter) to press a ~

spacecraft *n.* a manned ~ (see the Usage Note for **ship**)

spaceflight *n.* 1. a manned; unmanned ~ 2. a ~ to (a ~ to the moon)

space probe *n.* to launch a ~

space vehicle *n.* to launch a ~ (see the Usage Note for **ship**)

spacing *n.* (on a typewriter) double; single ~

span *n.* 1. a brief ~ 2. an attention; life; memory ~ 3. in a ~ (in the brief ~ of ten years)

spanking *n.* 1. to give smb. a (good) ~ 2. to get a ~ 3. (misc.) to deserve a ~

spanner *n.* a box ~ (BE; AE has *lug wrench*)

spare *v.* 1. (C) can you ~ a few minutes for me today? or: can you ~ me a few minutes today? 2. (O; can be used with one animate object) ~ us the details; he wanted to ~ you embarrassment

sparing *adj.* (cannot stand alone) ~ of

spark *n.* 1. to emit, produce a ~ 2. ~s fly

sparrow *n.* 1. ~s chirp 2. a flock of ~s

spasm *n.* a muscle ~

spat I *n.* ['quarrel'] to have a ~ with

spat II *v.* (D; intr.) ('to quarrel') to ~ with

speak *v.* 1. ('to talk') to ~ bluntly, candidly, frankly, freely; coherently; correctly; fluently; glibly; incorrectly; irresponsibly; loudly; openly; politely; quickly, rapidly; quietly, softly; responsibly; rudely; slowly; truthfully 2. (D; intr.) ('to talk') to ~ about, of (to ~ about politics) 3. (d; intr.) to ~ for ('to be a spokesperson for') (she spoke for all of us; who will ~ for the accused?) 4. (d; intr.) ('to talk') to ~ from (to ~ from the heart; to ~ from experience) 5. (d; intr.) ('to converse') to ~ in (they were ~ing in English; more usu. is: they were ~ing English) 6. (d; intr.) to ~ to ('to address') (she spoke to the crowd; to ~ to the subject; to ~ to the question on the agenda; don't ~ to him) 7. (D; intr.) ('to converse') to ~ to, with (she spoke to me about several things; I spoke with them for an hour) 8. (misc.) to ~ well of smb. ('to praise smb.'); to ~ ill of smb. ('to criticize smb.'); it ~s for itself ('it is self-evident') roughly ~ing ('approximately'); strictly ~ ('in concrete terms')

speaker n. ['one who speaks'] 1. a native ~ (of a language) 2. an effective, good; fluent ~ 3. a guest; public ~ (she is a good public ~) ['device that amplifies sound'] 4. an extension ~; loudspeaker

speaking n. public ~

speaking terms n. to be on ~ with smb.

speak out v. 1. (D; intr.) to ~ about, concerning, on (to ~ on a subject) 2. (d; intr.) to ~ against ('to oppose') (to ~ against a proposal) 3. (d; intr.) to ~ for ('to support') (to ~ for a proposal)

speak up see **speak out**

spear n. 1. to hurl, throw a ~ at 2. to thrust a ~ into

spearhead n. 1. to send out a ~ 2. an armored ~

special adj. ~ to

specialist n. 1. to call in; consult a ~ 2. a ~ in, on (a ~ in plastic surgery; a ~ on Milton)

specialize v. (D; intr.) to ~ in

species n. 1. an endangered ~ 2. a ~ becomes extinct, dies out; survives

specifications n. 1. to adhere to, meet ~ 2. rigid ~

specify v. 1. (D; tr.) to ~ by (to ~ smb. by name) 2. (L) the contract ~fies that a penalty must be paid if the work is not completed on time 3. (Q) the instructions ~ how the medicine is to be taken

specimen n. a blood; sputum; stool; urine ~

specs (colloq.) see **spectacles**

spectacle n. ['show, exhibition'] 1. to stage a ~ 2. a dramatic ~ ['object of curiosity'] 3. to make a ~ of oneself 4. a pitiful ~

spectacles n. (now esp. BE) a pair of ~

spectators n. to seat ~ (the stadium seats sixty thousand ~)

spectrum n. a broad, wide ~

speculate v. 1. (D; intr.) ('to meditate, think') to ~ about, on (to ~ about what might have been) 2. (D; intr.) ('to conduct business by taking risks') to ~ in; on (to ~ in oil shares; to ~ in gold; to ~ on the stock market) 3. (L) ('to assume, think') they ~d that the election results would be close

speculation n. ['meditation, thinking'] 1. to indulge in ~ 2. idle; wild ~ 3. a flurry of ~ 4. ~ about (~ about the upcoming elections) 5. ~ that + clause (there was ~ that a treaty would be signed) ['risky business methods'] 6. to engage in ~ 7. ~ in (~ in stocks and bonds)

speculator n. a property (BE), real-estate (AE); stock-market ~

speculum n. a nasal; vaginal ~

speech n. ['address, talk'] 1. to deliver, give, make a ~ 2. to ad-lib, improvise a ~ 3. a boring; brief, short; impromptu, unrehearsed; long; long-winded; passionate; rambling; rousing, stirring ~ 4. an acceptance; after-dinner; campaign; farewell; inaugural; keynote; political; welcoming ~ 5. a ~ about ['communication in words'] 6. free ~ ['pronunciation'] 7. clipped ~ 8. impaired; slurred ~

speechless adj. 1. to be left ~ 2. ~ with (~ with anger)

speed n. ['swiftness, velocity'] 1. to build up, pick up; maintain ~ 2. to reach a ~ (to reach cruising ~; to reach a ~ of one hundred miles an hour) 3.

breakneck, breathtaking, high, lightning; cruising; deliberate, full, top; low; moderate; steady; supersonic ~ 4. a burst of ~ 5. at a certain ~ (at top ~) 6. (misc.) full ~ ahead! ['amphetamine'] (slang) 7. to shoot; snort ~

speed limit n. 1. to enforce; establish a ~ 2. to observe a ~ 3. to exceed a ~

speed trap n. to set up a ~

spell n. ['incantation'] 1. to cast a ~ on, over 2. to break, remove a ~ 3. a magic ~ 4. under a ~

spellbinding adj. ~ to + inf. (it's ~ to read her memoirs)

spelling n. 1. phonetic ~ 2. in (phonetic) ~

spell out v. (B) they ~ed out their demands to us

spend v. 1. (D; tr.) to ~ for, on (to ~ a lot of money for a new car; to ~ a lot on repairs) 2. (D; tr.) to ~ in (to ~ a great deal of time in studying/ time studying)

spending n. deficit; defense; government ~

spider n. 1. ~s crawl 2. ~s spin webs

spill I n. ['accidental pouring'] 1. an oil ~ ['fall'] 2. to take a ~ (from a horse) 3. a nasty ~

spill II v. 1. (D; tr.) to ~ all over, on (I ~ed the milk all over her) 2. (d; intr.) ('to pour') to ~ into (the crowd was ~ing into the streets) 3. (d; intr.) ('to flow') to ~ out of (the liquid was ~ing out of the container)

spin n. ['fast drive'] (colloq.) to go for, take a ~ (let's go for a ~ around town)

spinal tap n. to do a ~ (on smb.)

spiral n. an inflationary; wage-price ~ (a vicious inflationary ~)

spirit I n. ['vigor'] ['enthusiasm'] 1. to display, show ~ 2. to catch the ~ (of the times) 3. to break smb.'s ~ (her ~ was broken) 4. (a) civic; class; college; competitive; dauntless, hardy; ecumenical; fighting; partisan; patriotic; rebellious; religious; school; scientific; team ~ 5. a guiding; moving ~ 6. (misc.) a ~ of good will pervaded the conversation ['supernatural being, ghost'] 7. to conjure up, evoke a ~ 8. an evil; holy ~ ['soul'] 9. a kindred ~ 10. in ~ (in body and in ~) ['attitude'] 11. in a ~ (in a ~ of cooperation)

spirit II v. (P; tr.) he was ~ed off to prison

spirits n. ['mood'] 1. to lift, raise smb.'s ~ 2. to dampen smb.'s ~ 3. good, high ~ 4. ~ droop, flag; rise 5. in ~ (in high ~) ['alcohol'] 6. to drink ~

spit v. 1. (D; intr.) to ~ at, on 2. (d; intr.) to ~ in, into (to ~ in smb.'s face) 3. (d; tr.) to ~ out of (to ~ smt. out of one's mouth)

spite n. 1. in ~ of 2. out of ~ (they did it out of ~)

spiteful adj. ~ to + inf. (it was ~ of him to say that)

splash n. (colloq.) ['vivid impression'] to make a (big) ~

spleen n. ['bad temper'] 1. to vent one's ~ on ['ductless organ near the stomach'] 2. a ruptured ~

splendid adj. ~ to + inf. (it was ~ of you to make the offer)

splendor, splendour n. 1. regal ~ 2. in ~ (to dine in regal ~)

splice v. (D; tr.) to ~ to (to ~ a wire to a cable)

splint n. 1. to apply a ~ to 2. a ~ for (a fractured

leg)

splinter *n.* 1. to get; have a ~ (in one's finger) 2. to extract, get out, remove a ~ (she got the ~ out of my finger)

split I *n.* ['breach'] 1. a formal; irreparable ~ 2. a ~ between 3. a ~ in (the party)

split II *v.* 1. (d; tr.) ('to divide') to ~ between; with (we split the profits with them) 2. (d; intr., tr.) ('to divide') to ~ into (they split into several factions; the teacher split the class into two groups)

split ticket *n.* (AE) to vote a ~ ('to distribute one's vote among candidates of more than one party')

split up *v.* (colloq.) (D; intr.) to ~ with (she split up with her boyfriend)

splurge *v.* (colloq.) (D; intr.) ('to spend extravagantly') to ~ on (to ~ on a new car)

spoil *v.* (d; intr.; usu. in a progressive form) to ~ for ('to seek') (to be ~ing for a fight)

spoils *n.* to divide the ~ (of war)

spokesman see **spokesperson**

spokesperson *n.* a ~ for (a ~ for the strikers)

spokeswoman see **spokesperson**

sponge I *n.* ['spongy substance'] 1. to squeeze a ~ ['symbol of surrender'] 2. to throw in, toss in the ~

sponge II *v.* (colloq.) 1. (D; tr.) ('to wheedle') to ~ from, off, off of (AE) (he ~d a cigarette from me) 2. (d; intr.) to ~ on ('to impose on') (to ~ on one's friends)

sponsor I *n.* 1. a radio; television, TV ~ 2. a ~ for, of

sponsor II *v.* (D; tr.) to ~ for (she ~ed me for membership)

sponsorship *n.* under smb.'s ~

spoon *n.* a dessert; measuring; soup ~; tablespoon; teaspoon

spoonful *n.* a heaping; level ~

sport *n.* ['person judged by her/his ability to take a loss or teasing'] 1. a bad, poor; good ~ 2. a ~ about (she was a good ~ about losing the bet) ['mockery'] 3. to make ~ of smb. ('to mock smb.') ['type of physical activity'] 4. a contact; spectator ~ 5. an exciting; strenuous, vigorous ~ (skiing is an exciting ~) ['physical activity'] (BE) 6. to go in for ~ 7. fond of ~; in the world of ~ (AE has *sports*)

sports *n.* ['physical activity'] (AE) 1. to go in for ~ 2. fond of ~; in the world of ~ (BE has *sport*) ['types of physical activity'] 3. amateur; aquatic, water; competitive; intercollegiate (AE), inter-university (BE); intramural; outdoor; professional; varsity (AE); winter ~ ['track meet'] (BE) 4. school ~; ~ day

sportsmanship *n.* to display, show ~

spot I *n.* ['mark, stain'] 1. to leave, make a ~ 2. to get out, remove a ~ 3. a grease ~ ['mark on the skin'] 4. a beauty ~ ['area, place'] 5. a high; isolated, secluded; low ~ 6. (soccer) the penalty ~ 7. at a ~ (let's meet at this same ~ tomorrow) ['place of entertainment'] (colloq.) 8. to hit ('visit') all the night ~s ['point, position'] 9. the high, low ~ (the high ~ of our visit) ['misc.'] 10. on the ~ ('immediately'); ('at the center of activity'); ('exposed to the worst danger'); to put smb. on the ~ ('to

expose smb. to danger'); a blind ~ ('an area that cannot be seen') (also fig.); to have a soft/tender/warm ~ (in one's heart) for ('to have a weakness for'); to be in a tight ~ ('to be in a difficult situation'); a trouble ~ (that reporter has been in many trouble ~s throughout the world); (BE; colloq.) a ~ of bother ('a bit of trouble')

spot II *v.* 1. (d; tr.) ('to identify') to ~ as (the police ~ted him as a known criminal) 2. (D) ('to see') we ~ted them going through the gate

spot check *n.* to do, make a ~

spotlight *n.* 1. to direct, focus, shine, turn a ~ on 2. (fig.) in the ~

spouse *n.* a beloved; faithful; unfaithful ~

spout *v.* (d; intr.) ('to spurt') to ~ from

sprawl I *n.* urban ~

sprawl II *v.* (P; intr.) to ~ on the sofa

sprawling *adj.* to send smb. ~

spread *v.* 1. to ~ smt. evenly (to ~ paint evenly) 2. to ~ quickly; unchecked (the epidemic spread unchecked) 3. (D; intr.) to ~ to (the epidemic spread to neighboring countries) 4. (misc.) to ~ like wildfire

spree *n.* 1. to go on a ~ 2. a spending; weekend ~

spring I *n.* ['season'] 1. an early ~ 2. in (the) ~ 3. (misc.) there is a touch of ~ in the air; a harbinger of ~ ['source of water'] 4. a hot, thermal; mineral; subterranean ~ ['bounce, elasticity'] 5. a ~ to (there was a ~ to her step)

spring II *v.* 1. (D; intr.) to ~ at (the lion sprang at the hunter) 2. (D; intr.) ('to arise, result') to ~ from 3. (D; tr.) ('to prepare') to ~ on (to ~ a surprise on smb.) 4. (d; intr.) ('to jump') to ~ to (to ~ to smb.'s defense; to ~ to one's feet)

springboard *n.* a ~ for (a ~ for a new campaign)

spring-clean *n.* (BE) to do a ~

spring-cleaning (esp. AE) see **spring-clean**

spruce up *v.* (D; refl.) to ~ for (they ~d themselves up for the big party)

spunk *n.* (colloq.) ['courage'] 1. to show ~ 2. the ~ to + inf. (she had the ~ to defend her rights)

spur I *n.* ['incentive, stimulus'] 1. a ~ to ['misc.'] 2. on the ~ of the moment ('without planning')

spur II *v.* 1. (D; tr.) to ~ to (to ~ smb. to action) 2. (H) what ~red her to do that?

spur on *v.* 1. (D; tr.) to ~ to (to ~ smb. on to greater effort) 2. (H) we ~red them on to make a greater effort

spurs *n.* ['recognition'] 1. to win one's ~ ['devices worn on a rider's heel'] 2. to dig, drive one's ~ (into the side of a horse) 3. ~ jingle

spurt I *n.* a growth ~

spurt II *v.* (D; intr.) to ~ from (blood ~ed from the wound)

sputum *n.* to cough up, produce ~

spy *v.* 1. (d; intr.) to ~ for (to ~ for a foreign power) 2. (D; intr.) to ~ on, upon 3. (J) we spied them coming through the gate

squabble I *n.* a ~ about, over; between; with

squabble II *v.* (D; intr.) to ~ about, over, with

squad *n.* 1. a demolition; firing; flying (BE) ~ 2. a vice ~

squalor *n.* in ~ (to live in ~)

squander *v.* (D; tr.) to ~ on (to ~ a fortune on bad

investments)

square I *n.* 1. to draw, make a ~ 2. (misc.) on the ~ ('honest'); back to ~ one ('back to the beginning')

square II *v.* (D; intr., tr.) to ~ with (their story doesn't ~ with the facts; to ~ one's account with smb.)

square root *n.* to find, extract the ~

squash I *n.* (BE) ['fruit drink'] lemon; orange ~

squash II *n.* (AE) ['marrow-like plant'] summer; winter ~ (BE has *marrow*)

squawk I *n.* to let out a ~

squawk II *v.* (colloq.) (D; intr.) ('to complain') to ~ about

squeak *n.* ['shrill cry'] 1. to emit, let out a ~ ['escape'] (colloq.) 2. a close ~

squeal I *n.* to emit, let out a ~

squeal II *v.* 1. (slang) (D; intr.) ('to inform') to ~ on; to (he ~ed on them to the police) 2. (D; intr.) to ~ in, with (to ~ with delight)

squeamish *adj.* ~ about

squeeze I *n.* (colloq.) ['hug'] 1. to give smb. a ~ ['misc.'] 2. in a tight ~ ('in difficulty')

squeeze II *v.* 1. (C) ~ some orange juice for me; or: ~ me some orange juice 2. (d; tr.) to ~ from, out of (~ some tooth paste out of the tube) 3. (d; intr., tr.) to ~ into (to ~ into a small room; to ~ juice into a glass) 4. (d; intr.) to ~ through (to ~ through a narrow passage) 5. (N; used with an adjective) ~ the mops dry

squelch *n.* (colloq.) ['crushing rebuke'] a perfect ~

squint *v.* (D; intr.) to ~ at

squirm *v.* (d; intr.) to ~ out of ('to evade') (to ~ out of an obligation)

squirt I *n.* ['instance of squirting'] 1. to give smt. a ~ ['insignificant person'] (colloq.) 2. a little ~

squirt II *v.* (d; intr.) to ~ out of (the liquid ~ed out of the bottle)

stab *n.* ['attempt'] (colloq.) 1. to have, make a ~ at ['sensation'] 2. a sharp; sudden ~ (of pain) ['thrust of a pointed weapon'] 3. a ~ in the back (also fig.)

stability *n.* 1. to lend ~ to 2. ~ in

stable *n.* 1. a livery; riding ~ 2. (misc.) (Greek mythology) to clean the Augean ~s

stack I *n.* 1. a bookstack; haystack; smokestack (esp. AE) 2. (misc.) to blow one's ~ ('to lose one's temper')

stack II *v.* 1. (esp. AE) (D; tr.) ('to arrange underhandedly') to ~ against (the cards were ~ed against her) 2. (d; tr.) to ~ with (the floor was ~ed with books)

stacks *n.* (in a library) closed; open ~

stack up *v.* (colloq.) (D; intr.) to ~ against, to ('to compare to') (how do we ~ to the competition?)

stadium *n.* 1. to crowd, fill, jam, pack a ~ 2. to empty a ~ 3. a baseball; football; Olympic ~ 4. a ~ empties; fills

staff *n.* ['personnel'] 1. an administrative; coaching; editorial; hospital; medical; nursing; office; teaching ~ 2. a skeleton ~ 3. on the ~ 4. (misc.) to join a ~ (she joined the ~ as an editor) ['group of officers serving a commander'] 5. a general;

joint; military; personal; special ~ 6. on a ~ (he was on the general ~) 7. (misc.) to assign smb. to a ~ (she was assigned to the ~ as an intelligence officer)

stag *adj., adv.* ['unaccompanied by a member of the opposite sex'] 1. to go ~ 2. (misc.) a ~ party

stage *n.* ['platform on which plays are performed'] 1. a revolving; sinking; sliding ~ 2. on (the) ~ (she has appeared many times on ~; to go on ~) ['scene, setting'] 3. to set the ~ for (the ~ was set for a showdown) ['level, degree, step'] 4. to reach a ~ 5. an advanced; beginning, elementary; closing, final; critical, crucial; intermediate; opening ~ 6. flood ~ 7. at a ~ (negotiations were at a crucial ~; the river was at flood ~) 8. in a ~ (in this ~ of one's development) ['portion, part'] 9. easy ~s 10. by, in ~s (to cover a distance by easy ~s; to learn a language in easy ~s)

stagger *v.* 1. (D; intr.) to ~ from; into (to ~ into a room) 2. (D; intr.) to ~ out of (to ~ out of a building) 3. (R) it ~ed me to learn of his defection 4. (misc.) to ~ to one's feet; to ~ under a heavy burden

staggered *adj.* 1. ~ at, by (~ at the news of the earthquake) 2. ~ to + inf. (she was ~ to learn of the fire)

staggering *adj.* ~ to + inf. (it was ~ to total up the losses)

stain I *n.* ['discolored spot'] 1. to leave a ~ 2. to remove a ~ 3. a stubborn ~ 4. (fig.) a ~ on (a ~ on one's reputation)

stain II *v.* (N; used with an adjective) we ~ed the wood dark brown

staircase *n.* a circular, spiral; winding ~

stairs *n.* 1. to climb, go up the ~ 2. to come down; go down the ~ 3. moving ~

stairway see **staircase**

stake I *n.* ['piece of wood'] 1. to drive a ~ (into the ground) 2. to plant a ~ (in the ground) ['post'] 3. (to burn smb.) at the ~ ['share'] 4. to have a ~ in smt. ['risk'] 5. at ~ (our whole future is at ~)

stake II *v.* (D; tr.) to ~ to (to ~ a claim to smt.)

stake out *v.* (D; tr.) to ~ on, to (AE) (to ~ a claim to a mine)

stakes *n.* ['wager'] ['prize'] 1. big, high ~ (to play for high ~) ['misc.'] (AE) 2. to pull up ~ ('to move elsewhere')

stalemate *n.* 1. to break a ~ 2. a continuing ~

stalk *v.* (P; intr.) to ~ out of the room

stall (BE) see **stand I 8**

stamina *n.* the ~ to + inf. (she lacked the ~ to finish the race)

stammer *v.* (B) she ~ed a few words to us

stamp I *n.* ['postage stamp'] 1. to put, stick a ~ on (an envelope) 2. to lick, moisten a ~ 3. to issue a ~ (the post office has issued a new commemorative ~) 4. to cancel a ~ 5. an airmail; commemorative; postage; revenue; tax ~ 6. a book; roll; sheet of ~s ['coupon'] 7. a food; trading ~ ['device for imprinting'] 8. a rubber ~

stamp II *v.* 1. (d; tr.) to ~ as ('to mark') (these revelations ~ed him as a cheat) 2. (d; intr.) to ~ on ('to crush') (to ~ on an insect) 3. (N; used with an adjective) she ~ed the document *secret*

stampede I *n*. to cause, create a ~
stampede II *v*. (D; tr.) to ~ into (they were ~d into selling their homes)
stand I *n*. 1. to make, put up a ~ 2. a last ~ ['position'] 3. to take a ~ 4. a firm, resolute, strong ~ 5. a ~ on (they took a resolute ~ on the issue of tax reform) ['rack, small table'] 6. a music ~ ['place taken by a witness'] 7. a witness ~ (AE; BE has *witness box)* ['small structure used for conducting business'] (BE often prefers *stall)* 8. a fruit; hot-dog ~; newsstand; vegetable ~ ['performance, engagement'] 9. a one-night ~ ['row'] 10. a taxi ~ (esp. AE; BE prefers *taxi rank)*
stand II *v*. 1. ('to hold oneself') to ~ firm; still 2. (BE) (d; intr.) ('to be a candidate') to ~ as (to ~ as a Labour candidate) 3. (d; intr.) ('to hold oneself erect') to ~ at (to ~ at attention; to ~ at ease) 4. (d; intr.) to ~ by ('to support') (her family stood by her throughout the trial) 5. (d; intr.) to ~ for ('to represent') (our party used to ~ for progress) 6. (BE) (d; intr.) to ~ for ('to be a candidate') (to ~ for Parliament) 7. (d; intr.) to ~ for ('tc tolerate') (we will not ~ for such conduct) 8. (d; intr.) to ~ on ('to insist on') (to ~ on one's rights; to ~ on ceremony) 9. (d; intr.) to ~ over ('to watch') (he always ~s over me when I work) 10. (d; intr.) ('to be regarded') to ~ with (how do you ~ with your boss?) 11. (E) ('to face') ('to have as a prospect') we stood to gain a great deal 12. (esp. BE) (E; usu. with cannot -- can't -- couldn't) ('to tolerate') she couldn't ~ to wait any longer 13. (G; usu. with cannot -- can't -- couldn't) ('to tolerate') she can't ~ waiting 14. (K; usu. with cannot -- can't -- couldn't) ('to tolerate') I can't ~ his boasting 15. (esp. BE) (O) ('to buy') can I ~ you another round of drinks? 16. (s) she stood first in her class; to ~ accused of murder 17. (misc.) to ~ by one's guns ('to defend one's viewpoint stubbornly'); to ~ on one's own feet ('to support oneself'); to ~ tall (esp. AE; colloq.) ('to be resolute')
standard *n*. 1. to establish, set a ~ 2. to apply a ~ 3. to adhere to, maintain a ~ 4. to lower; raise ~s/ a ~ (to raise the ~ of living; to raise academic ~s) 5. to abandon a ~ (the gold ~ was abandoned) 6. a high; low ~ 7. a double ~ (to apply a double ~) 8. the gold ~ (to go off the gold ~) 9. a living ~ (or: a ~ of living) 10. academic, scholastic ~s 11. on a ~ (on a gold ~)
standardization *n*. to achieve, bring about ~
standard of living *n*. 1. to raise the ~ 2. a high; low ~ 3. a ~ falls, goes down; goes up, rises
stand back *v*. (D; intr.) to ~ from
standby *n*. ['alert'] to be on ~
stand by *v*. (D; intr.) ('to be ready') to ~ with (they were ~ing by with additional supplies)
stand clear *v*. (d; intr.) to ~ of
stand for *v*. (K) ('to tolerate') I will not ~ their behaving like that
stand in *v*. (d; intr.) to ~ for ('to substitute for') (can anyone ~ for her?)
standing *n*. ['duration'] 1. of (long) ~ (a custom of long ~) ['status'] 2. academic; advanced ~ (at a university) 3. ~ among, with (~ among the voters) 4. the ~ to + inf. (who has the ~ to take over

the leadership of the party?) 5. (misc.) in good ~; (US; on a traffic sign) No Standing/No Stopping (GB has *No Waiting)*
stand out *v*. 1. (D; intr.) ('to be clearly visible') to ~ against (to ~ against a dark background) 2. (D; intr.) ('to be noticeable') to ~ among, from, in (to ~ among the others; to ~ in a crowd; to ~ from the rest of the group) 3. (D; intr.) ('to be noticeable') to ~ as (she ~s out as the leading cand date)
standpoint *n*. from a ~ (from a practical ~ from our ~)
stands *n*. ['benches for spectators'] in the ~
standstill *n*. 1. to bring smt. to a ~ 2. to come to a ~ 3. a complete, total ~ 4. at a ~ (negotiations were at a complete ~) 5. (misc.) to fight smt. to a ~
stand up *v*. 1.(d; intr.) to ~ for ('to defend') (to ~ for one's rights) 2. (d; intr.) to ~ to ('to oppose') (no one dared to ~ to the boss)
star I *n*. ['heavenly body'] 1. a bright ~ 2. a falling, shooting ~ 3. the evening; morning; north ~ 4. a distant ~ 5. ~s shine, twinkle ['prominent performer'] 6. a baseball; basketball; box-office; film, movie (AE); football; guest; rugby; soccer; track ~ ['fortune'] 7. a ~ rises; sets, wanes (her ~ was rising) 8. under a ~ (she was born under a lucky ~) ['medal'] 9. a battle ~
star II *v*. 1. (D; intr.) to ~ as (in his last film he ~red as a cowboy) 2. (D; intr.) to ~ in (to ~ in a new play)
starch I *n*. cornstarch; potato ~
starch II *v*. to ~ stiffly
stare I *n*. a haughty; icy; vacant ~
stare II *v*. 1. to ~ wide-eyed 2. (D; intr.) to ~ at
starlet *n*. a film ~
starlight *n*. by ~
start I *n*. 1. to get off to, make a ~ 2. a false; flying, running; fresh, new; head; promising ~ 3. at the ~ 4. for a ~ (for a ~ let's agree where we should meet) 5. from the ~
start II *v*. 1. (d; intr., tr.) to ~ as (she ~ed her career as a dancer) 2. (D; intr.) ('to leave') to ~ for (when did they ~ for the airport?) 3. (d intr.) ('to leave') to ~ from (we ~ed from Philadelphia) 4. (d; intr.) to ~ on (to ~ on another case) 5. (d; intr., tr.) to ~ with (we'll ~ with you) 6. (Ξ) she ~ed to cough 7. (G) she ~ed coughing 8. (J) what ~ed them drinking?
starter *n*. for ~s ('to begin with')
start in *v*. (d; intr.) to ~ on ('to put pressure on') (then they ~ed in on her)
startle *v*. (R) it ~d me to see them dressed like that
startled *adj*. 1. ~ at (~ at the news) 2. ~ to + inf (she was ~ to hear of their divorce)
startling *adj*. ~ to + inf. (it was ~ to realize that we were completely cut off from the rest of the world)
start off *v*. 1. (d; intr., tr.) to ~ as (she ~ed off her career as a dancer) 2. (D; intr.) ('to leave') to ~ for (to ~ for the airport) 3. (D; intr.) to ~ from ('to leave') (we ~ed off from our house) 4. (D intr., tr.) ('to begin') to ~ with (we ~ed our tour off with a visit to the zoo)

start out see **start off**

starve v. 1. (D; tr.) to ~ into (to ~ smb. into submission) 2. (misc.) to ~ to death; to ~ oneself to death

starved adj. ~ for, of (BE) (~ for company)

state I n. ['government'] 1. to establish, found, set up a ~ 2. to govern, rule a ~ 3. a buffer; client; garrison; independent; police; puppet; secular; sovereign; welfare ~ 4. a member ~ (the member ~s of the UN) ['condition'] 5. a comatose; good; moribund; nervous; poor; transitional; unconscious; unspoiled; weakened ~ 6. one's financial; mental ~ 7. a gaseous; liquid; solid ~ 8. in a ~ (in a good ~ of repair; in a poor ~ of health; in a highly nervous ~) 9. (misc.) the ~ of the art ('the level of development') ['nervous condition'] 10. in a ~ (she was in quite a ~) ['pomp'] 11. to lie in ~ ['one of the fifty American states'] 12. a dry ~ ('a state in which the sale of alcoholic beverages is prohibited') 13. (historical; US) a border; free; slave ~

state II v. 1. to ~ clearly; emphatically 2. (B) we ~d our views to them 3. (L; to) they ~ed (to the reporters) that a summit conference would take place soon 4. (Q) she did not ~ how she expected to win the election

statehood n. 1. to achieve ~ 2. to seek, strive for ~

statement n. ['act of stating'] ['something stated'] 1. to issue, make a ~ 2. to confirm a ~ 3. to deny; refute; retract, withdraw a ~ 4. a brief, short; clear; false; oral; rash; succinct; sweeping; terse; vague; written ~ 5. a ~ that + clause (she has issued a ~ that she intends to be a candidate) 6. (misc.) a ~ to the effect that... ['report'] 7. to issue a ~ 8. a bank; financial; official; public ~ 9. a ~ about (the government issued a ~ about the strike)

state's evidence n. to turn ~ (see also **King's evidence, Queen's evidence**)

statesman n. an elder, prominent ~

statesmanship n. to practice ~

static n. to produce ~

station I n. ['building or place used for a specific purpose'] 1. a broadcasting; bus; coaling; coastguard; comfort (AE); experimental; fire; freight (AE); hydroelectric, power; naval; police; polling; radar; radar-tracking; railroad (AE), railway (esp. BE); recruiting; space; television, TV; tracking; weather ~ ['place where motor vehicles are serviced'] 2. a filling, gas (AE), gasoline (AE), petrol (BE), service ~ ['place of duty'] 3. an action; battle ~ ['position'] 4. one's ~ in life

station II v. (P; tr.) they were ~ed in Germany

statistics n. 1. to collect, gather; tabulate ~ 2. to bandy ~ (about) 3. cold, hard ~ 4. vital ~ ('essential data about a population') 5. ~ indicate, show

statue n. 1. to carve; sculpt, sculpture a ~ 2. to cast a ~ (in bronze) 3. to unveil a ~ 4. an equestrian ~

stature n. 1. imposing ~ (a person of imposing ~) 2. the ~ to + inf. (does she have the ~ to run for national office?)

status n. 1. to achieve ~ 2. celebrity ~ 3. a most-favored nation ~ 4. legal ~ (to enjoy/have legal ~) 5. one's marital ~

status quo n. to maintain, preserve; restore the ~

statute n. a penal ~

statute of limitations n. the ~ takes effect, goes into effect (or: colloq. and illogically -- the ~ expires, runs out)

stay I n. ['delay'] (legal) 1. to issue; vacate a ~ 2. (misc.) a ~ of execution

stay II v. 1. (D; intr.) ('to remain') to ~ for (to ~ for dinner) 2. (d; intr.) to ~ off ('to keep off') (to ~ off the grass) 3. (d; intr.) to ~ out of ('to avoid') (to ~ out of trouble) 4. (d; intr.) to ~ with smb. ('to be smb.'s guest') (they ~ed with us) 5. (s) to ~ calm

stay abreast v. (D; intr.) to ~ of (to ~ of the news; the runners ~ed abreast of each other)

stay ahead v. (D; intr.) to ~ of

stay away v. (D; intr.) to ~ from (to ~ from smb.)

staying power n. the ~ to + inf. (does she have the ~ to finish the race?)

stead n. to stand smb. in good ~ ('to be useful to smb.')

steady adj. 1. (colloq.) (AE) to go ~ with smb. ('to be smb.'s boyfriend or girlfriend') 2. (misc.) (before a race) ready, ~, go! (BE; AE has get ready, get set, go!)

steak n. 1. to broil (AE), grill a ~ 2. a juicy; tender; tough ~ 3. to like one's ~ medium; rare; well-done 4. a beefsteak; club; cube; flank; minute; Porterhouse; rump; Salisbury; salmon; sirloin; Swiss; T-bone ~

steal v. 1. (D; tr.) ('to give surreptitiously') to ~ at (to ~ a glance at smb.) 2. (D; intr., tr.) ('to take illegally') to ~ from (to ~ from the rich; he stole money from his employer) 3. (d; intr.) ('to depart silently') to ~ from, out of (she stole out of the room)

stealth n. by ~ (to enter a building by ~)

steal up v. (D; intr.) ('to sneak up') to ~ on, to (he stole up on me in the dark)

steam I n. 1. to emit; produce ~ 2. ~ condenses; forms 3. (misc.) (colloq.) to let off ~ ('to vent one's feelings')

steam II v. 1. (d; intr.) to ~ into; out of (to ~ into harbor) 2. (N; used with an adjective) she ~ed the envelope open

steamed up adj. (colloq.) ['angry'] ~ about, over

steamer n. an oceangoing; tramp ~

steam out v. (d; intr.) to ~ to (to ~ to sea)

steel I n. 1. to make, produce ~ 2. to temper ~ 3. stainless ~ 4. a bar; ingot; sheet; slab; strip of ~ 5. (misc.) cold ~ ('bayonet, knife used in close combat')

steel II v. 1. (D; refl.) to ~ for (to ~ oneself for the next attack) 2. (H; refl.) to ~ oneself to face an ordeal

steeped adj. (cannot stand alone) ~ in (~ in local traditions)

steeple n. a church ~

steer I n. (colloq.) ['suggestion'] 1. to give smb. a (bum) ~ 2. a bum ('bad'); friendly ~

steer II n. ['castrated bovine'] to rope a ~

steerage n. ['section in a passenger ship'] 1. to travel ~ 2. in ~ (to cross the ocean in ~)

steer clear v. (d; intr.) to ~ of (to ~ of danger)

steering *n.* power ~
steering wheel *n.* 1. to turn a ~ 2. at the ~ (who was at the ~?) (see **wheel 7-9**)
stem I *n.* (ling.) a consonant; verb ~
stem II *v.* (d; intr.) to ~ from
stench *n.* a dreadful, horrible, unbearable ~
stencil *n.* to cut a ~
step I *n.* ['placing the foot'] 1. to make, take a ~ (to take a ~ backward) 2. to retrace one's ~s 3. a giant (usu. fig.); mincing ~ 4. (usu. fig.) ~ by ~ ['sequence of movements'] (dancing) 5. to execute, perform a ~ ['stride in marching'] (mil.) 6. to keep in ~ 7. to change ~ 8. an even, steady ~ 9. half; route ~ 10. in ~; out of ~ (also fig.: she was out of ~ with everyone else) ['action'] 11. to take a ~ 12. a bold; careful, prudent; critical; dangerous; decisive; drastic; false; fatal; forward; giant; historic; positive; precautionary; preventive; rash, risky ~ (to take a giant ~ forward) ['gait'] 13. a heavy ~ ['distance'] 14. a ~ from (their place is just a few ~s from the station)
step II *v.* 1. (d; intr.) to ~ between (the referee ~ped between the two boxers) 2. (d; intr.) to ~ into (to ~ into a room) 3. (d; intr.) to ~ off (to ~ off a train) 4. (d; intr.) to ~ on (she ~ped on my foot; to ~ on the brake) 5. (d; intr.) to ~ out of (to ~ out of the room) 6. (d; intr.) to ~ over (she ~ped over the body)
step aside *v.* (D; intr.) to ~ for (he ~ped aside for a younger person)
step back *v.* (D; intr.) to ~ from (to ~ from the abyss)
step down *v.* (D; intr.) to ~ from (to ~ from the presidency)
step out *v.* 1. (D; intr.) to ~ into (to ~ into the corridor) 2. (D; intr.) to ~ on ('to betray') (he was ~ping out on his wife)
steppingstone *n.* a ~ to (a ~ to advancement)
steps *n.* ['stairs'] 1. steep ~ 2. a flight of ~
step up *v.* (D; intr.) to ~ to (he ~ped up to me and told me who he was)
stereotype *n.* to perpetuate a ~
stern *adj.* ~ towards; with
stew *n.* beef; Irish; mulligan; veal ~
steward *n.* a shop ~
stick I *n.* 1. a hiking; hockey; pointed; walking ~ 2. a celery ~ 3. a composing ~ ('device for typesetting') 4. a swagger ~ (carried by a military officer) 5. (misc.) to carry a big ~ ('to threaten to use force to settle a dispute')
stick II *v.* 1. ('to remain fixed') to ~ fast (the car is stuck fast in the mud) 2. (d; intr.) to ~ by ('to be loyal to') (to ~ by one's friends) 3. (d; tr.) ('to thrust') to ~ into (to ~ a needle into a cushion; to ~ one's hands into one's pockets) 4. (d; tr.) ('to fasten, paste') to ~ on (to ~ a stamp on an envelope) 5. (d; tr.) ('to thrust') to ~ through (she stuck her head through the window) 6. (d; intr.) ('to adhere') to ~ to (the stamp didn't ~ to the envelope) 7. (d; intr.) ('to limit oneself') to ~ to (to ~ to the subject) 8. (d; intr.) to ~ to ('to be loyal to') (to ~ to one's principles) 9. (d; intr.) ('to remain') to ~ with (~ with me, and you will not get lost) 10. (misc.) to ~ in one's throat ('to be

hard to say'); ('to be a source of irritation')
sticker *n.* a bumper; price ~
stickler *n.* ['one who insists on exactness'] a ~ for (a ~ for protocol)
stick out *v.* 1. (D; intr.) ('to protrude') to ~ from; into (the nail stuck out from the wall; his feet stuck out into the aisle) 2. (D; tr.) ('to extend') to ~ to, towards (she stuck out her hand to us)
sticks *n.* (colloq.) ['rural area'] in the ~ (to live way out in the ~)
stick shift *n.* (colloq.) (AE) to operate a ~
stick up *v.* (colloq.) (d; intr.) to ~ for ('to defend') (to ~ for one's friend)
stiff *adj.* frozen ~
stigma *n.* 1. to attach a ~ to 2. a ~ attaches to (no ~ attaches to being poor) 3. a ~ about, to (there is no ~ to being poor)
stigmatize *v.* (D; tr.) to ~ as (to be ~d as a traitor)
still I *adj., adv.* deathly; perfectly ~ (to stand perfectly ~)
still II *n.* in the ~ of the night
stilts *n.* 1. (to walk) on ~ 2. a pair of ~
stimulate *v.* 1. (d; tr.) to ~ into 2. (H) to ~ smb. to do smt.
stimulating *adj.* ~ to + inf. (it is ~ intellectually to live in a large city)
stimulation *n.* 1. to provide ~ 2. erotic, sexual ~
stimulus *n.* 1. to give, provide a ~ 2. a powerful ~ 3. a ~ to
sting *n.* ['skin wound'] 1. a bee; wasp ~ ['trap'] ['police trap'] (colloq.) (AE) 2. to set up a ~
stingy *adj.* ~ with (~ with one's money)
stink *v.* (D; intr.) to ~ of (the place ~s of rotten fish)
stint *n.* ['period of service'] to do, serve one's ~ (he did his ~ as a soldier)
stipend *n.* 1. to receive a ~ 2. to pay a ~ 3. a modest ~ (to live on a modest ~)
stipulate *v.* 1. (L) the contract ~s that the work must be finished by the end of the year 2. (Q) did they ~ how the job was to be done?
stipulation *n.* 1. to make a ~ 2. a ~ that + clause (there was a ~ that court costs would be shared equally)
stir I *n.* ['disturbance'] 1. to cause, create, make a ~ 2. a big ~ 3. a ~ about, over
stir II *v.* 1. (D; tr.) to ~ into (to ~ one ingredient into another) 2. (D; tr.) to ~ to (the news ~red them to greater efforts) 3. (H; usu. refl.) they couldn't ~ themselves to act
stitch *n.* 1. to cast, make a ~ 2. to drop; pick up, take up a ~ 3. (med.) to put ~es in 4. (med.) to remove, take out ~es 5. a chain; knit, plain (BE); purl; running ~
stock *n.* ['inventory, supply'] 1. to take ~ 2. in ~; out of ~ (this item is not in ~) ['share, shares in a corporation'] 3. to issue; sell ~ 4. common ~ (AE; BE has *ordinary shares*) 5. blue-chip; over-the-counter; preferred (AE; BE has *preference shares*) ~ ['equipment'] 6. rolling ~ ('railway vehicles') ['confidence, trust'] 7. to put ~ in smb. ['evaluation'] 8. to take ~ (we must take ~ of the situation) ['stage productions'] 9. summer ~ ['livestock'] 10. to graze ~ ['lineage'] 11. of good

~ ['misc.'] 12. smb.'s ~ in trade ('smb.'s customary practice')

stock exchange see **stock market**

stocking *n.* 1. mesh; nylon; seamless; silk; surgical ~s 2. a pair of ~s 3. (misc.) she got a ladder (BE)/ run (esp. AE) in her ~

stocking feet *n.* in one's ~

stock market *n.* 1. to gamble, speculate on the ~ 2. the ~ closes; opens (the ~ closed strong)

stocks *n.* ['shares on the stock market'] (esp. AE; CE has *shares*) ~ close; open (did ~ close strong or weak?)

stock up *v.* (D; intr.) to ~ on (to ~ on supplies)

stockyards *n.* at, in the ~ (to work at/in the ~)

stoical *adj.* ~ about

stoicism *n.* to display ~

stole *n.* a fur ~

stomach *n.* ['digestive organ'] 1. to settle; turn, upset smb.'s ~ 2. an empty; full; queasy; sour; strong; upset; weak ~ 3. a ~ aches, hurts 4. on an empty ~ ['inclination'] 5. to have no ~ for smt.

stomachache *n.* to get a ~ (AE)/to get ~ (BE)

stone I *n.* ['rock'] 1. to hurl, throw a ~ 2. a foundation; paving ~ 3. (misc.) to leave no ~ unturned ('to try all methods of achieving an end') ['gem'] 4. to set a (precious) ~ 5. a precious ~ ['stony mass in the body'] 6. a gallstone; kidney ~

stone II *v.* to ~ smb. to death

stool *n.* a cucking, ducking; step ~

stoop *v.* (d; intr.) to ~ to ('to lower oneself to') (to ~ to cheating)

stop I *n.* ['halt'] ['cessation'] 1. to make a ~ 2. to put a ~ to (the teacher put a ~ to the cheating) 3. to bring to a ~ (the driver brought the bus to a ~) 4. to come to a ~ (the train came to a ~) 5. an abrupt, sudden; brief; dead; full; smooth ~ 6. a flag (AE), request (BE); regular, scheduled; unscheduled; whistle (AE) ('very brief') ~ 7. a bus; pit; streetcar (AE), tram (BE) ~ 8. (misc.) to miss one's ~ ['place for resting'] 9. a truck ~ (AE; BE has *transport cafe*) ['punctuation mark'] 10. a full ~ (BE; AE has *period*)

stop II *v.* 1. to ~ short 2. (D; tr.) to ~ from (to ~ smb. from doing smt.) 3. (G) they ~ped talking 4. (BE) (J) to ~ smb. doing smt. 5. (K) I can't ~ his interrupting 6. (misc.) to ~ dead in one's tracks; to ~ at nothing ('to allow no scruples to interfere with one's efforts to achieve an end'); they ~ped (in order) to chat

stop by *v.* (esp. AE) (D; intr.) to ~ at (we'll ~ at your place)

stop in *v.* (D; intr.) to ~ at (they ~ped in at my place)

stop off *v.* (D; intr.) to ~ at (we all ~ped off at a bar)

stopover *n.* to make a ~

stoppage *n.* a work ~

stopping see the Usage Note for **standing**

stop short *v.* (d; intr.) to ~ of (they ~ped short of imposing new taxes)

stop sign *n.* to go through, run a ~

storage *n.* ['storing'] 1. to put smt. into ~ 2. to take smt. out of ~ 3. cold ~ ['memory of a computer'] 4. external; internal; magnetic ~

store *n.* ['shop, establishment where goods are sold'] (esp. AE; see the Usage Note for **shop**) 1. to manage, operate, run a ~ 2. a bookstore; candy; chain, multiple (BE); clothing; company; convenience; department; discount ~; drugstore; five-and-dime (AE), five-and-ten-cent (AE); food, grocery; furniture; general; hardware; jewelry; music; retail; self-service; shoe; toy ~ 3. (AE) a dry-goods ~ (BE has *draper's shop*) 4. (AE) a liquor, package ~ (BE has *off licence*) 5. (AE) a variety ~ (BE has *haberdashery*) 6. at, in a ~ (she works at/in a ~) ['misc.'] 7. to set ~ by ('to attribute importance to'); to lie/be in ~ ('to be imminent'); to have smt. in ~ for smb. ('to have smt. prepared for smb.')

stores *n.* ['supplies'] 1. naval ~ 2. a cache of ~

storm I *n.* ['atmospheric disturbance'] 1. to ride out, weather a ~ (the ship finally rode out the ~) 2. a blinding; heavy, severe, violent ~ 3. a dust; electrical ~; firestorm; hailstorm; ice ~; rainstorm; sandstorm; snowstorm; thunderstorm; tropical ~ 4. a ~ hits, strikes; rages 5. a ~ blows itself out, blows over, subsides 6. a ~ was gathering (also fig.) ['disturbance, commotion'] 7. to raise, stir up a ~ 8. a ~ was brewing, gathering ['assault, attack'] (mil. and fig.) 9. to take by ~ (the new play took Broadway by ~) ['misc.'] 10. to talk up a ~ (colloq.) ('to talk a great deal')

storm II *v.* (d; intr.) ('to rush angrily') to ~ into; out of (to ~ out of a room)

story I *n.* ['tale'] 1. to narrate, tell a ~ 2. to carry, circulate, print, run a ~ (all the newspapers carried the ~ about the fire) 3. to edit; rewrite; write a ~ 4. to concoct, fabricate, invent, make up a ~ 5. to change, revise; embellish, embroider a ~ 6. to cover up, hush up, kill, suppress a ~ 7. a boring; charming; cock-and-bull, farfetched; coherent; complicated, involved; dirty, off-color, risque; funny, humorous; gripping; implausible; improbable; juicy; likely, plausible; long; sob; true; ugly; untold ~ 8. a bedtime, children's, fairy; detective; ghost; hard-luck; love ~ 9. a breaking ('very new'); cover; exclusive; feature; front-page; human-interest ~; the inside ~ 10. conflicting ~ries (they told conflicting ~ries to the police) 11. a shaggy dog ~ ('a long rambling joke with an illogical punch line') 12. a short ~ ('a short prose narrative') 13. the whole ~ (who knows the whole ~ of the incident?) 14. a ~ breaks ('becomes known'); circulates 15. a ~ about, of (she told charming ~ries about her travels; to narrate gripping ~ries of wartime heroism) 16. a ~ that + clause (have you heard the ~ that she intends to resign?) ['background information'] 17. to get the (whole) ~ ['misc.'] 18. the police could not make a coherent ~ out of his ravings; a success ~ ('a successful career')

story II **storey** *n.* ['floor level'] a lower; top; upper ~

stove *n.* 1. to light a ~ 2. a coal; gas; kerosene (AE), paraffin (BE); kitchen; oil; pot-belly ~

straight *adj.* (misc.) to go ~ ('to be law-abiding'); to set smb. ~ ('to disabuse smb.')

straight ticket *n.* (AE) to vote a ~ ('to vote for all

the candidates of one party')

strain I   *n.*   ['exertion'] ['tension'] 1. to impose, place, put a ~ on 2. to stand the ~ 3. to ease, relieve the ~ 4. an emotional, mental; physical ~ 5. back ~; eyestrain 6. a ~ on (a ~ on relations) 7. under a ~

strain II   *v.*   1. (d; intr.) to ~ at (the dog ~ed at the leash/BE lead) 2. (E) they were ~ing to get the car out of the mud

strain III   *n.*   ['variety of microorganism'] a strong, virulent; weak ~

straits   *n.*   ['difficulties'] 1. desperate, dire; financial ~ 2. in desperate ~

strange   *adj.*   1. ~ to 2. ~ to + inf. (it was ~ to work at night = it was ~ working at night) 3. ~ that + clause (it is ~ that she hasn't written for a whole month)

stranger   *n.*   1. a complete, perfect, total, utter ~ 2. a ~ to (she's no ~ to us)

strangle   *v.*   to ~ smb. to death

stranglehold   *n.*   to get a ~ on smb.

strap   *n.*   a chin; shoulder ~

stratagem   *n.*   1. to resort to, use a ~ 2. a subtle ~

strategist   *n.*   an armchair ('amateur') ~

strategy   *n.*   1. to adopt, map out, plan, work out a ~ 2. to apply, pursue a ~ 3. a global; grand, long-range, long-term ~ 4. military ~ 5. a matter point of ~

straw   *n.*   ['tube'] 1. (to drink) through a ~ 2. (misc.) to decide smt. by drawing ~s (also fig.) ['misc.'] 3. a ~ in the wind ('a hint of smt. to come'); to clutch at ~s ('to try in desperation'); the last ~, or: the ~ that broke the camel's back ('a final burden that exceeds one's endurance')

stray   *v.*   (D; intr.) 1. to ~ from (to ~ from the subject) 2. (d; intr.) to ~ into, onto (to ~ onto smb.'s property)

streak I   *n.*   ['tendency, trait'] (usu. derog.) 1. a cruel; jealous; mean ~ 2. a yellow ~ ('cowardice') ['series'] 3. a losing; winning ~

streak II   *v.*   (P; intr.) to ~ across a field

streaked   *adj.*   ~ with (~ with gray)

stream I   *n.*   1. to ford a ~ 2. a mountain; running; swollen ~ 3. a steady ~ (a steady ~ of refugees) 4. the jet ~ ('band of high-velocity winds moving from west to east')

stream II   *v.*   (P; intr.) people were ~ing towards the town square

street   *n.*   1. to cross a ~ 2. to name; number ~s 3. a bustling, busy; congested; crowded; deserted, lonely; quiet ~ 4. a back; broad, wide; cross; dead-end; high (BE), main (AE); narrow; one-way; through; winding ~ 5. in (esp. BE), on (esp. AE) the ~ (the children were playing in/on the ~) 6. (BE) in the high ~ 7. (AE) on (the) main ~

streetcar   *n.*   (AE) 1. to drive, operate a ~ 2. to go by ~; to ride a ~; to ride in a ~; to take a ~ (BE has *tram*)

strength   *n.*   ['power'] 1. to build up, develop one's ~ 2. to find; gain, gather; recoup, regain; save ~ 3. to sap smb.'s ~ 4. brute, great; inner; physical; tensile ~ 5. a show of ~ 6. the ~ to + inf. (do you have the ~ to lift this weight?) 7. in ~ ('in large numbers') ['number of personnel, units'] 8. full,

maximum ~ (to bring a department up to full ~) 9. at; below ~ (our staff was at full ~; it is now five officers below ~) ['misc.'] 10. on the ~ of smt ('relying on smt.') (on the ~ of your recommendation); on the ~ (BE; colloq.) ('on the full-time permanent staff')

stress I   *n.*   ['emphasis'] 1. to lay, place, put the ~ on 2. to shift the ~ from; to ['intensity of sound'] 3. to place, put the ~ on (a syllable) 4. to shift the ~ from; to 5. (a) dynamic; free; fixed; pitch; primary; qualitative; quantitative; secondary; strong; weak ~ 6. sentence; word ~ ['tension'] 7. to control ~ 8. mental; perceived; physical ~ 9. under ~

stress II   *v.*   (L) they ~ed that all regulations would be strictly enforced

stretch I   *n.*   ['final phase'] to fade in the ~

stretch II   *v.*   (N; used with an adjective) we ~ed the rope tight

stretcher   *n.*   (to carry smb.) on a ~

stretch out   *v.*   (D; tr.) to ~ to (she stretched her hand out to us in friendship)

strew   *v.*   (d; tr.) to ~ with (the field was strewn with bodies)

stricken   *adj.*   ['afflicted'] 1. ~ with 2. (misc.) grief-stricken; poverty-stricken

strict   *adj.*   1. ~ about, concerning, in 2. ~ towards, with

stricture   *n.*   a ~ against, on

stride I   *n.*   ['normal speed'] 1. to hit one's ~ ['progress'] 2. to make great ~s in 3. great, tremendous ~s ['misc.'] 4. to take smt. in ~ ('to confront a new problem calmly')

stride II   *v.*   1. to ~ confidently; purposefully 2. (P; intr.) she strode confidently into the room

strife   *n.*   1. to cause, create ~ 2. bitter; communal; domestic; factional; industrial; internal; internecine; sectarian ~ 3. ~ among, between; in (to create ~ between two sisters)

strike I   *n.*   ['refusal to work'] 1. to call, go (out) on; organize a ~ 2. to conduct, stage a ~ 3. to avert; break (up); settle a ~ 4. a buyers'; general; hunger; official (BE); rent; sit-down; sympathy; token; unofficial (BE), wildcat ~ (the prisoners went on a hunger ~) 5. on ~ (some of the workers were on ~) ['attack'] 6. to carry out a ~ 7. an air; first, preemptive; second; surgical ~ ['disadvantage'] (from baseball) (AE) 8. they have two ~s against them ('they are at a decided disadvantage')

strike II   *v.*   1. (D; intr.) ('to refuse to work') to ~ against; for (the workers struck against the company for higher pay) 2. (D; tr.) ('to hit') to ~ against, on (she struck her head against the door) 3. (d; tr.) ('to impress') to ~ as (the idea struck me as silly) 4. (d; intr.) to ~ at ('to attack') (to ~ at the root causes of poverty; to ~ at the enemy) 5. (N; used with an adjective) ('to make') to ~ smb. dead 6. (BE) (O) ('to give') he struck me a heavy blow

strike back   *v.*   (D; intr.) to ~ at (to ~ at the enemy)

strikebreaker   *n.*   to bring in ~s

strike out   *v.*   1. (d; intr.) ('to act') to ~ against, at (to ~ against injustice) 2. (d; intr.) to ~ for ('to set out for') (to ~ for shore) 3. (misc.) to ~ on one's own ('to begin an independent existence')

striking distance   *n.*   ['effective range'] within ~

string *n.* ['grouping of players according to ability'] first; second ~ (see also **strings)**

strings *n.* ['strips used for fastening'] 1. apron ~; shoestrings ['cords on a musical instrument'] 2. to pick (esp. AE), pluck ~ ['influence'] (colloq.) 3. to pull ~

strip I *n.* ['runway'] 1. an airstrip, landing ~ ['dividing patch'] 2. a centre (BE), median (AE) ~ (on a road)

strip II *v.* 1. (D; intr.) to ~ for (to ~ for a physical examination) 2. (d; tr.) to ~ of (to ~ smb. of all civil rights) 3. (D; intr., tr.) to ~ to (to ~ to the waist) 4. (N; used with an adjective) to ~ smb. naked

strip down *v.* (d; intr.) to ~ to (he ~ped down to his underwear)

stripe *n.* ['strip, band'] 1. a sergeant's ~s 2. a service ~ (worn on a soldier's sleeve to indicate length of service) ['sort'] (esp. AE) 3. of a certain ~ (people of their ~)

stripping *n.* 1. weather ~ 2. (BE) (commercial) asset ~

striptease *n.* to do a ~

strive *v.* 1. (d; intr.) to ~ for (to ~ for peace) 2. (formal) (E) we ~ to please

stroke *n.* ['apoplexy'] 1. to have, suffer a ~ 2. an apoplectic; crippling, massive, severe; slight ~ ['movement, series of movements'] 3. (tennis) a backhand; forehand ~ 4. (swimming) a backstroke; breast; butterfly ~; sidestroke ['sound of striking'] 5. at a ~ (at the ~ of midnight) ['movement of a piston'] 6. an exhaust; exhaust-suction; intake; suction ~ ['action'] 7. a brilliant ~ 8. (misc.) a ~ of genius; to reduce inflation at one ~; their hard-won freedoms were abolished with the ~ of a pen ['misc.'] 9. a ~ of luck

stroll I *n.* 1. to go for, take a ~ 2. to take smb. for a ~ (she took the children for a ~)

stroll II *v.* (P; intr.) to ~ through the park

stroller *n.* (esp. AE) to push a ~ (BE has *pushchair*)

structure *n.* 1. (ling.) to generate a ~ 2. (ling.) a deep; intermediate; surface ~ 3. (pol.) a power ~ 4. (physics) molecular ~ 5. a corporate; economic, financial; political; price; tax; wage ~

struggle I *n.* 1. to carry on, put up, wage a ~ 2. a bitter, desperate, fierce, frantic, violent; ceaseless, unending, unrelenting; internecine; life-and-death ~ 3. the class ~ 4. a ~ against, with; for (a ~ against poverty; a ~ for justice; a ~ with one's conscience) 5. a ~ to + inf. (it was a ~ to make ends meet = it was a ~ making ends meet) 6. in ~ (locked in ~) 7. (misc.) a ~ to the death

struggle II *v.* 1. to ~ bravely; desperately 2. (D; intr.) to ~ against, with (to ~ against tyranny) 3. (D; intr.) to ~ for (to ~ for freedom) 4. (E) they ~d to remain alive 5. (misc.) to ~ to one's feet

strut *v.* 1. (P; intr.) to ~ into (to ~ into a room) 2. (d; intr.) to ~ out of (to ~ out of a meeting)

stub *n.* 1. a pencil; ticket ~ 2. a check (AE), cheque (BE) ~

stubborn *adj.* ~ about

stubbornness *n.* 1. sheer ~ 2. ~ about 3. ~ to +

inf. (it was sheer ~ not to agree) 4. out of ~ (she refused to compromise out of ~)

stuck *adj.* (colloq.) ['burdened'] 1. ~ with (he always gets ~ with the worst jobs; I am ~ with the chore of breaking the bad news) ['infatuated'] 2. ~ on (he's ~ on her) ['fully involved'] (BE) 3. ~ into (there is no holding him once he gets ~ into smt.)

stud *n.* at ~ ('for breeding') (the retired racehorses are at ~)

student *n.* 1. an excellent, outstanding; good, strong ~ 2. a bad, poor, weak ~ 3. day; evening; foreign, overseas (BE); full-time; part-time; special; transfer ~ 4. a college, university; degree; graduate, postgraduate (esp. BE); high-school (AE); undergraduate ~ 5. (misc.) a student-teacher USAGE NOTE: In GB, *students* usu. refer to those in post-secondary education. Younger ones are usu. called *pupils*. However, secondary-school pupils in Britain have begun to call themselves *school students*. In the US, the term *students* is used for those at a university and in secondary school--*college students, high-school students*. Children at (BE)/in (esp. AE) primary schools are usu. called *pupils* in the US, and almost always in GB. In CE one can differentiate between a *student of Freud* ('a student of Freud's ideas') and *Freud's student* ('one who was taught personally by Freud').

studies *n.* 1. to complete; pursue one's ~ 2. advanced; graduate, postgraduate (esp. BE); undergraduate ~ 3. Black; peace; social; women's ~

studio *n.* an art; dance; film; recording; television, TV ~

study I *n.* ['investigation'] 1. to conduct, do, make a ~ 2. a careful, detailed, exhaustive, in-depth, intensive, rigorous, thorough; scientific ~ 3. a classic, classical; definitive ~ 4. a case; epidemiological; experimental; time-and-motion (AE), work (BE) ~ 5. under ~ (the matter is under ~) ['branch of learning, subject'] 6. nature ~ ['learning'] 7. supervised ~

study II *v.* 1. to ~ diligently, hard 2. (D; intr.) to ~ for (to ~ for a degree) 3. (d; intr.) to ~ under (to ~ under a well-known professor) 4. (Q) to ~ how to survive in the wilderness

study up *v.* (colloq.) (AE) (D; intr.) to ~ on (to ~ on a topic)

stuff I *n.* (colloq.) ['subject matter'] 1. to know one's ~ 2. heady ('exciting'); kid ('elementary') ~; the same old ~ ['knowledge, ability'] 3. to show one's ~ 4. (AE) the ~ to + inf. (she has the ~ to succeed) 5. (misc.) (esp. AE) the right ~ ['duties'] 6. to do one's ~

stuff II *v.* 1. (d; tr.) to ~ into (she ~ed her things into a suitcase) 2. (D; tr.) to ~ with (they ~ed their suitcases with all sorts of things)

stumble *v.* 1. (d; intr.) to ~ across, into, on, onto, upon ('to meet by chance') (to ~ across an old friend) 2. (D; intr.) to ~ over ('to trip over') (he ~d over every sentence)

stumbling block *n.* a ~ to (a ~ to progress)

stump I *n.* to remove a ~ (of a tree)

stump II *v.* (d; intr.) to ~ for ('to support by making speeches') (to ~ for a candidate)

stun v. (R) it ~ned me to see him drunk

stunned adj. ~ to + inf. (we were ~ to learn of his defection)

stunt n. 1. to do, perform a ~ 2. (colloq.) to pull a ~ ('to do smt. unexpected, probably for a bad purpose') 3. a publicity ~

stupid adj. 1. ~ about 2. ~ to + inf. (it was ~ of him to lie; I was ~ to agree)

stupidity n. 1. to display ~ 2. sheer ~ 3. the height of ~ 4. ~ to + inf. (it was sheer ~ to believe him) 5. ~ that + clause (it was sheer ~ that he decided to drop out of school)

stupor n. 1. to fall into a ~ 2. a drunken ~

style n. ['manner of expression'] 1. to develop; polish, refine one's ~ 2. an affected; classic classical; elegant; flowery, ornate; pedestrian; plain; vigorous ~ ['manner of acting'] 3. to cramp smb.'s ~ 4. an abrasive; grand ~ 5. in (a) ~ (to live in a/in grand ~) ['fashionable elegance'] 6. high ~ 7. in ~ (to live in ~) ['excellence of expression or behavior'] 8. to lack ~

suasion n. ['persuasion'] moral ~

subdivide v. (D; tr.) to ~ into

subject I adj. (cannot stand alone) ~ to (~ to change)

subject II n. ['topic, theme'] 1. to bring up, broach; pursue; tackle a ~ 2. to address, cover, deal with, discuss, take up, treat a ~ 3. to dwell on; exhaust; go into a ~ 4. to avoid; drop a ~ 5. to change the ~ 6. an appropriate, suitable; delicate, ticklish; favorite; inappropriate; pleasant; unpleasant; thorny ~ 7. a ~ comes up (for discussion) 8. a ~ for (a ~ for debate) 9. on a ~ (we have nothing to say on that ~) ['course of study'] 10. to study, tackle, take, take up a ~ 11. to master a ~ 12. an elective (AE), optional (BE); required ~ 13. a major (AE), main (BE); minor (AE), secondary (BE) ~ ['noun, noun phrase in a clause'] 14. a compound; grammatical; impersonal; logical; simple ~ ['citizen of a monarchy'] (esp. BE) 15. a British; loyal; naturalized ~

subject III v. (d; tr.) to ~ to (to ~ smb. to torture)

subjection n. ~ to

subject matter n. related; unrelated ~

subjugate v. (D; tr.) to ~ to

subjugation n. in ~

sublease see **sublet**

sublet v. 1. (B) to ~ an apartment to smb. 2. (D; tr.) to ~ from (to ~ a house from smb.)

sublimate v. (D; tr.) to ~ into, to

submarine n. 1. a conventional; midget; nuclear, nuclear-powered ~ 2. ~s dive; hunt in packs; surface

submission n. ~ to

submissive adj. ~ to

submit v. 1. (B) ('to present') they ~ted their report to us 2. (D; intr.) ('to yield') to ~ to (to ~ to superior force; to ~ to arbitration) 3. (usu. legal) (L) ('to claim') their lawyer ~s that there are no grounds for denying bail

subordinate I adj. ~ to

subordinate II v. (D; refl., tr.) to ~ to (they had to ~ their own needs to the needs of the group)

subordination n. ~ to

subpoena I n. 1. to issue a ~ 2. to serve a ~ on 3. a ~ to + inf. (he received a ~ to appear in court in two weeks)

subpoena II v. 1. (D; tr.) to ~ as (to ~ smb. as a witness) 2. (H) to ~ smb. to testify

subscribe v. 1. (D; intr.) to ~ for ('to agree to purchase') (they ~d for a large number of shares) 2. (D; intr.) to ~ to ('to receive regularly') (to ~ to a magazine) 3. (d; intr.) to ~ to ('to agree with') (to ~ to an opinion)

subscriber n. a ~ to (a ~ to a magazine)

subscription n. ['arrangement for receiving a periodical'] 1. to enter a ~ to 2. to renew a ~ 3. to cancel a ~ 4. a ~ to (a ~ to a magazine) ['amount of money pledged'] 5. a public ~

subsequent adj. (cannot stand alone) ~ to

subservience n. ~ to

subservient adj. ~ to

subsidiary adj. ~ to

subsidy n. 1. to provide a ~ for 2. to grant a ~ to 3. a government, state ~ 4. a ~ for; to

subsist v. (d; intr.) to ~ on

subsistence n. 1. (a) bare, hand-to-mouth ~ 2. a means of ~

substance n. ['drug'] 1. (AE) a controlled ~ ('a drug regulated by law') 2. (misc.) ~ abuse ['meaningful quality'] 3. ~ to (is there any ~ to their claim?) 4. (misc.) a person of ~ ['matter'] 5. a chemical; hard; oily; pure; toxic ~

substitute I n. 1. a poor ~ 2. a ~ for (a ~ for sugar)

substitute II v. (D; intr., tr.) to ~ for (the coach ~d Smith for Jones)

substitution n. 1. to make a ~ 2. a ~ for

subsume v. (formal) (d; tr.) ('to classify') to ~ under (to ~ an item under a more inclusive category)

subterfuge n. to resort to, use (a) ~

subtract v. (D; tr.) to ~ from (to ~ five from ten)

subtraction n. to do ~

suburb n. 1. a fashionable; residential ~ 2. in the ~s (to live in the ~s)

subvention see **subsidy**

subversion n. to engage in ~

subway n. (esp. US) ['underground railway'] 1. (to travel) by ~ 2. in the ~ (crime in the ~)

succeed v. 1. (D; tr.) ('to come after') to ~ as (she ~ed me as treasurer) 2. (D; intr.) to ~ in (to ~ in doing smt.; to ~ in business) 3. (D; intr.) to ~ to ('to inherit') (to ~ to the throne)

success n. 1. to achieve, attain (a) ~; to enjoy ~ 2. to score a ~ 3. to make a ~ of smt. 4. a brilliant, great, howling, huge, resounding, signal, thorough, total, tremendous, unequivocal, unqualified ~ 5. a box-office, commercial; critical ~ 6. (a) ~ in; with

successful adj. 1. highly ~ 2. ~ at, in; with (~ in business)

succession n. ['right to succeed to an office, position'] 1. the ~ to (the ~ to the throne) ['misc.'] 2. in ~ ('successively, one after the other'); in quick ~

successor n. a ~ to (the ~ to the throne)

succumb v. (D; intr.) to ~ to (to ~ to smb.'s urging; to ~ to a disease)

suck v. 1. (d; tr.) to ~ from (to ~ the juice from an orange) 2. (N; used with an adjective) (she ~ed the lemon dry)

sucker n. (colloq.) ['easily deceived person'] 1. to make a ~ out of smb. 2. a ~ for (she's a ~ for any hardluck story)

sue v. 1. (d; intr.) to ~ for ('to request') (to ~ for peace) 2. (D; intr., tr.) ('to seek in court') to ~ for (to ~ for damages; she ~d him for a large sum of money) 3. (E) ('to seek in court') they ~d to get their property back

suffer v. (D; intr.) to ~ from (to ~ from insomnia)

suffering n. 1. to inflict ~ on 2. to bear, endure ~ 3. to alleviate, ease, relieve ~ 4. chronic; great, incalculable, intense, untold ~

suffice v. 1. (D; intr.) to ~ for (my salary ~s for our basic needs) 2. (E) it should ~ to cite her previous accomplishments; my salary ~s to meet our basic needs 3. (misc.) ~ it to say that we will do our duty

sufficient adj. 1. ~ for 2. ~ unto oneself ('independent') 3. ~ to + inf. (it would have been ~ to send a brief note)

suffix n. a derivational; inflectional ~

suffrage n. 1. to extend, grant ~ 2. universal; women's ~

sugar n. 1. to produce; refine ~ 2. beet; brown; cane; confectioner's (AE), icing (BE); crude; demerara (BE); granulated; lump; maple ~ 3. (med.) blood ~ 4. a lump of ~ 5. (misc.) as sweet as ~

suggest v. 1. (B) she ~ed a compromise to us 2. (G) I ~ed waiting 3. (K) who ~ed his taking part? 4. (L; subj.; to) she ~ed (to us) that an exception be/should be made 5. (Q) did she ~ where we should meet?

suggestion n. 1. to advance, make, offer, put forward a ~ 2. to ask for, call for, invite ~s 3. to act on; adopt a ~ 4. to reject a ~ 5. an appropriate; helpful; pertinent; preposterous ~ 6. a ~ about, concerning 7. a ~ that + clause; subj. (she made a ~ that each worker contribute/should contribute one day's pay) 8. at smb.'s ~ (at my ~ we went on a picnic)

suggestive adj. ~ of

suicide n. 1. to commit ~ 2. to attempt; contemplate ~ 3. political ~

suit I n. ['legal claim'] 1. to bring, file, institute (a) ~ against 2. to contest; press a ~ 3. to lose; win a ~ 4. to dismiss a ~ 5. a civil; class-action; malpractice; pending ~ ['courtship'] (old-fashioned) 6. to plead, press one's ~ ['set of clothes'] 7. to have a ~ made 8. to put on; take off; try on a ~ 9. a bathing; business (AE), lounge (BE); custom-made, made-to-measure (BE); diving; double-breasted; dress; gym; leisure; pants (AE), trouser; ready-made; sailor; single-breasted; ski; space; sweat; tank; three-piece; two-piece; union (AE) ~ 10. (BE) a boiler ~ ('overalls') 11. a ~ fits (well) 12. (misc.) (humorous) in one's birthday ~ ('naked') ['set of similar playing cards'] 13. to follow ~ (also fig.) 14. a trump ~ ['trait'] 15. smb.'s

suit II v. 1. to ~ perfectly 2. (misc.) to ~ to a T ('to be perfectly appropriate for')

suitability n. ~ for

suitable adj. 1. eminently ~ 2. ~ for 3. ~ to + inf. (would it be ~ to discuss this matter at lunch?)

suitcase n. to pack; unpack a ~

suite n. ['group of connected rooms'] 1. a bridal; executive; hotel; luxury; office; penthouse ~ ['set of matched furniture'] 2. a bedroom; living-room ~

suited adj. 1. ~ for, to (~ for the job; ~ to each other) 2. ~ to + inf. (is he psychologically ~ to be a police officer?)

sulk v. (D; intr.) to ~ about, over

sum n. 1. to raise a ~ (of money) 2. a considerable, large, substantial, tidy; flat; lump; nominal; round ~

summarize v. (D; tr.) to ~ for (she ~d the plot for the class)

summary n. 1. to give, make a ~ 2. a brief ~ 3. a news ~

summer n. 1. Indian, St. Luke's (BE; rare), St. Martin's (BE; rare) ~ 2. during, over (esp. AE) the ~ 3. in (the) ~

summit n. ['peak'] (also fig.) 1. to reach a ~ 2. at a ~ (to stand at the ~) ['summit conference'] 3. to hold a ~ 4. at a ~ (we met at the ~ in Geneva)

summit conference n. 1. to hold a ~ 2. at a ~ (to meet at a ~)

summon v. 1. (D; tr.) to ~ before (to be ~ed before a judge) 2. (D; tr.) to ~ to (we were ~ed to the director's office) 3. (H) to ~ smb. to do smt.

summons n. 1. to issue a ~ 2. to serve a ~ on 3. a ~ to + inf. (I received a ~ to appear in court)

sums n. to do ~

sun n. 1. the blazing; bright; hot; midday; tropical ~ 2. the ~ beats down; rises; sets; shines 3. in, under the ~

sunburn n. 1. to get a ~ 2. a painful ~

sundae n. a butterscotch; cherry; chocolate; hot-fudge; strawberry ~

sundown n. at ~

sunlight n. 1. bright, brilliant, glaring ~ 2. in the ~ 3. a shaft of ~

sunrise n. at ~

sunset n. at ~

sunshine n. 1. to soak up ~ 2. bright, dazzling; warm ~

sunstroke n. to get, have ~

suntan n. to get a ~

supercilious adj. ~ about

superimpose v. (D; tr.) to ~ on (to ~ one image on another; to ~ a new way of life on old customs)

superintendent n. a building; school ~

superior I adj. 1. clearly, decidedly, definitely, far ~ 2. ~ in (~ in numbers) 3. ~ to (~ to all other competitors)

superior II n. an immediate ~

superiority n. 1. to achieve, establish ~ 2. to enjoy, hold ~ 3. clear ~ 4. ~ in; over, to

superlative n. (to express oneself) in ~s

supermarket n. at, in a ~ (to shop at/in a ~)

supersensitive adj. ~ to

superstition *n.* a ~ about
superstitious *adj.* ~ about
supervision *n.* 1. to exercise ~ of, over 2. to tighten ~ 3. to ease up on, relax ~ 4. lax, slack; strict ~ 5. under smb.'s ~
supper *n.* 1. to eat, have ~ 2. to make, prepare; serve ~ 3. at ~ (what did they discuss at ~?) 4. for ~ (what was served for ~?)
supplement *n.* 1. a literary; Sunday ~ (to a newspaper) 2. a vitamin ~ (to take a vitamin ~ every day) 3. a ~ to
supplementary *adj.* ~ to
supplicate *v.* (formal) (H) to ~ smb. to do smt.
supply I *n.* 1. to bring up, provide ~lies 2. to lay in, receive; replenish; store ~lies 3. an abundant, liberal, plentiful; fresh ~ 4. military; office; relief ~lies 5. the coal; money; water ~ 6. in short ~
supply II *v.* 1. (D; tr.) to ~ to (to ~ power to industry) 2. (D: tr.) to ~ with (to ~ industry with power)
supply lines *n.* 1. to overextend ~ 2. to cut ~
support I *n.* 1. to give, lend, offer, provide; pledge ~ 2. to enlist, line up, mobilize, round up ~ for 3. to derive, draw, get, receive ~ from 4. to gain, get, win ~ for 5. to have the ~ of 6. ardent, complete, firm, solid, strong, unflagging, unqualified, unstinting, unwavering; wholehearted ~ 7. active; liberal; loyal; lukewarm, qualified ~ (to give lukewarm ~ to a candidate) 8. government, state; popular, public ~ 9. farm; price ~s 10. ~ for; in 11. in ~ of (she came out in ~ of the party)
support II *v.* 1. to ~ completely, strongly, wholeheartedly 2. (K) we ~ed their seeking office
supporter *n.* 1. an ardent, enthusiastic, fervent, loyal, stalwart, steady, strong ~ 2. an athletic ~ (see also the Usage Note for **fan II**)
supportive *adj.* ~ of
suppose *v.* 1. (L) we ~ that the situation will improve 2. (formal) (M) we ~d him to be guilty
supposed *adj.* ~ to + inf. (it was ~ to rain; she was ~ to work today)
supposition *n.* 1. to make a ~ 2. a ~ that (I reject the ~ that she stole the money) 3. on (a) ~ (to condemn smb. on mere ~)
suppository *n.* 1. to insert a ~ 2. a rectal; vaginal ~
supremacy *n.* 1. to achieve, establish ~ 2. to acknowledge smb.'s ~ 3. military; naval ~ 4. (so-called) racial, white ~
supreme *adj.* to reign ~
surcharge *n.* 1. to add a ~ to 2. a ~ on
sure *adj.* 1. ~ about (are you ~ about this?) 2. ~ of (~ of success) 3. ~ to + inf. (she is ~ to pass the exam) 4. ~ that + clause (I am ~ that they will come; please make ~ that there will be enough light and heat)
surf *n.* to ride the ~
surface *n.* 1. a bumpy; even, smooth; frozen; plane; rough ~ 2. below, beneath, under the ~ (also fig.) 3. on the ~ (also fig.) 4. (misc.) to scratch, skim the ~ ('to treat superficially')
surge I *n.* (technical) a voltage ~
surge II *v.* (P; intr.) the crowd ~d around the entrance
surgeon *n.* 1. a flight; orthopedic (AE),

orthopaedic (BE); plastic; veterinary (BE) ~ 2. a tree ~ 3. a ~ performs operations, operates (on patients)
surgery *n.* ['branch of medicine'] 1. to perform ~ 2. to undergo ~ 3. elective; emergency; heroic; major; minor; radical; remedial ~ 4. bypass; cosmetic; open-heart; plastic ~ ['office'] (BE) 5. a doctor's ~ (CE has *doctor's office*) 6. an MP's ~ (to receive and listen to constituents) ['misc.'] 7. tree ~ (see the Usage Note for **office**)
surmise I *n.* (formal) ['conjecture'] 1. to express a ~ that + clause (she expressed a ~ that the situation would improve)
surmise II *v.* (L) I ~d that the situation would improve
surplus *n.* 1. to accumulate a ~ 2. to run ('have') a ~ 3. food ~es; war ~
surprise I *n.* 1. to spring, uncork a ~ on smb. 2. to achieve ~ 3. to express ~ 4. to show ~ 5. (a) complete, outright, total ~ (we achieved complete ~) 6. a pleasant; unpleasant ~ (they sprang an unpleasant ~ on us) 7. ~ at (to express ~ at recent events) 8. a ~ to (the results were a complete ~ to everyone) 9. a ~ to + inf. (it was a pleasant ~ to learn of her promotion) 10. a ~ that + clause (it was a ~ that he got here on time) 11. by ~ (our troops took the fortress by ~) 12. to smb.'s ~ (to our ~ he was not drunk)
surprise II *v.* 1. to ~ greatly, very much 2. (R) it ~d me to see them drunk; it ~d us that their party won the election
surprised *adj.* 1. ~ at (~ at the news) 2. ~ to + inf. (I was ~ to see her) 3. ~ that + clause (everyone was ~ that we attended the meeting)
surprising *n.* 1. ~ to + inf. (it was ~ to see her there) 2. ~ that + clause (it was ~ that she was nominated)
surrender I *n.* unconditional ~
surrender II *v.* (D; intr., tr.) to ~ to (to ~ to the enemy; to ~ a fortress to the invader)
surrounded *adj.* ~ by, with
surroundings *n.* austere; elegant; pleasant; unpleasant ~
surtax *n.* to impose a ~ (on)
surveillance *n.* 1. to conduct, maintain ~ 2. to keep; place smb. under ~ 3. around-the-clock, constant; close, strict ~ (she was placed under strict ~) 4. electronic ~ 5. under ~
survey *n.* 1. to conduct, do, make a ~ 2. a brief; comprehensive ~ 3. a geodetic; topographical ~
survival *n.* 1. to assure smb.'s ~ 2. (misc.) the ~ of the fittest
survivor *n.* to pick up ~s (at sea)
susceptibility *n.* ~ to (~ to disease)
susceptible *adj.* ~ to
suspect I *n.* 1. to arrest a ~ 2. to interrogate question a ~ 3. to place a ~ under surveillance 4. a prime ~
suspect II *v.* 1. to ~ strongly 2. (D; tr.) to ~ as (to be ~ed as an accomplice) 3. (D; tr.) to ~ of (the police ~ed him of participation in the robbery) 4. (L) we ~ strongly that she is guilty
suspend *v.* 1. (D; tr.) ('to hang') to ~ from (to ~ a hook from the ceiling) 2. (D; tr.) ('to bar tem-

porarily') to ~ from (to ~ smb. from duty)

suspenders *n.* (AE; BE has *braces*) a pair of ~ (that hold up trousers)

suspense *n.* 1. to bear the ~ 2. to break the ~ 3. in ~ over (everyone was in ~ over the outcome)

suspension *n.* independent ~ (on a car)

suspicion *n.* ['suspecting'] ['mistrust'] 1. to arouse, cause, create, evoke, sow, stir (a) ~ 2. to entertain, harbor, have a ~ 3. to confirm a ~ 4. to cast ~ on 5. to allay, dispel ~ 6. a groundless, unfounded ~ 7. a lingering, lurking; slight, sneaking; strong; vague ~ 8. a ~ about, of (there was some ~ about her motives) 9. ~ falls on smb. 10. a ~ that + clause (these events confirmed my strong ~ that he is guilty) 11. above ~ ('not suspected') 12. on ~ of (arrested on ~ of murder) 13. under ~ ('suspected') 14. (misc.) a cloud of ~ ['slight trace'] 15. a ~ of (not even the slightest ~ of scandal)

suspicious *adj.* 1. ~ about, of 2. ~ that + clause (it was ~ that no story appeared in the press)

suture *n.* 1. to put in a ~ 2. to remove, take out a ~

swallow *n.* ['act of swallowing'] to take a ~

swamp *v.* (d; tr.) to ~ by, with (they were ~ed with work)

swan *n.* as graceful as a ~

swap I *n.* ['exchange'] to make a ~ for

swap II *v.* 1. (D; tr.) to ~ for (she ~ped her bicycle for a hi-fi) 2. (O) I'll ~ you my bicycle for your hi-fi

swarm *v.* 1. (d; intr.) ('to crowd') to ~ around (the autograph seekers ~ed around the actor) 2. (d; intr.) ('to throng') to ~ into (to ~ into an auditorium) 3. (d; intr.) ('to throng') to ~ over, through (to ~ through the streets) 4. (d; intr.) ('to teem') to ~ with (the streets were ~ing with tourists)

swarming *adj.* ~ with

swath *n.* ['path'] to cut a ~ (to cut a wide ~ of destruction)

swathe *v.* (d; tr.) ('to wrap') to ~ in (she was ~d in mink)

sway I *n.* ['dominance'] 1. to hold ~ over 2. under smb.'s ~

sway II *v.* 1. to ~ gently 2. (D; intr.) to ~ to (to ~ to the music) 3. (misc.) to ~ from side to side; to ~ back and forth; to ~ in the breeze

swear *v.* 1. to ~ solemnly 2. (B) ('to promise solemnly') they swore allegiance to the government 3. (D) intr.) ('to curse') to ~ at (he swore at them) 4. (d; intr.) ('to rely completely') to ~ by (everyone ~s by her remedy for a cold) 5. (d; intr.) to ~ to ('to confirm solemnly') (to ~ to the truth of a statement) 6. (d; tr.) ('to bind solemnly') to ~ to (to ~ smb. to secrecy) 7. (E) ('to promise solemnly') she swore to tell the truth 8. (L; to) ('to promise solemnly') she swore (to us) that she would tell the truth 9. (misc.) to ~ on the Bible; to ~ like a trooper ('to use obscene language freely'); to ~ smb. into office

swear in *v.* (D; tr.) to ~ as (she was sworn in as president)

sweat *n.* 1. to break out in a cold ~ 2. beads of ~ 3. (misc.) by the ~ of one's brow ('by working very hard')

sweater *n.* 1. to crochet; knit a ~ 2. a light; warm ~ 3. a plaid; woolen ~

sweep I *n.* ['reconnaissance'] 1. to make a ~ (behind enemy lines) ['winning of a series of contests'] 2. to make a clean ~ (of a series) ['sweeper'] 3. a chimney ~

sweep II *v.* 1. (d; intr., tr.) ('to move overwhelmingly') to ~ into (the other party swept into office; they were swept into the sea) 2. (d; intr.) ('to move swiftly') to ~ through (our troops swept through the village) 3. (N; used with an adjective) ('to clean with a broom') to ~ a floor clean

sweep down *v.* (d; intr.) to ~ on (the storm swept down on the village)

sweep in *v.* (D; intr.) to ~ from (the hurricane swept in from the sea)

sweepstakes *n.* to win the ~

sweet *adj.* (colloq.) 1. ~ on ('in love with') (he is ~ on her) 2. ~ to + inf. (it was ~ of you to think of me)

swell I *n.* ['growing wave'] a ground ~ (a ground ~ of support was building up)

swell II *v.* (d; intr.) to ~ with (to ~ with pride)

swelling *n.* (the) ~ goes down, subsides (the ~ went down)

swerve *v.* (D; intr.) to ~ from; to (to ~ from a course; to ~ to the right)

swift *adj.* 1. (lit.) ~ of (~ of foot) 2. ~ to + inf. (she was ~ to react)

swig *n.* ['swallow'] to take a ~

swim I *n.* 1. to have, take a ~ 2. to go for a ~

swim II *v.* (D; intr.) to ~ for (to ~ for shore)

swindle *v.* (D; tr.) to ~ out of (to ~ smb. out of money)

swing I *n.* ['punch'] 1. to take a ~ at smb. 2. a wild ~ ['shift'] 3. a ~ to (in the last elections there was a ~ to the right) ['operation'] 4. in full ~ (the work was in full ~)

swing II *v.* 1. (D; intr., tr.) to ~ at (he swung at me; I swung the bat at the ball) 2. (D; intr.) to ~ from; to (to ~ from right to left)

swipe *n.* (colloq.) ['critical remark'] to take a ~ at

switch I *n.* ['change'] 1. to make a ~ 2. a ~ from; to ['device used to open or close an electrical circuit'] 3. to flick, throw a ~ 4. a master; power; time; toggle ~ ['movable section of railroad track'] (AE) 5. a railroad ~ (BE has *railway point*)

switch II *v.* (D; intr., tr.) to ~ from; into; to (to ~ to the metric system; she ~ed her support to the other candidate; to ~ from English into Russian)

switchboard *n.* at a ~ (to work at a ~)

switcheroo *n.* (slang) (AE) ['variation'] to pull a ~

switch over *v.* (D; intr.) to ~ to (we ~ed over to French)

swoon I *n.* to fall into a ~

swoon II *v.* 1. (d; intr.) to ~ over (to ~ over a new film idol) 2. (d; intr.) to ~ with (to ~ with joy)

swoop *n.* ['stroke'] at one fell ~ ('at one time')

swoop down *v.* (D; intr.) to ~ on (the hawk ~ed down on the sheep)

swop (colloq.) (BE) see **swap I, II**

sword *n.* 1. to draw, unsheathe a ~ 2. to wield a ~

3. to cross ~s with smb. (now usu. fig.) 4. to thrust a ~ into 5. to sheathe a ~ 6. (misc.) a double-edged, two-edged ~ ('smt. that can have opposite results to those intended')

syllable *n.* 1. to stress a ~ 2. a closed; open; stressed; unstressed ~

syllabus *n.* to draw up, make up a ~

symbol *n.* 1. a chemical; phallic; phonetic; religious; status ~ 2. (misc.) a ~ of authority

symbolic *adj.* ~ of

symmetrical *adj.* ~ to, with

sympathetic *adj.* ~ to, with

sympathize *v.* 1. to ~ deeply 2. (D; intr) to ~ with

sympathy *n.* 1. to arouse, stir up ~ for 2. to capture; command ~ 3. to express; feel, have ~ for 4. to display, show ~ for 5. to lavish ~ on 6. to accept smb.'s ~ 7. deep, deepest, great, heartfelt, profound, strong ~ (please accept our deepest ~) 8. little ~ for (to have little ~ for smb.) 9. one's ~ goes out to smb. 10. a token of one's ~ 11. ~ for (to have ~ for the underdog) 12. in ~ with (to be in complete ~ with smb.'s cause) 13. out of ~ (we did it out of ~ for your family)

symphony *n.* 1. to compose, write a ~ 2. to perform, play a ~

symposium *n.* to hold a ~ on

symptom *n.* 1. to have, manifest, show ~s (of) 2. an acute; chronic ~ 3. a specific ~ 4. withdrawal ~s

symptomatic *adj.* ~ of

synchronize *v.* (D; tr.) to ~ with

syndrome *n.* 1. the China; Stockholm ~ 2. premenstrual; toxic shock ~ (to suffer from premenstrual ~)

synonymous *adj.* ~ to, with

synopsis *n.* to give; make, prepare a ~

synthesis *n.* to make a ~

syphilis *n.* 1. to spread, transmit ~ 2. to catch, develop; have ~ 3. acquired; congenital; early; late; latent; primary; secondary; tertiary ~

syringe *n.* a hypodermic ~

syrup *n.* 1. chocolate; corn; maple ~ 2. cough ~

system *n.* ['group of items serving a common purpose'] 1. an air-conditioning; amplifying; brake; data-processing; filing; guidance; heating; highway (AE), motorway (BE), road; intercommunication; life-support; number; public-address; railroad (AE), railway (BE), steering; transit (esp. AE), transport (esp. BE) ['form of organization, principles pertaining to a form of organization'] 2. a capitalist; caste; communist; Copernican; economic; educational, school; electoral; governmental; hierarchical; honor; merit; multiparty; one-party; patronage; philosophical; political; quota; seniority; socialist; spoils; two-party ~ 3. (colloq.) (AE) a buddy ~ 4. under a ~ (under our political ~) 5. (misc.) to beat the ~ ('to circumvent established procedures') ['group of items forming a unified whole in nature'] 6. an ecosystem; mountain; river; solar ~ ['functionally related group of bodily elements or structures'] 7. the cardiovascular; central nervous; circulatory; digestive; excretory; genito-urinary; immune; reproductive; respiratory ~ ['classification'] ['type of measurement'] 8. a decimal; metric; monetary; taxonomic ~ ['group of substances in or approaching equilibrium'] (chemistry) 9. a binary; ternary ~ ['set of meteorological conditions'] 10. a high-pressure; low-pressure ~ 'procedure'] 11. the touch ~ (of typing) ['elements that allow the operation of a computer'] 12. to boot up; reboot a ~ 13. a disk operating, operating ~ ['misc.'] 14. ~s analysis; ~s theory

T

T *n.* to a ~ ('precisely') (you fit the role to a ~)

tab I *n.* ['tabulator, device for setting a margin'] 1. to set a ~ ['bill'] (colloq.) (AE) 2. to pick up the ~ for (she picked up the ~ for everyone) 3. the ~ for

tab II *v.* (colloq.) (AE) 1. (d; tr.) ('to identify') to ~ as (she was ~bed as a leading contender) 2. (d; tr.) ('to designate') to ~ for (large sums were ~bed for school construction)

tabernacle *n.* to build a ~

table *n.* ['piece of furniture'] 1. to lay (esp. BE), set (esp. AE) a ~ 2. to clear a ~ 3. a card; coffee; dining-room; dressing; drop-leaf; end; folding; kitchen; night; operating; ping-pong; pool; tray; writing ~ 4. (AE) a training ~ (for members of a team) 5. around, round a ~ (to sit around a ~) 6. at the ~/at ~ (BE) ('while eating') (we never discuss politics at the dinner ~) ['table for conducting discussions, negotiations'] ['negotiating session'] 7. a bargaining, conference, negotiating; round ~ 8. at the ~ (at the negotiating ~) ['enumeration, list'] 9. to compile, draw up a ~ 10. a conversion; genealogy; mortality; multiplication; periodic ~ 11. logarithmic ~s 12. in a ~ (to give data in ~s) ['level'] 13. a water ~ ['misc.'] 14. to turn the ~s on smb. ('to reverse the roles in a struggle with smb.'); under the ~ ('illegally')

tablespoon *n.* a heaping; level ~

tablet *n.* ['pad'] 1. a writing ~ ['pill'] 2. to take a ~ 3. an aspirin ~ 4. a scored ~ ['slab'] 5. a bronze; clay; marble ~

taboo *n.* 1. to break, violate a ~ 2. a rigid ~ 3. a ~ on 4. (to place smt.) under (a) ~

tabs *n.* (colloq.) ['watch, surveillance'] to keep ~ on

tack I *n.* ['short nail'] 1. a carpet; thumb (AE; BE has *drawing pin*) ~ ['direction of a sailing ship'] 2. the port; starboard ~ ['course of action'] ['direction'] 3. to change ~ 4. (misc.) to go off on the wrong ~

tack II *v.* (d; tr.) ('to attach') to ~ onto, to

tackle *n.* fishing ~

tact *n.* 1. to display, exercise, show; have ~ 2. considerable, great; subtle ~ 3. the ~ to + inf. (does she have the ~ to conduct the negotiations?)

tactful *adj.* ~ to + inf. (it was not ~ to mention that)

tactic *n.* a scare ~ (see **tactics**)

tactics *n.* 1. to devise; employ; use ~ 2. bullying; delaying; diversionary; pressure; questionable; roughhouse (AE); scare; smear; strong-arm; wily ~ (to employ questionable ~) 3. (esp. AE) Madison Avenue ~ ('reliance on sophisticated promotion, advertising') 4. salami ~ ('maneuvering by stages')

tactless *adj.* ~ to + inf. (it was ~ of him to speak like that)

taffy *n.* (esp. AE) 1. to make; pull ~ 2. saltwater ~

tag I *n.* ['children's game'] to play ~

tag II *n.* ['label, marker'] 1. to put a ~ on smt. 2. a name; price ~ 3. (AE) license ~s (on a car) 4. (AE) (mil.) dog (colloq.), identification ~s (BE has *identification disc*) ['short phrase'] (ling.) 5. a question ~

tag III *v.* (colloq.) 1. (d; intr.) to ~ after ('to follow') (the child ~ged after the others) 2. (d; tr.) ('to label') to ~ as (he was ~ged as a quitter) 3. (AE) (d; tr.) ('to fine') to ~ for (she was ~ged for going through a red light)

tag along *v.* 1. (D; intr.) to ~ behind (she would always ~ behind them) 2. (D; intr.) to ~ with

tag end *n.* ['very end'] at the ~ (of smt.)

tail *n.* ['rear appendage to an animal's body'] 1. to wag a ~ 2. to dock ('shorten') a ~ 3. a bushy ~ 4. (misc.) to turn ~ ('to flee') ['person who conducts surveillance'] (colloq.) 5. to put a ~ on smb.

tail end *n.* ['very end'] at the ~ (of smt.)

tailor I *n.* a custom; ladies'; men's ~

tailor II *v.* (d; tr.) to ~ for; to (to ~ an insurance policy to the needs of the insured)

tailor-made *adj.* ~ for (~ for the assignment)

tailspin *n.* to go into a ~

tainted *adj.* ~ by, with

take I *n.* (colloq.) ['reaction'] 1. a double ~ ('delayed reaction') (to do a double ~) ['illegal payments'] 2. on the ~ (they were all on the ~) ('they were all accepting bribes')

take II *v.* 1. to ~ (a matter) lightly; seriously 2. (A) ('to carry') she took a cup of tea to him; or: she took him a cup of tea 3. (d; intr.) to ~ after ('to resemble') (he ~s after his father) 4. (d; tr.) ('to construe') to ~ as (we took her gesture as a sign of friendship; I took his remark as a compliment) 5. (d; tr.) ('to grasp') to ~ by (she took him by the hand) 6. (D; tr.) ('to lead, accompany') to ~ for (she took her daughter for a walk; he took us for a ride) 7. (D; tr.) ('to obtain, secure') to ~ for (I took the book for him) 8. (d; tr.) to ~ for ('to assume to be') (do you ~ me for a fool?) 9. (D; tr.) ('to obtain'); ('to remove') to ~ from (he took the book from me; I took the money from the safe) 10. (d; tr.) ('to subtract') to ~ from (~ five from ten) 11. (d; tr.) ('to carry') to ~ into (~ the chairs into the house) 12. (d; tr.) to ~ into ('to bring into') (to ~ smb. into one's confidence; they took the prisoner into custody) 13. (d; tr.) to ~ into ('to include') (to ~ smt. into consideration; we took all the facts into account) 14. (d; tr.) ('to remove'); ('to deduct') to ~ off (I took the books off the shelf; they took ten pounds off the bill) 15. (d; tr.) ('to carry') to ~ out of (~ the chairs out of the house) 16. (d; intr.) to ~ to ('to like') (to ~ kindly to an offer; she took to them at once) 17. (d; intr.) to ~ to ('to begin'); ('to engage in') (to ~ to drink; she took to gambling at the casinos; he took to fishing with great gusto) 18. (d; intr.) ('to go'); ('to have recourse') to ~ to (to ~ to one's bed; to ~ to the streets; to ~ to the lifeboats; to ~ to the air-waves) 19. (d; tr.) ('to lead, accompany, trans-port') to ~ to (to ~ smb. to dinner; she took us to the art museum; we took them to the station) 20. (d; tr.) ('to carry') to ~ to (I took the books to the library; she took the money to the bank) 21. (d; tr.) ('to move, transfer') to ~ to (they took the case to the supreme court) 22. (D; tr.) ('to accept, bear') to ~ with (he took his punishment with a smile; to ~ a remark with a grain of salt) 23. (M) ('to consider'); ('to accept') I took him to be a friend; do you ~ this man to be your lawful wed-ded husband? 24. (O) ('to require') the job took us two hours 25. (O) ('to seize') we took him pris-oner; to ~ smb. hostage 26. (R) ('to demand, require') it sometimes ~s courage to tell the truth 27. (misc.) she took it on herself to break the news; to ~ five (esp. AE; colloq.) ('to have a five minute break'); they took the law into their own hands ('they dispensed justice without a trial'); to ~ smb. to court ('to sue smb.'); to ~ smb. under one's wing ('to protect and help smb.'); to ~ to one's heels ('to flee'); to ~ by storm ('to over-whelm completely'); to ~ by surprise ('to sur-prise'); to ~ smt. lying down ('to accept a defeat without protest'); to ~ smt. for granted (see **granted**)

take away v. (D; tr.) ('to remove') to ~ from (she took the scissors away from the child)

take back v. 1. (D; tr.) ('to accept') to ~ from (they took the furniture back from the customer) 2. (D; tr.) ('to return') to ~ to (she took the book back to the library)

take down v. (D; tr.) ('to write down') to ~ in (to ~ testimony down in shorthand)

take in v. (D; tr.) ('to accept') to ~ as (we took her in as a partner)

taken adj. ['impressed'] ['infatuated'] ~ with (he was very much ~ with her)

takeoff n. (colloq.) ['parody'] to do a ~ of (esp. BE), on

take off v. 1. (colloq.) (D; intr.) ('to leave') to ~ for (they took off for town) 2. (D; intr.) ('to begin flight') to ~ from (we took off from a small landing strip)

take out v. 1. (d; tr.) to ~ on (don't ~ your anger out on me) 2. (misc.) to ~ it out on smb. ('to make smb. else suffer for one's own problem')

takeover n. 1. a hostile ~ (of a firm) 2. (misc.) a ~ bid

take over v. (D; intr., tr.) to ~ from (the new gov-ernment has taken over from the outgoing govern-ment; we will ~ power from them)

take to v. (F) ('to resort to') they took to accepting bribes

take up v. 1. (d; tr.) to ~ on ('to accept, adopt') (he took me up on my offer) 2. (d; intr.) to ~ with ('to join') (he took up with a rough crowd)

taking n. for the ~ (it's there for the ~) ('it can be taken by anyone who wants it')

tale n. 1. to concoct, make up a ~ 2. to narrate, tell a ~ 3. an absorbing, exciting, fascinating, grip-ping; fanciful; grizzly; hair-raising, harrowing, shocking ~ 4. a fairy; folk ~ 5. a tall ('unbelieva-

ble') ~ 6. (misc.) to tell ~s out of school ('to reveal secrets')

talent n. 1. to demonstrate, display, show (a) ~ 2. to cultivate, develop a ~ 3. to squander one's ~(s) 4. (a) mediocre; outstanding ~ 5. (a) natural ~ 6. the ~ to + inf. (she has the ~ to go far) 7. (a) ~ for (a ~ for painting) 8. of ~ (a person of considerable ~)

talented adj. ~ at, in

talk I n. ['address, lecture'] 1. to give a ~ 2. a pep; sales ~ 3. a ~ about, on (she gave an interesting ~ on bringing up children) ['conversation'] ['chat-ter'] 4. to have a ~ (with) 5. blunt, plain; idle, small; loose; table ~ 6. a long ~ (she had a long ~ with him about his work) 7. sweet ~ ('flattery') 8. double, fast ~ ('deception') 9. a heart-to-heart ('frank') ~ 10. straight ('frank') ~ 11. (colloq.) big ~ ('boasting') 12. ~ about, of; with (there is ~ of her resigning) 13. ~ that + clause (there is ~ that there will be a strike) ['type of speech'] 14 baby ~ (to use baby ~)

talk II v. 1. to ~ bluntly, candidly, frankly, freely; loud, loudly; openly 2. (D; intr.) to ~ about, of, on (they were ~ing about the elections; she was ~ing of her trip; to ~ on a topic) 3. (d; tr.) to ~ into ('to persuade') (to ~ smb. into doing smt.) 4. (d; tr.) to ~ out of ('to dissuade') (to ~ smb. out of doing smt.) 5. (d; intr.) ('to speak') to ~ to, with (esp. AE) (I will ~ to them about this problem) 6. (misc.) to ~ big ('to boast'); to ~ oneself hoarse

talk back v. (D; intr.) to ~ to (to ~ to one's boss)

talk down v. (d; intr.) to ~ to (to ~ to the aud-ence)

talker n. (colloq.) a fast, smooth ~ ('one who speaks glibly, in a deceptive manner')

talking n. to do the ~ (she did all the ~)

talking-to n. (colloq.) ['scolding'] to give smb. a (good) ~

talk over v. (D; tr.) ('to discuss') to ~ with (we ~ed it over with them)

talks n. ['negotiations'] 1. to conduct, hold ~ about 2. to break off ~ 3. contract; exploratory; formal; high-level; informal; peace; top-level ~ 4. ~ about; with (~ about smt.; ~ with smb.)

tall adj. to stand ~ (esp. AE; colloq.) ('to be reso-lute')

tally I n. to make a ~

tally II v. (D; intr.) ('to correspond') to ~ with

tambourine n. to play (on) the ~

tamper v. (d; intr.) to ~ with (to ~ with a lock; one should not ~ with a jury)

tampon n. to insert a ~

tan I n. to get a ~

tan II v. (intr.) to ~ easily, readily

tandem n. in ~

tangent I adj. ~ to (~ to a circle)

tangent II n. ['digression'] to go off at, go off on a ~

tangential adj. (formal) ['incidental'] ~ to

tangle I n. to unravel a ~

tangle II v. (colloq.) (d; intr.) ('to quarrel') to ~ over; with (don't ~ with him)

tango n. to dance, do the ~

tank n. ['armored combat vehicle'] 1. to drive a ~

['receptacle, container'] 2. a fish; gas (AE), gasoline (AE), petrol (BE); oil; oxygen; septic; water ~ ['prison'] (slang) (esp. AE) 3. in the ~ ['misc.'] 4. a think ~ ('a group of thinkers, planners')

tanker *n.* an oil ~

tantamount *adj.* (cannot stand alone) ~ to

tantrum *n.* 1. to have, throw a ~ 2. a temper ~ (he threw a temper ~)

tap I *n.* 1. on ~ ('ready to be drawn') (beer on ~) 2. on ~ ('available'); ('imminent') (what's on ~ for tonight?) 3. see **faucet**

tap II *v.* 1. (d; tr.) ('to ask') to ~ for (to ~ smb. for information) 2. (D; tr.) to ~ on ('to strike lightly') (to ~ smb. on the shoulder)

tape *n.* ['narrow strip of material'] 1. adhesive, sticky (BE); friction; magnetic; masking; measuring; name; ticker ~ ['string stretched across the track at the end of a race'] 2. to reach the ~ (both runners reached the ~ together) ['tape recording'] 3. to make a ~ 4. to play, put on; play back a ~ 5. to rewind; wind a ~ 6. to erase a ~ (see also **red tape**)

taper *v.* (d; intr., tr.) to ~ to (~ed to a point)

tape recorder *n.* 1. to start; turn on a ~ 2. to operate, play a ~ 3. to stop; turn off a ~ 4. a cassette; reel-to-reel ~

tape recording *n.* 1. to make a ~ 2. to play, play back a ~

tapestry *n.* 1. to weave a ~ 2. (misc.) (BE) life's rich ~

taps *n.* ['signal played on a bugle'] 1. to play, sound ~ 2. at ~ (lights go out at ~)

tar *n.* coal ~

tardiness *n.* ~ in

target I *n.* 1. to aim at; hit; shoot at a ~ 2. to track a ~ 3. to miss; overshoot a ~ 4. a civilian; military; moving; stationary ~ 5. off ~ ('not accurate') 6. on ~ ('accurate') 7. (misc.) to use smt. as a ~

target II *v.* (d; tr.) to ~ as (he was ~ed as the next victim)

target practice *n.* to conduct ~

tariff *n.* 1. to impose, levy a ~ 2. to pay a ~ 3. a protective ~ 4. a ~ on (a stiff ~ was imposed on tobacco products)

tarpaulin *n.* to spread a ~

tarry *v.* to ~ long

task *n.* 1. to carry out, do, fulfill, perform; cope with; take on, undertake a ~ 2. to assign smb. a ~ 3. a delicate, ticklish; difficult; fruitless, hopeless; Herculean, monumental; irksome; menial; onerous; pleasant; unpleasant; unwelcome; welcome ~ 4. (misc.) to take smb. to ~ for smt. ('to criticize smb. for smt.')

taskmaster *n.* a hard, rigid, severe, stern ~

taste I *n.* ['appreciation'] ['sense of what is proper'] 1. to acquire, cultivate, develop a ~ 2. to demonstrate, display, show (a) ~ 3. (an) acquired; artistic; bad; discriminating; elegant, excellent, exquisite; good ~ (it is bad ~ to ignore an invitation to a wedding) 4. a ~ for (to develop a ~ for music) 5. ~ in (they showed good ~ in planning the decor; excellent ~ in music) 6. in (a certain) ~ (everything was done in good ~) 7.

(misc.) ~s differ; a sense of ~ ['sensation obtained from tasting, eating'] (also fig.) 8. to leave a ~ (the fruit left a pleasant ~ in my mouth; the whole affair left a bitter ~ in my mouth) 9. to spoil the ~ 10. a bad, foul; bitter; mild; nice, pleasant, sweet; sour; strong ~ 11. (misc.) the sense of ~ ['small amount tasted'] 12. to have, take (esp. AE) a ~ (of) 13. to give smb. a ~ of smt. (often fig.) (they gave him a ~ of his own medicine)

taste II *v.* 1. (d; intr.) to ~ of (the food ~s of garlic) 2. (s) the food ~s good

taster *n.* a wine ~

tattle *v.* (colloq.) (D; intr.) ('to inform') to ~ on

taunt I *n.* to hurl a ~ at smb.

taunt II *v.* 1. (D; tr.) to ~ about 2. (d; tr.) to ~ into (to ~ smb. into doing smt.)

tax I *n.* 1. to impose, levy, put a ~ on 2. to collect a ~ from 3. to pay a ~ (to pay a ~ on a new car; to pay a large sum in ~es; to pay a ~ to the government) 4. to increase, raise ~es 5. to cut, lower, reduce ~es 6. to rescind, revoke a ~ 7. an amusement; capital gains; cigarette; death (AE), inheritance (BE has *death duty*); direct; estate; excess-profits; excise; federal (AE); gasoline (AE), petrol (BE); gift; income; indirect; liquor; local; negative income; nuisance; personal-property; poll; property; real-estate; sales; state (US); transfer; value-added; windfall-profits (US); withholding (esp. AE; BE has *PAYE*) ~ 8. a flat; graduated, progressive ~ 9. a ~ on (a ~ on cigarettes) 10. delinquent ~es 11. (misc.) ~ evasion; a ~ haven ~; a ~ shelter; ~ relief

tax II *v.* (formal) (d; tr.) ('to accuse') to ~ with (to ~ smb. with a crime)

taxi *n.* 1. to take a ~ 2. to hire a ~ 3. (misc.) to go somewhere by ~

tax return *n.* to file, submit a ~

tea *n.* ['plant'] 1. to grow ~ ['beverage'] 2. to brew, make; steep ~ 3. to drink, have ~ 4. strong; weak ~ 5. decaffeinated; herbal; hot; iced; mint; scented ~ 6. (BE) high ~ ('early evening meal') 7. (BE) morning ~ 8. a cup; glass of ~ (bring us two cups of ~; or: bring us two ~s) USAGE NOTE: In Britain, *tea* can also mean 'a meal where tea is served'. *High tea* includes substantial food.

teach *v.* 1. (A) she taught history to us; or: she taught us history 2. (H) she taught them to swim 3. (L; may have an object) he taught (us) that the best policy is to tell the truth 4. (Q) she taught me how to drive

teacher *n.* 1. to certify; license; train a ~ 2. an exchange; practice, student ~ 3. (BE) a supply ~ (AE has *substitute*) 4. a ~ of (a ~ of English)

teaching *n.* 1. practice, student ~ 2. team ~ 3. health ~ 4. (misc.) to go into ~

teakettle *n.* 1. to put the ~ on 2. a ~ whistles

team *n.* 1. to field; organize a ~ 2. to coach; manage a ~ 3. to disband, split up a ~ 4. a home; opposing, rival; visiting ~ 5. a baseball; basketball; cricket; drill; football; soccer; track, track-and-field; volleyball ~ 6. (Am. professional football) a wild-card ~ 7. (mil.) a combat ~ 8. a negotiating ~ 9. (misc.) (AE) to make a ~ ('to succeed in becoming a member of a team')

USAGE NOTE: AE uses *team* more often than BE--Chicago has fielded a strong team for today's game; Chicago is the strongest team in the league. BE prefers *side* when referring to a competitive match--Liverpool have fielded a strong side for today's match. BE often uses *club* when referring to a team in general--Liverpool is the strongest club in the First Division. A player can be *on a team, in/on a side*. In references to international competition, *team* is standard in BE--the England team in the World Cup.

team up *v.* (D; intr.) to ~ against; with (we ~ed up with them against our common enemy)

teapot *n.* a storm (BE), tempest (AE) in a ~ ('a fuss over nothing')

tear I /tiy(r)/ *n.* ['drop of the fluid secreted by the lacrimal gland'] 1. to shed a ~ 2. to weep (bitter) ~s 3. bitter ~s 4. ~s flowed, rolled, streamed down their cheeks 5. ~s welled up in my eyes 6. (misc.) crocodile ('false') ~s; to be in ~s over smt.; to break into ~s; eyes fill with ~s; bored to ~s

tear II /tey(r)/ *n.* ['rip'] 1. to make a ~ 2. to mend a ~

tear III *v.* 1. (d; intr.) to ~ at (to ~ at the bandages) 2. (d; tr.) to ~ from, out of (she tore several pages out of the book) 3. (d; intr.) to ~ into ('to attack verbally') (he tore into his opponent) 4. (D; tr.) to ~ into, to (she tore the paper into/to pieces; to ~ an argument to shreds) 5. (d; tr.) to ~ off (she tore a button off the coat)

tear away *v.* (D; refl., tr.) to ~ from (she couldn't ~ herself away from the book)

tease *v.* 1. (D; tr.) to ~ about (they ~d her about her new hairdo) 2. (D; tr.) to ~ into (to ~ smb. into doing smt.)

teaspoon *n.* a heaping; level ~

teatime *n.* 1. at ~ 2. past ~

technicality *n.* on a ~ (we lost the case on a ~)

technician *n.* a dental; lab, laboratory; medical; radar; television, TV ~

Technicolor *n.* (T) in ~

technique *n.* 1. to acquire, develop, work out; perfect a ~ 2. to apply a ~ 3. an acting; dance ~ 4. relaxation ~s

technology *n.* 1. to create, develop (a) ~ 2. to apply, employ ~ 3. to export, transfer ~ (to developing countries) 4. high ~ (also *high tech*) 5. state-of-the-art ~

teed off *adj.* (colloq.) (AE) ['angry'] ~ about, at

teem *v.* (d; intr.) to ~ with ('to be full of') (the river was ~ing with fish)

teens *n.* in one's ~ (they are still in their ~)

teeth see **tooth**

telegram *n.* 1. to send a ~ 2. to get, receive a ~ 3. a ~ from; to (a ~ from London to Glasgow)

telegraph *v.* 1. (A) they ~ed 'the information to us; or: they ~ed us the information 2. (H; no passive) they ~ed us to leave immediately 3. (L; may have an object) she ~ed (us) that the manuscript had been received 4. (Q; may have an object) they ~ed (us) where we should meet

telepathy *n.* mental ~

telephone I *n.* 1. to hook up, install a ~ 2. to

answer a ~ 3. to tap a ~ 4. to disconnect a ~ 5. a cordless; dial; pay, public ~ 6. a ~ rings ~ by ~; on, over the ~ (she spoke to him by ~; I enjoyed our chat on/over the ~; to speak on/over the ~; he is always on the ~) 8. (misc.) to be wanted on the ~; to call smb. to the ~

telephone II *v.* 1. (B) they ~d the message to us 2. (H; no passive) she ~d us to return home 3. (L; may have an object) he ~d (us) that he would be late 4. (Q; may have an object) I ~d (them) when to come

telephone call *n.* see **call I, 12-17**

telephone receiver *n.* see **receiver 1-2**

telescope *n.* 1. to focus a ~ on 2. a reflecting; refracting ~

television *n.* 1. to put on, turn on the ~ 2. to watch ~ 3. to turn off the ~ 4. black-and-white; color ~ 5. cable, pay; closed-circuit; educational; local; national; peak-viewing-time (BE), prime-time (esp. AE); public ~ 6. on ~ (I saw her on ~)

television set *n.* 1. to put on, turn on a ~ 2. to turn off a ~

tell *v.* 1. (A; usu. without to) ('to relate') she told the news to everyone; or: she told everyone the news; he told me his name; she told them a story; ~ me the truth 2. (D; intr.) ('to be certain') to ~ about (you can never ~ about people like that) 3. (d; intr., tr.) ('to inform') to ~ about, of (he didn't want to ~ about the incident; ~ me about the game; she told everyone of her success) 4. (c; tr.) ('to ascertain') to ~ from (can you ~ anything from a quick examination?) 5. (d; tr.) to ~ from ('to differentiate') (can you ~ one twin from another?) 6. (colloq.) (d; intr., tr.) to ~ of (BE), on ('to inform on') (he told on her when the teacher returned; I'm going to ~ my father on you) 7. (D; intr.) to ~ on ('to affect') (the strain was beginning to ~ on her) 8. (H) ('to order') she told me to leave 9. (L; must have an object) ('to inform') we told them that we would be late 10. (Q; must have an object) ('to inform') ~ me how to get there 11. (Q) ('to ascertain') can you ~ from a quick examination where his injuries are?

teller *n.* (AE) a bank ~ (BE has *cashier*)

telling *n.* ['certainty'] there is no ~ what will happen

temerity *n.* the ~ to + inf. (he had the ~ to file a grievance)

temper *n.* 1. to control, keep one's ~ 2. to lose one's ~ 3. a bad, explosive, hot, nasty, quick, uncontrollable, ungovernable, violent ~ 4. a calm, even ~ 5. ~s flare (up) 6. a display, fit of ~ (she said that in a fit of ~)

temperament *n.* an artistic; poetic ~

temperance *n.* ~ in

temperate *adj.* ~ in

temperature *n.* ['degree of heat or cold'] 1. to take smb.'s ~ 2. a high; low; normal ~ 3. (smb.'s) body ~ 4. room ~ (at room ~) 5. a ~ drops, falls; goes down 6. a ~ goes up, rises 7. a ~ remains steady 8. at a (certain) ~ (water boils at a certain ~) ['excess over normal body heat'] 9. to have, run a ~ 10. a high; slight ~

tempo *n.* 1. to increase, step up the ~ 2. to slow

down the ~
tempt v. 1. (D; tr.) to ~ into (to ~ smb. into doing smt.) 2. (H) to ~ smb. to do smt.
temptation n. 1. to overcome, resist ~ 2. to be exposed to, face ~ 3. to succumb to ~ 4. to place, put ~ in smb.'s way 5. irresistible, strong ~
tenacity n. 1. to demonstrate, display, show ~ 2. bulldog; great ~ (to demonstrate great ~) 3. the ~ to + inf. (she had the ~ to finish the job)
tend v. 1. (AE) (d; intr.) to ~ to (to ~ to one's own business) (CE has *attend to*) 2. (d; intr.) to ~ towards 3. (E) he ~s to exaggerate
tendency n. 1. to demonstrate, display, show a ~ 2. a growing; pronounced; strong; universal ~ 3. homicidal; suicidal; vicious ~cies (for years he has displayed suicidal ~cies) 4. a ~ towards 5. a ~ to + inf. (she has a ~ to exaggerate)
tender I adj. ~ to, towards, with
tender II n. ['offer, bid'] (esp. BE) 1. to make, put in, send in, submit a ~ 2. to invite ~s 3. a ~ for ['currency'] 4. legal ~
tender III v. 1. (B) ('to offer') she ~ed her resignation to the government 2. (BE) (d; intr.) to ~ for ('to bid on') (to ~ for the construction of a new motorway)
tenderness n. ['kindness, care'] 1. to show ~ 2. ~ towards
tendon n. 1. to pull a ~ 2. an Achilles' ~
tenet n. 1. a basic, fundamental ~ 2. a ~ that + clause (our basic ~ is that all people are equal) 3. (misc.) to embrace the ~s of a new philosophy
tennis n. 1. to play ~ 2. lawn; paddle; table ~ 3. (misc.) a ~ match; a game of ~ (let's play a game of ~; she won the first game and went on to win the set and match)
tennis racket n. to restring; string a ~
tenor n. to sing ~
tenpins n. to play ~
tense I adj. ~ with (~ with anxiety)
tense II n. (grammar) the future; future perfect; past; past perfect; present; progressive ~
tension n. ['strained relations'] ['strain'] 1. to cause, create ~ 2. to heighten, increase ~ 3. to alleviate, ease, lessen, relieve ~ (to alleviate/ease ~ between the superpowers) 4. acute; mounting ~ 5. arterial; international; nervous; premenstrual; racial ~ 6. ~ builds up, mounts 7. ~ eases, subsides 8. ~ between ['tautness'] 9. fanbelt ~ ['voltage'] 10. high; low ~
tent n. 1. to erect, pitch, put up a ~ 2. to dismantle, take down a ~ 3. a circus; pup; pyramidal; wall ~ 4. a croup; oxygen ~
tenterhooks n. on ~ ('in suspense')
tenure n. ['permanence of employment as a teacher'] 1. to give, grant ~ 2. to acquire, get, receive ~ 3. academic ~
term I n. ['expression, word'] 1. abstract; bold; clear; flattering; general; glowing; vague ~s (she described him in glowing ~s) 2. a general; generic; legal; technical ~ 3. in ~s (to speak in general ~s) 4. (misc.) a contradiction in ~s ['period of time served'] 5. to serve a ~ (in office) 6. an unexpired ~ 7. a ~ expires, runs out 8. a jail, prison ~ ['division of a school year'] 9. the autumn (BE), fall

(AE); spring; summer ~ 10. at the end of a/of (BE) ~ ['time at which a normal pregnancy terminates'] 11. to have a baby at ~ (see also **terms**)
term II v. ['formal'] (N; used with a noun) ('to call') by what right does he ~ himself an artist?
terminal n. ['point on an electric circuit'] 1. a negative; positive ~ ['device by which information enters or leaves a computer'] 2. a computer ~; a Visual Display Terminal = VDT (AE; BE has *Visual Display Unit* = VDU) ['passenger, freight station'] 3. an airline; bus; freight; shipping; trucking ~ 4. at a ~ (let's meet at the bus ~)
termination n. ['cessation of employment'] voluntary ~
terminology n. 1. to codify, create, establish, standardize (a) ~ 2. basic; legal; scientific; technical ~
terms n. ['conditions, provisions'] 1. to dictate; set; state; stipulate ~ 2. easy; favorable ~ 3. surrender ~ (to stipulate surrender ~ to an enemy) 4. by the ~ (of an agreement) 5. on certain ~ (on one's own ~s; on our ~) 6. under (the) ~ of the agreement ['agreement'] 7. to come to ~ with smb. ['relationship'] ['footing'] 8. equal, even; familiar, intimate; speaking; unequal ~ 9. on certain ~ with (to be on speaking ~ with smb.; to negotiate with smb. on equal ~)
terrace n. from; on a ~
terrain n. harsh, rough; hilly; mountainous; smooth ~
terrible adj. 1. ~ to + inf. (it was ~ to work there = it was ~ working there) 2. ~ that + clause (it is ~ that she lost her wallet; I feel ~ that you cannot accept our invitation)
terrified adj. 1. ~ by, of 2. ~ that + clause (we are ~ that there may be another earthquake)
terrify v. (R) it ~fied me to contemplate the consequences of your actions; it ~ies us that there may be another earthquake
terrifying adj. 1. ~ to + inf. (it was ~ to watch) 2. ~ that + clause (it's ~ that there are so many drunk drivers on the road)
territory n. 1. to annex; occupy ~ 2. to cede ~ 3. a neutral; trust ~ 4. (an) occupied; unoccupied ~ 5. unexplored ~ 6. (misc.) to reconnoiter enemy ~
terror n. 1. to employ, engage in, resort to, sow, unleash ~ 2. to inspire ~; to strike ~ into (to strike ~ into the hearts of people) 3. sheer, stark ~ 4. (colloq.) a holy ~ 5. in ~ (to live in ~ of smt.) 6. (misc.) a campaign, reign of ~
terrorism n. 1. indiscriminate; state; urban ~ 2. an act of ~ 3. see **terror 1**
terrorist n. an armed; urban ~
terrorize v. (D; tr.) to ~ into
test I n. ['examination, set of questions'] 1. to administer, conduct, give a ~ 2. to draw up, make up, set (BE) a ~ 3. to take a ~ 4. to fail; pass a ~ 5. a demanding, difficult; easy ~ 6. an achievement; aptitude; intelligence; loyalty (esp. AE); placement; proficiency ~ 7. a completion; free-association; lie-detector; multiple-choice; objective; true-and-false ~ 8. a competency; means ~ 9. a ~ in, on (a ~ in mathematics; a ~ on new material) ['trial, experiment'] ['examination'] 10.

to carry out, conduct, do, run a ~ 11. exhaustive, extensive, thorough ~s 12. an acid, demanding, exacting, severe ~ 13. a blood; diagnostic; endurance; laboratory; litmus; means; nuclear; paraffin; Pap; patch; paternity; personality; psychological; road; saliva; screen; skin; tuberculin ~ 14. a ~ for (to do a skin ~ for tuberculosis) 15. a ~ on (they conducted a series of ~s on me at the health center) 16. (misc.) to stand the ~ of time. the ~ turned out to be positive; to put smb. to the ~

test II v. 1. (D; intr., tr.) to ~ for (to ~ for excessive air pollution; to ~ the urine for sugar) 2. (D; tr.) to ~ in (we ~ed them in English) 3. (P; intr.) some of our students ~ed in the top percentile 4. (esp. AE) (s) some students ~ high, others low

testament n. 1. the New; Old Testament 2. a ~ to 3. (misc.) smb.'s last will and ~

test flight n. to conduct a ~

testicle n. an undescended ~

testify v. 1. (D; intr.) to ~ about (to ~ about a case) 2. (D; intr.) to ~ against; for, on behalf of (to ~ for the plaintiff) 3. (d; intr.) to ~ to (the results ~ to the quality of their work) 4. (L) he ~fied that he had not seen the accident 5. (misc.) to ~ under oath

testimonial n. 1. to give, offer a ~ 2. an eloquent ~ 3. a ~ to (a ~ to smb.'s accomplishments)

testimony n. 1. to give, offer ~ 2. to cite ~ 3. to recant, repudiate, retract (one's) ~ 4. to contradict, discount, refute ~ 5. false, perjured; reliable ~ 6. ~ about 7. ~ against; for, on behalf of (she gave ~ against the plaintiff) 8. ~ that + clause (nothing could refute her ~ that the driver was drunk)

tetanus n. to develop ~

text n. 1. to set a ~ (in type) 2. to annotate a ~ 3. an annotated ~ (see also **textbook**)

textbook n. 1. an introductory ~ 2. a ~ of, on (a ~ on advanced grammar)

texture n. rough; smooth ~

thank v. 1. to ~ profusely; sincerely 2. (D; tr.) to ~ for (she ~ed me profusely for my help) 3. (colloq.) (H; no passive) I'll ~ you to make less noise in the future

thankful adj. 1. ~ for; to 2. ~ to + inf. (~ to be alive) 3. ~ that + clause (we were ~ that you offered to help)

thanks n. 1. to express; give one's ~; to say ~ 2. to accept smb.'s ~ 3. one's heartfelt, sincere, warm ~ 4. ~ for; to 5. (misc.) many ~; ~ a lot; I finished the whole job on time, no ~ to you; we completed the work on time, ~ to your help

that pronoun 1. at ~ ('in addition') (she was a thief and a clever one at ~) 2. (misc.) take ~! ('I'm going to punch you!')

thaw n. 1. the spring ~ 2. a ~ sets in (also fig.)

theater, theatre n. ['building in which plays are performed or films shown'] 1. to crowd, jam, pack a ~ 2. an art; dinner (esp. AE); movie (AE; BE has cinema); open-air; repertory ~ 3. at the ~ (we were at the ~ last night) ['theatrical profession'] 4. the legitimate ~ 5. in the ~ (she was well thought of in the ~) ['room equipped for surgical operations'] (BE) 6. an operating theatre

theft n. 1. to commit (a) ~; to practice ~ 2. petty ~ 3. a ~ from (a daring ~ from a museum)

theme n. 1. a basic; contemporary; dominant ~ 2. a ~ for (a ~ for discussion)

theorem n. 1. to deduce, formulate a ~ 2. to prove; test a ~ 3. a binomial ~

theorize v. 1. (D; intr.) to ~ about 2. (L) the police ~d that the burglar had entered through a window

theory n. 1. to formulate a ~ 2. to advance. advocate, present, propose, suggest a ~ 3. to confirm; develop; test a ~ 4. to disprove, explode, refute a ~ 5. a pet; scientific ~ 6. game; information number; political; quantum; systems ~ 7. the big bang; steady state ~ 8. the germ ~ (of disease) 9. a ~ evolves; holds up 10. a ~ that (she has a ~ that drinking milk prevents colds) 11. in ~ (in ~ their plan makes sense) 12. on a ~ (they proceeded on the ~ that the supplies would arrive on time) 13. (misc.) the ~ of relativity; to combine ~ and practice

therapist n. an occupational; physical ~; psychotherapist; speech ~

therapy n. 1. to employ, use ~ 2. art; dance electro-convulsive (BE), electro-shock (AE); group; inhalation; music; occupational; physical; radiation, X-ray; recreational; shock; speech ~ 3. ~ for 4. in ~ (she was in ~)

there adv. over ~

thermometer n. 1. a clinical; meat; oral; over; rectal ~ 2. a ~ shows a temperature

thermostat n. 1. to set a ~ 2. to calibrate a ~

thesis n. ['research paper'] 1. to write a ~ 2. a doctoral, Ph.D.; master's ~ ['proposition, hypothesis'] 3. to advance, propose; test a ~ 4. to challenge; refute a ~ 5. a ~ about, on 6. a ~ that + clause (these developments disprove their ~ that high taxes stifle investment) (see the Usage Note for **dissertation**)

thick I adj. (misc.) as ~ as thieves ('very closely allied'); to lay it on ~ ('to exaggerate')

thick II n. ['most intense part'] in the ~ (of the battle)

thick and thin n. ['all difficulties'] through ~ (to remain friends through ~)

thief n. a common, petty; sneak ~

thing n. ['deed'] ['event'] 1. to do a ~ (she did a nice ~ when she offered to help; to do great ~s; to do the right ~) 2. a bad; difficult; easy; good; mean; nasty; nice; sensible; strange; stupid; terrible ~; the right; wrong ~ 3. a ~ to + inf. (it was an easy ~ to do; it was the wrong ~ to do) 'object'] 4. to use a ~ for (don't use this ~ for removing paint) ['facts, details'] 5. to get a ~ out of smb. (I couldn't get a ~ out of her) 6. to know a ~ about (he doesn't know a ~ about music); to know a ~ or two ('to know quite a bit') ['fact, point'] colloq.) 7. the ~ is that + clause (the ~ is that I still have a great deal of work to do; the other ~ is that ●I really don't want to go) ['article of clothing'] 8. not to have a ~ to wear (I don't have a ~ to wear) 9. to put on; take off one's ~s ['possessions, effects'] 10. to pack one's ~s ['step'] 11. the first; next ~ (the next ~ is to submit your application) ['person of a certain type'] 12. a pretty; poor ~ (a pretty little thing; you poor thing) ['thought, idea'] 13. to say the right ~ ['matters'] (used in the plural) 14. to even ~s up 15. to see ~s (as they are) 16. (misc.) all ~s considered ('with everything taken into account'); ~s don't look good; ~s are looking up for us; how do ~s stand? how are ~s? ['utensils'] 17. to clear the (breakfast) ~s away ['individual'] 18. a living ~ (there wasn't a living ~ in sight) ['fear'] ['obsession'] (colloq.) 19. a ~ about (she has a ~ about flying) ['misc.'] 20. to do one's ~ ('to do what one feels competent or motivated to do'); any old ~ ('anything at all'); a sure ~ ('smt. that is certain to succeed'); of all ~s ('most surprisingly'); to tell smb. a ~ or two ('to tell smb. frankly what one thinks')

think I *n.* (colloq.) (BE) to have a ~ about

think II *v.* 1. to ~ aloud; clearly; hard (I thought hard and finally remembered the name) 2. (D; intr.) ('to reflect') to ~ about, of (I was ~ing about you; to ~ of the past) 3. (d; intr.) ('to be concerned') to ~ about, of (I was only ~ing of your welfare when I declined the offer) 4. (d; intr.) to ~ of ('to have an opinion of') (what do you ~ of this proposal?) 5. (d; intr.) to ~ of ('to consider; to intend') (she never thought of telephoning; to ~ of resigning) 6. (E) ('to remember') (she never thought to call) 7. (L) ('to anticipate') we thought that it would rain 8. (L) ('to believe') I ~ that he is a fool 9. (M; used in the passive) ('to consider') he is thought to be irreplaceable 10. (N; used with an adjective) ('to consider') many people ~ her charming 11. (misc.) I thought to myself that it would be nice to have some hot soup; he doesn't ~ of himself as a politician; to ~ better of doing smt. ('to change one's mind about doing smt.')

think about *v.* (J and K) ('to direct one's thoughts to') I thought about you/your working out there in the hot sun

think ahead *v.* (D; intr.) ('to direct one's thoughts ahead') to ~ to (to ~ to the future)

think back *v.* (D; intr.) ('to direct one's thoughts back') to ~ on, to (to ~ to the old days)

thinker *n.* a clear; great; logical; muddled; original ~

thinking *n.* clear; good; muddled; original; positive; quick; wishful ~

thinking cap *n.* (old-fashioned) to put on one's ~ ('to ponder a problem')

thinner *n.* paint ~

third degree *n.* (colloq.) ['brutal, harsh interrogation'] to give smb. the ~

thirst I *n.* 1. to experience ~; more usu. is: to be thirsty 2. to quench, slake one's ~ 3. unquenchable; unquenched ~ 4. a ~ for (a ~ for knowledge)

thirst II *v.* (d; intr.) to ~ for (to ~ for knowledge)

thorn *n.* 1. to remove a ~ (from one's finger) 2. (misc.) a ~ in one's side ('a source of irritation')

thorough *adj.* ~ in

thoroughfare *n.* a busy, crowded ~

thought *n.* ['reflection'] 1. to entertain, harbor, have; relish a ~ (to harbor ~s of revenge) 2. to express, present a ~ 3. to gather; sum up one's ~s 4. an evil; fleeting, passing; happy; intriguing;

refreshing; sober, sobering; ugly; upsetting ~ 5. the ~ struck me that... 6. a ~ about, on (what are your ~s on this matter?) 7. a ~ that + clause (the ~ that we would soon reach home gave us courage) 8. at a ~ (my mind boggles at the very ~) 9. in one's ~s (she was always in my ~s) 10. (misc.) that ~ has crossed my mind; to read smb.'s ~s; a train of ~; in ~ and deed ['consideration'] 11. to give ~ to 12. to abandon, give up all ~s (of doing smt.) 13. (misc.) perish the ~! ('one should not even consider the possibility!') ['ideas, principles'] 14. liberal; logical; modern ~ ['opinion'] 15. to express a ~ 16. a ~ about, on 17. a ~ that + clause (she expressed her ~ that the case should be settled without litigation) ['concentration'] 18. (deep) in ~ ['intention'] 19. to have no ~ (of doing smt.)

thoughtful *adj.* 1. ~ about 2. ~ to + inf. (it was ~ of her to do that)

thoughtless *adj.* ~ to + inf. (it was ~ of them to make noise)

thousand *n.* by, in the ~s (the crowd streamed into the stadium by the ~s)

thrall *n.* (formal) ['slavery'] in ~ to

thrash *v.* to ~ soundly

thrashing *n.* a sound ~

thread I *n.* ['fiber, cord'] 1. to make, spin; wind ~ 2. coarse; fine; heavy; thin ~ 3. cotton; lisle; nylon; polyester; rayon; silk ~ 4. a reel (BE), spool (AE) of ~ 5. (misc.) to hang by a ~ ('to be very uncertain') ['theme'] ['train of thought'] 6. to lose the ~ (of an argument) 7. the common ~ (of a story) 8. a tenuous ~

thread II *v.* (C) ~ a needle for me; or: ~ me a needle

threat *n.* 1. to issue, make, utter a ~ 2. to carry out, fulfill a ~ 3. to be, constitute, pose a ~ 4. a covert; dire, grave, serious; direct; empty, idle; explicit; imminent; implicit; terroristic; veiled ~ 5. a security ~ 6. a ~ to (to constitute a ~ to the party leadership) 7. a ~ to + inf. (she carried out her ~ to resign) 8. a ~ that + clause (she carried out her ~ that she would resign) 9. under ~ of (under ~ of reprisals)

threaten *v.* 1. (D; tr.) to ~ with (to ~ smb. with reprisals) 2. (E) she ~ed to resign

threshold *n.* ['entrance'] 1. (also fig.) to cross a ~ 2. (also fig.) on the ~ (to be on the ~ of a promising career) 3. (med.) a renal ~

thrift *n.* to practice ~

thrifty *adj.* ~ in

thrill I *n.* 1. to give, provide a ~ 2. to experience, get, have a ~ 3. a ~ for smb. 4. a ~ to + inf. (it was a ~ to ride in your new car = it was a ~ riding in your new car) 5. (misc.) to gamble for the ~ of it ('to gamble for the sheer excitement of gambling')

thrill II *v.* 1. (d; intr.) to ~ to (she ~ed to the sound of their voices) 2. (R) it ~ed me to learn of your success

thrilled *adj.* 1. ~ with (they were ~ with the gift) 2. ~ to + inf. (she was ~ to receive an invitation) 3. ~ that + clause (we were ~ that he would give a concert in our town)

thrilling *adj.* ~ to + inf. (it was ~ to see them)

thrive *v.* (D; intr.) to ~ on (to ~ on hard work)

throat *n.* 1. to clear one's ~ 2. to gargle one's ~ 3. a clear; inflamed, red, sore; scratchy; strep ~ 4. (misc.) to cut one's own ~ ('to ruin oneself'); to jump down smb.'s ~ ('to criticize smb.'); to ram smt. down smb.'s ~ ('to impose smt. on smb.'); the words stuck in her ~ ('she found it difficult to say'); to have a lump in one's ~ ('to be overcome by emotion'); to cut/slash/slit smb.'s ~

throes *n.* in the ~ (in the ~ of a severe economic crisis)

thrombosis *n.* a coronary ~

throne *n.* 1. to ascend, mount, succeed to a ~ 2. to seize, usurp a ~ 3. to occupy, sit on a ~ 4. to abdicate (from), give up a ~

throng *v.* (P; intr.) they all ~ed around the speaker

throttle *n.* 1. to open a ~ 2. at full ~ ('at full speed')

throw I *n.* 1. (basketball) a free ~ 2. (baseball) a wild ~

throw II *v.* 1. (A) ~ the ball to her; or: ~ her the ball 2. (D; tr.) to ~ across, over (to ~ a ball over a fence) 3. (D; tr.) to ~ at (he threw a stone at me) 4. (d; refl., tr.) to ~ into (he threw himself into his work; they threw the body into the river) 5. (d; refl., tr.) to ~ on (she threw herself on the mercy of the court; to ~ light on a subject) 6. (d; tr.) to ~ out of (they were thrown out of work) 7. (d; refl., tr.) to ~ to (I threw myself to the ground) 8. (misc.) to ~ smb. off balance

throw away *v.* (D; tr.) ('to squander') to ~ on (to ~ one's money on gambling)

throwback *n.* ['reversion'] a ~ to

throw back *v.* (B) she threw the ball back to me

throw up *v.* (B) ('to reproach') I was late, but she didn't ~ it up to me

thrust I *n.* 1. to make a ~ 2. a ~ into

thrust II *v.* 1. (d; tr.) to ~ at (she thrust the money at me) 2. (d; tr.) to ~ into (she thrust the money into my hand) 3. (misc.) to ~ one's way through a crowd

thud *n.* a dull ~

thumb *n.* ['finger'] 1. babies often suck their ~s ['misc.'] 2. under smb.'s ~ ('dominated by smb.'); to twiddle one's ~s ('to be idle'); to turn ~s down on ('to reject')

thunder *n.* 1. ~ booms, reverberates, roars, rolls 2. a clap, peal, roll of ~ (a deafening clap of ~) 3. (misc.) to steal smb.'s ~ ('to do first what smb. else was going to do')

thunderbolt *n.* a ~ struck (a tree)

thunderstruck *adj.* 1. ~ at (~ at the news) 2. ~ to + inf. (they were ~ to learn that the train had already left)

thwart *v.* (D; tr.) to ~ in

tic *n.* a nervous ~

tick I *n.* (colloq.) (esp. BE) ['credit'] on ~ (to let smb. have smt. on ~)

tick II *n.* (colloq.) (BE) ['moment'] in a ~ (she'll be down in a ~)

ticket *n.* ['document showing that a fare or admission fee has been paid'] 1. to issue a ~ 2. to buy; get a ~ 3. to honor ('accept') a ~ 4. a one-way

(AE), single (BE); return (BE), round-trip (AE) ~ 5. a commutation (AE); complimentary, free; library (BE); meal (AE; BE has *luncheon vouch-er);* pawn; platform (BE); season; valid ~ 6. an airplane; bus; train ~ 7. a ~ for, to (a ~ for a concert; a ~ to a game) ['list of candidates'] (pol.) (AE) 8. to split a ~ 9. a split; straight ~ ('to vote a split ~') ['printed card indicating participation in a game of chance'] 10. a winning ~ (she held the winning ~) 11. a lottery; sweepstakes ~ ['misc.'] 12. to write one's own ~ (esp. AE; colloq.) ('to have complete freedom of action') (see also **traffic ticket)**

tickled *adj.* (colloq.) (esp. AE) ['happy'] 1. ~ to + inf. (they would be ~ to come to the party) 2. ~ that + clause (we're ~ that you'll be at our party) 3. (misc.) ~ pink/silly ('very much pleased')

tide *n.* ['rising and falling of the surface of bodies of water'] 1. a daily; ebb; falling; flood high, spring; low, neap ~ 2. a ~ comes in; ebbs, goes out ['trend, tendency'] 3. to buck (AE), go against the ~ 4. to go with the ~ 5. to stem the ~

tidings *n.* 1. to bear, bring ~ 2. to receive ~ 3. glad; sad ~

tie I *n.* ['necktie'] 1. to tie one's ~ 2. (BE) an old-school ~ ('a tie showing which school the owner attended') ['draw'] (sports) 3. to break a ~ 4. a scoreless ~ 5. (to end) in a ~ ['match'] (BE) (sports) 6. a cup ~ ['link, bond'] 7. to establish ~s with 8. to cement, strengthen ~s 9. to cut, sever loosen ~s with 10. close, intimate, strong ~s 11. old school ~s 12. ~s between; to, with (~s to other nations) ['support for rails'] (AE) 13. a railroad ~ (BE has *sleeper)*

tie II *v.* 1. (D; tr.) ('to equal the score of') to ~ for (to ~ smb. for the lead) 2. (D; tr.) ('to fasten') to ~ to (they ~d him to a post) 3. (D; intr.) ('to equal the score') to ~ with (our team ~d with them for the lead) 4. (N; used with an adjective) she ~d the rope tight

tie down *v.* (D; tr.) to ~ to (he was ~d down to his job

tie-in *n.* (colloq.) ['relation'] a ~ between; with

tiers *n.* ['rows'] in ~

tie-up *n.* ['stoppage'] 1. to cause a ~ 2. a traffic ~ ['link'] 3. a ~ to; with

tiff *n.* ['quarrel'] 1. to have a ~ with 2. a minor ~

tiger *n.* 1. a Bengal; man-eating; saber-toothed; Siberian ~ 2. ~s growl, roar 3. a young ~ is a cub 4. a female ~ is a tigress 5. (misc.) to fight like a ~ ('to fight very fiercely'); a paper ~ ('one who only seems to pose a threat')

tight *adj.* ['stingy'] (colloq.) (esp. AE) 1. ~ with (~ with money) ['misc.'] 2. to sit ~ ('to maintain one's position')

tightrope *n.* to walk a ~ (also fig.)

tile *n.* ceramic; vinyl ~

till *n.* ['money drawer'] to have one's finger(s) in the ~ ('to steal from a money drawer')

tiller *n.* ['rudder'] to ship ('put in place for use') the ~

tilt I *n.* ['attack'] (colloq.) (BE) 1. to have, make a ~ at ['inclination'] 2. a ~ to, towards ['misc.'] 3. at full ~ ('at full speed')

tilt II *v.* 1. (D; intr.) to ~ to (to ~ to the right) 2. (misc.) to ~ at windmills ('to fight imaginary enemies')

timber *n.* 1. to float, raft ~ (down a river) 2. seasoned; unseasoned ~

time *n.* ['unlimited duration'] ['entire period of existence'] 1. ~ flies; passes 2. in ~ (we exist in ~ and space) ['unlimited future period'] 3. ~ will tell (~ will tell if we are right) 4. in ~ (in ~ everything will be forgotten) ['moment'] ['fixed moment'] ['appropriate moment'] 5. to fix, set, specify a ~ for (to fix a ~ for a meeting) 6. to bide ('wait patiently for') one's ~ 7. bedtime; curtain ~; lunchtime; starting ~ 8. the appointed; present; right; wrong ~ 9. a closing; opening ~ 10. a ~ for (it's ~ for lunch) 11. ~ to + inf. (it's ~ for us to leave) 12. ~ that + clause (it's high time that she returned home) 13. at a certain ~ (at a bad ~; at the present ~; at that ~; at any old ~) 14. by a certain ~ (by that ~ he had left) 15. (misc.) in good ~; in plenty of ~ ('early enough') ['duration'] ['period'] ['interval'] 16. to pass, spend ~ (she spends her ~ reading) 17. to gain, save ~ 18. to find ~ (she somehow finds ~ to jog every day) 19. to consume, take ~ (it takes quite a bit of ~ to get there; how much ~ will this job take?) 20. to lose; waste ~; to fritter away one's ~ 21. a long; short ~ 22. ancient; former; olden; prehistoric; recent ~s (in ancient ~s) 23. (AE) compensatory ~ ('free time given to an employee for previously worked overtime') (BE has *time off in lieu*) 24. (AE) equal ~ (for political candidates on TV and radio) 25. peak viewing (BE), prime ~ (what's on TV tonight during prime ~?) 26. (a) record ~ (she ran the distance in record ~) 27. released ~ ('time given for extracurricular activities') 28. travel ~ ('time spent in going to and returning from work') 29. (the) running ~ (of a film) 30. ~ drags 31. ~ for (will you have ~ for an interview?) 32. (misc.) to kill ~ ('to make time pass'); to play for ~ ('to seek delay'); to take one's ~ ('to act slowly'); for a ~; for the ~ being ('for now'); ~ hangs heavy on our hands ['conditions during a period'] 33. bad, difficult, hard, rough ~s (during/in hard ~s) ['available period'] 34. free, leisure, spare ~ (what do you do in your leisure ~?) 35. ~ to + inf. (there is no ~ to lose; will you have ~ to see me tomorrow?) 36. ~ for (~ for relaxation; I have no ~ for my family) ['period worked'] 37. full ~; overtime; part ~ (I work part ~) 38. lost ~ (to make up lost ~; or: to make up for lost ~) ['period of serving, service'] 39. to do, serve ~ (to do/serve ~ in prison) ['tempo, rhythm'] 40. to beat, keep ~ (to music, to a song) 41. (mus.) common ~ 42. (usu mil.) double; quick ~ (quick ~, march!) 43. in ~ to (the music) ['system of measuring duration'] 44. to keep, show, tell ~ (a clock tells ~; my watch keeps good ~) 45. central (US); daylight-saving (AE), summer (BE); eastern (US); Greenwich (mean); local; mountain (US); Pacific (US); solar; standard (AE) ~ ['schedule'] 46. ahead of ~ 47. behind ~ 48. in ~ for (we arrived in ~ for the concert) 49. on ~ (they got there on ~) ['experience'] 50. to have a (good) ~ 51. a good, great, lovely ~

(we had a great ~ on our trip) 52. a bad, rough, tough, unpleasant ~ ['timeout'] (sports) 53. to call ~ ['occasion'] 54. the first; last; next ~; that; this ~ ['end of pregnancy'] 55. her ~ is near ['misc.'] 56. at the same ~ ('however'); at ~s ('occasionally'); for the ~ being ('at present'); from ~ immemorial ('from the earliest period'); in good ~ ('when appropriate'); in no ~ ('very soon'); to have the ~ of one's life ('to enjoy oneself thoroughly'); to keep up with the ~s ('to keep abreast of the latest developments'); to make good ~ ('to travel quickly'); to make ~ with smb. (esp. AE; colloq.) ('to be successful in attracting smb.'); to mark ~ ('to be inactive'); ~ and ~ again; or ~ after ~ ('frequently'); to live on borrowed ~ ('to live beyond the expected time of death'); pressed for ~ ('in a hurry'); to work against ~ ('to work to meet a deadline'); the ~ is ripe for action ('it is time to act'); he died before his ~ ('he died prematurely') USAGE NOTES: 1. The phrase *in time* can mean 'eventually'--in time everything will be forgotten. 2. The phrase *in time* can also mean 'with some time to spare'--we arrived in time for the concert. 3. The phrase *on time* means 'neither early nor late'--they got there on time.

time bomb *n.* 1. to set off a ~ 2. a ~ ticks away

time clock *n.* to punch a ~

time limit *n.* to set a ~ for

timeout *n.* to take (a) ~

timer *n.* ['timing device'] to set a ~

timetable *n.* 1. to make up a ~ 2. to issue a ~ 3. to follow a ~ 4. to upset a ~ (see **schedule 3**)

timid *adj.* ~ about

timing *n.* bad; good ~

tinged *adj.* (cannot stand alone) ~ with (~ with regret)

tinker *v.* (colloq.) (D; intr.) to ~ with

tint *v.* (N; used with an adjective) the windshield is ~ed blue

tip I *n.* ['gratuity'] 1. to give, leave a ~ 2. a big, generous, handsome ~ (I left a generous ~ for the waitress)

tip II *v.* 1. to ~ generously, handsomely, liberally 2. (O) we ~ped the waiter five dollars

tip III *n.* ['information'] 1. give smb. a ~ 2. an anonymous; hot ~ 3. a ~ about, on

tip IV *n.* ['pointed end'] 1. a filter ~ ['end'] 2. on the ~ of smb.'s tongue (the word was on the ~ of my tongue; it was on the ~ of my tongue to say something)

tip off *v.* (D; tr.) ('to inform') to ~ about

tiptoe *n.* (to stand, walk) on ~

tirade *n.* 1. to launch into a ~ 2. a blistering, lengthy ~ 3. a ~ against

tire I *n.* 1. to deflate; inflate a ~ 2. to mount a ~ 3. to change; patch; repair; recap; retread a ~ 4. to crisscross, rotate ~s (to reduce wear) 5. to slash a ~ 6. a flat ~ (we had a flat ~ during our trip) 7. a worn ~ 8. a balloon; radial; snow; spare; steel-belted; studded; tubeless ~ 9. whitewall ~s 10. a ~ blows out; goes flat

tire II *v.* (d; intr.) to ~ of (to ~ of watching television)

tired *adj.* 1. dead ~ 2. ~ of (I'm ~ of waiting)

tiresome *adj.* ~ to + inf. (it's ~ to do the same thing every day = it's ~ doing the same thing every day)

tissue *n.* ['structural material'] 1. cellular; conjunctival; connective; fatty; granulation; muscular; scar ~ ['soft paper'] 2. cleansing; toilet ~ ['misc.'] 3. a ~ of lies

title *n.* ['appellation'] 1. to bestow, confer a ~ on 2. to renounce a ~ 3. an official ~ ['exclusive possession'] 4. to give smb. ~ to smt. 5. to hold ~ to smt. 6. clear ~ to 7. ~ to (they hold ~ to the property) 8. (misc.) there is a cloud on the ~ ['championship'] 9. to win a ~ 10. to hold a ~ 11. to clinch a ~ 12. to give up; lose a ~

toad *n.* a horned ~

toady up *v.* (d; intr.) to ~ to (he ~died up to the boss)

toast I *n.* ['browned bread'] 1. to make ~ 2. French; melba ~ 3. a piece, slice of ~

toast II *v.* (C) ~ two slices for me; or: ~ me two slices

toast III *n.* ['act of drinking to honor smb.'] 1. to drink; propose a ~ 2. a ~ to (we drank a ~ to her) 3. (misc.) to join smb. in a ~ ['highly admired person'] 4. the ~ of (the ~ of the town; the ~ of high society)

tobacco *n.* 1. to grow, raise ~ 2. to cure ~ 3. to chew ~ 4. strong ~ 5. chewing ~ 6. a plug of (chewing) ~

to-do *n.* ['fuss'] to make a (big) ~ over

toe *n.* 1. to stub one's ~ on 2. to curl one's ~s 3. the big; little ~ 4. (misc.) to keep on one's ~s ('to be alert') to tread on smb.'s ~s ('to offend smb.')

toehold *n.* ['footing'] to get a ~

toenail *n.* an ingrown ~

toil I *n.* ['hard work'] 1. arduous, unremitting ~ 2. physical ~

toil II *v.* (D; intr.) ('to work hard') to ~ over

toilet *n.* 1. to flush a ~ 2. a pay; public ~

token *n.* ['symbol, sign'] 1. to give, provide a ~ of 2. a tangible ~ 3. (misc.) by the same ~ ('for a similar reason'); in ~ of ('as evidence of') ['metal or plastic disc used as a substitute for money'] 4. to drop in, insert, put in a ~ (to insert a ~ into a slot) 5. a bus; subway (AE) ~

told *adj.* all ~ ('altogether')

tolerance *n.* 1. to display, show ~ 2. to have ~ 3. ~ for

tolerant *adj.* 1. ~ of (~ of criticism) 2. ~ towards

tolerate *v.* (K) I will not ~ his smoking

toleration *n.* 1. to display, show ~ 2. ~ for

toll I *n.* ['amount levied'] 1. to charge, exact, impose a ~ 2. to collect ~s (on a bridge, road) 3. a bridge; tunnel; turnpike (AE) ~ 4. (misc.) ~ free ['damage'] 5. to take a ~ (on) (the storm took a heavy ~; the earthquake took a heavy ~ on several villages) 6. a heavy ~ ['casualties'] 7. the death ~

toll II *v.* (D; intr.) to ~ for (the bell ~ed for those who had made the supreme sacrifice)

tomato *n.* 1. to grow ~es 2. to can ~es 3. a rotten ~ (also fig.)

tome *n.* ['volume'] a scholarly ~

tom-tom *n.* 1. to beat a ~ 2. the beat of the ~

ton *n.* 1. a gross; long; metric; short ~ 2. (misc.) (BE; slang) to do the ~ ('to go one hundred miles per hour') USAGE NOTE: The ton in GB is the *long ton* (two thousand two hundred forty pounds). In the US, the ton is the *short ton* (two thousand pounds). The *metric ton* is one thousand kilograms and is officially spelled *tonne* in GB.

tone *n.* ['style, trend'] 1. to set the ~ ['sound'] 2. dulcet, sweet; harsh; strident ~(s) ['manner of speaking that reveals the speaker's feelings'] 3. an abusive; angry; apologetic; arrogant; business-like; condescending, patronizing; decisive; emphatic; firm; flippant; friendly; imperious; ironic; querulous; serious; solemn; strident; subdued; threatening ~ (their ~ was friendly) 4. in a ~ (in angry ~s) 5. (misc.) don't take that ~ with me ['signal'] 6. a dial (AE), dialling (BE) ~ ['pitch'] (ling.) 7. a falling; high; low; rising ~

tongs *n.* 1. coal; curling; ice; sugar ~ 2. a pair of ~

tongue *n.* ['language'] 1. one's mother, native ~ ['organ of speech'] ['speech'] 2. to use one's ~ ('to speak') 3. to hold one's ~ ('to be silent') 4. to find one's ~ ('to begin to speak') 5. to stick one's ~ out (the child stuck out its ~ at me) 6. to click one's ~ 7. a coated ~ 8. (misc.) a ~ depressor; on everyone's ~ ('discussed by everyone'); on the tip of one's ~ ('not quite recalled'); ~s were wagging ('people were gossiping'); to speak with a forked ~ ('to be deceitful') ['manner of speaking'] 9. a caustic, foul, nasty, sharp; glib; loose ~ (he has a nasty ~)

tongue-lashing *n.* 1. to give smb. a (good) ~ 2. to get, receive a ~

tonic *n.* 1. to take a ~ 2. a ~ for 3. (misc.) a gin and ~ ('type of mixed drink')

tonnage *n.* dead-weight; displacement; gross; net, registered ~

tonsillectomy *n.* to do, perform a ~

tonsils *n.* 1. enlarged; inflamed ~ 2. (misc.) to have one's ~ out/removed/taken out

tool *n.* 1. to use a ~ 2. a garden; machine power ~ 3. burglar's ~s

toot *n.* (colloq.) to give a ~ (on a horn)

tooth *n.* 1. to cut, get teeth (babies are often fretful when they are cutting teeth) 2. to brush (esp. AE), clean one's teeth 3. to cap; drill; extract, pull, take out; fill a ~ 4. to pick one's teeth 5. to clench, gnash, grind, grit one's teeth 6. an artificial, false; baby (AE), milk; back; front; lower; permanent; upper; wisdom ~ 7. an abscessed; decayed ~ 8. teeth ache; chatter; decay, rot; erupt ('appear'); fall out; get discolored 9. a set of teeth 10. (misc.) to have a sweet ~ ('to love sweets'); to sink one's teeth into smt. ('to become completely engrossed in smt.'); to show one's teeth ('to show hostile intentions'); ~ and nail ('with all one's strength')

toothache *n.* to get, have a ~ (AE)/get, have (a) ~ (BE)

toothbrush *n.* to use a ~

top I *n.* ['device that spins'] 1. to spin a ~ ['misc.'] 2. to sleep like a ~ ('to sleep soundly')

top II *n.* ['highest point'] 1. to reach the ~ 2. a mountain ~; rooftop 3. from; to (the) ~ (from ~ to bottom; we climbed to the ~) 4. at the ~ ['cover, cap'] 5. to put on, screw on a ~ 6. to screw off, unscrew a ~ 7. a bottle; box; screw ~ ['misc.'] 8. to blow one's ~ ('to explode in anger'); to go over the ~ ('to begin a charge by going over a parapet'); ('to exceed a limit'); to be on ~ of a situation ('to be in control of a situation')

topic *n.* 1. to bring up, broach; discuss a ~ 2. a controversial; everyday ~ 3. (misc.) a ~ of conversation

topple *v.* (D; intr., tr.) to ~ from (he was ~d from the throne)

topsy-turvy *adv.* to turn smt. ~

torch *n.* ['portable electric light'] (BE; AE has *flashlight*) 1. to turn on a ~ 2. to flash, shine a ~ on ['burning stick'] 3. to light a ~ 4. to bear a ~ ['device used to produce a very hot flame'] 5. a welding ~ ['misc.'] 6. to put smt. to the ~ ('to set fire to smt.'); to carry a ~ for smb. (colloq.) ('to remain in love with smb. who does not return that love')

torment *v.* (D; tr.) to ~ into (to ~ smb. into doing smt.)

torn *adj.* ['divided'] (cannot stand alone) ~ between (he was ~ between his family and his job)

tornado *n.* a ~ strikes (the ~ struck several cities)

torpedo *n.* 1. to fire, launch a ~ 2. an acoustic; aerial; bangalore; magnetic ~ 3. a ~ explodes 4. a ~ hits; misses its target

torrent *n.* 1. an angry, raging ~ 2. a mountain ~ 3. (misc.) the rain came down in ~s

tort *n.* (legal) to commit a ~

torture I *n.* 1. to employ, resort to, use ~ 2. to inflict ~ on 3. to subject smb. to ~ 4. to undergo ~ 5. cruel; plain, sheer; sadistic; severe ~ 6. water ~ 7. ~ to + inf. (it was sheer ~ to listen to her sing = it was sheer ~ listening to her sing) 8. under ~ (he confessed under ~)

torture II *v.* (D; tr.) to ~ into (he was ~d into confessing)

toss I *n.* ['flipping of a coin to decide an issue'] to lose; win the ~

toss II *v.* 1. ('to turn and twist') to ~ restlessly (in one's sleep) 2. (A) ('to throw') ~ the ball to me; or: ~ me the ball 3. (D; intr., tr.) to ~ for ('to decide by flipping a coin') (let's ~ for it)

total *n.* 1. to add up, calculate, tally up a ~ 2. a combined; grand; sum ~

touch I *n.* ['social contact'] 1. to get; keep, stay in ~ 2. to lose ~ with 3. close ~ 4. in ~ with smb. (keep in close ~ with me) 5. out of ~ with (I am out of ~ with the present situation) ['feel'] 6. to the ~ (smooth to the ~) ['physical contact'] 7. a delicate; gentle, light, soft; heavy ~ ['sensitivity'] 8. to have the common ~ ('to have the ability to appeal to the common people') ['ability'] 9. to lose one's ~ ['manner'] 10. a bold; distinctive; magic; man's; personal; woman's ~ ['detail, stroke'] 11. the finishing ~es (to put the finishing ~es on/to smt.) ['misc.'] 12. a soft ~ ('an overly generous person')

touch II *v.* 1. (d; intr.) ('to stop briefly') to ~ at

(the ship will ~ at three ports) 2. (colloq.) (d; tr.) to ~ for ('to ask for') (to ~ smb. for a loan) 3. (d; intr.) to ~ on ('to treat briefly') (to ~ on a topic)

touchdown *n.* (esp. Am. football) to score a ~

touching *adj.* ~ to + inf. (it was ~ to watch)

touchy *adj.* (colloq.) ~ about (he's ~ about his appearance)

tough *adj.* (colloq.) ['strict'] 1. ~ on, with (they are ~ on drunk drivers) ['difficult'] 2. (cannot stand alone) ~ to + inf. (he is ~ to work with = it is ~ to work with him = it is ~ working with him = he is a ~ person to work with) ['unfortunate'] 3. ~ that + clause (it's ~ that you can't be with your family) ['misc.'] 4. to hang ~ (esp. AE; slang) ('to be very firm'); to talk ~ ('to take a very firm bargaining position')

tour *n.* 1. to conduct, operate; organize a ~ 2. to go on, make a ~ of 3. a barnstorming (AE); city; concert; Cook's; goodwill; guided; lecture; lightning; organized; package; sightseeing; speaking; student; study ~ 4. on ~ (to be on ~)

tournament *n.* 1. to conduct, hold a ~ 2. a bridge; chess; invitational; rapid-transit (for chess); tennis ~

tourniquet *n.* 1. to apply a ~ 2. to loosen; tighten a ~

tour of duty *n.* to do a ~

tout *v.* (colloq.) ('to praise') 1. (d; tr.) to ~ as (he was ~ed as the next middleweight champion) 2. (P; tr.) to ~ highly

tow I *n.* 1. a ski ~ 2. to take (a ship) in ~

tow II *v.* 1. (D; tr.) to ~ into (to ~ a barge into a port) 2. (D; tr.) to ~ out of (to ~ a boat out of a harbor) 3. (D; tr.) to ~ to (to ~ a car to a garage)

towel *n.* ['cloth, paper for drying'] 1. a bath; dish (AE), tea (esp. BE); face; guest; hand; linen; paper; roller; Turkish ~ 2. a sanitary ~ (AE has *sanitary napkin*) 3. a disposable ~ ['symbol of surrender'] 4. to throw, toss in the ~

tower I *n.* 1. a bell; conning; control; fire; TV; water ~ 2. a signal ~ (AE; BE has *signal box*) 3. a ~ stands (one hundred feet high)

tower II *v.* (d; intr.) to ~ above, over (as a thinker, she ~s over her colleagues)

town *n.* 1. a boom; ghost ('deserted'); jerkwater (AE; colloq.), one-horse, provincial, sleepy, small; market (BE) ~ (they live in a sleepy, little ~) 2. a company ~ 3. smb.'s hometown 4. a county ~ (BE; AE has *county seat*) 5. (misc.) to come to ~; to go to ~ (colloq.; fig.) ('to go all out'); to leave ~; to blow/skip ~ (esp. AE; colloq.) ('to leave town suddenly'); (out) on the ~ ('enjoying city nightlife') USAGE NOTE: In GB, many places are called *towns* that would be called *cities* in the US. In the US, many places are called *towns* or *small towns* that are *villages* in GB. AE rarely uses *village* for places in the US.

tow out *v.* (d; tr.) to ~ to (they ~ed the barge out to the freighter)

toy I *n.* 1. to make a ~ 2. an educational; mechanical; musical ~ (to wind a mechanical ~) 3. (misc.) to play with ~s; a ~ car; plane; train

toy II *v.* (d; intr.) to ~ with (to ~ with smb.'s affections; cats ~ with mice)

trace I *n*. 1. to leave a ~ 2. to show a ~ of (to show no ~ of remorse) 3. to lose (all) ~ of 4. a slight ~ (he didn't show the slightest ~ of intoxication)
trace II *v*. (D; tr.) to ~ to (the letter was ~d to its sender)
traceable *adj*. ~ to
trace back *v*. (d; tr.) to ~ to (she ~d her origins back to the twelfth century)
tracer *n*. ['inquiry'] (esp. AE) 1. to put out, send out a ~ on ['tracer bullet'] 2. to fire a ~ ['substance used to follow a reaction in the body'] (med.) 3. to inject, introduce a ~ (into the body) 4. to scan (for) a ~ 5. a radioactive ~
tracing *n*. to make a ~
track *n*. ['awareness'] 1. to keep ~ of (to keep ~ of expenses) 2. to lose ~ of 3. close ~ (to keep close ~ of smt.) ['course for racing'] 3. a fast; muddy; slow ~ 5. a cinder ~; racetrack; running ~ ['path, road'] 6. a cart ~ (BE; AE has *dirt road*) 7. (misc.) off the beaten ~ ('isolated') ['rail'] 8. to lay ~s 9. a double; main; railroad (AE), railway (BE); single ~ 10. (misc.) on the wrong side of the ~s (AE; colloq.) ('in the poor section of a city') ['recording'] 11. a sound ~ ['misc.'] 12. the inside ~ ('an advantageous position') USAGE NOTE: For footraces, *track* is CE. For horseracing, AE uses *track* and *racetrack;* BE prefers *course* and *racecourse.*
tracks *n*. ['trail'] 1. to leave ~ 2. to make ~ for ('to go directly to') 3. to cover one's ~ ['misc.'] 4. to stop (dead) in one's ~ ('to stop instantaneously')
tract *n*. ['system of organs'] the digestive; gastrointestinal; genitourinary; intestinal; respiratory ~
traction *n*. in ~ (her leg is in ~)
tractor *n*. to drive, operate a ~
trade I *n*. ['commerce, business'] 1. to carry on, conduct, engage in ~ 2. to build up, develop, drum up, promote; lose ~ 3. to restrain, restrict ~ 4. (a) brisk, lively ~ (they built up a lively ~) 5. fair ~ 6. domestic; export; foreign, international, overseas; free; illicit; maritime; retail; wholesale ~ (to promote international ~) 7. (the) slave ~ 8. the carriage ~ ('business with wealthy people') 9. ~ among, between; with (to conduct ~ with many countries) 10. ~ in 11. (misc.) (in) restraint of ~ ['exchange'] 12. to make a ~ with smb. 13. a fair ~ ['occupation'] 14. to ply, practice a ~ 15. to learn a ~ 16. by ~ (she is a bookbinder by ~) 17. (misc.) a jack of all ~s
trade II *v*. 1. (D; tr.) to ~ for (she ~d a knife for a hat) 2. (D; intr.) to ~ in (to ~ in furs) 3. (D; intr.) to ~ with (to ~ with various countries) 4. (O) she ~d me a knife for a spoon
trade in *v*. (D; tr.) to ~ for (she ~d in her old car for a newer one)
trademark *n*. 1. to issue a ~ 2. to receive, register a ~ 3. to bear; display a ~ 4. to infringe a ~
trader *n*. 1. a fur ~ 2. a ~ in
trade up *v*. (colloq.) (D; intr.) to ~ from; to (to ~ to a larger car)
trading *n*. brisk; slow, sluggish ~ (slow ~ on the stock market)
tradition *n*. 1. to hand down a ~ 2. to establish,

start a ~ (we started a new ~) 3. to cherish; maintain, preserve, uphold a ~ 4. to break with ~ 5. an ancient, old; cherished; deep-rooted, deep-seated, established; family; hallowed; popular; religious ~ 6. according to, by ~ (according to ancient ~; by popular ~) 7. in a ~ (in our ~)
traditional *adj*. ~ to + inf. (it's ~ around here to fly the flag on holidays)
traffic I *n*. ['movement of vehicles, aircraft'] 1. to direct ~ (the police officer was directing ~) 2. to block, hold up, obstruct, tie up ~ 3. bumper-to-bumper, heavy; light; rush-hour; slow-moving ~ 4. air; highway (AE), motorway (BE); inbound; local; long-distance; merging; one-way; through, thru (AE); two-way; vehicular ~ 5. (misc.) the flow of ~; an update on ~ conditions; a ~ report ['commerce, trade'] 6. brisk, lively ~ 7. illegal, illicit ~ 8. ~ in (illicit ~ in drugs) ['misc.'] 9. (colloq.) to charge what the ~ will bear ('to charge as much as people are willing to pay')
traffic II *v*. (d; intr.) to ~ in (to ~ in drugs)
traffic light *n*. see **light II 13-15**
traffic ticket *n*. (AE) ['summons for a traffic violation'] (CE has *ticket*) 1. to give smb. a ~ 2. to get; pay a ~ 3. to fix a ~ ('to arrange to have a traffic ticket nullified') 4. a ~ for (the police officer gave her a ticket for speeding)
tragedy *n*. ~ strikes (~ struck their family)
trail I *n*. 1. to blaze, make; lay out a ~ 2. to leave a ~ (the wounded animal left a ~ of blood) 3. to cover up a ~ 4. a steep; winding ~ 5. a hiking; ski; vapor ~ (to lay out a ski ~) 6. on smb.'s ~ (the police were on his ~) 7. (misc.) the ~ winds through the forest
trail II *v*. (D; intr.) to ~ behind (to ~ behind the leaders)
trailer *n*. 1. a house ~ (AE; BE has *caravan*) 2. a flatbed; truck (esp. AE; BE prefers *trailer*) ~
train I *n*. ['row of connected railroad cars'] 1. to drive a ~ 2. to shunt ~s (onto different tracks) 3. to board, get on; catch; get off; miss; take a ~ (we took a ~ to the city) 4. to change ~s (we'll have to change ~s in Chicago) 5. to flag down; hold; stop a ~ (to stop a ~ by pulling the communication/emergency cord) 6. a boat; commuter; down (BE) ('from a city'); electric; elevated; express; freight (AE), goods (BE); hospital; inbound; local; long-distance; outbound; passenger; shuttle; slow (BE); stopping (BE); suburban; through; up (BE) ('to a city') ~ 7. a ~ arrives, pulls in; derails; leaves, pulls out; stops 8. a ~ for, to; from (the ~ from Exeter to London) 9. by ~ (to travel by ~) 10. aboard, on a ~ (we met on the ~) ['column'] 11. a mule; supply; wagon ~ ['mechanism for transmitting power'] 12. a power ~
train II *v*. 1. (D; intr., tr.) to ~ for (to ~ for the Olympics) 2. (D; tr.) to ~ in (to ~ smb. in defensive driving) 3. (d; tr.) ('to aim') to ~ on (he ~ed his gun on the intruder) 4. (H) they were ~ed to react instantaneously to an attack; they ~ed the workers to be precise
trained *adj*. 1. ~ to + inf. (the dogs are ~ to attack) 2. (misc.) house-trained (esp. BE; AE prefers *house-broken);* potty-trained (BE); toilet-

trained
trainer *n*. an animal ~
training *n*. 1. to give, provide ~ 2. to get, receive ~ 3. intense; thorough ~ 4. assertiveness; basic; hands-on; in-service, on-the-job (AE); manual; military; physical; sensitivity; toilet; voice ~ 5. ~ in (hands-on ~ in the use of computers) 6. the ~ to + inf. (the soldiers did not have the necessary ~ to carry out the mission) 7. by ~ (she's an engineer by ~) 8. in ~ (he was in ~ for the big fight)
traipse *v*. (colloq.) (P; intr.) they were ~sing around in the park
trait *n*. an acquired; character; genetic, hereditary; negative; personality; positive ~
traitor *n*. 1. a ~ to (a ~ to one's country) 2. (misc.) to turn ~
tram (BE) see **streetcar**
tramcar (BE) see **streetcar**
tramp *v*. (P; intr.) to ~ through the woods
trample *v*. 1. (d; intr.) to ~ on, upon (to ~ on smb.'s rights) 2. (misc.) to ~ underfoot
trance *n*. 1. to fall into a ~ 2. (to be) in a ~
tranquillity, tranquility *n*. 1. to shatter the ~ 2. (misc.) an air of ~
tranquillizer *n*. 1. to take a ~ 2. to prescribe a ~ for
transaction *n*. 1. to conduct ~s 2. a delicate ~ 3. business, financial ~s 4. ~s between
transcribe *v*. 1. (D; tr.) to ~ from; to (to ~ testimony from a tape) 2. (D; intr., tr.) to ~ in (to ~ speech in phonetic script)
transcript *n*. 1. an official ~ 2. (AE) a grade ~ ('a student's record')
transcription *n*. 1. to make a ~ 2. (ling.) a broad; narrow; phonetic ~
transfer I *n*. ['act of transferring'] 1. to make a ~ 2. an electronic; technology ~ 3. a ~ from; to ['ticket allowing a passenger to change from one vehicle to another on public transportation'] (esp. AE) 4. a bus; streetcar; subway ~
transfer II *v*. (D; intr., tr.) to ~ from; to (she was ~red from New York to Toronto)
transform *v*. (D; tr.) to ~ from; into, to (to ~ current from one voltage to another)
transformation *n*. ['radical change'] 1. to undergo a ~ 2. a complete, radical, total ~ ['transformational rule'] (ling.) 3. to formulate a ~ 4. to apply a ~ 5. to order ~s 6. a dative-movement, indirect-object; imperative; insertion; negative; particle-movement; passive; question ~ 7. a ~ applies
transformer *n*. a step-down; step-up ~
transfuse *v*. (D; tr.) to ~ into, to
transfusion *n*. 1. to administer, give a ~ 2. to get, receive a ~ 3. a blood; bone-marrow; plasma ~
transgress *v*. (formal) (D; intr.) to ~ against
transgression *n*. to commit a ~ against
transistor *n*. a solid-state ~
transit *n*. 1. (esp. AE) mass, rapid ~ 2. in ~ (damaged in ~)
transition *n*. 1. to make a ~ 2. a gradual ~ 3. a ~ from; to 4. (misc.) in a state of ~
translate *v*. 1. (D; tr.) to ~ from; into, to (to ~ a book from French into Spanish) 2. (misc.) to ~ at sight; to ~ simultaneously

translation *n*. 1. to do, make a ~ 2. (a) close, literal, word-for-word; free, loose ~ 3. an authorized ~ 4. (a) loan ~ 5. (a) machine; running; simultaneous ~ 6. a ~ from; into, to (a ~ from Russian into English) 7. in ~ (to read a book in ~; the poem is very effective in free/in a free ~)
transliterate *v*. 1. (D; tr.) to ~ as (to ~ a Russian letter as *ch*) 2. (D; tr.) to ~ from; into (to ~ a text from Cyrillic into Roman letters)
transliteration *n*. to do a ~
transmission *n*. ['gearbox'] 1. an automatic; standard; synchronized ~ ['act of transmitting'] 2. a ~ from; to
transmit *v*. (D; tr.) to ~ from; to (the results were ~ted to all local stations from the network)
transmitter *n*. 1. a longwave; radar; radio; shortwave ~ 2. a television, TV ~
transmute *v*. (formal) (D; tr.) to ~ from; into (to ~ base metal into gold)
transpire *v*. (L) ('to become apparent, evident, known') it ~d that he had gone out of town before the crime occurred
transplant I *n*. 1. to do a ~ 2. to reject a ~ (her body rejected the ~) 3. a bone-marrow; corneal; gene; heart; kidney; organ ~
transplant II *v*. (D; tr.) to ~ from; to
transport I (esp. BE) see **transportation**
transport II *v*. 1. to ~ bodily 2. (d; tr.) to ~ from; to
transportation *n*. (esp. AE; BE usu. has *transport*) 1. to provide ~ 2. air; bus; ground, surface; mass, public ~ 3. ~ from; to (to provide ~ from the city to the airport)
transpose *v*. (D; tr.) to ~ from; into, to (to ~ a song into a different key)
transposition *n*. a ~ from; into, to
transship *v*. (D; tr.) to ~ from; to
trap *n*. ['device for catching animals or people'] ['stratagem for tricking unsuspecting people'] 1. to bait; set a ~ for 2. to spring a ~ on 3. to fall into a ~ 4. to lure smb. into a ~ 5. a booby; death ~; mousetrap; radar, speed ~; a sand ~ (in golf) ['mouth'] (slang) 6. to shut one's ~
trapeze *n*. 1. a flying ~ 2. on a ~
trapper *n*. an animal; fur ~
trash *n*. (AE; CE has *refuse, rubbish*) 1. to accumulate ~ 2. to dispose of, dump ~ (BE prefers *to tip refuse*) 3. (misc.) (derog.) white ~ ('poor white people in the southern US')
trauma *n*. 1. to cause (a) ~ 2. to suffer (a) ~ 3. (a) physical; psychological ~
travel I *n*. 1. air; foreign; sea ~ 2. ~ from; to (~ from the United States to Japan)
travel II *v*. 1. to ~ extensively, widely; far; far and wide 2. to ~ deluxe; first-class; incognito; light; second-class 3. (D; intr.) to ~ by (to ~ by air) 4. (D; intr., tr.) to ~ from; to (to ~ from London to Tokyo) 5. (D; intr.) to ~ across, in, through (to ~ in Canada; to ~ through the Rockies) 6. (d; intr.) to ~ with (to be ~ing with a group of students) 7. (misc.) to ~ on business; to ~ downstream; to ~ upstream
traveler, traveller *n*. 1. an experienced, seasoned ~ 2. an air ~ 3. a commercial traveller (BE; CE

has *traveling salesman*) 4. (misc.) a fellow ~ ('a Communist sympathizer')

travesty *n.* 1. to make a ~ of 2. a shocking ~ 3. a ~ of, on

tray *n.* a serving ~

treachery *n.* ~ to + inf. (it was ~ to reveal such secrets to the enemy)

tread I *n.* ['step'] 1. a firm; heavy; light ~ ['mark'] 2. tire ~s ['pattern of ridges'] 3. a worn ~ 4. a tire ~

tread II *v.* 1. (usu. fig.) (d; intr.) to ~ on, upon (to ~ on smb.'s toes) 2. (P; intr.) to ~ softly

treadle *n.* to work a ~

treadmill *n.* on a ~

treason *n.* 1. to commit; plot ~ 2. high ~ 3. an act of ~ 4. ~ to + inf. (it is ~ to sell military information to a foreign power)

treasonable see **treasonous**

treasonous *adj.* ~ to + inf. (it is ~ to deal with the enemy during wartime)

treasure *n.* 1. an art ~ 2. a priceless; real ~ 3. (a) buried; sunken ~ (to find buried/a buried ~; to raise sunken ~ from the bottom of the sea)

treat I *n.* ['source of joy'] 1. to provide a ~ 2. a ~ for (their visit was a real ~ for us) 3. a ~ to + inf. (it was a ~ to watch them dance) ['paying for the food or entertainment of others'] 4. to stand ~ 5. (misc.) it's my ~

treat II *v.* 1. ('to describe') to ~ (a subject) exhaustively, painstakingly, thoroughly 2. ('to deal with') to ~ badly; cruelly; fairly; unfairly 3. (d; tr.) to ~ as ('to deal with') (they ~ed us as honored guests) 4. (D; tr.) ('to cure') to ~ for; with (to ~ smb. for a cold with a new drug) 5. (d; tr.) to ~ like ('to deal with') (he ~ed him like his own brother) 6. (formal) (d; intr.) to ~ of ('to deal with') (her books ~ of economic problems) 7. (D; tr.) to ~ to ('to provide with at one's own expense') (to ~ smb. to a decent meal) 8. (d; tr.) to ~ with ('to deal with') (to ~ smb. with kindness)

treatise *n.* 1. to write a ~ 2. a scientific; theoretical ~ 3. a ~ on, upon

treatment *n.* ['care'] ['cure'] 1. to administer, give, provide ~ 2. to get, receive, undergo ~ 3. to respond to ~ 4. inpatient; medical; outpatient; radiation; shock ~ 5. ~ for (to undergo ~ for alcoholism) 6. under ~ ['method of dealing with'] 7. atrocious, brutal, cruel, harsh, inhumane ~ (brutal ~ of prisoners) 8. equal, equitable; fair; humane; kid-glove, preferential; kind; red-carpet; shabby; special; uneven; unfair ~ (to receive preferential ~) 9. (colloq.) the VIP ('special') ~ (they got the VIP ~) 10. the silent ~ (to give smb. the silent ~) ['description, study'] 11. a cursory; definitive; exhaustive, lengthy; superficial ~

treaty *n.* 1. to conclude, sign; negotiate, work out a ~ 2. to confirm, ratify a ~ (the senate confirms all treaties) 3. to break, violate a ~ 4. to abrogate, denounce a ~ 5. a bilateral; commercial, trade; nonaggression; peace; test-ban ~ 6. a ~ between; with (a ~ between former foes) 7. a ~ to + inf. (they signed a ~ to settle all border disputes by arbitration)

tree *n.* ['woody plant with a trunk'] 1. to grow; plant a ~ 2. to prune, trim a ~ 3. to chop down, cut down, fell a ~ 4. to uproot a ~ (the gale uprooted several ~s) 5. a Christmas; shade ~ 6. a ~ grows 7. in; on a ~ (monkeys live in ~s; fruit grows on ~s) 8. (misc.) to climb a ~; (colloq.) up a ~ (AE), up a gum ~ (BE) ('stymied'); to bark up the wrong ~ ('to be mistaken') ['something resembling a tree'] 9. a family, genealogical ~ 10. a clothes; shoe ~

trek I *n.* ['long trip'] to go on, make a ~ from; to

trek II *v.* (P; intr.) to ~ across the fields

tremble *v.* 1. (d; intr.) to ~ at (to ~ at the thought of going back to work) 2. (D; intr.) to ~ from, with (to ~ from the cold; to ~ with fear)

tremor *n.* 1. a nervous ~ 2. uncontrollable; violent ~s 3. an earth ~

trench *n.* 1. to dig a ~ 2. a slit ~ 3. (misc.) in the ~es (during World War I)

trend *n.* 1. to create, set, start a ~ 2. a discernible, noticeable; general; growing; marked; recent; unwelcome; welcome ~ 3. an economic; political ~ 4. a ~ towards

trespass I *n.* criminal ~

trespass II *v.* 1. (obsol.) (D; intr.) to ~ against 2. (D; intr.) to ~ on, upon (to ~ on a neighbor's property)

trespassing *n.* no ~!

trial *n.* ['legal proceedings'] 1. to conduct, hold a ~ 2. to bring smb. to ~; to put smb. on ~ 3. to stand ~ for (he stood ~ for embezzlement) 4. to go to ~ (the case went to ~) 5. to waive a jury ~ (the accused waived a jury ~) 6. a fair; speedy ~ (to get a fair ~) 7. a closed; court; jury (or a ~ by jury); open, public; show; summary; war-crimes ~ 8. at a ~ (she testified at his ~) 9. on ~ for (he was on ~ for murder) ['test, experiment'] 10. a field ~ 11. ~ by (~ by fire) 12. (misc.) by ~ and error ['source of worry'] 13. a ~ to (they are a ~ to their parents)

trial balloon *n.* to float, send up a ~

triangle *n.* 1. to draw, make a ~ 2. an acute; congruent; equilateral; isosceles; obtuse; right (AE), right-angled (BE); scalene ~ 3. (fig.) the eternal ~; a love ~

tribe *n.* 1. to lead a ~ 2. a native; nomadic, wandering; primitive ~ 3. (misc.) to belong to a ~; a member of a ~

tribulation *n.* 1. to bear, endure a ~ 2. (misc.) trials and ~s

tribunal *n.* a high ~

tribute *n.* ['money paid under duress'] 1. to exact ~ from 2. to pay ~ to ['testimonial'] 3. to pay (a) ~ to 4. a fitting; glowing; moving, touching ~ 5. a floral ~ ('a bunch of flowers') 6. a ~ to

trick I *n.* ['dexterous feat, sleight of hand'] 1. to do, perform a ~ 2. a card; hat ~ ['prank'] ['deceitful act'] 3. to play a ~ on smb. 4. a clever, dirty, low, mean, nasty, shabby, sneaky, snide ~ 5. a confidence ~ (BE; AE has *confidence game*) ['scoring unit in a card game'] 6. to lose; take, win a ~ ['misc.'] 7. to do the ~ ('to be exactly what is needed'); one's bag of ~s ('one's expertise'); ~ or treat! (at Halloween) (see also **tricks**)

trick II *v.* 1. (D; tr.) to ~ into (to ~ smb. into doing smt.) 2. (D; tr.) to ~ out of (she was ~ed out of her money)

trickle *v.* (P; intr.) stragglers kept ~ling into camp

trickle down *v.* (D; intr.) to ~ to (to ~ to the general population)

tricks *n.* (often pol.) dirty ~

trifle I *n.* a mere ~

trifle II *v.* (d; intr.) to ~ with

trigger *n.* ['device for releasing the hammer of a firearm'] 1. to press, pull, release, squeeze a (the) ~ 2. a hair ('delicate') ~ ['device that fires an explosive'] 3. a ~ for (a ~ for an H-bomb)

trim I *n.* ['good condition'] ['condition'] 1. fighting ~ (in fighting ~) 2. in ~ (to be in ~) ['ornamental metalwork on a car'] 3. chrome ~ (he scratched my chrome ~)

trim II *v.* (d; tr.) to ~ from (to ~ the fat from the budget)

trimmings *n.* ['garnishings'] with all the ~ (turkey with all the ~)

trip I *n.* 1. to go on, make, take a ~ (she went on a ~; I've made this ~ many times; we would like to take a ~) 2. to arrange, organize, plan a ~ 3. to cancel; postpone a ~ 4. an extended, long; short ~ 5. a business; camping; field; pleasure; return; round; round-the-world; wedding ~ (we are planning a round-the-world ~) 6. a ~ from; to (they went on a ~ to Canada; to take a ~ from England to Australia) 7. a ~ through (a ~ through the west) 8. on a ~ (she was away on a ~) 9. (misc.) an ego ~ ('an action that satisfies one's ego')

trip II *v.* (D; intr.) ('to stumble') to ~ on, over (to ~ on a rock; she was ~ping over every word)

triplets *n.* a set of ~

triplicate *n.* in ~ (to prepare all documents in ~)

tripod *n.* on a ~ (the camera rested on a ~)

triumph I *n.* 1. to achieve, score a ~ 2. a glorious, splendid; short-lived ~ 3. a ~ over (a ~ over evil) 4. in ~ (to return home in ~)

triumph II *v.* (D; intr.) to ~ over

triumphant *adj.* ~ in; over

Trojan *n.* (misc.) to work like a ~ ('to work very hard')

trolley *n.* ['small wheeled conveyance'] (BE) 1. a (shopping) ~ (in a supermarket) (AE has *shopping cart*) 2. a tea ~ (AE has *tea wagon*) 3. a sweet ~ (in a restaurant) ['streetcar, tram'] (AE) 4. see **streetcar** USAGE NOTE: Wheeled conveyances that are called *trolleys* in BE are often called *carts* in AE. In a library, books are moved on a *trolley* (BE) or on a *cart* (AE).

trombone *n.* to play the ~

troop I *n.* 1. a cavalry ~ 2. a Boy Scout; Girl Scout (AE) ~

troop II *v.* (P; intr.) the children ~ed into school

trooper *n.* 1. (AE) a state ~ 2. (misc.) to swear like a ~ ('to use vile language')

troops *n.* 1. to commit; deploy; dispatch; lead ~ 2. to review ~ 3. to station ~ (in a country) 4. green; seasoned ~ 5. defeated; demoralized; victorious ~ 6. airborne; armored; ground; irregular; motorized; mounted; regular; shock; ski ~

trophy *n.* 1. to award a ~ 2. to win a ~ 3. a sports;

war ~

tropic *n.* the Tropic of Cancer; Capricorn

tropics *n.* in the ~ (to live in the ~)

trot *n.* 1. at a ~ 2. (misc.) (BE; colloq.) on the ~ all day ('busy all day'); that horse won four races on the ~ ('that horse won four races in succession')

troth *n.* (formal) to plight one's ~ ('to make a promise of marriage')

trouble I *n.* 1. to cause, make, start, stir up ~ 2. to invite, look for ~ 3. to have ~ (she had a lot of ~ with her back) 4. to go to ~ (they went to a great deal of ~ to arrange the interview) 5. to get (smb.) into ~ (we got into ~ during our trip; she got herself into serious ~ with the police; they got me into ~ at school) 6. to take the ~ to do smt. (I took the ~ to check on her story) 7. to get (smb.) out of ~ (I got out of ~; she got herself out of ~; they got him out of ~) 8. to avoid, steer clear of ~ 9. real, serious ~ 10. back; engine; heart ~ (to develop engine ~) 11. ~ is brewing 12. ~ blows over 13. ~ about, over; with (we had ~ with our neighbors over the noise that they were making) 14. a bit of ~ 15. no ~ to + inf. (it's no ~ to call them) 16. in ~ (with) (they were in ~; he was in ~ with the police) 17. out of ~ (to keep out of ~) 18. (misc.) to put smb. to a lot of ~; it is not worth the ~; sending a telegram will save you the ~ of making a second trip; she has ~ going up steps; he had no ~ memorizing the material for the test

trouble II *v.* 1. (d; refl., tr.) to ~ about (don't ~ yourself about the arrangements) 2. (colloq.) (E; in neg. sentences) she didn't even ~ to lock the door 3. (colloq.) (H; in interrogative sentences; no passive) could I ~ you to open the window? 4. (R) it ~d me to read that no negotiations were scheduled; it ~d us that they did not write of their plans

troubled *adj.* ~ to + inf. (we were ~ to learn of her problems)

troublesome *adj.* ~ to + inf. (it is ~ to be without electricity)

trousers *n.* 1. to put on; wear ~ 2. to take off ~ 3. to button up; unbutton; unzip; zip up one's ~ 4. baggy; long; short ~ 5. a pair of ~ 6. (misc.) a trouser leg

trousseau *n.* a bridal ~

trowel *n.* a bricklayer's; gardener's; plasterer's ~

truant *n.* (esp. AE) 1. to play ~ 2. (misc.) a ~ officer

truce *n.* 1. to agree on, arrange, call, work out a ~ 2. to violate a ~ 3. to denounce a ~ 4. an armed; uneasy ~ 5. a ~ between

truck I *n.* ['vehicle'] 1. (esp. AE; BE often has *lorry, van*) to drive, operate a ~ 2. a delivery (AE); dump (esp. AE), dumper (BE); tipper (BE); garbage (AE); panel (AE; BE has *delivery van*); pickup (AE); sound; trailer (AE; BE has *articulated lorry*); trash (AE; BE has *dustcart*) ~ 3. a tow ~ (AE; BE has *breakdown lorry, breakdown van*) 4. a railway ~ (BE; AE has *flatcar*)

truck II *n.* ['dealings'] to have no ~ with

trudge *v.* (P; intr.) to ~ through the mud

true *adj.* 1. historically ~ 2. ~ to (~ to one's principles) 3. ~ that + clause (it is not ~ that she has resigned)

truly *adv.* (usu. at the close of a letter) (esp. AE) yours ~; yours very ~; very ~ yours (CE has *yours sincerely, sincerely yours*)

trump *n.* ['winning card'] 1. to play a ~ ['final resource'] 2. to have a ~ up one's sleeve

trump card *n.* ['final resource'] to play one's ~

trumpet *n.* to play the ~

trumps *n.* to lead ~ (when playing cards)

trunk *n.* ['main stem'] 1. a tree ~ ['large piece of luggage'] 2. to pack; unpack one's ~ 3. to ship a ~ 4. a steamer; wardrobe ~ USAGE NOTE: On cars, *trunk* is AE; *boot* is BE.

trunks *n.* bathing ~

trust I *n.* ['reliance'] 1. to place, put one's ~ in 2. to abuse smb.'s ~ 3. absolute; blind, unquestioning ~ 4. public ~ 5. on ~ (to sell on ~) ['cartel'] 6. to break up a ~ ['fund'] 7. to set up a ~ (for a child) 8. a unit ~ (BE; AE has *mutual fund*) 9. a blind; perpetual ~ (to place one's holdings in a blind ~ during one's term of office) 10. in ~ for

trust II *v.* 1. to ~ blindly, implicitly 2. (d; intr.) ('to believe') to ~ in (to ~ in God) 3. (d; intr.) to ~ to ('to rely on') (to ~ to memory) 4. (d; tr.) ('to entrust') to ~ with (to ~ smb. with one's savings) 5. (H) ('to entrust') I ~ed her to deposit the funds; ~ them to do smt. silly (ironic) 6. (L) ('to believe') we ~ that you will keep your word

trust fund *n.* to set up a ~ for smb.

truth *n.* 1. to ascertain, elicit, establish, find; face, face up to; search for, seek the ~ 2. to reveal; tell the ~ 3. to distort, stretch the ~ 4. the absolute, cold, gospel, naked, plain, sober, unvarnished ~ 5. the awful; bitter; ultimate ~ 6. (the) historical ~ 7. a grain, kernel of ~ 8. the ~ that + clause (the ~ is that he served in the army) 9. in ~

try I *n.* 1. to have, make a ~ at 2. (colloq.) to give it, smt. a ~ 3. (rugby) to score a ~ 4. a ~ at, for 5. a ~ to + inf. (they made another ~ to have the decision reversed) 6. (misc.) (AE; colloq.) to give it the old college ~ ('to make a determined effort')

try II *v.* 1. to ~ hard; to ~ one's best 2. (D; intr.) ('to attempt') to ~ for (to ~ for a prize) 3. (D; tr.) ('to subject to trial') to ~ for (they tried her for murder) 4. (E) ('to attempt') she tried to telephone us 5. (G) ('to attempt') he tried jogging, but his ankles would hurt USAGE NOTES: 1. The phrase *try and do smt.* is a colloq. variant of *try to do smt.*, but has no past tense. 2. The sentence *she tried to jog* usu. means that she never was able to jog; *she tried jogging* means that she was able to jog, but gave it up after a while.

tryout *n.* a ~ for

try out *v.* 1. (D; intr., tr.) to ~ for (to ~ for a major part in a play) 2. (D; tr.) to ~ on (to ~ a new drug on animals)

tryouts *n.* to hold ~ for

tryst *n.* 1. to keep a ~ 2. a ~ with

tsar (BE) see **czar**

tub *n.* ['bathtub'] (esp. AE; BE prefers *bath)* 1. to fill the ~ (for a bath) 2. to empty the ~ (after a bath) 3. to clean out; scrub (out) a ~

tube *n.* ['channel within a body'] 1. bronchial; Eustachian; Fallopian ~s ['rubber casing'] 2. an inner ~ ['hollow cylinder'] 3. an electron; picture, television; test ~ 4. a vacuum ~ (AE; BE has *valve)* 5. (slang) the boob ~ (television')

tuberculosis *n.* to contract, develop ~

tubing *n.* copper; glass; flexible; plastic; rubber ~

tuck *v.* (d; tr.) to ~ into (to ~ a child into bed; he ~ed his shirt into his trousers)

tug I *n.* ['pull'] 1. to give a ~ on ['tugboat'] 2. a seagoing ~

tug II *v.* (D; intr.) to ~ at (to ~ at a rope)

tuition *n.* ['instruction'] (BE) 1. to give ~ ['payment for instruction'] 2. to pay ~ for 3. free; half ~ (to receive free ~)

tumble I *n.* (colloq.) ['fall'] 1. to take a ~ 2. a bad, nasty ~ (she took a nasty ~) 3. a ~ from ['sign of recogniton'] 4. to give smb. a ~ (they wouldn't give us a ~)

tumble II *v.* 1. (d; intr.) to ~ into (to ~ into bed) 2. (d; intr.) to ~ out of (to ~ out of a chair) 3. (colloq.) (d; intr.) to ~ to ('to catch on to, comprehend') (they didn't ~ to the meaning of the clues)

tumor, tumour *n.* 1. to excise, remove a ~ 2. a benign; inoperable; malignant ~

tumult *n.* ['violent, noisy agitation'] 1. to cause ~ 2. in ~ over

tune I *n.* ['melody'] 1. to compose, write a ~ 2. to hum; play; sing; whistle a ~ (to play a ~ on the piano) 3. to carry ('sing the notes of') a ~ 4. a ~ of, to (the ~ to a song) 5. a catchy; lilting ~ 6. in ~; out of ~ (to sing in ~; she was playing out of ~) 7. to a ~ (to dance to a ~) ['agreement'] 8. in ~ with (in ~ with the times) 9. out of ~ with ['attitude'] (colloq.) 10. to change one's ~ ['misc.'] (colloq.) 11. to call the ~ ('to be in command'); to sing a different ~ ('to begin to act differently'); to the ~ of ('approximately')

tune II *v.* (d; tr.) to ~ to (we ~d our sets to the local station)

tune in *v.* (D; intr.) to ~ on, to (to ~ to a station)

tuner *n.* a piano ~

tune-up *n.* 1. to do a ~ (of an engine) 2. an engine ~

tuning *n.* fine ~

tunnel I *n.* 1. to bore, construct, dig a ~ 2. a pedestrian; railroad (AE); railway (BE); wind ~ 3. a ~ caves in 4. through a ~ (to drive through a ~) 5. (misc.) (fig.) the light at the end of the ~

tunnel II *v.* (D; intr.) to ~ under (to ~ under the Channel)

turbulence *n.* clear-air ~

turkey *n.* 1. to raise ~s 2. to carve; roast; stuff a ~ 3. a wild ~ 4. ~s gobble 5. a female ~ is a hen 6. a male ~ is a gobbler

turmoil *n.* in (a) ~ (the country was in ~)

turn I *n.* ['change of direction'] ['direction'] 1. to make, negotiate a ~ (to negotiate a difficult ~) 2. to take a ~ (the conversation took an interesting ~) 3. a left; right; sharp ~; U-turn (to make a U-turn) 4. a ~ to (a ~ to the right) ['proper order, opportunity'] 5. to take one's ~ 6. to take ~s at;

with (we took ~s with them standing/at standing guard) 7. to wait one's ~ 8. smb.'s ~ comes (my ~ came) 9. smb.'s ~ to + inf. (it's my ~ to drive) 10. by ~s 11. in ~; out of ~ ['change'] 12. to take a ~ (the situation took a ~ for the better) 13. a dramatic; favorable; unexpected; unfavorable ~ (events took a dramatic ~ for the worse) 14. at the ~ (of the century) ['short walk'] 15. to take a ~ (let's take a ~ around/round the park) ['shock'] 16. to give smb. a ~ (the revelation gave me quite a ~) ['misc.'] 17. at every ~ ('on every occasion'); to do smb. a good ~ ('to do smb. a favor')

turn II *v.* 1. ('to change direction') to ~ abruptly, sharply 2. (d; intr., tr.) to ~ against ('to become antagonistic towards'); ('to make antagonistic towards') (to ~ against one's friends; what ~ed him against us?) 3. (d; intr.) to ~ for; to ('to resort to') (she had to ~ to her family for help) 4. (d; intr.) ('to shift') to ~ from; to (let's ~ from this topic to a more pleasant one; to ~ to a new field) 5. (D; intr.) ('to change direction') to ~ into, onto (to ~ into a side street) 6. (d; intr., tr.) to ~ into, to ('to be converted, transformed into'); ('to convert, transform into') (caterpillars ~ into butterflies; freezing water ~s into ice; his love ~ed to hate; they ~ed the meeting into a brawl; the incident ~ed her into a better person) 7. (D; intr.) to ~ off ('to leave') (to ~ off the main road) 8. (d; intr.) to ~ on ('to attack') (to ~ on smb. in anger) 9. (d; intr.) to ~ on, upon ('to depend, hinge on') (everything ~s on the judge's interpretation of the law) 10. (D; intr.) ('to change direction') to ~ to (to ~ to the right) 11. (d; intr.) ('to direct one's attention, efforts') to ~ to (to ~ to a new subject; she ~ed to the study of art) 12. (d; tr.) ('to direct') to ~ to, towards (to ~ one's attention to a new problem; ~ your face towards the mirror; you should not ~ your back to the audience) 13. (D; intr.) to ~ towards ('to face') (~ towards me) 14. (N; used with an adjective) ('to cause to become') we ~ed the dog loose; worry ~ed her hair gray 15. (S) to ~ traitor; she ~ ed pale 16. (misc.) to ~ one's back on smb. ('to reject smb.') (see the Usage Note for **grow**)

turnabout *n.* ['reversal'] to do a ~

turn away *v.* (D; intr.) to ~ from

turn back *v.* (D; intr.) to ~ from; to

turn in *v.* (B) ('to hand over') they ~ed him in to the police; she ~ed the assignment in to the teacher; he refused to ~ himself in to the authorities

turning point *n.* 1. to mark a ~ (in history) 2. to reach a ~ 3. a ~ for 4. at a ~ (we are at a ~ in history)

turn off *v.* (D; intr.) to ~ from; into (we ~ed off from the main road into a side road)

turn on *v.* (slang) 1. (D; intr.) to ~ to ('to become excited about') (to ~ to Beethoven) 2. (D; tr.) to ~ to ('to excite about') (to ~ smb. on to Beethoven)

turnout *n.* ['attendance'] ['participation'] 1. to attract a (large) ~ 2. a big, enormous, heavy, large; good; record ~ 3. a light, poor, small ~ 4. (a) voter ~

turn out *v.* 1. (D; intr.) ('to appear') to ~ for (a large crowd ~ed out for her first concert) 2. (E) ('to prove') the test ~ed out to be positive 3. (L) it ~ed out that they were away on a trip 4. (s) the test ~ed out negative

turnover *n.* ['movement of goods'] 1. a brisk, rapid ~ ['filled pastry'] 2. an apple ~

turn over *v.* (B) ('to hand over') to ~ a thief over to the police

turnpike *n.* (AE) ['toll expressway'] 1. (to travel) by ~ 2. (to drive) on a ~

turn signal *n.* (AE) to put on, use a ~ (BE has *indicator*)

turnstile *n.* 1. to pass through a ~ 2. a subway (AE), underground (BE) ~

turn up *v.* 1. (D; intr.) ('to appear') to ~ in (she finally ~ed up in London) 2. (s) ('to appear') (he ~ed up drunk at/for work)

turpitude *n.* moral ~

turtle *n.* 1. a fresh-water; land; mud; snapping ~ 2. (misc.) to turn ~ ('to capsize')

tusk *n.* an elephant; walrus ~

tussle I *n.* (colloq.) 1. to get into, have a ~ 2. a ~ about, over; with

tussle II *v.* (colloq.) (D; intr.) to ~ with

tutelage *n.* under smb.'s ~

tutor I *n.* 1. a course (BE); private ~ 2. a ~ to

tutor II *v.* (D; tr.) to ~ in (to ~ smb. in physics)

tutorial *n.* ['course'] 1. to give smb. a ~ 2. to have a ~ with 3. a ~ about, on

TV see **television**

TV set see **television set**

twang *n.* 1. a nasal ~ 2. (misc.) to speak with a ~

tweed *n.* herringbone ~

tweezers *n.* a pair of ~

twilight *n.* in the ~ (in the ~ of one's career)

twine *v.* 1. (d; intr., refl.) to ~ around, round (the vines ~d around the tree) 2. (misc.) she has them ~d around her little finger ('they will do anything she wants them to do')

twinkle *n.* a ~ in smb.'s eyes

twins *n.* 1. fraternal; identical; Siamese ~ 2. a pair, set of ~

twist I *n.* ['type of dance'] 1. to dance, do the ~ ['act of twisting'] 2. to give smt. a ~ ['unexpected turn'] 3. an ironic; strange, unusual ~ ['interpretation'] 4. to give a (new) ~ (to the news) ['approach, method'] 5. a new ~

twist II *v.* 1. (D; tr.) to ~ into (to ~ smt. into a certain shape) 2. (D; tr.) to ~ out of (to ~ smt. out of shape) 3. (misc.) to ~ smb.'s arm ('to coerce smb.'); to ~ smb. around one's little finger ('to manipulate smb.'); the road ~s and turns

twitch I *n.* a nervous; uncontrollable ~

twitch II *v.* to ~ nervously; uncontrollably

two cent's worth *n.* (slang) (AE) ['opinion'] to get in, put in one's ~

type I *n.* ['metal blocks used in printing'] 1. to set ~ (to set ~ by hand) 2. boldface, boldfaced; elite; italic; pica; regular; Roman ~ 3. a font/fount of ~ 4. in ~ (to set a book in ~) ['sort, category'] 5. a blood ~ 6. of a certain ~ (a person of that ~ = that ~ of person)

type II *v.* 1. (C) ('to typewrite') ~ this letter for

me; or: ~ me this letter 2. (D; tr.) ('to assign to a type') to ~ as (that actor was ~d as a villain)

typecast *v.* (D; tr.) to ~ as; in (to be typecast in a certain role)

typeface see **type I 2**

typewriter *n.* 1. to operate, pound (colloq.) a ~ 2. an electric; electronic; manual; portable ~ 3. a ~ skips 4. on a ~ (I did the letter on my electric ~)

typhoid *n.* to contract, develop ~

typhoon *n.* the ~ hit/struck (several islands)

typhus *n.* to contract, develop ~

typical *adj.* 1. ~ of 2. ~ to + inf. (it was ~ of her to say such things)

typing *n.* to do (the) ~

typist *n.* 1. a shorthand ~ (BE; AE has *stenographer*) 2. a clerk-typist

tyranny *n.* 1. to impose ~ on 2. to overthrow a ~ 3. cruel, merciless; ruthless ~ 4. an act of ~ 5. ~ over

tyrant *n.* 1. to overthrow a ~ 2. a cruel, merciless; ruthless ~

tyre (BE) see **tire I**

U

UFO *n.* ['unidentified flying object'] 1. to sight a
~ 2. (misc.) a ~ sighting
ukase *n.* ['edict'] to issue a ~
ulcer *n.* a bleeding; duodenal; gastric, stomach;
mouth; peptic; perforated ~
ultimate *n.* ['acme'] 1. the ~ in (the ~ in comfort)
2. (carried) to the ~
ultimatum *n.* 1. to deliver, give, issue, present an
~ 2. to get, receive an ~ 3. to defy; ignore an ~ 4.
to withdraw an ~
umbilical cord *n.* 1. to tie (off) an ~ 2. to cut the ~
(also fig.)
umbrage *n.* ['offense'] 1. to give ~ 2. to take ~ at
umbrella *n.* 1. to open an ~ 2. to fold (up) an ~ 3.
a beach ~ 4. under an ~ (also fig.)
unable *adj.* (cannot stand alone) ~ to + inf. (she
is ~ to work today)
unacceptable *adj.* ~ to
unaccountable *adj.* ~ to
unaccustomed *adj.* (cannot stand alone) ~ to (~
to public speaking)
unaffected *adj.* 1. ~ by 2. to remain ~
unafraid *adj.* ~ of
unaided *adj.* ~ by; in
unamenable *adj.* (formal) ~ to
unanimity *n.* ~ in
unanimous *adj.* ~ in
unappreciative *adj.* ~ of
unasked *adj.* ~ for
unattended *adj.* to leave smt. ~
unaware *adj.* (cannot stand alone) 1. ~ of 2. ~
that + clause (they were ~ that the road had been
closed)
unawares *adv.* ['unexpectedly'] to catch smb. ~
unbalanced *adj.* mentally ~
unbeatable *adj.* ~ at, in (~ at chess)
unbecoming *adj.* ~ of; to (conduct ~ to an officer
= conduct ~ an officer)
unbeknown *adj.* (cannot stand alone) ~ to (~ to
us, they had already left)
unbeknownst *adj.* (formal) (cannot stand alone)
~ to
unbelievable *adj.* 1. ~ to 2. ~ that + clause (it's ~
to me that she would commit such a blunder)
unbending *adj.* ~ in (~ in one's manner)
unbiased *adj.* ~ towards
unburden *v.* 1. (B; refl.) he finally ~ed himself to
his family 2. (D; refl.) to ~ of (to ~ oneself of a
secret)
uncanny *adj.* 1. positively ~ 2. ~ to + inf. (it was
~ to see how closely they resemble each other) 3.
~ that + clause (it's ~ that we got here on the
same day after traveling for three months) 4.
(misc.) it's ~ how much the twins resemble each
other
uncensured *adj.* to go ~
uncertain *adj.* 1. ~ about, as to, of (~ about the
outcome) 2. (misc.) I am still ~ (as to) whether (or
not) they are coming

uncertainty *n.* ~ about, as to (there was no ~
about the matter; there is still some ~ as to
whether they are coming)
unchallenged *adj.* to go ~
unchanged *adj.* to remain ~
uncharacteristic *adj.* 1. ~ of 2. ~ to + inf. (it was
~ of her not to answer her correspondence)
uncharitable *adj.* 1. ~ of 2. ~ to + inf. (it was ~ of
her to say that)
unchecked *adj.* to go, remain ~
unclaimed *adj.* to go, remain ~
uncle *n.* (misc.) (colloq.) to say ~ ('to yield')
uncomfortable *adj.* (to feel) ~ about; with (I felt
~ about discussing this matter in public)
uncommitted *adj.* ~ to
uncommon *adj.* ~ to + inf. (it is not ~ to find
people here who know several languages)
uncommunicative *adj.* ~ about, regarding
uncompromising *adj.* ~ in; towards (~ in one's
attitude; ~ towards their proposal)
unconcern *n.* ~ for, over
unconcerned *adj.* ~ about, at, over, with
unconscious *adj.* 1. to remain ~ 2. ~ of
unconventional *adj.* ~ to + inf. (it is ~ to go to
work in shorts)
unconvinced *adj.* 1. to remain ~ 2. ~ of
uncooperative *adj.* ~ about; in; towards (~ in
working out a compromise)
uncorrected *adj.* to go, remain ~
uncritical *adj.* ~ of
unction *n.* (rel.) 1. to give ~ 2. to receive ~ 3.
Extreme Unction USAGE NOTE: The term
Anointing of the Sick is now preferred to *Extreme
Unction.*
undaunted *adj.* ~ by; in (~ in one's resolve)
undecided *adj.* 1. ~ about 2. ~ whether + inf. (he
is ~ whether to go) 3. to remain ~
undemonstrative *adj.* ~ towards
underbelly *n.* (fig.; historical) the soft ~ (of
Europe) ('the Balkans and Italy')
underbrush *n.* in the ~
undercoating *n.* (on a car) to apply ~
undercover *adv.* ['acting in secret'] 1. to work ~ 2.
to go ~
undergraduate *n.* a college, university ~
underground *adv.* to go ~
undergrowth *n.* 1. to clear the ~ 2. dense, heavy;
thick ~ 3. in the ~
understand *v.* 1. to ~ clearly, perfectly 2. (d; tr.)
to ~ by (what do you ~ by this term?) 3. (H) I
understood her to say that she would attend the
meeting 4. (K) I cannot ~ his behaving like that 5.
(L) I ~ that you will be moving here soon 6. (Q)
we do not ~ why she left 7. (misc.) they don't ~
anything about politics; she gave me to ~ that the
bill would be paid
understanding I *adj.* ~ about, of
understanding II *n.* ['agreement'] 1. to arrive at,
come to, reach an ~ 2. a clear; secret; tacit; ver-

bal; written ~ 3. an ~ about; with (we reached a tacit ~ with them about the matter) 4. an ~ to + inf. (to reach an ~ to keep a dispute out of the newspapers) 5. an ~ that + clause (it was my ~ that we would share the expenses) 6. on an ~ (we bought the supplies on the ~ that we would be reimbursed) ['harmony'] ['comprehension'] 7. to bring about, develop, promote ~ 8. deeper; mutual ~ 9. ~ between (promote deeper ~ between nations; to develop mutual ~)

understatement *n.* 1. to make an ~ 2. to go in for ~ 3. (misc.) a masterpiece of ~; the ~ of the year

understood *adj.* ~ that + clause (it was ~ that everyone would help)

undertake *v.* (E) she undertook to complete the project in six months

undertaking *n.* ['promise'] (esp. BE) 1. to give smb. an ~ 2. an ~ to + inf. (an ~ to complete a project in six months) ['task, enterprise'] 3. a joint; large-scale ~

underway *adv.* to get smt. ~

underwear *n.* thermal ~

underworld *n.* in the ~

underwriter *n.* an insurance ~

undeserving *adj.* ~ of

undesirable *adj.* 1. ~ to + inf. (it is ~ to raise taxes at this time) 2. ~ that + clause; subj. (it is ~ that they be/should be present)

undeterred *adj.* ~ by (~ by our advice)

undignified *adj.* ~ to + inf. (it was ~ to behave like that)

undiminished *adj.* ~ by; in (~ in stature)

undisturbed *adj.* ~ by (~ by the commotion)

undoing *n.* ['ruin'] to prove to be smb.'s ~ (alcohol proved to be his ~)

undone *adj.* to come ~ (her necklace came ~)

undreamed, undreamt *adj.* ~ of

uneasiness *n.* 1. to cause ~ 2. to allay one's ~ 3. ~ about

uneasy *adj.* ~ about

unemployed *n.* ['unemployed people'] the hard-core ~

unemployment *n.* 1. to cause, create ~ 2. to eliminate; reduce ~ 3. high; low; mounting; seasonal ~

unemployment compensation *n.* 1. to pay ~ 2. to draw, get, receive ~ 3. to be on ~ 4. to go on ~ 5. to apply for ~

unemployment insurance see **unemployment compensation 1, 2, 5**

unequal *adj.* ~ to

unequaled *adj.* ~ at, in

unerring *adj.* (usu. does not stand alone) ~ in (~ in her judgment)

unessential *adj.* ~ to

unethical *adj.* ~ to + inf. (it was ~ of them to do that)

unexcelled *adj.* ~ in

unfair *adj.* 1. ~ to (~ to certain groups) 2. ~ to + inf. (it was ~ to take advantage of the situation) 3. ~ that + clause (it's ~ that she has to work so hard)

unfaithful *adj.* ~ in; to

unfaithfulness *n.* ~ in; to

unfamiliar *adj.* ~ to; with (the area was ~ to me;

I was ~ with the situation)

unfamiliarity *n.* ~ with (my ~ with the area)

unfasten *v.* 1. (D; tr.) to ~ from 2. (misc.) to come ~ed

unfavorable, unfavourable *adj.* ~ to

unfed *adj.* to go ~

unfeeling *adj.* ~ towards

unfit *adj.* 1. mentally, psychologically; physically ~ 2. ~ for (~ for military service) 3. ~ to + inf. (~ to serve)

unfortunate *adj.* 1. ~ for 2. ~ in

unfriendly *adj.* ~ to, towards

ungrateful *adj.* ~ for; to (he was ~ to us for our help)

unhappy *adj.* 1. ~ about, at, over; in; with (she was ~ about/at/over the news) 2. ~ to + inf. (she was ~ to learn the news) 3. ~ that + clause (we are ~ that you cannot visit us)

unharmed *adj.* 1. to go ~ 2. ~ by

unhealthy *adj.* ~ to + inf. (it's ~ to smoke)

unheeded *adj.* 1. to go ~ (his advice went ~) 2. ~ by

unheedful *adj.* (cannot stand alone) ~ of (~ of threats)

unification *n.* to achieve, bring about ~ (to achieve ~ of a country)

uniform I *adj.* ~ in; with

uniform II *n.* 1. to don, put on; wear a ~ 2. to take off a ~ 3. a dress, full-dress; fatigue; military; naval; nurse's; parade; police; regulation ~ 4. in ~; out of ~ (he was out of ~ when he was picked up by the military police)

uniformity *n.* ~ in

unify *v.* 1. (D; tr.) to ~ into (they were ~fied into one nation) 2. (D; tr.) to ~ with

unimportant *adj.* ~ for; to

uninformed *adj.* ~ about, on

uninterested *adj.* ~ in (~ in politics)

uninvited *adj.* to appear, show up, turn up ~

union *n.* 1. to form a ~ 2. to break up, dissolve a ~ 3. a company; craft; credit; industrial; labor (AE), trade (BE); postal; student ~

union shop *n.* to introduce a ~

unique *adj.* 1. ~ in 2. ~ to (~ to a certain area)

unison *n.* in ~ with

unit *n.* ['single constituent of a whole'] 1. a basic, primary ~ ['military formation'] 2. to activate; form a ~ 3. to commit a ~ (to combat) 4. to deactivate; disband a ~ 5. an advance, advanced; airborne; armored; combat; crack, elite; mechanized, motorized; naval; tactical ~ (advance armored ~s have reached the river) ['standard'] 6. a message ~ (used for telephone calls) 7. a monetary ~ (the pound is the monetary ~ of Britain) ['single residence'] 8. a rental ~ ['computer terminal'] a Visual Display Unit = VDU; BE; AE has *Video Display Terminal* = VDT)

unite *v.* 1. (D; intr., tr.) to ~ against (to ~ against aggression; to ~ one's allies against the common foe) 2. (D; intr., tr.) to ~ for (we must ~ for the common good; the nation was ~d for the struggle against terrorism) 3. (D; intr., tr.) to ~ in (we must ~ in our struggle against terrorism; to ~ a nation in the fight against inflation) 4. (D; intr., tr.) to ~ into (we had to ~ the competing factions into a cohesive whole) 5. (D; intr.) to ~ with (our countries must ~ with each other against the common enemy)

united *adj.* ~ in

unity *n.* 1. to achieve, bring about ~ 2. to destroy, shatter ~ 3. national ~ (to achieve national ~) 4. in ~ (in ~ there is strength)

universals *n.* (ling.) linguistic ~

university *n.* 1. to establish, found a ~ 2. to go to a ~/to go to ~ (BE) (she goes to a good ~) 3. a free, open; people's ~ 4. an Ivy-League (US); redbrick (GB); state (US) ~ 5. at; in a ~ (to teach at a ~; there is a spirit of cooperation at/in our ~) USAGE NOTE: In BE, one goes *to university* or, as in AE, *to a university*. CE has only *to go to a good university*. See the Usage Notes for **college, school.**

unjust *adj.* 1. ~ of 2. ~ to 3. ~ to + inf. (it was ~ of him to accuse you without proof) 4. ~ that + clause (it's ~ that our side of the story was never heard)

unjustified *adj.* 1. completely, totally ~ 2. ~ in (she was ~ in complaining)

unkind *adj.* 1. ~ of 2. ~ to 3. ~ to + inf. (it was ~ of him to say that)

unknown *adj.* ~ to (the facts were ~ to us)

unlawful *adj.* ~ to + inf. (it's ~ to drive without a license)

unleash *v.* (D; tr.) to ~ against, on (to ~ a new arms race on the world)

unlikely *adj.* 1. (cannot stand alone) ~ to + inf. (they are ~ to accept our invitation) 2. ~ that + clause (it's ~ that she will attend)

unload *v.* (D; tr.) to ~ from (to ~ cargo from a ship)

unlucky *adj.* 1. ~ at, in; for (~ at cards; ~ in love; ~ for some people) 2. ~ to + inf. (some people feel that it is ~ to walk under a ladder)

unmarked *adj.* ~ by

unmarred *adj.* ~ by (the ceremony was ~ by any untoward incidents)

unmatched *adj.* ~ by; in

unmerciful *adj.* ~ to, towards

unmindful *adj.* (cannot stand alone) ~ of (~ of danger)

unnamed *adj.* to remain ~

unnatural *adj.* 1. ~ to + inf. (it's ~ of parents to reject their own children) 2. ~ that + clause (it's ~ that members of the same family should fight so much)

unnecessary *adj.* 1. ~ for 2. ~ to + inf. (it's ~ for us to wait) 3. ~ that + clause (it's ~ that you should get involved)

unnoticed *adj.* to go, pass ~ (the incident went/ passed ~)

unobserved *adj.* to go ~

unopposed *adj.* ~ to

unorthodox *adj.* ~ to + inf. (it is ~ to bypass the channels of command in the army)

unparalleled *adj.* ~ in (~ in ferocity)

unperturbed *adj.* ~ by (she was ~ by the loud noise)

unpleasant *adj.* 1. ~ to (he is ~ to everyone) 2. ~

to + inf. (it's ~ to talk to him = it's ~ talking to him = he's ~ to talk to = he's an ~ person to talk to)

unprepared *adj.* 1. ~ for 2. ~ to + inf. (I am unprepared to take on such a responsibility)

unpunished *adj.* 1. to go, remain ~ (the criminals went ~) 2. ~ for

unqualified *adj.* 1. ~ for 2. ~ to + inf. (she is ~ to work as a teacher)

unrealistic *adj.* ~ to + inf. (it is ~ to hope for an improvement so soon)

unreasonable *adj.* 1. ~ of (that was ~ of you) 2. ~ to + inf. (it is ~ to demand that employees work without a break)

unrecognized *adj.* 1. to go, remain ~ 2. ~ by

unreported *adj.* to go ~ (the story went ~)

unresponsive *adj.* ~ to

unrest *n.* 1. to foment, stir up ~ 2. civil; labor; political; social ~

unrivaled, unrivalled *adj.* ~ in

unsafe *adj.* ~ to + inf. (it's ~ to drive without putting on seat belts)

unsaid *adj.* to leave smt. ~

unsanctioned *adj.* ~ by (~ by custom)

unsatisfactory *adj.* 1. ~ in (they were ~ in their job performance) 2. ~ to (~ to all concerned)

unscathed *adj.* to go ~

unschooled *adj.* ~ in

unscrupulous *adj.* 1. ~ in (~ in his business dealings) 2. ~ to + inf. (it was ~ of their lawyer to withhold evidence)

unseemly *adj.* (formal) ~ to + inf. (it was ~ of them to show up at the reception without an invitation)

unseen *adj.* to remain ~

unselfish *adj.* ~ to + inf. (it was ~ of her to make the offer)

unsettle *v.* (R) it ~d me to see them quarrel

unsettling *adj.* ~ to + inf. (it was ~ to see them quarrel)

unshakable *adj.* ~ in (~ in one's faith)

unshaken *adj.* ~ in (~ in one's beliefs)

unshaven *adj.* to go ~ (he went ~ for a week)

unsightly *adj.* ['not pleasing to the sight'] it was ~ to behold

unskilled *adj.* ~ at, in

unsparing *adj.* ~ of (~ of praise)

unspoiled, unspoilt *adj.* ~ by (~ by success)

unstinting *adj.* (cannot stand alone) ~ in (~ in one's praise)

unstuck *adj.* ['ruined'] (slang) to come ~ (the whole scheme came ~)

unsuccessful *adj.* ~ at, in; with

unsuitable *adj.* ~ for

unsuited *adj.* ~ to

unsure *adj.* ~ of

unsurpassed *adj.* 1. ~ at, in (~ at learning languages) 2. ~ by (~ by any competitor)

unsusceptible *adj.* ~ to

unsuspicious *adj.* ~ of

unswerving *adj.* ~ in (~ in one's determination to stamp out corruption)

unsympathetic *adj.* ~ to

untainted *adj.* ~ by (~ by scandal)

untarnished *adj.* ~ by

unthanked *adj.* to go ~

unthinkable *adj.* 1. ~ to + inf. (it would be ~ to build a house so close to the river) 2. ~ that + clause (it is ~ that they would even make such an offer)

untiring *adj.* (usu. does not stand alone) ~ in (~ in one's efforts)

untold *adj.* to remain ~ (the story remained ~ for years)

untouched *adj.* ~ by

untreated *adj.* to go, remain ~ (the disease went ~)

untroubled *adj.* ~ by

untrue *adj.* ~ to

untruth *n.* to tell an ~

untruthful *adj.* ~ about

untutored *adj.* ~ in

untypical *adj.* ~ of

unused *adj.* ['unaccustomed'] (cannot stand alone) ~ to (they are ~ to hard work)

unusual *adj.* 1. ~ to + inf. (it is ~ to see snow in this region; it's ~ for two world records to be set in/on one day) 2. ~ that + clause (it's ~ that two world records should be set in/on one day)

unversed *adj.* (cannot stand alone) ~ in (~ in the ways of big business)

unwarranted *adj.* ~ by

unwavering *adj.* ~ in (~ in one's support)

unwilling *adj.* ~ to + inf. (she is ~ to participate)

unwillingness *n.* an ~ to + inf. (everyone deplored their ~ to compromise)

unwise *adj.* ~ to + inf. (it would be ~ to walk through the park at midnight)

unworthy *adj.* ~ of (~ of your help; such behavior is ~ of you)

unyielding *adj.* ~ in (~ in one's demands)

up *adj.* (cannot stand alone) ['abreast'] 1. ~ on (are you ~ on the news?) ['dependent'] 2. ~ to (the decision is ~ to you; it's ~ to you to decide; it's ~ to you whether we go)

upbraid *v.* (D; tr.) to ~ for (they ~ed him for his sloppy work)

upbringing *n.* smb.'s family; religious ~

update *n.* (colloq.) ['bringing up-to-date'] 1. to give an ~ on (I'll give you an ~ on the situation) 2. an ~ on (here is an ~ on the situation)

up front *adv.* ~ with ('candid with')

upgrade *v.* (D; tr.) to ~ to (our legation was ~d to an embassy)

upheaval *n.* 1. a violent ~ 2. a political; social ~

upholstery *n.* leather; plastic; vinyl ~

upkeep *n.* ['cost of maintenance'] the ~ of, on (the ~ on this machinery is very costly)

upper hand *n.* ['control'] (colloq.) 1. to gain, get; have the ~ 2. to lose the ~ 3. the ~ in; over (we gained the ~ over them in that contest)

uprising *n.* 1. to foment, incite an ~ 2. to crush, put down, quell, an ~ 3. an armed; peasant ~ 4. an ~ against

uproar *n.* 1. to create an ~ 2. an ~ over 3. in an ~

uproot *v.* (D; tr.) to ~ from (they were ~ed from their homes)

upset I *adj.* 1. to get ~ about, over 2. ~ with (she was ~ with me about my expenses) 3. ~ to + inf. (she was ~ to learn of their attitude)

upset II *n.* ['unexpected victory'] (sports) to score an ~ over

upset III *v.* (R) it upset me to learn of their attitude

upsetting *adj.* 1. ~ to (recent events have been very ~ to us) 2. ~ to + inf. (it was ~ to learn of their attitude)

upside down *adv.* to turn smt. ~

upstanding *adj.* (esp. BE) be ~ ('stand up') (be ~ for the judge; be ~ for a toast)

uptake *n.* ['comprehension'] (colloq.) (quick) on the ~

uptight *adj.* (colloq.) ~ about

upturn *n.* 1. a sharp ~ 2. an ~ in (a sharp ~ in the economy)

upwards *adv.* ~ of (~ of an hour) ('somewhat more than an hour')

uranium *n.* enriched ~

urge I *n.* 1. to feel an ~ 2. to satisfy an ~ 3. to control; stifle an ~ 4. an irrepressible, irresistible, uncontrollable; natural; sudden ~ 5. an ~ to + inf. (she felt an ~ to respond)

urge II *v.* 1. to ~ forcefully, strongly 2. (H) she ~d me to accept the compromise 3. (L; subj.) we ~d that the bill be/should be passed

urgency *n.* 1. ~ about, in (there is no ~ about this matter) 2. (misc.) a sense of ~

urgent *adj.* ~ that + clause; subj. (it is ~ that they all be/should be present)

urging *n.* at smb.'s ~ (at our ~ they accepted the invitation)

urn *n.* a burial; coffee ~

usable, useable *adj.* ~ for

use I /ju:s/ *n.* 1. to make ~ of 2. to put smt. to (good) ~ 3. to find a ~ for 4. to lose; regain the ~ of (she lost the ~ of one arm) 5. to deny (the) ~ of (the visitors were denied ~ of the library) 6. constant; daily; emergency; extensive; external; internal; official; practical; universal; wide ~ (they made extensive ~ of computers) 7. (legal) fair ~ 8. ~ for (do you have any ~ for this old paper?) 9. ~ in (is there any ~ in trying again?) 10. ~ of (what's the ~ of worrying?) 11. for ~ (for official ~ only) 12. in ~ (the copying machine is in ~) 13. of ~ to (it was of no earthly ~ to us; can I be of any ~ to you?) 14. (misc.) she has no ~ for them ('she dislikes them'); to come into ~; to go out of ~ USAGE NOTE: The following constructions are variants; the constructions with no prepositions are colloquial-- *is there any use in trying again?--is there any use trying again? what's the use of worrying?--what's the use worrying?*

use II /ju:z/ *v.* 1. to ~ widely 2. (D; tr.) to ~ as (she ~d the candlestick as a paperweight) 3. (D; tr.) to ~ for (let's ~ paper plates for the picnic) 4. (E; in positive sentences and neg. sentences with *never* this verb is used only in the past tense to denote a former practice or state; in interrogative sentences the infinitive of this verb occurs with *didn't, did not*) she ~d to work there; there ~d to be an open field here; she never ~d to work here; didn't he ~ to work here? USAGE NOTE: In neg. sentences with *didn't, did not,* this verb occurs with the infinitive and, colloquially, with the past tense--she didn't use/used to work there. In old-fashioned BE, constructions such as the following may occur--used she (not) to work there? she used not to work there.

used I /ju:st/ *adj.* (cannot stand alone) ['accustomed'] to be; get ~ to (she is ~ to working hard; to get ~ to hard work)

used II /ju:zd/ *adj.* ['employed'] ~ for (this machine is ~ for making copies)

useful *adj.* 1. ~ for, to (a combinatory dictionary is ~ for/to students) 2. ~ for, in (computers are ~ in compiling statistics) 3. ~ to + inf. (it's ~ to know several foreign languages when you are traveling abroad = it's ~ knowing several foreign languages when you are traveling abroad)

useless *adj.* ~ to + inf. (it's ~ to try to convince her)

usher *v.* 1. (d; tr.) to ~ into (they ~ed the guests into a large waiting room) 2. (d; tr.) to ~ out of 3. (d; tr.) to ~ to (we were ~ed to our seats)

usual *adj.* ~ to + inf. (it's ~ to ask for permission before visiting a class)

usury *n.* 1. to engage in, practice ~ 2. to condemn; outlaw ~

utensils *n.* cooking, kitchen ~

utility *n.* ['company providing a public service'] a public ~

utilize *v.* 1. to ~ fully 2. (D; tr.) to ~ for

utmost *n.* ['maximum effort'] to do one's ~ (we did our ~ to help)

utter *v.* (B) she ~ed a few words to them

utterance *n.* a prophetic ~

U-turn *n.* to make a ~

V

vacancy *n.* 1. to create a ~ 2. to fill a ~ 3. (misc.) no ~ (the sign reads *no vacancy)*

vacation *n.* ['period of rest'] (AE; CE has *holiday)* 1. to spend; take a ~ 2. to be on. go on ~ 3. an extended, long; paid; short ~ 4. a spring; summer; winter ~ 5. a ~ from 6. during a ~; on ~ (she was away on ~) ['period during which a college or university is closed'] 7. (BE) the long ~ USAGE NOTE: Soldiers and sailors go on *leave;* civilians go on *holiday* (BE) or on *vacation* (AE). British students go on *holiday* during the long *vacation/vac.*

vaccinate *v.* (D; tr.) to ~ against (to ~ smb. against a disease)

vaccination *n.* 1. to carry out, do a (mass) ~ (of the population) 2. (a) compulsory; mass ~ 3. a ~ against (to carry out a mass ~ against tuberculosis)

vaccine *n.* influenza; polio; Sabin; Salk; smallpox; tetanus; yellow-fever ~

vacillate *v.* (D; intr.) to ~ between; in

vacuum *n.* 1. to create, produce a ~ 2. to break; fill a ~ 3. a partial ~ 4. in a ~ (nothing can live in a ~)

vague *adj.* ~ about (she was ~ about her plans)

vain *adj.* 1. ~ about (~ about one's appearance) 2. ~ to + inf. (it is ~ to protest) 3. (misc.) in ~ ('without success') (to work in ~); to take the Lord's name in ~ ('to treat the Lord's name in a disrespectful manner')

valedictory *n.* ['farewell speech'] 1. to deliver, give a ~ 2. (misc.) a ~ address

valid *adj.* 1. ~ for (~ for one year) 2. ~ to + inf. (is it ~ to say that Olympic athletes are amateurs?)

valise *n.* to pack; unpack a ~

valley *n.* 1. a ~ between (high mountains) 2. in a ~ (they live down in the ~)

valor, valour *n.* 1. to demonstrate, display, show ~ 2. uncommon ~ 3. (misc.) the better part of ~

valuable *adj.* ~ to + inf. (it's ~ to know languages if you work in an export firm)

valuables *n.* to check one's ~ (esp. AE)

value I *n.* ['worth'] ['monetary, numerical worth'] 1. to attach ~ to 2. to place, put, set a ~ on 3. to acquire, take on ~ 4. an absolute; book; cash; face; fair; intrinsic; nominal; nuisance; numerical; strategic; token ~ 5. (economics) surplus ~ 6. (economics) present ~ 7. a (market) ~ goes down; goes up 8. at a certain ~ (at face ~) 9. of ~ (a discovery of great ~) ['principles, qualities'] 10. to cherish; foster ~s 11. enduring; moral; spiritual; traditional; uncorrupted ~s (to return to traditional ~s) 12. middle-class; Victorian ~s

value II *v.* 1. to ~ highly, very much 2. (d; tr.) to ~ as (to ~ smb. as a friend) 3. (d; tr.) to ~ at (~ a painting at five thousand pounds) 4. (D; tr.) to ~ for (to ~ smt. for sentimental reasons)

valve *n.* ['device that permits flow'] 1. to grind ~s 2. a ball; butterfly; check; exhaust; gate; globe;

needle; safety; shunt; suction ~ ['membranous fold that permits body fluids to flow in one direction'] (anat.) 3. a heart ~ (the patient has a defective heart ~)

van I *n.* ['road vehicle'] 1. to drive a ~ 2. a breakdown ~ (BE; AE has *tow truck)* 3. a delivery ~ (BE; AE has *delivery truck)* 4. a moving ~ (AE), removal (BE) ~ ['rail vehicle'] 5. a guard's ~ (BE; AE has *caboose)* 6. a luggage ~ (BE; AE has *baggage car)*

van II *n.* ['vanguard'] in the ~

vandalism *n.* to commit ~

vane *n.* a weather ~

vanguard *n.* in the ~

vanish *v.* 1. to ~ completely 2. (D; intr.) to ~ from (to ~ from sight) 3. (D; intr.) to ~ into (to ~ into thin air)

vanity *n.* to flatter, tickle smb.'s ~

vapor, vapour *n.* to emit a ~

vapor trail, vapour trail *n.* to leave a ~ (high flying aircraft leave ~s)

variable *n.* (math.) a dependent; independent; random ~

variance *n.* ['permission to bypass a regulation'] (legal) (US) 1. to grant a ~ 2. to apply for a ~ 3. a zoning ~ ['disagreement'] 4. at ~ with (a theory at ~ with the facts)

variation *n.* ['deviation, change'] 1. (a) wide ~ 2. ~ in ['modified repetition of a musical theme'] (mus.) 3. ~s on a theme

variety *n.* 1. to add, lend ~ to 2. (a) wide ~ 3. in a ~ of (in a ~ of roles)

varnish *n.* 1. to apply ~ 2. nail ~ (BE; AE has *nail polish)*

varsity *n.* ['college or secondary-school team'] (AE) 1. to make ('be selected to join') the ~ 2. the junior ~ 3. on the ~ (we play on the ~)

vary *v.* 1. to ~ considerably, greatly 2. (D; intr.) to ~ between 3. (D; intr.) to ~ from; to (prices ~ from ten to fifteen dollars) 4. (d; intr.) to ~ in size; they ~ in their opinions)

vault I *n.* 1. a bank ~ 2. (misc.) to keep one's valuables in a ~

vault II *v.* (d; intr.) to ~ over (he ~ed over the bar)

veal *n.* 1. to roast ~ 2. roast ~

veer *v.* 1. (D; intr.) to ~ from; to (to ~ from one's course; to ~ to the right)

veer away *v.* (D; intr.) to ~ from

vegetables *n.* 1. to grow ~ 2. green; leafy; root ~ 3. garden ~ 4. cooked; raw; steamed; stir-fried ~

vegetation *n.* dense, lush. rank ~

vehicle *n.* ['conveyance'] 1. to drive, operate a ~ 2. an all-purpose; amphibious; armored; half-tracked; motor; passenger; recreational; re-entry; space ~ 3. a hired (BE), rented, self-drive (BE) ~ ['means'] 4. a ~ for (a ~ for spreading propaganda)

veil *n.* 1. to draw a ~ (over) 2. to lift a ~ 3. a bridal

~ 4. (misc.) under a ~ of mystery

vein *n.* ['blood vessel'] 1. to open a ~ 2. the jugular ~ 3. varicose ~s ['mood'] ['manner'] 4. a gloomy; happy; humorous; lighter; melancholy; merry; serious ~ 5. in a certain ~ (let's continue our discussion in a lighter ~)

velocity *n.* 1. to develop; gain; lose ~ 2. muzzle ~ 3. at a certain ~ (at the ~ of sound)

velvet *n.* (misc.) as smooth as ~

vendetta *n.* 1. to conduct, lead a ~ 2. a personal ~ 3. a ~ against

vending machine *n.* to use a ~

vendor *n.* a street ~

veneer *n.* ['superficial gloss'] a thin ~

venerate *v.* (D; tr.) to ~ for

veneration *n.* 1. deep, profound ~ 2. ~ for

venetian blinds *n.* 1. to close, shut; lower; open; raise ~ 2. to install ~

vengeance *n.* 1. to exact, take, wreak ~ on, upon 2. to vow ~ 3. to seek ~ for 4. ~ for (to take ~ on smb. for smt.) 5. (misc.) with a ~ ('to an extreme degree') (it started snowing with a ~)

venom *n.* ['poison'] 1. to neutralize ~ ['malice'] 2. to spew, spout ~

vent *n.* ['outlet'] to give ~ to (he gave ~ to his pent-up feelings)

ventriloquism *n.* to practice ~

venture I *n.* 1. to undertake a ~ 2. a business ~ 3. (misc.) to join smb. in a ~

venture II *v.* (formal) (E) I ~ to suggest that your whole idea is unworkable

venue *n.* ['site of a trial'] a change of ~ (her lawyer requested a change of ~)

veracity *n.* to doubt smb.'s ~

veranda see **porch 1, 3**

verb *n.* 1. to conjugate, inflect; passivize a ~ 2. an auxiliary, helping; compound, phrasal; copular (esp. BE), copulative, linking; defective; irregular; main; modal; regular; strong; weak ~ 3. an active; passive ~ 4. an intransitive; reflexive; transitive ~ 5. an imperfective; perfective ~ 6. ~s agree (with); ~s govern, take a case (a ~ agrees with the subject in number) 7. a ~ has aspect; mood; tense; voice 8. ~s have complements; objects

verdict *n.* 1. to arrive at, reach a ~ 2. to announce; bring in, deliver, hand down, render, return a ~ 3. to sustain ('uphold') a ~ (the higher court sustained the ~) 4. to overturn, quash, set aside a ~ 5. to appeal a ~ 6. a fair; unfair ~ 7. an adverse, unfavorable; directed; favorable; sealed ~ 8. a ~ of guilty; or: a guilty ~; a ~ of not guilty; a ~ for the defendant; a ~ for the plaintiff (the jury brought in a ~ of not guilty) 9. a ~ that + clause (they appealed the court's ~ that fraud had been committed) 10. (misc.) to defy/ignore a ~

verge I *n.* ['brink'] 1. on the ~ of (he was on the ~ of a nervous breakdown) 2. (misc.) driven to the ~ of bankruptcy

verge II *v.* (d; intr.) to ~ on, upon (her actions ~d on the ridiculous)

verify *v.* (L) the police ~fied that she had an airtight alibi

vermin *n.* 1. to exterminate ~ 2. (misc.) infested with ~

vernacular *n.* in the ~ (to express oneself in the ~)

versatile *adj.* ~ at, in

versatility *n.* 1. to demonstrate ~ 2. ~ at, in

verse *n.* 1. to compose, write; recite ~(s) 2. to scan ~ 3. free; heroic; macaronic; rhymed, rhyming; unrhymed ~ 4. in ~ 5. (misc.) to cite/give/quote chapter and ~ ('to indicate one's sources very precisely')

versed *adj.* (cannot stand alone) ~ in

version *n.* 1. to give one's ~ (of a story) 2. to corroborate smb.'s ~ (of an event) 3. an abridged, condensed; authorized, official; censored; expurgated; unabridged, uncut; unauthorized, unofficial; uncensored; unexpurgated; written ~ (an uncut ~ of a film) 4. a movie (AE); stage ~ (of a novel)

vertebra *n.* a cervical; lumbar; sacral; thoracic ~

vessel *n.* ['tube in the body'] 1. a blood ~ ['ship, boat'] 2. to charter a ~ 3. to launch a ~ 4. a cargo; escort; oceangoing ~

vest I *n.* (AE) a bulletproof *jacket*; life (CE has *life jacket*) ~ USAGE NOTE: In BE, the basic meaning of *vest* is 'undershirt'; in AE, it is 'waistcoat'.

vest II *v.* (formal) 1. (d; tr.) to ~ in (to ~ power in smb.) 2. (d; tr.) to ~ with (to ~ smb. with power)

vested *adj.* (cannot stand alone) 1. ~ in (the power to impose taxes is ~ in Congress) 2. ~ with (Congress is ~ with the power to impose taxes)

vestiges *n.* ['traces'] 1. to lose all remaining ~ of 2. the last ~ of

veteran *n.* a disabled; war (AE) ~ (to retrain disabled ~s) USAGE NOTE: In BE, *veteran* means 'old soldier'; in AE, it means any former serviceman or servicewoman, young or old.

veto *n.* 1. to exercise, impose, use a ~ 2. to sustain a ~ 3. to override a ~ (Congress overrode the President's ~) 4. a pocket ~ 5. (legal) a heckler's ~ 6. a ~ of, over

vex *v.* (formal) (R) it ~es me to read such things in the newspapers; it ~es me that they are always late

vexed *adj.* (formal) 1. deeply ~ 2. ~ about, at, with (we were ~ at the mix-up) 3. ~ to + inf. (they were ~ to learn of the delay)

vexing *adj.* ~ to + inf. (it is ~ to read such things in the newspapers)

vice I *n.* commercialized; legalized ~

vice II (BE) see **vise**

vicinity *n.* 1. the close, immediate ~ 2. in the ~ (in the immediate ~ of the school)

vicious *adj.* ~ to + inf. (it was ~ of him to make such an accusation)

vicissitude *n.* the ~s of life

victim *n.* 1. an innocent; unsuspecting ~ (of) 2. an accident; amnesia; earthquake; flood; hurricane; storm ~ 3. (misc.) to fall ~ to

victory *n.* 1. to achieve, gain, pull off (colloq.), score, win a ~ 2. a clear, clear-cut, decisive, outright, resounding, stunning; upset ~ 3. a bloodless; cheap; glorious; hard-won; hollow; moral; Pyrrhic; signal; sweeping ~ 4. a ~ in; over (a ~ in a struggle; a ~ over an enemy) 5. (misc.) to snatch ~ from the jaws of defeat

videotape *n*. to make a ~ (of)

vie *v*. (formal) (d; intr.) to ~ against, with; for (she had to ~ for the prize against very strong competition)

view I *n*. ['opinion'] 1. to air, express, present, put forward, voice a ~ 2. to harbor, hold a ~ 3. to advance, advocate a ~ 4. to exchange ~s 5. to take a ~ 6. a cheerful, optimistic, rosy; dim, grave, pessimistic ~ (she took a dim ~ of the matter) 7. advanced; contrary; conservative; divergent; diverse; liberal; progressive; modern; old-fashioned; outdated, outmoded; philosophical; political; popular; radical; reactionary; slanted; sound; strong; unpopular ~s 8. a ~ about, on 9. a ~ that + clause (they disputed my ~ that taxes should be raised) 10. in smb.'s ~ (in my ~ the offer is unacceptable) ['sight'] 11. to get a ~ of 12. to block smb.'s ~ 13. a beautiful, breathtaking, magnificent, superb ~ 14. a clear, unhampered, unimpaired ~ 15. a bird's eye; close-up; full; full-length ~ 16. in, within ~ (in full ~ of the public) 17. (misc.) to come into ~ ['perspective'] 18. an exploded ~ ['what can be seen'] 19. a rear ~ 20. a ~ from (the ~ from the window) 21. (misc.) a room with a nice ~ (of the ocean) ['aim'] 22. with a ~ (with a ~ to reestablishing diplomatic relations) ['misc.'] 23. in ~ of ('in consideration of'); a point of ~

view II *v*. (d; tr.) to ~ as (she was ~ed as a serious threat to the party leadership)

viewpoint *n*. 1. a ~ that + clause (he explained his ~ that taxes should be increased) 2. from smb.'s ~

vigil *n*. 1. to hold a ~; to keep (a) ~ 2. an all-night ~ 3. a ~ over

vigilance *n*. 1. to display, show; exercise ~ 2. eternal ~

vigor, vigour *n*. 1. to regain one's ~ 2. to lose one's ~ 3. to sap smb.'s ~ 4. the ~ to + inf. (does he have enough ~ to get everything done?)

vile *adj*. (formal) ~ to + inf. (it was ~ of them to issue such a statement)

village *n*. a farming (esp. AE); fishing ~ (see the Usage Note for **town**)

village green *n*. on the ~

villain *n*. an arch, consummate ~ USAGE NOTE: In AE, *villain* is mostly literary or humorous; in BE slang, it still means 'criminal'.

vim *n*. ['energy'] with ~ and vigor; full of ~ and vigor

vindicate *v*. (B) ('to justify') can you ~ your actions to us?

vindictive *adj*. ~ of (that was ~ of him)

vinegar *n*. apple; cider; wine ~

vintage *n*. ['period'] 1. of a certain ~ (a mansion of prewar ~; a car of ancient ~) 2. (misc.) a ~ wine

viola *n*. to play the ~

violation *n*. 1. to commit a ~ 2. a brazen, flagrant; minor ~ 3. a moving ~ (by a motorist) 4. in ~ of (he acted in ~ of the law)

violence *n*. ['devastating force'] 1. to resort to, use ~ 2. excessive ~ 3. an act of ~ 4. ~ against ['distortion'] ['harm'] 5. to do ~ to (the decision does

~ to our whole judicial tradition) ['rioting'] 6 communal; continuing; racial; sporadic ~ 7. ~ breaks out

violin *n*. 1. to play the ~ 2. to string; tune a ~

virgin *n*. a vestal ~ (historical)

virtue *n*. ['admirable feature'] ['moral excellence'] 1. to have a ~ (our budget has the ~ of providing for a small surplus) 2. a cardinal ~ 3. (misc.) a paragon of ~ ['misc.'] 4. by ~ of ('because of'); of easy ~ (old-fashioned) ('sexually promiscuous'); to make a ~ of necessity ('to make the best of smt. bad')

virus *n*. an influenza; intestinal ~

visa *n*. 1. to grant, issue a ~ 2. to extend; renew a ~ 3. to get, receive a ~ 4. to apply for a ~ 5. to overstay; violate a ~ 6. to deny smb. a ~ 7. to cancel a ~ 8. an entry; exit; student; tourist; transit ~

vise, vice *n*. ['tool for holding an object being worked on'] 1. to loosen; tighten a ~ 2. in a ~ USAGE NOTE: The AE form is *vise;* the BE form is *vice*.

visibility *n*. ['degree of being visible'] 1. good; limited; poor; marginal; unlimited; zero ~ (all planes were grounded because of poor ~) ['exposure to publicity'] 2. high; low; maximum ~

visible *adj*. 1. clearly, plainly ~ 2. ~ to (~ to the naked eye)

vision *n*. ['sight'] 1. acute; blurred; dim; double; impaired; keen; normal; peripheral; tunnel ~ 2. (misc.) a field of ~ ['foresight'] 3. the ~ to + inf. (she had the ~ to make wise investments several years ago) 4. of ~ (a person of great ~) 5. (misc.) tunnel ~ ('narrow horizons')

visit I *n*. 1. to make, pay; schedule a ~ 2. to cancel; cut short a ~ 3. a flying ('very short'); formal; friendly; informal; official; return state; unscheduled; weekend ~ 4. a ~ to (this is my first ~ to your country) 5. on a ~ (on a ~ to South America)

visit II *v*. 1. (obsol. and formal) (d; tr.) to ~ on (the Lord's anger was ~ed on the people) 2. (AE) (d; intr.) to ~ with (we ~ed with several friends)

visitor *n*. 1. a frequent ~ 2. a weekend ~ 3. (BE) a prison ~ 4. (BE) a health ~ (AE has *public-health nurse*) 5. a ~ from (~s from abroad) 6. a ~ to (~s to our city)

vista *n*. ['view'] 1. to open up new ~s (of the future) 2. a broad, wide ~

visual aids *n*. to employ, use ~

visualize *v*. 1. (d; tr.) to ~ as (I cannot ~ him as a famous star) 2. (J) I cannot ~ him becoming a famous star 3. (K) I cannot ~ his becoming a famous star

vital *adj*. 1. ~ for, to (their aid is ~ to our success) 2. ~ to + inf. (it is ~ to be prepared for any eventuality) 3. ~ that + clause; subj. (it is ~ that we be/should be kept informed of all developments)

vital signs *n*. to check, take smb.'s ~

vital statistics *n*. to gather; record; report ~

vitamins *n*. to take ~

vocabulary *n*. 1. to command a ~ 2. to build, develop, enlarge one's ~ 3. an extensive, huge, large, rich ~ 4. a meager, restricted, small ~ 5 a basic; technical ~ 6. an active; passive ~

vocation *n*. to have missed one's ~ ('not to have chosen an occupation or vocation at which one is particularly adept')

vogue *n*. ['popularity'] ['current fashion'] 1. to be the ~ (home computers are the latest ~) 2. to be in ~; to come into ~; to have a ~ (BE) 3. to go out of ~ 4. the current; latest ~ 5. (misc.) to be all the ~

voice *n*. ['sound produced by vocal cords'] 1. to raise one's ~ 2. to drop, lower one's ~ 3. to lose one's ~ 4. a clear; deep; firm, steady; gentle, soft; gruff, harsh, raucous; guttural; high-pitched; hoarse; husky; loud; low, low-pitched; mellifluous, melodious; mellow; metallic; quaking, quivering, shaking, shaky, trembling; resonant; rich; shrill; stentorian; strident; subdued; thundering ~ 5. a ~ breaks, cracks; changes; drops, falls; quivers, shakes, trembles 6. in a certain ~ (in a loud ~) 7. (misc.) (to shout) at the top of one's ~ ['expression'] 8. to give ~ to ['verbal form indicating the relation of the verb to its subject'] 9. the active; middle; passive ~ ['misc.'] 10. an inner ~ ('conscience'); the ~ of reason

void I *adj*. ['devoid'] (cannot stand alone) ~ of

void II *n*. to fill a ~

volcano *n*. 1. an active; dead, extinct; dormant; intermittent ~ 2. ~s erupt

volition *n*. ['act of choosing'] of, on one's own ~ (they agreed of their own ~; to act on one's own ~)

volley *n*. ['simultaneous discharge of weapons'] 1. to fire a ~ ['tennis ball in flight'] 2. (to hit a ball) on the ~

volleyball *n*. to play ~

voltage *n*. 1. to step up (the) ~ 2. high; low ~ 3. (misc.) a ~ surge

volume *n*. ['loudness'] 1. to amplify; increase, turn up the ~ 2. to decrease, turn down the ~ ['space occupied in three dimensions'] 3. molecular ~ ['book'] 4. a rare ~ 5. a companion ~ (this work is a companion ~ to our first dictionary) 6. (misc.) to speak ~s ('to imply a lot') (a single glance can speak ~s)

volunteer I *n*. to recruit ~s

volunteer II *v*. 1. (D; intr.) to ~ as (to ~ as a tutor) 2. (D; intr.) to ~ for (who will ~ for this job?) 3. (E) she ~ed to water our plants

vomiting *n*. to cause, induce ~

voodoo, voodooism *n*. to practice ~

vortex *n*. to draw into a ~

vote I *n*. ['collective opinion as determined by voting'] 1. to take a ~ on (a motion) 2. to put a motion to a ~; to bring a motion to a ~ 3. to influence, swing a ~ (recent events swung the ~ in our favor; the press can influence the ~) 4. to count, tally the ~ 5. a close; lopsided; solid; unanimous ~ 6. a rising; straw; voice; write-in ~ 7. a ~ on (a ~ on an issue) 8. (esp. BE) a ~ to + inf. (we took a ~ to adjourn) 9. by a ~ (by a unanimous ~) 10.

(misc.) a ~ of censure; confidence; no-confidence; thanks ['individual expression of opinion, ballot'] 11. to cast a ~ 12. to change, switch one's ~ 13. to get, receive smb.'s ~ (you'll never get my ~) 14. the deciding ~ (to cast the deciding ~) 15. a write-in ~ 16. a ~ against; for; on (to cast a ~ for a proposal) 17. the ~s to + inf. (we have enough ~s to carry the state) ['group of voters'] 18. the conservative; floating (BE); ('unattached'); independent; labor; liberal; undecided ~ ['voters as a group'] 19. to deliver the ~(s); to get out the ~ (the party machine delivered the ~s; a series of interesting debates helped to get out the ~) 20. a heavy; light ~ ['right to vote, franchise, suffrage'] 21. to get, receive the ~ (in some countries women got the ~ after World War I)

vote II *v*. 1. (C; usu. used without *for*) Congress ~d him a pension 2. (D; intr.) to ~ against; for (to ~ against a bill) 3. (d; tr.) to ~ into (to ~ smb. into office) 4. (D; intr.) to ~ on, upon (to ~ on a resolution) 5. (d; tr.) to ~ out of (to ~ smb. out of office) 6. (E) the committee ~d to approve the report 7. (L; subj.) Parliament ~d that the allocation be/should be reduced 8. (N; used with an adjective, noun) she was ~d the most likely to succeed 9. (misc.) to ~ by a show of hands

voter *n*. 1. an absentee; floating (BE) ('unattached'); independent; registered ~ 2. a ~ registers (to vote)

voting *n*. 1. absentee; bloc ~ 2. (misc.) ~ irregularities

voting lists *n*. to tamper with ~

vouch *v*. (d; intr.) to ~ for (I can ~ for the truth of her statement)

voucher *n*. a gift (BE); hotel; luncheon (BE; AE has *meal ticket*); tuition (AE) ~

vouchsafe *v*. (formal) (E) ('to condescend') she ~d to help

vow I *n*. 1. to make, take a ~ 2. to keep one's ~ 3. to break, violate a ~ 4. a formal, solemn ~ 5. clerical; marriage; monastic; religious ~s (priests take religious ~s) 6. a ~ to + inf. (she made a solemn ~ not to smoke again) 7. a ~ that + clause (we took a ~ that we would always help each other) 8. (misc.) to exchange; renew marriage ~s

vow II *v*. 1. (E) she ~ed to return 2. (L; to) I ~ed (to them) that he would be avenged

vowel *n*. a back; closed; front; high; lax; long; middle; nasal; open; reduced; rounded; short; stressed; tense; unstressed ~

voyage *n*. ['journey by water'] 1. to go on a ~ 2. a long; maiden; ocean, sea; round-the-world ~ 3. a ~ to (a ~ to the islands)

V sign *n*. to give, make the ~

vulgar *adj*. ~ to + inf. (it's ~ to spit in public)

vulnerable *adj*. ~ to

vulture *n*. ~s feed on carrion

vying see **vie**

W

wad *n.* (slang) (AE) ['amount that one has available'] to shoot ('spend') one's ~

wade *v.* 1. (d; intr.) to ~ across (to ~ across a stream) 2. (d; intr.) to ~ into (to ~ into a river) 3. (d; intr.) to ~ into ('to attack') (the speaker ~d into the opposing candidate) 4. (d; intr.) to ~ through (to ~ through deep water) 5. (d; intr.) to ~ through ('to read through with difficulty') (to ~ through a long report)

wage I *n.* 1. to draw, earn a ~ 2. to pay a ~ 3. to freeze ~s 4. a decent, living; minimum; subsistence ~ (to pay workers a decent ~) 5. an annual, yearly; daily; hourly; monthly; weekly ~

wage II *v.* 1. (D; tr.) to ~ against (to ~ a campaign against smoking)

wage bracket *n.* in a ~

wager I *n.* 1. to lay, make, place a ~ or 2. a ~ that + clause (she made a ~ that her team would win)

wager II *v.* 1. (D; intr., tr.) to ~ on (did you ~ much money on that horse?) 2. (O; can be used with one, two, or three objects) we ~ed him ten dollars; we ~ed ten dollars; we ~ed him ten dollars that it would rain

wages *n.* 1. see **wage I** 2. starvation ~

waggon (BE) see **wagon**

wagon *n.* 1. a station ~ (AE; BE has *estate car*) 2. a tea ~ (AE; BE has *tea trolley*) 3. (esp. AE) a paddy, patrol ~ 4. (AE) a welcome ~ ('a car sent with gifts from local merchants to a family that has just moved into a neighborhood') 5. a Conestoga; covered ~ 6. a goods ~ (BE; AE has *freight car*) 7. (colloq.) (AE) a chuck ('food') ~ (on a ranch) 8. (misc.) on the ~ ('pledged not to drink alcoholic beverages')

waist *n.* 1. a slender, slim ~ 2. around, round the ~ (she wore a belt around her ~)

wait I *n.* 1. to lie in ~ for 2. to have a long ~ for (we had a long ~ for the bus)

wait II *v.* 1. (BE) (d; intr.) to ~ at (to ~ at table) (cf. 3) 2. (D; intr.) to ~ for (they ~ed for me; they ~ed for me to leave) 3. (AE) (d; intr.) to ~ on (to ~ on tables) (cf. 1) 4. (d; intr.) to ~ on, upon ('to attend to') (to ~ on smb. hand and foot) 5. (E) we are ~ing to go 6. (misc.) to keep smb. ~ing; they ~ed until she returned

wait for *v.* (H; no passive) we ~ed for them to leave

waiting *n.* (GB; on a traffic sign) no ~ (US has *no standing* or *no stopping*)

waiting list *n.* on a ~

wait up *v.* (D; intr.) to ~ for (they ~ed up for him until he returned)

waiver *n.* to agree to, sign a ~

wake I *n.* ['vigil over a corpse'] to hold a ~

wake II *n.* ['aftermath'] in the ~ (of (war brings misery in its ~; in the ~ of explorers came settlers)

wake III *v.* 1. (d; intr.) to ~ to (they woke to the sounds of music) 2. (d; intr.) (E) they woke to find themselves surrounded by the enemy) 3. (s) I

woke refreshed

wake up *v.* 1. (D; intr., tr.) to ~ from, out of (to ~ out of a sound sleep) 2. (d; intr.) to ~ to ('to the danger of inflation') 3. (E) I woke up to find the house on fire

walk I *n.* ['journey by foot'] 1. to have (BE: take a ~ 2. to take smb. for a ~ (BE also has: to take smb. a long ~ round the grounds) 3. to go for, go on a ~ 4. a brisk; easy; leisurely; long; nature; short ~ (to take a brisk ~) 5. a ~ from; to (we took a ~ from our house to the center of town; it's an easy ~ from here to school) ['profession'] ['class'] 6. from every ~ of life

walk II *v.* 1. to ~ fast; slow 2. (d; intr.) to ~ across (to ~ across the street) 3. (d; intr.) to ~ along (to ~ along a river bank) 4. (d; intr.) to ~ around, round (to ~ around a house) 5. (d; intr.) to ~ by, past (to ~ past the library) 6. (d; intr.) to ~ down (to ~ down the street) 7. (D; intr.) to ~ from; to (we ~ed from the park to the station) 8. (d; intr.) to ~ into (to ~ into a room; to ~ into an ambush) 9. (d; intr.) to ~ on, over (don't ~ on the wet floor!) 10. (d; intr.) to ~ out of (to ~ out of a meeting) 11. (d; intr.) to ~ (all) over ('to treat badly') (they ~ed all over us) 12. (d; intr.) to ~ through (to ~ through the park; to ~ through a puddle) 13. (d; tr.) to ~ through ('to help with smt. complicated') (she ~ed me through the procedure) 14. (misc.) she ~ed her dog in the park; they ~ed off the job in protest against the long hours

walk away *v.* 1. (D; intr.) to ~ from (he ~ed away from me without saying a word; to ~ from an accident) ('to survive an accident unhurt') 2. (d. intr.) to ~ with ('to win') (she ~ed away with all the top prizes)

walker *n.* a tightrope ~

walk in *v.* (d; intr.) to ~ on ('to come across unexpectedly') (I ~ed in on an interesting scene)

walking papers *n.* (colloq.) (AE) ['notice of dismissal'] to give smb. her/his ~ (BE has *marching orders*)

walk off *v.* (d; intr.) to ~ with ('to win') (she ~ed off with the first prize)

walkout *n.* 1. to stage a ~ 2. to end a ~ 3. a sympathy ~

walk out *v.* (D; intr.) to ~ on ('to leave') (she ~ed out on her husband)

walk over *v.* (d; intr.) to ~ to (he ~ed over to her table)

walk up *v.* (d; intr.) to ~ to (I ~ed up to them and said a few words)

wall *n.* 1. to build, erect, put up a ~ 2. to demolish, tear down a ~ 3. to climb, scale a ~ 4. to paint; panel; paper ~s 5. to line ~s (to line ~s with bookshelves) 6. a high; low ~ 7. a brick; fire, inside; outside; retaining ~; seawall; stone; supporting ~ 8. (also fig.) a ~ between (the ~ between church and state) 9. against the ~ (they were lined up/ stood up against the ~ and shot) 10. (misc.) we had our backs to the ~ ('we were in a desperate situation'); (slang) to drive smb. up the ~ ('to frustrate smb. completely')

wallet *n.* 1. a leather ~ 2. (misc.) his ~ was bulging with banknotes

wall off *v.* (D; tr.) to ~ from

wallop *n.* (colloq.) ['force'] to pack a ~ (the winds packed a real ~)

wallow *v.* (d; intr.) to ~ in (to ~ in the mud)

wallpaper *n.* 1. to hang ~ 2. a roll of ~

waltz *v.* (colloq.) (d; intr.) to ~ through ('to complete with ease') (she just ~ed through the test)

wand *n.* 1. to wave a ~ 2. a magic ~

wander *v.* (d; intr.) ('to stray') to ~ from (to ~ from the subject)

wander away *v.* (D; intr.) to ~ from (the children ~ed away from their parents)

wanderer *n.* a homeless ~

wane I *n.* ['decrease'] ['period of decrease'] on the ~ (the moon is on the ~)

wane II *v.* 1. (D; intr.) to ~ into (to ~ into insignificance) 2. (misc.) to wax and ~

wangle *v.* (colloq.) (C) could you ~ an invitation for me? or: could you ~ me an invitation?

want I *n.* ['need'] 1. to fill, meet, satisfy a ~ 2. to minister to smb.'s ~s 3. for ~ of (to die for ~ of medical care) 4. in ~ of (in ~ of a job) ['poverty'] 5. in ~ (to live in ~)

want II *v.* 1. to ~ badly, desperately, very much (they ~ed very badly to see us) 2. (d; intr.) to ~ for ('to be in need of') (they will never ~ for anything) 3. (D; tr.) ('to seek') to ~ for (he is ~ed for murder in three states) 4. (D; tr.) ('to desire') to ~ for (we ~ you for our team) 5. (E) ('to desire') I ~ to help 6. (BE) (G) ('to be in need of') your shirts ~ mending; the house ~s painting; her hair ~s cutting 7. (H; no passive) ('to desire') they ~ us to finish the job in two weeks 8. (colloq.) (J) I ~ them singing in tune! 9. (colloq.) (M) ('to desire') I ~ them to be kept busy at all times 10. (N; used with an adjective, past participle) ('to desire') we ~ the troublemakers removed; I ~ them ready in one hour; she ~s the house painted tomorrow

want ad *n.* (colloq.) (esp. AE) 1. to place a ~ 2. to answer a ~ 3. to follow, read the ~s

wanted *adj.* ['sought'] 1. ~ by (~ by the police) 2. ~ for (~ for murder)

wanting *adj.* ['deficient'] 1. ~ in 2. (misc.) to be found ~

war I *n.* 1. to conduct, fight, wage ~ against, with 2. to make ~ 3. to declare ~ on; to go to ~ over 4. to escalate, step up a ~ 5. to lose; win a ~ 6. to ban, outlaw ~ 7. to end a ~ 8. an all-out, full-scale, total; global, world ~ 9. a civil; cold; defensive; holy; hot, shooting; limited, local; offensive; revolutionary; world ~ 10. an atomic, nuclear, thermonuclear; conventional ~; star ~s 11. a gang; price ~ 12. a ~ of aggression; attrition; extermination; nerves 13. a ~ breaks out; rages; spreads (the ~ spread to the Balkans) 14. an act of ~ 15. a ~ against; between (a ~ against an aggressor; a ~ between former allies) 16. at ~ with (to be at ~ with one's neighbors) 17. (misc.) a theater of ~; a state of ~ (to be in a state of ~ with a country)

war II *v.* 1. (d; intr.) to ~ against, with (to ~ with one's neighbors) 2. (d; intr.) to ~ over (to ~ over disputed territory)

war clouds *n.* ~ gather

war crime *n.* 1. to commit a ~ 2. to prosecute ~s

ward *n.* ['hospital room'] 1. an emergency; maternity, obstetrics; pediatrics; private (BE) ('not under the National Health Service') ~ 2. in, on a ~ (to work in the emergency ~; who works in/on this ~?)

warden *n.* 1. a prison ~ (AE; BE has *governor*) 2. (BE) a traffic ~ 3. an air-raid ~ USAGE NOTE: An AE *prison warden* should not be confused with a BE *prison warder*, who in AE is a *prison guard*.

wardrobe *n.* ['clothes'] 1. an autumn (esp. BE), fall (AE); spring; summer; winter ~ 2. (misc.) I bought a whole new ~ for the cruise

warehouse *n.* a bonded ~

wares *n.* to hawk, peddle one's ~

warfare *n.* armored; atomic, nuclear; biological; chemical; conventional; desert; economic; germ; global; guerrilla; jungle; modern; naval; psychological; push-button; trench ~

war games *n.* to hold, stage ~

warhead *n.* a nuclear ~

warm *v.* (d; intr.) to ~ to ('to begin to like') (I was just ~ing to the task)

warm front *n.* a ~ approaches; forms

warmth *n.* body ~

warm up *v.* 1. (D; intr.) to ~ for (the players were ~ing up for the game) 2. (d; intr.) to ~ to (after a few drinks he ~ed up to the other guests)

warn *v.* 1. (D; tr.) to ~ about, against, of (they ~ed me about his bad temper; I ~ed him against driving on ice; the police ~ed us of the pickpockets) 2. (H) they ~ed him to be careful; I ~ed her not to go 3. (L; may have an object) she ~ed (us) that the winter would be severe

warning *n.* 1. to give, issue, send; shout a ~ 2. to heed; receive a ~ 3. an advance; cryptic; dire; tacit ~ 4. a storm ~ 5. a ~ to (a ~ to all; let this be a ~ to you) 6. a ~ to + inf. (a ~ to watch out for pickpockets) 7. a ~ that + clause (they issued a ~ that the escaped criminals were dangerous) 8. without ~

warpath *n.* (usu. colloq. and humorous) 1. to go on the ~ 2. to be on the ~ (they are on the ~ again)

warrant I *n.* 1. to issue a ~ (the court issued a search ~) 2. to swear out a ~ against smb. 3. to serve a ~ on (a ~ was served on her) 4. an arrest; bench; death; search ~ (to sign smb.'s death ~) (also fig.) 5. a ~ to + inf. (the police have a ~ to search the house) 6. (misc.) a ~ is out for his arrest

warrant II *v.* 1. (K) ('to justify') nothing ~ed his behaving like that 2. (L) ('to guarantee') I cannot ~ that the coins are genuine 3. (formal and rare) (M) I cannot ~ the coins to be genuine

warranty *n.* 1. to give a ~ 2. an implied; limited; special ~ 3. a ~ expires, runs out 4. a ~ on (a two-year ~ on a new car) 5. under ~ (the new car is still under ~)

warren *n.* a rabbit ~

warship *n.* 1. to commission; launch a ~ 2. to command a ~

wart *n.* to remove a ~

wartime *n.* during, in ~

wary *adj.* ~ of (be ~ of strangers)

wash I *n.* ['laundry'] 1. to do the ~ 2. to hang out the ~ 3. the weekly ~ ['installation for washing'] 4. a car ~

wash II *v.* 1. (D; tr.) to ~ for (would you please ~ the dishes for me?) 2. (misc.) to be ~ed overboard USAGE NOTE: In AE, *to wash up* means 'to wash one's hands and face'; in BE, it means 'to do the dishes'.

washcloth *n.* 1. to soap up a ~ 2. to wring out a ~

wash down *v.* (D; tr.) to ~ with (to ~ a meal with a glass of beer)

washing machine *n.* to run, use a ~

wasp *n.* ~s sting

waste *n.* 1. to cause ~ 2. to cut down on ~ 3. hazardous; nuclear; radioactive; solid; toxic ~s 4. (misc.) to go to ~ ('to be wasted'); to lay ~ to ('to destroy'); a terrible ~ of time and money

wasteful *adj.* 1. ~ of (~ of natural resources) 2. ~ to + inf. (it's ~ to use so much fuel)

wasteland *n.* 1. to reclaim ~ 2. a desolate ~

watch I *n.* ['timepiece'] 1. to set; wind (up) a ~ 2. to synchronize ~es 3. a pocket; self-winding; waterproof; wrist ~ 4. an analog; digital ~ 5. a ~ is fast; right; slow 6. a ~ goes; keeps time; runs down; stops ['surveillance'] 7. to keep, maintain a ~ on 8. a close ~ 9. on the ~ for (to be on the ~ for bargains) ['sailor's duty'] 10. to stand ~ 11. on ~ (several sailors were on ~) ['auxiliary police'] (esp. AE) 12. a crime; town ~ ['preliminary warning'] (esp. AE) 13. a storm ~

watch II *v.* 1. (d; intr.) to ~ for (to ~ for the postman) 2. (d; intr.) to ~ over (to ~ over one's property) 3. (I) we ~ed them enter the auditorium 4. (J) we ~ed them entering the auditorium 5. (Q) ~ how it's done

watcher *n.* ['observer'] a China (colloq.); Kremlin (colloq.); poll ~

watching *n.* ['observation'] 1. to bear ~ (his activities bear ~) ('his activities should be watched') ['act of watching'] 2. bird ~

watchman *n.* a night ~

watch out *v.* 1. (D; intr.) to ~ for 2. (esp. AE) (L; used in the imper.) ~ that she doesn't fool you

water I *n.* 1. to draw, run ~ (for a bath) 2. to add ~ 3. to drink; sip ~ 4. to pour; spill ~ 5. to splash; sprinkle; squirt ~ on 6. to boil, sterilize; chlorinate; distill; filter; fluoridate; purify; soften ~ 7. to drain ~ from 8. to pollute ~ 9. boiling; carbonated; clear; cold; contaminated, polluted; distilled; drinking, potable; fresh; hard; heavy; holy; hot; ice; mineral; murky; rain; rose; running; safe; salt; salty; sea; soda; soft; stagnant; tepid; warm ~ 10. ~ boils; evaporates; flows, pours, runs; freezes; leaks; oozes; rises; vaporizes 11. a body of ~ 12. by ~ (to travel by ~) 13. under ~ (after the flood our basement was under ~) 14. (misc.) to make/pass ~ ('to urinate'); to hold ~ ('to be valid') (your theory doesn't hold ~); to tread ~ (when swimming); ~ under the bridge ('past

events that are done with'); to pour cold ~ on ('to discourage'); to keep one's head above ~ ('to keep out of difficulty'); toilet ~ ('liquid used as a skin freshener')

water II *v.* (misc.) to make smb.'s mouth ~ ('to create a desire or appetite in smb.'); her mouth ~s at the sight of popcorn

watercolors *n.* to paint in ~

waterfront *n.* along, on the ~

waters *n.* 1. flood ~ (the flood ~ receded) 2. coastal; international; navigable; territorial ~ 3. in ~ (the ship was in international ~) 4. (misc.) to fish in muddy/troubled ~ ('to attempt to stir up trouble'); to take the ~ ('to take a water cure')

water table *n.* the ~ is high; low

waterway *n.* an inland ~

waterworks *n.* a municipal ~

wave I *n.* ['moving ridge on the surface of water'] 1. a high, tall; mountainous ~ 2. a tidal ~ 3. ~s break (on the rocks); crest ['upsurge'] 4. a crime ~ ['physical disturbance that is transmitted in the propagation of sound or light'] 5. light; radio; sound; transverse ~s 6. long; medium; short ~s ['brain rhythm'] 7. an alpha; brain ~ ['period of weather'] 8. a cold; heat ~ ['reaction'] 9. a shock ~ ['waviness of the hair'] 10. a permanent ~ USAGE NOTE: In colloq. BE, a *brain wave* can also mean a 'sudden bright idea', which in AE is a *brainstorm*. In colloq. BE, a *brainstorm* is a 'sudden mental aberration'. However, the verb *to brainstorm* (as in *a brainstorming session*) is now CE.

wave II *v.* 1. (A) ~ goodbye to them; or: ~ them goodbye 2. (D; intr., tr.) to ~ at, to (~ to them; she ~d her arm at me)

wave back *v.* (D; intr.) to ~ at, to (she ~d back at/ to us)

wavelength *n.* ['manner of thinking'] (colloq.) to be on the same ~; to operate on different ~s

waver *v.* (D; intr.) to ~ between (to ~ between two possibilities)

wax I *n.* sealing ~

wax II *v.* 1. (s) ('to become') to ~ indignant; to ~ eloquent over ('to express one's enthusiasm concerning') 2. (misc.) to ~ and wane

way *n.* ['path', route'] 1. to blaze, clear, pave, prepare; smoothe the ~ for (to pave the ~ for reform) 2. to take the (easy) ~ (out of a difficult situation) 3. to lead; point, show the ~ 4. to edge; elbow; fight; force; hack; jostle; make; muscle push; shove; squeeze; thread; tunnel; wedge work one's ~ through; to (to elbow one's ~ through a crowd; the battalion fought its ~ through enemy lines to the coast; he pushed his ~ through the mob; to shove one's ~ through the revelers; we made our ~ to the door; to tunnel one's ~ to freedom) 5. to twist; wend, wind one's ~ (the river winds its ~ to the sea) 6. to find one's ~ 7. to worm one's ~ (into smb.'s confidence) 8. to know the ~ to (do you know the ~ to the station?) 9. to lose one's ~ 10. (BE) a permanent ~ ('a railroad track') 11. the ~ from; to (he kept chattering all the ~ from our house to the airport) 12. the ~ into, to (the ~ into the park; can you show me the

~ to the station?) 13. the ~ out of (the ~ out of the city; show me the ~ out of this building; there is no easy ~ out of this mess) 14. on the ~ (a letter is on the ~; she is on her ~ to the airport) 15. (misc.) to work one's ~ through college; out of harm's ~; to make one's ~ in life; to see one's ~ clear to do smt.; they went their separate ~s; to come to a parting of the ~s; by ~ of ('via'); to go the ~ of all flesh ('to be mortal'); to know one's ~ around ('to be familiar with procedures') ['room for movement'] 16. to make ~ for 17. in the ~ (to be/stand in the ~; to get in smb.'s ~) 18. out of the ~ (to get out of the ~) ['progress'] 19. under ~ (an investigation is under ~) ['distance'] 20. to come; go a long ~ ['direction'] 21. this ~; that ~; the other ~ (she went that ~; please step this ~; they went the other ~) ['aspect, respect'] 22. in a certain ~ (in every ~; in no ~; in more ~s than one) ['manner, method'] 23. to find a ~ (they found a ~ to spend less money on electricity) 24. the proper, right; wrong ~ 25. charming, winsome ~s 26. that; this ~ (do it this ~) 27. the ~ to + inf. (show me the ~ to work this washing machine; that's the ~ to do it; there is no easy ~ to learn a new language) 28. in a certain ~ (in her own ~; in such a ~ that...; in a small ~) 29. (misc.) to my ~ of thinking; to mend one's ~s; to fall into evil ~s ['purpose'] 30. by ~ of (by ~ of apology; by ~ of example; by ~ of illustration) ['effective manner'] 31. to have a ~ with (she has a ~ with children) ['goal'] 32. to get, have one's ~ (she always gets her ~) ['misc.'] 33. to make one's ~ in the world; to get under ~ ('to start out'); in a ~ ('to some degree'); to go out of one's ~ ('to make a special effort'); to give ~ ('to collapse'); to pay one's own ~ ('to pay for oneself'); to be in the family ~ ('to be pregnant'); by the ~ ('incidentally'); on the ~ out ('becoming obsolescent'); there are no two ~s about it ('it is definitely true'); out our ~ ('where we live'); we are in a fair ~ to get our new library ('it appears as if we will get our new library'); this compromise goes a long ~ towards resolving our differences; the ~ to smb.'s heart USAGE NOTE: Constructions such as *to hack one's way through the jungle* cannot be passivized. Compare *they hacked a path through the jungle--a path was hacked (by them) through the jungle.*

weak *adj.* 1. ~ at, in (he's ~ in mathematics) 2. ~ from, with (~ with hunger)

weakened *adj.* ~ by

weakness *n.* ['quality of being weak'] 1. to reveal, show ~ 2. in (his ~ in mathematics) ['fondness'] 3. a ~ for (a ~ for chocolate)

wealth *n.* ['abundance of material possessions'] 1. to accumulate, acquire, amass, attain ~ 2. to dissipate, squander ~ 3. to flaunt one's ~ 4. fabulous, untold; hereditary ~ ['abundance of resources'] 5. mineral; natural ~ (the natural ~ of a country) ['abundance, profusion'] 6. a ~ of information

wean *v.* 1. (D; tr.) to ~ from (to ~ a calf from its mother) 2. (misc.) to ~ smb. away from bad company

weapon *n.* 1. to load a ~ 2. to fire a ~ 3. to brandish; carry; draw; handle a ~ 4. to calibrate; zero in a ~ 5. to lay down, throw down one's ~s 6. a concealed; deadly ~ 7. automatic; defensive; heavy; light; offensive; semiautomatic ~s 8. atomic, nuclear, thermonuclear; conventional ~s 9. (misc.) (they entered the building) with drawn ~s/with ~s drawn; the ultimate ~ ('nuclear missiles')

wear I *n.* ['clothing'] 1. beach; casual; children's; evening; everyday; ladies'; men's; sports ~ ['wearing out'] 2. to save ~ and tear (on)

wear II *v.* 1. (N; used with an adjective) she ~s her hair short 2. (s) my patience is ~ing thin

weary I *adj.* ~ of (they grew ~ of his preaching)

weary II *v.* (d; intr.) to ~ of (to ~ of one's job)

weasel *v.* (colloq.) (AE) to ~ out of ('to evade') (to ~ out of one's obligations)

weather *n.* 1. to forecast, predict the ~ 2. (good) beautiful; clear, fair; dry; fine, good, nice, pleasant; mild; seasonable ~ 3. (bad) atrocious, bad, beastly, bleak, foul, gloomy, inclement; threatening; ugly ~ 4. (rainy) cloudy, overcast; foggy; rainy; unsettled; wet ~ 5. (warm) hot; humid, muggy; sultry; sweltering; tropical; warm ~ 6. (cold) cold; cool; freezing; polar; windy; wintry ~ 7. the ~ clears up 8. ~ sets in (bad ~ set in) 9. in ~ (restaurants lose customers in bad ~)

weather forecast see **weather report**

weather report *n.* to give the ~

weather stripping *n.* to install, put on ~

weave I *n.* a plain; satin; twill ~

weave II *v.* 1. (C) she wove a basket for us; or: she wove us a basket 2. (d; tr.) to ~ around, round (she wove the story around a specific theme) 3. (d; tr.) to ~ from, out of (she wants to ~ a scarf from this wool) 4. (d; tr.) ('to insert') to ~ into (to ~ some humor into a plot) 5. (misc.) to ~ in and out of traffic

web *n.* 1. to spin; weave a ~ 2. an intricate, tangled ~ (a tangled ~ of intrigue) 3. a spider ~ USAGE NOTE: Spiders *spin* webs. People *weave* webs (the author wove a web of mystery).

wedded *adj.* (cannot stand alone) ~ to (~ to tradition)

wedding *n.* 1. to officiate at, perform a ~ 2. to attend a ~ 3. a big; (humorous) shotgun ~ 4. at a ~

wedding anniversary *n.* a diamond; golden; silver ~

wedding cake *n.* to cut the ~

wedding date *n.* to set a ~

wedding day *n.* on smb.'s ~

wedge I *n.* to drive a ~ between; into

wedge II *v.* 1. (d; intr., tr.) to ~ between; into 2. (N; used with an adjective) she ~d the door open

wedged *adj.* (cannot stand alone) ~ between

wedlock *n.* 1. to join in ~ 2. out of ~ (born out of ~)

weed out *v.* (D; tr.) to ~ from

weeds *n.* 1. to pull ~ 2. to kill ~

week *n.* 1. to spend a ~ (somewhere) 2. last; next; this ~ 3. a ~ from (Tuesday) 4. by the ~ (she is paid by the ~) 5. during the ~ 6. for a ~ (they came here for a ~) 7. for ~s (she hasn't been here for ~s; AE also has: she hasn't been here in ~s) 8.

in a ~ (they'll be here in a ~) 9. (misc.) (AE) freshman ~ USAGE NOTE: In the meaning 'a week from Tuesday', BE also has--a week on Tuesday, on Tuesday week. Note also the BE expressions--she arrived a week last Tuesday; she will arrive a week next Tuesday.

weekday *n.* on ~s; AE also has: ~s (she works on ~s)

weekend *n.* 1. to spend a ~ somewhere 2. at (BE), during, over (esp. AE) the ~ 3. on ~s (I work on ~s) 4. (AE) ~s (she works ~s) 5. (BE) at ~s (he works at ~s)

weeknight *n.* on ~s; AE also has: ~s (she works on ~s)

weep *v.* 1. (d; intr.) to ~ about, over (to ~ over one's misfortune) 2. (d; intr.) to ~ for (to ~ for joy) 3. (misc.) to ~ oneself to sleep; I wept on seeing them so poor

weevil *n.* an alfalfa; boll ~

weigh *v.* 1. to ~ heavily 2. (d; intr.) ('to count') to ~ against (his testimony will ~ heavily against you) 3. (d; tr.) ('to balance') to ~ against (to ~ one argument against another) 4. (d; intr.) ('to press') to ~ on (legal problems ~ed heavily on her mind) 5. (P; intr.) ('to have a weight') the suitcase ~s quite a lot

weigh down *v.* (D; tr.) to ~ with (we were ~ed down with packages)

weigh in *v.* (D; intr.) to ~ at (the boxer ~ed in at one hundred fifty pounds)

weight I *n.* ['amount weighed, heaviness'] 1. to gain, put on ~ 2. to lose, take off ~ 3. dead; gross; minimum; net ~ 4. atomic; avoirdupois; birth; molecular ~ 5. under a ~ (the table collapsed under the ~ of the food) ['device used for its heaviness in athletic exercises'] 6. to lift ~s 7. heavy; light ~s 8. a set of ~s ['importance'] 9. to carry ~ 10. to add; attach, give, lend ~ to 11. considerable ~ 12. (misc.) to throw one's ~ around/about (BE) ('to flaunt one's influence'); to pull one's ~ ('to do one's fair share')

weight II *v.* (D; tr.) ('to slant') to ~ against (the evidence was ~ed against me)

weird *adj.* (colloq.) 1. ~ about (there is smt. ~ about them) 2. ~ that + clause (it's ~ that you never noticed her)

welch see **welsh**

welcome I *adj.* 1. perfectly ~ 2. ~ to (you are ~ to my share) 3. ~ to + inf. (you are ~ to borrow my car at any time) 4. (misc.) to make smb. feel ~

welcome II *n.* 1. to bid, extend, give a ~ to 2. to receive a ~ 3. to overstay one's ~ 4. a cordial, enthusiastic, hearty, rousing, royal, warm ~ (we gave them a rousing ~) 5. a chilly, cool ~ 6. a ~ from; to (we received a warm ~ from the mayor; the immigrants received a cool ~ to their new country)

welcome III *v.* 1. to ~ cordially, enthusiastically, warmly 2. to ~ coolly 3. (D; tr.) to ~ to (we ~d them to our city)

welcome mat *n.* (colloq.) (esp. AE) to put out the ~ for smb.

welfare *n.* ['governmental financial aid'] 1. public ~ 2. (esp. US) on ~ (to be on ~; to go on ~)

['well-being'] 3. to promote the public ~ 4. the general; public ~ 5. for smb.'s ~

well I *adv.* 1. to leave ~ enough alone (AE)/to leave ~ alone (BE) ('not to interfere with smt that is satisfactory') 2. (misc.) are things going ~ with you?

well II *n.* ['hole dug to tap a supply of water'] 1. to bore, dig, drill, sink a ~ 2. an abandoned; deep ~ 3. an artesian; oil ~ 4. a ~ dries up

well-being *n.* 1. to threaten smb.'s ~ 2. material; physical; psychological ~

well-disposed *adj.* ~ towards

well-grounded *adj.* ~ in

well-informed *adj.* ~ about

well-intentioned *adj.* ~ towards

well-known *adj.* 1. ~ to 2. ~ that + clause (it's ~ that she intends to retire next year)

well up *v.* (D; intr.) to ~ with (her eyes ~ed up with tears)

welsh *v.* (this verb is offensive to Welsh people) (D; intr.) to ~ on (to ~ on a bet)

welt *n.* to raise a ~ (on the skin)

west I *adj., adv.* ~ of

west II *n.* 1. in, to the ~ 2. (US) the Wild West 3. (misc.) ~ (US) ('in the Am. west'); up ~ (London slang) ('to the West End of London from the East End'); to go ~ (esp. BE; old-fashioned) ('to die')

wet *adj.* 1. dripping, soaking ~ 2. ~ with (~ with dew) 3. (misc.) she got her shoes ~

whack I *n.* (colloq.) ['blow'] 1. to give smb. a ~ ['attempt'] 2. to take a ~ at 3. to have the first ~ at ['misc.'] 4. out of ~ (he threw his shoulder out of ~)

whack II *v.* (colloq.) (O) ('to strike') I'll ~ you one

whale *n.* ['sea mammal'] 1. to harpoon a ~ 2. a blue; bowhead; sperm, white ~ 3. a school of ~s 4. a young ~ is a calf 5. a female ~ is a cow 6. a male ~ is a bull ['misc.'] 7. a ~ of a good time ('a very good time')

whammy *n.* (slang) (AE) ['jinx'] to put a (the) ~ on smb.

wharf *n.* at; on a ~ (the ship was tied up at a ~)

what *determiner, pronoun* 1. ~ about, of ~ about them?) 2. (used in exclamatory sentences) ~ a (~ a day!) 3. (misc.) (colloq.) she has ~ it takes ('she is very capable'); to know ~'s ~ ('to understand clearly what the situation is'); ~ else is new? (esp. AE); so ~? ~ on earth can she mean?

wheat *n.* 1. to grow; harvest ~ 2. to grind; thresh ~ (to grind ~ into flour) 3. summer; winter ~ 4. club; common; drum; hybrid ~ 5. cracked; whole ~ USAGE NOTE: AE has *whole wheat bread, whole wheat flour;* BE has *wholemeal bread, wholemeal flour.*

wheedle *v.* 1. (d; tr.) to ~ from, out of (to ~ information from smb.) 2. (d; tr.) to ~ into (to ~ smb. into doing smt.)

wheel *n.* ['circular rim or solid disc joined to a hub that turns'] 1. to spin; turn a ~ 2. to align; balance; rotate ~s (on a car) 3. a balance; driving; front; idler; mill; paddle; potter's; ratchet; rear; retractable; roulette; spinning; sprocket; undershot;

water ~ 4. a big (BE), Ferris ~ (in an amusement park) 5. a ~ spins; turns 6. (misc.) to break on the ~; (humorous) to reinvent the ~ ['device that turns a car'] 7. to take the ~ 8. a steering ~ (to turn the steering ~) 9. (to be) at the ~ (who was at the ~ when the accident took place?) ['misc.'] 10. a big ~ ('an influential person')

wheelbarrow *n.* to push, roll a ~

wheelchair *n.* 1. to push a ~ 2. a motorized ~

wherewithal *n.* ['resources'] 1. the ~ for (to have the ~ for a trip abroad) 2. the ~ to + inf. (they didn't have the ~ to conduct a successful political campaign)

which *determiner, pronoun* ~ of (~ of them do you know?) USAGE NOTE: The use of the preposition *of* is necessary when a pronoun follows. When a noun follows, the use of *which of the* limits the meaning--which student(s) did you see? which of the students whom we had discussed did you see?

whiff *n.* (colloq.) ['smell, odor'] 1. to get, have; take a ~ of (to get a good ~ of tear gas) 2. to give smb. a ~ of smt. 3. at a ~ (she lost consciousness at the first ~ of ether)

whim *n.* 1. to pursue; satisfy a ~ 2. an idle; sudden ~ 3. on a ~ (they went there on a ~)

whine *v.* 1. (B) she ~d a few words to them 2. (D; intr.) to ~ about (he kept ~ing about his bad luck) 3. (L; to) he ~d (to us) that he had been cheated

whip I *n.* ['lash used for whipping'] 1. to crack, snap a ~ ['dessert made by whipping'] 2. a prune ~ ['member of a political party who enforces party discipline'] 3. a majority; minority; party ~

whip II *v.* 1. (d; tr.) ('to beat') to ~ into (to ~ eggs into a froth) 2. (colloq.) (d; tr.) ('to bring') to ~ into (the sergeant ~ped the recruits into shape) 3. (d; tr.) ('to incite') to ~ into (the speaker ~ped the crowd into a frenzy)

whip hand *n.* ['control'] to get; have the ~ over

whipping *n.* ['beating'] 1. to get, receive, take a ~ (from) 2. to give smb. a ~

whip-round *n.* (BE) ['collection'] to have a ~

whirl *n.* (colloq.) ['try'] 1. to give smt. a ~ ['hectic activity'] 2. the social ~

whirlpool *n.* to be drawn into a ~

whisk I *n.* an egg ~ (BE; AE has *eggbeater*)

whisk II *v.* (P; tr.) ('to move quickly') they were ~ed into the hotel; the important visitors were ~ed through customs

whisk away *v.* see **whisk off**

whiskers *n.* ['beard'] 1. to grow ~ 2. to shave off one's ~ 3. rough ~

whiskey, whisky *n.* 1. to age; distill, produce ~ 2. straight ('undiluted') ~ 3. blended; corn; Irish; rye; Scotch ~ 4. ~ ages USAGE NOTE: The spelling *whiskey* is usu. used in Ireland and the US.

whisk off *v.* (colloq.) (d; tr.) to ~ to (they were ~ed off to prison)

whisper I *n.* 1. a stage ~ 2. in a ~ (to speak in a ~)

whisper II *v.* 1. (B) he ~ed a few words to her 2. (d; intr.) to ~ about (what were they ~ing about?) 3. (L; to) she ~ed (to us) that she was preparing a surprise party

whistle I *n.* ['instrument that produces a whistling sound'] 1. to blow (on) a ~ 2. a bird; factory; police; referee's ~ 3. a ~ blows, sounds ['act of whistling'] 4. to give a ~ 5. a shrill ~ ['misc.'] 6. as clean as a ~ ('very clean'); to blow the ~ on smb. ('to reveal smb.'s evil intentions')

whistle II *v.* 1. (B) she ~d a song to me 2. (D; intr.) to ~ at; to (who ~d at you?) 3. (D; intr.) to ~ with (to ~ with surprise) USAGE NOTE: One whistles *to* smb. to attract her/his attention. One whistles *at* smb. to express one's feelings about that person.

white feather *n.* ['symbol of cowardice'] to show the ~

white flag *n.* ['symbol of surrender'] to show the ~

white paper *n.* ['official government report'] to issue a ~

white slavery *n.* to sell smb. into ~

whittle *v.* 1. (D; intr.) to ~ at (to ~ at a piece of wood) 2. (D; tr.) to ~ into (to ~ a reed into a whistle) 3. (D; tr.) to ~ out of (to ~ a whistle out of a reed)

whittle away *v.* (D; intr.) to ~ at (to ~ at smb.'s alibi)

whole *n.* 1. to constitute, form a ~ 2. as a ~ 3. on the ~ (the situation is, on the ~, satisfactory)

whole hog *n.* (colloq.) (esp. AE) ['the whole way'] to go (the) ~

wholesale *adv.* to buy; sell ~

whoop *n.* ['loud cry'] to emit, let out a ~

whoopee *n.* (colloq.) ['boisterous fun'] to make ~

whooping cough *n.* to catch (the) ~

wicked *adj.* 1. ~ of (that was ~ of him) 2. ~ to + inf. (it's ~ to lie)

wide *adj.* ['deviating'] (cannot stand alone) ~ of (you are ~ of the mark)

widow *n.* a grass; war ~

widower *n.* a grass ~

width *n.* in ~ (ten feet in ~)

wife *n.* 1. (old-fashioned) to take a ~ 2. to beat; desert, leave one's ~ 3. an abused, battered; common-law; estranged ~; ex-wife, former; jealous; unfaithful ~ 4. (misc.) he had two children by his first ~

wig *n.* 1. to wear a ~ 2. to put on; take off a ~

wild I *adj.* ['enthusiastic'] (colloq.) 1. (cannot stand alone) ~ about, over (audiences went ~ over the new play) ['furious'] 2. ~ with (~ with anger) ['out of control'] 3. to run ~

wild II *n.* ['wilderness'] in the ~ (to live in the ~)

wilderness *n.* 1. a desolate; trackless; unexplored ~ 2. in the ~

wildfire *n.* to spread like ~ ('to spread very quickly')

wild oats *n.* ['youthful excesses'] to sow one's ~

will I *n.* ['desire'] 1. to impose one's ~ (on) 2. to implement the ~ (of the majority) 3. the ~ to + inf. (the ~ to survive) 4. (misc.) a clash of (strong) ~s; against smb.s ~; with a ~ (to work with the ~ to succeed) ['attitude'] 5. to show good ~ 6. to bear no ill ~ ['choice'] 7. free ~ (of their own free ~) 8. at ~ (to fire at ~) ['legal document disposing of an estate'] 9. to draw up, make, make out a ~ 10. to change a ~ 11. to administer; execute a ~ 12. to probate, validate a ~ 13. to challenge, contest a ~ 14. to break, overturn a ~ 15. to repudiate a ~ 16. a deathbed ~ ['spirit'] ['power to make decisions'] 17. to break smb.'s ~ 18. an indomitable, iron, strong; inflexible ~

will II v. (A) he ~ed his entire estate to her; or: he ~ed her his entire estate

will III v. (auxiliary) (F) she ~ return

willies n. (colloq.) ['jitters'] 1. to get the ~ 2. to give smb. the ~ (her behavior gives me the ~)

willing adj. ~ to (she is ~ to help)

willingness n. 1. to demonstrate, show ~ 2. to express ~ 3. the ~ to + inf. (she expressed the ~ to work for us)

willpower n. 1. to demonstrate ~ 2. the ~ to + inf. (do you have the ~ to stick to the diet?)

wily adj. ~ of (that was ~ of him)

win I n. to chalk up a ~

win II v. 1. to ~ easily, hands down 2. (D; intr.) to ~ against (to ~ against considerable odds)

wince v. 1. (D; intr.) to ~ at (to ~ at the thought of going back to work) 2. (misc.) to ~ in pain

winch n. to operate, use a ~

wind I n. /wind/ ['movement, current of air'] 1. an adverse; balmy, gentle, light; biting, cold, cutting, icy; brisk, heavy, high, stiff, strong; fair, favorable; gale-force; gusty; head; raw; tail; trade ~ 2. the prevailing ~s 3. the ~ blows; falls, subsides; howls; picks up 4. a blast, gust of ~ 5. a down; up ~ 6. (misc.) as free as the ~ ['knowledge'] 7. to get ~ of smt. ['breath'] 8. to catch, get one's second ~ 9. out of ~ ['misc.'] 10. to break ~ ('to expel rectal gas'); in the ~ ('imminent'); to take the ~ out of smb.'s sails ('to deflate smb.'); to see how the ~ blows ('to see what is likely to happen'); to sow the ~ and reap the whirlwind

wind II v. /waynd/ 1. (d; tr.) to ~ around, round (she wound the string around her finger) 2. (P; intr.) the procession wound through the town 3. (misc.) to ~ smb. around one's little finger ('to manipulate smb.')

winded adj. ['out of breath'] easily ~

windfall n. ['good fortune'] 1. to get a ~ 2. a sudden, unexpected ~

windmill n. 1. a ~ turns 2. (misc.) to tilt at ~s ('to struggle with imaginary opponents')

window n. 1. to open a ~; to roll down a ~ (in a car) 2. to close, shut a ~; to roll up a ~ (in a car) 3. to clean, wash a ~ 4. a bay; bow; French; lattice; sash; shop; storm ~ 5. a ~ fogs up, sweats; frosts over

window shade n. (AE) 1. to lift, raise a ~ 2. to draw, drop, lower a ~ (BE has _blind_)

wind up v. ('to end up') 1. (d; intr.) to ~ with 2. (G) I wound up paying for everyone 3. (P; intr.) to ~ out in the cold 4. (s) he wound up worse off than when he started

wine n. 1. to make, produce ~ 2. dry; sweet ~ 3. cooking; dessert; mulled; red; rosé; sacramental; sparkling; table; vintage; white ~ 4. domestic; imported ~ 5. a house ~ (of a restaurant) 6. ~ ferments USAGE NOTE: The phrase _domestic wine_ seems to be reserved for wine produced in English-speaking countries. English-speakers in France or Italy, for example, usu. do not refer to

French or Italian wine as _domestic_.

wing n. ['faction of a political party'] 1. a conservative; liberal; radical ~ ['a bird's forelimb'] 2. to spread one's ~s (also fig.) (the bird spread its ~s and flew off) 3. (misc.) to clip smb.'s ~s ('to restrict smb.'s freedom') ['protection'] 4. to take smb. under one's ~ ['act of flying'] 5. to take ~ (also fig.) 6. on the ~ ['extension, annex of a building'] 7. to add a ~ (to a building) 8. see **fender** ['misc.'] 9. to wait in the ~s ('to await the opportunity to take over a job')

wink I n. 1. to give smb. a ~ 2. a suggestive ~ 3. (misc.) I didn't get a ~ of sleep last night; to take forty ~s ('to take a brief nap')

wink II v. (D; intr.) to ~ at (also fig.: the police ~ed at illegal gambling)

winner n. 1. a likely; sure ~ 2. (misc.) to be on to a (sure) ~ (at a racetrack)

win over v. (d; tr.) to ~ to (we won them over to our side)

winter n. 1. a cold, hard, harsh, severe; mild ~ 2. in, over (the) ~ 3. in the dead of ~

wipe v. 1. (d; tr.) to ~ off ('to erase from') (to ~ a city off the map) 2. (D; tr.) to ~ on (she ~d her hands on the towel) 3. (N, used with an adjective) he ~d the dishes dry

wipers n. 1. to turn on the ~ 2. windscreen (BE), windshield (AE) ~

wire I n. ['long metal thread'] 1. to string ~ 2. barbed; chicken; copper ~ 3. a trip ~ ['cable conducting electric current'] 4. to cross, jump ~s (in order to start a car) 5. to tap ~s 6. telephone ~s ['cablegram, telegram'] 7. to send a ~ ['finish line'] (also fig.) 8. (right) down to the ~ ('to the very end') 9. (misc.) to get in under the ~ ('to enter barely in time')

wire II v. 1. (A) ('to send by wire') we ~d the money to her; or: we ~d her the money 2. (d; intr.) ('to request by sending a wire') to ~ for (she ~d home for some money) 3. (D; tr.) ('to provide with wire') to ~ for (the auditorium was ~d for sound) 4. (d; tr.) ('to connect') to ~ to (the explosives were ~d to the door) 5. (H; no passive) ('to inform by wire') we ~d them to return home immediately 6. (L; may have an object) ('to inform by wire') she ~d (us) that the manuscript had arrived 7. (Q; may have an object) we will ~ (you) where to meet

wire back v. (L; to) they ~d back (to us) that they would attend the conference

wireless n. (BE) (now less common than _radio_) see **radio 1-4**

wiring n. 1. defective, faulty ~ 2. electric ~

wisdom n. 1. to impart ~ 2. to doubt, question smb.'s ~ (to question the ~ of an action) 3. (the) conventional ~; infinite ~ 4. the ~ to + inf. (will they have the ~ to make the correct choice? 5. of ~ (a person of great ~)

wise adj. ['sagacious'] 1. ~ to + inf. (it was ~ of you to remain silent = you were ~ to remain silent) ['aware of'] (colloq.) 2. ~ to (she was ~ to their scheme; I finally got ~ to their tricks; they put me ~ to his tricks)

wisecrack I n. ['flippant remark'] 1. to make a ~

2. a ~ about

wisecrack II *v.* (colloq.) (L) ('to remark flippantly') she ~ed that she could earn more money at home

wise up *v.* (colloq.) (AE) (D; intr.) to ~ to (I finally ~d up to his tricks)

wish I *n.* ['desire'] 1. to make a ~ 2. to fulfill, realize a ~ 3. to get one's ~ 4. to express a ~ 5. to respect smb.'s ~ 6. a fervent, strong; unfulfilled ~ 7. the death ~ 8. a ~ for (a ~ for peace) 9. a ~ to + inf. (they expressed a ~ to visit the museum) 10. a ~ that + clause; subj. (the editor respected her ~ that the contribution not be/should not be announced publicly) 11. against smb.'s ~es (the project was carried out against our ~es) 12. in accordance with smb.'s ~es ['greetings'] 13. to extend, offer, send one's (best) ~es 14. one's best, good, warm, warmest ~es 15. one's ~es for (one's best ~es for the New Year)

wish II *v.* 1. (A; usu. without *to)* they ~ed us good luck 2. (D; intr.) to ~ for (we were ~ing for cool weather) 3. (E) I ~ to lodge a complaint 4. (formal) (H; no passive) do you ~ me to stay? 5. (L) we ~ that he would settle down 6. (misc.) to ~ smb. well ('to hope that things will go well for smb.')

wit I *n.* 1. to display, show ~ 2. acid, keen, mordant, penetrating, rapier-like, sharp, sophisticated, trenchant ~ 3. dry; quick, ready; sly ~ 4. (misc.) at one's ~'s end (see also **wits)**

wit II to ~ ('namely')

witchcraft *n.* to practice ~

witch-hunt *n.* to conduct a ~ against

withdraw *v.* (D; intr., tr.) to ~ from; to (our troops have withdrawn from the border area; to ~ money from a bank; to ~ to a safer area)

withdrawal *n.* ['removal of funds'] 1. to make a ~ 2. mass ~s 3. a ~ from (a ~ from an account) ['retreat'] (often mil.) 4. to carry out, make a ~ 5. to complete a ~ 6. an orderly; precipitate; strategic; tactical; unilateral ~ 7. a ~ from; to (a ~ to higher ground)

withhold *v.* (D; tr.) to ~ from (to ~ information from the police)

witness I *n.* ['testimony'] 1. to bear ~ to 2. false ~ (to bear false ~) ['one who testifies'] 3. to produce a ~ (the district attorney finally produced a credible ~) 4. to cross-examine; examine, interrogate, question; interview a ~; to hear ~es 5. to lead a ~ (one should not lead a ~) 6. to swear in a ~ 7. to confuse; discredit; trap a ~ 8. a character; competent; credible; defense; expert; hostile; key, material; prosecution; reliable ~ 9. a ~ is sworn in = a ~ takes the oath; a ~ testifies (under oath) 10. a ~ steps down 11. a ~ against (a ~ against one's former accomplices) 12. a ~ for (a ~ for the prosecution) 13. a ~ to (a ~ to an accident)

witness II *v.* (K) who ~ed his signing the documents?

witness box *n.* (BE) to go into the ~

witness stand *n.* (AE) to take the ~

wits *n.* 1. to collect one's ~ 2. the ~ to + inf. (he didn't have enough ~ to realize what was happening) 3. (misc.) keep your ~ about you! ('stay

alert!'); to live by one's ~

witty *adj.* ~ of (that was ~ of her)

wizard *n.* 1. a financial; mathematical ~ 2. a ~ at (a ~ at solving crossword puzzles)

wizardry *n.* sheer ~

wolf *n.* 1. ~ves howl 2. ~ves hunt in packs 3. a pack of ~ves 4. a young ~ is a pup 5. (misc.) to cry ~ ('to give a false alarm'); to keep the ~ from the door ('to provide the necessities'); a ~ in sheep's clothing ('one who disguises hostile intentions')

woman *n.* 1. to deliver a ~ (of a baby) 2. an attractive, beautiful, pretty; average; fat; grown; handsome; middle-aged; old; short; tall; thin; ugly; wise; young ~ 3. a divorced; married; single ~ 4. a career; professional; self-made; working ~ 5. an anchor ~; businesswoman; newspaperwoman 6. (AE) a cleaning ~ (BE has *charwoman, char)* 7. (BE) a lollipop ~ (AE has *crossing guard)* 8. (AE) enlisted women (BE has *other ranks)* 9. the other ~ ('a married man's paramour') 10. (misc.) a ~ of letters; a ~ of action; a ~ of the world; the ~ of the year USAGE NOTE: The terms *career woman* and *working woman* are becoming old-fashioned. (see also the Usage Note for **girl)**

womanhood *n.* to reach ~

wonder I *n.* 1. to perform, work a ~ 2. to do ~s for 3. a natural ~ 4. a ~ that + clause (it's a ~ that we didn't get lost; it's no small ~ that they had so much trouble) 5. in ~ (to look around in ~) 6. (misc.) the seven ~s of the world; the eighth ~ of the world

wonder II *v.* 1. to ~ really, very much (I really ~ if they'll come) 2. (D; intr.) to ~ about, at (to ~ about a problem) 3. (Q) I ~ why they left

wonderful *adj.* 1. ~ to + inf. (it was ~ to visit our national parks) 2. ~ that + clause (it was ~ that we could see each other)

wonderland *n.* a scenic ~

wont *adj.* (obsol. and rare) ['accustomed'] (cannot stand alone) ~ to + inf. (she is ~ to call at any time)

wood *n.* 1. to chop, cut ~ 2. to gather ~ 3. firewood; kindling ~ 4. a cord of ~ 5. (misc.) out of the ~ (BE)/~s (AE) ('safe from danger')

wool *n.* 1. to produce ~ 2. to comb; process; sort ~ 3. lamb's; steel, wire (BE) ~ 4. (BE) cotton ~ (AE has *absorbent cotton)* 5. (misc.) to pull the ~ over smb.'s eyes ('to deceive smb.')

woozy *adj.* (colloq.) ['dazed, dizzy'] ~ from (~ from lack of sleep)

word I *n.* ['independent, meaningful linguistic form'] 1. to coin a ~ 2. to pronounce, say, utter; write a ~ (to say a few ~s about smt.) 3. to mispronounce a ~ 4. to distort smb.'s ~s 5. to not mince any ~s ('to speak frankly') 6. angry, cross, sharp; choice; fighting; harsh; hasty; heated, hot; high-sounding; hollow, hypocritical; sincere; weasel ~s 7. an archaic, obsolete; borrowed; compound; dialectal, regional; foreign; four-letter, obscene; function; ghost; monosyllabic; native; nonce; portmanteau; simple; taboo ~ 8. a guide ~ (at the top of a page in a dictionary, reference work) 9. (misc.) (upon) my ~ ('really'); to hang on (to) smb.'s ~s ('to listen to smb. very attentively');

in so many ~s ('precisely'); of few ~s ('not talkative'); ~ for ~ ('verbatim'); she took the ~s right out of my mouth ('she said exactly what I wanted to say'); a household ('common') ~; to get a ~ in edgewise (AE)/edgeways (BE) ('to manage to say smt. in a dispute'); to have the last ~ ('to conclude an argument'); to put in a good ~ for smb. ('to plead smb.'s case'); in a ~ ('briefly'); a play on ~s ('a pun'); begin at the ~ go; one's dying ~s ['promise'] 10. to give one's ~ 11. to take smb.'s ~; to take smb. at her/his ~ 12. to break one's ~ 13. one's solemn ~; one's ~ of honor 14. one's ~ that + clause (she gave me her ~ that she would deliver the message) 15. of one's ~ (she's a woman of her ~) ('she keeps her promises') ['command'] 16. to give the ~ ['information, news'] 17. to bring; send ~ 18. to breathe, say a ~ (don't breathe a ~ about it to anyone) 19. to get ~ (we got advance ~ that the contract would be signed) 20. the latest ~ 21. advance ~ 22. ~ about, of (there was no ~ of the incident in the newspapers; she would like to say a few ~s about the incident) 23. ~ that + clause (they sent ~ that they would be late) ['conversation'] 24. to have a ~ with smb. about smt. (see also **words**) USAGE NOTE: The construction *I'd like to have a word with you* usu. indicates that the conversation will be of a serious nature. Compare *I had words with him* 'I had an argument with him'.

word II *v.* to ~ smt. strongly

word order *n.* (a) fixed; flexible; normal; reverse ~

words *n.* ['text'] 1. ~ to (a song) ['argument, discussion'] 2. to have ~ with smb. 3. to weigh ('consider carefully') one's ~ 4. heated; threatening ~

work I *n.* ['labor'] 1. to do ~ (they never do any ~) 2. to begin; quit, stop ~ (they quit ~ at one o'clock) 3. to take on ~ 4. to undo smb.'s ~ 5. backbreaking, hard; delicate; demanding; dirty, scut; easy, light; exhausting, tiring; physical ~ 6. meticulous, precise; shoddy, slipshod, sloppy ~ 7. fieldwork; paper ~ 8. (misc.) he never does a lick/ stitch (AE)/stroke of ~; to make short ~ of smt. ('to dispose of smt. quickly') ['employment'] 9. to go to ~ 10. to return to ~ 11. to take off from ~ 12. to leave ~ (early) 13. at ~ (they are still at ~) 14. out of ~ (they have been out of ~ for a week) ['result of research, labor, artistic effort'] 15. to exhibit; hang one's ~s (in a gallery) 16. a literary; scholarly ~ 17. collected; published; selected ~s 18. (misc.) ~ in progress; a ~ of art ['service'] 19. social ~ (to do social ~) 20. undercover ~ (to do undercover ~ for the police) ['treatment'] 21. root-canal ~ (to do root-canal ~ on smb.) ['misc.'] 22. to go to ~ on smb. ('to put pressure on smb.') (see also **works**)

work II *v.* 1. ('to labor') to ~ hard, strenuously 2. (d; intr.) to ~ against ('to oppose') (to ~ against a proposed law) 3. (d; intr.) to ~ at, on (they were ~ing on a new book; you have to ~ at being friendlier with people) 4. (d; intr.) ('to be employed; to labor') to ~ for (she ~s for a large firm; to ~ for a living) 5. (d; intr.) to ~ for ('to support') (to ~ for a good cause) 6. (d; refl.) ('to

excite') to ~ into (she ~ed herself into a rage) 7. (d; tr.) to ~ into ('to insert') (she ~ed a few jokes into her speech) 8. (d; intr.) to ~ through ('to go through') (to ~ through difficult material) 9. (d. intr.) ('to progress') to ~ towards (to ~ towards a common goal) 10. (d; intr.) ('to collaborate') to ~ with (to ~ closely with one's colleagues) 11. (misc.) to ~ far into the night; to ~ one's way through college; to ~ one's way through a crowd; I slowly ~ed my way through the long report; the committee ~ed to reduce tension; to ~ against the clock

worked up *adj.* (colloq.) ~ about, over (he got himself all ~ over a trifle)

worker *n.* 1. to hire, take on a ~ 2. to retrain; train ~s 3. to organize, unionize ~s 4. to dismiss, fire, sack (colloq.) a ~; to make a ~ redundant (as by eliminating her/his job) (BE) 5. an efficient, hard, indefatigable; idle; meticulous ~ 6. a blue-collar (esp. AE); full-time; immigrant; migrant; office; part-time; skilled; social; undocumented (AE); unemployed; unskilled; white-collar ~

working hours *n.* regular; staggered ~ (during regular ~)

workmanship *n.* 1. conscientious; delicate, exquisite, fine; meticulous ~ 2. poor, shoddy ~

workout *n.* ['exercise'] 1. to get, have a ~ 2. a daily ~

works *n.* ['construction projects'] 1. public ~ ['preparation'] (colloq.) 2. in the ~ ['operations'] 3. to gum up, mess up the ~ ['everything available'] (colloq.) 4. to give smb. the ~

workshop *n.* ['working seminar'] 1. to conduct a ~ 2. a ~ on

workup *n.* ['series of tests'] 1. to do a ~ 2. a diagnostic ~

work up *v.* 1. (d; refl., tr.) ('to excite') to ~ into (he ~ed himself up into a rage) 2. (d; refl., tr.) ('to incite') to ~ to (the orator ~ed the crowd up to a fever pitch) 3. (misc.) she ~ed her way up to the top

world *n.* ['earth'] 1. around, round the ~ (to travel around the ~) 2. (misc.) to see the ~ ('to travel to many parts of the earth') ['area, part of the earth'] 3. the free; known; Third ~ (in the Third ~) ['domain, realm, sphere'] 4. the animal; financial; literary; physical; scientific ~ 5. the academic; outside; real ~ (out in the real ~) ['period'] 6. the ancient; medieval; modern ~ (there are many problems in the modern ~) ['life, being'] 7. to bring (smb.) into the ~ 8. to come into the ~ 9. the next ~ ('life after death') ['misc.'] 10. out of this ~ ('remarkable'); ~s apart ('very far apart')

world's fair *n.* to hold, stage a ~

worm *v.* 1. (d; tr.) to ~ into (how did they ~ their way into the meeting?) 2. (d; intr., tr.) to ~ out of (to ~ out of an obligation; to ~ information out of smb.) 3. (misc.) to ~ one's way into smb.'s confidence

worried *adj.* 1. ~ sick 2. ~ about 3. ~ that + clause (we were ~ that she might not arrive on time)

worry I *n.* 1. to cause ~ 2. deep, serious ~ 3. financial ~ries 4. ~ about, over

worry II *v.* 1. (D; intr.) to ~ about, over (they ~ about you; I ~ried about them working so hard; to ~ over trifles) 2. (R) it ~ried me that they did not answer the telephone

worse *adj.* any ~ (will it be any ~ living in the city?)

worship I *n.* 1. ancestor; hero; idol; nature; public ~ 2. (misc.) a house of ~

worship II *v.* 1. to ~ reverently 2. (D; tr.) to ~ as (to ~ smb. as a god) 3. (misc.) I ~ the ground you walk on

worst *n.* to prepare for the ~

worth I *adj., prep.* 1. well ~ (the cost) 2. ~ to (how much is it ~ to you?) 3. (misc.) ~ one's salt ('worthy of respect for one's work')

worth II *n.* 1. intrinsic ~ 2. net ~ 3. (legal) comparable ~ (the theory of comparable ~) 4. of ~ (books of great ~)

worthwhile *adj.* 1. ~ for 2. ~ to + inf. (it's ~ for you to visit the exhibit)

worthy *adj.* (usu. does not stand alone) ~ of (~ of praise)

would *v.* (F) ~ you do it?

wound *n.* 1. to inflict a ~ on/upon smb. 2. to receive a ~ 3. to clean; dress; suture; swab a ~ 4. a deep; fatal, mortal; festering; flesh; gaping; light, slight; self-inflicted; serious, severe; superficial ~ (to receive a slight ~) 5. a bullet, gunshot; knife ~ 6. a ~ festers 7. (misc.) to lick one's ~s ('to recover from a beating')

wounded *adj.* fatally, mortally; lightly, slightly; seriously ~

wracked *adj.* ~ with (~ with pain)

wrangle *v.* 1. to ~ constantly, incessantly 2. (D; intr.) to ~ about, over; with

wrangling *n.* constant, incessant ~

wrap I *n.* freezer; plastic ~

wrap II *v.* 1. (d; tr.) to ~ around (to ~ a blanket around oneself) 2. (d; tr.) to ~ in (to ~ a child in a blanket)

wrapped up *adj.* ['engaged, busy'] ~ in (they are all ~ in campaigning)

wrapper *n.* a cellophane ~

wraps *n.* to keep a plan under ~ (colloq.) ('to keep a plan secret')

wrath *n.* (formal) 1. to bring down, incur smb.'s ~ 2. to visit one's ~ upon smb. 3. one's righteous ~

wreak *v.* (D; tr.) to ~ with (to ~ havoc with smb.)

wreath *n.* 1. to make, weave a ~ 2. to lay, place a ~ (they laid a ~ at the Tomb of the Unknown Soldier) 3. a bridal; Christmas; floral ~

wreck *n.* ['wrecked car'] 1. to tow a ~ ['person who has suffered a breakdown'] 2. a nervous ~

wreckage *n.* 1. to strew ~ (over a wide area) 2. to clear, remove ~

wrench I *n.* 1. monkey ~ 2. (AE) a lug ~ (BE has box spanner)

wrench II *v.* (d; tr.) to ~ from (he ~ed the handbag from the old woman)

wrest *v.* (d; tr.) to ~ from (to ~ power from a dictator)

wrestle *v.* (D; intr.) to ~ with (to ~ with various problems)

wrestler *n.* to pin; throw a ~

wrestling *n.* arm; catch-as-catch-can; Greco-Roman; Indian ~

wretch *n.* a poor ~

wretched *adj.* ~ of (that was ~ of him)

wriggle *v.* (d; intr.) to ~ out of (he ~d out of my grip)

wring *v.* 1. (d; tr.) ('to extract') to ~ from, out of (the police finally succeeded in ~ing a confession from the prisoner) 2. (N; used with an adjective) ('to squeeze') to ~ a towel dry

wrinkle *n.* ['crease'] 1. to make a ~ 2. to iron out, press out ~s ['innovation'] (colloq.) 3. the latest ~ in (the latest ~ in marketing home computers)

wrist *n.* to sprain one's ~

writ *n.* ['legal order'] 1. to issue; serve a ~ (to serve a ~ on smb.) 2. to quash a ~

write *v.* 1. ('to form letters') to ~ illegibly; legibly 2. (A) ('to compose and send') she wrote a letter to me; or: she wrote me a letter 3. (C) ('to compose') he wrote a recommendation for me; or: (colloq.) he wrote me a recommendation 4. (d; intr.) to ~ about, of ('to describe') (to write about/ of the war) 5. (D; tr.) to ~ about ('to compose about') (she wrote a book about her experiences) 6. (D; intr.) ('to be a writer') to ~ for (she ~s for popular magazines) 7. (d; intr.) to ~ for ('to request') (she wrote for a recommendation; she wrote to me for a recommendation; AE also has: she wrote me for a recommendation) 8. (d; intr.) to ~ to ('to compose and send a letter to') (he ~s to her every day; AE also has: he ~s her every day) 9. (D; tr.) to ~ to ('to compose for') (to ~ words to a song) 10. (d; intr.) ('to order, command') to ~ to + to + inf. (she wrote to me to come home) 11. (AE) (H; no passive) ('to order, command') she wrote me to come home 12. (L; to; may have an object in AE) ('to inform') they wrote to us/wrote us (AE) that they would come home 13. (Q; to; may have an object in AE) ('to inform') she wrote to us/wrote us (AE) where we were to meet

write away *v.* (d; intr.) to ~ for (the children wrote away for a puzzle book)

write back *v.* 1. (A) ('to answer') she wrote a long letter back to me; or: she wrote me back a long letter 2. (D; intr.) to ~ to ('to answer') she wrote back to me

write off *v.* (D; tr.) to ~ as (he was written off as a has-been)

writer *n.* a free-lance; hack; professional; screen ~

write-up *n.* (colloq.) ['account'] to get a (good) ~ (in the newspapers)

write up *v.* (AE) (D; tr.) to ~ for (to ~ a story for a newspaper; to ~ smb. up for a decoration)

writhe *v.* (D; intr.) to ~ in (to ~ in pain)

writing *n.* 1. cuneiform; hieroglyphic; picture ~ 2. creative ~ 3. (misc.) to put smt. in/into ~

writing paper *n.* personalized ~

writings *n.* ['written works'] smb.'s collected; selected ~

wrong I *adj.* 1. completely, dead (colloq.), totally ~ 2. ~ in (I was ~ in going there) 3. ~ to + inf. (it was ~ of them to gossip = they were ~ to gossip;

I was ~ to disregard your advice; it is ~ to lie) 4. ~ with (what's ~ with her?) 5. (misc.) everything went ~

wrong II *adv.* to go ~

wrong III *n.* 1. to do (smb.) ~ 2. to redress, right, undo a ~ 3. a grievous; irreparable ~ 4. in the ~ (you were in the ~) 5. (misc.) two ~s do not make a right; to know right from ~

wrought up *adj.* ['upset'] ~ over (he gets ~ over trifles)

X

X ray *n.* 1. to do (colloq.), make, take an ~ (the doctor decided to take an ~ of my back) 2. to interpret, read an ~ (the radiologist will read your ~ before you leave) 3. to go for; have an ~ 4. to have an ~ taken

xylophone *n.* to play the ~

Y

Y *n.* (= YMCA, YWCA, YMHA, YWHA, which are abbreviations of Young Men's or Women's Christian or Hebrew Association) at the ~ (they are staying at the ~)

yacht *n.* 1. to sail a ~ 2. on a ~ (they spent the summer on their ~)

yammer *v.* (colloq.) (D; intr.) to ~ about; for

yank I *n.* ['tug'] to give a ~

yank II *v.* (colloq.) 1. (d; intr.) ('to tug') to ~ at, on (the small girl kept ~ing at her mother's apron) 2. (d; tr.) to ~ out of ('to withdraw') (they ~ed their children out of school)

yap I *n.* ['mouth'] (colloq.) to shut one's ~

yap II *v.* (colloq.) 1. (D; intr.) to ~ about 2. (d; intr.) to ~ at

yard I *n.* ['enclosed area'] a barnyard (esp. AE), farmyard; brickyard; coalyard; dockyard (BE), shipyard; graveyard; junkyard (esp. AE), scrapyard (BE); lumberyard (AE), timberyard (BE); navy (AE); prison; railroad (AE), railway (BE) ~ USAGE NOTE: In BE, such a plot adjoining a house is called a *garden* if grassy (a back garden, a front garden) or a *yard* if paved (a backyard, a front yard). In AE, such a plot is called a *yard*, whether grassy or paved; a large, grassy plot can also be called a *garden*.

yard II *n.* ['unit of measure'] 1. a cubic; square ~ 2. by the ~ (to sell carpeting by the square ~)

yardstick *n.* ['standard'] to apply a ~ to

yarn *n.* ['fiber'] 1. to spin ~ 2. to unsnarl ~ 3. wool(en); worsted ~ 4. (misc.) a ball; hank; skein of ~ ['tale, story'] (colloq.) 5. to spin, tell a ~ about

yawn I *n.* 1. to stifle, suppress a ~ 2. a loud ~

yawn II *v.* to ~ loudly

year *n.* 1. to spend a ~ (somewhere) 2. a bad, lean; banner (AE), good; happy; healthy; memorable; peak, record; profitable ~ (our firm had a very profitable ~; their team had a good ~) 3. smb.'s formative; golden ~s 4. every; last; next; this ~ 5. the coming; current; past ~ 6. an academic, school; calendar; election; fiscal; jubilee; presidential (US); sabbatical; tax ~ 7. a common; leap; light; lunar; sidereal; solar ~ 8. by the ~ (to be paid by the ~) 9. by ('before') a ~ (by the ~ 2000, the population in many countries will double) 10. for a ~ (they went abroad for a ~) 11. for, in (esp. AE) ~s (they have not been here for/ in ~s) 12. in a ~ (they'll be back in a ~) 13. in a (certain) ~ (he died in the ~ of the great flood; in

future ~s; in ~s to come) 14. (misc.) once a ~; ~ in, ~ out; the first time in (esp. AE), for (BE) a ~; she is five ~s old; light ~s away; for ~s to come; up to last ~; children of tender ~s; she had three ~s of college

yearn *v.* 1. (d; intr.) to ~ for (to ~ for freedom) 2. (E) she ~s to return home

yearning *n.* 1. to express; feel a ~ for 2. a strong ~ 3. a ~ for 4. a ~ to + inf. (she has a ~ to visit the village where she was born)

yeast *n.* brewer's ~

yell I *n.* 1. to give, let out a ~ 2. a bloodcurdling; rebel ~

yell II *v.* 1. (B) she ~ed smt. to them 2. (D; intr.) to ~ with (to ~ with fear) 3. (L; to) he ~ed (to us) that the house was on fire 4. (N; refl.; used with an adjective) he ~ed himself hoarse

yellow *n.* bright; pale ~

yellow fever *n.* to catch, contract ~

yelp I *n.* to give, let out a ~

yelp II *v.* (D; intr.) to ~ at

yen *n.* ['desire'] (colloq.) 1. to have a ~ for 2. a ~ to + inf. (she had a ~ to go bowling)

yield I *n.* ['earnings'] the current ~ (of an investment)

yield II *v.* 1. (B) I ~ed the right-of-way to the other driver 2. (D; intr.) to ~ to (they finally ~ed to our demands; to ~ to temptation)

yoga *n.* to practice ~

yoke I *n.* ['wooden frame'] 1. to put a ~ on (oxen) ['servitude, bondage'] 2. to cast off, throw off the ~ (of bondage) 3. a foreign ~ 4. under a (foreign) ~

yoke II *v.* (D; tr.) to ~ to (to ~ oxen to a cart)

young I *adj.* 1. ~ at heart 2. ~ in spirit

young II *n.* ['offspring of an animal'] 1. to bring forth ~ (wild animals bring forth their ~ in the wilderness) 2. with ~ ('pregnant')

yours *pronoun* 1. (at the close of a letter) ~ faithfully, sincerely, truly 2. (colloq.) ~ truly (I, myself') USAGE NOTE: At the end of letters, the following combinations occur--Yours (informal); Yours ever (BE; friendly); Yours faithful y (esp. BE); Yours sincerely; Sincerely yours (AE); Yours truly (AE); Very truly yours (AE). The formulas marked as 'informal' or 'friendly' are usu. used in letters beginning with *Dear George, Dear Sally*. The others are used in letters beginning with *Dear Mr./Mrs. Smith*.

youth *n.* 1. gilded ~ 2. in one's ~

Z

zeal *n.* 1. to demonstrate, display, show ~ 2. ardent, fervent, great; excessive; religious; righteous ~ 3. ~ for (to show ~ for one's work) 4. the ~ to + inf. (does she have enough ~ to finish the project?) 5. in one's ~ (in her ~ to impress others, she made many blunders)

zealot *n.* a religious ~

zealous *adj.* ~ about, in

zebra *n.* a herd of ~(s)

zenith *n.* 1. to attain, reach a ~ 2. at a ~ (at the ~ of their power)

zero *n.* 1. absolute ~ 2. (misc.) ~ gravity; ~ hour; ~ population growth

zero in *v.* (d; intr.) ('to concentrate') to ~ on (they all ~ed in on me)

zest *n.* 1. to add ~ to 2. a ~ for (a ~ for life)

zigzag *n.* to make a ~

zip I (BE), **zipper** (AE) *n.* (AE) 1. to do up (BE), zip up a ~ 2. to undo, unzip a ~ 3. a ~ gets stuck

zip II *v.* (P; intr.) they ~ped past us

zodiac *n.* the signs of the ~

zone I *n.* 1. to establish, set up a ~ 2. a climatic; frigid; temperate; time; torrid ~ 3. a buffer; combat; communications; danger; demilitarized; drop; neutral; no-parking; no-passing; occupation; postal; safety; school; security; towaway; war ~ 4. an erogenous ~ (of the body)

zone II *v.* (d; tr.) to ~ as (they ~d the area as residential)

zoning *n.* exclusionary ~

zoo *n.* at, in a ~ (she works at the ~; wild animals are well cared for in our ~)

zoom in *v.* (d; intr.) to ~ on (the camera ~ed in on the podium)